Welcome to Rick Steves' Europe

Travel is intensified living—maximum thrills per minute and one of the last great sources of legal adventure. Travel is freedom. It's recess, and we need it.

I discovered a passion for European travel as a teen and have been sharing it ever since—through my bus tours, public television and radio shows, and travel guidebooks. Over the years, I've taught millions of travelers how to best enjoy Europe's blockbuster sights—and experience "Back Door" discoveries that most tourists miss.

This book offers a balanced mix of Spain's lively cities and cozy towns, from trendy Barcelona and upbeat Madrid to Andalucía's romantic hill towns. It's selective: Rather than listing dozens of beach resorts, I recommend only my favorite (Nerja). And it's in-depth: My self-guided museum tours and city walks provide insight into the country's vibrant history and today's living, breathing culture.

I advocate traveling simply and smartly. Take advantage of my money- and time-saving tips on sightseeing, transportation, and more. Try local, characteristic alternatives to expensive hotels and restaurants. In many ways, spending more money only builds a thicker wall between you and what you traveled so far to see.

We visit Spain to experience it—to become temporary locals. Thoughtful travel engages us with the world, as we learn to appreciate other cultures and new ways to measure quality of life.

Judging by the positive feedback I receive from readers, this book will help you enjoy a fun, affordable, and rewarding vacation—whether it's your first trip or your tenth.

¡Buen viaje! Happy travels!

Rick Steves

CONTENTS

SPAIN

For the traveler, Spain means many things: bullfights, massive cathedrals, world-class art, Muslim palaces, whitewashed villages, delicious paella, sunny beaches, and lively nightlife. You'll find all of this, but the country's charm really lies in its people and their colorful lifestyle. From the stirring communal *sardana* dance in Barcelona to the sizzling rat-a-tat-tat of flamenco in Sevilla, this country creates its own beat amid the heat.

Spain's spread-out geography makes it seem more like a collection of distinct regions than a centralized nation. In the central plain sits the lively urban island of Madrid. Just south is holy Toledo, a medieval showpiece and melting-pot city with Christian, Muslim, and Jewish roots. Farther south is Andalucía, home to sleepy, whitewashed hill towns and three great cities: Granada (topped with a magnificent Moorish palace), Córdoba (with a massive medieval mosque), and Sevilla (where Holy Week is celebrated as if God were watching). Spain's south coast offers a palm-tree jungle of beach resorts along the Costa del Sol, a taste of British fish-and-chips in Gibraltar, and a launch pad to Morocco from Tarifa.

To Spain's far north is San Sebastián and the Basque Country, with sparkling beaches, cutting-edge architecture, and tasty *pintxos* (the local take on tapas). In nearby Pamplona, bulls and tourists run for their lives. Gregarious pilgrims hike across northern Spain on their long journey to the cathedral town of Santiago de Compostela. To the east, along the

Running with the bulls in Pamplona; Segovia's towering aqueduct

Mediterranean coast, Spain has an almost Italian vibe. Trendy Barcelona, where Antoni Gaudí's architecture makes waves, keeps one eye cocked toward trends sailing in from the rest of Europe.

Thanks to the Pyrenees Mountains, Spain is physically isolated from the rest of the Continent: It is in Europe, but not of Europe. For more than 700 years (711-1492), Spain's dominant culture was Muslim, not Christian. And after a brief golden age in the 16th century (financed by New World gold), Spain retreated into three centuries of isolation.

Spain's seclusion contributed to the creation of its distinctive customs—bullfights, flamenco dancing, elaborate Holy Week processions, and a national obsession with ham. Even as other countries opened up to one another in the 20th century, the fascist dictator Francisco Franco virtually sealed off Spain from the rest of Europe's democracies. But since Franco's death in 1975, Spaniards have swung almost to the opposite extreme, becoming wide open to new ideas, technologies, and visitors. Tourism is huge here. With 47 million inhabitants, Spain entertains 82 million visitors annually.

Spanish is spoken everywhere. But Catalans (around Barcelona) also speak their own Romance language, Catalan. The Galicians speak Galego. And in the far north the Basques keep alive the ancient tongue of Euskara. People think of themselves

Spain's Cuisine Scene

Fresh off a plane and headed to my first stop in Spain, I popped into a rustic truck stop for lunch. My traveling spirit did a little leap and I thought, *"Yes, España!"* My passport had been stamped, but I didn't really arrive until my teeth broke through the crisp crust of my fresh baguette... and hit *jamón*.

That ham, dry-cured and aged from happy, acorn-fed pigs, is an example of the rustic intensity of the Spanish culture. Cured ham hocks with pointed toes are found in every La Mancha bar. In Spain, *jamón* is more than a food; it's a way of life. Spaniards thinly slice ham hocks with the same reverence that Americans bring to roast turkey on Thanksgiving. Spain's dry central plain isn't that good for grazing, but it's perfect for raising black Iberian pigs.

To complement all that ham, 700 years of (porkless) Muslim rule left its mark on Spanish cuisine. The Moors, who were great horticulturists, introduced new herbs and spices. The Moorish legacy is well represented by paella, one of Spain's best-known dishes, combining the traditional Middle Eastern flavor of saffron with rice and seafood, sausage, and chicken.

Every region of Spain has specialties worth savoring. In Catalunya, in the northeast, there's *fideuà,* a flavor-infused noodle topped with seafood, and *arròs negre,* rice cooked in black squid ink. Along the North Atlantic coast, in Asturias, seafood is combined with hearty mountain grub, including giant white *faba* beans and the powerful Cabrales blue cheese.

Savor Spain's many flavors, from cured ham and fresh seafood to hearty beans.

Green, rainy Galicia in the northwest is known for octopus, chopped up ▶▶▶

and served dusted with paprika. The region's deep-fried green peppers de *Padrón* are tasty and tricky, offering a kind of tastebud roulette—about one in ten is spicy hot. For a snack, try *percebes*, salty crustaceans harvested from the rocky shore.

The cuisine of Andalucía, in the south, makes ample use of onion, tomatoes, and peppers. These combine deliciously in *sofrito*, a base for many dishes. The most famous Andalusian dish is gazpacho, the zesty chilled tomato soup. Other specialties are *pisto* (a ratatouille-like vegetable stew) and *salmorejo* (chilled tomato soup, garnished with ham and egg).

San Sebastián, in Basque Country, is arguably the culinary capital of Spain. Its inviting tapas bars display a stunning array of help-yourself goodies (they're called *pintxos* here). Top dishes include spider crab, tasty anchovies, and grilled octopus. Just grab what you like from the platters at the bar; when it's time to settle up, the server will count the toothpicks on your plate.

Many visitors find the Spanish eating schedule frustrating. Lunch, the largest meal of the day, is eaten between about 14:00 and 16:00. Because most Spaniards work late, a light supper at 21:00 or 22:00 is typical. Generally, no self-respecting restaurant serves lunch and dinner at American hours. But to eat well any time, and within even the tightest budget, duck into a tapas bar and build a light meal out of tasty snacks. ◼

Spice it up with peppers, refreshing chilled soup, and tempting tapas.

first and foremost as Basques, Catalans, Andalusians, Galicians, and so on...and only second as Spaniards. Each region hosts local festivals, whether parading Virgin Mary statues through the streets or running in front of a pack of furious bulls.

For a country its size, Spain has produced an astonishing number of talented artists with distinctive styles—from El Greco's mystical religiosity to the sober realism of Diego Velázquez. In the 20th century, Pablo Picasso shattered the two-dimensional picture plane, then pasted it back together to invent Cubism. Salvador Dalí created surreal juxtapositions, while Joan Miró picked up the Surrealist baton and ran with it. In music, Spain continues its long tradition of great guitarists—classical, flamenco, and Gipsy Kings-style "new flamenco."

Even as the country plunges forward, some things stay the same. Daily lives focus on friends and family, as they always have. Many people (especially in rural areas) still follow the siesta schedule: Spaniards tend to have a small, quick breakfast, grab a late-morning sandwich to tide them over, then gather with friends and family for a big midday meal. From around 1:00 to 4:00 p.m., many businesses close as people go home to eat lunch, socialize, and maybe take a quick nap. The siesta is not so much a time to sleep as it is an opportunity for everyone to shut down their harried public lives.

Enjoy Spain's street life, from sidewalk cafés to the daily paseo.

The resort town of Nerja overlooks the Mediterranean; sangria comes with a smile.

In the cool of the evening, Spain comes back to life. Whole families pour out of their apartments to stroll through the streets and greet their neighbors—a custom called the paseo. Even the biggest city feels like a rural village. People stop at bars for a drink and tapas or to watch a big soccer match on TV. Around 10:00 p.m. in the heat of summer, it's finally time for a light dinner. Afterward, even families with young children might continue their paseo or attend a concert.

Spaniards are notorious night owls. Many clubs and restaurants don't even open until after midnight. Dance clubs routinely stay open until the sun rises, and young people stumble out bleary-eyed and head for work. The antidote for late nights? The next day's siesta.

Travelers love Spain. You can see some European countries by just passing through, but Spain is a destination. Learn its history and accept it on its terms. Gain (or just fake) an appreciation for cured ham, dry sherry, and bull's tail stew, and the Spaniards will love you for it. If you go, go all the way. Immerse yourself in Spain.

Spain's Top Destinations

¡Bienvenido! There's so much to see in Spain and so little time. This overview categorizes the country's top destinations into must-see places (to help first-time travelers plan their trip) and worth-it places (for those with extra time or special interests). I've also suggested a minimum number of days to allow per destination.

PLACES COVERED IN THIS BOOK

▲▲▲ Must See
▲▲ Try Hard to See
▲ Worthwhile

100 Kilometers
100 Miles

Atlantic Ocean

FRANCE

BASQUE COUNTRY

ANDORRA

SANTIAGO DE COMPOSTELA

CAMINO DE SANTIAGO

Camino de Santiago

NEAR BARCELONA

N.W. OF MADRID

SALAMANCA

BARCELONA

P O R T U G A L

MADRID

TOLEDO

CÓRDOBA

SEVILLA

GRANADA

Mediterranean Sea

WHITE HILL TOWNS

SPAIN'S SOUTH COAST

TANGIER

ALGERIA

MOROCCO

MUST-SEE DESTINATIONS

Spain's four major cities—Barcelona, Madrid, Granada, and Sevilla—give you an excellent and diverse sampler of urban Spain. All are linked by train.

▲▲▲Barcelona (allow 2-3 days)

This trendy seaside city has an atmospheric old town, an elegant new town, strollable boulevards, and a Modernista skyline. Barcelona is the heart of Catalan culture, and hometown talents Gaudí, Picasso, and Miró all left their mark on this arty city. Barcelona's inviting beaches are linked by a promenade and dotted with beach bars, delightful at sunset.

▲▲▲Madrid (2 days)

Madrid is the country's dynamic capital. It's Spain on a grand scale, with a huge central square (Puerta del Sol), the Royal Palace (2,000 rooms), and top-notch art treasures, from Picasso's powerful *Guernica* to the Prado's many masterpieces. This livable city has an unsurpassed tapas scene, fun paseo, street markets, and flamenco shows.

▲▲▲Granada (1-2 days)

Granada pairs evocative history with good living. Its Moorish legacy shines brightest at the magnificent Alhambra palace, and the old town's Royal Chapel is the final resting place of Ferdinand and Isabel. The fun-to-explore city also has distinctive neighborhoods, from the bustling Alcaicería shopping lanes to the hilly Albayzín, with funky tea shops and sublime views of the Alhambra against the mountains.

Madrid's Retiro Park; dancing in Barcelona; Granada's Alhambra at sunset; visiting Madrid's Prado Museum

▲▲▲Sevilla (1-2 days)

This soulful city boasts a number of Spain's bests: flamenco, Holy Week fervor, bullfighting, and the late-night paseo. Sights include the tangled Barrio Santa Cruz neighborhood, a massive Gothic cathedral (with Columbus' tomb), and the Moorish Alcázar palace and gardens. And there's the nonstop city itself—a festival of color, music, and street life.

Spaniards turn out for festive events; Ronda clings to its cliff top; Sevilla comes alive at April Fair.

WORTH-IT DESTINATIONS

You can weave any of these destinations—rated ▲ or ▲▲—into your itinerary. Choose from a mix of small towns, pilgrim destinations, countryside stops, beach resorts, and historic cities, or go for a taste of Gibraltar or Tangier. It's easy to add some destinations based on proximity (if you're going to Madrid, Toledo is next door), but some out-of-the-way places can merit the journey, depending on your time and interests.

▲Near Barcelona (1 day)
Day-tripping from Barcelona, pilgrims and photographers head to the rugged mountain retreat of Montserrat, while fans of Salvador Dalí visit Figueres for its Dalí Theater-Museum and Cadaqués for the artist's house.

▲▲Basque Country (1-2 days)
The vibrant Basque region, which overlaps southwest France, is anchored on the Spanish side by the beach resort town of San Sebastián (pictured above) and neighboring Bilbao, with its striking Guggenheim modern art museum.

▲Camino de Santiago (4 days for drivers)
This centuries-old pilgrimage route traverses the top of Spain from France to Santiago de Compostela, with stops at charming villages and interesting cities (including Pamplona, famous for the Running of the Bulls).

▲Santiago de Compostela (1-2 days)
Tucked into the far northwest corner of Spain, this moss-covered city is the end of the trail for pilgrims walking the Camino de Santiago (the "Way of St. James"). Greet pilgrims

Bilbao's stunning Guggenheim museum; trekkers at Santiago's cathedral; sublime Toledo; Córdoba's vast Mezquita

as they arrive at the town's vast cathedral, home to the relics of St. James.

▲Salamanca (1 day)

Humming with a youthful vibe, this university town has the country's finest main square, where you can pull up front-row seats at a sidewalk café and enjoy a drink and tapas. Here and about town, bands of student musicians break into song, hoping for a few coins.

▲Northwest of Madrid (1-3 days)

Several different destinations make fine day trips (or a loop trip) from Madrid: El Escorial has an imposing royal palace, and nearby is the Valley of the Fallen, a monument to victims of the Spanish Civil War. The pleasant town of Segovia (also good for an overnight stop) is crossed by a towering Roman aqueduct. Little Ávila, the birthplace of St. Teresa, nestles within its well-preserved medieval wall.

▲▲Toledo (1-2 days)

Hill-capping Toledo has a wonderfully rich history (Roman, Jewish, Moorish, Christian), an outstanding cathedral, and works by hometown artist El Greco. An overnight visit is best to savor the town's evening tranquility, though Toledo also works well as a day trip from Madrid.

▲Córdoba (1 day)

This bustling city is home to Spain's top surviving Moorish mosque, the huge and marvelous Mezquita. Nearby are the quaint side lanes of the city's Jewish quarter, alive with history. Córdoba is an easy stop on the AVE train line between Madrid and Sevilla, or a quick day trip from Sevilla.

▲▲Andalucía's White Hill Towns (1-2 days)

Andalucía is the classic heartland of southern Spain, known for its windswept hills and scenically perched towns, including tiny Arcos de la Frontera and livelier Ronda, with its massive, gorge-straddling bridge. (If you want to visit more hill towns than these, you'll find it easier by car.)

▲Spain's South Coast (2-3 days)

Spain's beach-resort zone offers several vivid stops: the appealing village of Nerja (enjoy paella on the beach); the whitewashed hill town of Frigiliana; the intriguing Rock of Gibraltar (with English pubs in town and a colony of monkeys on the Rock); and the laid-back town of Tarifa, with daily ferries to Tangier, Morocco. A swing along the coast can include all these destinations (or choose your favorite).

▲▲Tangier, Morocco (1-2 days)

Tangier, Morocco's revitalized gateway, offers a fascinating look at North Africa and the Muslim culture, with its friendly, curious people. The bustling medina (old town) is a winding maze of shops and tea houses. A quick ferry ride from Spain, Tangier makes an unforgettable day trip (or you can stay the night).

Tangier at dusk; a sidewalk café in Tarifa; a timeless Andalusian hill town

Planning Your Trip

To plan your trip, you'll need to design your itinerary—choosing where and when to go, how you'll travel, and how many days to spend at each destination. For my best general advice on sightseeing, accommodations, restaurants, and more, see the Practicalities chapter.

DESIGNING AN ITINERARY

As you read this book and learn your options...

Choose your top destinations.

My recommended itinerary (see the sidebar on the next page) gives you an idea of how much you can reasonably see in 21 days, but you can adapt it to fit your own interests and time frame. Trendsetters linger in Barcelona, and art lovers are drawn to Madrid. If you like flamenco, Sevilla will shake your castanets. Historians travel back in time to Granada's sprawling Alhambra or to Toledo, with its concentrated mix of art and history within small-town walls. Pilgrims pay homage at Santiago de Compostela and Montserrat, while sun worshippers bask at coastal Nerja and San Sebastián (a city fun for foodies, too). If you're fond of quiet hill towns, get a good dose (or doze?) in Andalucía. For an exotic excursion, it's Tangier. Photographers want to go everywhere.

Decide when to go.

Spring and fall offer the best combination of good weather, lighter crowds, long days, and plenty of tourist and cultural activities.

Whirlwind Three-Week Trip of Spain

Day	Plan	Sleep
1	Arrive in Barcelona	Barcelona
2	Barcelona	Barcelona
3	Barcelona	Barcelona
4	More Barcelona, or day-trip to Dalí sights or Montserrat	Barcelona
5	Fly to Granada (1.5 hours)	Granada
6	Granada	Granada
7	More Granada; afternoon bus to Nerja (2.5 hours)	Nerja
8	Nerja beach day, or side-trip to Frigiliana	Nerja
9	Bus to Ronda (2-3 hours)	Ronda
10	Ronda	Ronda
11	Bus to Sevilla (3 hours)	Sevilla
12	Sevilla	Sevilla
13	More Sevilla, or day-trip to Córdoba, Arcos, or Jerez	Sevilla
14	Train to Toledo (4 hours)	Toledo
15	Toledo	Toledo
16	Travel to Madrid (30 minutes by train)	Madrid
17	Madrid	Madrid
18	Your choice of day trip: Segovia, El Escorial, or Salamanca	Madrid
19	Long train or bus (5 hours) to San Sebastián	San Sebastián
20	San Sebastián	San Sebastián
21	Day-trip to St-Jean-de-Luz or Bilbao; sleep in Bilbao if departure flight options are better from there	San Sebastián or Bilbao
22	Fly home	

July and August are the most crowded and expensive in the coastal areas, and less crowded but uncomfortably hot and dusty in the interior. Air-conditioning is essential.

Off-season, roughly November through March, expect shorter hours and fewer activities in smaller towns. Confirm your sightseeing plans locally.

Though Spain can be brutally hot in the summer, winters can be bitterly cold, and spring and fall can be crisp. For weather specifics, see the climate chart in the appendix.

With More Time: Tempting add-ons to this plan are a day (or more) for Tangier, Morocco (between days 8 and 9); spending a night or two in the Castilian cities of Salamanca or Segovia; and continuing from the Basque Country along the historic Camino de Santiago, across northern Spain, to Santiago de Compostela.

With a Car: Long distances between cities are best connected by train, but renting a car makes particular sense in the South Coast/ White Hill Towns area (pick up the car in Granada on day 7, drop it in Sevilla on day 11) and for touring the Basque Country (and possibly extending all the way west along the Camino de Santiago).

Connect the dots.

Link your destinations into a logical route. Determine which cities you'll fly into and out of. Begin your search for transatlantic flights at Kayak.com.

Decide if you'll travel by car or public transportation, or a combination. A car is particularly helpful for exploring Andalucía's hill towns or the Camino de Santiago, but it's useless in big cities (park it). If relying on public transit, you'll probably use a mix of trains and buses. Trains are faster, but buses can reach a few places that trains can't.

Back streets beckon and good times roll. Happy travels!

To determine approximate travel times between destinations, study the driving map in the Practicalities chapter or check Google Maps; visit Bahn.de or Renfe.com for train schedules. Spain's long distances make it worth considering a short flight for part of your trip; check Skyscanner.com for intra-European flights.

Write out a day-by-day itinerary.

Figure out how many destinations you can comfortably fit in your time frame. Don't overdo it—few travelers wish they'd hurried more. Allow enough days per stop (see estimates in "Spain's Top Destinations," earlier). Minimize one-night stands. It can be worth taking a late-afternoon drive or train ride to settle into a town for two consecutive nights—and gain a full uninterrupted day for sightseeing. Staying in a home base (like Madrid) and making day trips can save time over changing locations and hotels.

Take sight closures into account. Avoid visiting a town on the one day a week its must-see sights are closed. Check if any holidays or festivals fall during your trip—these attract crowds and close sights (for the latest, visit Spain's tourist website, www.spain.info). Note major sights where advance reservations are smart or a free Rick Steves audio tour is available.

Give yourself some slack. Every trip, and every traveler, needs downtime for doing laundry, picnic shopping, people-watching, and so on. Pace yourself. Assume you will return.

Trip Costs Per Person

Run a reality check on your dream trip. You'll have major transportation costs in addition to daily expenses.

Flight: A round-trip flight from the US to Barcelona or Madrid costs about $900-1,500, depending on where you fly from and when.

Public Transportation: For a three-week trip, allow $700 for buses and second-class trains ($1,000 for first class). Whether you get a rail pass in advance or buy train tickets as you go, you'll pay about the same—unless you take advantage of online discounts for advance purchases. In some cases, a short flight can be cheaper than taking the train.

Car Rental: Allow roughly $275 per week, not including tolls, gas, parking, and insurance.

AVERAGE DAILY EXPENSES PER PERSON

$200
Applies to cities, figure on less for towns

Lodging
Based on two people splitting the cost of a $170 double room
$85

Meals
$5 for breakfast, $15 for lunch, $25 for dinner, and $5 for ice cream
$50

City Transit
Buses, Metro, and taxis
$15

Sights and Entertainment
This daily average works for most people.
$50

Budget Tips

To cut your daily expenses, take advantage of the deals you'll find throughout Spain and mentioned in this book.

City transit passes (for multiple rides or all-day usage) decrease your cost per ride.

Avid sightseers buy combo-tickets or passes that cover multiple museums. If a town doesn't offer deals, visit only the sights you most want to see, and seek out free sights and experiences (people-watching counts).

Some businesses—especially hotels and walking-tour companies—offer discounts to my readers (look for the RS% ▶▶▶

Rick Steves Spain

▶▶▶ symbol in the listings in this book).

Reserve your rooms directly with the hotel. Some hotels offer a discount if you pay in cash and/or stay three or more nights (check online or ask). Rooms can cost less between roughly November and March. And even seniors can sleep cheaply in hostels (most have private rooms) for about $30 per person. Or check Airbnb-type sites for deals.

It's no hardship to eat inexpensively in Spain. You can get tasty, affordable meals at tapas bars, sandwich shops, and some local chains, too. Cultivate the art of picnicking in atmospheric settings.

When you splurge, choose an experience you'll always remember, such as a fun food-tasting tour or a dazzling flamenco show. Minimize souvenir shopping; focus instead on collecting wonderful stories and memories. ■

Sherry bodega tour in Jerez; artistic lamppost in Barcelona; catching the ferry to Morocco

BEFORE YOU GO

You'll have a smoother trip if you tackle a few things ahead of time. For more details on these topics, see the Practicalities chapter and RickSteves.com, which has helpful travel-tip articles and videos.

Make sure your travel documents are valid. If your passport is due to expire within six months of your ticketed date of return, you need to renew it. Allow six weeks or more to renew or get a passport (www.travel.state.gov). Check for current Covid entry requirements, such as proof of vaccination or a negative Covid-19 test result.

Arrange your transportation. Book your international flights. Overall, Kayak.com is the best place to start searching for flights. Figure out your transportation options: It's worth thinking about buying train tickets online in advance, getting a rail pass, renting a car, or booking cheap European flights. (You can wing it once you're there, but it may cost more.) Drivers: Consider bringing an International Driving Permit (sold at AAA offices in the US, www.aaa.com) along with your license.

Book rooms well in advance, especially if your trip falls during peak season or any major holidays or festivals.

Reserve ahead for key sights. It's crucial to reserve ahead far in advance for Granada's Alhambra to be assured of seeing its often sold-out Palacios Nazaríes. To beat the lines, reserve for Madrid's Prado Museum and Sevilla's two big sights: the cathedral and Alcázar. In Barcelona, reservations are required for the Sagrada Família and Palace of Catalan Music, and essential for the Picasso Museum, Casa Batlló, La Pedrera, Palau Güell, and Park Güell. Also in Barcelona, Casa Amat-

ller's English guided tour must be booked in advance. Reservations are required for the Salvador Dalí House near Cadaqués, and smart for the Dalí Theater-Museum in Figueres and the Altamira Caves in July and August.

Consider travel insurance. Compare the cost of insurance to the cost of your potential loss. Check whether your existing insurance (health, homeowners, or renters) covers you and your possessions overseas.

Call your bank. Alert your bank that you'll be using your debit and credit cards in Europe. Ask about transaction fees and, if you don't already have one, get a "contactless" credit card (request your card PIN, too). You don't need to bring euros for your trip; you can withdraw euros from cash machines in Europe.

Use your smartphone smartly. Sign up for an international service plan to reduce your costs, or rely on Wi-Fi in Europe instead. Download any apps you'll want on the road, such as maps, translators, transit schedules, and Rick Steves Audio Europe (see sidebar).

Pack light. You'll walk with your luggage more than you think. I travel for weeks with a single carry-on bag and a day pack. Use the packing checklist in the appendix as a guide.

Rick's Free Video Clips and Audio Tours

Travel smarter with these free, fun resources:

Rick Steves Classroom Europe, a powerful tool for teachers, is also useful for travelers. This video library contains about 500 short clips excerpted from my public television series. Enjoy these videos as you sort through options for your trip and to better understand what you'll see in Europe. Check it out at Classroom.RickSteves.com (just enter a topic to find everything I've filmed on a subject).

Rick Steves Audio Europe, a free app, makes it easy to download my audio tours and listen to them offline as you travel. For this book (look for the 🎧), these audio tours cover sights and neighborhoods in Barcelona, Sevilla, and Madrid. The app also offers interviews (organized by country) from my public radio show with experts from Europe and around the globe. Find it in your app store or at RickSteves.com/AudioEurope.

Travel Smart

If you have a positive attitude, equip yourself with good information (this book), and expect to travel smart, you will.

Read—and reread—this book. To have an "A" trip, be an "A" student. Note opening hours of sights, closed days, crowd-beating tips, and whether reservations are required or advisable. Check the latest at RickSteves.com/update.

Be your own tour guide. As you travel, get up-to-date info on sights, reserve tickets and tours, reconfirm hotels and travel arrangements, and check transit connections. Visit local tourist information offices. Upon arrival in a new town, lay the groundwork for a smooth departure; confirm the train, bus, or road you'll take when you leave.

Outsmart thieves. Pickpockets abound in crowded places where tourists congregate. Treat commotions as smokescreens for theft. Keep your cash, credit cards, and passport secure in a money belt tucked under your clothes; carry only a day's spending money in your front pocket or wallet. Don't set valuable items down on counters or café tabletops, where they can be quickly stolen or easily forgotten.

Minimize potential loss. Keep expensive gear to a minimum. Bring copies or take photos of important documents (passport and cards) to aid in replacement if they're lost or stolen. Back up photos and files frequently.

Beat the summer heat. If you wilt easily, choose a hotel with air-conditioning, start your day early, take a midday siesta, and resume your sightseeing later. Churches offer a cool haven (though dress modestly—no bare shoulders or shorts). Take

frequent ice cream breaks. Join the paseo, when locals stroll in the cool of the evening.

Guard your time and energy. Taking a taxi can be a good value if it saves you a long wait for a cheap bus or an exhausting walk across town. To avoid long lines, follow my crowd-beating tips, such as making advance reservations, or sightseeing early or late.

Be flexible. Even if you have a well-planned itinerary, expect changes, closures, sore feet, sweltering weather, and so on. Your Plan B could turn out to be even better.

Attempt the language. Many Spaniards—especially those in the tourist trade and in big cities—speak English. Still, many people don't, particularly in lesser-touristed areas. But if you learn some Spanish, even just a few pleasantries, you'll get more smiles and make more friends. Apps such as Google Translate work for on-the-go translation help, but you can get a head start by practicing the survival phrases near the end of this book.

Connect with the culture. Interacting with locals carbonates your experience. Enjoy the friendliness of the Spanish people. Ask questions; most locals are happy to point you in their idea of the right direction. Set up your own quest for the best paella, paseo, or tapas bar. When an opportunity pops up, make it a habit to say "yes."

Spain...here you come!

BARCELONA

If you're in the mood to surrender to a city's charms, let it be in Barcelona. The capital of Catalunya and Spain's second city, Barcelona bubbles with life—in its narrow lanes, pedestrian-friendly boulevards, elegant modern uptown, bohemian corners, bustling market halls, and along its long beach promenade spiked with inviting beach bars *(chiringuitos)*.

As the capital of the Catalan people, Barcelona is full of history—with ancient Roman ruins, medieval churches, twisty Gothic lanes, and monuments to Columbus and the sea trade. By the late 19th century, Barcelona had boomed into an industrial powerhouse. This thriving city became a showpiece of innovative art and architecture. Talented Catalan architects, including Antoni Gaudí, forged the Modernista style and remade the city's skyline with curvy, fanciful buildings, culminating in Gaudí's Sagrada Família, a gloriously avant-garde church under construction since 1882 (and slated for completion in 2026). Pablo Picasso lived in Barcelona as a teenager—just as he was on the verge of reinventing painting. Salvador Dalí and Joan Miró are among the other world-changing 20th-century artists with ties to the city.

Today's Barcelona is as vibrant as ever. Locals still join hands and dance the everyone-is-welcome *sardana* in front of the Barcelona Cathedral. Neighborhood festivals jam the events calendar. Restaurants serve dinner late by our standards, so do as the locals do, and dip into tapas bars in the early evening to enjoy Catalan small plates. Then, spill into the crowded streets to join the paseo when everyone strolls in the cool of the evening. Barcelona's engaging culture is on an unstoppable roll in Spain's most cosmopolitan and European corner.

PLANNING YOUR TIME

The following day-plans offer suggestions for how to maximize your sightseeing. You can adapt these itineraries to fit your own interests. To find out what days sights are closed, check "Helpful Hints," later. Note major sights where a free Rick Steves audio tour (𝛀) is available.

Reserve ahead for key sights. Every visitor wants to see the same sights in Barcelona—the Picasso Museum, La Pedrera (Casa Milà), Sagrada Família church, Casa Batlló, and Park Güell—so it's essential to book in advance. While technically you can try to buy tickets at these sights (except at the Sagrada Família), I consider reservations mandatory in Barcelona. Booking ahead is also a must to tour Barcelona's Palace of Catalan Music and Casa Museu Amatller.

Barcelona in One Day

For a relaxing day, stroll the Ramblas, visit the Sagrada Família and Picasso Museum and have dinner in the El Born district. Or, try the following ambitious plan (only possible with advance reservations).

9:00	From Plaça de Catalunya, follow my Barri Gòtic Walk and Barcelona Cathedral Tour. (Or follow my Barcelona City Walk audio tour.)
11:00	Starting near the cathedral, explore El Born while walking to the Picasso Museum, stopping midway for an early lunch at Santa Caterina Market.
12:30	Take my Picasso Museum Tour.
14:00	Catch a taxi or the Metro to the Sagrada Família.
14:30	Tour the Sagrada Família.
16:30	Hop a taxi or the Metro to the Diagonal Metro stop.
17:00	Walk to Passeig de Gràcia in the Eixample to see Modernista sights La Pedrera and Block of Discord, then head back to Plaça de Catalunya.
19:00	From Plaça de Catalunya, take my Ramblas Ramble to the harborfront.
Evening	From the harborfront (or any point along the Ramblas) take a taxi to a neighborhood with good tapas bars (which open early): Barceloneta (stroll the beach promenade), Barri Gòtic (around the cathedral), or lively El Born. Foodies can walk to nearby El Raval for cheaper, bohemian-chic eateries. Note that restaurants open late, around 21:00.

Barcelona in Two or More Days

With at least two days, divide and conquer the town geographically: Spend one day in the Old City (Ramblas, Barri Gòtic/ca-

thedral, Picasso Museum/El Born) and another on the Eixample and Gaudí sights (La Pedrera, Sagrada Família, Park Güell). With a third day, visit Montjuïc and/or side-trip to Montserrat (see the next chapter).

With extra time, consider taking a hop-on, hop-off bus tour for a sightseeing overview (for example, the Bus Turístic blue route links most Gaudí sights and could work well on Day 2).

Day 1: Old City

9:00	Follow my Barri Gòtic Walk and tour Barcelona Cathedral. (Or follow my free Barcelona City Walk audio tour.)
11:00	Browse the fun shops described in my Barri Gòtic Shopping Walk.
13:00	Starting near the cathedral, explore El Born. Drop into Santa Caterina Market for lunch.
15:00	Tour the Picasso Museum.
17:00	Stroll the Ramblas (follow my Ramblas Ramble, or just ramble).
Evening	For a tapas-bar dinner, choose among the neighborhoods listed in my one-day plan. Other possibilities include sightseeing (many sights are open late), concerts, or hanging out at a beach bar in Barceloneta.

Day 2: Modernisme

9:00	Spend the morning in the Eixample, touring La Pedrera and/or one of the Block of Discord houses— Casa Batlló or Casa Amatller. Have lunch along the way.
12:30	From Plaça de Catalunya, hop a taxi or Metro to the Sagrada Família.
13:00	Tour the Sagrada Família.
15:00	Choose among these options: Taxi to Park Güell for more Gaudí. Or take the bus to Montjuïc (if you're not going to Montjuïc on Day 3) to enjoy the city view and your pick of sights. Or explore the harborfront La Rambla de Mar, the Old Port, and the beach scene.
Evening	Choose among the evening activities listed earlier.

Day 3: Montjuïc and Barceloneta

Tour Montjuïc, stopping at Fundació Joan Miró, Catalan Art Museum, and CaixaForum. Take the scenic cable-car ride down from Montjuïc to the port and spend the rest of the day at Barceloneta— stroll the promenade, hit the beach, and find your favorite beach bar for dinner.

Day 4: Day Trip

Consider a day trip to the mountaintop monastery of Montserrat, the beach resort town of Sitges, or the Salvador Dalí sights at Figueres and Cadaqués (reserve both in advance; see the next chapter).

Connecting with the Rest of Spain

Located in the far northeast corner of Spain, Barcelona makes a good first or last stop for your trip. From the US, it's as easy to fly into Barcelona as it is to land in Madrid, Lisbon, or Paris. Or you could sandwich Barcelona between flights. Those who plan on renting a car later in their Spain trip can start in Barcelona, take the high-speed train to Madrid (3 hours), sightsee Madrid and Toledo, then pick up a car—cleverly saving on several days' worth of rental fees. For more on train travel and car rentals in Spain, see the Practicalities chapter.

Orientation to Barcelona

Bustling Barcelona is geographically big and culturally complex. Plan your time carefully, carving up the metropolis into manageable sightseeing neighborhoods. Use my day plans to help prioritize. For efficiency, learn to navigate Barcelona by Metro, bus, and taxi. Make reservations in advance for Barcelona's most popular sights—otherwise you might not get in at all. Armed with good information and a thoughtful game plan, you're  ready to go. Then you can relax, enjoy, and let yourself be surprised by all that Barcelona has to offer.

Apart from your geographical orientation, it's smart to orient yourself linguistically to a language distinct from Spanish. Although Spanish ("Castilian"/*castellano*) is widely spoken, the native tongue in this region is Catalan—nearly as different from Spanish as Italian (see the "You're Not in Spain, You're in Catalunya!" sidebar, later).

BARCELONA: A VERBAL MAP

Like Los Angeles, Barcelona is basically flat, sloping gently from the foothills down to the sea. A large central square, **Plaça de Catalunya,** divides the older and newer parts of town. Above the square is the modern part called the Eixample. Below the square is the Old City and hilly Montjuïc, overlooking the harbor.

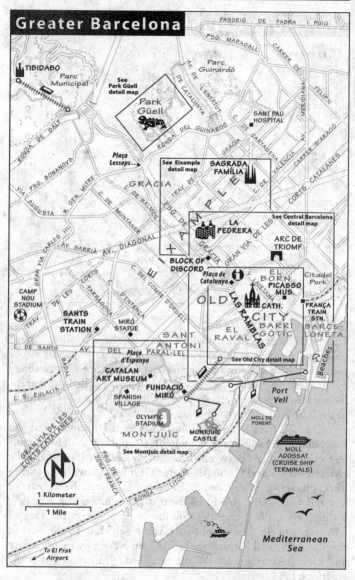

Greater Barcelona

TIBIDABO
Parc Municipal
PASSEIG DE FABRA I PUIG
PSG. MARAGALL
CARRER DE
Parc Guinardó
See Park Güell detail map
Park Güell
AV. DE ESTATUT
DE CATALUNYA
SANT PAU HOSPITAL
MERIDIANA
CARRER D'ARAGÓ
RONDA DE DALT
Plaça Lesseps
RONDA DEL GUINARDÓ
C. DE CARTAGENA
AV. DE VALÈNCIA
See Eixample detail map
SAGRADA FAMÍLIA
CORTS CATALANES
GRÀCIA
TRAV. DE GRÀCIA
VIA AUGUSTA
PSG. BONANOVA
C. DE BALMES
C. DE MUNTANER
R. GEN. MITRE
EIXAMPLE
PSG. DE GRÀCIA
GRAN VIA DE LES
See Central Barcelona detail map
LA PEDRERA
ARC DE TRIOMF
AV. SARRIÀ AV. DIAGONAL
C. DEL COMTE D'URGELL
BLOCK OF DISCORD
Plaça de Catalunya
EL BORN
PICASSO MUS.
Citadel Park
GRAN VIA CARLES III
DE LES CORTS
TARRAGONA
C. D'ENTENÇA
OLD
LAS RAMBLAS
CATH.
FRANÇA TRAIN STN.
CAMP NOU STADIUM
CITY
BARRI GÒTIC
BARCE-LONETA
SANTS TRAIN STATION
MIRÓ STATUE
SANT ANTONI
EL RAVAL
C. DE SANTS AV.
DEL PARAL·LEL
See Old City detail map
Beaches
BADAL
Plaça d'Espanya
CATALAN ART MUSEUM
FUNDACIÓ MIRÓ
Port Vell
C. S. EULÀLIA
SPANISH VILLAGE
MOLL DE PONENT
GRAN VIA DE LES CORTS CATALANES
OLYMPIC STADIUM
MONTJUÏC
MONTJUÏC CASTLE
MOLL ADOSSAT (CRUISE SHIP TERMINALS)
ZONA FRANCA
See Montjuïc detail map
PSG. DE LA
1 Kilometer
1 Mile
RONDA (LITORAL)
To El Prat Airport
Mediterranean Sea

BARCELONA

Barcelona is a big city (1.6 million people), but its major sights cluster in convenient zones. Travelers need only focus on a few areas: the Old City, the harbor/Barceloneta, the Eixample, and Montjuïc. Antoni Gaudí's Park Güell is north of the Eixample in the Gràcia district. Grouping your sightseeing, walks, dining, and shopping thoughtfully can save you lots of time and money.

BARCELONA

Barcelona Neighborhood Overview

TIBIDABO · Park Güell · GRÀCIA · BEYOND THE EIXAMPLE · SAGRADA FAMÍLIA · LA PEDRERA · PASSEIG DE GRÀCIA · BLOCK OF DISCORD · EIXAMPLE · CAMP NOU STADIUM · SANTS STATION · Plaça de Catalunya · LAS RAMBLAS · OLD CITY · CATHEDRAL · EL BORN · Citadel Park · VIA LAIETANA · PICASSO MUSEUM · BARRI GÒTIC · EL RAVAL · SANT ANTONI · GRAN VIA DE LES CORTS CATALANES · AV. DEL PARAL·LEL · Plaça d'Espanya · CATALAN ART MUSEUM · MONTJUÏC · Port Vell · BARCELONETA & BEACHES · Not to Scale · Mediterranean Sea · CRUISE PORT · To Airport

Old City (Ciutat Vella)

This is the compact core of Barcelona—ideal for strolling, shopping, and people-watching—where you'll probably spend most of your time. It's a labyrinth of narrow streets that once were confined by the medieval walls. The lively pedestrian drag called the **Ramblas** goes through the heart of the Old City from Plaça de Catalunya to the harbor.

The Old City is divided into thirds by the Ramblas and Via Laietana, a vehicle-heavy thoroughfare running roughly parallel to the Ramblas. Between the Ramblas and Via Laietana is the characteristic **Barri Gòtic** (BAH-ree GOH-teek), with the cathedral as its navel. Locals call it "El Gòtic" for short. To the east of Via Laietana is the trendy **El Born** district (a.k.a. "La Ribera"), a shopping, dining, and nightlife mecca centered on the Picasso Museum and the Church of Santa Maria del Mar. To the west of the Ramblas is **El Raval** (rah-VAHL), enlivened by its university and modern-art museum. While rough-edged in places, it is the emerging foodie zone.

Harborfront

The old harbor, Port Vell, gleams with landmark monuments and new developments. A pedestrian bridge links the Ramblas with the modern Maremagnum shopping/aquarium/entertainment complex. On the peninsula across the quaint sailboat harbor is Barceloneta, a traditional fishing neighborhood with gritty charm and

some good seafood restaurants. Beyond Barceloneta, a gorgeous man-made beach several miles long stretches east to the commercial and convention district called the Fòrum.

Eixample

Above the Old City, beyond the bustling hub of Plaça de Catalunya, is the elegant Eixample (eye-SHAM-plah) district, its grid plan softened by cutoff corners. Much of Barcelona's Modernista architecture is found here—especially along the swanky artery Passeig de Gràcia, an area called **Quadrat d'Or** (Golden Quarter). To the east is the Sagrada Família; to the north is the Gràcia district and Antoni Gaudí's **Park Güell**.

Montjuïc

The large hill overlooking the city to the southwest is Montjuïc (mohn-jew-EEK), home to a variety of sights, including some excellent museums (Catalan Art, Joan Miró) and the Olympic Stadium. At the base of Montjuïc, stretching toward Plaça d'Espanya, are the former **1929 World Expo Fairgrounds,** with additional fine attractions (including the CaixaForum art gallery and the bullring-turned-mall, Las Arenas).

TOURIST INFORMATION

Barcelona's TI has several branches (+34 932 853 834, www. barcelonaturisme.com). The primary TI is beneath the main square, **Plaça de Catalunya** (daily 8:30-20:30, entrance just across from El Corte Inglés department store—look for red sign and take stairs down). Other branches are scattered around the city and generally have the same hours (daily 8:30-20:30, some have shorter hours Sat-Sun). Locations include on **Pla de la Seu** in the Barri Gòtic (next to the Barcelona Cathedral), inside the base of the harborside **Columbus Monument,** at the **airport** (terminals 1 and 2B), and at the **Sants train station.**

Smaller info kiosks pop up in touristy locales: on **Plaça d'Espanya,** in the park across from the **Sagrada Família** entrance, near the **Columbus Monument** (where the shuttle bus from the cruise port arrives), seasonally at the **Nord bus station,** at the various **cruise terminals** along the port, and on **Plaça de Catalunya.** Throughout the summer, red-jacketed tourist-info helpers appear in touristy parts of town; although they work for the hop-on, hop-off Bus Turístic, they are happy to answer questions.

The free El Corte Inglés map, provided by most hotels and the El Corte Inglés customer service department at Plaça de Catalunya, is better than the TI's map.

TIs are handy places to buy the **Articket BCN** sightseeing

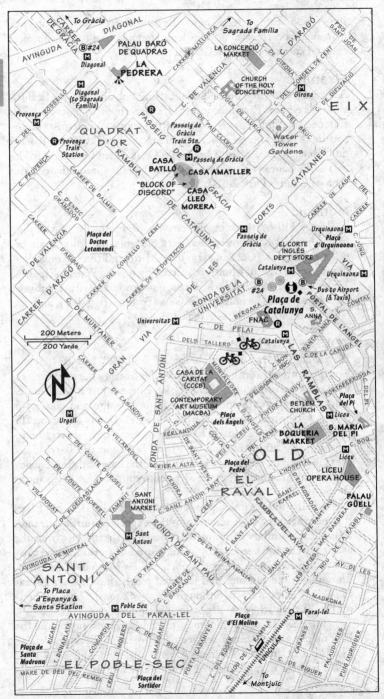

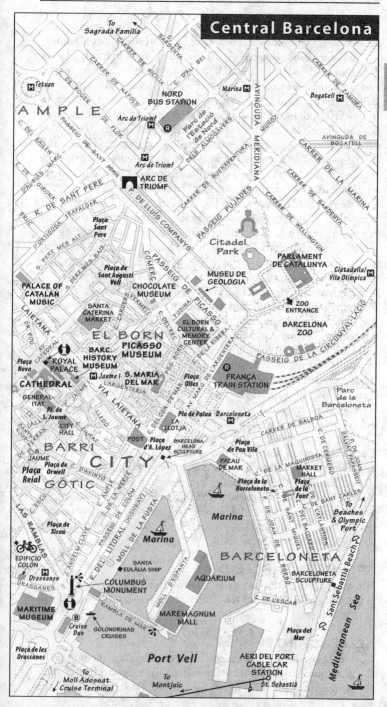

Central Barcelona

pass, or tickets for the Bus Turístic or TI-run walking tours (all described later). They also sell tickets to FC Barcelona soccer games.

Modernisme Route: A handy map showing all 116 of Barcelona's Modernista buildings is available online (www.rutadelmodernisme.com) or in person at the Institut Municipal del Paisatge Urbà, inside the Edificio Colón, the city's first skyscraper (Mon-Fri 9:00-14:00, closed Sat-Sun, Avinguda de les Drassanes 6, 21st floor, ajuntament.barcelona.cat/paisatgeurba). They also offer a sightseeing discount package (€12 for a great guidebook and 20-50-percent discounts at many Modernista sights—worthwhile if going beyond the biggies I cover in depth; for €18 you'll also get a guidebook to Modernista bars and restaurants).

Regional Catalunya TI: The all-Catalunya TI, inside a former palace, can help with travel and sightseeing tips for the entire region. They also have a relaxing café and a space for tasting regional treats (Mon-Fri 7:00-23:00, Sat-Sun from 11:00, closed at lunch, Palau Moja, midway along the Ramblas at #118, Portaferrisa 1, www.palaumoja.com).

Sightseeing Passes: The **Articket BCN** pass covers admission to six art museums and their temporary exhibits, letting you skip the ticket-buying lines. Sights include the recommended Picasso Museum, Catalan Art Museum, and Fundació Joan Miró (€35, valid 12 months; sold online, at participating museums, and at most TIs; www.articketbcn.org). If you visit three or more covered museums, this ticket can save you money and time. Just show your Articket BCN (to the ticket taker, at the info desk, or at a special Articket window), and you'll get your museum ticket, which you can use to enter at any time (especially useful for Picasso Museum).

For most travelers, the **Barcelona Card** and the **Barcelona Card Express** are not worth the trouble.

Digital Publications: Good pretrip planning tools include *Time Out BCN Guide* (concise but thorough day-by-day list of events, www.timeout.com/barcelona); *Barcelona Metropolitan* magazine (timely coverage of local topics and events, www.barcelonametropolitan.com); and *Barcelona Prestige* (upscale dining and shopping, www.bcn-guide.com).

ARRIVAL IN BARCELONA

For more information on getting to or from Barcelona by train, plane, bus, or cruise ship, see "Barcelona Connections" at the end of this chapter.

HELPFUL HINTS

Closed Days: Many sights are closed on Monday, including the Catalan Art Museum, Palau Güell, Barcelona History Museum, Fundació Joan Miró, Frederic Marès Museum, and the

Santa Eulàlia schooner (part of the Maritime Museum). On Sunday, the food markets are closed, and some sights close early—check hours when planning your day.

Sightseeing Tips: To ensure you'll see Barcelona's top (and very crowded) sights—the Picasso Museum, La Pedrera (Casa Milà), Sagrada Família (tickets sold only online), Casa Batlló, and Park Güell—book timed-entry tickets online in advance. It's easy, it's cheaper, and it's for your own good. For these sights, I list prices and details for online booking. For Barcelona's Casa Museu Amatller and Palace of Catalan Music, you'll need to reserve ahead for the guided tour in English, however, a self-guided tour using an audioguide is also available. Dalí's house in Cadaqués require a guided tour, which also must be reserved in advance. Once you make a reservation, you'll receive your ticket by email. (If you don't get it, check your junk folder.) You can either print the ticket or show the bar code on your mobile phone as you enter.

Theft and Scam Alert: You have a better chance of being pickpocketed here—especially on the Ramblas—than anywhere else in Europe. The Sagrada Família (both inside and out), with its hordes of tourists gawking skyward, is also popular with pickpockets. Leave valuables in your hotel and wear a money belt. Whenever you pay with cash, count your change carefully.

Street scams are easy to avoid if you recognize them. Most common is the too-friendly local who tries to engage you in conversation. If a super-friendly man acts drunk and wants to dance because his soccer team just won, he's a pickpocket. Beware of thieves posing as lost tourists who ask for your help. Don't fall for any street-gambling shell games. Beware of groups of women aggressively selling flowers, people offering to clean a stain from your shirt, and so on. If you stop for any commotion or show on the Ramblas, put your hands in your pockets before someone else does. Assume any scuffle is a distraction by a team of thieves. On pedestrian streets, thieves on bikes are adept at swooping by and grabbing a purse or day bag you've placed right at your feet. But don't be intimidated... just be smart.

Personal Safety: Some areas feel seedy and can be unsafe after dark. Most crime is nonviolent, but muggings do occur. Certain parts of the Barri Gòtic (basically the two or three blocks directly south and east of Plaça Reial) and El Raval (just west of the Ramblas) can be dicey. One block can separate a comfy tourist zone from the junkies and prostitutes. If you use common sense in avoiding dark and lonely lanes, you should be fine.

Baggage Storage: Locker Barcelona is located near the recommended Hotel Denit. For weekends and holidays, book a locker in advance (cost depends on size, daily 8:30-22:30, shorter hours in winter, Carrer d'Estruc 36, +34 933 028 796, www.lockerbarcelona.com).

Pharmacy: Pharmacies are sprinkled throughout the Barri Gòtic and Eixample: Look for a bright green illuminated cross. A 24-hour pharmacy is across from La Boqueria Market at #98 on the Ramblas.

Laundry: The clean-as-a-whistle **LavaXpres** is centrally located near recommended Plaça de Catalunya and Ramblas hotels (self-service, English instructions, daily 8:00-22:00, Passatge d'Elisabets 3, www.lavaxpres.com). **Wash 'n Dry,** just off the Ramblas, is in a seedier neighborhood just down the street past Palau Güell (self-service and full service, daily 9:00-22:00, Carrer Nou de la Rambla 19, +34 934 121 953). For both locations, see the map on page 134.

Bike Rental: Biking is a joy in Citadel Park, the Eixample, and along the beach, but is stressful in the city center. Bike-rental shops are in just about every part of the city; I've listed only a few.

Barcelona Rent-A-Bike is located near Plaça de Catalunya (in the courtyard at Carrer dels Tallers 45). Their bikes have three gears and helmets are included (€6/2 hours, €10/4 hours, €15/24 hours, daily 10:00-20:00, shorter hours in winter, e-bikes available at extra cost, +34 933 171 970, www.barcelonarentabike.com). Nearby at Carrer Jovellanos 1 you'll find **Color Bikes,** renting colorful Dutch bicycles for the same price as Barcelona Rent-A-Bike (+34 933 184 033, www.colorbikes.com).

Bike Rental Barcelona is near the Drassanes Metro stop, just a block from the Ramblas. It's pricier, but offers a wide variety, from comfortable retro models to e-bikes and touring bikes (€10/2 hours, €15.50/6 hours, €16.50/24 hours, daily 9:00-20:00, Carrer de Montserrat 8, +34 666 057 655, www.bikerentalbarcelona.com).

You'll see racks of government-subsidized "Bicing" **borrow-a-bikes** around town, but these are only for locals. Instead, check out the apps *Donkey Republic* and *Ridemovi* (e-bikes), which offer rental bikes all over town.

GETTING AROUND BARCELONA

Barcelona's Metro and bus system is run by **TMB**—Transports Metropolitans de Barcelona (+34 932 987 000 or +34 932 148 000, www.tmb.cat). It's worth asking for TMB's excellent printed Metro/bus map at the TI, larger stations, or the TMB information

counter in the Sants train station (not always available). **Google Maps** is a great route planner both for Metro and bus riders.

Tickets and Multiride Cards: A single-ride ticket *(bitllet senzill)* costs €2.40. The T-Casual card (€11.35 for 10 rides) is for an individual traveler only. The T-Familiar card (€10 for 8 rides) is shareable as long as you stay together the entire journey (you'll be fined fI riding without a ticket). Taking the Metro to or from the airport requires a separate €5.15 fare (more convenient by Aerobus shuttle).

Multiride cards show how many trips you've taken, with the time and date of each ride. One "ride" covers you for 1.25 hours of unlimited use on all Metro and local bus lines, as well as local rides on the Renfe and Rodalies de Catalunya train lines (including the ride to the train station) and the suburban FGC trains. Transfers made within your 1.25-hour limit are not counted as a new ride, but you must revalidate your multiride card whenever you transfer.

Multiday "Hola BCN!" travel cards cover unlimited travel for two or more days and include Metro service between the city and airport (€16.40/2 days, €23.80/3 days, €31/4 days, €38.20/5 days).

You can buy tickets from easy-to-use **ticket machines** at Metro stations. Most machines accept coins, bills, and credit/debit cards—just press "English" to start. With the **TMB app** you buy tickets for all forms of public transit and find your nearest station. On buses you can use **contactless** payment methods (credit card or phone) to buy a single ticket.

By Metro

The city's Metro, among Europe's best, connects just about every place you'll visit. Among the several color-coded Metro lines, most useful for tourists is the **L3 (green)** line. Handy city-center stops on this line include (in order):

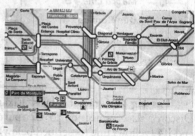

Sants Estació: Main train station

Espanya: Plaça d'Espanya, with access to the lower part of Montjuïc and trains to Montserrat

Paral·lel: Funicular to the top of Montjuïc

Drassanes: Bottom of the Ramblas, near Maritime Museum and Maremagnum mall

Liceu: Middle of the Ramblas, near the heart of the Barri Gòtic and cathedral

Plaça de Catalunya: Top of the Ramblas and main square with TI, airport bus, and lots of transportation connections

BARCELONA

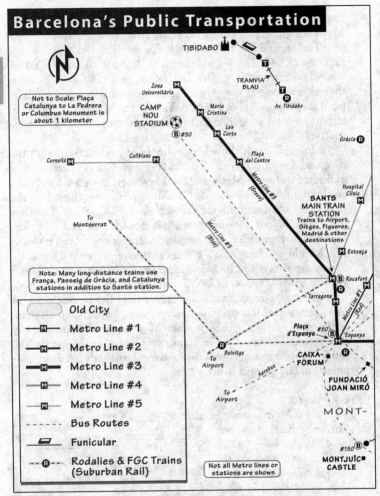

Barcelona's Public Transportation

Not to Scale: Plaça Catalunya to La Pedrera or Columbus Monument is about 1 kilometer

TIBIDABO

TRAMVIA BLAU

Av. Tibidabo

Zona Universitària

CAMP NOU STADIUM ⚽

Maria Cristina

Les Corts

Gràcia Ⓡ

Cornellà Ⓜ

Collblanc

Plaça del Centre

Metro Line #3 (Green)

Hospital Clinic

SANTS MAIN TRAIN STATION
Trains to Airport, Sitges, Figueres, Madrid & other destinations

To Montserrat

Metro Line #5 (Blue)

Entença Ⓜ

Rocafort

Note: Many long-distance trains use França, Passeig de Gràcia, and Catalunya stations in addition to Sants station.

Tarragona

Metro line #1 (Red)

Plaça d'Espanya   #50 Ⓑ

Espanya

	Old City
—Ⓜ—	Metro Line #1
—Ⓜ—	Metro Line #2
—Ⓜ—	Metro Line #3
—Ⓜ—	Metro Line #4
—Ⓜ—	Metro Line #5
- - - -	Bus Routes
⬒	Funicular
—Ⓡ—	Rodalies & FGC Trains (Suburban Rail)

To Airport   Belvitge Ⓡ

Aerobus

To Airport

CAIXA-FORUM

FUNDACIÓ JOAN MIRÓ

MONT-

Not all Metro lines or stations are shown

#150 Ⓑ

MONTJUÏC CASTLE

Passeig de Gràcia: Classy Eixample street at the Block of Discord; also connection to L2 (purple) line to Sagrada Família and L4 (yellow) line (described below)

Diagonal: Gaudí's La Pedrera

The **L4 (yellow)** line, which crosses the L3 (green) line at Passeig de Gràcia, has a few helpful stops, including **Alfons X** (near Park Güell), **Jaume I** (between the Barri Gòtic/cathedral and El Born/Picasso Museum), and **Barceloneta** (at the south end of El Born, near the harbor action).

Riding the Metro: Before boarding, study a map (posted at Metro entrances, platforms, and aboard Metro cars; available at TIs, and printed on some tourist city maps and in the back of this book) to get familiar with the system. Look for your line number

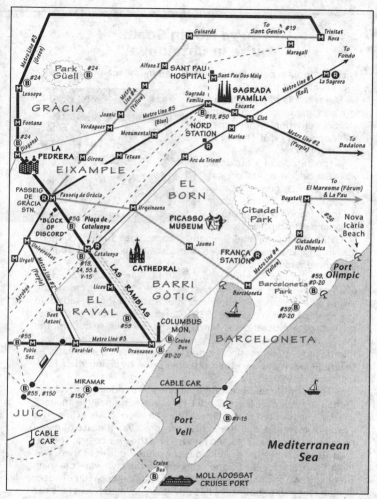

and color, and find the end stop for your direction of travel. Whatever type of ticket you use, enter the Metro by inserting your ticket into the turnstile (with the arrow pointing in), retrieve it, and pass through. Follow signs for your line and direction.

On board, most cars have handy lighted displays that indicate upcoming stops. Because the lines cross one another multiple times, there can be several ways to make any one journey. (It's a good idea to carry a general map with you—especially if you're transferring.) Keep your Metro ticket until you've exited the system, just in case an inspector asks to see it.

Watch your valuables. If I were a pickpocket, I'd set up shop along the made-for-tourists L3 (green) line.

"You're Not in Spain, You're in Catalunya!"

This is a popular nationalistic refrain you might see on T-shirts or stickers around town. Catalunya is *not* the land of bullfighting and flamenco that many visitors envision when they think of Spain (visit Madrid or Sevilla for those).

The region of Catalunya, with Barcelona as its capital, has its own language, history, and culture. Its people—eight million strong—have a proud, independent spirit. Historically, Catalunya ("Cataluña" in Spanish, sometimes spelled "Catalonia" in English) has often been at odds with the central Spanish government in Madrid.

The Catalan language and culture were discouraged or even outlawed at various times, as Catalunya often chose the losing side in wars and rebellions against the kings in Madrid. In the Spanish Civil War (1936-1939), Catalunya was one of the last pockets of democratic resistance against the military coup of the fascist dictator Francisco Franco, who punished the region with four decades of repression. During that time, the Catalan flag was banned—locals showed their regional pride by flying their football team's flag instead.

Three of Barcelona's monuments are reminders of royal and Franco-era suppression. Citadel Park was originally a military citadel, constructed in the 18th century to keep locals in line. The Castle of Montjuïc, built for similar reasons, was the site of many political executions, including hundreds in the Franco era. The Sacred Heart Church atop Tibidabo, completed under Franco, was meant to atone for Barcelona's sins during the civil war—the main sin being opposition to Franco. Today, Catalunya is still divided: Some favor independence, while others are loyal to Spain (see the "Independence for Catalunya?" sidebar on page 70).

By Bus

Given the excellent Metro service, it's unlikely you'll spend much time on local buses (covered by same tickets and passes as Metro; insert ticket in machine behind driver or use contactless pay options). Buses are useful, however, to get to Park Güell (bus #24), to connect the sights on Montjuïc, and to reach the beach.

By Taxi

Barcelona is one of Europe's best taxi towns. Save time by catching

To see real Catalan culture, look for the *sardana* dance or an exhibition of *castellers*. The main symbol of Catalunya is the dragon slain by St. George ("Jordi" in Catalan)—the region's patron saint. You'll find dragons all over Barcelona, along with the Catalan flag—called the Senyera—with four horizontal red stripes on a gold field. According to legend, Wilfred the Hairy—a count of Barcelona and one of the founding fathers of Catalunya—was wounded in a ninth-century battle. A grateful neighboring king rewarded Wilfred's bravery with a copper shield and ran Wilfred's four bloody fingers across its surface, leaving four red stripes.

The Catalan language is irrevocably tied to the history and spirit of the Catalan people. After the end of the Franco era in the mid-1970s, the Catalan language made a huge comeback. Schools are now required to conduct all classes in Catalan; most school-age children learn Catalan first and Spanish second. While all Barcelonans still speak Spanish, nearly all understand Catalan, three-quarters speak Catalan, and half can write it.

Most place names in this book are listed in Catalan. Here's how to pronounce some of the city's major landmarks:

Plaça de Catalunya	PLAH-sah duh kah-tah-LOON-yah
Eixample	eye-SHAM-plah
Passeig de Gràcia	PAH-sehj duh GRAH-see-ah
Catedral	KAH-tah-dral
Barri Gòtic	BAH-ree GOH-teek
Montjuïc	mohn-jew-EEK

When finding your way, these terms will be useful:

Exit	*sortida* (sor-TEE-dah)
Square	*plaça* (PLAH-sah)
Street	*carrer* (kah-REHR)
Boulevard	*passeig* (PAH-sehj)
Avenue	*avinguda* (ah-veen-GOO-dah)

a cab (figure €10 from Ramblas to Sants station). Taxis are plentiful and honest, and cab rates are reasonable (€2.30 drop charge; €1.21/kilometer during the day; €1.45/kilometer 20:00-8:00, Sun, and holidays; €1 surcharge per large suitcase; €2.50 surcharge to/from Sants train station; €4.30 surcharge for airport or cruise port). Similar to Uber (which doesn't run in Barcelona), the **Taxi Barcelona & AMB** app lets you order a car and offers a fixed-price ride to your destination.

Tours in Barcelona

ON FOOT

🎧 To sightsee on your own, download my free Barcelona City Walk and Eixample Walk audio tours, which illuminate some of the city's top sights and neighborhoods (see page 26).

TI Walking Tours

The TI at **Pla de la Seu** (next to the Barcelona Cathedral) offers great guided walks through the Barri Gòtic. You'll learn the medieval story of the city as you walk through the cathedral neighborhood (€25, small discount if you buy online, daily at 10:00, 2 hours, groups limited to 35, buy online in advance—especially in summer, otherwise buy ticket 15 minutes early at the TI desk—not from the guide, +34 932 853 832, www.barcelonaturisme.com).

The TI at **Plaça de Catalunya** offers a Picasso walk through the streets of his youth and early career, finishing in the Picasso Museum (€30, discount online, year-round Tue and Sat at 10:00 and 15:00, Thu at 10:00, 2 hours including museum visit). They also offer a Gaudí & Modernisme walk starting at the Palace of Catalan Music (next to the Jaume Plensa sculpture). The walk explains the facades of La Pedrera, Casa Batlló, Casa Amatller, and more (€18, discount online, daily at 15:00, 2 hours). It's smart to reserve these walks in advance and double-check departure times with the TI (www.barcelonaturisme.com).

Discover Walks

Discover Walks offers good walking tours in under two hours for €19-22. These include Gaudí (daily at 10:30, meet in front of KFC at Avinguda de Gaudí 2) and the Ramblas and Barri Gòtic (Tue, Thu, and Sat at 15:00, meet in front of Liceu Opera House on the Ramblas). The company uses exclusively native-born guides—no expats (+33 695 388 849, www.discoverwalks.com).

"Free" Walking Tours

A dozen or so companies offer "free" walks that rely on—and expect—tips to stay in business. Though led by young people who've memorized a clever script (rather than trained historians), these walks can be a fun, casual way to get your bearings. If you see a "free tour" gathering, and it seems like it may be fun and interesting, you're welcome to join in. **Runner Bean Tours,** run by Gorka, Ann-Marie, and a handful of local guides, is reliable and well established. They offer two 2.5-hour, English-only walks, one on the Old City and the other covering Gaudí (both tours depart from Plaça Reial daily at 11:00, March-Oct also at 16:30, mobile +34 636 108 776, www.runnerbeantours.com). They also do night tours (€16), family walks (€16), and more.

Local Guides

These are three reliable and good local guides that I've enjoyed working with for years: **Sònia Crespo** (+34 610 442 052, sonia@barcelonaexperts.com), **Mónica Sánchez Sabater** (+34 639 319 759, monicasandchezsabater@gmail.com), and **Mariona Prats** (+34 607 605 776, mariona@barcelonasustainabletours.com). Prices start around €250/3 hours, and they do both walking tours and visits to museums and sights.

José Soler is a great and fun-to-be-with local guide who enjoys tailoring a walk through his hometown to your interests (€275/half-day per group, mobile +34 615 059 326, details at www.pepitotours.com, info@pepitotours.com). He and his driver also take small groups by car, van, or minibus on four-hour Barcelona highlights tours and tours outside the city (from €495); they can meet you at your hotel, the cruise port, or airport.

Live Barcelona is a team of professional, enthusiastic guides led by Cristina Sanjuán since 1997. They offer a variety of walking or chauffeured tours, and can arrange cruise excursions and transfers (from €195/3 hours, mobile +34 609 205 844, www.livebarcelona.com).

ON WHEELS

Guided Bus Tours

Catalunya Bus Turístic runs excursions to nearby destinations, including some that are difficult to reach by public transportation. Trips run April-Oct and include Premium Montserrat & Gaudí (€72, Mon-Sat at 8:30, 8 hours, includes Gaudí's unfinished Colònia Güell development); Easy Montserrat (€50, Sun-Fri at 10:00, 6 hours, includes the rack railway); and Salvador Dalí sights in Figueres and Girona (€80, Tue-Sun at 8:30, 11 hours). Itineraries depart from Plaça de Catalunya in front of El Corte Inglés and from near the Nord bus station, close to the Triumphal Arch (live trilingual commentary in Catalan, Spanish, and English; €5 extra for a more in-depth English audioguide; less-frequent in winter, book online for 10 percent discount, +34 932 853 832, www.catalunyabusturistic.com).

Hop-On, Hop-Off Buses

The handy hop-on, hop-off **Bus Turístic** offers three multistop circuits in colorful double-decker buses that go topless in sunny weather and are useful as a once-over-lightly tour or simply to get around. The two-hour **blue route** covers north Barce-

Barcelona at a Glance

▲▲▲**Picasso Museum** Extensive collection offering insight into the brilliant Spanish artist's early years. **Hours:** Mon 10:00-17:00, Tue-Sun 9:00-20:30, Thu until 21:30; Nov-mid-March Tue-Sun 9:00-19:00, Thu until 21:30, closed Mon. See page 84.

▲▲▲**Sagrada Família** Gaudí's remarkable, unfinished church—a masterpiece in progress. **Hours:** Mon-Sat 9:00-20:00, Sun 10:30-20:00; March and Oct daily until 19:00, Nov-Feb until 18:00. See page 103.

▲▲**Ramblas** Barcelona's colorful, gritty, tourist-filled pedestrian thoroughfare. See page 51.

▲▲**Palace of Catalan Music** Best Modernista interior in Barcelona. **Hours:** Guided 50-minute tours in English run every hour 10:00-15:00, audioguide tours run every half-hour until 15:30, plus frequent concerts. See page 92.

▲▲**La Pedrera (Casa Milà)** Barcelona's quintessential Modernista building and Gaudí creation. **Hours:** Daily 9:00-20:30, Nov-Feb until 18:30; nighttime visits also available. See page 101.

▲▲**Park Güell** Colorful Gaudí-designed park overlooking the city. **Hours:** Daily April-Oct 9:30-19:30, rest of year 9:30 until sunset. See page 110.

▲▲**Catalan Art Museum** World-class showcase of this region's art, including a substantial Romanesque collection. **Hours:** Tue-Sat 10:00-20:00 (Oct-April until 18:00), Sun 10:00-15:00, closed Mon year-round. See page 119.

▲**La Boqueria Market** Colorful but touristy produce market, just off the Ramblas. **Hours:** Mon-Sat 8:00-20:30, best mornings after 9:00, closed Sun, many stalls shut down early on Mon. See page 57.

▲**Palau Güell** Exquisitely curvy Gaudí interior and fantasy rooftop. **Hours:** Tue-Sun 10:00-20:00, Nov-March until 17:30, closed Mon year-round. See page 76.

▲**Maritime Museum** A sailor's delight, housed in a medieval shipyard. **Hours:** Daily 10:00-20:00. See page 77.

▲**Barcelona Cathedral** Colossal Gothic cathedral ringed by dis-

tinctive chapels. **Hours:** Generally open Mon-Fri 10:00-18:00, Sat until 17:00, Sun 14:00-17:00. See page 80.

▲*Sardana* **Dances** Patriotic dance in which proud Catalans join hands in a circle. **Hours:** Every Sun at 11:15, many Sat at 18:00, no dances in Aug. See page 82.

▲**Frederic Marès Museum** Quirky museum highlighted by Marès' collection of bric-a-brac from 19th-century Barcelona. **Hours:** Tue-Sat 10:00-19:00, Sun until 20:00, closed Mon. See page 82.

▲**Barcelona History Museum—Plaça del Rei** One-stop trip through town history, from Roman times to today. **Hours:** Tue-Sat 10:00-19:00, Sun until 20:00, closed Mon. See page 83.

▲**Santa Caterina Market** Fine market hall built on the site of an old monastery and updated with a wavy Gaudí-inspired roof. **Hours:** Mon-Sat 7:30-15:30, Tue and Thu-Fri until 20:30, July-Aug shorter hours Tue and Thu, closed Sun. See page 93.

▲**Church of Santa Maria del Mar** Catalan Gothic church built by wealthy medieval shippers. **Hours:** Generally open to visitors daily 10:00-20:30. See page 93.

▲**Casa Batlló** Gaudí-designed home topped with fanciful dragon-inspired roof. **Hours:** Daily 9:00-20:00; nighttime visits also available. See page 96.

▲**Fundació Joan Miró** World's best collection of works by Catalan modern artist Joan Miró and his contemporaries. **Hours:** Tue-Sun 10:00-20:00, shorter hours in winter, closed Mon year-round. See page 118.

▲**Magic Fountains** Lively fountain spectacle near Plaça d'Espanya. **Hours:** June-Sept Wed-Sun 21:30-22:30, April-May and Oct Thu-Sat 21:00-22:00, winter Thu-Sat 20:00-21:00 (no shows Jan-Feb). See page 122.

▲**CaixaForum** Modernista brick factory, now occupied by a cultural center featuring good contemporary art exhibits. **Hours:** Daily 10:00-20:00. See page 122.

▲**Barcelona's Beaches** Fun-filled, man-made beaches reaching from the harbor to the Fòrum. See page 124.

lona (most Gaudí sights, departs from El Corte Inglés on Plaça de Catalunya). The two-hour **red route** covers south Barcelona (Barri Gòtic and Montjuïc, departs from the Ramblas side of Plaça de Catalunya). The 40-minute **green route** covers the beaches and modern Fòrum complex (runs April-Oct only, departs from Port Olímpic stop on Plaça dels Voluntaris). All have headphone commentary and free Wi-Fi (daily 9:00-20:00 in summer, off-season until 19:00, buses run every 20-30 minutes depending on season, www.barcelonabusturistic.cat). One-day (€30) and two-day (€40) tickets, which you can buy on the bus at the TI, or cheaper online, offer discounts on the city's major sights and walking tours. Another company, **Barcelona City Tour,** offers a nearly identical service (same price and discounts, two loops instead of three, www.barcelona.city-tour.com).

Bike Tours

Barcelona Ciclo Tour offers three-hour bike tours taking you from sight to sight, mostly on bike paths and through parks, with stop-and-go commentary in English (€22, includes water, daily at 11:00, reserve online, meet 10 minutes in advance outside the Hard Rock Café on Plaça de Catalunya, office at Carrer Tallers 45, +34 933 171 970, www.barcelonaciclotour.com).

Barcelona eBikes offers daily themed tours, including Gaudí Highlights (€39, daily at 11:00), Sagrada Família (€69, daily at 11:00, includes admission), and a Picasso and Bohemian tour (€39, daily at 16:00). Tours start at Carrer Montsío 10, a block past the restaurant Els Quatre Gats restaurant (office at Plaça San Agustín Well 16, +34 935 480 457, www.barcelonaebikes.com).

SPECIALTY TOURS AND ACTIVITIES
Spanish Civil War Tours

Nick Lloyd is the author of *Forgotten Places: Barcelona and the Spanish Civil War.* He and his partner, Catherine Howley, are passionate teachers who take small groups on walks through the Old City to explain the social context and significance of the Spanish Civil War (1936-1939) in Barcelona. History buffs really love this tour (€25/person, Mon-Tue and Thu-Sat mornings, fewer in winter, 3 hours with an hour-long stop in a café for a sit-down talk, English only, www.iberianature.com/barcelona).

Cooking Classes and Food Tours

Cook & Taste offers group cooking classes in which you'll make and eat traditional dishes paired with local wines (group classes daily at 11:00 and 17:00, €70/person, €12 extra for guided La Boqueria or Santa Caterina visit offered Tue-Sat morning or Fri afternoon before the cooking class, Carrer Paradís 3, +34 933 021 320, www.cookandtaste.net). They also offer private classes and a

chef-guided gastronomic tour of gourmet food and wine shops and La Boqueria.

Food Lovers Company's guides carefully select traditional and atmospheric spots where you can sample an abundance of high-quality seasonal specialties as they share personal insights on Barcelona and its cuisine (from €140/person, morning or evening tours, 4 hours, 6 people maximum, mobile +34 635 603 290, www.foodloverscompany.com, hello@foodloverscompany.com). They also offer an all-day private winery tour in the nearby Penedés region that includes stops at two traditional family-run wineries, with tastings, brunch, and transport in a private van.

The Barcelona Taste takes small groups on guided walks, making three to four stops in roughly three hours. They enthusiastically introduce you to lots of local taste treats and drinks. Options include a lunch tour (12:30-14:45) in the Eixample or evening tours (19:00-22:00) in the Poble Sec neighborhood at the foot of Montjuïc (from €99/person, Tue-Sat, reserve early in season, www.thebarcelonataste.com).

Walks in Barcelona

These two self-guided walks take you through the old town—down the main boulevard ("Ramblas Ramble") and through the cathedral neighborhood ("Barri Gòtic Walk").

∩ My free Barcelona City Walk audio tour covers the Ramblas (in part) and the Barri Gòtic neighborhood.

RAMBLAS RAMBLE

For more than a century, Barcelona's main boulevard has been a magnet for visitors. This one-hour stroll down the Ramblas goes from Plaça de Catalunya gently downhill to the waterfront, with an easy return by Metro.

Traditionally the Ramblas was the place where locals flocked to buy flowers, lottery tickets, and a daily newspaper, or to enjoy a spot of shade while watching the world go by. But over time much of the local charm of the Ramblas has been taken over by sightseers, tacky trinkets, and lousy eateries. Many shops now cater to visitors more than locals, and the old neighborhood population has fled to more affordable homes in the suburbs. Still, if you come to Barcelona...

you've got to ramble the Ramblas. (And if you stroll first thing in the morning, you'll find it more charming.)

The word "Ramblas" is plural; the street is actually a succession of five separately named segments. But street signs and addresses treat it as a single long street—"La Rambla," singular. This one-hour walk will help you see beyond the tourist crowds to discover the essence of the area. On the wide central sidewalk, you'll raft the river of tourism as you pass plenty of historic bits and pieces of this great city.

When to Go: The Ramblas is two different streets by day and by night. To fully experience its yin and yang, walk it once in the evening and again in the morning, grabbing breakfast on a stool in a market café. Note that the Ramblas can be rowdy and off-putting late at night or after the Barça soccer team wins a match. Saturday is the best time to see La Boqueria Market.

Pickpockets: The Ramblas is prime hunting ground for pickpockets. Keep only today's spending money in your front pocket; secure your credit/debit cards, extra cash, and passport in your money belt.

Services: You'll find WCs at La Boqueria, beneath the statue at Plaça del Teatre, and at the Maremagnum mall at the end of this walk.

Eating: The eateries here are tourist traps: Avoid them. But just off the street you'll find a few handy lunch spots, and the stalls of La Boqueria Market invite grazing. For details, see "Eating in Barcelona," later.

❷ Self-Guided Walk

• *Start your ramble on Plaça de Catalunya, at the top of the Ramblas.*

❶ Plaça de Catalunya

Dotted with fountains, statues, and pigeons, and ringed by grand buildings, this plaza is Barcelona's center. Plaça de Catalunya is the hub for the Metro, bus, airport shuttle, and Bus Turístic. Of the region's 7.4 million Catalans, more than half live in greater Barcelona. Plaça de Catalunya is their Times Square.

Geographically, the 12-acre square links the narrow streets of old Barcelona with the broad boulevards of the newer city (the Eixample). Four grand thoroughfares radiate from here: The Ramblas is the popular tourist promenade. Passeig de Gràcia, Barcelona's answer to Paris' Champs-Elysées, has fashionable shops and

BARCELONA

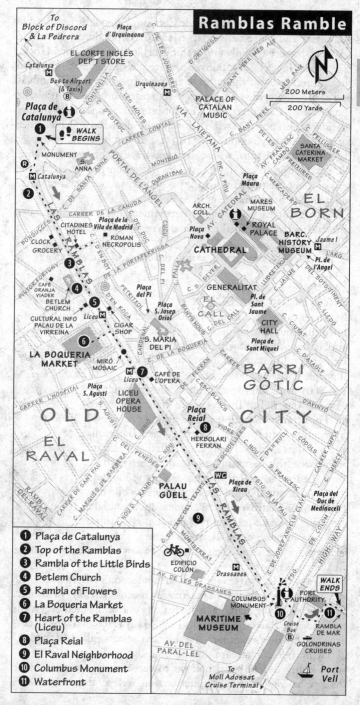

Ramblas Ramble

200 Meters
200 Yards

To Block of Discord & La Pedrera

Plaça d'Urquinaona

Catalunya

EL CORTE INGLÉS DEP'T STORE

Bus to Airport (& Taxis)

Urquinaona

PALACE OF CATALAN MUSIC

Plaça de Catalunya

❶ WALK BEGINS

SANTA CATERINA MARKET

MONUMENT

S. ANNA

❷ Catalunya

PORTAL DE L'ANGEL

EL BORN

CARRER DE LA CANUDA

ARCH. COLL.

MARÈS MUSEUM

Plaça de la Vila de Madrid

CITADINES HOTEL

Plaça Nova

ROYAL PALACE

Jaume I

BARC. HISTORY MUSEUM

ROMAN NECROPOLIS

CLOCK GROCERY

CATHEDRAL

Pl. de l'Angel

❸

CAFÉ GRANJA VIADER

Plaça del Pi

GENERALITAT

BETLEM CHURCH

❹

Plaça S. Josep Oriol

EL CALL

Pl. de Sant Jaume

❺ Liceu

CULTURAL INFO PALAU DE LA VIRREINA

CIGAR SHOP

S. MARIA DEL PI

CITY HALL

❻

LA BOQUERIA MARKET

MIRÓ MOSAIC

Plaça de Sant Miquel

Liceu ❼

CAFÉ DE L'OPERA

BARRI GÒTIC

OLD

Plaça S. Agusti

LICEU OPERA HOUSE

CITY

EL RAVAL

Plaça Reial

❽

HERBOLARI FERRAN

RAMBLA DEL RAVAL

PALAU GÜELL

WC

Plaça de Xirau

Plaça del Duc de Medinaceli

HIGH WAY

LAS RAMBLAS

❾

EDIFICIO COLÓN

Drassanes

WALK ENDS

PORT AUTHORITY

❶❶

COLUMBUS MONUMENT

❿

MARITIME MUSEUM

Cruise Bus

RAMBLA DE MAR

GOLONDRINAS CRUISES

AV. DEL PARAL·LEL

To Moll Adossat Cruise Terminal

Port Vell

❶ Plaça de Catalunya
❷ Top of the Ramblas
❸ Rambla of the Little Birds
❹ Betlem Church
❺ Rambla of Flowers
❻ La Boqueria Market
❼ Heart of the Ramblas (Liceu)
❽ Plaça Reial
❾ El Raval Neighborhood
❿ Columbus Monument
⓫ Waterfront

cafés (and noisy traffic). Rambla de Catalunya is equally fashionable but cozier and more pedestrian-friendly. Avinguda del Portal de l'Angel (shopper-friendly and traffic-free) leads to the Barri Gòtic.

While Plaça de Catalunya is the center of Barcelona, it's also the cultural heart of the entire Catalunya region. At the Ramblas end of the square, the odd, inverted-staircase **monument** represents the shape of Catalunya. An inscription honors one of its former presidents, Francesc Macià i Llussà, who declared independence for the breakaway region in 1931. (It didn't quite stick.) Sculptor Josep Maria Subirachs, whose work you'll see at the Sagrada Família, designed it. These days, Catalans gather on the square by the tens of thousands to demonstrate passionately about whether Catalunya should be independent from Spain.

The giant El Corte Inglés department store towering above the square (on the northeast side) has just about anything you might need.

• *Cross the street, head down about 30 yards, and pause to take in the scene.*

❷ Top of the Ramblas

The street called the Ramblas stretches before you. It slopes gently downhill from here to the harbor. It's dotted with trees and ironwork lampposts, lined with fanciful buildings, paved with colorful mosaics, and trod upon by thousands of people both day and night.

Start with the ornate, black and gold lamppost on your right. The base is a water tap called the **Fountain of Canaletes,** which has been a local favorite for more than a century. When Barcelona tore down its medieval wall and created this elegant promenade, this fountain was one of its early attractions. Legend says that a drink from the fountain ensures that you'll come back to Barcelona one day. The fountain is still a popular rendezvous spot and a gathering place for celebrations and demonstrations.

As you survey the Ramblas action, get your bearings for our stroll. You'll see the following features here and all along the way:

Wavy Tile Work: The pavement decorations represent the stream that once flowed here. *Rambla* means "stream" in Arabic, and this used to be a drainage ditch along one of the medieval walls enclosing the Barri Gòtic (to the left). Many Catalan towns, established where rivers approach the sea, have streets called "Ramblas." Today Barcelona's "stream" has become a river of humanity.

Skinny Balconies: Look up to see the city's characteristic shallow balconies. They're functional as well as decorative, with

windows opening from floor to ceiling to allow light and air into the tight, dark spaces of these cramped old buildings.

Hardy Plane Trees: The deciduous trees lining the boulevard are known for their peeling bark and toughness in urban settings. They're ideal for the climate, letting in maximum sun in the winter and providing maximum shade in the summer.

Fixed Chairs: Nearby, notice the chairs fixed to the sidewalk at jaunty angles. It used to be that you'd pay to rent a chair here to look at the constant parade of passersby. Seats are now free, and it's still the best people-watching in town. Enjoy these chairs while you can—you'll find virtually no public benches or other seating farther down the Ramblas, only cafés that serve beer and sangria in just one (expensive) size: *gigante.*

ONCE Booths: Across from the fountain and a few steps down, notice the first of many booths along this walk that sell lottery tickets in support of ONCE, Spain's organization for the blind.

Soccer Souvenirs: You'll see soccer paraphernalia, especially the scarlet and blue of FC Barcelona—known as Barça. The team motto, "More than a club" *(Mes que un club)*, suggests that Barça represents not only athletic prowess but also Catalan cultural identity.

• *Continue strolling.*

Walk 100 yards farther to #115, with an entrance flanked by two columns and a fine facade struggling to be noticed above the Ramblas ruckus. This marks the venerable **Royal Academy of Science and Arts building** (now home to a performing-arts theater). The building is emblematic of the city's striking architecture from the late 1900s—an industrial boom time that brought lots of construction. The **Carrefour** supermarket next door has cheap groceries (at #113).

• *Remember that each of the Ramblas segments has its own name. You're now standing at what was the...*

❸ Rambla of the Little Birds (RIP)

A generation ago the Ramblas had a different kind of commerce. Locals came here for their newspapers, flowers, and even domestic pets. Traditionally, kids brought their parents here to buy birds, but also turtles and hamsters. But the clientele stopped coming and animal-rights groups lobbied to cut back on the stalls. Today, none of the traditional pet kiosks survive—and there's not a bird in

sight. The commerce that remains is trinkets and drinks for hordes of tourists. Only the locals—and you—know the story behind the name for this stretch of the Ramblas, now lined with ice-cream and souvenir shops.

• *At #122 (the big, modern Citadines Hotel on the left), take a 100-yard detour through a modern passageway marked with the hotel's name to a restored...*

Roman Necropolis: Look down and imagine a 2,000-year-old road lined with tombs. Barcelona was founded about 10 BC by Romans, during the reign of Emperor Augustus, as the city of "Barcino," and this was the main road (Via Augusta) in and out of the walled town. (Today, the highway from Barcelona to France still follows the route laid out by this Roman thoroughfare.) In Roman cities, tombs were generally placed along roads outside the city walls. Emperor Augustus spent a lot of time on the Iberian Peninsula conquering new land, so the Romans were sure to incorporate Hispania into the empire's infrastructure. Looking down at these ruins, you can see that Roman Barcino was about 10 feet lower than today's street level.

• *Return to the Ramblas and continue down 100 yards or so to the next cross street, Carrer de la Portaferrissa (on the left), to see the* **decorative tile** *over a fountain still in use by locals. The scene shows what this spot looked like three centuries ago: There's the original city wall with its gate, and merchants are busy selling flowers, bananas, and, I believe, Barça T-shirts. Now cross the boulevard to the front of the big church.*

❹ Betlem Church

This imposing church is dedicated to Bethlehem, and for centuries locals have flocked here at Christmastime to see nativity scenes.

The church's diamond-shaped stonework is 17th-century Baroque: Check out the sloping roofline, ball-topped pinnacles, corkscrew columns, and scrolls above the entrance. This Baroque style, so common elsewhere in Europe, is unusual in Barcelona. That's because during the Baroque and Renaissance eras (1500-1800), Barcelona was broke. The city enjoyed two heydays: in the 1300s as a medieval sea-trading power, and in the 1800s during the prosperous Industrial Age. In between, Barcelona languished as New World discoveries shifted lucrative trade to the Atlantic, and the Spanish crown kept unruly Catalunya on a short leash.

The church interior is stark, having been burned during Spain's civil war in the 1930s.

For a sweet treat, head around to the narrow lane on the far side of the church (Carrer d'en Xucla) to the recommended **Café Granja Viader**.

• *Continue down the boulevard, through the stretch called the...*

❺ Rambla of Flowers

Pause at this charming section of the Ramblas to admire the nice apartment facades. This colorful block is lined with flower stands.

Besides admiring the blossoms on display, gardeners will covet the seeds sold here for varieties of radishes, greens, peppers, and beans seldom seen in the US—including the iconic green *Padrón* pepper of tapas fame (note that if you buy seeds, you're obligated to declare them at US customs when returning home).

At #99 (on the right), the **cultural center** in Palau de la Virreina sells tickets to dance and musical concerts (easier to buy here than at the main TI).

At #97 (right), the **Casa Beethoven** shop is a cultural throwback to an earlier era, sedately selling music books, sheet music, and antiques like vinyl records.

On the left, at #100, **Tabacs Gimeno** has been selling cigars since the 1920s. Step inside and appreciate the dying art of cigar boxes and hand-crafted pipes.

• *A little farther on, across the street (opposite the Erotic Museum) is the arcaded entrance to Barcelona's great covered market, La Boqueria.*

❻ La Boqueria Market

This lively market hall (worth ▲) is an explosion of chicken legs, bags of live snails, stiff fish, delicious oranges, and odd odors.

The market was originally located just outside the city, as were many in medieval times. It later expanded into the colonnaded courtyard of a monastery before being covered with a colorful arcade in 1850.

While tourists are drawn to the area around the main entry, locals know that the stalls up

front pay the highest rent—and therefore inflate their prices and cater to out-of-towners. Skip the tempting but more expensive juices sold here and head to a booth farther in or along the sides (market open Mon-Sat 8:00-20:30, best mornings after 9:00, closed Sun, many stalls shut down early on Mon).

Stop at the **Pinotxo Bar**—it's just inside the market, under the sign—and snap a photo of animated Juan. He and his family are always busy feeding shoppers. Getting Juan to crack a huge smile and a thumbs-up for your camera makes a great shot...and he loves it.

Fresh, Local Produce: Stands show off seasonal fruits and vegetables that you'll see on menus. The focus here is on Spanish specialties like olives and saffron. The tubs of little green peppers that look like jalapeños are lightly fried for the dish called *pimientos de Padrón*. In a culinary form of Russian roulette, a few of these mild peppers sometimes turn out to be hot—greeting the eater with a fiery jolt. In the fall, you'll see lots of mushrooms; in the winter, artichokes.

Ham: Full legs of *jamón* (ham) abound. The many varieties of *jamón serrano* are distinguished by the type of pig they come from and what that pig ate. Top quality are *ibérico* (Iberian) and *bellota* (acorn eaters). Even by the slice these are very expensive, but gourmets pay €300 or more to go whole hock (see the "Sampling *Jamón*" sidebar on page 978).

Sausage: You'll see many types of the Catalan *botifarra* sausage. Some are ready to eat, while others must be cooked. *Chorizo* is the red Spanish sausage that's sometimes spicy (a rare bit of heat in an otherwise mild cuisine). A few meats are less common in American dishes, like rabbit and suckling pig. Beware: *Huevos de toro* means bull testicles—surprisingly inexpensive...and oh so good.

Seafood: The fishmonger stalls could double as a marine biology lab. In this Mediterranean city, people have come up with endless ways to harvest the sea. Fish is sold whole, not filleted—local shoppers like to look their dinner in the eye to be sure it's fresh. Count the many different types of shrimp (*gamba, langostino,*

clawed *cigala*). Another popular treat is the tubular razor clam *(navaja)*.

Cod: Some stalls specialize in dried salt cod *(bacalao)*. Historically, codfish—preserved in salt and dried—provided desperately needed protein on long sea voyages as Catalan merchants ventured far from their homes. Before it can be eaten, salt cod must be rehydrated, so it's sold either covered in salt or already submerged in water, to hasten the time between market and plate.

Olives: These are a keystone of the Spanish diet. Take a look at the 25 kinds offered at the Graus Olives i Conserves shop (center, at the back).

• *After you've scoped out the market, head back to the street and continue down the Ramblas.*

On your left, you're skirting the old Barri Gòtic neighborhood. Glance left through a modern cutaway arch for a glimpse of the medieval church tower of **Santa Maria del Pi,** a popular venue for guitar concerts (see "Nightlife in Barcelona," later). This marks the Plaça del Pi and a great shopping street, Carrer Petritxol, which runs parallel to the Ramblas. Also nearby is the **Taverna Basca Iratí,** one of many user-friendly, Basque-style tapas bars in town.

On the right side of the Ramblas (at #83), find the highly regarded **Escribà bakery,** with its appealing Modernista facade: Look for the *Antigua Casa Figueras* sign arching over the doorway, mosaics of twining plants, a stained-glass peacock displaying his tail feathers, and undulating woodwork. In the sidewalk in front of the door, a plaque dates the building to 1902. Step inside the fine interior and indulge in a unique edible treat before continuing your ramble.

• *After another block, you reach the Liceu Metro station, marking the...*

❼ Heart of the Ramblas

At the Liceu Metro station's elevators, the Ramblas widens a bit into a small, lively square (Plaça de la Boqueria). Liceu marks the midpoint of the Ramblas between Plaça de Catalunya and the waterfront.

Underfoot, find the much trod-upon **Joan Miró mosaic** in red, white, yellow, and blue. The mosaic's black arrow represents an anchor, a reminder of the city's attachment to the ocean and a welcome to visitors arriving by sea. Miró's simple, colorful designs are found all over the city, from murals to mobiles to the La Caixa bank logo. The best place to see

his work is in the Fundació Joan Miró at Montjuïc (described later, under "Sights in Barcelona").

The surrounding buildings have playful ornamentation typical of the city. The **Chinese dragon** holding a lantern (at #82) decorates a former umbrella shop (notice the fun umbrellas perched high up). While the dragon may seem purely decorative, it's actually an important symbol of Catalan pride for its connection to the local patron saint, St. George (Jordi).

A few steps down (on the right) is the **Liceu Opera House** (Gran Teatre del Liceu), which hosts world-class opera, dance, and theater (box office left of main entrance, open Mon-Fri 10:00-19:00, Sat until 18:00, closed Sun). Opposite the opera house is **Café de l'Opera** (#74), an elegant stop for an expensive beverage. This bustling café, with Modernista decor and a historic atmosphere, boasts that it's been open since 1929, even during the Spanish Civil War.

• *We've seen the best stretch of the Ramblas; to cut this walk short, you could catch the Metro from here back to Plaça de Catalunya. Otherwise, let's continue to the port.*

Thirty yards along, pause and look left down a wide, straight street (Carrer de Ferran). Enjoy the view of elegant lamps, facades, and balconies as it leads to Plaça de Sant Jaume, the governmental center for both Barcelona and the region of Catalunya.

Head down the Ramblas another 50 yards (to #46), and turn left down an arcaded lane (Carrer de Colom) to the square called...

❽ Plaça Reial

Dotted with palm trees, surrounded by an arcade, and ringed by yellow buildings with white Neoclassical trim, this elegant square has a colonial ambience. It's a lively hangout by day or by night. You'll find old-fashioned taverns (*cervecerías*), modern bars with patio seating, and a Sunday coin-and-stamp market. Completing the picture are Gaudí's first public works (the two colorful helmeted lampposts).

• *Head back out to the Ramblas.*

Across the boulevard, a half-block detour down Carrer Nou de la Rambla brings you to **Palau Güell,** designed by Antoni Gaudí (on the left, at #3). Even from the outside, you get a sense of this innovative apartment, the first of Gaudí's Modernista buildings. As this is early Gaudí (built 1886-1890), it's darker and more Neo-Gothic than his more famous later work. The two parabolic-arch doorways and elaborate wrought-iron work signal his emerging

BARCELONA

nonlinear style. Completely restored in 2011, Palau Güell offers an informative look at a Gaudí interior (see the listing on page 76).

• *Return to the Ramblas and keep heading down.*

❾ El Raval Neighborhood

The neighborhood on the right side of this stretch of the Ramblas was nicknamed the Barri Xinès—the world's only Chinatown with nothing even remotely Chinese in or near it. The name was a prejudiced term broadly applied to any foreigner—whether from abroad or another part of Spain. The neighborhood's actual inhabitants were poor Spanish, North African, and Roma (Gypsy) people. At night, the Barri Xinès was frequented by sex workers, drug pushers, and thieves, many of whom catered in one way or another to sailors wandering up from the port. Today, the Raval neighborhood is rapidly gentrifying.

The skyscraper to the right of the Ramblas is the Edificio Colón. When built in 1970, the 28-story structure was Barcelona's first high-rise. Near the skyscraper is the Maritime Museum, housed in what were the city's giant medieval shipyards.

• *Near the bottom of the Ramblas, take note of the Drassanes Metro stop, which can take you back to Plaça de Catalunya when you're ready. Up ahead is the...*

❿ Columbus Monument

The 200-foot column honors Christopher Columbus, who came to Barcelona in 1493 after journeying to America. This Catalan answer to Nelson's Column on London's Trafalgar Square (right down to the lions, perfect for posing with at the base) was erected for the 1888 Universal Exposition, an international fair that helped vault a surging Barcelona onto the world stage.

The base of the monument, ringed with four winged victories (taking flight

to the four corners of the earth), is loaded with symbolism: statues and reliefs of mapmakers, navigators, early explorers preaching to subservient Native Americans, and (enthroned just below the winged victories) the four regions of Spain. The reliefs near the bottom illustrate scenes from Columbus' fateful voyage. A tiny elevator ascends to the top of the column, lifting visitors to a covered observation area for fine panoramas over the city (the entrance/ticket desk is in the TI, inside the base of the monument; elevator-€6, daily 8:30-20:30, when crowded the line cuts off up to an hour early).

• *Scoot across the busy traffic circle and continue straight ahead to the water's edge. Turn left, walk 50 yards, and find a pedestrian bridge that juts out over the harbor (with a wavy design and a wooden floor). Walk onto the bridge, then turn back and face the Columbus statue. This is a good spot to check out the...*

⓫ Waterfront

Survey Barcelona's bustling maritime zone. For more than 2,000 years, this harbor's trade has been the reason Barcelona is on the world map.

The wooden pedestrian **bridge** you're standing on is a modern extension of the Ramblas, called La Rambla de Mar ("Rambla of the Sea"). The bridge can swing out to allow boat traffic into the marina.

As you face Columbus, take in the sights. At the foot of the Ramblas are the docks with the *golondrinas* harbor-cruise boats

(for details, see listing under "Sights in Barcelona," later). To the left of Columbus is the big Maritime Museum. Farther left, in the distance, is the majestic, 570-foot bluff of parklike **Montjuïc**, with sights and museums reachable by cable car (as you can see). To the right of the Columbus statue, the fanciful yellow Modernista-style building (that may be under renovation) is the former port authority. Stretching to the right of that is a delightful promenade along the seawall of Barcelona's Old Port (Port Vell); it's worth a stroll. Along the promenade is a permanently moored historic schooner, the ***Santa Eulàlia*** (part of the Mari-

time Museum). Finally, over your right shoulder is Maremagnum, a modern shopping mall with a huge aquarium, restaurants, and piles of people. Its nighttime scene is rollicking and trendy.

• *Your ramble is over. To get to other points in town, your best bet is to backtrack to the Drassanes Metro stop. Alternatively, you can catch bus #59 from the waterfront on Avenue Passeig de Colom (or take a cab) back to Plaça de Catalunya (where my "Barri Gòtic Walk," next, begins).*

To extend this walk, it's fun to stroll the length of the promenade to the iconic Barcelona Head sculpture (by American Pop artist Roy Lichtenstein). This puts you right at the edge of El Born's shopping and restaurant area. Or, from the Barcelona Head, circle back through Maremagnum, making a nice pedestrian loop around the marina.

BARRI GÒTIC WALK

Barcelona's Barri Gòtic (Gothic Quarter) is a bustling world of shops, bars, and nightlife packed into narrow, winding lanes and undiscovered courtyards. This is Barcelona's birthplace—where the ancient Romans built a city, where medieval Christians built their cathedral, where Jews gathered together, and where Barcelonans lived within a ring of protective walls until the 1850s, when the city expanded.

Treat this 1.5-hour self-guided walk from Plaça de Catalunya to Plaça del Rei as a historical scavenger hunt. You'll focus on the earliest chunk of Roman Barcelona, right around the cathedral, and explore some legacy sights from the city's medieval era.

When to Go: If you plan to enter the museums mentioned on this walk, avoid Monday, when some sights are closed.

Eating: For restaurants and tapas bars along the way, see page 146.

❷ Self-Guided Walk

• *Start on Barcelona's grand main square, **Plaça de Catalunya**. From the northeast corner (between the giant El Corte Inglés department store and the Banco de España), head down the broad pedestrian boulevard called...*

❶ Avinguda del Portal de l'Angel

For much of Barcelona's history, this street was home to a major city gate. A medieval wall enclosed the city, and the entrance here—the "Gate of the Angel"—gave the street its name. An angel statue atop the gate purportedly kept Barcelonans safe from plagues and bid voyagers safe journey as they left the security of the city. Imagine the fascinating scene here at the Gate of the Angel, where Barcelona stopped and the Iberian wilds began.

Much later, this same boulevard (and much of the city) got a

facelift in preparation for the 1888 Universal Exposition, the first international fair held in Spain.

Picture the traffic congestion here in the 1980s, before this street was closed to most motorized vehicles (if you visit in the morning you'll still dodge delivery trucks supplying stores). Today, you're elbow to elbow with shoppers cruising through some of the most expensive retail space in town.

Although today this street has been globalized and sanitized, a handful of businesses with local roots survive. On the right at the first corner (at #25), a green sign and appetizing display window mark **Planelles Donat**—long appreciated for its sweet *turró* (or *turrón*, an almond-and-honey candy), ice cream, refreshing *orxata* (or *horchata*, an almond-flavored drink), and *granissat* (or *granizado*, ice slush). Imagine how historic shops like this started, with artisans from villages camping out here in a vestibule of some big building, selling baskets of their homemade goodies—and eventually evolving into real shops.

• *A block farther down, pause at Carrer de Santa Anna to admire the Art Nouveau awning at another* **El Corte Inglés** *department store. From here, take a half-block detour to the right on Carrer de Santa Anna. At #32 go through a large entryway to the pleasant courtyard of the...*

❷ Church of Santa Anna

This austere Catalan Gothic church—a 12th-century gem—was part of a convent and still has its marker cross standing outside. To the left of the cross, approach the gate, where you can peek inside the fine cloister—an arcaded walkway around a leafy courtyard. Climb the modern stairs across from the church for views of the bell tower. Inside the church you'll find a bare Romanesque interior, topped with an octagonal wooden roof. At the back of the nave, the recumbent-knight tomb is of Miguel de Boera, renowned admiral of Charles V. (Let's hope his hands were not that large.)

Take a moment here on Carrer de Santa Anna to look around and notice little details. Look up at pulleys (handy in buildings with no elevators). Take in the ironwork buildings with fine old entrances and cheaper facades (with plasterwork fashioned into fake col-

umns). Note how the buildings maxed out their late-19th-century height limits. Here (and around town), you may see the *estelada flag*—red and gold with a blue triangle and white star—a symbol of Catalan separatists.

• *Backtrack to Avinguda del Portal de l'Angel and continue down the street. At Carrer de Montsió (on the left), just past the United Colors of Benetton store, side-trip a half-block to...*

❸ Els Quatre Gats

This restaurant (at #3) is a historic monument, tourist attraction, nightspot, and recommended eatery (closed Mon, see listing on page 147). It's famous for being the circa-1900 bohemian-artist hangout where Picasso nursed drinks with friends and had his first one-man show. The building itself, by prominent architect Josep Puig i Cadafalch, represents Neo-Gothic Modernisme. Take a look around the corner from the entrance—it looks more like a medieval church or a castle, with pointed arches, windows with stone tracery, and gargoyles peeking from the stonework.

Stepping inside, you feel the turn-of-the-century vibe. Even if you don't eat or drink here, you can check out the vintage photos on the wall and take a quick look around (ask *"Solo mirar, por favor?"*). Rich Barcelona elites and would-be avant-garde artists looked to Paris (not Madrid) for cultural inspiration. This place was clearly influenced by Paris' Le Chat Noir, a cabaret/café and the hangout of Montmartre intellectuals. Like Le Chat Noir, Els Quatre Gats even published its own artsy magazine for a while. The story of the name? When the proprietor told his friends that he'd stay open 24 hours a day, they said, "No one will come." Using a popular Catalan phrase, they told him, "It'll just be you and four cats."

• *Return to and continue down Avinguda del Portal de l'Angel. You'll soon reach a fork in the road and a building with a...*

❹ Fountain

The blue-and-yellow tilework, a circa-1918 addition to this even older fountain, depicts ladies with big jugs of water. Picture the scene here back in the 17th century. No one had indoor plumbing, and the neighborhood ladies would gather to fill their big crocks and take them home. This particular fountain was especially important as the last watering stop for horses before leaving town.

• *Shoppers will feel the pull of wonderful little shops down the street to the right. But be strong and take the left fork, down Carrer dels Arcs. Rounding the corner, you'll pass the **Reial Cercle Artístic**, hosting exhibitions by Catalan artists (free, daily 10:00-14:00 & 15:00-20:00). Continue and enter the large square called...*

BARCELONA

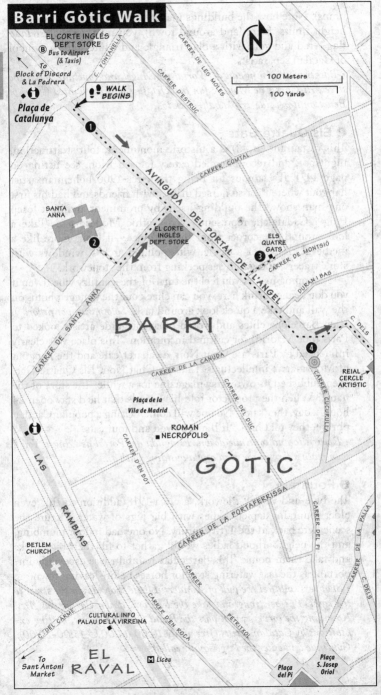

Barri Gòtic Walk

EL CORTE INGLÉS DEP'T STORE

Ⓑ Bus to Airport (& Taxis)

To Block of Discord & La Pedrera

C. FONTANELLA

Plaça de Catalunya

WALK BEGINS

①

CARRER D'ESTRUC

CARRER DE LES MOLES

N

100 Meters

100 Yards

CARRER COMTAL

AVINGUDA DEL PORTAL DE L'ANGEL

SANTA ANNA

②

EL CORTE INGLÉS DEPT. STORE

ELS QUATRE GATS

③

CARRER DE MONTSIÓ

DURAN I BAS

CARRER DE SANTA ANNA

BARRI

C. DELS

④

REIAL CERCLE ARTISTIC

CARRER DE LA CANUDA

Plaça de la Vila de Madrid

ROMAN NECROPOLIS

CARRER DEL DUC

CARRER CUCURULLA

GÒTIC

CARRER D'EN BOT

LAS

RAMBLAS

CARRER DE LA PORTAFERRISSA

CARRER DEL PI

CARRER DE LA PALLA

BETLEM CHURCH

CARRER

C. DEL CARME

CULTURAL INFO PALAU DE LA VIRREINA

CARRER D'EN ROCA

PETRITXOL

C. DEL PI

To Sant Antoni Market

EL RAVAL

Ⓜ Liceu

Plaça del Pi

Plaça S. Josep Oriol

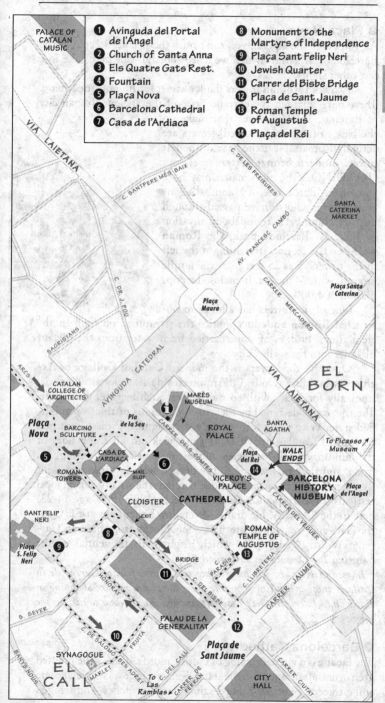

① Avinguda del Portal de l'Angel
② Church of Santa Anna
③ Els Quatre Gats Rest.
④ Fountain
⑤ Plaça Nova
⑥ Barcelona Cathedral
⑦ Casa de l'Ardiaca
⑧ Monument to the Martyrs of Independence
⑨ Plaça Sant Felip Neri
⑩ Jewish Quarter
⑪ Carrer del Bisbe Bridge
⑫ Plaça de Sant Jaume
⑬ Roman Temple of Augustus
⑭ Plaça del Rei

PALACE OF CATALAN MUSIC

VIA LAIETANA

C. SANTPERE MÉS BAIX

C. DE LES FREIXURES

SANTA CATERINA MARKET

AV. FRANCESC CAMBÓ

C. DE J. POU

CARRER MERCADERS

Plaça Maura

Plaça Santa Caterina

SAGRISTANS

AVINGUDA CATEDRAL

VIA LAIETANA

EL BORN

ARCS

CATALAN COLLEGE OF ARCHITECTS

MARÈS MUSEUM

CARRER DELS COMTES

ROYAL PALACE

SANTA AGATHA

To Picasso Museum

Plaça Nova

BARCINO SCULPTURE

Pla de la Seu

⑤

Plaça del Rei

WALK ENDS

⑭

BARCELONA HISTORY MUSEUM

Plaça de l'Angel

CASA DE L'ARDIACA

⑦ ⑥

ROMAN TOWERS

MAIL SLOT

VICEROY'S PALACE

CATHEDRAL

CARRER DEL VEGUER

SANT FELIP NERI

CLOISTER

EXIT

ROMAN TEMPLE OF AUGUSTUS

⑬

CARRER JAUME

Plaça de l'Angel

⑧

⑨

Plaça S. Felip Neri

BRIDGE

⑪

C. PARADÍS

C. LLIBRETERIA

HONORAT

C. DEL BISBE

S. SEVER

C. DE SALOMÓ BEN ADRET

FRUITA

⑩

PALAU DE LA GENERALITAT

⑫

CARRER CIUTAT

BANYS NOUS

MARLET

SYNAGOGUE

EL CALL

To Las Ramblas

C. DEL CALL

CARRER DE FERRAN

Plaça de Sant Jaume

CITY HALL

❺ Plaça Nova

As you enter the square, you can't miss the prickly steeple of the Barcelona Cathedral (which we'll see shortly). But first, take in a few other sights.

Two bold **Roman towers** flank a street leading off the square. These once guarded the entrance gate of the ancient Roman city of Barcino. The big stones that make up the base of the (reconstructed) towers are actually Roman. Near the base of the left tower, **modern bronze letters** spell out "BARCINO." The city's name may have come from Barca, one of Hannibal's generals, who is said to have passed through during Hannibal's roundabout invasion of Italy. At Barcino's peak, the **Roman wall** (see the section stretching to the left of the towers) was 25 feet high and a mile around, with 74 towers. It enclosed a population of 4,000.

One of the towers has a bit of reconstructed **Roman aqueduct** (notice the streambed on top). In ancient times, bridges of stone carried fresh water from the distant hillsides into the walled city.

Opposite the towers is the modern **Catalan College of Architects** building (Collegi d'Arquitectes de Barcelona), which is, ironically for a city with so much great architecture, quite ugly. The frieze was designed by Picasso (1962) in his distinctive simplified style. With just a few squiggly stick-figures, Picasso captured traditional Catalan activities. If you check out all three sides of the building, you'll see scenes suggesting music, bullfighting, sea trade, and the *sardana* dance. The branch-waving kings represent the giant puppets *(gegants)* paraded through the streets during local festivals. Picasso spent his formative years (1895-1904, age 14-23) here in the Old City. He drank with fellow bohemians at Els Quatre Gats and frequented brothels a few blocks from here on Carrer d'Avinyó ("Avignon")—which inspired his influential Cubist painting *Les Demoiselles d'Avignon*.

• *Immediately to the left as you face the Picasso frieze,* **Carrer de la Palla** *is another inviting shopping street (described under "Shopping in Barcelona," later). But let's head left through Plaça Nova to take in the mighty...*

❻ Barcelona Cathedral

The **facade** is a virtual catalog of Gothic motifs. There's the pointed arch over the entrance and the stained-glass windows with elaborate stone tracery. Statues of robed saints stand in niches, and winged

angels teeter on the octagonal bell towers. And the whole thing is topped with three tall steeples. These pointy spires are meant to give the impression of a church flickering with spiritual fires. This was the Gothic style called Flamboyant—meaning "flame-like."

This has been Barcelona's holiest spot for 2,000 years. The Romans built their temple of Jupiter right here. In AD 343, that pagan temple was replaced by a Christian cathedral. Around the year 1000, that building was replaced again, this time by a Romanesque-style church. The current Gothic structure was started around 1300, during the medieval glory days of the Catalan nation, and finished in 1450. But the much newer facade, dating from the 1800s, is in the Neo-Gothic style of Modernisme. That part of the construction was capped in 1913 with the central spire, 230 feet tall. So, in a way, the cathedral is evidence of Barcelona's two "golden ages"—its seaport heyday in the 1300s, and its 19th-century revival.

The square in front of the cathedral is **Pla de la Seu,** which is flanked on the left by a building housing a small TI and the Diocesan Museum of Barcelona. The area in front of the cathedral is where Barcelonans dance the patriotic dance called the *sardana* on weekends.

The cathedral's **interior**—with its vast space, peaceful cloister, and many ornate chapels—is worth a visit (see listing under "Sights in Barcelona," later). If you interrupt this tour to visit the cathedral now, you'll exit the cloister a block down Carrer del Bisbe. From there you can circle back to the right, following the wall of the cathedral to visit stop #7—or skip #7 and step directly into stop #8.

As you stand in the square facing the cathedral, look far to your left to see the multicolored, wavy canopy marking the roofline of the **Santa Caterina Market.** The busy street between here and the market—called Via Laietana—is the boundary between the Barri Gòtic and the funkier, edgier **El Born** neighborhood.

• *For now, return to the Roman towers and pass between them to head up Carrer del Bisbe. Take an immediate left, up the ramp to the entrance of...*

❼ Casa de l'Ardiaca

It's free to enter this mansion that was once the archdeacon's residence and now functions as the city archives (closed Sun). The elaborately carved doorway is Renaissance. To the right of the doorway is a carved mail slot by 19th-century Modernista architect Lluís Domènech i Montaner. Enter a small courtyard with a fountain. Notice how the century-old palm tree seems to be held captive by urban man. Next, step inside the air-conditioned lobby of the city archives, where—along the back of the ancient Roman wall—there are often free exhibits. At the left end of the lobby, go

Independence for Catalunya?

In much of Spain, you'll find four languages on ATM screens, and all are native to Spain: Spanish—spoken by most of the population; Euskara—used by the Basques in the far north; Galician—used by the Celtic people of the northwest; and Catalan—the language of the northeast Catalunya region, including Barcelona. The country is more complicated than many realize.

For decades, the ETA, a Basque group, dominated separatist news from Spain. But that group dissolved in 2018, laying down its weapons after an almost 50-year and, at times, violent struggle for independence. More recently Catalunya has been in the news, with its own bold independence movement, and Spain, for its hard stance against Catalan separatists.

Pro-independence Catalans explain the situation to me like this: Tensions rose in 2017 when Catalunya wanted the right to put a referendum on independence before voters (like Scotland). The central government in Madrid said "no" and sent 4,000 police officers to Barcelona to enforce a ban on the vote. But in October the Catalan people held the referendum anyway: stay or leave.

Despite peaceful demonstrations (even in the face of police violence), Spain maintained the vote to leave was illegal and charged several Catalan leaders with rebellion and sedition. The Catalan president fled the country rather than go to jail.

Many Europeans were shocked by the harsh reaction from Madrid. Many Spaniards were upset that it wasn't stronger. And Catalunya itself is sadly divided. Those who oppose Catalan independence still feel loyal to the region—they're just not in favor of splitting away. And those passionate for a completely independent Catalunya consider those who oppose them to be turncoats.

Catalunya has lived as part of Spain for centuries. So why did the Catalans decide to break? They tell me it's because the central government in Madrid has become

through the archway and look down into the stairwell for a peek at more impressive Roman stonework. Back in the courtyard, climb to the balcony for views of the cathedral steeple and gargoyles. From this vantage point, note the small Romanesque chapel on the right (the only surviving 13th-century bit of the cathedral) and how it's dwarfed by the towering cathedral.

• *Return to Carrer del Bisbe and turn left. After a few steps, you reach a small square with a bronze statue ensemble.*

right-wing and regressive—repeatedly overriding domestic initiatives better left to the Catalan people.

Just as Vermont is more liberal than Wyoming, Catalunya is more liberal than mainstream Spain. Catalan laws that would have prohibited bullfighting, banned fracking, protected Catalunya's cultural heritage, and taxed nuclear energy, corporations, and banks in creative ways to help society (common initiatives among other European nations) were opposed and overturned by Madrid. The central government even decreed that if one child in a Catalan school asks that the Spanish language be used, the entire class must be taught in Spanish rather than Catalan. From a Barcelona perspective, national news coverage of these issues is biased in favor of Madrid. And in much of the Catalan press, it's biased in the other direction.

Catalunya has become a divided society, split by the question: Are you for independence or are you a Spanish nationalist? In Catalunya, pro-independence is politically correct, and Spanish nationalists are often insulted as "fascists." Catalans who want to stay with Spain feel that the separatists are driving a wedge between themselves and the rest of society. Many very patriotic Catalans believe they can be adequately autonomous without leaving Spain. It's an awkward discussion (not unlike the political dynamic in the US today).

The unfortunate thing about independence votes is that they are all or nothing. Most people would like something in the middle—which so far hasn't been an option. Madrid's aggressive response to this latest surge for Catalan independence is driving many longtime Spanish nationalists and moderates into the independence camp.

It's a bit like David and Goliath. But David is not always right. A Catalan friend who is against separating makes the case that the real victim is Catalan society, as now there is no longer a single "Catalan people." The society is losing its ability to talk together. He misses the good old days when, on the feast of St. George (Jordi, Catalunya's patron saint), the roses given in his honor were all red—not (as now) yellow, the color of protest. Only time will tell what the future holds for Catalunya.

❽ Monument to the Martyrs of Independence

Five Barcelona patriots—including two priests—calmly receive their last rites before being garroted (strangled) for resisting Napoleon's occupation of Spain in the early 19th century. They'd been outraged by French atrocities in Madrid (depicted in Goya's famous *Third of May* painting in Madrid's Prado Museum). According to the plaque marking their mortal remains, these martyrs to independence gave their lives in 1809 *"por Dios, por la Patria, y por el Rey"*—for God, country, and king.

• Exit the square down tiny Carrer de Montjuïc del Bisbe (to the right as you face the martyrs). This leads to the cute...

❾ Plaça Sant Felip Neri

This shaded square serves as the playground of an elementary school and is often bursting with energetic kids speaking Catalan (just a couple of generations ago, this would have been illegal and they would be speaking Spanish). It's a fun scene to enjoy at a respectful distance (no photos of the children, please).

The Church of Sant Felip Neri, which Gaudí attended, is still pocked with bomb damage from the Spanish Civil War. As a stronghold of democratic, anti-Franco forces, Barcelona saw a lot of fighting. The shrapnel that damaged this church was meant for the nearby Catalan government building (Palau de la Generalitat, which we'll see later on this walk).

Just as the Germans practiced their new air force technology in Guernica in the years leading up to World War II, the fascist friends of Franco (both German and Italian) also helped bomb Barcelona from the air. As was the fascist tactic, a second bombing followed the first as survivors combed the rubble for lost loved ones. A plaque on the wall (left of church door) honors the 42 killed—mostly children—in that 1938 aerial bombardment.

The buildings here were paid for by the guilds that powered the local economy. The shoemakers guild (to the right of the arch where you entered the square) is decorated above the windows with reliefs depicting boots.

*• Exit the square past the fun **Sabater Hermanos** artisanal soap shop, and head down Carrer de Sant Felip Neri. At the T-intersection, turn right onto Carrer de Sant Sever, then immediately left on Carrer de Salomó Ben Adret. You've entered the...*

❿ Jewish Quarter (El Call)

In Catalan, a Jewish quarter goes by the name El Call—literally "narrow passage," for the tight lanes where medieval Jews were forced to live, under the watchful eye of the nearby cathedral. (Some believe El Call comes from the Hebrew *kahal*, which means congregation.) At the peak of Barcelona's El Call, some 4,000 Jews were crammed into just a few alleys in this neighborhood.

Walk down Carrer de Salomó Ben Adret, and pass through the charming little square (a gap in the dense tangle of medieval buildings cleared by another civil war bomb), where you will find a

rust-colored sign displaying a map of the Jewish Quarter. Take the next lane to the right (Carrer de Marlet). On the right is the (literally) low-profile, four-foot-high entrance to what in the Middle Ages was likely Barcelona's **main synagogue** (Antigua Sinagoga Mayor, €2 to enter Tue-Fri 11:00-14:00 and Sun 11:00-15:00, free to enter Sun 16:00-19:00, closed Mon and Sat, shorter hours off-season).

The structure dates from the third century, but it was destroyed during a brutal pogrom in 1391. The city's remaining Jews were expelled in 1492, and artifacts of their culture—including this synagogue—were forgotten for centuries. In the 1980s, a historian tracked down the synagogue using old tax-collection records. Another clue that this was the main synagogue: In accordance with Jewish traditions, it stubbornly faces east (toward Jerusalem), putting it at an angle at odds with surrounding structures. You can visit the synagogue interior (admission includes a little tour by the attendant if you ask). The sparse interior includes access to two small subterranean rooms with Roman walls topped by a medieval Catalan vault. Look through the glass floor to see dyeing vats used for a shop that later occupied this site, run by former Jews who had been forcibly converted to Christianity.

• *From the synagogue, start back the way you came but then continue straight ahead, onto Carrer de la Fruita. At the T-intersection, turn left, then right, to find your way back to the Martyrs statue. From here, we'll turn right down Carrer del Bisbe to the...*

⑪ Carrer del Bisbe Bridge

This has been a main street since the days of ancient Barcino. The Romans built straight streets on a rectangular grid plan, and this one led to their town center.

Arching across Carrer del Bisbe is a medieval-looking sky-bridge. This structure—reminiscent of Venice's Bridge of Sighs—connects the Catalan government building (on the right) with what was the Catalan president's ceremonial residence (on the left). Though the bridge appears to be centuries old, it was constructed in the 1920s by Catalan architect Joan Rubió (a follower of Gaudí), who also did the carved ornamentation on the buildings.

• *Continue along Carrer del Bisbe to...*

⑫ Plaça de Sant Jaume

This stately central square of the Barri Gòtic takes its name from the Church of St. James (in Catalan: Jaume, JOW-mah) that once stood here. After the church was torn down in 1823, the square was fixed up and rechristened "Plaça de la Constitució" in honor of the then decade-old Spanish constitution. But the plucky Catalans

never embraced the name, and after Franco, they went back to the original—even though the church is long gone.

Set at the intersection of ancient Barcino's main thoroughfares, this square was once a Roman forum. In that sense, it's been the seat of city government for 2,000 years.

For more than six centuries, the **Palau de la Generalitat** (on the uphill side of the square) has housed the offices of the autonomous government of Catalunya. It always flies the Catalan flag next to the obligatory Spanish one. Above the building's doorway is Catalunya's patron saint—St. George (Jordi), slaying the dragon. The dragon (which you'll see all over town) is an important Catalan symbol. From these balconies, the nation's leaders (and soccer heroes) greet the people on momentous days. The square is often the site of festivals or demonstrations.

Facing the Generalitat across the square is the **Barcelona City Hall** (Casa de la Ciutat). It sports a statue (in the niche to the left of the door) of a different James—"Jaume el Conqueridor." The 13th-century King Jaume I is credited with freeing Barcelona from French control, granting self-government, and setting it on course to become a major city. He was the driving force behind construction of the Royal Palace (which we'll see shortly).

Look left and right down the main streets branching off the square; they're lined with ironwork streetlamps and balconies draped with plants. Carrer de Ferran, which leads to the Ramblas, is classic Barcelona.

In ancient Roman days, when Plaça de Sant Jaume was the town's central square, two main streets converged here—the Decumanus (Carrer del Bisbe—bishop's street) and the Cardus (Carrer de la Llibreteria/Carrer del Call). The forum's biggest building was a massive temple of Augustus, which we'll see next.

• *Facing the Generalitat, exit the square going up the second street to the right of the building, on tiny Carrer del Paradís.*
Follow this street as it turns right. When it swings left, pause at #10, the entrance to the...

⑬ Roman Temple of Augustus (Temple Roma d'August)

You're standing at the summit of Mont Tàber, the Barri Gòtic's highest spot. A plaque on the wall by the entrance reads: "Mont Tàber, 16.9 meters" (elevation 55 feet). At your feet, a millstone inlaid in the pavement also marks a momentous spot. It was here that the ancient Romans founded the town of Barcino around 12 BC. They built a *castrum* (fort) on

the hilltop, protecting the harbor, and this temple to honor their emperor, Augustus.

Go inside for a peek at the last vestiges of the imposing Roman temple (free, Tue-Sat 10:00-19:00, Sun until 20:00, Mon until 14:00). All that's left are four columns and some fragments of the transept and its plinth (good English info on-site). The huge columns, dating from the late first century BC, are as old as Barcelona itself. They were part of the ancient town's biggest structure, dedicated to Augustus, who was worshipped as a god. These Corinthian columns (with deep fluting and topped with leafy capitals) were the back corner of a 120-foot-long temple that extended from here to Barcino's forum...Plaça de Sant Jaume (where you just were).

• *Continue down Carrer del Paradís one block. When you bump into the back end of the cathedral, pause to notice how amazingly well-preserved the cityscape is here, under an assembly of gargoyles.*

Take a right, going down Carrer de la Pietat/Baixada de Santa Clara. (Is that a unicorn gargoyle on the side of the church? A unigoyle?) Go 100 yards until you emerge into a square called...

⑩ Plaça del Rei

This square is a great place to end our walk, as it calls up Barcelona's medieval golden age. The buildings enclosing the square recall the city's medieval past. The central section (topped by a five-story addition) was the core of the **Royal Palace** (Palau Reial Major). A vast hall on its ground floor once served as the throne room and reception room. From the 13th to the 15th century, the Royal Palace housed Barcelona's counts as well as the resident kings of Aragon. One of those kings of Aragon, Ferdinand, married Isabel, queen of Castile, creating the united country of Spain. In 1493, here in this Royal Palace, they hosted a triumphant Christopher Columbus, accompanied by six New World natives (whom he called "*indios*") and several pure-gold statues. King Ferdinand and Queen Isabel welcomed him home and honored him with the title "Admiral of the Oceans."

To the right is the palace's church, the 14th-century **Chapel of Santa Agatha,** where royalty worshipped. The venerable church sits atop the foundations of a Roman wall (entrance included in Barcelona History Museum admission; see page 84).

To the left is the **Viceroy's Palace** (Palau del Lloctinent). It was built in the 1500s for the right-hand man of the Spanish monarch, who was now located in far-off Castile. So, in a way, this building represents the rise of Spain and the decline of Aragon, Catalunya, and the city of Barcelona. Catalunya was swallowed up into greater Spain, the Royal Palace was demoted to a small regional residence, and Barcelona declined.

Step into the interior courtyard, a delightful Renaissance

space with a fine staircase and coffered wood ceiling. Over the years, this building served as the local headquarters of the Spanish Inquisition. It currently houses the historical archives of the crown of Aragon. Among their treasures is the so-called **Santa Fe Capitulations**—the 1492 contract between Columbus and the Catholic Monarchs that set the terms for his upcoming sea voyage. (The document is rarely on display but there's often a poster of it on the courtyard wall.)

• *Our walk is over. While you're here, you could check out the Plaça del Rei branch of the **Barcelona History Museum**, starring some excavated Roman ruins. (For a peek at the Roman streets without going in, look through the low windows lining the street.)*

It's easy to get your bearings by backtracking to either Plaça de Sant Jaume or the cathedral. The Jaume I Metro stop is two blocks away (leave the square on Carrer del Veguer and turn left). From here, you could head over to the Santa Caterina Market or simply wander through more of this area, enjoying Barcelona at its Gothic best.

Sights in Barcelona

For the most popular sights (the Picasso Museum and the big Modernista sights—Sagrada Família, Park Güell, Casa Batlló, and La Pedrera), make online reservations well in advance. For general tips, see the "Sightseeing" section in the Practicalities chapter.

∩ Many of the following sights are also covered in my free Barcelona City Walk and Eixample Walk audio tours.

NEAR THE RAMBLAS

The Ramblas, Barcelona's most famous boulevard, flows from Plaça de Catalunya, past the core of the Barri Gòtic, to the harborfront Columbus Monument. Several sights located along this main boulevard are covered in my "Ramblas Ramble" self-guided walk, including the booming La Boqueria Market (worth ▲ and described on page 57) and the Columbus Monument (page 61). The following sights are located just off the Ramblas.

▲Palau Güell

Just as the Picasso Museum reveals a young genius on the verge of a breakthrough, this early building by Antoni Gaudí (completed in 1890) shows the architect taking his first tentative steps toward what would become his trademark curvy style. Dark and masculine, with castle-like rooms, Palau Güell (pronounced "gway")

BARCELONA

was custom built to house the wealthy Güell family and gives an insight into Gaudí's artistic genius. The rooftop has his signature colorful tile mosaic chimneys and offers a panorama of the city. While some people will find this redundant if also visiting La Pedrera, others will appreciate this exquisite building for its delightfully loopy rooftop and far fewer crowds.

Cost and Hours: €12 timed-entry ticket includes good audioguide—buy in advance online, free first Sun of the month; open Tue-Sun 10:00-20:00, Nov-March until 17:30, closed Mon year-round; last entry one hour before closing, rooftop closes when raining; guided tour in English Sat at 10:30; a half-block off the Ramblas at Carrer Nou de la Rambla 3, Metro: Liceu or Drassanes, +34 934 725 775, www.palauguell.cat.

▲Maritime Museum (Museu Marítim)

Barcelona's medieval shipyard, the best preserved in the entire Mediterranean, is home to an excellent museum near the bottom of the Ramblas. The museum's per-

manent collection covers the salty history of ships and navigation from the 13th to the 18th century (restoration projects on their permanent collection will eventually reveal pieces from the 18th to the 20th century). Even if you choose not to pay for a full visit, the building is worth a look; interesting free exhibits are in the lobby (inside the main entrance facing the water), where you can get a glimpse of the building's interior.

Cost and Hours: €10, free Sun from 15:00 and for kids 16 and under, ticket includes visit to *Santa Eulàlia* boat; open daily 10:00-20:00, last entry one hour before closing; nice café with seating inside or out on the museum courtyard (free to enter), Avinguda de les Drassanes, Metro: Drassanes, +34 933 429 920, www.mmb.cat.

Visiting the Museum: The building's cavernous halls evoke the 14th-century days when Catalunya was a naval and shipbuilding power, cranking out 30 huge galleys each winter. As in the US today, military and commercial ventures mingled as Catalunya built its trading empire.

Start your visit by going up the ramp to the right and into

BARCELONA

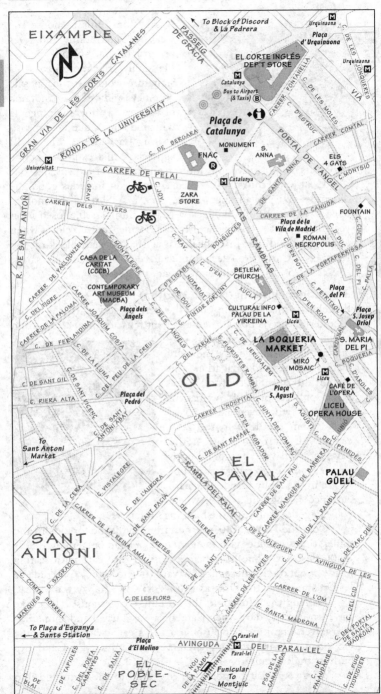

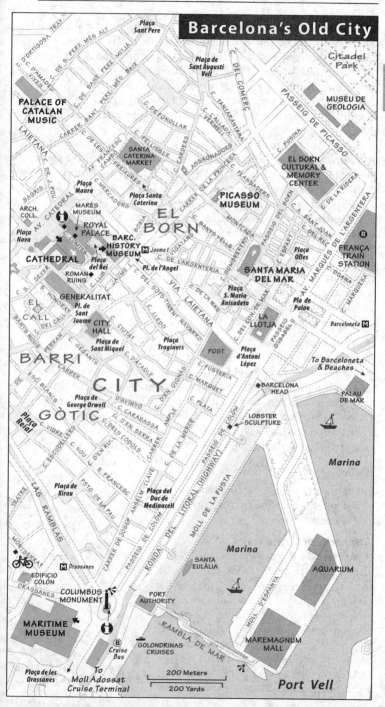

BARCELONA

Barcelona's Old City

Plaça Sant Pere

Plaça de Sant Augustí Vell

Citadel Park

MUSEU DE GEOLOGIA

PASSEIG DE PICASSO

C. D'ORTIGOSA, TRAF.
C. DE S. PERE MÉS ALT
C. DAMADEU VIVES
C. DE SANT PERE MÉS BAIX

PALACE OF CATALAN MUSIC

CARRER SANT PERE MÉS MITJA
C. DE LES
AV. FRANCESC CAMBÓ
C. DE FONOLLAR
C. L'ALLADA TERMEL
C. TANTARANTANA
C. PELLISSER
C. DE LES FREIXURES

SANTA CATERINA MARKET

C. MERCADERS
C. ASSAONADORS
C. CARDERS

EL BORN CULTURAL & MEMORY CENTER

C. DE LA RIBERA
C. DE LA PRINCESA
C. FLASSADERS
C. FUSINA

Plaça Maura

Plaça Santa Caterina

C. DE LA PRINCESA

PICASSO MUSEUM

C. DE LES CAPUTXES

ARCH. COLL.
MARÈS MUSEUM
AV. CATEDRAL

EL BORN

C. BANYS VELLS
C. MONTCADA
PASSEIG DEL BORN
C. A. SANT-JOAN

Plaça Nova

ROYAL PALACE

COMTES
C. VIGATANS

C. DE REC
C. DE REC COMERÇ

R
FRANÇA TRAIN STATION

CATHEDRAL

BARC. HISTORY MUSEUM
Jaume I
Plaça del Rei
C. L'ARGENTERIA
Pl. de l'Angel

C. DE L'ESPART
AV. MARQUES DE L'ARGENTERA
C. DUANA
C. MARQUESA

ROMAN RUINS
C. SEVER
C. S. HONORAT
C. LLIBRE
C. JAUME
GENERALITAT
C. DEL BOTS-TINENT NAVARRO

VIA LAIETANA

SANTA MARIA DEL MAR
Plaça S. Maria Anisadeta
Pla de Palau
Plaça Olles

Barceloneta M

EL CALL
BANYS NOUS
C. DEL CALL
Pl. de Sant Jaume
C. LLEDÓ
C. DE LA MAR
C. DE LA NAU

C. FERRAN

CITY HALL
C. CIUTAT
Plaça de Sant Miquel
C. DATAULF
Plaça Traginers

C. DEL CON DE MAR
LA LLOTJA
PASSEIG D'ISABEL II

BARRI
C. GEGANTS
C. N'EN GIGNAS
C. MARQUET

POST

Plaça d'Antoni López

To Barceloneta & Beaches

CITY
C. D'AVINYO
C. CARABASSA
C. PLATA
C. FUSTERIA

BARCELONA HEAD

PALAU DE MAR

Plaça de George Orwell
C. N'EN SERRA
C. DE LA MERCE

GÒTIC
C. DELS CODOLS
C. N'EN RULL
C. AMPLE

LOBSTER SCULPTURE

Plaça Reial
C. VIDRE
C. ESCUDELLERS
C. NOU

PASSEIG DE COLÓM

Marina

LAS RAMBLAS
C. S. FRANCESC
PSTG. DE LA PAU
PASSEIG DE JOSEP ANSELM CLAVÉ

Plaça de Xirau
Plaça del Duc de Medinaceli

MOLL DE LA FUSTA

MONTSERRAT
M Drassanes
RONDA DEL LITORAL (HIGHWAY)

Marina

EDIFICIO COLÓN
DRASSANES

SANTA EULÀLIA

AQUARIUM

COLUMBUS MONUMENT
PORT AUTHORITY

MOLL D'ESPANYA

MARITIME MUSEUM

Plaça de les Drassanes

B Cruise Bus
To Moll Adossat Cruise Terminal

GOLONDRINAS CRUISES
RAMBLA DE MAR

MAREMAGNUM MALL

200 Meters
200 Yards

Port Vell

a movie-screening room, where a **film** (in Castilian and Catalan) tells the history of shipyards and galleys. In the next room is a model of the *drassanes* (shipyards) building, which today contains the Maritime Museum. Head into the next room and, on the far right, find a **model** of 15th-century Barcelona's waterfront. Notice the shipyard all the way to the left, the old medieval walls surrounding the city, and the Church of Santa Maria del Mar to the right.

Then head to the highlight: the impressively huge and richly decorated replica of the royal galley *Juan de Austria,* which fought in the 1571 Battle of Lepanto. Displays describe its history and daily life on a galley. To get a seagulls' eye view, go up the stairs to a raised platform at the bow and midship.

Nearby: Your museum ticket includes entrance to the *Santa Eulàlia,* an early 20th-century schooner docked a short walk from the Columbus Monument (otherwise €3, Tue-Fri and Sun 10:00-20:30, Sat 14:00-20:30, shorter hours Nov-March, closed Mon year-round). On Saturday mornings, you can sail around the harbor on the schooner for three hours—reserve well in advance (Sat 11:00-13:00, €15 for adults, €9 for kids 7-14, +34 933 429 920, reserves.mmaritim@diba.cat).

Golondrinas Cruises

At the harbor near the Columbus Monument, tourist boats called *golondrinas* offer two unguided trips, giving you a view of Barcelona's (unimpressive) skyline from the water. The shorter version goes around the harbor in 40 minutes (€7.70, departures Sat-Sun 11:15-17:15). The hour-long cruise goes beyond the harbor (€9.50, departures daily 12:00-17:00, Sat-Sun also at 18:00, more in summer, fewer in winter, +34 934 423 106, www.lasgolondrinas.com).

BARRI GÒTIC

For more details on this area and several of the following sights, see the Barri Gòtic Walk, earlier.

▲Barcelona Cathedral (Catedral de Barcelona)

The city's 14th-century, Gothic-style cathedral (with a Neo-Gothic facade) has played a significant role in Barcelona's history—but as far as grand cathedrals go, this one is relatively unexciting. Still, it's worth a visit to see its richly decorated chapels, finely carved choir, tomb of Santa Eulàlia, and restful cloister with gurgling fountains and resident geese. Minor sights within in-

clude an ornately carved choir, a rooftop terrace, and an altarpiece museum.

Cost and Hours: €9 includes cathedral, choir, terrace, museum, and cloister. Cathedral open Mon-Fri 10:00-18:00, Sat until 17:00, Sun 14:00-17:00. Note that access may be limited during services.

Information: +34 933 428 262, www.catedralbcn.org.

Dress Code: The dress code is strictly enforced; don't wear tank tops, shorts, or skirts above the knee.

Tours: An audioguide is included and handed out at the entrance.

🎧 Download my free Barcelona City Walk audio tour, which includes a tour of the cathedral interior.

Visiting the Cathedral: This has been Barcelona's holiest spot for 2,000 years. The Romans built their Temple of Jupiter here. In AD 343, the pagan temple was replaced with a Christian cathedral. That building was supplanted by a Romanesque-style church (11th century). The current Gothic structure was started in 1298 and finished in 1450, during the medieval glory days of the Catalan nation. The facade was humble, so in the 19th century the proud local bourgeoisie (enjoying a second golden age) redid it in a more ornate, Neo-Gothic style. Construction was capped in 1913 with the central spire, 230 feet tall.

The nave is ringed with 28 **chapels.** Besides creating worship spaces, the walls defining these chapels serve as interior buttresses supporting the roof (which is why the exterior walls are smooth, without the normal Gothic buttresses outside). Barcelona honors many of the homegrown saints found in these chapels with public holidays. In the middle of the nave, the 15th-century choir *(coro)* features ornately carved stalls. During the standing parts of the Mass, the chairs were folded up, but VIPs still had those little wooden ledges to lean on. Each was creatively carved and—since you couldn't sit on sacred things—the artists were free to enjoy some secular and naughty fun here.

Look behind the **high altar** (beneath the crucifix) to find the bishop's chair (cathedra). As a cathedral, this church is the bishop's seat—hence its Catalan nickname of *La Seu.* To the left of the altar is the organ and the elevator up to the terrace. To the right of the altar, the wall is decorated with Catalunya's yellow-and-red coat of arms.

Steps beneath the altar lead to the **crypt,** featuring the marble-and-alabaster sarcophagus (1327-1339) containing the remains of Santa Eulàlia. The cathedral is dedicated to this saint. Thirteen-year-old Eulàlia, daughter of a prominent Barcelona family, was martyred by the Romans for her faith in AD 304. Murky legends say she was subjected to 13 tortures.

The **elevator** in the left transept takes you up to the rooftop **terrace** for an expansive city view.

Otherwise, exit through the right transept to enter the cloister. Its arcaded walkway surrounds a lush circa-1450 courtyard. Ahhhh. It's a tropical atmosphere of palm, orange, and magnolia trees; a fish pond; trickling fountains; and squawking geese.

As you wander the cloister (clockwise), check out the **coats of arms** as well as the **tombs** in the pavement. These were for rich merchants who paid good money to be buried as close to the altar as possible. A few pavement stones here and there have the symbols of their trades: scissors, shoes, bakers, and so on. The resident **geese** have been here for at least 500 years. There are always 13, in memory of Eulàlia's 13 years and 13 torments.

The little museum has the six-foot-tall 14th-century **Great Monstrance**—a ceremonial display case for the communion wafer that's paraded through the streets during the Corpus Christi festival.

▲*Sardana* Dances

If you're in town on a weekend, you can see the *sardana*, a patriotic dance in which Barcelonans link hands and dance in a circle (Sun at 11:15, many Sat at 18:00, no dances in Aug, event lasts 1-2 hours, in Pla de la Seu square in front of the cathedral; see sidebar).

▲Frederic Marès Museum (Museu Frederic Marès)

This delightful museum, adjacent to the cathedral, features the eclectic collection of Frederic Marès (1893-1991), a local sculp-

tor and packrat. The museum sprawls through several old Barri Gòtic buildings around a peaceful courtyard. It offers a fascinating look at ancient Roman statues from this region and is an exquisite warehouse of Romanesque and Gothic Christian art from Catalunya.

Cost and Hours: €4.20, free first Sun of the month and all other Sun from 15:00; open Tue-Sat 10:00-19:00, Sun until 20:00, closed Mon; essential audioguide-€1, Plaça de Sant Iu 5, Metro: Jaume I, +34 932 563 500, www.museumares.bcn.cat.

Eating: The tranquil courtyard café offers a pleasant break, even when the museum is closed (café open spring and summer only, until 22:00).

Circle Dances in Squares and Castles in the Air

From circle dancing to human towers, Catalans are proud of their distinctive, cultural traditions.

For many, the slow-motion *sardana* dance is a patriotic display of Catalan unity, while for others, it's a fun chance to kick up their heels. To dance the *sardana*, partici-  pants form a circle, often on a public square. Holding hands with their arms raised, they gracefully step and hop to the music. The band consists of a long flute, oboes, strange-looking brass instruments, and a bongo-like drum.

All are welcome to join in, even tourists cursed with two left feet. Dances are held in the square in front of the cathedral on Sundays at 11:15 and many Saturdays at 18:00 (none in August). Put your day bag in the center of your circle, as other participants do, to guard against theft.

Another Catalan tradition is the castell, a tower erected solely of people. Towers can be up to 10 humans high. The burliest form the base, supporting the *manilles* ("handles") who help haul others to the top, including the smallest of all, who becomes the steeple. Spotters cluster around the base in case anyone falls. *Castelleres* are judged on how quickly they build their towers and how fast they dismantle them. Castells pop up at festivals (such as Festa Major de Gràcia in mid-August and La Mercè in late September) and usually in the cathedral square on spring and summer Saturdays at 19:30.

Both traditions—the *sardana* and castells—require group participation, which is fitting for Catalunya, known for its community spirit. Keeping its traditions and language alive, Catalans proudly say, *"Visca Catalunya!"* (Long live Catalunya!)

▲Barcelona History Museum—Plaça del Rei (Museu d'Història de Barcelona)

At the Plaça del Rei branch of the city history museum (MUHBA for short), you'll see objects gathered from archaeological digs around Barcelona. But the real highlight is an underground labyrinth of excavated Roman ruins. Though the museum is housed in part of the former Royal Palace complex, you'll see only a bit of that grand space. Instead, the focus is on the exhibits on the basement level. The included audioguide provides informative, if dry, descriptions of the exhibits; you'll also find abundant English

handouts and a handful of video screens showing what this site must have once looked like in ancient times.

Cost and Hours: €7; includes audioguide and other MUHBA branches; free first Sun of month and all other Sun from 15:00—but no audioguide during free times; open Tue-Sat 10:00-19:00, Sun until 20:00, closed Mon; Plaça del Rei, enter on Carrer del Veguer, Metro: Jaume I, +34 932 562 122, www.barcelona.cat/museuhistoria/en.

Visiting the Museum: Start with the 10-minute introductory video in the **theater** (at the end of the ground floor). Then take an elevator down 65 feet (and 2,000 years—see the date spin back as you descend) to the **basement** to stroll the now-underground streets of Roman Barcino—founded by Emperor Augustus around 10 BC.

The history is so strong here, you can smell it as you stroll across walkways over the excavated ruins of Roman Barcelona. This was a working-class part of town. The route leads through areas used for laundering clothes and dyeing garments, the remains of a factory that salted fish and produced *garum* (a fish-derived sauce used extensively in ancient Roman cooking), and facilities for winemaking. Next, wander through bits of a seventh-century early Christian church and an 11th-century bishop's palace that show Barcelona through its glory days in the Middle Ages. The final section downstairs takes you through Visigothic remains, including the octagonal font where Christians were baptized.

Finally, head upstairs (or ride the elevator to floor 0) to see a **model** of the city from the early 16th century. From here, you can enter **Tinell Hall** (part of the Royal Palace), with its long, graceful, rounded vaults and displays on local medieval history in a Mediterranean context. The nearby 14th-century **Chapel of St. Agatha** sometimes has free temporary exhibits.

EL BORN

El Born (Metro: Jaume I) is home to the Picasso Museum, with narrow lanes sprouting from the neighborhood's main artery, Passeig del Born.

▲▲▲Picasso Museum (Museu Picasso)

Pablo Picasso may have made his career in Paris, but the years he spent in Barcelona—from age 14 through 23—were among the most formative of his life. It was here that young Pablo mastered the realistic painting style of his artistic forebears—and it was also here that he first felt the freedom that allowed him to leave that all behind and give in to his creative, experimental urges. When he left Barcelona, Picasso headed for Paris...and revolutionized art forever.

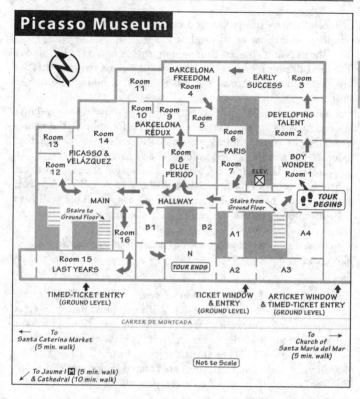

The pieces in this excellent museum capture that priceless moment just before this bold young thinker changed the world. You'll also see works from his twilight years. It's the top collection of Picassos in his native country.

Cost and Hours: €12 for timed-entry ticket to permanent collection; free Thu evening 16:00-19:00 and all day first Sun of month, note you must also reserve free hours (up to four days in advance); open Mon 10:00-17:00, Tue-Sun 9:00-20:30, Thu until 21:30; Nov-mid-March Tue-Sun 9:00-19:00, Thu until 21:30, closed Mon; audioguide-€5, Carrer de Montcada 15, +34 932 563 000, www.museupicasso.bcn.cat.

Reservations and Ticketing Tips: Buy a timed-entry ticket in advance at the museum website. While tickets are sold at the door, there's nearly always a long line, and the museum often sells out.

The museum's website can be temperamental—keep trying; if you're unsuccessful, buy an **Articket BCN** when you arrive (for pass details, see page 38). An Articket BCN allows you to enter the galleries whenever you wish (stop first at the Articket window

to receive a museum ticket; you can also buy an Articket at this window—there may be a short line).

The museum's busiest times are mornings before 13:00, all day Tue, and during free entry times. Day-of tickets (when available) are also sold online (must purchase at least 2 hours before your visit).

Getting In: The galleries sit one floor above a free-to-enter courtyard with several entrances. Tickets are sold at the center ground-floor entry; those with timed tickets can enter to either side. Articket BCN-holders enter to the right.

Getting There: It's on Carrer de Montcada; the general ticket office is in the courtyard at #19, and the Articket BCN booth is at #23. From the Jaume I Metro stop, it's a five-minute walk. It's a 10-minute walk from the cathedral and many parts of the Barri Gòtic.

Services: The ground floor has a required bag check, a bookshop, and WC.

◒ Self-Guided Tour

The Picasso Museum's collection of nearly 300 paintings is presented more or less chronologically. With good text panels in every room providing context, it's easy to follow the evolution of Picasso's work. This tour (like the museum itself) is arranged by the stages of his life and art. Don't be surprised if a painting described here is not on view. Individual paintings are rotated in and out constantly (to keep it interesting for locals and repeat visitors). But the themes and chronology remain constant.

Boy Wonder (Room 1)

Pablo's earliest art is realistic and earnest. His work quickly advanced from childish pencil drawings (from about 1890), through a series of technically skilled **art-school works** (copies of plaster feet and arms), to oil paintings of impressive technique. Pablo was born in 1881, so you can easily calculate how amazingly young he was when he painted these works. His **portraits**—of grizzled peasants, family members, and himself (at age 15)—demonstrate surprising psychological insight. Though Pablo dabbled in landscapes, still lifes, and everyday scenes, he was always, first and foremost, a painter of people.

Developing Talent (Room 2)

Pablo moved to Barcelona at age 14. During a summer trip to Málaga (his birthplace and boyhood home) in 1896, he experimented with a series of fresh, Impressionistic-style landscapes (relatively rare in Spain at the time). As a 15-year-old, Pablo dutifully entered art-school competitions. A case along the wall shows off his art-school studies, Barcelona scenes from 1896 (allowing you to see

the city through Picasso's eyes), and classical studies of the human body.

His first big work, *First Communion*, tackled a prescribed religious subject, but Picasso made it an excuse to paint his family. His sister Lola was the model for the communicant, and the man beside her has the face of Picasso's father.

You may find a touching portrait of his mother, with a cameo-like face and fine details in her white blouse. Find the portrait of his aunt **Tía Pepa,** painted in Málaga in 1896 (this and other family portraits are frequently rotated). It's said Picasso painted this in less than a day. Notice how ably he captured the toughness of his aunt.

Early Success (Room 3)

In the large, classically painted *Science and Charity* (1897), Picasso used realistic means to represent subjects of social concern—a technique typical of the social realism movement of the late 19th century. The doctor (modeled on Pablo's father) represents science. The nun represents charity and religion. From the hopeless face and lifeless hand of the sick woman, it seems that Picasso believes nothing will save her from death.

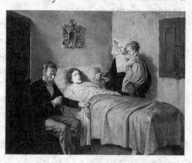

Science and Charity won second prize at a fine-arts exhibition, earning Picasso the chance to study in Madrid. Stifled by the stuffy art school there, he hung out instead in the Prado Museum and learned by copying earlier Spanish masters, especially Diego Velázquez, with whom he developed a virtual friendship. An example of Picasso's impressive mimicry is sometimes displayed in this room—a nearly perfect copy of a **portrait of Philip IV** by Velázquez. (Near the end of this tour, we'll see a much older Picasso riffing on another Velázquez painting.)

In this room you'll also see outdoor views of Madrid (mostly in Retiro Park) and rural village scenes. In 1898 Pablo fell sick and was sent to convalesce in the mountain village of Horta de Sant Joan. Away from his father and the conservative art establishment in Madrid, his creative spirit was freed. You can sense that Picasso was finding his artistic independence as he painted these landscapes and scenes of village life.

Barcelona Freedom (Room 4)

After regaining his health, Picasso returned to Barcelona in 1900. Art Nouveau was all the rage there. He quit art school and fell in with an avant-garde crowd. These bohemians congregated daily

at Els Quatre Gats ("The Four Cats," a popular restaurant to this day—see page 65). Picasso even created the **menu cover** for this favorite hangout. Further establishing his artistic freedom, he painted often dark and brooding **portraits** of his new friends (including Carlos Casagemas and Jaume Sabartés, who later became Picasso's personal assistant and donated the foundational works of this museum). Still a teenager, Pablo exhibited his first one-man show—a series of neighborhood sketches in the style of Toulouse-Lautrec—at Els Quatre Gats in 1900.

Paris (Rooms 6-7)

In 1900 Picasso made his first trip to Paris, a city bursting with life, light, and love. He began sampling the contemporary art styles around him: He painted **cancan dancers** like Toulouse-Lautrec, **still lifes** like Paul Cézanne, brightly colored **Fauvist** works like Henri Matisse, and Impressionist **landscapes** like Claude Monet (you may see examples on the walls of this room). In *The Waiting (Margot)*, the subject—with her bold outline and strong gaze—pops out from the vivid, mosaic-like background.

Blue Period (Room 8)

Picasso would travel to Paris several times before settling there in 1904. The suicide of his best friend Casagemas, his own poverty, and the influence of new ideas linking color and mood led Picasso to abandon jewel-bright color for his Blue Period (1901-1904). Now the artist was painting not what he saw, but what he felt. Painting misfits and street people, Picasso, like Velázquez and Toulouse-Lautrec before him, revealed the beauty in ugliness.

During a visit back to Barcelona, Picasso painted a nighttime view over the **rooftops** of the city. His palette is still blue, but here we see proto-Cubism...five years before the first real Cubist painting.

Rose Period

Picasso finally lifted out of his funk after meeting a new lady, Fernande Olivier (a bronze bust of her from 1906 may be on view). He moved out of the blue and into the happier Rose Period (1904-1907), dominated by soft pink and reddish tones. Other than the *Portrait of Bernadetta Bianco*, the museum is weak on Rose Period works.

Cubism

Pablo's role in the invention of the groundbreaking Cubist style (with his friend Georges Braque) is well known—at least I hope so, since this museum has no true Cubist paintings. The technique of "building" a subject with "cubes" of paint simmered in Picasso's artistic stew for years. The idea was to simultaneously see several 3-D facets of the subject.

Barcelona Redux (Rooms 9-10)

Picasso spent six months back in Barcelona in 1917 (yet another girlfriend, a Russian ballet dancer, had a gig in town). The paintings in these rooms demonstrate the artist's irrepressible versatility: He had already developed Cubism, but he also continued to play with other styles. In *Woman with Mantilla*, we see a little Post-Impressionistic Pointillism in a portrait that is as elegant as a classical statue. Nearby, *Gored Horse* has all the anguish and power of his iconic *Guernica* (painted years later).

Remember that this museum has very little from the most famous and prolific "middle" part of Picasso's career—basically, from his adoption of Cubism to his sunset years on the French Riviera. (To fill in the gaps in his middle career, see the sidebar on the next page.)

Picasso and Velázquez (Rooms 12-14)

Whoosh. We've skipped ahead a few decades in Picasso's life, and suddenly he is 40 years older. We left him at age 36 in 1917. Now it's 1957 and he's 76. As a mature artist, Picasso had few peers. He turned to the great Old Masters for inspiration.

He decided to make a series of works related to what many consider the greatest painting by anyone, ever: Diego Velázquez's *Las Meninas*. The 17th-century original (in Madrid's Prado Museum) depicted the young maids of honor (or *meninas*) of the Spanish royal court. Heralded as the first completely realistic painting, *Las Meninas* became, centuries later, an obsession for Picasso.

Pablo, who had great respect for Velázquez, painted more than **40 interpretations** of the masterwork, and donated all of them to

Velázquez's Las Meninas *(left) inspired many versions by Picasso (right).*

Pablo Picasso (1881-1973)

Pablo Picasso was the most famous and, for me, the greatest artist of the 20th century. Always exploring, he became the master of many styles (Cubism, Surrealism, Expressionism) and of many media (painting, sculpture, prints, ceramics, assemblages). Still, he could make anything he touched look unmistakably like "a Picasso."

Born in Málaga, Spain, Picasso was the son of an art teacher. At a very young age, he quickly advanced beyond his teachers. Picasso's teenage works are stunningly realistic and capture the inner complexities of the people he painted. As a youth in Barcelona, he fell in with a bohemian crowd that mixed wine, women, and art.

In 1900, at age 19, Picasso started making trips to Paris, and he moved there four years later. He absorbed the styles of many painters (especially Henri de Toulouse-Lautrec) while searching for his own artist's voice. His paintings of beggars and other social outcasts show the empathy of a man who was himself a poor, homesick foreigner. When his best friend, Spanish artist Carlos Casagemas, committed suicide, Picasso plunged into a **Blue Period** (1901-1904)—so called because the dominant color in these paintings matches their melancholy mood and subject matter (emaciated beggars, hard-eyed pimps).

In 1904, Picasso got a steady girlfriend (Fernande Olivier) and suddenly saw the world through rose-colored glasses—the **Rose Period.** He was further jolted out of his Blue Period by the "flat" look of the Fauve paintings being made around him. Not satisfied with their take on 3-D, Picasso played with the "building blocks" of line and color to find new ways to reconstruct the real world on canvas.

At his studio in Montmartre, Picasso and his neighbor Georges Braque worked together, in poverty so dire they often didn't know where their next bottle of wine was coming from. And then, at age 25, Picasso reinvented painting. Fascinated by the primitive power of African tribal masks, he sketched human faces with simple outlines and almond eyes. Intrigued by his girlfriend's body, he sketched Fernande from every angle, then experimented with showing several different views on the same canvas. A hundred paintings and nine months later, Picasso gave birth to a monstrous canvas of five nude, fragmented prostitutes with mask-like faces—*Les Demoiselles d'Avignon* (1907).

This bold new style was called **Cubism.** With Cubism, Picasso shattered the Old World and put it back together in a new way. The subjects are somewhat recognizable (with the help of the titles), but they're built with geometric shards (let's call them "cubes")—it's like viewing the world through a kaleidoscope of brown and gray. Cubism presents several different angles of the subject at once—say, a woman seen from the front and side si-

multaneously, resulting in two eyes on the same side of the nose. Cubism showed the traditional three dimensions, plus Einstein's new fourth dimension—the time it takes to walk around the subject to see other angles.

In 1918, Picasso married his first wife, Olga Kokhlova. He then traveled to Rome and entered a **Classical Period** (1920s) of more realistic, full-bodied women and children, inspired by the three-dimensional sturdiness of ancient statues. While he flirted with abstraction, throughout his life Picasso always kept a grip on "reality." His favorite subject was people. The anatomy might be jumbled, but it's all there.

Though he lived in France and Italy, Picasso remained a Spaniard at heart, incorporating Spanish motifs into his work. Unrepentantly macho, he loved bullfights, seeing them as a metaphor for the timeless human interaction between the genders. The horse—clad with blinders and pummeled by the bull—is just a pawn in the battle between bull and matador. To Picasso, the horse symbolizes the feminine, and the bull, the masculine. Spanish imagery—bulls, screaming horses, a Madonna—appears in Picasso's most famous work, *Guernica* (1937). The monumental canvas of a bombed village summed up the pain of Spain's brutal civil war (1936-1939) and foreshadowed the onslaught of World War II.

At war's end, Picasso left Paris, his wife, and his emotional baggage behind, finding fun in the **south of France.** Sun! Color! Water! Freedom! Senior citizen Pablo Picasso was reborn, enjoying worldwide fame. He lived at first with the beautiful young painter Françoise Gilot, mother of two of his children, but it was another young beauty, Jacqueline Roque, who became his second wife. Dressed in rolled-up white pants and a striped sailor's shirt, bursting with pent-up creativity, Picasso often cranked out a painting a day. Picasso's Riviera works set the tone for the rest of his life. They're sunny, lighthearted, and childlike; filled with motifs of the sea, Greek mythology (fauns, centaurs), and animals; and freely experimental in their use of new media. His simple drawing of a dove holding an olive branch became an international symbol of peace.

Picasso made collages, built "statues" out of wood, wire, ceramics, papier-mâché, or whatever, and even turned everyday household objects into statues (like his famous bull's head made of a bicycle seat with handlebar horns). **Multimedia** works like these have become so standard today that we forget how revolutionary they once were. His last works have the playfulness of someone much younger. As it is often said of Picasso, "When he was a child, he painted like a man. When he was old, he painted like a child."

the museum, which rotates the version on display. Picasso deconstructed Velázquez and then injected light, color, and perspective as he improvised on the earlier masterpiece. In Picasso's big, black and white version, he more or less re-created Velázquez's painting in its entirety. But here, the king and queen (reflected in the mirror in the back of the room) are hardly seen, while the painter—the great Velázquez—towers above everyone. In other paintings in the series, Picasso uses vibrant color and focuses on details—one maid of honor or a pair of them, or zeroes in on just their faces.

Last Years (Room 15)
Picasso spent the last 36 years of his life living simply in the south of France. With simple black outlines and Crayola colors, Picasso painted sun-splashed nature, peaceful doves, and the joys of the beach.

His last works have the playfulness of someone much younger. As is often said of Picasso, in his youth he was taught to see the world like an adult, and in his golden years he enjoyed seeing and portraying the world with the freedom of a child.

Nearby (in Rooms B1, N, and B2), you'll see how in his later years Picasso became a master of other media besides painting. With his **ceramics,** he made bowls and vases in fun animal shapes, decorated with simple motifs.

Picasso died with brush in hand, still growing as an artist. Sadly, since he vowed never to set foot in fascist, Franco-ruled Spain, Picasso never returned to his homeland...and never saw this museum. But to the end, Picasso continued exploring and loving life through his art.

Other Sights in El Born
▲▲Palace of Catalan Music (Palau de la Música Catalana)
This concert hall, built in just three years, was finished in 1908. Its tall facade has many beautiful decorations, but its location—on a narrow street that offers little perspective—makes it hard to appreciate. Still, the building boasts my favorite Modernista interior in town (by Lluís Domènech i Montaner). Its inviting arches lead you into the 2,138-seat hall, which is accessible only with a tour (or by attending a concert). A kaleidoscopic skylight features a choir singing around the sun, while playful carvings and mosaics celebrate music and Catalan culture. If you're interested in Modernisme, this tour is one of the best—and helps balance the hard-to-avoid focus on Gaudí as "Mr. Modernisme."

Cost and Hours: €20 for a 50-minute **guided tour** in English, runs daily on the hour 10:00-15:00, tour times may vary based on performance schedule; €14 **self-guided** tour offered daily every

30 minutes 10:00-15:30—you'll download an audioguide to your phone (50 minutes, bring your own earbuds/headphones).

Information: +34 932 957 200, www.palaumusica.cat.

Advance Reservations: Buy tickets in advance to get a spot on the English-language guided tour (sells out early, 20 percent discount online if you book more than 30 days ahead—purchase yours at least two days before, though they're sometimes available the same day or the day before—especially Oct-March). If the guided tour is sold out, the self-guided tour is a good alternative; tickets are sold on the website and just inside the ornate entrance on Carrer de Sant Pere Més (daily 9:30-15:30).

Getting There: It's a 10-minute walk from the Barcelona Cathedral or Picasso Museum, Carrer Palau de la Música 4, Metro: Urquinaona.

Concerts: An excellent way to see the hall is by attending one of its frequent concerts (€20-175, see website for details, box office +34 932 957 207). To see the Modernista main concert hall, be sure the show is being held in the **Sala de Concerts**—not the new Petit Palau hall.

▲Santa Caterina Market (Mercat de Santa Caterina)

This eye-catching market hall was built on the ruins of an old Dominican monastery, then renovated in 2006 with a wildly colorful, swooping, Gaudí-inspired roof and shell built around its original white walls (a good exhibition at the rear entrance provides a view of the foundations and English explanations).

Come for the outlandish architecture but stay for the food and the local color (it lacks the tourist logjam of La Boqueria). It's one of my favorite lunch spots in town—either at the recommended **Cuines Santa Caterina** (with inviting restaurant seating inside and out) or at one of several tapas bars in the market. These tapas bars epitomize all that is good with this kind of eating in Spain.

Cost and Hours: Free; Mon-Sat 7:30-15:30, Tue and Thu-Fri until 20:30, closed Sun; shorter hours Tue and Thu in July-Aug; Avinguda de Francesc Cambó 16, +34 933 195 740, www.mercatdesantacaterina.com.

▲Church of Santa Maria del Mar (Basílica de Santa Maria del Mar)

This so-called "Cathedral of the Sea" was built entirely with local funds and labor, in the heart of the wealthy merchant El Born quarter. Proudly independent, the church features a purely Catalan Gothic interior that was forcibly uncluttered of its Baroque decor by civil war belligerents. On the big front doors, notice the figures of workers who donated their time and sweat to build the church. The stone they used was quarried at Montjuïc and carried across town on the backs of porters called *bastaixos*.

BARCELONA

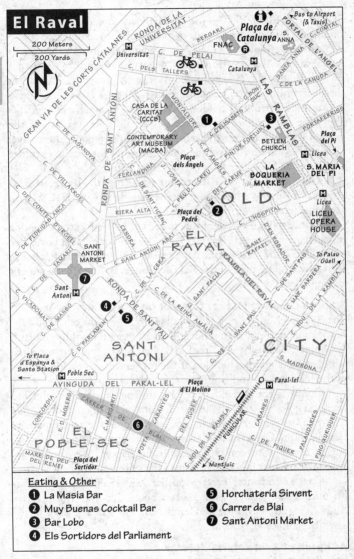

El Raval

200 Meters
200 Yards

Eating & Other
1 La Masia Bar
2 Muy Buenas Cocktail Bar
3 Bar Lobo
4 Els Sortidors del Parliament
5 Horchatería Sirvent
6 Carrer de Blai
7 Sant Antoni Market

Cost and Hours: Free entry during worship daily 10:00-12:00 & 17:00-20:30. Entry is €5 (€10 to visit the terrace) when the interior is illuminated and you have access to the choir and the crypt (Mon-Sat 12:00-17:00, Sun 13:30-17:00). Guided rooftop tours generally run Sat-Sun on the hour during paid-entry times (€14, 1 hour, check for English tours and sign up at the door or on the website). Plaça Santa Maria, Metro: Jaume I, +34 933 102 390, www.santamariadelmarbarcelona.org).

EL RAVAL

Historically edgy El Raval is Barcelona's "new El Born"—a bohemian-chic magnet for the young and trendy and the foodie crowd. This formerly dark, dangerous, and foreboding "wrong" side of the Ramblas is booming. The new Museum of Contemporary Art (MACBA) and the massive Sant Antoni market hall are gentrifying the area like the Picasso Museum and Santa Caterina Market did in El Born. Once congested streets are becoming pedestrian-only, lined with creative and fun-loving shops, cafés, bars, and restaurants.

Visiting El Raval: To explore the area, I'd follow this route: From the top of the Ramblas take a right on Carrer del Bonsuccés, which becomes Carrer d'Elisabets and leads to the **Museum of Contemporary Art (MACBA)** and Casa de la Caritat (a cultural center). Then turn left on Carrer dels Àngels to reach Carrer del Carme, where a right takes you to the community square at Plaça del Pedró. Continue down Carrer de Sant Antoni Abat to the **Sant Antoni Market**—a massive 19th-century hall that's just inside the Sant Antoni neighborhood. Then follow tree-lined Ronda de Sant Pau to Carrer del Parlament, which ends at the Poble Sec Metro stop on wide Avinguda del Paral-lel. Cross this busy street into the El Poble-Sec neighborhood at the base of the Montjuïc hill. Follow the pedestrian street Carrer de Blai (with cheap tapas bars—see next) and Carrer del Roser to Metro Paral-lel.

Eating and Drinking in El Raval: Try **La Masia Bar,** a very local, tight, and rough dive (cheap salads and tapas, Carrer d'Elisabets 16); **Muy Buenas Cocktail Bar,** with a charming 1928 interior (tapas from 20:00, Carrer del Carme 63); **Bar Lobo,** a modern, bright place for tapas (Carrer del Pintor Fortuny 3); **Els Sortidors del Parlament,** a rustic but high-end, trendy tapas bar with an inviting menu (Carrer del Parlament 53); or **Horchatería Sirvent,** famous for its *horchata* and ice cream (Carrer del Parlament 56). **Carrer de Blai** is a long stretch of thriving bars and youthful restaurants where €1 tapas are the norm—half what you'd pay in El Born.

THE EIXAMPLE

For many visitors, Modernista architecture is Barcelona's main draw. And at the heart of the Modernista movement was the Eixample, a carefully planned "new town," just beyond the Old City with wide sidewalks, hardy shade trees, and a rigid grid plan cropped at the corners to create space and lightness at each intersection. Conveniently, this new construction provided a generation of Modernista architects with a blank canvas for creating boldly experimental designs.

Block of Discord

At the center of the Eixample is the Block of Discord, where three colorful Modernista facades compete for your attention: Casa Batlló, Casa Amatller, and Casa Lleó Morera (all on Passeig de Gràcia—near the Metro stop of the same name—between Carrer del Consell de Cent and Carrer d'Aragó). All were built by well-known Modernista architects at the end of the 19th century. Because the mansions look as though they are trying

to outdo each other in creative twists, locals nicknamed the noisy block the "Block of Discord." Of the three houses, two are open to visitors—Casa Batlló and the less-crowded Casa Amatller.

🎧 Download my free Eixample Walk audio tour for a tour of this neighborhood.

▲Casa Batlló

While the highlight of this Gaudí-designed residence is the roof, the interior is also interesting—and much more over-the-top than

La Pedrera's. The house features a funky mushroom-shaped fireplace nook on the main floor, a blue-and-white, ceramic-slathered atrium, an attic with parabolic arches, and a dragon-inspired rooftop. There's barely a straight line in the house. The "Gold" ticket includes a good (if long-winded) virtual-reality guide on a tablet that depicts the rooms as they may have been.

Cost and Hours: €35 "Blue" ticket includes audioguide; €43 "Gold" skip-the-line ticket includes a hall with period furniture, virtual-reality tablet, and dizzying "Gaudí Dome" experience at the end; €45 early-entrance ticket promises fewer crowds (offered Fri-Sun at 8:30 or 8:45). All tickets are timed entry—buy online in advance (€4 more at the door). Open daily 9:00-20:00, Passeig de Gràcia 43, +34 932 160 306, www.casabatllo.es.

Nighttime Visits & Concerts: "Magic Night" tickets include the same features as the "Gold" and "Blue" tickets above, but also a rooftop concert and a glass of *cava* (Wed-Sun at 20:00, €49 "Blue" ticket, €59 "Gold" ticket gets you a better seat.

Modernisme and the Renaixença

Modernisme is Barcelona's unique contribution to the Europe-wide Art Nouveau movement. Meaning "a taste for what is

modern"—such as streetcars, electric lights, and big-wheeled bicycles—this free-flowing organic style lasted from 1888 to 1906.

Broadly speaking, there were two kinds of Modernisme (otherwise known as Catalan Art Nouveau). Early Modernisme has a Neo-Gothic flavor, clearly inspired by medieval castles and towers—logically, since architects wanted to recall the days when Barcelona was at its peak. From that starting point, Antoni Gaudí branched off on his own, adding the color and curves we most associate with the look of Barcelona's Modernisme.

The aim was to create buildings that were both practical and decorative. To that end, Modernista architects experimented with new construction techniques. Their most important material was concrete, which they could mold to curve and ripple like a wave and enliven with brightly colored glass and tile. Their structures were fully modern, but the decoration was a clip-art collage of natural images, exotic Moorish or Chinese themes, and fanciful Gothic crosses and knights to celebrate Catalunya's medieval glory days.

It's ironic to think that Modernisme was a response against

the regimentation of the Industrial Age—and that all those organic shapes were only made possible thanks to Eiffel Tower-like iron frames. As you wander through the Eixample looking at all those fanciful facades and colorful, leafy, blooming shapes in doorways, entrances, and ceilings, remember that many of these homes were built at the same time as the first skyscrapers in Chicago and New York City.

Underpinning Modernisme was the Catalan cultural revival movement, called the Renaixença. Across Europe, it was a time of national resurgence. It was the dawn of the modern age, and downtrodden peoples—from the Basques to the Irish to the Hungarians to the Finns—were throwing off the cultural domination of other nations and celebrating what made their own culture unique. Here in Catalunya, the Renaixença encouraged everyday people to get excited about all things Catalan—from their language, patriotic dances, and inspirational art to their surprising style of architecture.

Barcelona's Eixample

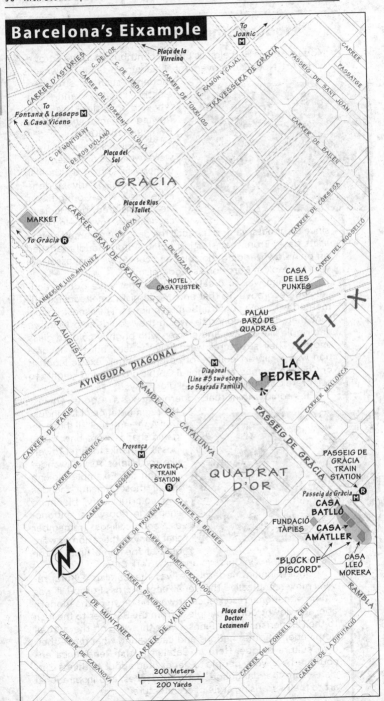

To Joanic Ⓜ

Plaça de la Virreina

CARRER D'ASTÚRIES
C. DE L'OR
C. DE VERDI
CARRER DE TORRIJOS
C. RAMÓN Y CAJAL
TRAVESSERA DE GRÀCIA
PASSEIG DE SANT JOAN
CARRER
PASSATGE
CARRER DEL TORRENT DE L'OLLA

To Fontana & Lesseps Ⓜ & Casa Vicens

C. DE MONTSENY
C. DE ROS D'OLANO
CARRER DE BAILÉN

Plaça del Sol

GRÀCIA

CARRER DE CÓRSEGA

Plaça de Rius i Tallet

MARKET
CARRER GRAN DE GRÀCIA
C. DE GOYA
C. DE MOZART
CARRER DEL ROSSELLÓ

To Gràcia Ⓡ

CARRER DE LUIS ANTÚNEZ

HOTEL CASA FUSTER

CASA DE LES PUNXES

VIA AUGUSTA

PALAU BARÓ DE QUADRAS

EIX

AVINGUDA DIAGONAL

RAMBLA DE CATALUNYA

Diagonal Ⓜ (Line #5 two stops to Sagrada Família)

LA PEDRERA

PASSEIG DE GRÀCIA

CARRER MALLORCA

CARRER DE PARÍS
CARRER DE CÓRSEGA
Provença Ⓜ

PROVENÇA TRAIN STATION Ⓡ

QUADRAT D'OR

PASSEIG DE GRÀCIA TRAIN STATION

CARRER DEL ROSSELLÓ
CARRER DE PROVENÇA
CARRER DE BALMES

Passeig de Gràcia Ⓡ Ⓜ

CASA BATLLÓ

FUNDACIÓ TÀPIES

CASA AMATLLER

CARRER D'ENRIC GRANADOS

"BLOCK OF DISCORD"

CASA LLEÓ MORERA

RAMBLA

C. DE MUNTANER
CARRER D'ARIBAU
CARRER DE VALÈNCIA
CARRER DEL CONSELL DE CENT
CARRER DE LA DIPUTACIÓ

Plaça del Doctor Letamendi

CARRER DE CASANOVA

200 Meters
200 Yards

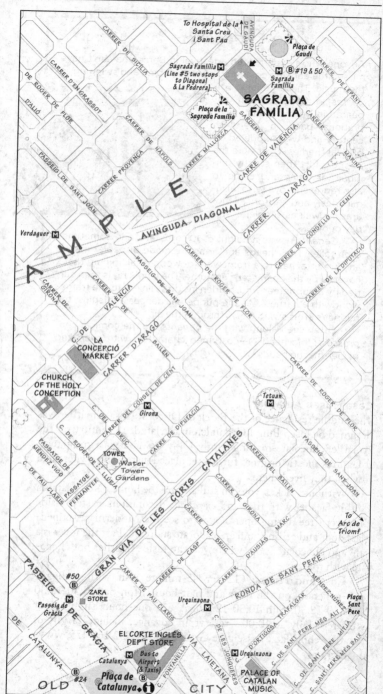

To Hospital de la
Santa Creu
i Sant Pau

Plaça de
Gaudí

CARRER DE SICILIA

CARRER D'ENGRASSOT

DE ROGER DE FLOR

CARRER DE GAUDÍ

CARRER DE LEPANT

Sagrada Família M
(Line #5 two stops
to Diagonal
& La Pedrera)

M B #19 & 50
Sagrada
Família

CARRER DE LA MARINA

SAGRADA
FAMÍLIA

Plaça de la
Sagrada Família

CARRER DE NÀPOLS

CARRER DE MALLORCA

SARDENYA

CARRER DE VALÈNCIA

PASSEIG DE SANT JOAN

CARRER PROVENÇA

CARRER D'ARAGÓ

A M P L E

AVINGUDA DIAGONAL

CARRER

CARRER DEL CONSELL DE CENT

Verdaguer M

CARRER DE GIRONA

CARRER DE
VALÈNCIA

PASSEIG DE SANT JOAN

CARRER DE ROGER DE FLOR

CARRER DE LA DIPUTACIÓ

DE PALIÓ

DE ROGER DE FLOR

CARRER DE ROGER DE FLOR

LA
CONCEPCIÓ
MARKET

CARRER D'ARAGÓ
BAILEN

CHURCH
OF THE HOLY
CONCEPTION

C. DE

C. DEL BRUC

Girona

CARRER DEL CONSELL DE CENT

Tetuan
M

CARRER DE DIPUTACIÓ

PASSATGE DE
MÉNDEZ VIGO

C. DE ROGER DE T. LLUÏA

TOWER
Water
Tower
Gardens

PASSATGE
PERMANYER

C. DE PAU CLARIS

CARRER DE LES CORTS CATALANES

CARRER DEL BRUC

CARRER DE GIRONA

CARRER DEL BAILEN

PASSEIG DE SANT JOAN

To
Arc de
Triomf

GRAN VIA DE LES CORTS CATALANES

CARRER DE CASP

CARRER D'AUSIAS MARC

RONDA DE SANT PERE

PASSEIG

#50
B

ZARA
STORE

Passeig de
Gràcia M

CARRER DE PAU CLARIS

Urquinaona
M

C. MÉNDEZ-NÚÑEZ

Plaça
Sant
Pere

DE CATALUNYA

DE
CATALUNYA

EL CORTE INGLÉS
DEP'T STORE

M
Catalunya

Bus to
Airport
(& Taxis)

VIA LAIETANA

C. DE LES JONQUERES

C. FONTANELLA

Urquinaona
M

D'ORTIGOSA TRAFALGAR

C. DE SANT PERE MÉS ALT

C. DE SANT PERE MITJA

C. SANT PERE MÉS BAIX

B
#24

Plaça de
Catalunya

B

PALACE OF
CATALAN
MUSIC

OLD

CITY

Gegants

Anyone who's experienced a festival in Barcelona can't have missed the dancing costumed giants bobbing and swinging to the music. These gegants (*gi-gantes* in Castilian) first appeared in Corpus Christi celebrations back in the 14th century and were modeled on biblical themes. Over time the puppets lost their strictly religious identities and came to also represent royalty, local luminaries, and historical figures, as well as simple, everyday people.

Gegants rise to a height of 10 to 12 feet, and sometimes even taller. Their heads and arms are made of papier-mâché and are attached to a framework of wood or aluminum that's covered by the character's costume. The whole rig is then carried by a puppeteer who, hidden inside, is linked to the framework with a harness. As the puppeteer dances and spins, the puppet's arms swing freely through the air.

Often seen along with the *gegants* are the comical *cap-grossos* ("big heads")—costumed characters with oversized papier-mâché heads.

Casa Museu Amatller

The middle residence of the Block of Discord, Casa Amatller was designed by Josep Puig I Cadafalch in the late 19th century for the Amatller chocolate-making family. Only viewable via a group tour, it features mostly original furniture, placed just as the owners had it when they lived there.

Without a ticket, you can still admire the home's Neo-Catalan Gothic facade, with tiles and *esgrafiado* decoration, or step inside the foyer (free during open hours) to see the Modernista stained-glass door and ceiling, and an elaborate staircase. Past the foyer is a café and chocolate shop, where you can taste Amatller hot chocolate with toast.

Cost and Hours: €12 for 45-minute visit with audioguide—generally on the hour and half-hour (Mon-Sat 10:30-12:30 & 17:30-18:30, Sun 10:30-12:30). A €15 one-hour English tour is offered daily at 10:00—reserve in advance, includes a gift of Amatller chocolate; Passeig de Gràcia 41, +34 932 160 175, www.amatller.org.

Casa Lleó Morera

This Modernista house, at Passeig de Gràcia 35, is not open to the public, but you can admire its paella-like mix of styles from the outside. It's the work of architect Lluís Domènich i Montaner, who also designed the Palace of Catalan Music. The lower floors have classical columns and a bay window reminiscent of a Greek temple. Farther up are Gothic balconies of rosettes and tracery, while the upper part has faux Moorish stucco work.

▲▲La Pedrera (Casa Milà)

One of Gaudí's trademark works, this house—built between 1906 and 1912—is an icon of Modernisme. The wealthy industrialist Pere Milà i Camps commissioned it, and while some still call it Casa Milà, most call it La Pedrera (The Quarry) because of its jagged, rocky facade. While it's fun to ogle from the outside, it's also worth going inside, as it's arguably the purest Gaudí interior in Barcelona—executed at the height of his abilities (unlike his earlier Palau Güell)— and contains period furnishings.

While Casa Batlló has a Gaudí facade and rooftop, these were appended to an existing building; La Pedrera, on the other hand, was built from the ground up according to Gaudí's plans. Your ticket includes entry to the interior (with the furnished apartment) and to the delightful rooftop, with its forest of tiled chimneys.

Cost and Hours: €25 timed-entry ticket includes good audioguide, buy online in advance, €3 more at the door; open daily 9:00-20:30, Nov-Feb until 18:30, nighttime visits available—see below; roof may close when it rains; at the corner of Passeig de Gràcia and Provença (visitor entrance at Provença 261), Metro: Diagonal, +34 932 142 576, www.lapedrera.com.

Avoiding Lines: Buy in advance online to guarantee entry. The €32 premium ticket allows you to arrive whenever you wish (no entry time, valid 6 months from purchase) and skip all lines, including those for audioguides and the elevator (often up to a 30-minute wait). There's also an early bird La Pedrera Exclusive guided tour at 8:00 (€39, certain days in peak season, details online).

Nighttime Visits: After-hours visits dubbed "La Pedrera Night Experience" include a guided tour of the building (but not the apartment), along with a rooftop light show and glass of *cava* (€35, usually daily 21:00-23:00, Nov-Feb 19:00-21:00, book ahead). A nighttime combo-ticket (€45) includes the rooftop night experience plus the regular timed-entry daytime admission.

BARCELONA

Concerts: On summer weekends, an evening rooftop concert series, "Summer Nights at La Pedrera," features live jazz and the chance to see the rooftop illuminated (€35, June-mid-Sept Fri-Sat at 20:15, book ahead).

Visiting the House: A visit covers three sections—the rooftop, the attic, and the apartment. Enter, pass through security, pick

up your audioguide, and walk through the fanciful, nature-inspired courtyard. Notice how the windows gradually get smaller as you look up to the top floors, allowing an equivalent amount of light and air to enter on the top floor as on the bottom floor.

Head up the elevator to the jaw-dropping **rooftop,** where 30 chimneys and ventilation towers play volleyball with the clouds. (It could be that George Lucas got his inspiration for his Darth Vader helmet from the chimneys.) Look for the archway that frames the Sagrada Família in the distance, and grasp the layout of the city from mountain to sea. For a great view of Eixample city planning, look over into this block's central area, filled with gardens.

Follow the signs to go down to the **attic,** which houses a sprawling multimedia exhibit tracing the history of the architect's career, with models, photos, and videos of his work. It's all displayed under distinctive parabola-shaped arches. While evocative of Gaudí's style in themselves, the arches are formed this way partly to support the multilevel roof above. This area was also used for ventilation, helping to keep things cool in summer and warm in winter. Tenants had storage spaces and did their laundry up here. In the 1940s there were actually 13 apartment units in this attic space.

Continue the visit by going downstairs to the bourgeois **apartment,** decorated as it might have been when the building was first occupied by middle-class urbanites (a short video explains Barcelona society at the time). Notice Gaudí's clever use of the atrium to maximize daylight in all the apartments.

Back at the **ground level** of La Pedrera, poke into the dreamily painted original entrance courtyard.

▲▲▲Sagrada Família (Holy Family Church)

Gaudí's grand masterpiece sits unfinished in a residential Eixample neighborhood 1.5 miles north of Plaça de Catalunya. An icon of the city, the Sagrada Família boasts bold, wildly creative, unmistakably organic architecture and decor inside and out—from its melting Glory Facade to its skull-like Passion Facade to its rain forest-esque interior.

Cost and Hours: All tickets are timed-entry and must be purchased online in advance (no tickets sold on-site at the church). €26 ticket includes church and audioguide (via app), €30 ticket includes church and 50-minute guided tour with live guide. Open Mon-Sat 9:00-20:00, Sun 10:30-20:00; March and Oct daily until 19:00, Nov-Feb until 18:00; +34 932 080 414, www. sagradafamilia.org.

La Sagrada Família App: When you book online, you'll receive an email with your ticket attached and a link to the official La Sagrada Família app. You'll need to download the app to your phone to use the audioguide. You can also access your ticket on your phone (or buy tickets) via the app.

Getting There: The Metro stop Sagrada Família (on lines L2 and L5) puts you right on the church's doorstep. Exiting toward Plaça de Gaudí (follow silhouette logos of the church) will save a little walking.

Getting In: Carefully note your assigned entry time. You can enter the church starting 15 minutes before the time on your ticket and up to 30 minutes after. Make your way to the Nativity Facade side, show your ticket (either on your phone or printed out), and go through the airport-style security. *Access B* is for individuals, and *Access A* is sometimes open just for groups. Sharp items like pocketknives must be checked (you'll get a claim number to pick up your items upon exiting through this side). All hats must be removed.

Church Services: Mass (in various languages) is held every Sunday at 9:00; those who actually want to worship here are admitted at no charge. Entry to the church begins at 8:30, but lines can form as early as 6:30.

Towers: Access to the towers may be covered by a separate ticket; a guided-tour combo-ticket includes access to one tower. Check the website for details. Towers can close when windy or rainy (if that happens, the tower portion of your ticket will be refunded).

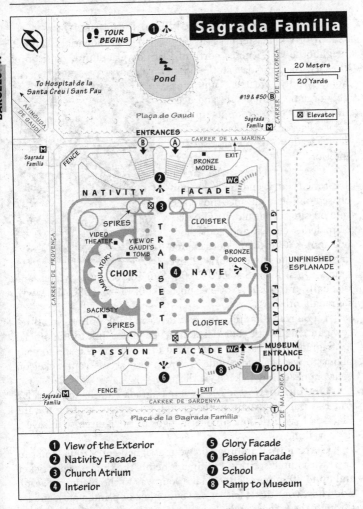

Sagrada Família

TOUR BEGINS

Pond

Plaça de Gaudí

To Hospital de la Santa Creu i Sant Pau

20 Meters
20 Yards

#19 & #50 Ⓑ

⊠ Elevator

ENTRANCES
Ⓑ Ⓐ   CARRER DE LA MARINA

BRONZE MODEL   EXIT

WC

N A T I V I T Y   F A C A D E

SPIRES   ⊠ ❸   CLOISTER

VIDEO THEATER   VIEW OF GAUDI'S TOMB

AMBULATORY   CHOIR   T R A N S E P T   ❹ N A V E   BRONZE DOOR   ❺

SACRISTY   SPIRES   CLOISTER

⊠   MUSEUM ENTRANCE

P A S S I O N   F A C A D E   WC   ❼ SCHOOL

❻   ❽

FENCE   EXIT

CARRER DE SARDENYA

Plaça de la Sagrada Família

G L O R Y   F A C A D E

UNFINISHED ESPLANADE

❶ View of the Exterior
❷ Nativity Facade
❸ Church Atrium
❹ Interior
❺ Glory Facade
❻ Passion Facade
❼ School
❽ Ramp to Museum

Elevators on opposite sides of the church take you partway up the towers—one on the Passion Facade, and one on the Nativity Facade. The elevators go up only—to get down, you'll use a tightly wound, narrow staircase. The **Passion Facade elevator** takes you up a touch higher, and the stairs to come down are slightly wider than those descending from the **Nativity Facade elevator**. The facades are not joined, so it isn't possible to cross from one facade to the other, but you can cross a dizzying bridge between towers on the same facade.

Baggage Check: Day bags are allowed in the church but are scanned. Small lockers are available at each elevator when the tow-

ers are open (backpacks are not allowed in towers). Though intended for those riding the elevators, the lockers can be used by anyone.

Background

Gaudí labored on Sagrada Família for 43 years, from 1883 until his death in 1926. Nearly a century on, people continue to toil to bring Gaudí's designs to life. There's something inspirational about a community of committed people with a vision, who've worked on a church that wouldn't be finished in their lifetimes—as was standard in the Gothic age. The progress of this remarkable building is a testament to the generations of architects, sculptors, stonecutters, fundraisers, and donors who shared Gaudí's astonishing vision. After paying the admission price (becoming a partner in this building project), you will actually feel good. If there's any building on earth I'd like to see, it's the Basílica de la Sagrada Família... finished.

❷ Self-Guided Tour

• *Before entering the church, start on the far side of the pond in the park that faces the Nativity Facade (east side, where entry lines are located). From there, you're back far enough to take in the entire towering facade.*

❶ View of the Exterior from Beyond the Pond

Stand and imagine how grand this church will be when completed. The eight 330-foot spires topped with crosses are just a fraction of this mega-church. When  finished, it will have 18 spires. Four will stand at each of the three entrances. Rising above those will be four taller towers, dedicated to the four Evangelists. A tower dedicated to Mary (expected to be completed soon) rises still higher—400 feet. And in the very center of the complex will stand the grand 560-foot Jesus tower, topped with a cross that will shine like a spiritual lighthouse, visible even from out at sea.

The Nativity Facade—where tourists enter today—is only a side entrance to the church. The grand main entry will be around to the left. To accommodate the church's planned entrance esplanade, a nine-story apartment building will have to be torn down. (This is an ongoing controversy as authorities negotiate with landowners.)

The three facades—Nativity, Passion, and Glory—will chronicle Christ's life from birth to death to resurrection. Inside and out, a goal of the church is to bring the lessons of the Bible to the world. Despite his boldly modern architectural vision, Gaudí was

fundamentally traditional and deeply religious. He designed the Sagrada Família to be a bastion of solid Christian values in the midst of what was a humble workers' colony in a fast-changing city.

When Gaudí died, the only section that had been completed was the Nativity Facade (with its themes of birth and new life). Notice the dove-covered Tree of Life on top, with playful little creatures carved into nooks and crannies throughout, and a white pelican at the bottom. Because it was believed that this noble bird would feed its young with its own blood, the pelican was a common symbol in the Middle Ages for the self-sacrifice of Jesus.

The Nativity Facade's four spires are dedicated to apostles, and they repeatedly bear the word "sanctus," or holy. Their colorful ceramic caps symbolize the miters (formal hats) of bishops. The shorter spires (to the left) symbolize the Eucharist (communion), alternating between a chalice with grapes and a communion host with wheat.

The rest of the church, while inspired by Gaudí's long-range vision, has been designed and executed by others. This artistic freedom was amplified in 1936, when civil war shelling burned many of Gaudí's blueprints. Supporters of the ongoing work insist that Gaudí, who enjoyed saying, "My client [God] is not in a hurry," knew he wouldn't live to complete the church and recognized that later architects and artists would rely on their own muses for inspiration.

• *Keep an eye on the time. About 15 minutes before your assigned timeslot, join the line to enter the church complex. Pass through security, put your belt back on, then walk up the stairs to the viewing plaza in front of the Nativity Facade. Check out the small **bronze model** of how the church might look when completed. Then stand as far back as you can to take in this facade.*

❷ Nativity Facade

This is the only part of the church essentially finished in Gaudí's lifetime (although the architect had intended for this facade to be painted). The four spires decorated with his naturalistic sculpture mark this facade as unmistakably part of his original design. Mixing Gothic-era symbolism, images from nature, and Modernista asymmetry, the Nativity Facade is the best example of Gaudí's original vision, and it established the template for future architects. Cleverly, this attractive facade was built and finished first to bring in financial support for the project.

The theme of the facade, which faces the rising sun, is Christ's birth. A statue above the doorway shows Mary, Joseph, and Baby Jesus in the manger, while a curious cow and donkey peek in. It's the Holy Family—or "Sagrada Família" (literally "sacred family")—to whom this church is dedicated. Flanking the doorway are

the three Magi and adoring shepherds. Other statues at this height show Jesus as a young carpenter (right), the Holy Family fleeing to Egypt (left), and angels playing musical instruments. Much higher up, in the arched niche, Jesus crowns Mary triumphantly.

The doors in the middle of the facade (covered with small colorful bugs and leaves) were designed by head sculptor Etsuro Sotoo. Born in Japan, Sotoo visited Barcelona for the first time in 1978 and fell in love with the project. He worked hard to become a part of it and even converted to Catholicism.

• *If your ticket includes a tower or a guided tour, a guard will direct you to your elevator or tour meeting point. Otherwise, enter the ❸ church atrium through Sotoo's doors. Continue to the center of the church, near the altar, to survey the magnificent...*

❹ Interior

Typical of even the most traditional Catalan and Spanish churches, the floor plan is in the shape of a Latin cross, 300 feet long and 200 feet wide. Ultimately, the church will accommodate 8,000 worshippers. The crisscross arches of the ceiling (the vaults) show off Gaudí's distinctive engineering. The church's roof and flooring were only completed in 2010—just in time for Pope Benedict XVI to arrive and consecrate the church.

Part of Gaudí's religious vision included a love for nature. He said, "Nothing is invented; it's written in nature." Like the trunks of trees, these **columns** (56 in all) blossom with life, complete with branches, leaves, and knot-like capitals. The columns vary in color and material—brown clay, gray granite, dark gray basalt.

Light filtering through the stained-glass windows has the dappled effect of a rainforest canopy. Notice how splashes of color breathe even more life into this amazing space. The morning light shines in through blues, greens, and other cool colors, whereas the evening light glows through reds, oranges, and warm tones. Gaudí envisioned an awe-inspiring symphony of colored light to encourage a contemplative mood.

At the center of the church stand four main columns, each marked with an Evangelist's symbol and name in Catalan: angel (Mateu), lion (Marc), bull (Luc), and eagle (Joan). These columns support a ceiling vault that's 200 feet high—and eventually will

also support the central steeple (the Jesus tower with the shining cross).

The Holy Family is looking down from on high: Jesus is above the altar, Mary is in the left transept, and Joseph in the right transept.

Behind the high altar, peer down to see a surprisingly traditional space—the 19th-century Neo-Gothic building that Gaudí was originally hired to finish. Today this is a **crypt** holding the tomb of Gaudí himself. A few steps away are two small theaters in adjacent side chapels. One shows a short **video** about the architect and his work.

• *Walk through the forest of massive columns to the opposite end of the church. The view from here is best for appreciating the majesty of the building's interior. (A big mirror is placed here to make admiring the ceiling easier.) Notice the row of statues representing, once again, the four Evangelists. These are models of the sculptures that will eventually be placed on the pinnacles of the four exterior towers dedicated to each Evangelist. Suspended high above the nave, the U-shaped* **choir** *can seat a thousand singers, who will eventually be backed by four organs.*

Doors here will one day open to the...

❺ Glory Facade

While you can't go out what will one day be the main entrance, you can study a life-size image of the **bronze door** intended for this spot, emblazoned with the Lord's Prayer in Catalan and surrounded by "Give us this day our daily bread" in 50 languages. If you were able to exit through the actual door, you'd be face-to-face with drab, doomed apartment blocks. In the 1950s, the mayor of Barcelona, figuring this day would never really

come, sold the land destined for the church project. Now the city must buy back these buildings in order to complete Gaudí's vision of a grand esplanade leading to this main entry. Four towers will rise. The facade's sculpture will represent how the soul passes through death, faces the Last Judgment, avoids the pitfalls of hell, and finds its way to eternal glory with God.

• *Head back up the nave and exit through the left transept. To the left, notice the second* **elevator** *up to the towers. Before exiting, look down at the fine porphyry floor with scenes of Jesus' entry into Jerusalem. To the right, stroll through the* **sacristy**, *where you will find benches, candelabras, and sacristy furniture designed by Gaudí. Now head outside and down the ramp. Step away to take in the...*

❻ Passion Facade

Judge for yourself how well Gaudí's original vision has been carried out by later artists. The Passion Facade's four spires were designed

by Gaudí and completed (quite faithfully) in 1976. But the lower part was only inspired by Gaudí's designs. The sculptures intended for this facade were interpreted freely and sternly (also controversially) by Josep Maria Subirachs (1927-2014), who completed the work in 2005.

Subirachs tells the story of Christ's torture and execution. The various scenes—Last Supper, betrayal, whipping, and so on—zigzag up from bottom to top, culminating in Christ's crucifixion over the doorway. The style is severe and unadorned, quite different from Gaudí's signature naturalism. Large letters spell out "Iesus Nazarenus Rex Iudæorum" (Jesus the Nazarene, King of the Jews). The bone-like archways are closely based on Gaudí's original designs. And Gaudí had made it clear that this facade should be grim and terrifying.

• *Now, for a fun little break from all this church architecture, head into the small building outside the Passion Facade. This is the...*

❼ School

Gaudí erected this school for the children of the workers building the church. Today, it displays a replica classroom and old photos of school activities during Gaudí's time.

• *Back outside, head down the ramp, where you'll find WCs and the entrance to the...*

❽ Museum

Housed in what will someday function as the church crypt, the museum takes you through the past, present, and future of Sagrada Família's development.

It starts with a photo of the master himself and a timeline illustrating how construction has progressed from Gaudí's day until now. Walking the hall, you'll pass pieces of Gaudí's original plaster model of the church (damaged during Spain's civil war; on the left), and his reconstructed studio (also on the left). Compare Gaudí's old-fashioned space with a nearby photo of the current team, working with the latest technology.

In a room at the end of the hall, four plaster models show the evolution of Gaudí's thinking (clockwise from left): 1) the Neo-Gothic design by the church's first architect, Francisco de Paula del Villar; 2) Gaudí's re-envisioned plan, with a nave formed of narrow parabolic arches; 3) a plan with the middle story opened up; and

4) finally, an even more open plan with tree-like columns fanning out at the top.

Exploring further, you'll find a small theater showing a worthwhile nine-minute movie. You'll also find an intriguing "hanging model" for Gaudí's unfinished Church of Colònia Güell (in a suburb of Barcelona), with a design similar to that of Sagrada Família.

Gaudí lived on the site of Sagrada Família for more than a decade and is buried here in the Neo-Gothic 19th-century crypt. You can look (steeply) down at his tomb. There's a move afoot to beatify Gaudí and make him a saint.

Back in the main hall, peer into the actual workshop where artists employ the latest technology (such as 3-D printing) to test ideas and create models.

• *Our tour is over. From here, you have a few options. To **return to central Barcelona**, it's simple to hop on the Metro. Bus #50 goes to the heart of the **Eixample** (corner of Gran Via de les Corts Catalanes and Passeig de Gràcia), then continues on to Plaça Espanya (**Montjuïc** sights). Or you can take a taxi to **Park Güell**, two (uphill) miles to the northwest.*

BEYOND THE EIXAMPLE
▲▲Park Güell

Designed as an upscale housing development for early 20th-century urbanites, this park is home to some of Barcelona's most famous symbols, including a dragon guarding a whimsical staircase and a wavy bench bordering a panoramic view terrace supported by a forest of columns. Gaudí used vivid tile fragments to decorate much of his work, creating a playful, pleasing effect. You'll pay to enter the **park** and you must choose an entry time for the **Monumental Zone**—the part visitors want to see—with all the iconic Gaudí features. Also in the park is the Gaudí House Museum, where Gaudí lived for a time—but it's not worth the separate entry fee for most travelers.

Gaudí intended this 30-acre garden to be a high-end community, with 60 upscale residences. Funded by his frequent benefactor Eusebi Güell, he began work on the project in 1900; however, the project stalled in 1914, with the outbreak of World War I, and it never resumed. Only two houses were built, neither designed by Gaudí (one is now the Gaudí House Museum). Be thankful that the housing development faltered—as a park, this place is a delight. It offers a novel peek into Gaudí's eccentric genius in a setting that's wonderfully in keeping with the naturalism that pervades his work. Even without its Gaudí connection, Park

Güell is simply a fine place to enjoy a break from a busy city where green space is relatively rare.

Cost: €10 for park admission and timed-entry into the Monumental Zone. You have 30 minutes from your designated time to enter the zone. The only smart way to visit is to buy your ticket online in advance (tickets are sold at the park, but you'll wait in a long line).

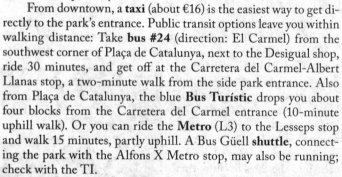

Hours: Daily April-Oct 9:30-19:30, rest of year 9:30 until sunset.

Information: +34 934 091 831, www.parkguell.barcelona.

When to Go: To avoid the biggest crowds, visit as early in the day as possible or after 18:00.

Getting There: Park Güell is about 2.5 miles from Plaça de Catalunya, beyond the Gràcia neighborhood in Barcelona's foothills. If asking for directions, ask for "Park Gway" (sounds like "parkway").

From downtown, a **taxi** (about €16) is the easiest way to get directly to the park's entrance. Public transit options leave you within walking distance: Take **bus #24** (direction: El Carmel) from the southwest corner of Plaça de Catalunya, next to the Desigual shop, ride 30 minutes, and get off at the Carretera del Carmel-Albert Llanas stop, a two-minute walk from the side park entrance. Also from Plaça de Catalunya, the blue **Bus Turístic** drops you about four blocks from the Carretera del Carmel entrance (10-minute uphill walk). Or you can ride the **Metro** (L3) to the Lesseps stop and walk 15 minutes, partly uphill. A Bus Güell **shuttle**, connecting the park with the Alfons X Metro stop, may also be running; check with the TI.

Getting In: The park has three entrances: two at the front and one on the side. No matter where you enter, you'll finish up at the palm-frond gate (the historical front entrance, now exit-only) after visiting the Monumental Zone. I prefer starting at the side entrance on Carretera del Carmel—from there it's a nice walk through the park past some of Gaudí's fanciful viaducts before visiting the Monumental Zone. At all entrances you'll find a ticket office, WCs nearby, and plenty of park staff to help orient you. Hang on to your ticket; you'll need to show it when you exit.

Visiting the Park: Spend 30-60 minutes (or more) in the park strolling around the viaducts and grounds before heading to the Monumental Zone for the grand finale. Be at the terrace and its Monumental Zone entrance at your scheduled time (or up to 30 minutes after).

BARCELONA

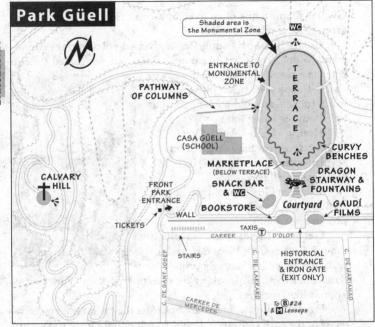

Park Güell

Shaded area is the Monumental Zone

WC

TERRACE

ENTRANCE TO MONUMENTAL ZONE

PATHWAY OF COLUMNS

CASA GÜELL (SCHOOL)

CURVY BENCHES

MARKETPLACE (BELOW TERRACE)

DRAGON STAIRWAY & FOUNTAINS

SNACK BAR & WC

CALVARY HILL

FRONT PARK ENTRANCE

BOOKSTORE

Courtyard

GAUDÍ FILMS

TICKETS

WALL

TAXIS

D'OLOT

C. DE SANT JOSEP

STAIRS

CARRER

C. DE LARRARD

HISTORICAL ENTRANCE & IRON GATE (EXIT ONLY)

C. DE MARIAHAÓ

CARRER DE MERCEDES

To B #24 & M Lesseps

After entering the Monumental Zone, the **view terrace** (Nature Square) boasts one of Barcelona's best views. (Find the Sagrada Família in the distance.)
Functioning as both a seat and a balustrade, the 360-foot-long bench is designed to fit your body just so. To Gaudí, this terrace evoked ancient Greek theaters that burrowed scenically into the sides of hills—but it is more like an ancient Greek agora, a wide-open meeting place, jammed with people feasting on the view.

Facing the city, continue down the right-hand staircase. The big pink house flanking the stairs is where Eusebi Güell lived. Now a **school,** this house predates the park project and was not designed by Gaudí. As you walk down the stairs, notice the playful **Pathway of Columns** to your right. Gaudí drew his inspiration from nature, and this arcade is like a surfer's perfect tube. Both structural and aesthetic, it is one of many clever double-decker **viaducts** that Gaudí designed for the grounds: vehicles up top, pedestrians in the portico below.

Continue through the **marketplace** (Hypostyle Room), which was designed to house a **produce market** for the neighborhood's

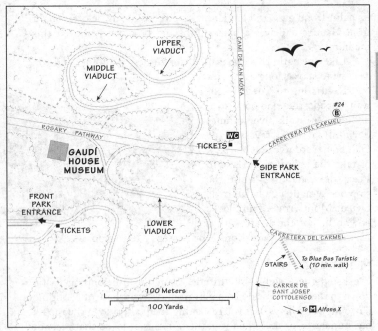

UPPER VIADUCT

MIDDLE VIADUCT

CAMI DE CAN MORA

#24
(B)

CARRETERA DEL CARMEL

ROSARY PATHWAY

WC
TICKETS

SIDE PARK ENTRANCE

GAUDÍ HOUSE MUSEUM

FRONT PARK ENTRANCE

TICKETS

LOWER VIADUCT

CARRETERA DEL CARMEL

STAIRS

To Blue Bus Turístic (10 min. walk)

CARRER DE SANT JOSEP COTTOLENGO

To M Alfons X

100 Meters

100 Yards

inhabitants. Eighty-six Doric columns—each lined at the base with white ceramic shards—populate the marketplace and add to its vitality. (Their main job, though, is to hold up the view terrace above.) Shards of white ceramic also cover the multiple domes of the ceiling. The four giant mosaic decorations overhead represent the four seasons.

At the top of the dragon stairs, twin staircases curve downward, separated by three **fountains** stacked between them. The first, at the top of the steps, is an icon of the park—and of Barcelona: a smiling dragon, slathered in colorful tile. Next is a red-and-gold Catalan shield, with the head of a serpent poking out. The third fountain is rocky and leafy, typical of Gaudí's naturalism.

Walk down to the courtyard (but keep in mind that once you leave the Monumental Zone, you can't return). Look back and notice the two grottos flanking the stairs: One was a garage for Eusebi Güell's newfangled automobiles; the other was a cart shelter.

Enjoy Gaudí's **historical front entrance** (now exit only) with

its palm-frond **gate** and gas lamps on either side, made of wrought iron. Gaudí's dad was a blacksmith, and he always enjoyed this medium.

Like any park, this one is made for aimless rambling, and you are free to stay as long as you like.

Returning to Town: Taxis wait outside the exit on Carrer d'Olot. Or, walk five minutes downhill to the Travessera de Dalt boulevard to catch bus #24, or take the blue Bus Turístic to Plaça de Catalunya from the stop on Avinguda de la Mare de Déu de Montserrat—four blocks downhill. For the Metro, it's a 15-minute walk to the Alfons X or Lesseps Metro stops.

MONTJUÏC

I've listed these sights by altitude, from the hill-topping castle down to the 1929 World Expo Fairgrounds at the base of Montjuïc ("Mount of the Jews"). If you're visiting them all, ride to the top by bus, funicular, or taxi, then visit them in this order so that most of your walking is downhill.

Here's one simple plan: From Metro Paral-lel, take the funicular up (included in your Metro ticket). Walk five minutes (left from exit) gradually downhill to the big white Fundació Joan Miró, five minutes more to the Olympic Stadium, and five more to the Catalan Art Museum. From there, descend the stairs to the Magic Fountains. Detour left (if interested) to the CaixaForum. Then return to the Magic Fountains and continue to Plaça d'Espanya, Las Arenas mall, and a Metro stop to the rest of Barcelona.

Getting to Montjuïc: You have several choices. The simplest is to take a **taxi** directly to your destination (about €12 from downtown).

Buses also take you up to Montjuïc. From Plaça de Catalunya, bus #55 goes as far as Montjuïc's cable-car station/funicular. To get higher (to the castle), ride the Metro or bus #50 from Plaça de Catalunya to Plaça d'Espanya, then make the easy transfer to bus #150 to ride all the way up the hill. Alternatively, the red Bus Turístic will get you to the Montjuïc sights.

Another option is the **funicular** (covered by Metro ticket, runs every 10 minutes 9:00-22:00). To reach it, take the Metro to the Paral-lel stop, then follow signs for *Parc Montjuïc* and the funicular icon—you can enter the funicular without using another ticket. (If the funicular is closed, you'll find a shuttle bus.) From the top of the funicular, turn left and walk gently downhill for the

Fundació Joan Miró, Olympic Stadium, and Catalan Art Museum. If you're heading all the way up to the Castle of Montjuïc, you can catch a bus or cable car from the top of the funicular (see castle listing, later).

For a scenic (if slow) approach to Montjuïc, you can ride the fun circa-1929 Aeri del Port **cable car** *(telefèric)* from the tip of

the Barceloneta peninsula (across the harbor, near the beach) to the Miramar viewpoint park in Montjuïc. (Another station, along the port near the Columbus Monument, is closed.) The cable car is expensive, loads excruciatingly slowly (especially coming from the beach), and goes between two relatively remote parts of town, so it's really not an efficient connection. It's only worthwhile for its sweeping views over town or to head back down to Barceloneta at the end of the day. Lines are shorter if you board in Montjuïc (€11 one-way, €16.50 round-trip, 3/hour, daily 10:30-19:00, June-Sept until 20:00, Nov-Feb 11:00-17:30, closed in high wind, +34 934 304 716, www.telefericodebarcelona.com).

If you're only visiting the Catalan Art Museum and/or CaixaForum, you can take the Metro to Plaça d'Espanya and **walk** up (primarily riding handy escalators).

Getting Around Montjuïc: Up top, it's easy and fun to walk between the sights—especially downhill. You can also connect the sights using the red Bus Turístic or one of the public buses: Bus #150 does a loop around the hilltop and is the only bus that goes to the castle; on the way up, it stops at or passes near the CaixaForum, Catalan Art Museum, Olympic Stadium, Fundació Joan Miró, the lower castle cable-car station/top of the funicular, and finally, the castle. On the downhill run, it loops by Avinguda Miramar, the cable-car station for Barceloneta. Bus #55 connects only the funicular/cable-car stations, Fundació Joan Miró, and the Catalan Art Museum.

Castle of Montjuïc (Castell de Montjuïc)

The castle, which is pretty empty, is mostly worthwhile for the great city views from its ramparts. It was built in the 18th century with a Vauban-type star-fortress design by the central Spanish government to keep an eye on Barcelona and stifle citizen revolt. Until the late 20th century, the place functioned more to repress the people of Barcelona than to defend them. When the 20th-century dictator Franco was in power, the castle was the site of hundreds of political

BARCELONA

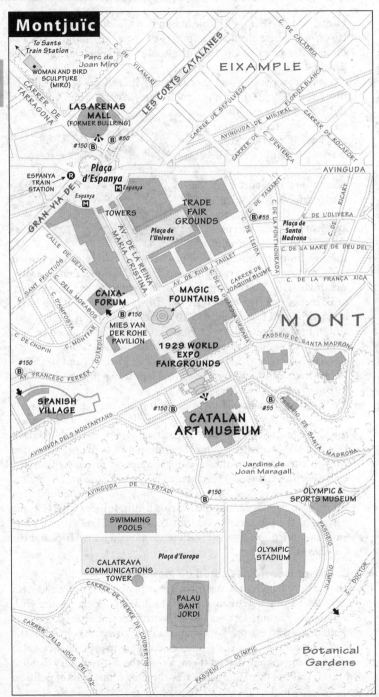

Montjuïc

To Sants Train Station

Parc de Joan Miró

EIXAMPLE

WOMAN AND BIRD SCULPTURE (MIRÓ)

LAS ARENAS MALL (FORMER BULLRING)

CARRER DE TARRAGONA

C. DE VILAMARI

C. DE CALABRIA

LES CORTS CATALANES

CARRER DE SEPULVEDA

FLORIDA BLANCA

CARRER DE MISTRAL

AVINGUDA DE MISTRAL

CARRER DE C. D'ENTENÇA

CARRER DE ROCAFORT

#150 (B)

(B) #50

Plaça d'Espanya

AVINGUDA

ESPANYA TRAIN STATION (R)

Espanya (M)

GRAN VIA DE

(M) Espanya

TOWERS

AV. DE LA REINA MARIA CRISTINA

Plaça de l'Univers

TRADE FAIR GROUNDS

(B) #55

CARRER DE TAMARIT

C. DE LA FONT HONRADA

C. DE L'OLIVERA

CARRER DE LLEIDA

Plaça de Santa Madrona

C. DE LA MARE DE DEU DEL

C. DE LA FRANÇA XICA

CALLE DE MEXIC

C. SANT FRUCTUOS

C. DELS MORABOS

C. D'AMPOSTA

C. DE CHOPIN

C. DE MONTFAR

CAIXA-FORUM

(B) #150

MIES VAN DER ROHE PAVILION

AV. DE RIUS I TAULET

MAGIC FOUNTAINS

CARRER DE JOAQUIM BLUME

AV. DE LA GRAN VIA URBANA

1929 WORLD EXPO FAIRGROUNDS

M O N T

PASSEIG DE SANTA MADRONA

(B) #150

AV. FRANCESC FERRER I GUARDIA

SPANISH VILLAGE

AVINGUDA DELS MONTANYANS

#150 (B)

CATALAN ART MUSEUM

(B) #55

PASSEIG DE SANTA MADRONA

Jardins de Joan Maragall

OLYMPIC & SPORTS MUSEUM

AVINGUDA DE L'ESTADI

#150 (B)

PASSEIG OLIMPIC

C. DOCTOR

SWIMMING POOLS

Plaça d'Europa

CALATRAVA COMMUNICATIONS TOWER

OLYMPIC STADIUM

CARRER DE PIERRE DE COUBERTIN

PALAU SANT JORDI

CARRER DELS JOCS DEL 32

PASSEIG OLIMPIC

Botanical Gardens

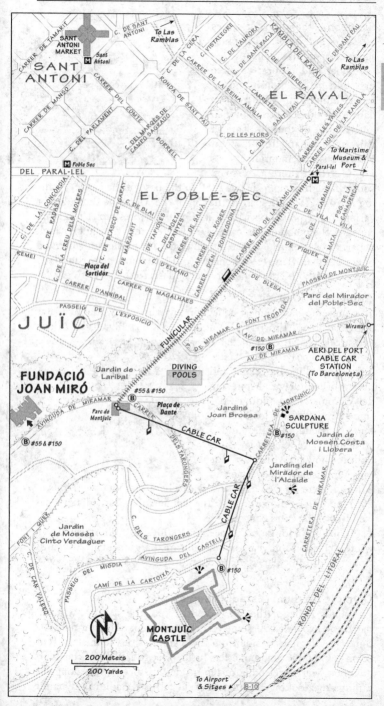

executions. These days it serves as a park and host to a popular summer open-air cinema.

Cost and Hours: €5, free first Sun of the month and all other Sun from 15:00; open daily 10:00-20:00, Nov-Feb until 18:00; €4 tours in English daily at 11:00 and 15:00; www.bcn.cat/castelldemontjuic.

Getting There: To spare yourself the hike up, ride bus #150 to the base of the castle, catching it from Plaça d'Espanya, the top of the Montjuïc funicular, or various other points on Montjuïc. Or if the lines aren't too long, consider the much pricier **cable car** (Telefèric de Montjuïc), which departs from near the upper station of the Montjuïc funicular and offers excellent views (€9.40 one-way, €14.20 round-trip, runs daily June-Sept 10:00-21:00, shorter hours off-season).

▲Fundació Joan Miró

This museum has the best collection anywhere of works by Catalan artist Joan Miró (ZHOO-ahn mee-ROH, 1893-1983). Born

in Barcelona, Miró divided his time between Paris and Catalunya (including Barcelona and his favorite village, Mont-roig del Camp). This building—designed in 1975 by Josep Lluís Sert, a friend of Miró and a student of Le Corbusier—was built to show off Miró's art. The museum displays an overview of Miró's oeuvre (as well as generally excellent temporary exhibits of 20th- and 21st-century artists). The wonderful multimedia guide is well worth the extra charge.

Cost and Hours: €13; Tue-Sun 10:00-20:00, shorter hours in winter, closed Mon year-round; multimedia guide-€5; 200 yards from top of funicular, Parc de Montjuïc, +34 934 439 470, www.fmirobcn.org/ca.

Olympic Stadium (Estadi Olímpic)

Originally built for the 1929 World Expo, the stadium was updated and expanded 50-some years later in preparation for the 1992 Summer Olympics. Aside from the memories of the medals, Barcelona's Olympic Stadium offers little to see today. But if the doors are open, you're welcome to step inside. History panels along the railings overlooking the playing field tell the stadium's dynamic

story and show the place in happier times.

Nearby: Across the street, the **Olympic and Sports Museum** is high-tech but hokey—worth the time and money only for those nostalgic for the '92 Games. Hovering over the stadium is the futur-istic **Montjuïc Communications Tower** (designed by prominent Spanish architect Santiago Calatrava), originally used to transmit Olympic highlights and lowlights around the world.

▲▲Catalan Art Museum
(Museu Nacional d'Art de Catalunya)

The mission of this wonderful museum is to showcase Catalan art from the 10th century through the mid-20th century. Often called

"the Prado of Romanesque art" (and "MNAC" for short), it holds Europe's best collection of Roman-esque frescoes and offers a good sweep of modern Catalan art—fitting, given Catalunya's astonishing contribution to the Mod-ern. It's all housed in the grand Palau Nacional (National Palace), an emblematic building from the 1929 World Expo, with magnificent views over Barce-lona, especially from the building's rooftop terrace.

Cost and Hours: €12, free Sat from 15:00 and first Sun of month; open Tue-Sat 10:00-20:00 (Oct-April until 18:00), Sun 10:00-15:00, closed Mon year-round; above Magic Fountains near Plaça d'Espanya—take escalators up; +34 936 220 360, www.museunacional.cat.

Eating: The museum hosts the chic and pricey Oleum restau-rant with vast city views (€28 lunch *menu*, open until 23:30, until 15:30 in winter). There's also a comfy outdoor terrace café near the museum entrance (serving snacks with more city views; open Tue-Sun 10:00-19:30, closing time varies with Magic Fountains sched-ule—as late as 23:00 in summer).

Rooftop Terrace: The rooftop terrace offers views across the city. It's free with your museum ticket (otherwise €2; same hours as museum except Fri-Sat until 23:00 May-Sept). To reach the terrace from the main entrance, pass the WCs on the left and show your

ticket to ride the elevator most of the way, then climb a few flights of stairs up to the terrace. To take an elevator the whole way, go to the far end of the museum, through the huge dome room, to the far-right corner.

Visiting the Museum: As you enter, pick up a map, and download the audioguide app *Second Canvas Museo Nacional;* bring your own earbuds or headphones. The left wing is Romanesque, and the right wing is Gothic, Renaissance, and Baroque. Upstairs is more Baroque, plus modern art, photography, coins, and more.

Romanesque: The MNAC's world-class collection of Romanesque (Romànic) art gives a rare glimpse into the medieval mind.

Most pieces came from a handful of Catalan village churches clustered in a remote valley in the Pyrenees that thrived c. 1000-1300.

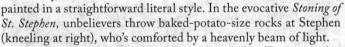

In **Room 1,** you're greeted by a fresco of Mary painted in a re-created apse of one of the churches.

Room 2 has the collection's most lively and colorful murals, painted in a straightforward literal style. In the evocative *Stoning of St. Stephen,* unbelievers throw baked-potato-size rocks at Stephen (kneeling at right), who's comforted by a heavenly beam of light.

In **Room 4,** one apse features saints in halos (Peter with his keys alongside Mary with a flaming chalice) and the countess who paid for the painting (lower right). The other apse has winged angels (seraphim) who appear to the prophets Isaiah (lower left) and Ezekiel (right), alongside Ezekiel's vision of the four-wheeled flaming chariot.

Rooms 5-7 focus on one of the most popular images in the medieval world: Christ in Majesty (a.k.a. the Pantocrator, or All Powerful). Jesus is depicted inside an almond-shaped halo, seated on a throne, with one hand raised in blessing, the other holding an open Bible. He's surrounded by either seraphim or the four symbols of the Evangelists. Christ is always easy to identify—he's the only one with a cross in his halo. Room 7 puts all the Romanesque elements together for a great in situ experience—a replica church, with Christ in Majesty in the apse and other Romanesque themes.

Browse through **Rooms 8-16** seeing leafy column capitals, wooden crucifixes, and statues of Mary and the saints, until you spill back out into the main hall.

• *Cross the hall to the rooms of...*

Gothic Art: Picking up where Romanesque left off (c. 1300), fresco murals give way to vivid 14th-century wood-panel paintings

of Bible stories. Make your way to **Room 26** (straight in, then to the left) and find the collection's highlight: a half-dozen paintings by the Catalan master Jaume Huguet (1412-1492), particularly his *Consagració de San Agustín (Consecration of Saint Augustine)*.

These paintings (impressive enough on their own) were once part of a huge altarpiece—an estimated 40 feet tall and 30 feet wide—with some 20 paintings, done for a church in El Born. Huguet labored on the project for more than 20 years. The theme was the life of St. Augustine. It started with the painting of young Augustine (in black robe and red cap) dropping his pagan books to the floor as he realizes the truth and converts to Christianity. In other scenes Augustine wears his golden robes and bishop's hat as he's shown preaching at a pulpit, or disputing a heretic (in green, who tumbles to the ground before the power of Augie's words), or kneeling to wash the feet of a pilgrim (who turns out to be Christ in disguise), or greeting a boy (who turns out to be a vision of young Jesus).

Huguet's masterpiece was the *Consecration* scene, where Augustine becomes bishop and is crowned with the hat. The details are incredible: the bright colors and gold leaf, the sober expressive faces, the brocaded robe with pictures of saints, and the early attempt at 3-D created by the floor tiles. Notice that this isn't simply a "painting"—it has a raised surface, like a cameo. It's a sheet of wood topped with molded stucco, then covered with paints and gold leaf. Nearby is Huguet's *Last Supper*, which was also part of the Augustine altarpiece.

• *The Gothic collection leads into...*

Renaissance and Baroque: Browse several rooms, watching as Renaissance artists make altarpieces more balanced and serene, with distant realistic backgrounds. You'll see Spain's golden age (Zurbarán, heavy religious scenes, and Spanish royals with their

endearing underbites) and examples of Romanticism (dewy-eyed Catalan landscapes). Room 32 has El Greco's *Christ Carrying the Cross* and José de Ribera's saints with wrinkled foreheads. In addition, you'll find minor works by major—if not necessarily Catalan—masters like Velázquez, Goya, Tintoretto, Rubens, and Titian.

Rest of the Museum: The Gothic/

Renaissance/Baroque exit spills out by the room of the huge **dome,** which has a cafeteria. From here, you can ride the glass elevator upstairs to the **modern art** section, where a big chronological clockwise circle from Room 1 covers Symbolism, Modernisme, fin de siècle fun, Art Deco, and more.

1929 WORLD EXPO FAIRGROUNDS AND NEARBY

Nearly everything you see here dates from the 1929 World Expo (the exceptions are CaixaForum and Las Arenas mall). The expo's theme was to demonstrate how electricity was about more than lightbulbs: Electricity powered the funicular, the glorious expo fountains, the many pavilion displays, and even the flame atop the fountain marking the center of Plaça d'Espanya.

Getting There: The fairgrounds sprawl at the base of Montjuïc, from the Catalan Art Museum's doorstep to Plaça d'Espanya. It's easiest to see these sights on your way down from Montjuïc. Otherwise, ride the Metro to Espanya, then use the series of stairs and escalators to climb up through the heart of the fairgrounds (eventually reaching the Catalan Art Museum).

▲Magic Fountains (Font Màgica)

Music, colored lights, and huge amounts of water make an artistic and coordinated splash in the evening near Plaça d'Espanya.

Cost and Hours: Free 20-minute shows start every half-hour; June-Sept Wed-Sun 21:30-22:30, April-May and Oct Thu-Sat 21:00-22:00, winter Thu-Sat 20:00-21:00 (no shows Jan-Feb); from the Espanya Metro stop, walk toward the towering National Palace.

▲CaixaForum

The CaixaForum Social and Cultural Center is housed in one of Barcelona's most important Art Nouveau buildings. In 1911, Josep Puig i Cadafalch (a top architect often overshadowed by Gaudí) designed the Casaramona textile factory, using Modernista design in an industrial rather than a residential context. It functioned as a factory for less than a decade, then later served a long stint as a police station under Franco. Beautifully refurbished in 2002, the

facility reopened as a great center for bringing culture and art to the people of Barcelona.

Cost and Hours: €6, daily 10:00-20:00, Avinguda de Francesc Ferrer i Guàrdia 6, +34 934 768 600, www.caixaforum.es/barcelona.

Visiting the Center: From the lobby, signs point to *Sala 2, 3, 4,* and *5;* each typically hosts an outstanding temporary exhibition. Ride the escalator to the first floor, which features a modest but interesting exhibit about the history and renovation of the building. Then head into the appealing red-brick courtyard to access the exhibition halls. The sight features some English descriptions. Take the stairs or elevator up to the Modernista Terrace (*Planta 2,* or look for signs to *Aula 1*). This terrace, boasting a wavy floor and bristling with fanciful brick towers, offers views over the complex and to Montjuïc.

Las Arenas (Bullring Mall)

The grand Neo-Moorish Modernista *plaça de toros* functioned as an arena for bullfights from around 1900 to 1977, and then reopened in 2011 as a mall.

The **rooftop terrace,** with stupendous views of Plaça d'Espanya and Montjuïc, is ringed with eateries (reachable by external glass elevator for €1 or from inside escalators/elevators for free). Besides getting a bird's-eye perspective of the fairgrounds, you can gaze down at Parc de Joan Miró, which includes the giant sculpture *Woman and Bird (Dona i Ocell)*. Miró's sense of humor is evident—if the sculpture seems phallic, keep in mind that the Catalan word for "bird" is also slang for "penis."

Cost and Hours: Free, daily 10:00-22:00, Oct-May 9:00-21:00, outside elevator and restaurants open late year-round, Gran Via de les Corts Catalanes 373, Metro: Espanya, exit following *Sortida Tarragona* signs, www.arenasdebarcelona.com.

BEACHES & NEARBY
▲Barcelona's Beaches

Barcelona has created a summer tourist trade by building a huge stretch of beach east of the town center. From Barceloneta, an uninterrupted band of sand tumbles three miles northeast to the Fòrum.

The overall scene is great for sunbathing and for an evening paseo before dinner. It's like a resort island—complete with lounge chairs, volleyball, showers, WCs, bike paths, and inviting beach bars called *chiringuitos*. Each beach segment has its own vibe: Sant Sebastià (closest, popular with older beachgoers and families), Barceloneta (with many seafood restaurants), Nova Icària (pleasant family beach), and Mar Bella (attracts a younger crowd, clothing-optional).

Getting There: The Barceloneta Metro stop leaves you a long walk from the sand. To get to the beaches without a hike, take the bus. From the Ramblas, bus #59 will get you as far as Barceloneta Park; bus #D20 leaves from the Columbus Monument and follows a similar route. Bus #V15 runs from Plaça de Catalunya to the tip of Barceloneta (near the W Hotel).

Biking the Beach: For a break from the city, rent a bike (for rental shops, see page 40) and take the following little ride: Explore Citadel Park, filled with families enjoying a day out. Then roll through Barceloneta. This artificial peninsula was once the home of working-class sailors and shippers. From the Barceloneta beach, head up to the Olympic Village, where the former apartments for 13,000 visiting athletes now house permanent residents. From here you'll come to a series of man-made crescent-shaped beaches, each with trendy bars and cafés. You might find yourself pedaling past people working on an all-over tan. In the distance is the huge solar panel marking the Fòrum shopping and convention center.

Citadel Park (Parc de la Ciutadella)

In 1888, Barcelona's biggest, greenest park, originally the site of a much-hated military citadel, was transformed for a Universal Exhibition (world's fair). The stately Triumphal Arch at the top of the park, celebrating the removal of the citadel, was built as the main entrance. Inside you'll find wide pathways, plenty of trees and grass, a zoo, a museum of geology, and a castle-like former restaurant for the fair (closed to the public).

Enjoy the ornamental fountain that the young Antoni Gaudí

BARCELONA

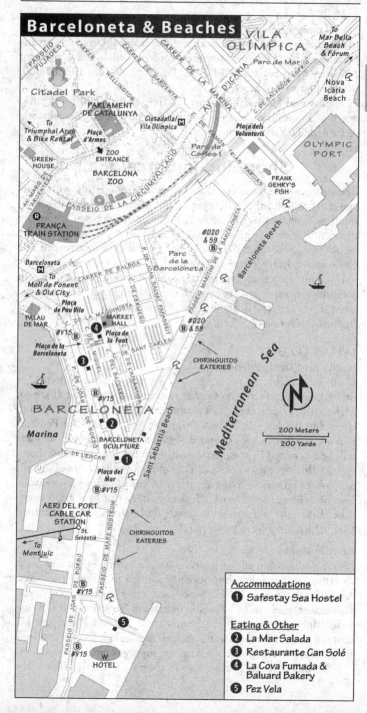

Barceloneta & Beaches

VILA OLÍMPICA

To Mar Bella Beach & Fòrum

PASSEIG PUJADES

CARRER DE WELLINGTON

CARRER DE SARDENYA

CARRER DE LA MARINA

AV. D'ICARIA

Parc de Mar

C. DE SALVADOR ESPRIU

Nova Icària Beach

Citadel Park

PARLAMENT DE CATALUNYA

To Triumphal Arch & Bike Rental

Plaça d'Armes

Ciutadella/ Vila Olímpica Ⓜ

C. DE RAMON TRIAS FARGAS

Plaça dels Voluntaris

OLYMPIC PORT

GREEN-HOUSE

ZOO ENTRANCE

Parc de Carles I

AV. MARQ DE L'ARGENTERA

BARCELONA ZOO

FRANK GEHRY'S FISH

PASSEIG DE LA CIRCUMVAL·LACIÓ

Ⓡ FRANÇA TRAIN STATION

#D20 & 59 Ⓑ

Barceloneta Ⓜ

Barceloneta Beach

To Moll de Ponent & Old City

CARRER DE BALBOA

P. DE JOAN SALVAT PAPASSEIT

Parc de la Barceloneta

C. DE CERMEÑO

PASSEIG MARÍTIM DE LA BARCELONETA

PALAU DE MAR

Plaça de Pau Vila

C. DE LA MAQUINISTA

❹ MARKET HALL

#V15 Ⓑ

Plaça de la Barceloneta

❸

C. DE SANT MIGUEL

Plaça de la Font

#D20 & 59 Ⓑ

C. DE SANT CARLES

C. DE LA LLANTIA

Mediterranean Sea

CHIRINGUITOS EATERIES

❷ #V15 Ⓑ

P. DE JOAN DE BORBÓ

C. DEL BALUARD

BARCELONETA

Marina

❷

BARCELONETA SCULPTURE

❶

Sant Sebastià Beach

Plaça del Mar

Ⓑ #V15

Ⓝ

200 Meters
200 Yards

AERI DEL PORT CABLE CAR STATION

St. Sebastià

CHIRINGUITOS EATERIES

To Montjuïc

PASSEIG DE MARE NOSTRUM

PASSEIG DE JOAN DE BORBÓ

Ⓑ #V15

❺

Ⓦ HOTEL

Accommodations
❶ Safestay Sea Hostel

Eating & Other
❷ La Mar Salada
❸ Restaurante Can Solé
❹ La Cova Fumada & Baluard Bakery
❺ Pez Vela

helped design, and consider a jaunt in a rental rowboat on the lake in the center of the park. Check out the tropical Umbracle greenhouse and the Hivernacle winter garden, which has a pleasant café-bar (Mon-Sat 10:00-14:00 & 17:00-20:30, Sun 10:30-14:00, shorter hours off-season).

Cost and Hours: Park entry is free, daily 10:00 until dusk, north of França train station, Metro: Arc de Triomf, Barceloneta, or Ciutadella/Vila Olímpica.

Shopping in Barcelona

The streets of the Barri Gòtic and El Born are bursting with characteristic hole-in-the-wall shops and delightful neighborhood boutiques, while the Eixample is the upscale "uptown" shopping district. The area around Avinguda del Portal de l'Angel (at the northern edge of the Barri Gòtic) has a number of department and chain stores. Large stores and some smaller shops in touristy zones may remain open through the afternoon—but don't count on it. On Saturdays, many shops are open in the morning only. On Sundays, most shops are closed (though the Maremagnum complex on the harborfront is open).

WHAT TO BUY
Home and Design Goods
Consider picking up prints, books, posters, decorative items, or other keepsakes featuring works by your favorite artist (Picasso, Dalí, Miró, Gaudí, etc.). Gift shops at major museums are open to the public (such as the Picasso Museum and Gaudí's La Pedrera) and are a bonanza for art and design lovers. Model-ship builders will be fascinated by the offerings at the Maritime Museum shop.

In this design-oriented city, home decor shops are abundant and fun to browse, offering a variety of euro-housewares unavailable back home. Decorative tile and pottery can be a good keepsake. Eixample sidewalks are paved with distinctively patterned tiles, which are sold in local shops.

Foodie Items
Home cooks might enjoy shopping for olive oil, wine, spices (such as saffron or sea salts), high-quality canned foods and preserves, torró (Catalan nougat), dried beans, and other Spanish food items. Remember, these must be sealed to make it back through US customs. But keep in mind that cured meat can never get past US customs, even if it is vacuum-packed and sealed. Cooks can look for European-style gadgets at kitchen-supply stores.

Market halls are great places to shop for Catalan edibles. The

best are La Boqueria (just off the Ramblas) and Santa Caterina in El Born (both described earlier).

Clothing and Jewelry

Department and chain stores can be fun places to browse for clothing. An *espardenya* (or *alpargata* in Spanish) is a soft-canvas, rope-soled shoe (known in the US as an espadrille). A few shops in Barcelona (including La Manual Alpargatera, in the Barri Gòtic) still make these the traditional way.

Jewelry shops are popular here. While the city doesn't have a strictly local style, finding a piece with a Modernista flourish gives it a Barcelona vibe.

Catalan Pride

If you're drawn to Catalunya's culture, consider a Catalan flag (gold and red stripes). And if you're a fan of Catalunyan independence, pick up one with the blue triangle and star.

Sports fans love jerseys, scarves, and other gear associated with the wildly popular Barça soccer team. As you wander, you'll likely see official football team shops. Knockoffs can be found at any tourist gift shop for less.

SHOPPING SPOTS

Barri Gòtic

The wide Carrer de la Portaferrissa, between the Barcelona Cathedral and the Ramblas, is lined with mostly international clothing stores (H&M, Mango, etc.). For more interesting streets lined with little local shops—plunge into some lanes just to the south.

Carrer de la Palla is ideal for antiques. On **Carrer dels Banys Nous,** the sprawling **Oliver** shop sells home decor, women's clothing, and accessories. Directly across the lane, **Artesania Catalunya** is a large market-space run by the city, featuring handmade items from Catalan artisans.

Plaça del Pi has some worthwhile shops and often local food and crafts markets. On **Carrer de Petritxol**, lined with art galleries and fancy jewelry shops, stop into **Xurreria** for *churros con chocolate;* or try **Vicens,** a fancy sweets shop specializing in *torró*, a nougat confection. **Carrer Ample** feels local but with little bursts of trendy energy. Skinny **Carrer de Bonsuccés,** on the other side of the Ramblas, has some fine boutiques.

El Born

This area is bohemian-chic, with funky shops and unique boutiques. The neighborhood centers on the long boulevard called Passeig del Born and the Church of Santa Maria del Mar. Look for interesting shops in the area around **Carrer del Rec** (boutiques), on **Carrer de l'Esparteria** (off Carrer del Rec), and the streets be-

tween **Carrer dels Banys Vells** and **Carrer de l'Argenteria** (artisan workshops and handmade clothing, accessories, and bags).

The Eixample

This ritzy "uptown" district is home to some of the city's top-end shops. In general, you'll find a lot of big international names along **Passeig de Gràcia,** the main boulevard that runs from Plaça de Catalunya to the Gaudí sights—an area fittingly called the "Golden Quarter" (Quadrat d'Or). Appropriately enough, the "upper end" of Passeig de Gràcia has the fancier shops—Gucci, Luis Vuitton, Escada, Chanel, and so on—while the southern part of the street is relatively "low-end" (Zara, Mango, H&M). One block to the west, **Rambla de Catalunya** holds more local (but still expensive) options: fashion, home decor, jewelry, perfume, and so on. The streets that connect Rambla de Catalunya to Passeig da Gràcia are also home to some fine shops, including some fun kitchen stores: Try **Gadgets & Cuina** (Carrer d'Aragó 249).

Department Stores

Plaça de Catalunya has a gigantic **El Corte Inglés** with a supermarket in the basement and a ninth-floor view cafeteria (Mon-Sat 9:00-21:00, until 22:00 in summer, closed Sun). Across the square is **FNAC**—a French department store that sells electronics, music, books, and tickets for major concerts and events (Mon-Sat 9:30-21:00, until 22:00 in summer, closed Sun).

Nightlife in Barcelona

Like all of Spain, Barcelona is extremely lively after hours. People head out for dinner at 22:00, then barhop or simply wander the streets until well after midnight. Some days it seems that more people are out and about at 2:00 in the morning (party time) than at 2:00 in the afternoon (lunch time). The most "local" thing you can do here after sunset is to explore neighborhood watering holes and find your favorite place to enjoy a glass of wine.

Information: Check out online guides *Time Out BCN Guide* (www.timeout.com/barcelona) and *Visit Barcelona* (www.visitbarcelona.com), both in English with descriptions of each day's main events and ticket information. The TI's culture website is also helpful: www.barcelona.cat/barcelonacultura. *Guía del Ocio* is a Spanish-language entertainment website with a section on Barcelona (www.guiadelocio.com/barcelona).

Palau de la Virreina, an arts-and-culture information office, provides details on Barcelona cultural events—music, opera, and theater (Tue-Sun 11:00-20:00, closed Mon, Ramblas 99, see the "Ramblas Ramble" map, earlier, +34 933 161 000, www.lavirreina.bcn.cat). A ticket desk is next door.

Getting Tickets: Most venues sell tickets through their web-sites, or you can book through TicketMaster or Eventbrite. You can also get tickets through the box offices in the main El Corte Inglés department store or the giant FNAC electronics store (both on Plaça de Catalunya, extra booking fee), or at the ticket desk in Palau de la Virreina (see above).

MUSIC AND DANCE
Concerts

The **Palace of Catalan Music** (described under "Sights in Barcelona," earlier) offers a full slate of performances, ranging from symphonic to Catalan folk songs to chamber music to flamenco (€20-175 tickets, box office open Mon-Sat 9:30-21:00, Sun 10:00-15:00, Carrer Palau de la Música 4, Metro: Urquinaona, box office +34 933 957 207, www.palaumusica.cat). Look for shows held in the Sala de Concerts in order to see the Modernista main concert hall (not in the new Petit Palau hall).

The **Liceu Opera House** (Gran Teatre del Liceu), right in the heart of the Ramblas, is a pre-Modernista, sumptuous venue for opera, dance, children's theater, and concerts (tickets from €10, buy tickets online up to 1.5 hours before show or in person, Ramblas 51, box office just around the corner at Carrer Sant Pau 1, Metro: Liceu, info +34 934 859 900 www.liceubarcelona.cat).

Some of Barcelona's top sights host good-quality concerts. On summer weekends, a classy option is a **"Summer Nights at La Pedrera"** jazz concert at Gaudí's Modernista masterpiece in the Eixample (see page 101). Also try the **Fundació Joan Miró** and **CaixaForum** (for details, check their websites).

Touristy Performances of Spanish Clichés

Two famously Spanish types of music—flamenco and Spanish guitar—have little to do with Barcelona or Catalunya, but are performed here to keep visitors happy. If you're headed for other parts of Spain where these musical forms are more typical (such as Andalucía for flamenco), you might as well wait until you can experience the real deal.

Flamenco: While flamenco is foreign to Catalunya (locals say that it's like going to see country music in Boston), there are some good places to view this unique Spanish artform. Head to **Palau Dalmases,** in an atmospheric old palace courtyard in the heart of El Born, for the highest-quality performances I've found (€30 includes a drink, Fri-Wed at 19:30 and 21:30, Thu at 19:30 only, also hosts opera and jazz, Carrer de Montcada 20, +34 933 100 673, www.palaudalmases.com).

Tarantos, on Plaça Reial in the heart of the Barri Gòtic, puts on brief (30 minutes), riveting flamenco performances several times

nightly—an easy and inexpensive way to see it. Performances are in a touristy little bar/theater with about 50 seats (€17; nightly at 19:30, 20:30, and 21:30; Plaça Reial 17, https://tarantosbarcelona. com).

Another option is the pricey (and relatively high-quality) **Tablao Cordobés** on the Ramblas (€45 includes a drink, €80 includes mediocre buffet dinner and better seats, 3 performances/day, Ramblas 35, +34 933 175 711, www.tablaocordobes.es).

For flamenco in a concert-hall setting, try one of the Palace of Catalan Music's regular performances (see listing earlier, under "Concerts").

Spanish Guitar: "Masters of Guitar" concerts are offered nearly nightly at 21:00 in the Barri Gòtic's Church of Santa Maria del Pi (€23 at the door, €4 less if you buy online or at least 3 hours ahead—look for ticket sellers in front of church, Plaça del Pi 7; +34 647 514 513, www.maestrosdelaguitarra.com). The same company also does occasional concerts in the **Palace of Catalan Music** (€39-45).

AFTER-HOURS HANGOUT NEIGHBORHOODS
El Born
Passeig del Born, a broad parklike strip stretching from the Church of Santa Maria del Mar up to the old market hall, is lined with inviting bars and nightspots. Right on Passeig del Born is **Miramelindo,** a local favorite—mellow yet convivial, with two floors of woody ambience and a minty aura from all those mojitos the bartenders are mashing up (Passeig del Born 15). **Palau Dalmases,** in the atmospheric courtyard of an old palace, slings cocktails when it's not hosting flamenco shows (described earlier). **La Vinya del Senyor** is a fine place for a glass of high-quality wine on the square in front of the Church of Santa Maria del Mar.

Plaça Reial and Nearby
This elegant-feeling square, just off the Ramblas in the Barri Gòtic, has a trendy charm. It bustles with popular bars and restaurants offering pleasant outdoor tables and inflated prices. While not a great place to eat, this is a great place to sip a before- or after-dinner drink. **Bar Club Ocaña,** at #13, has a dilapidated-mod interior, a see-through industrial kitchen, rickety-chic secondhand tables out on the square, and another cocktail bar downstairs (open nightly, can reserve a table online at www.ocana.cat). Or there's always

the student option: Buy a cheap €1 beer from a convenience store (you'll find several just off the square, including a few along Carrer dels Escudellers, just south of Plaça Reial), then grab a free spot on the square, either sitting on one of the few fixed chairs, perched along the rim of the fountain, or simply leaning up against a palm tree.

Wandering the streets near the square leads to other nightlife options. **Carrer de Escudellers** is a significantly rougher scene—a few trendy options are mixed in with several sketchy dives. Much closer to the harbor, **Carrer de la Mercè** (described later, under "Eating in Barcelona") has its share of salty sailors' pubs and more youthful bars. The next street up, **Carrer Ample,** has a similar scene.

Barceloneta

A broad beach stretches for miles from the former fishermen's quarter at Barceloneta to the Fòrum. Every 100 yards or so is a *chiringuito*—a shack selling drinks and light snacks. Originally these sold seafood, but now they keep locals and tourists well-lubricated. It's a very fun, lively scene on a balmy summer evening and a nice way to escape the claustrophobic confines of the Old City to enjoy some sea air and the day's final sun rays.

Barceloneta itself has a broad promenade facing the harbor, lined with interchangeable seafood restaurants. But the best beach experience is beyond the tip of Barceloneta. From here, a double-decker boardwalk runs the length of the beach, with a cool walkway up above and a series of fine seafood restaurants with romantic candlelit beachfront seating tucked down below.

Montjuïc

With a little hustle, in summer it's possible to string together a fun evening of memorable views from the Montjuïc hilltop. Start with sweeping city vistas as you ride the Aeri del Port cable car (catch it at the tip of the Barceloneta peninsula) up to the park's Miramar viewpoint. From there, head up to Montjuïc Castle on foot for more breathtaking views. Finally, wind your way around the hilltop to the Catalan Art Museum and reward yourself with a drink at its terrace café—a prime spot for taking in the Magic Fountains show (for details, see the museum listing earlier, under "Sights in Barcelona").

The Eixample

Barcelona's upscale uptown isn't quite as lively or funky as some other neighborhoods, but a few streets have some fine watering holes. Walk along the inviting, parklike **Rambla de Catalunya,** or a couple of blocks over, along **Carrer d'Enric Granados** and **Carrer d'Aribau** (near the epicenter of the Eixample's gay commu-

nity); these streets are speckled with cocktail bars offering breezy outdoor seating. In the opposite direction (east of Passeig de Gràcia), **Bar Dow Jones**—popular with the American expat student crowd—has a clever gimmick: Drink prices rise and fall like the stock market (Carrer del Bruc 97).

Sleeping in Barcelona

Choosing the right neighborhood in Barcelona is as important as choosing the right hotel. All of my recommended accommodations are in safe areas convenient to sightseeing. The area around Plaça de Catalunya, Barcelona's central square, is filled with business-class hotels. Near the Ramblas—the city's pedestrian boulevard—you'll find cheaper, less-refined places with more character. For Old World charm, stay in Barcelona's Old City. For an uptown feel, sleep in the Eixample.

Despite being Spain's most expensive city, Barcelona has reasonably priced rooms. Cheap places are more crowded in summer; fancier business-class hotels fill up in winter and may offer discounts on weekends and in summer. When considering relative hotel values, in summer and on weekends you can often get modern comfort in centrally located business-class hotels for about the same price (€130) as you'll pay for ramshackle charm. For some travelers, short-term, Airbnb-type rentals can be a good alternative; search for places in my recommended hotel neighborhoods.

I rank accommodations from $ budget to $$$$ splurge. For the best deal, contact hotels directly by phone or email. When you book direct, the owner avoids a commission and may be able to offer a discount. Book well in advance for peak season or if your trip coincides with a major holiday or festival (see the appendix). Note, though, that Barcelona can be busy any time of year. For more details on reservations, short-term rentals, and more, see the "Sleeping" section in the Practicalities chapter.

NEAR PLAÇA DE CATALUNYA

These modern hotels are on big streets within two blocks of Barcelona's exuberant central square, where the Old City meets the Eixample. As business-class hotels, they have hard-to-pin-down prices that fluctuate with demand. In summer and on weekends, supply often far exceeds the demand, and many of these places cut prices. Some of my recommended hotels are on Carrer Pelai, a busy street; for these, request a quieter room in back.

$$$$ Hotel Catalonia Plaça Catalunya has four stars, an elegant old entryway with a modern reception area, splashy public spaces, slick marble and hardwood floors, 150 comfortable rooms, and a garden courtyard with a pool a world away from the big-city

noise. It's a bit pricey for the quality of the rooms—you're paying for the posh lobby (air-con, elevator, a half-block off Plaça de Catalunya at Carrer de Bergara 11, Metro: Catalunya, +34 933 015 151, www.cataloniahotels.com, booking@cataloniahotels.com).

$$$$ Hotel Midmost is an oasis a little west of Plaça de Catalunya. It has 56 rooms with luxurious, four-star style; a seaside-lounge-inspired rooftop terrace; and a mini pool to relax (family rooms, air-con, elevator, Carrer de Pelai 14, Metro: Universitat, +34 935 051 100, www.hotelmidmost.com, info@hotelmidmost.com).

$$$ Hotel Ginebra is a modern version of the old-school *pension,* with 18 rooms in a classic, well-located building at the corner of Plaça de Catalunya (RS%—use code "HGinebra-Rick-Steves" and print voucher, family rooms, breakfast extra, laundry, air-con, elevator, Rambla de Catalunya 1, Metro: Catalunya, +34 932 502 017, www.hotelginebra.com.es, info@hotelginebra.com.es, Brits Alfred and Ivon).

$$$ Hotel Reding Croma, on a quiet street a 10-minute walk west of the Ramblas and the Plaça de Catalunya action, is a slick and sleek place renting 44 basic but mod rooms on color-themed floors at a reasonable price (RS%, air-con, elevator, Carrer de Gravina 5, Metro: Universitat, +34 934 121 097, www.hotelreding.com, reservas@hotelreding.com).

$$$ Hotel Lleó (YAH-oh) is well-run, with 92 big, bright, and comfortable rooms; a great breakfast room; and a generous lounge (air-con, elevator, small rooftop pool, Carrer de Pelai 22, midway between Metros: Universitat and Catalunya, +34 933 181 312, www.hotel-lleo.com, info@hotel-lleo.com).

$$ Hotel Atlantis is solid, with 50 big, nondescript, slightly dated rooms and fair prices for the location (includes breakfast, air-con, elevator, Carrer de Pelai 20, midway between Metros: Universitat and Catalunya, +34 933 189 012, www.hotelatlantis-atbcn.com, info@hotelatlantis-bcn.com).

$$ Hotel Denit is a small, stylish, 36-room hotel on a pedestrian street two blocks off Plaça de Catalunya. It's chic, minimalist, and fun: Guidebook tips decorate the halls, and the rooms are sized like T-shirts, from small to extra-large (includes breakfast, air-con, elevator, Carrer d'Estruc 24, Metro: Catalunya, +34 935 454 000, www.denit.com, info@denit.com).

ON OR NEAR THE RAMBLAS

These places are generally family-run, with ad-lib furnishings, more character, and lower prices.

$$$ Hotel Continental Barcelona, in a building overlooking the top of the Ramblas, offers classic, tiny view-balcony opportunities if you don't mind the street noise. Its 40 rooms are quite

BARCELONA

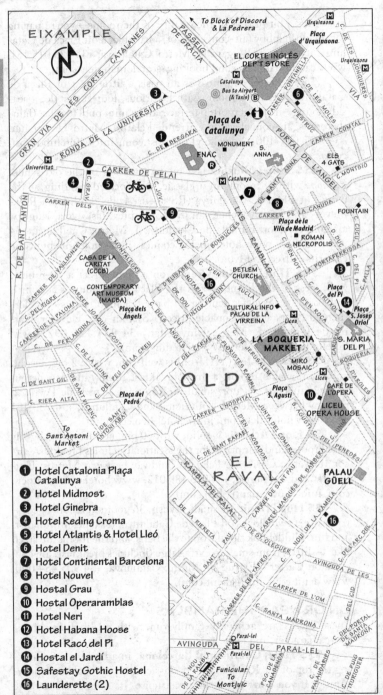

1 Hotel Catalonia Plaça Catalunya
2 Hotel Midmost
3 Hotel Ginebra
4 Hotel Reding Croma
5 Hotel Atlantis & Hotel Lleó
6 Hotel Denit
7 Hotel Continental Barcelona
8 Hotel Nouvel
9 Hostal Grau
10 Hostal Operaramblas
11 Hotel Neri
12 Hotel Habana Hoose
13 Hotel Racó del Pi
14 Hostal el Jardí
15 Safestay Gothic Hostel
16 Launderette (2)

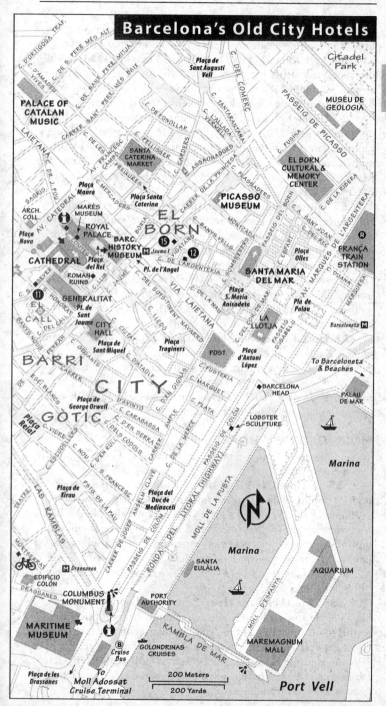

Barcelona's Old City Hotels

comfortable and the staff is friendly. Choose between your own little Ramblas-view balcony (where you can eat your breakfast) or a quieter back room. J. M.'s (José María's) free breakfast and all-day snack-and-drink bar are a plus (RS%, air-con, elevator, quiet terrace, Ramblas 138, Metro: Catalunya, +34 933 012 570, www.hotelcontinental.com, barcelona@hotelcontinental.com).

$$$ Hotel Nouvel, in an elegant, Victorian-style building on a handy pedestrian street, is less business oriented and offers more character than the others listed here. It boasts royal lounges and 78 comfy rooms (air-con, elevator, Carrer de Santa Anna 18, Metro: Catalunya, +34 933 018 274, www.hotelnouvel.es, info@hotelnouvel.com).

$$ Hostal Grau is a homey, family-run, and extremely eco-conscious hotel with custom recycled furniture and organic bedding. It has 25 crisp, impeccable, and cheery rooms a few blocks off the Ramblas in the colorful university district. Double-glazed windows keep it quiet (some rooms with balconies, family rooms, strict cancellation policy, air-con, kitchen available for guests, elevator, 200 yards up Carrer dels Tallers from the Ramblas at Ramelleres 27, Metro: Catalunya, +34 933 018 135, www.hostalgrau.com, bookgreen@hostalgrau.com, Monica).

$$ Hostal Operaramblas, with 68 simple rooms 20 yards off the Ramblas, is clean, modern, and a great value. The street can feel a bit seedy at night, but it's safe, and the hotel is very secure (RS%—use code "operaramblas," air-con in summer, elevator, Carrer de Sant Pau 20, Metro: Liceu, +34 933 188 201, www.operaramblas.com, info@operaramblas.com).

MORE OLD CITY HOTELS

These accommodations are buried in Barcelona's Old City, mostly in the Barri Gòtic.

$$$$ Hotel Neri is posh, pretentious, and sophisticated, with 22 rooms spliced into the ancient stones of the Barri Gòtic, overlooking an overlooked square (Plaça Sant Felip Neri) a block from the cathedral. It has pricey modern art on the bedroom walls, dressed-up people in its gourmet restaurant, and high-class service (air-con, elevator, rooftop tanning deck, Carrer de Sant Sever 5, Metro: Liceu or Jaume I, +34 933 040 655, www.hotelneri.com, info@hotelneri.com).

$$$$ Hotel Habana Hoose, a modern, boutique-type place, has a people-to-people ethic and refreshingly straight prices. Its 43 restful rooms are located in the El Born district on a pedestrianized street between the cathedral and Church of Santa Maria del Mar (air-con, elevator, Carrer de l'Argenteria 37, 50 yards from Metro: Jaume I, +34 935 956 505, www.chicandbasic.com/barcelona/en, habanahoose@chicandbasic.com).

$$$ Hotel Racó del Pi, part of the H10 hotel chain, is a quality, professional place with generous public spaces and 37 modern, bright, quiet rooms. It's located on a wonderful pedestrian street immersed in the Barri Gòtic (air-con, around the corner from Plaça del Pi at Carrer del Pi 7, three-minute walk from Metro: Liceu, +34 933 426 190, www.h10hotels.com, h10.raco.delpi@h10hotels.com).

$$ Hostal el Jardí offers 40 remodeled rooms on a breezy square. Many of the tight, plain, comfy rooms come with petite balconies (for an extra charge) and enjoy an almost Parisian feel. It's a good deal only if you value the quaint-square-with-Barri-Gòtic ambience—you're paying for the location. Book well in advance (air-con, elevator, some stairs, halfway between Ramblas and cathedral at Plaça Sant Josep Oriol 1, Metro: Liceu, +34 933 015 900, www.eljardi.com, reservations@eljardi.com).

EIXAMPLE

For an uptown, boulevard-like neighborhood, sleep in the Eixample, a 10-minute walk from the Ramblas action. Most of these places use the Passeig de Gràcia or Catalunya Metro stops. Because these stations are so huge—especially Passeig de Gràcia, which sprawls underground for a few blocks—study the maps posted in the station to establish which exit you want before surfacing.

$$$$ Hotel Granvía, filling a palatial, brightly renovated 1870s mansion, offers a large, peaceful sun patio, several comfortable common areas, and 58 spacious, modern, business-style rooms (RS%—free breakfast for Rick Steves readers who book direct, family rooms, air-con, elevator, Gran Via de les Corts Catalanes 642, Metro: Passeig de Gràcia, +34 933 181 900, www.hotelgranvia.com, hgranvia@nnhotels.com).

$$$$ Hotel Yurbban Trafalgar is a small, classy boutique hotel with 56 rooms and a masculine-minimalist decor. Their rooftop bar, tiny pool, and views alone are worth the price of your stay (air-con, free self-service laundry, gym, near the Palace of Catalan Music at Carrer de Trafalgar 30, a long block from Metro: Urquinaona, +34 932 680 727, www.yurbban.com, trafalgar@yurbban.com).

$$$ Hotel Continental Palacete, with 22 rooms (some tiny), fills a 100-year-old chandeliered mansion. With flowery wallpaper and ornately gilded stucco, it's gaudy in the city of Gaudí, but it's also friendly, quiet, and well located. Guests have unlimited access to the outdoor terrace and a fruit, veggie, and drink buffet (RS%, includes breakfast, air-con, two blocks northwest of Plaça de Catalunya at corner of Rambla de Catalunya and Carrer de la Diputació, Rambla de Catalunya 30, Metro: Passeig de Gràcia, +34 934 457 657, www.hotelcontinental.com, palacete@hotelcontinental.com).

Hotels & Restaurants in the Eixample

$$ BacHome B&B has two bright and comfortable locations in traditional Eixample buildings on Carrer Bruc. BacHome Terrace (at #14, +34 620 657 810) has 10 rooms and a pleasant outdoor terrace. BacHome Gallery (#96, +34 608 350 965) has seven rooms and common areas with big windows looking out onto the city (includes breakfast, air-con, elevator, Metro: Urquinaona, www.bachomebarcelona.com, reservations@bachomebarcelona.com).

$$ Hostal Oliva, family-run with care, is a spartan, old-school place with 16 basic, bright, high-ceilinged rooms. It's on the fourth floor of a classic old Eixample building—with a beautiful mahogany elevator—in a perfect location, just a couple of blocks above Plaça de Catalunya (corner of Passeig de Gràcia and Carrer de la Diputació, Passeig de Gràcia 32, Metro: Passeig de Gràcia, +34 934 880 162, www.hostaloliva.com, info@hostaloliva.com).

BARCELONA

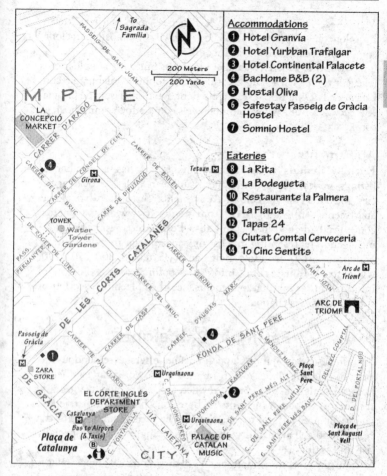

Accommodations
1. Hotel Granvía
2. Hotel Yurbban Trafalgar
3. Hotel Continental Palacete
4. BacHome B&B (2)
5. Hostal Oliva
6. Safestay Passeig de Gràcia Hostel
7. Somnio Hostel

Eateries
8. La Rita
9. La Bodegueta
10. Restaurante la Palmera
11. La Flauta
12. Tapas 24
13. Ciutat Comtal Cerveceria
14. To Cinc Sentits

OTHER ACCOMMODATIONS

Hostels

¢ **Safestay Hostels:** Barcelona has a terrific chain of well-run hostels—in the Eixample, in the Barri Gòtic, and near the beach—offering plenty of opportunities to meet other backpackers (www.safestay.com). All three locations enforce quiet hours after 23:00. **Safestay Gothic Hostel** rents 130 beds a block from the Picasso Museum (roof terrace, Carrer Vigatans 5, Metro: Jaume I, reception +34 932 687 808, safestaygothic@safestay.com). **Safestay Passeig de Gràcia Hostel** rents 400 beds in the heart of the Eixample (bar, kitchen, Passeig de Gràcia 33, Metro: Passeig de Gràcia, +34 932 156 538, receptionbcnpdg@safestay.com). **Safestay Sea Hostel** has 70 beds by the beach (closed roughly Nov-Feb, Plaça del

Mar 4—see the "Barceloneta & Beaches" map, earlier, Metro: Barceloneta, reception +34 634 354 499, www.seahostelbarcelona. com, hello@seahostelbarcelona.com).

¢ **Somnio Hostel,** a smaller place, has nine very simple rooms (cheaper rooms with shared bath, private rooms available, air-con, Carrer de la Diputació 251, second floor, Metro: Passeig de Gràcia, +34 932 725 308, www.somniohostels.com, info@somniohostels. com).

Apartments

Friendly Rentals (www.friendlyrentals.com) has a number of listings in Barcelona (and other European cities). Local agencies include **Top Barcelona Apartments** (http://top-barcelona-apartments.com) and **MH Apartments** (www.mhapartments. com). I've had good luck with **Cross-Pollinate,** a reputable booking agency representing B&Bs and apartments in a handful of European cities, including Barcelona (US tel. +1 800 270 1190, www.cross-pollinate.com, info@cross-pollinate.com). For more information on renting apartments, see the "Sleeping" section of the Practicalities chapter.

Eating in Barcelona

Barcelona, the capital of Catalan cuisine, offers a tremendous variety of colorful places to eat, ranging from workaday eateries to homey Catalan bistros *(cans)*, crowded tapas bars, and avant-garde restaurants. Good restaurants in Barcelona benefit from talented chefs who aren't afraid to experiment, the relative affluence of the region, and the availability of good, fresh ingredients—especially fish and seafood.

In my recommendations, I've distinguished tapas places (which serve small plates throughout the afternoon and evening) from more formal restaurants (with generous portions, no tapas, and service that starts much later than the American norm). Most of my recommended eateries—grouped by neighborhood and handy to the sights—are practical, characteristic, affordable, and lively, with a busy tapas scene at the bar, along with restaurant tables where larger plates can be enjoyed family-style. To avoid bad, overly touristy restaurants, a good rule of thumb is not to eat (or drink) on the Ramblas or Passeig de Gràcia.

Catalan tapas menus most often include seafood (cod, hake, tuna, squid, and anchovies), delicious local olives, and a traditional sausage called *butifarra*. In restaurants, you'll see Catalan favorites such as *fideuà*, a thin, flavor-infused noodle served with seafood—a kind of Catalan paella—and *arròs negre*, black rice cooked in squid ink. *Pa amb tomàquet* is the classic Catalan way to eat bread—

toasted white bread with olive oil, tomato, and a pinch of salt. It's often served free with your plate and also used to make sandwiches. While the famous cured *jamón* (ham) is more Spanish than it is Catalan, you'll still find lots of it in Catalunya (see the "Sampling *Jamón*" sidebar in the Practicalities chapter). All this food is accompanied by local beers, wines, and, of course, the beloved sweet vermouth.

EATING TIPS

I rank eateries from $ budget to $$$$ splurge. For more advice on eating in Spain, including ordering, tipping, adapting to the Spanish eating schedule, and typical cuisine and beverages, see the "Eating" section of the Practicalities chapter. I've tried to make this information appropriately Catalan—as opposed to just Spanish with a Barcelona accent.

Hours: As in the rest of Spain, the people of Catalunya eat late—lunch around 14:00 (and as late as 16:00), and dinner after 21:00. The earliest you can go to a restaurant for dinner is about 20:30, when the place is empty or filled with tourists. Going after 21:00 is better, but if you wait until 22:00, it can be hard to get into popular restaurants. Note that many restaurants close in August (or July), when the owners take a vacation.

Although tapas are served throughout the day, the real action begins late—21:00 or after. For less competition at the bar, go early or on Monday and Tuesday (but check to see if the place is open, as many close on Sunday or Monday). For advice on adapting to the Spanish eating schedule, see page 975.

Bread and Water: Most places don't automatically give you bread with your meal. If you ask for it, you'll usually receive *pa amb tomàquet* (bread with tomato spread), and you will be charged. Barcelona's tap water is safe to drink and free, but some bar owners are rather insistent on not serving it to their clientele, as it doesn't taste particularly good. For details on how to ask for water, see page 985.

Local-Style Tapas: Catalans have an affinity for Basque culture, so you'll find a lot of Basque-style tapas places here, where they

lay out bite-size tapas (called *pintxos*, or *pinchos*) on the countertop. These places are user-friendly, as you are free to take what you want, and you don't have to look at a menu or wait to be served; just grab what looks good, order a drink, and save your toothpicks (they'll count them up at the end to tally your bill). I've listed several of these bars (including Taverna Basca Irati and Sagardi Euskal Taberna), but there are many others. Look for

vasco or *euskal* (both mean "Basque")—or just keep an eye out for places with lots of toothpicks. You'll also find traditional Catalan tapas bars and *bodegas* (originally a name denoting wine cellars but preserved as many *bodegas* evolved into restaurants).

Catalan in Restaurants: Catalan and Spanish (in that order) are the official languages of Barcelona. While menus are usually in both languages, and many times English as well, these days—with the feisty spirit of independence stoked—you may find some menus in just Catalan, or Catalan and English without Spanish. I've given most food terms in Spanish and added Catalan where helpful. For terms in Spanish and Catalan, consult the "Tapas Menu Decoder" on page 982 and the list of drink terms on page 981.

In any Catalan bar or restaurant, an occasional *"si us plau"* (please) or *"moltes gràcies"* (thank you very much) goes a long way with the locals. An *"adéu"* (goodbye), *"que vagi bé"* (have a good one!), or, in the evening, *"bona nit"* (good evening/night) on your way out the door will certainly earn you a smile. And, as they say in Catalan, *"Bon profit!"* (Bon appétit!)

NEAR THE RAMBLAS

The entire length of the Ramblas itself is a tourist trap with bad food, weak drinks, and rip-off prices. But within a few steps of the Ramblas, you'll find several handy lunch places, an inviting market hall, and some good vegetarian options.

Lunching Simply yet Memorably near the Ramblas

Although these places are enjoyable for a lunch break from sightseeing, many are also open for dinner.

$$ Taverna Basca Irati serves 40 kinds of hot and cold Basque *pintxos* for €2.10 each. These are small open-faced sandwiches—a baguette slice topped with something tasty. Muscle in through the hungry crowd, get an empty plate from the waiter, and then help yourself. Every few minutes, waiters circulate with platters of new, still-warm munchies. Grab one as they pass by...it's addictive (you'll be charged by the number of toothpicks left on your plate when you're done). For drink options, look for the printed menu on the wall in the back. Wash down your food with Rioja (full-bodied red wine), Txakolí (sprightly Basque white wine), or *sidra* (apple wine). Open daily (11:00-24:00, a block off the Ramblas, behind arcade at Carrer del Cardenal Casanyes 17, Metro: Liceu, +34 933 023 084).

$$ Restaurant Elisabets is a rough little neighborhood eatery packed with antique radios. It's popular with young locals and tourists alike for its €13.50 "home-cooked" three-course lunch special (13:00-17:30 only). Stop by for lunch, survey what those around you are enjoying, and order what looks best. Locals put up

with the brusque service for the tasty food (Mon-Sat 7:30-23:00, closed Sun and Aug, reservations smart for lunch, 2 blocks west of Ramblas on far corner of Plaça del Bonsuccés at Carrer d'Elisabets 2, Metro: Catalunya, +34 933 175 826).

$$ Café Granja Viader is a quaint time capsule, family-run since 1870. They boast about being the first dairy business to bottle and distribute milk in Spain. Specializing in baked and dairy treats, toasted sandwiches, and light meals, this place is ideal for a traditional breakfast. Or indulge your sweet tooth: Try a glass of *orxata* (or *horchata*—*chufa*-nut milk, summer only), *llet mallorquina* (Majorca-style milk with cinnamon, lemon, and sugar), *crema catalana* (crème brûlée, their specialty), or *suis* ("Swiss"—hot chocolate with a snowcap of whipped cream). *Mel i mató* is fresh cheese with honey...very Catalan (Mon-Sat 9:00-13:00 & 17:00-21:00, closed Sun, a block off the Ramblas behind Betlem Church at Carrer d'en Xuclà 4, Metro: Liceu, +34 933 183 486).

Cafeteria on Plaça de Catalunya: For a quick, affordable lunch with an almost 360-degree view, the ninth-floor cafeteria at **$$ El Corte Inglés** can't be beat. Grab a tray and browse; there's always fresh paella, and the food is often cooked to order (Mon-Sat 9:30-21:00, until 22:00 in summer, closed Sun, Metro: Catalunya, +34 933 063 800).

Picnics: Shoestring tourists buy groceries at **El Corte Inglés** (supermarket in basement) and **Carrefour Market** (Mon-Sat 10:00-22:00, closed Sun, Ramblas 113, Metro: Liceu).

La Boqueria Market: If you're in La Boqueria and ready for lunch, a snack, or a drink, several high-energy bars would love to take your money. The **Pinotxo Bar** (just to the right as you enter) has a waiter beloved for his smile and his double thumbs up. If you see fun-loving Juan, give him a wink and a double thumbs up yourself. For more on La Boqueria, see the "Ramblas Ramble," earlier. For a less-touristy market hall, try Santa Caterina in El Born (described later).

Vegetarian Eateries near the Ramblas

$$ Biocenter, a Catalan soup-and-salad restaurant busy with local vegetarians, takes its cooking very seriously. They serve a generous portion of *pa amb tomàquet* (weekday lunch specials include soup or salad and plate of the day, Mon-Sat 13:00-23:00, Sun until 16:00, two blocks off the Ramblas at Carrer del Pintor Fortuny 25, Metro: Liceu, +34 933 014 583).

$$ Flax & Kale is a top-end vegetarian place; the nearby campus gives it a university vibe. As its name suggests, this place serves seriously healthy dishes and juices in a delightful, spacious indoor setting (Mon-Fri 12:00-23:00, Sat-Sun from 10:00, five-minute walk from the top of the Ramblas at Carrer Tallers 74, +34 933 175

BARCELONA

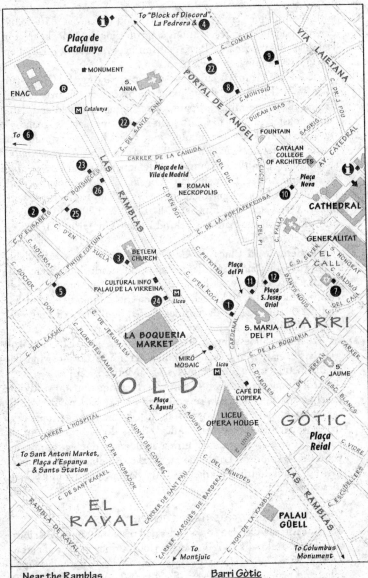

Near the Ramblas
1. Taverna Basca Irati
2. Restaurant Elisabets
3. Café Granja Viader
4. To El Corte Inglés
5. Biocenter
6. To Flax & Kale, Teresa Carles & Mucci's Pizza

Barri Gòtic
7. La Vinateria del Call
8. Els Quatre Gats
9. Onofre Vinos y Viandas
10. Bilbao Berria Pintxos & Tapas
11. Bar del Pi
12. El Drac de Sant Jordi
13. Carrer de la Mercè Tapas Bars

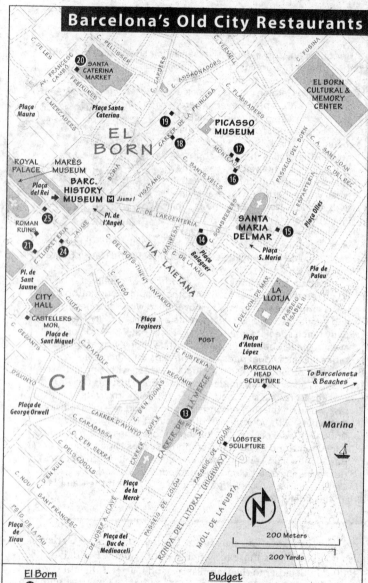

Barcelona's Old City Restaurants

El Born
14 Sagardi Euskal Taberna
15 Vegetalia
16 El Xampanyet
17 Tapeo
18 Can Cisa/Bar Brutal
19 Bar del Pla
20 Cuines Santa Caterina & Tapas Bars

Budget
21 Conesa Entrepans
22 El Mós (2)
23 Mucci's Pizza
24 Wok to Walk (2)
25 Buenas Migas (2)
26 Supermarket

Budget Meals Around Town

Bright, clean, and inexpensive **sandwich shops** proudly hold the cultural line against the fast-food invasion that has hamburgerized the rest of Europe. You'll see two big Catalan chains (Bocatta and Pans & Company) everywhere, serving mass-produced McBaguettes ordered from a multilingual menu. I've had better luck with hole-in-the-wall sandwich shops—virtually as numerous as the chains—where you can see exactly what you're getting. Good alternatives include **Conesa Entrepans** (on Plaça de Sant Jaume) and the good local chain **El Mós,** with speedy service, fresh ingredients, and long hours daily (two locations near Plaça de Catalunya, at Carrer Comtal 12 and Carrer Santa Anna 9).

Kebab places are also a good, super-cheap standby; you'll see them all over town. Another popular budget option is the **empanada**—a pastry turnover filled with seasoned meat and vegetables. In basic restaurants and bars, you'll often find **daily lunch specials** (*menú del día*) for about €12. And you can always graze cheaply in bars offering an array of affordable **tapas** and individual bites called ***pintxos*** (or *pinchos*).

For other options, try **Mucci's Pizza,** with good, fresh pizza slices and empanadas (two locations just off the Ramblas, at Bonsuccés 10 and Tallers 75). **Wok to Walk** makes tasty food on the run, serving up noodles and rice in takeaway containers with your choice of meat and/or veggies and finished with a savory sauce (convenient branches near Plaça de Sant Jaume and Liceu Metro station). **Buenas Migas** is another Barcelona chain serving focaccia, quiche, salads, and pastas (locations include behind the cathedral at Baixada de Santa Clara 2, at Plaça de la Sagrada Família 17, and off the Ramblas at Plaça del Bonsuccés 6).

664). Its sister location, named for the founder, **Teresa Carles,** is also good but has a more forgettable setting (daily 12:00-17:00 & 19:00-23:00, closer to the Ramblas, just off Carrer Tallers at Carrer Jovellanos 2, Metro: Universitat or Catalunya, +34 933 171 829).

BARRI GÒTIC

These eateries populate Barcelona's atmospheric Gothic Quarter, near the cathedral.

Restaurants

$$$ La Vinateria del Call, buried deep in the Jewish Quarter, is one of the oldest wine bars in town. It offers a romantic restaurant-style meal of tapas with fine local wines. Eating at the small bar by the entrance is discouraged, so I'd settle in at a candlelit table. They have more than 100 well-priced wines, including a decent selection of Catalan wines at €2.50 a glass. Three or four plates of their classic tapas will fill two people (daily 19:30-24:00; with back to church, leave Plaça de Sant Felip Neri and walk two short blocks to Carrer de Salomó Ben Adret 9; Metro: Jaume I, +34 933 026 092).

$$$ Els Quatre Gats ("The Four Cats") was once the haunt of the Modernista greats—including a teenaged Picasso and architect Josep Puig i Cadafalch, who designed the building. You can snack or drink at the bar, or head to the back for a sit-down meal after 19:00. While touristy (less so later), the food and service are good, and the prices are fair (weekday lunch specials, Tue-Sun 11:00-24:00, closed Mon, just steps off Avinguda del Portal de l'Angel at Carrer de Montsió 3, Metro: Catalunya, +34 933 024 140).

$$$ Onofre Vinos y Viandas, owned and run by Marisol and Ángel, is a tiny wine bar (20 wines by the glass) with a handful of simple tables behind walls of wine bottles. Foodie but without pretense, it has few tourists and a fun, creative, accessible menu—be adventurous and try the brandy foie shavings (Mon-Sat 10:00-16:30 & 19:30-24:00, closed Sun, near the Palace of Catalan Music, Carrer de les Magdalenes 19, +34 933 176 937).

$$ Bilbao Berria Pintxos and Tapas is a hardworking tapas bar, like its Basque sisters around town. It faces the cathedral, with tables outside on the square (15 percent surcharge to sit there) and sells little open-faced sandwiches and fun bites buffet-style for around €2.50 per toothpick. Grab a plate and pick what you want (Plaça Nova 3, +34 933 170 124).

On Plaça de Sant Josep Oriol: To enjoy the most inviting square in the Gothic Quarter with a meal, consider these simple eateries, both with a few tables on the square: **$$ Bar del Pi** is a hardworking bar serving salads, sandwiches, and tapas (daily 9:00-23:00). **$ El Drac de Sant Jordi** has a fun budget formula—€12 for any four tapas, a drink, and a tiny dessert (daily 13:00-23:00).

Tapas on Carrer de la Mercè in the Barri Gòtic

This area lets you experience a rare, unvarnished bit of old Barcelona with great *tascas*—colorful local tapas bars. Get small plates (for maximum sampling) by asking for "tapas," not the bigger "*raciones*." Glasses of red wine *(vino tinto)* go for about €1. And though trendy uptown restaurants are safer, better-lit, and come with English menus and less grease, these places will stain your journal. The neighborhood's dark, the regulars are rough-edged, and you'll get

a glimpse of a crusty Barcelona from before the affluence hit.

Of the many bars on Carrer de la Mercè, I'd visit these three: **$ Bar Celta** (marked *la pulpería*, at #9); **$ La Plata** (#28); and **$ Bodega del Gòtic**, at the north end of Carrer de la Mercè (#46).

EL BORN

El Born sparkles with eclectic and trendy as well as subdued and classy little restaurants hidden in the small lanes surrounding the Church of Santa Maria del Mar. Consider starting off your evening with a glass of fine wine at one of the *enotecas* on the square facing the church (such as La Vinya del Senyor). Many restaurants and shops in this area are closed on Mondays. For all of these eateries, use Metro: Jaume I.

(If El Born feels too touristy, I feel your pain. The "next El Born" is El Raval. For a quick review of places you might eat there, see the brief overview on page 95.)

Near the Church of Santa Maria del Mar

$$ Sagardi Euskal Taberna offers an array of Basque goodies—tempting *pintxos* and *montaditos* (small open-faced sandwiches) at €2.10 each—along its huge bar. Ask for a plate and graze (just take whatever looks good). You can sit on the square with your plunder for about 20 percent extra. Wash it down with Txakolí, a Basque white wine poured from the spout of a huge wooden barrel into a glass as you watch. Study the two price lists—bar and terrace—posted at the bar

(daily 12:00-24:00, Carrer de l'Argenteria 62, +34 933 199 993). Note that Sagardi serves the same *pintxos* as Taverna Basca Irati, described earlier.

$$ Vegetalia, facing the Monument of Catalan Independence and the Church of Santa Maria del Mar, is a basic vegetarian diner with a cheery, healthy-feeling interior (good three-course lunch special, daily from 11:00, +34 930 177 256).

Near the Picasso Museum

$$ El Xampanyet ("The Little Champagne Bar"), a colorful family-run bar with a fun-loving staff (Juan Carlos, his mom, and other

relatives). They specialize in tapas and anchovies—and their cheap homemade *cava* (Spanish champagne) goes straight to your head. Don't be put off by the seafood from a tin: Catalans like it this way. A *sortido de fumats* (assorted plate of small fish) with *pa amb tomàquet* makes for a fun meal. This place is filled with tourists by day, but jam-packed with locals after dark. The scene is great, but can be tough without a little Spanish-language skill. When I asked about the price, Juan Carlos said, "Who cares? The ATM is just across the street" (same price at bar or table, Tue-Sun 12:00-15:30 & 19:00-23:00, closed Sun evening and Mon, a half-block beyond the Picasso Museum at Carrer de Montcada 22, +34 933 197 003).

$$ Tapeo is a mod, classy alternative to the funky Xampanyet across the street. It serves high-end tapas at a long, sit-down bar and tiny tables with stools. This small space fills quickly so go early to get a seat (daily 12:00-16:00 & 19:00-24:00, Carrer de Montcada 29, +34 933 101 607).

$$$ Can Cisa/Bar Brutal is a creative and edgy bohemian-chic place with a young, local following. It serves a mix of Spanish and Italian dishes with an emphasis on wines—especially natural wines, with plenty available by the glass (Mon-Sat 13:00-24:00, closed Sun, Carrer de Princesa 14, +34 932 954 797).

$$$ Bar del Pla is a favorite near the Picasso Museum. This classic diner/bar—overlooking a tiny crossroads next to Barcelona's oldest church—serves traditional Catalan dishes, *raciones*, and tapas. Their *croquetas*, mushrooms with wasabi, and crispy oxtail with foie gras are highlights. Prices are the same at a table or at the bar, which puts you in the middle of a great scene (Mon-Sat 12:00-23:00, closed Sun, reservations smart, local IPA; leaving the Picasso Museum, head right two blocks past Carrer de la Princesa to Carrer de Montcada 2; +34 932 683 003; www.bardelpla.cat).

At Santa Caterina Market

$$ Cuines Santa Caterina, bright and modern, has shared tables under the open rafters of a modern market hall. There's also a handy tapas bar and fine self-service outdoor seating on the square. Their menu—with vegetarian, international, and Mediterranean dishes, all made from market-fresh and seasonal ingredients—cross-references everything on an innovative grid (outside tables OK for both restaurant and tapas bar, daily 12:30-16:00 & 19:30-23:00, Avinguda de Francesc Cambó 16, +34 932 689 918, no reservations).

$ Tapas Bars: Several lively tapas bars in the market are great for a quick and characteristic bite. Sitting here at one of these bars, immersed in the local scene, nets you a cheap and wonderful meal along with great market memories.

EIXAMPLE

The people-packed boulevards of the Eixample are lined with appetizing eateries featuring breezy outdoor seating. Choose between a real restaurant or an upscale tapas bar (for the best variety, I prefer Rambla de Catalunya). For locations, see the map on page 138.

Restaurants

$$ La Rita is a fresh and dressy little restaurant serving Catalan and Mediterranean cuisine near the Block of Discord. Their €13 lunch and €19 dinner *menú* specials are a great value. Arrive early... or wait (daily 13:00-16:00, Tue-Sat also 20:30-23:00, near corner of Carrer de Pau Claris and Carrer d'Aragó at d'Aragó 279, a block from Metro: Passeig de Gràcia, +34 934 872 376).

$$ La Bodegueta is an atmospheric below-street-level bodega serving hearty wines, homemade vermouth, *anchoas* (anchovies), tapas, and *flautas*—sandwiches made with flute-thin baguettes. On a nice day, it's great to eat outside, sitting in the median of the boulevard under shady trees. Its €16 three-course lunch special with wine is a deal (Mon-Fri only, 13:00-16:00). A long block from Gaudí's La Pedrera, this makes a fine sightseeing break (Mon-Sat 7:00-24:00, Sun from 18:00, at intersection with Carrer de Provença, Rambla de Catalunya 100, Metro: Provença, +34 932 154 894).

$$$ Restaurante la Palmera serves a mix of Catalan, Mediterranean, and French cuisine in an elegant room with bottle-lined walls. This untouristy place offers great food, service, and value—for me, a very special meal in Barcelona. They have three zones: the classic main room, a more forgettable adjacent room, and a few outdoor tables. I like the classic room. Reservations are smart (creative €26 six-plate *degustation* sampler; Mon 13:00-16:00, Tue-Sat 13:00-16:00 & 19:30-23:00, closed Sun; Carrer d'Enric Granados 57, at the corner with Carrer Mallorca, Metro: Provença, +34 934 532 338, www.lapalmera.cat).

$$ La Flauta fills two floors with enthusiastic eaters (I prefer the ground floor). It's fresh and modern, with a fun, no-stress menu featuring small plates, creative *flauta* sandwiches, and a €15 three-course lunch deal. Consider the list of *tapas del día*. Good wines by the glass are listed on the blackboard, and solo diners get great service at the bar (Mon-Sat 7:00-24:00, closed Sun, upbeat and helpful staff, no reservations, just off Carrer de la Diputació at Carrer d'Aribau 23, Metro: Universitat, +34 933 237 038).

Tapas Bars

Many trendy and touristic tapas bars in the Eixample offer a cheery welcome and slam out the appetizers. These two are particularly handy to Plaça de Catalunya and the Passeig de Gràcia artery (closest Metro stops: Catalunya and Passeig de Gràcia).

$$$ **Tapas 24** makes eating fun. This local favorite, with a few street tables, fills a spot a few steps below street level with happy energy, funky decor, and good yet pricey tapas. Along with daily specials and fine breakfasts, the menu has all the typical standbys and quirky inventions. The *tapas del día* list is particularly good. The owner, Carles Abellan, is one of Barcelona's hot chefs; although his famous fare is pricey, you can enjoy it without going broke. Prices are the same whether you dine at the bar, a table, or outside. Come early or wait; no reservations are taken (daily 9:00-24:00, just off Passeig de Gràcia at Carrer de la Diputació 269, +34 934 880 977).

$$ **Ciutat Comtal Cerveceria** is an Eixample favorite with an elegant bar and tables plus good seating out on the Rambla de Catalunya for all that people-watching action. It's packed after 21:00, when you'll likely need to put your name on a list and wait. While it has no restaurant-type menu, the varied list of tapas and *montaditos* is easy, fun, high-quality, and includes daily specials (daily 8:00-24:00, facing the intersection of Gran Via de les Corts Catalanes and Rambla de Catalunya at Rambla de Catalunya 18, +34 933 181 997).

Out-of-the-Way Splurge

$$$$ **Cinc Sentits** ("Five Senses"), a 20-minute walk southwest of the Eixample, toward Montjuïc, is my gourmet recommendation for those who want to dress up and spend more money. At this chic, minimalist, snooty place, all the attention goes to the fine service and beautifully presented avant-garde cuisine inspired by Catalan traditions and ingredients. Expect *menús* only—no à la carte. The *menú curt* includes 8 courses (€119) and the *menú degustació* has 10 courses (€139); both are unforgettable extravaganzas. Each comes with a wine-pairing option (€69-79 extra). Reservations are essential (Tue-Sat 13:30-15:00 & 20:30-22:00, closed Sun-Mon, Carrer d'Entença 60, Metro: Rocafort line 1, or a 5-minute walk from Metro: Plaça de Espanya, +34 933 239 490, www.cincsentits.com).

BARCELONETA AND THE BEACH

The nearest Metro stop to this former sailors' quarter is Barceloneta; the bus will get you closer—the best ones are #V15 (catch it at Plaça de Catalunya or along Via Laietana), #59 (from the top of the Ramblas), or #D20 (from the Columbus Monument). For the locations of these eateries, see the "Barceloneta & Beaches" map on page 125.

At the Center of Barceloneta

The main square of Barceloneta (Plaça del Poeta Boscà) is homey, with a 19th-century iron-and-glass market, families at play in the park, and lots of hole-in-the-wall eateries and bars. The main drag,

Passeig de Joan de Borbó, faces the city and is lined with many interchangeable seafood restaurants and cafés.

$$$$ La Mar Salada is a traditional seafood restaurant with a slightly modern twist and both indoor and outdoor seating (weekday lunch *menú*, open Wed-Mon 13:00-16:00 & 20:00-23:00, closed Tue, Passeig de Joan de Borbó 59, +34 932 212 127).

$$$$ Restaurante Can Solé, serving seafood since 1903, hides on a nondescript lane between the square and the marina one block off the harborfront promenade. This venerable yet homey restaurant draws a celebrity crowd, judging by the autographed pictures of the famous and not-so-famous that line the walls (Tue-Sat 13:30-16:00 & 20:30-23:00, closed Sun-Mon, Carrer de Sant Carles 4, +34 932 215 012, www.restaurantcansole.com).

$$ La Cova Fumada, at the far end of the main square from the big market hall, is a popular, good-value choice for tapas in a neighborhood family setting (outdoor tables, Mon-Fri 9:00-15:00, Tue and Fri also 18:00-20:00, Sat 9:00-13:00, closed Sun, Carrer del Baluard 56, +34 932 214 061).

$ Baluard, one of Barcelona's most highly regarded artisan bakeries, faces one side of the market. Line up with the locals to get a loaf of heavenly bread, a pastry, or a slice of pizza (Mon-Sat 8:00-21:00, closed Sun, Carrer del Baluard 38, +34 932 211 208).

On the Beach

The *chiringuito* tradition of funky eateries lining Barcelona's beach now has serious competition from trendy bars and restaurants. My favorites are at the far south end near the towering Hotel W.

$$$$ Pez Vela is the top-end option with a fashionable local crowd and its own DJ (daily 13:00-23:30, Passeig del Mare Nostrum 19, +34 932 216 317).

Barcelona Connections

BY PLANE

Most flights use Barcelona's primary **Josep Tarradellas Barcelona-El Prat Airport;** a few budget flights use a smaller airstrip 60 miles away, called **Girona–Costa Brava Airport.** Information on Barcelona's airports can be found on the official Spanish airport website, www.aena.es.

Josep Tarradellas Barcelona-El Prat Airport

Generally referred to as El Prat, the airport is eight miles southwest of town (code: BCN, info +34 913 211 000). It has two large terminals linked by shuttle buses. Terminal 1 serves Air France, Air Europa, American, British Airways, Delta, Iberia, Lufthansa, United, Vueling, and others. EasyJet, Ryanair, and minor airlines

use the older Terminal 2, which is divided into sections A, B, and C.

Terminal 1 and the bigger sections of Terminal 2 (A and B) each have a post office, a pharmacy, a left-luggage office, plenty of good eateries in the gate areas, and ATMs.

Getting Between El Prat Airport and Downtown

To get downtown cheaply and quickly, take the bus or train (about 30 minutes on either). You can also connect by Metro (more transfers) or taxi (more expensive).

By Bus: At either terminal, follow *Intercity* bus signs to catch the Aerobus (#A1 and #A2, corresponding with Terminals 1 and 2). It makes several stops downtown, including at Plaça de Catalunya and near many of my recommended hotels (returning from downtown, buses leave from in front of El Corte Inglés). Either way it's very easy: Buses depart about every five minutes (runs 24/7, fewer departures after midnight, 30- to 40-minute ride, buy €6 ticket from driver, +34 902 100 104, www.aerobusbcn.com).

By Train: The Renfe train (on the "R2 Nord" Rodalies line) leaves from Terminal 2 and involves more walking. Head up the escalators and down the long orange-roofed skybridge to reach the station (2/hour at about :08 and :38 past the hour, 20 minutes to Sants station, 25 minutes to Passeig de Gràcia station—near Plaça de Catalunya; €4.60, purchase from machines at the airport train station). If you're arriving or departing from Terminal 1, you'll need to use the airport shuttle bus to connect with the train station, so leave extra time (10 buses/hour, 7-minute ride between terminals).

By Metro: Take Metro's L9 Sud (orange) line from either Terminal 1 or 2 to the Zona Universitária stop, then transfer to the L3 (green) line and ride to a downtown stop (Passeig de Gràcia, Plaça de Catalunya, or Liceu). To reach the airport from downtown via Metro, take line L3 to Zona Universitária, and transfer to line L9 in the direction of Aeroport T1 (runs about every 10 minutes 5:00 until late; 25-30 minute ride). Use the €5.15 *Bitllet Aeroport* ticket or any "Hola BCN!" travel card (single-ride Metro tickets and T-Casual and T-Familiar multiride cards do not cover this trip).

By Taxi: A taxi between the airport and downtown costs about €40 (including €4.30 airport supplement). To get to the cruise port, ask for *"tarifa cuatro"*—a €39 flat rate between the airport and the cruise port, all fees included.

Girona-Costa Brava Airport

Some budget airlines use this airport, located 60 miles north of Barcelona near Girona (code: GRO, +34 972 186 600, www.aena.es). If you arrive on a Ryanair flight, you can take a **bus** (#604), run by Ryanair and operated by Sagalés, to the Barcelona Nord bus

station (departs airport about 20 minutes after each arriving flight, 1.25 hours, €16, +34 902 130 014, www.sagales.com). You can also take a Sagalés bus (#602, about every 10 minutes, 1.5 hours, €2.75) or a taxi (€25) to the town of Girona, then catch a train to Barcelona (at least hourly, 1.5 hours, €15-20). A taxi between the Girona airport and Barcelona costs at least €130.

BY TRAIN

Virtually all trains end up at Barcelona's **Sants train station,** west of the Old City. AVE trains from Madrid go only to Sants station. But many other trains also pass through other stations en route, such as **França train station** (between the El Born and Barceloneta neighborhoods), or the downtown **Passeig de Gràcia** or **Plaça de Catalunya** stations (which are also Metro stops—and very close to most of my recommended hotels). Figure out which stations your train stops at (ask the conductor) and get off at the one most convenient to your hotel.

Sants Train Station

Barcelona's big white main train station offers many services. In the large lobby area, you'll find a TI, ATMs, a world of handy

shops and eateries, pay WCs, car-rental kiosks, and, in the side concourse, a classy, quiet Sala Club lounge for travelers with first-class reservations. Sants is the only Barcelona station with luggage storage (€6/up to 2 hours, €10/day, daily 5:30-23:00, follow signs to *consigna;* go toward track 14, then exit the main building toward parking lot and go down to level -1).

In the vast main hall is a very long wall of ticket windows. Figure out which one you need before you wait in line (all are labeled in English). Generally, windows 1-7 (on the left) are for local commuter and *media distancia* trains, such as to Sitges; windows 8-21 handle advance tickets for long-distance *(larga distancia)* trains beyond Catalunya; windows 22-26 give information—go here first if you're not sure which window you want; and windows 27-31 sell tickets for long-distance trains leaving today. These window assignments can shift in the off-season. The information booths by windows 1 and 21 can help you find the right line and can provide some train schedules.

Scattered nearby are train-ticket vending machines. The red-and-gray machines sell tickets for local and *media distancia* trains

within Catalunya. The purple machines are for national Renfe trains; these machines can also print out reserved tickets if you have a confirmation code. And the orange machines sell local *Rodalies* train tickets. There are usually attendants around the machines to help you.

An easier option for English-speaking travelers is to buy your tickets at the travel agencies inside El Corte Inglés department stores. See page 478 for more info.

Getting Downtown: To reach the center of Barcelona, take the Metro or a train. To ride the subway, follow signs for the Metro (red *M*), and hop on the L3 (green) or L5 (blue) line, both of which link to useful points in town. Purchase tickets for the Metro at touch-screen machines near the tracks.

To zip downtown even faster (just 5 minutes), you can take any Rodalies de Catalunya suburban train from track 8 (R1, R3, or R4) to Plaça de Catalunya (departs at least every 10 minutes). Your long-distance Renfe train ticket comes with a complimentary ride on Rodalies, as long as you use it within three hours before or after your travels. Look for a code on your ticket labeled *Combinat Rodalies* or *Combinado Cercanías*. Go to the orange commuter ticket machines, touch *Combinat Rodalies*, type in your code, and the machine will print your ticket.

Train Connections

Unless otherwise noted, all trains listed below depart from Sants station; some trains also stop at other stations more convenient to the downtown tourist zone: França station, Passeig de Gràcia, or Plaça de Catalunya. Figure out if your train stops at these stations (and board there) to save yourself the trip to Sants.

If departing from the downtown Passeig de Gràcia station, where three Metro lines converge with the rail line, you might find the underground tunnels confusing. You can't access the Renfe station directly from some entrances. Use the northern entrances to this station (rather than the southern "Consell de Cent" entrance, which is closest to Plaça de Catalunya). Train info: +34 912 320 320, www.renfe.com.

From Barcelona by Train to Madrid: The **AVE** train to Madrid is faster and more comfortable than flying (especially when you consider that you're zipping from downtown to downtown). The train departs at least hourly. The nonstop train is a little more expensive but faster (€130, 2.5 hours) than the train that makes a few stops (€110, 3 hours). Regular reserved AVE tickets can be purchased in advance (often with a discount) at the Renfe website and printed from an email or at the station. You can also download a ticket QR code to your phone. If you have a rail pass, most trains

require paid reservations; see the "Transportation" section of the Practicalities chapter.

Avlo, a new line of low-cost high-speed trains, offers fares as low as €20 for the Barcelona-Zaragoza-Madrid route. It's a good budget option, but comes with less leg room and no food service (vending machines only, pay extra for seat reservation and larger suitcases, www.avlorenfe.com).

From Barcelona by Train to: Sitges (departs from both Passeig de Gràcia and Sants, 4/hour, 40 minutes), **Montserrat** (departs from Plaça d'Espanya—*not* from Sants, 1-2/hour, 1 hour, €23.50 round-trip, includes cable car or rack train to monastery—see details on page 160), **Figueres** (hourly, 1 hour via AVE or Alvia to Figueres-Vilafant; hourly, 2-3 hours via local trains to Figueres station), **Sevilla** (2/day direct, more with transfer in Madrid, 5.5 hours), **Granada** (3/day via AVE, 1 direct, 2 with change in Madrid, 6-7.5 hours—1.5-hour flight is better), **Córdoba** (6/day direct, 5.5 hours, many more with transfer in Madrid), **Salamanca** (6/day, 7 hours, change in Madrid from Atocha station to Chamartín station via Metro or *cercanías* train; also 1/day with a change in Valladolid, 8.5 hours), **San Sebastián** (2/day direct, 6 hours), **Málaga** (7/day via AVE, 6.5 hours; some with transfer), **Lisbon** (no direct trains, best to fly).

From Barcelona by Train to France: Direct high-speed trains run to **Paris** (2/day, 6.5 hours), **Lyon** (1/day, 5 hours), and **Toulouse** (1/day, 3 hours), and there are more connections with transfers.

BY BUS

Most buses depart from the Nord bus station at Metro: Arc de Triomf, but confirm when researching schedules (www.barcelonanord.barcelona). Destinations served by Alsa buses (www.alsa.es) include **Madrid** and **Madrid's Barajas Airport** (nearly hourly, 8 hours), and **Salamanca** (2/day, 12 hours). Moventis Sarfa buses (https://compras.moventis.es) serve many **coastal resorts,** including **Cadaqués** (1-2/day, 3 hours). Reservations are smart for long-distance destinations, especially during the busy summer season.

BUS Garraf leaves from the university and Plaça d'Espanya in downtown Barcelona to **Sitges** (2/hour, 1 hour, www.busgarraf.cat). One bus departs daily for the **Montserrat** monastery, leaving from Carrer de Viriat near Sants station (1.5 hours, www.autocaresjulia.com, see page 162).

BY CRUISE SHIP

Cruise ships arrive in Barcelona at one of three ports, all just southwest of the Old City, beneath Montjuïc. If your trip includes cruis-

ing beyond Barcelona, consider my guidebook, *Rick Steves Mediterranean Cruise Ports*.

Most cruise ships arrive in Barcelona at the **Moll Adossat/ Muelle Adosado** port, about two miles from the bottom of the Ramblas. This port has four modern, airport-like terminals (lettered A through D); most have a café, shops, and TI kiosk; some have Wi-Fi and other services. Two other terminals are far less commonly used: the **World Trade Center**, just off the southern end of the Ramblas (a 10-minute walk from the Columbus Monument), and **Moll de la Costa**, tucked just beneath Montjuïc (ride the free, private shuttle bus to World Trade Center; from there, it's a short walk or taxi ride to the Columbus Monument).

Getting Downtown: From any of the cruise terminals, it's easy to reach the Ramblas. **Taxis** meet arriving ships outside terminal building exits (about €15-20 to downtown, as much as €10 more in heavy traffic; expect a cruise-port surcharge). To get to the airport, ask for *"tarifa cuatro"*—a €39 flat rate between the airport and the cruise port, all fees included.

You can also take a **shuttle bus** from Moll Adossat/Muelle Adosado to the bottom of the Ramblas, then walk or hop on public transportation to various sights. The blue Cruise Bus departs from the parking lot in front of each of the port's four terminals and drops you right on the waterfront near the Columbus Monument (€4.50 round-trip, cash only, 2/hour, timed to cruise ship arrival, 5-15 minutes). The return bus to the port leaves from where you were dropped off (look for a covered bus stop bench and blue-and-white sign reading *Cruise Bus*).

NEAR BARCELONA

Montserrat • Figueres • Cadaqués • Sitges

Four fine sights are day-trip temptations from Barcelona. Pilgrims with hiking boots head 1.5 hours into the mountains for the most sacred spot in Catalunya: Montserrat. Fans of Surrealism can enjoy a fantasy in Dalí-land by combining a stop at the Dalí Theater-Museum in Figueres (1-2 hours from Barcelona) with a day or two in the classy, often sleepy port-town getaway of Cadaqués (pictured above, an hour from Figueres). Or for a quick escape from the city, head 35 minutes south to the charming and free-spirited beach town of Sitges.

Montserrat

Montserrat—the "serrated mountain"—rockets dramatically up from the valley floor northwest of Barcelona. With its unique

rock formations, a mountaintop monastery (also called Montserrat), and spiritual connection with the Catalan people, it's a popular day trip. This has been Catalunya's most important pilgrimage site for a thousand years. Hymns explain how the mountain was carved by little angels with golden saws. Geologists blame nature at work.

Once upon a time, there was no mountain. A river flowed

here, laying down silt that solidified into sedimentary layers of hard rock. Ten million years ago, the continents shifted, and the land around the rock massif sank, exposing this series of peaks that reach upward to 4,000 feet. Over time, erosion pocked the face with caves and cut vertical grooves near the top, creating the famous serrated look.

The monastery is nestled in the jagged peaks at 2,400 feet, but it seems higher because of the way the rocky massif rises out of nowhere. The air is certainly fresher than in Barcelona. In a quick day trip, you can view the mountain from its base, ride a funicular up to the top of the world, tour the basilica and museum, touch a Black Virgin's orb, hike down to a sacred cave, and listen to Gregorian chants by the world's oldest boys' choir.

Montserrat's monastery is Benedictine, and its 30 monks carry on its spiritual tradition. Since 1025, the slogan *"ora et labora"* ("prayer and work") has pretty much summed up life for a monk here.

GETTING TO MONTSERRAT

Barcelona is connected to the valley below Montserrat by a convenient train; from there, a cable car or rack railway transports you up to the mountaintop. Decide which to take (they are similar in cost and travel time) when you buy your ticket in Barcelona—see the "Tickets to Montserrat" sidebar. Altogether, it's about 1.5 hours each way from downtown Barcelona to the monastery. Other options are driving or taking the bus.

By Train Plus Cable Car or Rack Railway

Trains to Montserrat leave from Barcelona's Plaça d'Espanya. Take the Metro to Espanya, then follow signs for Montserrat (which show a graphic of a train and the *FGC* symbol—for Ferrocarrils de la Generalitat de Catalunya) through the tunnels to the FGC station. Once there, check the overhead screens or ask for help (staff are usually at the ticket machines) to find the track for train line R5 (direction: Manresa, 1-2/hour—usually at :36 and/or :56).

Hang on to your train ticket; you'll need it to exit the FGC station when you return to Plaça d'Espanya. You'll ride about an hour on the train. For the cable car, get off at the Montserrat-Aeri station; for the rack railway, continue another few minutes to the next station, Monistrol de Montserrat (or simply "Monistrol de M.").

Cable Car or Rack Train? For the sake of scenery and fun, I enjoy the little German-built cable car more than the rack railway. Departures are more frequent (4/hour rather than hourly on the railway), but because the cable car is small, you may wait a while to get on (up to an hour when crowded). If you dislike heights, take the rack train. If you'd like to try both, buy a one-way ticket to Montserrat including the cable car, and buy the return ticket for the rack railway and train back to Barcelona from the Cremallera station in Montserrat.

Cable Car, from Montserrat-Aeri Station: Departing the train, follow signs to the cable car station (covered by your train or combo-ticket; 4/hour, 5-minute trip, mid-April-Oct daily 9:30-19:00, shorter hours in winter, www.aeridemontserrat.com). Don't linger on the platform: Make your way to the cable car quickly, as you may have to wait to go up. On the way back down, cable cars depart from the monastery every 15 minutes; make sure to give yourself enough time to catch a Barcelona-bound train (these leave at :05 and :45 past the hour Mon-Fri, only at :45 Sat-Sun).

Tickets to Montserrat

Various combo-tickets cover your journey to Montserrat, as well as some sights there. All begin with the train from Barcelona's Plaça d'Espanya and include either the cable car or the rack railway—you'll be asked to specify one or the other when you buy the ticket (same price for either round-trip).

The basic option is to buy a **train ticket** to Montserrat (€23.50 round-trip, includes cable car or rack railway to monastery, see timetable at www.fgc.cat). Note that if you decide at Montserrat that you want to use the funiculars to go higher up the mountain or to the Sacred Cave, you can buy a €16.50 ticket covering both funiculars at the TI or at either funicular. Two combo-tickets offered by the train company cover transportation and various admissions (€34 **Trans Montserrat** and €53 **Tot Montserrat,** www.cremallerademontserrat.cat).

You can get advice about your ticket choice and return schedules at the Montserrat Cremallera (rack railway) or cable car info booths at Plaça d'Espanya station (daily 8:00-14:00). Then purchase any of these options from a ticket machine—if you need help, ask one of the TI officials standing by in the morning. To use your included round-trip Metro ride to get *to* the station, buy your Montserrat ticket in advance at the Plaça de Catalunya TI. You can also buy your ticket at www.montserratvisita.com (€28, includes cable car or rack railway and entrance to the Museum of Montserrat—described later) but you must take your purchase voucher to the Cremallera rack railway info booth during open hours (daily 8:00-14:00) to receive an actual ticket. Combo-tickets are also available at the Barcelona TI's online shop (http://bcnshop.barcelonaturisme.com).

Rack Railway (Cremallera), from Monistrol de Montserrat Station: From this station you can catch the Cremallera rack railway up to the monastery (covered by your train or combo-ticket; hourly, 20-minute trip, www.cremallerademontserrat.cat). On the return trip, this train departs the monastery at :15 past the hour, allowing you to catch the Barcelona-bound train leaving Monistrol de Montserrat at :45 past the hour. The last connection leaves the monastery at 19:15. Confirm the schedule when you arrive. Note that there is one intermediate stop on this line (Monistrol-Vila, at a large parking garage), but—either coming or going—you want to stay on until the end of the line.

By Car

Once drivers get out of Barcelona (Road A-2, then C-55), it's a short 30-minute drive to the base of the mountain, then a 10-minute series of switchbacks to the actual site (where you can find park-

ing for €5/day). It may be easier to park your car down below and ride the cable car or rack railway up; there's plenty of free parking at the Monistrol-Vila rack railway station (cable car—€8 one-way, €12 round-trip; rack railway—€6.90 one-way, €11.50 round-trip).

By Bus

One bus per day connects downtown Barcelona directly to the monastery at Montserrat (departs from Carrer de Viriat near Barcelona's Sants station daily at 9:15, returns from the monastery to Barcelona at 18:00 June-Sept, at 17:00 Oct-May, €5 each way, 1.5 hours, operated by Autocares Julià, www.autocaresjulia.com). Since the other options are scenic, fun, and relatively easy, the only reason to take a bus is to avoid transfers.

Orientation to Montserrat

When you arrive at the base of the mountain, look up the rock face to find the cable car line, the monastery near the top, and the tiny building midway up (marking the Sacred Cave).

However you make your way up to the Montserrat monastery, it's easy to get oriented once you arrive at the top. Everything is within a few minutes' walk of your entry point. All the transit options—including the rack railway and cable car—converge at one big station. Above that are the funicular stations: one up to the ridge top, the other down to the Sacred Cave trail. Across the street is the TI, and above that (either straight up the stairs or up the ramp around the left side) is the main square.

Crowd-Beating Tips: Arrive early or late, as tour groups mob the place midday. Crowds are less likely on weekdays and worst on Sundays.

TOURIST INFORMATION

The square below the basilica houses a helpful TI, right across from the rack railway station (daily from 9:00, closes just after last train heads down—roughly 18:45, Sat-Sun until 20:00; +34 938 777 701, www.montserratvisita.com). A good audioguide, available only at the TI, describes the general site and basilica (€7 includes book; €18 includes entrance to museum, bland audiovisual presentation, and book). If you're a hiker, ask for the handout outlining hiking options here. Trails offer spectacular views (on clear days) to the Mediterranean and even (on clearer days) to the Pyrenees.

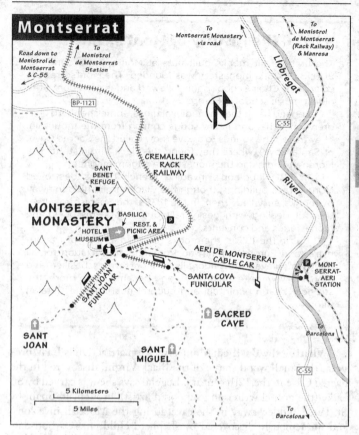

Sights in Montserrat

▲▲Basilica

Although there's been a church here since the 11th century, the present structure was built in the 1850s, and the facade only dates from 1968. The decor is Neo-Romanesque, so popular with the Romantic artists of the late 19th century. The basilica itself is ringed with interesting chapels, but the focus is on the Black Virgin (La Moreneta) sitting high above the main altar.

Cost and Hours: Basilica—free, daily 7:50-10:50 & 12:00-20:00. La Moreneta—free, viewable daily 8:00-10:30 & 12:00-18:25, must reserve timed-entry ticket online in advance at www.abadiamontserrat.cat—select "English," then "Booking," then "Image of the Virgin." Mass is held daily at 11:00 (also requires a timed-entry ticket booked in advance). If you arrive without a timed-entry ticket for La Moreneta or Mass, head directly to the church (on the right side of the courtyard) and get it there.

The History of Montserrat

The first hermit monks built huts at Montserrat around AD 900. By 1025, a monastery was founded. The Montserrat Escolania, or Choir School, soon followed and is considered the oldest music school in Europe.

Legend has it that in medieval times, some shepherd children saw lights and heard songs coming from the mountain. They traced the sounds to a cave (now called the Sacred Cave, or Santa Cova), where they found the Black Virgin statue (La Moreneta)—making the monastery a pilgrim magnet.

In 1811 Napoleon's invading French troops destroyed Montserrat's buildings, though the Black Virgin, hidden away by monks, survived. Then, in the 1830s, the Spanish royalty—tired of dealing with pesky religious orders—dissolved the monasteries and convents.

But in the 1850s, the monks returned as part of Catalunya's (and Europe's) renewed Romantic appreciation for all things medieval and nationalistic. Montserrat's basilica and monastery were reconstructed and became, once more, the strongly beating spiritual and cultural heart of the Catalan people.

Visiting the Basilica: Montserrat's top attraction is **La Moreneta,** the small wood statue of the Black Virgin, discovered in the Sacred Cave in the 12th century. Legend says she was carved by St. Luke (the gospel writer and supposed artist), brought to Spain by St. Peter, hidden away in the cave during the Moorish invasions, and miraculously discovered by shepherd children. (Carbon dating says she's 800 years old.) "Moreneta" is usually translated as "black" in English, but the Spanish name actually means "tanned." The statue was originally lighter, but it darkened over the centuries from candle smoke, humidity, and the natural aging of its original varnish.

Though Mary is behind a protective glass case, the royal orb she cradles in her hands is exposed. Pilgrims touch Mary's orb with one hand and hold their other hand up to show that they accept Jesus. Newlyweds in particular seek Mary's blessing.

Immediately after La Moreneta, to the right, is the delightful Neo-Romanesque **chapel** where worshippers can sit behind the Virgin and pray. The ceiling, painted in the Modernista style in 1898 by Joan Llimona, shows Jesus and Mary high in heaven. The trail connect-

ing Catalunya with heaven seems to lead through these serrated mountains.

You'll leave by walking along the **Ave Maria Path** (along the outside of the church), with thousands of colorful votive candles. Before you leave the inner courtyard and head out into the main square, pop in to the humble little room with the many votive offerings left as part of a prayer request or as thanks for divine intercession.

Museum of Montserrat

This bright, shiny, and cool collection of paintings and artifacts was mostly donated by devout Catalan Catholics. While it's nothing earth-shaking, you'll enjoy an air-conditioned wander past lots of antiquities and fine artwork. Head upstairs first to see some lesser-known works by the likes of Picasso, Caravaggio, Monet, Renoir, Pissarro, Degas, and local Modernista artists. Down on the main floor, you'll see ecclesiastical gear, a good icon collection, and more paintings.

Cost and Hours: €8, covered by Tot Montserrat combo-ticket, daily 10:00-17:45, Sat-Sun until 18:45, +34 938 777 745.

▲Sant Joan Funicular and Hikes

This funicular climbs 820 feet above the monastery in five minutes. At the top of the funicular, you are at the starting point of a 20-minute walk that takes you to the Sant Joan Chapel (follow sign for *Ermita de St. Joan*). Other hikes also begin at the trailhead by the funicular (get details from TI before you ascend; basic map with suggested hikes posted by upper funicular station).  For a quick and easy chance to get out into nature and away from the crowds, simply ride up and follow the most popular hike—a 45-minute, mostly downhill loop through mountain scenery back to the monastery. To take this route, go left from the funicular station; the trail—marked *Monestir de Montserrat*—will first go up to a rocky crest before heading downhill.

Cost and Hours: €9.10 one-way funicular ride, €14 round-trip, €16.50 combo round-trip for both Sant Joan and Santa Cova, covered by Trans Montserrat and Tot Montserrat combo-tickets, goes every 20 minutes, more often with demand.

Sacred Cave (Santa Cova)

The statue known as La Moreneta was originally discovered in the Sacred Cave (or Sacred Grotto), a 40-minute hike down from the monastery (then another 50 minutes back up). The path (c. 1900) was designed by devoted and patriotic Modernista architects, including Gaudí and Josep Puig i Cadafalch. It's lined with Modernista statues depicting scenes corresponding to the Mysteries of the Rosary—prayers that reflect on the life and death of Jesus. While the original Black Virgin statue is now in the basilica, a replica sits in the cave. A three-minute funicular ride cuts 20 minutes off the hike. (The funicular may be closed for repairs—check locally.) If you're here late in the afternoon, check the schedule before you head into the Sacred Cave to make sure you don't miss the final ride back down the mountain.

Cost and Hours: €3.50 one-way funicular ride, €5.50 round-trip, €16.50 combo round-trip for both Sant Joan and Santa Cova, covered by Trans Montserrat and Tot Montserrat combo-tickets, goes every 20 minutes, more often with demand.

Choir Concert

Montserrat's Escolania, or Choir School, has been training voices for centuries. Fifty young boys, who live and study in the monastery itself, make up the choir, which performs daily except Saturday. The boys sing for only 10 minutes, the basilica is jam-packed, and it's likely you'll see almost nothing. Also note that if you attend the evening performance, you'll miss the last train or cable car ride down the mountain.

Cost and Hours: Free, reservation required, generally Mon-Fri at 13:00, Sun at 11:00, Sun-Thu at 19:00, choir on vacation late June-late Aug, check schedule and reserve at www.escolania.cat/en/cuando-cantamos.

Eating in Montserrat

Montserrat is designed to feed hordes of pilgrims and tourists. You'll find a cafeteria along the main street (across from the train station) and a grocery store and bar with simple sandwiches where the road curves on its way up to the hotel. In the other direction, follow the covered walkway below the basilica to reach the Mirador dels Apòstols, with a bar, cafeteria, restaurant, and picnic area. The Hotel Abat Cisneros also has a restaurant, and the Montserrat-Aeri train station has a ramshackle but charming family-run bar with outdoor tables, simple food, and views of the mountain and the cable cars. The best option is to pack a picnic from Barcelona, especially if you plan to hike.

Figueres

The town of Figueres (feeg-YEHR-ehs)—conveniently connected by train to Barcelona—is of sightseeing interest mainly for its Dalí Theater-Museum. In fact, the entire town seems Dalí dominated. But don't be surprised if you also see bargain-hunting French shoppers. Some of the cheapest shops in Spain—called *ventas*—are here to lure French visitors.

GETTING TO FIGUERES

Figueres is an easy day trip from Barcelona or a handy stopover en route to France. It has two train stations on opposite sides of town: **Figueres-Vilafant** (served by the high-speed train from Barcelona's Sants station, about hourly, 1 hour) and **Figueres** (served by the less expensive but slower regional train; departs from Barcelona's Sants station or from the Renfe station at Metro: Passeig de Gràcia; hourly, 2.5-3 hours; slightly more expensive *media distancia* trains take closer to 2 hours). If you're on your way to Paris, it's possible to take the high-speed train from Barcelona in the morning, visit the Dalí Theater-Museum, and catch the late-afternoon TGV train (also called "InOui") to Paris. Neither train station has baggage storage, but the bus station (across from Figueres station) and the Dalí Theater-Museum do. For bus connections to Cadaqués, see "Getting to Cadaqués," later.

Orientation to Figueres

You'll find the town's museums and sights clustered within a couple of blocks of one another—the Rambla shopping street, church, city hall, toy museum (Museu del Joguet), and Catalan art museum (Museu Empordà)—as well as the only sight that matters for most visitors: the Dalí Theater-Museum.

Tourist Information: The TI is at Plaça de l'Escorxador 2 (Mon-Sat 9:30-19:00—until 20:00 July-Aug, Sun 10:00-14:00, +34 972 503 155, www.turismefigueres.com). An info desk sometimes opens at the Figueres TGV train station.

Arrival in Figueres: To reach the Dalí museum from Figueres-Vilafant station, take the **bus** marked *Estació AVE-Figueres* (€1.75, departs only with the arrival of each train, buy ticket from driver), and get off at the Rambla stop—ask the driver for the museum. From there, it's a five-minute walk uphill to the museum. **Taxis** charge about €12 to and from the station.

To get to the museum from Figueres station, simply follow *Museu Dalí* signs (and the crowds) for the 15-minute walk to the museum.

Sights in Figueres

DALÍ THEATER-MUSEUM

This ▲▲▲ museum is *the* essential Dalí sight—and, if you like his work, one of Europe's most enjoyable museums, period. Inaugurated in 1974, the Dalí Theater-Museum (Teatre-Musei Dalí) is a work of art in itself. Ever the entertainer and promoter, Dalí personally conceptualized, designed, decorated, and painted it to showcase his life's work. The museum fills a former theater and contains the artist's mausoleum (his tomb is in the crypt below center stage). It's also a kind of mausoleum to Dalí's creative spirit.

Dalí worked here over many years and personally designed the core of the museum (Rooms 1 through 18). Even the building's exterior—painted pink, studded with golden loaves of bread, and topped with monumental eggs and a geodesic dome—exudes the artist's outrageous public persona. The Dalí Theater-Museum is called the largest Surrealist object in the world.

Cost: €14; purchase a timed-entry ticket online in advance. Your ticket includes free entry to the nearby Museu Empordà (Catalan paintings) and discounted entry to the Museu del Joguet de Catalunya (toys).

Hours: July-Aug daily 9:00-20:00; Sept-June Tue-Sun 10:30-18:00, occasionally open Mon—call or confirm online; last entry 45 minutes before closing, +34 972 677 500, www.salvador-dali.org.

Reservations Recommended: It's important to reserve ahead online for this museum, which can be a mob scene, especially when bad weather drives beach crowds here (they let in no more than 250 people each half-hour). You can make a reservation as little as two hours in advance.

Bag Check: The free and required bag check will have your belongings waiting for you at the exit. It's OK to leave checked backpacks and small suitcases here while you browse the town.

Sightseeing Tip: Much of Dalí's art is movable and coin-operated—bring a few €0.20 and €1 coins and keep an eye out for the machines where you insert them.

❍ Self-Guided Tour

The museum has two parts—the theater-mausoleum and the "Dalí's Jewels" exhibit in an adjacent building. There's no logical order for a

Salvador Dalí (1904-1989)

Born in Figueres to a well-off family, Dalí showed talent early. After a breakthrough art exhibit in Barcelona in 1925, Dalí moved to Paris. He hobnobbed with fellow Spaniards Pablo Picasso and Joan Miró, along with a group of artists exploring Sigmund Freud's theory that we all have a hidden part of our mind, the unconscious "id," which surfaces when we dream. Dalí became the best-known spokesman for this group of Surrealists, channeling his id to create photore-alistic dream images (melting watches, burning giraffes) set in bizarre dreamscapes.

His life changed forever in 1929, when he met an older, married Russian woman named Gala who would become his wife, muse, model, manager, and emotional compass. Dalí's popularity spread to the US, where he (and Gala) weathered the WWII years.

In the prime of his career, Dalí's work became less Surre-alist and more classical, influenced by past masters of painted realism (Velázquez, Raphael, Ingres, Vermeer) and by his own study of history, science, and religion. He produced large-scale paintings of historical events (e.g., Columbus discover-ing America, the Last Supper) that were collages of realistic scenes floating in a surrealistic landscape, peppered with thought-provoking symbols.

Dalí—an extremely capable technician—mastered many media, including film. *An Andalusian Dog* (*Un Chien Andalou*, 1929, with Luis Buñuel) was a cutting-edge montage of dis-turbing, eyeball-slicing images. He designed Alfred Hitch-cock's big-eye backdrop for the dream sequence of *Spell-bound* (1945). He made jewels for the rich and clothes for Coco Chanel, wrote a novel and an autobiography, and pio-neered what would come to be called "installations." He also helped develop "performance art" by showing up at an open-ing in a diver's suit or by playing the role he projected to the media—a super-confident, waxed-mustached artistic genius.

visit (that would be un-Surrealistic). Dalí said there are two kinds of visitors: those who don't need a description, and those who aren't worth a description. At the risk of offending Dalí, I've written this loose commentary to attach some meaning to your visit.

Courtyard (Ground Floor): Step into the courtyard (with its audience of golden statues) and face the stage (visible through the window wall). You know how you can never get a cab when it's

raining? Pop a coin into Dalí's personal 1941 Cadillac and it rains inside the car. Look above, atop the tire tower: That's the boat Dalí enjoyed with his soul mate, Gala—his emotional life preserver, who kept him from going overboard. When she died, so did he (for his last seven years). Blue tears made of condoms drip below the boat.

Stage/Cupola (Ground Floor): Now cross through the courtyard and go up to the stage. On the left, squint at the big digital Abraham Lincoln, and president #16 comes into focus. Approach the painting to find that Abe's facial cheeks are Gala's butt cheeks—or use the coin-operated telescope (at the far end) or your phone's camera to focus on his face.

Treasures Room (Ground Floor): Under Lincoln, a door leads to the **Treasures Room** (Room 4), with the best collection of

original Dalí oil paintings in the museum. (Many of the artworks displayed elsewhere in the building are prints.) You'll see Cubist visions of Cadaqués and dreamy portraits of Gala. One portrays her half nude, as if her arms are a woven basket supporting her exposed breast like a crust of bread. Dalí said, "She has become my basket of bread." In the tiny-but-powerful *Specter of Sex Appeal*, crutches—a recurring Dalí theme—also represent Gala, who kept him supported whenever a meltdown threatened.

Downstairs Crypt (Lower Level): Make your way downstairs, below the stage, and pay respect at the artist's crypt, within dimly lit rooms filled with golden sculptures. True to the irreverent spirit of Dalí, the public toilets are right next to his tomb.

Mae West Room (First Floor): Back upstairs and to the right (as you face the stage), head into the famous Mae West Room (Room 11), a tribute to the sultry seductress. Dalí loved

her attitude. Saying things like, "Why marry and make one man unhappy, when you can stay single and make so many so happy?" Mae West was to conventional morality what Dalí was to conventional art. Climb to the vantage point where the sofa lips, fireplace nostrils, painting eyes, and drapery hair come together to make the face of Mae West.

Smoking Lounge (First Floor): Circle around to Room 15, with purple walls, labeled "Palace of the Wind" (just above the

entrance). Formerly the theater's smoking lounge, it displays portraits of Gala and Dalí (with a big eye, big ear, and a dark side) bookending a Roman candle of creativity. The fascinating ceiling painting shows the feet of Gala and Dalí as they bridge the earth and the heavens. Dalí's drawers are wide open and empty, indicating that he gave everything to his art. It was in this hall that the young Dalí first exhibited his art to the public.

Final Section (First Floor): Circle clockwise around the theater and pass above the stage once more, then go through the Bramante's Temple Room, followed by several more exhibits in Rooms 19 to 22. You'll be routed back downstairs and through the gift shop.

Nearby: As you leave the theater through the turnstile gate, hook right around the corner to pop into the adjacent, not-to-be-missed Dalí's Jewels exhibit (*Dalí-Joies*, covered by your theater ticket). It shows sketches and paintings of jewelry Dalí designed, and the actual pieces jewelers made from those surreal visions.

Cadaqués

Since the late 1800s, Cadaqués (kah-dah-KEHS) has served as a haven for intellectuals and artists alike. The fishing village's craggy coastline, sun-drenched colors, and laid-back lifestyle inspired Fauvists such as Henri Matisse and Surrealists such as René Magritte, Marcel Duchamp, and Federico García Lorca.

Even Picasso, drawn to this enchanting coastal haunt, painted some of his Cubist works here.

The Salvador Dalí House at Port Lligat, a 20-minute walk from the Cadaqués town center, is the main sightseeing attraction (reservations required). Dalí, raised in nearby Figueres, brought international fame to this sleepy Catalan port in the 1920s. As a kid Dalí spent summers here in the family cabin, where he was inspired by the rocky landscape that would later be the backdrop for many Surrealist canvases. In 1929, he met his future wife, Gala, in Cadaqués. Together they converted a fisherman's home in nearby Port Lligat into their semipermanent residence, dividing their time between New York, Paris, and Cadaqués. It was here that Dalí did his best work.

In spite of its fame, Cadaqués is mellow and feels off the beaten path. At the easternmost tip of Spain, it's remote, with no train service and only a tiny access road that dead-ends, making it less developed than it might otherwise be. If you want a peaceful beach-town escape near Barcelona, this is it.

GETTING TO CADAQUÉS

Reaching Cadaqués is very tough without a car. There are no trains and only a few buses a day. A taxi from Figueres is another option.

By Car: Cadaqués is about an hour's drive from Figueres. To visit the town center, park in the big lot just above the city—don't try to park near the harborfront. The handiest free parking is on Riera de Sant Vicenç, the long, generally dry riverbed that flows through the center of town (but steer clear on Monday when the town market happens here).

To drive to the Salvador Dalí House, carefully track *Port Lligat* signs at the big, elongated roundabout as you enter Cadaqués (as you approach from Figueres, you'll loop all the way around the roundabout and exit at its top corner—near where you entered). A big parking lot is just past the Salvador Dalí House, an easy five-minute walk along a gravel beach.

By Bus: Moventis Sarfa buses serve Cadaqués from **Figueres** (4/day weekdays, 2/day weekends, 1 hour) and from **Barcelona** (1-2/day, 3 hours). You can buy tickets in Barcelona at the TI on Plaça de Catalunya. Bus info: +34 972 258 713 (Cadaqués), https://compras.moventis.es. On busy summer days, it's wise to buy your ticket in advance.

By Taxi: A one-way taxi from Figueres costs about €70. It's just a little more for a round-trip—including the drive to Port Lligat and a couple of hours' wait. You can arrange a ride over the phone in advance (+34 972 505 043; good Spanish skills help—or ask your hotelier), or in person at the taxi stand on the Rambla in Figueres (from the Dalí Theater-Museum, walk down Carrer Sant

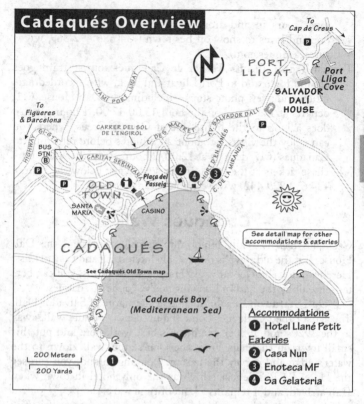

Cadaqués Overview

To Cap de Creus

PORT LLIGAT

Port Lligat Cove

SALVADOR DALÍ HOUSE

CAMÍ PORT LLIGAT

To Figueres & Barcelona

CARRER DEL SOL DE L'ENGIROL

C. DES MALTRET

AV. SALVADOR DALÍ

BUS STN.

AV. CARITAT SERINYANA

OLD TOWN

Plaça del Passeig

C. D'ORT D'EN SANÉS

C. DE LA MIRANDA

SANTA MARIA

CASINO

CADAQUÉS

See detail map for other accommodations & eateries

See Cadaqués Old Town map

Cadaqués Bay (Mediterranean Sea)

C. DE S. BARTOMEUS

200 Meters
200 Yards

Accommodations
❶ Hotel Llané Petit

Eateries
❷ Casa Nun
❸ Enoteca MF
❹ Sa Gelateria

NEAR BARCELONA

Pere to the Rambla). Driver Josep María has an official taxi-and-van service and offers the same rates (+34 696 906 476).

Orientation to Cadaqués

TOURIST INFORMATION
The TI is near the waterfront at Carrer Cotxe 2 (July-Sept Mon-Sat 9:00-21:00, shorter hours Sun and off-season plus closed for lunch, +34 972 258 315, www.visitcadaques.org).

HELPFUL HINTS
Electric Golf Carts and Bikes: EcoCar has a handful of electric golf carts and drivers that can take you around, including to the Dalí House in Port Lligat (€4/person) and to the spectacular clifftop views at Cap de Creus (€8/person). They also rent carts and electric bikes by the hour, half-day, or day (cash only, Avinguda Caritat Serinyana 10, +34 618 883 656, www. ecocarcadaques.com, Diego speaks English).
Local Guide: Simply a delight to be with, **Mercè Donat** orga-

nizes tours in and around Cadaqués. Mercè knows everyone and loves to show off her town (+34 686 492 369, www.rutescadaques.com).

Tourist Train: The **Es Trenet de Cadaqués** tourist train goes around town and to Port Lligat and back, with recorded narration and a few photo stops—including the Dalí House (€11, departs at 11:00 and on the hour 15:00-17:00, 1 hour). It also does a loop to the lighthouse at Cap de Creus, where you can enjoy the views for about 20 minutes before returning to Cadaqués (€17, departs at 12:00, 2 hours; for either tour, purchase tickets at the booth in the square just below the casino, +34 653 829 442, www.estrenetdecadaques.cat).

Cadaqués Walk

Cadaqués has no really important "sights" other than the Dalí House. But the old town is remarkably interesting and easy to miss. Here's a quick eight-point walk. Having strolled this, you can better relax along the harbor knowing you've "done" Cadaqués.

Dalí Statue on Beach: Start near the statue of Salvador Dalí. The artist called Cadaqués home (he lived a 20-minute walk away in the 1920s and 1930s). He did his best work here and put this small town on the map. From the Dalí statue, walk down to the water's edge and survey the harbor. Looking inland, you can see the Hotel La Residencia. This was the only hotel in town when Dalí arrived, and it remains a kind of time warp.

• *Notice the street that runs below grade, beneath a short bridge that's nearly at the water's edge.*

Riverbed Street: This street, just in front of the casino building, is actually a paved and usually dry riverbed. A couple of times each year, after big rains, this big drain becomes a raging river, saving the city from flash floods—which washed out several earlier bridges. Old-timers remember previous bridges on this spot, which separates the old town from the new. Traditionally, the bridge was where people hung out on benches, but the new bridge is too narrow to host loungers. Now people make do with the wide windowsills of the casino.

• *Walk over to the casino entrance.*

Casino: This place feels like the timeless clubhouse of the town, where the old boys gather to play cards and pool. Wander inside. There's a public WC next to the pool table. Enjoy the old photos on the walls.

• *Just past the casino is a small park with three...*

Cuba Trees: These stubby "elephant trees" were imported by locals who left Cuba when it won its independence from Spain in 1897. These trees are a reminder that lots of Catalans moved to

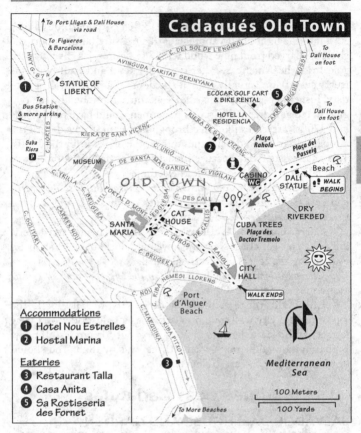

Cadaqués Old Town

To Port Lligat & Dalí House via road
To Figueres & Barcelona
C. DEL SOL DE L'ENGIROL
To Dalí House on foot
AVINGUDA CARITAT SERINYANA
STATUE OF LIBERTY
To Bus Station & more parking
ECOCAR GOLF CART & BIKE RENTAL
HOTEL LA RESIDENCIA
To Dalí House on foot
C. HORTES
Saba Riera P
RIERA DE SANT VICENÇ
RIERA DE SANT VICENÇ
C. UNIÓ
Plaça Rahola
Plaça del Passeig
MUSEUM
C. DE SANTA MARGARIDA
C. VIGILANT
CASINO WC
Beach
DALÍ STATUE
WALK BEGINS
OLD TOWN
C. TRILLA
CARRER NOU
PORTAL D'MONT
C. DES CALL
C. IGLESIA
CAT HOUSE
SANTA MARIA
PR. CALLS
CUBA TREES
Plaça des Doctor Tremolo
DRY RIVERBED
C. SOLITARI
C. BRUGERA
C. CURÓS
C. RAHOLA
C. BRUGERA
CITY HALL
WALK ENDS
C. NOU
RIBA NEMESI LLORENS
Port d'Alguer Beach
C. MARGUINA
RIBA PITXOT
N
Mediterranean Sea
To More Beaches
100 Meters
100 Yards

Accommodations
1 Hotel Nou Estrelles
2 Hostal Marina

Eateries
3 Restaurant Talla
4 Casa Anita
5 Sa Rostisseria des Fornet

Cuba in the 19th century and came back home when Spanish rule ended. Just uphill from the top tree are bits of the beloved (and well-used) old bridge benches. From here, try to imagine when Cadaqués was a small walled town filling the bluff above you.

• *Climb uphill to the right, through the old gate, into the...*

Old Town and Jewish Quarter: Stepping through the main gate, you enter a different world. Climb up Carrer des Call, the old Jewish street. There was a strong Jewish community in Spain from the first century until 1492. That's when Christian fanaticism (gone wild with the final Reconquista victory) led to the expulsion of Jews and Muslims from Catholic Spain. Notice the characteristic slate pavers underfoot.

• *Keep climbing until the T-intersection. There, at the top, turn left to the church.*

Church of Santa Maria: Enjoy the commanding view from in front of the church. This spot marks the high point of the old town. If the church is open, step inside to enjoy its amazing Baroque

altar from the 1700s (generally 10:00-13:00 & 16:00-20:00). Pop a euro into the light box to appreciate this treasure (and support the church). Carved from pine wood with 365 figures, it's covered with gold from the Americas. Peter (with the keys) and Paul (with his trusty sword) are actually part of the doors that lead into the sacristy. Fishermen paid for this altar—as you're reminded by the two guys in red and green, dressed as fishermen would have been in the mid-1700s. Treasures like this throughout Spain survived until the rampant destruction of churches during the civil war in the 1930s. This altar exists today because industrious locals built a protective wall in front of it all the way to the ceiling.

• *From the church, walk steeply down Carrer Curós. But first, on the left, notice the Cat House, a one-woman mission to care for the town's homeless cats. (She lives here with 20 cats and one dog.)*

Carrer Curós, or Gallery Street: This characteristic lane is lined with art galleries. Near the lower end, local painters show off by painting the covers on electrical panels.

• *The street bottoms out at* City Hall *(on the left) and a small terrace overlooking the harbor.*

City Hall: You're at the Casa de la Vila, or City Hall. The top of the old city wall here now serves as a balustrade for a view terrace, and it's a delightful spot to look out for pirates. The last Barbary pirate raid (from North Africa) was in 1828. You should be safe. Hey...it's cerveza-o'clock!

Sights near Cadaqués

SALVADOR DALÍ HOUSE AND GARDEN

Once Dalí's home and worth ▲▲▲, this house (Casa Salvador Dalí) in Port Lligat gives fans a chance to explore a labyrinthine compound. This is the best artist's house I've toured in Europe. It shows how a home can really reflect the creative spirit of an artistic genius and his muse. The ambience, both inside and out, is perfect for a Surrealist hanging out with his creative playmate. The bay is ringed by sleepy islands. Fishing boats are jumbled  on the beach. After the fishermen painted their boats, Dalí asked them to clean their brushes on his door—creating an abstract work of art he adored (which you'll see as you line up to get your ticket).

Cost and Hours: House-€13, garden only-€7; mid-June-mid-Sept daily 9:30-20:30; rest of year Tue-Sun 10:30-18:00, often closed Mon—see website; closed early Jan-mid-Feb. Last tour de-

parts 50 minutes before closing. No bags are allowed in the house; the baggage check is free.

Reservations Required: You must reserve in advance to visit the house (+34 972 251 015, www.salvador-dali.org). In summer, book at least a week in advance. You must arrive 30 minutes early to pick up your ticket, or they'll re-sell it. Really! For a full visit, see the home (with a timed entry and escorted tour) followed by the garden.

No Reservation? Those without a ticket to the home can easily get a garden ticket and see all the exteriors (including the pool).

Getting There: Parking is free nearby. There is no public bus service to the house, but from Cadaqués you can arrange a ride to and from in an **EcoCar** (see "Helpful Hints," earlier). On foot, the house is a 20-minute, one-mile walk over the hill from Cadaqués to Port Lligat. (The path, which cuts across the isthmus, is simple: straight up and over. It's much shorter than the road.) Follow signs to *Casa S. Dalí*.

Visiting the House

Only eight people are allowed inside the house every 10 minutes. There are five sections, each with a guard who gives you a brief explanation and then turns you loose for a few minutes. The entire visit takes 50 minutes. Before or after your tour, enjoy the 15-minute video (alternates in four languages) that plays in the waiting lounge—with walls covered in Dalí media coverage—just across the lane from the house.

The **house's interior** is left almost precisely as it was in 1982, when Gala died and Dalí moved out—never to return. (He died in 1989.) You'll see Dalí's studio (the clever easel cranks up and down to allow the artist to paint while seated, as he did eight hours a day); the bohemian yet divine living room (complete with a mirror to reflect the sunrise onto their bed each morning); and the painter's study (with his favorite mustaches all lined up). Like Dalí's art, his home is offbeat, provocative, and fun.

Visiting the Garden

While you'll get a guided tour of Dalí's home, you're on your own in his playful garden—which is where your house tour ends. It's a one-way circle (following numbered signs, 14-20). Here's what to look for:

Dalí's **patio** is where you can enjoy a little playful Dalí hide-and-seek, with crickets in cages, a horseshoe-shaped, slate dining table, and cool corridors leading to the olive garden out back (#14-16). From a platform, you'll view *Christ of the Rubbish*, a huge **statue** (#17) that sprawls on the ground, created from collected junk.

In the **olive grove** (#18), relax on Dalí's six-legged chairs

("they never fall"). And then enjoy a commanding view of the bay, including an island where hippies slept back in the 1960s. At the top of the garden is a theater with video documentaries (rarely with English subtitles).

Descend through Dalí's "historic garden," noting that he preserved this oasis to honor the hard labor and time it took to create. At a little patio you reach a broken eggshell sculpture (symbolizing how Dalí and Gala were "hatched")—climb in for some photo fun.

Next you enter the **"egg terrace"** (#19, the egg symbolizes fertility), protected from the steady wind. Above, in a niche is a sink—a reminder of Dalí's belief (or joke) that to gain salvation you must be clean. He was ambiguous about his religion.

Now it's party time, and you're poolside. Dalí's penis-shaped **pool** (#20) is surrounded by stylish kitsch (Mae West lips sofa, fountain with cheap Spanish sherry bottles)—decor as eclectic as his circle of friends. Imagine the parties.

Your exit was Dalí's **entry**. Dalí had a national phone booth placed here for the convenience (and expense) of friends who needed to make a call. Notice the white sculpture of a warrior with a small child (see the two little feet) emerging from it. The message: Leave your warrior outside and let your inner child enter.

NEAR CADAQUÉS
Cap de Creus
The top excursion for nature lovers is the easternmost point of mainland Spain—Cap de Creus. The cape, marked by a lighthouse, is a popular nine-mile round-trip hike (get details at the Cadaqués TI). There are swimming coves along the way and a restaurant at the lighthouse. The easy way to get there is via Eco-Car or tourist train (see "Helpful Hints," earlier).

Sleeping in Cadaqués

$$ Hotel Llané Petit, with 32 spacious rooms (half with view balconies), is a small resort-like hotel with its own little beach, a 10-minute walk south of the town center (some view rooms, air-con, elevator, RS%—free breakfast, pay parking, Carrer del Doctor Bartomeus 37, +34 972 251 020, www.llanepetit.com, info@llanepetit.com).

$ Hotel Nou Estrelles is a big, concrete exercise in efficient, economic comfort. Facing the bus stop a few blocks in from the waterfront, this family-run hotel offers 15 rooms at a great value (air-con, elevator, Carrer Sa Tarongeta 3, +34 972 259 100, www.hotelnouestrelles.com, reservas@hotelnouestrelles.com, Emma).

$ Hostal Marina is run by a local family with care and en-

thusiasm and has 30 fresh rooms at a great location a block from the harborfront main square (RS%—use code "Rick Steves," some rooms with balcony, family rooms, no elevator, Riera de Sant Vicenç 3, +34 972 159 091, www.hostalmarinacadaques. com, info@hostalmarinacadaques.com, Pau and Isabel).

Eating in Cadaqués

$$$$ Restaurant Talla, grandly situated across from the old town with a harbor view, serves modern Mediterranean top-end cuisine. It has a rustic yet elegant interior and some fine harborside tables outside. Call ahead to reserve a seating at this popular place (open 12:00-23:00, closed Tue-Wed mid-April-May, Riba Pitxot 18, +34 972 258 739).

$$$ Casa Nun, serving wonderful traditional Catalan dishes and the freshest seafood, has been run by Paco since 1979 (fun photos in the back). Its cozy interior is whitewashed and tiled, and the little front porch gives a few tables great harbor views. Portions are big—don't hesitate to split first courses family-style (Wed-Sun 12:00-24:00, closed Mon-Tue, Plaça Portixó 6, +34 972 258 856).

$$ Casa Anita is good for an entertaining meal. You'll sit with others around a big table and enjoy fresh local fish and homemade *helado* (ice cream). There's no menu—you'll just eat what they serve you. Finish your meal with a glass of sweet Muscatel (closed Mon, Carrer Miquel Rosset 16, +34 972 258 471, Joan and family).

$$$ Enoteca MF is popular for their creative tapas and *raciones,* prepared with local ingredients that they mostly produce or catch themselves (Riba des Poal, +34 972 258 954).

$ Sa Rostisseria des Fornet is a very simple deli designed mostly for takeout but with a couple of humble tables. There's no atmosphere, but it's cheap (you pay by weight), fast, and tasty (Carrer Miquel Rosset 3, +34 972 258 501).

For Dessert: The venerable ice cream shop **Sa Gelateria** faces the harbor (east of the center). Along with gelato, they serve homemade popsicles. Speaking of popsicles, pop in for the interesting historic photos of Cadaqués and its people.

Sitges

Sitges (SEE-juhz) is one of Catalunya's most popular resort towns. Because the town beautifully mingles sea and light, it's long been an artists' colony. Here you can still feel the soul of the Modernistas...in the architec-

ture, the museums, the salty sea breeze, and the relaxed rhythm of life. Today's Sitges is a world-renowned vacation desti- nation among the gay commu- nity. Despite its jet-set status, the Old Town has managed to retain its charm. With a much slower pulse than Barcelona, Sitges is an enjoyable break from the big city.

To reach Sitges, you can take the train or bus. Southbound trains depart Barcelona from the Sants and Passeig de Gràcia sta- tions (take frequent Rodalies train on the dark-green line R2sud toward Sant Vicenç de Calders, 35 minutes). The TI is to the left after you exit the train station. They can provide information about beaches and the town in general (Plaça Eduard Maristany 2, +34 938 944 251, www.sitgesanytime.com). BUS Garraf runs an easy and frequent bus from downtown Barcelona (with stops near the university and Plaça d'Espanya) that stops at Barcelona's airport en route to Sitges (1 hour, www.busgarraf.cat).

Visiting Sitges: Sitges basically has two attractions—its tight-and-tiny Old Town (with a couple of good museums) and its long, luxurious beaches.

Take time to explore the **Old Town**'s narrow streets. They're crammed with cafés, boutiques, and all the resort staples. The focal point, on the waterfront, is the 17th- century Baroque-style **Sant Bartomeu i Santa Tecla Church.** The terrace in front of the church will help you get the lay of the land. Poke into the Old Town or take the grand staircase down to the beach promenade.

The town's two appealing museums share one entrance and fee and are located along the water behind the church (+34 938 940 364, www.museusdesitges.cat). The **Museu Maricel,** which began as an eclectic display of art from a local collector, proudly shows works from the 10th century through the first half of the

20th, including pieces by Sitges artists. The **Museu del Cau Fer-rat** bills itself as a "temple of Modernism," as collected by local artist and intellectual Santiago Rusiñol.

Nine **beaches,** separated by breakwaters, extend about a mile southward from town. Stroll down the seaside promenade, which stretches from the town to the end of the beaches (beach chairs available for rent). The crowds thin out about halfway down, and the last three beaches are more intimate and cove-like. Along the way, restaurants and *chiringuitos* (beach bars) serve tapas, paella, and drinks.

BASQUE COUNTRY

Euskal Herria

Straddling two nations on the Atlantic Coast—stretching about 100 miles from Bilbao, Spain, north to Bayonne, France—lies the ancient, free-spirited land of the Basques. The Basque Country is famous for its beaches, culinary scene, and scintillating modern architecture...and for its feisty, industrious natives. It's also simply beautiful: Bold stone houses and bright white chalet-style homes with deep-red and green shutters scatter across lush, rolling hills; the Pyrenees Mountains soar high above the Atlantic; and surfers and sardines share the waves.

Insulated from mainstream Europe for much of their history, the plucky Basques have wanted to be left alone for more than 7,000 years. An easily crossed border separates the French *Pays Basque* from the Spanish *País Vasco,* allowing you to sample both sides from a single base (in Spain, I prefer fun-loving San Sebastián; in France, I hang my beret in cozy St-Jean-de-Luz).

Much unites the Spanish and French Basque regions: They share a cuisine, Union Jack-style flag (green, red, and white), and common language (Euskara), spoken by about a half-million people. (Virtually everyone also speaks Spanish and/or French.) And both have been integrated by their respective nations, sometimes forcibly. The French Revolution quelled French Basque ideas of independence; 130 years later, Spain's fascist dictator, Generalísimo Francisco Franco, attempted to tame his own separatist-minded Basques.

But over the past few generations, things have started looking up. The long-suppressed Euskara language is enjoying a resurgence. And, as the European Union celebrates ethnic regions rather than nations, the Spanish and French Basques are feeling

Basque Country at a Glance

▲▲**San Sebastián (Spain)** Relaxing upscale city with beach-front promenade wrapped around chic shopping neighborhood and tasty tapas bars. See page 189.

▲▲**Bilbao (Spain)** Revitalized regional capital with architectural gem—Guggenheim Bilbao—and atmospheric old town. See page 222.

▲▲**St-Jean-de-Luz (France)** Sleepy seaside retreat in the French *Pays Basque* that serves as home base for countryside exploration. See page 239.

▲**Guernica (Spain)** Village at the heart of Basque culture that was devastated by bombs during the Spanish Civil War—later immortalized by a Picasso masterpiece. See page 217.

▲**Bayonne (France)** Urban French scene with a Basque twist, home to impressive cultural museum, scenic ramparts, and lots of ham. See page 253.

Biarritz (France) Beach resort known for its mix of international glitz and surfer dudes. See page 260.

BASQUE COUNTRY

more united. This heavily industrialized region is experiencing a striking 21st-century renaissance. In Spain, the dazzling architecture of the Guggenheim Bilbao modern-art museum and the glittering resort of San Sebastián are drawing enthusiastic crowds. And, in France, long-ignored cities such as Bayonne and the surfing mecca of Biarritz are being revitalized. At the same time, traditional small towns—like Spain's Lekeitio and France's St-Jean-de-Luz and nearby mountain villages—are also thriving, making the entire region colorful, fun, welcoming...and unmistakably Basque.

PLANNING YOUR TIME

One day is enough for a quick sample of the Basque Country, but two or three days lets you breathe deep and hold it in. Where you go depends on your interests: Spain or France? Cities (such as Bilbao and Bayonne) or resorts (such as San Sebastián and St-Jean-de-Luz)?

If you want to slow down and focus on Spain, spend one day relaxing in San Sebastián and the second side-tripping to Bilbao (and Guernica, if you have a car).

Better yet, take this easy opportunity to dip into France. Sleep in one country, then side-trip into the other, devoting one day to

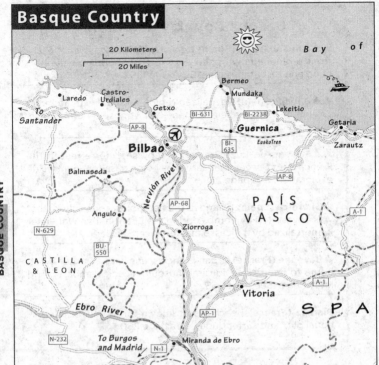

Basque Country

Spain (either San Sebastián or Bilbao), and a second day to France (St-Jean-de-Luz and Bayonne).

Wherever you go, your Basque sightseeing should be a fun blend of urban, rural, cultural, and culinary activities.

GETTING AROUND THE BASQUE COUNTRY

The tourist's Basque Country—from Bilbao to Bayonne—stays close to the coastline. Everything is connected by good roads and public transportation. If traveling between Spain and France, carry your passport, as police might ask for identification at border crossings.

By Bus and Train: From San Sebastián, the bus is the best way to reach Bilbao (and from there, bus or train to Guernica). To go between San Sebastián and France, you have a choice of train or bus. Trains offer more frequent departure times but require a transfer in Hendaye; buses can sometimes be faster and more convenient (check schedules and compare). Once in France, the three main towns—St-Jean-de-Luz, Bayonne, and Biarritz—are connected by bus and by train (and Bayonne and Biarritz by the electric Tram'bus). Even if you rent a car, I'd do these three towns by

public transit due to the insane traffic during high season. Specific connections are explained in each section.

Note that a few out-of-the-way areas—Spain's Bay of Biscay and France's Basque villages of the interior—are impractical by public transportation...but worth the trouble by car.

By Car: San Sebastián, Bilbao, St-Jean-de-Luz, and Bayonne are connected by a convenient expressway, called AP-8 in Spain and A-63 in France (rough timings: Bilbao to San Sebastián, 1.5 hours; San Sebastián to St-Jean-de-Luz, 45 minutes; St-Jean-de-Luz to Bayonne, 30 minutes).

Language on Road Signs: At the start of each section, I list place names using the Spanish or French spelling first and the Euskara spelling second; throughout the rest of the section, I default to the spelling that prevails locally. While most people refer to towns by their Spanish or French names, many road signs list places in Euskara. (In Spain, signs are usually posted in both Euskara and Spanish, either on the same sign or with dual signage on opposite sides of the street. In less separatist-minded France, signs are often only in French.) The Spanish or French version is sometimes scratched out by locals, so you might have to navigate by Euskara names.

Who Are the Basques?

To call the Basques "mysterious" is an understatement. Before most European nations had ever set sail, Basque whalers competed with the Vikings for control of the sea. During the Industrial Revolution and lean Franco years, Basque steel kept the Spanish economy alive. In the last few decades, the separatist group ETA gave the Basque people an unwarranted reputation for violence. And through it all, the Basques have spoken a unique language that to outsiders sounds like gibberish or a secret code.

So just who are the Basques? Even for Basques, that's a difficult question. According to traditional stereotypes, Basques are thought of as having long noses, heavy eyebrows, floppy ears, stout bodies, and a penchant for wearing berets. But widespread Spanish and French immigration has made it difficult to know who actually has Basque ethnic roots. (In fact, some of the Basques' greatest patriots have had no Basque blood.) And so today, anyone who speaks the Basque language, Euskara, is considered a "Basque"—as are the many people who grew up under Franco and never had the chance to learn the language.

Euskara, related to no other surviving tongue, has been used since Neolithic times—making it, very likely, the oldest European language that's still spoken. With its seemingly impossible-to-pronounce words filled with k's, tx's, and z's (restrooms are *komunak: gizonak* for men and *emakumeak* for women), Euskara makes speaking Spanish suddenly seem easy. Try greeting locals with *kaixo* and saying goodbye with *agur*. (Some tips: *tx* is pronounced "ch" and *tz* is pronounced "ts." Other key words: *kalea* is "street," and *ostatua* is a cheap hotel.) Kept alive as a symbol of Basque cultural identity, Euskara typically is learned proudly as a second or third language. Many locals can switch effortlessly from Euskara to Spanish or French.

The Basque economy has historically been shaped by three factors: the sea, agriculture, and iron deposits.

Basque sailors were some of the first and finest in Europe, as they built ever-better boats to venture farther and farther into the Atlantic in search of whales and cod. By the mid-15th century, Basque sailors were venturing a thousand miles from home into the far northern Atlantic Ocean. Despite lack of physical evidence, many historians surmise that the Basques must have sailed to Newfoundland before Christopher Columbus landed in the Caribbean.

When the "Spanish" era of exploration began, Basques continued to play a key role, as sailors and shipbuilders. Columbus' *Santa María* was likely Basque built, and his crew included many

Basques. History books teach that Ferdinand Magellan was the first to circumnavigate the globe, with the footnote that he was killed partway around. Who took over the helm for the rest of the journey, completing the circle? It was his Basque captain, Juan Sebastián de Elcano. And a pair of well-traveled Catholic priests, known for their far-reaching missionary trips that led to founding the Jesuit order, were also Basques: St. Ignatius of Loyola and St. Francis Xavier.

Later, the Industrial Age swept Europe, gaining a foothold in Iberia when the Basques began using their rich iron deposits to make steel. Pioneering Basque industrialists set the tempo as they dragged Spain into the modern world. Cities such as Bilbao were heavily industrialized, sparking an influx of workers from around Spain (which gradually diluted Basque blood in the Basque Country).

The independence-minded Basques are notorious for their stubbornness. In truth, as a culturally and linguistically unique is-

land surrounded by bigger and stronger nations, the Basques have learned to compromise. Historically Basques have remained on good terms with outsiders, so long as their traditional laws, the *Fueros,* were respected. Though outdated, the *Fueros* continue to symbolize a self-governance that the Basques hold dear. It is only when foreign law has been placed above the *Fueros*—as many of today's Basques feel Spanish law is—that the people have become agitated.

In recent years, much of the news of the Basques—especially in Spain—was made by the terrorist organization ETA, whose goal had been to establish an independent Basque state. (ETA stands for the Euskara phrase *"Euskadi Ta Askatasuna,"* or "Basque Country and Freedom.") ETA is thought to have been responsible for more than 800 deaths since 1968. The group gradually disarmed and finally announced its dissolution in April 2018, with apologies to victims and their families.

This is only a first glimpse into the important, quirky, and fascinating Basque people. To better understand the Basques, there's no better book than Mark Kurlansky's *The Basque History of the World*—essential pretrip reading for historians. And various museums in this region also illuminate Basque culture and history, including the Museum of San Telmo in San Sebastián, the Assembly House and Basque Country Museum in Guernica, and the Museum of Basque Culture in Bayonne (all described in this chapter).

Also note that in terms of linguistic priority (e.g., museum information), Euskara comes first, Spanish and French tie for second, and English is a distant fourth...and it often doesn't make the cut.

BASQUE COUNTRY CUISINE SCENE

Mixing influences from the mountains, sea, Spain, and France, Basque food is reason enough to visit the region. The local cuisine—dominated by seafood, tomatoes, and red peppers—offers some spicy dishes, unusual in most of Europe. And though you'll find similar specialties throughout the Basque lands, Spain is still Spain and France is still France. Here are some dishes you're most likely to find in each area.

Spanish Basque Cuisine: Hopping from bar to bar sampling *pintxos*—the local term for tapas—is a highlight of any trip (for details, see the "Do the *Txikiteo*" sidebar, later). You'll want to try the famous *pil-pil*, made from emulsifying the skin of *bacalao* (dried, salted cod) into a mayonnaise-like sauce with chili and garlic. Another tasty dish is *kokotxas*, usually made from hake *(merluza)* fish cheeks, prepared like *pil-pil*, and cooked slowly over low heat so the natural gelatin is released, turning it into a wonderful sauce—*¡qué bueno!* Look also for white asparagus from Navarra. Local brews include *sidra* (hard apple cider) and *txakolí* (chah-koh-LEE, a light, sparkling white wine—often theatrically poured from high above the glass for aeration). Wine-wise, I prefer the reds and rosés from Navarra. Finish your dinner with *cuajada*, a yogurt-like, creamy milk dessert that's sometimes served with honey and nuts. Another specialty, found throughout Spain, is *membrillo*, a sweet and *muy* dense quince jelly. Try it with cheese for a light dessert, or look for it at breakfast.

French Basque Cuisine: The red peppers (called *piments d'Espelette*) hanging from homes in small villages give foods a distinctive flavor and often end up in *piperade*, a dish that combines peppers, tomatoes, garlic, ham, and eggs. Peppers are also dried and used as condiments. Look for them with the terrific Basque dish *axoa* (a veal or lamb stew on mashed potatoes). Look also for anything "Basque-style" *(à la basquaise)*—cooked with tomato, eggplant, red pepper, and garlic. Don't leave without trying *ttoro* (tchoo-roh), a seafood stew that is the Basque Country's answer to bouillabaisse and cioppino. *Marmitako* is a hearty tuna stew. Local cheeses come from Pyrenean sheep's milk *(pur brebis)*, and the local ham *(jambon de Bayonne)* is famous throughout France. After dinner try a shot of *izarra* (herbal-flavored brandy). To satisfy your sweet tooth, look for *gâteau basque*, a local tart filled with pastry cream or cherries from Bayonne. Hard apple cider is a tasty and local beverage. The regional wine Irouléguy comes in red, white, and rosé, and is the only wine produced in the French part of

Basque Country (locals like to say that it's made from the smallest vineyard in France but the biggest in the Northern Basque Country).

Spanish Basque Country

Four of the seven Basque territories lie within Spain, where they're known as El País Vasco. Many consider Spanish Basque culture to be feistier and more colorful than the relatively assimilated French Basques—you'll hear more Euskara spoken here than in France.

For nearly 40 years, beginning in 1939, the figure of Generalísimo Franco loomed large over the Spanish Basques. Franco depended on Basque industry to keep the floundering Spanish economy afloat. But even as he exploited the Basques economically, he so effectively blunted their culture that the language was primarily Spanish by default. Franco kicked off his regime by offering up the historic Basque town of Guernica as target practice to Hitler's air force. The notorious result—the wholesale slaughter of innocent civilians—was immortalized by Pablo Picasso's mural *Guernica*.

But Franco is long gone, and today's Basques are looking to the future. The iron deposits have been depleted, prompting the Basques to reimagine their rusting cities for the 21st century. True to form, they're rising to the challenge. Perhaps the best example is Bilbao, whose iconic Guggenheim Museum—built on the former site of an industrial wasteland—is the centerpiece of a bold new skyline.

San Sebastián is the heart of the tourist's País Vasco, with its sparkling, picturesque beach framed by looming green mountains and a charming old town with gourmet *pintxos* (tapas) spilling out of every bar. On-the-rise Bilbao is worth a look for its landmark Guggenheim and its atmospheric old town. For small-town fun, drop by the fishing village of Lekeitio (near Bilbao). And for history, Guernica has some intriguing museums.

This chapter focuses on Basque destinations on or near the ocean. Some inland Basque towns and cities—most notably Pamplona—are covered in the Camino de Santiago chapter.

San Sebastián / Donostia

Shimmering above the breathtaking Concha Bay, elegant and prosperous San Sebastián (Donostia in Euskara, which locals lovingly shorten to Donosti) has a favored location, with golden beaches capped by twin peaks at either end and a cute little island offshore. A delightful beachfront promenade runs the length of the bay, with

a charismatic old town at one end and a smart shopping district in the center. It has 186,000 residents and almost that many tourists in high season (July-Sept). With a romantic setting, a soaring statue of Christ gazing over the city, and a late-night lively old town, San Sebastián has a mini Rio de Janeiro aura.

Though the actual "sightseeing" isn't much, the scenic city itself provides a pleasant introduction to Spain's Basque Country. As a culinary capital of Spain—with many local restaurants getting international attention—competition is tight to dish up some of the top tapas anywhere.

In 1845, Queen Isabel II's doctor recommended she treat her skin problems by bathing here in the sea. (For modesty's sake, she would go inside a giant cabana that could be wheeled into the surf—allowing her to swim far from prying eyes, never having to set foot on the beach.) Her visit mobilized Spain's aristocracy, and soon the city was on the map as a seaside resort. By the turn of the 20th century, San Sebastián was the toast of the belle époque, and a leading resort for Europe's beautiful people. Before World War I, Queen María Cristina summered here and held court in her Miramar Palace overlooking the crescent beach (the turreted, red-brick building partway around the bay). Hotels, casinos, and theaters flourished. Even Franco enjoyed 35 summers in a place he was sure to call San Sebastián, not Donostia.

PLANNING YOUR TIME

San Sebastián's sights can be exhausted in a few hours, but it's a great place to be on vacation for a full, lazy day (or longer). Stroll the two-mile-long promenade with the locals and scout the place you'll grab to work on a tan. The promenade leads to a funicular that lifts you to the Monte Igueldo viewpoint, unless you're up for hiking to the top. After exploring the old town and port, walk up to the hill of Monte Urgull. If you have more time, enjoy the delightful aquarium or the free history museum inside Monte Urgull's old castle. Or check out the Museum of San Telmo, the largest of its kind on Basque culture, which tracks the evolution of this unique society with state-of-the-art displays. A key ingredient of any visit to San Sebastián is enjoying tapas *(pintxos)* in the old-town bars.

Orientation to San Sebastián

The San Sebastián that we're interested in surrounds Concha Bay (Bahía de la Concha). It can be divided into three areas: Playa de la Concha (best beaches), Centro (the shopping district), and the old town (the skinny, grid-planned streets north of Centro called Parte Vieja). Centro, just east of Playa de la Concha, has beautiful turn-of-the-20th-century architecture, but no real

sights. A busy drag called the Boulevard stands where the city wall once ran, and separates the Centro from the old town.

It's all bookended by small mountains: Monte Urgull on the east end of the bay, and Monte Igueldo to the west. The river (Río Urumea) divides central San Sebastián from the district called Gros, with a lively night scene and surfing beach.

TOURIST INFORMATION

The main **TI** in San Sebastián is located right on the Boulevard (Mon-Sat 9:00-20:00, off-season until 19:00; Sun 10:00-19:00, off-season until 14:00, Boulevard 8, +34 943 481 166, www.sansebastianturismo.eus). You can pick up a free city map, or get it on your phone by scanning a QR code outside the building. If you have a car, ask for the general road map (free), which provides a useful driving map and a guide to essential experiences in the region. The TI also offers a handy brochure (€1) with self-guided walking tours—the Old Town/Monte Urgull walk is best—as well as guided walking tours (see "Tours in San Sebastián," later).

A seasonal **TI** by the Renfe train station is open in summer (22 Paseo de Francia; check website for schedule). **Regional info** about the surrounding province of Gipuzkoa (Guipúzcoa, in Spanish) can be found online at www.gipuzkoaturismoa.eus.

Sightseeing Cards: The **San Sebastián Card** gives you small discounts for some restaurants, museums, and shops; half-price on the TI's guided tour; and public transit (6 rides-€9, 12 rides-€16, shareable with one other person). It's not worth the cost unless you expect to ride public transit a lot—and the city is small enough that you probably won't. If you're exploring the larger region, the TI also sells the **Basque Card,** but for most travelers it's also not worth it.

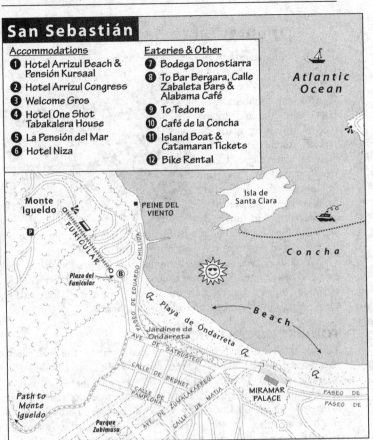

San Sebastián

Accommodations
1. Hotel Arrizul Beach & Pensión Kursaal
2. Hotel Arrizul Congress
3. Welcome Gros
4. Hotel One Shot Tabakalera House
5. La Pensión del Mar
6. Hotel Niza

Eateries & Other
7. Bodega Donostiarra
8. To Bar Bergara, Calle Zabaleta Bars & Alabama Café
9. To Tedone
10. Café de la Concha
11. Island Boat & Catamaran Tickets
12. Bike Rental

ARRIVAL IN SAN SEBASTIÁN

By Train: The town has two train stations (neither has baggage storage, but you can leave bags nearby—see "Helpful Hints," later).

If you're coming on a regional train from Hendaye/Hendaia on the French border, get off at the **Amara EuskoTren station** (five stops before the end of the line, which is called Lasarte-Oria). It's a level 15-minute walk to the center: Exit the station and walk across the long plaza, then veer right and walk eight blocks down Calle Easo (toward the statue of Christ hovering on the hill) to the beach. The old town will be ahead on your right, with Playa de la Concha to your left. To speed things up, exit the station to the right, catch bus #21, #26, or #28 along Calle Easo, and take it to the Boulevard stop, near the TI at the bottom of the old town.

If you're arriving by train from elsewhere in Spain (or from France after transferring in Irún), you'll get off at the main **Renfe station.** It's just across the river from the Centro shopping district.

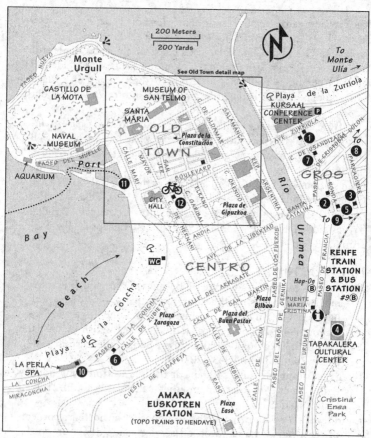

To get to the old town, catch bus #9 from the city side of the station to the Boulevard stop (€1.80, pay driver) or catch a taxi (they wait out front, about €7 to downtown). Alternatively, just walk (about 10-15 minutes)—beyond the tree-lined plaza, cross the fancy dragon-decorated María Cristina Bridge, turn right onto the busy avenue called Paseo de los Fueros, and follow the Urumea River until the last bridge. The modern, blocky Kursaal Conference Center across the river serves as an easy landmark.

By Bus: A few buses—such as those from the airport—can let you off at pretty Plaza de Gipuzkoa (first stop after crossing the river, in Centro shopping area, one block from the Boulevard, TI, and old town). But most buses—including those from Bilbao—take you instead to San Sebastián's underground bus station, next to the Renfe train station. To get to the old town from here, cross the María Cristina Bridge and follow the walking directions above.

By Plane: **San Sebastián Airport** is beautifully situated along the harbor in the nearby town of Hondarribia, 12 miles east of

the city, just across the bay from France (airport code: EAS, www.
aena.es). An easy regional bus (#E21) connects the airport to San
Sebastián's Plaza de Gipuzkoa, just a block south of the Boulevard
and TI (€2.75, pay driver, 6/day, 35 minutes, https://ekialdebus.
eus). Other buses connect the airport to San Sebastián's Plaza
Gipuzkoa, but #E21 is much faster. A taxi into town costs about
€38.

By Car: Take the Amara freeway exit, follow *Centro Ciudad* signs into the city center, and park in a pay lot (many are well
signed—the Kursaal underground lot is the most central). If you're
picking up or returning a rental car, you'll find Avis at the Renfe
train station (+34 943 461 556) and Sixt at the Kursaal Conference
Center (Avenida de Zurriola 1, +34 871 180 192). Take a taxi to
reach the less centrally located Hertz (Centro Comercial Garbera,
Travesía de Garbera 1, +34 943 392 223) and Europcar (Plaza de
Irún 6, +34 664 091 328).

HELPFUL HINTS

Bookstore: Elkar, an advocate of Basque culture and literature,
  has two branches on the same street in the old town. Both
  have a collection of Basque literature, and one has a wide selection of guidebooks, maps, and books in English (Mon-Sat
  10:00-13:30 & 16:00-20:00, closed Sun, Calle Fermín Calbetón 21 and 30, +34 943 420 080).

Baggage Storage: It's €5/24 hours at the **bus station** (long hours
  daily) or at **Navi.net,** an internet café (daily 10:00-21:00,
  Calle Narrica 12).

Laundry: In the old town, try **5 à Sec,** opposite the northern corner
  of the Bretxa Market (drop-off service, same day if dropped
  off by 12:00; open Mon-Sat 9:30-14:30 & 17:00-20:00, closed
  Sun; Calle Aldamar 24, +34 943 432 044). Self-service **Garbi-
  matik** is on a side street half a block from the Bretxa Market
  (daily 9:00-22:00, San Lorenzo 6, mobile +34 635 739 795).

Bike Rental: The city has some great bike lanes and is a good place
  to enjoy on two wheels. You can access San Sebastián's **dBizi**
  bike-sharing program through their website, www.dbizi.eus
  (must load €5.30 credit, valid 30 days, standard bike-€1.55/
  hour, e-bike-€3.30/hour). Or, try **Sanse Bikes** near the City
  Hall (€7/2 hours, €10/4 hours, €15/8 hours, Boulevard 25,
  +34 943 045 229). Another option is **La Bicicleta Gros** (€13/4
  hours, €22/24 hours; Avenida de Zurriola 22, three blocks
  across river from TI, mobile +34 943 442 233).

Marijuana: While Spain is famously liberal about marijuana laws,
  the Basque Country is even more so. Walking around San
  Sebastián, you'll see "grow shops" sporting the famous green
  leaf (shopkeepers are helpful if you have questions). The sale

of marijuana is still illegal, but marijuana consumption is decriminalized, and people are allowed to grow enough for their personal use at home. With the town's mesmerizing aquarium and delightfully lit bars filled with enticing munchies, it just makes sense.

GETTING AROUND SAN SEBASTIÁN

By Bus: Along the Boulevard at the bottom edge of the old town, you'll find a line of public buses ready to take you anywhere in town; give any driver your destination, and they will tell you the number of the bus to catch (€1.80, €2.10 after midnight, pay driver).

Some handy bus routes: #21, #26, and #28 connect the Amara EuskoTren station to the TI (get off at the Boulevard stop); #5, #16, and #25 begin at the Boulevard/TI stop, go along Playa de la Concha and through residential areas; #16 eventually arrives at the base of the Monte Igueldo funicular. Bus info: www.dbus.eus.

By Taxi: Taxis start at about €7, which covers most rides in the center. You can't hail a taxi on the street—you must call one (+34 943 404 040 or +34 943 464 646) or find a taxi stand (most convenient along the Boulevard).

Tours in San Sebastián

Walking Tours

The **TI** runs an English-language walking tour called Essential San Sebastián (€15, 2 hours, covers both the old town and the city center). Schedules vary—reserve at the TI or at www.sansebastianturismo.eus.

Local Guides

Based in San Sebastián, **Agustin Ciriza** leads walking tours of his hometown and guided tours through the Spanish and French Basque Country, with destinations including Bilbao, Hondarribia, Biarritz, and the Biscay Coast. He also offers guided Camino walks, mountain treks, and Rioja region wine tours, as well as *txakolí* tastings (€180/group for city tours, from €25/person for hiking options, mobile +34 686 117 395, https://agustinciriza.com).

Gabriella Ranelli, an American who's lived in San Sebastián for more than 30 years, specializes in culinary tours. She can take you on a sightseeing spin around the old town, along with a walk through the market and best *pintxo* bars (€165/person, 2-person minimum, less for 4 or more people), or on an excursion to nearby towns and wine regions (from €750/day, transportation included for up to 4 people, +34 943 422 163, www.tenedortours.com). Gabriella also organizes cooking classes—where you shop at the market, then join a local chef to cook up some tasty *pintxos* of your own

(€275/person, 2-person minimum, less for 4 or more people)—as well as wine tastings (starting at €195/person).

James in Spain, run by James Scanlan, an American settled in San Sebastián, offers a variety of tours in the city and the greater Basque Country. Options range from city walks and *pintxos* tours to themed tours focused on regional history, maritime culture, or in-depth wine experiences (€180/3 hours). He also offers cycling tours for all levels, both in town and on quiet, charming Basque roads (mobile +34 688 607 545, www.jamesinspain.com).

Itsaso Petrikorena leads food and cultural tours of the city and countryside villages in both the French and Spanish regions of the Basque Country. He also arranges visits to wineries and cider houses (mobile +34 647 973 231, betitsaso@yahoo.es).

Gastronomic Tours

Mimo San Sebastián offers a half-day gourmet cooking class (from €190/person, including ingredients and wine) and *pintxo* tours that have you hopping from bar to bar (€130, includes food and wine, Calle Okendo 1 bajo, +34 943 062 018, https://mimo.eus).

Tours on Wheels

Most travelers won't find it necessary in this walkable city, but the **"txu-txu"** tourist train gives you a good overview of San Sebastián (€5, daily 11:00-20:00, mid-Sept-June until 18:30, closed Jan-Feb and Mon off-season, 40-minute round-trip, +34 943 422 973, http://sansebastian.city-tour.com). A faster **hop-on, hop-off bus** with several stops is run by the same company. Buy an all-day €12 ticket on the bus, at the TI, or online (daily 10:30-20:00, shorter hours off-season, handy stop in front of Renfe train station for day-trippers).

Sights in San Sebastián

IN THE OLD TOWN

Huddled in the shadow of its once-protective Monte Urgull, the old town (Parte Vieja, worth ▲▲) is where San Sebastián was born about 1,000 years ago. Because the town burned down in 1813 (as Spain, Portugal, and England fought the French to get Napoleon's brother off the Spanish throne), the architecture you see is generally Neoclassical and uniform. Still, the grid plan of streets hides heavy Baroque and Gothic churches, surprise plazas, and fun little shops, including venerable pastry stores, rugged produce markets, Basque-independence souvenir shops, and seafood-to-go delis. The highlight of the old town is its array of incredibly lively tapas bars—though here these snacks are called *pintxos* (PEEN-chohs; see "Eating in San Sebastián," later). To see the fishing industry in action, wander out to the port (described later).

Throughout the old town, flagpoles mark **"private eating clubs"** (you might occasionally see a club's name displayed, but most are otherwise unmarked). The clubs used to be exclusively male; women are now allowed as invited guests...but never in the kitchen, which remains the men's domain. Basque society is matrilineal and very female-oriented. A husband brings home his paycheck and hands it directly to his wife, who controls the house's purse strings (and everything else). Basque men felt they needed a place where they could congregate and play "king of the castle," so they formed these clubs where members could reserve a table and cook for their friends.

▲Plaza de la Constitución

The old town's main square is where bullfights used to be held. Notice the seat numbering on the balconies: Even if you owned

an apartment here, the city retained rights to the balconies, which it could sell as box seats. (Residents could peek over the paying customers' shoulders.) Above the clock, notice the seal of San Sebastián: a merchant ship with sails billowing in the wind. The city was granted trading rights by the crown—a reminder of the Basque Country's importance in Spanish seafaring. Inviting café tables crowd the square from all corners.

▲▲Museum of San Telmo (San Telmo Museoa)

This fascinating museum innovatively wrapped a modern facade around a 16th-century Dominican convent and its peaceful cloister. It's now the largest museum of Basque culture in the country and is well worth a visit. Exhibits of archaeological and ethnographic artifacts demonstrate the traditional folkways of Basque life and vividly tell the history of the region. Its art collection features a few old-school gems (El Greco, Rubens, Tintoretto), while 19th- and 20th-century paintings by Basque artists offer an interesting glimpse into the spirit, faces, and natural beauty of these fiercely independent people. QR codes posted near the exhibits provide English explanations.

Cost and Hours: €6, includes free downloadable multimedia guide, free to enter on Tue; open Tue-Sun 10:00-20:00, closed Mon; Plaza Zuloaga 1, +34 943 481 580, www.santelmomuseoa. eus.

Visiting the Museum: The museum's layout takes you through the temporary exhibitions first—often focusing on Basque art movements. Or you can enter directly into Section 1, within the

BASQUE COUNTRY

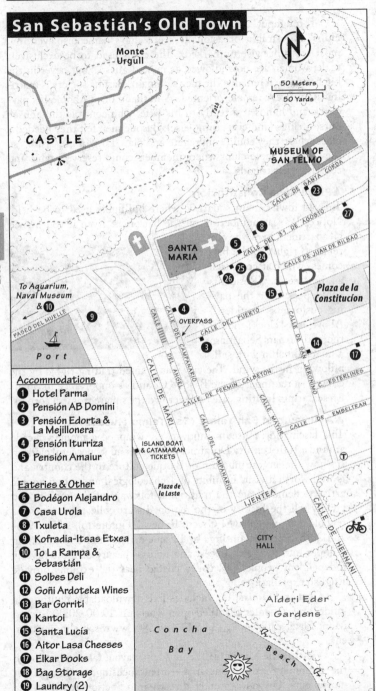

San Sebastián's Old Town

Monte Urgull

N

50 Meters
50 Yards

CASTLE

MUSEUM OF SAN TELMO

CALLE DE SANTA CORDA

23

CALLE DEL 31 DE AGOSTO

27

8

SANTA MARIA

5

CALLE DE JUAN DE BILBAO

24

O L D

26 25

15

Plaza de la Constitución

4

OVERPASS

CALLE DEL PUERTO

To Aquarium,
Naval Museum
& 10

9

3

CALLE DEL CAMPANARIO

CALLE DEL ANGEL

CALLE DE SAN JERONIMO

14

PASEO DEL MUELLE

Port

CALLE DE MARI

CALLE DE FERMIN CALBETON

CALLE MAYOR

17

C. ESTERLINES

CALLE DE EMBELTRAN

T

ISLAND BOAT
& CATAMARAN
TICKETS

CALLE DEL CAMPANARIO

Plaza de
la Lasta

IJENTEA

CITY
HALL

CALLE DE HERNANI

Alderi Eder
Gardens

Concha
Bay

Beach

Accommodations
1 Hotel Parma
2 Pensión AB Domini
3 Pensión Edorta &
   La Mejillonera
4 Pensión Iturriza
5 Pensión Amaiur

Eateries & Other
6 Bodégon Alejandro
7 Casa Urola
8 Txuleta
9 Kofradia-Itsas Etxea
10 To La Rampa &
   Sebastián
11 Solbes Deli
12 Goñi Ardoteka Wines
13 Bar Gorriti
14 Kantoi
15 Santa Lucía
16 Aitor Lasa Cheeses
17 Elkar Books
18 Bag Storage
19 Laundry (2)

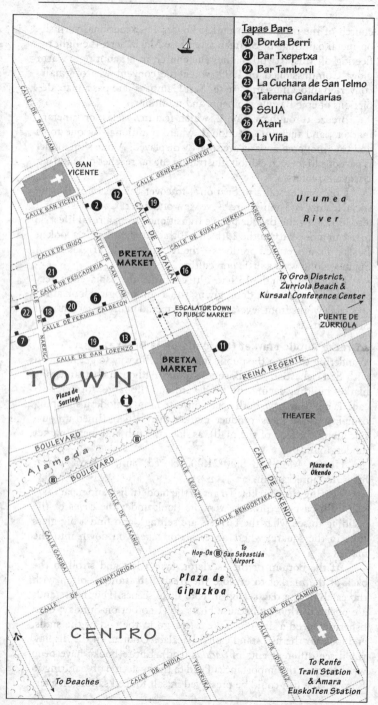

Tapas Bars
20 Borda Berri
21 Bar Txepetxa
22 Bar Tamboril
23 La Cuchara de San Telmo
24 Taberna Gandarías
25 SSUA
26 Atari
27 La Viña

BASQUE COUNTRY

church of the original convent. It houses 11 exceptional varnish-on-metal paintings by Spanish artist José María Sert; the light reflecting off this artwork bathes the church in a hauntingly warm glow. Commissioned in 1929, when the convent was originally converted into a museum, these "Sert Canvases" are passionate depictions of epic Basque moments and traditions.

Breeze through Section 2, which features steles, or funerary markers, and tuck into Section 3, where traditional Basque tools and time-honored apparel are smartly displayed. A fine ship model is part of a high-tech exhibit illustrating the far reaches of seafaring Basque explorers.

Continue upstairs to Section 4 to cover the basics of Basque social history and gain a bird's-eye view of the Sert Canvases. You'll also learn how the Basque people transitioned from a rural lifestyle to urban modernity in the 19th and 20th centuries. Enjoy a look at Basque-manufactured products—the Kenmores and Frigidaires of Spain—along with a little pop culture.

Paintings from the 15th to 19th centuries are displayed in Section 5 on the top-most floor, giving you a chronological look at respectable works from several well-known (and many lesser-known) Spanish artists.

▲Bretxa Public Market (Mercado de la Bretxa)

Wandering through the public market is a fun way to get in touch with San Sebastián and Basque culture. Although the sandstone market building facing the Boulevard and the large, former Pescadería building have both been converted into a modern shopping complex, the farmers' produce market thrives here (lined up outside along the side of the mall), as does the fish and meat market (underground).

Hours: Mon-Sat 8:00-21:00, closed Sun, Bretxa Plaza, https://cclabretxa.com.

Visiting the Market: To get to the modern fish and meat market, walk past the produce vendors (look under the eaves of the building to see what the farmers are selling), and find a big glass cube in the square, where an escalator takes you down into the market.

At the bottom of the escalator, take a left and stroll to the back of the market to explore the **fresh-fish stands**—often with the catch of the day set up in cute little scenes. Few fish stands are open on Monday because boats don't go out on Sunday; even fishermen need a day off. Take a left, go to the end of the stalls, and look for the fish stand called Bacalaos Uranzu. In the display, you'll see different cuts of *bacalao* (cod). Entire books have been written about the importance of cod to the evolution of seafaring in Europe. The fish could be preserved in salt to feed sailors on ever-

longer trips into the North Atlantic, allowing them to venture beyond the continental shelf (into deeper waters where they couldn't catch fresh fish). Cod was also popular among Catholic landlubbers on Fridays. Today cod remains a Basque staple. People still buy the salted version, which must be soaked for 48 hours (and the water changed three times) to become edible. If you're in a rush, you can buy desalted cod...but at a cost in flavor. There's a free **WC** in the market—just ask *"¿Dónde está el servicio, por favor?"*

When you're done exploring, take the escalator up, turn left, and cross the street to the **Aitor Lasa** cheese shop at Aldamar 12 (closed Sun, +34 943 430 354). Pass the fragrant piles of mushrooms at the entrance and head back to the display case, showing off the Basque specialty of *idiazábal*—raw sheep's milk cheese. Notice the wide variety, which depends on the specific region it came from, whether it's smoked or cured, and for how long it's been cured *(curación)*. If you're planning a picnic, this is a very local (and expensive) ingredient. To try the cheese that won first prize a few years back in the Ordizia International Cheese Competition, ask for *"El queso con el premio de Ordizia, por favor."* The owners are evangelical about the magic of combining the local cheese with walnuts and *dulce de manzana* homemade apple jam.

AT THE PORT
At the west end of the old town, protected by Monte Urgull, is the port. Take the passage through the wall at the appropriately named Calle Puerto, and jog right along the level, portside promenade, Paseo del Muelle. You'll pass fishing boats unloading the catch of the day (with hungry locals looking on), salty sailors' pubs, and fishermen mending nets. Also along  this strip are the skippable Naval Museum and the entertaining aquarium. Trails to the top of Monte Urgull are just above this scene, near Santa María Church (or climb the stairs next to the aquarium).

Cruises
Small boats cruise from the old town's port to the island in the bay (Isla de Santa Clara), where you can hike the trails and have lunch at the lone café, or pack a picnic before setting sail. **Motoras de la Isla** offers two options: the direct red *(roja)* route to the island (€4 round-trip, small ferry departs June-Sept only, every half-hour 10:00-20:00) and the blue *(azul)* route, which cruises the bay

for 30 minutes in a glass-bottom boat before dropping passengers off (€7 round-trip, hourly 12:00-19:30, +34 943 000 450, www. motorasdelaisla.com). The *Ciudad San Sebastián* catamaran gives 40-minute tours of the bay from Monte Urgull to Zurriola Beach (€12, hourly in summer 12:00-20:00, fewer in spring and fall, none in winter; +34 943 287 932, www.ciudadsansebastian.com).

Naval Museum (Museo Naval)

This small museum is mostly interesting for its 18th-century building—one of the few that survived the 1813 siege of the city and where port activities were monitored. Its two floors house temporary exhibits related to the city's connection to the sea.

Cost and Hours: €3, free on Thu, Tue-Sat 10:00-14:00 & 16:00-19:00, Sun 11:00-14:00, closed Mon, borrow English description at entry, Paseo del Muelle 24, +34 943 430 051, www. itsasmuseoa.eus.

▲▲Aquarium

San Sebastián's aquarium is surprisingly good. Upstairs are displays on whaling, shipbuilding, legal versus illegal pirating, fishing, and local oceanography (with thorough English descriptions). Downstairs, a mesmerizing 45-foot-long tunnel is filled with more than 30 local species of sea life, flopping and flying over you in a tank holding nearly 400,000 gallons of water. Several smaller tanks are homes to octopus, slowly tumbling jellyfish, and tropical species—local kids see them and holler, "Nemo!"

Cost and Hours: €13, €6.50 for kids ages 4-12; daily 10:00-21:00, closes earlier off-season, last entry one hour before closing; stuffy-yet-helpful audioguide-€3, at the end of Paseo del Muelle, +34 943 440 099, www.aquariumss.com.

▲Monte Urgull

Green and leafy, this city park watches over the old town. The once-mighty castle (Castillo de la Mota) atop the hill deterred most attackers, allowing the city to prosper in the Middle Ages.

The **Casa de la Historia** museum within the castle covers San Sebastián history; it has mildly interesting displays on the ground floor and access to the statue of Christ's view over the city. There are also 13 delightful videos available in English—created for the 200th anniversary of the city's devastating fire of 1813, each eight-minute film features San Sebastián youth sharing their city's important historical moments (free to enter museum, English pamphlet, Wed-Sun 10:00-17:30, closed in winter and Mon-Tue year-round, +34 943 428 417).

Maps scattered throughout the **park** provide good and basic information about the fortress. Seek out the crumbling memorial to British soldiers who gave their lives to defend the city from Na-

poleon. The best views from the hill are not from the statue of Christ, but from the **Battery of Santiago** ramparts (to Christ's far right), just above the port's aquarium. Picnickers can enjoy their lunch along the walls and on benches peppering the grassy battery park, or walk to the westernmost point of the battery to the free-spirited **Café El Polvorín** for simple salads, sandwiches, good sangria, and picturesque vistas.

A walkway allows you to stroll the mountain's entire perimeter near sea level. This route is continuous from Hotel Parma to the aquarium and offers an enjoyable after-dinner wander. You can also walk a bit higher up over the port (along the white railing)—called the *paseo de los curas*, or "priest's path," where the clergy could stroll unburdened by the rabble in the streets below (access from just behind the aquarium). These paths are technically open only from sunrise to sunset (daily 8:00-21:00, Oct-April until 19:30), but you can often access them even later.

THE BEACH AND BEYOND
▲▲La Concha Beach and Promenade
The shell-shaped Playa de la Concha, the pride of San Sebastián, has one of Europe's loveliest stretches of sand. Lined with a two-mile-long promenade, it allows even backpackers to feel aristocratic. Although it's pretty empty off-season, sunbathers pack its shores in summer. But year-round it's surprisingly devoid of eateries and money-grubbing businesses. There are free  showers, and *cabinas* provide lockers, showers, and shade for a fee. For a century, the lovingly painted wrought-iron balustrade that stretches the length of the promenade has been a symbol of the city; it shows up on everything from jewelry to headboards. It's shaded by tamarisk trees, with branches carefully pruned into knotty bulbs each winter that burst into leafy shade-giving canopies in the summer—another symbol of the city. The **Miramar Palace and Park** divides the crescent beach in the middle at Pico de Loro (Parrot's Beak). This is where Queen María Cristina held court when she summered here in the early 1900s. Today the palace is home to summer classes for the Basque Studies University, as well as a music school. The gardens are open to the public.

For a meal overlooking the beach, **$$ Café de la Concha** serves reasonably priced, mediocre food, but you can't beat the lo-

cation of its terrace (daily 9:00-24:00, on the beach at the center of the crescent, Paseo de la Concha, +34 943 473 600).

La Perla Spa

The spa overlooking the beach attracts a less royal crowd today and appeals mostly to visitors interested in sampling "the curative properties of the sea." You can enjoy its Talasso Fitness Circuit, featuring a hydrotherapy pool, a relaxation pool, a panoramic hot tub, cold-water pools, a seawater steam sauna, a dry sauna, and a relaxation area.

Cost and Hours: 2-hour fitness circuit-€32.50, Mon-Sat 9:00-21:00, Sun until 15:00, €3 caps and €1.20 rental towels, bring a swimsuit or buy one there, on the beach at the center of the crescent, Paseo de la Concha, +34 943 458 856, www.la-perla.net.

Monte Igueldo

For commanding city views (if you ignore the tacky amusements on top), ride the funicular or hike up Monte Igueldo, a mirror image of Monte Urgull. The  views over San Sebastián, along the coast, and into the distant green mountains are sensational day or night. The entrance to the funicular is on the road behind the tennis club on the far western end of Playa de Ondarreta, which extends from Playa de la Concha to the west.

Cost and Hours: Funicular—€4 round-trip, runs every 15 minutes; changeable hours but roughly April-Sept daily 10:00-21:00; Oct-March Mon-Fri 11:00-18:00, Sat-Sun until 20:00. If you drive to the top, you'll pay €2.50 to enter.

Getting There: Bus #16 takes you from Plaza de Gipuzkoa in the old town to the base of the funicular in about 10 minutes. If you'd rather do the half-hour hike to the top, start at the Tenis bus stop before the funicular and follow the yellow arrows uphill along a road and then on a smaller path. It can be muddy after a rainy day, but it's well worth the walk through the lush forest. Near the top, take a right at the asphalt road to reach the viewpoint.

Peine del Viento

Besides the gorgeous view from the top of Monte Igueldo, another classic San Sebastián scene is at this group of three statues by native son Eduardo Chillida (1924-2002). From the base of the Monte Igueldo funicular, walk around the tennis court complex to the edge of the beach. Curly steel prongs "comb the wind" (as the sculptures' name means) among crashing waves. Chillida lived and died on Monte Igueldo, so these sculptures are now considered a

memorial to one of Spain's most internationally recognized modern sculptors.

IN GROS
Gros and Zurriola Beach

The district of Gros, just east across the river from the old town, offers a distinctly Californian vibe. Literally a dump not long ago (gross indeed), today it has a surfing scene on Zurriola Beach (popular with students and German tourists) and a futuristic conference center (described next).

▲Kursaal Conference Center and Kubo-Kutxa Gallery

These two Lego-like boxes mark the spot of what was once a grand casino, torn down by Franco to discourage gambling. Many locals wanted to rebuild it as it once was, in a similar style to the turn-of-the-20th-century buildings in the Centro, but—in an effort to keep up with the postmodern trends in Bilbao—city leaders opted instead for Rafael Moneo's striking contemporary design. The complex is supposed to resemble the angular rocks that make up the town's breakwater. The Kursaal houses a theater, conference facilities, some gift shops and travel agencies, and a restaurant; it also hosts many events for the San Sebastián Film Festival. The Kubo-Kutxa Gallery, located in a small cube farthest from the river, offers temporary exhibits by international artists and promotes contemporary Basque artists. Each exhibit is complemented by a 10-minute video that plays continuously in the gallery theater (free, Tue-Sun 12:00-14:00 & 16:00-20:00, closed Mon, no-midday break on summer weekends, +34 943 251 939, www.sala-kubo-aretoa.eus.

Tabakalera International Culture Center

An old tobacco factory next to the Renfe train station has been converted into an international center for contemporary culture oozing with a young, artistic vibe. The center hosts the Basque Language Institute, various contemporary art exhibitions from both local and international artists, and screenings during the San Sebastián Film Festival. There are shops and a café on the bottom floor, and the roof terrace on the top floor has knockout views of the river and city skyline. To get there, take bus #9 from the Boulevard stop in the old town and get off at the Frantziskotarrak stop (free, Mon-Fri 9:00-21:00, Sat 10:00-22:00, Sun 10:00-21:00, Andre Zigarrogileak Plaza 1, +34 943 118 855, www.tabakalera.eus).

Sleeping in San Sebastián

Rates in San Sebastián are some of the highest in Spain. They can skyrocket in summer and during the town's film festival in September. During peak season, hotels often require a minimum stay

of two to three nights. Since breakfast is often not included, I've recommended some good options elsewhere in town (see "Eating in San Sebastián," later).

IN OR NEAR THE OLD TOWN

For locations, see the "San Sebastián's Old Town" map, earlier.

$$$$ Hotel Parma is a business-class place with 26 fine rooms and family-run attention to detail and service. It stands stately on the edge of the old town, away from the bar-scene noise, and overlooks the river and a surfing beach (RS%, air-con, modern lounge, pay parking nearby, Paseo de Salamanca 10, +34 943 428 893, www.hotelparma.com, hotelparma@hotelparma.com; Iñaki, Pino, Eider, and Francisco).

$$$ Pensión AB Domini neighbors Bretxa Market and San Telmo Museum. It delightfully mixes traditional, bare-stone walls with contemporary decor. Three of its six rooms have views toward the museum—unique in the narrow-laned old town. With only two *pintxo* bars nearby, it's one of the quieter hotels in town, but bring earplugs for Saturdays (some rooms with shared bath, discounted parking, San Juan 8, second floor, +34 943 420 431, www.abpensiones.es, reservas@abpensiones.es).

$$ Pensión Edorta ("Edward"), family owned and run with care deep in the old town, elegantly mixes wood, brick, and color in nine stylish rooms (elevator, Calle del Puerto 15, +34 943 423 773, www.pensionedorta.com, info@pensionedorta.com, Javier).

$$ Pensión Iturriza is no Old World *pensión*—its six small, minimalist rooms have modern fixtures and were designed with feng shui in mind. This is a restful and quiet place. A more luxurious penthouse apartment is also available (Calle Campanario 10, +34 943 562 959, www.pensioniturriza.com, info@pensioniturriza.com, Ibon).

$$ Pensión Amaiur, in the oldest building in the old town, has tilting wooden stairs that lead to a flowery interior with long, narrow halls and five great-value rooms. Some rooms face a *frontón* (*pelota* court), while a couple have private balconies facing the street. There's a common room to prepare meals—a great spot to hang out and share travel tips. Bring earplugs to block out noise from the tapas-going crowd, or ask for an interior room (cheaper rooms with shared bath, next to Santa María Church at Calle 31 de Agosto 44, +34 943 429 654, www.pensionamaiur.com, info@pensionamaiur.com).

ACROSS THE RIVER, IN GROS

The pleasant Gros district—San Sebastián's "uptown"—is marked by the super-modern, blocky Kursaal conference center. The nearby Zurriola Beach is popular with surfers and has a thriving *pintxos*

scene and good restaurants. Most of these hotels are less than a five-minute walk from the old town. For locations, see the "San Sebastián" map, earlier.

$$$$ Hotel Arrizul Beach is bright and fresh, with fashionable, minimalist decor in each of its 12 rooms (air-con, elevator, pricey nearby underground parking, Peña y Goñi 1, +34 943 322 804, www.arrizul.com, info@hotelarrizulbeach.com). Just up the street, closer to the train and bus stations, **$$$$ Hotel Arrizul Congress** is run by the same friendly staff and has a similar style (family rooms, air-con, elevator, Ronda 3, +34 943 327 026, www.hotelarrizulcongress.com, info@hotelarrizulcongress.com).

$$$ Welcome Gros is five blocks from the beach and has 15 rooms with minimal but stylish decor, plus 11 apartments with daily cleaning (air-con, elevator, Iparraguirre 3, +34 943 326 954, www.welcomegros.com; for apartments see www.groscity.com, info@welcomegros.com).

$$$ Hotel One Shot Tabakalera House is an artsy hotel in the same building as the Tabakalera Culture Center, the city's old tobacco factory. It is conveniently located next to the Renfe train station and is a 20-minute walk from the old town. The rooms are hip and contemporary with a colorful design (air-con, breakfast, discounted parking, fitness room, Mandasko Dukearen 52, +34 943 930 028, www.hoteloneshottabakalerahouse.com, tabakalerahouse@oneshothotels.com).

$$ Pensión Kursaal has 21 basic, contemporary, and crisp rooms in a historic building just across from the beach (elevator, pay parking, Peña y Goñi 2, +34 943 292 666, www.pensionkursaal.com, info@pensionkursaal.com).

$$ La Pensión del Mar has six bright rooms on a quiet street just a 10-minute walk from the old town. There is small common kitchen and free coffee and tea (elevator, discounted parking, two rooms with shared bathroom, Tomas Gros 3, +34 943 359 970, www.lapensiondelmar.es, info@lapensiondelmar.es).

ON THE BEACH
$$$$ Hotel Niza, set in the middle of Playa de la Concha, is often booked well in advance. Half of its 40 rooms (some with balconies) overlook the bay. From its chandeliered and plush lounge, a classic 1911 elevator takes you to comfortable pastel rooms with wedding-cake molding (only streetside rooms have air-con, fans on request, pay parking—must reserve in advance, Zubieta 56—see the "San Sebastián" map, +34 943 426 663, www.hotelniza.com, reservas@hotelniza.com). The breakfast room has a sea view and doubles as a bar with light snacks throughout the day (Bar Narru, long hours daily).

Eating in San Sebastián

Basque food is regarded as some of the best in Spain, and San Sebastián is the culinary capital of the Basque Country. (For tips on Basque cuisine, see the "Basque Country Cuisine Scene" section at the beginning of this chapter.) San Sebastián is proud of its many Michelin-rated fine-dining establishments, but they require a big commitment of time and money. Most casual visitors will prefer to hop from pub to pub through the old town, following the crowds between Basque-font signs. I've listed a couple of solid traditional restaurants, but for the best value and memories, I'd order top-end dishes with top-end wine in top-end bars. Some places close for siesta in the late afternoon and early evening.

IN THE OLD TOWN
For locations of old town eateries, see the "San Sebastián's Old Town" map, earlier.

Pintxo Bar-Hopping
San Sebastián's old town provides the ideal backdrop for tapas-hopping; just wander the streets and sidle up to the bar in the liveliest spot. Calle Fermín Calbetón has the best concentration of bars; the streets San Jerónimo and 31 de Agosto are also good. I've listed these top-notch places in order as you progress deeper into the old town. Note that there are plenty of other options along the way. Before you begin, study the *txikiteo* sidebar, later.

Unless otherwise noted, these places are open from around noon to 15:00, close for the afternoon, then reopen in the evening.

$$ Borda Berri (loosely, "New Mountain Hut") features a more low-key ambience and top-quality *pintxos*. There are only a few items at the bar; check out the chalkboard menu for today's options, order, and the two chefs/owners will cook it fresh. The specialty here is melt-in-your-mouth beef cheeks *(carrillera de ternera)* in a red-wine sauce, risotto with wild mushrooms, and foie gras (grilled goose liver) with apple jelly, which is even better paired

with a glass of their best red wine (closed Mon, Calle Fermín Calbetón 12, +34 943 430 342).

$$ Bar Txepetxa is *the* place for anchovies. A plastic circle displaying a variety of *antxoas* tapas makes choosing your anchovy treat easy. These fish are fresh—not cured and salted like those most Americans hate (Sun lunch only, Tue dinner only, closed Mon, Calle Pescadería 5, +34 943 422 227).

$$ Bar Tamboril is a traditional spot right on the main square, favored for its seafood, mushrooms *(txampis tamboril)*, and anchovy tempura along with its good prices. Their list of hot *pintxos* (grab the little English menu on the bar) makes you want to break the one-tapa-per-stop rule (closed Sun, Calle Pescadería 2, +34 943 423 507).

$$$ La Cuchara de San Telmo, whose cooks are taught by big-name Basque chef Alex Mondiel, is a cramped place that devotes as much space to its thriving kitchen as its bar. It has nothing precooked and set on the bar—order your mini gourmet plates with a spirit of adventure from the constantly changing blackboard. Their foie gras with apple jelly is rightfully famous (lunch only on weekends, closed Mon, tucked away on a lonely alley called Santa Corda behind Museum of San Telmo at Calle 31 de Agosto 28, +34 943 420 840).

$$ Taberna Gandarías is a great place for savory traditional *pintxos* in a lively but easygoing atmosphere. The personable blueshirted fellas tending to you will patiently explain the food options. Consider a *media ración* (half-order) of the perfectly done *ibérico* ham. They serve food more hours than most (some gluten-free options, daily 11:00-24:00, Calle 31 de Agosto 23, +34 943 426 362).

$$$ SSUA is cool and upscale compared to the others, with an edgier vibe. You'll find an ambitious menu with both *pintxos* and creative dishes based on local recipes. Try their *foie mi-cuit* and *vieira a la parrilla* (grilled scallop) for a unique taste bud experience (Wed-Sun 12:30-24:00, closed Mon-Tue, Calle 31 de Agosto 31, mobile +34 686 015 479). Inviting small tables in the back make this a sit-down dining opportunity.

$$ Atari offers a handful of comfortable tables and large windows. In warm weather, sit at outdoor tables across from Santa María Church. They have *pintxos* and *raciones: Pulpo con piment Espelette* (octopus with Espelette peppers) and *foie a la plancha* (grilled duck liver) are just a couple of the delights on the menu (daily 12:00-23:30, closed Tue-Wed in winter, Calle Mayor 18, can also enter on corner of Calle 31 de Agosto, +34 943 440 792).

$$ La Mejillonera is famous among students for its big, cheap beers, *patatas bravas,* and mussels (*"tigres"* are the spicy favorite). A long, skinny stainless-steel bar and lots of photos make ordering easy—this is my only recommended bar where you pay when

Do the *Txikiteo:* A Tapas Cheat Sheet

Txikiteo (chih-kee-TAY-oh) is the Basque word for hopping from bar to bar, enjoying small sandwiches and tiny snacks (*pintxos*, PEEN-chohs) and glasses of wine. Local competition drives small bars to lay out the most appealing array of *pintxos*. The selection is amazing, but the key to eating well here is going for the *pintxos calientes*—the hot tapas advertised on blackboards and cooked to order. Tapas are best, freshest, and accompanied by the most vibrant crowd from 12:00 to 14:00 and from 20:00 to 22:30. Watch what's being served—the locals know each bar's specialty. No matter how much you like a place, just order one dish; you want to be mobile.

Later in the evening, bars get more crowded and challenging for tourists. To get service amid the din, speak loudly and directly (little sweet voices get ignored), with no extra words. Expect to share everything. Double-dipping is encouraged. It's rude to put a dirty napkin on the table; it belongs in the small bins or directly on the floor.

Basque tapas bars distinguish themselves by laying out big platters of help-yourself goodies. This user-friendly system lets you point to—or simply take—what looks good, rather than navigating a menu. If you can't get the bartender's attention to serve you a particular *pintxo*, don't be shy—watch other people; if they are serving themselves, grab what you want and a napkin, and munch away. You pay when you leave; just keep a mental note of the tapas you've eaten. There's a code of honor. Everyone is part of the extended Basque family. In fact, places that have you fill

served. Throw your mussel shells on the floor like the boisterous locals (Calle del Puerto 15, +34 943 428 465).

$$ La Viña is a reliable option for a mix of traditional and modern *pintxos*. Rub elbows with locals and top off your meal with an airy and decadent slice of cheesecake that's big enough to share (Tue-Sun 10:30-16:30 & 18:30-24:00, closed Mon, also closed Nov and last week of June, Calle 31 de Agosto 3, +34 943 427 495).

Restaurants in the Old Town

$$$ Bodégon Alejandro is a good spot for modern Basque cuisine in a sleek-yet-cozy cellar setting (Wed-Sun 13:00-15:30 & 20:30-22:30, closed Mon-Tue, in old town on Calle Fermín Calbetón 4, +34 943 427 158).

$$$ Casa Urola is a must for San Sebastián gastronomy enthusiasts. Chef Pablo's updated versions of traditional Basque dishes even persuade other local chefs to eat here after finishing their shifts. Much of the exquisite menu changes seasonally. The peaceful upstairs dining room has a contemporary elegance (reservations

your plate and pay before eating are generally to be avoided.

If you want a meal instead of *pintxos,* some bars—even ones that look only like bars from the street—have attached dining rooms, usually in the back.

For a full list of Spanish tapas terms (which work here in Basque Country, too), see the "Tapas Menu Decoder" sidebar on page 982 of the Practicalities chapter. Here are a few terms unique to Basque bars:

pintxos: tapas (small plates)

antxoas: anchovies (not the cured, heavily salted kind you always hated)

txampis (CHAHM-pees): mushrooms

txangurro (chan-GOO-roh): spider crab (or imitation crab), often mixed with onions, tomatoes, and wine, served hot or made into a spread to put on bread

marmitako: tuna stew

ttoro: seafood stew

cazuelas: hot meal-size servings (like *raciones* in Spanish)

txakolí (chah-koh-LEE): fresh white wine, poured from high to aerate it and to add sparkle. Good with seafood, and therefore fits the local cuisine well.

zurito (thoo-REE-toh): small beer

Zenbat da?: "How much?" (to ask for the bill)

recommended). Without reservations, go downstairs—there are few tables, so most diners eat standing at the bar (*media ración*—half-portion—available for several dishes, extensive wine list; Wed-Mon 13:00-16:00 & 20:00-23:30, bar open until late, closed Tue; Fermín Calbetón 20, +34 943 441 371, www.casaurolajatetxea.es).

$$ Txuleta is tucked away on a small plaza near Santa Maria Church. While the service is hit or miss, this restaurant excels at grilled meats and seasonal *pintxos* that are worth the hefty price. Be adventurous and try the *kokotxas* (hake cheeks). The glass-enclosed terrace provides lots of seating (closed Mon evening and Tue, Plaza de la Trinidad 2, +34 943 441 007, www.txuletarestaurante.com).

Seafood Along the Port: For seafood with a salty sailor's view, check out **$$ Kofradia-Itsas Etxea,** the "House of the Basque Fishermen." This seafood-only restaurant has a bar area serving *pintxos,* and a gourmet dining area serving *pescado del día* (the daily catch) prepared in the local style (bar area Wed-Thu 11:30-19:00, Fri-Sat until 22:30, Sun until 17:00; dining area Wed-Sun 13:00-

15:15, Fri-Sat also 20:00-22:30; both closed Mon-Tue; reserve online for dining area, https://kofradia.eus).

Farther along the harbor on the way to the aquarium are a half-dozen hardworking, local-feeling restaurants. **$$$$ La Rampa** is an upscale eatery, specializing in crab *(txangurro)* and lobster dishes and seafood *a la parrilla* (closed Wed, Paseo del Muelle 26, +34 943 421 652, www.restaurantelarampa.com). Also along here, locals like **$$$ Sebastián** (more traditional, closed Tue).

RESTAURANTS AND PINTXO BARS IN GROS

For locations, see the "San Sebastián" map, earlier.

$$ Bodega Donostiarra has been a San Sebastián institution since 1928. Locals flock here for sit-down meals with freshly made Spanish tortillas, meats of the grilled and cured varieties, and seafood. For a quick bite, head to their original zinc bar for *pintxos* or a *sandwich completo* with tuna, onions, and anchovies (Mon-Sat 9:00-24:00, closed Sun, Calle Peña y Goñi 13, +34 943 011 380).

$$ Bar Bergara serves refined *pintxos* in a casually cool setting. Originally run by *chef-savante* Patxi Bergara, his nephews Monty and Esteban now continue the ethic of serving award-winning *pintxos* that are "eye-catching, original, and petite enough to eat in two bites." Cold snacks are artfully displayed on the bar, while *pintxos calientes* are made when ordered. Ask for an English menu (daily 12:00-16:00 & 19:00-23:00, to-go sandwiches available, General Artetxe 8, +34 943 275 026).

Tedone is one of the few quality vegetarian options in this city of *gastronomía*. Hiding out on a tiny lane, this health-conscious eatery dishes up flavorful organic options that are truly Basque (daily 13:00-15:30 & 20:15-23:00, Corta 10, +34 943 273 561).

Thursday Night Party Scene: Every Thursday in Gros, university students and those who want to save some euros brave the masses for *pintxo-pote* (PEEN-cho POH-teh). Because of the increased popularity of gastronomy in San Sebastián, locals, who often eat out regularly, want a good deal for food and drinks. Bars, particularly along **Calle Zabaleta** (between Gran Vía and Avenida Navarra) and parallel streets, offer a drink (usually beer or wine) and a basic *pintxo* for €2-3. It's basically a happy-hour scene that spills out onto the streets. Just follow the crowds and remember that this isn't just sustenance, it's a social event (19:00-23:00).

PICNICS AND TAKEOUT

A picnic on the beach or atop Monte Urgull is a tempting option. You can assemble a bang-up spread at the **Bretxa Public Market** at Plaza de Sarriegi (described earlier).

Solbes, just across the street from the Bretxa Public Market, has a reputation as *the* gourmet deli store in the old town. There's

a remarkable wine selection in the back cellar, plus high-quality cured meats and cheeses out front. Be sure to price fruits and veggies on the scale yourself to avoid confusion at checkout (Mon-Sat 9:00-20:30, Sun until 14:30, Calle Aldamar 4—see the "San Sebastián's Old Town" map, +34 943 427 818).

For wine, head to **Goñi Ardoteka,** with its ample selection of quality Spanish wines. The three owners (and brothers) Asier, Nerea, and Hamaya are true wine lovers and are happy to give their recommendations (Mon-Fri 10:00-14:00 & 16:30-19:30, Sat 10:30-14:00, closed Sun, Calle Aldamar 3—see the "San Sebastián's Old Town" map, +34 943 211 597).

BREAKFAST

If your hotel doesn't provide breakfast—or even if it does—consider one of these old-town places. The first is a traditional stand-up bar, the second is a small café, and the third is a greasy spoon. If you're staying in Gros, consider the Alabama Café. For locations, see the "San Sebastián's Old Town" map, earlier.

$$ Bar Gorriti, delightfully local, is packed with market workers and shoppers starting their day. You'll stand at the bar and choose a hot-off-the-grill *francesca jamón* omelet (fluffy, tiny omelet sandwich topped with a slice of ham) and other goodies. This and a good cup of coffee make for a very Basque breakfast. By the time you get there for breakfast, many market workers will be taking their midmorning break (breakfast served Mon-Sat 7:00-10:00, closed Sun, facing the side of the big white market building at San Juan 3, +34 943 428 353).

$$ Kantoi is a plain café with brisk service and perhaps some of the best coffee in the old town. They serve a small selection of sandwiches, cakes, and toast with cheese or ham (Mon-Fri 8:00-16:00, Sat from 9:00, closed Sun, Calle Mayor 10).

$$ Santa Lucía, a 1950s-style diner, is ideal for a cheap old-town breakfast or *churros* break (*churros* are like deep-fried doughnut sticks that can be dipped in pudding-like hot chocolate). Photos of two dozen different breakfasts decorate the walls, and plates of fresh *churros* keep patrons happy (daily 8:30-21:30, Calle del Puerto 6, +34 943 425 019).

In Gros: $$ Alabama Café is a solid breakfast option with a mix of healthy and less-healthy alternatives. Set breakfast combos (€6-9) include coffee or tea, a glass of fresh orange juice, and toast with various toppings. There are a few tables downstairs and plenty more upstairs in this artsy eatery (Tue-Fri 8:00-21:00, Sat-Sun from 8:30, closed Mon, Calle San Francisco 45—see the "San Sebastián" map, +34 943 104 694, https://alabamacafe.es).

San Sebastián Connections

BY TRAIN

San Sebastián has two train stations: Renfe and Amara EuskoTren (described under "Arrival in San Sebastián" on page 192). The station you use depends on your destination.

Renfe Station: This station handles long-distance destinations within Spain (most of which require reservations). Due to construction on the AVE line, train departures might be reduced or replaced with buses; check online at www.renfe.com. Connections include **Irún** (4/day, 30 minutes), **Madrid** (6/day, 5-8 hours), **Burgos** (6/day, 3 hours), **León** (1/day direct, 5 hours, more with transfer), **Pamplona** (2/day, 2 hours), **Salamanca** (6/day, some direct, 7 hours), **Barcelona** (2/day, 6 hours), **Santiago de Compostela** (2/day direct, 10.5 hours).

Amara EuskoTren Station: If you're going into France, take the regional Topo train (which leaves from Amara EuskoTren station) over the French border into **Hendaye** (usually 2/hour, 35 minutes). From Hendaye, you can connect to France's SNCF network (www.sncf.com), with connections to **Paris** (4/day direct, 5 hours, more with transfer in Dax or Bordeaux). Unfortunately, the Amara EuskoTren station doesn't have information on Paris-bound trains from Hendaye. EuskoTren tickets to Hendaye must be used within two hours of purchase.

Also leaving from San Sebastián's Amara EuskoTren station are slow regional trains to destinations in Spain's Basque region, including **Bilbao** (hourly, 2.5 hours—the bus is faster). Although the train ride from San Sebastián to Bilbao takes twice as long as the bus, it passes through more interesting countryside. The Basque Country shows off its trademark green and gray: lush green vegetation and gray clouds. It's an odd mix of heavy industrial factories, homegrown veggie gardens, streams, and every kind of livestock you can imagine. EuskoTren info: +34 902 543 210, www.euskotren.eus.

BY BUS

The underground bus station is conveniently located next to the Renfe train station (across the river, just east of the Centro district).

Different companies offer services to different destinations, with some overlap. Pesa serves most of the region, from Bayonne to Bilbao (www.pesa.net). Alsa serves a few Basque Country destinations, Madrid, Burgos, and León (www.alsa.es). MonBus serves Barcelona (www.monbus.es).

From San Sebastián, buses go to **Bilbao** (2/hour, hourly on weekends, 1.5 hours, Pesa; morning buses fill with tourists, commuters, and students—buy your ticket the day before; once in

Bilbao, buses leave you at the Intermodal station with easy tram connections to the Guggenheim modern-art museum); **Bilbao Airport** (hourly, 1.5 hours, Pesa), **Pamplona** (6/day, 1 hour, Alsa), **León** (2/day, 6-7 hours, Alsa), **Madrid** (8/day, 6 hours direct, otherwise 7 hours; a few departures direct to Madrid's Barajas Airport, 5.5 hours; Alsa), **Burgos** (7/day, 3.5 hours, Alsa), **Barcelona** (1/day plus 1/night, 7 hours, MonBus).

Buses to French Basque Country: French company BlaBla-Bus runs buses to **St-Jean-de-Luz,** which then continue on to **Biarritz** and **Bayonne** (4/day, fewer on Sun, depart from outside the Renfe train station—not underground, www.blablacar.fr/bus), as do Spanish companies Pesa (2/day) and Alsa (5/day). General travel times from San Sebastián are 45 minutes to St-Jean-de-Luz, 1.25 hours to Biarritz, and 1.5 hours to Bayonne.

Bay of Biscay

Between the Spanish Basque cities of San Sebastián and Bilbao is a beautiful countryside of rolling green hills and a scenic, jagged coastline that looks almost Celtic. Aside from a scenic joyride, this area merits a visit for the cute fishing and resort town of Lekeitio.

FROM SAN SEBASTIÁN TO BILBAO

San Sebastián and Bilbao are connected in about 75 minutes by the AP-8 toll road. While speedy and scenic, this route is nothing compared with some of the free, but slower, back roads with lots of twists and turns that connect the two towns.

If side-tripping from San Sebastián to Bilbao, you can drive directly there on AP-8 in the morning. But going home to San Sebastián, consider this more scenic route: Take AP-8 until the turnoff for Guernica (look for *Amorebieta/Gernika-Lumo* sign), then head up into the hills on BI-635. After visiting Guernica, follow signs along the very twisty BI-2238 road to Lekeitio (about 40 minutes). Leave Lekeitio on the road just above the beach; after crossing the bridge, take the left fork and follow BI-3438 to Markina/Ondarroa (with a striking modern bridge and nice views back into the steep town; follow *portua* signs for free 30-minute parking at the port). Continue to Mutriku and Deba as you hug the coastline east toward San Sebastián. There's a good photo-op pullout as you climb along the coast just after Deba. Soon after, you'll have

two opportunities to get on the AP-8 (blue signs) for a quicker approach to San Sebastián; but if you've enjoyed the scenery so far, stick with the coastal road (white signs, N-634) through Zumaia and Getaria, rejoining the expressway at the high-class resort town of Zarautz.

Lequeitio/Lekeitio

More commonly known by its Euskara name, Lekeitio (leh-KAY-tee-oh)—rather than the Spanish version, Lequeitio—this small

fishing port has an idyllic harbor and a fine beach. It's just over an hour by bus from Bilbao and an easy stop for drivers, and it's protected from the Bay of Biscay by a sand spit that leads to the lush and rugged little San Nicolás Island. Hake boats fly their Basque flags, and proud Basque locals black out the Spanish translations on street signs.

Lekeitio is a teeming resort during July and August (when its population of 7,000 triples as big-city Basque folks move into their vacation condos). Isolated from the modern rat race by its location down a long, windy little road, it's a backwater fishing village the rest of the year.

Sights here are humble, though the 15th-century St. Mary's Parish Church is a good example of Basque Gothic, with an im-

pressive altarpiece. The town's back lanes are reminiscent of the old days when fishing was the only industry. Fisherwomen sell their husbands' catches each morning along the port. The golden crescent beach is as inviting as the sandbar, which—at low tide—challenges you to join the seagulls out on San Nicolás Island.

The best beach in the area for surfers and sun lovers is Playas Laga (follow signs off the road from Bilbao to Lekeitio). Relatively uncrowded, it's popular with body-boarders.

Getting There: Bizkaibus #A3523 connects Lekeitio with **Bilbao** (8/day, 1.5 hours; same bus stops at **Guernica**, 40 minutes, https://web.bizkaia.eus/es/web/bizkaibus). Lurraldebus connects Lekeitio and **San Sebastián** (5/day Mon-Fri, 4/day Sat-Sun, 1.5

hours, www.lurraldebus.eus). But this destination is most logical for those with a car. Drivers can park most easily in the lot near the bus station. Exit the station left, walk along the road, then take the first right (down the steep, cobbled street) to reach the harbor. There is no baggage storage in town.

Tourist Information: The TI faces the fish market next to the harbor (daily 10:00-15:00 & 16:00-19:00, shorter hours and closed Mon Sept-June, +34 946 844 017, www.lekeitio.org).

Eating in Lekeitio: Although it's sleepy off-season, the harbor promenade is made-to-order in summer for a slow meal or a tapas crawl.

Guernica / Gernika

The workaday market town of Guernica (GEHR-nee-kah) is near and dear to Basques and pacifists alike. This is the site of the Gernikako Arbola—the oak tree of Gernika, which marked the assembly point where the regional Basque leaders, the Lords of Bizkaia, met through the ages to assert their people's freedom. Long the symbolic heart of Basque separatism, it was also a natural target for Franco (and Hitler) in the Spanish Civil War—resulting in an infamous bombing raid that left the town in ruins (see "The Bombing of Guernica" sidebar), as immortalized by Picasso in his epic work, *Guernica*.

Today's Guernica, rebuilt after being bombed flat in 1937 and nothing special at first glance, holds some of the Basque Country's more compelling museums. And Basque bigwigs have maintained the town as a meeting point—they still elect their figurehead leader on that same ancient site under the oak tree.

Orientation to Guernica

Guernica is small (about 17,000 inhabitants) and compact, focused on its large market hall (Monday market 9:00-14:00).

Tourist Information: The TI is in the town center (Mon-Sat 10:00-19:00, Sun until 14:00, shorter hours in winter, Artekalea 8, +34 946 255 892, http://turismo.gernika-lumo.net). If you'll be visiting both the Peace Museum and the Basque Country Museum, buy the €6 combo-ticket here. Called a "Unified Ticket," it's a great deal but you can only get it at the TI.

Arrival in Guernica: Drivers will find a handy parking lot near the train tracks at the end of town. Buses drop off passengers along the main road skirting the town center. The train station also sits on the main road. No matter how you enter, the TI is well marked (look for yellow *i* signs)—head there first to get your bearings and pick up a handy town map.

Sights in Guernica

I've listed Guernica's sights in the order of a handy sightseeing loop from the TI.

• *Exit the TI to the left, cross the street, and walk up the left side of the square, where you'll find the...*

▲Gernika Peace Museum

Because of the brutality of the Guernica bombing, and the powerful Picasso painting that documented the atrocities of war, the name "Guernica" has become synonymous with pacifism. This thoughtfully presented exhibit has taken a great tragedy of 20th-century history and turned it into a compelling cry for peace in our time.

Cost and Hours: €6, free Sat 16:00-19:00; open Sun-Mon 10:00-15:00, Tue-Sat 10:00-19:00, closed Mon off-season; Foru Plaza 1, +34 946 270 213, www.museodelapaz.org.

Visiting the Museum: Borrow the English translations at the entry, request an English version of the audio presentation upstairs, and head up through the two-floor exhibit. The first floor begins by considering different ways of defining "peace." You'll then enter an apartment and hear a local woman, Begoña, describe her typical Guernica life in the 1930s...until the bombs dropped (a mirror effect shows you the devastating aftermath). You'll exit through the rubble into an exhibit about the town's history, with a special emphasis on the bombing. Finally, a 10-minute movie shows grainy footage of the destruction and ends with a collage of peaceful reconciliations in recent history—in Ireland, South Africa, Guatemala, Australia, and Berlin. On the second floor, Picasso's famous painting is superimposed on three transparent panels to highlight different themes. The exhibit concludes with a survey of the recent history of conflicts in the Basque Country.

• *Exit left up the stairs and continue uphill to the big church. At the road above the church, you can turn right and walk one block to find a tile replica of **Picasso's Guernica** (left-hand side of the street). Or you can head left to find the next two attractions.*

▲Basque Country Museum (Euskal Herria Museoa)

This well-presented exhibit offers a good overview of Basque culture and history (though some floors may be closed for restoration). Start in the ground-floor theater (Room 4) and see the overview

The Bombing of Guernica

During the civil war, Guernica was the site of one of history's most reviled wartime acts.

Monday, April 26, 1937, was market day, when the town was filled with farmers and peasants from the countryside selling their wares. At about 16:40 in the afternoon, a German warplane appeared ominously on the horizon and proceeded to bomb bridges and roads surrounding the town. Soon after, more planes arrived. Three hours of relentless saturation bombing followed, as the German and Italian air forces pummeled the city with incendiary firebombs. People running through the streets or along the green hillsides were strafed with machine-gun fire. As the sun fell low in the sky and the planes finally left, hundreds—or possibly thousands—had been killed, and many more wounded. (Because Guernica was filled with refugees from other besieged towns, nobody is sure how many perished.)

Hearing word of the attack in Paris, Pablo Picasso—who had been commissioned to paint a mural for the 1937 world's fair—was devastated at the news of what had gone on in Guernica. Inspired, he painted what many consider the greatest antiwar work of art, ever. (For more on this great painting, now displayed in Madrid, see page 468.)

Why did the bombings happen? Reportedly, Adolf Hitler wanted an opportunity to try out his new saturation-bombing attack strategy. Spanish dictator Francisco Franco, who was fed up with the independence-minded Basques, offered up their historic capital as a candidate for the experiment.

There's no doubt that Guernica, a gateway to Bilbao, was strategically located. And yet, a small munitions factory that supplied anti-Franco forces with pistols oddly wasn't hit by the bombing. Historians believe most of the targets here were far from strategic. Why attack so mercilessly, during the daytime, on market day, when innocent casualties would be maximized? Like the famous silent scream of Picasso's *Guernica* mother, this question haunts pacifists everywhere to this day.

video (request English). Follow the suggested route and climb chronologically up through Basque history, with the necessary help of an included audioguide. You'll find exhibits about traditional Basque architecture and landscape, lots of antique maps, and a region-by-region rundown of the Basque Country's seven territories. One interesting map shows Basque emigration over the centuries—including to the US. The top floor is the most engaging, highlighting Basque culture: sports, dances, cuisine, myths and legends, music, and language. For a breath of fresh air, step out back into the **Peoples of Europe Park** and enjoy a peaceful respite.

Cost and Hours: €3.50, free on Sat, includes audioguide ex-

cept on Sat; open Tue-Sat 10:00-14:00 & 16:00-19:00, Sun 10:30-14:30, closed Mon except July-Aug 10:30-14:30; Allende Salazar 5, +34 946 255 451.

▲▲Gernika Assembly House and Oak Tree

In the Middle Ages, the meeting point for the Basque general assembly was under the old oak tree on the gentle hillside above Guernica. The tradition continues today, as the tree stands at the center of a modest but interesting complex celebrating Basque culture and self-government.

Cost and Hours: Free 45-minute visit, must reserve a timed-entry slot online in advance; daily 10:00-14:00 & 16:00-19:00, Oct-May until 18:00; on Allende Salazar, +34 946 251 138, www.jjggbizkaia.eus—click "EN" for English, then "reserve appointment."

Visiting the Assembly House: As you enter the grounds past the guard hut, on the right you'll see an **old tree trunk** in the small colonnade dating from the 1700s. Basque traditions have lived much, much longer than a single tree's life span. When one dies, it's replaced with a new one. This is the oldest surviving trunk.

The exhibit has four parts: a stained-glass window room, the oak-tree courtyard, the assembly chamber, and a basement theater (request the 10-minute video in English that extols the virtues and beauties of the Basque Country).

Inside the main building, pick up a copy of the English brochure that describes in detail the importance of this site. First find the impressive **stained-glass window room.** The computer video here gives a good six-minute overview of the exhibit. The gorgeous stained-glass ceiling is rife with Basque symbolism. The elderly leader stands under the oak holding a book with the "Old Law" *(Lege Zarra)*, which are the laws by which

the Basques lived for centuries. Below him are groups representing the three traditional career groups of this industrious people: sailors and fishermen; miners and steelworkers; and farmers. Behind them all is a classic Basque landscape: On the left is the sea, and on the right are rolling green hills dotted with red-and-white homes. Small, square panels around the large window represent all the important towns in the region, with Guernica's oak tree easy to pinpoint. Step into the wood-paneled library off the main room, and peek into the head honcho's office in the corner.

Out back, a Greek-style tribune surrounds the fateful **oak**

tree, a descendant of the nearly century-old ancestor, and possibly of all the trees here since ancient times. This little fella is the fifth tree to stand here—it started growing in 2000 and was planted here in 2015. The previous tree struggled to survive after standing here for just 10 years.

Basque leaders have met in solidarity at this location for centuries. In the Middle Ages, after Basque lands became part of Castile, Castilian kings came here to pledge respect to the old Basque laws. When Basque independence came under fire in the 19th century, patriots rallied by singing a song about this tree ("Ancient and holy symbol / Let thy fruit fall worldwide / While we gaze in adoration / Upon thee, our blessed tree"). After the 1937 bombing, in which this tree's predecessor was miraculously unscathed, hundreds of survivors sought refuge under its branches. Today, although official representatives in the Spanish government are elected at the polls, the Basques choose their figurehead leader, the Lehendakari ("First One"), in this same spot.

Step back inside to enter the **assembly chamber**—like a mini parliament for the region of Bizkaia ("Vizcaya" in Spanish, "Biscay" in English; one of the seven Basque territories). Notice the holy water and the altar—a sign that there was no separation of church and state in Basque politics. The large paintings above the doors show the swearing of allegiance to the Old Law. Portraits of 26 former Lords of Bizkaia maintain a watchful eye over the current assembly's decisions.

• *Exiting the grounds of the Assembly House, walk back to the front of the Basque Country Museum, and take the public school staircase on your right down to Pasealekua Square. At the bottom of the stairs, pop into a café (on your left) known to locals as the...*

Bar de los Jubilados (Old Bomb Shelter)

This unmarked café, part of the retirement community center housed in the same building, is a good place for a quick coffee and snack—but its main claim to fame is that it was a bomb shelter during the 1937 bombing. Ask the bartender, *"¿Dónde está el túnel, por favor?"* You'll be directed toward the women's restroom (gentlemen, don't worry, you can go, too). Walk down the hall, turn right into the women's restroom, and go past the stalls into a small, cold, two-part room. While it's not much to look at these days, imagine dozens of panicked people scrambling to take shelter here, hoping and praying that they would live through the devastating aerial attack (daily 10:30-21:30, Pasealekua Square).

Guernica Connections

Guernica is well connected to **Bilbao** (2 EuskoTren trains/hour, 50 minutes, arrive at Bilbao's Atxuri station; also 4 buses/hour, 40 minutes) and to **Lekeitio** (8/day, 40 minutes). Connections are sparser on weekends. The easiest way to connect to San Sebastián is via Bilbao, though you can also get there on the slow but scenic "Topo" EuskoTren train (transfer in Lemoa, about 2 hours).

Bilbao / Bilbo

Bilbao (bil-BOW, rhymes with "cow") has seen a transformation like no other Spanish city. Entire sectors of the industrial city's long-depressed port have been cleared away to allow construction of a new convention center, shops, apartment buildings, and the stunning Guggenheim Museum.

Today's Bilbao mingles beautiful old buildings with eyesore high-rise apartment blocks, super-modern additions to the skyline (such as the Guggenheim and its neighbor, the 40-story Iberdrola Tower), and—scattered in the lush hillsides all around the horizon—typical whitewashed Basque homes with red roofs. Bilbao enjoys a vitality and Old World charm befitting its status as a regional capital of culture and industry.

PLANNING YOUR TIME

For most visitors, the Guggenheim is the main draw (and many could spend the entire day there). But with a little more time, it's also worth hopping on a tram to explore the atmospheric old town or walk along the Nervión River promenade. With even more time, ride the Mount Artxanda funicular for a breathtaking overview of the entire area. Don't bother coming to Bilbao on Monday, when virtually all its museums—including the almighty Guggenheim—are closed (except July-Aug).

Orientation to Bilbao

When you're in the center, Bilbao feels smaller than its population of 350,000. The city, nestled amidst green hillsides, hugs the Nervión River as it curves through town. The Guggenheim is more or less centrally located near the top of that curve; the bus station is to the west; the old town (Casco Viejo) and train stations are to the

east; and a super-convenient and fun-to-ride green tram called the EuskoTren Tranbia ties it all together.

TOURIST INFORMATION

Bilbao's main TI is housed in a former bank next to the Renfe station at Plaza Circular; look for the red *i* sign above the door (daily 9:00-20:00, +34 944 795 760, www.bilbaoturismo.net). If you're interested in something beyond the Guggenheim, ask about their city and themed walking tours in English (described later, under "Tours in Bilbao"). The TI also has a ticket machine for buying EuskoTren tram tickets and the *Barik* public transport card (see "Arrival in Bilbao," below).

Another handy TI is near the main entrance of the Guggenheim; it's a good place to pick up the bimonthly *Bilbao Pocket Guide* (daily 11:00-19:00, Alameda Mazarredo 66). The Basque Country regional TI office at the airport can help you with information about Bilbao and the entire region (daily 9:00-21:00, +34 944 031 444, https://turismo.euskadi.eus).

ARRIVAL IN BILBAO

Most travelers—whether arriving by train, bus, or car—will want to go straight to the Guggenheim. Thanks to a perfectly planned **tram system** (EuskoTren Tranbia), this couldn't be easier. Simply buy a €1.35 single-ride ticket at a user-friendly green machine. If you're planning multiple tram rides or traveling with a small group, consider the *Barik* **public transport card,** which cuts the cost of a single ride to €0.66 (nonrefundable €3 for the card itself, €5 minimum to reload; sold at the airport, Metro stations, the TI on Plaza Circular, kiosks, and the Atxuri EuskoTren train station). *Barik* can be used for up to 10 people riding together on the Metro, buses (including the airport bus), and tram. Activate your ticket or card at the machine just before boarding (follow the red arrow); you can't do it once on board.

Hop on a green-and-gray tram, enjoy the Muzak, and head for the Guggenheim stop (there's only one line, trams come every 10 minutes). If you get lost, ask: "*¿Dónde está el Guggenheim?*" (DOHN-deh eh-STAH el "Guggenheim"). Note that the only baggage storage in town is at the Intermodal bus station (not at either train station). Don't confuse the green tram with the slow, scenic, blue train to San Sebastián. And while Bilbao has a slick

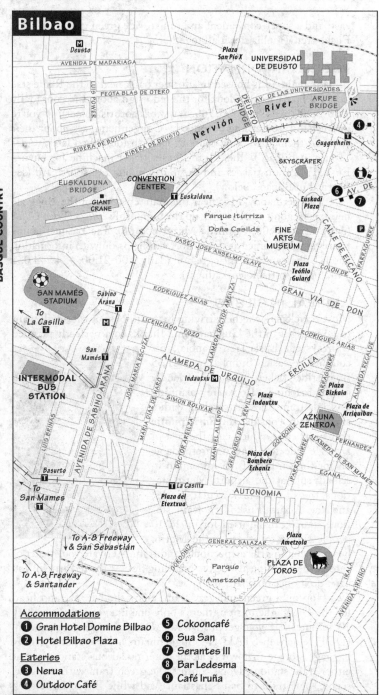

Bilbao

BASQUE COUNTRY

Accommodations

1 Gran Hotel Domine Bilbao
2 Hotel Bilbao Plaza

Eateries

3 Nerua
4 Outdoor Café
5 Cokooncafé
6 Sua San
7 Serantes III
8 Bar Ledesma
9 Café Iruña

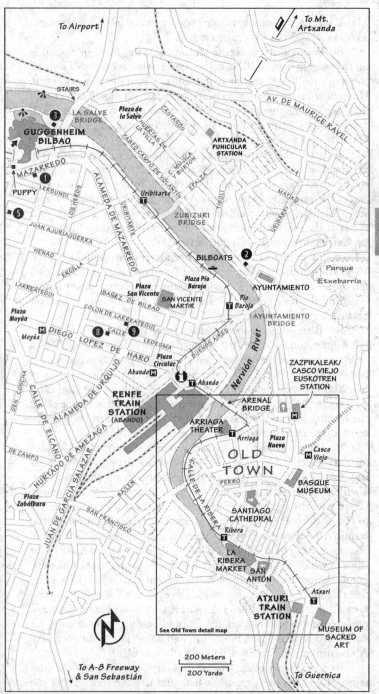

To Airport

To Mt. Artxanda

STAIRS

LA SALVE BRIDGE

Plaza de la Salve

AV. DE MAURICE RAVEL

❸

GUGGENHEIM BILBAO

CASTAÑOS

PUERTAS DE LA VILLA

PASEO CAMPO DE VOLANTÍN

C. MÚJICA Y BURTON

ARTXANDA FUNICULAR STATION

MAZARREDO

❶

LERSUNDI

LOS HEROS

ALAMEDA DE MAZARREDO

URIBITARTE

EPALZA

IBOLI

TIBOLI

MATIKO

PUPPY

❺

Uribitarte Ⓣ

ZUBIZURI BRIDGE

URIBARRI

JUAN AJURIAGUERRA

HENAO

ERCILLA

BILBOATS

❷

Parque Etxebarria

LARREATEGUI

IBAÑEZ DE BILBAO

Plaza San Vicente

Plaza Pío Baroja

SAN VICENTE MÁRTIR

Pío Baroja Ⓣ

AYUNTAMIENTO

Plaza Moyúa

Ⓜ

DIEGO LOPEZ DE HARO

COLÓN DE LARREATEGUI

CALLE

❽   ❾

LEDESMA

AYUNTAMIENTO BRIDGE

Nervión River

Moyúa

BUENOS AIRES

Plaza Circular

ZAZPIKALEAK/ CASCO VIEJO EUSKOTREN STATION

CALLE DE URQUIJO

Abando Ⓜ

Ⓘ Abando

ARENAL BRIDGE

Ⓜ

GEN. CONCHA

CALLE DE ELCANO

ALAMEDA DE URQUIJO

HURTADO DE AMEZAGA

RENFE TRAIN STATION (ABANDO)

ARRIAGA THEATER

Ⓣ Arriaga

Plaza Nueva

Casco Viejo

DE CAMPO

BAILEN

OLD TOWN

PERRO

BASQUE MUSEUM

JUAN DE GARCIA SALAZAR

Plaza Zabálburu

SAN FRANCISCO

CALLE DE LA RIBERA

SANTIAGO CATHEDRAL

Ⓣ Ribera

LA RIBERA MARKET

SAN ANTÓN

Atxuri Ⓣ

ATXURI TRAIN STATION

MUSEUM OF SACRED ART

N

To A-8 Freeway & San Sebastián

See Old Town detail map

200 Meters
200 Yards

To Guernica

Metro system, most tourists won't need it to get around. Tram info: +34 944 333 333, www.euskotren.eus.

By Train: Bilbao's **Renfe station** (serving most of Spain) is on the river in central Bilbao. The train station is on top of a small shopping mall (a Europcar rental office is upstairs at track level). Unfortunately, the tram stop nearest the train station has no ticket machine and neither does the Renfe station—to board here you'll need to buy a *Barik* card or a single-ride ticket at the TI on Plaza Circular next to the station.

To reach the tram, descend into the stores. Leave from the exit marked *Hurtado de Amézaga* and go right to find the TI and the Abando tram stop. (If the TI is closed, follow the tram tracks across the bridge and around the Arriaga Theater to the next tram stop, Arriaga, where single-ride tickets are sold.) Activate your ticket at the machines at the tram stop before boarding (direction: La Casilla, to reach the Guggenheim).

Trains from San Sebastián arrive at the **Zazpikaleak/Casco Viejo station** in the old town near Plaza Nueva. From here, it's a few minutes' walk to the Arriaga tram stop; buy a ticket before boarding the tram (direction: La Casilla), which follows the river to the Guggenheim stop.

By Bus: Buses stop at the **Intermodal station** (www. bilbaointermodal.eus) on the western edge of downtown, about a mile southwest of the Guggenheim. This new underground station houses a ticket office, WCs, lockers, and a cafeteria. The tram (stop: San Mamés) is on the road by the station —look for the steel *CTB* sign and follow the *EuskoTren* signs (not the escalator that leads to the Metro). Buy and validate a ticket at the machine and hop on the tram (direction: Atxuri) to the Guggenheim or old town.

By Plane: Bilbao's compact, modern, user-friendly airport (airport code: BIO, www.aena.es/en/bilbao-airport) is about six miles north of downtown. Everything branches off the light-and-air-filled main hall, designed by prominent architect Santiago Calatrava. The handy, green Bizkaibus (#3247) takes you directly to the city center—look for a sign outside the far-right exit of the terminal (€3, buy ticket or *Barik* card at the tiny ticket office before boarding, daily 6:00-24:00, 2-3/hour, 20-minute trip, makes four stops downtown—the first one at Recalde is closest to the Guggenheim—before ending at the Intermodal bus station). A 15-minute taxi ride into town costs about €25. To get to San Sebastián, you can take a direct bus from Bilbao Airport (€17, buy at ticket machine or on Lurraldebus's LurTicket app before boarding, runs hourly, 1.5 hours, drops off at Plaza Pío XII in San Sebastián, www.pesa.net). A taxi directly to San Sebastián will run you €150.

By Car: A big underground parking garage is near the museum; if you have a car, park it here and use the tram. From the

freeway, take the exit marked *Centro* (with bull's-eye symbol), follow signs to *Guggenheim* (you'll see the museum), and look for the big *P* that marks the garage.

HELPFUL HINTS

Sightseeing Cards: The **Bilbao Bizkaia Card** is sold at TIs and online (www.bilbaobizkaiacard.com). It covers transportation, including the Artxanda funicular, and two TI walking tours, and allows you to skip the line when buying tickets at the Guggenheim and the Fine Arts Museum (€10/24 hours, €15/48 hours, €20/72 hours).

Baggage Storage: The Intermodal bus station on the west side of the city is your best option (Gurtubay 1, +34 944 395 077).

Laundry: The self-service **Lavandería Autoservicio Adei** is handy for visitors staying in the old town. You don't even have to buy detergent—it's already dispensed in the machines (daily 8:00-22:00, last load at 21:00, Ribera 9, mobile +34 665 710 082).

Tours in Bilbao

Walking Tours

Bilbao Walking Tours offers 1.5-hour tours on Saturdays and Sundays (more often in summer), including an old-town tour at 10:00 and a modern-city tour at 12:00 showing the city's history since the 19th century (both start at the Plaza Circular TI). Tours are in Spanish and English, and it's best to reserve in advance. The walks are timed so that you can do both in a single day (€4.50, free with Bilbao Bizkaia Card, +34 944 795 760, www.bilbaoturismo. net).

Tram Tour

Riding the EuskoTren round-trip between the Atxuri and Euskalduna stops is a great way to see the city's oldest and newest neighborhoods, especially on rainy days. For more on the tram, see "Arrival in Bilbao," earlier.

Boat Tour

For a different view of the city, try the **Bilboats** one-hour tour along the river, offering plenty of architectural photo ops. The tour begins near Ayuntamiento Bridge (€13, daily in spring and summer at 13:00, 16:00, 17:30, and 19:00, fewer departures off-season; reserve ahead, canceled if fewer than 10 people buy tickets; tram stop: Pío Baroja; Plaza de Pío Baroja, +34 946 424 157, www.bilboats.com). For hardcore sailors, a two-hour version goes all the way to the Bay of Biscay, passing under the unique suspension bridge in Portugalete (€19, daily July-Aug at 10:30, Sat-Sun only rest of year).

Bike Tour

Although Bilbao is not the most bike-friendly city, bike lanes close to both sides of the Nervión River offer a pleasant ride. At **Tourné Bilbao,** you can rent bikes (€8/2 hours, €10/4 hours) or join their daily city tour at 10:30 (€32/3 hours, includes bottle of water; €7.50 extra for two *pintxos* and a drink after the tour with the guide; Villarías Kalea 1, near the Renfe station and TI, +34 944 249 465, www.tournebilbao.com).

Local Guide

Knowledgeable Bilbao native and licensed guide **Iratxe Muñoz** offers tours of the city, including the Guggenheim, as well as coastal towns and inland areas of the Basque Country (rates vary, +34 607 778 072, iratxe.m@apite.eu).

Sights in Bilbao

▲▲▲Guggenheim Bilbao

Although the collection of art in this museum is no better than those in Europe's other great modern-art museums, the build-

ing itself—designed by Frank Gehry and opened in 1997—is reason enough for many travelers to happily splice Bilbao into their itineraries. Even if you're not turned on by contemporary art, the Guggenheim is a must-see experience. Its 20 galleries, on three floors, are full of surprises, and it's well worth the entry fee just to appreciate the museum's structural design, which is a masterpiece in itself.

Cost and Hours: €16 online in advance, €18 onsite, both prices include audioguide; Tue-Sun 10:00-19:00, closed Mon except July-Aug, same-day reentry allowed; café; tram stop: Guggenheim, Avenida Abandoibarra 2, +34 944 359 080, www.guggenheim-bilbao.eus.

Tours: A free and excellent audioguide is included with a regular entry ticket (scan QR code at the museum to get it on your phone). The museum offers a 30-minute guided tour in English describing the art on exhibit (Sat-Sun at 12:00, in summer sometimes Mon-Fri at 17:00, confirm online). Show up at least 30 minutes early to put your name on the list at the information desk (to the left as you enter). Private 60-minute guided tours in English are available by reservation (€85 in addition to admission fee, book online).

Background: Frank Gehry's groundbreaking triumph offers a fascinating look at 21st-century architecture. Using cutting-edge

technologies, unusual materials, and daring forms, he created a piece of sculpture that smoothly integrates with its environment and serves as the perfect stage for some of today's best art. Clad in limestone and titanium, the building connects the city with its river. Gehry meshed many visions. To him, the building's multiple forms jostle like a loose crate of bottles. The building is inspired by a silvery fish...and also evokes wind-filled sails heading out to sea. Gehry keeps returning to his fish motif, reminding visitors that, as a boy, he was inspired by carp...even taking them into the bathtub with him.

Visiting the Museum: The audioguide will lead you room-by-room through the collection, but this information will get you started.

Guarding the main entrance is artist Jeff Koons' 42-foot-tall **West Highland Terrier.** Its 60,000 plants and flowers, which blossom in concert, grow through steel mesh. A joyful structure, it brings viewers back to their childhoods—perhaps evoking human-kind's relationship to God—or maybe it's just another notorious Koons hoax. One thing is clear: It answers to "Puppy." Although the sculpture was originally intended to be temporary, the people of Bilbao fell in love with *Puppy*—so they bought it.

Descend to the **main entrance,** where you can show or buy your ticket and get the audioguide. At the information desk, pick up the small English brochure explaining the architecture and mu-seum layout, and the seasonal *Guggenheim Bilbao* magazine that details the art currently on display.

Enter the **atrium.** This acts as the heart of the building, pump-ing visitors from various rooms on three levels out and back, always returning to this central area before moving on to the next. The architect invites you to caress the sensual curves of the walls. There are virtually no straight lines (except the floor). Notice the sheets of glass that make up the staircase and elevator shafts—overlap-ping each other like a fish's scales. Each glass and limestone panel is unique, designed by a computer and shaped by a robot...as will likely be standard in constructing the great buildings of the future.

From the atrium, step out onto the riverside **terrace.** The "water garden" lets the river symbolically lap at the base of the building. This pool is home to four unusual sculptures (the first two appear occasionally throughout the day): Yves Klein's five-part "fire fountain" (notice the squares in the pool to the right); Fujiko Nakaya's "fog sculpture" that billows up from below; another piece by Jeff Koons, *Tulips,* which is a colorful chrome bouquet of in-flated flowers; and the most recent addition, *Tall Tree and the Eye* by British artist Anish Kapoor. Composed of 73 reflective spheres ar-ranged vertically, the sculpture endlessly reflects the Guggenheim, the river, and the beholder.

Still out on the terrace, notice the museum's commitment to public spaces: On the right, a grand **staircase** leads under a big green bridge to a tower; the effect wraps the bridge into the museum's grand scheme. The 30-foot-tall **spider,** called *Maman* ("Mommy"), is French American artist Louise Bourgeois' depiction of her mother: She spins a beautiful and delicate web of life... which is used to entrap her victims. (It makes a little more sense if you understand that the artist's mother was a weaver. Or maybe not.)

Step back inside. Gehry designed the vast **ground floor** mainly to house often-huge modern-art installations. Computer-controlled lighting adjusts for different exhibits. Surfaces are clean and bare, so you can focus on the art. While most of the collection comes and goes, Richard Serra's huge *Matter of Time* sculpture in the largest gallery (#104) is permanent. Who would want to move those massive metal coils? The intent is to have visitors walk among these metal walls—the "art" is experiencing this journey.

Because this museum is part of the Guggenheim "family" of museums, the **collection** perpetually rotates among the sister Guggenheim galleries in New York and Venice. The best approach to your visit is simply to immerse yourself in a modern-art happening, rather than to count on seeing a particular piece or a specific artist's works.

You can't fully enjoy the museum's architecture without taking a circular stroll up and down each side of the river along the handsome promenade and over the two modern **pedestrian bridges.** The building's skin—shiny and metallic, with a scale-like texture—is made of thin titanium, carefully created to give just the desired color and reflective quality. The external appearance tells you what's inside: The blocky limestone parts contain square-shaped galleries, and the titanium sections hold nonlinear spaces.

As you look out over the rest of the city, think of this: Gehry designed his building to reflect what he saw here in Bilbao. Now other architects are, in turn, creating new buildings that complement his. It's an appealing synergy for this old city.

Leaving the Museum: To get to the old town from the Guggenheim, you can take the tram that leaves from the river level beside the museum, just past the kid-pleasing fountain (ride it in direction: Atxuri). Hop off at the Arriaga stop, near the dripping-Baroque riverfront theater of the same name. From here, cross the street to enter the heart of the old town.

Or, for a pleasant 20-minute walk, exit the museum and go behind it to the river. Head toward the spider *Maman*, passing under her and the tall bridge *La Salve*, which is incorporated into the museum. Continue along the river, passing the white, harp-shaped Santiago Calatrava bridge *(Zubizuri)*, a second bridge

(Ayuntamiento), and finally crossing at the third bridge *(Arenal)* to arrive at the old town. (Bridges are labeled on city maps.)

NEAR THE GUGGENHEIM
Fine Arts Museum (Museo de Bellas Artes)
Often overshadowed by the Guggenheim, the Fine Arts Museum contains a thoughtfully laid out collection arranged chronologically from the 12th century to the present. Find minor works by many Spanish artists, such as Goya, El Greco, Picasso, Murillo, Zurbarán, Sorolla, Chillida, Tàpies, and Barceló—along with a handful of local Basque painters. International artists in the collection include Gauguin, Klee, Bacon, Cassatt, and more. The museum is at the edge of the lovely Doña Casilda Iturrizar Park, perfect for a stroll after your visit. A major renovation, expected to continue into 2024, may mean they are showing a very limited collection of a few classics and some contemporary art by Spanish artists (and entry may be free). Check online before you visit.

Cost and Hours: €10, includes audioguide, Wed-Mon 10:00-20:00, closed Tue, a short walk from the Guggenheim at Museo Plaza 2, +34 944 396 060, www.museobilbao.com.

Azkuna Zentroa (Alhóndiga Bilbao)
Bilbao's culture and leisure center, designed by French architect Philippe Starck, is worth a quick visit or a lazy afternoon. Not one of the 43 interior columns is alike—the designs are meant to represent the entirety of materials and styles from antiquity to today. The center houses a cinema, auditorium, exhibition spaces, and restaurant—so it functions as a community gathering space. Most impressive is its glass-bottomed rooftop pool—from the atrium below, visitors can gaze up at the backstrokers in the water above.

Cost and Hours: Free entry to the center itself, €9 day pass gives you access to the pool and sundeck, daily 8:30-23:00, 10-minute walk from the Guggenheim at Plaza Arriquibar 4, +34 944 014 014, www.azkunazentroa.eus.

Funicular de Artxanda
Opened in 1915, this funicular still provides *bilbainos* with a green escape from their somewhat grimy city. The three-minute ride offers sweeping views of the city on the way to the top of Mount Artxanda, where there's a park, restaurants, and a sports complex. Bring a picnic on a sunny afternoon, and take a moment to ponder the giant thumbprint sculpture dedicated to Basque soldiers who fought against Franco during the civil war.

Cost and Hours: €4.30 round-trip, covered by Bilbao Bizkaia Card; departs every 15 minutes, daily 7:15-22:00, until 23:00 Fri-Sat in summer; cross the Zubizuri Bridge and walk two blocks

along Calle Mújica y Burton to the cable-car station, Plaza del Funicular, +34 944 454 966, https://funicularartxanda.bilbao.eus.

IN THE OLD TOWN

Bilbao's old town (Casco Viejo), with tall, narrow lanes lined with thriving shops and tapas bars, is worth a stroll. Because the weather is wetter here than in many other parts of Spain (hence the green hillsides), the little balconies that climb the outside walls of buildings are glassed in, creating cozy little breakfast nooks. Various museums (including those dedicated to diocesan art and the Holy Week processions) are in or near the old town, but on a quick visit only the Basque Museum is worth considering.

Santiago Cathedral

Whether you want to or not, you'll eventually wind up at old Bilbao's centerpiece, the Santiago Cathedral. This 14th-century Gothic church has a tranquil interior that has been scrubbed clean inside and out.

Cost and Hours: €6 combo-ticket includes audioguide and entry to the San Anton Church next to La Ribera Market, daily July-Aug 10:00-21:00, Sept-June until 20:00, Plaza Santiago 1, +34 944 153 627, www.catedralbilbao.com.

Basque Museum (Euskal Museoa)

This museum, in a 16th-century convent, was closed in 2021 for renovation. If it has reopened, you'll find lovingly assembled artifacts of Basque heritage. English pamphlets scattered throughout offer helpful summaries of the displays.

Cost and Hours: €3, Mon and Wed-Fri 10:00-19:00, Sat 10:00-13:30 & 16:00-19:00, Sun 10:00-14:00, closed Tue, Miguel de Unamuno Plaza 4, +34 944 155 423, www.euskalmuseoa.eus.

Visiting the Museum: The main sight in the ground-floor cloister is the Iron Age *El Mikeldi*, a stone animal figure. The first floor centers on the maritime activities of the seafaring Basques, as well as the pastoral lifestyle of the region's shepherds. The second floor has exhibits covering porcelain, timeworn tools, and ironworks that helped spur the economic prominence of the Basque region.

On the top floor are fragments from two oak trees from Guernica—cherished relics of Basque nationalism (see the Guernica section, earlier). The Arbol Viejo and the Arbol Nuevo each stood for 150 years in front of the Gernika Assembly House until their

"clinical death." This floor also has exhibits on the social, political, and economic impact of Bilbao over three centuries.

La Ribera Market

There's been a market here since Bilbao was founded in 1300. As part of an urban renewal plan, the 1929 La Ribera city market re-opened in 2011 to an enthusiastic public. Stroll the stalls for the freshest fish (look for the busiest sellers), shop for produce, and ad-mire a series of Art Deco stained-glass panels on the top floor. The city's coat-of-arms, with two wolves, can be found in the largest panels. Consider returning in the afternoon or evening to the styl-ish *cervecería* and the few *pintxo* bars on the ground floor (Mon-Sat 8:00-14:30, also Tue-Fri 17:00-20:00, closed Sun; bars open Mon 9:00-16:00, Tue-Sat until 24:00, Sun 11:00-24:00; public WC, +34 944 231 019).

Sleeping in Bilbao

Bilbao merits an overnight stay. Even those who are interested only in the Guggenheim find that there's much more to see in this his-toric yet quickly changing city.

NEAR THE GUGGENHEIM MUSEUM

For locations, see the "Bilbao" map on page 224.

$$$$ Gran Hotel Domine Bilbao is *the* place for well-heeled modern-art fans looking for a splurge close to the museum. It's right across the street from the main entrance to the Guggenheim and Jeff Koons' *Puppy*. The hotel is gathered around an atrium with a giant "stone tree" and other artsy flourishes, and its decor (by a prominent Spanish designer) was clearly inspired by Gehry's mas-terpiece. The 145 plush rooms are distinctly black, white, steel, and very postmodern (air-con, elevator, free gym with wet and dry sau-nas, pay parking, Alameda Mazarredo 61, +34 944 253 300, www. hoteldominebilbao.com, info@hoteldominebilbao.com). Breakfast on the hotel's great museum-view terrace is a treat open even to nonguests (served daily 7:00-11:00, Sat-Sun until 12:00). If arriv-ing by tram, take the main museum steps up by the fountains to reach the hotel.

$$ Hotel Bilbao Plaza has 53 bright and modern rooms, pleasant public spaces, and a friendly staff. With a great location on the river, it's a 10-minute walk to the Guggenheim and a five-minute walk to modern Bilbao or the edge of the old town—so it's away from the bar noise at night (air-con, elevator, pay parking, Paseo Campo Volantín 1, at the Ayuntamiento bridge, +34 946 856 700, www.hotelbilbaoplaza.com, info@hotelbilbaoplaza.com).

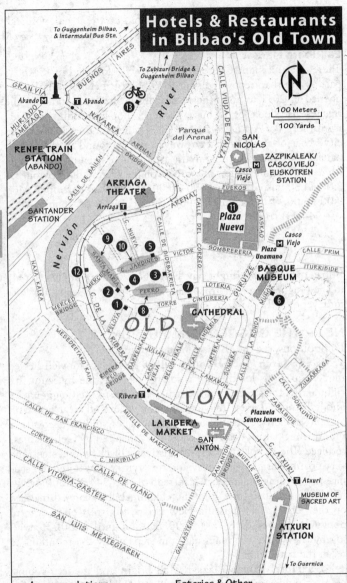

Hotels & Restaurants in Bilbao's Old Town

Accommodations

1 Basque Boutique
2 Iturrienea Ostatua
3 Casual Gurea Bilbao
4 7Kale Bed & Breakfast
5 Hotel Bilbao Jardines
6 La Estrella Ostatu

Eateries & Other

7 Baster
8 Calle del Perro Eateries
9 Calle Santa María Eateries
10 Calle Jardines Eateries
11 Plaza Nueva Eateries
12 Launderette
13 Bike Rental

IN AND NEAR THE OLD TOWN

To reach the old town, take the tram to the Arriaga stop.

$$ Basque Boutique offers eight classy rooms with petite balconies. All rooms are designed with Basque themes, such as the "El Caserío" room with traditional Basque furniture and the "Gernika" room inspired by the painting by Pablo Picasso. The shared space has free coffee and tea, and you can try on traditional Basque clothing to take a fun photo (air-con, no elevator, Calle de la Torre 2, second floor, +34 944 790 788, www.basqueboutique.es, info@basqueboutique.es).

$ Iturrienea Ostatua is a polished, quaint version of a traditional *pensión* with nine rooms, a breakfast room, rustic decor, and mini fridges. Double-pane windows help with the noise, but if you are sensitive, bring earplugs or ask for an interior room (Calle Santa María 14, first floor, +34 944 161 500, www.iturrieneaostatua.com, iturrienea@outlook.es).

$ Casual Gurea Bilbao has 26 clean, well-priced rooms and a welcoming staff. Double-pane windows keep the rooms quiet despite being on a busy street. A common area has coffee and vending machines (elevator, Calle Bidebarrieta 14, third floor, +34 944 163 299, www.casualgurea.com, reservas@casualhoteles.com).

$ 7Kale Bed & Breakfast, across the street from Iturrienea Ostatua, has a similar concept. They have 12 bright rooms with private bathrooms, and a small breakfast room. Balcony rooms are lovely, but the hotel is on a pedestrian street that's lively at night and can be noisy—ask for a quiet room away from the street (Calle Santa María 13, first floor, +34 946 402 011, www.7kalebnb.com, 7kale@7kalebnb.com).

$ Hotel Bilbao Jardines is a slumbermill buried in the old town with 32 modern but basic rooms and squeaky floors (air-con, elevator, free loaner bicycles, Calle Jardines 9, +34 944 794 210, www.hotelbilbaojardines.com, info@hotelbilbaojardines.com; Marta, Félix, and Mónica).

$ La Estrella Ostatu is a family-run establishment with 26 simple but neat rooms up a twisty staircase near the Basque Museum. It's on a busy pedestrian street with several bars—bring earplugs (María Muñoz 6, +34 944 164 066, www.la-estrella-ostatu.com, laestrellabilbao@yahoo.es, just enough English spoken, Jesus and Begoña).

Eating in Bilbao

Bilbao has a thriving restaurant and tapas-bar scene. And with several Michelin-star restaurants, Bilbao seems poised to give San Sebastián a run for its money as culinary capital of the Basque Country. For pointers on Basque food, see "Basque Country Cui-

sine Scene" section at the beginning of this chapter. While each neighborhood has a clustering of bars and restaurants, the best spots are in the old town, and in the new town area between the Guggenheim and old town. The area around the Guggenheim also has several good options.

NEAR THE GUGGENHEIM MUSEUM

The easiest choice is the good **$$$ bar** in the museum itself, which features *pintxos*, salads, and sandwiches (upper level, separate entry above museum entry; Tue-Sun 9:30-20:30, also open Mon July-Aug). Adjacent to the bar is the museum's more chic **$$$ Bistro,** with an express lunch (reservations smart, fixed-price meal offered all day, open for dinner Fri-Sat, closed Mon, +34 944 239 333, www.bistroguggenheimbilbao.com). The finest dining experience is at the one-Michelin-star restaurant **$$$$ Nerua,** with waiters almost as fancy as the food (riverfront access upstairs outside museum, Tue-Sun 13:00-15:00, evening service Fri-Sat 20:30-22:00, closed Mon, +34 944 000 430, www.neruaguggenheimbilbao.com).

The circular structure outside the museum by the playgrounds and fountains is a pleasant **outdoor café** serving sandwiches. If the tables are full, you can take your food to one of the stone benches nearby. In the evenings, they sometimes have live music.

The streets in front of the museum have a handful of **$$** sit-down and takeout eateries. **Cokooncafé** serves a mouthwatering brunch and good coffee (Calle Iparraguirre 5, Tue-Sat 9:00-15:00, Sun until 14:00, closed Mon). **Sua San** has *pintxos*, salads, and sandwiches in addition to their daily menu; takeout available—perfect for a picnic in front of the Guggenheim (Alameda Mazarredo 79, Mon-Fri 8:00-23:00, Sat 9:00-24:00, Sun until 16:30, +34 944 987 751, https://suasan.com). At **Serantes III,** the food is heartier, more local, and homemade (Mon-Sat 9:00-16:00 & 18:00-24:00, Sun from 10:00; Alameda Mazarredo 75, +34 944 248 004, www.restauranteserantes.com). For locations, see the "Bilbao" map on page 224.

IN THE OLD TOWN

You'll find plenty of options on the lanes near the cathedral or on Plaza Nueva. Most restaurants around the old town advertise a fixed-price lunch for around €13; some close for siesta between 16:00 and 20:00. For locations, see the "Hotels & Restaurants in Bilbao's Old Town" map.

Calle Correo: The hip little bar **$$ Baster** is just behind the cathedral. Sit in the small interior or delightful outdoor area for late breakfast, *pintxos*, their well-known *patatas bravas*, or a *ver-*

mut preparado (Tue-Thu 9:30-22:00, Fri-Sat until 23:00, Sun until 16:00, closed Mon, Calle Correo 22, +34 944 071 228).

Calle del Perro: This street is tops for tasty *pintxos*. **$$ Xukela Bar** is my favorite, with its inviting atmosphere, good wines, and an addictive array of tapas spread along its bar. The adventurous might try their specialty—*cresta de gallo*, a.k.a. fried rooster comb (tables generally only for clients eating hot dishes, Calle del Perro 2, +34 944 159 772). Calle del Perro is also good for sit-down restaurants. Browse the menus and interiors and choose your favorite. Well-regarded options include three **$$** places virtually next door to each other: **Egiluz** (meals served in small restaurant up steep spiral staircase in the back); **Río-Oja** (focus on shareable traditional dishes called *cazuelitas*); and **Rotterdam** (also has *cazuelitas* displayed on the bar; try the *chipirones en su tinta*—squids in their own ink). Across from Río-Oja, **$$ Restaurante Mandoya** is a charming sit-down place with a friendly staff and appealing interior. They specialize in both fish and meat, serving up hearty lunch portions. It gets busy, so come early or make a reservation (Tue-Sun 13:30-16:30, Fri-Sat also 20:30-23:30, closed Mon, Calle del Perro 3, +34 944 157 984, www.restaurantemandoya.com).

Calle Santa María: This street caters to a younger crowd, with softer lighting and a livelier atmosphere, and has several bars and restaurants worth considering: Gatz, Santa María, Kasko, Con B de Bilbao, and Amarena. **$$$ Kasko** is a good sit-down option, with a pianist and an interesting fixed-price lunch and dinner (daily, Santa María 16, +34 944 160 311). **$$ Con B de Bilbao** serves beautiful and hearty *pintxos* or *montaditos* in a trendy, eclectic setting (closed Sun for dinner, Calle Santa María 9, +34 944 158 776). Busy **$$ Amarena** is probably the best choice if you want a full restaurant meal (daily, on the corner at Calle Santa María 18, +34 944 169 421).

Calle Jardines: Eateries also abound on Jardines street, including the popular **$$ Berton** and its sister bar/dining room **$$ Berton Sasibil,** across the lane (at #11 and #8, closed Mon, +34 944 167 035). **$ Charamel Gozotegia** has coffee, tea, and pastry to follow your *pintxo* lunch. Ask for the traditional *pastel vasco* (Basque cake) or their specialty *milhoja artesana*, all homemade by a group of young, creative bakers (daily until 20:30, Calle Jardines 2, +34 944 165 984).

Plaza Nueva and Calle del Arenal: The old town's living room, Plaza Nueva is full of outdoor café tables, lively *pintxo* bars, kids playing ball, and a stamp, coin, and used-book market on Sunday morning. It's a great local scene to take in. For good *pintxos*, check out the award-winning **$$ Gure Toki** and its neighbor bar **$$ Sorginzulo,** both with outdoor seating.

IN THE NEW TOWN

You'll see cafés, restaurants, and *pintxo* bars scattered along the way from the Guggenheim to the old town in the neighborhood parallel to the Nervión River. The most concentrated and accessible area is on and near the pedestrian street Calle Ledesma, which runs parallel to Gran Vía de Don Diego López de Haro. On a busy night, you won't be able to tell where people ordered their drinks as they flow up and down the street. The classic **$$ Bar Ledesma,** at #14, draws a crowd, but most of the places on this strip have similar *pintxos* and drinks. Around the corner, on the large inviting square called Jardines de Albia, is **$$ Café Iruña,** a café-bar-restaurant with Andalusian decor serving breakfast as well as *pintxos* and full meals (fixed-price weekday meal, long hours daily, +34 944 237 021). For locations see the "Bilbao" map on page 224.

Bilbao Connections

From Bilbao by Bus to: San Sebastián (2/hour, hourly on weekends, 1.5 hours, Pesa), **Guernica** (4/hour, fewer on weekends, 40 minutes, Bizkaibus), **Lekeitio** (hourly, 1.5 hours, Bizkaibus), **Pamplona** (6/day, 2 hours), **Burgos** (6/day, fewer on weekends, 2-3 hours, Alsa), **Santander** (hourly, 1.5 hours, Alsa, transfer there to bus to **Santillana del Mar** or **Comillas**). These buses depart from Bilbao's Intermodal station (tram stop: San Mamés, www.bilbaointermodal.eus).

By Renfe Train to: Madrid (2/day direct, more with transfer, 5-7 hours), **Barcelona** (1/day, 7 hours), **Burgos** (3/day direct, more with transfer, 3 hours), **Salamanca** (1/day, 5.5 hours), **León** (1/day, 5 hours). Remember, these trains leave from the Renfe station, across the river from the old town (tram stop: Abando).

By EuskoTren to: San Sebastián (hourly, long and scenic 2.5-hour trip to San Sebastián's Amara EuskoTren station, departs from Bilbao's Zazpikaleak/Casco Viejo station just east of Plaza Nueva), **Guernica** (2/hour, 50 minutes, take Bilbao-Bermeo line from Atxuri station, just beyond the Ribera Market, direction: Bermeo). EuskoTren info: www.euskotren.eus.

French Basque Country

Compared with the Spanish lands across the border, the French Basque Country (Le Pays Basque) seems French first and Basque second. You'll see less Euskara writing than in Spain, but these destinations have their own special spice, mingling Basque and

French influences with beautiful rolling countryside and gorgeous beaches.

Just 45 minutes apart by car, San Sebastián and St-Jean-de-Luz bridge the Spanish and French Basque regions. Between them you'll find the functional towns of Irún (Spain) and Hendaye (France).

My favorite home base here is the central, comfy, and manageable resort village of St-Jean-de-Luz. It's a stone's throw to Bayonne (with its "bigger-city" bustle and good Basque museum) and the snazzy beach town of Biarritz. A drive inland rewards you with a panoply of adorable French Basque villages. And St-Jean-de-Luz is a relaxing place to "come home" to, with its mellow ambience, fine strolling atmosphere, and good restaurants.

BASQUE COUNTRY

St-Jean-de-Luz / Donibane Lohizune

St-Jean-de-Luz (san zhahn-duh-lewz) sits cradled between its small port and gentle bay. The days when whaling, cod fishing, and pirating made it wealthy are long gone, but don't expect a cute Basque backwater. Tourism has become the economic mainstay, and it shows. Pastry shops serve Basque specialties, and store windows proudly display berets (a Basque symbol). Ice-cream lickers stroll traffic-free streets, while soft, sandy beaches tempt travelers to toss their itineraries into the bay. The knobby little mountain La Rhune towers above the festive scene. Locals joke that if it's clear enough to see La Rhune's peak, it's going to rain, but if you can't see it, it's raining already.

The town has little of sightseeing importance, but it's a good base for exploring the Basque Country and a convenient beach and port town that provides the most enjoyable dose of Basque culture in France. The town fills with French tourists in July and August—especially the first two weeks of August, when it's practically impossible to find a room without a reservation made long in advance...or even to walk down the main street.

Orientation to St-Jean-de-Luz

St-Jean-de-Luz's old city lies between the train tracks, the Nivelle River, and the Atlantic. The main traffic-free street, Rue Gambetta, channels walkers through the center, halfway between the train tracks and the ocean.

The only sight worth entering in St-Jean-de-Luz is the church where Louis XIV and Marie-Thérèse tied the royal knot. St-Jean-de-Luz is best appreciated along its pedestrian streets, lively squares, and golden, sandy beaches. With nice views and walking

It Happened at Hendaye

If taking the train between the Spanish and French Basque regions, you'll change trains at the nondescript little Hendaye station. While it seems innocent enough, this was the site of a fateful meeting between two of Europe's most notorious 20th-century dictators.

In the days before World War II, Adolf Hitler and Francisco Franco maintained a diplomatic relationship. But after the fall of France, they decided to meet secretly in Hendaye to size each other up. On October 23, 1940, Hitler traveled through Nazi-occupied France, then waited impatiently on the platform for Franco's delayed train. The over-eager Franco hoped the Führer would invite him to join in a military alliance with Germany (and ultimately share in the expected war spoils).

According to reports of the meeting, Franco was greedy, boastful, and misguided, leading Hitler to dismiss him as a buffoon. Franco later spun the situation by claiming that he had cleverly avoided being pulled into World War II. In fact, his own incompetence is what saved Spain. Had Franco made a better impression on Hitler here at Hendaye, it's possible that Spain would have entered the war, which could have changed the course of Spanish, German, and European history.

trails, the park at the far eastern end of the beachfront promenade at Pointe Ste. Barbe makes a good walking destination.

The small, untouristed town of Ciboure, across the river from St-Jean-de-Luz, holds little of interest (although fans of Maurice Ravel can hunt down his birthplace at Quai Maurice Ravel 27).

TOURIST INFORMATION

The helpful TI is next to the big market hall, along the busy Boulevard Victor Hugo (July-Aug Mon-Sat 9:00-12:30 & 14:00-18:00, Sun 10:00-13:00 & 15:00-18:00; shorter hours rest of the year, closed Sun Jan-March; 20 Boulevard Victor Hugo, +33 5 59 26 03 16, town info: www.saint-jean-de-luz.com, regional info: www.en-pays-basque.fr).

ARRIVAL IN ST-JEAN-DE-LUZ

By Train or Bus: From the train station, the pedestrian underpass leads to the bus station. From there, it's easy to get to the TI and the center of the old town (just a few blocks away).

By Car: Follow signs for *Centre-Ville*, then *Gare* and *Office de Tourisme*. The old town is not car-friendly, with one-way lanes that cut back and forth across pedestrian streets. It's best to park your car in the free parking lot next to the train tracks.

By Plane: The nearest airport is Biarritz-Anglet-Bayonne

Airport, 10 miles to the northeast near Biarritz. The tiny airport is easy to navigate, with a useful TI desk (airport code: BIQ, www.biarritz.aeroport.fr). To reach St-Jean-de-Luz, you can take bus #3 (€2, hourly on weekdays, half as many on weekends, 45 minutes, get off at the Halte Routière stop near the train station, www.transports-atcrb.com) or a 25-minute taxi ride (about €30).

HELPFUL HINTS

Market Days: The Les Halles covered market is open daily from 7:00 to 13:00 and offers everything from fresh fish and produce to regional specialty dried goods. On Tuesday and Friday mornings (and summer Saturdays) until about 13:00, there's also a street market. Farmers' stands spill through the streets from the market on Boulevard Victor Hugo, giving everyone a rustic whiff of "life is good."

Pharmacies: Several can be found on Rue Gambetta. Look for the green cross.

Laundry: Laverie Automatique du Port is at 4 Boulevard Thiers (self-service daily 7:00-21:00, change machine; full-service available Wed-Fri 9:30-12:00 & 14:30-18:00, Sat 9:30-12:00, mornings only in winter; mobile +33 6 80 06 48 36).

Car Rental: Avis, at the train station, is handiest (Mon-Sat 9:00-12:00 & 14:00-17:30, closed Sun, +33 5 59 26 79 66).

Tours in St-Jean-de-Luz

Tourist Train

A little tourist train does a 30-minute trip around town (€7, departs every 45 minutes from the port, runs April-Oct 10:30-19:00, no train Nov-March). It's only worth the money if you need to rest your feet.

Bus Excursions

Le Basque Bondissant runs day-trip excursions, including a Wednesday-only jaunt to the Guggenheim Bilbao (€40 round-trip, includes museum admission, departs 9:00 from green bus terminal across the street from train station, returns 19:15). You can get information on other tours and buy tickets at the TI or online (+33 5 59 26 25 87, www.basque-bondissant.com). Reservations are recommended in winter, when trips are canceled if not enough people sign up.

Boat Trips

Le Passeur, at the port, offers bay crossings to Socoa and Ciboure, with departures every 40 minutes (€3 each way, €20/10 trips—shareable among groups, runs mid-April-Sept). They also have guided tours of the bay by Zodiac (€15, 1 hour, June-Aug only) or

BASQUE COUNTRY

Dipping into France

If you're heading from Spain to France, you don't have to worry about currency changes—both use the euro—or lengthy border stops (although police might ask to see your passport on buses or trains going into Spain). Here are a few other practicalities:

Hours: France typically does not enjoy as substantial a "siesta" as Spain; shops may close for an afternoon break, but usually only for an hour. The French eat lunch and dinner closer to the European mainstream time (around 12:00-13:30 & 19:00-21:00)—much earlier than Spaniards do.

Hotel Tips: The French have a simple hotel-rating system based on amenities, indicated in this chapter by asterisks. One star is modest, two has most of the comforts, and three is generally a two-star place with a fancier lobby and more elaborately designed rooms. Four or five stars offer more luxury than you'll probably have time to appreciate.

Restaurant Tips: In France, if you ask for the *menu* (muh-new), you won't get a list of dishes; you'll get a fixed-price meal. *Menus,* which include three or four courses, are generally a good value if you're hungry: You'll get your choice of soup, appetizer, or salad; your choice of a few main-course options with vegetables; plus a cheese course and/or a choice of desserts. Service is included (*service compris* or *prix net*), but wine and

with a regular boat including a drink at the end (€20, 1 hour, April-Oct; reservations required, Quai Maréchal Leclerc, +33 6 11 69 56 93, buruxkan@hotmail.com). **Nivelle V** offers mini Atlantic cruises and excursions, including 3.5-hour fishing trips (€36, 3.5 hours), a Basque Coast to Spain tour (€19, 2 hours), and a Sea Cliff tour (€11, 45 minutes). Get tickets at their portside kiosk (runs April-mid-Oct, reservations required July-Aug, Quai Maréchal Leclerc, mobile +33 6 09 73 61 81, www.croisiere-saintjeandeluz.com).

St-Jean-de-Luz Walk

To get a feel for the town, take this hour-long self-guided stroll. You'll start at the port and make your way to the historic church.

Port: Begin at the little working port (at Place des Corsaires, just beyond the parking lot). Pleasure craft are in the next port over, in Ciboure. Whereas fishing boats used to catch lots of whales and anchovies, now they take in sardines and tuna—and take tourists out on joyrides. Anchovies were once a big part of the fishing business, but were overfished nearly into extinction and have been protected by the EU for the last few years, leading to a gradual rebound.

other drinks generally are extra.

French Survival Phrases: Although some French Basques speak Euskara, most speak French in everyday life. You'll find these phrases useful:

English	French
Good day	*Bonjour* (bohn-zhoor)
Mrs. / Ma'am	*Madame* (mah-dahm)
Mr. / Sir	*Monsieur* (muhs-yuh)
Please	*S'il vous plaît* (see voo play)
Thank you	*Merci* (mehr-see)
I'm sorry	*Désolé* (day-zoh-lay)
Excuse me	*Pardon* (par-dohn)
Yes / No	*Oui / Non* (wee / nohn)
How much is it?	*Combien?* (kohn-bee-an)
Cheers!	*Santé!* (sahn-tay)
Goodbye	*Au revoir* (oh ruh-vwahr)
women / men	*dames/hommes* (dahm / ohm)
one / two / three	*un/deux/trois* (uhn / duh / trwah)
Do you speak	*Parlez-vous* (par-lay voo)
English?	*Anglais?* (ahn-glay)

St-Jean-de-Luz feels cute and nonthreatening now, but in the 17th century it was home to the Basque Corsairs. With the French government's blessing, these pirates who worked the sea—and enriched the town—moored here.

• *After you walk the length of the port, on your right is the tree-lined...*

Place Louis XIV: The town's main square, named for the king who was married here, is a hub of action that serves as the town's communal living room. During the summer, the bandstand features traditional Basque folk music and dancing at 21:00 (almost nightly July-Aug, otherwise Sun, schedule usually posted on bandstand). Facing the square is the City Hall (Herriko Etchea) and the **House of Louis XIV** (he lived here for 40 festive days in 1660). A visit to this house is worthwhile only if you like period furniture, though it's only open for part of the year; the rest of the time the privately owned mansion is occupied by the same family that's had it for over three centuries (€7, generally June-Aug Wed-Mon 10:30-12:30 & 14:30-18:30, Sept-mid-Oct 11:00-15:00 & 16:00-17:00, closed Tue and Nov-mid-April, visits by 40-minute guided tour only, 4/day, in French with English handouts, +33 5 59 26 27 58, www.maison-louis-xiv.fr).

The king's visit is memorialized by a small black equestrian

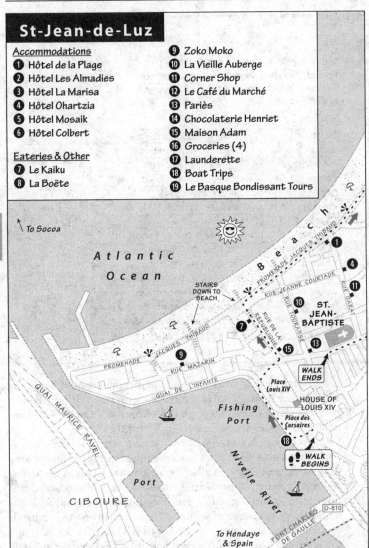

St-Jean-de-Luz

Accommodations

1 Hôtel de la Plage
2 Hôtel Les Almadies
3 Hôtel La Marisa
4 Hôtel Ohartzia
5 Hôtel Mosaik
6 Hôtel Colbert

Eateries & Other

7 Le Kaiku
8 La Boëte
9 Zoko Moko
10 La Vieille Auberge
11 Corner Shop
12 Le Café du Marché
13 Pariès
14 Chocolaterie Henriet
15 Maison Adam
16 Groceries (4)
17 Launderette
18 Boat Trips
19 Le Basque Bondissant Tours

BASQUE COUNTRY

statue at the entrance of the City Hall (a miniature of the huge statue that marks the center of the Versailles courtyard). The plane trees, with truncated branches looking like fists, are cut back in the winter so that in the summer they'll come back with thick, shady foliage.

• *Opposite the port on the far side of the square is...*

Rue de la République: This historic lane leads from Place Louis XIV to the beach. Once the home of fishermen, today it's lined with mostly edible temptations. Facing the square, **Maison**

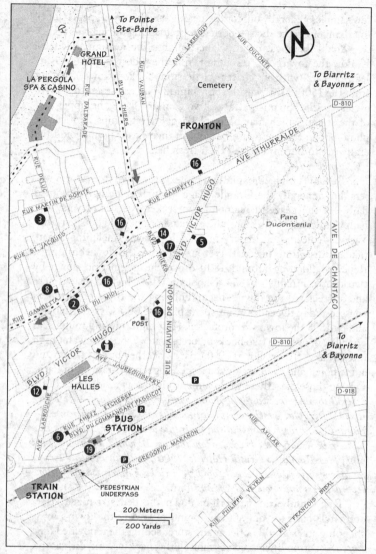

Adam (at #4) still uses the family recipe to bake the chewy, almond-rich *macarons* Louis XIV enjoyed during his visit to wed Princess Marie-Thérèse in 1660. Get one for €1 or grab other sweets, such as the less historic but just as tasty *gâteau basque*—a baked tart with a cream or cherry filling. Their gourmet shop next door (at #6) has more of the same.

Don't eat your fill of dessert just yet, though, because farther down Rue de la République you'll find **Pierre Oteiza,** stacked with rustic Basque cheeses and meats from mountain villages (with a

few samples generally out for the tasting, and handy €4 paper cones of salami or cheese slices—perfect for munching during this walk).

You'll likely eat on this lane tonight. The recommended **Le Kaiku,** the town's top restaurant, fills the oldest building in St-Jean-de-Luz (with its characteristic stone lookout tower), dating from the 1500s. This was the only building on the street to survive a vicious 1558 Spanish attack. Two cannons flank the upper end of the street, which may be from Basque pirate ships. Notice the photo of fisherwomen with baskets on their heads, who would literally run to Bayonne to sell their fresh fish.

• *Continue to the...*

Beach: A high embankment protects the town from storm waters, but generally the Grande Plage—which is lovingly groomed daily—is the peaceful haunt of sun-seekers, soccer players, and happy children. Walk along the elevated promenade (to the right). Various tableaux tell history in French. Storms (including a particularly disastrous one in 1749) routinely knocked down buildings. Repeated flooding around 1800 drove the population down by two-thirds. Finally, in 1854, Napoleon III—who had visited here and appreciated the town—began building the three breakwaters you see today. Decades were spent piling 8,000 fifty-ton blocks, and by 1895 the town was protected. (But high tide and rough seas often break over the two bookend breakwaters, spraying water high into the sky.) To develop their tourist trade, they built a casino and a fine hotel, and even organized a special getaway train from Paris. During those days there were as many visitors as residents (3,000).

• *Stroll through the seaside shopping mall fronting the late–Art Deco-style* **La Pergola,** *which houses a casino, lots of shopping, expensive restaurants, and the* **Hélianthal spa** *(entrance around back). Anyone in a white robe strolling the beach is from the spa. Beyond La Pergola is the pink, Neo-Romantic* **Grand Hôtel** *(c. 1900), with an inviting terrace for an expensive coffee break. From here circle back into town along Boulevard Thiers until you reach the bustling...*

Rue Gambetta: Turn right down the pedestrianized street and circle back to your starting point, following the town's lively shopping strip. You'll notice many stores selling the renowned *linge Basque*—cotton linens such as tablecloths, napkins, and dishcloths, in the characteristic Basque red, white, and green. There are as many candy shops as there are tourists. Keep an eye open for a local branch of the British auction house Christie's, which specializes in high-end real estate. Video screens in the window advertise French castles for a mere €2 million, while local vacation homes go for considerably less.

• *Just before Place Louis XIV, you'll see the town's main church.*

Eglise St. Jean-Baptiste: The marriage of Louis XIV and Marie-Thérèse put St-Jean-de-Luz on the map, and this church

BASQUE COUNTRY

Pelota

In keeping with the Basque people's seafaring, shipbuilding, and metalworking heritage, Basque sports are often feats of

strength: Who can lift the heaviest stone? Who can row the fastest and farthest?

But the most important Basque sport of all is *pelota*—similar to what you might know as jai alai. Players in white pants and red scarves or shirts use a long, hook-shaped wicker basket (called a *txistera* in Euskara) to whip a ball (smaller and far bouncier than a baseball) back and forth off walls at more than 150 miles per hour. This men's-only game can be played with a wall at one or both ends of the court. Most matches are not professional, but betting on them is common. It can also be played without a racket—this handball version is used as a starter game for kids. Children use a bouncy rubber ball, while adults use a ball with a wooden center that's rather rough on the hands and needs a lot of strength to keep moving.

It seems that every small Basque town has two things: a church and a *pelota* court (called a *frontón*). While some *frontónes* are simple and in poor repair, others are freshly painted as a gleaming sign of local pride.

The TI in St-Jean-de-Luz sells tickets and has a schedule of matches throughout the area; you're more likely to find a match in summer (almost daily at 21:00 July-mid-Sept, afternoon matches sometimes on Sat-Sun). Matches are held throughout the year (except for winter) in the villages (ask for details at TI). The professional *cesta punta* matches on Tuesdays and Fridays often come with Basque folkloric halftime shows.

is where it all took place. The ultimate in political marriages, the knot tied between Louis XIV and Marie-Thérèse in 1660 also cinched a reconciliation deal between Europe's two most powerful countries. The king of Spain, Philip IV—who lived in El Escorial palace—gave his daughter in marriage to the king of France, who lived in Versailles. This marriage united Europe's two largest palaces, which helped end a hundred years of hostility and forged an alliance that enabled both to focus attention on other matters (like England). Little St-Jean-de-Luz was selected for its 15 minutes of fame because it was roughly halfway between Madrid and Paris, and virtually on the France-Spain border. The wedding cleared out

both Versailles and El Escorial palaces, as anyone who was anyone attended this glamorous event.

The church, centered on the pedestrian street Rue Gambetta, seems modest enough from the exterior...but step inside

(free, Mon-Sat 8:00-12:00 & 14:00-18:30, Sun 8:00-12:00 & 15:00-19:00). The local expertise was in shipbuilding, so the ceiling resembles the hull of a ship turned upside-down. The dark wood balconies running along the nave segregated the men from the women and children (men went upstairs until the 1960s, as they still do in nearby villages) and were typical of Basque churches. The number of levels depended on the importance of the church, and this church, with three levels, is the largest Basque church in France.

The three-foot-long paddle-wheel ship hanging in the center was a gift from Napoleon III's wife, Eugènie. It's a model of an ill-fated ship that had almost sunk just offshore when she was on it. The box seats across from the pulpit were reserved for leading citizens who were expected to be seen in church and set a good example. Today the mayor and city council members sit here on festival Sundays.

The 1670 Baroque altar feels Franco-Spanish and features 20 French saints, with the city's patron saint—St. John the Baptist—placed prominently in the center. Locals in this proud and rich town call it the finest altar in the Basque Country. To see it better, pay €1 to switch on the automatic light (box next to the scene of the Crucifixion in the nave, on the right). The place has great acoustics, and the 17th-century organ is still used for concerts (a handful of concerts a year, get schedule at TI).

Leaving the church, turn left to find the bricked-up doorway—the church's original entrance. According to a quaint but untrue legend, it was sealed after the royal marriage (shown on the wall to the right in a photo of a painting) to symbolize a permanent closing of the door on troubles between France and Spain.

Sleeping in St-Jean-de-Luz

Hotels are more expensive here and breakfast costs extra. Those wanting to eat and sleep for less will do slightly better just over the border, in San Sebastián.

$$$$ Hôtel de la Plage*** has the best location, right on the ocean. Its 29 rooms—23 with ocean view and hardwood

floors—have pleasant, fresh decor. The contemporary seaview breakfast room sits next to a comfortable lounge (family rooms, air-con, elevator, pay parking, 33 Rue Garat, +33 5 59 51 03 44, www.hoteldelaplage.com, reservation@hoteldelaplage.com, run by friendly Pierre, Mehdi, and Gerome).

$$$ Hôtel Les Almadies,* on the main pedestrian street, is a bright boutique hotel with seven flawless rooms (4 with a balcony), comfy public spaces with clever modern touches, a pleasant breakfast room and lounge, an inviting sun deck, and a caring owner (good fans, pay parking—reserve in advance, 58 Rue Gambetta, +33 5 59 85 34 48, www.hotel-les-almadies.com, hotel.lesalmadies@orange.fr, Jen and Matthieu).

$$$ Hôtel La Marisa* is located on a quiet street just a few steps away from the beach. Its 16 rooms are filled with hardwood furniture and have maritime touches and a lavish feel. Enjoy its charming flower patio and small library (elevator, pay parking, some rooms have air-con, 16 Rue Martin de Sopite, +33 5 59 26 95 46, www.hotel-lamarisa.com, info@hotel-lamarisa.com, Frédéric and Oliver).

$$ Hôtel Ohartzia** ("Souvenir"), one block off the beach, is comfortable, clean, and peaceful, with the most charming facade I've seen. It comes with 14 updated and well-cared-for rooms, generous and homey public spaces, plus a delightful garden. Upper rooms with a balcony have town and mountain views. Several rooms are 21st-century modern with vivid colors, and two have small interior terraces (elevator, 28 Rue Garat, +33 5 59 26 00 06, www.hotel-ohartzia.com, hotel.ohartzia@wanadoo.fr). Their front desk is technically open only 8:00-21:00, but owners Madame and Monsieur Audibert (who speak little English) live in the building; their son Benoît speaks English well.

$$ Hôtel Mosaik,* on a major street a couple of blocks above the old town's charm, is simple, bright, and *très sympa* (very nice), with 22 tidy rooms and an accommodating staff (family rooms, 4 apartments, air-con, limited pay parking, closed last half of Dec, 56 Boulevard Victor Hugo, +33 5 59 26 11 90, https://mosaikhotel.com, mosaikhotel@orange.fr). To get a room over the quieter courtyard, ask for *côté cour* (koh-tay koor).

$ Hôtel Colbert* has 34 modern, tastefully appointed rooms across the street from the train station (family rooms, air-con, elevator, pay parking or park for free at lot next to train station, 3 Boulevard du Commandant Passicot, +33 5 59 26 31 99, www.hotelcolbertsaintjeandeluz.com, contact@hotelcolbertsaintjeandeluz.com).

BASQUE COUNTRY

Eating in St-Jean-de-Luz

St-Jean-de-Luz restaurants are known for offering good-value, high-quality cuisine. You can find a wide variety of eateries in the old center. For forgettable food with unforgettable views, choose from several places overlooking the beach. Most places serve from 12:15 to 14:00, and from 19:15 on. Remember, in France, *menu* means a fixed-price, multicourse meal (generally not including wine or other drinks).

The traffic-free Rue de la République, which runs from Place Louis XIV to the ocean promenade, is lined with hardworking restaurants (one of which is recommended next). Places are empty at 19:30, but packed at 20:30. Making a reservation, especially on weekends or in summer, is wise. Or consider a fun night of bar-hopping for dinner in San Sebastián instead (an hour away in Spain).

$$$$ Le Kaiku is *the* gastronomic experience in St-Jean-de-Luz. They serve modern, creatively presented cuisine, and specialize in wild seafood (rather than farmed). This dressy place, which owns a Michelin star, is the most romantic in town but manages not to be stuffy (weekday fixed-price meals, closed Sun-Mon except July-Aug, 17 Rue de la République, +33 5 59 26 13 20, www.kaiku.fr, Nicolas). For the best experience, talk with your server about what you like best and your price limits (about €85 will get you a three-course meal *à la carte* without wine).

$$$ La Boëte does seafood and fish only...and does it well. Popular with locals, it's a bustling spot just off Rue Gambetta with a small, inviting terrace (Tue-Sat 10:00-14:30 & 18:00-22:00, closed Sun-Mon, 3 Rue Jean Bague, +33 5 59 22 54 76).

$$$$ Zoko Moko offers Mediterranean nouvelle cuisine, with artistic creations on big plates. Get an *amuse-bouche* (an appetizer chosen by the chef) and a *mignardise* (a fun bite-sized dessert) with each main plate ordered. The lunchtime *menu du marché* changes weekly, depending on what's fresh in the market (€29 lunch *menu* and €56 four-course *menu;* daily except closed Sun-Mon in winter; 6 Rue Mazarin, +33 5 59 08 01 23, www.zoko-moko.com, owner Charles).

$$$ La Vieille Auberge serves up hearty, homemade, traditional Basque dishes. Their Basque egg casserole together with braised pig cheeks in wine was a highlight of my day. Choose from the reasonably priced €23.90 *menu,* or splurge on à la carte selections. The friendly staff makes it a convivial experience (Wed-Sun 12:00-14:00 and 19:00-21:00, closed Mon-Tue, reservations not accepted, 22 Rue Tourasse).

Fast and Cheap: Peruse the takeaway crêpe stands on Rue Gambetta. For a more elaborate crêpe, sit-down salad, or cheese-

and-meat platter, try **$ Corner Shop** (daily 10:00-20:00, shorter hours in winter, 22 Rue Garat, +33 6 75 42 76 73).

Breakfast: For a French-style breakfast together with a handful of locals, head to the market house and find **$ Le Café du Marché,** across from the market's main entrance (reasonable coffee, croissant, and fresh orange juice; Mon-Sat from 7:00, Sun from 9:30, 15 Avenue Labrouche, +33 5 59 26 10 75).

Sweets: Pariès is a favorite for its traditional sweets. Locals like their fine chocolates, *tartes, macarons,* fudge *(kanougas),* and *touron* (like marzipan, but firmer), which comes in a multitude of flavors—brought by Jews who stopped here just over the border in 1492 after being expelled from Spain. Their delectable *gâteau basque* is worth a try (9 Rue Gambetta, +33 5 59 26.01 46).

Chocolaterie Henriet has been a regional favorite since 1946. Walk into this quaintly elegant confectionary world and take your pick. Chocolates are priced per gram. My favorite is the *Rochers de Biarritz*—chocolate-covered roasted almonds with just a hint of orange (daily 10:00-19:00, Sun until 13:00, 10 Boulevard Thiers—just off Rue Gambetta, +33 5 59 22 08 42).

Supermarkets: There are two small groceries: **L'epicerie Gambetta** is at the east end of Rue Gambetta near Boulevard Thiers (Mon-Sat 9:30-20:00, Sun from 10:00) and **Petit Casino** is at Victor Hugo #46, a block from the post office (Mon-Sat 8:00-13:00 & 15:00-19:30, closed Sun). **Monop',** a mini grocery store at 74 Rue Gambetta, has more selection and longer hours (Mon-Sat 8:30-late, Sun until 13:00). The bigger **Carrefour City** is at the intersection of Rue Gambetta and Boulevard Victor Hugo, near the recommended Hôtel Mosaik (Mon-Sat 7:00-21:00, Sun until 13:00).

St-Jean-de-Luz Connections

The train station in St-Jean-de-Luz is called St-Jean-de-Luz-Ciboure. Buses leave from the green building across the street; use the pedestrian underpass to get there. Bus and rail service is reduced on Sundays and off-season.

From St-Jean-de-Luz by Train to: Biarritz (nearly hourly, 10 minutes), **Bayonne** (2/hour, 30 minutes), **St-Jean-Pied-de-Port** (5/day, 2.5 hours with transfer in Bayonne), **Paris** (5/day direct via high-speed TGV, 4.5 hours; more with transfer in Bordeaux, 6 hours), **Bordeaux** (6/day direct, 2.5 hours), **Sarlat** (3/day, 5-6 hours, transfer in Bordeaux), **Carcassonne** (5/day, 5-7 hours, transfer in Bordeaux or Toulouse).

By Train to San Sebastián: First, take the 10-minute train to the French border town of Hendaye (about 10/day). Or get to Hen-

daye by Car Express bus #3 (about hourly, 55 minutes, described next); check the schedule to see which leaves first.

Leave the Hendaye SNCF train station to the right and look for the small building on the same side of the street, where you'll catch the commuter EuskoTren into San Sebastián (usually 2/hour, runs about 7:00-22:30, 35 minutes).

By Bus: Chronoplus's Car Express #3 buses leave from the bus station directly across from the train station. Buy tickets from the driver or a ticket machine. The bus connects St-Jean-de-Luz to **Biarritz**'s train station (change to Chronoplus bus #5 to get into town) and **Bayonne** (2/hour, 55 minutes). It also goes the opposite direction to **Hendaye** about hourly. Be sure to check times and final destinations on the timetable at the bus stop post, or pick up the schedule at the TI (fewer departures on weekends, www. chronoplus.eu). Another bus (#45) connects St-Jean-de-Luz to **Sare** (Mon-Fri almost hourly, fewer Sat-Sun, 35 minutes, https:// hegobus.fr). BlaBlaBus runs buses to **San Sebastián** (Mon-Sat 5/ day, www.blablacar.fr/bus). Buses stop on the street in front of the green kiosk next to the bus station and take about 50 minutes.

By Excursion: If you're without a car, consider using **Le Basque Bondissant**'s day-trip excursions to visit otherwise difficult-to-reach destinations, such as the Guggenheim Bilbao (see "Tours in St-Jean-de-Luz," earlier).

By Taxi to San Sebastián: This will cost you about €75 for up to four people, but it's convenient (+33 5 59 26 10 11 or mobile +33 6 25 76 97 69).

ROUTE TIPS FOR DRIVERS

A one-day side trip to both Bayonne and Biarritz is easy from St-Jean-de-Luz. These three towns form a sort of triangle (depending on traffic, each one is less than a 30-minute drive from the other). Hop on the autoroute to Bayonne, sightsee there, then take D-810 into Biarritz. Leaving Biarritz, continue along the coastal D-810. In Bidart, watch (on the right) for the town's proud *frontón* (*pelota* court) and stop for a photo of the quaint Town Hall. Consider peeling off to go into the village center of Guéthary, with another *frontón* and a massive Town Hall. If you're up for a walk on the beach, cross the little bridge in Guéthary, park by the train station, and hike down to the walkway along the surfing beach (lined with cafés and eateries). When you're ready to move on, you're a very short drive from St-Jean-de-Luz.

Bayonne / Baiona

To feel the urban pulse of French Basque Country, visit Bayonne—modestly but honestly nicknamed "your anchor in the Basque Country" by its tourist board. With frequent, fast train and bus connections with St-Jean-de-Luz, Bayonne makes an easy half-day side trip.

Come here to browse through Bayonne's atmospheric and well-worn-yet-lively old town, and to admire its impressive Museum of Basque Culture. Known for establishing Europe's first whaling industry and for inventing the bayonet, Bayonne is more famous today for its ham *(jambon de Bayonne)* and chocolate.

Get lost in Bayonne's old town. In pretty Grand Bayonne, tall, slender buildings, decorated in Basque fashion with green-and-red shutters, climb above cobbled streets. Be sure to stroll the streets around the cathedral and along the banks of the smaller Nive River, where you'll find the market (Les Halles).

Orientation to Bayonne

Bayonne's two rivers, the grand Adour and the petite Nive, divide the city into three parts: St-Esprit, with the train station, and the more interesting Grand Bayonne and Petit Bayonne, which together make up the old town.

TOURIST INFORMATION

The modern TI sits alongside a lengthy parking lot one block off the mighty Adour River, on the northeastern edge of Grand Bayonne. They have very little in English other than a map and a town brochure, but there's always someone on staff who speaks English (July-Aug Mon-Sat 9:30-18:30, Sun 10:00-13:00; shorter hours and closed Sun off-season; Place des Basques, +33 5 59 46 09 00, www.visitbayonne.com). In summer, they sometimes offer a two-hour tour in English (€8, leaves at 15:00).

ARRIVAL IN BAYONNE

By Train: The TI and Grand Bayonne are a 15-minute walk from the train station. Walk straight out of the station, cross the parking lot and traffic circle, and then cross the imposing bridge (Pont St. Esprit). Once past the big Adour River, continue across a smaller

bridge (Pont Mayou), which spans the smaller Nive River. Stop on Pont Mayou to orient yourself: You just left Petit Bayonne (left side of Nive River); ahead of you is Grand Bayonne (spires of cathedral straight ahead, TI a few blocks to the right). The Museum of Basque Culture is in Petit Bayonne, facing the next bridge up the Nive River.

By Car or Bus: The handiest parking is also where buses (and the electric Tram'Bus connecting Bayonne and Biarritz) arrive in Bayonne: next to the TI at the modern parking lot on the edge of Grand Bayonne. To reach the town center from here, walk past the war memorial and through the break in the ramparts. Follow the walkway until you reach a fancy gate that leads through a tunnel. After the tunnel, turn right at the next street; the cathedral should immediately come into view. Continue behind the cathedral and walk down, down, down any of the atmospheric streets to find Les Halles (the market) and the Nive River.

To reach this parking lot, **drivers** take the *Bayonne Sud* exit from the autoroute, then follow green *Bayonne Centre* signs, then white *Centre-Ville* signs (with an *i* for tourist information). You'll see the lot on your right. Payment machines accept coins and cards. In high season, when this lot can be full, use one of the lots just outside the center (follow signs to *Glain*—€1/day—or *Porte d'Espagne* as you arrive in town), then catch the little orange *navette* (shuttle bus) to get into the center (free, find route maps posted at stops in town, every 8 minutes, Mon-Sat 7:30-19:30, none on Sun).

HELPFUL HINTS

Laundry: Laverie is under a colonnade directly across the street from the TI (self-service, daily 7:00-21:00, 8 Place des Basques, mobile +33 6 08 46 02 51). **Le Spot du Linge,** a combined laundry and café, is a few blocks from the train station (self-service and drop-off, daily 9:30-20:30, 22 Place de la Republique, www.lespotdulinge.fr).

Local Guide: Fun and energetic **Claire Lohiague** can take you on a walking tour of Bayonne (€65/person for 2-3 hours, half-day tours available), or to nearby cities or villages in the French Basque Country (hotel pickup in her minivan, mobile +33 6 85 35 96 30, argibiliak@gmail.com).

Sights in Bayonne

▲Museum of Basque Culture (Musée Basque)

This museum (in Petit Bayonne, facing the Nive River at Pont Marengo) explains French Basque culture from cradle to grave—in French, Euskara, and Spanish. Ask to borrow the pamphlets with museum descriptions in English. Artifacts and videos take

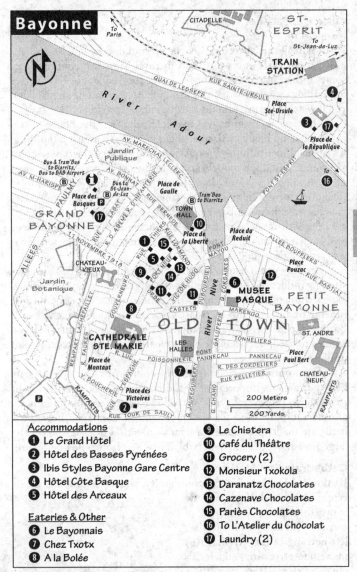

Bayonne

(Map legend:)

Accommodations
1 Le Grand Hôtel
2 Hôtel des Basses Pyrénées
3 Ibis Styles Bayonne Gare Centre
4 Hôtel Côte Basque
5 Hôtel des Arceaux

Eateries & Other
6 Le Bayonnais
7 Chez Txotx
8 A la Bolée

9 Le Chistera
10 Café du Théâtre
11 Grocery (2)
12 Monsieur Txokola
13 Daranatz Chocolates
14 Cazenave Chocolates
15 Pariès Chocolates
16 To L'Atelier du Chocolat
17 Laundry (2)

BASQUE COUNTRY

you into traditional Basque villages and sit you in the front row of time-honored festivals, letting you envision this otherwise hard-to-experience culture.

Cost and Hours: €8, free first Sun of month and Thu 18:00-20:00; open Tue-Wed and Fri-Sun 10:00-18:30, Thu 13:00-20:00, closed Mon except mid-July–mid-Aug, last entry one hour before closing; for audioguide download the Musée Basque app in ad-

vance, 37 Quai des Corsaires, +33 5 59 59 08 98, www.musee-basque.com.

Visiting the Museum: On the ground floor, you'll begin with a display of carts and tools used in rural life, then continue past some 16th-century gravestones. Look for the *laiak*—distinctive forked hoes used to work the ground. At the end of this section you'll watch a grainy film on Basque rural lifestyles.

The next floor up begins by explaining that the house *(etxea)* is the building block of Basque society. More than just a building, it's a social institution—Basques are named for their houses, not vice versa. You'll see models and paintings of Basque houses, then domestic items, a giant door, kitchen equipment, and furniture (including a combination bench-table, next to the fireplace). After viewing an exhibit on Basque clothing, you'll move into the nautical life, with models, paintings, and actual boats. The little door leads to a large model of the port of Bayonne in 1805, back when it was a strategic walled city.

Upstairs you'll learn that the religious life of the Basques was strongly influenced by the Camino de Santiago pilgrim trail, which passes through their territory. One somber space explains Basque funeral traditions. The section on social life includes a video of Basque dances (typically accompanied by flute and drums). These are improvised, but according to a clearly outlined structure—not unlike a square dance.

The prominence given to the sport of *pelota* (see sidebar, earlier) indicates its importance to the Basque people. One dimly lit room shows off several types of *txistera* baskets (*chistera* in French), gloves, and balls used for the game; videos show you how these items are made. The museum wraps up with a brief lesson on the large Jewish population here (which had fled from a hostile Spain).

Cathédrale Ste. Marie

Bankrolled by the whaling community, this cathedral sits dead-center in Grand Bayonne and is worth a peek. Centuries of construction and two major fires left nothing of the original Romanesque structure, and locals obtained stones from two different quarries (compare the colors in the facade). Find the unique keystones—reminders of British rule here in Aquitaine—on  the ceiling along the nave, then circle behind the church to find the peaceful and polished 13th-century cloister. Restoration of this

church will take several years, so expect some scaffolding and a few closed chapels.

Cost and Hours: Free, Mon-Sat 9:30-11:30 & 15:00-17:45, Sun 16:00-17:45; cloister usually accessible one hour after church opens.

Sweets Shops

With no more whales to catch, Bayonne turned to producing mouthwatering chocolates and marzipan; look for shops on the arcaded Rue du Port Neuf (running between the cathedral and the Adour River). **Daranatz** is Bayonne's best chocolate shop, with bars of chocolate blended with all kinds of flavors—one with a general mix of spices (lots of cardamom), one with just cinnamon, and another with *piments d'Espelette* (15 Arceaux Port Neuf, +33 5 59 59 03 55). **Cazenave,** founded in 1854, is a fancy *chocolaterie* with a small café in the back. Try their foamy hot chocolate with fresh whipped cream on the side, served with buttered toast for €10. You can also share one order of toast and two chocolates (Tue-Sat 9:00-12:00 & 14:00-19:00, closed Sun-Mon, 19 Rue Port Neuf, +33 5 59 59 03 16). **Pariès,** well-known throughout France, got its start in Bayonne. Their bonbons rank among the best, but for something different try the cherry-jam-filled *gâteau basque* (Mon-Sat 9:00-19:00, Sun until 13:00, 14 Rue Port Neuf, +33 5 59 59 06 29).

Chocolate Workshops

L'Atelier du Chocolat is a chocolate factory and boutique in an industrial part of town, accessible by bus. You'll see a detailed exhibit on the history and making of chocolate, some workers making luscious goodies (until 17:00), and a video in English on request. The generous chocolate tasting at the end is worth the ticket price for chocoholics.

Cost and Hours: €6.50, Mon-Fri 9:30-13:00 & 14:00-18:30, closed Sat-Sun, July-Aug no lunch break, last entry one hour before closing, 7 Allée de Gibéléou, +33 5 59 55 70 23, www.atelierduchocolat.fr. They also have a shop on Rue Port Neuf, along with the *chocolateries* mentioned earlier.

Getting There: Take city bus #4 from the TI or the Mairie stop across from the Town Hall (buy €1.20 ticket at the stop or on board), and get off at the Stade D. Deschamps stop. Backtrack and walk left onto Rue Gleizé, then head right on Allée de Gibéléou until you come to the workshop.

In-Town Option: To save time but still see a chocolate workshop, head to the much smaller **Monsieur Txokola** just a block behind the Basque Museum (Tue-Sat 10:00-18:00, closed Sun-Mon, staff may be able to provide English explanations, 11 Rue Jacques Laffitte, www.monsieurtxokola.fr).

Ramparts

The ramparts around Grand Bayonne are open for walking and great for picnicking (access from park at far end of TI parking lot). However, the ramparts do not allow access to either of Bayonne's castles—both are closed to the public.

Sleeping in Bayonne

$$$ **Le Grand Hôtel,****** with 54 rooms, is the best of the limited options in Bayonne—it's well located in Grand Bayonne, with all the comforts and a pleasant staff. While renovating their old building, the owners took care to maintain the original, classic decor (RS%—free breakfast for readers with this book, elevator, pay parking, 21 Rue Thiers, +33 5 59 59 62 00, www.legrandhotelbayonne. com, ha0y1@accor.com).

$$ **Hôtel des Basses Pyrénées****** took an ageing, turn-of-the-century hotel and added plush, modern comforts. Their 26 rooms, including 3 suites in a medieval tower, are suitably chic. Located on an open square, its adjoining restaurant also has a good reputation with locals (elevator, reserved pay parking, 12 Rue Tour de Salut, +33 5 59 25 70 88, www.hotel-bassespyrenees-bayonne. com, contact@hoteldesbassespyrenees.com).

$$ **Ibis Styles Bayonne Gare Centre***** sits next to the Pont Saint Esprit, near the train station. Some of its 45 white, bright rooms overlook the river (includes breakfast, elevator, pay parking at train station lot, 1 Place de la République, +33 5 59 55 08 08, www.ibis.com, h8716@accor.com).

$ **Hôtel Côte Basque**** is conveniently located by the train station in the Saint Esprit neighborhood, just across the river from the old town. It's on a busy street, so its 40 small-but-comfortable rooms have double-paned windows to cut the noise (family rooms, elevator, pay parking, 2 Rue Maubec, +33 5 59 55 10 21, www. hotel-cotebasque.fr, contact@hotel-cotebasque.fr).

$ **Hôtel des Arceaux,**** run by friendly Frédéric, is a B&B-style establishment with 13 rooms on a small pedestrian street in Grand Bayonne. It's just across the street from recommended chocolate shops (family room, 26 Rue Port Neuf, +33 5 59 59 15 53, hotel.arceaux@wanadoo.fr).

Eating in Bayonne

The Grand Bayonne riverside has several tapas restaurants, a couple of easy *bistrots,* and a pizza place. The Petit Bayonne riverside has some *bistrots* and a few more proper sit-down restaurants. The pedestrian streets surrounding the cathedral in Grand Bayonne offer

casual dining spots serving crêpes, *tartines*, quiches, and salads. Most places have outdoor tables in nice weather.

$$$ Le Bayonnais, next door to the Museum of Basque Culture, serves traditional Basque specialties à la carte. Sit in the blue-tiled interior or out along the river (weekday lunch specials and dinner *menu*, closed Sun-Mon, 38 Quai des Corsaires, +33 5 59 25 61 19).

$$ Chez Txotx (pronounced "choch") has a very Spanish-bodega ambience under a small chorus line of hams. You can also sit outside, along the river, just past the market hall (daily, 49 Quai Amiral Jauréguiberry, +33 5 59 59 16 80).

$$ A la Bolée serves up inexpensive sweet and savory crêpes in a cozy atmosphere along the side of the cathedral (daily, 10 Place Pasteur, +33 5 59 59 18 75).

$$$ Le Chistera proudly serves traditional Basque dishes made with market-fresh ingredients. Try the *poulet* with Basque sauce or one of their soups, and polish off your meal with home-made *gâteau basque* (good-value lunch *menu*, Tue-Sun 12:00-14:00, Thu-Sun also 19:30-21:00, closed Mon, 42 Rue Port Neuf, +33 5 59 59 25 93).

$$ Café du Théâtre has pleasant outdoor tables on a square by the river. Try it for a simple early breakfast or a delightful lunch with locals and office workers (daily 8:00-22:00, 8 Place de la Liberté, +33 5 59 59 60 00).

Picnic Supplies: If the weather's good, consider gathering a picnic from the shops along the pedestrian streets, at Les Halles market (daily, 7:00-13:30), in the Spar Supermarché (daily 7:30-21:00, 2 Rue Port de Castets, also entrance on Rue Victor Hugo), or at the Monoprix (Mon-Sat 8:30-20:00, Sun 9:00-12:45, 8 Rue Orbe). Don't forget the chocolate, then head for the park around the ramparts below the *Jardin Botanique* (benches galore).

Bayonne Connections

Chronoplus operates regular buses, a Car Express bus, and an electric Tram'bus throughout the area. Most lines run two to three times an hour from about 7:00 to 23:00 (less frequent Sat-Sun). For regular buses and the Car Express bus, buy a ticket at the stop or on the bus (regular bus-€1.20, Car Express-€2). For the Tram'bus, tickets (€1.20) can only be bought at the stop; if you plan to ride twice or more in one day, buy the 24-hour ticket for €2.20 (www.chronoplus.eu). A handy public transport map can be picked up at the TI.

From Bayonne by Bus to: BAB (Biarritz-Anglet-Bayonne) Airport (2-3/hour, 15 minutes, Car Express bus #3 or #4), **Biarritz** (Tram'bus, 4/hour, fewer on Sun, 30 minutes, line T1 from just

behind the TI near Place des Basques or from the Mairie stop at the Town Hall), **St-Jean-de-Luz** (2/hour, 55 minutes, Car Express bus #3 from in front of the TI), **Espelette** (bus #14, 1/hour, 50 minutes), **Ainhoa** (bus #3 to St-Jean-de-Luz, then bus #47; 1/hour, 45 minutes, https://hegobus.fr).

From Bayonne by Bus to San Sebastián: BlaBlaBus departs from 22 Quai de Lesseps on the opposite side of the river from the TI (5/day, fewer on Sun, 2.5 hours, www.blablacar.fr/bus). You can also take Car Express bus #3 to Hendaye and ride the EuskoTren from there (www.euskotren.eus).

By Train to: St-Jean-Pied-de-Port (4/day, 1.5 hours).

By Taxi to: Biarritz (20 minutes, about €30), **St-Jean-de-Luz** (30 minutes, about €50—or more if traffic is heavy, +33 5 59 59 48 48).

Biarritz

A glitzy resort town steeped in the belle époque, Biarritz (bee-ah-ritz) is where the French Basques put on the ritz. In the 19th cen-

tury, this simple whaling harbor became, almost overnight, a high-class aristocrat magnet dubbed the "beach of kings." Although St-Jean-de-Luz and Bayonne are more fully French and more fully Basque, the made-for-international-tourists, jet-set scene of Biarritz is not without its charms. Perched over a popular surfing beach, anchored by grand hotels and casinos, hemmed in by jagged and picturesque rocky islets at either end, and watched over by a lighthouse on a distant promontory, Biarritz is a striking beach resort. However, for sightseers with limited time, it's likely more trouble than it's worth.

Orientation to Biarritz

Biarritz feels much bigger than its population of 30,000. The town sprawls, but virtually everything we're interested in lines up along the waterfront: the beach, the promenade, the hotel and shopping zone, and the TI.

Tourist Information: The TI is in a little pink castle two blocks up from the beach (July-Aug daily 9:00-19:00; shorter hours rest of the year; Square d'Ixelles, +33 5 59 22 37 10, www.tourisme.biarritz.fr). It's just above the beach and casino, hiding behind the City Hall—look for *hôtel de ville* signs.

Arrival in Biarritz: If coming by **car,** follow signs for *Centre-Ville,* then carefully track signs for specific parking garages. The most central garages are called *Grande Plage, Casino, Bellevue,* and *St. Eugénie* (closest to the water). Signs in front of each tell you whether it's full *(complet);* if it is, move on to the next one.

Biarritz's **train** station is about two miles from town—you can connect to the city center (Mairie) on the Car Express bus #5 (€2, buy ticket from machine or driver, 3-4/hour). **Buses** from Bayonne (the electric Tram'bus) stop at "Biarritz Mairie" near the TI. Car Express bus #3 from **Hendaye** and **St-Jean-de-Luz** stops at the Biarritz train station. From there, take bus #5 into town as described above. There is no baggage storage in Biarritz.

Sights in Biarritz

There's little of sightseeing value in Biarritz. The TI can fill you in on the town's four museums (Marine Museum—described below; Chocolate Planet and Museum—intriguing, but a long walk from the center; Oriental Art Museum—large, diverse collection of art from across Asia; and Biarritz Historical Museum—really?).

Your time is best spent strolling along the various levels that climb up from the sea. (Resist the urge to check out the pebble beach for now.) From the TI, you can do a loop: First head west on the lively **pedestrian streets** that occupy the plateau above the water, which are lined with restaurants, cafés, and high-class, resorty window-shopping. (Place Georges Clemenceau is the grassy "main square" of this area.) Biarritz is picnic-friendly, with *beaucoup* benches facing the waves. Consider stocking up before continuing this walk.

Work your way past the Église Sainte Eugénie out to the point with the **Marine Museum** (Musée de la Mer). The most convenient of Biarritz's attractions, this pricey Art Deco museum/aquarium wins the "best rainy-day option" award, with a tank of seals and a chance to get face-to-teeth with live sharks (€15, generally daily 9:30-20:00, closes later in summer and earlier  in winter, last entry one hour before closing, +33 5 59 22 75 40, www.aquariumbiarritz.com).

Whether or not you're visiting the museum, it's worth hiking down to the entrance, then wandering out on the walkways that

connect the big offshore rocks. These lead to the so-called **Virgin of the Rock** (Rocher de la Vierge), topped by a statue of Mary.

From here stick along the water as you head back toward the TI. After a bit of up and down over the rocks, don't miss the trail down to **Fisherman's Wharf** (Port des Pêcheurs), a little pocket of salty authenticity that clings like barnacles to the cliff below the hotels. The remnants of an aborted construction project from the town's glory days, this little fishing settlement of humble houses and rugged jetties seems to faintly echo the Basque culture that thrived here before the glitz hit. Many of the houses have been taken over by the tourist trade (gift shops and restaurants).

Continuing along the water (and briefly back up to street level), make your way back to the town's centerpiece, the **big beach** (Grande Plage). Dominating this inviting stretch of sand is the Art Deco casino, and the TI is just above that. If you haven't yet taken the time to splash, wade, or stroll on the beach...now's your chance.

Eating in Biarritz

If you arrive early, head for **Les Halles,** a covered market great for picking up items for a picnic. Enjoy its bustling market vibe (daily 7:30-14:00, mid-July-Aug also open 18:00-21:00, 11 Rue des Halles). Many eateries surround the market, including **$$ Le Café du Commerce,** a good place for breakfast. A **Carrefour City** grocery store is also next to the market.

For lunch or a sit-down dinner, try **$$$ Le Clos Basque,** on a side street just a couple of blocks from the TI. The restaurant has an inviting terrace and an enjoyable atmosphere, and cooks up tasty Basque dishes (Thu-Sat 12:00-13:30 & 19:30-21:30, Sun lunch only, closed Mon, 12 Avenue Louis Barthou, reservations smart—call +33 5 59 24 24 96). For a meal by the sea, **$$ Casa Juan Pedro** serves up fresh seafood and meat dishes at the Fisherman's Wharf (generally daily 12:15-14:00 & 19:30-22:00, can get busy in high season, 48 Allée Port des Pêcheurs, +33 5 59 24 00 86).

Biarritz Connections

From Biarritz by Bus to: Bayonne (4/hour on Chronoplus's Tram'bus T1, fewer on Sun, 30 minutes). See details under "Bayonne Connections," earlier.

By Train to: St-Jean-de-Luz (nearly hourly, 20 minutes; from the center, take Car Express bus #5 to Biarritz train station, 3-4/hour; www.sncf.fr).

Villages in the French Basque Country

Traditional villages among the green hills, with buildings colored like the Basque flag, offer the best glimpse of Basque culture. Cheese, hard cider, and *pelota* players are the primary products of these villages, which attract few foreigners but many French summer visitors. Most of these villages have welcomed pilgrims bound for Santiago de Compostela since the Middle Ages. Today's hikers trek between local villages or head into the Pyrenees. The most appealing villages lie in the foothills of the Pyrenees, spared from beach-scene development.

Use St-Jean-de-Luz as your base to visit the Basque sights described below. For information on another French Basque village a bit farther away—St-Jean-Pied-de-Port (Donibane Garazi), the starting point of the Camino de Santiago pilgrim trail—see the next chapter. You can reach some of these places by public transportation, but the hassle outweighs the rewards.

Do a circuit of these towns in the order they're listed here (and, with time, add St-Jean-Pied-de-Port at the end). Assuming you're driving, I've included route instructions as well.

• *Only 15 minutes from St-Jean-de-Luz, follow signs for Ascain, then Sare. On the twisty-turny road toward Sare, you'll pass the station for the train up to...*

La Rhune/Larrun

Between the villages of Ascain and Sare, near the border with Spain, a small cogwheel train takes tourists to the top of La Rhune, the region's highest peak (2,969 feet). You'll putt-putt up the hillside for 35 minutes in a wooden, open-air train car to reach panoramic views of land and sea (€20 round-trip, April-mid-Sept daily 8:00-17:00, shorter hours in winter, departures weather-dependent—the trip is worthless if it's not clear, goes every 35 minutes when busiest July-Aug, buy ticket ahead in summer, +33 5 59 54 20 26, www.rhune.com). For those traveling without a car, buses run from St-Jean-de-Luz (take #45 from the bus station and get off at Col de Saint-Ignace; 8/day Mon-Sat, 3/day Sun, 20 minutes, https://hegobus.fr).

• *Continue along the same road and look for pull-offs with room for a couple of cars, typically placed at the most scenic spots. Stop to smell the grass before the next stop...*

Sare/Sara

Sare, which sits at the base of the towering mountain La Rhune, is among the most picturesque villages—and the most touristed. It's easily reached from St-Jean-de-Luz by bus or car. The small TI is on the main square; pick up a map for suggested walking routes in

town (Mon-Fri 9:00-12:30 & 14:00-17:30, closed Sat-Sun, +33 5 59 54 20 14, www.en-pays-basque.fr). Nearby is a cluster of hotels and the town church (which has an impressive interior, with arches over the gold-slathered altar and Basque-style balconies lining the nave). Reforms in the 18th century prohibited burials at or near Catholic churches, but Basque-style tombstones still surround the main church. At the far end of the square is the town's humble *frontón* (*pelota* court).

• *Leaving Sare, first follow signs for* toutes directions, *then St–Pée, and watch for the turnoff to...*

Ainhoa/Ainhoa

Ainhoa is a colorful, tidy, picturesque one-street town that sees fewer tourists (which is a good thing). Its chunks of old walls and gates mingle with red-and-white half-timbered buildings. The 14th-century church—with a beautiful golden *retable* (screen behind the altar)—and the *frontón* share center stage. Parking is plentiful; resist the urge to turn off at the *frontón*—it's better to continue on for parking near the TI. At the TI, pick up

a town map and ask to see the free 25-minute movie about Ainhoa (Mon-Fri 9:00-12:30 & 14:00-17:30, closed Sat-Sun, +33 5 59 29 93 99).

Ainhoa is also a popular starting point for hikes into the hills. For a spectacular village-and-valleys view, drive five minutes (or walk 60 sweaty minutes) up the steep dirt road to the Chapelle de Notre-Dame d'Aranazau ("d'Aubepine" in French). Start in the central parking lot directly across the main street from the church, then head straight uphill into the clouds. Follow signs for *oratoire*, then count the giant white crosses leading the way to the top. The chapel is occasionally closed, and cloudy days don't offer spectacular views, but the ethereal experience is worth the steep detour for drivers.

• *As you leave Ainhoa, you'll have to backtrack the way you came in to find the road to...*

Espelette/Ezpeleta

Espelette won't let you forget that it's the capital of the region's AOC red peppers (*piments d'Espelette*), with strands of them dangling like good-luck charms from many houses and storefronts. Start by visiting the Red Pepper Interpretive Center (Centre d'Interprétation du Piment), and watch the worthwhile 15-min-

ute video explaining the history and the planting process (Mon-Fri 10:00-13:00 & 14:00-17:00, closed Sat-Sun, 25 Merkatu Plaza, +33 5 59 93 88 86, www.pimentdespelette.com).

Afterward, head to the well-restored château and medieval tower of former local barons, which now houses the Town Hall, exhibition space, and the TI (Mon-Fri 9:00-12:30 & 14:00-18:00, Sun 10:00-13:00, shorter hours in winter, +33 5 59 93 95 02, www.en-pays-basque.fr). From here, stroll through the charming, cobbled center, or wander downhill toward the pink *frontón*, following the *église* signs past houses constructed in the 1700s and a captivating stream, to find the town church. Climb up into the church balconies for some fancy views.

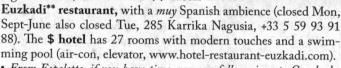

Sleeping and Eating: For a good regional meal, consider the **$$ Hôtel Euzkadi** restaurant,** with a *muy* Spanish ambience (closed Mon, Sept-June also closed Tue, 285 Karrika Nagusia, +33 5 59 93 91 88). The **$ hotel** has 27 rooms with modern touches and a swimming pool (air-con, elevator, www.hotel-restaurant-euzkadi.com).

• *From Espelette, if you have time, you can follow signs to Cambo les Bains, then St-Jean-Pied-de-Port (40 minutes, covered in the next chapter).*

BASQUE COUNTRY

THE CAMINO DE SANTIAGO

St-Jean-Pied-de-Port • Pamplona • Burgos • León •
O Cebreiro • Lugo • Cantabria

The Camino de Santiago—the "Way of St. James"—is Europe's ultimate pilgrimage route. Since the Middle Ages, humble pilgrims have trod hundreds of miles across the north of Spain to pay homage to the remains of St. James in his namesake city, Santiago de Compostela. After several lonely centuries, the route has been rediscovered, and more and more pilgrims are traveling—by foot, bike, and horse—along this ancient pathway.

While dedicating a month of your life to walk the Camino is admirable, you might not have that kind of time. But with a car (or public transportation), any traveler can use the Camino as a sightseeing spine—a string of worthwhile cities, towns, and countryside sights—and an opportunity to periodically "play pilgrim."

There were many ancient pilgrimage routes across Europe to Santiago de Compostela, but the most popular one across Spain—and the route described here—has always been the so-called "French Road" (Camino Francés), which covers nearly 500 miles across northern Spain from the French border to Santiago.

The route begins in the French foothills of the Pyrenees, in the Basque village of St-Jean-Pied-de-Port. Twist up and over rugged Roncesvalles Pass into Spain, and on to Pamplona—the delightful Basque-flavored capital of Navarre, famous for its Running of the Bulls. From here, head west through the fertile hills of Navarre to the vineyards of La Rioja, then across the endless wheat fields and rough, arid plains of northern Castile to Burgos and León, with their beautiful dueling Gothic cathedrals—one a riot of architectural styles, the other gracefully simple but packed with stained glass.

As the path crosses into Galicia near the time-passed stony mountain village of O Cebreiro, the terrain changes, becoming lush and green. This last leg of the journey, in Galicia, is the most popular: Pilgrims pass simple farms, stone churches, moss-covered homes with slate roofs, apple orchards, flocks of sheep, dense forests of oak, sweet chestnut, and eucalyptus...and plenty of other pilgrims. Just before Santiago, the ancient walled Roman city of Lugo is a worthwhile detour for car travelers.

Whether undertaken for spiritual edification or sightseeing pleasure, the Camino de Santiago ties together some of Spain's most appealing landscape, history, architecture, and people.

And if you're traveling between the Basque Country (see previous chapter) and Galicia (Santiago de Compostela), consider several interesting stops in the province of Cantabria, along Spain's northern coast. These include the appealing town of Santillana del Mar (close to the prehistoric Altamira Caves); Comillas, a beach town with fine examples of Modernista architecture (even a Gaudí); and the dramatic Picos de Europa mountains.

GETTING AROUND THE CAMINO DE SANTIAGO

By Car: This chapter is geared for car pilgrims who want to trace the Camino and linger at the highlights. Italicized directions marked by a bullet point are designed for drivers (with specific route tips, road numbers, and directional signs). To supplement these instructions, it's essential to have GPS and carry a good road map (most TIs can give you a free map covering just their province, or you can buy a better one by Michelin or Mapa Total for about €6). Driving the full Camino nonstop would take about 12 hours. Assuming you're taking the most direct (expressway/*autovía*) route, figure these estimated times for specific legs of the Camino by car (these times don't take into account stops or detours, such as the Rioja Wine Loop):

- St-Jean-Pied-de-Port to Pamplona—1.5 hours
- Pamplona to Burgos—2.5-3 hours (depending on route)
- Burgos to León—2 hours
- León to Astorga—1 hour
- Astorga to O Cebreiro—1-1.5 hours (depending on route)
- O Cebreiro to Lugo—1 hour
- Lugo to Santiago—1.75 hours

Many freeways are marked *Autovía Camino de Santiago* to keep you on track. But be warned that *Camino de Santiago* directional signs in small towns can be misleading, since they're sometimes intended for foot pilgrims, not drivers. Navigate by town names and road numbers instead.

By Public Transportation: Most of the Camino route can be done by bus and/or train. However, it can be difficult, or even im-

The Camino de Santiago at a Glance

These attractions are listed in the order you'll reach them as you traverse the Camino de Santiago.

▲**St-Jean-Pied-de-Port** Tranquil French mountain village clustered along a babbling stream—the perfect springboard for the Camino. See page 271.

Roncesvalles Middle-of-nowhere spot where Camino walkers catch their collective breath after the exhausting first leg over the Pyrenees. See page 275.

▲▲**Pamplona** Thriving Basque town (a.k.a. Iruña) with atmospheric narrow lanes, fine churches, and world-famous Running of the Bulls. See page 279.

▲**Puente la Reina** Classic Camino pilgrim town with a perfectly picturesque bridge. See page 297.

Irache Monastery Legendary "wine fountain" lifting pilgrims' spirits in the middle of nowhere. See page 298.

▲**La Rioja** A detour (near skippable city of Logroño) into pastoral wine country, worthwhile for oenophiles and those intrigued by charming wine towns (Laguardia) and contemporary architecture (with wineries by Gehry and Calatrava). See page 298.

possible, to reach some of the out-of-the-way stops between the big cities (such as O Cebreiro). Where feasible, I've listed train and bus connections for each of the main stops. Trains cover all the major cities, and Alsa buses also link the main stops (www.alsa.es).

The Old-Fashioned Way: If you're walking or biking the entire Camino, don't rely exclusively on my coverage in this chapter (which describes the major towns and cities but ignores so much more). Equip yourself with a good day-by-day guidebook with details on each leg, and get good advice about what to pack. For starters, see the "Walking the Way" sidebar on page 312.

Santo Domingo de la Calzada Dusty village with fun legends and pilgrim amenities. See page 299.

▲**Burgos** Sprawling but walkable city centered on its glorious Gothic cathedral, with loads of quirky touches. See page 302.

▲▲**León** Bustling city with grand Gothic cathedral (crammed with Spain's best stained glass), fresco-slathered Romanesque chapel (in the San Isidoro Museum), and lively tapas-bar scene. See page 315.

▲**Astorga** Historic chocolate town graced with Antoni Gaudí's visit-worthy Bishop's Palace. See page 326.

Villafranca del Bierzo Sleepy pilgrim town perched on rugged hills at the edge of Galicia. See page 330.

▲▲**O Cebreiro** Quintessential Galician mountain village, with stone *palloza* hobbit houses, a pre-Romanesque church, and oodles of pilgrim ambience. See page 332.

▲**Lugo** Atmospheric Galician city just off the Camino, lassoed by stout, mossy walls. See page 335.

▲▲**Santiago de Compostela** Destination of all those pilgrims, with an invigorating cityscape and a dramatic cathedral that's not a letdown, even after a 500-mile walk. See the next chapter.

PLANNING YOUR TIME

Drivers begin in Basque Country (San Sebastián in Spain or St-Jean-de-Luz in France), where you can pick up your rental car. If you're in a hurry or don't plan to visit France, you can skip St-Jean-Pied-de-Port and connect easily to Pamplona from Spain's Basque Country.

Day 1: Drive through the French Basque villages (see previous chapter) to St-Jean-Pied-de-Port, then over Roncesvalles Pass to Pamplona. Sleep in Pamplona.

Day 2: Explore Pamplona, then drive westward to Burgos (stopping en route at Puente la Reina, and detouring for the Rioja Wine Loop if you have time and a healthy interest in wine). Sleep in Burgos.

Day 3: Sightsee Burgos this morning, then drive to León and dip into the cathedral there. Sleep in León—or, if you're tired of big cities, continue an hour farther to sleep in Astorga.

Day 4: Continue westward to Galicia, stopping at O Cebreiro and Lugo before arriving at Santiago de Compostela.

ORIENTATION TO THE CAMINO

The term "Camino de Santiago" actually refers to many different routes across Europe. All travel from east to west. For my description of the popular "French Road" (Camino Francés), we'll begin in the French Basque town of St-Jean-Pied-de-Port, cross over the Pyrenees at Roncesvalles, then pass through three northern Spanish cities (Pamplona, Burgos, León), before climbing into green Galicia, ending at Santiago de Compostela.

Tourist Information: Pilgrims will find no shortage of helpful resources along the way. In addition to TIs in each town (listed in this chapter), you'll also find "Pilgrim Friend" associations and other offices (often attached to an *albergue* or *refugio*) that offer kind advice to the weary traveler.

Holy Year: The Compostela Holy Year *(Año Xacobeo)* occurs when the Feast of St. James (July 25) falls on a Sunday (next in 2027); during a Holy Year, traffic on the trails doubles, and the pilgrim atmosphere is even more festive.

Tours: Iberian Adventures runs guided and self-guided walking and hiking tours in English for individuals and small groups along the Camino de Santiago and on Spain's northern

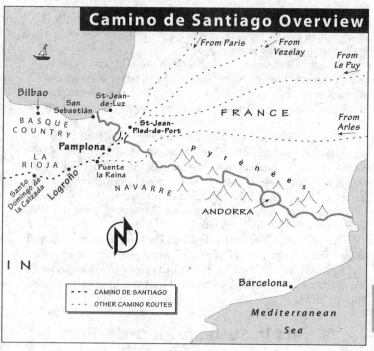

Camino de Santiago Overview

From Paris   From Vezelay

From Le Puy

Bilbao

San Sebastián   St-Jean-de-Luz

St-Jean-Pied-de-Port

BASQUE COUNTRY

FRANCE

From Arles

Pamplona

LA RIOJA

Santo Domingo de la Calzada

Logroño

Puente la Reina

NAVARRE

P y r é n é e s

ANDORRA

IN

Barcelona

--- CAMINO DE SANTIAGO
--- OTHER CAMINO ROUTES

Mediterranean Sea

coast, as well as through major mountain ranges, such as the Pyrenees and Picos de Europa. Company owner Jeremy Dack highlights each area's natural environment, history, culture, cuisine, and wine, and emphasizes environmental awareness and respect for local customs (+34 620 939 116, www.iberianadventures.com, info@iberianadventures.com).

St-Jean-Pied-de-Port

Just five miles from the Spanish border, the walled town of St-Jean-Pied-de-Port (san-zhahn-pee-ay-duh-por) is the most popu-

lar village in all the French Basque countryside (you may also see it labeled as Donibane Garazi, its Basque name). Traditionally, St-Jean-Pied-de-Port has been the final stopover in France for Santiago-bound pilgrims, who gather here to cross the

Pyrenees together and continue their march through Spain. The scallop shell of "St. Jacques" (French for "St. James") is etched on walls throughout the town.

About half the visitors to this town are pilgrims; the rest are mostly French tourists. Gift shops sell a strange combination of pilgrim gear (such as quick-drying shirts and shorts) and Basque souvenirs. This place is packed in the summer (so come early or late).

Tourist Information: The TI is on the main road along the outside of the walled old town (Mon-Sat 9:30-12:30 & 14:00-18:00, closed Sun except July-Aug Sun 10:00-13:00; +33 5 59 37 03 57, www.en-pays-basque.fr). For Camino information, you'll do better at the Pilgrim Friends Office (described later). Ask the TI about weekly *pelota vasca* games (usually Mon at 17:00 at the *trinquet* court on Place du Trinquet).

Arrival in St-Jean-Pied-de-Port: Parking is ample and well signed from the main road. If arriving by **train,** exit the station to the left, then follow the first road to the right (Avenue Renaud). Signs for the TI and the Camino will lead you uphill to a gate in the city wall.

Sights in St-Jean-Pied-de-Port

There's little in the way of sightseeing here, other than pilgrim-spotting. But St-Jean-Pied-de-Port feels like the perfect "Welcome to

the Camino" springboard for the upcoming journey. Many modern pilgrims begin their Camino in this traditional spot because of its easy train connection to Bayonne, and because—as its name implies ("St. John at the Foot of the Pass")—it offers a very challenging but rewarding first leg: up, over, and into Spain.

After passing through the gate in the city wall, follow Rue de France to the main drag, Rue de la Citadelle. Head left, uphill, and stop at #39, the **Pilgrim Friends Office** (Les Amis du Chemin de Saint-Jacques, daily 7:30-12:00 & 14:00-20:00, Fri and Sun until 22:00, +33 5 59 37 05 09). This is where pilgrims check in before their long journey to Santiago.

For €2, pilgrims can buy the official credential (*credenciel* in French, *credencial* in Spanish) that they'll get stamped at each stop between here and Santiago to prove they walked the whole way and thereby earn their *compostela* certificate. Pilgrims also

receive a warm welcome, lots of advice (like a handy chart breaking down the walk into 34 stages, with valuable distance and elevation information), and help finding a bunk (the well-traveled staff swears that no pilgrim ever goes without a bed in St-Jean-Pied-de-Port).

A few more steps up, on the left, you'll pass the skippable Bishop's Prison (Prison des Evêques). Continue on up to the **citadel,** dating from the mid-17th century—when this was a highly strategic location for keeping an eye on the easiest road over the Pyrenees between Spain and France. Although this stout fortress is not open to the public (as it houses a school), the grounds around it offer sweeping views over the French Basque countryside.

Now backtrack downhill toward the river. With rosy-pink buildings and ancient dates above doorways, this lane simply feels old. Notice lots of signs for *chambres* (rooms) and *refuges*—humble, hostel-like pilgrim bunkhouses. The **Notre-Dame Gate,** which was once a drawbridge, is straight ahead. Cross the old bridge over the Nive River (the same one that winds up in Bayonne) and head up **Rue d'Espagne** to restaurant row—Rue d'Uhart—for a break before your Camino begins.

Sleeping and Eating in St-Jean-Pied-de-Port

Sleeping: Lots of humble pilgrim lodgings line the main drag, Rue de la Citadelle. If you're looking for a bit more comfort, consider these options (stars are based on the French rating system).

$$ Hotel Ramuntcho** is the only real hotel option in the old town, located partway up Rue de la Citadelle. Its 17 rooms, above a spacious breakfast room, are straightforward but modern (1 Rue de France, +33 5 59 37 03 91, www.hotel-ramuntcho.com, hotel.ramuntcho@wanadoo.fr).

$ Itzalpea,** a café and teahouse, rents five rooms along the main road just outside the old town (closed Sat off-season, air-con, 5 Place du Trinquet, +33 5 59 37 03 66, www.hotel-itzalpea.com, itzalpea@wanadoo.fr).

$ Maison Simonenia has five clean and bright rooms along the main drag. A small breakfast is served on the patio (12 Rue de la Citadelle, +33 5 59 37 56 10, https://hommetelsa.wixsite.com/simonenia, simonenia@orange.fr).

Eating: Tourists, pilgrims, and locals alike find plenty of **$$** places to eat along Rue de la Citadelle (heading up to the citadel), Rue du Trinquet (the main traffic street into town), and Rue d'Uhart. Consider **Café de Navarre** (1 Place Juan de Huarte, +33 5 59 37 01 67), **Cafe Ttipia** (2 Place Charles Floquet, +33 5 59 37

Best Stages for a Short Walk

The Camino de Santiago is divided into 34 stages of about 12 to 15 miles apiece (approximately one day's walk). Even if you're doing most of the Camino by car, consider taking an extra day or two to walk one of these recommended stages (to get back to your car, catch a bus—TIs have schedules—or, where buses aren't an option, take a taxi). These stages are scattered throughout the Camino and are listed from east to west.

Roncesvalles to Zubiri (21.5 km/13.5 miles): This is the first stage in Spain, after the arduous trek over the Pyrenees. It's mostly (though not entirely) downhill, through rolling hills and meadows, amidst sheep and charming villages.

Puente la Reina to Estella (19 km/12 miles): Here the Camino becomes a bit more level and arid. This leg begins in an appealing pilgrim town, then passes through gentle farm fields and along a three-and-a-half-mile stretch of Roman road (from Cirauqui to Lorca).

Pieros to Villafranca del Bierzo (7.5 km/5 miles): For this stretch, the Camino ascends through the hilly El Bierzo region, en route to Galicia. The last bit of this leg takes you through vineyards and vegetable patches into Villafranca, entering the town at the Romanesque church of Santiago.

Ambasmestas to O Cebreiro (13.2 km/8.2 miles): If you're not intimidated by a steep uphill hike, this leg is a gorgeous introduction to Galicia—culminating at a perfect little hilltop village.

Sarria to Portomarin (21.5 km/13.5 miles): Because it's about 100 kilometers (62 miles) from Santiago (the minimum to qualify for a *compostela certificate*), Sarria is a popular starting point for short-haul pilgrims. From here you can make it to Santiago in less than a week. The terrain: pretty Galicia.

11 96), or **Restaurant Oillarburu** (8 Rue de l'Eglise, +33 5 59 37 06 44), all very popular with locals. If you're lucky enough to land here on a Monday morning, shop at the **weekly market,** where farmers, cheesemakers, and winemakers bring their products from the countryside.

St-Jean-Pied-de-Port Connections

A scenic train conveniently links St-Jean-Pied-de-Port to **Bayonne** (4/day, 1 hour) and from there to **St-Jean-de-Luz** (about 45 minutes beyond Bayonne, www.sncf.fr). It's about a 1.5-hour drive to St-Jean-de-Luz. There is also limited bus service from St-Jean-Pied-de-Port to **Pamplona** (bus stop at Place Juan de Huarte

near Hôtel Les Remparts, 1/day, 1.5 hours, run by the Spanish line Alsa, www.alsa.es). NavarVIP offers taxi service to Pamplona for about €100 (+34 948 102 100, www.navarvip.com, Luis).

From St-Jean-Pied-de-Port to Pamplona

The first stretch of the Camino, crossing the Pyrenees from France into Spain, is among the most dramatic. There's little in the way of civilization, but this stretch from St-Jean-Pied-de-Port to Pamplona is a memorable start for the journey.

• *From St-Jean-Pied-de-Port, look for green signs to* Pamplona, *then follow road signs to* **Arnéguy** *on road D-933. (But be warned that the road signs for* Camino de Santiago *take a much more roundabout high-mountain, one-lane road instead of the direct road to the border.)*

As you go over the **stone bridge** in the village of Arnéguy, you're passing from France into Spain. For centuries this bridge was the site of a delicate dance between nervous smugglers and customs police. Today you'll barely notice you've crossed a border, except for the gigantic *ventas*—large duty-free malls catering to a mainly Spanish clientele. Along the drive, keep a watchful eye out for stone pillars with crosses—old trail markers for pilgrims.

The road meanders through a valley before twisting up to the pass called **Puerto de Ibañeta** (also known as the Roncesvalles Pass). This scrubby high-mountain pass is one of the Basque Country's most historic spots. The most accessible gateway through the Pyrenees between France and Spain, this pass has been the site of several epic battles. According to a popular medieval legend, Charlemagne's nephew Roland was killed fighting here. Vengeful Basque tribes, seeking retribution for Charlemagne's sacking of Pamplona, followed the army as it began its return to France—and felled the mighty Roland along this very road. Several centuries later, Napoleon used the same road to invade Spain.

Coming down from the pass, you reach **Roncesvalles/Orreaga** ("Valley of Pines"), which gave this area its name. This jumble of buildings surrounding a monastery is sort of a pilgrim depot, where travelers can pause to catch their collective breath after clearing the first arduous leg of the Camino. The big building on the right is a simple *refugio,* filled with

The History of the Camino

The first person to undertake the Camino de Santiago was...Santiago himself. After the death of Christ, the apostles scattered to the corners of the earth to spread the Word of God. Supposedly, St. James went on a missionary trip from the Holy Land all the way to the northwest corner of Spain, which at that time really was the end of the Western world. (For more on St. James, see the sidebar on page 357.)

According to legend, St. James' remains were discovered in 813 in the town that would soon bear his name. This put Santiago de Compostela on the map, as one of three places—along with Rome and Jerusalem—where remains of apostles are known to be buried. In 951 the bishop of Le Puy in France walked to Santiago de Compostela to pay homage to the relics. As other pilgrims followed his example, the Camino de Santiago informally emerged. Then, in the 12th century, Pope Callistus II decreed that any person who walked to Santiago in a Holy Year, confessed their sins, and took Communion at the cathedral would be forgiven. This opportunity for a cheap indulgence made the Camino de Santiago one of the most important pilgrimages in the world.

It's probably no coincidence that St. James' remains were "discovered" and promoted just as the Reconquista was in full swing. The pope's decree helped to consolidate the Christians' hold over lands retaken from the Moors. Pilgrims were ideal candidates to repopulate and defend northern Spain. Many of those who made the journey to Santiago stuck around somewhere along the route (often because of privileges granted them by local rulers who needed help rebuilding). It became a self-sustaining little circle: Pilgrims came along the Camino, saw great sights, and decided to stay...to build even greater sights for the next pilgrims to enjoy.

The Christian monarchy designated an old Roman commercial road from France across northern Iberia as the "official" route, and soon churches, monasteries, hostels, hospitals, blacksmiths, and other pilgrims' services began to pop up. Religious-military orders such as the Knights of Santiago and the Knights Templar protected the route from bandits and fought alongside Christian armies against the Moorish resurgence, allowing the evolving Catholic state to gather strength in the safe haven created by the Camino.

In the Middle Ages, pilgrims came to Santiago from all over Europe. Many prominent figures embarked on the journey, includ-

ing St. Francis of Assisi, Dutch painter Jan van Eyck, and the Wife of Bath in Chaucer's *Canterbury Tales.*

This steady flow of pilgrims from around Europe resulted in a rich exchange of knowledge, art, and architecture. Even today you'll find magnificent cathedrals along the Camino in cities such as Burgos and León, which incorporated and improved on the latest in cathedral design from France at that time.

By 1130 the trek was so popular that it prompted a French monk named Aimery Picaud to pen (likely with the help of some ghostwriters) a chronicle of his journey, including tips on where to eat, where to stay, the best way to get from place to place, and how to pack light and use a money belt. This Codex Calixtinus (Latin for "Camino Through the Back Door") was the world's first guidebook—the great-great-granddaddy of the one you're holding right now.

In the age of Columbus, the Renaissance, and the Reformation, interest in the Camino dropped way off. When the Moors were finally defeated in 1492, the significance of Reconquista icon St. James fell by the wayside. The discovery of the New World in the same year led both the Church and the monarchy to turn their attention across the Atlantic, and the pilgrimage began to wane. That was followed by a century of religious wars pitting Catholics against Protestants, which also distracted potential pilgrims. Feeling threatened by the pirate Francis Drake (not considered "sir" in Spain), the church hid the remains of St. James so thoroughly that they were lost for generations. Meanwhile, the rise of humanism during the Renaissance diminished the mystique of the pilgrimage. For the next centuries, and as recently as a few decades ago, only a few hardy souls followed the route.

In the late 1960s, a handful of parish priests along the Camino began working to recover the route, establishing associations of "friends of the Camino" that would eventually agree on a path and mark it. They received help from none other than Generalísimo Francisco Franco, who decided that Catholicism and nationalism went hand-in-hand. By reviving the Camino, he reasoned, Spain was assured to relive its most glorious days. In 1982, and again in 1989, Pope John Paul II visited Santiago de Compostela, reminding the world of the town's historic significance. In 1987 the European Union designated the Camino as Europe's first Cultural Itinerary. And after the success of the 1992 Expo in Sevilla, the Galician government decided to pour funds into reviving the tradition for the Holy Year in 1993.

The plan worked, and now—aided by European Union funding—the route has enjoyed a huge renaissance of interest, with more than 200,000 pilgrims each year trekking to Santiago. Cyclists and horse riders are now joining hikers on the journey, and these days it's "in" to follow the seashells to Santiago.

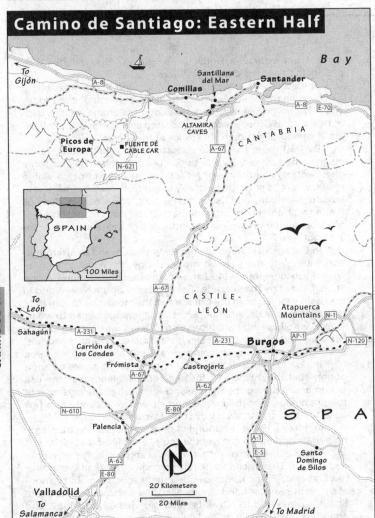

Camino de Santiago: Eastern Half

Bay

To Gijón

A-8

Comillas

Santillana del Mar

Santander

A-8

E-70

ALTAMIRA CAVES

CANTABRIA

A-67

Picos de Europa

FUENTE DÉ CABLE CAR

N-621

SPAIN

100 Miles

A-67

CASTILE-LEÓN

To León

Atapuerca Mountains

N-1

Sahagún

A-231

A-231

Burgos

AP-1

N-120

Carrión de los Condes

Frómista

A-67

Castrojeriz

A-62

N-610

E-80

S P A

Palencia

A-1

E-5

Santo Domingo de Silos

A-62

E-80

20 Kilometers

20 Miles

Valladolid

To Salamanca

To Madrid

bunk beds. In the afternoon, you might see pilgrims washing their clothes at the spigots in front, then hanging them to dry amid the cows and knobby trees out back. The big church (on the left) has a tourable cloister and museum (€5 for both, daily 10:00-14:00 & 15:30-19:00, off-season until 18:00, includes audioguide, guided tours but no fixed times or guarantee of English). As you leave town, you pass the first sign for Santiago de Compostela...790 kilometers (490 miles) straight ahead.

From here to Pamplona, the Camino passes through some pretty rolling hills and meadows, and several appealing villages.

CAMINO DE SANTIAGO

The first after Roncesvalles, picture-perfect **Auritz/Burguete,** was supposedly Hemingway's favorite place to fish for trout when he needed to recover from a Pamplona bender.

Zubiri marks the halfway point between the pass and Pamplona, with two powerful reminders of the old Basque Country: a Guardia Civil bunker built to withstand separatist bomb attacks, and a giant magnetite quarry mined for steel production.

• *Around that next bend is the first big city on the Camino: Pamplona.*

Pamplona

Proud Pamplona, with stout old walls standing guard in the Pyrenees foothills, is the capital of the province of Navarre ("Navarra" in Spanish). At its peak in the Middle Ages, Navarre was a grand kingdom that controlled parts of today's Spain and France. (The king of Spain, Felipe VI, is a descendant of the French line of Navarre royalty.) After the French and Spanish parts split, Pamplona remained the capital of Spanish Navarre.

Today Pamplona—called "Iruña" in the Basque language—feels at once affluent (with the sleek new infrastructure of a town on the rise), claustrophobic (with its warren of narrow lanes), and fascinating (with its odd traditions, rich history, and ties to Hemingway). Culturally, the city is a lively hodgepodge of Basque and Navarro. Locals like to distinguish between Vascos (people of Basque citizenship—not them) and Vascones (people who identify culturally as Basques—as do many Navarros). Pamplona is also an important seat for a controversial wing of the Catholic Church, Opus Dei, founded in Spain in 1928 by the Catholic priest Josemaría Escrivá. He established the private Pamplona-based University of Navarra, and Opus Dei also runs a hospital and several schools in the city.

Of course, Pamplona is best known as the host of one of Spain's (and Europe's) most famous festivals: the Running of the Bulls (held in conjunction with the Fiesta de San Fermín, July 6-14). For latecomers, San Fermín Txikito ("Little San Fermín") offers a less touristy alternative in late September. But there's more to this town than bulls—and, in fact, visiting at other times is preferable to the crowds and 24/7 party atmosphere that seize Pamplona during the festival. Contrary to the chaotic or even backward image that its famous festival might suggest, Pamplona generally feels welcoming, sane, and enjoyable.

Orientation to Pamplona

Pamplona has about 200,000 people. Most everything of interest is in the tight, twisting lanes of the old town *(casco antiguo)*, centered on the main square, Plaza del Castillo. The newer Ensanche ("Expansion") neighborhood just to the south—with a sensible grid plan—holds several good hotels and the bus station.

TOURIST INFORMATION

Pamplona's TI is located next to City Hall (daily 9:00-14:00 & 15:00-20:00, shorter hours off-season, on Plaza Consistorial at Calle San Saturnino 2, +34 948 420 700, www.pamplona.es/turismo).

ARRIVAL IN PAMPLONA

You can store bags at the bus station, but not at the train station.

By Bus: The sleek, user-friendly bus station is underground along the western edge of the Ensanche area at Calle Yanguas y Miranda 2, about a 10-minute walk from the old-town sightseeing zone. The station has a multilingual information desk that makes trip planning a breeze (Mon-Fri 10:00-14:00 & 15:00-19:00, Sat-Sun 10:00-13:00 & 16:00-19:00, +34 948 203 566). On arrival, go up the escalators, cross the street, turn left, and walk a half-block, where you can turn right down the busy Conde Oliveto street. Along this street, you're near several of my recommended accommodations—or you can walk two blocks to the big traffic circle called Plaza Príncipe de Viana. From here, turn left up Avenida de San Ignacio to reach the old town.

By Train: The Renfe station is farther from the center, across the river to the northwest. It's easiest to hop on public bus #9 (€1.35, pay driver, every 15 minutes), which stops at the big Plaza Príncipe de Viana traffic circle south of the old town—look for a roundabout with a fountain in the center—as well as Paseo de Sarasate near Plaza del Castillo.

By Car: Everything is well marked: Simply follow the bull's-eyes to the center of town, where individual hotels are clearly signposted. There's also handy parking right at Plaza del Castillo and Plaza de Toros, where the bullring is (close to several recommended hotels).

By Plane: Pamplona Airport is located about four miles outside the city (code: PNA, +34 913 211 000, www.aena.es). A regular taxi from the airport to the city center costs around €12. A shared taxi with a fixed schedule goes between the airport and Paseo de Sarasate 1 (fares as low as €1, 1/hour, daily 10:00-24:00, call ahead to reserve, +34 948 232 300 or +34 948 351 335).

HELPFUL HINTS

No Bull—There's Another Fiesta: The last weekend in September, Pamplona celebrates **San Fermín Txikito** ("Little San Fermín"), a bull-free and practically tourist-free festival centered on the church of San Fermín de Aldapa (located behind the Mercado Santo Domingo on Calle Aldapa). Used only for Mass the rest of the year (and housing little of interest except a small statue of the saint), this church opens its doors each fall to become the heart of a celebration involving concerts, brass-band and food competitions, and parades of giant mannequins.

Laundry: Lavandería de lo Viejo is conveniently located just a block off the main square (daily 8:00-22:00, Calle Zapatería 28, +34 616 332 233).

Local Guide: Francisco Glaría is a top-notch guide and simply a

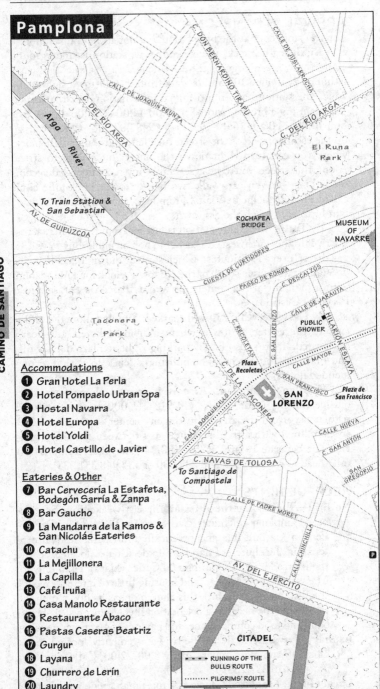

CAMINO DE SANTIAGO

Pamplona

Arga River

To Train Station & San Sebastian

AV. DE GUIPÚZCOA

C. DON BERNARDINO TIRAPU

CALLE DE JOAQUÍN BEUNZA

C. DEL RÍO ARGA

CALLE DE JUSLARROCHA

C. DEL RÍO ARGA

El Runa Park

ROCHAPEA BRIDGE

MUSEUM OF NAVARRE

CUESTA DE CURTIDORES

PASEO DE RONDA

C. DESCALZOS

CALLE DE JARAUTA

Taconera Park

C. RECOLETAS

C. SAN LORENZO

PUBLIC SHOWER

C. HILARIÓN ESLAVA

Plaza Recoletas

C. DE LA TACONERA

CALLE MAYOR

C. SAN FRANCISCO

SAN LORENZO

Plaza de San Francisco

GALLE BOSQUECILLO

CALLE NUEVA

C. SAN ANTÓN

SAN GREGORIO

C. NAVAS DE TOLOSA

To Santiago de Compostela

CALLE DE PADRE MORET

CALLE CHINCHILLA

AV. DEL EJERCITO

P

Accommodations
1. Gran Hotel La Perla
2. Hotel Pompaelo Urban Spa
3. Hostal Navarra
4. Hotel Europa
5. Hotel Yoldi
6. Hotel Castillo de Javier

Eateries & Other
7. Bar Cervecería La Estafeta, Bodegón Sarría & Zanpa
8. Bar Gaucho
9. La Mandarra de la Ramos & San Nicolás Eateries
10. Catachu
11. La Mejillonera
12. La Capilla
13. Café Iruña
14. Casa Manolo Restaurante
15. Restaurante Ábaco
16. Pastas Caseras Beatriz
17. Gurgur
18. Layana
19. Churrero de Lerín
20. Laundry

CITADEL

- - - RUNNING OF THE BULLS ROUTE
.... PILGRIMS' ROUTE

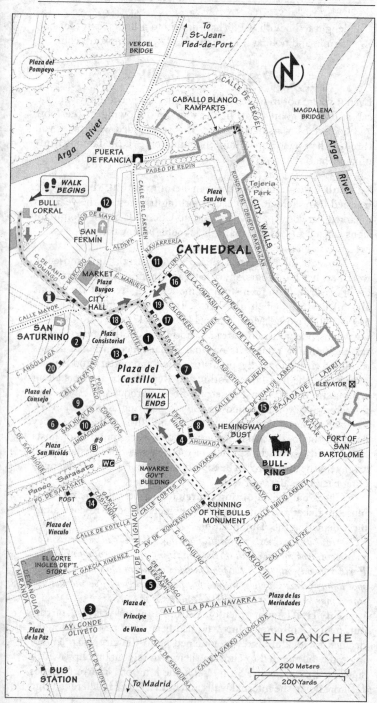

delight to be with (€140/half-day up to 4 hours, extra for San Fermín and holidays, +34 629 661 604, www.novotur.com).

Pamplona Walk

Even if you're not in town for the famous San Fermín festival, you can still get a good flavor of the town by following in the foot- and hoof-steps of its participants. This self-guided walk takes you through the town center along the same route of the famous Running of the Bulls.

• *Begin by the river, at the...*

Bull Corral: During the San Fermín festival, the bulls are released from here at 8:00 each morning (the rest of the year, it's a parked-car corral). They first run up Cuesta de Santo Domingo; signs labeled *El Encierro* mark their route. Follow them.

• *A few blocks ahead on the right is the...*

Museum of Navarre (Museo de Navarra): This museum, worth ▲, has four floors of artifacts and paintings celebrating the art of Navarre, from prehistoric to modern (€2, free Sat afternoons and all day Sun; open Tue-Sat 9:30-14:00 & 17:00-19:00, Sun 11:00-14:00, closed Mon; Santo Domingo 47, +34 848 426 492, www.museodenavarra.navarra.es). Formerly a 16th-century hospital, the building retains its original Renaissance entrance. Art is displayed chronologically: prehistoric tools and pottery and Roman mosaics on the first floor, Gothic and Renaissance artifacts along with castle frescoes on the second floor, Baroque and 19th- and 20th-century works (including Goya's painting *Retrato de Marqués de San Adrián*) on the third floor, and 20th- and 21st-century paintings by local artists on the top floor. The ground floor hosts free rotating exhibitions, often of modern art. Spacious and well arranged, the museum can be toured within an hour—consider circling back here after our walk.

Check out the **adjoining church** (on the left as you exit, show museum ticket), with its impressive golden Baroque-Rococo altarpiece depicting the Annunciation.

• *Continue along Cuesta de Santo Domingo. Embedded in the wall on your right, look for the small shrine containing an image of San Fermín. Farther up on your left is the food market of Santo Domingo, a handy spot to buy picnic supplies, including fine local cheeses (supermarket upstairs, market stalls downstairs). Ahead in the square is...*

City Hall (Ayuntamiento): When Pamplona was just starting out, many Camino pilgrims who had been "just passing through" decided to stick around. They helped build the city you're enjoying today but tended to cling to their own regional groups, which squabbled periodically. So in 1423, the king of Navarre (Charles III) tore down the internal walls and built a City Hall here to unite

the community. This version (late Baroque, from the 18th century) is highly symbolic: Hercules demonstrates the city's strength, while the horn blower trumpets Pamplona's greatness.

The festival of San Fermín begins and ends on the balcony of this building (with the flags). Next to the TI are some of the barricades used during festivities. Look in the direction you just came

from (the route of the bulls), and find the line of metal squares in the pavement—used to secure barricades for the run. There are four rows on this square, creating two barriers on each side. The inner space is for journalists and emergency medical care; spectators line up along the outer barrier. This first stretch is uphill, allowing the bulls to use their strong hind legs to pick up speed.

• *Follow the route of the bulls two blocks down Calle de Mercaderes and do a short detour half a block up the skinny lane called Calle Curia to...*

Pastas Caseras Beatriz: At #16, this shop (most locals just call it "Beatriz") makes the best treats in Pamplona. Anything with chocolate is good, but the mini croissants are sensational. They come in three types: *garrotes de chocolate,* filled with milk chocolate; *cabello de angel,* filled with sweet pumpkin fibers; and *manzana,* apple. So simple...but oh so good.

• *Note that if you want to side-trip to the cathedral—described later, under "Sights in Pamplona"—it's straight ahead two more blocks. If not, backtrack and turn left onto...*

Calle de la Estafeta: At this turn, the bulls—who are now going downhill—begin to lose their balance, often sliding into the barricade. Once the bulls regain their footing, they charge up the middle of La Estafeta. Notice how narrow the street is: No room for barricades...no escape for the daredevils trying to outrun the bulls.

On days that the bulls aren't running, La Estafeta is one of the most appealing streets in Pamplona. It's home to some of the best tapas bars in town (see "Eating in Pamplona," later). Because the old town was walled right up until 1923, space in here was at a premium—making houses tall and streets narrow.

Halfway down the street, notice the alley on the right leading to the main square (we'll circle back to the square later).

• *La Estafeta eventually leads you right to Pamplona's...*

Bullring (Plaza de Toros): Here's where the bulls meet their fate, but it's used for bullfights only nine days each summer (during the festival). The original arena from 1923 was expanded in the

The Symbols of Santiago

The pilgrim route leading to Santiago de Compostela—and the city itself—are rife with symbolism. Here are a few of the key items you'll see along the way.

St. James: The Camino's namesake is also its single biggest symbol. St. James can be depicted three ways: as a pilgrim, as an apostle, and as a Crusader (slaughtering Moors).

Scallop Shell (Vieira): The scallop shell is the symbol of St. James. Figuratively, the various routes from Europe to Santiago come together like the lines of a scallop shell. And literally, scallops are abundant on the Galician coast. Though medieval pilgrims carried shells with them only on the return home—to prove they'd been here and to scoop water from wells—today's pilgrims also carry them on the way to Santiago. The yellow sideways shell that looks like a starburst marks the route for bikers.

Gourd: Gourds were used by pilgrims to drink water and wine.

Yellow Arrow: These arrows direct pilgrims at every intersection from France to Santiago.

Red Cross: This long, skinny cross with curly ends at the top and sides, and ending in a sword blade at the bottom, represents the Knights of Santiago. This 12th-century Christian military order had a dual mission: to battle Muslim invaders while providing hospice and protection to pilgrims along the Camino de Santiago.

Tomb and Star: St. James' tomb (usually depicted as a simple coffin or box), and the stars that led to its discovery, appear throughout the city of Santiago, either together or separately.

1960s (see the extension at the top), doubling its capacity and halving its architectural charm.

Look for the big bust of **Ernest Hemingway,** celebrated by Pamplona as if he were a native son. Hemingway came here for the first time during the 1923 Running of the Bulls. Inspired by the spectacle and the gore, he later wrote about the event in his classic *The Sun Also Rises.* He said that he enjoyed seeing two wild animals running together: one on two legs, and the other on four. This literary giant put Pamplona and its humble, obscure bullfighting festival on the world map; visitors come from far and wide even today, searching for adventure in Hemingway's Pamplona. He came to his last Running of the Bulls in 1959 and reportedly regretted the

attention his writing had brought to what had been a simple local festival. But the people of Pamplona appreciate "Papa" as one of their own. At the beginning of the annual festival, young people tie a red neckerchief around this statue so Hemingway can be properly outfitted for the occasion.

If you've always wanted to **tour a bullring,** this is your chance. The exhibit (worth ▲) gives a behind-the-scenes look at this iconic space (€7, includes audioguide; mid-July-Aug daily 10:30-20:00; shorter hours and usually closed Mon in spring and fall; closed mid-June-mid-July and off-season—confirm hours online; +34 948 225 389, www.feriadeltoro.com). At the start, you'll go down the same ramp and through the same red door that the bulls do during the festival. Once inside, you'll view a video showing historic and modern footage from the running of the bulls. Then you'll enter the corral where the bulls are held prior to the bullfight. In the stable, another video portrays the life of a bull from its simple *Ferdinand* existence in the countryside to its sudden end. The displays also explain the different stages of a bullfight and its major players. Just before you enter the arena, walk by the chapel where the toreadors say their prayers before entering the ring. Once you're out on the sand, go to the center and yell "Olé!" to test the great acoustics. Look for section number 2, where Hemingway used to sit so he could hear the workers comment on the strengths and weaknesses of the different bulls

During the festival, **bullfights** start at 18:30, and tickets are expensive. But the price plummets if you buy tickets from scalpers after the first or second bull. The audience at most bullfights is silent, but Pamplona's spectators are notorious for their raucous behavior. They're known to intentionally spill things on tourists just to get a reaction...respond with a laugh and a positive attitude, and you'll earn their respect—and you'll probably have the time of your life.

• *For a peek at some of the old city fortifications that define Pamplona, take a detour behind the bullring to see the Fort of San Bartolomé (described on page 292). Otherwise, walk 20 yards while keeping the bullring on your left, then cross the busy street and walk a block into the pedestrian zone (on Avenida de Roncesvalles) to the life-size...*

Running of the Bulls Monument (Monumento al Encierro): This statue (pictured on the next page) shows 6 bulls, 2 steers, and 10 runners in action. Find the self-portrait of the sculptor (bald, lying down, and about to be gored). The statue has quickly become a local favorite but is not without controversy: There are 10 *mozos* but no *mozas*—where are the female runners?

• *Facing the monument, you can turn right and walk two blocks up the street to the main square...*

Plaza del Castillo: While not as grand as Spain's top squares, Pamplona's has something particularly cozy and livable about it. It's dominated by the Navarre government building (sort of like a

The Running of the Bulls: Fiesta de San Fermín

"A San Fermín pedimos, por ser nuestro patrón, nos guíe en el encierro, dándonos su bendición."

"We ask San Fermín, because he is our Patron, to guide us through the Running of the Bulls, giving us his blessing."

-Song sung before the run

For nine days each July, a million visitors pack into Pamplona to watch a gang of reckless, sangria-fueled adventurers thrust themselves into the path of an oncoming herd of furious bulls. Locals call it El Encierro (literally, "the enclosing"—as in, taking the beasts to be enclosed in the bullring)...but everyone else knows it as the "Running of the Bulls."

The festival begins at City Hall at noon on July 6, with various events filling the next nine days and nights. Originally celebrated as the feast of San Fermín—who is still honored by a religious procession through town on July 7—it has since evolved into a full slate of live music, fireworks, general revelry, and an excuse for debauchery. After dark the town erupts into a rollicking party scene. To beat the heat, participants chug refreshing sangria or kalimotxo (*calimocho* in Spanish)—half red wine, half cola. The town can't accommodate the crowds, so some visitors day-trip in from elsewhere (such as San Sebastián), and many young tourists simply pass out in city parks overnight (public showers are on Calle Hilarión Eslava in the old town).

The Running of the Bulls takes place each morning of the festival and is broadcast nationwide on live TV. The bulls' photos

appear in the local paper beforehand, allowing runners to size up their opponents. If you're here to watch, stake your claim at a vantage point along the outer barrier by 6:30 or 7:00 in the morning. Don't try to stand along the inner barrier—reserved for press and medical personnel—or you'll be evicted when the action begins.

Before the run starts, runners sing a song to San Fermín (see lyrics above) three times to ask for divine guidance. Soon the bulls will be released from their pen near Cuesta de Santo Domingo. From here they'll stampede a half-mile through the town center...with thrill-seekers called *mozos* (male) or *mozas* (female) running in front of the herd, trying to avoid a hoof or horn in the rear end.

Runners traditionally wear white with strips of red tied

around their necks and waists, and carry a newspaper to cover the bull's eyes when they're ready to jump out of the way. Two legends explain the red-and-white uniform: One says it's to honor San Fermín, a saint (white) who was martyred (red); the other says that the runners dress like butchers, who began this tradition. (The bulls are color-blind, so they don't care.)

At 8:00, six bulls are set loose. The beginning of the run is marked by two firecrackers—one for the first bull to leave the pen, and another for the last bull. The animals charge down the street, while the *mozos* and *mozas* run in front of them for as long as possible before diving out of the way. The bulls are kept on course by fencing off side-streets (with openings just big enough for runners to escape). Shop windows and doors are boarded up.

A bull becomes most dangerous when separated from the herd. For this reason, a few steers—who are calmer, slower, have bigger horns, and wear a bell—are released with the bulls, and a few more trot behind them to absorb angry stragglers and clear the streets. (There's no greater embarrassment in this *muy* macho culture than to think you've run with a bull...only to realize later that you actually ran with a steer.)

The bulls' destination: the bullring...where they'll be ceremonially slaughtered as the day's entertainment. (For more on bullfighting, see page 951.)

If you're considering running with the bulls, it's essential to equip yourself with specific safety information not contained in this book. Locals suggest a few guidelines: First, understand that these are very dangerous animals, and running with them is entirely at your own risk. Be as sober as possible, and wear good shoes to protect your feet from broken glass and from being stepped on by bulls and people. (Runners wearing sandals might be ejected by police.) You're not allowed to carry a backpack, as its motion could distract the bulls. If you fall, wait for the animals to pass before standing up—it's better to be trampled by six bulls than to be gored by one. Ideally, try to get an experienced runner to guide you.

Cruel as this all seems to the bulls—who scramble for footing on the uneven cobblestones as they rush toward their doom in the bullring—the human participants don't come away unscathed, either. Each year, dozens of people are gored, trampled, or otherwise injured. Over the last century, at least 16 runners have been killed at the event. But far more people have died from overconsumption of alcohol.

The festival ends at midnight on July 14, when the townspeople congregate in front of the City Hall, light candles, and sing their sad song, "Pobre de Mí": "Poor me, the Fiesta de San Fermín has ended."

CAMINO DE SANTIAGO

state capitol). Several Hemingway sights surround this square. The recommended Gran Hotel La Perla, in the corner, was his favor-

ite place to stay. It recently underwent a head-to-toe five-star renovation, but Hemingway's room was kept exactly as he liked it, right down to the furniture he used while writing...and two balconies overlooking the bull action on La Estafeta street. He also was known to frequent Bar Txoko at the corner opposite La Perla (as well as pretty much every other bar in town) and the venerable Café Iruña. The recommended Café Iruña actually has a separate "Hemingway Corner" room, with a life-size statue of "Papa" to pose with.

• *You've survived the run. Now enjoy the rest of Pamplona's sights.*

Sights in Pamplona

▲Pamplona Cathedral (Catedral de Pamplona)

The Camino de Santiago is lined with great cathedrals, making Pamplona's feel like an architectural also-ran. However, after an expensive makeover, it looks like new and holds an interesting museum with a thoughtful message for pilgrims and tourists alike.

Cost and Hours: Cathedral and museum—€5, daily 10:30-19:00, until 17:00 in winter, museum closed Sun and during church services, last entry one hour before closing, let ticket office know if you want to do the 11:15 bell tower climb (best to arrive at 10:30 and take a number), +34 948 212 594, www.catedraldepamplona.com.

Visiting the Cathedral: The cathedral—a Gothic core wrapped in a Neoclassical shell—is shiny and clean from the outside, but the interior is dark and mysterious. Follow signs for *entrada* at the left side of the main entrance, buy your ticket, and go inside.

The prominent **tomb** dominating the middle of the nave holds Charles III (the king of Navarre who united the disparate groups of Pamplona) and his wife. The blue fleur-de-lis pattern is a reminder that the kings of Navarre once controlled a large swath of France. Notice that Charles' face is realistic, indicating that it was sculpted while he was still alive, whereas his wife's face is idealized—done after she died. Around the base of the tomb, monks from various orders mourn the couple's death.

In the **choir,** look for the silver and gold statue nicknamed "Mary of the Adopted Child." The Baby Jesus was stolen from this statue in the 16th century and replaced with a different version...

which looks nothing like his mother. (The mother, dating from the 13th century, is the only treasure surviving from the previous church that stood on this spot.)

In the back-left corner chapel, dedicated to San Juan Bautista, find the Renaissance **crucifix**—shockingly realistic for a no-name artist of the time (compare it with the more typical one in the next chapel). The accuracy of Christ's musculature leads some to speculate that the artist had a model. (When you drive a nail through a foot, toes splay as you see here...but this is rarely seen on other crucifixes of the time.) It's said that if the dangling lock of hair touches Jesus' chest, the world will end.

Leave the cathedral and head to the **museum**, in the former cloister and attached buildings. The exhibits document the origins of Western thought and religion without focusing on one particular civilization or geographic area. Pass the spiral staircase into a room that chronicles the stages of cathedral construction. Next, wander through the Gothic cloister to the Archaeology Hall and the main exhibit.

Ramparts View: Exit to the left of the cathedral, walking through the tree-lined square and down picturesque Calle del Redín. Continue to the small viewpoint overlooking the Caballo Blanco ramparts. This is your best chance to see part of Pamplona's imposing **city walls**—designed to defend against potential invaders from the Pyrenees, still 80 percent intact, and now an inviting parkland. Belly up to the overlook, with views across the city's suburban sprawl. Beyond those hills on the horizon to the left are San Sebastián and the Bay of Biscay. Camino pilgrims enter town through the Puerta de Francia gate below and on the left. This area is popular with people who are in town for the Running of the Bulls but didn't make hotel reservations. Sadly, it was not unusual for people to fall asleep on top of the wall...then roll off to their deaths. The hodgepodge fencing here is designed to prevent that from happening during the next festival.

Church of San Saturnino

As a prominent town on the Camino route, Pamplona has its share of other interesting pilgrim churches. This one, the most important of the bunch, is an architectural combination: a 15th-century Gothic body with an 18th-century Baroque altar. Duck inside: This is where pilgrims can get their credential stamped (someone's usually on duty in the pews). At the end across from where you enter, you'll see an altar with the silver-bodied, golden-haloed Holy Virgin of the Camino. As you continue your journey, you'll notice that most churches along the Camino are dedicated to Mary. According to legend, when St. James himself came on a missionary trip through northern Spain, he suffered a crisis of faith around

Zaragoza (not far from here). But, inspired by the Virgin, he managed to complete his journey to Galicia. Pilgrims following in his footsteps find similar inspiration from Mary today.

Cost and Hours: Free, Mon-Sat 9:15-12:00 & 18:00-19:30, Sun 10:00-13:30 & 18:30-19:30, Calle San Saturnino 3 (just off City Hall Square) +34 948 221 194, http://iglesiasansaturnino. com.

Church of San Lorenzo

San Fermín is a big name in town, and you'll find him in a giant side chapel of this church. Enter the church and turn right down the transept to find the statue of San Fermín, dressed in red and wearing a gold miter (tall hat). Pamplona was founded by the Roman emperor Pompey (hence the name) in the first century BC. Later, a Roman general here became the first in the empire to allow Christians to worship openly. The general's son—Fermín—even preached the word himself...until he was martyred. Fermín has been the patron saint here ever since. Just below the statue's Adam's apple, squint to see a reliquary holding Fermín's actual finger. The statue—gussied up in an even more over-the-top miter and staff—is

paraded around on Fermín's feast day, July 7, which was the origin of today's bull festival. This chapel is the most popular place in town for weddings.

Cost and Hours: Free, daily 8:15-12:30 & 17:30-20:30, overlooking the ring road at the edge of the old town at Calle Mayor 74, +34 629 443 777, www.capillasanfermin.com.

Fort of San Bartolomé (Fortín de San Bartolomé)

Pamplona is still defined by its remarkably preserved fortifications, considered some of the finest in Europe. A stroll through the city center often brings walls and gates into view. A large citadel protects the hard-to-defend southwest corner of the old town and has become one of the city's most enjoyed green spaces. The city walls, originally dividing three separate towns, were combined under the reign of Charles III. Centuries later, a constant threat from nearby France forced the city to adopt French defensive measures: a star-shaped wall inspired by France's Vauban fortifications.

Cost and Hours: Interior likely closed for renovation—check with TI for the latest, Calle Arrieta, www.pamplona.es.

Sleeping in Pamplona

Because Pamplona is a business-oriented town, prices go up during the week; on weekends, you can usually score a discount. All prices go way, way up for the San Fermín festival, when you must book as far in advance as possible.

$$$$ Gran Hotel La Perla is the town's undisputed top splurge. Hemingway's favorite hotel, sitting right on the main square, offers 44 posh rooms at Pamplona's best address (air-con, elevator, restaurant, Plaza del Castillo 1, +34 948 223 000, www.granhotellaperla.com, informacion@granhotellaperla.com). Well-heeled lit lovers can drop a bundle for a night in the Hemingway room, still furnished as it was when "Papa" stayed there (with a brand-new bathroom grafted on the front).

$$ Hotel Pompaelo Urban Spa has 30 modern rooms located just next to the City Hall. The hotel has a sky-bar with *vistas buenas*, and a spa for hotel guests in the basement. The reception area and some of the rooms include historical walls from the old city tower (air-con, elevator, Plaza Consistorial 3, +34 848 473 137, www.hotelpompaelo.com, reservas@hotelpompaelo.com).

$ Hostal Navarra is the best value in Pamplona, with 14 modern, well-maintained, clean rooms. Near the bus station, but an easy walk from the old town, it's well run by well-spoken Miguel (RS%, check-in from 14:00, reception closes at 22:00—notify if you'll be arriving later, Calle Tudela 9, +34 627 374 878, www.hostalnavarra.com, info@hostalnavarra.com).

$ Hotel Europa, a few blocks off the square, offers 25 rooms with reasonable prices for its green-marble elegance and ideal location (air-con, elevator, Calle Espoz y Mina 11, +34 948 221 800, www.hoteleuropapamplona.com, europa@hreuropa.com). The ground-floor restaurant is a well-regarded splurge among locals.

$ Hotel Yoldi is a comfortable business-style hotel in a 19th-century building. Well located just off Plaza Príncipe de Viana, its 50 modern rooms are handy for travelers arriving by bus from the train station (elevator, café, Avenida de San Ignacio 11, +34 948 224 800, www.hotelyoldi.com, yoldi@hotelyoldi.com).

$ Hotel Castillo de Javier, right on the bustling San Nicolás bar street (request a quieter back room), rents 19 small, simple yet lovely rooms (air-con, elevator, Calle San Nicolás 50, +34 948 203 040, www.hotelcastillodejavier.com, info@hotelcastillodejavier.com). This is a step up from the several cheap *hostales* that line the same street.

Eating in Pamplona

Typical specialties in Pamplona are *piquillo* (red peppers), white asparagus, and *menestra* (vegetable stew). Try the Navarran *Roncal* cheese and finish off your meal with a local dessert: *pantxineta* (a custard and almond tart) or *txantxigorri* (a cake made of lard, bread dough, and sugar). Try these with a fine Navarran wine or the local, sloe-flavored *pacharán* liqueur—considered a good digestif.

All the eateries listed here are within a couple minutes' walk of one another, and the tapas bars make a wonderful little pub crawl.

TAPAS CRAWL

On Calle de la Estafeta: The best concentration of trendy tapas bars is on and near the skinny drag called La Estafeta. My favorites here are **$$ Bar Cervecería La Estafeta** (try the *gulas*—baby eels—stuffed in a red pepper, daily, at #54, +34 948 222 157); **$$ Bodegón Sarría**, where you'll lick your lips for *escombro*, a hot sandwich with Iberian ham and chorizo (dining room to enjoy Navarran dishes, at #50, +34 948 227 713); and **$$ Zanpa**, which serves *pintxos* in the front and has sit-down dining in the back (look for their grilled meat and *tortilla de patatas,* at #48, +34 948 484 848).

Near Plaza del Castillo: A proud little prizewinning place, **$$ Bar Gaucho** serves gourmet tapas cooked to order. You could sit down, enjoy three tapas, and have an excellent meal. I never pass up the *huevo con trufo*—stir the truffle into the egg to get the full effect of the flavors (daily, just a few steps off the main square at Calle Espoz y Mina 7, +34 948 225 073).

The narrow and slightly seedy Calle San Nicolás has more than its share of hole-in-the-wall tapas joints, with an older, more traditional clientele and homier, more straightforward tapas. **$$ La Mandarra de la Ramos** ("Ramos' Apron"), at #9, is a pork lover's paradise, where cured legs dangle enticingly over your head. Ham it up with a couple of *tostadas de jamón,* best washed down with a glass of the local *vino tinto* (daily, just around the corner from Café Roch, +34 948 212 654).

$$ Catachu serves ample portions in a simple but eclectic setting (menus more expensive on weekends, open daily, Calle Lindachiquia 16, +34 948 226 028).

Near the Cathedral: Seafood lovers can go to **$$ La Mejillonera**, where they can enjoy a *caña* (small draft beer) and *media* (half-portion) *de calamares bravos* in a simple, homey atmosphere. The deep-fried mini calamari are the perfect vehicle for picking up all that mayo and hot sauce (daily, Mon dinner only, Calle Navarrería 12, +34 948 229 184).

$$ La Capilla transformed a former chapel into a pristine,

white dining space. Step into the restaurant to peek at the grand chandelier, but stay at the bar for some of the most innovative tapas in the city. Go early to grab a seat facing the plaza (closed Sun for dinner and Mon-Tue all day, Calle Dos de Mayo 4, +34 948 987 404).

RESTAURANTS

$$$ Café Iruña, which clings to its venerable past and its connection to Hemingway (who loved the place), serves up drinks out on the main square and food in the delightful old 1888 interior. While the food is mediocre, the ambience is great. Find the little "Hemingway's Corner" (El Rincón de Hemingway) side eatery in back, where the bearded one is still hanging out at the bar (accessible only on weekends). Enjoy black-and-white photos of Ernesto, young and old, in

Pamplona (open daily, Plaza del Castillo 44, +34 948 222 064, www.cafeiruna.com).

$$$ Casa Manolo Restaurante is a white-tablecloth place, elegant and inviting, situated upstairs in a building that was once a cafeteria for workers. It's an excellent spot to try out traditional food from Navarra, such as *espárragos frescos* (fresh asparagus) and Navarran beef (Tue-Sat 13:00-16:00 & 21:00-23:00, Sun lunch only, closed Mon, reservations smart, across from the fancy Zara store at Calle de García Castañón 12, +34 948 225 102, www. restaurantecasamanolo.com).

$$$$ Restaurante Ábaco, run by top chef Jesús Íñigo, is a special splurge, having received a Michelin Bib Gourmand award for quality and value. It offers an inspiring menu of creative *pintxos* and larger dishes. A mixed interior of wood and steel gives the place a hip yet traditional feel that goes well with the food. Try the specialty *pintxo, esponja de anchoa*—an amazing anchovy sandwich (Tue-Sat 13:30-15:30 & 21:00-22:30, Sun 13:30-15:30, closed Mon, Calle Juan de Labrit 19, +34 948 855 825, www. abacorestaurante.com).

SWEETS

To satisfy a sugar craving, visit the **Pastas Caseras Beatriz** shop on Calle Curia, which sells delicious mini croissants *(garrotes)* with various sweet fillings (closed Sun, Calle Curia 16, +34 948 783 564, described earlier in my self-guided walk). Nearby on Calle Estafeta is **Gurgur** (named for the rumbling sound of a hungry belly),

where you can find specialties such as *chorizo de Pamplona*, coffee caramels, *txantxigorri* cake, the local *pacharán* liqueur, and *Roncal* cheese—ask the owner Nacho to slice it up (daily until 21:00, Calle Estafeta 21, +34 948 207 992).

Layana summons passersby with the thick scent of sugar and butter. A line of locals often spills out the doors because they know that both the *pasta de nata* and the *pasta de mermelada* (cream-filled and marmalade-filled cookies) are worth the wait (closed Sun, Calle Calceteros 12, +34 948 221 124).

Churrero de Lerín serves the best *churros y chocolate* in Pamplona. The doughnut-like hoops are perfect with the thick, hot chocolate. Cleanse your palate with a free swig of sweet brandy from the *porrón*, a glass dispenser with a spout like a hummingbird's beak. Be sure to pour from high up and avoid touching your mouth to the spout. You're welcome to add graffiti to the walls...as long as you don't write about politics or religion (daily, Calle de la Estafeta 5, +34 618 434 976).

Pamplona Connections

Note that the bus station is closer to the old town than the train station, and that some connections are faster by bus.

From Pamplona by Bus to: St-Jean-Pied-de-Port (1/day, 1.5 hours, Alsa), **San Sebastián** (6/day, 1 hour, Alsa), **Bilbao** (6/day, 2 hours, La Burundesa), **Madrid** (almost hourly—most with transfer, 6 hours, Alsa and Jiménez Movilidad), **Madrid Barajas Airport** (4/day, 5-6 hours, Alsa, buy online in advance—tickets sell out). Bus info: Alsa (www.alsa.es), La Burundesa (www.laburundesa.com), Jiménez Movilidad (https://jimenezmovilidad.es).

By Train to: Burgos (5/day, 2.5 hours—direct, faster trains in afternoon), **San Sebastián** (2/day, 2 hours), **Madrid** (4/day direct, 3.5 hours).

From Pamplona to Burgos

The stretch of the Camino between Pamplona and Burgos is particularly appealing, with several tempting stopovers. As you finish your descent from the rugged Pyrenees, you enter the flatter, more cultivated landscape that typifies the long middle stretch of the Camino (basically from here to Galicia). The two best stops along here are the small town of Puente la Reina (with an iconic old bridge and fun pilgrim vibes) and a potential detour for wine lovers through La Rioja wine country.

• *Begin by taking the A-12 expressway west from Pamplona (toward* Logroño). *Consider stopping in Puente la Reina, as it's a very easy detour—the exit* (Puente la Reina norte) *is well marked from the ex-*

pressway. Approaching town, watch for the first bell tower; parking is on the left.

PUENTE LA REINA/GARES

The Camino de Santiago's two French routes converge in this cozy sun-baked village, just one walking stage (about 12 miles) west of Pamplona. Named for a graceful 11th-century stone bridge at the far end of town, the village retains a pilgrims' vibe. All the sights here fall on a straight axis: church, main street, and bridge with built-in **TI** (Tue-Sat 10:00-14:00 & 16:00-19:00, Sun 11:00-14:00; shorter hours off-season, closed Mon year-round; Calle Puente de los Peregrinos 1, +34 948 341 301). Parking the car where the town starts and wandering to the bridge gives "car hikers" a whiff of Camino magic.

As you enter the town, watch for the **Church of the Crucifixion** (Iglesia del Crucifijo), with a stork's nest on its steeple. The Knights of St. John, who came to protect pilgrims from the Moors, founded this church in the 12th century. Inside you'll find a distinctive Y-shaped crucifix that shows a Christ who's dead, yet still in pain (by a German craftsman—a reminder of the rich influx of pan-European culture the Camino enjoyed). It was likely carried by German pilgrims all the way across Europe to this spot. Across the street is a pilgrims' *refugio* run by a contemporary religious order—Padres Reparadores—offering bunks and credential stamps to Camino walkers. The TI can also give pilgrims that coveted stamp.

The straight, wide **Calle Mayor** connects the church and *refugio* with the bridge. Classic Camino towns feature main drags like this one. They were born as a collection of services flanking the path. Pilgrims needed to eat, sleep, pray, and deal with health problems. The more stone a house showed off (rather than brick), the wealthier the owner. You may see modern flooring being stripped away to reveal now-trendy river-pebble cobbles inside.

The main street leads directly to the most interesting sight in town (and its namesake), the **"Bridge of the Queen"** (which you can also see on the right as you drive across the modern bridge near the end of town). With a graceful seven-arch Romanesque design (one arch is hidden) that peaks in the middle, the bridge represents a life span: You can't quite see where you're going until you get there. The extra holes were designed to let high water

through, so that water pressure wouldn't push the stone construction over—clever 11th-century engineering. Pilgrims enjoy congregating on the riverbank under the arches of this bridge (ramp on right side)—a great place to stop and stretch your legs. Ponder this scene: the bridge, the pilgrims, the flowing river, the happy birdsong...it's timeless.

• *From here, hop immediately back on the A-12 expressway (toward Estella) to speed along. As you pass by Estella/Lizarra (home to the imposing Romanesque Palace of the Kings of Navarre), you'll begin to notice that you're entering wine country with scrubby vegetation, red soil, and hill towns dotting the landscape. Take exit 44, direction: Ayegui, and follow signs to Irache Monastery, a worthwhile, quick, and fun detour.*

IRACHE MONASTERY AND WINE FOUNTAIN

This monastery (Monasterio de Irache), immersed in vineyards, has a unique custom of offering free wine to pilgrims. From the parking lot near the monastery, consider briefly wandering through the large, barren church and odd, double-decker cloister (get your credential stamped inside). Then go inside the Museo del Vino to purchase a €1 cup (if you didn't bring your own). Walk down, following signs for *fuente de vino,* to find a faucet that dispenses free wine (daily 8:00-20:00; also one for water). The Spanish poem on the sign explains, "To drink without abusing, we invite you happily; but to be able to take it along, you must pay for the wine." In other words, pilgrims are allowed to drink as much wine as they like...provided they don't take any with them.

If you do want to bring some along, you're in luck: The wine for sale inside the Museo del Vino is of much better quality and costs half as much as comparable wines elsewhere in Spain (€2-3 for an average red, €9 for the really good stuff). At the faucet, note the webcam—text friends to look for you at www.irache.com. Hi, Mom!

• *Continuing south, you can choose your route: To save time, zip on the A-12 expressway right to Logroño. But for a scenic and only slightly slower meander through some cute villages (El Busto, Sansol) and larger towns (Los Arcos and Viana, with its ornate cathedral), take the expressway only as far as Los Arcos, then follow NA-1110/N-111 from there. Either way, you'll end up at...*

LOGROÑO AND LA RIOJA

Just before the skippable big city of Logroño, you'll cross the Ebro River. Today, as in centuries past, this river marks the end of the Basque territory (and Navarre) and the beginning of the rest of

Spain. With more than 150,000 residents, Logroño is the largest city in La Rioja. Renowned for its robust wines, the Rioja region has historically served as a buffer between the Basques and the powerful forces to the south and east (the Moors or the Castilian Spaniards).

• *Again, choose your route from here. If you have time and a healthy interest in wine (and vineyard scenery), detour off the Camino by heading north on N-232a to the village of Laguardia, rejoining the expressway—and the Camino—later (see "La Rioja Wine Loop" sidebar). Otherwise, stick with the expressway to Santo Domingo de la Calzada.*

Note that west of Logroño, the expressway does a big jog to the north (AP-68, then AP-1). You'll save miles (though not necessarily time) and stick closer to the Camino if instead you take the N-120 highway from here to Burgos. Along the way is...

SANTO DOMINGO DE LA CALZADA

This Rioja town, a larger version of Puente la Reina, has a fine cathedral, oodles of historic buildings, tranquil squares, and all the trappings of a pilgrim zone (seashells in the pavement, *refugios*, vending machines, and launderettes). You'll see images of a rooster and a hen everywhere in town, thanks to a colorful local legend: A chaste pilgrim refused to be seduced by the amorous daughter of an innkeeper. For revenge she hid a silver cup in his bed and accused him of theft. The judge, eager to hang the lad, proclaimed that the pilgrim was as dead as the roasted rooster and hen the judge was about to eat. The charred birds suddenly stood up and began to crow and cluck, saving the pilgrim from certain death.

CAMINO DE SANTIAGO

• *Soon after Santo Domingo de la Calzada, you pass into the region of...*

CASTILLA Y LEÓN

Welcome to Spain's largest "state" (about the size of Indiana). If you've always wanted to see the famous plains of Spain...this is it. This vast, arid, high-altitude Meseta Central ("Inner Plateau") stretches to hilly, rainy Galicia in the northwest and all the way past Madrid to the south coast. Those walking the entire Camino find this flat, dry stretch to be either the best part (getting away from it all with a pensive stroll) or the worst part (boring and potentially blistering hot).

• *The next big city on the Camino is just around the bend: Burgos.*

La Rioja Wine Loop

Serious wine lovers enjoy detouring off the Camino at Logroño to visit the wine village of **Laguardia,** tour some unique wineries, and sample Rioja wine.

For many lovers of Spanish wines, it just doesn't get better than Rioja (ree-OH-hah). Rioja wine is a D.O.C. product, meaning that it can only be produced in the Rioja region. Protected from  the elements by the Cantabrian Mountains to the north (which you'll see from Laguardia), vineyards have thrived in the valley of the Ebro River since Roman times. Rioja wines, which can be red, white, or rosé, grow in a variety of soil types dominated by red clay and limestone. The reds, made primarily from the tempranillo grape (Spain's "noble grape"), are medium- to full-bodied in the Bordeaux style and characterized by aging in oak barrels—infusing them with overtones of vanilla. You'll see four types of Rioja wines, depending on how long they've been aged (from shortest to longest, and cheapest to most expensive): simply Rioja (or sometimes cosecha, "harvest," or joven, "young"), crianza, reserva, and gran reserva.

Be warned that the Rioja region is not well set up for impromptu visitors. All wineries prefer reservations, and most require them, especially if you want a visit in English. If you're serious about your Rioja, set up here for a day or two, pick your designated driver, do some homework (www.laguardia-alava.com is helpful), and reserve at the wineries of your choice. Although Laguardia is connected by bus to Pamplona (via Logroño), most of the experience here lies in the countryside—workable only by car.

• *From Logroño follow N-232a northwest to Laguardia. Adventurous drivers should consider taking a small detour from N-232a: Get off at A-4202 (toward Lapuebla de Labarca), then head north to Laguardia on A-3216. Your reward is pulling off and examining grapes that are planted up to the roadside. In Laguardia, follow signs to a pay parking garage or continue to the Navaridas lot for free parking outside the town wall.*

Laguardia is the scenic center of the Rioja wine-tasting country. This walled town—literally "The Guard," for its position watching out for potential invaders coming in from the mountains—is perched on a promontory with fine views of the surrounding region. There's not much in the way of sightseeing, but poke around a bit. Under your feet are more than 200 wine cellars (bodegas) where Rioja quietly ages. If you'd like to visit, here are two: **El Fabulista** (€8 for two tastes and a one-hour guided visit, book in advance for visit in English, Plaza San Juan, +34 945 621 192, www.bodegaelfabulista.com, Alonso) and **Carlos San Pedro** (€5 for one taste and a half-hour tour, book in advance for tour in English,

Calle Páganos 44, +34 945 621 111, www.bodegascarlossanpedro. com). Laguardia's TI can give you information on wine tastings in town and nearby (TI open Mon-Fri 10:00-14:00 & 16:00-19:00, Sat 10:00-14:00 & 17:00-19:00, Sun 10:45-14:00, Calle Mayor 52, +34 945 600 845, www.laguardia-alava.com).

The countryside around Laguardia is blanketed with vineyards. For those just passing through, three wine-related attractions are worth considering. All are within a few minutes' drive of Laguardia. Note that Ysios and Marqués de Riscal are architectural gems worth dropping by to see even if you couldn't care less about the wine.

Villa Lucía, a food-and-wine event space, has a wine museum about La Rioja's favorite product as well as its traditional architecture. Call ahead to join a tour or do some wine tasting (€12-20, Tue-Sun 10:00-20:00, closed Mon, no tours Sun afternoon, on the right as you reach the edge of town, +34 945 600 032, www.villa-lucia.com).

Ysios is a modern winery with an undulating silver roof designed by the bold and prolific Spanish architect Santiago Calatrava. Wine lovers enjoy the 90-minute tours of the cellar, in which

countless casks age under the wavy ceiling (€25, includes two tastes; daily at 10:00, 11:00, and 12:30, call ahead to ensure a space in an English tour, if available, +34 945 600 640, www.bodegasysios.com). But even from the outside, it's a worthwhile photo op for anyone (just a three-minute drive behind Laguardia, toward the mountains—behind the town, look for Ysios signs; you'll see the building from far off).

• From the Laguardia area, follow signs south to **Elciego** (on A-3210, pull off into town and walk up to the church for a great photo op), then head to...

Marqués de Riscal, in the village of Elciego, was one of the pioneer winemakers of the Rioja wine industry. Its winery features a distinctive hotel designed by Frank Gehry (of Bilbao Guggenheim fame). The wine cellar is tourable daily (€19, 1.5 hours, includes three tastes plus local sausage and chorizo, call or book online first to request an English tour, +34 945 606 000, www. marquesderiscal.com). The hotel (a double room costs €400-1,000), with its colorful, wavy design, seems out of place in this otherwise humble village.

• If you're ready to move along, you can head south from Elciego toward Cenicero. In Cenicero, you can join the AP-68 expressway or continue down (following signs for Nájera) to highway N-120 (turn off at A-12, which is also confusingly called N-120; avoid signs to N-120a) to rejoin the Camino road into Burgos.

Burgos

Burgos (BOOR-gohs) is a pedestrian-friendly city lined up along its pretty river. Apart from its epic history and urban bustle, Burgos has one major claim to touristic fame: its glorious Gothic-style cathedral, packed to the gills with centuries' worth of elaborate decorations.

The burg of Burgos was founded during the Reconquista to hold on to land that had been won back from the Moors. Its position on the Camino de Santiago, and the flourishing trade in wool, helped it thrive. Beginning in 1230, it became the capital of the kingdom of Castile for half a millennium (having usurped the title from León). The town's favorite son is the great 11th-century Spanish hero El Cid (locals say "el theeth"), who valiantly fought against the Moors. The 20th century saw the town decline, even as it briefly became the capital of Franco's forces during the Spanish Civil War (1936-1939). Later the dictator industrialized Burgos to even out the playing field (Catalunya and the Basque Country had previously been the centers of industry).

Today the outskirts of Burgos still feel workaday, but the old town gleams with a hint of elegance. The city constantly tries to improve itself—new public sculpture decorates nearly every plaza, greeting strollers on their evening paseo. Old architecture blends with the new (for example, find the public library at the end of Calle San Juan). Wealthy, well-dressed locals fill Burgos' churches on weekends for weddings, christenings, and First Communions. Stately plane trees line up along the riverside promenade. And watching over everything is that grand cathedral.

Orientation to Burgos

With about 180,000 inhabitants, Burgos is bisected by the Arlanzón River. The old town is centered on the huge cathedral. The city center is mostly pedestrianized and very manageable.

TOURIST INFORMATION

...s' main TI is just off Plaza del Rey, near the cathedral (daily
...:00, Oct-May 10:00-14:00 & 16:00-19:30, Calle Nuño
... +34 947 288 874, http://turismo.aytoburgos.es). A sec-

Accommodations

❶ Hotel Silken Gran Teatro
❷ Crisol Mesón del Cid
❸ Hotel Centro Burgos Los Braseros
❹ El Hotel Jacobeo
❺ Pensión Peña

Eateries & Other

❻ Calle Sombrerería Eateries
❼ Calle San Lorenzo Eateries
❽ Casa Ojeda
❾ Rincón de España
❿ Taberna Urbana Maneli
⓫ Renfe Train Tickets

ond TI on Plaza de Alonso-Martínez covers the entire province of Castile and León (daily, www.turismocastillayleon.com).

Tours: Rosalía Lopez Murillo offers tours of Burgos and villages in the region (info@burgosvisitasguiadas.es).

ARRIVAL IN BURGOS

By Bus: The bus station is just across the river from the cathedral. Exit the station to the left, then turn right at the busy street and cross the bridge (you'll see the large arch and spires).

By Train: Burgos' Rosa Manzano station is a long 45-minu

walk from town. Unless you're poor or a pilgrim, catch a taxi for €11. Bus service into town isn't much help to tourists (€1.20, bus #25 or #43, direction: Plaza de España, then a 10-minute walk to cathedral, 2/hour Mon-Fri, hourly Sat-Sun). The bus stop and taxi stand are both at the station's main entrance. The Renfe office at Calle Moneda 21 sells train tickets (Mon-Fri 9:30-13:30 & 17:00-20:00, closed Sat-Sun).

By Car: Burgos is easy and well signed. Simply follow signs to the city center *(centro ciudad)*, then look for a pay garage when you see the cathedral spires. Plaza Mayor and Plaza de España are the most central garage locations.

Sights in Burgos

▲▲BURGOS CATHEDRAL

Burgos is rightfully famous for its showpiece Gothic cathedral (Catedral de Burgos). With its soaring, frilly spires and an interior that's been augmented across the centuries, Burgos' cathedral is an impressive sight. Unfortunately, the church's cultural and spiritual significance is badly presented; what little English information is provided is stilted and boring. Use this self-guided tour to make the place meaningful.

Cost and Hours: €9, €5 for pilgrims, downloadable audioguide; daily 9:30-19:30, shorter hours off-season, last entry one hour before closing; free lockers, +34 947 204 712, www.catedraldeburgos.es.

❍ Self-Guided Tour: Begin by facing the main facade of the grand church, which was built over the course of a century.

Exterior: You can read the building's history in its architecture: It was started in the 13th century by French architects, who used a simple, graceful style much like Paris' famous Notre-Dame (mentally erase the tops of the spires and you'll recognize that famous cathedral). In the 14th century, German cathedral builders took over, adding the flamboyant fringe to the tops of the towers (similar to the cathedral in Cologne, Germany).

The entrance on this side is open only for worshippers, who ~~ha~~ve access to two chapels at the back of the cathedral (where ~~dai~~ly Mass takes place). Tourists head around the right side of ~~ch~~urch to buy tickets and enter. As you walk there, you'll real~~ize~~ this "front door" facade is only one small part of the vast ~~church~~—more spires and frills lie beyond.

~~Buy your~~ ticket and enter through the side door. After you show your

ticket and download the audioguide to your mobile device, turn left and do a clockwise spin around the church, stopping at many of the...

Chapels: The cathedral's 18 chapels were added over many centuries, in different styles, and were decorated in creative ways by a wide range of benefactors. (To aid with navigation for certain stops, I've listed the numbers that are posted for audioguide users.) The first few chapels are just a warm-up: The Chapel of St. John of Sahagún (#6) features Baroque relic altars and some frescoes (unusual in this church), while the Chapel of the Presentation (#8) features a painting by an Italian Renaissance master, Il Piombo.

At the back of the church, the barriers separate the worship area from the tourist zone. But look high up, just to the right of the rose window, to see the church mascot: the **"Fly-Catcher" clock** (El Papamoscas), which rings out every quarter-hour. Above the clock is a whimsical statue of its German maker, whose mouth opens and closes when the bell rings at the top of each hour. (The tourists who congregate here and crane their necks to gape up at the show seem to be imitating the clockmaker.)

Continue to the chapel dedicated to **St. Anne** (Santa Ana, #12). Here you'll find a spectacular Gothic altar, showing the family tree of Jesus springing out of a reclining Jesse. (The sculptor included his self-portrait as one of the evangelists—find the bespectacled guy, the second from left in the bottom row.) Facing the altar is a Flemish tapestry and some original 15th-century vestments.

• You've now circled back around to the...

Transept: On your left are the sumptuous **Golden Stairs** (#13, designed by a Flemish Renaissance master who had studied under Michelangelo) and an ornate, silver processional stand. Opposite the stairs you can enter the choir area. Step into the very center of the choir—also the very center of the cathedral—and place yourself directly under the sumptuous Plateresque dome, then look up and spin. Look back down

again to see the **tomb of El Cid** (Rodericus Didaci Campidoctor) and his wife (#15). El Cid's well-traveled remains were interred in Valencia, then in various points in Burgos, before being brought here in the early 20th century.

Take a look at the **main altar,** with a fine statue of Mary slathered in silver. Also poke around the carved wooden **choir**—much like the choir in Toledo's cathedral—with a giant 16th-cent

songbook for Gregorian chants and two organs (used only for special occasions).

• *Directly behind the main altar, enter the cathedral's best chapel, the...*

Chapel of the High Constable (#22): Because it has its own altar, two side naves, and a choir and organ (in the back), it's been called "the cathedral within the cathedral." A high constable is a knight who won a crown in battle for his king or queen—the highest of VIPs in the Middle Ages. And yet, this chapel shows the influence not of a powerful man but of a powerful woman. It was commissioned by the high constable's wife (who's entombed with him at the center of the chapel). She wanted the chapel decorations to demonstrate equality of the sexes (a bold statement in the late 15th century). Notice that most of the decorations on "his" side (left) are male oriented, including the two brutes holding the coat of arms and the figures on the side altar. But "her" decorations (right) are more feminine—damsels holding the coat of arms, and mostly women decorating the side altar. The yin and yang of the sexes is even suggested by the black-and-white flooring. Also notice a pair of grand paintings here (unrelated to the sexual politics): on "his" side a beautiful Flemish depiction of a woman in a red dress (likely from the school of Hans Memling); and on "her" side Mary Magdalene, by a favorite pupil of Leonardo da Vinci (who probably put his own touches on the work as well).

• *Continuing around, you'll walk past the beautifully carved main sacristy (#23), then enter the...*

Upper Cloister (#24): The tour route takes you counterclockwise around this cloister, to a few more chapels and museum exhibits: The Corpus Christi Chapel (#26) features stairs up to the library (closed to the public) and access to the chapter house (#27), where the monks would meet.

Continuing to the Chapel of St. John the Baptist and St. James (#29), you find the cathedral's museum collection, including ecclesiastical items (such as some exquisitely detailed crosses and chalices), an emotive statue of Christ being whipped, and an altar depicting St. James the Moor Slayer.

• *Finally you'll head downstairs to the...*

Lower Cloister (#33): At the foot of the stairs is a schmaltzy [statue] of El Cid, and straight ahead is a series of three chambers [off] to the right. In the first is a model of the original Romanesque church (with the current Gothic footprint around it for [comparison]), Romanesque capitals from cathedral columns, and a

sarcophagus. The second chamber emphasizes the Gothic aspects of the cathedral and contains a large model of the entire cathedral complex. Farther down the cloister, Renaissance exhibits include a restored heraldic stained-glass window and a carved nativity scene. The third chamber on the right is a cinema showing a 15-minute film documenting the history of the cathedral and its recent restorations (Spanish only, 2/hour).

Backtrack to El Cid, and then continue around the cloister to see glass cases displaying several original statues and carvings retrieved during the restoration work (and replaced with copies). The patio often houses contemporary art exhibitions (open May-Sept only).

• *Exit through the ticket office, which also contains the gift shop and the lockers. Go in peace—and if you're carrying a pilgrim's credential, stamp it yourself here. You've earned it.*

OTHER SIGHTS IN BURGOS

On a short visit, the cathedral is the main sight. But if you have the time, a few other attractions might be worth a look.

▲Museum of Human Evolution (Museo de la Evolución Humana)

This museum, housed in a glass building by the river, was inspired by discoveries of Pleistocene-era remains in the nearby Atapuerca Mountains, about nine miles east of Burgos. The remains constitute one of the most important settlements of the first Europeans and continue to yield information about our earliest human ancestors. Flanking the museum are a research center and a large conference center. In front of the museum is a sculpture of a naked man walking hand-in-hand with a child, surrounded by various metal tubes symbolizing their evolution...a surprising topic for a city with such a conservative religious history.

Highlights include re-creations of the Atapuerca sites (which can be visited via a shuttle from the museum; see listing under "Near Burgos," later) and the 400,000-year-old skull of "Miguelón"; a full-size mock-up of the ship that carried Charles Darwin around the world—HMS *Beagle;* and exhibits on the development of early technology and artistic expression as seen in cave paintings. The museum also hosts interesting temporary exhibits.

Cost and Hours: €6; free Wed 16:30-20:00; open Tue-Sat

CAMINO DE SANTIAGO

10:00-20:00, Sun until 15:00, closed for lunch Oct-June, closed Mon year-round; Paseo Sierra de Atapuerca, +34 947 421 000, www.turismocastillayleon.com.

▲Church of St. Nicholas (Iglesia de San Nicolás)

This impressive little church is tucked away behind the Burgos Cathedral, along the pilgrimage route to Santiago de Compostela. It's one of the oldest in Burgos, but too often skipped by visitors. The highlight is the main altarpiece from 1505, carved with 64 motifs of saints and Bible scenes. Pick up the English info sheet at the entrance that explains the interior and the church history.

Cost and Hours: €2; Tue-Sat 11:30-13:30 & 17:00-19:00, closed Sun-Mon; Calle de Fernán Gonzáles, +34 947 260 539.

Other Museums

On the hill behind the cathedral, **Centro de Arte Caja de Burgos** is a contemporary art museum with temporary exhibits (free, Tue-Fri 11:00-14:00 & 17:30-20:00, Sat until 21:00, Sun until 14:30, closed Mon, Calle Saldaña, +34 947 256 550, https://portal.cajadeburgos.com). Just across the river, near the bus station, the **Burgos Museum** (Museo de Burgos) celebrates the cultural heritage of Burgos province. Its five floors of painting and sculpture and two floors of archaeological exhibits ring the gorgeous courtyard of a fine old 1540 convent. The somewhat-hard-to-appreciate museum features La Tizona, the famous sword of El Cid (€1.20, free Sat-Sun; open Tue-Sat 10:00-14:00 & 17:00-20:00, Oct-June until 19:00; year-round Sun 10:00-14:00, closed Mon; Calle Miranda 13, +34 947 265 875, www.museoscastillayleon.jcyl.es—click "Museos Provinciales" then "Museo de Burgos").

Plaza Mayor and Promenade

Burgos' main square, a long block from the cathedral, feels strangely uninviting, with long marble benches. The stone building with two clock towers is the Town Hall; if you walk under here you'll emerge at the city's delightful riverside promenade. Lined with knobby plane trees and outdoor cafés, it has an almost Provençal ambience. Going left along the promenade takes you to **Plaza del Mío Cid,** with an equestrian statue celebrating Burgos' favorite son, "My El Cid." Going right along the promenade leads you to the impressive **Arco de Santa María** (Virgin Mary's Gate), one of 12 original gates to this stout-walled city, six of which survive. Built in the 13th century and decorated in 16th-century Renaissance style, the gate's

interior is open to the public. Although there isn't much to see inside—temporary art exhibits and old pharmacy artifacts—it's free (Tue-Sat 11:00-14:00 & 17:00-21:00, Sun until 14:00, closed Mon). After climbing through, go outside to look up at the gate, and in a deep, strong voice, declare: "Burgos." Passing through this gate takes you directly to the cathedral.

▲Las Huelgas Monastery (Monasterio de las Huelgas)

In addition to its grand cathedral, Burgos has a pair of impressive monasteries. The Cistercian monastery of Las Huelgas is the easiest to reach (though still a bit of a walk from the cathedral). Entrance is by one-hour tour only, and English tours are rare. Inside you'll see a "pantheon" of royal tombs, a Gothic cloister with Mudejar details, a chapter house with 13th-century stained glass,

and a Romanesque cloister. The highlight is a statue of St. James with an arm that could be moved to symbolically "knight" the king by placing a sword on his shoulders (since only a "saint"—or statue of a saint—was worthy of knighting royalty). Finally, you'll tour a museum of rare surviving clothes from common people (not just religious vestments) from the 13th and 14th centuries.

Cost and Hours: €6 required guided tour; 5-8 tours/day (almost exclusively in Spanish) Tue-Sat 10:00-18:00, Sun 10:30-15:00; reserve online at www.patrimonionacional.es—go to "Tickets," then "Buy tickets for visit," then scroll down to find the Burgos monastery; Plaza Compás, +34 947 201 630.

Getting There: It's about a 20-minute walk west of the city center, or you can take bus #5, #7, or #39 (catch the bus across the bridge from the cathedral).

Cartuja Monastery (Cartuja de Miraflores)

Unless you adore monasteries, seeing both Las Huelgas and Cartuja is redundant—and Cartuja is farther out of town. However, the Cartuja Monastery is a nice destination for a pleasant two-mile walk (bring a picnic), and explanatory brochures are available in English. To get there, cross the river by Plaza del Mío Cid and turn left, following the river until you reach the monastery. Or take a €10 taxi ride (or bus #26 or #27) and walk back.

Cost and Hours: Free, Mon-Sat 10:15-15:00 & 16:00-18:00, Sun from 11:00, +34 947 252 586, www.cartuja.org.

CAMINO DE SANTIAGO

NEAR BURGOS
Atapuerca Archaeological Site
Nine miles out of Burgos sit the Sierra de Atapuerca Mountains, where archaeologists discovered human remains dating back over a million years. Scholars drool over the find, which continues to offer significant new insights into the lives of prehistoric humans—well explained by the Museum of Human Evolution in Burgos (described earlier). To visit the Atapuerca site, take a shuttle bus from the Museum of Human Evolution (reservations essential, get details at TI or the museum).

Cost and Hours: €6; tour frequency varies seasonally, but usually Tue-Fri at 11:00 and 17:00; Sat-Sun at 10:00, 11:00, 12:00, and 13:00; plus Sat at 16:00 and 17:00; +34 947 421 000, www.atapuerca.org).

Santo Domingo de Silos
This unassuming village—about 40 miles (an hour's drive) south of Burgos—has a fine Benedictine monastery that's become a quirky footnote in popular music. The monastery's monks are famous for their melodic Gregorian chants, which were recorded and released as the hugely popular album *Chant* in 1994. (It went on to sell six million copies.) Although the monks don't perform concerts, some of their daily services—which are free and open to the public—include chanting. The lengthy vespers *(visperas)* service is entirely chanted (daily at 19:00 except Thu at 20:00 in July-Sept, 2.5 hours); there's also some chanting at the shorter Eucharist service (Mon-Sat at 9:00, Sun at 11:00). You can also tour the cloister and museum (€3.50, open to the public Tue-Sat 10:00-13:00 & 16:30-18:00, Sun 12:00-13:00 & 16:00-18:00, closed Mon). Call to confirm before making the trip (+34 947 390 049, www.abadiadesilos.es).

Sleeping in Burgos

$ Hotel Silken Gran Teatro is comfortable, modern, and well located beside the river (connected by a footbridge to the Museum of Human Evolution complex). Prices for its 117 rooms vary wildly depending on season and view—book well in advance for a good deal (air-con, elevator, café, restaurant, free gym, pay parking, Avenida del Arlanzón 8, +34 947 253 900, www.hoteles-silken.com, recepcion.granteatro@hoteles-silken.com).

$ Crisol Mesón del Cid enjoys Burgos' best location, gazing across a quiet square at the cathedral's front facade (full-frontal cathedral views are worth the extra euros). The 49 rooms in two buildings come with classy tile floors and old-fashioned furniture (air-con, elevator, Plaza de Santa María 8, +34 947 208 715, www.mesondelcid.es, mesondelcid@mesondelcid.es).

$ Hotel Centro Burgos Los Braseros, set back a little from the street, offers modern class for reasonable prices. Its lobby and 59 rooms are slick and stylish (air-con, elevator, request quiet room, restaurant, café, Avenida del Cid 2, +34 947 252 958, www. hotelcentroburgos.com, reservas@hotelcentroburgos.com).

¢ **El Hotel Jacobeo** is a cheaper option, with 14 modern rooms along a lively pedestrian street (all rooms face the back—so it's quiet, Calle de San Juan 24, +34 947 260 102, www.hoteljacobeo. com, hoteljacobeo@hoteljacobeo.com).

¢ **Pensión Peña** is Burgos' best budget option. Lively Loli, who speaks no English, rents eight simple but bright and well-maintained rooms (sharing three bathrooms) on the second floor of an old apartment building with a newish elevator (Calle de la Puebla 18, +34 947 206 323, +34 639 067 089, no website—reserve on Booking.com or by calling directly).

Eating in Burgos

TAPAS

On Calle Sombrerería: Several good eateries are on this somewhat touristy street near the cathedral.

$$ Bar Gaona Jardín, at #29 (+34 947 206 191), has a leafy interior and cooks up nice, hot tapas. Across the street at #27, **$$ Cervecería Morito** offers a more chaotic ambience—one tight room with tables and a bar, or pay a little more to eat at the terrace across the road (daily, +34 947 267 555).

At the end of the street, **$$ Pecaditos,** at #3, is a local favorite for its tasty tapas and bargain prices (daily, +34 947 278 466), and **$$ Rimbombín,** at #6, wins awards for their *tortilla española* and speedy service (daily, +34 947 261 200).

On Calle San Lorenzo: Calle San Lorenzo has charm and a more diverse tapas scene. Begin your crawl from the narrow access to the street on Plaza Mayor, working your way from traditional to modern cuisine. To sample a good Spanish wine with your tapas, try a glass of the strong local red, Ribera del Duero, or a refreshing white Albariño from Galicia.

$$ Casa Pancho has a long, inviting bar and friendly staff who churn out tapas as old-school as many of their clientele (the menu's photos of dishes are described in English). Their specialty is *cojonuda*—quail egg, blood sausage, and red pepper on bread (table service extra, daily, at #13, +34 947 203 405).

Next, cross the street to **$$ Mesón Los Herreros,** with an excellent wine selection, larger tapas than most, and a *cojonuda* that's the spiciest thing I've eaten in Spain. Do a comparison taste test (daily, at #20, +34 947 202 448).

When you're finished, continue up to the brighter, whiter

Walking the Way

The Camino by car? Purists cringe at the thought—arguably, it contradicts the whole point of the Camino to do it in a rush. If you have a month of your life to devote to the trek, consider following the Camino the intended and traditional way.

As walking the Camino is in vogue, there's no shortage of good Camino guidebooks and maps. Try *Walking the Camino de Santiago* by Bethan Davies and Ben Cole, *A Pilgrim's Guide to the Camino de Santiago* by John Brierly, or *Buen Camino* by Jim and Eleanor Clem. For a more philosophical take, check out *Following the Milky Way* by Elyn Aviva and *On Pilgrimage* by Jennifer Lash. The Spanish national tourism office has posted good online resources at www.spain.info.

Get a good book. Read and study it. Pack carefully. Solicit advice from people who've done it. Then enjoy the journey.

The procedure for walking the Camino has remained the same throughout history (though a cloak, floppy hat, walking stick, and gourd for drinking are no longer strictly required). The route of the Camino is marked with yellow arrows or scallop shells at every intersection. (For more on the significance of these items and others, see sidebar on page 286.)

Early in the journey, pilgrims buy their "credential" *(credencial)*—a sort of passport, which they get stamped and dated at churches and lodgings along the way. (They can also show it to stay at cheap *refugios* and to get a reduced pilgrim's rate at many museums and churches en route.) At the end, they present their stamped credential in Santiago and receive a special certificate called a *compostela*. Only those who meet the two principal criteria qualify: You must do the pilgrimage for "spiritual" reasons, and you must walk at least the last 100 kilometers (about 62 miles, roughly from Sarria) or ride your bike or horse the last 200 kilometers (124 miles) into Santiago.

Doing the entire French Road from the border to Santiago takes about four to six weeks on foot (averaging 12-15 miles per day, with an occasional rest day—32 days is a typical Camino). Bikers can do it in about two weeks. Many of the trails, originally dirt paths, are now being paved. The journey itself is a type of hut-hopping: At regular intervals along the route (about every 5-10 miles), pilgrims can get a bunk for the night at humble little hostels called *albergues* (ahl-BEHR-gehs), *refugios* (reh-FOO-hee-ohs), or *hospitales* (oh-spee-TAH-lehs). Some of these are run by

the government (€5-10/bunk, closer to €3 in Galicia, even if they're "free" a donation is requested; no reservations taken—first-come, first-served, with priority given to credential-holding pilgrims arriving on foot). Others are privately run (typically a bit

more expensive—€10-20—and sometimes take reservations). A wide variety of other accommodations are available for those who prefer more comfort, ranging from simple *hostales* to grand hotels and *paradors* (I've listed my favorites in this chapter).

What began as a religious trek to atone for one's sins has evolved into a journey undertaken by anyone—spiritual or secular—who just wants some time to think. Although some pilgrims do the trip for "fun," those who take it seriously caution that it's one of the most wrenching things you can do. After a few weeks on the Camino, many pilgrims begin to develop a telltale limp... you'll notice it getting more pronounced as you move west. (There's a reason old pilgrim hostels are sometimes called "hospitals.")

But there are worse things than blisters and sore muscles. The Camino can take a psychological toll on pilgrims. Trudging step after step across endless plains toward an ever-receding horizon, you're forced to introspection. Religious or not, you can't help but come to terms with your regrets, demons, "sins," or anything else that's on your conscience.

This process of self-reflection is symbolized by picking up a small stone somewhere early on the Camino, then depositing it at the Iron Cross near the end of the trek—releasing yourself from whatever's been weighing you down. The absolution of sins that awaited medieval pilgrims isn't so different from the "find myself" motives of today's smartphone-toting tourists. Whether you're pardoned by the Church or simply unburdened of what's been nagging you, it's liberating all the same.

A wonderful pilgrim camaraderie percolates along the length of the Camino, as a United Nations of vagabonds—young and old—swap stories and tips. Driving, on foot, or on bike, you'll cross paths with the same pilgrims again and again...the guy who checked in before you at the hotel last night is at the cathedral with you the next morning. Along the way, the standard greeting (like a Jacobean "Happy Travels") is *"Buen Camino!"*

No matter how you get to Santiago, you'll share in the jubilation pilgrims have felt through the ages when—four miles out of town—the spires of the cathedral come into view.

CAMINO DE SANTIAGO

$$ La Quinta del Monje. Choose among the tapas on display under glass or pick up a picture menu for something made to order. Their chef offers playful variations on tried-and-true favorites (daily, at #19, +34 947 208 768). To wet your whistle, **$$ El Pez de San Lorenzo** makes great mint-orange vermouths (daily, at #31, +34 653 662 129).

RESTAURANT DINING

$$$ Casa Ojeda is a venerable institution that's a reliable choice for a real restaurant meal. Specializing in Burgos cuisine, they offer seating at the bar downstairs (only tapas and *raciones* served here) or in the upstairs dining room (meals served 20:30-23:00). Relax and enjoy the subdued, rapidly aging ambience (closed Sun evening and Mon, Calle Vitoria 5, +34 947 209 052).

$$$ Rincón de España has a great location on Plaza del Rey, close to the cathedral. It's popular with locals for its regional dishes, including *cochinillo* (roast suckling pig) and *cordero* (roast lamb) cooked in a wood-fired oven. The restaurant's two indoor rooms often are filled with wedding parties on weekends, and its outdoor terrace sports views of the cathedral spires. Brothers Javi and Fernando (who speaks English) are sommeliers and have a good local wine list. Try their *morcilla* (blood sausage, an area specialty) and, for dessert, the traditional *leche frita*—fried milk (daily 10:00-23:00, closed Mon-Tue evenings off-season, Calle Nuño Rasura 11, +34 947 205 955).

$$ Taberna Urbana Maneli, a popular spot for both locals and visitors on the street behind the cathedral, has a bar for tapas and a sit-down restaurant for lunch and dinner. Parts of the interior incorporate the old city wall dating from the 11th century. The food is homestyle and well priced—try their house specialty, roasted lamb for two (Wed-Sat 11:00-16:00 & 19:00-23:00, Tue and Sun lunch only, closed Mon, Calle Fernán González 36, +34 947 205 957).

Burgos Connections

From Burgos by Bus to: León (3/day, 2-3 hours), **Bilbao** (8/day, fewer on weekends, 2-3 hours), **Santiago de Compostela** (1/day, 8 hours), **San Sebastián** (6/day, 3-4 hours), **Salamanca** (3/day, 3.5 hours), **Madrid** (hourly, 10/day go directly to T4 at Barajas Airport, 3 hours). Keep in mind that Sunday connections are very sparse. Bus info: Alsa (www.alsa.es).

By Train to: Pamplona (5/day, 2.5 hours, faster trains in afternoon), **León** (4/day, 2 hours), **Bilbao** (5/day, 2.5 hours), **San Sebastián** (5/day, 3 hours), **Salamanca** (7/day, 2.5-5 hours), **Madrid** (6/day, 2.5-4.5 hours).

From Burgos to León

While there are some worthwhile stops between Burgos and León, this is a good place to put some serious miles under your belt: Follow signs for the A-231 expressway and zip between the cities in less than two hours. Sticking with the true Camino—a confusing spaghetti of roads without a single straight highway to keep you on track—takes you through a poorer, very humble countryside with few sights. Some travelers enjoy dipping into towns along here such as **Castrojeriz, Frómista,** and **Carrión de los Condes**—or the slightly larger town of **Sahagún,** with its impressive monastery and massive bell tower—but on a tight itinerary, your time is better spent in Burgos or our next stop, León.

León

With a delightfully compact old town (surrounded by ugly sprawl), León (lay-OWN) has an enjoyable small-town atmosphere. But most importantly, it has a pair of sights that serve as a textbook for medieval European art styles: Romanesque (the San Isidoro Monastery, with astonishingly well-preserved frescoes) and Gothic (the cathedral, with the best stained glass outside France).

León means "lion" in Spanish—but in this case, the name derives from Rome's seventh legion *(legio)*, which was stationed here. Founded as a Roman camp at the confluence of two rivers in AD 68, León gradually grew prosperous because of the gold that passed through (mined in the Las Médulas hillsides to the west). In 910, as the Moors were pushed ever southward, the capital of the Reconquista moved here from Oviedo, and for three centuries León was the capital of a vast kingdom (until it was supplanted by Burgos). Today, León is the capital of one of Spain's biggest provinces, making it an administrative and business center. It's also a major university town, with some 15,000 students who imbue it with an enjoyable vitality.

Orientation to León

The big city of León, with 130,000 people (200,000 in the metro area), sits along the Bernesga River. On a short visit, tourists can ignore everything outside the rectangular old town, which is set a few blocks up from the river.

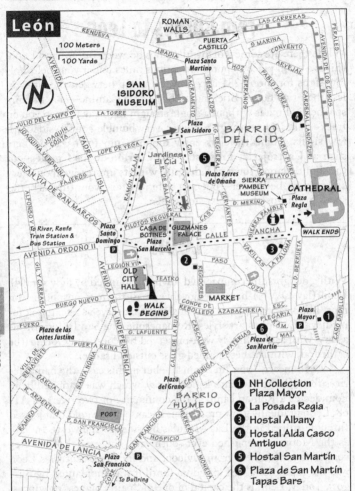

León

100 Meters
100 Yards

RENUEVA

ROMAN WALLS

LAS CARRERAS

PUERTA CASTILLO

S. MARINA

CONVENTO

ABADIA

AVENIDA DE LOS CUBOS

PERALES

AVENIDA DE LOS CUBOS

CARDENAL LANDAZURI

Plaza Santo Martino

SAN ISIDORO MUSEUM

JULIO DEL CAMPO

LA TORRE

SACRAMENTO

DESCALZOS

LA HOZ

SERRANOS

PABLO FLOREZ

ARVEJAL

AVENIDA DE

PADRE

JOAQUIN COSTA

JOAQUIN VERDURA

FAJEROS

ISLA

LOPE DE VEGA

RAMON Y CAJAL

R. DE SALAZAR

CID

Plaza San Isidoro

Jardines El Cid

F.G. REGUERAL

CERVANTES

BARRIO DEL CID

SAN PELAYO

PABLO FLOREZ

GRAN VIA DE SAN MARCOS

ALFONSO V

Plaza Torres de Omaña

SIERRA PAMBLEY MUSEUM

D. MERINO

SIERRA PAMBLEY

CATHEDRAL

Plaza Regla

WALK ENDS

To River, Renfe Train Station & Bus Station

Plaza Santo Domingo

PILOTOS REGUERA

CASA DE BOTINES

GUZMANES PALACE

CALLE ANCHA

CAST.

CERVANTES

VARILLAS

LA PALOMA

M. D. BERRUETA

AVENIDA ORDOÑO II

GIL Y CARRASCO

Plaza San Marcelo

LEGIÓN VII

OLD CITY HALL

TEATRO

RESIDORES

PASO

POZO

BURGO NUEVO

AVENIDA DE LA INDEPENDENCIA

WALK BEGINS

CONDE DE REBOLLEDO

AZABACHERIA

ESC.

PLEGARIA

MAT.

Plaza Mayor

CARO BADILLO

FUERO

Plaza de las Cortes Justina

G. LAFUENTE

CALLE DE LA RUA

CASCALERIA

ZAPATERIAS

Plaza de San Martín

J.M.

PUERTA REINA

CAPONIGA

Plaza del Grano

BARRIO HUMEDO

HERREROS

C. SAN FRANCISCO

HOSPICIO

F. MONEDA

VILLA DE BENAVENTE

GARCIA I.

R. ARGENTINA

RAMIRO II.

P. SAN FRANCISCO

POST

AVENIDA DE LANCIA

Plaza San Francisco

To Bullring

1 NH Collection Plaza Mayor

2 La Posada Regia

3 Hostal Albany

4 Hostal Alda Casco Antiguo

5 Hostal San Martín

6 Plaza de San Martín Tapas Bars

CAMINO DE SANTIAGO

TOURIST INFORMATION

León's TI is on the square facing the cathedral (Mon-Sat 9:30-14:00 & 17:00-20:00, shorter hours mid-Sept-June; Sun 9:30-17:00 year-round; Plaza de Regla 2, +34 987 237 082, www.leon.es).

Local Guide: Blanca Lobete is an excellent, energetic teacher who shares León's architectural gems with travelers (€100/3 hours, +34 669 276 335, guiaslegio@hotmail.com).

ARRIVAL IN LEÓN

By Train or Bus: The train and bus stations are almost next to each other along the river, about a 15-minute walk from the town center. A **taxi** can take you into town for about €6. To **walk** to the old town

from the stations, cross the big bridge, continue in the same direction through a roundabout, and walk straight up Avenida Ordoño II. You'll hit the turreted Gaudí building, marking the start of the old town. From here, the San Isidoro Museum is to the left and the cathedral is straight ahead (up Calle Ancha).

By Car: Compared with the other cities in this chapter, León is not well signed. Do your best to follow directions to the city center *(centro ciudad)*; once there, you can park in a very convenient underground parking garage at Plaza Santo Domingo, right at the start of the old town (and within a three-minute walk of all my recommended accommodations). Nearby Plaza Mayor also has a parking garage.

León Walk

León's two most worthwhile sights complement each other perfectly: the remarkable Romanesque frescoes at San Isidoro and the gorgeous stained glass of the cathedral. To connect these major sights, follow this self-guided walk through León's city center. (If you're rushed, head straight for the cathedral.)

• *Start at...*

Plaza San Marcelo: The old **City Hall** (Casa Consistorial) sports a variety of flags, from national to provincial. Next to the column in the plaza's small park (at the north end of the square), you'll find a **relief map** depicting León's development during three major periods. León began as a Roman military camp nearly 2,000 years ago—we'll see some Roman defensive walls later in this walk. After the Moorish occupation of the Iberian Peninsula, the city fell into decline, but it later reemerged as the capital of a Christian kingdom. Medieval walls enlarged the city, and as evidenced by the modern street plan, León prospers to this day.

• *From the park, head left to the Plaza Santo Domingo roundabout. Walk up Calle Ramón y Cajal (checking out the modern cityscape and keeping the church tower in sight), then head to the base of the bell tower and up the stairs to...*

Plaza San Isidoro: On this square, you'll find the 11th-century **San Isidoro Church** and its excellent **museum.** The church is free, so go into the entrance facing the plaza and take a peek. If you want to visit the museum—with its gorgeous Romanesque frescoes (described later)—turn right as you exit the church. On the same square, looking far to the left you can see a 92-foot-tall, Roman-inspired column. It was put up in 1968 to commemorate the Seventh Legion of the Imperial Roman Army, whose soldiers are considered the founders of the city. On top of the column is a bird's nest—the home of a white stork that returns every year.

Continue this walk from Plaza San Isidoro down Calle Cid.

At the big portico, look for the plaque dedicated to León's favorite son, Guzmán el Bueno. This hero of the Reconquista was born in this mansion (for more on Guzmán, see page 886).

• *Follow Calle Cid through the gardens, taking some time to sit down under the olive tree and listen to the birds sing. At the end of the gardens, turn right to the...*

Casa de Botines: This is one of few works by Antoni Gaudí outside Catalunya (another is the Bishop's Palace in Astorga, de-

scribed later in this chapter). Now the Casa de Botines is a bank and generally not open to visitors unless there's a special exhibition. Gaudí preferred to use local materials, such as slate for the roof (typical in León province). The rough stone exterior is intended to hang on to falling snow to create an atmospheric effect. Over the door is St. George, the patron saint of Gaudí's native Catalunya. Notice the architect himself on the bench across the square, designing his work.

Before you leave the square, peek into Guzmánes Palace on the corner next to Casa de Botines (free entry to the courtyard). Today this is the headquarters of the Provincial Government of León. Notice the big, round rock in the corner—a Celtic gravestone found in a nearby village.

• *At the end of the square, you reach an important thoroughfare. Turn left onto...*

Calle Ancha: This "Wide Street" cuts through the heart of the old town. It was widened in the mid-19th century to create an appropriate pathway to the cathedral and is lined with grand mansions of local wealthy people who wanted to live close to God.

It's only been pedestrianized for the last decade, creating a much-enjoyed people zone.

As you walk up Calle Ancha toward the cathedral, the neighborhood to the left is called **Barrio del Cid** (for a supposed former resident). The area to the right is known as the **Barrio Húmedo,** or "Wet Quarter," for all the bars that speckle its streets (see "Eating in León," later). Deep in the Barrio Húmedo is the appealing main square, **Plaza Mayor** (which transforms into a

market every Wed and Sat morning), overshadowed by the **cathedral** a few blocks away.

• *The end of Calle Ancha is also the end of your walk—at León's monumental cathedral (described next).*

Sights in León

▲▲LEÓN CATHEDRAL

León's 13th-century Gothic cathedral (Catedral de León) is filled with some of the finest stained glass in all of Europe. Pray for a sunny day when you can see its gorgeous colors scattered across this monumental space.

Cost and Hours: Cathedral and cloister-€7, museum-€3, QR codes throughout link to descriptions; open Mon-Sat 9:30-13:30 & 16:00-20:00, Sun 9:30-11:00 & 14:00-20:00, shorter hours off-season; +34 987 875 770, www.catedraldeleon. org.

Window Restoration: The cathedral's 737 stained-glass panels recently underwent a painstaking restoration. Each window was carefully removed from its old lead frame, dry-cleaned (with minimal use of liquid solvents), and reset. Restoring the 20,450 square feet of glass included preventive steps. A solid, clear pane of glass was set in the original's place, so that the freshly cleaned stained glass could sit inside, protected from the elements. A mesh metal panel was also installed on the exterior for an added layer of protection. Historians created an extensive photographic record of the process—which is of vital importance, since the last restoration in the 19th century misplaced some panels.

❷ Self-Guided Tour: Before going inside, stop and take a look at the facade.

Exterior: If you've just seen Burgos' cathedral, León's—while impressive—might seem a letdown. But reserve judgment until you get inside. León's cathedral was actually built in response to the one in Burgos, to keep León on the map after Burgos wrested capital status from it in 1230. But, whereas Burgos' was built over two centuries, this cathedral took only about 50 years to complete. The focus was on creating a simple, purely Gothic cathedral to showcase its grand stained-glass windows. The three porticos (doorways with pointed arches) are textbook Gothic. Notice the gap between the two towers and the main facade, which allows even more light

CAMINO DE SANTIAGO

to reach those windows. This also gives the cathedral a feeling of lightness. The one exception to the pure-Gothic construction: Notice the tower on the right is a bit taller—it was capped in the 15th century with a frilly spire to keep up with what was going on in Burgos.

• *Now approach the **main door**, above which is a carving of the Last Judgment.*

Above Mary, St. Michael weighs souls to determine who is going to party with the musicians of heaven (left; his scale bar is missing) or burn with the cauldrons and demons of hell (right). If you look carefully you'll see that all of those kicking back in heaven are members of the clergy or royalty. This subtle message made the Camino de Santiago even more appealing to pilgrims: If you weren't a priest or an aristocrat, completing the Camino was your only ticket to eternal bliss.

Before entering, ponder the crucial role that **light** plays in this house of holy glass. Like all cathedrals, the main door faces the west, and the altar (at the far end) faces east—toward Jerusalem. But that also means that the sun rises behind the altar (where Jesus symbolically resides) and sets at the Last Judgment. This theme is continued again and again inside.

• *Speaking of which, go on in and let your eyes adjust to the light.*

Interior: Notice how the purely Gothic structure—extremely high, with columns and pointed arches to direct your gaze ever heavenward—really allows the stained glass to take center stage. Of all this glass (the second most glass in any European cathedral, after Chartres in France), 70 percent is original, from the 13th through 16th centuries.

Imagine how the light in here changes, like living inside a kaleidoscope, as the sun moves across the sky each day. Notice that the colors differ thematically in various parts of the cathedral. Above the main door, the rose window (dedicated, like the cathedral itself, to the Virgin Mary, with 12 angels playing instruments around her) is the most colorful, as it receives the most light at the end of the day. Turning to face the front altar, notice that the glass on the left (north) side of the church, which gets less light, symbolizes darkness and obscurity—blue dominates this side. The glass on the right (south) side of the church, which is bathed in light much of the day, symbolizes brightness and has a greater variety of colors.

Now trace the layers of Gothic **cathedral construction** from the bottom up, as the building (like your eyes) stretches ever higher, closer to God. The lowest level is the stone foundation (with pointed archways embedded in the walls), symbolic of the mineral world. The first windows show flowers, trees, and animals—the natural world. At the top of each nature window are three me-

dallions showing the human world: common people doing their thing—demonstrating both vices and virtues.

Above this first row of windows, notice the stone gallery (used for window maintenance). The **tall windows** at the very top show biblical characters. On the left (north) side—the "darkness" side, before Christ—is the Old Testament; on the right (south) side—the "light" side, after Christ—is the New Testament. The two sides meet at the window (above the main altar) of Jesus—who is illuminated by the rising sun each morning, enlightening the entire cathedral.

• *Head for the **transept**.*

Unfortunately, this part of the cathedral almost didn't survive a well-intended but botched Baroque-era reconstruction. A heavy dome placed over the transept proved too heavy for the four graceful main pillars, causing a significant chunk of the church to collapse. The transept's blue (north) rose window, featuring Christ, survives from the 13th century, while the red (south) one, with Mary, is from the 19th century.

Walk into the carved wooden **choir** at the center of the nave. The curved wooden part over the top of each chair is a "sounding board" *(tornavóz)*, helping voices carry. The giant glass door replaced a solid wooden one in the early 20th century—opening up the church even more to God's light.

Circling back directly behind the main altar, you'll find a chapel with the **"White Virgin"** on the right, the original 13th-century statue (whose face was painted white) from the front facade of the church. Note the differences between the 16th-century stained glass above the Virgin (with one large, multipaneled scene) and the 13th- and 14th-century glass in the flanking chapels (with one scene per panel—and even tinier bits of glass).

• *For a close-up look at all the decorative bits missing from the cathedral's interior, exit on the north side to visit the cloister and museum (separate €3 admission for museum).*

Cloister and Museum: The **cloister** offers a good view of the flying buttresses that make the stained glass structurally possible. By removing the weight from the walls and transferring it to these buttresses, medieval engineers could build higher and make larger and larger windows. Also on display are some giant discarded Baroque elements (such as turret tops and sculptures) that were added to the facade in the 16th century and later removed because they cluttered up the architectural harmony.

Confusingly, the **museum** is divided into two parts; the staff will open the door to each section and then lock you in—supposedly to preserve temperature and humidity conditions. Don't worry. When finished with the first part, return to the door and wait pa-

tiently. Security cameras show them you need to be released. You'll let yourself out of the second section.

The first room you'll see is the Stone Room *(Sala de Piedra)*, with sculpted objects from the cathedral and around town. Find the unique Jewish tombstones and early tiles in the display case. Continue upstairs to the Ivory Room, then head to the *Torreón* to see one of the more interesting pieces—a Visigothic antiphonary, the most complete surviving liturgical book of chants from Spain's early-Christian days. How the chants sounded remains a mystery—modern musicians cannot transcribe them because pitches weren't indicated. In the second section of the museum, other interesting items include a Mudejar armoire from the 13th century, studies of the cathedral's stained glass, textiles, and some modern-day artwork. In the last room, *sala del románico,* there is an overwhelming collection of almost 50 simple yet endearing versions of Santa María.

In the museum's second part, head to the right and down the stairs. Here you'll find St. James *Matamoros* on his horse and, at the end, an impressive Mudejar cabinet. Don't get scared by the mummy glaring at you, or by the tools that look like torture instruments but are really just candle cutters. On the second floor is a collection of unimpressive modern religious art. On your way to the exit you'll pass a display case with several porcelain containers used for storing herbal medicine and samples of fabrics and patterns from the dioceses of León through the centuries.

OTHER SIGHTS IN LEÓN
Sierra Pambley Museum

This nondescript house facing the cathedral contains the well-preserved living quarters of a 19th-century businessman and some fascinating reminders of early education in Spain. Those interested in 19th- and 20th-century decorative arts must pay to tour the rooms, but the education exhibit is free.

At the age of 60, Francisco Blanco y Sierra Pambley created a foundation to educate students; classes were to be free of religious or political dogma. Several schools were founded, and the students thrived in this environment, supported by the latest technological innovations. You'll see a Kodak movie projector and a typewriter used to instruct girls—as this was one of the very few places in Spain where girls could receive any kind of formal education.

Unfortunately, Sierra Pambley was ahead of his time. When the Second Republic gained control of Spain in 1931, the foundation's humanist views came under suspicion. In 1936, all funds and property were confiscated; one director was even executed by a firing squad. The schools eventually came under the jurisdiction of the Catholic Church. After the death of Franco, the foundation

was reinstituted and its remaining funds returned to the organization.

Cost and Hours: Apartment-€5, education exhibit-free; Wed-Sun timed entrances at 11:00, 13:00, 17:00, and 19:00, closed Mon-Tue; no English descriptions, Calle Sierra Pambley 2, +34 987 276 775, www.sierrapambley.org/museo.

▲▲San Isidoro Museum (Museo de San Isidoro)

San Isidoro is an 11th-century Romanesque church that's been gradually added on to over the centuries. The church itself is free and always open to worshippers, but the attached museum is the real attraction. Inside you'll see a library, a cloister, a chapter house, and a "pantheon" of royal tombs featuring some of the most exquisite Romanesque frescoes in Spain.

Cost and Hours: €5 required guided tour, reserve English tour online or by email (reservas@museosanisidoro.com), timetable varies; May-mid-July Mon-Thu 10:00-14:00 & 16:00-19:00, Fri-Sat until 20:00, Sun 10:00-15:00; mid-July-mid-Sept Mon-Sat 9:00-21:00, Sun until 15:00; shorter hours off-season; Plaza de San Isidoro 4, +34 987 876 161, www.museosanisidorodeleon.com.

Visiting the Museum: After you buy your ticket, staff will escort you up the tight spiral staircase to the **chapter house.** This is a showcase for a glittering assortment of Romanesque reliquary chests and Asian silk embroidery—an amazing luxury for medieval kings. The frescoes here are more recent than those in the Royal Pantheon you'll visit later.

Next you'll be led to the evocative old **library** (an interesting mix of Gothic design and Renaissance decoration). Marvel at the size of all those Gregorian chant books as well as a giant Mozarabic Bible from 960—you can page through a facsimile in the gift shop.

In the **tower** alongside the library sits one solitary piece—an agate chalice decorated with gold and assorted gemstones. Some believe this to be the vessel used by Jesus at the Last Supper.

Now descend the stairs and enter the **Royal Pantheon** (Pantéon Real). This area, enclosed in the middle of the complex, was once the portico in front of the west door of the church. In 2002, historians discovered the tombs of 23 medieval kings and queens (which are now held in the stone tombs), 12 *infantes* (children of the monarch), and 9 counts. But who's buried here pales in comparison to the beautiful, vivid **frescoes** on the vaulting above them. Created in the late 11th and early 12th centuries, these frescoes have never been repainted—they're incredibly well preserved. While most Romanesque frescoes have been moved to museums, this is a rare opportunity to see some in situ (where the artist and patrons originally intended).

Follow along as the frescoes trace the **life of Christ** (go clock-

wise, starting on the wall in the front right corner with the cloister on your left). In the scene of the Annunciation, you'll notice a sense of motion (Mary's billowing clothes) that's unusual for typically stiff and unlifelike Romanesque art. Above that, on the ceiling in the corner, an angel appears to shepherds dressed in traditional 11th-century Leonese clothing. There's even a Leonese mastiff dog, lapping at his master's milk (while he's distracted by the angel).

In the next ceiling section (closer to the entry), Roman soldiers carry out the gruesome slaughter of the innocents. Then it's time for the **Last Supper** (middle section of the ceiling). As you take in the bold colors, notice that only 11 of the apostles have halos...all but Judas (under the table). In this fresco's corner, find the black rooster (gallus), a symbol of Jesus, who harkened the dawn of a new day for God's people. But in the next section we see the rooster used as a different symbol—as Peter denies Christ three times before the cock crows. Also see Jesus' arrest, Simon helping Jesus carry the cross, and Pontius Pilate washing his hands of the whole business. Finally (on wall, left of main altar) we see Jesus nailed to the cross.

The final panel, in the middle of the room, is the most artistically and thematically impressive: **Jesus returning triumphant** to judge the living and the dead. He's depicted here as Pantocrator ("All Powerful"). Over his shoulders are the symbols for alpha and omega, and he's surrounded by the four evangelists, depicted—according to the prophecy of Ezekiel—as winged creatures: angel, bull, eagle, and lion. The most interesting detail is the calendar running along the archway near Jesus' right hand. The 12 medallions—one for each month (labeled in Latin)—are symbolized by people's activities during that month. In January, the man closes one door (or year) while he opens the next. He proceeds to warm himself by the fire (February), prune (March), plant his crops (April), harvest (July), forage (September), slaughter the fattened pig (October), and bless his bread by the fire at Christmas (December). The message: Jesus is present for this entire cycle of life.

There's more to the museum. Continue left into the **cloister,** with its spectacular ceiling tracery. You'll find a small room with a giant 12th-century rooster weathervane that used to top the nearby tower (now replaced by a replica)—a symbol of the city.

Sleeping in León

These listings are inside the old town.

$$$ NH Collection Plaza Mayor is the old-town splurge, with 51 rooms right on Plaza Mayor (some with views for a small extra charge). Part of a classy chain, this place offers modern four-star comfort at reasonable prices (air-con, elevator, Plaza Mayor 15,

+34 987 344 357, www.nh-hotels.com, nhplazamayor@nh-hotels. com).

$$ La Posada Regia is a creaky little hotel with 36 rooms in two buildings just off the main walking street. The old-fashioned, pleasant decor is a combination of wood beams and patches of stone (Regidores 9, +34 987 213 173, www.regialeon.com, marquitos@ regialeon.com).

$ Hostal Albany offers 19 very mod rooms at a good price, just a few steps off the main walking street and cathedral square (air-con, elevator, Calle La Paloma 13, +34 987 264 600, www. hostalalbanylastermas.com, info@grupoalbany.com.

¢ Hostal Alda Casco Antiguo is situated on a quiet street just next to the cathedral. The hotel has 14 inviting rooms, a common area, and a kitchen for guests (air-con, elevator, laundry service, Calle Cardenal Landázuri 11, +34 987 620 050, www. aldacascoantiguo.es, cascoantiguo@aldahotels.com).

¢ Hostal San Martín is a good budget option run by friendly Esperanza and Fernando. Popular with pilgrims, it has 11 rooms; some quiet ones overlook a small square in the old town (request quiet room in back, cozy lounge; Plaza Torres de Omaña 1—located up the stairs on the second floor; +34 987 875 187, www. sanmartinhostales.es, sanmartinhostal@hotmail.com).

Eating in León

León is one of few Spanish cities whose bars still honor the old tradition of giving a free (if modest) tapa to anyone buying a drink. In many bars the menu includes *limonada*, a Leónese drink of chilled red wine mixed with cinnamon, lemon, sugar, and sometimes other fruit.

Your best bet for finding eats in León is to stroll the **Barrio Húmedo** area, south of Calle Ancha. This zone is packed with restaurants and bars offering good food and ambience.

Plaza de San Martín Tapas Crawl: In the "Wet Quarter," locals head for Plaza de San Martín to eat and drink. Survey the many little bars on or near the square, noting how locals know each bar's specialty and generally stick to that dish when ordering. Consider these joints: **$$ Tabierna Los Cazurros** offers a stylish hangout with delicious meat pies, called empanadas (+34 987 252 233). **$ Mesón Jabugo** has a wide range of tapas—try the local specialty *cecina de León*—beef that has been salted, sun-dried, and smoked (+34 620 982 186). If you're still hungry, **$$ Mesón el Tizón** fills one tight room with a bar in front and seating in back—order hot *raciones* from its chalkboard menu (Calle de las Carnicerías 1, +34 987 256 049). Just off Plaza San Martín are two more options offering tasty local cured meats and hearty regional stews: **$$ La**

Bodega del Húmedo (Calle Plegarias 8, +34 987 076 128) and
$$ Bar El Altar (Calle Plegarias 7, +34 987 031 028).

León Connections

From León by Bus to: Astorga (hourly, 50 minutes), **Burgos** (3/
day, 2-3 hours), **Lugo** (8/day, 4.5 hours), **Santiago de Compostela**
(1/day, 6 hours), **Madrid** (10/day to Estación Sur, 4 hours; 6/day
direct to Moncloa and Madrid Barajas Airport, 4 hours). Bus info:
Alsa (www.alsa.es).

By Train to: Burgos (4/day, 2 hours), **San Sebastián** (2/day,
5-6 hours), **Pamplona** (2/day, 4.5 hours), **Santiago de Compostela**
(1/day direct, 4.5 hours; 2/day with transfer in Ourense, 6.5 hours),
Madrid (8/day, 2.5-5 hours).

From León to Galicia

This section, arguably the most diverse stretch of the Camino,
begins in the flatness of the Meseta Central around León. Then,
around Astorga, the landscape gradually becomes more varied and
lush, as the Camino approaches the mountainous El Bierzo region
(the northwest fringe of Castile and León).

In its final stretch, the Camino leaves the broad expanse of the
Meseta Central and climbs steeply into Galicia (gah-LEE-thee-
ah). Green and hilly, Galicia shatters visitors' preconceptions about
Spain. There's something vaguely Irish about Galicia—and it's not
just the mossy stonework and green, rolling hills. The region actu-
ally shares a strain of Celtic heritage with its cousins across the
Cantabrian Sea. People here are friendly, and if you listen hard
enough, you might just hear the sound of bagpipes.

• *Begin by making your way west, to Astorga. You can stay on the N-120
highway, or pay a toll to zip there more quickly on the AP-71 expressway.*

ASTORGA

Astorga (ah-STOR-gah) sits at the intersection of two ancient
roads: the Camino and a north-south trade route from Sevilla to
the north coast. When León was a humble Roman camp, "As-
turica" was the provincial capital. But today the fortunes are re-
versed, as welcoming, laid-back, sleepy Astorga (with about 11,000
people)—just big enough to have some interesting sightseeing and
good hotels and restaurants—is a nice small-town alternative to
the big city of León. The main attraction here is the memorable
Bishop's Palace by Antoni Gaudí. On a sweet side note, Astor-
ga's connection to chocolate dates back to the 16th century, when
Hernán Cortés brought the cocoa bean from Central America to
Spain. Some even claim that Astorga is the European birthplace

of chocolate. The local industry peaked in 1925 with 51 chocolate makers in business. Today there are only a few left, but chocolate can be found everywhere.

Tourist Information: Astorga's TI shares a square with the Bishop's Palace and cathedral (daily 10:00-14:00 & 16:00-19:00, shorter hours off-season and closed Sun afternoon and all day Mon, Plaza Eduardo de Castro 5, +34 987 618 222, www.turismoastorga. es).

Arrival in Astorga: The **bus** station is just outside the old town, behind the Bishop's Palace. **Drivers** follow signs for *Centro Ciudad* and *Centro Urbano,* drive through the middle of town, and park in front of the TI and cathedral (to park in a blue-painted spot, prepay at the meter and put the ticket on your dashboard). Or park below the cathedral outside the Roman wall for free.

Sights in Astorga: The striking **Bishop's Palace** (Palacio Epis-copal), rated ▲, is a fanciful Gothic-style castle, similar to Gaudí's

Casa de Botines in León (€6, daily May-Oct 10:00-14:00 & 16:00-20:00, shorter hours off-season, +34 987 616 882, www.palaciodegaudi.es). In-side you'll see Gaudí's genius in the bishop's fine rooms, decorated with frescoes. The palace hosts a museum that vaguely describes the Cami-no and the history of Astorga, and provides a safe place for some of the region's fine medieval church art. You'll see a 17th-century statue of Pilgrim James, a few historical Camino documents, ecclesiastical gear, and a gal-lery of contemporary Spanish art from the surrounding region. Overall, the museum is not as good as it should be, but it's worth-while mostly for a chance to see a medieval-inspired Gaudí interior. Throw in an extra euro to get the multimedia tablet in English, which will enhance the experience.

Next to (and upstaged by) the palace is Astorga's light-filled Gothic **cathedral,** with a marvelously carved choir and a chapel to St. James that is popular with pilgrims. Tourists can only get in by paying for the attached museum, which shows off a substantial collection of paintings, altarpieces, and vestments (€5, includes au-dioguide, daily 10:00-20:30, shorter hours Nov-March, closed Sun mornings for Mass).

If you have extra time and love chocolate, the 10-minute walk from the cathedral to the **Chocolate Museum** (Museo del Choco-late) is well worth it. Follow the signs on Avenida de la Estación to a yellow house and the museum (€2, Tue-Sat 10:30-14:00 &

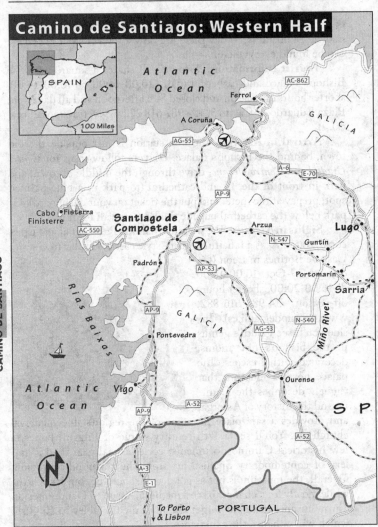

Camino de Santiago: Western Half

SPAIN

100 Miles

Atlantic Ocean

Ferrol

AC-862

GALICIA

A Coruña

AG-55

A-6

E-70

AP-9

Cabo Finisterre

Fisterra

AC-550

Santiago de Compostela

Arzua

Lugo

N-547

Guntín

Padrón

AP-53

Portomarín

Sarria

Rías Baixas

AP-9

GALICIA

AG-53

N-540

Miño River

Pontevedra

Atlantic Ocean

Vigo

Ourense

S P

AP-9

A-52

A-52

N

A-3

E-1

To Porto & Lisbon

PORTUGAL

16:30-19:00, Sun morning only, closed Mon, Avenida de la Estación 16, +34 987 616 220). Inside, the exhibits explain the cocoa bean and give an introduction to artisanal chocolate production in the region. Watch a video and inspect the collection of tools and machines. On your way out, try a couple of the samples in the little shop—it'll be hard to resist buying a bar or two. You can find several small stores selling artisanal chocolate (along with *mantecadas*, local muffin-like pastries) on the street leading from the cathedral to Plaza España.

Sleeping in Astorga: If you prefer to sleep in a small town,

Astorga is a good alternative to the big city of León (though values here are no better than in the city).

$ Hotel Gaudí has 35 woody rooms over a restaurant across from the cathedral; some have views of the Bishop's Palace (air-con in most rooms, elevator, pay parking, Plaza Eduardo de Castro 6, +34 987 615 654, www.gaudihotel.es, reservas@gaudihotel.es).

$ Hotel Astur Plaza, which feels more business-class, has 40 rooms right on the main square. Choose between a room overlooking the square—with a clock tower that clangs every 15 minutes—or a quieter back room. They offer spa facilities at their sister hotel for weary pilgrims (air-con; pay parking—first-come, first-

served; Plaza de España 2, +34 987 617 665, www.hotelasturplaza.
es, info@hotelasturplaza.es).

$ Ciudad de Astorga Hotel has 33 business-class rooms with
contemporary decor, a pleasant patio, and a spa with garden terrace.
It's about three blocks from the cathedral (air-con, pay parking,
Calle de los Sitios 7, +34 987 603 001, www.hotelciudaddeastorga.
com, reservas@hotelciudaddeastorga.com).

Eating in Astorga: A couple of blocks from the cathedral
right along the Camino, **$$ Restaurante Las Termas** is well re-
garded for its food—especially the traditional stew, *cocido maragato*
(open for lunch only, closed Mon, Calle Santiago 1, +34 987 602
212). **$$ Hotel Gaudí,** listed earlier, has an atmospheric bar with
tapas and *raciones,* as well as a restaurant (open daily).

Connections: Astorga is well connected by bus to **León**
(hourly, 50 minutes), **Ponferrada** (hourly, 1 hour), **Villafranca del
Bierzo** (3/day, 2 hours), **Lugo** (8/day, 2-3 hours), and **Santiago de
Compostela** (5/day, 5 hours).

• *After Astorga, you can either zip up to Galicia on the A-6 expressway
(toward Ponferrada) or stick with the Camino a bit farther south on
much slower regional roads (LE-142). These two routes converge again
at the small city of Ponferrada. Soon after, A-6 climbs up into the hills
and to the town of Villafranca del Bierzo.*

If you're sticking with the Camino, you'll pass near the...

IRON CROSS (CRUZ DE FERRO)

Near the top of Mount Irago is an iron cross atop a tall wooden
pole, set in a huge pile of stones built up over the years by pilgrims
unloading their "sins" brought from home (or picked up en route).
It's a major landmark for Camino pilgrims but difficult to reach for
drivers (figure an hour's hike off the main road). From the cross it's
a 30-minute walk to the nearly ruined stone village of Foncebadón.

VILLAFRANCA DEL BIERZO

Villafranca is the capital of the westernmost part of León, El Bierzo, which is trying to build a good reputation for its wine and
culinary specialties. Dubbed
"Little Compostela" for its array
of historical buildings, this town
is set in an attractive hilly terrain
strewn with grapevines, cherry
trees, and vegetable patches.
Though hardly thrilling, Villafranca del Bierzo is worth a
quick stop for its pilgrim ambience.

Tourist Information: The TI is at Avenida Díaz Ovelar 10

(daily 10:00-14:00 & 16:00-20:00, off-season until 19:00 and closed Mon, +34 987 540 028, www.villafrancadelbierzo.org). Plenty of free parking is available near the TI, just past the large church on the right when entering town.

Sights in Villafranca: To play pilgrim, hike from the main square up to the town's stout 14th-century castle (not open to the public). Then follow signs for *Iglesia Románica*, the Romanesque 12th-century Church of St. James (Santiago). The church has a "gate of forgiveness" (*puerta del perdón*, on the side facing the town). Thanks to a 16th-century papal ruling, if a pilgrim had come this far, fell ill, and couldn't continue over the rugged terrain to Santiago, he or she was pardoned anyway. (Handy loophole.)

Next to the church is the Villafranca ¢ *albergue*, a funky pilgrims' dorm with oodles of pilgrims bonding. It was built on the site of a medieval clinic that cared for those who needed to take advantage of the *puerta del perdón* (at the time, the clinic here was the only source of medical aid for 300 miles). Today this 80-bed *albergue* provides bunks to 10,000 pilgrims a year. They even have a separate room for snorers. If you'd like to learn about the system (or buy a scallop shell), stop in. It's run by Jesús, whose father began helping pilgrims here in the 1930s. Jesús welcomes curious non-pilgrims, albeit with the motto "The tourist demands, the pilgrim thanks" (you can reserve a bed here ahead of time, +34 987 540 260, www.alberguedelapiedra.com, amigos@alberguedelapiedra.com).

Sleeping and Eating in Villafranca: $ MicroHostal La Puerta del Perdón, warmly run by Herminio, is just the place for fancy pilgrims or anyone needing a comfortable and economical place to sleep and eat in Villafranca. A couple of the seven rooms have low, angled ceilings, so taller travelers may need to duck. The fine little restaurant is open to the public for lunch but only to hotel guests for dinner (facing the castle on the uphill side a block below the Church of St. James at Plaza de Prim 4, +34 987 540 614, www.lapuertadelperdon.com, info@lapuertadelperdon.com).

• *Just after Villafranca del Bierzo on the A-6 expressway, you cross into the final region on the Camino: Galicia.*

Shortly after entering Galicia, take the freeway exit and follow signs to Pedrafita do Cebreiro. *From Pedrafita, a well-maintained mountain road (LU-633) twists its way up to the classic Galician pilgrim village of O Cebreiro. The road has plenty of pullouts for photo ops. The town itself is not well marked; turn off at* Conxunto Histórico-Artístico *for parking.*

O Cebreiro

An impossibly quaint hobbit hamlet perched on a ridge high above
nothing, O Cebreiro (oh theh-
BRAY-roh) whispers, "Wel-
come to Galicia." This rustic village evokes an uncomplicated,
almost prehistoric past, when
people lived very close to nature,
in stone igloos with thatched
roofs. With sweeping views
across the verdant but harsh
Galician landscape, O Cebreiro

is constantly pummeled by some of the fiercest weather in Spain.
And it's all within a five-minute drive of the freeway.

Wander around. Enjoy the remoteness. O Cebreiro smells like
wood fires, manure, and pilgrim B.O. Get a snack or drink at a bar,
or browse through a gift shop. A few townspeople (who jabber at
each other in Galego—see page 347) share the town with weary
pilgrims on an adrenaline high after finally reaching Galicia. The
town's dogs, who've known each other their whole lives, still bark at
each other territorially from across the street, completely ignoring
the backpackers who regularly trudge through town.

Sights in O Cebreiro

▲Pallozas

From Celtic times 1,500 years ago, right up until the 1960s, the
villagers of O Cebreiro lived in humble round stone huts with
peaked thatched roofs, called
pallozas. One of the nine surviving *pallozas* has been turned into
a loosely run museum, where an
attendant is paid by the government to welcome visitors and
answer questions.

Cost and Hours: Free,
hours vary with hut caretaker's
schedule, generally Tue-Sat
8:30-14:30, mid-Sept-mid-June 11:00-18:00, closed Sun-Mon
year-round, https://museos.xunta.gal. If a door of a round hut is
open, poke inside.

Visiting the Huts: Here visitors can learn about the lifestyle
of the people who lived in *pallozas* until not so long ago. Upon
entering a *palloza,* you'll find the only "private" room in the house,
belonging to the parents. Beyond that is a living area around a

humble fire. (Notice there's no chimney—smoke seeps out through the thatch.) Ponder the ancient furniture. Surrounding the fire are clever benches (which were also used, by the kids, as very hard beds) with pull-down counters so they could double as a table at mealtime. The big beam with the chain could be swung over the fire for cooking. Looking up, you'll see the remains of a wooden ceiling that prevented sparks from igniting the thatch. The giant black-metal spirals suspended from the ceiling were used to smoke chorizo sausage—very efficient.

Attached to this living area is a miniature "barn." Animals lived on the lower level, while people slept on the upper level (which has been removed, but you can still see on the wall where the floor was once supported)—kept warm by all that livestock body heat. About a dozen people (and their animals) lived in one small hut. But thanks to the ideal insulation provided by the thatch, and the warmth from the fire and animals, it was toasty even through the difficult winter.

▲Royal St. Mary's Church (Santa María la Real)

All roads lead to the village church. Founded in the year 836—not long after the remains of St. James were found in Santiago—this

pre-Romanesque build-ing is supposedly the old-est church on the entire French Road of the Cami-no.

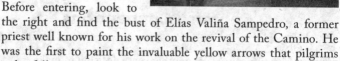

Cost and Hours: Free, daily 9:00-13:00 & 15:00-20:00.

Visiting the Church: Before entering, look to the right and find the bust of Elías Valiña Sampedro, a former priest well known for his work on the revival of the Camino. He was the first to paint the invaluable yellow arrows that pilgrims today follow.

Inside the church, observe how the interior is surprisingly spacious but very simple. Notice the sunken floor: The building is actually embedded into the ground for added protection against winter storms. At the desk inside they stamp pilgrims' credentials and sell votive candles. (I don't think there's anything wrong with giving your guidebook an O Cebreiro stamp—I did.)

The baptistery, in a tiny side room near the entrance, is separate from the main part of the church, as dictated by ancient tradition. It has a giant and very rough font used for immersion baptisms.

In the chapel to the right of the main altar is a much-revered 12th-century golden chalice and reliquary, which holds items

relating to a popular local miracle: A peasant from a nearby village braved a fierce winter snowstorm to come to this church for the Eucharist. The priest scoffed at his devotion, only to find that the host and wine had physically turned into the body and blood of Christ, staining the linens beneath them, which are now in the silver box.

Sleeping and Eating in O Cebreiro

The only businesses in town are a half-dozen very humble pub-restaurants, which feed pilgrims and other visitors hearty Galician cuisine in a communal atmosphere. You'll see signs offering a stick-to-your-ribs €10 "pilgrim menu." Many of these places also rent a few rooms upstairs. With inclement weather, doors are often closed—don't be shy; just walk right in. Be warned that these rooms are very rustic, English can be tricky, and reservations are only by phone.

Try **$ Hotel O Cebreiro**—run by Doña Pilar Valiña, the niece of Camino advocate Elias Valiña Sampedro—which has five comfortable rooms and a bar/restaurant downstairs (+34 982 367 182, www.hotelcebreiro.com, informacion@hotelcebreiro.com). On the small main square, find ¢ **Casa Navarro**—a *casa rural* with a handful of cozy, second-floor rooms—run by friendly owner José, who happens to be the nephew of Doña Pilar (+34 982 367 007, www.casaturismoruralnavarro.com, info@casaturismoruralnavarro.com). Other options include ¢ **Casa Carolo** (laundry service, +34 982 367 168) and ¢ **Mesón Antón** (also offers mountain bike rental, +34 638 350 753, https://hostal-meson-anton.negocio.site). The ¢ *albergue*, which is open only to pilgrims, is perched on a hill at the edge of town.

O Cebreiro Connections

BY CAR

From O Cebreiro you've got another route decision to make.

To stick with the Camino, you'll continue on LU-633, along twisty roads, toward Santiago. Along the way you'll pass through some interesting larger towns. **Samos** has a gigantic monastery and perfectly manicured cloister garden. **Sarria** is forgettable, but it's just over 100 kilometers (62 miles) from Santiago, making it a popular place to begin a truncated pilgrimage (since you need to walk at least that far to earn your *compostela* certificate). **Portomarín** is a relatively new town, built only after the River Miño was flooded to create a reservoir in the 1950s. The stout and blocky late-Romanesque Church of San Juan was moved to a new site, stone by stone—and if you look closely enough you can see how the stones were numbered to keep track of where they fit.

I prefer the faster expressway route (backtrack to A-6, which you'll take north, following signs for *A Coruña*), which offers the opportunity to dip into the appealing walled city of Lugo.

Lugo

While not technically on the French Road of the Camino de Santiago, the midsized city of Lugo (pop. 98,000) warrants a detour for car travelers. Boasting what are arguably the best-preserved Roman walls in Spain—a mile and a third long, completely encircling the town, draped with moss, and receding into the misty horizon—Lugo offers an ideal place for an evocative stroll. Lugo feels like a poor man's Santiago, with a patina of poverty and atmospherically crumbling buildings. Quirky chimneys thrust up through rickety old slate roofs. And yet there's something proud and welcoming about the town. Aside from the walls, Lugo has a cathedral and gregarious Galician charm, making it a fine place to spend some time.

Orientation to Lugo

Tourist Information: The TI is a few steps up a pedestrian street off the main square, Plaza Maior—look for the yellow signs (daily 10:00-20:00, shorter hours off-season; Praza do Campo 11, +34 982 251 658, www.lugo.gal). Inside the TI is an interpretive center describing the city's history and Roman walls.

Arrival in Lugo: The bus station is just outside the town walls; once inside the old town, the main square and TI are a block away. The train station is two blocks east of the town walls. Drivers follow signs to *Centro Ciudad* and *Centro Urbano*. Once you enter the town walls, parking garages are signed for *Plaza de Santo Domingo* or *Anxel Fole*—both are centrally located.

Sights in Lugo

In addition to the ancient walls and the cathedral (described on the next page), Lugo has a provincial museum and a Roman museum.

Roman Walls (Murallas Romanas)

The town's walls provide a kind of circular park where locals and visitors can stroll at rooftop level. You can access the walls at various points around town (you'll find stairs near most of the gates where traffic enters the old town), walk the entire way around in about 45 minutes. With less time the most interesting stretch is along the west side of town: Walk up the ramp behind the cathedral and turn right, watching behind you for tingly views of the walls and cathedral spires.

Cost and Hours: Free and always open.

Lugo Cathedral (Catedral de Lugo)

Lugo's cathedral is vast, dark, and dusty, with an unexpected Rococo altarpiece glittering with silver. While it's a lovely cathedral, it pales in comparison to Santiago's.

Cost and Hours: Cathedral, cloister, and museum—€6; open Mon-Sat 10:30-18:00, shorter hours off-season, closed Sun year-round; guided tour of roofs and towers offered Thu-Sat; +34 683 166 703, www.catedraldelugo.es.

Sleeping in Lugo

Sleeping in Lugo is worth considering to break up the long journey to Santiago from Cantabria or León. Budget *hostales* cluster just southeast of the town walls (near the bus station). The following two hotels are the only ones inside the old town. They may be willing to make a deal—ask for their best price.

$$ Pazo de Orban e Sangro is the town splurge, renting 12 rooms with hardwood floors, flat-screen TVs, slippery rates, and luxurious furnishings. It's just inside the town walls near the cathedral (air-con, elevator, pay parking, Travesía Miño, +34 982 240 217, www.pazodeorban.es, info@pazodeorban.es).

$ Hotel Méndez Núñez, right in the heart of the old town, has a classy old lobby, a medieval-feeling lounge, and 70 renovated rooms (air-con, elevator, Rúa da Raiña 1, +34 982 230 711, www.hotelmendeznunez.com, hotel@hotelmendeznunez.com).

Lugo Connections

Lugo is connected by Alsa bus to **Santiago de Compostela** (5/day, 2.5 hours), **Astorga** (8/day, 2-3 hours), and **León** (8/day, 4.5 hours).

• *After Lugo, the end is in sight. You have one final route decision to make: The fastest way (about 1.5 hours to Santiago) is to stick with the A-6 expressway north to A Coruña, then pay to take the AP-9 tollway south to Santiago. But if you'd like to rejoin the Camino for the last stretch—following in the footsteps (or tire treads) of a millennium of pil-*

grims—*follow signs from* Lugo *toward* Ourense *(on N-540/N-640, about 20-30 minutes longer than expressway). In* Guntín, *split off on N-547 and head for* Santiago de Compostela *(see next chapter). Buen Camino!*

Cantabria

CAMINO DE SANTIAGO

ON THE NORTH COAST
If you're connecting the Basque Country and Galicia (Santiago de Compostela) along the coast, you'll go through the provinces of Cantabria and Asturias. Both are interesting, but Cantabria (kahn-TAH-bree-ah) has a few villages and sights that are especially worth a visit. A drive through the Cantabrian countryside comes with endless glimpses of charming stone homes. And a night or two in this region is a good way to break up the long drive between Bilbao and Santiago (figure over seven hours straight through).

The dramatic peaks of the Picos de Europa and their rolling, green foothills define this region, giving it a more rugged feel than the "northern Riviera" ambience of the Basque region. The quaint town of Santillana del Mar makes a fine home base for visiting the prehistoric Altamira Caves. Comillas is a pleasant beach town with a surprising abundance of Modernista architecture.

Though it's largely undiscovered by Americans, Cantabria is heavily touristed by Europeans and very crowded in July and August. For information on the area, go to www.turismodecantabria.es and select English in the drop-down menu.

Towns and Sights in Cantabria

SANTILLANA DEL MAR
Every guidebook imparts the same two tidbits about Santillana del Mar: One is that it's known as the "town of three lies," as it's neither holy *(Santi)*, nor flat *(llana)*, nor on the ocean *(del Mar)*. The other is that the existentialist philosopher Jean-Paul Sartre once called it the "prettiest village in Spain."

The town is worth the fuss—it's what Spaniards would call *preciosa*. The proud little stone village consists of three cobbled streets and

a collection of squares, climbing up over mild hills from where the village meets the main road.

Tourist Information: The modern TI is right at the entrance to the town (open daily, Jesús Otero 20, +34 942 818 251). Only residents (and guests of hotels that offer parking) are allowed to drive in the center; instead, leave your car in one of the two big parking lots (pay in-season, free off-season)—one by the TI, and the other just to the south, at Plaza del Rey.

Sleeping in Santillana: Two swanky, arrogant paradors hold court on the main square—**$$ Parador de Santillana del Mar** and **$$ Parador de Santillana Gil Blas** (www.parador.es for both). Other options include **$ Hotel Altamira** (www.hotelaltamira.com) and **¢ Hospedaje Octavio** (https://hospedajeoctavio.negocio.site).

▲ALTAMIRA CAVES

Not far from Santillana del Mar, the Altamira Caves (Cuevas de Altamira) contain some of the best examples of prehistoric art anywhere (and are worth ▲▲▲ for those who love prehistoric caves). In 1879, the young daughter of a local archaeologist discovered several 14,000-year-old paintings in a limestone cave. By the 1960s and 1970s, it became a tremendously popular tourist destination. The number of visitors became too much for the delicate paintings, and the cave was closed. Now a replica cave and museum sit near the original site, allowing visitors to experience these facsimiles of prehistoric artwork in something approximating the original setting.

Cost and Hours: €3, free Sat after 14:00 and all day Sun; open Tue-Sat 9:30-20:00, Nov-April until 18:00; Sun 9:30-15:00 and closed Mon year-round; +34 942 818 005, www.culturaydeporte. gob.es—enter "Altamira Caves" in the search bar.

Reservations: In July and August, consider reserving entry to the replica cave through Banco Santander. To book ahead at no extra charge, you drop by any Santander bank branch or book online (in Spanish only, no online reservations possible for free Saturday afternoon and Sunday visits, find advance ticket link at website listed above). Request a specific date and time (one-hour window) for your visit. Take your ticket or confirmation number to the information counter, where you can schedule a guided tour (explained next).

Tours: You can visit the caves on your own or ask to join a free 30-minute guided tour when you purchase your ticket. Note that spaces are limited and the tours fill up fast in the busy summer season (get there when it opens to schedule a tour). The last tour departs 30 minutes before closing.

Getting There: The caves are on a ridge in the countryside a little over a mile southwest of Santillana del Mar. There's no public

transportation to the site. To get from Santillana del Mar to the caves without a car, it's either a 30-minute walk or a cheap taxi ride.

Visiting the Caves: Your visit starts at the museum and then moves on to the replica cave. The fine **museum** (to the right of the information desk) has good English descriptions, featuring models and reproductions of the cave dwellers who made these drawings (and their clothes, tools, and remains). The exhibit also has an account of the cave's discovery and its eventual acceptance by the scientific community (who were initially skeptical that "primitive" people were capable of such sophisticated art).

Next, you'll visit the highly detailed **replica cave** (either on your own or with a tour). You'll see an excavation site with the implements used by modern scientists to dig up ancient relics from three layers: On the bottom are hunting tools and chips of flint from Solutrean cavemen (18,500 years ago); above that is mostly clay, with the remains of a cave bear; and the top layer holds hearths and tools from the Magdalenian period (14,000 years ago). A workshop area demonstrates the techniques and tools of the prehistoric artists. Finally, you'll reach the great cave, decorated with 16 bison, a few running boars, some horses, and a giant deer—plus a few handprints and several mysterious symbols.

What's amazing about these paintings is simply that they were made by Cro-Magnon cave people. And yet the artists had an incredible grasp of delicate composition, depicting these animals with such true-to-life simplicity. Some of them are mere outlines, a couple of curvy lines—masterful abstraction that could make Picasso jealous.

So why did they make these paintings? Nobody knows for sure. The general agreement is that it wasn't simply for decoration and that the paintings must have served some religious or shamanistic purpose.

COMILLAS

Just 15 minutes west of Santillana del Mar, perched on a hill overlooking the Atlantic, you'll find quirky Comillas. Comillas presides over a sandy beach but feels more like a hill town, with twisty lanes clambering up away from the sea. Comillas makes a good home base if you prefer beach access, fascinating architecture, and a more lived-in feel to the touristy quaintness of Santillana del Mar.

Tourist Information: The TI is in the Town Hall on Plaza Joaquín del Piélago, the town's westernmost square (daily 9:00-21:00, shorter hours off-season, +34 942 722 591, www.comillas.es).

Sights in Comillas: Comillas enjoys a surprising abundance of striking Modernista architecture. (For more on this unique, Barcelona-born take on Art Nouveau, see page 97.) There are three

biggies: El Capricho and Palacio de Sobrellano line up along a ridge at the west end of town (just beyond the town center and parking lot, over the big park), while Universidad Pontificia faces them from a parallel ridge.

El Capricho was designed by the great Catalan architect Antoni Gaudí. As one of Gaudí's very first creations, the house attracts architecture fans from around the world. The building's sunflower-dappled exterior alludes to Gaudí's plan for it: His "sunflower design" attempted to maximize exposure to light by arranging rooms to get sun during the part of the day they were most used (€7, daily July-Sept 10:30-21:00, shorter hours off-season, +34 942 720 365, www.elcaprichodegaudi.com).

Designed by Gaudí's mentor, Joan Martorell i Montells, the **Palacio de Sobrellano** hints at early Barcelona-style Modernisme. Guided tours in Spanish are the only way to visit the spectacular home, but it's worth it to see how the other half lived (€3, grounds open daily at 10:00; 25-minute guided visits leave on the hour June-Sept 10:30-14:30 & 15:30-19:30; shorter hours and closed Mon off-season, last tour one hour before closing; +34 942 720 339, http://centros.culturadecantabria.com).

The huge building of the **Universidad Pontificia** was also designed by Joan Martorell i Montells. Originally built as a Jesuit seminary in 1883, today the building is used by the Fundación Comillas to teach Spanish and Hispanic culture along with business and law (€3.50, guided visits—Spanish only—at the top of each hour, daily 10:00-13:00, June-Sept also 17:00-20:00, +34 942 715 500, +34 630 256 767, www.fundacioncomillas.es).

The beachside road below the Universidad Pontificia, lined with a few hotels, is worth a stroll, especially to get a glimpse of a guardian angel. Famed Modernisme architect Lluís Domènech i Montaner converted old church ruins into an interesting cemetery with one spectacular tomb: His vault for the **Piélago family** depicts an angel riding the surf atop a giant wave.

On the opposite hill, look for an Art Nouveau statue, donated by the town, portraying the **First Marquis of Comillas.** He proudly stands atop a column, carried by one of his ships.

The town center, a two-minute walk inland, is just as pleasant—with an odd jumble of squares surrounding the big Parochial Church. A final bit of Modernisme is the Domènech i Montaner **lamppost/fountain** (near the TI), which commemorates Comillas as the first town in Spain to have electricity.

Sleeping in Comillas: In the town center, south of the big Parochial Church, near the long, skinny, restaurant-lined Plaza de Primo de Rivera (also known as "El Corro"), try **$ Hotel Marina de Campíos** (www.marinadecampios.com) or **$ Pasaje San Jorge** (www.pasajesanjorge.com).

▲PICOS DE EUROPA

The Picos de Europa—comprising one of Spain's most popular national parks—are a relatively small stretch of cut-glass mountain peaks (the steepest in Spain, some taller than 8,500 feet) just 15 miles inland from the ocean. These dramatic mountains are home to goats, brown bears, eagles, vultures, wallcreepers (rare birds), and happy hikers. Outdoorsy types could spend days exploring this dramatic patch of Spain, which is packed with visitors in the summer.

The Picos de Europa cover an area of about 25 miles by 25 miles. They're located where three of Spain's regions converge: Cantabria, Asturias, and León. (Frustratingly, each region's tourist office pretends that the parts of the park in the other regions don't exist—so it's very hard to get information, say, about Asturias' Cares Gorge when you're in Potes, Cantabria.) In addition to three regions, the park contains three different limestone massifs—large masses of rock—separated by rivers.

I'll focus on the Cantabrian part of the Picos, which contains the region's most accessible and enjoyable bits: the scenic drive through La Hermida Gorge, the charming mountain town of Potes, and the ride on the Fuente Dé cable car up to sky-high mountaintop views. This part of the Picos is doable as a long day trip from Santillana del Mar or Comillas (but is easier if you stay in Potes). The next-best activity is to hike the yawning chasm of the Cares Gorge, which is deeper in the park and requires another full day.

Getting Around the Picos de Europa

The Picos de Europa are best with a car. If you don't have wheels, skip them, because bus connections are sparse, time-consuming, and frustrating.

The A-8 expressway squeezes between the Picos and the north coast of Spain; roads branch into and around the Picos, but beware: Many of them traverse high-mountain passes—often on bad roads—and can take longer to drive through than you expect. *Puerto* means "pass" (slow going) and *desfiladero* means "gorge" (quicker but often still twisty).

Assuming you're most interested in Potes and Fuente Dé, you'll focus on the eastern part of the park, approaching from the A-8 expressway (or from Santillana del Mar and Comillas). You'll go through Unquera and catch N-621 into the park (follow signs for *Potes*). Wind your way through La Hermida Gorge (Desfiladero de la Hermida) and stop for a photo en route to Potes (about one hour, depending on traffic). The road crisscrosses between both banks of the Río Deva for spectacular scenery. Count on 30 more minutes to arrive at Fuente Dé.

The Cares Gorge, officially in Asturias, can be approached from either the south (the village of Caín, deep in the mountains beyond Potes) or the north (Puente Poncebos, with easier access)—but note that there's no direct road between the gorge and Potes.

Visiting the Picos de Europa

I've arranged these sights as you'll come to them if you approach from the coast (that is, from the expressway, Santillana del Mar, or Comillas).

Potes

This quaint mountain village, at the intersection of four valleys, is the hub of Cantabria's Picos de Europa tourist facilities. It's got an impressive old convent and a picturesque stone bridge spanning the Río Deva. It's a good place to buy maps and books, mainly geared toward UK tourists who arrive by ferry in Santander. Free parking can be found all around the church. Check in at the **TI** with any travel questions (unpredictable hours, but generally July-Sept daily 10:00-14:00 & 16:00-20:00, shorter hours off-season, Plaza la Serna, +34 942 730 787).

Sleeping in Potes: Overlooking the river, **$ Casa Cayo** has 17 cozy rooms and a fine restaurant (closed Christmas-mid-March, Calle Cántabra 6, +34 942 730 119, www.casacayo.com, informacion@casacayo.com).

▲▲Fuente Dé Cable Car (Teleférico Fuente Dé)

Perhaps the single most thrilling activity in the Picos de Europa is to take the cable car at Fuente Dé. The longest single-span cable car in Europe zips you up 2,600 feet in just four ear-popping minutes. Once at the top (altitude 6,000 feet), you're rewarded with a breathtaking panorama of the Picos de Europa. The huge, pointy, Matterhorn-like peak on your right is Peña Remoña (7,350 feet).

The cable car station on top has WCs, a cafeteria (commanding views, miserable food), and a gift shop (limited hiking guides—equip yourself before you ascend).

Cost and Hours: €20 round-trip, €11 one-way (if you're hiking down—explained later), purchase at ticket office or online (see next), runs every 30 minutes (more frequent with demand); daily July-mid-Sept 9:00-20:00, mid-Sept-Dec and Feb-June 10:00-18:00—until 19:00 or 20:00 on June weekends, closed Jan unless weather is unseasonably good. Every 100 hours, the cable car must be closed briefly for maintenance, so it's a good idea to check ahead before making the drive.

Advance Tickets Recommended: In summer you may have to wait in long lines both to ascend and to descend, since the cable car carries only 20 people. To reserve a spot, buy a timed ticket online at least 24 hours in advance (https://entradas.telefericofuentede. com).

Information: Cable car +34 942 736 610; you'll find links to *teleférico* hours at www.cantur.com. The Picos de Europa National Park runs a helpful information kiosk in the parking lot during peak season (July-Aug), with handouts and advice on hikes (including the one listed below). Even better, stop at the big National Park office in Sotama, just before Potes on the way to Fuente Dé (daily 9:00-18:00, in summer may be open until 20:00, +34 942 738 109, http://parquenacionalpicoseuropa.es).

Hiking Back Down: Once you're up there, those with enough time and strong knees should consider hiking back down. From the cable car station at the top, follow the yellow-and-white signs to *Espinama*, always bearing to the right. You'll hike gradually uphill (gain about 300 feet), then down (3,500 feet) the back side of the mountain, with totally different views than the cable car ride up: green, rolling hills instead of sharp, white peaks. Once in Espinama, you'll continue down along the main road back to the parking lot at the base of the cable car (signs to *Fuente Dé*). Figure about four hours total (nine miles) at a brisk pace from the top back to the bottom. Note that the trails are covered by snow into April and sometimes even May; ask at the ranger station near Potes about conditions before you hike (see "Information," earlier).

▲Cares Gorge (Garganta del Cares)

This impressive gorge hike—surrounded on both sides by sheer cliff walls, with a long-distance drop running parallel to (and sometimes under) the trail—is ideal for hardy hikers. The trail was built in the 1940s to maintain the hydroelectric canal that runs through the mountains, but today it has become a very popular summer hiking destination. The trail follows the Río Cares seven miles between the towns of Caín (in the south) and Camarmeña (near Puente Poncebos, in the north). Along the way, you'll cross harrowing bridges and take trails burrowed into the rock face. Because it's deeper in the mountains and requires a good six hours (13 miles round-trip, with some ups and downs), it's best left to those who are really up for a hike and not simply passing through the Picos.

Getting There: To reach Caín from Potes, you'll drive on rough, twisty roads (N-621) over the stunning Puerto de San Gloria pass (5,250 feet, watched over by a sweet bronze deer), into a green, moss-covered gorge. Just past the village of Portilla de la Reina, turn right (following signs for *Santa Marina de Valdeón*) to reach Caín. Note that this is a very long day trip from Potes, and almost brutal if home-basing in Comillas or Santillana del Mar.

SANTIAGO DE COMPOSTELA

The best destination in the northwestern province of Galicia, Santiago de Compostela rivals Granada as the most magical city in Spain. While Granada reminds visitors of Spain's Moorish past, Santiago de Compostela offers one of the most significant cathedrals in the Christian world—and a glimpse back through centuries of pilgrimage. The Santiago Cathedral has long had a powerful and mysterious draw on travelers: More than a thousand years' worth of Christian pilgrims have trod the desolate trail across the north of Spain just to peer up at its glorious facade.

But there's more to this city than pilgrims and the remains of St. James. Contrary to what you've heard, the rain in Spain does *not* fall mainly on the plain—it falls in Galicia. This "Atlantic Northwest" of Spain is like the Pacific Northwest of the United States, with hilly, lush terrain that enjoys far more precipitation than the interior, plus dramatic coastal scenery, delicious seafood, fine local wines, and an easygoing ambience. The Spanish interior might be arid, but the northwest requires rain gear. Even the tourists here have a grungy vibe: Packs of happy hipster pilgrims seek to find themselves while hiking the ancient Camino de Santiago from France (described in the previous chapter).

Santiago is the capital of Galicia, so there are government workers here in addition to the many locals who serve the constant flow of tourists. It's a sturdy city that, in its day, was one of Europe's most important religious centers, built of granite and later turned mossy green by the notorious weather.

As a pilgrim mecca, the city features accommodations, eateries, and sights geared toward low-budget travelers. Santiago's top sight—the cathedral—is free to enter, as are many of its other at-

tractions. Santiago has a generally festive atmosphere, full of travelers from every corner of the globe celebrating the end of a long journey.

PLANNING YOUR TIME

Santiago's biggest downside is its location: Except by air, it's a very long trip from any other notable stop in Spain. But if you decide to visit, you—like a millennium's worth of pilgrims before you—will find it's worth the trek. You can get a good feel for Santiago in a day, but a second day relaxing on the squares makes the long trip here more worthwhile.

The city has one real sight: the cathedral, with its fine museum and the surrounding squares. The rest of your visit is for munching seafood, pilgrim-watching, and browsing the stony streets. The highlight of a visit just may be hanging out on the cathedral square at about 10:00 to welcome pilgrims completing their long journey.

Orientation to Santiago

Santiago is built on hilly terrain, with lots of ups and downs. The tourist's Santiago is small: You can walk across the historical center, or Zona Monumental, in about 20 minutes. There you'll find the city's centerpiece—the awe-inspiring cathedral—as well as several other churches, a maze of pretty squares, a smattering of small museums, a bustling restaurant scene, and all of my recommended hotels.

The historical center is circled by a busy street that marks the former location of the town wall (easy to see on a map). Outside of that is the commercial city center—a modern, urban district called Céntrico. A 10-minute walk through Céntrico takes you to the train station.

TOURIST INFORMATION

The **Santiago de Compostela TI** is at Rúa do Vilar 63 (daily 9:00-20:00, Nov-April until 19:00 and closed Sat-Sun 14:00-16:00, +34 981 555 129, www.santiagoturismo.com). The TI rents city audioguides and runs walking tours of the cathedral and surrounding plazas (most afternoons in summer), and may also offer gastronomy tours and nighttime tours. I'd skip the tourist train, which does a pointless little loop around the outskirts.

On the same street, closer to the cathedral, you'll find **Turismo do Porto e Norte de Portugal,** which offers information about destinations just across the border in Portugal, plus tips on how to get there (Tue-Sat 10:00-17:30, closed Sun-Mon, +34 981 565 590, www.portoenorte.pt).

Nearby, at Praza de Mazarelos 15, the **regional TI** gives visi-

The Galego Language

Like Catalunya and the Basque Country, Galicia has its own distinctive language. Galego (called *"Gallego"* in Spanish, and sometimes called "Galician" in English) is a cross between Spanish and Portuguese. Historically, Galego was closer to Portuguese. But Queen Isabel imported the Spanish language to the region in the 15th century, and over time, the language has come to sound more and more like Spanish. In an attempt at national unity, dictator Francisco Franco banned Galego for official communications in the mid-20th century (along with Catalan and the Basque language, Euskara). During this time, Galicians often spoke Spanish in public—and Galego at home. Since the end of the Franco era, Galego has reemerged as a proud part of this region's cultural heritage. Street signs and sight names are posted in Galego, and I've followed suit in this chapter.

If you don't speak Spanish, you'll hardly notice a difference. Most apparent is the change in articles: *el* and *la* become *o* and *a*—so the big Galician city La Coruña is known as "A Coruña" around here. You'll also see a lot more *x*'s, which are pronounced "sh" (such as *Xacobeo*, "shah-koh-BAY-oh," the local word for St. James' pilgrimage route). The Spanish greeting *buenos días* becomes *bos días* in Galego. The familiar *plaza* becomes *praza*. And if you want to impress a local, change your *gracias* to *grazas* (GRA-thas)—a Galego thank-you.

tors several options to explore Galicia outside of Santiago (Mon-Sat 10:00-17:00, Sun until 14:30, +34 881 866 397, www.turismo.gal).

ARRIVAL IN SANTIAGO DE COMPOSTELA

There's luggage storage at the bus station, but not the train station.

By Train: Santiago's train station is on the southern edge of the modern Céntrico district. You'll find ATMs, a cafeteria, car-rental offices, and a helpful train information office. To reach the center of town, leave the station and walk up the grand granite staircase, jog right, cross the busy Avenida de Lugo, and walk uphill for 10 minutes on Rúa do Hórreo to Praza de Galicia, a few steps from the historical center. It's about €8 for a taxi from the station to your hotel.

By Bus: Santiago's bus station (Estación Intermodal) is right next to the train station.

By Plane: Santiago's small airport (SCQ, www.aena.es/en/santiago-airport) is about six miles from the city center. Bus #6A (*not* #6) connects the airport to the bus station (€1, runs 7:00-23:00, 2-3/hour, 40 minutes). A taxi into town costs €21.

SANTIAGO DE COMPOSTELA

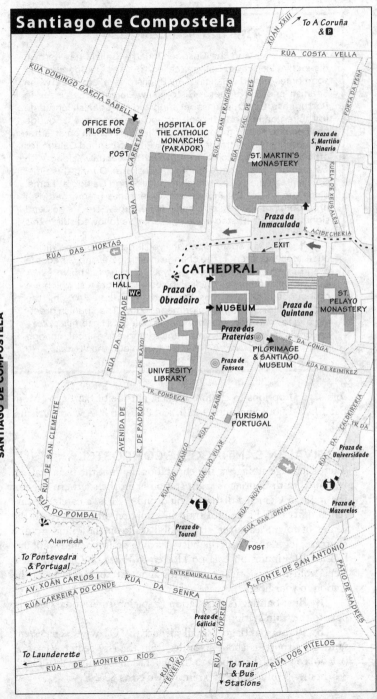

Santiago de Compostela

To A Coruña & P

XOÁN XXIII

RÚA COSTA VELLA

RÚA DOMINGO GARCIA SABELL

PORTA DA PENA

OFFICE FOR PILGRIMS

POST

RÚA DAS CARRETAS

HOSPITAL OF THE CATHOLIC MONARCHS (PARADOR)

RÚA DE SAN FRANCISCO

RÚA DO VAL DE DEUS

ST. MARTIN'S MONASTERY

Praza de S. Martiño Pinario

RUELA DE XEUSALEN

Praza da Inmaculada

R. ACIBECHERIA

RÚA DAS HORTAS

EXIT

CATHEDRAL

CITY HALL

WC

Praza do Obradoiro

MUSEUM

Praza da Quintana

ST. PELAYO MONASTERY

RÚA DA TRINDADE

AV. DE RAXOI

Praza das Praterías

R. DA CONGA

UNIVERSITY LIBRARY

Praza de Fonseca

PILGRIMAGE & SANTIAGO MUSEUM

RÚA DE XEIMIREZ

TR. FONSECA

AVENIDA DE

R. DE PADRÓN

RÚA DA RAIÑA

RÚA DO FRANCO

RÚA DO VILAR

TURISMO PORTUGAL

RÚA DA. CALDERERIA

TR DA

Praza de Universidade

RÚA DE SAN CLEMENTE

RÚA NOVA

Praza de Mazarelos

RÚA DO POMBAL

RÚA DAS ÓRFAS

Alameda

To Pontevedra & Portugal

Praza do Toural

POST

AV. XOÁN CARLOS I

R. ENTREMURALLAS

R. FONTE DE SAN ANTONIO

PATIO DE MADRES

RÚA DA SENRA

RÚA CARREIRA DO CONDE

Praza de Galicia

RÚA DO HÓRREO

RÚA DOS PITELOS

To Launderette

RÚA D TEIXEIRO

RÚA DE MONTERO RÍOS

To Train & Bus Stations

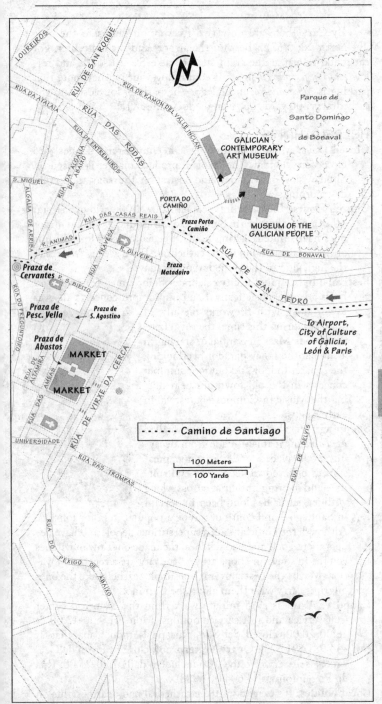

LOUREIROS

RÚA DE SAN ROQUE

RÚA DA ATALAIA

RÚA DE RAMON DEL VALLE INCLAN

RÚA DAS RODAS

RÚA DE ENTREMUROS

RÚA DE ALGALIA DE ABAIXO

S. MIGUEL

S. ALGALIA DE ARRIBA

R. ANIMAS

RÚA DAS CASAS REAIS

RÚA TRAVESA

R. OLIVEIRA

PORTA DO CAMIÑO

Praza Porta Camiño

Praza Matadoiro

Parque de Santo Domingo de Bonaval

GALICIAN CONTEMPORARY ART MUSEUM

MUSEUM OF THE GALICIAN PEOPLE

RÚA DE BONAVAL

RÚA DE SAN PEDRO

Praza de Cervantes

R. S. BIEITO

RÚA DO PREGUNTOIRO

Praza de Pesc. Vella

Praza de S. Agostino

Praza de Abastos

RÚA DE ALTAMIRA

RÚA DAS AMEAS

MARKET

MARKET

RÚA DE VIRXE DA CERCA

UNIVERSIDADE

RÚA DAS TROMPAS

RÚA DO PEXIGO DE ABAIXO

RÚA DE BELVIS

To Airport, City of Culture of Galicia, León & Paris

- - - - - Camino de Santiago

100 Meters

100 Yards

SANTIAGO DE COMPOSTELA

By Car: There are only two freeway off-ramps to the city. The north exit (#67) is best for the airport and the old center. For car-rental return at the train station, take SC-20 south and follow *estación ferrocarril* signs. If continuing your journey, note that parking is *"aparcadoiro"* in Galego. The parking lot closest to the cathedral is 400 yards up Avenida de Xoán XXIII.

HELPFUL HINTS

Closed Days: Many museums (except church-related ones) are closed on Monday. The colorful produce market is closed on Sunday, slow on Monday, and busiest on Thursday and Saturday mornings.

Church Hours: The cathedral is open 7:00-21:00 without a siesta; other major churches in Santiago open around 9:00, and minor ones have limited visiting hours. Special Masses for pilgrims are held daily at noon in the cathedral. There are big Masses at the high altar of the cathedral on Sunday.

Festivals: In late July the city celebrates Saint James' feast day and hosts a world music festival and impromptu concerts all over town, along with fireworks on July 24 and 31. During this time, the royal family attends Mass in Santiago, staying in a suite at the fancy parador overlooking the square. Indoor and outdoor summer concerts in the old town are held during the Music in Compostela festival in early August.

Shopping: Jet, the black gemstone (called *azabache* in Spanish) made from decaying wood placed under extreme pressure, is believed to keep away evil spirits—and to bring in tourist euros. Along with jet, silver has long been important in Santiago—and continues to be a popular item for tourists. Although the Galicians are a superstitious people and have beliefs about good and bad witches, the made-in-Taiwan witches you see in souvenir shops around the city are a recent innovation. Maybe the best souvenir is a simple seashell, like the ones pilgrims carry with them along the Camino.

Laundry: Axiña is a 15-minute walk from the historical center (self-service and full-service options, Mon-Fri 9:00-13:00 & 16:00-20:00, closed Sat-Sun, Rúa de Ramón Cabanillas 1, +34 981 591 323). Or try **Waterproof,** close to Praza de Cervantes (self-service only, soap included, daily 7:30-23:00, Rúa do Preguntoiro, +34 604 001 988).

Local Guides: It's easy to visit the cathedral and nearby sights on

your own with the information in this book, but if you have the extra cash, you could hire a guide. **Manuel Ruzo** is a good one (€140/2-3 hours, +34 639 888 064, manoloruzo@gmail. com).

Best Views: There are beautiful views back toward the cathedral from Alameda Park. From the cathedral, follow Rúa do Franco to the end. Swing right into the park and continue up Paseo de Santa Susana to the viewpoint (mirador) along Paseo da Ferradura. You can enjoy another excellent view from the very top of the park (clearly marked on TI maps).

Sights in Santiago

▲▲SANTIAGO CATHEDRAL

Santiago's cathedral (Catedral de Santiago) isn't the biggest in Spain, nor is it the most impressive. Yet it's certainly the most mys-

tical, exerting a spiritual magnetism that attracts people from all walks of life and from all corners of the globe. (To more fully appreciate the pilgrim experience, read the first part of the Camino de Santiago chapter before visiting the cathedral.)

Exploring one of the most important churches in Christendom, you'll do some time travel, putting yourself in the well-worn shoes of the millions of pilgrims who have trekked many miles to this powerful place.

Cost and Hours: Free, daily 7:00-21:00, www. catedraldesantiago.es.

Tours: One-hour guided tours, usually in Spanish only, allow visits to separate areas (portico-€10, combo-ticket with museum-€12, offered daily on the hour 10:00-13:00 & 16:00-18:00, book up to 90 days in advance online).

Baggage Check: Large backpacks aren't allowed in the church, and small bags require a security check. Leave large bags at your hotel or check them at the bus station. Pilgrims with a certificate will find free baggage storage downhill at the Office for Pilgrims (official address is Rúa das Carretas 33, but entrance is around the corner on Rúa Domingo García Sabell; see map).

➔ Self-Guided Tour
• *Begin facing the cathedral's main facade, in the big square called...*

SANTIAGO DE COMPOSTELA

Praza do Obradoiro

Find the pavement stone with the scallop shell right in the middle of this square. For more than a thousand years, this spot has been

where millions of tired pilgrims have taken a deep breath and thought to themselves: "I made it!" To maximize your chance of seeing pilgrims, be here at about 10:00—the last stop on the Camino de Santiago is two miles away, and pilgrims try to get to the cathedral in time for the 12:00 Mass. It's great fun to

chat with pilgrims who've just completed their journey. They seem to be very centered, content, and tuned in to the important things in life...like taking time to talk with others. You'll likely see ecstatic reunions between pilgrims who met along the way and then lost track of each other until the grand finale. Every time I visit, I find myself taking photos for people. Even if you're shy, a fun and easy way to meet pilgrims is by offering to capture their personal triumphs.

• *Take a spin around the square (start facing the cathedral).*

To your left is the **Hospital of the Catholic Monarchs** *(Hostal dos Reis Católicos),* now a fancy hotel. Isabel and Ferdinand

came to Santiago in 1501 to give thanks for successfully forcing the Moors out of Granada. When they arrived, they found many sick pilgrims at the square. (Numerous pilgrims came to Santiago to ask for help in overcoming an illness, and the long walk here often only made their condition worse.) Isabel and Ferdinand decided to build this hospital to give pilgrims a place to recover on arrival (you'll see their coats of arms flanking the intricately carved entryway). It remained a working, free hospital until 1952—many locals were born there—when it was converted into a fancy

parador and restaurant (see "Sleeping in Santiago" and "Eating in Santiago," later). The modern white windows set against the old granite facade might seem jarring—but this contrast is very common in Galicia, maximizing the brightness that accompanies any sunny spells in this notoriously rainy region.

A walkway from the parador leads to the **Office for Pilgrims** (Rúa das Carretas 33, daily April-Oct 8:00-21:00, Nov-March 10:00-19:00, entrance around the corner on Rúa Domingo García

Sabell). This is where pilgrims pick up their *compostela*, the certifi-cate that documents their successful *camino*. While tourists aren't welcome, you can peek into the gardens while chatting at the door with happy pilgrims.

Another 90 degrees to the left is the Neoclassical **City Hall** *(Concello)*. Notice the equestrian statue up top. That's St. James, rid-ing in from heaven to help the Spaniards defeat the Moors. All over town, Santiago's namesake and symbol—a Christian evangelist on a horse, killing Muslims with his sword—is out doing his bloody thing. See any police on the square? There's a reason for their pres-ence. In its medieval day, Santiago's cathedral was one of the top three pilgrimage sites in the Christian world (after Jerusalem and Rome). It remains important today, and with St. James taking such joy in butchering Muslims, it is considered a high-profile target for Islamic fundamentalists.

Completing the square (90 more degrees to the left) is the **university** building (its rectory faces the square; the tower behind with the flags marks the original building, which is now the li-brary). Santiago has Spain's third-oldest university, with more than 30,000 students (medicine and law are especially popular).

You'll likely see Spanish school groups on the square, field-tripping from all over the country. Teachers love to use this spot for an architecture lesson, since it features four architectural styles (starting with the cathedral and spinning left): 18th-century Ba-roque; 16th-century Plateresque; 18th-century Neoclassical; and medieval Romanesque (the door of the rectory).

• *Take a look at the...*

Cathedral Facade

Twelve hundred years ago, a monk followed a field of stars (prob-ably the Milky Way) to the little Galician village of San Fiz de Solovio and discovered what appeared to be the long-lost tomb of St. James. On July 25, 813, the local bishop declared that St. James' remains had been found. They set to building a church here and named the place Santiago (St. James) de Compostela (*campo de es-trellas*, or "field of stars," for the celestial bodies that guided the monk).

The little church was soon overwhelmed by visitors—and so were its larger replacements over the next century and a half—so in 1075, construction began on a Romanesque cathedral that would be grand enough to receive the throngs of pilgrims. (The granite workers who built it set up shop on this very square, still called Praza do Obradoiro—literally, "Workshop Square.") Much of the design is attributed to a palace artist named Maestro Mateo, whom we'll meet a little later. The work took nearly 150 years, and sub-

sequent alterations added elements of Gothic, Renaissance, and Baroque styles.

The exterior of the cathedral you see today is *not* the one that medieval pilgrims saw (though the interior is much the same). In the mid-18th century, Santiago's bishop—all fired up from a trip to Baroque-slathered Rome and wanting to improve the original, now-deteriorating facade—decided to spruce up the building with a new Baroque exterior in the Churrigueresque style. He also replaced the simple stonework in the interior with gaudy gold.

Study the facade. Atop the middle steeple is St. James (dressed like the pilgrim he was). Beneath him is his tomb, marked by a star—one of the many symbols you'll see all over the place (to decipher the symbols, see sidebar on page 286). On either side of the tomb are Theodorus and Athanasius, James' disciples who brought his body to Santiago. On the side pillars are, to the left, James' father, Zebedee; and to the right, his mother, Salomé.

Don't you wish you had a miniature replica of this beautiful facade to carry around with you? Actually, you probably do. Check your pocket for a copper-colored euro coin worth €0.01, €0.02, or €0.05. There it is! Of all the churches in Spain, they chose this one as their representative in euro-land. Sevilla and Toledo may have bigger cathedrals, but Santiago has the symbolism to propel its church into EU currency.

The cathedral also houses a museum with three parts; as you face this facade, the door to the main museum is to the right, the entry to the crypt is dead ahead (under the staircase), and the door on the left leads to the Gelmírez Palace and the cathedral rooftop (see Gelmírez Palace listing, later).

• *Enter the cathedral's main entrance. Once inside, enjoy the space, then make your way to the rear of the nave and find the display about the...*

Portico of Glory

Take a step back in time. Remember, this used to be the main facade of the cathedral, sculpted in about 1180 by Maestro Mateo. Pretend you're a medieval pilgrim and you've just walked 500 miles from the Frankish lands to reach this cathedral. You're here to request the help of St. James in recovering from an illness or to give thanks for a success. Maybe you've come to honor the wish of a dying relative or to be forgiven for your sins. Whatever the reason, you came here on foot.

You can't read, but you can tell from the carved images that this magnificent door represents the glory of God. Old Testament prophets on the left announce Christ's coming. New Testament apostles on the right spread his message. Jesus reigns directly above, approachable to the humble Christian pilgrim via St. James with his staff.

Theologically, pilgrims are coming not for St. James but to get to Christ via St. James. Look for Jesus, front and center, surrounded by Matthew, Mark, Luke, and John.

Beside them are angels carrying tools for the Crucifixion—the cross, the crown of thorns, the spear, and a jug of vinegar. Arching above them are 24 musicians playing celestial music—each one with a different medieval instrument.

Below St. James is a column with the Tree of Jesse—showing the genealogy of Jesus, with Mary near the top and, above her, the Holy Trinity: Father, Son, and a dove representing the Holy Spirit.

As a pilgrim, you would walk to the column in the middle of the entryway. Trembling with excitement at the culmination of your long journey, you'd place your hand into the well-worn finger holes on the column (see five grooves at about chest level) and bow your head, giving thanks to St. James for having granted you safe passage.

Then you'd go around to the other side of the post and, at knee level, see Maestro Mateo, who carved this fine facade. What a smart guy! People used to kneel and tap their heads against his three times to improve their intelligence (a ritual among university scholars here)—until a metal barrier was erected. (Grades have dropped recently.) Such a high-profile self-portrait of an artist in the 12th century was unprecedented. In Santiago he was something like the Leonardo da Vinci of his day.

• *Now turn around to appreciate the...*

Nave

Look up to take in the barrel vault and the heavy, dark Romanesque design of the church. (The original freestanding church had about 80 glorious alabaster windows. They were mostly bricked up when a complex of buildings was built around the church.) Up near the top, notice the gallery. This is where sweaty, smelly pilgrims slept. Check out the most modern addition to the side naves: TV monitors.

Now when crowds fill the cathedral for Mass, everyone has a good view of the service.

• *Continue up the nave until you reach the high altar, where you'll see a thick rope hanging from a pulley system high in the dome, which is attached to the...*

Botafumeiro

This huge silver-plated incense burner (120 pounds and about the size of a small child), suspended from the ceiling, is used about 12 times a year (ask at TI if a special Mass with the *botafumeiro* is sched-

SANTIAGO DE COMPOSTELA

uled during your visit). It also fills the cathedral with incense when a pilgrim pays about €300 to see it in action. During Holy Years, it swings nearly daily at the end of each pilgrims' Mass at 12:00. Supposedly the custom of swinging this giant incense dispenser began in order to counteract the stench of the pilgrims. After communion, eight men (called *tiraboleiros*) pull on the rope, and this huge contraption swings in a wide arc up and down the transept, spewing sweet-smelling smoke. If you're here to see it, the most impressive view is from either side of the main altar. From this position, the *botafumeiro* seems to whiz directly over your head. A replica is kept on display in the cathedral library (see "Cathedral Museum," later).

• *Stand in the center of the nave, in front of the...*

Altar

The big gold altar has all three representations of St. James in one place (see sidebar): Up top, on a white horse, is James the *Matamoros*—Moor Slayer; below that (just under the canopy) is pilgrim James; and below that is the original stone Apostle James by Maestro Mateo—still pointing down to his tomb after all these centuries.

The dome over the altar was added in the 16th century to bring some light into this dark Romanesque church.

On the columns up and down the nave and transept, notice the symbols carved into the granite. These are the markings of the masons who made the columns—to keep track of how many they'd be paid for.

• *Following the pilgrims' route, go down the ambulatory on the left side of the altar—passing where the* botafumeiro *rope is moored to the pillar—and walk down the little stairway on your right (see the green light of the* Entrada *sign) to the level of the earlier, 10th-century church and the...*

Tomb of St. James

There he is, in the little silver chest, marked by a star: Santiago. Pilgrims kneel in front of the tomb and make their request or say their thanks.

• *Continue through the little passage and up the stairs, turn left, and wander around the ambulatory, noticing the sumptuous chapels (built by noblemen who wanted to be buried close to St. James). At the very back of the church (behind the altar) is the greenish...*

St. James

James and his brother John, sons of Zebedee and Salomé, were well-off fishermen on the Sea of Galilee. One fateful day, a charismatic visionary came and said to them, "Come with me, and I will make you fishers of men." They threw down their nets and became apostles.

Along with Peter, James and John were supposedly Jesus' favorites—he called them the "sons of thunder." After Jesus' death, the apostles spread out and brought his message to other lands. St. James spent a decade as a missionary bringing Christianity to the farthest reaches of the known world—which, back then, was northwest Spain. The legend goes that as soon as he returned home to the Holy Land, in AD 44, James was beheaded by Herod Agrippa. Before his body and head could be thrown to the lions—as was the custom in those days—they were rescued by two of his disciples, Theodorus and Athanasius.

These two brought his body back to Spain in a small boat and entombed it in the hills of Galicia— carefully hiding it from the Roman authorities. There it lay hidden for almost eight centuries. In 813, a monk—supposedly directed by the stars—discovered the tomb, and the local bishop proudly exclaimed that St. James was in Galicia. Santiago de Compostela was born.

But is this the *real* story? Historians figure the "discovery" of the remains of St. James in Spain provided a way to rally Europe against the Moors, who had invaded Spain and were threatening the rest of Europe. The "marketing" of St. James was further bolstered by his miraculous appearance, on horseback and wielding a sword, to fight for the Christian army in the pivotal battle of Clavijo during the Reconquista. With St. James *Matamoros* ("Moor Slayer") in Iberia, all of Europe was inspired to push the Muslims back into Africa...which they finally did in 1492. James eventually became Spain's patron saint, and for centuries, Spanish armies rode into battle with the cry *"Santiago y cierra, España!"* (roughly: "For St. James! Spaniards strike!").

Sure, the whole thing was likely a propaganda hoax to get the populace to support a war. But yesterday's and today's pilgrims may not care whether the body of St. James actually lies in this church. The pilgrimage to Santiago is a spiritual quest powered through the ages by faith.

Holy Door

This special door is open only during Holy Years, when pilgrims use it to access the tomb and statue of the apostle. The door, sculpted by a local artist for the 2004 Holy Year, shows six scenes from the life of St. James: the conversion moment when Jesus invited those Galilean fishermen to become "fishers of men"; Jesus with the 12 apostles (James is identified by his scallop shell); James doing

his "fishing" in Spain; his return to Jerusalem in AD 44 to be be-headed; the ship taking his body back to Spain; and the discovery of James' body in 813. At the bottom, the little snail is the symbol of the pilgrim...slow and steady, with everything on its back.

Hug St. James

There's one more pilgrim ritual to complete. Opposite the Holy Door, find a little door—perhaps with a line of pilgrims (closed 13:30-16:00 and after 20:00). Climb the stairs under the huge ba-bies and find Maestro Mateo's stone statue of St. James—gilded and caked with precious gems. Embrace him from behind and enjoy a saint's-eye view of the cathedral...under the vigilant eye of a cathedral watchman, there to ensure you're not overcome by the unholy temptation to pry loose a jewel.

• *Congratulations, pilgrim! You have completed the Camino de Santiago. Now go in peace.*

OTHER SIGHTS AT THE CATHEDRAL
▲▲Cathedral Museum (Museo Catedral de Santiago)

The cathedral's museum shows off some interesting pieces from the fine treasury collection and artifacts from the cathedral's history. Your admission ticket includes a look inside Gelmírez Palace and its exhibit about recent restoration efforts.

Cost and Hours: €6, Tue-Sat 10:00-14:00 & 16:00-19:00, Sun 10:00-14:00, closed Mon, last entry one hour before closing, ticket office at entrance to the right of the main stairs into cathe-dral, www.catedraldesantiago.es.

Visiting the Museum: The museum is laid out chronologically from bottom to top.

Crypt: Wander into the small crypt to the right of the ticket counter and see some serious medieval engineering. Because the church was built on a too-small hill, the crypt was made to support the part of the nave that hung over the hillside. The Romanesque vaulting and carved decoration is more Maestro Mateo mastery.

Ground Floor: Here you'll find the remaining pieces of Mae-stro Mateo's original stone choir (stone seats for priests that filled the center of the nave in the 12th century), assembled as part of a new replica. Nearby, look for a miniature model of the choir. No-tice the expressive faces Mateo carved into the granite. Working in the Romanesque style, he was well ahead of his time artistically. Consider the cultural value of a place in Europe where people from all corners came together, shared, and then dispersed.

In some ways, the concept of Europe as a civilization was being born when Santiago was in its 12th-century heyday. You'll also see fragments of Roman settlements, dating from before the

tomb of St. James was discovered here, as well as some fabulous spiral columns of solid marble from Mateo's workshop.

First Floor: The four statues of a pregnant Mary illustrate a theme that's unusual in most of Europe but common in Galicia and neighboring Portugal in the 15th century.

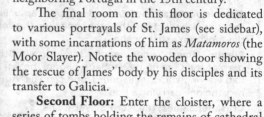

The final room on this floor is dedicated to various portrayals of St. James (see sidebar), with some incarnations of him as *Matamoros* (the Moor Slayer). Notice the wooden door showing the rescue of James' body by his disciples and its transfer to Galicia.

Second Floor: Enter the cloister, where a series of tombs holding the remains of cathedral priests line the floor. Pass by the ornate chapel and enter the courtyard to see a fountain (which once stood in front of the cathedral and was used by pilgrims to cleanse themselves) and the original church bells (replaced with new models in 1989). As you walk left (clockwise) around the cloister, the second door leads to the Royal Chapel, with a beautiful-smelling cedar altar that houses dozens and dozens of relics. The centerpiece, at eye level, holds the remains—likely the skull—of St. James the Lesser (the *other* Apostle James). Look up to find St. James riding heroically out of the woodwork to rally all of Europe to reconquer the Iberian Peninsula. This altarpiece was restored after a fire around 1900.

• *Cross the hall to the...*

Treasury: An altar dedicated to King Ferdinand III takes center stage. The fancy solid-gold monstrance is used for carrying the communion host around the cathedral on Corpus Christi (the wafer sits in the little round window in the middle). Other bits of religious finery await your inspection. Don't miss the intimate 18th-century Madonna and Child carving in the glass case. The nursing *Virgen de la Leche* looks out at us as she feeds her son.

• *Stroll around the cloister for tower views, then return through the door you entered to the...*

Library/Archive: This is where they store old books, a funky rack for reading those huge tomes ("turn pages" by spinning the rack), and a replica of the *botafumeiro* (gigantic incense burner).

• *Leave the library and go up one more floor to enjoy views from a fine balcony overlooking Praza do Obradoiro.*

Third Floor: Take a look inside the dark room to the right of the stairs. Here you'll find the painstakingly restored *gallardete* (long, triangular standard) flown from the Spanish captain's ship during the 1571 Battle of Lepanto. *Don Quixote* author Miguel de Cervantes was wounded in this battle—and likely saw this very

The Three Santiagos

Santiago is Spanish for "St. James." You'll see three different depictions of St. James in the cathedral and throughout the city:

Apostle James: James dressed in typical apostle robes, often indistinguishable from the other apostles (he sometimes carries a pilgrim's stick or shell).

Pilgrim James: James wearing some or all of the traditional garb of the Camino de Santiago pilgrim: brown cloak, floppy hat, walking stick, shell, gourd, and sandals. Among pilgrims, he's the one carrying a book.

Crusader James, the Moor Slayer *(Matamoros)*: Centuries after his death, the Spaniards called on St. James for aid in various battles against the Moors. According to legend, St. James appeared from the heavens on a white horse and massacred the Muslim foes. Locals don't particularly care for this depiction, especially these days, when they worry it might provoke attacks by fringe Islamic fundamentalist elements—which is probably why the cathedral chapel dedicated to this version of James conveniently has floral displays that cover the slain Moors.

flag—as Spain fought to victory over the Turks, gaining control of the Mediterranean.

Next, step out on the balcony to appreciate the grandness of the Praza do Obradoiro and watch pilgrims arrive. You'll then walk through several rooms of restored tapestries. The first room is from designs by Rubens. The two middle rooms show idealistic 18th-century peasant life—wives helping their men to be less moronic (but there's still a man peeing in the corner). The last room has a series of 12 tapestries, designed by Goya, with exacting details of life around 1790.

Nearby: Also included in your museum ticket is **Gelmírez Palace** (Pazo de Xelmírez), the medieval home and traditional residence of the archbishop. Show your ticket to access the palace through the doorway to the left of the crypt. This space houses an exhibit detailing the cathedral's restoration.

CATHEDRAL SQUARES

There is a square on each side of the cathedral. You've already visited Praza do Obradoiro, in the front. Here are the other three, working

clockwise (to reach the first one, go up the passage—which street musicians appreciate for its acoustics—to the left as you're facing the main cathedral facade).

Praza da Inmaculada

This was the way most medieval pilgrims using the French Road actually approached the cathedral. Across the square is **St. Martin's Monastery** (Mosteiro de San Martiño Pinario), one of two monasteries that sprang up around the church to care for pilgrims. It grew quickly and became the second-largest monastery in Spain after El Escorial, and the Baroque altar continues to make jaws drop. Today the monastery houses an enormous museum of ecclesiastical artifacts and special exhibits (€5, daily 11:00-14:00 & 16:00-19:00, entrance on the right corner of the building).

Walk to the corner of the Praza da Inmaculada with the arcade, and go to the post with the sign for *Rúa da Acibechería* (under the streetlight). If you look to the roof of the cathedral, between the big dome and the tall tower, you can make out a small white cross. This is where the clothes of medieval pilgrims were burned when they finally arrived at Santiago. This ritual was created for hygienic reasons in an age of frightful diseases...and filthy pilgrims.

• *Continue along the arcade and around the corner, and you'll enter...*

Praza da Quintana

The door of the cathedral facing this square is the Holy Door, only opened during Holy Years. There's St. James, flanked by the disciples who brought his body back to Galicia. Below them are more biblical characters, perhaps the 12 apostles and 12 prophets. Tip: Old Testament prophets hold scrolls. New Testament apostles hold books.

Across the square from the cathedral stands the imposing **St. Pelayo Monastery** (Mosteiro San Paio). The windows of its cells (now used by Benedictine sisters—notice the bars and privacy screens) face the cathedral. The church at the north end of this monastery is worth a peek. It has a frilly Baroque altar and a statue with a typical Galician theme: a pregnant Mary (to the left as you face the main altar). The nuns sing at the evening vespers following the 19:30 Mass (Mon-Fri; 30 minutes earlier Sat-Sun). Just off this sanctuary is the entrance to the monastery's **Sacred**

Art Museum (Museo de Arte Sacra), with a small but interesting collection (modest entry fee, closed Mon). The nuns of St. Pelayo make Galicia's famous *tarta de Santiago*—almond cake with a cross of Santiago in powdered sugar dusted on top. To buy one, exit the church to the right, head up the stairs, and walk all the way around the monastery to find the green doors on Travessa de San Paio de Antealtares. Once inside, go to the small window on the left (closed during siesta and all day Sun; they only sell entire cakes—a big one for €11.50 and a very big one for €19.50; ring bell and remember that patience is a virtue).

• *Circle right to return where you entered the cathedral at...*

Praza das Praterías

This "Silversmiths' Square" is where Santiago's silver workers used to have their shops (and some still do). Overlooking the square is a tall **tower.** Imagine the fortified, typically Romanesque cathedral complex before the decorative Baroque frills were added; it looked more like a hulking fortress for fending off invading enemies, from Normans to Moors to English pirates.

The **fountain** features a woman sitting on St. James' tomb, holding aloft a star—a typical city symbol. The mansion facing the cathedral is actually a collection of buildings with a thin yet effective Galician Baroque facade built to give the square architectural harmony. Its centerpiece even copies the fountain's star. Facing the fountain is the **Pilgrimage and Santiago Museum** (described on page 364).

MORE SIGHTS IN SANTIAGO

▲▲Market (Mercado de Abastos)

This wonderful market, housed in Old World stone buildings, offers a good opportunity to do some serious people-watching (Mon-Sat 8:00-14:00, closed Sun). It's busiest and best on Saturday, when villagers from the countryside come to sell things. (Monday's the least interesting day, since the fishermen don't go out on Sunday.)

The market was built in the 1920s (to consolidate Santiago's many small markets) in a style perfectly compatible with the medieval wonder that surrounds it. Today it offers an opportunity to get up close and personal with some still-twitching seafood. Keep an eye out for the specialties you'll want to try later—octopus, shrimp, crabs, lobsters, and expensive-as-gold *percebes* (barnacles;

Percebes = Barnacles

Local gooseneck barnacles, called *percebes,* are a delicacy. *Percebes* grow only on rocks that see a lot of dangerous waves. It takes specialists to harvest them: a team of two gatherers, one with a rope tied to his waist, the other spotting him from above. Because of the danger, *percebes* are really expensive. You'll see them stacked in the windows of seafood bars, where you'll pay about €8 for 100 grams ($35/lb). Check the price carefully when you order, as there are varieties that can cost many times that much. Two beers and a small 100-gram plate to split with your travel partner make for a wonderful snack. Just twist, rip, and bite: It's a bit like munching the necks off butter clams. I ask for toasted bread on the side.

For the freshest *percebes* at half the price—and twice the experience—buy them at the market, then let **Mariscomanía** boil them for you right there in their market café. They'll boil up any seafood (or meat) you buy in the market (it takes just a few minutes), charging €5 per person for table service (Tue-Sat 9:00-15:00, closed Sun-Mon, aisle 5 in the market, +34 981 560 982).

see sidebar). You'll also see large loaves of country bread, chicken the color it should be, and the local *chorizo* (spicy sausage).

Grelos, local turnip greens with thick stalks and long, narrow leaves, are used in the *caldo galego* soup. The little green *pimientos de Padrón* (in season June-Oct) look like jalapeños but lack the kick... sometimes. Now and then you'll find an impromptu stand outside cooking up fresh octopus. (See the "Santiago Specialties" sidebar, later.)

In the cheese cases you'll see what look like huge yellow Hershey's Kisses...or breasts—in fact, this creamy cheese is called *tetilla* ("small breast" in Galego). According to legend, artists at the cathedral sculpted a very curvaceous woman and the townspeople loved it. The bishop made them redo the statue with fewer sexy lines, so the locals got even by making their cheese look like breasts. Through the centuries since, Santiago has been full of tasty reminders of a woman's physical beauty. A smoked version of the cheese, called *San Simón da Costa,* can be found as well.

A perfect place to enjoy your goodies is **A Viñoteca do Mercado,** in the center of the market by the fountain. They specialize in regional wines, a perfect match to market products. Claim a

stand-up table, open your picnic, have a glass of Ribeiro, and watch the world go by (Mon-Sat 10:00-15:00, closed Sun year-round plus Mon in off-season, +34 663 883 635).

▲Pilgrimage and Santiago Museum (Museo das Peregrinacións e de Santiago)

This museum examines various aspects of the pilgrimage phenomenon. You'll see a map of pilgrimage sites around the world and then learn more about the pilgrimage that brings people to Santiago. There are models of earlier versions of the cathedral, explanations of the differing depictions of St. James throughout history (apostle, pilgrim, and Crusader), and coverage of the various routes to Santiago and stories of some prominent pilgrims. This well-arranged place lends historical context to all of those backpackers you see in the streets.

Cost and Hours: €2.40, Tue-Fri 9:30-20:30, Sat 11:00-19:30, Sun 10:15-14:45, closed Mon, Praza das Praterías 2, +34 881 867 401, http://museoperegrinacions.xunta.gal.

Museum of the Galician People (Museo do Pobo Galego)

This museum gives insights into rural Galician life. As you tour this collection, remember that if you side-trip a few miles into the countryside, you'll find tradi-

tional lifestyles thriving even today. Beautifully displayed around an 18th-century cloister, the museum springs from a unique triple staircase, which provided privacy to various hierarchies of the Dominican monks who lived here, depending on which stairway you climbed. The collection shows off boat-building and fishing techniques, farming implements and simple horse-drawn carts, tools of trade and handicrafts (including carpentry, pottery, looms, and baskets), traditional costumes, unique regional architecture, and a collection of musical instruments, with an emphasis on the bagpipes *(gaitas)*. If the farm tools seem old-fashioned, there's a reason: Old inheritance laws mean that plots have gotten smaller, so modern farming machinery is impractical—keeping traditional equipment alive. Don't miss access to the church (cloister corner directly ahead of entrance) and the Pantheon of Illustrious Galicians, where important writers, artists, and politicians are buried. Occasional pamphlets describe each section, but otherwise there is no English.

Cost and Hours: €4; Tue-Sat 11:00-18:00, Sun until 14:00, closed Mon; at northeast edge of historical center in monastery of

San Domingos de Bonaval, just beyond Porta do Camiño, +34 981 583 620, www.museodopobo.gal.

Nearby: Behind the museum is a plush and peaceful **park**—once crowded with tombstones. Next door, in a striking modern building, is the **Galician Contemporary Art Museum** (Centro Galego de Arte Contemporánea), with continually rotating exhibits—mostly by local artists (free, Tue-Sun 11:00-20:00, closed Mon).

Street Music

You'll likely hear bagpipes *(gaitas)* being played in the streets of Santiago. Nobody knows for certain how this unlikely instrument caught on in Galicia, but supposedly the tradition has been passed down since the Celts lived here. (Bagpipes are commonly thought to be unique to Celts like the Scottish and Irish, but nearly all European ethnic groups have bagpipes in their past. If anything, the Celts just endured their sound more willingly.) Some singers use bagpipes, too, including Milladoiro (a group popular with middle-aged Galicians) and Carlos Nuñez (trendy with younger people). Caped university students, called *tunas,* can be seen singing traditional songs (without bagpipes) around town every night during the summer.

Sleeping in Santiago

To cater to all those pilgrims, Santiago has a glut of cheap, basic accommodations, but the current popularity of the Camino means there are also very good hotel options. High season is roughly Easter through September; most places charge more during this time. The trickiest dates to book are Easter Sunday weekend and the days around the Feast of St. James (July 25), so if you plan to be in town around these times, reserve your rooms well ahead. The *hostales* speak enough English to make a reservation by phone (though sometimes not much more).

$$$$ Parador Santiago de Compostela is also known as Hostal dos Reis Católicos (Hospital of the Catholic Monarchs); it occupies the former hospital founded by the Catholic Monarchs at the beginning of the 16th century to care for pilgrims arriving from the Camino. It was converted into an upscale parador in 1952 and inaugurated by Franco (when royal family members are in town, they stay in his former suite overlooking the square). This grand building has 137 rooms surrounding a series of four courtyards packed with Santiago history. It has the best address in Santiago... and prices to match (check website or call for deals, pay parking, Praza do Obradoiro 1, +34 981 582 200, www.parador.es).

Still remembering its roots, the parador follows Ferdinand and

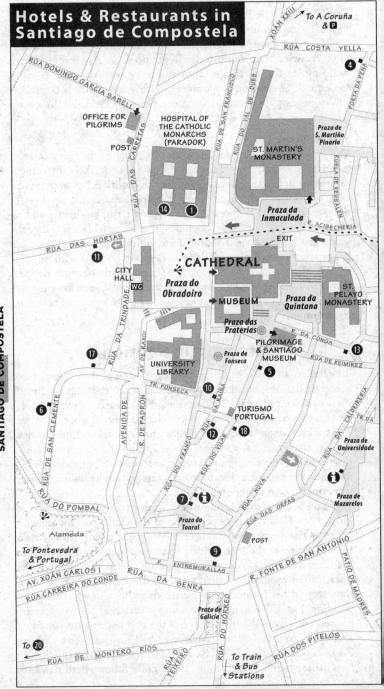

Hotels & Restaurants in Santiago de Compostela

RUA DOMINGO GARCÍA SABELL

XOÁN XXIII

To A Coruña & P

RUA COSTA VELLA

4

PORTA DA PENA

OFFICE FOR PILGRIMS

POST

RUA DAS CARRETAS

HOSPITAL OF THE CATHOLIC MONARCHS (PARADOR)

RUA DE SAN FRANCISCO

RUA DO VAL DE DUES

ST. MARTIN'S MONASTERY

Praza de S. Martiño Pinario

RUELA DE XEUSALEN

14 1

Praza da Inmaculada

R. ACIBECHERIA

RUA DAS HORTAS

11

CITY HALL

WC

Praza do Obradoiro

EXIT

CATHEDRAL

MUSEUM

Praza da Quintana

ST. PELAYO MONASTERY

RUA DA TRINDADE

AV. DE RAXOI

UNIVERSITY LIBRARY

Praza das Praterías

Praza de Fonseca

PILGRIMAGE & SANTIAGO MUSEUM

R. DA CONGA

RUA DE XEIMIREZ

13

17

TR. FONSECA

10

AVENIDA DE

R. DE PADRÓN

RUA DA RAIÑA

RUA DO FRANCO

RUA DO VILAR

TURISMO PORTUGAL

12 18

RUA DA CALDEIRERIA

TR DA

Praza de Universidade

RUA DE SAN CLEMENTE

6

RUA DO POMBAL

7

Praza do Toural

RUA NOVA

RUA DAS ORFAS

Praza de Mazarelos

Alameda

To Pontevedra & Portugal

9

R. ENTREMURALLAS

POST

R. FONTE DE SAN ANTONIO

PATIO DE MADRES

AV. XOÁN CARLOS I

RUA CARREIRA DO CONDE

RUA DA SENRA

RUA DOS PITELOS

Praza de Galicia

To 20

RUA DE MONTERO RÍOS

RUA DO TEIXEIRO

RUA DO HÓRREO

To Train & Bus Stations

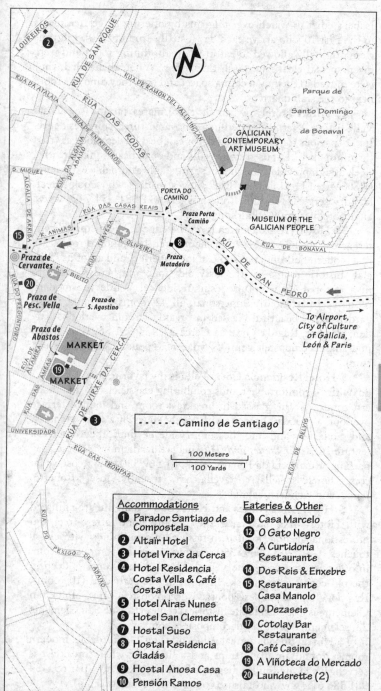

SANTIAGO DE COMPOSTELA

Parque de
Santo Domingo
de Bonaval

GALICIAN
CONTEMPORARY
ART MUSEUM

PORTA DO
CAMIÑO

Praza Porta
Camiño

MUSEUM OF THE
GALICIAN PEOPLE

RÚA DE BONAVAL

Praza de
Cervantes

Praza
Matadoiro

RÚA DE SAN PEDRO

Praza de
Pesc. Vella

Praza de
S. Agostino

To Airport,
City of Culture
of Galicia,
León & Paris

Praza de
Abastos

MARKET

MARKET

UNIVERSIDADE

RÚA DAS TROMPAS

- - - - - Camino de Santiago

100 Meters
100 Yards

Accommodations
1 Parador Santiago de Compostela
2 Altaïr Hotel
3 Hotel Virxe da Cerca
4 Hotel Residencia Costa Vella & Café Costa Vella
5 Hotel Airas Nunes
6 Hotel San Clemente
7 Hostal Suso
8 Hostal Residencia Giadás
9 Hostal Anosa Casa
10 Pensión Ramos

Eateries & Other
11 Casa Marcelo
12 O Gato Negro
13 A Curtidoría Restaurante
14 Dos Reis & Enxebre
15 Restaurante Casa Manolo
16 O Dezaseis
17 Cotolay Bar Restaurante
18 Café Casino
19 A Viñoteca do Mercado
20 Launderette (2)

Isabel's edict to watch over pilgrims by offering three free meals to the first 10 who arrive each day (usually around 8:00). Pilgrims were originally allowed to eat in the main dining room and were given special cloaks to quash their odor. When that failed, they were moved to their own eating space, and now they dine in a room next to the staff quarters.

$$ Altaïr Hotel, owned by the Liñares family (see Costa Vella listing, later), is located in a renovated three-story residence. Its 11 spacious rooms and mod decor can best be described as "rustic minimalist." Exposed stone walls and open beams mixed with a sleek design provide a unique yet surprisingly affordable experience (RS%—free breakfast for Rick Steves readers who book direct, laundry service, Rúa dos Loureiros 12, +34 981 554 712, www.altairhotel.net, info@altairhotel.net).

$$ Hotel Virxe da Cerca is on the edge of the historical center, across the busy street from the market. Its standard rooms are in a modern building, but some of its "superior" and all of its "special" historic rooms—with classy old stone and hardwoods—are in a restored 18th-century Jesuit residence. While the modern rooms feel particularly impersonal, all 42 rooms surround a lush garden oasis (beautiful glassed-in breakfast room overlooks garden, elevator, Rúa da Virxe da Cerca 27, +34 981 569 350, www.pousadasdecompostela.com, vdacerca@pousadasdecompostela.com).

$ Hotel Residencia Costa Vella is my favorite spot in Santiago, with 14 comfortable rooms combining classic charm and modern comforts. The glassed-in breakfast room and lounge terrace overlook a peaceful garden, with lovely views of a nearby church and monastery and into the countryside beyond. They deserve a feature in *Better Stones and Tiles* magazine (laundry service, pay parking, Rúa Porta da Pena 17, +34 981 569 530, www.costavella.com, hotelcostavella@costavella.com, friendly José, Roberto, Anna, and wonderful staff).

$ Hotel Airas Nunes and **Hotel San Clemente** are affiliated with Hotel Virxe da Cerca. They're both good, stress-free, and professional feeling, located in restored old buildings with classy touches (+34 981 569 350, www.pousadasdecompostela.com, info@pousadasdecompostela.com). Hotel Airas Nunes is deep in the old center a few blocks in front of the cathedral (10 rooms, Rúa do Vilar 17, anunes@pousadasdecompostela.com). Hotel San Clemente is just outside the historical center (Rúa de San Clemente 28, sclemente@pousadasdecompostela.com).

$ Hostal Suso is a great value, offering 14 affordable, modern rooms around an airy atrium and a little bar where breakfast is served. It's located in the heart of Santiago (Rúa do Vilar 65, +34 981 586 611, www.hostalsuso.com, info@hostalsuso.com).

$ Hostal Residencia Giadás, tucked away just beyond the market, faces a tidy little square as if it owns it. The eight rooms, some with slanted floors, are simple but charming (elevator, next to Porta do Camiño at Praza do Matadoiro 2, reception in downstairs café, +34 981 587 071, www.hostalgiadas.com, info@hostalgiadas. com, Giadás family).

$ Hostal Anosa Casa, on a quiet street, is a five-minute walk to the cathedral and 10 minutes to the train station. Its nine compact rooms are nicely decorated (breakfast included, laundry service, Rúa de Entremurallas 9, +34 981 585 926, www.anosacasa. com, reservas@anosacasa.com).

¢ Pensión Ramos rents nine big, tasteful, clean rooms right in the center. It has lots of stairs, which is a blessing, since they take you farther away from the night noise (closed Nov-Easter, Rúa da Raiña 18, +34 981 581 859, Josefa speaks no English but her younger staff does).

Eating in Santiago

Restaurants generally serve lunch from 13:00 to 16:00 and dinner from 20:00 until very late (Spaniards don't start dinner until about 21:00). It's frustrating to try to eat before the locals do. If you find a restaurant serving before 13:00 or 21:00, you'll be all alone with a few sorry-looking tourists. Early-bird eaters should know that ordering a drink at any bar will generally get you a free tapa—Santiago is one of the few places in Spain that still honor this tradition.

For a quick meal on the go, grab a traditional meat pie, or *empanada*, which comes *de carne* (with pork), *de bonito* or *de atún* (tuna), *de bacalao* (salted cod), *de zamburiñas* (tiny scallops), *de berberechos* (cockles)—and these days, even *de pulpo* (octopus).

GOURMET DINING

$$$$ Casa Marcelo, Santiago's elite gourmet option, earned a Michelin star for its international cuisine. If you want to dine elegantly, this dressy 11-table restaurant is the place. For €60 (plus wine), you get a fixed-price meal featuring the chef's seasonal specials. The ever-changing menu fuses Galician food traditions with elements from all over the world. The kitchen is in plain view, so you'll get caught up in the excitement of cooking (open for lunch and dinner Tue-Sat 13:30-15:45 & 20:30-23:45, closed Sun-Mon, reservations only possible for groups of eight or more—get in line for a fair chance to enter, down the steep lane below the cathedral, Rúa das Hortas 1, +34 981 558 580).

Santiago Specialties

Strolling through the streets of Santiago is like visiting a well-stocked aquarium: Windows proudly display every form of edible sea life, including giant toothy fish, scallops and clams of every shape and size, monstrous shrimp, gooseneck barnacles (*percebes;* see sidebar, earlier), and—most importantly—octopus. The fertile fjords of the Galician coast are just 20 miles away, and the region's many fishing villages keep the capital city swimming in seafood. As the seafood is so fresh, the focus here is on purity rather than sauces. The seafood is served simply—generally just steamed or grilled, and seasoned only with a little olive oil, onions, peppers, and paprika.

Tasting octopus *(pulpo)* is obligatory in Galicia. It's most often prepared *a la gallega* (also called *pulpo a feira*): After the octopus is beaten to tenderize it, then boiled in a copper pot, its tentacles are snipped into bite-size pieces with scissors. It's topped with virgin olive oil, coarse sea salt, and a mixture of sweet and spicy paprika, then served on a round wooden plate. Eat it with toothpicks, never a fork. It's usually accompanied by large hunks of country bread to sop up the olive oil and washed down by local red *mencia* or white Ribeiro wine, often served in a little saucer-like ceramic cup *(cunca)*.

Not a fan of seafood? You can slurp the *caldo galego,* a traditional broth that originally came from the leftover stock used to prepare an elaborate Sunday feast (cabbage or *grelos,* potatoes, and so on—not too exciting, but providing comfort on a rainy day). Starting in June, look for *pimientos de Padrón*—miniature green peppers sautéed in olive oil with a heavy dose of rock salt.

And for dessert: Locals enjoy *queixo con mel* (cheese with honey) at the end of a meal. In the tourist zones, bakeries push samples of *tarta de Santiago,* the local almond cake. (Historically, the cake was baked by sisters in Santiago's convents.) The Galician version of firewater, *orujo,* is a popular after-dinner drink, thought to aid digestion. A somewhat lighter and tastier option is *licor de hierbas,* a distilled, Mountain Dew-colored blend of *orujo* flavored with local herbs.

RÚA DO FRANCO RESTAURANT ROW

Since hungry pilgrims first filled the city in the Middle Ages, Rúa do Franco (named not for the dictator but for the first French pilgrims) has been lined with eateries and bars. Today this street, which leads away from the cathedral, remains lively with foreign visitors—both tourists and pilgrims. There are dozens of seafood places, a few time-warp dives, and several lively bars with little €1.50 *montaditos* (sandwiches) for the grabbing. I'd stroll it once to see what appeals, and then go back to eat.

$$ O Gato Negro, a no-frills seafood tapas bar stuck in the

past and filled with loyal locals, is worth seeking out. It's one of the last places to serve Ribeiro wine in a ceramic cup (Tue-Sat 12:30-15:00 & 19:00-late, closed Mon and Sun evening, near Rúa do Franco on side street Rúa da Raiña—look for black cat sign outside, +34 981 583 105).

MEMORABLE EATING IN THE OLD CENTER

$$$ A Curtidoría Restaurante ("The Tannery") is a modern, spacious, and romantic place in the old town, rare for its open feeling. While the food is nothing exceptional, the setting is enjoyable and it's a solid value for a midday meal (good paella and fish plates, Rúa da Conga 2, +34 981 554 342, www.acurtidoria.com).

The fancy old **Parador Santiago de Compostela,** sharing the square with the cathedral, has two fine restaurants downstairs. The main restaurant, **$$$ Dos Reis,** fills a former stable with a dramatic stone vault. It offers international dishes—often with live piano and nearly dead guests. A typical parador restaurant, it comes with stiff tuxedoed service, white tablecloths, and not a hint of fun (daily, +34 981 582 200). Surprisingly, a few steps away is a wonderful alternative: **$$ Enxebre** has a livelier, easygoing tavern vibe, good traditional Galician food, and reasonable prices (daily, +34 981 050 527).

$ Restaurante Casa Manolo serves only one thing: a €10 fixed-price meal consisting of two generous courses, water, bread, and a packaged dessert. It's popular with students on a tight budget who want a classy meal out. This smart little family-run eatery combines sleek contemporary design, decent Galician and Spanish food, and excellent prices. The service is rushed (a good thing if you're in a hurry), but the value is unbeatable (arrive when they open or plan on waiting; Mon-Sat lunch 13:00-16:00, dinner 19:30-23:00, Sun lunch only, at the bottom of Praza de Cervantes, +34 981 582 950).

GOOD VALUES AWAY FROM THE TOURIST CENTER

$$$ O Dezaseis ("The Sixteen") is every local's favorite (and mine, too).

As soon as you walk down into its sprawling, high-energy vaulted dining room, you know this is the best place in town. In-the-know diners enjoy friendly service under stone walls, heavy beams, and modern art. You can choose from meat and fish plates, but simply ordering one *ración* per person and splitting their hearty mixed salad

for some veggies makes a fine and inexpensive meal. They do octopus just right here and have nice wines at good prices (Mon-Sat 13:30-16:00 & 20:00-24:00, closed Sun, reservations smart, Rúa de San Pedro 16, +34 981 577 633, www.dezaseis.com).

$$ Cotolay Bar Restaurante and two adjacent bar-restaurants are a hit with locals for drinks with free tapas. They are good budget bets for a meal of *raciones* without the tourists (€5-15 *raciones,* Mon-Sat 12:30-16:00 & 20:00-23:30, Sun lunch only, Rúa de San Clemente 8, +34 981 573 014).

CAFÉS
$ Café Costa Vella, in the breakfast room and garden of the highly recommended Hotel Residencia Costa Vella, is a little Eden tucked just beyond the tourist zone. The café welcomes nonguests for coffee and a relaxing break in a poetic time-warp garden with leafy views (great toasted sandwiches, plus a wide array of drinks, daily 8:00-23:00, Rúa Porta da Pena 17, +34 981 569 530).

$ Café Casino, a former private club, is a tired taste of turn-of-the-20th-century elegance with occasional live piano music. Local tour guides recommend this café to their timid British groups, who wouldn't touch an octopus with a 10-foot pole. While they have sandwiches and salads, I would just consider this an elegant coffee or tea stop (Sun-Thu 9:00-22:30, Fri-Sat until late, Rúa do Vilar 35, +34 981 577 503).

Santiago Connections

From Santiago de Compostela by Train to: Madrid (6/day, 6 hours, longer with connections in Palencia, León, or Pontevedra), **Salamanca** (1/day, 8 hours, transfer in Segovia), **León** (1/day direct, 4.5 hours; 2/day with transfer in Ourense, 6.5 hours), **Bilbao** (1/day, no direct service, 10.5 hours), **San Sebastián** (2/day, 11 hours), **Lugo** (3/day, 3.5 hours, requires transfer in Ourense or A Coruña—bus is better), **Porto,** Portugal (1/day via Vigo, 6 hours, better by bus—see below). Train info: +34 912 320 320, www.renfe.com.

By Bus to: Lugo (5/day, 2.5 hours), **Madrid** (5/day to Estación Sur, 9 hours, includes night bus that leaves at 21:30, most also serve Madrid's Barajas Airport Terminal 4; 2/day to Moncloa, 9 hours), **Salamanca** (1/day, 7.5 hours), **Astorga** (5/day, 5 hours), **León** (1/day, 6 hours), **Burgos** (1/day, 9 hours), **Bilbao** (2/day continue to **San Sebastián,** includes 1 night bus, 12 hours to Bilbao, 1.5 hours more to San Sebastián), **Porto,** Portugal (3/day, 4 hours, stops at Porto's airport before arriving in city center, www.flixbus.eu). All long-distance destinations are served by the Alsa bus company (www.alsa.es).

SALAMANCA

This sunny sandstone city boasts Spain's grandest plaza, its oldest university, and a fascinating history, all swaddled in a strolling, college-town ambience. A youthful, less touristy, less hilly version of Toledo, Salamanca is home to a fine ensemble of monuments, a pair of buttress-sharing cathedrals from different centuries, clusters of cloisters, and some surprisingly good museums. It's also affordable, as the many students help keep prices down.

Prestigious yet remote, Salamanca has that unusual mix of pride, pretense, and provinciality often found in old university towns. While Spaniards adore Salamanca, it feels undiscovered by tourists. That's probably because it's a bit far (1.5 hours each way) for an easy day trip from Madrid and not really on the way to other big destinations. But Salamanca rewards those who make the trip.

Enjoy strolling Salamanca's elegant streets and squares, watching the bright sunlight hit the golden sandstone just so. At day's end, join the paseo with the local crowd through Plaza Mayor, down Calle de Rúa Mayor, and out to the river. In Salamanca, young people congregate until late in the night, chanting and cheering, talking and singing. When I asked a local woman why young men here suddenly break into song, she said, "Doesn't it happen where you live?"

PLANNING YOUR TIME

Salamanca is feasible as a long day trip from Madrid (1.5 hours via high-speed train). By car or bus, it's 2.5 hours from Madrid. If you're bound for Santiago de Compostela or Portugal, Salamanca

Salamanca Area

To Santiago

Palencia

N-122

Esla Ricobayo
Reservoir

N-630

N-601

A-6

A-62
E-80

PORTUGAL

Valladolid

A-11

E-82

Zamora

Duero River

Tordesillas

A-601

Almendra
Reservoir

Douro River

SPAIN

A-66

A-62

Medina
del Campo

N-601

N-403

A-6

E-80

Tormes R.

Salamanca

A-62

A-50

E-80

To
Guarda,
Lisbon &
Coimbra

Ciudad
Rodrigo

BULL
BILLBOARD

To
Segovia

A-6

To
Madrid

To
Cáceres
& Mérida

A-66

N-110

Ávila

N-403

SPAIN

20 Kilometers

20 Miles

100 Miles

N-110

High-Speed Rail Line

is a natural stop. For those with more time in Spain, Salamanca is worth a full day and two nights.

Begin on the stunning Plaza Mayor, following my self-guided walk on Calle de Rúa Mayor through the heart of town to the university and cathedrals. After lunch, tour the Art Nouveau and/or automobile museums, and—if you're not churched out—visit the Church of San Esteban. Have a pre- or post-dinner drink on Plaza Mayor. To enjoy local tapas scenes, head out to Calle Van Dyck for a progressive dinner; for a sit-down

meal, splurge at a quality restaurant in the center. If you're staying overnight, be sure to take one last stroll through Plaza Mayor before bedtime.

Orientation to Salamanca

Salamanca's sights cluster in a barbell shape, with its magnificent town square (Plaza Mayor) at the north end and the cathedrals and university a 10-minute walk south. The surrounding streets are lively with eateries, shops, and people. It's fun to just get lost browsing the beautiful, mostly traffic-free back lanes of Salamanca's old town, embraced by a ring road.

TOURIST INFORMATION

The TI is on **Plaza Mayor** (Mon-Fri 9:00-19:00, Sat from 10:00, Sun 10:00-14:00, Plaza Mayor 32, +34 923 218 342). The TI website (www.salamanca.es) is a good source of practical information; you can also check the regional TI website (www.turismocastillayleon.com) to find out about events and festivals in and around Salamanca.

Museum Combo-Ticket: If you plan to visit both the Automobile History Museum and Art Nouveau Museum, stop at the TI first to buy a €5 combo-ticket—cutting your entry costs in half (not sold at sights).

ARRIVAL IN SALAMANCA

From either Salamanca's train or bus station to Plaza Mayor, it's a 25-minute walk, an easy bus ride (€1.05, pay driver), or a €10 taxi trip. The train station has no lockers; day-trippers can store bags at the bus station (*consignas;* at bay level facing main building on your left).

By Train: Most trains arrive at Salamanca's main train station. To walk from here into the center, exit left and head down to the ring road. Cross it at Plaza de España, then angle slightly left up Calle Azafranal. To go by bus, exit the front of the station, cross the street, and take bus #1, which lets you off just past the Plaza del Mercado (the market), next to Plaza Mayor.

Some slower trains continue to the town's second station, Salamanca Alamedilla station, which is a bit closer to the center. If you arrive here, walk down Avenida Alamedilla past a park to Plaza de España, then to Calle Azafranal. Note that you cannot depart from or buy tickets at Salamanca Alamedilla station.

By Bus: To walk into the center from the bus station, exit right and walk down Avenida Filiberto Villalobos; take a left on the ring road and the first right on Ramón y Cajal, head through Plaza de las Augustinas, and continue on Calle Prior to reach Plaza Mayor. Or take bus #4 (exit station right, catch bus on same side of the street as the station) to the city center; the closest stop is on Gran Vía, about two blocks east of Plaza Mayor (ask the driver or a fellow passenger, "*¿Para Plaza Mayor?*").

By Car: The old center is ringed by underground parking garages (around €20/day). Convenient options are at Plaza Santa Eulalia, Parking Plaza del Campillo, Parking Le Mans, and Parking Colón (for locations, see the "Salamanca" map, later). If you're overnighting, many hotels offer garages or valet parking for comparable fees.

HELPFUL HINTS

Book Ahead for Easter and September: During Easter week, bullfighting events, and the first half of September (Salamanca's Feria patron-saint celebration), hotels fill up and room prices increase.

Bike Rental and Tours: Juanjo and Javi from **Bikecicletas Salamanca** offer bike rentals and guided and unguided bike tours (reserve tours at least a day in advance, Calle Traviesa 18—around the corner from university facade, +34 923 216 940, +34 699 210 939, www.alquilerbicisalamanca.com).

Travel Agency: Viajes Salamanca books flights, trains, and some buses, including buses to Coimbra, Portugal (appointment only, Plaza Mayor 26, +34 923 211 414, marco@viajessalamanca.es).

Local Guide: Inés Criado Velasco, a good English-speaking guide, is happy to tailor a town walk to your interests (weekdays-€100/3 hours, 10 percent more on weekends and holidays, €150/5 hours for groups of 1-30, +34 609 557 528, www.inescriado.com, guia@inescriado.com).

Salamanca Walk

This stroll through the heart of Salamanca—worth ▲▲—connects all of the town's main sights in about an hour (not counting the time to enter museums). We'll begin on Spain's finest square, then walk south to one of its finest cathedrals and one of its most historic universities, before ending at a scenic viewpoint along the river.

• *Start on Salamanca's main square.*

❶ Plaza Mayor

Built from 1729 to 1755 by brothers Alberto and Nicolas Churriguera, Spain's ultimate plaza is worth ▲▲▲. It's a lovely place to simply hang out, enjoy a cup of coffee, and watch the world go by.

Plaza Mayor has long been Salamanca's community living room. It seems to continually be hosting some kind of party. Imagine the excitement of the days (until 1893) when bullfights were held in the square. Old-timers who gather here each day remember an earlier era, when teenage girls would promenade clockwise around the colonnade while the boys cruised counterclockwise.

Today, if you're lucky, you may find local student *tuna* musicians performing on the square—most likely on summer weeknights (see sidebar). Perhaps the best time for people-watching is Sunday after Mass (13:00-15:00), when the grandmothers gather here in their Sunday best.

The **Town Hall,** with the clock, grandly overlooks the square. While most Town Halls in Spain fly three or four flags, Salamanca's flies five. In order, from left to right: the province of Salamanca (purple with coat of arms); the state of Castile-León (red-and-white checkerboard, with castles and lions); Spain (red and yellow); the city of Salamanca (red with coat of arms); and the EU (blue with circle of gold stars).

Appreciate the harmonious architecture and the unique feel of this grand square—carved, like much of Salamanca, from a lemony, local sandstone called *piedra de Villamayor*. When first quarried, this stone is easy to carve, but over time it hardens—ideal for delicate but durable architectural decoration. Notice the square's perfectly symmetrical arches (hiding a pleasantly shaded arcade), its three levels of charming little balconies with matching shutters, and its artful lampposts. The square's designers, the Churriguera brothers, pioneered the intricately decorative look of the buildings that surround you. That look became a style all its own, called "Churrigueresque," which became popular around Spain and throughout its New World colonies.

While most European squares honor a single king or a saint, Plaza Mayor—ringed by famous Castilians—is for all the people. The **medallions** above the colonnade surrounding the plaza depict writers (Miguel de Cervantes), heroes and conquistadors (Christopher Columbus and Hernán Cortés), as well as numerous kings. Immediately to the right of the Town Hall, find Juan Carlos I, who abdicated in 2014, with Queen Sofía. Fascist dictator Francisco Franco was featured in a medallion until 2017.

You could spend all day noticing details around the square, but before we take off, here's just one more: Here on Plaza Mayor and throughout Salamanca, keep an eye out for **scallop shells.** Salamanca sits on the Camino de Santiago pilgrimage route from Seville to Galicia. The shell—a symbol of St. James (Santiago)—is used to mark pilgrimage routes to his tomb in Santiago de Compostela, whose famous cathedral is also in the Churrigueresque style.

Facing the Town Hall, look to the right, where you'll find the

Salamanca

To Bus Station (1/4 mile)

AV DE FILIBERTO VILLALOBOS

AV DE LOS MARISTAS

PASEO DE SAN VICENTE

AV. DE CARMEN

C. DE CARMEN

Campo de San Francisco

CALLE RAMÓN Y CAJAL

C. DE OSCAR PEYRA

C. ESPOZ Y MINA

C. PRIOR

PRADO

CALLE GARCÍA TEJADO

CUESTA DE SAN BLAS

CALLE ANCHA

CALLE DE LA COMPAÑÍA

Plaza de las Augustinas

N

200 Meters

200 Yards

CALLE DE CERVANTES

MELÉNDEZ

C. RABANAL

CASA DE LAS CONCHAS

3

CALLE DE LA EMPEDRADA

CALLE PALMA

C. PLACENTINOS

SERRANOS

CLERECÍA TOWERS

Plaza de San Isidro

CALLE LA RÚA MAYOR

CALLE

To E-3 Ciudad Rodrigo & Coimbra (Portugal) and N-501 to Segovia

C. RAVIESA

FRAY LUIS DE LEÓN STATUE

Patio de Escuelas

4

UNIVERSITY

S. SEB.

Plaza de Anaya

CALLE DE BALMES

C. CALDERÓN DE LA BARCA

5

NEW CATHEDRAL

OLD CATHEDRAL

CALLE MAZAS

CALLEJOS LIBREROS

Plaza Juan XXIII

CLOISTER

CATHEDRAL EXIT

C. TENTENECIO

GIBRALTAR

CATHEDRAL EXIT

CALLE DE SAN GREGORIO

CIVIL WAR ARCHIVE

ART NOUVEAU MUSEUM (CASA LIS)

VERRACO BULL STATUE

C. TESO DE SAN NICOLÁS

ROMAN BRIDGE

WALK ENDS

6

AUTOMOBILE HISTORY MUSEUM

AV. REYES DE

Río

Tormes

SALAMANCA

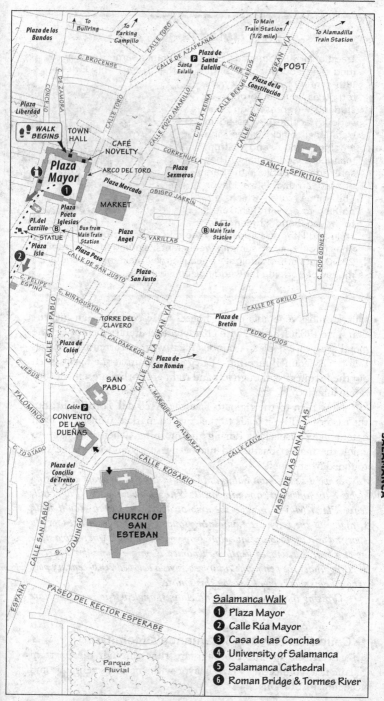

SALAMANCA

Salamanca Walk
1. Plaza Mayor
2. Calle Rúa Mayor
3. Casa de las Conchas
4. University of Salamanca
5. Salamanca Cathedral
6. Roman Bridge & Tormes River

Tuna Music

Traditionally, Salamanca's poorer students earned money to fund their education by singing in the streets. This 15th-to-18th-century tradition survives today, as musical groups of students (representing the various faculties)—dressed in traditional black capes and leggings—sing and strum mandolins and guitars. They serenade the public in the bars on and around Plaza Mayor. The name *tuna*, which has nothing to do with fish, refers to a vagabond student life-  style and later was applied to the music these students sing. They're out only on summer weeknights (singing for tips from 22:00 until after midnight), because they make more serious money performing for weddings on weekends.

square's most venerable coffee house, **Café Novelty**—an institution since 1905. It's filled with character and literary memories. The metal sculpture depicts a famous local writer, Torrente Ballester. Before city council meetings, delegates line up at the bar to hash out their strategies; though left and right are both represented, they rarely interact.

Now turn to the right to face the **Arco del Toro** (built into the eastern wall)—it leads to the covered market. Consider a brief detour here—especially during the morning, when it's busy—to enjoy the market bustle and maybe nurse a stand-up coffee surrounded by shoppers.

• *Now we'll head down Salamanca's main drag to its most interesting sights—the university and cathedrals. With your back to the Town Hall, leave Plaza Mayor through the arch at about one o'clock. You'll walk straight up the busy little adjoining square, called* **Plaza del Corillo** *(passing a stout, Romanesque church on your left), until you reach a statue of a bearded, stooped gentleman named Remigio González Martín. Writing under the pen name Adares, he was a beloved 20th-century poet who sold his works right here on this square.*

Crossing the busy street behind Adares, angle left to reach the start of...

❷ Calle Rúa Mayor—Salamanca's Main Drag

This lively and lovable thoroughfare runs through the heart of Salamanca, connecting Plaza Mayor with the city's religious and academic institutions.

Start walking down Calle Rúa Mayor toward the cathedral spire. This is a prime strip to window-shop restaurants for lunch or dinner. The second street on the left, Calle Felipe Espino, is lined with tempting tapas bars (described later, under "Eating in Salamanca"). Just past that, on the left at #13, notice the historic facade being held up by concrete and metal beams. The protected nature of Salamanca's historic old center makes it extremely expensive to renovate—you can't just tear down and build from scratch. So this has been a virtual ruin for years. At the end of the facade, at #17, notice the Mudejar-style double keyhole arches. (Mudejar is the Romanesque-Islamic Moorish design style made in Spain after the Christian conquest.)

Soon you'll pop out at a triangular little square with a monument honoring maestro Francisco de Salinas, a blind musicologist who taught at the University of Salamanca in the 16th century...one of many former professors you'll see celebrated around town. The building on the right is the ❸ **Casa de las Conchas.** One of Salamanca's most famous landmarks, its facade is encrusted with more than 300 scallop shells of St. James—again honoring the Camino de Santiago pilgrimage route that passes along here.

Circle around to the right, to the other side of the Casa de las Conchas, to see even more shells. Facing that facade are the twin towers of **La Clerecía Church**—nicknamed the "Stairway to Heaven." You can climb up these 200 steps for grand views (details later, under "Sights in Salamanca").

• *From here, let's detour from the main drag for a look at the key landmarks of Salamanca's famous university.*

Head up the street to the left of La Clerecía Church, through the wide Plaza de San Isidro. Take the second street on your left—the one on the right side of the building with the oversized door. This is Calle los Libreros, sprinkled with cafés and bars. Follow this for three short blocks, through the heart of the student zone, until a glorious facade opens up on your left. This is the historical main building of the...

❹ University of Salamanca

This university, the oldest in Spain (Universidad de Salamanca, est. 1218), was one of Europe's leading centers of learning for 400 years. Columbus came here for travel tips. Today, though no longer so prestigious, it's laden with history and popular with Americans, who enjoy its excellent summer program.

While you can pay to enter its historic lecture halls, the most interesting features of the university—worth ▲▲—are free to view and ring this square.

Duck into the plaza (Patio de Escuelas) opposite the university and face the ornately decorated grand **entrance facade.** Dating from the 16th century, this is the textbook example of Spain's

Plateresque style—named for its delicate, detail-packed, filigree-like carvings that resemble fine jewelry (*plata* means silver). The people studying the facade aren't art fans. They're trying to find a tiny frog on a skull that students look to for good luck. But forget the frog (for now)—follow the facade's symbolic meaning. It was made in three sections by Charles V. The bottom band—with the giant medallion—celebrates the Catholic Monarchs. Ferdinand and Isabel saw that the university had no facilities befitting its prestige, and they granted the money for this building.

The immodest middle section celebrates the grandson of Ferdinand and Isabel, Charles V. He appears with his queen, the Habsburg double-headed eagle, and the complex coat of arms of the mighty Habsburg Empire. Since this is a Renaissance structure, it features Greek and Roman figures in the shells. And, as a statement of intellectual independence from medieval Church control, the top shows the pope flanked by Hercules and Venus.

Dominating the square opposite the facade is a statue of **Fray** (Friar) **Luis de León** (1527-1591). In his role as an academic here, Luis de León challenged the Church's control of the word of God by translating part of the Bible into Castilian. For this he was denounced to the Inquisition and jailed for nearly five years. Upon being released, he started his first post-imprisonment lecture with, "As we were saying..." Such courageous men of truth believed the forces of the Inquisition were not even worth acknowledging. Salamantinos admire Fray Luis de León for maintaining the independence of academia in the face of questionable political mores.

At the end of the plaza behind Fray Luis de León, skip the modest Museum of the University (a humble art gallery), but do dip into the beautiful courtyard at the left corner of the square, with pillars shaped like parting curtains. In one of these rooms, look for Fernando Gallego's fanciful 15th-century *Sky of Salamanca* ceiling mural—a depiction of the night sky of constellations, illustrated with mythological figures.

Can't forget about the frog? Head back out and face the facade. It's on the right pillar, nearly halfway up, on the leftmost of three skulls.

You've already seen the most important parts of the university (including, yes, the frog). But if you like, you can also pay to visit the lecture halls, which are austere and pricey but contain a lot of history (enter through the door under the facade; for details, see below).

• *When you're ready to move on, face the facade and turn right down Calle los Libreros. Take the first left, on Calle de Calderón de la Barca. You'll run right into...*

❺ Salamanca Cathedral

Salamanca's cool-on-a-hot-day cathedral is two-in-one: a 12th-century Romanesque church (the "Old Cathedral," hiding behind the tower on your right) adjoining the much larger, newer "annex" that you're facing now (the "New Cathedral," completed in the 18th century).

Turn left and circle around to the main **facade,** facing the park. Like the university, it's decorated Plateresque—Spain's version of Flamboyant Gothic. You may notice tourists making a fuss over the entrance door (the one on the right, as you face this side of the cathedral). They're looking for the astronaut added by a capricious restorer in 1993. At first this caused an outrage, but now locals shrug and say, "He's the person closest to God." I'll give you a chance to find him on your own...

Meanwhile, turn around and survey the lovely garden square the cathedral faces, **Plaza de Anaya.** The cathedral buttresses face the stern, Neoclassical facade of the university's philology faculty. Genteel spaces like this help give Salamanca its "Spanish Oxford" vibe.

Now's a good time to tour the worthwhile cathedral interior (described later, under "Sights in Salamanca").

Oh, yeah—still looking for that **astronaut?** Here's some help: He's just a little guy, about the size of a Ken-does-Mars doll, entwined in the stone trim to the left of the New Cathedral side door, roughly 10 feet up. If you like that, check out the dragon (an arm's length below, and just to the right). Historians debate whether he's eating an ice-cream cone or singing karaoke.

• *Facing the astronaut, turn right, then left, circling all the way to the downhill side of the cathedral complex. (If you're touring the cathedral, you'll pop out at the same place.) From there, head downhill on Calle Tentenecio (passing the Sercotel Puerta de la Catedral hotel on your right). After one block, you'll see the fine facade of Spain's **General Ar-***

SALAMANCA

chive of the Civil War—an important documentation center for that still-poignant era of Spanish history. If you turn left here, the building next to the archive is Salamanca's excellent **Art Nouveau Museum**, which is well worth a visit (described later, under "Sights in Salamanca").

Bear right (downhill) at the archive to curl down one more block to a busy road along Salamanca's riverbank, Calle de San Gregorio. Bear right and cross the street to reach our final stop, the...

❻ Roman Bridge and Tormes River

This low-slung bridge (Puente Romano), with its elegantly simple arches, dates back to the late first century AD. Until the 20th cen-

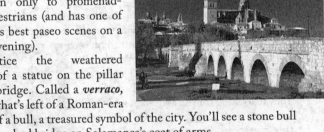

tury, it remained Salamanca's primary river crossing; today it's open only to promenading pedestrians (and has one of the city's best paseo scenes on a warm evening).

Notice the weathered stump of a statue on the pillar by the bridge. Called a *verraco*, this is what's left of a Roman-era statue of a bull, a treasured symbol of the city. You'll see a stone bull and an arched bridge on Salamanca's coat of arms.

Salamanca's river is the **Río Tormes**, well known among Spaniards thanks to *Lazarillo de Tormes*—a 16th-century novella that, in the Spanish literary pantheon, takes a backseat only to Cervantes. Young Lazarillo's tale, which every young Spanish student reads in school, begins here on the Tormes riverbank, then winds through Spain as he embarks on various adventures. *Lazarillo de Tormes* is credited with creating a whole new literary form: the picaresque novel, in which a *picaro* (rascal) travels around on a series of humorous adventures, outsmarting everyone he meets...the literary inspiration for everyone from Huck Finn to Pippi Longstocking to Hunter S. Thompson.

• *Our walk is finished. If the weather's nice and people are out strolling, join them and head across the bridge, where you'll look back to see the classic view of Salamanca's sandstone cityscape.*

If you stand with the bridge and its bull to your back, you can head straight up the way you came to reach the cathedral and the main route through town; or you can turn right and walk just a couple of minutes to Salamanca's surprisingly good **Automobile History Museum**. And just beyond that is one more worthwhile sight: the fine **Church of San Esteban** is about a 10-minute walk from here. Both are described under "Sights in Salamanca."

SALAMANCA

Sights in Salamanca

CATHEDRAL AND UNIVERSITY AREA

This zone is about a 10-minute walk south of Plaza Mayor. These are listed in the order you'll reach them on my "Salamanca Walk," outlined earlier.

▲Clerecía Towers/Stairway to Heaven (Torres de La Clerecía/Scala Coeli)

The twin spires of La Clerecía Church offer a bird's-eye view of the city and a panorama of the Old and New cathedrals. The church is behind the Casa de las Conchas, just off the Calle Rúa Major. You'll huff up 200 steps—the last stretch of which is the original bell-tower staircase, which has been restored. I'd skip the attached museum, and just climb the towers.

Cost and Hours: €3.75, daily 10:00-20:00, Dec-Feb until 18:00, last entry 45 minutes before closing, Calle Compañia 5, +34 923 277 174.

University of Salamanca Lecture Halls

The best features of Salamanca's prestigious university—its glorious facade and starry-skied old ceiling fresco—are free, and described in my self-guided "Salamanca Walk," earlier. But for a hefty fee, you can also enter the old lecture halls around the cloister, where many of Spain's golden age heroes studied. The lecture halls are interesting for academics and those with a serious interest in Salamanca's university history. But they're expensive, pretty stark, and difficult for a casual visitor to appreciate.

Cost and Hours: €10, Mon-Sat 10:00-20:00, Sept-March until 19:00, Sun 10:00-14:00 year-round, +34 923 294 400, ext. 1150, www.usal.es.

Visiting the Lecture Halls: Buy a ticket at the cash-only machine, enter the courtyard, and turn left to make a clockwise loop—following the good, posted English information for each room. You'll pass several different lecture halls, all of them quite austere—even monastic—and each one named for an important university figure. For example, the namesake of the second lecture hall, **Miguel de Unamuno** (1864-1936), was a Basque-born playwright, poet, novelist, philosopher, and University of Salamanca rector from the so-called "Generation of '98" (a creative and intellectual blossoming in turn-of-the-century Spain). He served here right up until the civil war. Following a heated debate with one of Franco's generals, he condemned both sides of the conflict, was stripped of his rectorship, and died in disgust under house arrest 10 weeks later.

The next lecture hall—for **Fray Luis de León**—is the most historic. The narrow wooden-beam tables and benches, whittled

down by centuries of studious doodling, are originals. Professors spoke from the Church-threatening *cátedra* (pulpit). This was where the friar boldly resumed his lectures, right where he left off, following five years of Inquisition punishment (see page 382).

Continuing around the courtyard, look up to appreciate the colorful Mudejar-style decorations between the ceiling beams. Step into the **chapel,** where the main altarpiece depicts professors swearing to Mary's virginity—an example of the conflict between academia and religion. (How did they know?)

Climb upstairs beside the Plateresque banister for a peek into the oldest **library** in Spain. Outside the library, look into the courtyard at the American sequoia, brought here 150 years ago and standing all alone. Continuing around the upper courtyard, look up at the cathedral's adjacent bell tower. See any giant nests? Storks stop here from February through August on their annual journey from Morocco to northern Europe. There are hundreds of these stork nests in Salamanca.

▲▲Salamanca Cathedral (Catedral de Salamanca)

Salamanca's cathedral is a two-fer: When constructing a spacious new cathedral (built 1513-1733), Church fathers put it right next to the town's 12th-century Romanesque church. The "New Cathedral," a towering mix of Gothic, Renaissance, and Baroque, shares buttresses with its older partner.

Cost and Hours: Cathedrals, cloister, and museum—€6, includes audioguide, free Tue 9:00-10:30 (but museum closed during free hours); open Mon-Sat 11:00-18:00, Sun until 16:00, last entry 45 minutes before closing; tower—€3.75, free Sun 17:00-19:00, open daily 10:00-20:00, Jan-Feb until 18:00, last entry one hour before closing.

Information: Cathedral +34 923 217 476, tower +34 923 226 701, www.catedralsalamanca.org.

Visiting the Cathedrals: To get to the old, you have to walk through the new.

New Cathedral (Catedral Nueva): Before entering the New Cathedral, check out its ornate **front door** (west portal on Calle Rúa Mayor—described earlier on my self-guided "Salamanca Walk").

Head inside. The **interior** is vast and majestic—architecturally rivaling any in Spain (but lacking the famous art that singles out others, like Toledo's). Fancy stone trim is everywhere, and the dome decoration is particularly wonderful. Occasionally the music is live,

not recorded. The *coro*, or choir, blocks up half of the church (normal for Spanish Gothic), but its wood carving is sumptuous; look up to see the recently restored, elaborate organ.

• *Enter the Old Cathedral through the San Lorenzo Chapel, to the left of the New Cathedral's main door.*

Old Cathedral (Catedral Vieja): Sit in a front pew to study the altarpiece's 53 scenes from the lives of Mary and Jesus (by the Italian Florentino, 1445) surrounding a precious 12th-century statue of the Virgin of the Valley. High above, notice the dramatic Last Judgment fresco of Jesus sending condemned souls into the literal jaws of hell.

Enter the **cloister** (off the right transept) and explore the chapels, notable for their unusual tombs, ornate altarpieces, and ceilings with leering faces at the bases of the supports. In the Capilla de Santa Bárbara (second on the left), you can sit as students once did for their tests. During these final exams, a stern circle of professors formed around the students at the tomb of a Salamanca bishop. (The university originated in the cathedral school, with a group of teacher-priests who met in this room.)

As you continue through the cloister, you'll find the chapterhouse *(salas capitulares)*, home to the **museum.** Immediately on your right, look for a 13th-century sculpture of the Virgin that opens to show scenes of Mary's life. Beyond that, pass under a beautiful 16th-century coffered ceiling to see a fine collection of 15th- and 16th-century Castilian paintings, mostly church altarpieces.

Continuing around the cloister, the Capilla de Santa Catalina was used as the university's library until 1610. The room is lined with tombs and paintings from the 15th to 17th century. The Capilla de Anaya, farthest from the cloister entrance, has a gorgeously carved 16th-century alabaster tomb (look for the dog and lion making peace—or negotiating who gets to eat the worried-looking rabbit—at the foot of the tomb) and a wooden 16th-century Mudejar organ.

At the end of your visit you will exit onto Calle Gibraltar across from the Casa Lis Art Nouveau Museum and the civil war archives. To loop back up to the tower and where you entered the cathedral, take your first right and go uphill on Calle Tentenecio.

Tower: For a fantastic view of the upper floors and terraces of both cathedrals, and a look at the inside passages with small exhibits about the cathedrals' history and architecture, visit the tower

(marked *Jeronimus*). It was sealed after Lisbon's 1755 earthquake to create structural support, and not opened again until 2002. The tower entrance is to the right as you exit the Old Cathedral.

▲Church of San Esteban

Salamanca's "second church" rivals the first church of many Spanish cities. It sits a few blocks east of the cathedral. Dedicated to St. Stephen (Esteban) the martyr, this complex contains a restored cloister, tombs, museum, sacristy, and church.

Cost and Hours: €4, church open daily 10:00-14:00 & 16:00-20:00, until 18:00 in winter, last entry 45 minutes before closing, museum closed Sun afternoons and all day Mon, +34 923 215 000, www.conventosanesteban.es.

Visiting the Church: The visitors entrance is to the right of the church entrance (which is closed except during services).

Before you enter, notice the Plateresque **facade** and its bas-relief of the stoning of St. Stephen. The Crucifixion above is by Italian Renaissance artist Benvenuto Cellini. As you enter the building, look at the large poster explaining the facade's many characters.

After buying your ticket, enter the **cloister,** turn right, and circle around—enjoying the serenity. About three-quarters of the way around, you'll enter a hall where signs indicate ways to the church *(iglesia),* sacristy *(sacristía),* choir *(coro),* and museum *(museo).* Head to the church first. Once inside, follow the free English pamphlet.

The nave is overwhelmed by a 100-foot, 4,000-piece wood **altarpiece** by José Benito Churriguera (1665-1725) that replaced the original Gothic one in 1693. You'll see St. Dominic on the left, St. Francis on the right, and a grand monstrance holding the Communion wafers in the middle, all below a painting of St. Stephen being stoned. This is a textbook example of the intricately detailed Churrigueresque style that influenced many South American mission buildings. Quietly ponder the dusty, gold-plated cottage cheese, as tourists shake their heads and say "too much" in their mother tongues.

Go up the architecturally unique staircase, built without any interior support; you'll notice that when you walk, you definitely lean inward. Turn left and make a loop around the upper level of the cloister, enjoying the calm, then visit the **museum** with its illustrated 14th-to-16th-century Bibles and choir books. Notice also how the curved ivory Filipino saints all look like they're carved out of an elephant's tusk. And don't miss the fascinating "chocolate box reliquaries" on the wall in the back (on the right), from the 16th and 17th centuries. Survey whose bones are collected between all the inlaid ivory and precious woods. Before leaving, take a quick

look at the collection of 19th-to-20th-century pharmacy-related pieces.

Exit the museum and step into the balcony **choir loft** for a fine overview of the nave. The big, spinnable book holder in the middle of the room held giant music books—large enough for all to chant from in an age when there weren't enough books for everyone. Amen.

Convento de las Dueñas

Located next door to the Church of San Esteban, the much simpler *convento* is a joy (enter by the door facing the busy roundabout). It consists of a double-decker cloister with a small museum of religious art. Check out the stone meanies exuberantly decorating the capitals on the cloister's upper deck. No English information is displayed, but an English booklet is available for a small fee. The nuns also sell sweets—their specialty is *amarguillos* (almonds, egg whites, and sugar; no assortments possible even though their display box raises hopes).

Cost and Hours: €2, generally Mon-Sat 10:30-12:45 & 16:30-19:30, off-season until 17:30, closed Sun year-round, +34 923 215 442.

NEAR THE RIVER

The Art Nouveau Museum and the Automobile History Museum sit a couple of steep blocks below the cathedral area, just above Salamanca's riverbank. A €5 combo-ticket sold only at the TI on Plaza Mayor covers both sights.

▲▲Art Nouveau Museum (Museo Art Nouveau y Art Deco)

Located in the turn-of-the-century Casa Lis, this museum displays a stunning collection of stained glass, paintings, vases, furniture, jewelry, cancan statuettes, and toy dolls. Nowhere else in Spain will you enjoy an Art Nouveau collection in a building from the same era. A visit here offers a welcome, lighter-than-air change of pace from Salamanca's heavy, somber, sandstone cityscape.

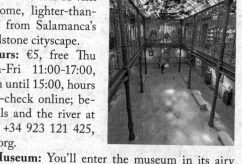

Cost and Hours: €5, free Thu 11:00-14:00; Mon-Fri 11:00-17:00, Sat until 20:00, Sun until 15:00, hours subject to change—check online; between the cathedrals and the river at Calle Gibraltar 14, +34 923 121 425, www.museocasalis.org.

Visiting the Museum: You'll enter the museum in its airy atrium, bathed in colorful light from the stained-glass skylight.

SALAMANCA

The 19 themed exhibits—highlighting various media and an international pantheon of talented artists—fill two floors. The English brochure translates the posted Spanish text.

First, tour the ground floor counterclockwise, beginning with porcelain, including fine works from Hungary's Zsolnay factory, which revolutionized porcelain for architectural use. You'll see a collection of bronzes from Vienna, exquisite jewelry by René Lalique, and paintings. Look for a playful series of chryselephantines—slinky statuettes made from a combination of gold *(chrysos)*, ivory *(elephas)*, and other precious materials, a style dating from ancient Greece. The chryselephantine collection includes fanciful, exotic, imaginative works by Austria's Ferdinand Preiss, and stylized dancers and well-to-do ladies by Romania's Demétre Chinarus. Also on this floor is a lovely café, with reasonably priced drinks and light bites in a fine Art Nouveau interior, looking out from inside the stained-glass facade.

Then head to the upper floor, which you'll also tour counterclockwise beginning with exquisite French dolls...and creepy German ones. You'll see sleek, Bauhaus-inflected figurines by Karl Hagenhauer, and a fascinating collection of "characters"—more like caricatures, with exaggerated features reminiscent of early Hummels. Rounding out this floor are bronzes, jewelry, fans, furniture, and glass, with an entire room devoted to the delicate works of French glass artist Émile Gallé.

For one more look at Art Nouveau beauty, exit the museum to the left and go down toward the busy road; turning left here, you can look back up to see the stained glass of the beautiful main facade.

▲Automobile History Museum
(Museo de Historia de la Automoción)

This museum—worth ▲▲▲ for gearheads—has three floors showcasing about 100 vehicles in chronological order from 1886 to the present. There's no posted English information, but at least you'll know the make, model, and year of each automobile. You'll begin in the basement, then work your way up through the vehicles. Find the 1899 Catalan three-wheeled car that was shown at the World's Fair in Paris, a 1930 fire truck, a big black 1970 Caddie used for shuttling heads of state (including Franco), and Formula 1 race cars driven by Fernando Alonso (2009) and Michael Schumacher (1995). The exhibit finishes with a collection of motorcycles.

Cost and Hours: €5, Tue-Sun 10:00-14:00 & 17:00-20:00 (17:30-20:30 in July-Aug), closed Mon year-round; audioguide-€2.50, download using on-site Wi-Fi; Plaza del Mercado Viejo, near the river immediately below the Art Nouveau Museum, +34 923 260 293, www.museoautomocion.com.

Sleeping in Salamanca

Salamanca, a student town, has plenty of good eating and sleeping values. Prices tend to go up on weekends. Most of my listings are on or within a three-minute walk of Plaza Mayor (Hotel Rector, Sercotel Puerta de la Catedral, and Microtel Placentinos are a little farther). The city is noisy on the weekends, so if you're a light sleeper, ask for an interior room.

$$$$ Hotel Rector is the place to splurge in Salamanca. Sitting at the bottom edge of town, just above the riverbank, it has 14 rooms with high-end touches—such as fresh flowers in every room—and a staff that hustles to please (air-con, elevator, pay parking, Paseo Rector Esperabé 10, +34 923 218 482, www.hotelrector. com, Julián and Ricardo).

$$$ Sercotel Puerta de la Catedral is a business-class hotel on a quiet pedestrian street around the corner from the cathedral entrance. While part of a chain, it has only 37 rooms, giving it a boutique feel. It's worth the extra euros for a room with a great view of the cathedral (air-con, elevator, pay parking, Plaza de Juan XXIII 5, +34 923 280 829, www.sercotelhoteles.com, reservas@sercotel.com).

$$ Sercotel Las Torres is a chain hotel with 53 modern, spacious rooms (several with see-through bathroom doors) and all the amenities. It's nothing special...except that it's located right on Plaza Mayor (some view rooms, air-con, elevator, exit Plaza Mayor at 11 o'clock to find hotel entry just off square at Calle Concejo 4, +34 923 212 100, www.sercotelhoteles.com, reservas@sercotel. com).

$$ Microtel Placentinos is quaint and intimate, with nine rustic rooms buried deep in the streets near the university buildings. A bit idiosyncratic, it has personality and class (air-con, elevator, Calle Placentinos 9, +34 923 281 531, www.microtelplacentinos. com, reservas@microtelplacentinos.com).

$ Hostal Plaza Mayor, with 19 small, simple, older rooms, has a homey feel and a good location practically on Plaza Mayor—but with no views (air-con, most rooms served by elevator, pay parking, Plaza del Corrillo 20, +34 923 262 020, www.hostalplazamayor.es, info@hostalplazamayor.es).

$ Hostería Casa Vallejo is a welcoming, family-run place, with 12 rustic but modernized rooms a block away from Plaza Mayor. The attached, recommended tapas bar/restaurant serves up tasty deals (air-con, elevator, San Juan de la Cruz 3, +34 923 280 421, www.hosteriacasavallejo.com, info@hosteriacasavallejo.com, Amparo and Jesús).

$ Hostal Los Angeles rents 10 simple but cared-for rooms, four of which overlook the square. Stand on the balcony and in-

SALAMANCA

Salamanca Hotels & Restaurants

To Parking Le Mans →

To Bus Station (1/4 mile) →

AV. DE FILIBERTO VILLALOBOS

C. DE CARMEN

Campo de San Francisco

PASEO DE SAN VICENTE

AV. DE LOS MARISTAS

CALLE RAMÓN Y CAJAL

CALLE DE LA COMPAÑÍA

C. DE ISCAR. PEYRA

C. DE ESPOZ Y MINA

PRADO

C. PRIOR

CUESTA DE SAN BLAS

CALLE ANCHA

Plaza de las Augustinas

CALLE GARCIA TEJADO

CALLE DE CERVANTES

CALLE DE LA EMPEDRADA

200 Meters

200 Yards

C. RABANAL

MELENDEZ

8

CASA DE LAS CONCHAS

CLERECÍA TOWERS

16

CALLE PALMA

C. PLACENTINOS

SERRANOS

C. TRAVIESA

Plaza de San Isidro

CALLE RÚA MAYOR

CALLE MAYOR

4

22

To E-3 Ciudad Rodrigo & Coimbra (Portugal) and N-501 to Segovia

FRAY LUIS DE LEÓN STATUE

Patio de Escuelas

S. SEB.

CALLE DE BALMES

UNIVERSITY

Plaza de Anaya

CALLE MAZAS

C. CALDERÓN DE LA BARCA

NEW CATHEDRAL

CALLE LOS LIBREROS

Plaza Juan XXIII

2

OLD CATHEDRAL

CLOISTER

C. TENTENECIO

GIBRALTAR

CATHEDRAL EXIT

CALLE DE SAN GREGORIO

CIVIL WAR ARCHIVE

ART NOUVEAU MUSEUM (CASA LIS)

1

C. TESO DE SAN NICOLÁS

VERRACO BULL STATUE

AUTOMOBILE HISTORY MUSEUM

AV. REYES DE

ROMAN BRIDGE

Río

Tormes

SALAMANCA

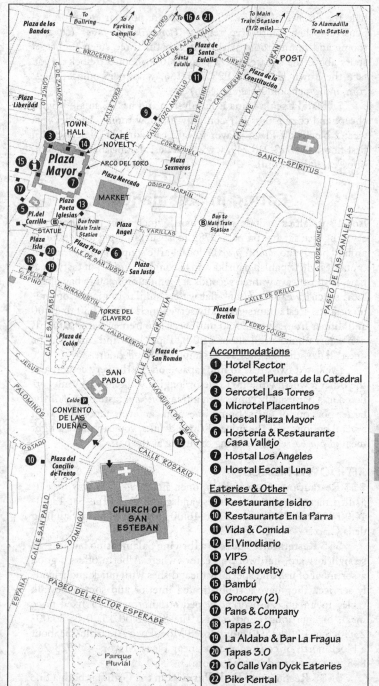

Accommodations
1. Hotel Rector
2. Sercotel Puerta de la Catedral
3. Sercotel Las Torres
4. Microtel Placentinos
5. Hostal Plaza Mayor
6. Hostería & Restaurante Casa Vallejo
7. Hostal Los Angeles
8. Hostal Escala Luna

Eateries & Other
9. Restaurante Isidro
10. Restaurante En la Parra
11. Vida & Comida
12. El Vinodiario
13. VIPS
14. Café Novelty
15. Bambú
16. Grocery (2)
17. Pans & Company
18. Tapas 2.0
19. La Aldaba & Bar La Fragua
20. Tapas 3.0
21. To Calle Van Dyck Eateries
22. Bike Rental

hale the essence of Spain. View rooms are popular and more expensive—when you reserve, request *"Con vista, por favor"* (cheaper rooms and family room with shared bath, three steep flights of stairs above the square, Plaza Mayor 10—about 3 o'clock as you face the Town Hall, +34 923 218 166, www.pensionlosangeles.com, info@pensionlosangeles.com).

$ Hostal Escala Luna is family-run and has 22 small, bright, cheap, and cozy rooms (air-con only in a few rooms, laundry service; 2 blocks off Plaza Mayor toward cathedral at Meléndez 13, first floor; +34 923 218 749, www.hostalescalalunasalamanca.com, info@escalaluna.com).

Eating in Salamanca

Local specialties include *serrano* ham, which is in just about everything (see sidebar on page 978); roast suckling pig (called *tostón* around here); and *sopa de ajo,* the local garlic soup. *Patatas meneadas* (potatoes with Spanish paprika and bacon) is a simple but tasty local tapa. If you always wanted seconds at Communion, buy a bag of the local specialty called *obleas*—flat wafers similar to giant Communion hosts. Restaurants generally serve lunch from 13:30 to 16:00 and dinner from about 20:30 until very late (remember, Spaniards don't start dinner until about 21:00). Tapas bars and cafés may be open all day, though they serve simpler food off-hours.

I've listed two areas to find tapas—one in the very center, and the other a worthwhile taxi ride or longish walk away. Drinks ordered at a bar usually come with a free *pincho,* a taste of one of the larger portions of tapas. Sometimes you can even choose between several options. For the price of three drinks, you can make a light meal of *pinchos* while standing or sitting at the bar.

SIT-DOWN MEALS

$$$ Restaurante Casa Vallejo, open since 1941, is known for its grilled meats, traditional dishes, and good wine (Tue-Sat 13:30-16:00 & 21:00-23:00, Sun 13:30-16:00 only, closed Mon, San Juan de la Cruz 3, +34 923 280 421).

$$$ Restaurante Isidro is a thriving Salamantino favorite—a straightforward, hardworking eatery where Alberto offers a good assortment of fish and specialty meat dishes with quick and friendly service. They have a sophisticated interior and some sidewalk tables in an upscale-workaday pedestrian zone (€15 fixed-price meal, big portions, good roasts, Tue-Sat 13:00-15:30 & 20:00-23:30, Sun 13:00-15:30 only, closed Mon, Pozo Amarillo 23, about a block north of covered market near Plaza Mayor, +34 923 262 848, restauranteisidro.atspace.com).

$$$$ Restaurante En la Parra ("On the Grill") is both a fine

splurge and an excellent value. Chef Rocío Parra Haro brings high-end, creative Spanish cooking at small-town prices. The interior is sleek yet welcoming, and the €45 *menú degustación* is a memorable experience for those with time to celebrate a special occasion (no à la carte, Tue-Sun 13:45-15:15 & 21:00-22:15, closed Mon, Calle San Pablo 80, +34 923 064 783, www.restaurantenlaparra.com).

$$$ Vida & Comida feels fresh and modern, serving a fusion of traditional and creative cuisine. It combines sit-down tablecloth ambience with an informal, fun menu of small plates (Tue-Sat 14:00-16:00 & 21:00-24:00, Sun 14:00-16:00 only, closed Mon, Plaza Santa Eulalia 11, +34 923 281 236).

$$ El Vinodiario is tucked away on a delightful square in the streets near the Church of San Esteban and Convento de las Dueñas. Their wine selection includes their own vintages, and tapas and meals are proudly made with local ingredients (daily 12:00-17:00 & 20:00-24:00, Plaza Basilios 1, +34 923 614 925).

$$ VIPS is the Spanish answer to a diner, with long hours, takeout, and an easy menu of burgers, club sandwiches, salads, and American-style breakfasts (daily 9:00-23:00, Plaza del Poeta Iglesias 6, +34 923 050 929).

CASUAL EATERIES ON PLAZA MAYOR

Enjoy a meal sitting on the finest square in Spain and savor some of Europe's best people-watching. The bars, with little tables spilling onto the square, serve *raciones* and €2 glasses of wine. A *ración de embutidos y quesos* (a mixed plate of hams, sausages, and cheese), a *ración* of *patatas bravas* (chunks of potatoes with a slightly spicy tomato sauce), and two glasses of wine make up a nice dinner for two for about €25—one of the best eating values in all of Europe. The places here are basically interchangeable—just find the view you like best and don't expect high cuisine. For dessert, stroll with an ice-cream cone from **$$ Café Novelty,** Plaza Mayor's Art Nouveau café. Dating from 1905, it's the oldest café in Salamanca—and has some customers who look like they've been there since it opened (daily 8:00-24:00, +34 923 219 990).

Just Off the Square: Bright, energetic, family-friendly **$$ Bambú** is a fresh, modern change from all the traditional woody bars, but with similarly delicious tapas. Look for a black-and-white sign, then go downstairs to the bar or the sit-down restaurant, which serves grilled meats, several salads, and varied *raciones* (Wed-Sun 13:00-16:00 & 20:00-24:00, Mon lunch only, closed Tue, Calle Prior 4, +34 923 260 092).

PICNIC FOOD

The beautiful covered market on Plaza Mercado has fresh fruits and veggies, as well as a bar to enjoy a morning coffee in the mid-

dle of the shopping action (Mon 8:00-19:00, Tue-Sat until 14:30, closed Sun, on east side of Plaza Mayor).

Supermarkets: A small **Carrefour Express** grocery, on the main drag between Plaza Mayor and the cathedrals, has just the basics (daily 9:00-23:00, Calle Rúa Mayor 35). For variety, the big **Carrefour Market** supermarket is your best bet, but it's a six-block walk north of Plaza Mayor on Calle Toro (Mon-Sat 9:00-22:00, closed Sun, across from Plaza San Juan de Sahagún and its church).

Sandwiches: The **Pans & Company** fast-food sandwich chain is always easy, with a branch on Calle Prior across from Burger King (daily 10:00-23:00).

TAPAS NEAR CALLE RÚA MAYOR

The main drag connecting Plaza Mayor to the cathedral and university zone—Calle Rúa Mayor—is packed with eateries that mostly cater to tourists. But a few steps away, you can find some eateries offering better values. One good place to browse is **Calle Felipe Espino** (the second cross-street you reach, on the left, after leaving Plaza Mayor). Along here a strip of places offer both indoor and outdoor seating. The first one, **$$ Tapas 2.0,** is a "gastrotasca" that tries for updated versions of classic Spanish tapas at reasonable prices (closed Tue, at #10). A few steps down is **$$$ La Aldaba,** with a pricey, atmospheric sit-down restaurant in back, affordable tapas at the bar in front where locals gather, and outdoor tables where diners can eat from the restaurant menu or the tapas menu (closed Sun dinner, at #6). Farther along, the more lowbrow **$$ Bar La Fragua** is a basic, traditional spot that feels like a throwback (closed Sun, at #2). Sister to Tapas 2.0, with a similar concept, **$$$ Tapas 3.0** is one street up at Calle Sánchez Barbero 9 (a little more expensive, creative, and formal).

OFF THE BEATEN PATH ON CALLE VAN DYCK

Locals and students head outside the old town to hit the tapa/*pincho* scene along a main artery called **Calle Van Dyck.** It's about a 20-minute walk or a short taxi ride from the edge of the old town, but it's worth the effort. You'll spend, on average, €2.50 for a *caña* (small beer), which comes with a small tapa. To get there on foot, go to the end of Calle Toro, cross the main drag (Avenida de Mirat), and go up Calle Maria Auxiliadora; after crossing the wide Avenida de Portugal, take the third left onto Calle Van Dyck. Unless otherwise noted, these places are open nightly for dinner, and often also open for lunch on weekends.

Start at the neighborhood classic, which has been around for more than 40 years—**$ Cafe Bar Chinitas** at #18—where Victorio, Manoli, and their son Javi serve up a delicious selection of 45 tapas. This feels like a very local scene, where Salamantino fami-

lies drop in with their kids mid-paseo (closed Sun June-July and Mon year-round; also closed all of Aug, +34 923 229 471). Or try the Galician seafood eatery **$$$ Bodega Chicho,** farther down the street at #34 (or enter around corner at Alfonso de Castro 15). You can either dine at their bar or sit down in the restaurant for grilled fish and seafood *raciones* galore. They don't do free *pinchos* with drinks—come here to commit to a quality meal (Wed 20:00-23:30, Thu-Sat 14:00-16:00 & 20:00-23:30, Sun 13:30-16:00, closed Mon-Tue, +34 923 123 775).

Farther down, **$$ Slainte Cervecería** (at #28)—sort of a hybrid between an Irish pub and a Spanish tapas bar—has forgettable food and a long chalkboard list of microbrews on tap from around Spain and other countries. **$ Bar El Montadito** at #51 has a memorable sign with a cowboy mounting his *montadito* (mini-sandwich). A couple of doors beyond, the traditional **$$ La Parilla** is dominated by its namesake grill—sizzling up both *pinchos* and belt-busting, meaty *raciones* (closed Wed, at #55).

Salamanca Connections

From Salamanca by Train to: Madrid Chamartín (4/day on speedy Alvia, 1.75 hours), **Ávila** (7/day, 1-1.5 hours), **Segovia** (4/day on speedy Alvia to Segovia's Guiomar station—a 20-minute bus ride to downtown, about 1.5 hours total), **Barcelona** (5-6/day, 5-7 hours, change in Madrid from Chamartín or Principe Pio station to Atocha station via Metro or *cercanías* train), **Santiago** (1/day, 8 hours; faster to train to Zamora and change to bus), **Burgos** (7/day, 2.5-5 hours, transfer in Valladolid or Ávila). Train info: +34 912 320 320, www.renfe.com.

By Bus to: Madrid (hourly express, 2.5-3 hours, arrives at Madrid's Estación Sur or airport terminals T1 or T4, Avanza bus), **Segovia** (1/day, 3 hours, Avanza—train connection is much faster), **Ávila** (4/day, 1.5 hours, Avanza), **Santiago** (1 night bus, 7 hours, Alsa), **Barcelona** (2/day with transfer in Burgos, 11.5 hours, Alsa), **Burgos** (3/day, 3-4 hours, Alsa), **Coimbra,** Portugal (1/day, 5 hours; same bus continues to **Lisbon** in about 9 hours total, Alsa). Bus info: Alsa (www.alsa.es), Avanza (www.avanzabus.com); also try www.movelia.es for multiple company listings.

MADRID

Today's Madrid is upbeat and vibrant. You'll feel it. Look around—just about everyone has a twinkle in their eyes.

Madrid is the hub of Spain. This modern capital—Europe's second-highest, at more than 2,000 feet above sea level—is home to more than 3 million people, with about 6 million living in greater Madrid.

Like its population, the city is relatively young. In medieval times, it was just another village, wedged between the powerful kingdoms of Castile and Aragon. When newlyweds Ferdinand and Isabel united those kingdoms in 1469, Madrid—sitting at the center of Spain—became the focal point of a budding nation. By 1561, Spain ruled the world's most powerful empire, and King Philip II moved his capital from cramped, medieval Toledo (and the influence of its powerful bishop) to spacious Madrid.

Successive kings transformed the city into a European capital. By 1900, Madrid had 575,000 people, concentrated within a small area. In the mid-20th century, the city exploded with migrants from the countryside, creating modern sprawl. Today Madrid is working hard to make itself more livable. Massive urban-improvement projects—pedestrianized streets, new parks, extended commuter lines, and renovated Metro stations—are transforming the city. Once-dodgy neighborhoods are turning trendy, and the traffic chaos is subsiding. Madrid feels orderly and welcoming.

Fortunately for tourists, the historic core survives intact and is easy to navigate. Dive headlong into the grandeur and intimate charm of Madrid. Feel the vibe in Puerta del Sol, the pulsing heart of modern Madrid and of Spain itself. The lavish Royal Palace, with its gilded rooms and frescoed ceilings, rivals Versailles. The

Prado has Europe's top collection of paintings, and nearby hangs Picasso's chilling masterpiece, *Guernica*. Retiro Park invites you to take a shady siesta and hopscotch through a mosaic of lovers, families, skateboarders, pets walking their masters, and expert bench-sitters. On Sundays, cheer for the bull at a bullfight or bargain like mad at a megasize flea market. Swelter through the hot, hot summers or bundle up for the cold winters. Save some energy for after dark, when Madrileños pack the streets for an evening paseo and *tapeo* (tapas crawl) that can continue past midnight. Lively Madrid has enough street-singing, bar-hopping, and people-watching vitality to give any visitor a boost of youth.

PLANNING YOUR TIME

Madrid is worth two days and three nights on even the fastest trip. Divide your time among the city's top three attractions: the Royal Palace (worth two hours), the Prado Museum (worth a half-day or more), and the contemporary bar-hopping scene.

Here's a two-day plan that hits Madrid's highlights. If the weather's iffy on Day 1, you can reverse this plan. With more time, Madrid has several days' worth of other museums to choose from (archaeology, city history, tapestries, the cultures of the Americas, clothing, local artists, and so on). Or, for good day-trip possibilities, see the Northwest of Madrid and Toledo chapters.

Day 1

Morning: Get your bearings with my self-guided city walk, which loops from Puerta del Sol to the Royal Palace and back—with a tour through the Royal Palace in the middle.

Afternoon: Your afternoon is free for other sights, shopping, or exploring—consider my self-guided walk of the glitzy Gran Vía or self-guided bus tours of the busy Paseo de la Castellana or the funky Lavapiés district. Be out at the golden hour—just before sunset—for the evening paseo, when beautifully lit people fill Madrid.

Evening: End your day with a progressive tapas dinner at a series of characteristic bars.

Day 2

Morning: Take a brisk good-morning-Madrid walk along Calle de las Huertas to the Prado, where you'll enjoy some of Europe's best art (purchase your ticket in advance). Art lovers can then head across the street to the Thyssen-Bornemisza Museum.

Afternoon: Enjoy an afternoon siesta in Retiro Park. Then tackle modern art at the Reina Sofía, which displays Picasso's *Guernica* (closed Tue).

Evening: Take in a flamenco or zarzuela performance.

Madrid

To A-6 Freeway, El Escorial & Segovia

To Clothing Museum

To Temple of Debod

Parque de la Montaña

MADRID TOWER

SPAIN TOWER

MUSEO CERRALBO

Plaza de España

Plaza de España

CERVANTES MON.

MALASAÑA

GRAN VÍA

CALLE DE MANZANA

CALLE DE SAN BERNARDO

CALLE DE LA LUNA

CALLE DEL PEZ

CALLE SILVA

CALLE DE LA MADERA

ESCORIAL

TUDESCOS CORK BAJA SAN PABLO

To Príncipe Pío Stn. & Goya's Tomb

PALACIO DEL SENADO

SATE POLICE STATION

See Central Madrid detail maps

CUESTA

Jardines de Sabatini

LA ENCARNACIÓN

Plaza Marina Española

CALLE TORIJA

Plaza de Santo Domingo

Plaza de Santo Domingo

GRAN VÍA

EL CORTE INGLÉS

Plaza del Callao

Callao

S. QUINTÍN

Campo del Moro

ROYAL PALACE

Plaza de la Amería

Plaza de Oriente

FELIPE V

CARLOS II

ROYAL THEATER

Plaza de Isabel II

Ópera

ROYAL MONASTERY

Plaza S. Martín

EL CORTE INGLÉS

Plaza del Carmen

SOL

Plaza Ramales

REQUENA

Plaza Herradores

SAN GINÉS

CALLE DEL ARENAL

Puerta del Sol

Sol

KM ZERO

ALMUDENA CATHEDRAL

FORMER TOWN HALL

Plaza de la Villa

CONVENT

MERCADO DE SAN MIGUEL

Plaza Mayor

CALLE MAYOR

POSTAS

CENTRO

ZARAGOZA

C. BOLSA

Plaza Benavente

CUESTA DE LA VEGA

CALLE

DE

SEGOVIA

Plaza Puerta Cerrada

CONCEPCIÓN JERÓNIMA

CALLE COLEGIADA

C. ATOCHA

Tirso de Molina

Plaza Tirso de Molina

SAN ISIDRO

La Latina

C. DUQUE DE ALBA

Jardines Vistillas

CALLE DON PEDRO

CALLE CAVA BAJA

Plaza de San Francisco

CRA. S. FRANCISCO

SAN FRANCISCO EL GRANDE

GRAN VÍA DE SAN FRAN.

CALLE HUMILLADERO

CALLE DEL ÁGUILA

CALLE STA ANA

Plaza de Cascorro

ABADES

MESÓN DE PAREDES

LAVAPIÉS

EL RASTRO FLEA MARKET

200 Meters

200 Yards

R. D. SEGOVIA

CALLE DE SAN FRAN.

LA PALOMA

CALLE CARGANZUELA

CARLOS ARNICHES

CALLE RIBERA DE CURTIDORES

CALLE MIRA EL SOL

CALLE DEL CASINO

PROVISIONES

SOMBRERETE

Puerta de Toledo

Glorieta de Puerta de Toledo

Plaza Campillo Mundo Nuevo

RONDA DE TOLEDO

EMBAJADORES

Glorieta de Embajadores

Embajadores

LOS PONTONES

CALLE DE TOLEDO

To Madrid Río Park & Toledo

MADRID

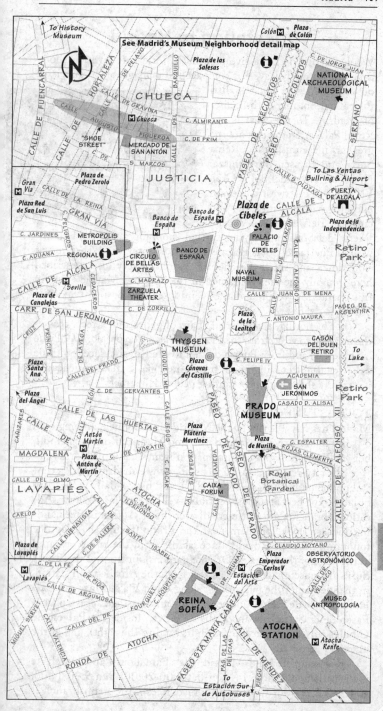

Orientation to Madrid

While Madrid is a massive city, its historic core—which short-time visitors rarely leave—is compact and manageable. Frame it off on your map: The square called Puerta del Sol marks the center of Madrid. To the west is the Royal Palace. To the east are the great art museums: Prado, Reina Sofía, and Thyssen-Bornemisza. North of Puerta del Sol is Gran Vía, a broad east-west boulevard bubbling with elegant shops and cinemas. Between Gran Vía and Puerta del Sol is a lively pedestrian shopping zone. And southwest of Puerta del Sol is Plaza Mayor, the center of a 17th-century, slow-down-and-smell-the-cobbles district. Everything described here (roughly the area contained in the "Central Madrid" map in this chapter) is within about a 20-minute stroll or a €10 taxi ride of Puerta del Sol.

For exploring, a wonderful chain of pedestrian streets crosses the city east to west, from the Prado to Plaza Mayor (along Calle de las Huertas) and from Puerta del Sol to the Royal Palace (on Calle del Arenal). Stretching north from Gran Vía, Calle de Fuencarral is a trendy shopping-and-strolling pedestrian street.

TOURIST INFORMATION

Madrid has city TIs run by the Madrid City Council, and regional TIs run by the privately owned Turismo Madrid. Both are helpful, but you'll get more biased information from Turismo Madrid.

The city-run TIs share a website (www.esmadrid.com), a central phone number (+34 915 787 810), and hours (daily 9:30-20:30 or later). The best and most central city TI is on **Plaza Mayor.** Additional branches are scattered all over the city, often in freestanding kiosks. Look for them near the **Prado** (facing the Neptune fountain), near the **Royal Palace** (across from the group entrance at the edge of the Plaza de Oriente gardens), in front of the **Reina Sofía** art museum (across the street from the Atocha train station, in the median of the busy road), along Gran Vía at **Plaza del Callao,** at **Plaza de Colón** (in the underground passage accessed from Paseo de la Castellana and Calle de Goya), inside the **Palacio de Cibeles** cultural center (up the stairs, and to the right), and at the **airport** (Terminals 2 and 4).

Regional Turismo Madrid TIs share hours and a website www.turismomadrid.es) (Mon-Sat 8:00-20:00, Sun 9:00-14:00, +34 912 723 400, www.turismomadrid.es). The main branch is

just east of Puerta del Sol at **Calle de Alcalá 31;** branches are also inside the **Sol Metro station** (inside the underground corridor), at **Atocha train station** (AVE arrivals side; this branch open Mon-Sat 8:00-15:30, Sun 9:00-14:00), and at the **airport** (Terminals 1 and 4).

At most TIs and online, you can get the *Es Madrid* English-language monthly, which includes a map and event listings (at www.esmadrid.com, select English, and search for "Magazine"). Themed *Madrid for You* booklets on various topics (families, museums, viewpoints, gastronomy, and so on) are also available. The regional TIs hand out a handy public transportation map.

Entertainment Guides: For arts and culture listings, the TI's printed material is good, but you can also pick up the more practical Spanish-language weekly entertainment guide *Guía del Ocio* (sold cheap at newsstands) or visit www.guiadelocio.com. It lists daily live music *("Conciertos")*, museums (under *"Arte"*—with the latest times, prices, and special exhibits), restaurants (an exhaustive listing), TV schedules, and movies ("V.O." means original version, *"V.O. en inglés sub"* or *"V.O.S.E."* means a movie is played in English with Spanish subtitles rather than dubbed).

ARRIVAL IN MADRID

For more information on arriving at or departing from Madrid, including stations and connections, see "Madrid Connections," at the end of this chapter.

By Train: Madrid's two train stations, Chamartín and Atocha, are on both Metro and *cercanías* (suburban train) lines with easy access to downtown Madrid. Chamartín handles most international trains and the AVE (AH-vay) train to and from Segovia. Atocha generally covers southern Spain, as well as AVE trains to and from Barcelona, Córdoba, Granada, Sevilla, and Toledo. Many train tickets include a *cercanías* connection to or from the train station.

Traveling Between Chamartín and Atocha Stations: You can take the Metro (€2, line 1, 30-40 minutes; see "Getting Around Madrid," later), but the *cercanías* trains are faster (€1.70 plus €0.50 for a "+Renfe & Tú" card purchased at the ticket counters or machines, 6/hour, 13 minutes, Atocha-Chamartín lines C1, C3, C4, C7, C8, and C10 each connect the two stations, lines C3 and C4 also stop at Sol—Madrid's central square). If you have a rail pass or any regular train ticket to Madrid, you can get a free transfer within three hours of your ticket times. At the *cercanías* ticket machine, choose *combinado cercanías,* then either scan the bar code on your train ticket or punch in a code (labeled *combinado cercanías*), and choose your destination. These trains depart from Atocha's track

MADRID

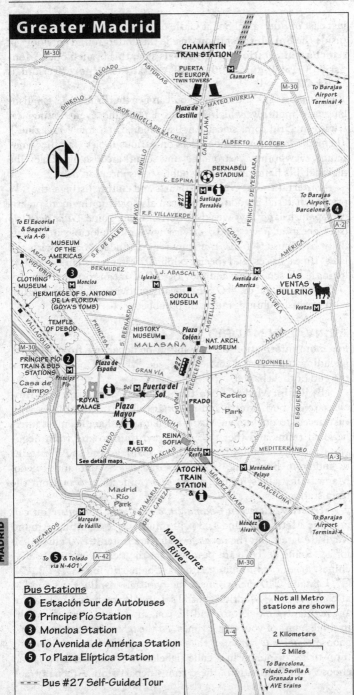

Greater Madrid

M-30

DELGADO

ASTURIAS

CHAMARTÍN
TRAIN STATION

PUERTA
DE EUROPA
"TWIN TOWERS"

Chamartín

M-30

To Barajas
Airport
Terminal 4

GINESIO

SOR ANGELA DE LA CRUZ

Plaza de
Castilla

MATEO INURRIA

CASTELLANA

ALBERTO ALCOCER

MURILLO

BERNABÉU
STADIUM

C. ESPINA

PRÍNCIPE DE VERGARA

#27

Santiago
Bernabéu

To Barajas
Airport,
Barcelona & 4

A-2

BRAVO

R.F. VILLAVERDE

J. COSTA

AMÉRICA

To El Escorial
& Segovia
via A-6

ARCO DE LA

VICTORIA

MUSEUM
OF THE
AMERICAS

S.F. DE SALES

BERMUDEZ

J. ABASCAL

Iglesia

3

Moncloa

CLOTHING
MUSEUM

HERMITAGE OF S. ANTONIO
DE LA FLORIDA
(GOYA'S TOMB)

TEMPLE
OF DEBOD

VALLADOLID

PRINCESA

S. BERNARDO

SOROLLA
MUSEUM

Avenida de
América

LAS
VENTAS
BULLRING

F SILVELA

Ventas

ALCALÁ

M-30

PRÍNCIPE PÍO
TRAIN & BUS
STATIONS

2

Príncipe
Pío

HISTORY
MUSEUM

MALASAÑA

Plaza de
España

GRAN VÍA

#27

Plaza
Colón

NAT. ARCH.
MUSEUM

CASTELLANA

RECOLETOS

O'DONNELL

D. ESGUERDO

Casa de
Campo

ROYAL
PALACE

Sol
Puerta del
Sol

Plaza
Mayor
&

PRADO

ATOCHA

PRADO

Retiro
Park

A-3

TOLEDO

EL
RASTRO

ACACIAS

REINA
SOFÍA

Atocha
Renfe

MEDITERRÁNEO

See detail maps

ATOCHA
TRAIN
STATION
&

Menéndez
Pelayo

BARCELONA

Madrid
Río
Park

STA. MARÍA

DE LA CABEZA

MÉNDEZ ALVARO

MADRID

Marqués
de Vadillo

G. RICARDOS

Manzanares
River

Méndez
Alvaro

1

To Barajas
Airport
Terminal 4

To 5 & Toledo
via N-401

A-42

M-30

A-4

To Barcelona,
Toledo, Sevilla &
Granada via
AVE trains

Bus Stations

1 Estación Sur de Autobuses
2 Príncipe Pío Station
3 Moncloa Station
4 To Avenida de América Station
5 To Plaza Elíptica Station

--- Bus #27 Self-Guided Tour

Not all Metro
stations are shown

2 Kilometers

2 Miles

6 and generally Chamartín's track 1, 3, 8, or 9—check the *salidas inmediatas* board to be sure).

By Bus: Madrid has several bus stations, each one handy to a Metro station: Estación Sur de Autobuses (for Ávila, Salamanca, and Granada; Metro: Méndez Álvaro); Plaza Elíptica (for Toledo, Metro: Plaza Elíptica); Moncloa (for El Escorial, Metro: Moncloa); and Avenida de América (for Pamplona and Burgos, Metro: Avenida de América). From any of these, just ride the Metro or a taxi to your hotel.

By Plane: See "Madrid Connections" at the end of this chapter.

HELPFUL HINTS

Sightseeing Tips: The Prado and Royal Palace are open daily. The Reina Sofía (with Picasso's *Guernica*) is closed on Tuesday, and many other sights are closed on Monday, including the Monasterio de San Lorenzo de El Escorial, a popular day trip outside of Madrid (see next chapter). If you're here on a Sunday, consider visiting the famous El Rastro flea market (year-round) and/or a bullfight (most Sun and holidays in March-mid-Oct plus almost daily during the San Isidro festival in early May-early June).

Theft Alert: Be wary of pickpockets—anywhere, anytime, but especially in crowded areas such as Puerta del Sol, the busy street between the Puerta del Sol and the Prado (Carrera de San Jerónimo), El Rastro flea market, Gran Vía (especially the paseo zone: Plaza del Callao to Plaza de España), anywhere on the Metro, bus #27, and at the airport. Be alert to the people around you: Someone wearing a heavy jacket in the summer is likely a pickpocket. Kids may dress like Americans and work the areas near big sights; anyone under 18 can't be charged in any meaningful way by the police. Assume any commotion is a scam to distract people about to become victims of a pickpocket. Wear your money belt. For help if you get ripped off, see the next listing.

Tourist Emergency Aid: SATE is an assistance service for tourists who need help with anything from canceling stolen credit cards to reporting a crime (central police station, daily 9:00-24:00, near Plaza de Santo Domingo at Calle Leganitos 19). They can act as an interpreter if you have trouble communicating with the police. Or you can call in your report to the SATE line (24-hour +34 902 102 112, follow automated instructions in English to connect to a live person).

Sex Work: While it's illegal to make money from someone else selling sex (i.e., pimping), sex workers over 18 can solicit legally. Calle de la Montera (leading from Puerta del Sol to Plaza

Central Madrid

To Plaza de España

CALLE TORIJA

To Plaza de España

GRAN VIA

Jardines de Sabatini

PALACIO DEL SENADO

Plaza de Santo Domingo

JACOMETREZO

Callao Ⓜ

LA ENCARNACIÓN

S. QUINTÍN

CALLE DE LA BOLA

STO. DOMINGO

Santo Domingo Ⓜ

PRECIADOS

CALLE ARRIETA

C. CAMPOMANES

C.D. FERAL

PST. S. MARTIN

ROYAL PALACE

CALLE DE BAILÉN

Plaza de Oriente

FELIPE V

CARLOS II

ROYAL THEATER

Plaza de Isabel II

FLORA

Plaza San Martín

Plaza de la Armería

REQUENA

VERGARA

C. SEN LUZON

INDEPENDENCIA

ESCALINATA

Ⓜ Ópera

CALLE DEL

CALLE HILERAS

SAN GINES

Plaza Ramales

SAN NICOLAS

FACTOR

Plaza Herradores

C. BORD.

COLOR

ALMUDENA CATHEDRAL

MAYOR

CALLE

Plaza de la Villa

MERCADO DE SAN MIGUEL

Plaza Mayor ℹ

ZARAGOZA

FORMER TOWN HALL

CONVENT

PUÑONROSTRO

MESONES BARS

CALLE SACRAMENTO

C. SAN JUSTO

Plaza Conde Barajas

CUCHILLEROS

200 Meters

200 Yards

CALLE DE SEGOVIA

C. DE SEGOVIA

Plaza Puerta Cerrada

C. DE TOLEDO

CONCEPCIÓN

C. COLEGIATA

C. MORERIA

C. REDONDILLA

C. DE S. ANDRES

Plaza Paja

C. NUNGIO

C. ALMENDRO

Y. ALM.

BAJA

GRAFAL

S. BRUNO

CALLE DE LOS ESTUDIOS

SAN ISIDRO

CALLE DON PEDRO

CALLE CAVA

CALLE CAVA ALTA

La Latina Ⓜ

CALLE

DUQUE

Plaza de San Francisco

CRA. S. FRANCISCO

C. JUANELO

C. CEBADA

Plaza de Cascorro

C. ANGEL

C. AGUILA

C. D. CALATRAVA

CALLE DE TOLEDO

CALLE ST. ANA

EL RASTRO FLEA MARKET (SUNDAYS)

C. RIBERA CURT

CALLE EMBAJADORES

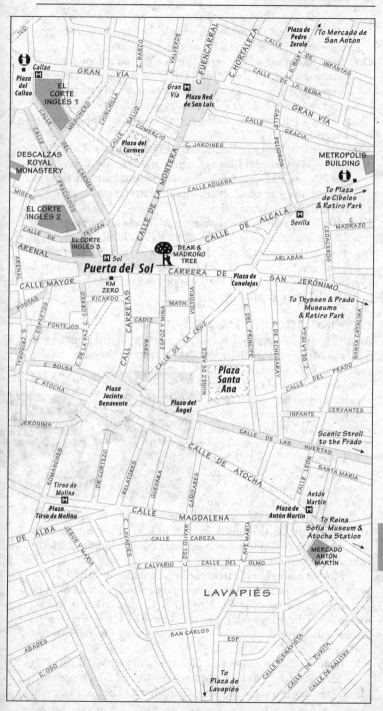

Red de San Luis) is lined with what looks like a bunch of high-schoolers skipping school for a cigarette break.

One-Stop Shopping at El Corte Inglés: Madrid's dominant department store, El Corte Inglés, fills three huge buildings in the pedestrian zone just off Puerta del Sol. From groceries and event tickets to fashion and housewares, El Corte Inglés has it all. For a building-by-building breakdown, see "Shopping in Madrid," later.

Bookstores: For books in English, try **FNAC Callao** (Calle Preciados 28), **Casa del Libro** (English on basement floor, Gran Vía 29), and **El Corte Inglés** (guidebooks and some fiction, in its Building 3 Books/Librería branch kitty-corner from main store, fronting Puerta del Sol).

Laundry: For a self-service laundry, try **Colada Express** at Calle Campomanes 9 (free Wi-Fi, daily 9:00-22:00, +34 657 876 464) or **Lavandería** at Calle León 6 (self- and full-service Mon-Fri 9:00-14:00 & 16:30-20:30, Sat 12:00-15:00, closed Sun; +34 914 299 545). For locations see the "Madrid Center Hotels" map on page 486.

GETTING AROUND MADRID

Madrid has excellent public transit. Pick up the Metro map (free at TIs or at Metro info booths in stations with staff); for buses get the fine, free *Public Transport* map (available at some TIs). The metropolitan Madrid transit website (www.crtm.es) covers all public transportation options (Metro, bus, and suburban rail).

By Metro: Madrid's Metro is simple, speedy, and cheap. Distances are short, but the city's broad streets can be hot and exhausting, so a subway trip of even a stop or two saves time and energy. The Metro runs from 6:00 to 1:30 in the morning. At all times, be alert to thieves, who thrive in crowded stations. Metro info: www.metromadrid.es.

Tickets: A **single-ride ticket** within zone A costs €1.50-2, depending on the number of stops you travel; zone A covers most of the city, but not trains to the airport. A **10-ride ticket** is €12.20 and valid on the Metro and buses; it can be shared by several travelers with the same destination (two people taking five rides should get one).

To buy either a single-ride or 10-ride ticket, you'll first buy a rechargeable red **Multi Card** *(tarjeta)* for €2.50 (nonrefundable—consider it a souvenir). The first Metro ticket you buy will

cost at least €4 and be issued on the card; thereafter, you can reload the card with additional rides *(viajes)*. Ticket machines ask you to punch in your destination from the alphabetized list (follow the simple prompts) to load up the correct fare. You can also buy or reload Multi Cards at newspaper stands and Estanco tobacco shops.

I'd skip the tourist ticket *(billete túristico)* you may see advertised, which covers all Metro and bus rides for a designated time period; unless you're riding transit like crazy, it's unlikely to save you money over the 10-ride ticket.

Riding the Metro: Study your Metro map—the simplified "Madrid Metro" map in this chapter can get you started. Lines are color-coded and numbered; use end-of-the-line station names to choose your direction of travel. When entering the Metro system, touch your Multi Card against the yellow pad to open the turnstile (no need to touch it again to exit). Once in the Metro station, signs direct you to the train line and direction (e.g., Linea 1, *Valdecarros*). To transfer, follow signs in the station leading to connecting lines. Once you reach your final stop, look for the green *salida* signs pointing to the exits. Use the helpful neighborhood maps to choose the right *salida* and save yourself lots of walking.

By Bus: City buses, though not as easy as the Metro, can be useful. You can use a **Multi Card** loaded with a 10-ride ticket (see details earlier). But for **single rides,** you'll buy a ticket on the bus, paying the driver in cash (€1.50; bus maps at TI or info booth on Puerta del Sol, poster-size maps usually posted at bus stops, buses run 6:00-24:00, much less frequent *Buho* buses run all night). The EMT Madrid app finds the closest stops and lines and gives accurate wait times (there's a version in English). Bus info: www.emtmadrid.es.

By Taxi or Uber: Madrid's taxis are reasonably priced and easy to hail. A green light on the roof and/or the word *Libre* on the windshield indicates that a taxi is available. Foursomes travel almost as cheaply by taxi as by Metro; for example, a ride from the Royal Palace to the Prado costs about €12. After the drop charge (about €3), the per-kilometer rate depends on the time: *Tarifa 1* (€1.15/kilometer) is charged Mon-Fri 6:00-21:00; *Tarifa 2* (€1.40/ kilometer) is valid after 21:00 and on Saturdays, Sundays, and holidays. If your cabbie uses anything other than *Tarifa 1* on weekdays (shown as an isolated "1" on the meter), you're being cheated.

Rates can be higher outside Madrid. There's a flat rate of €30 between the city center and any one of the airport terminals. Other legitimate charges include a €3 supplement for leaving any train or bus station, €20 per hour for waiting, and €5 if you call to have the taxi come to you. Make sure the meter is turned on as soon as you get into the cab so the driver can't tack anything on to the official rate. If the driver starts adding up "extras," look for the sticker

MADRID

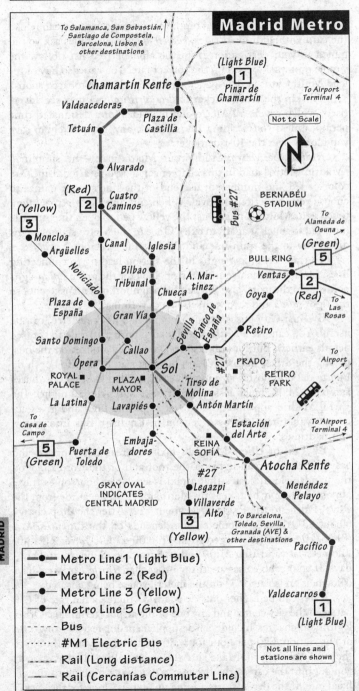

Madrid Metro

To Salamanca, San Sebastián, Santiago de Compostela, Barcelona, Lisbon & other destinations

(Light Blue) 1 Pinar de Chamartín

To Airport Terminal 4

Chamartín Renfe

Valdeacederas

Plaza de Castilla

Tetuán

Not to Scale

Alvarado

(Red) 2 Cuatro Caminos

BERNABÉU STADIUM

(Yellow) 3 Moncloa

Argüelles

Canal

Iglesia

(Green) 5

BULL RING

Ventas

To Alameda de Osuna

Noviciado

Bilbao Tribunal

A. Martinez

Goya

2 (Red)

To Las Rosas

Plaza de España

Chueca

Santo Domingo

Gran Vía

Banco de España

Retiro

To Airport

Ópera

Callao

Sol

PRADO

RETIRO PARK

ROYAL PALACE

PLAZA MAYOR

Tirso de Molina

La Latina

Lavapiés

Antón Martín

To Casa de Campo

Embaja-dores

Estación del Arte

To Airport Terminal 4

REINA SOFÍA

5 (Green) Puerta de Toledo

#27

Atocha Renfe

GRAY OVAL INDICATES CENTRAL MADRID

Menéndez Pelayo

Legazpi

Villaverde Alto

3 (Yellow)

To Barcelona, Toledo, Sevilla, Granada (AVE) & other destinations

Pacífico

Valdecarros

1 (Light Blue)

Legend

- ● Metro Line 1 (Light Blue)
- ● Metro Line 2 (Red)
- ● Metro Line 3 (Yellow)
- ● Metro Line 5 (Green)
- --- Bus
- ⋯ #M1 Electric Bus
- --- Rail (Long distance)
- ⁓ Rail (Cercanías Commuter Line)

Not all lines and stations are shown

MADRID

detailing all legitimate surcharges (it should be on the passenger window).

Uber works in Madrid pretty much like it does at home. Outside of peak times, an Uber ride can be slightly cheaper than a taxi.

Tours in Madrid

∩ To sightsee on your own, download my free Madrid City Walk audio tour.

LOCAL GUIDES

Across Madrid is run by Almudena Cros, a well-traveled art history professor. She offers several specialized tours, including one on the Spanish Civil War that draws on her family's history, and one on mythology in the Prado (generally €70/person, maximum 7 people, book well in advance, also gives good tours for children, +34 652 576 423, www.acrossmadrid.com).

Stephen Drake-Jones, an eccentric British expat, has led walks of historic old Madrid almost daily for decades. A historian with a passion for the Duke of Wellington (the general who stopped Napoleon), Stephen loves to teach history. For €100 you get a 3.5-hour tour with three stops for drinks and tapas—call it lunch (daily at 11:30, maximum 8 people). He offers a private version (€200/2 people) and themed tours covering the Spanish Civil War and Hemingway's Madrid, and has even written a book, *Drake-Jones' Madrid*, about the city's juicy history (+34 609 143 202, https://wellsoc.org).

Inés Carriedo and her all-women team of licensed guides eloquently take you through Madrid and its monuments and museums (€170/2 hours, €220/4 hours, +34 655 433 992, icscher@gmail.com).

Amanda Buttinger, an American living in Spain, has been a Rick Steves guide for close to two decades and can be your "friend in Europe," offering orientation, travel tips, city walks, and food tours (€50/hour, +34 649 933 035, www.gathertotravel.com, amanda@gathertotravel.com).

GROUP TOURS

Assemble your own group to share the cost of these tours.

Federico and his team of licensed guides lead city walks and museum tours in Madrid and nearby towns. They specialize in family tours and engaging kids and teens in museums, and size their city tours like cups of hot chocolate (small-€150/2 hours, medium-€200/4 hours, large-€250/6 hours, extra large-€300/8 hours; +34 649 936 222, www.spainfred.com). Federico rents his

Madrid at a Glance

▲▲▲**Royal Palace** Spain's sumptuous, lavishly furnished national palace. **Hours:** Daily 10:00-19:00, Oct-March until 18;00. See page 435.

▲▲▲**Prado Museum** One of the world's great museums, loaded with masterpieces by Diego Velázquez, Francisco de Goya, El Greco, Hieronymus Bosch, Albrecht Dürer, and more. **Hours:** Mon-Sat 10:00-20:00, Sun until 19:00. See page 448.

▲▲▲**Centro de Arte Reina Sofía** Modern art museum featuring Picasso's epic masterpiece *Guernica.* **Hours:** Mon and Wed-Sat 10:00-21:00, Sun until 14:30, closed Tue. See page 466.

▲▲▲**Paseo** Evening stroll among the Madrileños. **Hours:** Sundown until the wee hours. See page 481.

▲▲**Puerta del Sol** Madrid's lively central square. See page 415.

▲▲**Plaza Mayor** Historic cobbled square. See page 422.

▲▲**Thyssen-Bornemisza Museum** A great complement to the Prado, with lesser-known yet still impressive works and an especially good Impressionist collection. **Hours:** Mon 12:00-16:00, Tue-Sun 10:00-19:00. See page 464.

▲▲**Retiro Park** Festive green escape from the city, with rental rowboats and great people-watching. **Hours:** Closes at dusk. See page 470.

▲▲**National Archaeological Museum** Traces the history of Iberia through artifacts. **Hours:** Tue-Sat 9:30-20:00, Sun until 15:00, closed Mon. See page 471.

▲▲**Sorolla Museum** Delightful, intimate collection of portraits and landscapes by Spanish artist Joaquín Sorolla. **Hours:** Tue-Sat 9:30-20:00, Sun 10:00-15;00, closed Mon. See page 473.

MADRID

centrally located top-floor apartment exclusively to Rick Steves readers (sleeps up to 4 people, includes free Madrid Welcome tour).

Letango Tours offers private tours, travel consulting, packages, and stays all over Spain with a focus on families and groups. Their team of guides in Madrid offer a kid-friendly "Madrid Discoveries" tour that mixes a market walk and history with a culinary-and-tapas introduction (€295/group of up to 5, kids free, 3-plus

▲▲**Flamenco** Captivating music and dance performances, at various venues throughout the city. **Hours:** Shows nightly, but some places closed on Sun. See page 484.

▲**Royal Botanical Garden** A relaxing museum of plants, with specimens from around the world. **Hours:** Daily May-Aug 10:00-21:00, April and Sept until 20:00, shorter hours off-season. See page 464.

▲**Naval Museum** Seafaring history of a country famous for its Armada. **Hours:** Tue-Sun 10:00-19:00, until 15:00 in Aug, closed Mon. See page 470.

▲**Museum of the Americas** Pre-Columbian and colonial artifacts from the New World. **Hours:** Tue-Sat 9:30-15:00, Thu until 19:00, Sun 10:00-15:00, closed Mon. See page 472.

▲**Hermitage of San Antonio de la Florida** Church with Goya's tomb, plus frescoes by the artist. **Hours:** Tue-Sun 9:30-20:00, closed Mon. See page 473.

▲**Madrid History Museum** The city's story told through old paintings, maps, fascinating photos, and historic artifacts. **Hours:** Tue-Sun 10:00-20:00, closed Mon. See page 474.

▲**Bullfight** Spain's controversial pastime. **Hours:** Most Sundays and holidays March-mid-Oct, plus almost daily early May-early June. See page 477.

▲**El Rastro** Europe's biggest flea market, filled with bargains and pickpockets. **Hours:** Sun 9:00-15:00, best before 11:00. See page 479.

▲**Zarzuela** Madrid's delightful light opera. **Hours:** Evenings. See page 481.

MADRID

hours). They also lead tours to Barcelona, whitewashed villages, wine country, and more (www.letango.com).

Madridivine guides enthusiastically share their passion for Spanish culture through food and walking tours of historic Madrid. They connect you with locals, food, and wine from an insider's perspective (€200/group of up to 6, 3 hours, food and drinks extra—usually around €40, www.madridivine.com).

BY BUS

Hop-On, Hop-Off Bus

Madrid City Tour makes two different hop-on, hop-off circuits through the city: historic and modern (each with 16-21 stops, 1.5 hours, buses depart every 15 minutes). The two routes intersect at the south side of Puerta del Sol and in front of Starbucks across from the Prado. Your ticket covers both loops (€23/1 day, €27/2 consecutive days; discount if bought online, otherwise pay driver; recorded narration, daily 9:30-22:00, Nov-Feb 10:00-18:00, +34 917 791 888, https://madrid.city-tour.com).

Big-Bus City Sightseeing Tours

Julià Travel offers bus tours in Madrid and side trips to nearby destinations. Their 2.5-hour Madrid tour is narrated by a live guide in two or three languages (€29, one shopping stop, no museum visits, usually at 9:00 and 15:00, check website for schedule, no reservation required—just show up 15 minutes before departure). Tours leave from their office at Calle San Nicolás 7 near Plaza de Ramales, just south of Plaza de Oriente (+34 915 599 605, www.juliatravel.com).

Self-Guided Tours by Bus or Minibus

A ride on public **bus #27** from the museum neighborhood up Paseo del Prado and Paseo de la Castellana to the Puerta de Europa and back gives visitors a glimpse of the modern side of Madrid (see page 474), while a ride on electric **minibus #M1** takes you through the characteristic, gritty old center (see page 475).

Walks in Madrid

Two self-guided walks provide a look at two sides of Madrid. For a taste of old Madrid, start with my "Historic Core Walk," which winds through the center. My "Gran Vía Walk" lets you glimpse a more modern side of Spain's capital.

⌂ Download my free Madrid City Walk audio tour, which complements this section.

HISTORIC CORE WALK

Madrid's historic center is pedestrian-friendly and filled with spacious squares, a trendy market, bulls' heads in a bar, and a cookie-dispensing convent. Allow about two hours for this self-guided, mile-long walk that loops from Madrid's central square, Puerta del Sol, to the Royal Palace and back to the square (Metro: Sol).

• *Start in the middle of the square, by the equestrian statue of King Charles III, and survey the scene.*

❶ Puerta del Sol

The bustling Puerta del Sol, rated ▲▲, is Madrid's—and Spain's—center. In recent years, the square has undergone a facelift to become a fully pedestrianized and wide-open gathering place. For Spaniards, this place (with its iconic *Tío Pepe* sign) is probably the most recognizable spot in the country. It's a popular site for political demonstrations and national celebrations. For Madrileños,

Puerta del Sol is a transportation hub for the Metro, regional trains, and several main roads. It's also a magnet for strolling locals, sightseers, pickpockets, revelers, and locals dressed as cartoon characters who pose for photos for a fee. In many ways, it's the soul of the city.

The equestrian statue in the middle of the square honors the man who established the Puerta del Sol as an urban hub—**King Charles III** (1716-1788). His enlightened urban policies earned him the affectionate nickname "the best mayor of Madrid." He decorated city squares with beautiful fountains, got those meddlesome Jesuits out of city government, established the public-school system, mandated underground sewers, opened his private Retiro Park to the public, built the Prado, made the Royal Palace the wonder of Europe, and generally cleaned up Madrid. (For more on Charles, see page 440.)

Head to the slightly uphill end of the square and find the black **statue of a bear** pawing a tree. This image has been a symbol of Madrid since medieval times. Bears used to live in the royal hunting grounds outside the city. And the *madroño* trees produce a berry that makes the traditional *madroño* liqueur.

Charles III faces a red-and-white building with a bell tower. This was Madrid's first post office, which Charles III founded in the 1760s. Today it's the **county governor's office,** home to the "president" who governs greater Madrid. The building is notorious for having once been dictator Francisco Franco's police headquarters. A tragic number of those detained and interrogated by the Franco police tried to "escape" by jumping out its windows to their deaths.

Appreciate the **harmonious architecture** of the buildings that circle the square—yellow-cream, four stories, balconies of iron, shuttered windows, and balustrades along the rooflines.

Crowds fill the square on New Year's Eve as the rest of Spain watches the Times Square-style action on TV. The bell atop the

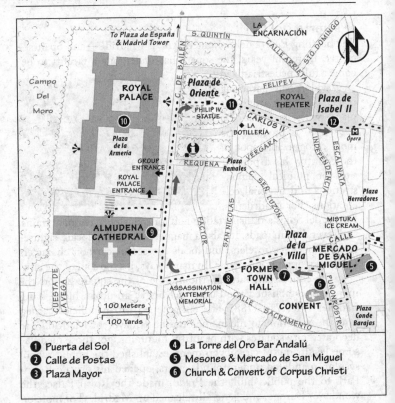

❶ Puerta del Sol	❹ La Torre del Oro Bar Andalú
❷ Calle de Postas	❺ Mesones & Mercado de San Miguel
❸ Plaza Mayor	❻ Church & Convent of Corpus Christi

governor's office chimes 12 times, while Madrileños eat one grape for each ring to bring good luck through each of the next 12 months.
• *Cross the square and street to the governor's office.*

Look down at the sidewalk directly in front of the entrance to the governor's office. The plaque marks **"kilometer zero,"** the symbolic center of Spain, from which the country's six main highways radiate (as the plaque shows). Standing on the zero marker with your back to the governor's office, get oriented visually: Directly ahead, at 12 o'clock, is the famous **Tío Pepe sign.** This big neon billboard—25 feet high and 80 feet across—pictures a jaunty Andalusian *caballero* with a sombrero and guitar. He's been busy advertising a local sherry wine since the 1930s.

Beyond the sign is a thriving **pedestrian commercial zone,** anchored by the huge department store, El Corte Inglés. At two o'clock starts the seedier Calle de la Montera, a street (with shady characters and prostitutes after dark) that leads to the trendy, pedestrianized Calle de Fuencarral. At three o'clock is a big Apple store; the Prado is about a mile farther to your right. Back over at 10 o'clock is the pedestrianized street called Calle del Arenal... where we'll finish this walk.

Madrid's Historic Core Walk

⑦ Former Town Hall
⑧ Assassination Attempt Memorial
⑨ Almudena Cathedral

⑩ Royal Palace
⑪ Plaza de Oriente
⑫ Plaza de Isabel II
⑬ Calle del Arenal

Now turn around. On the walls flanking the entrance to the governor's office are several **white marble plaques.** These commemorate three significant and painful experiences for Madrileños. The plaque on the right marks an event from 1808. An angry crowd gathered here to rise up against an invasion by France. Suddenly, French soldiers stormed the square and began massacring the Spaniards. The event galvanized the country, which eventually drove out the French. The painter Francisco de Goya, whose studio was not far from here, captured the event in his famous painting *The Third of May* (now in the Prado museum).

The plaque to the left of the entry remembers the horrific terrorist bombings on March 11, 2004, when brave Spanish citizens helped fellow citizens. Americans have our 9/11—Spain has its 3/11.

The plaque on the far left commemorates the victims of Covid-19, especially those who died alone. It's dated October 2020—far from the end of the pandemic.

Finally, notice the civil guardsmen at the entry. Traditionally, they wore wearing curious hats with square backs, which (it's said)

were cleverly designed so that the guards could lean against the wall while enjoying a cigarette.

On the corner of Puerta del Sol and Calle Mayor (downhill end of Puerta del Sol) is the busy, recommended *confitería* **La Mallorquina,** "*fundada en 1.894.*" A crowded takeaway section is in front (enter from the Puerta del Sol), a stand-up bar is in back (enter from the side door), and a more genteel sit-down tearoom with nice views of the square is upstairs—a red-letter sign at the bottom of the stairs indicates if it is full (*completo*). Go inside for a tempting peek at racks with goodies hot out of the oven. Enjoy observing the churning energy of Madrileños popping in for a fast coffee and a sweet treat. The shop is famous for its *Napolitana* pastry (like a flat croissant filled with custard or chocolate). Or sample Madrid's answer to doughnuts, *rosquillas* (*tontas* means "silly"—plain, and *listas* means "all dressed up and ready to go"—with icing).

Before leaving the shop, find the tiles above the entrance door and above the bar with the 18th-century views of Puerta del Sol. This was before the square was widened, when a church stood at its top end. Compare this with today's view out the door.

Puerta del Sol ("Gate of the Sun") is named for a long-gone gate carved with a rising sun, which once stood at the eastern edge of the old city. From here, we begin our walk through the historic town that dates back to medieval times.

• *Head west on busy Calle Mayor, just past McDonald's. Go a few steps up the side street on the left, then angle right on the pedestrian-only street called...*

❷ Calle de Postas

The street sign shows the post coach heading for that famous first post office. Medieval street signs posted on the lower corners of buildings included pictures so the illiterate (and monolingual tourists) could "read" them.

• *Continue up Calle de Postas, and take a slight right on Calle de la Sal through the arcade, where you emerge into...*

❸ Plaza Mayor

This vast, cobbled square (worth ▲▲) dates back to Madrid's glory days, the 1600s. Back then, this—not Puerta del Sol—was Madrid's main square (*plaza mayor*). The **equestrian statue** (wearing a ruffled collar) honors Philip III, who made this square the centerpiece of the budding

capital in 1619. Philip's dad (Philip II) made Madrid the country's capital and the son transformed a former marketplace into this state-of-the-art Baroque plaza.

The square is 140 yards long and 100 yards wide, enclosed by four-story buildings with symmetrical windows, balconies, slate roofs, and steepled towers. Each side of the square is uniform, as if a grand palace were turned inside-out. This distinct look, pioneered by architect Juan de Herrera (who finished El Escorial), is found all over Madrid.

This site served as the city's 17th-century open-air theater. On this stage, much Spanish history has been played out. The square's lampposts have reliefs on the benches below illustrating major episodes: bullfights fought here, dancers and masked revelers at Carnaval, royal pageantry, a horrendous fire in 1790, and events of the gruesome **Inquisition** (see sidebar on the next page). During the Inquisition, many were tried here—suspected heretics, Protestants, Jews, tour guides without a local license, and Muslims whose "conversion" to Christianity was dubious. The guilty were paraded around the square before their executions, wearing placards listing their many sins (bleachers were built for bigger audiences, while the wealthy rented balconies). The heretics were burned, and later, criminals were slowly strangled as they held a crucifix, hearing the reassuring words of a priest as the life was squeezed out of them with a garrote. Up to 50,000 people could crowd into this square for such spectacles.

The square's buildings are mainly private apartments. Want one? Costs run from €450,000 for a tiny attic studio to €2 million and up for a 2,500-square-foot flat. The square is painted a democratic shade of burgundy—the result of a citywide poll. Since the end of decades of dictatorship in 1975, Spain has had a passion for voting. Three different colors were painted as samples on the walls of this square, and the city voted for its favorite.

The building to Philip's left, on the north side beneath the twin towers, was once home to the bakers guild and now houses the **TI**, which is wonderfully air-conditioned.

A stamp-and-coin market bustles at Plaza Mayor on Sundays (10:00-14:00). Day or night, Plaza Mayor is a colorful place to enjoy an affordable cup

of coffee or overpriced food. Throughout Spain, lesser *plazas mayores* provide peaceful pools in the whitewater river of Spanish life.

MADRID

The Spanish Inquisition

Throughout Spain, you'll encounter palaces, plazas, and historic sites associated with the Spanish Inquisition—a court system run by the Catholic Church to ferret out unorthodoxy and arrest, try, and punish suspected sinners and heretics. Religious inquisitions had existed in Europe since medieval times, but in Spain the Inquisition took on an intensity and violence that seared itself into the European consciousness.

Ironically, it arose in what was once Europe's most diverse country—Spain—where Jews, Muslims, and Christians had for centuries lived side by side. But in the 1300s, Christians began to conquer Muslim lands and confine Jews behind ghetto walls. In 1478, Ferdinand and Isabel, "the Catholic Monarchs," founded the Spanish branch of the Inquisition as part of their campaign to unify the country under Christian rule. In 1492, when Moorish Granada was conquered and Judaism was banned, all remaining Muslims and Jews were forced to convert. It became the Inquisition's job to ensure that these *conversos* really meant it.

Things got ugly.

There were mass rallies, where suspected backsliders were tried and punished. In Sevilla, thousands were burned at the stake in front of the cathedral. Other atrocities took place on Madrid's Plaza Mayor, Toledo's Plaza de Zocodover, and Granada's Plaza de Bib-Rambla.

By the 1500s, the Inquisition had a new enemy—Protestants. Spain's ultra-Catholic kings made it their mission to fight heresy throughout Europe and the New World. Their palace at El Escorial (see next chapter) became the movement's de facto global headquarters. In its heyday, the Inquisition prosecuted (or should I say persecuted?) Protestants, Jews, Muslims, unorthodox Catholics, political enemies, scientists, and free-thinkers—anyone who dared question the establishment.

The Spanish Inquisition became notorious for its cruelty and kangaroo courts. The accused were not allowed lawyers. They were tortured to extract bogus confessions. Those found guilty were whipped, hanged, sliced up, or burned at the stake. Some executions were held in banquet halls for nobles' amusement. How many victims were there? Probably many thousands, but it's hard to know, because the atrocities were likely exaggerated by later anti-Catholic propaganda.

By the 1700s, the Inquisition was dying down—except in Spain. Legends grew of dank dungeons, cruel Grand Inquisitors, and daring Don Juans who fought against it. Even the unconventional artist Goya was questioned. Though the Inquisition was officially abolished in 1821, its ominous presence lingered on in Spain for decades. The modern saying, "I didn't expect the Spanish Inquisition!" when questioned (and the hilarious *Monty Python* sketch) are witty reminders of Spain's painful past.

• *Head to #26, which is under the arcade just to the left of the twin towers. This is a bar called...*

❹ La Torre del Oro Bar Andalú

For some *Andalú* (Andalusian) ambience, an entertaining (if gruff) staff, and lots of fascinating (if gruesome) bullfighting lore, step

inside. Order a drink at the bar and sightsee while you sip. Warning: First check the price list posted outside the door to understand the price tiers: "*barra*" indicates the price at the bar; "*terraza*" is the price at an outdoor table. A *caña* (small draft beer), Coke, or *agua mineral* should cost about €3. Your drink may come with a small, free tapa, per the old Spanish tradition. But to avoid being charged by surprise, clarify, "*Gratis?*"

The interior is a temple to bullfighting, festooned with gory decor. Notice the breathtaking action captured in the many photographs. Look under the stuffed head of Barbero the bull (center, facing the bar). At eye level you'll see a *puntilla*, the knife used to put poor Barbero out of his misery at the arena. The plaque explains: weight, birth date, owner, date of death, which matador killed him, and the location.

Just to the left of Barbero is a photo of longtime dictator Franco with the famous bullfighter Manuel Benítez Pérez—better known as El Cordobés, the Elvis of bullfighters and a working-class hero.

At the top of the stairs going down to the WC (on the right), find the photo of El Cordobés and Robert Kennedy—looking like brothers. Just above RFK find the photo of the famous matador, Paquirri, that captures a poignant moment: about to take his last breath after being gored, he smiles at the camera.

Below and left of the Kennedy photo is a picture of El Cordobés' illegitimate son being gored. Disowned by El Cordobés senior, yet still using his dad's famous name after a court battle, the junior El Cordobés is one of this generation's top fighters.

At the end of the bar, in a glass case, is the "suit of lights" the great El Cordobés wore in an ill-fated 1967 fight, in which the bull gored him. El Cordobés survived; the bull didn't.

In the case with the "suit of lights," notice the photo of a matador (not El Cordobés) horrifyingly hooked by a bull's horn. Take a slow browse along the length of the bar, past photos of matadors having both very good and very bad days. You can play "spot the

celebrity"—there's Bruce Springsteen…and Jimmy Carter. Bull fighting attracted the most macho of aficionados from Hemmingway… to the Latin American revolutionary, Che Guevara.

And with all the literally gory encounters with bulls, you can understand why religion and superstition followed matadors into the ring. Between Che and the door you'll find a small shrine to the Virgin Mary.

Leaving the bull bar, turn right and notice the **La Favorita hat shop** (at #25). See the plaque in the pavement honoring the shop, which has served the public since 1894.

Consider taking a break at one of the tables on Madrid's grandest square. Cafetería Magerit (nearby) occupies Plaza Mayor's sunniest corner and is a good place to enjoy a coffee with the view. The scene is easily worth the extra euro you'll pay for the drink.

• *Leave Plaza Mayor on Calle de Ciudad Rodrigo (at the northwest corner of the square), passing a series of solid turn-of-the-20th-century storefronts and sandwich joints, such as* **Casa Rúa** *(to the left), famous for their cheap* bocadillos de calamares—*fried squid rings on a small baguette.*

Mistura Ice Cream *(across the lane at Ciudad Rodrigo 6) serves fine coffee and quality ice cream. Its cellar is called the "chill zone" for good reason—an oasis of cool and peace, ideal for enjoying your treat.*

Emerging from the arcade, turn left and head downhill toward the iron-covered market hall. Before entering the market, look downhill to the left, down a street called Cava de San Miguel.

❺ *Mesones* and Mercado de San Miguel

Lining the street called Cava de San Miguel is a series of traditional dive bars called *mesones.* If you like singing and sangria, come back after 22:00 to visit one. These cave-like bars, stretching far back from the street, get packed with Madrileños out on dates who—emboldened by wine and the setting—are prone to suddenly breaking out in song. It's a lowbrow, electric-keyboard, karaoke-type ambience, best on Friday and Saturday nights. The

odd shape of these bars isn't a contrivance for the sake of atmosphere—Plaza Mayor was built on a slope, and these underground vaults are part of a structural system that braces the leveled plaza.

For a more refined setting, pop into the **Mercado de San Miguel** (daily 10:00-24:00). This historic iron-and-glass structure from 1916 stands on the site of an even earlier marketplace. Renovated in the 21st century, the city's oldest surviving market hall

now hosts some 30 high-end vendors of fresh produce, gourmet foods, wines by the glass, tapas, and full meals. Tourists pause here for its food, natural-light ambience, and social scene.

Go on an edible scavenger hunt by simply grazing down the center aisle. You'll find a variety of tapas, including croquettes, fish, artisan cheeses, and lots of olives. Skewer them on a toothpick and they're called *banderillas*—for the decorated spear a bullfighter thrusts into the bull's neck. You'll find a draft *vermut* (Vermouth) bar, along with sangria and sherry (V.O.R.S. means, literally, very old rare sherry—dry and full-bodied). Finally, the San Onofre bar is for your sweet tooth. You'll probably hear *"Que aproveche!"*—the Spanish version of bon appétit.

• *Exit the market at the far end and turn left, heading downhill on Calle del Conde de Miranda. At the first corner, turn right and cross the small plaza to the brick church in the far corner.*

❻ Church and Convent of Corpus Christi

The proud coats of arms over the main entry announce the rich family that built this Hieronymite church and convent in 1607. In 17th-century Spain, the most prestigious thing a noble family could do was build and maintain a convent. To harvest all the goodwill created in your community, you'd want your family's insignia right there for all to see. (You can see the donating couple, like a 17th-century Bill and Melinda Gates, kneeling before the communion wafer in the central panel over the entrance.) Inside is a cool and quiet oasis with a Last Supper altarpiece.

Now for a unique shopping experience. A dozen steps to the right of the church entrance is its associated convent—it's the big brown door on the left, at Calle del Codo 3 (Mon-Sat 9:30-13:00 & 16:30-18:30, closed Sun). The sign reads *Venta de Dulces* (Sweets for Sale). To buy goodies from the cloistered nuns, buzz the *monjas* button, then wait patiently for the sister to respond over the intercom. Say *"dulces"* (DOOL-thays), and she'll let you in. When the lock buzzes, push open the door. It will be dark—look for a glowing light switch to turn on the lights. Walk straight in and to the left, then follow the sign to the *torno*—the lazy Susan that lets the sisters sell their baked goods without being seen. Scan the menu, announce your choice to the quiet sister (she may tell you she has only one or two of the options available), place your money on the *torno*, and your goodies (and change) will appear. *Galletas* (shortbread cookies) are the least expensive item (a *medio*-kilo costs about €10). Or try the *pastas de almendra* (almond cookies).

• *Continue uphill on Calle del Codo, where, in centuries past, those in need of bits of armor shopped (as depicted on the tiled street sign on the building). Bend sharply left with the street—named "Elbow Street"—and head toward the Plaza de la Villa. Before entering the square, notice*

*an **old door** to the left of the* **Real Sociedad Económica** *sign, made of wood lined with metal. This is considered the oldest door in town on Madrid's oldest building—inhabited since 1480. It's set in a Mudejar keyhole arch. Remember, for many centuries (from 711 to 1492), Spain was largely Muslim, and that influence lived on in its Mudejar crafts-people. Look up to see a tower, once used as a prison.*

Now continue into the square called Plaza de la Villa, dominated by Madrid's...

❼ Former Town Hall

The impressive structure features Madrid's distinctive architectural style—symmetrical square towers, topped with steeples and a slate roof...Castilian Baroque. The build-ing was Madrid's Town Hall. Over the doorway, the three coats of arms sport many symbols of Madrid's rul-ers: Habsburg crowns on each, castles of Castile (in center shield), and the city symbol—the berry-eating bear (shield on left). This square was the ruling center of medieval Madrid in the centuries before it became an im-portant capital.

Imagine how Philip II took this city by surprise in 1561 when he decided to move the capital of Europe's largest empire (even big-ger than ancient Rome) from Toledo to humble Madrid. Madrid proved to be a perfect choice. It was located in the geographical center of the country. It united the two great kingdoms of Phil-ip's great-grandparents, Ferdinand and Isabel. And with plenty of room to grow, Madrid became the ideal spot to administer the growing Spanish empire.

Philip II went on a building spree, and his son Philip III con-tinued it. This particular building reflects the hasty development. It's glorious, yes—but like much of Madrid, it's built with inexpen-sive brick rather than costly granite.

The venerable Town Hall also bore witness to the decline of Spain's fortunes after the golden age. The statue in the little gar-den is of Philip II's admiral, Don Alvaro de Bazán, who defeated the Turkish Ottomans at the battle of Lepanto in 1571. This was Spain's last great victory. Mere months after Bazán's death in 1588, his "invincible" Spanish Armada was destroyed by England...and Spain's empire began its slow fade.

• *By the way, a charming little shop selling traditional monk- and nun-made pastries from around Spain is just down the lane (**El Jardín del Convento**, at Calle del Cordón 1, on the back side of the cloistered con-vent you dropped by earlier).*

From the top of the square, turn left on Calle Mayor, which leads downhill (along the right side of the old Town Hall) toward the Royal Palace. You'll pass a fine little shop specializing in books about Madrid (at #80, on the right). A few blocks down Calle Mayor, where the street opens up a bit on the left, is a small plaza in front of a church, where you'll find the...

❽ Assassination Attempt Memorial

This statue memorializes a 1906 assassination attempt. The targets were Spain's King Alfonso XIII and his bride, Victoria Eugenie, as they paraded by on their wedding day. While the crowd was throwing flowers, an anarchist (as terrorists used to be called) threw a bouquet lashed to a bomb from a balcony at #84 (across the street). He missed the royal newlyweds, but killed 28 people. The king and queen went on to live to a ripe old age, producing many great-grandchildren, including the current king, Felipe VI.

• *Continue down Calle Mayor one more block to a busy street, Calle de Bailén. Take in the big, domed...*

❾ Almudena Cathedral

Madrid's massive, gray-and-white cathedral (Catedral de Nuestra Señora de la Almudena, 110 yards long and 80 yards high) opened

in 1993, 100 years after workers started building it. This is the side entrance for tourists. Climbing the steps to the church courtyard, you'll come to a monument to Pope John Paul II's 1993 visit, when he consecrated Almudena—ending Madrid's 300-year stretch of requests for a cathedral of its own.

Unlike in most Spanish cities, Madrid's churches aren't its most interesting sights. Madrid was built as a capital, so its main landmarks are governmental rather than religious. This cathedral is worthwhile, but if you're running out of steam, it's skippable.

If you go in (€1 donation requested), stop in the center, immediately under the dome, and face the altar. Beyond it, colorful paintings—rushed to completion for the pope's '93 visit—brighten the apse. In the right transept the faithful venerate a 15th-century

Gothic altarpiece with a favorite statue of the Virgin Mary—a striking treasure considering the otherwise 20th-century Neo-Gothic interior. Peer down at the glittering 5,000-pipe organ in the rear of the nave.

The church's historic highlight is directly behind the altar: a 13th-century coffin. It's made of painted leather on wood, and depicts scenes of cows, horses, and strolling people. The coffin is now empty, but it once held Madrid's patron saint, Isidro. The story goes that Isidro was only a humble farmer, but he was exceptionally devout. One day, he was visited by angels. They agreed to plow his fields so he could devote himself to praying. When Isidro died, he was buried in this simple coffin. Forty years later, the coffin was opened, and his body was still perfectly preserved. This miracle convinced the pope to canonize Isidro. He is now the patron saint of farmers, and of the city of Madrid.

• *Leave the church from the transept where you entered. Head back to the street, and turn left. Hike around the church to its rarely used front door. Climb the cathedral's front steps and face the imposing...*

⑩ Royal Palace

Since the ninth century, this spot has been Madrid's center of power: from Moorish castle to Christian fortress to Renaissance palace to the current structure, built in the 18th century. With its expansive courtyard surrounded by imposing Baroque architecture, it represents the wealth of Spain before its decline. Its 2,800 rooms, totaling nearly 1.5 million square feet, make it Europe's largest palace. Stretching toward the mountains on the left is the vast Casa del Campo (a former royal hunting ground, now a city park).

• *You could visit the palace now, using my self-guided tour (see page 435).*

Or, to follow the rest of this walk back to Puerta del Sol, continue north up Calle de Bailén (walking alongside the palace). In the distance you'll see the **Madrid Tower** *skyscraper. This was a big deal in the 1950s when it was one of the tallest buildings in Europe (460 feet) and the pride of Franco and his fascist regime. The tower marks Plaza de España, and the end of my "Gran Vía Walk" (see page 431). To Spaniards, it symbolizes the boom time the country enjoyed when it sided with the West during the Cold War (allowing the US and not the USSR to build military bases in Spain).*

You'll pass the group entrance (on your left), and a TI (on your right). When you reach the large side entrance to the palace (on your left; note the palace guards), turn right. You'll find yourself facing a **statue** *of a king on a horse and the Royal Theater.*

⑪ Plaza de Oriente

As its name suggests, this square faces east. The grand yet people-friendly plaza is typical of today's Europe, where energetic gov-

ernments are converting car-congested wastelands into inviting public spaces. Where's the traffic? Under your feet. A former Madrid mayor who spearheaded the project earned the nickname "The Mole" for all the digging he did.

Notice the quiet. You're surrounded by more than three million people, yet you can hear the birds, bells, and fountain. The park is decorated with statues of Visigothic kings who ruled from the fifth to eighth century. Romans allowed them to administer their province of Hispania on the condition that they'd provide food and weapons to the empire. The Visigoths inherited real power after Rome fell, but lost it to invading Moors in 711. Throughout Spain's history, the monarchs have traced their heritage back to these distant Visigothic ancestors.

The fine bronze equestrian **statue of Philip IV** was a striking technical feat in its day, as the horse rears back dramatically balanced atop its fragile ankles. It was only made possible with the help of Galileo's clever calculations (and by using the tail for extra support).

The king faces the 1,700-seat **Royal Theater** (Teatro Real), built in the mid-1800s and rebuilt in 1997. It hosts traditional opera, ballets, concerts, and that unique Spanish form of light opera called zarzuela.

• *Continue through the square and then walk along the right side of the Royal Theater to...*

⑫ Plaza de Isabel II

This square is marked by a statue of Isabel II, who ruled Spain in the 19th century and was a great patron of the arts. Although she's immortalized here, Isabel had a rocky reign. She was a conservative out of step with Spain's march toward democracy. A revolution in 1868 forced her to abdicate—bringing Spain its first (brief) taste of democracy—and Isabel lived out her life in exile. Today, Isabel's statue stands before her most lasting legacy—the Royal Theater she built.

• *From here, follow Calle del Arenal (on the right side of the square), walking gradually uphill. You're heading straight back to Puerta del Sol.*

⑬ Calle del Arenal

As depicted on the tiled street signs, this was the "street of sand"— where sand was stockpiled during construction. Each cross street is

Spain's Royal Families: From Habsburg to Bourbon

Spain as we know it was born when four long-established medieval kingdoms were joined by the 1469 marriage of Ferdinand, ruler of Aragon and Navarre, and Isabel, ruler of Castile and León. The so-called "Catholic Monarchs" (Reyes Católicos) wasted no time in driving the Islamic Moors out of Spain (the Reconquista)—and expelled the Jews and explored the oceans, to boot. By 1492, Isabel and Ferdinand had conquered a fifth kingdom, Granada, establishing more or less the same borders that Spain has today.

This was an age when "foreign policy" was conducted, in part, by marrying royal children into other royal families. Among the dynastic marriages of their children, Isabel and Ferdinand arranged for their third child, Juana "the Mad," to marry the crown prince of Austria, Philip "the Fair." This was a huge coup for the Spanish royal family. A member of the Habsburg dynasty, Philip was heir to the Holy Roman Empire, which then encompassed much of today's Austria, Czech Republic, Slovakia, Hungary, Transylvania, the Low Countries, southern Italy, and more. When Juana's brothers died, making her ruler of the kingdoms of Spain, it paved the way for her son, Charles, to inherit the kingdoms of his four grandparents—creating a vast realm and famously making him the most powerful man in Europe. He ruled as Charles I (king of Spain, from 1516) and Charles V (Holy Roman Emperor, from 1519).

He was followed by Philip II, Philip III, Philip IV, and finally Charles II. Over this period, Spain rested on its golden age laurels, eventually squandering much of its wealth and losing some of its holdings. Arguably the most inbred of an already very inbred dynasty (his parents were uncle and niece), Charles II was weak, sickly, and unable to have children, ending the 200-year Habsburg dynasty in Spain with his death in 1700.

Charles II willed the Spanish crown to the Bourbons of France, and his grandnephew Philip of Anjou, whose granddaddy was the "Sun King" Louis XIV of France, took the throne. But the rest of

named for a medieval craft that, historically, was plied along that lane (for example, "Calle de Bordadores" means "Street of the Embroiderers"). Wander slowly uphill. As you stroll, imagine this street as a traffic inferno—which it was until the city pedestrianized it (and now monitors it with police cameras atop posts at intersections). Notice also how orderly the side streets

Europe feared allowing the already powerful Louis XIV to add Spain (and its vast New World holdings) to his empire. Austria, the Germanic States, Holland, England, and Catalunya backed a different choice (Archduke Charles of Austria). So began the War of Spanish Succession (1700-1714), involving all of Europe. The French eventually prevailed, and with the signing of the Treaty of Utrecht (1713), Philip gave up any claim to the French throne. This let him keep the Spanish crown but ensured that his heirs—the future Spanish Bourbon dynasty—couldn't become too powerful by merging with the French Bourbons.

In 1714, the French-speaking Philip became the first king of the Bourbon dynasty in Spain (with the name Philip V). He breathed much-needed new life into the monarchy, which had grown ineffectual and corrupt under the Habsburgs. After the old wooden Habsburg royal palace burned on Christmas Eve of 1734, Philip (who was born at Versailles) built a new and spectacular late-Baroque-style palace as a bold symbol of his new dynasty. This is the palace that wows visitors to Madrid today. Construction was finished in 1764, and Philip V's son Charles III was the palace's first occupant (you'll see his decorations if you visit the palace's interior). Charles III also renovated the Bourbon Palace rooms at El Escorial.

The Bourbon palace remained the home of Spain's kings from 1764 until 1931, when democratic elections led to the Second Spanish Republic and forced King Alfonso XIII into exile. After Francisco Franco took power in 1939, he sidelined the royals by making himself ruler-for-life. But later he handpicked as his successor Alfonso XIII's grandson, the Bourbon Prince Juan Carlos, whom Franco believed would continue his hardline policies. When Franco died in 1975, Juan Carlos surprised everyone by voluntarily turning power over to Spain's parliament. Today Spain is a constitutional monarchy with a figurehead Bourbon king, Felipe VI, son of Juan Carlos I (who abdicated in 2014).

are. Where a mess of cars once lodged chaotically on the sidewalks, orderly bollards *(bolardos)* now keep vehicles off the walkways. The fancier facades (such as the former International Hotel at #19— look up to see the elaborate balconies) are in the "eclectic" style (the Spanish version of Historicism—meaning a new interest in old styles) of the late 19th century.

Continue 200 yards up Calle del Arenal to a brick church on the right. As you walk, consider how many people are simply out strolling. The paseo is a strong tradition in this culture—people of all generations enjoy being out, together, strolling. And local

governments continue to provide more and more pedestrianized boulevards to make the paseo better than ever.

The brick **St. Ginés Church** (on the right) means temptation to most locals. It marks the turn to the best *chocolatería* in town. From the uphill corner of the church, look to the end of the lane where—like a high-calorie red-light zone—a neon sign spells out *Chocolatería San Ginés*...every local's favorite place for hot chocolate and *churros* (always open; see listing on page 502). Also notice the charming bookshop clinging like a barnacle to the wall of the church. It's been selling books on this spot since 1650.

Next door is the **Teatro Eslava,** famous for operettas in the Gilbert and Sullivan days and now a popular club and theater. In Spain, you can do it all when you're 18 (buy tobacco, drink, drive, and serve in the military).

Farther up on the left, in a little mall (at #8), are a couple of sights celebrating Spain's answer to Mickey Mouse, called **"Ratón Pérez"**—Perez the Mouse. First, find the six-inch-tall bronze statue of the beloved rodent in the lobby. Ratón Pérez first appeared in a children's book in the late 1800s, and kids have adored him ever since. He also serves as Spain's tooth fairy, leaving money under kids' pillows when they lose a tooth. Upstairs is the fanciful Casita Museo de Ratón Pérez (€3, daily, Spanish only) with a fun window display. A steady stream of adoring children and their parents pour through here to learn about this wondrous mouse.

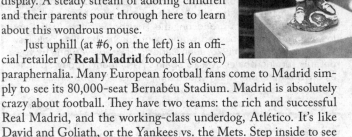

Just uphill (at #6, on the left) is an official retailer of **Real Madrid** football (soccer) paraphernalia. Many European football fans come to Madrid simply to see its 80,000-seat Bernabéu Stadium. Madrid is absolutely crazy about football. They have two teams: the rich and successful Real Madrid, and the working-class underdog, Atlético. It's like David and Goliath, or the Yankees vs. the Mets. Step inside to see posters of the happy team posing with the latest trophy.

Across the street at #5 is **Pronovias,** a famous Spanish wedding-dress shop that attracts brides-to-be from across Europe. These days, the current generation of Spaniards often just shack up without getting married. Those who do get married are more practical—preferring a down payment on a condo to a fancy wedding with a costly dress.

• *You're just a few steps from where you started this walk, at Puerta del Sol. Back in the square, you're met by a statue popularly known as* **La Mariblanca.** *The statue, which is at least 400 years old, represents a kind of Spanish Venus, possibly a fertility goddess. At her feet, she has*

Madrid's coat of arms, with our old friend, the bear and the berry tree. Today, La Mariblanca *stands tall amid all the modernity, as she blesses the people of this great city.*

GRAN VÍA WALK

For a walk down Spain's version of Fifth Avenue, stroll the Gran Vía. Built primarily between 1910 and the 1930s, this boulevard,

worth ▲, affords a fun view of early-20th-century architecture and a chance to be on the street with workaday Madrileños. As you walk, you'll notice that Madrid's main boulevard was renovated with wide sidewalks and traffic is mostly limited to buses and taxis. I've broken this self-guided walk into five sections, each of which was the ultimate in its day, starting near Plaza de Cibeles and ending at Plaza de España.

• *Start at the skyscraper at Calle de Alcalá #42 (Metro: Banco de España).*

❶ Circulo de Bellas Artes

This 1920s skyscraper has a venerable café on its ground floor (free entry to enjoy its belle époque-style interior) and the best roof-

top view around. Ride the elevator (€5, daily 12:00-24:00) to the seventh-floor Azotea roof terrace/lounge and bar, a fine place to nurse a scenic drink on a sunny day.

On the roof, stand under a black Art Deco statue of Minerva, perhaps put here to associate Madrid with this mythological protectress of culture and high thinking, and survey the city. Start in the far left and work your way around the perimeter for a clockwise tour.

Looking down to the left, you'll see the gold-fringed dome of the landmark Metropolis building (inspired by Hotel Negresco in Nice), once the headquarters of an insurance company and now being converted into a luxury space with a hotel, restaurants, and a spa. It stands at the start of the Gran Vía and its cancan of proud facades celebrating the good times in pre-civil war Spain. On the horizon, the Guadarrama Mountains hide Segovia. Farther to the

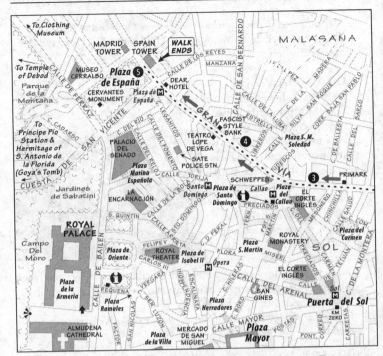

right, in the distance, skyscrapers mark the city's north gate, Puerta de Europa (with its striking slanted twin towers peeking from behind other towers). Round the terrace corner. The big traffic circle and fountain below are part of Plaza de Cibeles, with its ornate and bombastic cultural center and observation deck (Palacio de Cibeles—built in 1910 as the post-office headquarters, and since 2006 the Madrid City Hall). Behind that is the vast Retiro Park. Farther to the right (at the next corner of the terrace), the big low-slung building surrounded by green is the Prado Museum.

• *Take the elevator back down and cross the busy boulevard immediately in front of Círculo de Bellas Artes to reach the start of Gran Vía.*

❷ 1910s Gran Vía

This first stretch, from the Banco de España Metro stop to the Gran Vía Metro stop, was built in the 1910s as a strip of luxury stores. The Bar Chicote (at #12, on the right, marked *Museo Chicote*) is a classic cocktail bar that welcomed Hemingway and the stars of the day. While the people-watching and

Gran Vía Walk

1. Circulo de Bellas Artes
2. 1910s Gran Vía (Banco de España to Gran Vía Metro)
3. 1920s Gran Vía (Gran Vía to Callao Metro)
4. 1930s Gran Vía (Callao to Plaza de España Metro)
5. Plaza de España

window-shopping can be enthralling, be sure to look up and enjoy the beautiful facades, too.

By the way, as you stroll along Gran Vía (or anywhere in Madrid), tune in to the pedestrian traffic lights. In honor of Pride Day, in 2017 a progressive mayor replaced dozens of these with a version showing two men or two women holding hands as they wait or cross (see photo).

❸ 1920s Gran Vía

The second stretch, from the Gran Vía Metro stop to the Callao Metro stop, starts where two recently pedestrianized streets meet up. To the right, Calle de Fuencarral is the trendiest pedestrian zone in town, with famous brand-name shops and a young vibe. To the left, Calle de la Montera is known for prostitution. The action pulses from the McDonald's down a block or so. Some find it an eye-opening little detour.

The 14-story **Telefónica skyscraper** (on the right) is nearly 300 feet tall. Perched here at the highest point around, it seems even taller. It was one of the city's first skyscrapers (the tallest in Spain until the 1950s) with a big New York City feel—and with a tiny Baroque balcony, as if to remind us we're still in Spain. Telefónica was Spain's only telephone company through the Franco age (and was notorious for overbilling people, with nothing itemized

MADRID

and no accountability). Today it's one of Spain's few giant blue-chip corporations.

With plenty of money and a need for corporate goodwill, the building houses the free **Espacio Fundación Telefónica** (Tue-Sun 10:00-20:00, closed Mon), with an art gallery, kid-friendly special exhibits, and a fun permanent exhibit telling the story of telecommunications, from telegraphs to iPhones. This exhibit fills the second floor amid exposed steel beams—a space where a thousand "09 girls," as operators were called back then, once worked.

Farther along is a strip of fashion stores, including **Primark** at #32, which occupies the building that held the first modern department store in town. Farther along and just before the Callao Metro station, on the left at #37, stands a 1928 building that used to be the elegant **movie theater** *Cine Avenida*. Many pause here and mourn the loss of another cultural space turned commercial.

❹ 1930s Gran Vía

The final stretch, from the Callao Metro stop to Plaza de España, is considered the "American Gran Vía," built in the 1930s to emulate the buildings of Chicago and New York City. The **Schweppes** building (Art Deco in the Chicago style, with its round facade and curved windows) was radical and innovative in 1933. This section of Gran Vía is the Spanish version of Broadway, with all the big theaters and plays. These theaters survive thanks to Spanish translations of Broadway shows, productions that get a huge second life here and in Latin America.

Head a few blocks down the street. Across from the Teatro Lope de Vega (on the left, at #60) is a quasi-fascist-style building (on the right, #57). It's a **bank** from 1930 capped with a stern statue that looks like an ad for using a good, solid piggy bank. Looking up the street toward the Madrid Tower, the buildings become even more severe.

The **Dear Hotel** (at #80) has a restaurant on its 14th floor and a rooftop lounge and small bar above that. (Walk confidently through the hotel lobby, ride the elevator to the top, pass through the restaurant, and climb the stairs from the terrace outside to the rooftop.) The views from here are among the best in town.

❺ Plaza de España

The end of Gran Vía is marked by Plaza de España (with a Metro station of the same name). Statues of the epic Spanish characters Don Quixote and Sancho Panza (part of a Cervantes monument) grace the park, and two Franco-era buildings do their best to scrape the sky above. Franco wanted to show he could keep up with America, so he had the Spain Tower (shorter) and Madrid Tower

(taller) built in the 1950s. But they reminded people more of Moscow than the USA.

Sights in Madrid

▲▲▲ROYAL PALACE

Spain's Royal Palace (Palacio Real) is Europe's third-greatest palace, after Versailles and Vienna's Schönbrunn. It has arguably the

most sumptuous original interior, packed with tourists and royal antiques. For three centuries, Spain's royal family has called this place home.

The palace is the product of many kings over several centuries. Philip II (1527-1598) made a wooden fortress on this site his governing center when he established Madrid as Spain's capital. When that palace burned down, the current structure was built by King Philip V (1683-1746). Philip V wanted to make it his own private Versailles, to match his French upbringing: He was born in Versailles—the grandson of Louis XIV—and ordered his tapas in French. His son, Charles III (whose statue graces Puerta del Sol), added interior decor in the Italian style, since he'd spent his formative years in Italy. These civilized Bourbon kings were trying to raise Spain to the cultural level of the rest of Europe. They hired foreign artists to oversee construction and established local Spanish porcelain and tapestry factories to copy works done in Paris or Brussels. Over the years, the palace was expanded and enriched, as each Spanish king tried to outdo his predecessor.

Today's palace is ridiculously supersized—with 2,800 rooms, tons of luxurious tapestries, a king's ransom of chandeliers, frescoes by Tiepolo, priceless porcelain, and bronze decor covered in gold leaf. While these days the royal family lives in a mansion several miles away, this place still functions as the ceremonial palace, used for formal state receptions, royal weddings, and tourists' daydreams.

Cost and Hours: Palace-€12, royal kitchen-€6, palace and kitchen combo-ticket-€16, buy online to avoid long ticket-buying lines, all tickets are timed-entry. Open daily 10:00-19:00, Oct-March until 18:00, last entry one hour before closing; from Puerta del Sol, walk 15 minutes down pedestrianized Calle del Arenal (Metro: Ópera); palace can close for royal functions—confirm in advance.

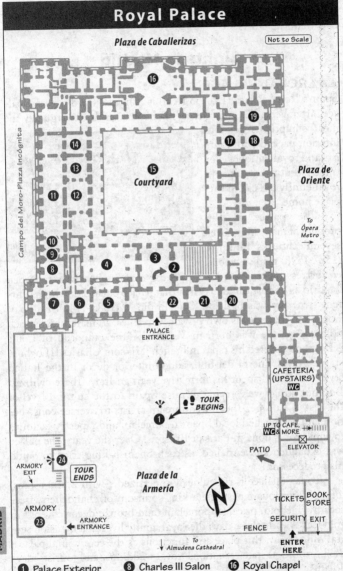

Royal Palace

Not to Scale

Plaza de Caballerizas

Campo del Moro-Plaza Incógnita

Courtyard

Plaza de Oriente

To Ópera Metro

PALACE ENTRANCE

CAFETERIA (UPSTAIRS) WC

TOUR BEGINS

UP TO CAFE, WC & MORE

PATIO

ELEVATOR

ARMORY EXIT

TOUR ENDS

Plaza de la Armería

ARMORY

ARMORY ENTRANCE

TICKETS

BOOK-STORE

SECURITY   EXIT

FENCE

ENTER HERE

To Almudena Cathedral

MADRID

❶ Palace Exterior	❽ Charles III Salon	⓲ Royal Chapel
❷ Palace Lobby (Ground Floor) & Grand Stairs	❾ Porcelain Room	⓱ Queen's Boudoir
	❿ Yellow Room	⓲ Stradivarius Room
❸ Hall of Halberdiers	⓫ Gala Dining Room	⓳ Crown Room
❹ Hall of Columns	⓬ Cinema Room	⓴ Official Antechamber
❺ Drawing Room	⓭ Silver Room	㉑ Official Waiting Room
❻ Antechamber	⓮ Crockery & Crystal Rooms	㉒ Throne Room
❼ Gasparini Room	⓯ Courtyard	㉓ Royal Armory
		㉔ View of the Gardens

Information: +34 914 548 800, www.patrimonionacional.es.

Crowd-Beating Tips: The palace is free for EU citizens—and most crowded—Monday-Thursday 17:00-19:00 in summer and 16:00-18:00 in winter. On any day, it's best to go early or late to avoid crowds.

Visitor Information: Short English descriptions posted in each room complement what I describe in my tour. The museum guidebook demonstrates a passion for meaningless data.

Tours: The €5 **audioguide** is good. Or download in advance the helpful Royal Palace of Madrid **app** (€4). The dry English **guided tour** (€4) runs infrequently and is not worth a long wait.

Length of This Tour: Allow 1.5 hours.

Services: Free lockers, a WC, and a gift shop are just past the ticket booth. Upstairs you'll find a more serious bookstore with good books on Spanish history.

Eating: Though the palace has a refreshing air-conditioned **$ cafeteria** upstairs in the ticket building, I prefer to walk a few minutes and find a place near the Royal Theater or on Calle del Arenal. The recommended **$$$ La Botillería,** boasting lunch specials and fin-de-siècle elegance, is pricey but memorable, in a delightful park setting opposite the palace off Plaza de Oriente; for location see map on page 492.

➔ Self-Guided Tour

You'll follow a simple one-way circuit on a single floor covering more than 20 rooms.

• *Pass through the ticket check and metal detector, proceed outside, stand in the middle of the vast open-air courtyard, and face the palace entrance.*

❶ Palace Exterior

The palace sports the French-Italian Baroque architecture so popular in the 18th century—heavy columns, classical-looking statues, a balustrade roofline, and a false-front entrance. The entire building is made of gray-and-white local stone (very little wood) to prevent the kind of fire that leveled the previous castle. This became Spain's center of power; notice how the palace of the king faces the palace of the bishop (the cathedral). Now, imagine the place in its heyday, with a courtyard full of soldiers on parade, or a lantern-lit scene of horse carriages arriving for a ball.

• *Enter the palace. Here you'll find an info desk, cloakrooms, and the meeting point for guided tours and the **Royal Kitchen** visit (if your ticket includes the Royal Kitchens, a guide will take you downstairs to the high- ceiling kitchens where you'll see copper pots, stove tops, cauldrons, and tables where meals for up to 140 people would be prepared).*

MADRID

❷ Palace Lobby and Grand Stairs

In the old days, horse-drawn carriages would drop you off inside this covered arcade. Today, stretch limos do the same thing for gala events. When you reach the foot of the Grand Stairs, you'll see a statue of a toga-clad Charles III—the man most responsible for the lavish rooms we're about to see (see the "Charles III" sidebar, later).

Stand at the base of the Grand Stairs and take in the scene. Gazing up the imposing staircase, you can see that Spain's kings wanted to make a big first impression.

Whenever high-end dignitaries arrive, fancy carpets are rolled down the stairs (notice the little metal bar-holding hooks).

Begin your ascent, up steps that are intentionally shallow, making your climb slow and regal. At the first landing, the burgundy coat of arms represents the current king, Felipe VI. He's part of a long tradition of kings stretching directly back to the Bourbon King Philip V, and even further back to Ferdinand and Isabel—and (according to legend) all the way back to the Visigothic kings who arrived after the fall of Rome. Overhead, the white-and-blue ceiling fresco opens up to a heavenly host of graceful female Virtues perched on a mountain of clouds, bestowing their favors on the Spanish monarchy.

Continue up to the top of the stairs. Before entering the first room, look to the right of the door to find a white marble bust of Felipe VI's great-great-g-g-g-g-great-grandfather Philip V, who began the Bourbon dynasty in Spain in 1700 and had this palace built. He was a direct descendant of France's "Sun King" Louis XIV...in case you couldn't tell from the curly wig.

• Now enter the first of the rooms. These were part of King Charles III's apartments, and even today, they belong to Charles' descendants. A big modern portrait of today's royal family seems to welcome visitors to their home: "Mi casa es su casa."

❸ Hall of Halberdiers (Royal Guard)

Immediately you get a sense of the palace's opulence, brought to you by the man portrayed over the fireplace: Charles III. Charles also appears overhead in the ceiling fresco (in red, with his distinctive narrow face) as the legendary hero Aeneas, standing in the clouds of heaven. Charles gazes up at his mother (as Venus), the sophisticated Italian duchess who raised her son to decorate the palace with Italian Baroque splendor. Charles hired the great Venetian painter Giambattista Tiepolo to do this room and others in the palace (see the "Tiepolo's Frescoes" sidebar, later). The fresco's

theme, of Vulcan forging Aeneas's armor, relates to the room's function as the palace guards' lounge.

Notice the two fake doors painted on the wall to give the room a more regal symmetry. The old clocks, still in working order, are the first of several we'll see—part of a collection of hundreds amassed as a hobby by Spain's royal family. Throughout the palace, pay attention to the carpets. They're part of a long tradition. Some are from the 18th century and others are new, but all were produced by the same Madrid royal tapestry factory and woven the traditional way—by hand.

The giant **portrait** depicts Spain's royal family: the current king Felipe (right), his dad and mom Juan Carlos I and Sofía (center), and his two sisters (left). It was Juan Carlos who resumed the monarchy in the 1970s after Francisco Franco's dictatorial regime. Rather than end up "Juan the Brief" (as some were nicknaming him), he steered the country toward democracy. (His image appears on older Spanish €1 and €2 coins.) Unfortunately, J. C. showed poor judgment in flaunting his wealth during Spain's recent economic crisis and was pressured to hand over the crown to his son, Felipe. Juan Carlos had commissioned this family portrait way back in 1993...and it was completed just in time for his abdication in 2014. (You can imagine the artist adding a few more wrinkles with each passing year.) Notice how Felipe stands apart from the rest of his family—a grouping that's open to interpretation. Perhaps he's the baby bird, being nudged from the nest, ready to shoulder the massive responsibility of a proud nation? Felipe's wife and Spain's current queen, Letizia Ortiz, isn't pictured—when this portrait was begun, they had not yet met.

• *Proceed into the...*

❹ Hall of Columns

In Charles III's day, this sparkling, chandeliered venue was the grand ballroom and dining room. The tapestries (like most you'll see in the palace) are 17th-century Belgian, from designs by Raphael. Appropriately, the ceiling fresco (by Jaquinto, following Tiepolo's style) depicts a radiant young Apollo driving the chariot of the sun, while Bacchus enjoys wine, women, and song with a convivial gang. The message: A good king drives the chariot of state as smartly as Apollo, so his people can enjoy life to the fullest.

Today this space is used for intimate concerts as well as important ceremonies. This is where Spain formally joined the European Union in 1985, where Spaniards honored their national soccer team after their 2010 World Cup victory, and where Juan Carlos I signed his abdication in 2014.

• *The next several rooms were the living quarters of King Charles III (r. 1759-1788). First comes his* ❺ *drawing room (with red-and-gold*

MADRID

Charles III (1716-1788)

Of the many monarchs who've enlarged or redecorated the Royal Palace, it was Charles III who set the tone for its Baroque-Rococo interior. Charles' mother was Italian, and he spent his formative years in Italy. When he became Spain's king, he brought along sophisticated Italian artists to decorate his new home—the painter Tiepolo, the architect Sabatini, and the decorator Gasparini. They created some of the most elaborate, jaw-dropping rooms tourists see in the palace today.

Charles was an enlightened ruler who tried to reform Spain along democratic principles. He failed. After his death, Spain dwindled into repressive irrelevance. But over the centuries, each of his successors labored to top Charles in ostentatious decoration, making Madrid's Royal Palace his greatest legacy.

walls), where the king would enjoy the company of a similarly great ruler—the Roman emperor Trajan—depicted "triumphing" on the ceiling. The heroics of Trajan, one of two Roman emperors born in Spain, naturally made the king feel good. Next, you enter the blue-walled...

❻ Antechamber

This was Charles III's dining room. The gilded decor you see here and throughout the palace is bronze with gold leaf. The furnishings reflect the tastes of various kings and queens who've inhabited this palace. The four paintings are of Charles III's son and successor, King Charles IV (looking a bit like a dim-witted George Washington), and his wife, María Luisa (who wore the pants in the palace). They're by Francisco de Goya, who also made duplicates of these portraits (now in the Prado) to meet the demand for his work. Velázquez's famous painting, *Las Meninas* (also in the Prado), originally hung in this room.

The 12-foot-tall clock—in porcelain, bronze, and mahogany—sits on a music box. Reminding us of how time flies, it depicts Chronus, the god of time, both as a child and as an old man. The palace's clocks are wound—and reset—once a week to keep them accurate.

❼ Gasparini Room

(Gasp!) The entire room is designed, top to bottom, as a single gold-green-rose ensemble: from the frescoed ceiling to the painted

stucco figures, silk-embroidered walls, chandelier, furniture, and multicolored marble floor. Each marble was quarried in, and therefore represents, a different region of Spain. Birds overhead spread their wings, vines sprout, and fruit bulges from the surface. With curlicues everywhere (including their reflection in the mirrors), the room dazzles the eye and mind. It's a triumph of the Rococo style, with exotic motifs such as the Chinese people sculpted into the corners of the ceiling. (These figures, like many in the palace, were formed from stucco, or wet plaster, that was molded into shape and painted.) The fabric gracing the walls was recently restored. Sixty people spent three years replacing the rotten silk fabric and then embroidering the original silver, silk, and gold threads back on.

Note the table. The Roman temple, birds, and flowers in the design are a micro-mosaic of teeny stones and glass. This was a typical souvenir from any aristocrat's trip to Rome in the mid-1800s. The chandelier, the biggest in the palace, is mesmerizing, especially with its glittering canopy of crystal reflecting in the wall mirrors.

The mirrors mark this as the king's dressing room. For a divine monarch, dressing was a public affair. The court bigwigs would assemble here as the king, standing on a platform—notice the height of the mirrors—would pull on his leotards and adjust his wig.

• *In the next small room, the silk wallpaper is clearly from modern times—note the intertwined "J. C. S." of the former monarchs Juan Carlos I and Sofía. Pass through the silk room to reach the...*

❽ Charles III Salon

This was Charles III's grand bedroom, and he died here in his bed in 1788. His grandson, Ferdinand VII, redid the room to honor the great man. The room's color scheme recalls the blue robes of the religious order of monks Charles founded here. A portrait of Charles on the wall shows him also in blue. The ceiling fresco shows Charles (kneeling, in armor) establishing his order, with its various (female) Virtues. Along the bottom edge (near the harp player), find the baby in his mother's arms—that would be Ferdy himself, the long-sought male heir, preparing to continue Charles' dynasty.

The chandelier is in the shape of the fleur-de-lis (the symbol of the Bourbon family) capped with a Spanish crown. As you exit the room, notice the thick walls between rooms. These hid service corridors for servants, who scurried about mostly unseen.

❾ Porcelain Room

This tiny but lavish room is paneled with green-white-gold porcelain garlands, vases, vines, babies, and mythological figures. The entire ensemble was disassembled for safety during the civil war. (Find the little screws in the greenery that hides the seams between

Tiepolo's Frescoes

In 1762, King Charles III invited Europe's most celebrated palace painter, Giambattista Tiepolo (1696-1770), to decorate three rooms in the newly built palace.  Sixty-six-year-old Tiepolo made the trip from Italy with his two well-known sons as assistants. They spent four years atop scaffolding decorating in the fresco technique, troweling plaster on the ceiling and quickly painting it before it dried.

Tiepolo's translucent ceilings seem to open up to a cloud-filled heaven, where Spanish royals cavort with Greek gods and pudgy cherubs. Tiepolo used every trick to "fool the eye" (trompe l'oeil), creating dizzying skyscapes of figures tumbling at every angle. He mixes 2-D painting with 3-D stucco figures that spill over the picture frame. His colorful, curvaceous ceilings blend seamlessly with the flamboyant furniture of the room below. Tiepolo's Royal Palace frescoes are often cited as the final flowering of Baroque and Rococo art.

panels.) Notice the clock in the center with Atlas supporting the world on his shoulders.

⑩ Yellow Room

This was a study for Charles III. The chandelier was designed to look like a temple with a fountain inside. Its cut crystal shows all the colors of the rainbow. Stand under it, look up, and sway slowly to see the colors glitter. This brilliantly lit room gives a glimpse of what the entire palace would look like whenever it was lit up for an occasion.

• *And if it were a special occasion, the next room is where everyone would gather and be dazzled.*

⑪ Gala Dining Room

This vast venue—perhaps the grandest room in the palace—is the main party room. The parquet floor was the preferred dancing surface when balls were held in this fabulous room. The room is lined with golden vases from China and fine tapestries. The ceiling fresco depicts the historical event that made Spain rich and made this opulent palace possible: Christopher Columbus kneels before Ferdinand and Isabel, presenting exotic souvenirs and his new, native friends (depicted with red skin).

Imagine this hall in action when a foreign dignitary dines here. Up to 12 times a year, the king entertains as many as 144 guests at this bowling lane-size table. If needed, the table can be extended the entire length of the room. The king and queen preside from the center. Find their chairs (slightly higher than the rest, and pulled out from the table a bit). The tables are set with fine crystal and cutlery. And the whole place glitters as the 15 chandeliers (and their 900 bulbs) are fired up.

• *Pass through the next room, originally where the royal string ensemble played for parties next door, but now known as the* ⓬ *Cinema Room because the royal family once enjoyed Sunday afternoon movies here. From here, move into the...*

⓭ Silver Room

Some of this 19th-century silver tableware—knives and forks, bowls, salt and pepper shakers, and the big punch bowl—is used in the Gala Dining Room on special occasions. If you look carefully, you can see quirky royal accessories, including a baby's silver rattle and fancy candle snuffers.

⓮ Crockery and Crystal Rooms

Each display case has a different style from a different period and made by a different factory. The oldest and rarest pieces belonged to the man who built this palace—Philip V. His china actually came from China, before that country was opened to the West. Soon, other European royal families were opening their own porcelain works (such as France's Sèvres or Germany's Meissen) to produce high-quality knockoffs (and cutesy Hummel-like figurines). The porcelain technique itself was kept a royal secret. As you leave, check out Isabel II's excellent 19th-century crystal ware.

• *Exit to the hallway and notice the interior courtyard you've been circling one room at a time.*

⓯ Courtyard

Like so many traditional Spanish homes, this palace was built around an open-air courtyard. The royal family lived on this spacious middle floor, staff lived upstairs, and the kitchens, garage, and storerooms were on the ground level. In 2004, this courtyard took on a new use when it was decorated to host King Felipe VI's royal wedding reception. Felipe married journalist Letizia Ortiz, a commoner (for love), and the two make it a point to be approachable with their subjects—they're very popular. (But then, so was Juan Carlos I, not long before his abdication. Royal life is fickle.)

• *Between statues of two of the giants of Spanish royal history (Isabel and Ferdinand), you'll enter the...*

MADRID

⑯ Royal Chapel

This huge domed chapel is best known among Spaniards as the place for royal funerals. When a monarch dies, the royal coffin lies in state here before making the sad trip to El Escorial to join the rest of Spain's past royalty (see next chapter). The glass coffin straight ahead contains the entire body of St. Felix, given to the Spanish king by the pope in the 19th century. Note the glassed-in "crying room" to the left for royal babies. While the royals rarely worship here (they prefer the cathedral adjacent to the palace), the thrones are here just in case.

• *Continue around the courtyard, then pass through the green* ⑰ *Queen's Boudoir—where royal ladies hung out—and into the...*

⑱ Stradivarius Room

Of all the instruments made by the renowned Italian violin maker Antonius Stradivarius (1644-1737), only 300 survive. This is the world's best collection and the only matching quartet set: two violins, a viola, and a cello. Charles III, a cultured man, fiddled around with these. Today, a single Stradivarius instrument might sell for $15 million.

• *The next room (on the left) is the...*

⑲ Crown Room

This room is kind of like the palace's "crown jewels" sanctuary. It displays the precious objects related to the long tradition of crowning a new monarch. In the middle of the room is the scepter of the last Spanish king of the Habsburg family, Charles II, from the 17th century. Alongside is the stunning crown of Charles III, from the succeeding (and current) dynasty, the Bourbons. There's a lion-footed chair, one of Charles III's thrones. Nearby is a golden necklace of the Order of the Golden Fleece, an exclusive club of European royalty (to which all Spanish monarchs belong) that dates back to medieval times. Many of these venerable objects are brought out whenever a new monarch is proclaimed, but today's constitutional monarchs don't go through an elaborate coronation ceremony or don a crown.

There are also more recent royal symbols, such as Juan Carlos I's wooden military baton (a traditional symbol of royal power). There's the 2014 proclamation from when Juan Carlos abdicated, and another from when Felipe VI accepted. Notice which writing implement each man chose to sign with: Juan Carlos' traditional classic pen and Felipe VI's modern one. The fine inlaid marble table in this room was used when King Juan Carlos signed the treaty finalizing Spain's entry into the European Union in 1985.

• *Walk back through the Stradivarius Room and into the courtyard hallway, passing the skippable Stucco Room. Cross over the top of the Grand Stairs, then continue your visit in the blue-wallpapered...*

MADRID

⑳ Official Antechamber

Here, amid royal portraits, ambassadors would wait for their big moment when they met the king in the (upcoming) Throne Room. Tiepolo's ceiling fresco, of Jason returning with the Golden Fleece, would remind them of the exclusive company the Spanish monarch kept, as a Knight of the Golden Fleece. Notice Tiepolo's skill at creating a seemingly three-dimensional space with a two-dimensional painting. He makes a castle tower seem to tower upward, and a trumpeting angel flies directly away from us.

• *After waiting here, the anticipation would build as ambassadors were called into the next room, the red-wallpapered...*

㉑ Official Waiting Room

Here dignitaries would have to wait a bit longer—awed by the rich tapestries, paintings, and Tiepolo's reverent ceiling fresco of the Spanish monarchy. It depicts Spain as a woman in white (with her lion and castle symbols), being crowned by wing-footed Mercury and adored by the gods, while an angel plunges dramatically downward. Even today, officials are received in this room by royalty for an official photo op to remember their big moment.

• *And now we've reached the grand finale, as you finally enter the...*

㉒ Throne Room

This room, where the Spanish monarchs preside, is one of the palace's most glorious.

The throne stands under a gilded canopy, on a raised platform, guarded by four lions (symbols of power found throughout the palace). The coat of arms above the throne shows the complexity of the Spanish empire across Europe—which, in the early 18th century, included Naples, Sicily, parts of the Netherlands, and more. Though the room was decorated under Charles III (late 18th century), the throne itself dates only from 2014. Traditionally, a new throne is built for each king or queen, complete with a gilded portrait on the back. Felipe VI decided to keep things simple, so his throne has only a crown.

Today, this room is where the king's guests salute him before they move on to state dinners. He receives them relatively informally...standing at floor level, rather than seated up on the throne.

The room holds many of the oldest and most precious things in the palace: silver-and-crystal chandeliers (from Venice's Murano Island), elaborate lions, and black bronze statues from the fortress that stood here before the 1734 fire. The 12 mirrors, impressively large in their day, each represent a different month.

The ceiling fresco (1764) is the last great work by Tiepolo, who died in Madrid in 1770. His massive painting (88 feet by 32 feet) celebrates the vast Spanish empire—upon which the sun also never set. The Greek gods look down from the clouds, overseeing Spain's

empire, whose territories are represented by the people and exotic animals ringing the edges of the ceiling. Follow the rainbow to the macho red-caped conquistador who motions toward the big bale of booty and the people he's conquered—feather-wearing Native Americans.

Admire Tiepolo's skill: At the far end of the room, he makes a pillar seem to shoot straight up into the sky. The pillar's pedestal has an inscription celebrating Tiepolo's boss, Charles III ("Carole Magna"). Notice how the painting spills over the gilded wood frame, where 3-D statues recline alongside 2-D painted figures. A woman's painted robe spills over the edge to become a hem made of stucco. Two fish have 2-D bodies but 3-D tails. All of the throne room's decorations—the fresco, gold garlands, mythological statues, wall medallions—unite in a multimedia extravaganza dedicated to the glory of Spain.

• *Your tour of the palace interior is done. Permission granted to call it a tour. But if you want one more interesting collection, you'll find it back outside. Exit the palace down the same grand stairway you climbed at the start. Cross the big courtyard, heading to the far-right corner to the...*

㉓ Royal Armory

Here you'll find weapons and armor belonging to many great Spanish historical figures. While some of it was for battle, kings also wore armor for royal hunts, sporting events (such as jousting tournaments), and official ceremonies. Much of this armor dates from Habsburg times, before this palace was even built. Circle the big room clockwise.

In the three glass cases on the left, you'll see the oldest pieces in the collection. In the central case (case III) are the shield, sword, belt, and dagger of Boabdil, the last Moorish king, who surrendered Granada in 1492. In case IV, the armor and swords belonged to Boabdil's conqueror, King Ferdinand.

The center of the room is filled with knights in armor on horseback. Many of the pieces belonged to the two great kings who ruled Spain at its 16th-century peak, Charles V (a.k.a. the Holy Roman Emperor) and his son, Philip II.

The long wall on the left displays a full array of Charles V's personal armor. At the far end, the mannequin of Charles on horseback wears the same armor and assumes the same pose as in Titian's famous painting of him (in the Prado).

The opposite wall showcases the armor and weapons of Philip II, the king who impoverished Spain with his wars against the Protestants, beginning the country's downward slide. Philip anticipated that debt collectors would ransack his estate after his death and specifically protected his impressive collection of armor by founding this armory.

The tapestries above the armor once warmed the walls of the otherwise stark palace that predated this one. Back when kings had to travel from palace to palace, they packed tapestries to make their home "fit for a king."

Find the stairs near the entrance and head down. You'll see more armor, a mixed collection mostly from the 17th century, plus early guns and Asian armor. The pint-size armor you may see wasn't for children to fight in. Rather, it's training armor for noble youngsters, who as adults would be expected to ride, fight, and play gracefully in these clunky getups. Before you leave, notice the life-saving breastplates dimpled with bullet dents (to right of exit door).

• *Climb the steps from the armory exit to the viewpoint.*

㉔ View of the Gardens

Looking down from this high bluff, it's clear why rulers have built on this strategically located spot since the ninth century. The vast palace backyard, once the king's hunting ground, is now a city park, dotted with fountains. Take in this grand vista, as kings and queens have for centuries, and—at least for a moment—you can feel like the ruler of all you survey.

• *Whew. After all those rooms, frescoes, chandeliers, knickknacks, kings, and history, consider a final stop in the palace's upstairs café for a well-deserved rest.*

BETWEEN THE ROYAL PALACE AND PUERTA DEL SOL

Descalzas Royal Monastery (Monasterio de las Descalzas Reales)

Madrid's most visit-worthy monastery was founded in the 16th century by Philip II's sister, Joan of Habsburg (known to Spaniards as Juana and to Austrians as Joanna). She's buried here. The monastery's chapels are decorated with fine art, Rubens-designed tapestries, and the heirlooms of the wealthy women who joined the order (the nuns were required to give a dowry). Because this is still a working Franciscan monastery, tourists can enter only when the nuns vacate the cloister, and the number of daily visitors is limited. The scheduled tours often sell out, so buy your ticket right at 10:00 for morning tours or 16:00 for afternoon tours (advance tickets available online, but for Spanish-language tours only; check www.patrimonionacional.es).

Cost and Hours: €6, visits guided in Spanish or English depending on demand, Tue-Sat 10:00-14:00 & 16:00-18:30, Sun 10:00-15:00, closed Mon, last entry one hour before closing, Plaza de las Descalzas Reales 1, near the Ópera Metro stop and just a short walk from Puerta del Sol, +34 914 548 800.

MADRID'S MUSEUM NEIGHBORHOOD

Three great museums, all within a 10-minute walk of one another, cluster in east Madrid. The Prado is Europe's top collection of paintings. The Thyssen-Bornemisza sweeps through European art from old masters to moderns. And the Centro de Arte Reina Sofía has a choice selection of modern art, starring Picasso's famous *Guernica.*

Combo-Ticket: If visiting all three museums, you can skip ticket lines and save a few euros with the **Paseo del Arte** combo-ticket (€32, sold at all three museums and on the Thyssen and Reina Sofía websites, good for a year). To save time, buy it online or at the less-crowded Thyssen or Reina Sofía.

Free Entry: The Prado is free to enter every evening, the Thyssen-Bornemisza's permanent collection is free on Monday afternoons, and the Reina Sofía has free hours daily except Tuesday (when it's closed).

▲▲▲Prado Museum (Museo Nacional del Prado)

With more than 3,000 canvases, including entire rooms of masterpieces by superstar painters, the Prado (PRAH-doh) is my vote for the greatest collection anywhere of paintings by the European masters. Centuries of powerful Spanish kings (and lots of New World gold) funded art from all across Europe, so you'll see first-class works from the Italian Renaissance (Raphael, Titian) as well as Northern art (Rubens, Dürer, and Bosch's fantastical *Garden of Earthly Delights*). Mainly, the Prado is *the* place to enjoy the holy trinity of Spanish painters—El Greco, Velázquez, and Goya—including Velázquez's *Las Meninas,* considered by some to be the

world's finest painting, period. Because the Prado is so huge, my tour zeroes in on the "Top Ten" stops (featuring about three dozen paintings in all). Allow at least two hours to speed through these highlights—but many spend three hours or more.

Cost and Hours: €15/1 day, €22/2 days, additional (obligatory) fee for occasional temporary exhibits, free Mon-Sat 18:00-20:00 and Sun 17:00-19:00 (even at free times you must have a physical ticket—save time and get it online in advance), temporary exhibits discounted during free hours, under age 18 always free; open Mon-Sat 10:00-20:00, Sun until 19:00.

Information: +34 913 302 800, www.museodelprado.es.

Crowd-Beating Tips: The only place to buy tickets on-site is the ground level of the Goya Entrance, where ticket-buying lines

Madrid's Museum Neighborhood

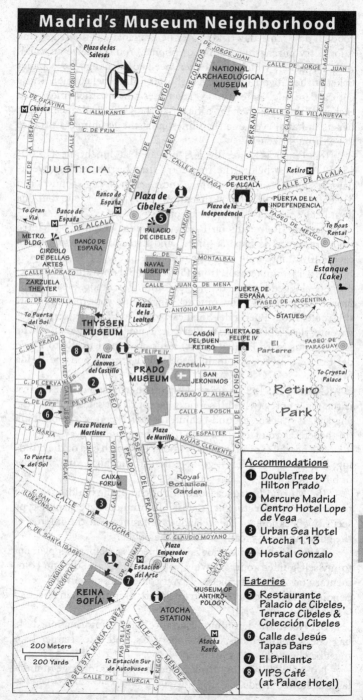

Plaza de las Salesas

NATIONAL ARCHAEOLOGICAL MUSEUM

C. DE JORGE JUAN

CALLE DE JORGE JUAN

CALLE DE LAGASCA

C. DE GRAVINA

Chueca

C. ALMIRANTE

C. DE PRIM

CALLE DEL

CALLE DE LA LIBERTAD

BARQUILLO

CALLE DE CLAUDIO COELLO

CALLE DE CLAUDIO DE VILLANUEVA

CALLE SERRANO

JUSTICIA

PASEO DE RECOLETOS

CALLE B. OLOZAGA

Retiro

CALLE DE ALCALÁ

Banco de España

Plaza de Cibeles

PUERTA DE ALCALÁ

Plaza de la Independencia

PUERTA DE LA INDEPENDENCIA

To Gran Via

METRO. BLDG.

Banco de España

C. DE ALCALÁ

BANCO DE ESPAÑA

PALACIO DE CIBELES

PASEO DE MEXICO

To Boat Rental

CIRCULO DE BELLAS ARTES

CALLE MADRAZO

ZARZUELA THEATER

C. DE ZORRILLA

C. DE MONTALBÁN

NAVAL MUSEUM

CALLE RUIZ DE ALARCÓN

CALLE JUAN DE MENA

CALLE ALFONSO XI

PUERTA DE ESPAÑA

El Estanque (Lake)

To Puerta del Sol

THYSSEN MUSEUM

Plaza de la Lealtad

C. ANTONIO MAURA

PASEO DE ARGENTINA

STATUES

C. DEL PRADO

C. DUQUE D. MEDINACELI

Plaza Cánovas del Castillo

C. FELIPE IV

CASÓN DEL BUEN RETIRO

PUERTA DE FELIPE IV

El Parterre

PASEO DE PARAGUAY

C. DE CERVANTES

CALLE DE VEGA

PRADO MUSEUM

ACADEMIA

SAN JERONIMOS

To Crystal Palace

C. DE LOPE

JESÚS

Plaza Platería Martínez

CASADO D. ALISAL

CALLE A. BOSCH

Retiro

C. S. MARIA

Plaza de Murillo

C. ESPALTER

ROJAS CLEMENTE

CALLE DE ALFONSO XII

Park

To Puerta del Sol

C. FÚCAR

CALLE SAN PEDRO

PASEO DEL PRADO

Royal Botanical Garden

CAIXA FORUM

C. SAN ILDEFONSO

CALLE DE ATOCHA

ALAMEDA

C. DE SANTA ISABEL

C. CLAUDIO MOYANO

Plaza Emperador Carlos V

FOURQUET

C. HOSPITAL

DR. DRUMAN

Estación del Arte

CALLE DR. VELASCO

MUSEUM OF ANTHROPOLOGY

REINA SOFÍA

ATOCHA STATION

Atocha Renfe

200 Meters

200 Yards

PASEO STA MARIA CABEZA

PAS DE LAS DELICIAS

CALLE DE MENDEZ

To Estación Sur de Autobuses

CALLE DE

MURCIA

Accommodations

1 DoubleTree by Hilton Prado

2 Mercure Madrid Centro Hotel Lope de Vega

3 Urban Sea Hotel Atocha 113

4 Hostal Gonzalo

Eateries

5 Restaurante Palacio de Cibeles, Terrace Cibeles & Colección Cibeles

6 Calle de Jesús Tapas Bars

7 El Brillante

8 VIPS Café (at Palace Hotel)

MADRID

can be long. To save time, buy your ticket online in advance (ticket good all day, same-day tickets may be available—if the ticket line is long, try purchasing from your phone). You'll receive an email with a voucher, which you'll then need to exchange for a paper ticket at the Goya Entrance (use shorter online-ticket line). Those with a Paseo del Arte combo-ticket (described earlier) must also exchange their voucher for a ticket at the Goya Entrance. Paper tickets in hand, everyone then lines up at the Jerónimos Entrance to go through security.

The Prado is generally less crowded at lunchtime (13:00-15:00), an hour before the free-entry time begins, and on weekdays. It's busiest on free evenings and weekends. Big spenders can pay €50 for a one-day ticket that allows entry with a group tour one hour before the museum officially opens.

Getting There: It's on Paseo del Prado. The nearest **Metro** stops are Banco de España (line 2) and Estación del Arte (line 1), each a 10-minute walk from the museum.

It's a 15-minute **walk** from Puerta del Sol on traffic-and-pick-pockets-clogged Carrera de San Jerónimo. For a more pleasant approach (which takes a few minutes longer), use your map to follow this route: From Puerta del Sol, head south to Plaza de Jacinto Benavente, then a block east, to Plaza del Ángel. From here, Calle de Las Huertas (with limited traffic) leads characteristically to Paseo del Prado, between the main Jerónimos Entrance and the Reina Sofía.

Getting In: The **Jerónimos Entrance,** where our tour begins, is the main entry (with all services except ticket sales/voucher exchange). It's tucked around behind the north end of the building (to the left, as you face the Prado from the main road).

The nearby **Goya Entrance,** also at the north end of the building, has the ticket office—go here first to exchange your voucher or buy a ticket.

The Murillo Entrance (south/right end of the building, as you face it) is mostly for student groups. All entrances have airport-type security checkpoints. The Velázquez Entrance—in the middle of the building—is typically closed to the public.

Tours: If the audioguide is available, it's a helpful supplement to my self-guided tour, allowing you to wander and dial up commentary on 250 masterpieces as you come across them (€4-6 depending on if there's a temporary exhibit). Skip the Prado's Second Canvas app.

Services: The Jerónimos Entrance has an information desk, bag check, audioguides, bookshop, WCs, and café. Larger bags must be checked.

No-no's: No photos, drinks, food, backpacks, or large umbrellas are allowed inside.

Cuisine Art: The museum's self-service **$ cafeteria/restaurant** is just inside the Jerónimos Entrance (Mon-Sat 10:00-19:30, Sun until 18:30, hot dishes served only 12:30-16:00). Across the street from the Goya Entrance, you'll find **$$ VIPS,** a popular but characterless chain restaurant, handy for a cheap and filling salad or sandwich, with some outdoor tables facing the Neptune fountain (daily 9:00-24:00, across the boulevard from northern end of Prado at Plaza de Canova del Castillo, under Palace Hotel). Next door is Spain's first Starbucks, opened in 2001. A strip of wonderful **$$ tapas bars** is just a few blocks west of the museum, lining Calle de Jésús (see page 496).

➲ Self-Guided Tour

Thanks to Gene Openshaw for writing the following tour.

The vast Prado Museum sprawls over four floors. This tour is designed to hit the highlights with a minimum of walking and in a (roughly) chronological way. We'll see altarpieces of early religious art, the rise of realism in the Renaissance, the royal art of Spain's golden age, and the slow decline of Spain—bringing us right up to the cusp of the modern world.

Paintings are moved around frequently, and rooms may be renumbered—if you can't find a particular work, ask a guard or at information desks.

• *Enter at the Jerónimos Entrance. Pick up a museum map—you'll need it. Locate where you are on the map—on Level 0, at the Jerónimos Entrance. Our first stop should be nearby, in Room 56A.*

To get there, find the corridor (near the security checkpoint) to the Edificio Villanueva. *Head down the corridor about 30 yards and turn right into Room 55, then immediately right again (into 55A), then left into Room 56A. Let's kick off this tour of artistic delights with a large three-panel painting of* The Garden of Earthly Delights.

❶ Hieronymus Bosch

In his cryptic triptych ***The Garden of Earthly Delights*** (*El Jardín de las Delicias,* c. 1505), the early Flemish painter Bosch (c. 1450-1516) paints a wonderland of eye-pleasing details. The message is that the pleasures of life are fleeting, and we'd better avoid them or we'll wind up in hell. Take your time here to unpack this dense masterpiece.

This altarpiece has a central scene and two hinged outer panels. All the images work together to teach a religious message. Imagine the altarpiece closed (showing the back side). The world is gray and bare, before God's creation. Now open it up, bring on the people, and splash into this colorful *Garden of Earthly Delights.*

The left panel is Paradise, showing naked Adam and Eve before original sin. Everything is in its place, with animals behaving

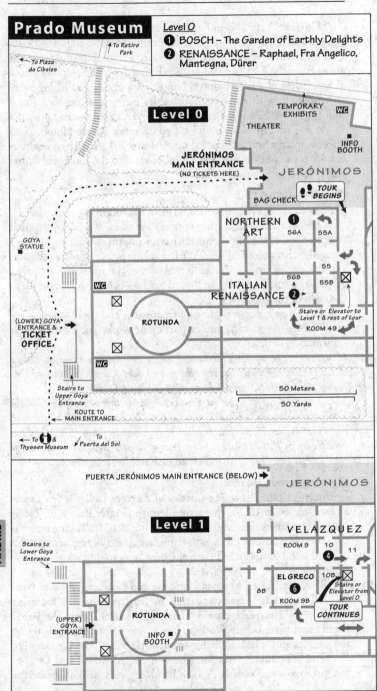

Prado Museum

Level 0
1. BOSCH – The Garden of Earthly Delights
2. RENAISSANCE – Raphael, Fra Angelico, Mantegna, Dürer

Level 0

↑ To Retiro Park

← To Plaza de Cibeles

TEMPORARY EXHIBITS
THEATER
WC
INFO BOOTH

JERÓNIMOS MAIN ENTRANCE
(NO TICKETS HERE) →

JERÓNIMOS

BAG CHECK

TOUR BEGINS

NORTHERN ART ❶ 56A 55A

GOYA STATUE

ITALIAN RENAISSANCE ❷ 56B 55B 55

WC

Stairs or Elevator to Level 1 & rest of tour

ROOM 49

(LOWER) GOYA ENTRANCE & TICKET OFFICE.

ROTUNDA

WC

50 Meters
50 Yards

Stairs to Upper Goya Entrance

ROUTE TO MAIN ENTRANCE

← To 🛈 & Thyssen Museum

↙ To Puerta del Sol

PUERTA JERÓNIMOS MAIN ENTRANCE (BELOW) →

JERÓNIMOS

Level 1

VELAZQUEZ

Stairs to Lower Goya Entrance

8 ROOM 9 10 ❹ 11

EL GRECO ❻ 10B

Stairs or Elevator from Level 0

8B

ROOM 9B

TOUR CONTINUES

(UPPER) GOYA ENTRANCE →

ROTUNDA

INFO BOOTH

MADRID

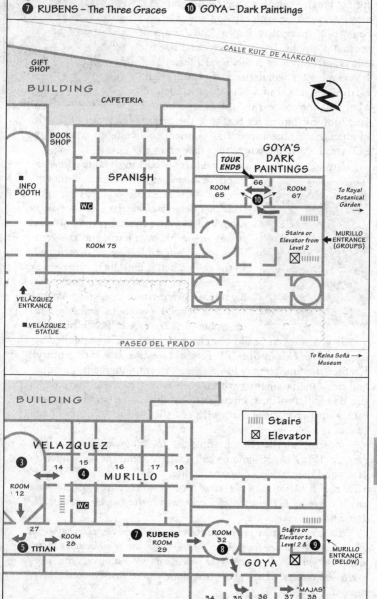

Level 1
3 VELÁZQUEZ – Las Meninas
4 More Velázquez
5 TITIAN – Court Paintings
6 EL GRECO – Various Works
7 RUBENS – The Three Graces

8 GOYA – The Family of Charles IV;
Nude Maja & Clothed Maja
9 GOYA – Tapestry Cartoons
(upstairs on Level 2)
Level 0
10 GOYA – Dark Paintings

CALLE RUIZ DE ALARCÓN

GIFT SHOP

BUILDING

CAFETERIA

BOOK SHOP

INFO BOOTH

SPANISH

WC

ROOM 75

VELÁZQUEZ ENTRANCE

VELÁZQUEZ STATUE

TOUR ENDS

GOYA'S DARK PAINTINGS

ROOM 65

10

ROOM 67

To Royal Botanical Garden

Stairs or Elevator from Level 2

MURILLO ENTRANCE (GROUPS)

PASEO DEL PRADO

To Reina Sofia → Museum

BUILDING

Stairs
Elevator

VELÁZQUEZ

3

14 15 16 17 18

4

MURILLO

ROOM 12

27

5 TITIAN

ROOM 28

WC

7 RUBENS
ROOM 29

ROOM 32

8

GOYA

Stairs or Elevator to Level 2 & 9

MURILLO ENTRANCE (BELOW)

34 35 36 37 "MAJAS" 38

MADRID

virtuously. Innocent Adam and Eve get married, with God himself performing the ceremony.

The central panel is a riot of naked men and women, black and white, on a perpetual spring break—eating exotic fruits, dancing, kissing, cavorting with strange animals, and contorting themselves into a *Kama Sutra* of sensual positions. In the background rise the fantastical towers of a medieval Disneyland. It's seemingly a wonderland of pleasures and earthly delights. But where does it all lead? Men on horseback ride round and round, searching for but never reaching the elusive Fountain of Youth. Humankind frolics in earth's "Garden," oblivious to where they came from (left) and where they may end up...

Now, go to hell (right panel). It's a burning Dante's *Inferno*-

inspired wasteland where genetic-mutant demons torture sinners. Everyone gets their just desserts, like the glutton who is eaten and re-eaten eternally, the musician strung up on his own harp, and the gamblers with their table forever overturned. In the center, hell is literally frozen over. A creature with a broken eggshell body hosting a tavern, tree-trunk legs, and a hat featuring a bagpipe (symbolic of hedonism) stares out—it's the face of Bosch himself.

If you want more Bosch, check out the nearby table featuring his **Seven Deadly Sins** (*Los Pecados Capitales*, late 15th century). Each of the four corners has a theme: death, judgment, paradise, and hell. The fascinating wheel, with Christ in the center, names the sins in Latin (lust, envy, gluttony, and so on), and illustrates each with a vivid scene that works as a slice of 15th-century Dutch life.

Nearby, another Bosch triptych, **The Haywain** (*El Carro de Heno*, c. 1516), has still more vivid imagery about the consequences of sin and the transience of earthly life.

• *The clock is ticking to see the rest of this museum's delights, so let's move on. We're going to the source of European painting as we know it: the Italian Renaissance.*

Backtrack the way you came. Reaching the corridor, turn right and go past the elevators (remember them—we'll use the elevators later). About 30 yards along, turn right into Room 49—a large, long, sage-green hall labeled XLIX *above the door you've just entered. You've reached...*

❷ The Renaissance

During its golden age (the 1500s), Spain may have been Europe's richest country, but Italy was still the most cultured. Spain's kings loved how Italian Renaissance artists captured a three-dimensional world on a two-dimensional canvas, bringing Bible scenes to life and celebrating real people and their emotions.

• *Start midway down Room 49, on the right-hand wall, with a guy in red painted by Raphael.*

Raphael (1483-1520) was the undisputed master of realism. When he painted *Portrait of a Cardinal* (*El Cardenal*, c. 1510-11), he showed the sly Vatican functionary with a day's growth of beard and an air of superiority, locking eyes with the viewer. The cardinal's slightly turned torso is as big as a statue. Nearby are several versions of *Holy Family* and other paintings by Raphael.

• *Now climb the four stairs in the middle of the room, up to Room 56B.*

Fra Angelico's *The Annunciation* (*La Anunciación*, c. 1426) is half medieval piety, half Renaissance realism. In the crude Garden of Eden scene (on the left), a scrawny, sinful First Couple hovers unrealistically above the foliage, awaiting eviction. The angel's Annunciation to Mary (right side) is more Renaissance, both with its upbeat message (that Jesus will be born to redeem sinners like Adam and Eve) and in the budding photorealism, set beneath 3-D arches. (Still, aren't the receding bars of the porch's ceiling a bit off? Painting three dimensions wasn't that easy.)

Also in Room 56B, the tiny *Death of the Virgin (El Tránsito de la Virgen;* also known as *The Dormition of the Virgin)*, by **Andrea Mantegna** (c. 1431-1506), shows his mastery of Renaissance perspective. The apostles crowd into the room to mourn the last moments of the Virgin Mary's life. The receding floor tiles and open window in the back create the subconscious effect of Mary's soul finding its way out into the serene distance.

• *To see how the Italian Renaissance spread to northern lands, step into the adjoining Room 55B (to the left, as you face the main hall).*

Albrecht Dürer's *Self-Portrait (Autorretrato)*, from 1498, is possibly the first time an artist depicted himself. The

MADRID

artist, age 26, is German, but he's all dolled up in a fancy Italian hat and permed hair. He'd recently returned from Italy and wanted to impress his countrymen with his sophistication. Dürer (1471-1528) wasn't simply vain. He'd grown accustomed, as an artist in Renaissance Italy, to being treated like a prince. Note Dürer's signature, the pyramid-shaped "A. D." (D inside the A), on the windowsill.

Nearby are Dürer's 1507 panel paintings of *Adam* and *Eve*—the first full-size nudes in Northern European art. Like Greek statues, they pose in their separate niches, with three-dimensional, anatomically correct bodies. This was a bold humanist proclamation that the body is good, man is good, and the things of the world are good.

• *The down-to-earth realism of Renaissance art soon spread to Europe's richest country—Spain.*

Backtrack down the four steps into Room 49, and make a U-turn to the left, to reach those elevators we saw earlier. Take the elevator up to level 1 and turn left into Room 11. A painting here (by Velázquez) of a radiant Apollo surprising the cuckold Vulcan and a gang of startled workmen introduces us to the main feature of Spanish art—unflinching realism.

Let's begin next door, in the large, lozenge-shaped Room 12.

❸ Velázquez, *Las Meninas*

Diego Velázquez (vel-LAHTH-keth, 1599-1660) was the photojournalist of court painters, capturing the Spanish king and his court in formal portraits that take on aspects of a candid snapshot. Room 12 is filled with the portraits Velázquez was called on to produce. Kings and princes prance like Roman emperors. Get up close and notice that his remarkably detailed costumes are nothing but a few messy splotches of paint—the proto-Impressionism Velázquez helped pioneer.

The room's centerpiece, and perhaps the most important painting in the museum, is Velázquez's *Las Meninas* (Maids of Honor,

c. 1656). It's a peek at nannies caring for Princess Margarita and, at the same time, a behind-the-scenes look at Velázquez at work. One hot summer day in 1656, Velázquez (at left, with paintbrush and Dalí moustache) stands at his easel and stares out at the people he's painting—the king and queen. They would have been standing about where  we are, and we see only their reflection in the mirror at the back of the room. Their daughter (blonde hair, in center) watches her par-

ents being painted, joined by her servants *(meninas)*, dwarves, and the family dog. At that very moment, a man happens to pass by the doorway at back and pauses to look in. Why's he there? Probably just to give the painting more depth.

This frozen moment is lit by the window on the right, splitting the room into bright and shaded planes that recede into the distance. The main characters look right at us, making us part of the scene, seemingly able to walk around, behind, and among the characters. Notice the exquisitely painted mastiff—annoyed by the little girl, but staying put...for now.

If you stand in the center of the room, the 3-D effect is most striking. This is art come to life.

• *Let's see more of Velázquez, whose work covers a wide range of subjects and emotions. Facing this painting, leave to the left, pass through Room 11, and enter Room 10.*

❹ More Velázquez

Velázquez enjoyed capturing light—and capturing the moment. *The Feast of Bacchus* (*Los Borrachos*, c. 1628-29) is a group selfie in a blue-collar bar. A couple of peasants mug for a photo-op with a Greek god—Bacchus, the god of wine. This was an early work, before Velázquez got his court-painter gig, and shows off his admiration for "real" people. Hardworking farmers enjoying the fruit of their labor deserved portraits, too. Notice the almost-sacramental presence of the ultrarealistic bowl of wine in the center, as Bacchus, with the honest gut, crowns a fellow hedonist.

• *Backtrack through the big gallery with* Las Meninas, *and continue straight ahead into Room 14.*

Velázquez's boss, King Philip IV, had an affair, got caught, and repented by commissioning *The Crucified Christ* (*Cristo Crucificado*, c. 1632). Christ hangs his head, humbly accepting his punishment. Philip would have been left to stare at the slowly dripping blood, contemplating how long Christ had to suffer to atone for Philip's sins. This is an interesting death scene. There's no anguish, no tension, no torture. Light seems to emanate from Jesus as if nothing else matters. The crown of thorns and the cloth wrapped around his waist are particularly vivid. Above it all, a sign reads in three languages: *"Jesus of Nazareth, King of the Jews."*

• *Continue on through Room 15 (with Velázquez's insightful portraits of the royal court dwarves) and detour into Rooms 16 and 17.*

Take a moment to appreciate these paintings by one of Velázquez's admirers: Bartolomé Murillo. **Murillo** (1618-1682) soaked up Velazquez's unflinching photorealism, but added a spoonful of sugar. In his most famous works—called *The Immaculate Conception*—Murillo put a human face on the abstract Catholic doctrine that Mary was conceived and born free of original sin. His "immaculate" virgins float in a cloud of Ivory Soap cleanliness, radiating youth and wholesome goodness. Mary wears her usual colors—white for purity and blue for divinity. (For more on Murillo, see page 694.) Murillo's sweet and escapist work must have been very comforting to the wretched people of his hometown of Sevilla, which was ravaged by plague in 1647-1652.

• *Backtrack to the* Meninas *room (12) and turn left. You'll exit into the museum's looooong grand gallery (Rooms 25-29) and come face-to-face with a large canvas of a knight on horseback.*

❺ Titian's Court Paintings

Spain's golden age kings Charles V and Philip II both hired Europe's premier painter—Titian the Venetian (c. 1485-1576)—to paint their portraits.

In *The Emperor Charles V at Mühlberg* (*Carlos V en la Batalla de Mühlberg*, 1548), the king rears on his horse, points his lance at a jaunty angle, and rides out to crush an army of Lutherans. Charles, having inherited many kingdoms and baronies through his family connections, was the world's most powerful man in the 1500s. (You can see the suit of armor depicted in the painting in the Royal Palace.)

In contrast (just to the right), Charles I's son, *Philip II* (*Felipe II*, c. 1550-1551), looks pale, suspicious, and lonely—a scholarly and complex figure. He moved Spain's capital from Toledo to Madrid and built the austere, monastic palace at El Escorial. These are the faces of the Counter-Reformation, as Spain took the lead in battling Protestants. Father and son had one thing in common: underbites, a product of royal inbreeding (which Titian painted... delicately).

• *The ultra-Catholic Philip II amassed a surprisingly large collection of Titian's Renaissance playmates, which you could seek out elsewhere on this floor. But let's turn to a quite different painter that Philip hired—El Greco.*

Facing Charles and Philip, turn right, walk about 30 yards, and turn right at the first door, into Room 9B.

❻ El Greco

El Greco (1541-1614) was born in Greece (his name is Spanish for "The Greek"), trained in Venice, then settled in Toledo—60 miles

MADRID

from Madrid. His paintings are like Byzantine icons drenched in Venetian color and fused in the fires of Spanish mysticism. (For more on El Greco, see page 585.) The El Greco paintings displayed here in Rooms 8B, 9B, and 10B rotate, but they all glow with his unique style.

In *Christ Carrying the Cross* (*Cristo Abrazado a la Cruz*, c. 1602), Jesus accepts his fate, trudging toward death with blood running down his neck. He hugs the cross and directs his gaze along the crossbar. His upturned eyes (sparkling with a streak of white paint) lock onto his next stop—heaven.

The Adoration of the Shepherds (*La Adoración de los Pastores*, c. 1614), originally painted for El Greco's own burial chapel in Toledo, has the artist's typical two-tiered composition—heaven above, earth below. The long, skinny shepherds are stretched unnaturally in between, flickering like flames toward heaven.

El Greco's portraits of Spanish nobles and saints (such as *The Nobleman with His Hand on His Chest*, *El Caballero de la Mano al Pecho*, c. 1580) focus on their aristocratic expressions. A man's hand with his fingers splayed out, but with the middle fingers touching, was El Greco's trademark way of expressing elegance (or was it the 16th-century symbol for "Live long and prosper"?). Though the identity of the nobleman is unknown, some have suggested it's El Greco himself. Several paintings have El Greco's signature written in faint Greek letters—"Doménikos Theotokópoulos," El Greco's real name.

• *While El Greco was painting austere Christian saints, other European artists were painting sensual Greek gods, in a dramatic new style—Baroque.*

Return to the main gallery, turn left, pass by Charles and Philip again, and proceed to the gallery's far end (technically Rooms 28 and 29) for the large, colorful, fleshy canvases by...

MADRID

❼ Rubens

A native of Flanders, Peter Paul Rubens (1577-1640) painted Baroque-style art meant to play on the emotions, titillate the senses, and carry you away. His paintings surge with Baroque energy and ripple with waves of figures. Surveying his big, boisterous

canvases, you'll notice his trademarks: sex, violence, action, emotion, bright colors, and ample bodies, with the wind machine set on full. Gods are melodramatic, and nymphs flee half-human predators. Rubens painted the most beautiful women of his day—well-fed, no tan lines, squirt-gun breasts, and very sexy.

Rubens' *The Three Graces* (*Las Tres Gracias*, c. 1630-1635) celebrates cellulite. The ample, glowing bodies intertwine as the women exchange meaningful glances. The Grace at the left is Rubens' young second wife, Hélène Fourment, who shows up regularly in his paintings.

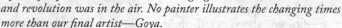

• *Rubens, El Greco, Titian, and Velázquez had all made their living working for Europe's royalty. But that world was changing, and revolution was in the air. No painter illustrates the changing times more than our final artist—Goya.*

From Rubens, continue to the end of the long main gallery and enter the round Room 32, where you'll see royal portraits by Goya.

❽ Goya—Court Painter

Follow the complex Francisco de Goya (1746-1828) through the stages of his life—from dutiful court painter, to political rebel and scandal maker, to the disillusioned genius of his "black paintings." The museum's exciting Goya collection is displayed on three different levels: classic Goya on this level; early cartoons upstairs; and his dark and political work downstairs.

In the group portrait *The Family of Charles IV* (*La Familia de Carlos IV*, 1800), the royals are all decked out in their Sunday best. Goya himself stands at his easel to the far left, painting the court (a tribute to Velázquez in *Las Meninas*) and revealing the shallowness beneath the fancy trappings. Charles, with his ridiculous hairpiece and goofy smile, was a vacuous, henpecked husband. His toothless yet domineering queen upstages him, arrogantly stretching her swan-like neck. The other adults, with their bland faces, are bug-eyed with stupidity.

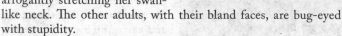

Surrounding you in this same room are other portraits of the king and queen. Also notice the sketch paintings, quick studies

done with the subjects posing for Goya. He used these for reference to complete his larger, more finished canvases.

• *Exit to the right across a small hallway, turn left, and walk through to Room 38, where you'll find Goya's most scandalous works.*

Rumors flew that Goya was fooling around with the vivacious Duchess of Alba, who may have been the model for two

similar paintings, **Nude Maja** (*La Maja Desnuda*, c. 1800) and **Clothed Maja** (*La Maja Vestida*, c. 1808). A *maja* was a trendy, working-class girl. Whether she's a duchess or a *maja*, Goya painted a naked lady—an actual person rather than some mythic Venus. And that was enough to risk incurring the wrath of the Inquisition. The nude stretches in a Titian-esque pose to display her charms, the pale body with realistic pubic hair highlighted by cool green sheets. (Notice the artist's skillful rendering of the transparent fabric on the pillow.) According to a believable legend, the two paintings were displayed in a double frame, with the *Clothed Maja* sliding over the front to hide the *Nude Maja* from Inquisitive minds.

• *Just off Room 37, you'll find an elevator and a staircase (farther down the hall). Use one of them to head up to level 2, to Rooms 85-87 and 90-94, for more Goya.*

❾ Goya—Tapestry Cartoons

These rooms display Goya's designs for tapestries (known as "cartoons") for nobles' palaces. Dressed in their gay "Goya-style" at-

tire, nobles picnic, dance, fly kites, play paddleball and Blind Man's Bluff, or just relax in the sun—as in the well-known **The Parasol** (*El Quitasol*, Room 86). It's clear that, while revolution was brewing in America and France, Spain's lords and ladies were playing, blissfully ignorant of the changing times.

• *Goya's later paintings took on a darker edge. To see them, take the stairs or elevator down to level 0. From the stairs, take a right into Room 66; from the elevator, go up and down the stairs (across the Murillo Entrance) to Room 66. Entering, start to the left, in Room 65, with powerful military scenes.*

⑩ Goya—Dark Paintings

Despite working for Spain's monarchs, Goya became a political liberal and a champion of the Revolution in France. But that idealism was soon crushed when the supposed hero of the Revolution, Napoleon, morphed into a tyrant and invaded Spain. Goya, who lived on Madrid's Puerta del Sol, captured the chaotic events that unfolded there.

In *The Second of May, 1808* (*El 2 de Mayo de 1808*, 1814), Madrid's citizens rise up to protest the occupation in Puerta del Sol, and the French send in their dreaded Egyptian mercenaries.

They plow through the dense tangle of Madrileños, who have nowhere to run. The next day, *The Third of May, 1808* (*El 3 de Mayo de 1808*, 1814), the French rounded up ringleaders and executed them. The colorless firing squad—a faceless machine of death—mows them down, and they fall in bloody, tangled heaps. Goya throws a harsh prison-yard floodlight on the main victim, who spreads his arms Christ-like to ask, "Why?"

Politically, Goya was split—he was a Spaniard, but he knew France was leading Europe into the modern age. His art, while political, has no Spanish or French flags. It's a universal comment on the horror of war. Many consider Goya the last classical and first modern painter...the first painter with a social conscience.

• *Finish the tour with Goya's final, late-in-life paintings. Turn about-face to the "black paintings" in Room 67.*

Depressed and deaf from syphilis, Goya retired to his small home and smeared its walls with his **"black paintings"**—dark in color and in mood. During this period in his life, Goya would paint his nightmares...literally. The style is considered Romantic—emphasizing emotion over beauty—but it foreshadows 20th-century Surrealism with its bizarre imagery, expressionistic and thick brushstrokes, and cynical outlook.

Stepping into Room 67, you are surrounded by art from Goya's dark period. These paintings are the actual murals from the walls of his house, transferred onto canvas. Imagine this in your living room. Goya painted what he felt with a radical technique unburdened by reality—a century before his time. And he painted without being paid for it—perhaps the first great paintings done not for hire or for sale. We know frustratingly little about these works because Goya wrote nothing about them.

Dark forces convened continually in Goya's dining room, where *The Great He-Goat* (*El Aquelarre/El Gran Cabrón*, c. 1820-

MADRID

1823) hung. The witches, who look like skeletons, swirl in a frenzy around a dark, Satanic goat in monk's clothing who presides over the obscene rituals. The black goat represents the devil and stokes the frenzy of his wild-eyed subjects. Amid this adoration and lust, a noble lady (far right) folds her hands primly in her lap ("I thought this was a Tupperware party!"). Or, perhaps it's a pep rally for her execution, maybe inspired by the chaos that accompanied Plaza Mayor executions. Nobody knows for sure.

In *Fight to the Death with Clubs* (*Duelo a Garrotazos*, c. 1820-1823), two giants stand face-to-face, buried up to their knees, and flail at each other with clubs. It's a standoff between superpowers in the never-ending cycle of war.

In *Saturn* (*Saturno,* c. 1820-1823), fearful that his progeny would overthrow him, the god eats one of his offspring. Saturn, also known as Kronus (*Chronus,* or time), may symbolize how time devours us all. Either way, the painting brings new meaning to the term "child's portion."

The Drowning Dog (*Perro Semihundido,* c. 1820-1823) is, according to some, the hinge between classical art and modern art. The dog, so full of feeling and sadness, is being swallowed by quicksand...much as, to Goya, the modern age was overtaking a more classical era. And look closely at the dog. It also can be seen as a turning point for Goya. Perhaps he's bottomed out—he's been overwhelmed by depression, but his spirit has survived. With the portrait of this dog, color is returning.

• *Keep that hope alive for one more painting. Head back to Room 65 or 66 and look for the portrait of a seated young woman gazing downward.*

The last painting we have by Goya is *The Milkmaid of Bordeaux* (*La Lechera de Burdeos,* c. 1827). Somehow, Goya pulled out of his depression and moved to France, where he lived until his death at 82. As an old man, color returned to his palette. His social commentary, his passion for painting what he felt (more than what he was hired to do), and, as you see here, the freedom of his brushstrokes explain why many consider Francesco de Goya to be the first modern artist. This is a good place to reflect on all we've seen in the Prado. Goya combined the vivid imagination of Bosch, Renaissance techniques, the sober realism of Velázquez, and the emotion of El Greco to pave the way to the future of art.

• *There's a lot more to the Prado, but there's also a lot more to Madrid. For a nature break from all this art, exit through the Jeronimo Entrance*

MADRID

(where you came in), walk to the other end of the museum building, and you'll reach the delightful Royal Botanical Garden, described next.

▲Royal Botanical Garden (Real Jardín Botánico)

After your Prado visit, you can take a lush and fragrant break in this sculpted park. Wander among trees from around the world, originally gathered by—who else?—the enlightened King Charles III. This garden was established when the Prado's building housed the natural science museum. A flier in English explains that this is actually more than a park—it's a museum of plants.

Cost and Hours: €6, free Tue from 14:00; open daily May-Aug 10:00-21:00, April and Sept until 20:00, shorter hours off-season; entrance opposite the Prado's Murillo/south entry, Plaza de Murillo 2, +34 914 203 017.

▲▲Thyssen-Bornemisza Museum (Museo del Arte Thyssen-Bornemisza)

Locals call this stunning museum simply the Thyssen (TEE-sun). It displays the impressive collection that Baron Thyssen (a wealthy German married to a former Miss Spain) sold to Spain for $350 million. The museum offers a unique chance to enjoy the sweep of all of art history—including a good sampling of the "isms" of the 20th century—in one collection. It's basically minor works by major artists and major works by minor art-

ists. (Major works by major artists are in the Prado.) But art lovers appreciate how the good baron's art complements the Prado's collection by filling in where the Prado is weak—such as Impressionism, which is the Thyssen's forte.

Cost and Hours: €13, includes some temporary exhibits (timed ticket may be required), free on Mon; permanent collection open Mon 12:00-16:00, Tue-Sun 10:00-19:00; temporary exhibits open Sat until 21:00; audioguide-€5 for permanent collection, €4 for temporary exhibits, €7 for both; Second Canvas Thyssen is a decent free app that explains major works—use museum's free Wi-Fi to access; +34 917 911 370, www.museothyssen.org.

Getting There: It's located kitty-corner from the Prado at Paseo del Prado 8 in Palacio de Villahermosa (Metro: Banco de España).

Services: The museum has free baggage storage (bags must fit through a small x-ray machine), a cafeteria and restaurant, and a shop/bookstore.

Connecting the Thyssen and Reina Sofía: It's about a 15-minute, slightly downhill walk. You can hail a cab at the gate to zip straight there. Or take bus #27: Catch it in the square with the Neptune fountain in front of the Starbucks, ride to the end of Paseo del Prado, get off at the McDonald's, and cross the street (going away from the Royal Botanical Garden) to reach Plaza Sánchez Bustillo and the museum.

⊘ Self-Guided Tour

After purchasing your ticket, pick up a museum map at the info desk. The museum's permanent collection is divided into the Carmen Thyssen Collection on the ground floor, and the Thyssen Collection on the first and second floors.

Ground Floor: Walk down the wide main hall to see the four larger-than-life paintings of former monarchs Juan Carlos I and Sofía, and the baron (who died in 2002) and his art-collecting baroness, Carmen. Then head to the entrance to the Carmen Thyssen Collection, where you can see the baroness's additions since the 1980s. The works are arranged in chronological order, from the 17th century to the 20th. Carmen Thyssen's collection is intriguing, but don't linger—the Thyssen Collection has the heavyweight artists.

• *Ascend to the second floor and work your way back down, taking a delightful walk through art history. The numbered rooms lead you from Primitive Italian (Room 1) to Surrealism and Pop Art (Rooms 41-43). Here's a breezy stroll that hits the highlights:*

Floor 2: The second floor focuses on the Old Masters of the 17th-19th centuries. Start where Western art did—with religious altarpieces from Italy depicting holy people in the golden realm of heaven (Rooms 1-2). Meanwhile, Flemish painters were discovering oil paints, allowing them to give their Virgin Marys more detail and human tenderness (Room 3). The Italians pioneered 3-D realism, to bring heavenly scenes down into the real world (Room 4).

Turn the corner into the long hallway, featuring portraits of famous Europeans circa 1500, including King Henry VIII (Room 5). Pop into Room 6 for a few fine El Grecos. In Room 12, begin the Baroque with Caravaggio, then turn the corner into Room 13 and pass through the 1600s, a time of very forgettable canvases. In Room 17, look for Canaletto's views of Venice, and find portraits by Rubens in Room 19. As you continue through Rooms 22-28, notice how, while Italians painted myths and goddesses, the practical Dutch enjoyed down-to-earth portraits, group portraits, everyday scenes, landscapes, seascapes, and detailed still-lifes of fruit and flowers. A proud self-portrait by Rembrandt may be on display when you visit. In Room 29, experience Goya's Romanticism.

• *Now go downstairs to...*

Floor 1: On the first floor you will find the Modern Masters, from Impressionism to the 20th century. In the 1800s, the French led the march toward modernism (Room 30). Artists painted in the open air to capture rural landscapes and the working poor with increasing spontaneity.

In Room 31, the movement culminates in Impressionism. The museum has a laudable collection of works by Manet, Monet, and their Impressionist contemporaries, who painted landscapes, Parisian street scenes, a night at the ballet (Degas), or backstage scenes of the Moulin Rouge (Toulouse-Lautrec).

As Impressionism becomes Post-Impressionism, and Expressionism bursts in (Rooms 32-33), note the variety of painters who used Impressionist techniques but with brighter colors, thicker paint, and more furious brushwork. Increasingly, they simplified reality and flattened the 3-D.

Simplified reality led to abstraction, and artists like Kandinsky began creating beautiful patterns of pure line and color (Room 33). The Spaniard Picasso and his Parisian roommate Georges Braque invented Cubism—a revolutionary style many others would imitate (Room 34). As artists increasingly turned away from photorealism, Mondrian experimented with simple rectangular grids of the primary colors—red, yellow, blue—on a white canvas (Room 35).

• *Continue straight down the hall; the numbers skip from 36 to 40.*

Marc Chagall used modern art techniques to create a dreamlike world of weightless lovers and fiddler-on-the-roof villages (Room 40). In Rooms 41-42, we see more varieties of Cubism—including collage, in which artists literally glued things onto the canvas to produce a kind of sculpture—as well as Surrealism and other "isms," explored by Picasso, Dalí, and Miró.

• *Backtrack to room 36, then go left down a hall to Rooms 37-39.*

Here we see how the world wars affected the art world. Artists "expressed" their emotions in big, minimal "abstract" canvases—Abstract Expressionism. Francis Bacon captured the horror of World War II's destruction with his screaming, caged, isolated figures in a barren landscape (Room 39).

• *Whew. That's five centuries of Western Art. Now you're ready for Madrid's museum of modern art, the Reina Sofía.*

▲▲▲Centro de Arte Reina Sofía

Home to Picasso's *Guernica*, the Reina Sofía is one of Europe's most enjoyable modern-art museums. Its exceptional collection of 20th-century art maps the development of Modernism from its origins in the late 19th century until today. The focus is on 20th-century Spanish artists—Picasso, Dalí, Miró, and Gris—but you'll also find works by Kandinsky, Braque, Magritte, and other giants

of modern art. Many works are displayed alongside contemporaneous documents—letters, newspaper clippings, gallery invitations—that place the art into social context. Those with an appetite for modern and contemporary art can spend several delightful hours in this museum.

Cost and Hours: €12 (includes most temporary exhibits); open Mon and Wed-Sat 10:00-21:00, Sun until 14:30, closed Tue.

Free Entry: The museum is free—and often crowded—Mon and Wed-Sat 19:00-21:00 and Sun 12:30-14:30 (must pick up a ticket to enter).

Information: +34 917 741 000, www.museoreinasofia.es.

Getting There: It's a block from the Estación del Arte Metro stop, on Plaza Sánchez Bustillo at Calle de Santa Isabel 52. In the Metro station, follow signs for the Reina Sofía exit. Emerging from the Metro, walk straight ahead a half-block and turn right on Calle de Santa Isabel. The museum is housed in two connected buildings the historic 18th-century Sabatini building and the Nouvel building, added in 2005. You'll see the tall, exterior glass elevators that flank the museum's main entrance.

A second entrance in the newer section of the building sometimes has shorter lines, especially during the museum's free hours. To get there, face the glass elevators and walk left around the old building to the large gates of the red-and-black Nouvel building.

Tours: A "tour" of *Guernica*—a discussion of the painting—is given in English about twice weekly, with no reservation needed but limited spots. Inquire at the information desk for times.

Services: Bag storage is free, but you need a €0.50 or €1 coin to use the locker. You get the coin back when you retrieve your belongings. The *librería* just outside the Nouvel wing has a larger selection of Picasso and Surrealist reproductions than the main gift shop at the entrance.

Cuisine Art: The museum's **$$ café** (a long block around the left from the main entrance) is a standout for its tasty cuisine. The square immediately in front of the museum is ringed by fine places for a simple meal or drink. My favorite is **$$ El Brillante,** a classic dive offering pricey tapas and baguette sandwiches. But everyone comes for the fried squid sandwiches. Sit at the simple bar or at an outdoor table (long hours daily, two entrances—one on Plaza Sánchez Bustillo, the other at Plaza del Emperador Carlos V 8, see the "Madrid's Museum Neighborhood" map, +34 915 286 966). And

just a 10-minute walk north is my favorite strip of **tapas bars,** on Calle de Jesús (see page 496).

Visiting the Museum

The collection is displayed thematically in eight sections (called "episodes"), which can be visited in any order. The museum's curators devised the themes (e.g., "Avant-garde Territories," "Art and the Cold War," "Enclosed Field") for maximum flexibility in the galleries, but visitors might find it hard to know where to start. For most, though, the place to begin is on **level 2** of the Sabatini building, where Pablo Picasso's *Guernica* (1937) is displayed (Room 205.10).

Guernica—**Background:** Perhaps the single most impressive piece of art in Spain, the monumental *Guernica* canvas—one of Europe's must-see sights—is not only a piece of art but a piece of history, capturing the horror of modern war in a modern style.

While it's become a timeless classic representing all war, it was born in response to a specific conflict—the Spanish Civil War (1936-1939), which pitted the democratically elected Second Republican government against the fascist general Francisco Franco. Franco won and ended up ruling Spain with an iron fist for the next 36 years. At the time Franco cemented his power, *Guernica* was touring internationally as part of a fundraiser for the Republican cause. With Spain's political situation deteriorating and World War II looming, Picasso in 1939 named New York's Museum of Modern Art as the depository for the work. It was only after Franco's death, in 1975, that *Guernica* ended its decades of exile. In 1981 the painting finally arrived in Spain (where it had never before been), and it now stands as Spain's national piece of art.

Guernica—**The Bombing:** On April 26, 1937, Guernica—a Basque market town in northern Spain and an important Republican center—was the target of the world's first saturation-bombing raid on civilians. Franco gave permission to his fascist confederate Adolf Hitler to use the town as a guinea pig to try out Germany's new air force. The raid leveled the town, causing destruction that was unheard of at the time (though by 1944, it would be commonplace). For more on the town of Guernica and the bombing, see the Guernica section of the Basque Country chapter.

News of the bombing reached Picasso in Paris, where coincidentally he was just beginning work on a painting commission awarded by the Republican government. Picasso scrapped his earlier plans and immediately set to work sketching scenes of the destruction as he imagined it. In a matter of weeks, he put these bomb-shattered shards together into a large mural (286 square feet). For the first time, the world could see the destructive force of the rising fascist movement—a prelude to World War II.

Guernica—**The Painting:** The bombs are falling, shattering the quiet village. ❶ A woman howls up at the sky (far right), ❷ horses scream (center), and ❸ a man falls from a horse and dies, while ❹ a wounded woman drags herself through the streets. She tries to escape, but her leg is too thick, dragging her down, like trying to run from something in a nightmare. ❺ On the left, a bull—a symbol of Spain—ponders it all, watching over ❻ a mother and her dead baby...a modern pietà. ❼ A woman in the center sticks her head out to see what's going on. The whole scene is lit from above by the ❽ stark light of a bare bulb. Picasso's painting threw a light on the brutality of Hitler and Franco, and suddenly the whole world was watching.

Picasso's abstract, Cubist style reinforces the message. It's as if he'd picked up the shattered shards and pasted them onto a canvas. The black-and-white tones are as gritty as the black-and-white newspaper photos that reported the bombing. The drab colors create a depressing, almost nauseating mood.

Picasso chose images with universal symbolism, making the work a commentary on all wars. Picasso himself said that the central horse, with the spear in its back, symbolizes humanity succumbing to brute force. The fallen rider's arm is severed and his sword is broken, more symbols of defeat. The bull, normally a proud symbol of strength and independence, is impotent and frightened. Between the bull and the horse, the faint dove of peace can do nothing but cry.

The bombing of Guernica—like the entire civil war—was an exercise in brutality. As one side captured a town, it might systematically round up every man, old and young—including priests—line them up, and shoot them in revenge for atrocities by the other side.

Thousands of people attended the Paris exhibition, and *Guernica* caused an immediate sensation. They could see the horror of modern war technology, the vain struggle of the Spanish Republicans, and the cold indifference of the fascist war machine. Picasso

vowed never to return to Spain while Franco ruled (the dictator outlived him).

With each passing year, the canvas seemed more and more prophetic—honoring not just the hundreds or thousands who died in Guernica, but also the estimated 500,000 victims of Spain's bitter civil war and the 55 million worldwide who perished in World War II. Picasso put a human face on what we now call "collateral damage."

More Art on Level 2: After seeing Guernica, browse your way through the rest of level 2 and its rich display of Modern, Cubist, and Surrealist works. You may see early works by young Pablo Picasso and his Paris roommate Georges Braque, as well as a host of Spanish moderns (Salvador Dalí, Juan Gris, and Joan Miró).

NEAR THE PRADO (AND BEYOND)

Several other worthy sights are located in and around the museum neighborhood (see the "Madrid's Museum Neighborhood" map, earlier). This is also where my self-guided bus tour along Paseo de la Castellana to the modern skyscraper part of Madrid starts (see page 481).

▲▲Retiro Park (Parque del Buen Retiro)

Once the private domain of royalty, this majestic park has been a favorite of Madrid's commoners since Charles III decided to share it with his subjects in the late 18th century. Siesta in this 300-acre green-and-breezy escape from the city. At midday on Saturday and Sunday, the area around the lake becomes a street carnival, with jugglers, puppeteers, and lots of local color. These peaceful gardens offer great picnicking and people-watching (closes at

dusk). From the Retiro Metro stop, walk to the big lake (El Estanque), where you can rent a rowboat. Enjoy the 19th-century glass-and-iron Crystal Palace, which often hosts free exhibits and installations. Past the lake, a grand boulevard of statues leads to the Prado.

▲Naval Museum (Museo Naval)

This museum tells the story of Spain's navy, from 1492 to today, in a plush and fascinating-to-boat-lovers exhibit. Given Spain's importance in maritime history, there's quite a story to tell. A good English brochure is available. Access to the Wi-Fi-based English audioguide can be unreliable, but give it a try. This is a military

facility, so you may see people in uniform. Backpacks are not allowed, and no baggage storage is available.

Cost and Hours: €3, Tue-Sun 10:00-19:00, until 15:00 in Aug, closed Mon, a block north of the Prado, across boulevard from Thyssen-Bornemisza Museum, Paseo del Prado 5, +34 915 238 789, http://fundacionmuseonaval.com.

CaixaForum

Across the street from the Prado and Royal Botanical Garden, this impressive exhibit hall has sleek architecture and an outdoor hanging garden—a bushy wall festooned with greens designed by a French landscape artist. The forum, funded by La Caixa Bank, features world-class temporary art exhibits—generally 20th-century art, well described in English. Ride the elevator to the top, where you'll find a café and sperm-like lamps dangling from the ceiling; from here, explore your way down.

Cost and Hours: €6, daily 10:00-20:00, audioguide-€2, Paseo del Prado 36, +34 913 307 300.

Palacio de Cibeles

This former post-office headquarters, now a cultural center and the Madrid City Hall, features mostly empty exhibition halls, an auditorium, and public hangout spaces—and is called the CentroCentro Cibeles for Culture and Citizenship. (Say that five times fast!) Skip the temporary exhibits: The real attraction lies in the gorgeous 360-degree rooftop views from the eighth-floor observation deck (ticket office outside to the right of the main entrance). Visit the recommended sixth-floor Restaurante Palacio de Cibeles and bar for similar views from its two terraces. Entering the Palacio itself is free—take advantage of its air-conditioning and free Wi-Fi.

Cost and Hours: Building free and open Tue-Sun 10:00-20:00, closed Mon; observation deck-€3, limited number of visitors allowed every half-hour 10:30-14:00 & 16:00-19:30, ticket office opens at 10:00 and in afternoon at 15:00, advance tickets available online; Plaza de Cibeles 1, +34 914 800 008, www.centrocentro.org.

▲▲National Archaeological Museum (Museo Arqueológico Nacional/MAN)

This well-curated, rich collection of artifacts and tasteful multimedia displays tells the story of Iberia. You'll follow a chronological walk through the wonders of each age: Celtic pre-Roman, Roman, a fine and rare Visigothic section, Moorish, Romanesque, and beyond. A highlight is the Lady of Elche (Room 13), a prehistoric Iberian female bust and a symbol of Spanish archaeology. You may also find underwhelming replica artwork from northern Spain's Altamira Caves (big on bison), giving you a faded peek at the skill

of the cave artists who created the originals 14,000 years ago. (For more on the real Altamira Caves, see the Camino de Santiago chapter.)

Cost and Hours: €3, free on Sat after 14:00 and all day Sun; open Tue-Sat 9:30-20:00, Sun until 15:00, closed Mon; multimedia guide-€2; 20-minute walk north of the Prado at Calle Serrano 13, Metro: Serrano or Colón, +34 915 777 912, www.man.es.

AWAY FROM THE CENTER

To locate these sights, see the "Greater Madrid" map at the beginning of this chapter.

▲Museum of the Americas (Museo de América)

Thousands of pre-Columbian and colonial artworks and artifacts make up the bulk of this worthwhile museum, though it offers few English explanations. Covering the cultures of the Americas (North and South), its exhibits focus on language, religion, and art, and provide a new perspective on the cultures of our own hemisphere. Highlights include one of only four surviving Mayan codices (ancient books) and a section about the voyages of the Spanish explorers, with their fantastical imaginings of mythical creatures awaiting them in the New World.

Cost and Hours: €3, free on Sun; open Tue-Sat 9:30-15:00, Thu until 19:00, Sun 10:00-15:00, closed Mon; Avenida de los Reyes Católicos 6, Metro: Moncloa, +34 915 492 641, http://museodeamerica.mcu.es.

Getting There: The museum is a 15-minute walk from the Moncloa Metro stop: Take the Calle de Isaac Peral exit, cross Plaza de Moncloa, and veer right to Calle de Fernández de los Ríos. Follow that street (toward the shiny Faro de Moncloa tower), and turn left on Avenida de los Reyes Católicos. Head around the base of the tower, which stands at the museum's entrance.

Clothing Museum (Museo del Traje)

In a cool and air-conditioned chronological sweep, this museum's exhibits illustrate the history of clothing from the 18th century through today. Displays cover regional ethnic costumes, the influence of bullfighting and the French, accessories through the ages, and Spanish flappers. The only downside of this marvelous, modern museum is its remote location.

Cost and Hours: €3, free on Sat after 14:30 and all day Sun; open Tue-Sat 9:30-19:00, Thu until 22:30 in July-Aug, Sun 10:00-15:00, closed Mon; Avenida de Juan Herrera 2; Metro: Moncloa and a longish walk, bus #46, or taxi; +34 915 497 150, http://museodeltraje.mcu.es.

▲Hermitage of San Antonio de la Florida (Ermita de San Antonio de la Florida)

In this simple little Neoclassical chapel from the 1790s, Francisco de Goya's tomb stares up at a splendid cupola filled with his own proto-Impressionist frescoes. He used the same unique technique that he employed for his "black paintings" (described earlier, under the Prado Museum listing). Use the mirrors to enjoy the drama and energy he infused into this marvelously restored masterpiece.

Cost and Hours: Free, Tue-Sun 9:30-20:00, closed Mon, Glorieta de San Antonio de la Florida 5; Metro: Príncipe Pío, then eight-minute walk down Paseo de San Antonio de la Florida; +34 915 420 722, www.esmadrid.com (search for "Ermita de San Antonio de la Florida").

Temple of Debod (Templo de Debod)

In 1968, Egypt gave Spain its own ancient temple. It was a gift of the Egyptian government, which was grateful for the Spanish dictator Franco's help in rescuing monuments that had been threatened by the rising Nile waters above the Aswan Dam. Consequently, Madrid is the only place I can think of in Europe where you can actually wander through an intact original Egyptian temple—complete with fine carved reliefs from 200 BC. Set in a romantic park that locals love for its great city views (especially at sunset), the temple—as well as its art—is well described.

Cost and Hours: Free, open Tue-Fri 10:00-20:00 in summer, shorter hours off-season, closed Mon year-round, north of the Royal Palace in Parque de Montaña, +34 913 667 415, www.esmadrid.com (search for "Templo de Debod").

▲▲Sorolla Museum (Museo Sorolla)

The delightful, art-filled home of painter Joaquín Sorolla (1863-1923) is one of Spain's most enjoyable museums. Sorolla is known for his portraits, landscapes, and use of light. Imagine the mansion, back in 1910, when it stood alone—without the surrounding high-rise buildings. With the aid of the essential audioguide, stroll through his home and studio, zeroing in on whichever painting grabs you. Sorolla captured wonderful slices of life—his wife/muse, his family, and lazy beach scenes of his hometown Valencia. He was a late Impressionist—a period called Luminism in Spain. And it was all about nature: water, light, reflection. The collection is intimate, and you can cap it with a few restful minutes in Sorolla's Andalusian gardens. Visit in the morning to experience the works with the best natural light.

Cost and Hours: €3, free on Sat 14:00-20:00 and all day Sun; open Tue-Sat 9:30-20:00, Sun 10:00-15:00, closed Mon; last entry 45 minutes before closing, General Martínez Campos 37, Metro: Iglesia, +34 913 101 584, www.museosorolla.es.

▲Madrid History Museum (Museo de Historia de Madrid)

This building, a hospital from 1716 to 1910, has housed a city history museum since 1929. The entrance features a fine Baroque door by the architect Pedro de Ribera, with a depiction of St. James the Moor-Slayer. Work your way up through the four-floor collection. The history of Madrid is explained through old paintings that show the city in action, maps, historic fans, jeweled snuffboxes, etchings of early bullfighting, and fascinating late-19th-century photographs.

Don't miss Goya's *Allegory of the City of Madrid* (c. 1810), an angelic tribute to the rebellion against the French on May 2, 1808. The museum is in the trendy Malasaña district, near the Plaza Dos de Mayo, where some of the rebellion that Goya painted occurred.

Cost and Hours: Free, Tue-Sun 10:00-20:00, closed Mon, Calle de Fuencarral 78, Metro: Tribunal, +34 917 011 863, www.esmadrid.com (search for "Museo de Historia").

Experiences in Madrid

▲Self-Guided Bus Tour: Paseo de la Castellana

Many visitors leave Madrid without ever seeing the modern "Manhattan" side of town. But it's easy to find. From the museum neighborhood, bus #27 makes the trip straight north along Paseo del Prado and then Paseo de la Castellana, through the no-nonsense skyscraper part of this city of more than three million. The line ends at the leaning towers of Puerta de Europa (Gate of Europe). This trip is simple and cheap (€1.50 or a single ride on a 10-ride Multi Card ticket, buses run every 10 minutes, see the "Greater Madrid" map at the beginning of this chapter for route). If starting from the Prado, catch the bus from the museum side to head north; from the Reina Sofía, the stop is a couple of blocks away at the Royal Botanical Garden, at the end of the garden fence. You'll joyride for 30-45 minutes to the last stop, get out at the end of the line when everyone else does, ogle the skyscrapers, and catch the Metro for a 20-minute ride back to the city's center (to Puerta del Sol). The ride is particularly enjoyable at twilight, when fountains and facades are floodlit. Possible stops of interest along the way are Plaza de Colon (National Archaeological Museum) and Bernabéu (massive soccer stadium).

Historic District: Bus #27 rumbles from the end of the Paseo del Prado at the Royal Botanical Garden (opposite McDonald's) and the Velázquez entrance to the Prado. Immediately after the Prado you pass a number of grand landmarks: a square with a fountain of Neptune (left); an obelisk and war memorial (right, with the stock market behind it); the Naval Museum (right); and Plaza de Cibeles—with the fancy City Hall and cultural center. From Plaza

de Cibeles, you can see the 18th-century Gate of Alcalá (the old east entry to Madrid), the Bank of Spain, and the start of the Gran Vía (left). Then you can relax for a moment while driving along Paseo de Recoletos.

Modern District: Just past the National Library (right) is a roundabout and square **(Plaza de Colon)** with a statue of Columbus in the middle and a giant Spanish flag. This marks the end of the historic town and the beginning of the modern city. (Hop out here for the National Archaeological Museum.)

At this point the boulevard changes its name (and the sights I mention are much more spread out). Once named for Franco, this street is now named for the people he no longer rules—*la Castellana* (Castilians). Next, you pass high-end apartments and embassies. Immediately after an underpass with several modern sculptures comes the **American Embassy** (right, hidden behind its fortified wall). Near a roundabout with a big fountain, watch on the left for some circa-1940s buildings that once housed Franco's ministries (typical fascist architecture, with large colonnades). You'll pass under a second underpass and see 1980s business sprawl on the left. One of these is the distinctive **Picasso Tower,** resembling one of New York's former World Trade Center towers with its vertical black-and-white stripes (it was designed by the same architect). Just after the Picasso Tower is the huge **Bernabéu Stadium** (right, home of Real Madrid, one of Europe's most successful soccer teams; bus stops on both sides of the stadium).

Your trip ends at **Plaza de Castilla,** where you can't miss the avant-garde Puerta de Europa, consisting of the twin "Torres Kios," office towers that lean at a 15-degree angle (look for the logo designed for the CaixaBank by Joan Miró: a blue star dropping a coin into a piggy bank). In the distance, you can see the five tallest buildings in Madrid. The plaza sports a futuristic golden obelisk by contemporary Spanish architect Santiago Calatrava.

It's the end of the line for the bus—and for you. You can return directly to Puerta del Sol on the Metro, or cross the street and ride bus #27 along the same route back to the Prado Museum or Atocha train station.

▲**Electric Minibus Joyride through the Lavapiés District**
For a relaxing ride through the characteristic old center of Madrid, hop the little electric **minibus #M1** (€1.50, or a single ride on a 10-ride Multi Card ticket, 5/hour, 20-minute trip, Mon-Sat 8:20-20:00, none on Sun). These are designed especially for the difficult-to-access streets in the historic heart of the city, and are handy for seniors (offer your seat if you see a senior standing).

The Route: Catch the minibus near the Sevilla Metro stop at the top of Calle Sevilla, and simply ride it to the end (Metro:

Embajadores). Enjoy this gritty slice of workaday Madrid—both people and architecture—as you roll slowly through Plaza Santa Ana, down a bit of the pedestrianized Calle de las Huertas, past gentrified Plaza Tirso de Molina (its junkies now replaced by a faded family-friendly flower market), and through Plaza de Lavapiés and a barrio of African and Bangladeshi immigrants. Jump out along the way to explore Lavapiés on foot, or stay on until you get to Embajadores just a few blocks away. From there, you can catch the next #M1 minibus back to the Sevilla Metro stop (it returns along a different route) or descend into the subway system (it's just two stops back to Sol).

The Lavapiés District: In the Lavapiés neighborhood, the multiethnic tapestry of Madrid enjoys seedy-yet-fun-loving life on the streets. Neighborhoods like this typically experience the same familiar evolution: Initially they're so cheap that only immigrants, the downtrodden, and counterculture types live there. The diversity and color they bring attracts those with more money. Businesses erupt to cater to those bohemian/trendy tastes. Rents go up. Those who gave the area its colorful energy in the first place can no longer afford to live there. They move out...and here comes Starbucks.

For now, Lavapiés is still edgy, yet comfortable enough for most. To help rejuvenate the area, the city built the big Centro Dramático Nacional Theater just downhill from Lavapiés' main square.

The district has few tourists. (Some think it's too scary.) Old ladies with their tired bodies and busy fans hang out on their tiny balconies, watching the scene. Shady types lurk on side streets (don't venture off the main drag, don't show your wallet or money, and don't linger late on Plaza de Lavapiés).

If you're walking, start from Plaza de Antón Martín (Metro: Antón Martín) or Plaza Santa Ana. Find your way to Calle del Ave María (on its way to becoming Calle del Ave Allah) and on to Plaza de Lavapiés (Metro: Lavapiés), where you'll find that a mosaic of cultures treat this square as a communal living room. Then head up Calle de Lavapiés to the Plaza Tirso de Molina (Metro stop). Once plagued by drug addicts, this square is now home to flower kiosks and a playground—a good example of Madrid's vision for reinvigorating its public spaces.

For food, you'll find plenty of tapas bars, plus gritty Indian (almost all run by Bangladeshis) and Moroccan eateries lining Calle de Lavapiés. For Spanish fare, try **$ Bar Melos,** a thriving dive jammed with a hungry and nubile crowd. It's famous for its giant patty melts called *zapatillas de lacón y queso* (because they're the size and shape of a *zapatilla*, or slipper—feeds at least two, daily 13:00-16:30 & 19:30-late, Calle del Ave María 44).

▲Bullfight

Madrid's Plaza de Toros hosts Spain's top bullfights on most Sundays and holidays from March through mid-October, and nearly every day during the San Isidro festival (early May–early June—often sold out long in advance). Fights start between 17:00 and 19:00 (early in spring and fall, late in summer). The bullring is at the Ventas Metro stop (a 25-minute Metro ride from Puerta del Sol, +34 913 562 200,

www.las-ventas.com). For more on this tradition, see the "Bullfighting" section of the Spain: Past & Present chapter.

Tickets: Bullfight tickets range from €5.50 to €160. There are no bad seats at Plaza de Toros; paying more gets you in the shade and/or closer to the gore. (The action often intentionally occurs in the shade to reward the expensive-ticket holders.) To be close to the bullfighters, choose areas 8, 9, or 10; for shade: 1, 2, 9, or 10; for shade/sun: 3 or 8; for the sun and cheapest seats: 4, 5, 6, or 7. Note these key words: *corrida*—a real fight with professionals; *novillada*—rookie matadors, younger bulls, and cheaper tickets.

Booking offices sell tickets online and in person. When buying online, read conditions carefully: The purchase voucher usually must be exchanged for a ticket at the booking office. The easiest place is **Bullfight Tickets Madrid** at Plaza del Carmen 1 (Mon-Sat 9:00-13:00 & 16:30-19:00, Sun 9:30-14:00, +34 915 319 131, www.bullfightticketsmadrid.com; run by José and his English-speaking son, also José, who also sells soccer tickets; will deliver tickets to your hotel).

Getting tickets through your hotel or a booking office is convenient, but they add 20 percent or more and don't sell the cheapest seats. To save money, you can stand in the ticket line at the bullring. Except for important bullfights—or during the San Isidro festival—there are generally plenty of seats available. About a thousand tickets are held back to be sold in the five days leading up to and on the day of a fight. People do scalp tickets, but beware: Those buying scalped tickets are breaking the law and can lose the ticket with no recourse.

For a dose of the experience, you can buy a cheap ticket and just stay to see a couple of bullfights. Each fight takes about 20 minutes, and the event consists of six bulls over two hours. Or, to keep your distance but get a sense of the ritual and gore, tour the bull bar on Plaza Mayor (see page 421).

Bullfighting Museum (Museo Taurino): This museum, located at the back of the bullring, is not as good as the ones in Sevilla or Ronda (free, daily 10:00-18:00, +34 917 251 857).

"Football" and Bernabéu Stadium

Madrid, like most of Europe, is enthusiastic about soccer (which they call *fútbol*). The Real ("Royal") Madrid team plays to a spirited crowd Saturdays and Sundays from September through May (tickets from €50—sold at bullfight box offices listed earlier). One of the most popular sightseeing activities among European visitors to Madrid is touring the 80,000-seat stadium. The €25 unguided visit includes the box seats, dressing rooms, technical zone, playing field, trophy room, and a big panoramic stadium view (Mon-Sat 9:30-19:00, Sun 10:00-18:30, shorter hours on game days, ticket office closes 14:30-15:30, bus #27—see self-guided bus tour on page 481—or Metro: Santiago Bernabéu, +34 913 984 300, www.realmadrid.com). Even if you can't catch a game, you'll see plenty of Real Madrid's all-white jerseys and paraphernalia around town.

Shopping in Madrid

Madrileños have a passion for shopping. It's a social event, often incorporated into the afternoon paseo, which eventually turns into drinks and dinner. Most shoppers focus on the colorful pedestrian area between and around Gran Vía and Puerta del Sol. Here you'll find H&M and Zara clothing, Imaginarium toys, FNAC books and music, and a handful of small local shops. The fanciest big-name shops (Gucci, Prada, and the like) tempt strollers along Calle Serrano, northwest of Retiro Park. For trendier chains and local fashion, head to pedestrian Calle Fuencarral, Calle Augusto Figueroa, and the streets surrounding Plaza de Chueca (north of Gran Vía, Metro: Chueca). Here are some other places to check out:

El Corte Inglés Department Store

The giant El Corte Inglés, with several buildings strung between Puerta del Sol and Plaza del Callao, is a handy place to pick up just about anything you need. **Building 3,** full of sports equipment, books, and home furnishings, is closest to Puerta del Sol and has a rooftop bar with views of the square. **Building 2,** a block up from Puerta del Sol on Calle Preciados, has a travel agency/box office for local events, souvenirs, toiletries, a post office, men's and women's fashions, a boring cafeteria, and a vast basement supermarket with a fancy "Club del Gourmet" section for edible souvenirs. Farther north on Calle del Carmen toward Plaza del Callao is **Building 1,** with electronics, another travel agency/box office, and the "Gour-

met Experience"—a floor filled with fun eateries and a rooftop terrace for diners (described on page 501).

The **travel agencies** in buildings 1 and 2 are fast and easy
places to buy AVE and other train tickets (plus airline tickets) with
a €6 service fee, but they don't sell reservations for rail-pass holders. (Another El Corte Inglés travel agency is in the Atocha train
station.)

All El Corte Inglés department stores are open daily (Mon-
Sat 10:00-22:00, Sun 11:00-21:00, +34 913 798 000, www.
elcorteingles.es). Salespeople wear flag pins indicating which languages they speak. If doing serious shopping here, ask about their
discounts (10 percent for tourists) and VAT refund policy (21 percent but with a minimum purchase requirement that you can ac-
cumulate over multiple shopping trips.

▲El Rastro Flea Market

Europe's biggest flea market is a field day for shoppers, people-
watchers, and pickpockets (Sun only, 9:00-15:00). It's best before

11:00, though bargain shoppers like to go around 14:00,
when vendors are more willing to strike end-of-day deals.
Thousands of stalls titillate
more than a million browsers
with mostly new junk. Locals
have lamented the tackiness of
El Rastro lately—on the main
drag, you'll find cheap underwear and bootleg CDs, but no
real treasures.

For an interesting market day (Sun only), start at Plaza Mayor,
where Europe's biggest stamp and coin market thrives. Enjoy this
genteel delight as you watch old-timers paging lovingly through
each other's albums, looking for win-win trades. When you're done,
head south or take the Metro to Tirso de Molina. Walk downhill,
wandering off on the side streets to browse antiques, old furniture,
and garage sale-style sellers who often simply throw everything out
on a sheet. Find a fantastic scene on Plaza del Campillo del Mundo
Nuevo where kids and adults leaf through each other's albums of
soccer cards and negotiate over trades.

A typical Madrileño's Sunday could involve a meander
through the Rastro streets with several stops for *cañas* (small beers)
at the gritty bars along the way, then a walk to the Cava Baja area
for more beer and tapas (see page 497). El Rastro offers a fascinating chance to see gangs of young thieves overwhelming and rip-
ping off naive tourists while plainclothes police officers circulate

and do their best. Don't even bring a wallet. The pickpocket action is brutal.

Specialty Shops

These places are fun to browse for Spanish specialties and locally made goods.

Ceramics: Antigua Casa Talavera has sold hand-made ceramics from Spain's family craftsmen since 1904. They can explain the various regional styles and colors of pottery and tiles, based on traditional designs from the 11th to 19th century (Mon-Fri 10:00-13:30 & 17:00-20:00, closed Sat-Sun, Calle Isabel La Católica 2, +34 915 473 417, www.antiguacasatalavera.com).

Leather: Taller Puntera is a workshop and store where the new generation carries on a longtime family tradition of Madrileño leather artisans. They design and create all of their products on-site, from bags to shoes and more (Mon-Sat 10:00-14:30 & 16:00-20:30, closed Sun, Plaza Conde de Barajas 4, +34 913 642 926, www.puntera.com).

Shoes: For *the* shoe street in Madrid head up Calle Fuencarral and take a right onto Calle Augusto Figueroa. Walk a couple of blocks down to find one local *zapatería* after another. On Gran Vía, Calle Arenal, or Calle Preciados, you'll also find **Camper** shoes, launched in 1975 on the Spanish island of Mallorca. This popular brand is now relatively easy to find around the world, though here in Madrid you may see more styles (daily, Calle Preciados 23, +34 915 317 897, www.camper.com).

Souvenirs: Casa de Diego sells *abanicos* (fans), *mantones* (typical Spanish shawls), *castañuelas* (castanets), *peinetas* (hair combs), and umbrellas. Even if you're not in the market, it's fun to watch the women flip open their final fan choices before buying—for them it is not a souvenir but an important piece of their wardrobe (Mon-Sat 9:30-20:00, closed Sun, Puerta del Sol 12, +34 915 226 643).

Guitars: Spain makes some of the world's finest classical guitars. Several of the top workshops, within an easy walk of Puerta del Sol, offer inviting little showrooms that give a peek at their craft and an opportunity to strum the final product. Consider the workshops of **José Romero** (Calle de Espoz y Mina 30, +34 915 214 218) and **José Ramirez** (Calle de la Paz 8, +34 915 314 229). **Union Musical** is a popular guitar shop off Puerta del Sol (Calle de Cedaceros 3, +34 914 293 877). If you're looking to buy, be prepared to spend €1,000.

Nightlife in Madrid

Those into clubbing may have to wait until after midnight for the most popular places to even open, much less start hopping. Spain has a reputation for partying very late and not stopping until offices open in the morning. (Spaniards, who are often awake into the wee hours of the morning, have a special word for this time of day: *la madrugada*.) If you're out early in the morning, it's hard to tell who is finishing their day and who's just starting it. Even if you're not a party animal after midnight, make it a point to be out with the happy masses, luxuriating in the cool evening air between 22:00 and midnight. The scene is absolutely unforgettable.

▲▲▲Paseo

Just walking the streets of Madrid seems to be the way the Madrileños spend their evenings. Even past midnight on a hot summer night, entire families with little kids are strolling, enjoying tiny beers and tapas in a series of bars, licking ice cream, and greeting their neighbors. Good areas to wander include from Puerta del Sol to Plaza Mayor and down Calle del Arenal until you hit Plaza de Isabel II; the pedestrianized Calle de las Huertas from Plaza Mayor to the Prado; along Gran Vía from about Plaza del Callao to Plaza de España, following the last section of my "Gran Vía Walk"; and, to window shop with the young and trendy, up Calle de Fuencarral (keep going until you hit traffic).

▲Zarzuela

For a delightful look at Spanish light opera that even English speakers can enjoy, try zarzuela. Guitar-strumming Napoleons in red capes; buxom women with masks, fans, and castanets; Spanish-speaking pharaohs; melodramatic spotlights; and aficionados clapping and singing along from the cheap seats, where the acoustics are best—this is zarzuela...the people's opera. Originating in Madrid, zarzuela is known for its satiric humor and surprisingly good music. Performances occur evenings at Teatro de la Zarzuela, which alternates between zarzuela, ballet, and opera throughout the year. The TI's monthly guide has a special zarzuela section. Be aware that not all shows at the Teatro de la Zarzuela are zarzuelas.

Tickets: Prices range from €18-50, less for restricted-view seats, 50 percent off for those over 65, buy online at http://teatrodelazarzuela.mcu.es) or in person at the Teatro de la Zarzuela box office (open Mon-Fri 12:00-20:00 and Sat-Sun 14:30-18:00 for advance tickets, or until showtime for same-day tickets, near the Prado at Jovellanos 4, Metro: Sevilla or Banco de España, +34 915 245 400).

MADRID

Madrid Shopping & Nightlife

To Plaza de España & ⑮

PALACIO DEL SENADO

CALLE TORIJA

To Plaza de España & ⑲

GRAN VÍA

❸

JACOMETREZO

Plaza de Santo Domingo

Callao Ⓜ

Jardines de Sabatini

CALLE DE LA BOLA

LA ENCARNACIÓN

CALLE ARRIETA

STO. DOMINGO

C. CAMPOMANES

Santo Domingo Ⓜ

PRECIADOS

TETN.

P ST. S. MARTÍN

ROYAL PALACE

S. QUINTÍN

Plaza de Oriente

FELIPE V

ROYAL THEATER

CARLOS II

Plaza de Isabel II

C.D. PERAL

FLORA

Plaza San Martín

Plaza de la Armería

CALLE DE BAILÉN

REQUENA

Plaza Ramales

VERGARA

C. SAN JUZON

Plaza de la Villa

CARLOS II

INDEPENDENCIA

ESCALINATA

Ópera Ⓜ

CALLE HILERAS

CALLE DEL

SAN GINÉS

THEATER

Plaza Herradores

C. BORD

COLOR.

ALMUDENA CATHEDRAL

SAN NICOLÁS

FACTOR

MAYOR

CALLE

FORMER TOWN HALL

Plaza de la Villa

MERCADO DE SAN MIGUEL

Plaza Mayor

ⓘ

ZARAGOZA

CONVENT

FUNONROSTRO

MESONES BARS

⑯

CALLE SACRAMENTO

⑭

❹

Plaza Conde Barajas

CUCHILLEROS

200 Meters

200 Yards

C. SAN JUSTO

C. DE TOLEDO

CONCEPCIÓN

CALLE DE SEGOVIA

C. DE SEGOVIA

Plaza Puerta Cerrada

C. COLEGIATA

MORERÍA

C. REDONDILLA

C. DE S.

Plaza Paja

C. NUNCIO

F. ALM.

GRAFAL

CAVA BAJA

S. BRUNO

C. DE TOLEDO

C. DE LOS ESTUDIOS

SAN ISIDRO

C. ALMENDRO

CALLE CAVA ALTA

La Latina Ⓜ

DUQUE

C. CEBADA

C. JUANELO

Plaza de Cascorro

C. DE TOLEDO

EL RASTRO FLEA MARKET (SUNDAYS)

❷

CALLE STA ANA

C. RIBERA CURTI

CALLE EMBAJADORES

Shopping

❶ El Corte Inglés Dep't Store (3)
❷ El Rastro Flea Market
❸ Antigua Casa Talavera Ceramics
❹ Taller Puntera Leather
❺ To Calle A. Figueroa Shoe Shops
❻ Camper Shoes
❼ Casa de Diego Souvenirs
❽ Romero Guitars
❾ Ramirez Guitars
❿ Union Musical Guitars
⓫ FNAC Callao Books
⓬ Casa del Libro Books

MADRID

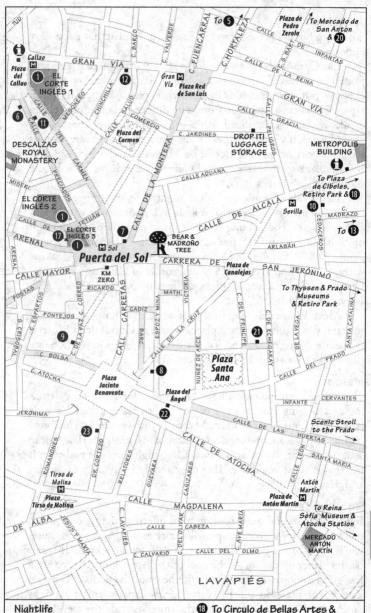

MADRID

▲▲Flamenco

Although Sevilla is the capital of flamenco, Madrid has a few easy options.

Las Carboneras is an easygoing, folksy little place a few steps from Plaza Mayor with two hour-long flamenco shows nightly; check website for times (€42 includes entry plus a drink and a small tapa, €80 gets you a table up front with dinner and unlimited cheap drinks if you reserve ahead, RS%—manager Enrique promises a second drink if you book directly and show this book, reservations recommended, Plaza del Conde de Miranda 1, +34 915 428 677, www.tablaolascarboneras.com). Dinner is served one hour before showtime.

Las Tablas Flamenco offers nightly shows respecting the traditional art of flamenco. You'll sit in a plain room with a mix of tourists and cool, young Madrileños in a modern, nondescript office block just over the freeway from Plaza de España (€32 with drink, €66-76 dinner and show, reasonable drink prices, shows daily at 19:00 and 21:00, 1.25 hours, corner of Calle de Ferraz and Cuesta de San Vicente at Plaza de España 9, +34 915 420 520, www.lastablasmadrid.com).

More Flamenco: Regardless of what your hotel receptionist may tell you, other flamenco places—such as Corral de la Morería (Calle de Morería 17) and Torres Bermejas (off Gran Vía)—are filled with tourists and pushy waiters.

Mesones

These long, skinny, cave-like bars, famous for customers drinking and singing late into the night, line the lane called Cava de San Miguel, just west of Plaza Mayor. If you were to toss lowbrow barflies, Spanish karaoke, electric keyboards, crass tourists, cheap sangria, and greasy calamari into a late-night blender and turn it on, this is what you'd get. They're generally lively only on Friday and Saturday.

Rooftop Bars

Madrid has several great rooftop bars, offering slightly overpriced drinks with views over the sprawling city center. At most of these, you'll pay €5 for a beer or wine, and €8-10 for a cocktail. This can be fun either by day, or in the cool of the late evening. Here are a few good options: To be right in the heart of the action, **Taberna Puertalsol** sits atop the El Corte Inglés department store right on Puerta del Sol; just head into the store and ride the elevator to Floor 5 (daily 12:30-late, Puerta del Sol 10). The classic **Circulo de Bellas Artes** skyscraper is capped with the Azotea cocktail bar, offering reasonably priced drinks overlooking the start of Gran Vía (€5 to ride the elevator; described on page 431). Near the Plaza de España end of Gran Vía, the **Dear Madrid** hotel has a rooftop

bar—called "Nice to Meet You"—on its 14th floor (Gran Vía 80). If you're seeking untouristy ambience rather than views, head to the Chueca district, where the locals-packed **Mercado de San Antón** has a fine rooftop bar (market described on page 502). Just north of the Prado, the Palacio de Cibeles (City Hall) has a sixth-floor **Terrace Cibeles;** it feels a little swankier, with lesser views (see page 494).

Bars and Jazz

If you're just picking up speed at midnight and looking for a place filled with old tiles and a Gen-X crowd, power into **Bar Viva Madrid** (daily 13:00-late, downhill from Plaza Santa Ana at Calle Manuel Fernández y González 7, +34 914 293 640). The same street has other bars filled with music. Or hike on over to Chocolatería San Ginés (described on page 502) for a dessert of *churros con chocolate.*

For live jazz, **Café Central** is the old town favorite. Since 1982 it's been known as the place where rising stars get their start (around €20, nightly at 21:00—reserve online, stop by to reserve your table, or come early to score one of the unreserved seats by the bar, food and drinks available, great scene, Plaza del Ángel 10, +34 913 694 143, www.cafecentralmadrid.com).

Sleeping in Madrid

Madrid has plenty of centrally located budget hotels and *pensiones.* Most of the accommodations I've listed are within a few minutes' walk of Puerta del Sol.

You should be able to find a sleepable double for €70, a good double for €100, and a modern, air-conditioned double with all the comforts for €150. Prices vary dramatically throughout the year at bigger hotels but remain about the same for the smaller hotels and *hostales.* It's almost always easy to find a place. Anticipate full hotels only in May (the San Isidro festival, celebrating Madrid's patron saint with bullfights and zarzuelas—especially around his feast day on May 15), around Easter, during LGBT Pride Week at the end of June, and in September (when conventions can clog the city). During the hot months of July and August, prices can be soft—ask for a discount.

With all of Madrid's street noise, I'd request the highest floor possible. Cheaper places have very thin walls and doors, so you might get noise from inside and outside (pack earplugs). Twin-bedded rooms are generally a bit larger than double-bedded rooms for the same price. During slow times, drop-ins can often score a room in business-class hotels for just a few euros more than the budget

MADRID

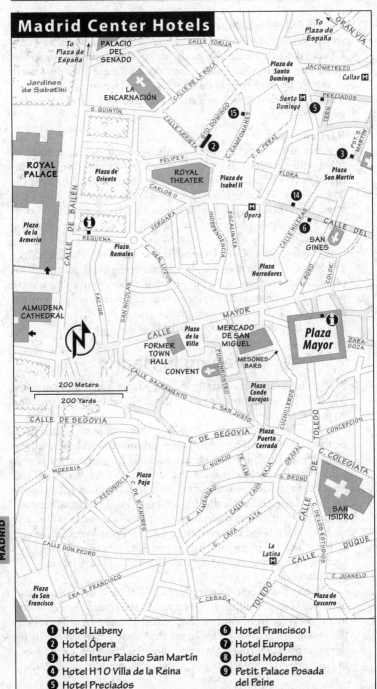

Madrid Center Hotels

1. Hotel Liabeny
2. Hotel Ópera
3. Hotel Intur Palacio San Martín
4. Hotel H10 Villa de la Reina
5. Hotel Preciados
6. Hotel Francisco I
7. Hotel Europa
8. Hotel Moderno
9. Petit Palace Posada del Peine

MADRID

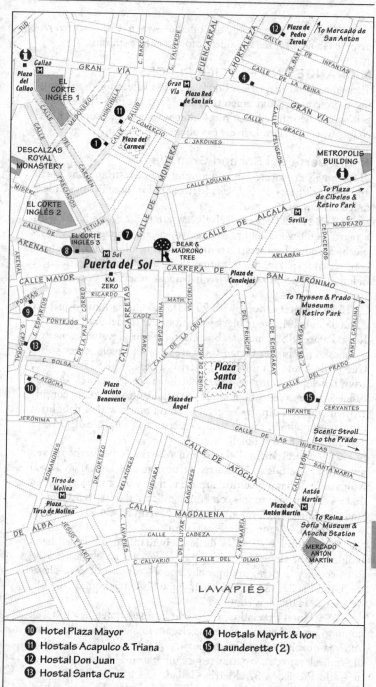

MADRID

10 Hotel Plaza Mayor	**14** Hostals Mayrit & Ivor
11 Hostals Acapulco & Triana	**15** Launderette (2)
12 Hostal Don Juan	
13 Hostal Santa Cruz	

hotels. Breakfast is generally not offered—when it is, it's often expensive (about €15; see the sidebar for breakfast options).

MIDRANGE AND FANCIER PLACES

These mostly business-class hotels are good values for those wanting more comfort and amenities than *hostales* offer. Their formal prices may be inflated, but most offer weekend and summer discounts when it's slow. Drivers pay about €24 a day in garages.

Near Puerta del Sol and Gran Vía

These hotels are located in and around the pedestrian zone north and west of Puerta del Sol. Use Metro: Sol for these listings unless noted otherwise.

$$$$ Hotel Liabeny feels like a grand Old World hotel, with a marble-and-wood lobby, an eager-to-please concierge, and 213 plush, spacious, business-class rooms offering all the comforts (air-con, elevator, pay parking, sauna, gym, off Plaza del Carmen at Salud 3, +34 915 319 000, www.liabeny.es, reservas@hotelliabeny.com).

$$$$ Hotel Ópera, with 79 classy rooms, is located just off Plaza de Isabel II, a four-block walk from Puerta del Sol toward the Royal Palace (RS%, includes breakfast, air-con, elevator, sauna and gym, ask for a higher floor—there are nine—to avoid street noise, Cuesta de Santo Domingo 2, Metro: Ópera, +34 915 412 800, www.hotelopera.com, reservas@hotelopera.com). Hotel Ópera's cafeteria is deservedly popular. If you're here on a weekend, consider their "musical dinners"—great operetta music with a delightful dinner (around €60, Sat at 21:30, reservations smart, call +34 915 426 382 or reserve at hotel).

$$$ Hotel Intur Palacio San Martín is perfectly tucked away from the hustle of the center next to the Descalzas Royal Monastery. It has a beautiful atrium lounge with a vertical garden and 94 comfortable rooms combining modern flair with respect for tradition (air-con, elevator, Plaza San Martín 5, +34 917 015 000, www.intur.com, sanmartin@intur.com).

$$$ Hotel H10 Villa de la Reina, filling a former bank building right along the pulsing Gran Vía, has an elegant, early-20th-century drawing-room lobby and 74 rooms (air-con, elevator, Gran Vía 22, +34 915 239 101, www.h10hotels.com, H10.villa.delareina@H10hotels.com).

$$$ Hotel Preciados, a four-star business hotel, has 100 welcoming, modern rooms as well as elegant lounges. It's well located and reasonably priced for the luxury it provides (free mini-bar, air-con, elevator, pay parking, just off Plaza de Santo Domingo at Calle Preciados 37, Metro: Callao, +34 914 544 400, www.preciadoshotel.com, preciadoshotel@preciadoshotel.com).

MADRID

$$$ Hotel Francisco I is on a lively pedestrian street midway between the Royal Theater and Puerta del Sol. It has a mod lobby and 93 rooms (air-con, elevator, Calle del Arenal 15, +34 915 480 204, www.hotelfrancisco.com, info@hotelfrancisco.com).

$$ Hotel Europa, with sleek marble, red carpet runners along the halls, happy Muzak charm, and an attentive staff, is a solid value. It rents 100 squeaky-clean rooms, many with balconies overlooking the pedestrian zone or an inner courtyard. The hotel has an honest ethos and offers a straight price (family rooms, air-con, elevator, Calle del Carmen 4, +34 915 212 900, www.hoteleuropa.eu, info@hoteleuropa.eu, run by Antonio and Fernando Garaban and their helpful and jovial staff, Javi, Jim, and Tomás. The recommended **$$ Restaurante-Cafeteria Europa** is a lively and convivial scene—fun for breakfast.

$$ Hotel Moderno, renting 90 rooms, has a quiet, professional, and friendly atmosphere. There's a comfy first-floor lounge and a convenient location close to Puerta del Sol (air-con, elevator, Calle del Arenal 2, +34 915 310 900, www.hotel-moderno.com, info@hotel-moderno.com).

Near Plaza Mayor

Both of these are in a bustling area a block off Plaza Mayor.

$$$ Petit Palace Posada del Peine feels like part of a big, modern chain (which it is), but fills its well-located old building with fresh, efficient character. Behind the ornate Old World facade is a comfortable business-class hotel with 67 rooms (air-con, elevator, Calle Postas 17, +34 915 238 151, www.petitpalace.com, posadadelpeine@petitpalace.com.

$$ Hotel Plaza Mayor, with 41 solidly outfitted rooms, is tastefully decorated and beautifully situated a block off Plaza Mayor. It occupies an enticing middle ground between pricey business-class hotels and the basic *hostales* (air-con, elevator, Calle de Atocha 2, +34 653 651 246, www.hotel-bb.es, hotel.plazamayor@hotelbb.com).

Near the Prado

For locations, see the "Madrid's Museum Neighborhood" map on page 449.

$$$$ DoubleTree by Hilton Prado has the predictable class of an American chain, but feels more like a European boutique hotel—with 61 rooms, an attentive staff, and a handy location tucked down a quieter side street near the Prado (air-con, elevator, Calle San Agustín 3, +34 913 600 820, www.doubletree3.hilton.com).

$$$ Mercure Madrid Centro Hotel Lope de Vega offers good business-class hotel value near the Prado. It is a "cultural-

Breakfast in Madrid

Many hotels don't include (or even offer) breakfast, so you may be out on the streets first thing looking for a place to eat. Nontouristy cafés only offer a hot drink and a pastry, with perhaps a potato omelet and sandwiches (toasted cheese, ham, or both). I like **Restaurante-Cafeteria Europa** just off Puerta del Sol for its classic breakfast scene, with a long bar, plenty of locals, and an easy-access menu (described on page 500). Touristy places will have a *desayuno* menu with various ham-and-eggs deals. Try *churros* at least once (see the listings on page 502 for my favorite places); if you're not in the mood for heavy chocolate in the morning, go local and dip your *churros* in a *café con leche*. If all else fails, a Starbucks is often nearby (just like home). Get advice from your hotel staff for their favorite breakfast place. My typical breakfast, found at any corner bar: *café con leche, tortilla española* (a slice of potato omelet), and *zumo de naranja natural* (fresh-squeezed orange juice).

themed" hotel inspired by 17th-century writer Lope de Vega. With 59 rooms, it feels cozy and friendly for a formal hotel (family rooms, air-con, elevator, very limited pay parking—reserve ahead; Calle Lope de Vega 49, +34 913 600 011, www.accor.com, H9618@accor. com).

CHEAP SLEEPS
Near Puerta del Sol

The first two listings are in the same building at Calle de la Salud 13, north of Puerta del Sol. The building overlooks Plaza del Carmen—a little square with a sleepy, almost Parisian ambience. The last listing, Hostal Don Juan, is a stone's throw from Gran Vía at the top of Calle de la Montera, which some dislike because of the prostitutes who hang out here, though the zone is otherwise safe and comfortable.

$ **Hostal Acapulco,** a cheery oasis, rents 16 bright rooms with a professional, hotelesque feel. The neighborhood is quiet enough that it's smart to request a room with a balcony (family room, air-con, elevator, fourth floor, reasonable laundry service, overnight luggage storage, parking—reserve ahead, +34 915 311 945, www. hostalacapulco.com, hostal_acapulco@yahoo.es, Ana, Marco, and Javier).

$ **Hostal Triana,** also a good deal, is bigger—with 40 rooms—and offers a little less charm for a little less money (most rooms have air-con, others have fans; elevator and some stairs, first floor,

+34 915 326 812, www.hostaltriana.com, triana@hostaltriana. com, Victor González).

$ Hostal Don Juan sits on a quiet-by-day, busy-by-night square just off the Gran Vía in the beginning of the Chueca neighborhood. Its 44 rooms are sleek and modern, contrasting with the Baroque explosion of varnish and gold in the common areas. It's a charmingly run time warp (air-con, elevator, Plaza Pedro Zerolo 1—former Plaza Vázquez de Mella, second floor, +34 915 223 101, www.hostaldonjuan.net, hshostaldonjuan@gmail.com).

Near Plaza Mayor

$ Hostal Santa Cruz, simple and well located, has 16 rooms at a good price (air-con, elevator, Plaza de Santa Cruz 6, second floor, +34 915 222 441, www.hostalsantacruz.com, info@ hostalsantacruz.com).

$ Hostal Mayrit and **Hostal Ivor** rent 28 rooms with thoughtful touches on pedestrianized Calle del Arenal. It's in a very handy location, so prices are at the higher end of this range (air-con, elevator, near Metro: Ópera at Calle del Arenal 24, reception on third floor, +34 915 480 403, www.hostalivor.com, reservas@hostalivor. com).

Near the Prado

For locations, see the "Madrid's Museum Neighborhood" map on page 449.

$$ Urban Sea Hotel Atocha 113 is a basic but contemporary option with 36 minimalist, well-worn rooms between the Prado and the Reina Sofía, near the Atocha train station (small rooftop terrace, self-service snacks, Calle de Atocha 113, +34 913 692 895, www.blueseahotels.com, recepcionatocha@blueseahotels.es).

$ Hostal Gonzalo has 15 basic but comfortable rooms. Well run by friendly and helpful Javier and Antonio, it's popular with European budget travelers (air-con, elevator, Cervantes 34, third floor, Metro: Antón Martín—but not handy to Metro, +34 914 292 714, www.hostalgonzalo.com, hostal@hostalgonzalo.com).

Eating in Madrid

In Spain, only Barcelona and the Basque Country rival Madrid for taste bud thrills. You have three dining choices: a memorable, atmospheric sit-down meal in a well-chosen restaurant; a forgettable, basic sit-down meal; or a meal of tapas at a bar or two...or four. Unless otherwise noted, restaurants start serving lunch at 13:00 or 13:30 and dinner around 20:30. Depending on what time you show up, the same place may seem forlorn, touristy, or thriving with local eaters. Many restaurants close in August. Madrid has

MADRID

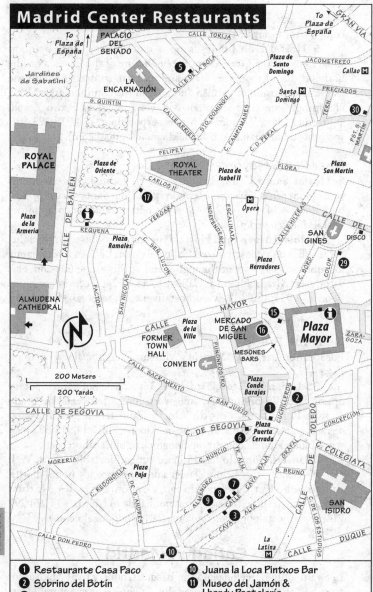

Madrid Center Restaurants

1 Restaurante Casa Paco
2 Sobrino del Botín
3 Casa Lucio
4 El Caldero
5 La Bola Taberna
6 El Madroño
7 Taberna de los Castizos
8 Taberna Los Huevos de Lucio
9 Taberna Tempranillo

10 Juana la Loca Pintxos Bar
11 Museo del Jamón &
   Lhardy Pastelería
12 La Casa del Abuelo
13 La Oreja de Jaime
14 Casa Toni
15 Casa Rúa
16 Mercado de San Miguel
17 La Botillería

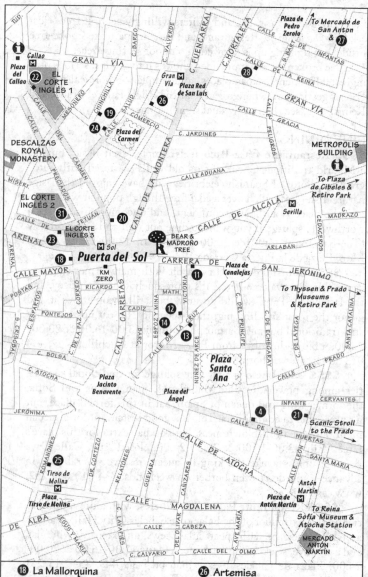

⑱ La Mallorquina	㉖ Artemisa
⑲ Restaurante Puerto Rico	㉗ To Chueca Area Eateries
⑳ Restaurante-Cafeteria Europa	㉘ Angelita Wine Bar
㉑ Casa Gonzalez	㉙ Chocolatería San Ginés
㉒ El Corte Inglés Cafeteria	㉚ Chocolaterías Valor
㉓ Casa Labra Taberna Restaurante	㉛ El Corte Inglés Supermarket
㉔ Takos Al Pastor	
㉕ Yatai Market	

MADRID

famously good tap water, and waiters willingly serve it free—just ask for *agua del grifo*. Restaurants and bars in Spain are smoke-free inside, but lighting up is allowed in outdoor seating areas.

I've broken my recommended choices into groups: serious dining establishments, tapas places, and simple, economical venues. For suggestions on where to eat near the Royal Palace, Prado, and Reina Sofía, see their individual sight listings.

FINE DINING

$$$$ Restaurante Casa Paco feels simple, even basic, but it's a Madrid tradition. Check out its old walls plastered with autographed photos of Spanish celebrities who have enjoyed their signature dish—ox grilled over a coal fire. Though popular with tourists, the place is authentic, confident, and uncompromising. It's a worthwhile splurge if you want to dine out well and carnivorously (Tue-Sat 13:00-16:00 & 20:00-24:00, Sun 13:00-16:00, closed Mon, Plaza de la Puerta Cerrada 11, +34 913 663 166).

$$$$ Sobrino del Botín is a hit with many Americans because "Hemingway ate here." It's grotesquely touristy, pricey, and the last place "Papa" would go now...but still, people love it and go for the roast suckling pig, their specialty. I'd eat upstairs for a still-traditional but airier atmosphere (daily 13:00-16:00 & 20:00-24:00, a block downhill from Plaza Mayor at Cuchilleros 17, +34 913 664 217, www.botin.es).

$$$$ Casa Lucio is a favorite splurge for traditional specialties among power-dressing Madrileños. Juan Carlos and Sofía, the former king and queen of Spain, eat in this formal place, but it's accessible to commoners. This is a good restaurant for a special night out and a full-blown meal, but you pay extra for this place's fame (daily 13:00-16:00 & 20:30-24:00, closed Aug, Calle Cava Baja 35; unless you're the king or queen, reserve several days in advance—and don't even bother on weekends; +34 913 653 252, www.casalucio.es).

$$$$ Restaurante Palacio de Cibeles, with a dress-up interior on the sixth floor of the Palacio de Cibeles (City Hall), features an outdoor terrace with spectacular views, an extensive wine list, and a creative, seasonal Spanish menu (daily 13:00-16:00 & 20:00-24:00, Plaza de Cibeles 1—see map on page 449, +34 915 231 454, http://palaciodecibeles.com). The neighboring and swanky **$$$ Terrace Cibeles** serves drinks and pricey light bites on its outdoor terrace late into the night (open only in good weather, daily 13:00-24:00). The second-floor **$$ Colección Cibeles** offers a simplified and less-expensive version of Restaurante Palacio's fare (€15 fixed-price meal, daily 10:00-24:00).

$$$ El Caldero ("The Pot") is a romantic spot and a good place for paella and other rice dishes. A classy, in-the-know crowd

appreciates its subdued elegance and crisp service. The house specialty, *arroz al caldero* (a variation on paella), is served with panache from a cauldron hanging from a tripod. Most of the formal rice dishes come in pots for two. Wash it all down with the house sangria (Tue-Sat 13:30-16:30 & 20:30-24:00, Sun-Mon 13:30-16:30, Calle de las Huertas 15, +34 914 295 044).

$$$$ La Bola Taberna, touristy but friendly, cozy, and tastefully elegant, specializes in *cocido Madrileño*—Madrid stew. The stew, made of various meats, carrots, and garbanzo beans in earthen jugs, is a winter dish, prepared here for the tourists all year. It's served as two courses: First enjoy the broth as a soup, then dig into the meat and veggies. Curious about how it's made? Ask to take a peek in the kitchen. Reservations are smart (cash only, daily lunch seatings at 13:30 and 15:30, Mon-Sat dinner 20:30-23:00, closed Sun for dinner, midway between Royal Palace and Gran Vía at Calle Bola 5, +34 915 476 930, http://labola.es).

Treating Tapas Bars as Restaurants: Of the many recommended *tabernas* and tapas bars listed next, several have tables and menus that lend themselves to fine dining. If you don't mind the commotion of the nearby bar action, you can order high on the menu in these places and, I'd say, eat better and more economically than in the more formal restaurants listed earlier.

TAPAS BAR-HOPPING

For maximum fun, people, and atmosphere, go mobile for dinner: Do the *tapeo*, a local tradition of going from one bar to the next, munching, drinking, and socializing. If done properly, a pub crawl can be a highlight of your trip. Before embarking upon this culinary adventure, study and use the tapas tips in the Practicalities chapter. Try speaking a little Spanish: You'll get a much better (and less expensive) experience. While tiny tapas plates are standard in Andalucía, these days most of Madrid's bars offer bigger plates for around €6 (vegetables) to €15 (fish). Called *raciones*, these are ideal for a small group to share. The real action begins late (around 21:00). While the energy is fun and local later in the evening, you may find it easier to get service and a spot by dining earlier—which is still late by American standards.

You'll occasionally find a bar that gives a free tapa to anyone ordering a drink, but it's a dying tradition in Madrid. If the bartender brings you one, consider it a bonus. To improve your odds, begin by ordering just a drink and see if something comes free. Once you get it (or don't), order additional food as you like.

There are tapas bars almost everywhere, but two areas in the city center are particularly rewarding for a bar-crawl meal: **Calle de Jesús** (near the Prado) is the easiest, with several wonderful and diverse places in a two-block row, while trendy **Calle Cava Baja** has

fancier offerings and feels most energetic. A third area, between **Puerta del Sol** and **Plaza Santa Ana,** is more central but overrun with tourists.

The Great Tapas Row on Calle de Jesús

This two-block stretch of tapas bars across the boulevard from the Prado offers a variety of fun places (for location, see the "Madrid's Museum Neighborhood" map on page 449). While the offerings are pretty similar, each has its own personality. Most have chaotic bars in front and small and inviting sections with tables in back. Make the circuit and eyeball each place to see which appeals—you'll see that there's no reason to spend all your time  and appetite at your first stop. Calle de Jesús stretches between Calle de Cervantes and Calle de las Huertas, behind the Palace Hotel. In the middle is the Plaza de Jesús, so named because this is the location of the Basilica of Jesús de Medinaceli (home to a relic that attracts huge crowds of pilgrims on special days). Start near the church at the first recommended bar, Cervecería Cervantes. These places are generally open every day for long hours.

$$ Cervecería Cervantes serves hearty *raciones,* specializes in octopus, and has both a fine bar and good restaurant seating (intersection of Plaza de Jesús and Calle de Cervantes, +34 914 296 093).

$$ Taberna de la Daniela Medinaceli, part of a local chain, is popular for its specialty *cocido madrileño*—a rich chickpea-based soup. It has a lovely dining area if you want to settle in for a while (Plaza de Jesús 7, +34 913 896 238).

$$ La Dolores, with a rustic little dining area, has been a hit since 1908 and is still extremely popular. Its canapés are listed on the wall (Plaza de Jesús 4, +34 914 292 243).

$$ Cervezas La Fabrica packs in seafood lovers at the bar; a quieter back room is available for those preferring a table. Prices are the same in both spots. They serve a nice *cava* (Spanish sparkling wine), which goes well with seafood (Calle de Jesús 2, +34 913 690 671).

$$ Cervecería Los Gatos is a kaleidoscope of Spanish culture, with chandeliers swinging above wine barrels in the intense bar area and characteristic tables in the more peaceful zone behind (Calle de Jesús 2, +34 914 293 067).

$$$ Taberna Maceira, perhaps the best of the bunch, feels like Northern Spain. It's a Galician place with a wonderfully woody and rustic energy. A sit-down restaurant (not a bar), it specializes

in octopus, cod, *pimientos de Padrón*, and *caldo gallego* (white bean soup)—all classic Galician specialties of northwest Spain. The *We're out of Coca-Cola (No hay Coca-Cola)* sign is up every single day (Mon-Sat 13:00-16:00 & 20:30-24:00, closed Sun, Calle de Jesús 7, +34 914 291 584).

Tapas on Calle Cava Baja

A few minutes' walk south of Plaza Mayor, Calle Cava Baja fills each evening with a young, professional crowd prowling for chic tapas and social fun. Come at night only and treat the entire street as a destination. I've listed a few standards, but excellent new eateries are always opening up. For a good, authentic Madrid dinner experience, survey the options, then choose

your favorites. Remember, it's easier and touristy early, and jammed with locals later. (For a formal dining experience on this street, come early and pick a place you like with tables in the back, or see the places recommended under "Fine Dining," earlier. Taberna Tempranillo or Juana la Loca would be my first choices.)

These tapas bars, listed in the order you'll reach them as you walk from Plaza Mayor up Calle Cava Baja, are worth special consideration.

$$$ El Madroño ("The Berry Tree," a symbol of Madrid), more of a cowboy bar, serves all the clichés. If Knott's Berry Farm was Spanish, this would be its restaurant. Preserving a bit of old Madrid, a tile copy of Velázquez's famous *Drinkers* grins from its facade. Inside, look above the stairs for photos of 1902 Madrid. Study the coats of arms of Madrid through the centuries as you try a *vermut* (vermouth) on tap. Or ask for a small glass *(chupito)* of the *licor de madroño*. Indoor seating is bright and colorful; the sidewalk tables come with good people-watching. Munch *raciones* at the bar or front tables to be in the fun scene, or have a quieter sit-down meal at the tables in the back (daily 8:00-24:00, a block off the top of Calle Cava Baja at Plaza de la Puerta Cerrada 7, +34 913 645 629).

$$ Taberna de los Castizos is bustling with *castizos* (people and objects that are truly "of Madrid," with all its traditions and style). They serve the classic Spanish fare: *tortilla de patatas* (potato omelette), *patatas bravas* (potatoes with spicy sauce), *albondigas* (meatballs), *pulpo* (octopus), croquettes, and so on. Small tapas are served with your drink (Calle Cava Baja 34, +34 607 578 021).

$$ Taberna Los Huevos de Lucio, owned by the same family as the reputable Casa Lucio (described under "Fine Dining," earlier), is a jam-packed bar serving good tapas, salads, *huevos estrellados* (fried eggs over fried potatoes), and wine. For a sit-down meal, head to the tables in the back (Calle Cava Baja 30, +34 913 662 984).

$$ Taberna Tempranillo, ideal for hungry wine lovers, offers fancy tapas and fine wine by the glass (see the board or ask for their English menu). While there are a few tables, the bar is just right for hanging out. With a spirit of adventure, use their fascinating menu to assemble your dream meal. When I order high on their menu, I'm generally very happy (closed Aug, Calle Cava Baja 38, +34 913 641 532).

$$ Juana la Loca Pintxos Bar ("Crazy Juana") overlooks a lonely square at the top end of Calle Cava Baja (on the left). It feels more sophisticated and civilized, with elegant *raciones,* refined-yet-tight seating, gorgeously presented dishes from a foodie menu, and reasonable prices considering the quality. Their classic is the runny *tortilla de patatas* with piles of decadently caramelized onions. To settle in for a sit-down meal, arrive early to snare a table (Plaza Puerta de Moros 4, +34 913 665 500).

Central Pub-Crawl Tapas Route

The little streets between Puerta del Sol, San Jerónimo, and Plaza Santa Ana are submerged in a flood of tourism. But they're also very central...and hold some tasty surprises. If you can get past the touristy trappings, this loop offers a handy, no-brainer intro to Spanish tapa-hopping.

• *Start at the intersection of Carrera de San Jerónimo and Calle Victoria.*

$$ Museo del Jamón ("Museum of Ham"), festooned with ham hocks, is a fun place to see—unless you're a pig (or a vegetarian). Its frenetic, cheap, stand-up bar (with famously rude service) is an assembly line of fast-and-simple *bocadillos* and *raciones.* If you order anything, get only a cheap sandwich, because the staff is not honest. Take advantage of the easy photo-illustrated menus that show various dishes and their prices. The best ham is the pricey *jamón ibérico*—from pigs who led stress-free lives in acorn-strewn valleys. Point clearly to what you want and be very specific to avoid being served a pricier meal than you intended. For a small sandwich, ask for a *chiquito* (daily 9:00-24:00, air-con).

• *Across the street is the touristy and overpriced bull bar* **La Taurina.** *(I*

wouldn't eat here, but you're welcome to ponder the graphic photos that celebrate the gory art of bullfighting.) Next door, take a detour from your pub crawl with something more suited to grandmothers.

$$ Lhardy Pastelería offers a genteel taste of Old World charm in this district of rowdy pubs. This peaceful time warp has been a fixture since 1839 for Madrileños wanting to duck in for a cup of consommé or a light snack. Step right in, and pretend you're an aristocrat back between the wars. Appreciate the line of elegant bottles (each a different Iberian fortified wine: sherry, port, and so on), revolving case of meaty little pastries, and fancy soup dispenser (chicken broth consommé, try it with a splash of sherry; Mon-Sat 10:00-22:00, Sun until 15:00; Carrera de San Jerónimo 8, +34 915 222 207). A very classy **$$$$** dinner-only restaurant hides upstairs.

• *Next, forage up Calle Victoria. The bars on this street and nearby lanes offer bloated prices and all the clichés. Near the end of the street, you'll find...*

$$ La Casa del Abuelo serves sizzling plates of tasty little *gambas* (shrimp) and *langostinos* (prawns), with bread to sop up the delightful juices. Try *gambas a la plancha* (grilled shrimp) or *gambas al ajillo* (ah-HEE-yoh, a small clay dish of shrimp cooked in oil and garlic that'll burn the roof of your mouth if you're not careful). Wash it down with a glass of sweet red house wine (Calle Victoria 12). The original,

characteristic, stand-up bar is on the right side of the street; their sit-down annex is on the left.

• *Just beyond, at the intersection with Calle de la Cruz, is...*

$$ La Oreja de Jaime is known for its sautéed pigs' ears *(oreja)*. While pig ears are a Madrid dish (fun to try, hard to swallow), this place is Galician—they offer *pimientos de Padrón* and the distinctive *ribeiro* (ree-BAY-roh) wine, served Galician-style, in characteristic little ceramic bowls to disguise its lack of clarity (Calle de la Cruz 12).

• *A few steps up Calle de la Cruz on the right is...*

$$ Casa Toni is good for classic dishes like *patatas bravas* (fried potatoes in a spicy sauce), *berenjena* (deep-fried slices of eggplant), *champiñones* (sautéed mushrooms), and gazpacho—the cold tomato-and-garlic soup that is generally served only during the hot season, but available here year-round just for tourists like you (Calle de la Cruz 14).

EATING REASONABLY
On or near Plaza Mayor

Madrileños enjoy a bite to eat on Plaza Mayor (without its high costs) by grabbing food to go from a nearby bar and just planting themselves somewhere on the square to eat (squid sandwiches are popular). But for many tourists, dinner at a sidewalk café right on Plaza Mayor is worth the premium price (consider Cervecería Pulpito, southwest corner of the square at #10).

Calamari Sandwiches: Plaza Mayor is famous for its *bocadillos de calamares*. For a tasty squid-ring sandwich, line up at **$ Casa Rúa** at Plaza Mayor's northwest corner, a few steps up Calle Ciudad Rodrigo. Hanging up behind the bar is a photo-advertisement of Plaza Mayor from the 1950s, when the square contained a park (daily 11:00-23:00).

$$ Mercado de San Miguel: This early-20th-century market sparkles after a recent renovation and bustles with a trendy food circus of eateries (daily 10:00-24:00). While it's expensive, touristy, and often crowded, it's also fun and accessible. You can stroll while you munch, hang out at bars, or try to find a seat at one of the market's food-court-style tables. For tips on grazing here, see page 422.

Facing the Royal Palace: $$$ La Botillería is recommended mostly for its location next to the National Theater and overlooking Plaza de Oriente. It's a venerable and elegant (and expensive) opera-type café with fine tables on the square. The menu is quite expensive, but they have a decent €19 weekday lunch special (more interesting menu after 20:00, Plaza de Oriente 2, +34 915 484 620, www.botilleria.es).

Near Puerta del Sol and Plaza Mayor

$$ La Mallorquina ("The Girl from Mallorca"), on the downhill end of Puerta del Sol, is a venerable pastry shop serving the masses at the bar (cheap *Napolitana* pastries and *rosquillas*—doughnuts) and takeout on the ground floor. But upstairs is a refined little 19th-century café—popular for generations. It offers an accessible menu and a relative oasis of quiet (daily 9:00-21:00, closed mid-July-Aug).

$$ Restaurante Puerto Rico, a simple, no-nonsense place, serves good meals for great prices to smart Madrileños in a long, congested hall (daily 13:00-24:00, Chinchilla 2, between Puerta del Sol and Gran Vía, +34 915 219 834).

$$$ Restaurante-Cafeteria Europa is a fun, high-energy scene with a mile-long bar, old-school waiters, local cuisine, and a fine €12 fixed-price lunch special (inside only). The menu lists three price levels: **bar** (inexpensive), **table** (pricey), or **terrace** (sky-high but with good people-watching). Your best value is to stick

to the lunch menu if you're sitting inside, or order off the plastic *barra* menu if you sit at the bar—the ham-and-egg toast or the homemade *churros* make a nice breakfast (daily 7:00-24:00, next to Hotel Europa, 50 yards off Puerta del Sol at Calle del Carmen 4, +34 915 212 900).

$$$ Casa Gonzalez is a revered gourmet cheese-and-wine shop with a circa-1930s interior and friendly service. Away from the tourist scene, it offers a genteel opportunity to enjoy a first-class cheese plate and a glass of wine in a fun setting recalling the happy days of the Republic of Spain—after the monarchy but before Franco. Their €20 assortment of five Spanish cheeses—more than enough for two—is a cheese lover's treat (40 wines by the glass, Mon-Sat 9:30-24:00, Sun 11:30-17:00, Calle de León 12, +34 914 295 618, Francisco and Luciano).

$$$ El Corte Inglés' "Gourmet Experience," a ninth-floor cafeteria, houses a specialty grocery mart and 10 mini restaurants with a wide range of cuisines—from burgers and Basque tapas to Mexican to Japanese. This snazzy and wildly popular complex is fresh, modern, and not particularly cheap. Take a seat at any of the indoor tables, or out on the open terrace—and ideally grab a table (inside or out) with a grand view over all of Madrid, from Gran Vía and Plaza de España to the Royal Palace (daily 10:00-24:00, in Building 1 at the top of Calle del Carmen, a half-block below Plaza del Callao).

$ Casa Labra Taberna Restaurante is famous as the birthplace of the Spanish Socialist Party in 1879...and as a spot for great cod. Their tasty little *tajada de bacalao* dishes put them on the map. Packed with Madrileños, it manages to be both dainty and rustic. It's a wonderful scene with three distinct sections: the inexpensive stand-up **bar** (line up for cod and croquettes, power up to the bar for drinks); a peaceful little **sit-down area** in back (still cheap); and a fancy, more expensive **restaurant.** Consider the outdoor tables self-serve. The waiters are fun to joke around with (daily 11:00-15:30 & 18:00-23:00, a block off Puerta del Sol at Calle Tetuán 12, +34 915 310 081).

$ Takos Al Pastor is a hip, cheap, authentic taquería, which often has a long line out front (Tue-Sun 13:30-24:00, closed Mon, Calle de la Abada 2, +34 680 247 217).

Asian: The trendy **$$ Yatai Market** food court gathers a variety of Asian street food counters under one roof—pad thai, sushi, ramen, bao steamed-bun sandwiches, and so on—with neon signs and shared tables (daily 12:00-24:00, just off Plaza de Tirso de Molina at Calle del Doctor Cortezo 10).

Vegetarian: $$ Artemisa is a hit with vegetarians and vegans who like good, healthy food without any hippie ambience (weekday lunch specials, open daily 13:30-16:00 & 20:30-23:30, north of

Puerta del Sol at Tres Cruces 4, a few steps off Plaza del Carmen, +34 915 218 721).

In the Chueca District

Chueca, just a short walk north of Gran Vía, in the past decade has gone from a sleazy no-go zone to a trendy and inviting neighborhood. Riding the Metro to the Chueca stop, you'll emerge right on Plaza de Chueca. The square feels like today's Madrid...without the tourism. A handful of places offer relaxing tables on the square, the neighborhood's San Antón market hall (Mercado de San Antón, just a block away) is now a fun food circus, and nearby streets hold plenty of hardworking, creative new eateries. Here are some good options:

$$ **Antigua Casa Angel Sierra Vermouth Bar** offers an old-time ambience that almost takes you back to 1917, when it opened. Belly up to the bar in its tight front room facing the square or, for more space, use the side entrance to reach a back room filled with giant barrels of vermouth and more spacious tables. They offer a simple menu of light, basic tapas—come here for the ambience, not the food (on Plaza de Chueca, Calle Gravina 11, +34 915 310 126).

$$ **Mercado de San Antón,** with three bustling floors of edible temptations, is flat-out fun for anyone who likes food (daily 10:00-late). There's a supermarket in the basement, and a produce-and-fish market on the ground floor. The first floor is a circle of tapas joints with shared tables looking down on the market action and sample dishes on display for easy ordering. The top floor is a more formal restaurant: $$$ **11 Nudos Terraza Nordés** offers classic Spanish dishes with a creative twist, cocktails, and a nice rooftop terrace (Augusto Figueroa 24, +34 913 300 294).

$$$ **Angelita Wine Bar** is a dressy little restaurant with spacious seating, a short food menu designed to go with the wines, and a long list of wines by the glass. An elegant place for a fine meal, it draws a smart local crowd (Mon 20:30-24:00, Tue-Sat 13:30-17:00 & 20:30-24:00, closed Sun, 100 yards from Gran Vía Metro station at Calle de la Reina 4, +34 915 216 678).

Churros con Chocolate

Those not watching their calories will want to try the deep-fried doughy treats called *churros* (or the thicker *porras*), best enjoyed by dipping them in pudding-like hot chocolate. Though many *chocolaterías* offer the dunkable fritters, *churros* are most delicious when consumed fresh out of the greasy cauldron at a place that actually fries them. Two Madrid favorites are near Puerta del Sol.

Chocolatería San Ginés is a classy institution, beloved for a century by Madrileños for its *churros con chocolate*. While busy all day, it's packed after midnight; the popular club and theater Teatro

Eslava is next door. Order at the counter, get a ticket, find a seat, and give your ticket to the server who delivers your order (open 24 hours; from Puerta del Sol, take Calle del Arenal 2 blocks west and turn left on bookstore-lined Pasadizo de San Ginés—you'll

see the café at #5, behind the big brick church; +34 913 656 546).

Chocolaterías Valor, a modern chain and Spanish chocolate maker, does *churros* with pride and gusto. A few minutes' walk from nearly all my hotel recommendations, it's a fine place for breakfast (daily 8:00-22:30, Fri-Sat until 24:00, a half-block below Plaza del Callao and Gran Vía at Postigo de San Martín 7, +34 915 229 288). You can also buy powdered Valor chocolate at **supermarkets** (like the one at El Corte Inglés Building 2) to make the drink at home.

Madrid Connections

BY TRAIN

Madrid has two main train stations: Chamartín and Atocha. Both stations offer long-distance trains *(largo recorridos)* as well as smaller local trains (*regionales* and *cercanías*) to nearby destinations.

Buying Train Tickets: Train station ticket counters can have long lines, especially during high season or holidays. Consider buying tickets online or at a travel agency. There's an El Corte Inglés travel agency at Atocha station (Mon-Fri 8:00-22:00, Sat 10:00-14:00, closed Sun, small fee, on ground floor of AVE side at the far end); you'll also find travel agencies at the El Corte Inglés department store (see the listing in the "Shopping in Madrid" section, earlier) and at the airport.

Train Information: +34 912 320 320, www.renfe.com.

Chamartín Station

The impressively large information, ticket, and customer-service office is at track 11. You can relax in the Sala VIP Club if you have a first-class rail pass and first-class seat or sleeper reservations (between tracks 13 and 14, cooler of free drinks). Baggage storage *(consigna)* is across the street, opposite track 17. The station's Metro stop is also called Chamartín (not "Pinar de Chamartín"). Train connections from here are listed later.

Atocha Station

The station is split in two: the AVE side (mostly long-distance

trains) and the *cercanías* side (mostly local trains to the suburbs—called *cercanías*—and the Metro for connecting into downtown). The two parts are connected by a corridor of shops and eateries. Each side has separate schedules and customer-service offices. The station's Metro stop is called Atocha Renfe.

Ticket Offices: The *cercanías* side has two offices—a small one for local trains and a big one for major trains (such as AVE). The AVE side has a pleasant, airy office that sells tickets for AVE and other long-distance trains. In the ticket hall, there are three types of sales points: *venta anticipada* (tickets in advance), *salida inmediata* (immediate departures—only tickets for certain designated trains, leaving soon, can be purchased here), and *salidas hoy* (departures today, but only for certain destinations—for example, Toledo). When you enter the ticket office, grab a number from a machine. If the line at one office is long, check the other offices. Ticket machines in the ticket office and scattered around the station usually don't work with American credit cards.

AVE Side: Located in the cavernous old brick station building, the AVE area boasts a lush, tropical garden filling its grand hall. It's used by AVE trains and other fast trains (Grandes Líneas). Here you'll find a customer service and information office (under the escalators), a spacious

ticket office (facing the garden, on the right side), a long-hours pharmacy (just past the ticket office), a handful of cafés and restaurants, and a pay WC. Baggage storage *(consignas)*, if open, is at the far end of the garden. Be clear on which level to catch your train: Some departures leave from the lower level (*planta baja* on departure boards); others leave from the "first floor" (*plta. primera*, ride up the escalators or elevators). Within the first-floor departure zone (past security) is the Club AVE/Sala VIP lounge for AVE business-class travelers and for first-class ticket holders or Eurailers with a first-class reservation (free drinks, newspapers, showers, and info service).

Cercanías **Side:** This is where you'll find the local *cercanías* trains, *regionales* trains, some eastbound faster trains, and the Atocha Renfe Metro stop. The *Atención al Cliente* office in the *cercanías* section has information only on trains to destinations near Madrid. Clearly marked signs lead you to a direct route to the *cercanías* train that goes to the airport, or to the Metro, taxi stand, or back to the AVE side.

Terrorism Memorial: The terrorist bombings of March 11, 2004, took place in Atocha and on local lines going into and out of the station. Security is understandably tight here. A moving memorial is in the *cercanías* part of the station (on the upper level, above the Atocha Renfe Metro stop). Walk inside and under the cylinder to read the thousands of condolence messages in many languages. The 36-foot-tall cylindrical glass memorial towers are visible from outside on the street.

AVE Trains

Spain's bullet trains open up good itinerary options. You can get from Madrid's Atocha station to **Barcelona** nonstop in 2.5 hours (at nearly 200 mph), with trains running almost hourly. The AVE train is faster and easier than flying, but not necessarily cheaper. Second-class tickets are about €110-130 one-way; first-class tickets are €180. Advance purchase and online discounts are available through the national rail company (Renfe) but sell out quickly. Save by not traveling on holidays. Your ticket includes one commuter-train transfer in Madrid or Barcelona. Avlo, a low-cost bullet train run by Renfe, is an option for the Madrid-Barcelona route (check www.renfe.com for status).

The AVE is also handy for visiting **Sevilla** (and, on the way, **Córdoba**). Consider this exciting, exhausting day trip: 7:00-depart Madrid, 8:45-12:40-in Córdoba, 13:30-20:45-in Sevilla, 23:15-back in Madrid.

Other AVE destinations include **Granada, Toledo, Segovia, Valencia, Alicante,** and **Malaga.** Prices vary with times, class, and date of purchase—they're usually cheapest up to two months ahead. Eurail Pass holders pay a seat reservation fee (for example, Madrid to Sevilla is €13 second class, and Madrid to Toledo is €4; must purchase at Renfe ticket windows—not available at ticket machines). Reserve each AVE segment ahead.

Train Connections

Below I've listed both non-AVE and (where available) AVE trains.

From Madrid by Train to: Toledo (AVE or cheaper Avant: nearly hourly, 30 minutes, from Atocha), **El Escorial** (*cercanías*, 2/hour, from Atocha and Chamartín, but bus is better—see next chapter), **Segovia** (best on AVE, up to 4/hour, 30 minutes plus 20-minute city bus to Segovia center, from Chamartín, take train going toward Valladolid), **Ávila** (nearly hourly, 1.5-2 hours, from Madrid's Príncipe Pío station; also 2/day, 1.5-2 hours, from Chamartín), **Salamanca** (4/day on speedy Alvia, 1.5 hours; or 7/day on much slower regional Media Distancia train, 3 hours; both from Chamartín), **Valencia** (AVE: nearly hourly, 2 hours, from Atocha; in Valencia, AVE passengers arrive at Joaquín So-

rolla station), **Santiago de Compostela** (nearly hourly, 3-4 hours, longer trips transfer in Ourense), **Barcelona** (AVE: at least hourly, 2.5-3 hours, from Atocha), **San Sebastián** (6/day, 5-8 hours, from Chamartín), **Bilbao** (2-4/day, 5-7 hours, some transfer in Zaragoza, from Chamartín), **Pamplona** (4/day direct, 3.5 hours, from Atocha), **Burgos** (6/day, 2.5-4.5 hours, from Chamartín), **León** (8/day, 2.5-5 hours, from Chamartín), **Granada** (AVE: 3/day, 3.5 hours, from Atocha, **Sevilla** (AVE: hourly, 2.5 hours, departures from 16:00-19:00 can sell out far in advance, from Atocha), **Córdoba** (AVE: almost hourly, 2 hours; Altaria trains: 4/day, 2 hours; all from Atocha), **Málaga** (AVE: hourly, 2.5-4 hours, from Atocha), **Algeciras** (2/day, 1 direct, 5.5-6 hours, from Atocha), **Lisbon,** Portugal (1/day, 11 hours, two transfers, from Atocha, bus or plane is better), **Marseille,** France (1/day direct, 8 hours, from Atocha; also stops at Montpellier, Nîmes, Avignon, and Aix-en-Provence).

BY BUS

Madrid has several major bus stations with good Metro connections. There are also several routes serving Barajas Airport's Terminal 4. Multiple bus companies operate from these stations, including Alsa (www.alsa.es) and Avanza (www.avanzabus.com). If you take a taxi from any bus station, you'll be charged a legitimate €3 supplement (not levied for trips to the station).

Plaza Elíptica Station: Served by Alsa. Buses to Toledo leave from here (2/hour, 1-1.5 hours, *directo* faster than *ruta*, Metro: Plaza Elíptica).

Estación Sur de Autobuses (South Station): Served by Alsa, Socibus, Avanza, and Interbus. From here, buses go to **Ávila** (nearly hourly, 6/day on weekends, 1.5 hours, Avanza), **Burgos** (2/day, 3.5 hours, Alsa), **Salamanca** (hourly express, 2.5-3 hours, Avanza), **León** (10/day, 4 hours, Alsa), **Santiago de Compostela** (4/day, 9 hours, includes 1 night bus, Alsa), **Granada** (nearly hourly, 5-6 hours, Alsa), **Algeciras** (1/day, overnight, 9 hours, Interbus) and **Lisbon** (2/day, 9 hours, Alsa). The station sits squarely on top of the Méndez Álvaro Metro (has TI, +34 914 684 200, www.estacionautobusesmadrid.com).

Moncloa Station: This station, in the Moncloa Metro station, serves **León** (6/day, 3.5-4.5 hours, Alsa), **Santiago de Compostela** (3/day, 9 hours, Alsa), **El Escorial** (4/hour, fewer on weekends, 1 hour, see next chapter), and **Segovia** (about 2/hour, La Sepulvedana). To reach the **Valley of the Fallen,** it's best to connect via El Escorial.

Avenida de América Station: Served by Alsa. Located at the Avenida de América Metro, buses go to **Lisbon** (4/day, 9

hours), **Burgos** (hourly, 3 hours), **Granada** (3/day, 6 hours), and **Pamplona** (almost hourly, most with transfer, 6 hours).

BY PLANE

Both international and domestic flights arrive at Madrid's Barajas Airport. Options for getting into town include public bus, *cercanías* train, Metro, taxi, and minibus shuttle.

Adolfo Suárez Barajas Airport

Ten miles east of downtown, Madrid's massive airport (code: MAD, www.aena.es) has four terminals. Terminals 1, 2, and 3 are connected by long indoor walkways (about a 10-minute walk apart); the newer Terminal 4 is farther away, and also has a separate satellite terminal called T4S. Be clear on which terminal your flight uses before heading to the airport. To transfer between Terminals 1-3 and Terminal 4, you can take a 10-minute shuttle bus (free, leaves every 10 minutes from departures level), or ride the Metro (stops at Terminals 2 and 4). Make sure to allow enough time if you need to travel between terminals (and then for the long walk within Terminal 4 to the gates).

Services: At the Terminal 1 arrivals area, you'll find the helpful Turismo Madrid TI (Mon-Sat 8:00-20:00, Sun 9:00-14:00, +34 913 058 656), ATMs, a flight info office, a post office window, a pharmacy, eateries, and car-rental agencies. Upstairs at the check-in level, Terminal 1 has an El Corte Inglés travel agency. The super-modern Terminal 4 offers essentially the same services, as well as a Renfe office (where you can get train info and buy long-distance train tickets, long hours daily). You'll find baggage storage *(consigna)* in Terminals 1, 2, and 4.

Handy Domestic Flights: Consider flying between Madrid and other cities in Spain (see "Flights" in the Practicalities chapter). Domestic airline Vueling (www.vueling.com) is popular for its discounts (e.g., Madrid-Barcelona flight as cheap as €40 if booked in advance).

Getting Between the Airport and Downtown

By Public Bus: The yellow **Exprés Aeropuerto** runs between all terminals of the airport and downtown, making three stops: O'Donnell, Plaza de Cibeles, and Atocha train station (€5, pay driver in cash—largest bill €20—or with tap-to-pay credit card, departs from arrivals level every 15-20 minutes, ride takes about 40 minutes, runs 24 hours a day). Once at Atocha, you can take a taxi or the Metro to your hotel. The bus back to the airport leaves Atocha from near the taxi stand on the *cercanías* side. From 23:30

MADRID

to 6:00, the bus only goes to Plaza de Cibeles, not all the way to Atocha.

Bus #200 (from all terminals) is less handy than the express bus because it leaves you farther from downtown (at the Metro stop at Avenida de América, northeast of the historical center). This bus departs from the arrivals level about every 10 minutes and takes about 20 minutes to reach Avenida de América (runs 6:00-24:00, buy €1.50 ticket from driver, or get a Multi Card with 10 shareable rides—see page 408).

By *Cercanías* Train: From Terminal 4, passengers can ride a *cercanías* train to either of Madrid's stations (€2.60, 2/hour, 25 minutes to Atocha, 12 minutes to Chamartín). Those returning to Madrid's airport by AVE train from elsewhere in Spain can transfer for free to the *cercanías* at Atocha: Scan your AVE ticket at the *cercanías* ticket machine to receive a ticket for the airport train. Be sure to board a train labeled T-4. For terminals 1, 2, or 3, the bus is a more convenient choice.

By Metro: Considering the ease of riding the Exprés Aeropuerto bus in from the airport, I wouldn't recommend taking the Metro. The subway involves two transfers to reach the city; it's not difficult, but usually involves climbing some stairs (for Metro tips, see page 409).

By Taxi or Uber: With cheap and easy alternatives available, there's not much reason to take a taxi or Uber unless you have lots of luggage or just want to go straight to your hotel. If you do take a taxi between the airport and downtown, the flat rate is €30 (no charge for luggage). Uber also serves the airport, and the fare is usually about the same (but can go higher with demand). Plan on getting stalled in traffic.

Getting Between the Airport and Other Towns

Some buses leave from the airport to far-flung destinations, such as Pamplona (see www.alsa.es; buy ticket online or from driver).

BY CAR

Avoid driving in Madrid. If you're planning to rent a car, pick it up as you depart the city.

Route Tips for Drivers

To leave Madrid, follow signs for *A-6* (direction *Villalba* or *A Coruña*) for Segovia, El Escorial, or the Valley of the Fallen (see next chapter for details). For Madrid-Toledo routes, see page 599.

From Madrid to Segovia (60 miles/97 km): After leaving Madrid on A-6, exit 39 gets you to Segovia via a slow, wind-

ing route over the scenic mountain. Exit at 60 (after a long toll tunnel) or get there more quickly by staying on the toll road all the way to Segovia. At the Segovia aqueduct, follow *casco histórico* signs to the old town (on the side where the aqueduct adjoins the crenellated fortress walls).

NORTHWEST OF MADRID

El Escorial • Valley of the Fallen • Segovia • Ávila

Spain's lavish, brutal, and complicated history is revealed throughout Old Castile. This region, northwest of Spain's capital city, is where the dominant Spanish language *(castellano)* originated, and is named for its many castles—battle scars from the long-fought Reconquista. Before slipping out of Madrid, consider several fine side trips here, all conveniently reached by car, bus, or train.

An hour from Madrid, tour the imposing palace at El Escorial. Nearby, at the awe-inspiring Valley of the Fallen, pay tribute to the countless victims of Spain's bloody civil war. Segovia, an altogether lovely burg with a remarkable Roman aqueduct, fine cathedral, and romantic castle, is another worthwhile destination. And Ávila warrants a quick stop to walk its perfectly preserved medieval walls.

All of these sights are located in the rugged, mountainous part of Castile in and near the Sierra de Guadarrama range. Be prepared for hilly terrain, cooler temperatures (thanks to the altitude), and often-snowcapped mountains on the horizon...giving this area an almost alpine flavor.

PLANNING YOUR TIME

History buffs can see **El Escorial** and the **Valley of the Fallen** in less than a day—but don't go on a Monday, when both sights are closed. By bus, see them as a day trip from Madrid; by car, see them en route to Segovia.

If you just like nice towns,

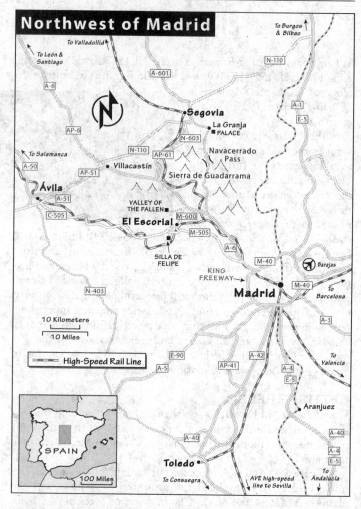

Segovia, also easy to reach from Madrid, is worth a half-day of sightseeing (and potentially more for lingering). If you have time, spend the night—the city is a joy in the evenings. **Ávila,** while charming, merits only a quick stop to marvel at its medieval walls and, perhaps, St. Teresa's finger.

Thanks to speedy train connections, it's possible to see Segovia on the way from Madrid to Salamanca. It's trickier but doable to also squeeze in Ávila: Take the fast train (or bus) to Segovia, then bus from Segovia to Ávila, and finally continue to Salamanca by bus or train.

Note that **Toledo** and **Salamanca** (covered in separate chapters) are also popular and doable side trips from Madrid.

El Escorial

When Spain defeated France in a crucial 1557 battle, a grateful King Philip II (1527-1598) vowed to build a grand structure to the glory of God: the Monasterio de San Lorenzo de El Escorial (worth ▲▲).

The sprawling complex would serve God in several ways: as a monastery to further the Catholic faith, a school to promote knowledge, a mausoleum to honor Spanish royalty, and a palace to provide respite from the bustle of Madrid. For two decades (1563-1584), Philip poured Spain's wealth into building El Escorial. The result was a massive structure, 30 miles northwest of Madrid, packed with art and history. Because of this bully in the national budget, Spain has almost nothing else to show from this most powerful period of her history.

You'll see grandiose buildings, colorful frescoes, quiet cloisters, somber tombs, a towering altarpiece, chandeliered rooms, canvases by Titian and El Greco, an ingenious model of the cosmos, and King Philip's bedpan. El Escorial is a time capsule of Spain's golden age—and its glorious decline.

GETTING THERE

From Madrid, El Escorial is less than an hour by car (and can easily be combined with a visit to the nearby Valley of the Fallen). By public transportation, the bus gets you closer to the palace than the train.

By Bus: At Madrid's Moncloa bus station, follow signs to Terminal 1 (blue), go up to the platforms in the blue hallway, and find platform 11 (#664 and #661, 4/hour, fewer on weekends, 1 hour, €4.20 one-way, buy ticket from driver, Alsa, +34 911 779 951).

Either bus drops you downtown in San Lorenzo de El Escorial, a pleasant 10-minute stroll from the palace (see map): Exit the bus station from the back ramp that leads over the parked buses (note that return buses to Madrid leave from platform 3 or 4 below; schedule posted by info counter inside station). Once outside, turn left and follow the cobbled pedestrian lane, Calle San Juan, as it veers right and becomes Calle Juan de Leyva. A few short blocks later, it dead-ends at Duque de Medinaceli, where you'll turn left and see the palace. Stairs lead past several decent eateries, through a delightful square, past the TI, and directly to the tourist entry of El Escorial. The **TI** has a free mini museum—including a monas-

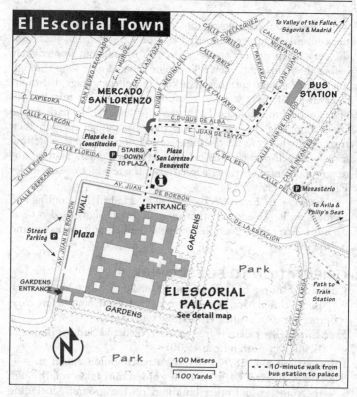

El Escorial Town

To Valley of the Fallen,
Segovia & Madrid

CALLE VELAZQUEZ

C. COELLO

CALLE CAÑADA NUEVA

C. F. MUÑOZ

CALLE LAS POZAS

CALLE BRIZ

C. PATRIARCA

C. SAN JUAN

BUS STATION

MERCADO SAN LORENZO

CALLE CALVARIO

C. LAPIEDRA

C.F. MUÑOZ

C. DUQUE MEDINACELI

C. DUQUE DE ALBA

CALLE ALARCÓN

C. DUQUE DE ALBA

C. JUAN DE LEYVA

CALLE JUAN DE TOLEDO

Plaza de la Constitución

STAIRS DOWN TO PLAZA

Plaza San Lorenzo / Benavente

C. DEL REY

CALLE INFANTES

CALLE FLORIDA

CALLE RUBIO

AV. JUAN DE BORBÓN

C. DEL REY

Monasterio

CALLE SERRANO

ENTRANCE

To Ávila & Philip's Seat

WALL

GARDENS

C. DE LA ESTACIÓN

AV. JUAN DE BORBÓN

Street Parking

Plaza

GARDENS ENTRANCE

EL ESCORIAL PALACE
See detail map

Park

Path to Train Station

GARDENS

CALLE CALLEJA LARGA

Park

100 Meters

100 Yards

- - - 10-minute walk from bus station to palace

tery model made of sugar—and offers maps of two lovely and easily accessible hiking routes (Mon-Sat 10:00-14:00 & 15:00-18:00, Sun 10:00-15:00, +34 918 905 313, www.sanlorenzoturismo.org).

By Train: Local trains run to El Escorial from Madrid's Atocha and Chamartín stations (*cercanías* line C-3A, 1-2/hour). From the El Escorial station, the palace is a 20-minute walk straight uphill through Casita del Príncipe park. Or you can take a shuttle bus (L1) from the station (2/hour, usually timed with train arrival, €1.30) or a taxi (€7.50) to the town center and the palace.

By Car: It's quite simple and takes just under an hour. Head out of Madrid on highway A-6 (watch for signs to *A Coruña*). At kilometer 18, stay on A-6, skipping an exit for El Escorial. Later, around kilometer 37, you'll see the cross marking the Valley of the Fallen ahead on the left. Keep going and exit at kilometer 47 to M-600 (following signs toward *El Escorial/Guadarrama*). The road goes right past the entrance to the Valley of the Fallen (after a half-mile, see a granite gate on right, marked *Valle de los Caídos*), then continues to El Escorial (follow signs to *San Lorenzo de El Escorial*, and then *centro histórico*).

Parking: After driving through the drab town of El Escorial,

you have several parking options near the monastery. To park in the convenient garage beneath Plaza de Constitución, watch for the very sharp turnoff on the right at a roundabout immediately before the monastery, then follow blue *P* signs on a loop through town to the garage entrance. Walking out of the garage, the monastery is just across the street and down the stairs (or turn left out of the garage to reach the TI in two short blocks). To park on the street alongside the monastery, bypass the garage turnoff, then turn right when you hit the monastery. Loop around it, watching for pay-and-display parking on your right. In a pinch, another underground garage (Parking Monasterio) is a few blocks east, under Parque Felipe II.

Leaving El Escorial: To return to Madrid (or continue to Segovia/Ávila, Toledo, or other points), follow signs to *A-6 Guadarrama.* After about six miles you pass the Valley of the Fallen and hit the freeway.

ORIENTATION TO EL ESCORIAL

Cost and Hours: €12, Tue-Sun 10:00-20:00, Oct-March until 18:00, closed Mon year-round, last entry one hour before closing. For even a quick visit, allow two hours.

Free Entry: The palace is free to enter Wed and Sun beginning at 17:00 (Oct-March from 15:00).

Information: +34 918 905 904, www.patrimonionacional.es.

Tours: For an extra €4, a 1.5-hour **guided tour** takes you through the complex and other buildings on the grounds, including the House of the Infante and House of the Prince. There are very few tours in English; if nothing's running soon, go on your own: Follow my self-guided tour, or rent the €5 handheld **multimedia guide.**

Visitor Information: English descriptions are scattered throughout the palace. For more information, get the *Guide: Monastery of San Lorenzo El Real de El Escorial,* which follows the general route you'll take (€9, available at shops in the palace).

Weather: At an elevation of nearly 3,500 feet, it can be very cold. Dress appropriately.

Services: Backpacks must be checked in cloakroom **lockers** (€1 coin required).

Eating: True to its austere orientation, El Escorial doesn't even have a simple café; for food or drinks, you must venture across the street, into town. The **Mercado San Lorenzo,** a four-minute walk from the palace, is a good place to shop for a picnic (Mon-Fri 9:30-13:30 & 18:00-20:30, Sat 9:30-14:00, closed Sun, Calle del Rey 9). **Plaza Jacinto Benavente** and **Plaza de la Constitución,** two blocks north of the palace complex, host

a handful of nondescript but decent restaurants serving fixed-price lunches or tapas, often at shady outdoor tables.

⊘ SELF-GUIDED TOUR
Exterior

The building is huge, a symbol of power rather than elegance—like a penitentiary. At about 700 feet long and 500 feet wide, it covers eight acres and has 2,600 windows, 1,200 doors, more than 100 miles of passages, and 1,600 overwhelmed tourists.

It was designed by the architect Juan de Herrera (inspired by his mentor, Juan Bautista de Toledo). El Escorial was classic Herrera: grid-like windows, austere granite, slate roofs, corner towers with pyramid-shaped spires, and geometrical simplicity with little ornamentation. Its monumental scale captured the grandiose political and spiritual aspirations of King Philip II. El Escorial inspired countless *Herreresque* buildings across Spain, including Madrid's Plaza Mayor.

If El Escorial seems, well, severe, consider that it was shaped by a kind of bunker mentality: Spain's Catholics were in the fight of their lives battling the Protestants of northern Europe. But to Philip, El Escorial also embodied how progressive Catholics could merge Renaissance humanism with Catholic spirituality. To Protestants, on the other hand, it epitomized the evil of closed-minded Catholicism. To architects, the building—on the cusp between styles—exudes both Renaissance simplicity and Counter-Reformation grandeur.

All in all, El Escorial feels less like a luxurious palace and more like an austere fortress—a fortress for God.

• *Let's go in. Pass through security, buy your ticket, and follow the signs to the beginning of the tour. The vast complex may seem daunting, but the* visita *arrows and signs will guide you. You'll first go through a series of courtyards and stone halls that lead you into a big courtyard. Turn around and face the six statues of the biblical kings who gave the name to...*

The Courtyard of the Kings (El Patio de los Reyes)

Here in the central courtyard of the complex, get oriented. The building with the six kings is the basilica. Beneath the basilica (not visible from here) are the royal tombs, and behind it are the royal residences. The building to your right is the monastery,

El Escorial—Ground Floor

- To Train Station
- HABSBURG PALACE (UPSTAIRS)
- ROYAL PANTHEON (STAIRS LEAD DOWN TO CRYPT)
- WALKING GALLERY
- 50 Meters
- 50 Yards
- Gardens
- PANTHEON OF ROYAL CHILDREN (DOWNSTAIRS)
- EXIT FROM BOURBON PALACE TOUR ENDS
- CHARLES V CENOTAPH
- ALTAR
- PHILIP II CENOTAPH
- HALL OF BATTLES (UPSTAIRS)
- DOME
- CHAPTER ROOMS
- SHOP
- BASILICA
- CLOISTER
- Gardens
- CELLINI'S CHRIST
- WC
- MAIN STAIRCASE
- ENTRANCE
- TICKETS
- GATE HOUSE
- OLD CHURCH
- To Town & Bus Station
- TOUR BEGINS
- Courtyard of the Kings
- COLLEGE (CLOSED TO THE PUBLIC)
- MONASTERY (CLOSED TO THE PUBLIC)
- AV. JUAN DE BORBÓN
- STAIRS DOWN TO COURTYARD
- STAIRS UP TO LIBRARY
- LIBRARY (UPPER FLOOR)
- N
- Plaza
- WALL
- GARDEN ENTRANCE
- AV. JUAN DE BORBÓN

where you'll see the cloisters. To your left is the school (which you won't visit), and behind you is the library.

Imagine being a 16th-century visitor arriving in this immense courtyard, awed by Philip II, the most powerful man in Europe. The six shiny-crowned kings of the tribe of Judah underscored his divine kingship. Philip—enigmatic, introverted, ascetic, and extremely religious—used El Escorial to rule his vast empire and to champion the Catholic cause.

• A crucial part of Philip's plan was education. Let's go see the library. Turn your back to the kings, find the stairs in the corner (near the exit), and head up. Before you enter the library, look above the fancy door with the plaque warning "Excomunión..."—you'll be excommunicated if you steal a book (or fail to show the guard your ticket).

Royal Library (Biblioteca Real)

This long, sumptuous, book-lined room makes it clear that Philip valued learning. Monks here devoured the world's knowledge, the better to understand God and battle Protestant "heresies." The

library's location—link-ing the school with the monastery—symbolized the dovetailing of secular and religious thought. The books on the carved book-cases (designed by Herre-ra) are shelved spine-first to allow the golden pages to breathe and to create a royal aesthetic.

The big globe in the room is an armillary sphere—an elabo-rate model of the solar system. When you turned a (now missing) crank, it spun like a gyroscope, demonstrating how the heavenly bodies revolved around Earth (with a misshapen North America still mostly unexplored by Europeans). Designed by a math profes-sor from Pisa, this device was state-of-the-art science circa 1580... until the man's colleague, Galileo, established the sun as the center of the universe.

In the burst-of-color ceiling fresco (by Pellegrino Tibaldi), robed women symbolize the subjects taught here: geometry, gram-mar, astronomy, and so on. They led the eager student to the ul-timate goal (at the far end of the room): "Philosophia," or love of wisdom.

• *Exit (wiser) at the far end and head downstairs. You'll pass a WC, then go through a souvenir shop, before walking back across the Courtyard of the Kings. You are now entering the stretch of the tour focusing on El Es-corial's religious side: the church, cloisters, and religious art. Go through the central arch under the six kings into the...*

Basilica

This church is the spiritual centerpiece and beating heart of this en-tire faith-driven enterprise. Herrera designed the cavernous space as a perfect 50-meter square with four equal arms, symbolizing divine perfection. Soaring overhead is a 100-meter-high central dome inspired by the one being built at the same time at St. Peter's in Rome. The vast ceiling frescoes (by the prolific Luca Giordano) are like visions of heaven, including a choir of angels above the basilica's choir loft.

Approach the high altar. It's a towering, 100-foot-tall, four-tiered frame of red marble and green jasper. It holds gilded bronze statues (like Jesus crucified on the top) and dramatic paintings (like the angels who mourn him). At the base is the temple-like taber-nacle (by Herrera), for the Communion wafers. In the very center of the altar is its most important painting—of St. Lawrence, or San Lorenzo. It shows the Christian martyr being literally roasted atop a flaming grill. The reclining saint is taking "turn the other

cheek" to new extremes. Lorenzo was so cool, he reportedly told his Roman executioners, "You can turn me over now—I'm done on this side."

The basilica, the monastery, and the town adjoining El Escorial are all named for San Lorenzo. And the entire complex of El Escorial is built on a grid-like floorplan in honor of St. Lawrence's grill.

The golden statues flanking the altar mark royal tombs in the crypt below (which you'll visit later). To the left is the great Charles V (with his family), who built Spain's mighty empire and ushered in its golden age. To the right is his son, Philip II, who used that wealth to build El Escorial. From here, you can't see the faces of Charles or Philip...but you're not the target audience. Later on, you'll see a place with a view of the back of the altar, where Spain's monarchs could privately attend Mass while gazing upon these statues of their illustrious ancestors.

As you make your way back outside, browse some of the church's 36 Baroque altars, then detour to the right corner for Benvenuto Cellini's marble masterpiece, *The Crucifixion* (1562). Jesus is stark naked (though he's sometimes given a loincloth), with a face supposedly modeled after the Shroud of Turin. Cellini carved this from Carrara marble for his own tomb in Florence, but instead ended up selling it to the Medicis, who diplomatically gave it to Philip.

• *Exit to your left and continue to the Gate House* (Portería), *which served as a waiting room for people visiting the monks. From here, you'll enter the...*

Cloister (Claustro)

Turn right and work your way around the cloister, which glows with bright paintings by Pellegrino Tibaldi (who also did the library). The pavilion in the courtyard is by (who else?) Herrera.

Detour briefly up the main staircase to marvel at Luca Giordano's awe-inspiring ceiling fresco, *The Glory of the Spanish Monarchy.* The heavens open, revealing Jesus (near his cross), along with the God the Father, the dove of the Holy Spirit, and countless saints and angels reclining on plush clouds. Just below the Trinity, find Philip II kneeling before them, holding two crowns they've blessed him with. To the right is his dad, Charles (holding the globe of his empire), and to the left is an adoring San Lorenzo. At the very bottom, a mortal on a balcony tells his

friends, "Yep, that's my family!" Luca Giordano painted this and a dozen other mammoth frescoes in the monastery in a mere 22 months—a testament to his nickname, "Speedy Luca!"

• *Let's see more art. At the end of the cloister's first corridor, on the right, step into the...*

Old Church (Iglesia Vieja)

This venerable space, predating El Escorial, had been used to inter several kings, and was where Philip lived during construction. Among the many paintings, look above the main altar for the powerful *Martyrdom of St. Lawrence* by Titian. Titian was Philip's favorite painter, and this was supposed to be the glorious centerpiece of the basilica's high altar. With its dramatic dark background and glowing coals, it was a masterpiece...but it turned out to be the wrong size.

• *Continue circling the cloister. Along the next corridor, on the right, are the...*

Chapter Rooms (Salas Capitulares)

These gloriously frescoed rooms, where monks gathered to do church business, evolved into a small art gallery.

As you enter, you're face-to-face with **El Greco's *Martyrdom of St. Maurice and the Theban Legion*** (1580-82). Obsessed with saintly sacrifice, Philip II commissioned this scene to grace the basilica. But Philip was so disappointed, it wound up here. Why? Because El Greco made the actual beheading of the saint (lower left) an afterthought, while he focused on a moment he personally found more moving—when St. Maurice convinces his comrades not to give up on their Christian faith. Disappointed as Philip was, artistry wins out: Today, this is the most significant painting at El Escorial.

In the room on the left, look for another painting Titian did for his patron Philip—a *Last Supper*.

• *Now head underground, to the land of the dead. Head into the room on the right and go down the stairs at the far end. You'll pass a wall of wooden archive boxes, then go through a shop, then continue into the...*

Pantheon of the Princes (Panteón de los Principes)

These corridors are filled with the tombs of lesser (nonruling) members of the royal family. Each bears that person's name (in Latin), relationship to the king, and slogan or epitaph.

You'll pass the evocative, wedding-cake **Pantheon of Royal Children** (Panteón de los Infantes), which holds the remains of royal children who died before the age of seven (and their first

Communion). This is a poignant reminder of the scourge of child mortality back in those days, even among the super-wealthy.

• *Continue down another hall, with more tombs of lesser royals. You'll walk up a flight of stairs, then down a long stairway to reach the...*

Royal Pantheon (Panteón Real)

This octagonal, marble-and-bronze-paneled room is the gilded resting place of 26 kings and queens...four centuries' worth of Spanish monarchy in uniform gray-marble coffins, labeled with bronze plaques. In the room's postmortem filing system, rulers are on the left, consorts on the right.

On the top shelf to the left of the altar is the great Charles (*Carolvs*) V, who ruled as Holy Roman Emperor during Spain's golden age. He's flanked by his Queen Isabel (labeled in German, *Elisabeth*). Their son and the builder of El Escorial, Philip II, rests below Charles, opposite his wife—the one (of four) who produced a ruling heir.

There are plenty of other illustrious kings, like Philip IV, who patronized Velázquez, and Charles III, the so-called "mayor" who beautified Madrid. The only female ruler buried on the left side is Isabel II, the backward-looking 19th-century queen who was toppled by a liberal revolution. The most recent tomb is Victoria Eugenia (bottom left, as you face the door), the great-grandmother of Spain's current king, Felipe VI.

Will more recent royalty be buried here? There are two empty niches (above the door) ready to be filled. But this prime real estate comes with a waiting process. Before a royal corpse can rest here, it needs to decompose in a nearby room (closed to tourists) for at least 25 years. The deceased grandparents of the current king, Johannes III and Maria de Mercedibus, have been penciled in for burial as soon as their remains are ready. After that, where does that leave Felipe's parents, Juan Carlos and Sofía, and Felipe himself, and monarchs still to come? This hotel seems to be *completo*.

• *Head back up the stairs. As you ascend, consider this: El Escorial's lower level was reserved for the dead. The middle level (with the basilica and cloisters) was for the Church. You're now headed for the upper level—the royal residences.*

Habsburg Palace (Palacio de los Austrias)

Among its many functions, El Escorial was a royal palace—a popular retreat from the heat and politics of Madrid, a place to meditate in the monastery and hunt in the mountains. This part of the palace is named for the Habsburg family dynasty—Charles V, Philip II, and so on—who ruled Spain for 200 years.

You begin in **Philip II's apartment.** Look at the king's humble bed...barely queen-size. Philip was notoriously austere, and

when he stayed here he dropped royal trappings to focus on God. Speaking of God, remember (when we were in the basilica) that there was a private place for monarchs to attend Mass, with a view of the back of the altar and the front of the ancestors' faces. Peek through the window.

The red box next to Philip's pillow holds the royal bedpan. But don't laugh—he's looking down from the wall to your left. Philip lived a long and productive life and left El Escorial as his legacy. And at age 71, now gout-ridden and overseeing a dying empire, he died at his beloved El Escorial, here in this bed.

Continue on to the **King's Antechamber,** with its fine inlaid-wood door, one of a set of five (a gift from the German emperor that celebrates the exciting humanism of the age). The slate strip angling across the room on the floor is a sundial from 1755. It lined up with a (now plugged) hole in the wall so that at noon a tiny beam hit the middle of the three lines. Palace clocks were set by this. Where the ray crossed the strip indicated the date and sign of the zodiac.

In the **Walking Gallery** that follows, the royals got their exercise privately, with no risk of darkening their high-class skins with a tan. Here and in the next rooms you find galleries filled with portraits of the—let's be honest—quite unattractive Habsburg royals. Note the family resemblance: the jutting Habsburg jaw and lips. That's the kind of thing you get when you mix blue blood with more blue blood (a common problem among Europe's royals).

Find **Charles V** (1500-1558, King Charles I in Spain) over the fireplace mantel. As Holy Roman Emperor, Charles ruled over not only Spain but also Germany, Austria, the Low Countries, much of Italy, and the Americas. The guy with the red tights to the right of Charles is his illegitimate son, **Don Juan de Austria**—famous for his handsome looks, thanks to a little fresh blood.

But during Philip II's reign, Spain was drained by war—including the naval defeat of the Spanish Armada by England (1588)—and went into decline. Later Habsburg rulers were ineffectual and inbred. **Charles II** (1665-1700, to the right of the door you came in), who suffered from epilepsy, had a severe underbite. Dubbed "Charles the Mad," he was the last of the Spanish Habsburgs. He died without an heir in 1700, ushering in the War of the Spanish Succession, the dismantling of Spain's empire, the rise of France's Bourbon dynasty...and the need for a new wing in El Escorial. (But we're getting ahead of ourselves.)

For now, continue through the Habsburg wing, noticing the adjustable **sedan chair** that Philip II, thick with gout, was carried in (for seven days) on his last trip from Madrid to El Escorial. He wanted to be here when he died.

Go through the **Guards' Room** to the **King's Apartments** and

find the small portrait of Philip II flanked by two large paintings of his daughters. The palace was like Philip: austere. Notice the simple floors, plain white walls, and bare-bones chandelier. Peek into the bedroom of one of his daughters, Isabel Clara Eugenia. The sheet warmer beside her bed was often necessary during the winter. If the bed curtains are drawn, bend down to see the view from her bed... of the high altar in the basilica next door. The entire Habsburg Palace was built in a U-shape around that venerated altar.

• *Go up several stairs to the...*

Hall of Battles (Sala de Batallas)

The paintings celebrate Spain's great military victories—including the one that brought us El Escorial. It was the Battle of San Quentin, won on the feast day of St. Lawrence (August 10, 1557), that inspired Philip II to construct El Escorial. The sprawling series of paintings (1590) helped teach later kings the elements of military tactics and formations. (To follow along, note that Spain flew the white-and-red flags, France the blue.)

• *Continue through a door next to the one you entered to the...*

Bourbon Palace (Palacio de los Borbones)

These royal apartments—the frilly yin to the Habsburgs' austere yang—housed Spain's next (and current) dynasty, the Bourbons.

Around 1700, the Habsburgs were defeated by Europe's rising power, France, and the French grandson of Louis XIV became king of Spain. The Bourbons turned this wing into a mini Versailles: chandeliers, mirrors, heavy drapes, and elaborate Baroque furniture. They also loved high-art tapestries, for both insulation and decoration. Hunting scenes were popular, as this was their main activity when they retreated here. Many tapestries came from the Royal Tapestry Factory in Madrid (which you can still visit today).

In the first room (the Banqueting Hall), the *Dance on the Banks of the Manzanares Canal* was designed by the great painter Goya. Continuing on, you'll find more Goya tapestries depicting cheery scenes of Bourbon aristocrats frolicking in their carefree lives, while Europe's poor plotted revolution. As you pass through room after sumptuous room, listen for the ticking of the royal clock collection...while you ponder the ticking of Time. How Philip II built El Escorial, then passed it down through the later Habsburgs, to the Bourbons...to today's King Felipe VI, the great-great-great-great-great-great-great-great-great grandson of France's "Sun King," Louis XIV.

• *Our tour is done. From here, you can check out temporary exhibits just past the cloakroom, or head outside. To get a nice view of El Escorial from its fine gardens—rather than the stark plaza that surrounds it on two sides—you can head to...*

El Escorial Gardens

To reach the gardens (free to enter), circle all the way around the right side of the building as you face it. Going beneath the arcade running over the road, look left for the garden entrance. While the gardens are as stark and geometrical as the building itself (with sharply manicured hedges rather than flowers and trees), this is where you'll enjoy the best views of El Escorial—especially in the afternoon light. Listen for a nagging peacock and enjoy the views over the wooded hillsides to the distant skyscrapers of Madrid.

NEAR EL ESCORIAL: PHILIP'S SEAT

Drivers can visit the nearby Silla de Felipe II (Philip's Seat), a rocky viewpoint where the king would come to admire his palace as it was being built. It's well marked from M-505, which runs between Madrid and Ávila. If you leave El Escorial by first heading back toward Madrid and then turning off for Ávila, you'll see the turnoff to Philip's Seat on your left after about a mile. It's a couple minutes' drive up a twisty road to a hill adjacent to the monastery.

Valley of the Fallen

Six miles from El Escorial, high in the Sierra de Guadarrama Mountains, is the Valley of the Fallen (Valle de los Caídos). A 500-foot-tall granite cross marks this immense and powerful underground monument to the victims of Spain's 20th-century nightmare—the Spanish Civil War (1936-1939). That conflict is still extremely controversial in Spain today—rarely commemorated by monuments or even discussed in museums. Considering that, the Valley of the Fallen is a must for those interested in 20th-century history (or fascist architecture).

Until recently, the Valley of the Fallen was also the final resting place of Generalísimo Francisco Franco, Spain's dictator from 1939 until his death in 1975. But in late 2019, after years of debate, Franco's remains were exhumed and moved to his wife's mausoleum in the Mingorrubio Cemetery in El Pardo, a suburb of Madrid.

GETTING THERE

Most visitors side-trip to the Valley of the Fallen from El Escorial. If you don't have your own wheels, the easiest way to get between these two sights is to negotiate a deal with a **taxi** to take you from El Escorial to Valley of the Fallen, wait 30-60 minutes, and then bring you back to El Escorial (figure €45 total). There is a local **bus** that leaves from El Escorial's bus station, but it's not very frequent or convenient, as it drops you three miles from the Valley of the Fallen site.

Drivers can find tips under El Escorial's "Getting There—By Car," earlier. Pay at the booth as you enter from the main road, then drive about three miles through a pine forest to the site itself. A big parking lot is next to the café, a short walk from the basilica.

ORIENTATION TO THE VALLEY OF THE FALLEN

Cost and Hours: €9, Tue-Sun 10:00-19:00, Oct-March until 18:00, closed Mon year-round, +34 918 905 902, www.patrimonionacional.es.

Mass: You can enter the basilica during Mass, but you can't sightsee the central area or linger afterward. One-hour services run Tue-Sat at 11:00 and Sun at 11:00, 13:00, and 17:30 (17:00 in winter). During services, the entire front of the basilica (altar and tombs) is closed. Mass is usually accompanied by the resident boys' choir, the "White Voices" (Spain's answer to the Vienna Boys' Choir).

Visitor Services: There's a **$$** café with WCs at the site's main parking lot.

VISITING THE VALLEY OF THE FALLEN

The main thing to see at the Valley of the Fallen is the basilica interior. While the cross at the top of the monument is undergoing a lengthy restoration, there is no access to it by funicular or by foot along the trail (marked *Sendero de la Cruz*). Given that, an hour is enough for a quick visit.

Approaching by car or bus, you enter the sprawling park through a granite gate. The best views of the cross are from the bridge (but note that it's illegal for drivers to stop anywhere along this road). On the right, tiny chapels along the ridge mark the stations of the cross, where pilgrims stop on their hike to this memorial.

In 1940, prison workers dug 220,000 tons of granite out of the hill to form an underground basilica, then used the stones to erect the cross (built like a chimney, from the inside). Since it's built directly over the dome of the subterranean basilica, a seismologist keeps a careful eye on things.

The stairs that lead to the imposing **monument** are grouped in

sets of tens, meant to symbolize the Ten Commandments (including "Thou shalt not kill"—hmm). The emotional pietà draped over the basilica's entrance is huge—you could sit in the palm of Christ's hand. The statue was sculpted by Juan de Ávalos, the same artist who created the dramatic figures of the four Evangelists at the base of the cross. It must have had a powerful impact on mothers who came here to remember their fallen sons.

A solemn silence and a stony chill fill the **basilica.** At 300 yards long, it was built to be longer than St. Peter's...but the Vatican had the final say when it blessed only 262 of those yards. It's nearly empty inside, making it feel much larger.

After walking through the two long vestibules, stop at the iron gates of the actual basilica. The line of torch-like lamps adds to the shrine-like ambience. Franco's prisoners, the enemies of the right, spent a decade digging this memorial out of solid rock. (Though it looks like bare rock still shows on the ceiling, it's just a clever design.) The sides of the monument are lined with copies of 16th-century Brussels tapestries of the Apocalypse, and alabaster statues of the Virgin Mary perch above the arches of the side chapels. Notice the hooded figures peering out at you all over the space.

Take the long walk down the nave, then up 10 steps into the main part of the church, populated with rough wooden pews. Under a glittering mosaic dome is the high altar. At the base of the dome, four gigantic bronze angels look down over you.

Interred behind the high altar and side chapels (marked "RIP, 1936-1939, died for God and country") are the remains of approximately 34,000 people, including both Franco's Nationalists and the 12,000 or so anti-Franco Republicans who lost their lives in the war (the urns are not visible). This is also where Franco was interred until his body was moved to Madrid in 2019—you might still see flowers strewn on the site of Franco's original grave.

In front of the altar is the grave of José Antonio Primo de Rivera (1903-1936), the founder of Spanish fascism, who was killed by Republicans during the civil war; as one of the fallen, he remains buried in the basilica. Next to the fascist's grave, the statue of a crucified Christ is lashed to a timber Franco himself is said to have felled. The seeping stones seem to weep for the victims.

Today, families of the buried Republicans and Nationalists, along with many Spaniards, remain conflicted about the Valley of the Fallen. The war is still a deep wound in Spanish society, and

The Spanish Civil War (1936-1939)

Thirty-three months of warfare killed roughly 500,000 Spaniards. Unlike America's Civil War, which split the US north and south, Spain's war was between classes and ideologies, dividing every city and village, and many families. It was especially cruel, with atrocities and reprisals on both sides.

The war began as a military coup to overthrow the democratically elected Republic, a government that the army and other conservative powers considered too liberal and disorganized. The rebel forces, called the Nationalists (Nacionalistas), consisted of the army, monarchy, Catholic Church, big business, and rural estates, with aid from Germany, Italy, and Portugal. Trying to preserve the government were the Republicans (Republicanos), also called Loyalists: the government, urban areas, secularists, small business, and labor unions, with aid from the United States (minimal help) and the "International Brigades" of communists, socialists, and labor organizers.

In the summer of 1936, the army rebelled and took control of its own garrisons, rejecting the Republic and pledging allegiance to Generalísimo Francisco Franco (1892-1975). These Nationalists launched a three-year military offensive to take Spain region by region, town by town. The Republican government cobbled together an army of volunteers, local militias, and international fighters. The war pitted conservative Catholic priests against socialist factory workers, rich businessmen against radical students, farmers loyal to the old king against small businessmen.

Spain's civil war attracted international attention. Adolf Hitler and Benito Mussolini sent troops and supplies to their fellow fascist Franco. It was Hitler's Luftwaffe that helped Franco bomb the town of Guernica (April 1937), an event famously captured on canvas by Pablo Picasso (for more on the bombing, see sidebar on page 219; to read about the painting, see page 468). On the Republican side, hundreds of Americans (including Ernest Hemingway) steamed over to Spain, some to fight for democracy as part of the "Abraham Lincoln Brigade."

By 1938, only Barcelona and Madrid held out. But they were no match for Franco's army. On April 1, 1939, Madrid fell and the war ended, beginning 36 years of iron-fisted rule by Franco.

the sight inspires heavy emotions and controversy about what the future of the monument should really be.

As you leave, stare into the eyes of those angels with swords and think about all the "heroes" who keep dying "for God and country," at the request of the latter.

The expansive **view** from the monument's terrace includes the peaceful, forested valley and sometimes snow-streaked mountains.

Segovia

A beautiful city built along a ridge, Segovia is one of Madrid's most tempting day trips...and even better overnight. Fifty miles from Madrid, this town of 55,000 boasts a thrilling Roman aqueduct, a grand cathedral, and a historic castle. In days past, Segovia was a Roman town, a medieval trade center, and a perennial favorite of the kings and queens of Castile.

With its echoes of that history, Segovia remains one of Spain's most pleasant towns. Since the city is more than 3,000 feet above sea level and just northwest of a mountain range, it's exposed to cool northern breezes, and people come here from Madrid for a break from the summer heat. It's a fun place to simply hang out and enjoy some low-impact sightseeing.

Day-Tripping from Madrid: Considering the easy train and bus connections, Segovia makes a fine day trip from Madrid (30 minutes one-way by AVE train, 1.5 hours by bus; see "Segovia Connections" for details). The disadvantages of this plan are that you spend the coolest hours of the day (early and late) en route, you miss the charming evening scene in Segovia, and you'll pay more for a hotel in Madrid than in Segovia. If you have time, spend the night. But even if you just stay the day, Segovia offers a rewarding and convenient break from the big-city intensity of Madrid.

Orientation to Segovia

Segovia is a medieval "ship" ready for your inspection. Start at the stern—the aqueduct—and stroll up Calle de Cervantes and Calle Juan Bravo to explore the tangle of narrow streets around playful Plaza Mayor, head for the prickly Gothic masts of the cathedral, and then descend to the Alcázar at the bow.

Tourist Information: The TI at Plaza del Azoguejo, at the base of the **aqueduct,** specializes in Segovia and has friendly staff, two wooden models of Segovia helpful for orientation, a €5 city audioguide, pay WCs, and a gift shop (Mon-Sat 10:00-18:30, Sun until 17:00, +34 921 466 720, www. turismodesegovia.com). A different TI, on **Plaza Mayor,** covers both Segovia and the surrounding region (at #10; Mon-Sat 9:30-14:00 & 16:00-19:00, Sun 9:30-17:00, shorter hours mid-Sept-

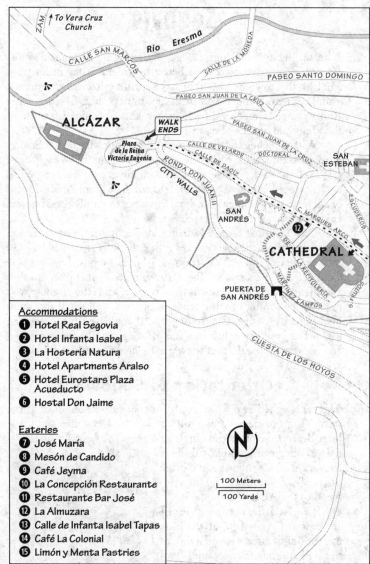

Accommodations
1 Hotel Real Segovia
2 Hotel Infanta Isabel
3 La Hostería Natura
4 Hotel Apartments Aralso
5 Hotel Eurostars Plaza Acueducto
6 Hostal Don Jaime

Eateries
7 José María
8 Mesón de Candido
9 Café Jeyma
10 La Concepción Restaurante
11 Restaurante Bar José
12 La Almuzara
13 Calle de Infanta Isabel Tapas
14 Café La Colonial
15 Limón y Menta Pastries

June, +34 921 460 334, www.turismocastillayleon.com). A smaller TI at the **AVE train station** opens for weekend day-trippers (Sat-Sun 10:00-13:30 only, +34 921 447 262).

ARRIVAL IN SEGOVIA

If day-tripping from Madrid, confirm the return schedule when you arrive here.

By Train: There's no luggage storage at the AVE train station

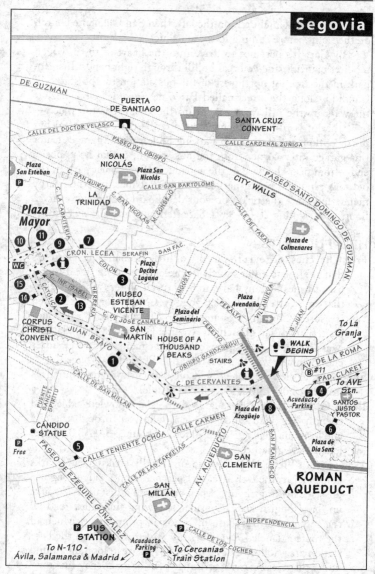

(called Guiomar). From the station, ride bus #11 for 20 minutes to the base of the aqueduct. Bus #12 also takes you into town, but it drops you off at the bus station, a 10-minute walk to the aqueduct.

By Bus: You'll find luggage storage near the exit from the bus station (tokens sold daily 9:00-14:00 & 16:00-19:00, gives you access to locker until end of day). It's a 10-minute walk from the bus station to the town center: Exit left out of the station, continue straight across the street, and follow Avenida Fernández Ladreda,

passing San Millán church on the left, then San Clemente church on the right, before coming to the aqueduct.

By Car: It's best not to drive into the heart of town, which requires maneuvering your car uphill through tight bends. Instead, park in the free lot northwest of the bus station by the statue of Cándido, along the street called Paseo de Ezequiel González. If the walk up the hill from this lot to the Alcázar is too much—or if the lot is full (which happens often)—there's a central but pricey option: the Acueducto Parking underground garage. Enter this garage kitty-corner from the bus station, or—at its opposite end—from near the base of the aqueduct. If you must park in the old town, look for spots marked with blue stripes, pay the nearby meter, and place the ticket on your dashboard (pay meter every 2 hours; free parking 20:00-9:00, Sat afternoon, and all day Sun).

HELPFUL HINTS

Free Churches: Segovia has plenty of little Romanesque churches that are free to enter shortly before or after Mass (see TI for a list of times). Many have architecturally interesting exteriors that are worth a look. Keep your eyes peeled for these hidden treasures: Church of Santos Justo y Pastor, above the aqueduct; San Millán church on Avenida Fernández Ladreda; San Martín church, on a square of the same name; and San Andrés church on the way to the Alcázar on Plaza de la Merced.

Shopping: A flea market is held on Plaza Mayor on Thursdays (roughly 8:00-15:00, food also available).

Local Guide: Leticia Pascual Valero is a knowledgeable and friendly Segovian guide who can take you through the city and its monuments (€120-180 for 2-4 hours, +34 653 028 088, leticiapscl@gmail.com).

Walk with a View: With its trio of visually striking landmarks (aqueduct, cathedral, Alcázar) perched atop a ridge, Segovia boasts a striking skyline when seen from a distance. If you're up for a longish walk, consider following the valley road all the way around the base of Segovia's promontory. Much of the route is labeled *Ruta Turística Panorámica.* From the bus-station area, follow Cuesta de los Hoyos west, looping around under the Alcázar (with striking views of its Disney-like towers). Then, when you cross the river, turn right and hook back around the north side of town—detouring to the Vera Cruz church. From there, you can take the steep trail back up to the Alcázar, or continue all the way along the river, then cut back up to the aqueduct.

Segovia Walk

Most people park outside town, ogle the Roman aqueduct, and make a beeline for the Alcázar. There's lots to see along the way, though, so I've narrated the route in this 30-minute self-guided walk. We'll start at the Roman aqueduct, hike uphill along the pedestrian-only street to the main square (with the cathedral and collection of sights), then continue down to the Alcázar.

While you can use this walk to visit Segovia's main sights during daylight hours, it's also enjoyable just before dinner, when the town is cool and filled with strolling Segovians.

• *Start where Segovia's history did, at...*

Plaza del Azogüejo and the Roman Aqueduct

This lively square, often made livelier by a cheery carousel, is named "small market" (compared to the big market—Plaza Mayor—at the end of this walk).

The square is dominated by Segovia's defining feature: its 2,000-year-old *acueducto romano*—worth ▲▲. Ancient Segóbriga was approximately the same size as today's Segovia—with some 50,000 inhabitants, including soldiers at a military base, all of whom needed a reliable water supply. Emperor Trajan's engineers built a nine-mile aqueduct to channel water from the Río Frío to the city, culminating at the Roman castle (today's Alcázar). Though most of that conduit was underground, this elegant, double-arched bridge was needed to keep the precious stream of water flowing evenly across this stretch of valley. It's an impressive structure: 2,500 feet long and 100 feet high, with 118 arches, made from 24,000 granite blocks without any mortar, and still carrying a stream of water.

The aqueduct was damaged in the Reconquista warfare of the

11th century and was later rebuilt by Queen Isabel. It functioned until the late 19th century. Notice the cross at the base and the statue in the high niche of the Virgen de la Fuencisla—Segovia's patron saint. (In Roman days this held a statue of Hercules.)

Strolling Through Segovia's History

On this walk, you'll see sights from the many layers of Segovia's 2,000-year past.

Roman Prosperity (1-700 AD): Segovia appeared in recorded history when the Romans conquered the indigenous Celts (c. 80 BC). The massive aqueduct the Romans built just to bring fresh water to Segovia testifies to the importance of this prosperous trading hub (pop. 50,000) in their Europe-wide empire.

Moorish Dormancy (700-1100): The city crumbled and snoozed through the Islamic years. After Reconquering around 1100, Christian colonists reinvigorated the sleepy village, erecting churches like San Martín to affirm their faith. This ushered in the next period.

Medieval Golden Age (1100-1500): Enriched by the manufacture and export of flannel, Segovia built impressive mansions with soaring towers, blending Gothic and Moorish styles. The castle (the Alcázar) became a popular residence for the local kings of Castile. Alfonso the Wise attracted scholars, artists, and poets who popularized the Castilian language and culture. Cosmopolitan Segovia became home to a diverse populace from across Spain—Castilians, Andalusians, Christians, Muslims, and a large community of Jews—planting the seed of a common "Spanish" culture.

Isabel and Greater Spain (1500-1600): The future Queen Isabel I grew up in Segovia, making the Alcázar her home from age 10 to 22. After being crowned queen (on Plaza Mayor), she restored the aqueduct and used Segovia as a nucleus for her growing Spanish realm. Later, the city remained a proud center of Castilian resistance (led by Juan Bravo) against German encroachment under Isabel's successor, Charles V. Segovia's soaring cathedral is a legacy of this prosperous century.

Decline (1600-1800): A nasty plague and a depressed wool market dropped Segovia's population from 27,000 to 8,000 in a single century. The royals visited the Alcázar less, though the nearby palace of La Granja became a popular summer retreat. Segovia hit rock bottom in 1808, when Napoleon's French troops sacked the city.

Romantic Recovery (1800-Today): As Spain itself slowly stabilized and modernized, Segovia recovered. Blessed with a legacy of historic-if-crumbling structures, the Segovians began restoring them in the fanciful Romantic style, attracting tourist dollars and reviving the spirit—and bringing Segovia to the cultural center it is today.

From the square, a grand stairway leads from the base of the aqueduct to the top—offering close-up looks at the imposing work and a sweeping water's-eye-view panorama over the length of the aqueduct. Back at ground level, as you walk through Segovia's streets, keep an eye out for small plaques depicting the arches of the aqueduct, which tell you where the subterranean channel runs through the city.

Facing the square is the flashy **Mesón de Cándido**—the most famous of many Segovia restaurants serving the local specialty, roast suckling pig *(cochinillo asado)*. (For recommendations of places to try this specialty, see "Eating in Segovia," later.) On the other side of the aqueduct is a practical little roundabout where buses zip to and from the train station.

• *You'll now move on from Segovia's Roman birthplace to its medieval core. Head up...*

Segovia's Main Street

With the aqueduct at your back, head uphill on **Calle de Cervantes,** appreciating the workaday nature of the town and some of its more imaginative architecture. This street is known as the Calle Real—the "Royal Street"—because it leads, eventually, to the Alcázar.

Pause after about a block, at the gap in the buildings on the left, and enjoy the **viewpoint** (Mirador de la Canaleja). Survey the rooftops of Segovia's lower neighborhood, San Millán, and notice how the city is carved out of a very hilly terrain. On the horizon are the often-snowcapped Sierra de Guadarrama mountains that separate Segovia and Madrid.

Continue up the street, where there's a reminder of the next phase of Segovia's history—the medieval mix of Islamic and Christian elements. Just uphill on the right is the unmistakably prickly facade of the so-called **"house of a thousand beaks"** (Casa de los Picos). This building's original Moorish design is still easy to see, despite the wall just past the door that blocks your view from the street. This wall, the architectural equivalent of a veil, hid this home's fine courtyard—Moors didn't flaunt their wealth. You can step inside to see art students at work and perhaps an exhibit, but it's most interesting from the exterior.

Notice the house's truncated **tower**—one of many fortified towers that marked the homes of feuding local noble families. In medieval Spain, clashing loyalties led to mini civil wars. In the 15th century, as Ferdinand and Isabel centralized authority in Spain, nobles were required to lop their towers. You'll see the once-tall, now-stubby towers of 15th-century noble mansions all over Segovia.

Continue up the main drag (which has now become Calle de

Juan Bravo). Another example of a once-fortified, now-softened house with a cropped tower is about 50 yards farther up, on the left, at tiny Plaza del Platero Oquendo.

Continue uphill until you come to the complicated **Plaza de San Martín,** a commotion of history surrounding a striking statue of Juan Bravo. When Spain's King Charles V, a Habsburg who didn't even speak Spanish, took power, he imposed his rule over Castile. This threatened the local nobles, who, inspired and led by Juan Bravo, revolted in 1521. Although Juan Bravo lost the battle—and his head—he's still a symbol of Castilian pride. This statue was erected in 1921, on the 400th anniversary of his death.

In front of the Juan Bravo statue stands the bold and bulky **House of Siglo XV.** Its fortified *Isabelino* style was typical of 15th-century Segovian houses. Later, in a more peaceful age, the boldness of these houses was softened with the decorative stucco work called *esgrafiado*—Arabic-style floral and geometrical patterns—that you see today (for example, in the big house behind Juan Bravo). The 14th-century Tower of Lozoya, behind the statue, is another example of the lopped-off towers.

On the same square, the 12th-century **Church of St. Martín** was built as Christians were reinhabiting the formerly Islamic city. The style is Segovian Romanesque: a mix of Christian Romanesque (clustered columns with narrative capitals) and Moorish styles (minaret-like towers built with bricks).

• *Although our walk doesn't stop here, fans of modern art should consider at some point checking out the nearby...*

Museo de Arte Contemporáneo Esteban Vicente

A collection of abstract art by local artist Esteban Vicente (1903-2001) is housed in two rooms of the remodeled remains of the 1455 palace of Isabel's half-brother Henry IV. Wilder than Rothko but more restrained than Pollock, Vicente's vibrant work influenced post-WWII American art. The place is a good reminder that Segovia's long cultural heritage lives on.

Cost and Hours: Free; Tue-Fri 11:00-14:00 & 16:00-19:00 (July-Sept 17:00-20:00), Sat 11:00-20:00, Sun until 15:00, closed Mon; +34 921 462 010, www.museoestebanvicente.es.

• *Continue up the street another 100 yards, until you reach a triangular square.*

Corpus Christi Convent and Jewish Quarter

The Gothic arch on the left is the entrance to the **Corpus Christi Convent.** For €1, you can pop in to see the Franciscan church, which was once a synagogue, which was once a mosque (closed Tue and Fri). It is sweet and peaceful, with lots of art featuring St. Francis, and allows you to see the layers of religious history here.

Also in the building's entryway, look for the little window where cloistered nuns sell the treats they make on the premises.

Back out on the little square, notice the narrow street forking off to the left, which leads to Segovia's **former Jewish quarter.** For two centuries (c. 1200-1400), Segovia hummed with a vibrant community of Jews. (Still, as throughout Europe, Jews were relegated to the less-desirable land—lower on the hill, and therefore more vulnerable to attackers.) This neighborhood thrived until anti-Jewish sentiment bubbled up across Spain, culminating in Isabel's expulsion of all Jews from Spain in 1492. While there's not much left from this time, those with a special interest can follow this street a couple of blocks down. The columned building on the left (at #12) was once the house of Abraham Seneor, who was a rabbi and an accountant for Spain's royal family. This building now holds municipal offices, as well as an information center about the Jewish story of Segovia.

• *From the Corpus Christi Convent, take the right fork up to inviting...*

Plaza Mayor

As Segovia's main square for centuries, this has been the scene of colorful spectacles of all sorts. In medieval times there were executions and performances of religious theater. In 1474, Isabel was proclaimed Queen of Castile here. (It was at the San Miguel church—since replaced with a Renaissance structure—opposite the twin-spired City Hall and behind the TI.) Bullfights were also staged here, with spectators jamming the balconies. When the bullfights ended in the 19th century, grumbling Segovians were given a gentler form of entertainment—bands in the gazebo. To bring Segovia's history full-circle, find the symbol of Segovia's aqueduct—where you started—in the seals on the Theater Juan Bravo and atop the City Hall.

Today, the very best entertainment is simply enjoying some tapas and a drink in your choice of the many restaurants and cafés lining the square. Finally, treat yourself to the town's specialty pastry, *ponche segoviano* (marzipan cake), at the recommended Limón y Menta, the bakery on the corner where you entered Plaza Mayor.

• *Our walk now continues toward two of Segovia's greatest sights. The first has its prickly hind end abutting Plaza Mayor—the massive...*

Segovia Cathedral (Catedral de Segovia)

Segovia's cathedral (worth ▲▲) is the grandest legacy of the city's peak of prosperity in the 1500s. Built from 1525 through 1768 (the third on this site), it was Spain's last major Gothic building. Embellished to the hilt with pinnacles and flying buttresses, the exterior is a great example of the final, overripe stage of Gothic, called Flamboyant. Yet the Renaissance arrived before it was finished—as

evidenced by the fact that the cathedral is crowned not by a spire but by a dome. The spacious and elegantly simple interior provides a delightful contrast to the frilly exterior.

Cost and Hours: Cathedral-€3, combo-ticket with tower-€7, free on Sun mornings 9:00-10:00 and in Nov-March 9:30-10:30 (cathedral access only—no cloisters); open daily 9:30-21:30, Nov-March until 18:30; tower visits by guided tour only, tours depart every 90 minutes 10:30-19:30 (fewer in winter), English tour at 15:00; +34 921-462-205, https://catedralsegovia.es.

Visiting the Cathedral: As you enter, angle right to the **choir,** which features finely carved wooden stalls from the previous church (1400s). The *cátedra* (bishop's chair) is in the center rear of the choir.

The many side chapels are mostly 16th-century and come with big locking gates—a reminder that they were the private sacred domain of the rich families and guilds that "owned" them. They could enjoy private Masses here with their names actually spoken in the blessings and a fine burial spot close to the altar.

Find the **Capilla La Concepción** (as you face the choir, it's the last chapel ahead on the right, just inside the door to the ter-

race). Its many 17th-century paintings hang behind a mahogany wood gate imported from colonial America. The painting, *Tree of Life,* by Ignacio Ries (left of the altar), shows hedonistic mortals dancing atop the Tree of Life. As a skeletal Grim Reaper prepares to receive them into hell (by literally chopping down the tree...timberrrr), Jesus rings a bell imploring them to wake up before it's too late. The chapel's center statue is Mary of the Apocalypse (as described in Revelations, standing on a devil and half-moon, which looks like bull's horns). Mary's pregnant, and the devil licks his evil chops, waiting to devour the baby Messiah.

Opposite from where you entered, a fine **portal** (which leads into the cloister) is crowned by a painted Flamboyant Gothic pietà in its tympanum.

Step through that portal into the **cloister,** turn right, and circle counterclockwise. The first room you'll come to is a nice little museum containing paintings and silver reliquaries. Continuing around the cloister, the next door leads into the sumptuous, gilded

chapter room—draped with precious Flemish tapestries. Out in the bottom of the stairwell, notice the gilded wagon. The Holy Communion wafer is placed in the top of this temple-like cart and paraded through town each year during the Corpus Christi festival. At the top of the stairs is a collection of tapestries and vestments under delicate fan vaulting. Back out in the cloister, hanging on the wall between rooms, a glass case displays keys to the 17th-century private chapel gates. Circle the rest of the way around the cloister, enjoying the peace. From the cloister courtyard, you can see the Renaissance dome rising above the otherwise Gothic rooftop.

The 290-foot tower offers stunning views of the city and the surrounding area. You can climb 190 steps to the top on a guided tour several times a day (enter directly opposite the Capilla La Concepción).

• *The final stop on our walk is the Alcázar, which is 10 minutes from the cathedral along Calle Marques del Arco (which becomes Calle Daoíz). You approach the Alcázar through a small park with a monument to those "heroes of May 2" who bravely but vainly resisted the 1808 invasion of Spain by the French (symbolized by the pesky eagle). Until 1808, Segovia had never been overrun, thanks to its mighty...*

Alcázar

Segovia has one of the most fanciful, striking castles in all of Spain, thanks to a Romantic Age faux-medieval remodel job. It's the clos-est thing Spain has to its own Neuschwanstein. A castle has stood on this spot since around 1100. Throughout the Middle Ages, this fortified palace was one of the favorite residences of the monarchs of Castile and a key fortress for controlling the region.

The ▲▲ Alcázar grew through the ages, and its function changed many times: After its stint as a palace, it was a prison for 200 years, and then a royal artillery school. It burned in 1862, after which it was remodeled in the eye-pleasing style you see today. First ogle the exterior. Then visit the finely decorated interior and view terrace. And finally—if you don't mind the steps—you can climb to the top of the tower for the only 360-degree city view in town. This description quickly covers the highlights, but the audioguide is a good investment if you'd like the full story.

Cost and Hours: Palace-€6, tower-€3, daily 10:00-20:00, Nov-March until 18:00, €3 audioguide describes each room (45

minutes, €5 deposit), tower closed in windy or rainy weather, +34 921 460 759, www.alcazardesegovia.com.

Visiting the Alcázar: Buy your ticket in the building on the left as you face the Alcázar (and ask for a map near the ticket desk). Then head over the **drawbridge.** Peer down into the deep, deep "moat," and appreciate the strategic smarts of building a castle on a promontory at the tip of Segovia's ridge.

Once inside, follow signs to the start of the tour. You'll enjoy a one-way route through 11 **royal rooms.** What you see today inside the Alcázar is rebuilt, like the outside—a Disney-esque exaggeration of the original. Still, its fine Moorish decor and historic furnishings are fascinating. The sumptuous ceilings are accurately restored in Mudejar style.

Entering the exhibit, you'll be greeted by knights on horseback, then find your way to the Throne Room, whose ceiling is the artistic highlight of the palace. Facing the throne are portraits of Ferdinand and Isabel, whose union made Spain a medieval powerhouse. Imagine teenage Isabel before her famous marriage, growing up in this castle: reading, embroidering, taking music lessons, and learning the strategy of chess.

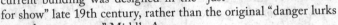

Next, in the Gallery Room—with another fine ceiling—is a big mural of Queen Isabel the Catholic being proclaimed Queen of Castile and León in Segovia's main square in 1474. Enjoying the views of the countryside from the huge windows, it's clear the current building was designed in the "just for show" late 19th century, rather than the original "danger lurks around every corner" Middle Ages.

Continue through more rooms, including the Pine Cone Room, where 392 pinecone-shaped adornments hang from the Mudejar ceiling. The Royal Bedroom is made cozy by hanging tapestries on the stony walls.

Pause to savor the striking Hall of the Monarchs. The upper walls feature statues of the 52 rulers of Castile and León who presided during the long and ultimately successful Reconquista (711-1492) and the two decades afterward: from Pelayo (the first, over the room's exit door and a bit to the left), clockwise to Juana VII (the last). Alfonso VI reconquered Castile from the Moors, turning Segovia Christian. Alfonso the Wise was one of several monarchs who made Segovia's Alcázar their home. Another resident, Henry IV, "The Impotent," died childless, paving the way for his halfsister Isabel to assume the throne and change history. There were only seven queens during the period (the numbered ones).

From here, head through the small, window-lined Cord Room (decorated with the cord-like belts of the Franciscan order) to reach the chapel. As you face the main altar, notice the painting in the center of the altar on your left: A scene of St. James the Moor-Slayer—with Muslim heads literally rolling at his feet. James is the patron saint of Spain. His name was the rallying cry in the centuries-long Christian crusade to push the Muslim Moors back into Africa.

Exiting the royal rooms, step into the modest **armory.** The finest item is the 16th-century, ornately carved ivory crossbow, with a hunting scene shown in the accompanying painting.

From the armory, step out onto the **terrace** (the site of the original Roman military camp, circa AD 100; may be closed in winter and in bad weather). Taking in its vast views, marvel at the natural fortification provided by this promontory cut by the confluence of two rivers. The Alcázar marks the end (and physical low point) of the gradual downhill course of the nine-mile-long Roman aqueduct. Can you find the mountain nicknamed *Mujer Muerta* ("dead woman")?

On your way back out, you can cut through the Museum of Artillery, recalling the period (1764-1862) when this was the royal artillery school. It shows the evolution of explosive weaponry, with old photos and prints of the Alcázar.

Finally, back at the drawbridge, you can choose to climb the **tower.** Hiking 152 steps up a tight spiral staircase rewards you with sweeping views over the town and the countryside...all in all, a satisfying end to our Segovia walk.

Sights near Segovia

The three big sights in Segovia are its aqueduct, cathedral, and the Alcázar—all covered on the "Segovia Walk," earlier. Two sights nearby are worth knowing about.

▲Vera Cruz Church

Perched on a ridge below the Alcázar is this unusual, historic church. Built in the 13th century by an order of chivalric knights (possibly the Knights Templar), this 12-sided Romanesque church once supposedly housed a piece of the "true cross." Pick up an English flier at the entrance and step into the simple, nearly unadorned interior, where you'll find a unique floor plan: a circular nave ringing a giant central column called an edicule. The inner chamber was used for chivalrous ceremonies. (While this architecture was typical of churches built by knights' orders, few survive today.) You'll see the red Maltese cross, signifying that the church is linked with the Knights Hospitaller, who still use it from time to time. With its

unique shape and history, the space carries a mystical feeling. And the views back up to the Alcázar from here are excellent as well.

Cost and Hours: €2.50, Tue 16:00-19:00, Wed-Sun 10:30-13:30 & 16:00-19:00, off-season until 18:00, closed Mon and when caretaker takes an autumn holiday; outside town beyond the castle, 25-minute walk from main square; +34 921 431 475.

▲La Granja de San Ildefonso Palace

This "little Versailles," six miles south of Segovia, is another royal residence, more pastoral than Segovia's Alcázar and cozier than El Escorial. La Granja's palace and gardens were a favorite of Spain's Bourbon rulers, whose family roots were in France. It was built by a homesick Philip V, the grandson of Louis XIV. Today it's restored to its original 18th-century splendor, with its royal collection of tapestries, clocks, and crystal (actually made at the palace's royal crystal factory). Plumbers and gardeners imported from France and Italy made Philip a garden that rivaled Versailles'. The Bourbon Philip chose to be buried

here (in the adjacent church) rather than with his Habsburg predecessors at El Escorial.

Cost and Hours: Palace—€9, Tue-Sun 10:00-20:00, Oct-March until 18:00, closed Mon year-round, last entry one hour before closing, audioguide-€3 (available Fri-Sun only), guided tour-€4 (ask for one in English—you might need to wait); park—free except when fountains are running (when you may need a palace ticket or €4 fountains-only ticket to enter), daily 8:00-20:30, until 21:30 in summer, shorter hours off-season; +34 921 470 019, www.patrimonionacional.es.

Getting There: Linecar buses make the 25-minute trip from Segovia (catch at the bus station) to San Ildefonso-La Granja (check schedule online, +34 921 427 705, www.linecar.es). Drivers find the palace at the top of town, facing a peaceful park; there's no official parking lot but plenty of free street parking nearby.

Visiting the Palace and Gardens: The **palace** interior ranks low on a European scale (nearby, Madrid's Royal Palace and El Escorial's Bourbon Palace are better). And it's hard to appreciate without the audioguide. After touring three large rooms of tapestries, you'll circulate through the typical lineup of royal apartments—ceiling frescoes, glittering chandeliers, gilded furniture, marble floors, and lots of paintings by little-known artists. The ground-floor halls are lined with Neoclassical statues and garden views.

You'll exit the palace into the real draw: the **gardens.** (You can also enter the gardens directly—for free—by circling all the way around the right side of the palace.) The sprawling grounds radiate from the palace in a Versailles-like grid-and-axis layout, with a more rugged section just beyond. The pine trees and snow-capped peaks on the horizon contribute to an almost alpine feel. The gardens are decorated with fanciful fountains, most featuring mythological stories. However, the fountains run only on certain days (check the website for the schedule and entry details).

Sleeping in Segovia

The best places are on or near the central Plaza Mayor. This is where the city action is—the best bars, most tourist-friendly and *típico* eateries, and the TI. During busy times—on weekends and in July and August—reserve in advance.

NEAR PLAZA MAYOR

$$ Hotel Real Segovia is a classic hotel (quick to brag about the many old-time movie stars who stayed here). They rent 37 beautifully updated rooms with all the modern amenities right along the main drag, between the aqueduct and Plaza Mayor. In spite of its central location, many of its rooms face the quiet countryside, and its top-floor terrace has some of Segovia's best views (air-con, elevator, pay parking, Juan Bravo 30, +34 921 462 663, www.hotelrealsegovia.com, info@hotelrealsegovia.com).

$$ Hotel Infanta Isabel, right on Plaza Mayor, has 38 elegant rooms—some with plaza views—and a welcoming staff. It faces both the main square and a popular tapas bar-lined street—it's smart to request a quiet room (air-con, elevator, pay parking, Plaza Mayor 12, +34 921 461 300, www.hotelinfantaisabel.com, admin@hotelinfantaisabel.com).

$ La Hostería Natura is a *hostal* with more personality. Their 18 colorful, tiled rooms—accessed by an old wooden staircase—are a few short blocks away from Plaza Mayor (air-con, Calle Colón 5, +34 921 466 710, www.naturadesegovia.com, info@naturadesegovia.com).

NEAR THE AQUEDUCT

$$$ Hotel Eurostars Plaza Acueducto has little character but provides the comforts of a business-class hotel. It's right at the foot of the aqueduct and next to the bus stops for the AVE train station. Some of its 72 rooms have full or partial views of the aqueduct (air-con, elevator, gym, pay parking; Avenida Padre Claret 2, +34 921 413 403, www.eurostarshotels.com, reservas@eurostarsplazaacueducto.com).

$ **Hotel Apartments Aralso** is a practical choice—a 10-minute hike below the aqueduct, near the bus station. This solidly built guesthouse in a workaday residential area rents 12 well-appointed, functional rooms with fully equipped kitchens. Sweetly run by André and María, it's a good choice for those who don't mind being a bit outside the creaky old center (family rooms, air-con, elevator, nearby pay parking, Calle Teniente Ochoa 8, +34 921 444 816, www.apartamentosaralso.com, reservas@apartamentosaralso. com).

$ **Hostal Don Jaime,** on a gentle hill just above the aqueduct, is a friendly, family-run place with 38 basic, older yet well-maintained rooms in two buildings (a few single rooms with shared bath, family rooms, breakfast included for Rick Steves readers, pay parking, Ochoa Ondategui 8, +34 921 444 787, www.hostaldonjaime. com, hostaldonjaime@hotmail.com).

Eating in Segovia

Look for Segovia's culinary claim to fame, roast suckling pig (*cochinillo asado*: 21 days of mother's milk, into the oven, and onto your plate—oh, Babe). It's salty and tender, wrapped in crispy skin, and worth a splurge here (or in Toledo or Salamanca).

For slightly lighter fare, try *sopa castellana*—soup mixed with eggs, ham, garlic, and bread—or warm yourself up with the *judiones de La Granja*, a popular soup made with flat white beans from the region. Segovia also has a busy tapas bar scene, featuring small bites served up with every drink you order.

Ponche segoviano, a dessert made with an almond-and-honey *mazapán* base, is heavenly after an earthy dinner or with a coffee in the afternoon (at the recommended Limón y Menta).

PLACES TO EAT ROAST SUCKLING PIG

While some of the places listed later also serve this classic local dish, these two are the most renowned options for those who really want to pig out in the old town.

$$$$ **José María** doesn't have the history or fanfare of Cándido (see next), but Segovians claim this high-energy place serves the best roast suckling pig in town. It thrives with a hungry mix of tourists and locals. The bar leading into the restaurant is a scene in itself.

Muscle up to the bar and get your drink and tapa before going into the dining room. It's smart to reserve ahead (daily 12:30-24:00,

air-con, a block off Plaza Mayor at Cronista Lecea 11, +34 921 466 017, www.restaurantejosemaria.com).

$$$$ Mesón de Cándido, one of the top restaurants in Castile, is famous for its memorable dinners. Even though it looks like a ye-olde tourist trap at the base of the aqueduct, it's a grand experience. Take time to wander around and survey the photos of celebs—from Juan Carlos I to Antonio Banderas and Melanie Griffith—who've dined here. Try to get a table in a room with an aqueduct view (daily 13:00-16:30 & 20:00-23:00, reservations recommended, Plaza del Azogüejo 5, air-con, under aqueduct, +34 921 428 103, www.mesondecandido.es). Three gracious generations of the Cándido family still run the show.

OTHER OPTIONS IN THE OLD CENTER

Plaza Mayor, the main square, provides a great backdrop for a light lunch, dinner, or drink. Compare menus and views and choose your best. Things here are fairly interchangeable, and you'll pay a premium for the location, but café prices are generally reasonable, and many offer a good selection of tapas and *raciones*. Grab a table at the place of your choice and savor the scene. Good options include **$$$ Café Jeyma,** with a great cathedral view (but the worst reputation for food); **$$$ La Concepción Restaurante,** closer to the cathedral; and **$$$ Restaurante Bar José.**

$$ La Almuzara is a garden of veggie and organic delights: whole-wheat pizzas, pastas, tofu, seitan, and even a few dishes with meat (Wed-Sun 12:30-16:00 & 20:00-24:00, closed Mon-Tue, between cathedral and Alcázar at Marques del Arco 3, +34 921 460 622).

Segovia's Trendy Tapas Strip: Many of the eateries described above have good tapas bars up front. But to sample several bars in one go, stroll down **Calle de Infanta Isabel** (angling off Plaza Mayor). The places here skew young and trendy, but inside you'll find a mixed-ages crowd.

Breakfast: In the morning, I like to eat on Plaza Mayor (many choices) while enjoying the cool air and the people scene. Or, 100 yards down the main drag toward the aqueduct, **$$ Café La Colonial** serves good breakfasts (with seating on a tiny square or inside, Plaza del Corpus).

Nightlife: After hours, the bars on Plaza Mayor, Calle de Infanta Isabel, and Calle de Isabel la Católica are packed. There are a number of late-night dance clubs along the aqueduct.

Dessert: Limón y Menta offers a good, rich *ponche segoviano* (marzipan) cake by the slice—or try the lighter, crunchy, honey-and-almond *crocantinos* (Mon-Fri 9:00-20:30, Sat-Sun until 21:00, seating inside, Calle de Isabel la Católica 2, +34 921 462 141).

Market: An outdoor produce market thrives on Plaza Mayor

on Thursday (roughly 8:00-15:00). Nearby, on Calle del Cronista Ildefonso Rodríguez, a few stalls are open daily except Sunday. **Carrefour Express,** a small supermarket, is across from the Casa de los Picos (daily 9:00-21:00, Calle Juan Bravo 54).

Segovia Connections

BY PUBLIC TRANSPORTATION

From Segovia to Madrid: Choose between the fast AVE train and the bus. Even though the 30-minute AVE train takes less than half as long as the bus, the train stations in Segovia and Madrid are less convenient, so the total time spent in transit is about the same. (Skip the *cercanías* commuter trains, as they take two hours and don't save you much money.)

The **AVE train** goes between Segovia's Guiomar station (labeled "Segovia AV" on booking sites) and **Madrid's Chamartín station** (up to 4/hour, 30 minutes). An Alvia train goes from the same station to **Salamanca** (4/day, 1.5 hours). To get to Guiomar station, take city bus #11 from the base of the aqueduct (20 minutes, buses usually timed to match arrivals).

Buses run from Madrid's Moncloa station to Segovia. If arriving at Moncloa station in Madrid, follow the signs for the color-coded terminals to Terminal 1 (blue). From there, signs marked *Taquillas Segovia* lead you to the ticket office, or look for the ticket machines, which accept cash or chip-and-PIN credit cards (2/hour, 1.5 hours, www.avanzabus.com).

When riding the bus from Madrid to Segovia, about 30 minutes after leaving Madrid you'll see—breaking the horizon on the left—the dramatic concrete cross of the Valley of the Fallen. Its grand facade marks the entry to the mammoth underground memorial.

From Segovia by Bus to: Ávila (4/day, 2/day on weekends, 1 hour, Avanza, www.avanzabus.com). Some Ávila buses continue to **Salamanca** (3.5 hours)—but the train is much faster.

ROUTE TIPS FOR DRIVERS

From Segovia to Salamanca (100 miles/160 km): Leave Segovia by driving around the town's circular road, which offers good views from below the Alcázar. Then follow signs for *Ávila* (road N-110). Notice the fine Segovia view from the three crosses at the crest of the first hill. You could stay on N-110 all the way to Ávila, but it's cheap to hop on the speedy AP-51 tollway at Villacastín,

about halfway to Ávila. If time allows, exit at **Ávila** for a look at the town walls and to stretch your legs. Continuing from Ávila to Salamanca, be ready to pull over for the best views of the Ávila walls: Just after you cross the river at the far end of the town wall, watch for the *Cuatro Postes* pullout on the right (it's just uphill from the river). Soon after, hop on the speedy and free A-50 expressway, which zips you to Salamanca in under an hour.

About 20 miles before Salamanca, you'll spot a huge bull on the left side of the road. As you get closer, it becomes more and more obvious it isn't alive. (It's not realistic to pull over for a photo if you're on the expressway, but it's reachable if you take the slower N-501.) Soon you'll see the massive church towers of **Salamanca** on the horizon and enjoy great panoramic views of the city from across the river as you get closer.

Ávila

Ávila is famous for its perfectly preserved medieval walls, as the birthplace of St. Teresa, and for its yummy *yema* treats. For more than 300 years, Ávila was on the battlefront between the Muslims and Christians, changing hands several times—hence its heavily fortified appearance. But today, perfectly peaceful Ávila has a charming old town that weathers only occasional incursions of day-trippers from Madrid, Segovia, or Salamanca (each about an hour away by car). Ávila doesn't quite crack the top tier of great walled European cities—it's sort of a wannabe Carcassonne. But it's handy to reach, has several fine churches and monasteries, and makes for an enjoyable quick stop between Segovia and Salamanca.

Orientation to Ávila

Surrounded by modern sprawl, Ávila's walled old center is shaped like an elongated, backwards "D." The flat side of the "D"—facing east—is where you'll find the TIs, parking, and most of the sights (including two points to access the top of the walls). On a quick visit, most people focus on this busy little zone. Inside the walls, Ávila is sleepy: From the cathedral (which abuts the eastern wall), it's a 10-minute walk on the main drag, Calle de los Reyes Católicos, past the market to the humble main square, Plaza Mercado Chico. A five-minute walk south of there is the only other important sight within the walls, the Convent of St. Teresa.

Tourist Information: Ávila's city TI is just outside the northeast corner of the walls, facing the Basilica of San Vicente (daily 9:00-20:00, Nov-March until 18:00, free WCs, well-equipped

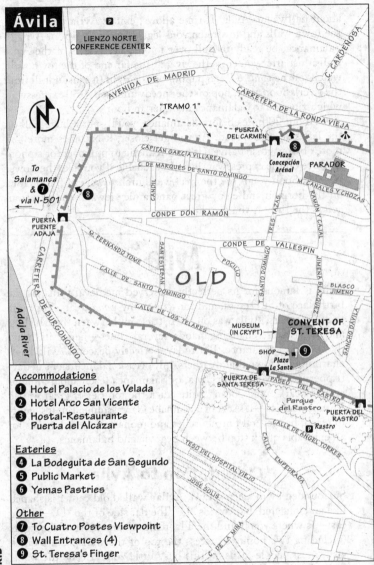

Ávila

LIENZO NORTE
CONFERENCE CENTER

AVENIDA DE MADRID

CARRETERA DE LA RONDA VIEJA

C. CARDEÑOSA

"TRAMO 1"

PUERTA
DEL CARMEN

Plaza
Concepción
Arénal

PARADOR

CAPITÁN GARCIA VILLAREAL

C. DE MARQUES DE SANTO DOMINGO

To
Salamanca
& 7
via N-501

M. CANALES Y CHOZAS

CANDIL

CONDE DON RAMÓN

TRES TAZAS

T. SANTO DOMINGO

T. RAMÓN Y CAJAL

PUERTA
PUENTE
ADAJA

M. FERNANDO TOME

SAN ESTEBAN

POCILLO

CONDE DE VALLESPIN

JIMENA BLÁZQUEZ

BLASCO
JIMENO

CALLE DE SANTO DOMINGO

OLD

CARRETERA DE BURGOHONDO

Adaja River

CALLE DE LOS TELARES

MUSEUM
(IN CRYPT)

CONVENT OF
ST. TERESA

SANCHO DAVILA

SHOP

Plaza
La Santa

9

PUERTA DE
SANTA TERESA

PASEO DEL RASTRO

Parque
del Rastro

PUERTA DEL
RASTRO

CALLE DE ANGEL YORRES

Rastro

Accommodations
1 Hotel Palacio de los Velada
2 Hotel Arco San Vicente
3 Hostal-Restaurante
  Puerta del Alcázar

Eateries
4 La Bodeguita de San Segundo
5 Public Market
6 Yemas Pastries

Other
7 To Cuatro Postes Viewpoint
8 Wall Entrances (4)
9 St. Teresa's Finger

TESO DEL HOSPITAL VIEJO

JOSÉ SOLIS

CALLE EMPEDRADA

C. DE LA MINA

shop, helpful wooden models of the town and important wall sections, +34 920 350 000 ext. 370, www.avilaturismo.com). A less helpful regional TI is inside the wall ticket office, near the cathedral (Mon-Sat 9:30-14:00 & 17:00-20:00, Sun 9:30-17:00, shorter hours mid-Sept-May, +34 920 211 387).

Sightseeing Pass: The ÁvilaCard is €15 and valid for 48 hours. It includes the wall, cathedral, museum of St. Teresa, and

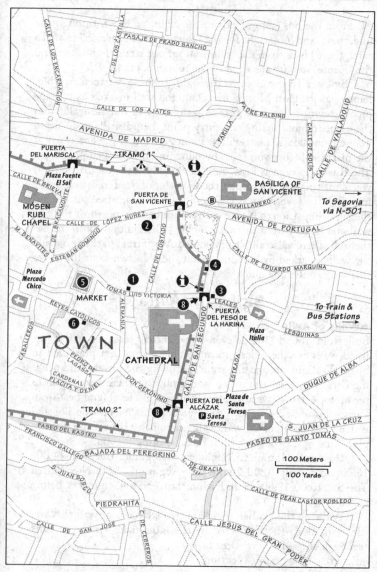

a handful of other sights. If you plan on seeing them all, you can save a few euros.

ARRIVAL IN ÁVILA

By Bus or Train: Ávila's bus and train stations sit kitty-corner from each other about a mile east of the wall. There are lockers at Ávila's bus station, but not at the train station. To reach the Basilica of San Vicente, you can walk (allow 15-20 minutes) or take city bus #4 or

#1. From the bus station, exit to the right, go down through the underpass, and look right for the "Puente de la Estación" stop. To catch these buses from the train station, exit straight ahead to find the "Renfe" stop (to the right of the roundabout).

By Car: To get close to the sights, choose between two big, handy pay garages: Most convenient (and well marked as you approach town) is the **Sta. Teresa garage,** a five-minute walk from the cathedral and main wall entry point, beneath Plaza de Santa Teresa (your license plate will be photographed as you enter; pay at the machine before you leave by punching in your plate number). The **Rastro garage** is just south of the city wall (use this only if you're making a quick stop at the Convent of St. Teresa and nothing else). To save money, you could use the big, free lot behind the sprawling **Lienzo Norte conference center,** north of the city wall and farther from the main sights (20-minute walk to the cathedral). There's also ample pay-and-display **street parking** outside the walls (marked by blue lines), but there's a two-hour limit—so this works only for a quick visit.

Sights in Ávila

▲Walls of Ávila

Built from around 1100 on even-more-ancient remains, Ávila's fortified walls are the oldest, most complete, and best preserved in Spain. Walking around the walls, climbing the towers, and peeking between crenellations is a fun stroll. But there's not much to see up top—the views are better from ground level (and best from Cuatro Postes, across the river—see next). If it's blazing hot and you're short on time, the wall walk is skippable. But if you want to play "king of Castile"...it's right there, waiting for you.

Cost and Hours: €5, includes audioguide, free Tue 14:00-16:00; open daily 10:00-20:00, July-Aug until 21:00; Nov-March Tue-Sat 10:00-18:00, closed Mon; last entry 45 minutes before closing.

Walking the Walls: There are two stretches of wall that you can walk along (both covered by the same ticket—but you can't reenter a section you've already entered). The **main section** (called "Tramo 1")—stretching eight-tenths of a mile, one-way—is along the north side. Enter the wall by the gate closest to the cathedral (Puerta del Peso de la Harina). From here, you can head up to the northeast corner, then curve left and go all

the way along the north side. There are two other entrances/exits for this stretch: Puerta del Carmen (about halfway along the north side) and Puerta Puente Adaja (on the far west end, opposite the cathedral). Go as far as you like. Then, either exit at one of those two points and return to ground level, or go back the way you came on top of the wall. The **shorter section** ("Tramo 2"), just about 300 yards one-way, can be accessed at the Puerta del Alcázar, just off Plaza de Santa Teresa.

Viewing the Walls: The best views of the walls themselves are actually from street level. If you're wandering the city and see arched gates leading out of the old center, pop out to the other side and take in the impressive wall from the ground. Drivers can see the especially impressive north side as they circle to the right from Puerta de San Vicente.

Paseo Outside the Walls: An interesting paseo scene takes place along the outside of the walls each night—make your way along the southern wall (Paseo del Rastro) to Plaza de Santa Teresa for spectacular vistas across the plains.

Viewing Ávila from Cuatro Postes

The best overall view of the walled town of Ávila is about a mile away on the Salamanca road (N-501), at a clearly marked turnout for the Cuatro Postes (four posts). Drivers should keep an eye out on the right, after they cross the river and are on their way uphill. If you're without wheels, you have a few options: You could walk or take a public bus to the far west end of the wall (to the bridge called Ponte de Allaja), then hike uphill for about 10-15 minutes to Cuatro Postes. Or you can catch a tourist trolley (€5.50, www. eltranvia.es) or tuk-tuk (€6.75, www.tuktukavila.com) for a little loop tour around town, which includes a sweat-free ride up to the viewpoint. All run infrequently—confirm your options at the TI.

Ávila Cathedral (Catedral de Ávila)

While it started as Romanesque, Ávila's cathedral, finished in the 16th century, is considered the first Gothic cathedral in Spain. Its position—with its granite apse actually part of the fortified wall—underlines the "medieval alliance between cross and sword." The cathedral interior doesn't rank very high on a Spanish scale (and even just in Ávila, San Vicente's is more interesting). It's weighty, stony, and bottom-heavy, with delicate Gothic windows illuminating a much lighter (and light-filled) top half. The focal point is the exquisitely carved outer stone wall of the choir ("retrochoir")—with Plateresque carvings of Jesus' life. In the right transept, find your way into the sacristy, cloister, and museum (including a minor painting by El Greco).

Cost and Hours: €6, includes audioguide, Mon-Sat 10:00-

21:00, Sun from 12:30, generally closes 2-3 hours earlier off-season, Plaza de la Catedral.

Basilica of San Vicente

Sitting just outside the northeast corner of the wall (facing the TI), this hulking church—with its distinctive Romanesque-arch arcade facing the busy street—is worth a peek. The 12th-century interior oozes history, with rough tombstones embedded in the floor, heavy columns framing round windows, a glittering altarpiece, and a huge, canopied, colorfully painted tomb holding three local fourth-century martyrs.

Cost and Hours: €3, includes audioguide, Mon-Sat 10:00-19:00, Sun 16:00-18:00, off-season closed for lunch 14:00-16:00.

Convent of St. Teresa

Built in the 17th century on the spot where the saint was born, this convent is a big hit with pilgrims (10-minute walk from cathedral). St. Teresa (1515-1582)—reforming nun, mystic, and writer—bought a house in Ávila and converted it into a convent with more stringent rules than the one she belonged to. She faced opposition in her hometown from rival nuns and those convinced her visions of heaven were the work of the devil. However, with her mentor and fellow mystic St. John of the Cross, she established convents of Discalced (shoeless) Carmelites throughout Spain, and her visions and writings led her to sainthood (she was canonized in 1622).

Inside the humble convent **church,** a lavishly gilded side chapel marks the actual place of her birth (left of main altar, door may be closed).

The finger is housed in the little **Sala de Reliquias** at the back of the church shop (as you face the church, it's on your right). You'll see Teresa's finger, complete with a fancy emerald ring, along with one of her sandals and two bones of St. John of the Cross.

A **museum** dedicated to the saint is in the crypt (around the left side as you face the church). Inside under heavy stone vaults, you'll see a wide collection of items relating to Teresa, including replicas of her spartan bedroom and items she might have used. There's also an extensive collection of books, portraits, stamps, and coins of St. Teresa—helping explain why this woman and this convent are so important to so many people around the world.

Cost and Hours: Convent—free, daily 10:00-13:30 & 17:00-19:00, no photos of finger allowed; museum—€2, Tue-Sun 10:00-14:00 & 16:00-19:00, shorter hours off-season, closed Mon year-round.

Yemas

These pastries, made by local nuns, are more or less soft-boiled egg yolks that have been cooled and sugared (*yema* means yolk). They're

sold all over town. The shop **Las Delicias del Convento** is a retail outlet for the cooks of the convent (€4 for a small box, Mon-Sat 10:30-20:00, Sun until 18:00, between the TI and convent at Calle de los Reyes Católicos 12, +34 920 220 293).

Sleeping and Eating in Ávila

Sleeping: With Salamanca and Segovia so close, you're unlikely to need a bed in Ávila, but here are a few possibilities. Consider **$$ Hotel Palacio de los Velada** (in a five-centuries-old palace at Plaza de la Catedral 10, +34 920 255 100, www.veladahoteles. com); **$ Hotel Arco San Vicente** (one block from the Basilica of San Vicente at Calle López Núñez 6, +34 920 222 498, www. arcosanvicente.com), or **$ Hostal Puerta del Alcázar** (next to the Puerta del Peso de la Harina, just outside the wall at San Segundo 38, +34 920 211 074, www.puertadelalcazar.com).

Eating: Restaurants around Plaza del Mercado Chico, the main square of the old center, are good spots to try Ávila specialties called *chuletón*, a thick steak, and *judías del Barco de Ávila*, big white beans often cooked in a meaty stew. Other good eating options include **$$$ Restaurante Puerta del Alcázar** (filled with more locals than hotel guests, San Segundo 38, +34 920 211 074) and **$$$ La Bodeguita de San Segundo** (good for a light lunch, outside the wall near the cathedral at San Segundo 19, +34 920 257 309). For a coffee or hot chocolate, try the courtyard café of the recommended **$$ Hotel Palacio de los Velada.** For **picnic** supplies, head to the town's market house between Plaza del Mercado Chico and the cathedral, or the Friday-morning farmers market on Plaza del Mercado Chico.

Ávila Connections

The bus terminal is closed on Sundays, but you can purchase tickets when you board. Bus info: Avanza (www.avanzabus.com), Jiménez Dorado (www.jimenezdorado.com). Train info: +34 912 320 320, www.renfe.com.

From Ávila to: Segovia (4 buses/day, 2/day weekends, 1 hour, Avanza), **Madrid Chamartín** (2 trains/day, 1.5-2 hours), **Madrid Príncipe Pío** (nearly hourly trains, 1.5-2 hours), **Madrid Estación Sur** (nearly hourly buses, 6/day on weekends, 1.5 hours, Jiménez Dorado), **Salamanca** (7 trains/day, 1-1.5 hours; 4-5 buses/day, 1.5 hours, Avanza).

TOLEDO

About an hour south of Madrid, Toledo teems with tourists, souvenirs, and great art by day, and delicious dinners, echoes of El Greco, and medieval magic by night. Incredibly well preserved and full of cultural wonder, the entire city has been declared a national monument. To keep the city's historic appearance intact, the Spanish government has forbidden any modern exteriors.

Toledo was once Spain's capital and packs 2,500 years of tangled history—Roman, Jewish, Visigothic, Moorish, and Christian—onto a rocky perch protected on three sides by the Tajo River. This rich mix of heritages makes Toledo one of Europe's cultural highlights and a great way to sample Spain's cultural layers all in one place.

Today, Toledo thrives as a provincial capital and tourist destination—it's a slick 30-minute train ride from Madrid. And whether you arrive by car, train, or bus, getting into town is easy. You'll find an old city center that's largely traffic-free.

Despite its tremendously kitschy tourist vibe, this stony wonderland remains the historic, artistic, and spiritual center of Spain. Toledo sits enthroned on its history, much as it was when Europe's most powerful monarch, the Holy Roman Emperor Charles V (King Charles I in Spain), and its most famous resident artist, El Greco, called it home. Be sure to get off the main walkways and explore some of the back streets. In just a few steps, you'll find a corner of Toledo all your own.

PLANNING YOUR TIME

To see Toledo's top sights—including its museums (great El Greco) and cathedral (best in Spain)—and to experience its medieval at-

mosphere (wonderful after dark), you'll need at least a night and a day. A second day offers a more relaxing visit and lets you see more than the highlights. (Even Toledo's "second-tier" sights rank high on a Spain-wide scale.) Keep in mind that early and late trains tend to sell out to commuters and other day-trippers. After dark, Toledo is the rare Spanish city that feels downright sleepy.

Here's a good one-day plan: Upon arrival, head to the main square, Plaza de Zocodover, and get oriented by following my self-guided walk. Then visit the cathedral interior and the finest El Greco, inside Santo Tomé church. With any remaining time, consider the Army Museum (for history aficionados), the Santa Cruz Museum (for art lovers), the El Greco Museum (the artist's life and times), two remarkably well-preserved historic Mudejar synagogues (Tránsito and Santa María Blanca), or the royal burial church at San Juan de los Reyes. Thorough visits to all of these would take two days, but selective sightseers can mix and match to fill one memorable day. In the evening—or before returning to Madrid—wander the back lanes, sample sweet *mazapán*, people-watch at Plaza de Zocodover, and dine well—*carcamusas* (pork stew), anyone?

Orientation to Toledo

Toledo sits atop a circular hill, with the cathedral roughly dead-center. Lassoed into a tight tangle of streets by the sharp bend of

the Tajo River (called the "Tejo" in Portugal, where it hits the Atlantic at Lisbon), Toledo has Spain's most confusing medieval street plan. But it's a small town within its walls, with only 10,000 inhabitants (84,000 live in greater Toledo, including its modern suburbs). The major sights are well signed, and locals will politely point you in the right direction. (You are, after all, the town's bread and butter.)

The top sights stretch from the main square, Plaza de Zocodover (zoh-koh-doh-VEHR), southwest along Calle del Comercio (nicknamed Calle Ancha, "Wide Street") to the cathedral, and beyond that to Santo Tomé and more. Most tourists never stray from this axis. Make a point to get lost. The town is compact. When it's time to return to someplace familiar, pull out your map or ask, "*¿Para Plaza de Zocodover?*" From the far end of town, handy bus #12 circles back to Plaza de Zocodover.

Although the city is very hilly (in Toledo, they say everything's

TOLEDO

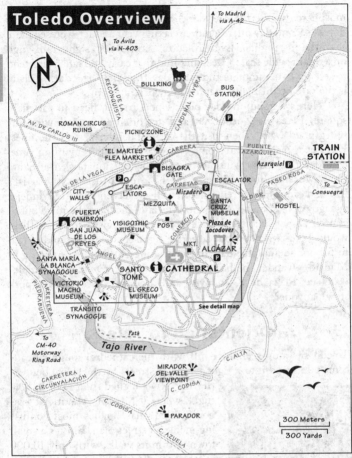

uphill—it certainly feels that way), nothing is more than a short hike away.

TOURIST INFORMATION

Toledo's TIs share a website at Toledo-turismo.com. Look for TIs in a freestanding building in the park just across from **Bisagra Gate** (Mon-Sat 10:00-18:00, Sun until 14:00, +34 925 211 005) and inside **City Hall** on Plaza del Ayuntamiento, facing the cathedral (daily 10:00-15:30, +34 925 254 030).

Sightseeing Passes: Skip the Toledo Pass or Toledo Card—neither save you money over individual tickets.

The **Pulsera Turística** wristband (€10, sold at participating sights) doesn't cover the cathedral, Santa Cruz Museum, or the Army Museum, but it makes sense if you plan to see at least four of the monuments and churches it does cover: Santo Tomé, Santa

María la Blanca Synagogue, Monastery of San Juan de los Reyes, Mezquita del Cristo de la Luz, Church of El Salvador, Real Colegio de Doncellas Nobles, and Church of San Ildefonso/Jesuitas (no time limit as long as it stays on your wrist, nontransferable).

ARRIVAL IN TOLEDO

Since the train and bus stations are below the town center, and parking can be a challenge, "arriving" in Toledo means getting up-hill to Plaza de Zocodover. This involves a taxi (affordable), a city bus (cheap), or a walk plus a ride up a series of escalators.

By Train: Toledo's early-20th-century train station is Neo-Moorish and a national monument itself for its architecture and art, both of which celebrate the three cultures that coexisted here.

Early and late trains can sell out; reserve ahead. If you haven't yet bought a ticket for your departure from Toledo, get it before you leave the Toledo station. Choose a specific time rather than leave it open-ended. (If you prefer more flexibility, take the bus.)

From the train station to Plaza de Zocodover, a **taxi** is about €5 (the ride to individual hotels might cost a bit more). It's easy to take **city bus** #5, #61, or #62; leaving the station, the bus stop is 30 yards to the right (€1.40, pay on bus, confirm by asking, *"¿Para Plaza de Zocodover?"*). Skip the red-and-purple tourist buses that meet arriving day-trippers at the station—they're a bad value.

It costs very little to take the public bus, or even a taxi, so there's little reason to **walk** (especially in warm weather). But if you feel the need, allow 25 minutes and turn right as you leave the station and follow the fuchsia line on the sidewalk labeled *Up Toledo, Follow the Line*. Track this line (and periodic escalator symbols) past a bus stop, over the bridge, around the roundabout to the left, and into a bus parking area. From here, go up a series of escalators: You'll emerge about a block downhill from Plaza de Zocodover.

By Bus: At the bus station, buses park downstairs. Before leaving the station, confirm your departure time (around 2/hour to Madrid). Buses don't often book up, and you can put off buying a return ticket until just minutes before you leave Toledo.

From the bus station, Plaza de Zocodover is a €4.50 **taxi** ride or a short **bus** ride (catch #5 or #12 downstairs; €1.40, pay on bus). It's also possible to **walk:** Exit the bus station, go straight through the roundabout, and continue straight ahead. Look for a tunnel burrowed into the cliff (below the big, blocky convention center), where you can ride a series of escalators into town, letting you off just below Plaza de Zocodover.

By Car: Arriving by car, you can enjoy a scenic big-picture orientation by following the *Ronda de Toledo* signs on a circular drive around the city. You'll see the city from many angles along the Circunvalación road across the Tajo Gorge. Stop at a viewpoint

Toledo at a Glance

▲▲▲**Toledo Cathedral** One of Europe's best, with a marvelously vast interior and great art. **Hours:** Mon-Sat 10:00-18:30, Sun from 14:00. See page 573.

▲▲**Santo Tomé** Simple chapel with El Greco's masterpiece, *The Burial of the Count of Orgaz.* **Hours:** Daily 10:00-18:45, off-season until 17:45. See page 583.

▲**Army Museum** Covers all things military; located in the imposing fortress, the Alcázar. **Hours:** Tue-Sun 10:00-17:00, closed Mon. See page 569.

▲**Santa Cruz Museum** Renaissance building housing wonderful artwork, including eight El Grecos. **Hours:** Mon-Sat 10:00-18:00, Sun until 15:00. See page 567.

▲**El Greco Museum** Small collection of paintings, including the *View and Plan of Toledo,* El Greco's panoramic map of the city. **Hours:** Tue-Sat 9:30-19:30 (off-season until 18:00), Sun 10:00-15:00, closed Mon. See page 584.

▲**Tránsito Synagogue and Sephardic Jewish Museum** A look at Toledo's Jewish past. **Hours:** Tue-Sat 9:30-19:30 (off-season until 18:00), Sun 10:00-15:00, closed Mon. See page 586.

▲**Victorio Macho Museum** Collection of 20th-century Toledo sculptor's works, with expansive river-gorge view. **Hours:** Sun-Wed 10:00-14:00, Thu-Sat 11:00-18:00. See page 587.

▲**Monastery of San Juan de los Reyes** Church/monastery intended as final resting place of Isabel and Ferdinand. **Hours:** Daily 10:00-18:45, off-season until 17:45. See page 589.

▲**Visigothic Museum** Romanesque church housing the only Visigothic artifacts in town. **Hours:** Tue-Sat 10:00-14:00 & 16:00-18:00, Sun 9:00-15:00, closed Mon. See page 581.

or drive to Parador de Toledo, just south of town, for an expansive city view from the hotel's balcony. The best time for this trip is the magic hour before sunset, when the top viewpoints are busy with tired old folks and frisky young lovers.

A car is useless within Toledo's city walls, where the narrow, twisting streets are no fun to navigate (watch your mirrors). Many hotels offer discounted parking rates at nearby garages; ask when making your reservation.

The most convenient place to park is the big underground

Miradero Garage at the convention center (€21/day; drive through Bisagra Gate, go uphill half a mile, look for sign on the left directing you to *Plaza del Miradero*). From here you can ride an escalator into town. Farther into town, there's parking at the **Alcázar Garage** (just past the Alcázar—€2/hour, €22/day). There are also two big, free, **uncovered parking lots:** the one between the river and the bus station is best if you want to use the escalators to get up to the center; the other lot is between the river and the train station. North of the city walls, you'll find pay parking and another set of escalators going up near the **Glorieta de la Reconquista roundabout,** but at the top you'll still be far from Plaza de Zocodover.

HELPFUL HINTS

Taxis: There are three taxi stands in the old center: Plaza de Zocodover, Bisagra Gate, and Santo Tomé. For around €15, taxis routinely give visitors scenic circles around town with photo stops.

Nightlife: Toledo is sleepy after dark. If there's something going on, it's likely at **Circulo del Arte,** a bar and music venue that fills a jaw-dropping 12th-century Mudejar hall—with keyhole brick arches—hiding in back streets near the top of town. It offers a diverse slate of musical events—some free, others with a cover (schedule at www.circuloartetoledo.org, Plaza San Vicente 2, +34 925 256 653).

Local Guidebook: *Toledo de la Mano* (*Toledo Hand-in-Hand*, €12) has helpful walking tours and sight descriptions that delve into the city's history and traditions. It's sold at gift shops in the cathedral, at sights such as Santa María la Blanca Synagogue and the Mezquita del Cristo de la Luz, and at the bookstore Librería Hojablanca (Calle Martín Gamero 6, +34 925 297 746).

Tours in Toledo

In this chapter, I've covered all the sightseeing information you'd need for up to two days in Toledo. The main reason to take a tour is to reach the Mirador del Valle viewpoint, on a hilltop across the river. Avoid tourist buses—most sightseeing is in Toledo's walkable old core, where buses can't go, and it's cheaper to pay for a taxi into town and then hop on the tourist train (described next).

Tourist Train

For a pleasant city overview, take the **TrainVision Tourist Train**— a 45-minute putt-putt through Toledo and around the Tajo River Gorge. It's a cheesy but fine way for nondrivers to enjoy views of the city from across the Tajo Gorge (€7, buy ticket from kiosk on

TOLEDO

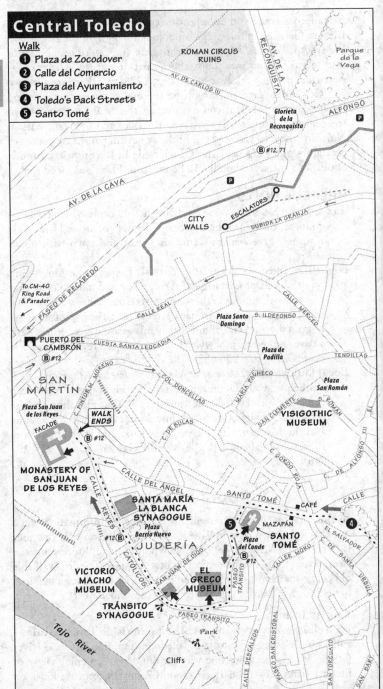

Central Toledo

Walk
1. Plaza de Zocodover
2. Calle del Comercio
3. Plaza del Ayuntamiento
4. Toledo's Back Streets
5. Santo Tomé

ROMAN CIRCUS RUINS

AV. DE CARLOS III

AV. DE LA RECONQUISTA

Parque de la Vega

ALFONSO

Glorieta de la Reconquista

P

(B) #12, 71

P

AV. DE LA CAVA

CITY WALLS

ESCALATORS

SUBIDA LA GRANJA

To CM-40 Ring Road & Parador

PASEO DE RECAREDO

CALLE REAL

CALLE MERCED

Plaza Santo Domingo

S. ILDEFONSO

PUERTO DEL CAMBRÓN

(B) #12

CUESTA SANTA LEOCADIA

Plaza de Padilla

TENDILLAS

SAN MARTÍN

C. PINTOR M. MORENO

COL. DONCELLAS

MARÍA PACHECO

SAN ELEMENTE

Plaza San Román

S. ROMÁN

Plaza San Juan de los Reyes

WALK ENDS

FACADE

C. DE BULAS

VISIGOTHIC MUSEUM

C. GORDO ROJA

C. DE ALFONSO XII

(B) #12

MONASTERY OF SAN JUAN DE LOS REYES

CALLE REYES

CALLE DEL ÁNGEL

SANTO TOMÉ

CAFÉ

CALLE

4

SANTA MARÍA LA BLANCA SYNAGOGUE

Plaza Barrio Nuevo

#12 (B)

CALLE CATÓLICOS

SAN JUAN DE DIOS

5

MAZAPÁN

SANTO TOMÉ

EL SALVADOR

C. DE SANTA URSULA

Plaza del Conde

JUDERÍA

EL GRECO MUSEUM

PASEO TRÁNSITO

(B) #12

TALLER MORO

VICTORIO MACHO MUSEUM

TRÁNSITO SYNAGOGUE

PASEO TRÁNSITO

Park

PASEO SAN CRISTOBAL

CALLE DESCALZOS

SAN TORCUATO

SAN BART.

Tajo River

Cliffs

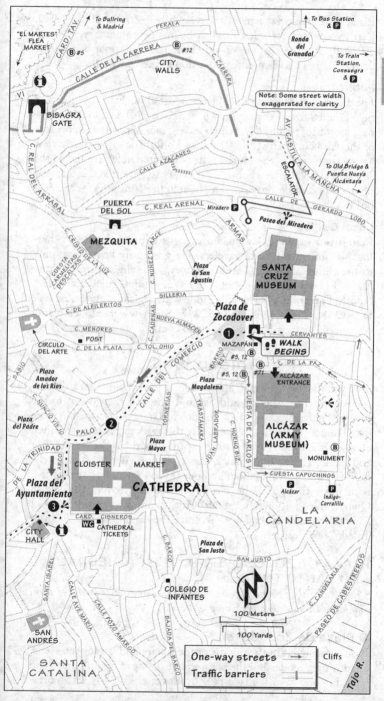

Plaza de Zocodover, where it leaves daily 1-2/hour 10:00-18:30, later in summer, recorded English/Spanish commentary, +34 625 301 890). For the best views, sit on the right side, not behind the driver. There's a five-minute photo stop at the viewpoint.

Public Buses

For the cheapest tour, use public transportation. Take my "Bus #12 Self-Guided Tour" through town (see page 590). Or, for a "gorgeous" loop trip, try bus #71, which leaves from opposite the entrance of the Alcázar (hourly 7:45-21:45) and offers the same classic view across the gorge as the tourist train; its route circles around to the Mirador del Valle viewpoint, where you can get off and snap some photos, then while away about an hour at the same stop for the next bus to take you back.

Local Guides

Juan José Espadas (a.k.a. Juanjo) is a good guide who enjoys sharing his hometown with travelers. He gracefully brings meaning to the complex mix of Toledo's history, art, religion, and culture (€150/3 hours, mobile +34 667 780 475, juanjo@guiadetoledo.es). **Adolfo Ferrero** is a personable guide with a background in art history (€155/3 hours, mobile +34 629 177 810, www.toledodelamano.com, adolfo.ferrero@toledodelamano.com).

Toledo Walk

This walk snakes through the center of town from Plaza de Zocodover to the cathedral and Santo Tomé and then down to the Jewish Quarter, linking all of Toledo's top sights (described in more detail under "Sights in Toledo"). Use this walk to get oriented, then choose which sights appeal to you (prioritize the cathedral interior and Santo Tomé). On a quick day trip from Madrid, stick to the first half of this walk (about an hour if you don't enter any sights); with more time, add the second half, which covers the Jewish Quarter (an additional half-hour). At the end, you can ride bus #12 back to Plaza de Zocodover. To trace the route, see the "Central Toledo" map, earlier.

PLAZA DE ZOCODOVER TO THE CATHEDRAL AND SANTO TOMÉ

• *Begin at Toledo's main square, where taxis and buses from the train and bus stations drop off arriving visitors.*

❶ Plaza de Zocodover

Position yourself in the middle of the square and survey the scene. Surprisingly modest for the main square of one of Spain's finest and most historic towns, Plaza de Zocodover is Toledo's transporta-

tion hub and your gateway to the old town. The word "Zocodover" derives from the Arabic for "livestock market." This was once the scene of Inquisition judgments and bullfights, but it's now a lot more peaceful. Older people arrive in the morning, and young people come in the evening.

The tourist train to the panoramic Mirador del Valle viewpoint south of town leaves from here, as do city buses #5, #61, and #62 to the train station. Just uphill, near the taxi stand, is the stop for bus #12, which travels around the old town to Santo Tomé (and works as a good self-guided tour—described at the end of this section), and for bus #71, which heads out to the viewpoint.

Toledo is the capital of Castile-La Mancha, and the orange-hued **government building**—sort of the "state capitol"—overlooks Plaza de Zocodover. Look for the three flags: one for Europe, one for Spain, and one for Castile-La Mancha. And speaking of universal symbols, find the low-key McDonald's. A source of controversy, it was finally allowed...with only one small golden arch. Next came the bigger Burger King, which no one blinked at.

Notice the **double-headed eagle** emblem emblazoned on bus windows (you'll find it all over town). It symbolizes the Habsburg monarchs, who briefly made their home here, but has been appropriated as Toledo's city seal.

The "square" has an oddly triangular footprint. In the 16th century, King Philip II—one of those Habsburgs—tried in vain to knock down some buildings and create a more typical square, like the showcase Plaza Mayor in Madrid. But key buildings were owned by the Church, which refused to grant permission. The cathedral in Toledo—Spain's most important—has always exerted an oversized influence on civic life. And that's one of the many reasons Philip II decided to relocate his capital (in 1561) to Madrid, where he could build whatever he liked. The throne's departure left Toledo a forgotten historic backwater...exactly why it's so beloved by visitors today.

Notice the colorful scenes on the tiled **benches** in the square, illustrating events from Cervantes' *Don Quixote*. Cervantes' wife came from near Toledo, and he knew the city well, often mentioning it in his writings. *Don Quixote* even includes a tongue-in-cheek mention that Cervantes didn't write the work—he just translated it from an Arabic manuscript found in Toledo.

Now walk to the edge of the square along the busy street and

Toledo's History

Perched strategically in the center of Iberia, Toledo was for centuries a Roman transportation hub with a thriving Jewish population. After Rome fell, Toledo became a Visigothic capital (AD 554). In 711 the Moors (Muslims) made it a regional center. Because of its importance, Toledo was the first city in the crosshairs of Christian forces. It fell in 1085, marking the beginning of the end of Muslim Spain, which culminated in the fall of Granada in 1492. A local saying goes,  "A carpet frays from the edges, but the carpet of al-Andalus (Muslim Spain) frayed from the very center"—Toledo.

Though the city was now dominated by Christians, many Moors remained, tolerated and respected as scholars and craftsmen. During its medieval heyday (c. 1350), Toledo was a city of the humanities, where God was known by many names. People of different faiths lived in harmony. The Jewish community—educated, wealthy, and cosmopolitan—thrived (relatively) from the city's earliest times. Jews of Spanish origin are called Sephardic Jews.

The city reached its peak in the 1500s, when Spain was in its golden age, Toledo's bishops wielded vast political power, Emperor Charles V made it his "Imperial City," and artists like El Greco called it home. All of Spain considered Toledo to be the heart of what was becoming a budding nation-state.

Then suddenly, in 1561, Philip II decided to move the capital to a small town north of here—Madrid. Some say that Madrid was the logical place for a capital in the geographic center of newly formed *España*. Others think Philip wanted more room to grow, or to separate politics from religion. Whatever the reason, Toledo—though still Spain's religious capital—began a slow decline. Its medieval structures were never rebuilt, leaving it mothballed. In the 19th century, Romantic travelers rediscovered it and wrote of it as a mystical place, which it remains today.

face the big governmental building. Look uphill to your right to see two of the four corner turrets of the **Alcázar**—the mighty fortress that was for a time (in the 16th century, before Philip left in a huff) Spain's seat of power. During the Spanish Civil War, Franco's Nationalists holed up inside the Alcázar, and the Republicans laid siege to the fortress (see "The History of the Alcázar" sidebar, later in this chapter). Most of the area around the Alcá-

zar was destroyed—this part of town, including much of Plaza de Zocodover, has been rebuilt (notice the *Restaurado 1945* sign on the governmental building). Today the Alcázar houses the Army Museum, a sprawling exhibit on Spain's military history. (I'll point out the entrance in a moment.)

Dodge buses as you cross the street and look right to see an outpost of **Santo Tomé,** one of Toledo's top shops for the delicious almond candy called *mazapán* (the shops are named for the famous chapel). If you're ready for a treat, stop in and buy an assortment to munch. (For more on *mazapán*, and tips on shopping, see "Shopping in Toledo" later.)

Continue down the stairs straight past the *mazapán* shop, head through the arch, and snap a selfie with the statue of **Cervantes** (who's looking down the street named for him).

Looking back above Cervantes' head, notice that the archway you just came through has a distinctive keyhole shape—a classic feature of **Mudejar** architecture, the hybrid Moorish/Christian style of Muslim craftspeople who stayed behind after the Moors were forced out of Spain. Toledo—which was the first major town retaken by the Reconquista, in 1085—is *the* top Mudejar city in Spain. (For more on the Reconquista, see the Spain: Past and Present chapter.) Cities farther south, like Granada, remained Moorish for centuries longer. In many ways, Toledo is a hinge between the Moorish-flavored south and the distinctly Christian north. Throughout the city, keep an eye out for the distinctly Mudejar look.

A few steps beyond Cervantes, look right up the street to the big, blocky building. This is the entrance to the **Army Museum,** inside the Alcázar fortress. Then continue 30 paces straight ahead (downhill on Cervantes Street) and look left to see the frilly Plateresque entrance to the **Santa Cruz Museum,** with a fine collection of art, including some top El Grecos.

• *Retrace your steps past Cervantes, back through that keyhole arch, and cross the street into Plaza de Zocodover. Continue straight through the middle of the square and carry on (past a row of ATMs) along Toledo's main shopping artery, the aptly named...*

❷ Calle del Comercio

This main drag, connecting Plaza de Zocodover with the cathedral, is jammed with day-trippers. But *Toledanos* still shop here, too, and you'll notice a mix of local businesses (clothing stores, banks, lotto shops) and tourist-oriented shops (offering knives, leather, *mazapán*, and damascene—fine inlaid work). Many visitors never break free of this gauntlet, but make sure you do—some of Toledo's most appealing back streets lie just above and below here.

As you stroll and browse, you may wonder: Why are knives

Toledo's Muslim Legacy

You can see the Moorish influence in these sights:

- Mezquita del Cristo de la Luz, the last of the town's mosques
- Tránsito Synagogue's Mudejar plasterwork
- Santa María la Blanca Synagogue's mosque-like horseshoe arches and pinecone capitals
- Puerta del Sol (Gate of the Sun) and other surviving gates (with horseshoe arches) along the medieval wall
- The city's labyrinthine, medina-like streets

---

such a big deal in Toledo? In the Middle Ages, Toledo made the very best steel—using know-how imported from the Middle East via Muslim craftsmen. Don Quixote-type knights of the age considered having a Toledo-cast sword to be *the* top status symbol.

After one block, at the Starbucks, look up the intersecting street to the right (above the yogurt shop) for the most-photographed street sign in town: **Calle de Toledo de Ohío**...in honor of "the other Toledo." Elsewhere in Toledo, a similar sign adorns a suburban street called Calle de Corpus Christi—for the Texan town named for Toledo's biggest religious celebration.

Walk a few blocks along Calle del Comercio as it winds through the heart of town. Where the street widens, take the right fork (Calle del Hombre del Palo). Soon you're walking along the bulky wall of the **cathedral** complex, on your left. At the next fork—at the lovely building with the double-headed eagle on top—take a sharp left and continue downhill alongside the cathedral.

As you walk along the cathedral, look about 20 feet up to see metal girders. These support priceless Flemish tapestries—some dating back to the 16th century—during the annual celebration of **Corpus Christi,** 60 days after Easter. On that day, the communion host is paraded around town in a gigantic gold monstrance (you can see it inside the cathedral). For a month leading up to the big day, the 1.5-mile procession route is rigged with a cloth canopy and hung with ceremonial lights.

You'll pass under a skybridge that connects the cathedral to the bishop's palace—the gigantic, hulking building on your right.
• *Just below that, you pop out into the square called...*

❸ Plaza del Ayuntamiento

This square is named for Toledo's **City Hall**—the mini Alcázar straight ahead, with a TI inside. Notice that this building flies not three flags but four: the EU, Spain, Castile-La Mancha (purple-and-white), and the city flag of Toledo (purple). The low-profile

modern fountain in front of the City Hall—designed to resemble the Tajo riverbed—runs every 30 minutes. Look around and see how many double-headed eagles you can count on this very proudly *Toledana* square.

Now turn around to appreciate the **view of the cathedral**—it's hard not to be impressed. The tower rocketing up is capped with three crowns—signifying this cathedral's primacy over all other Spanish churches. On the right side, notice the stubby base of what was planned to be a matching second steeple. As work progressed, the foundation began to crumble (you can see the damage). It was being built on the artificially leveled-out square rather than the angled rock at the base of the existing tower. So plans were scaled back and a domed chapel was built instead.

Study the **facade**. The tympanum (over the door) illustrates the founding story of the cathedral: In the seventh century, the local Bishop Ildefonso wrote a book about the Virgin Mary—who rewarded him by miraculously appearing and offering him a holy vestment, legitimizing Toledo as the leading Christian city of Spain. The original carvings in soft, white limestone were later protected by a harder layer of gray granite carvings. Looking up, you can see how workers created a granite canopy over the limestone rose window (which now peeks out a little window of its own). Between the rose window and the tympanum, granite Apostles peer out from the ledge in a Last Supper scene.

The **cathedral interior** is undoubtedly the top sight in town. To enter, head up the lane on the right side of the cathedral. The ticket office is on the right side of the street. (A self-guided tour of the interior is outlined later, under "Sights in Toledo.")

• *When you're ready to move on, we'll take a stroll through...*

❹ Toledo's Back Streets

Leave Plaza del Ayuntamiento on the narrow, uphill lane to the right of the City Hall. Continuing straight ahead, you'll go under an arch, then through a little passage and out a door on the other side onto a fine little square.

Turn right, then right again, and curl steeply uphill. You'll be walking along the apse (on your left) of the Mudejar-style Santa Ursula convent from the 13th century (notice the keyhole arches), once home to *mazapán*-making nuns. They've moved out, but there are still several active nunneries in Toledo.

Cresting the hill on Camino el Salvador, notice the wide-open space on your right. In Toledo's medieval cityscape—where streets are tight and buildings are close together—open space like this is a sure sign that something once here is now gone. Sure enough, this was a site of yet another monastery, which collapsed. Now it's a rare

park. The modern, bunker-like building behind the park (cleverly lit with skylights) is an archive.

Reaching the end of the park, jog left slightly to continue along Calle Santo Tomé—toward the rectangular steeple. At the start of this street are two more opportunities to sample *mazapán*. On the right is the endearing **El Café de las Monjas,** which sells desserts created by nuns living in Toledo's convents (notice the adorable-slash-creepy window display of nun-dolls hard at work in the kitchen). Across the street, ahead on the left, is the original branch of the **Santo Tomé** *mazapán* **shop** that we saw on Plaza de Zocodover. The goodies are made at this location.

• *Continue on Calle Santo Tomé. When you reach the tall, rectangular tower, turn left down the narrow lane just past it. You'll emerge at the long square marking...*

❺ Santo Tomé

This otherwise unexceptional church is home to the masterpiece of Toledo's great medieval painter, El Greco. *The Burial of the Count of Orgaz* illustrates the attendants of a local bigwig's funeral, both in heaven and here on earth. You'll likely see a line at the ticket office (facing the long square), but the wait is worth it. (For details and a description of the painting, see the "Santo Tomé" listing under "Sights in Toledo.")

The square extending behind Santo Tomé—**Plaza del Conde**—is the terminus for handy bus #12 (bus stop at far end of square). This marks the end of the first half of this walk. If your time in Toledo is short, visit San Tomé, then hightail it back to Plaza Zocodover on the bus (or walk back via the back streets instead of the clogged Calle del Comercio).

• *With more time, continue through...*

TOLEDO'S JEWISH QUARTER

You've already entered Toledo's former Jewish Quarter, where up until the Middle Ages, Jews were allowed to live, work, and practice their religion. But in 1492, Isabel and Ferdinand expelled the Jews (except for those who converted to Christianity). Most synagogues and other Jewish institutions were destroyed or repurposed as churches, but two very rare synagogue buildings survived.

To reach the heart of the Jewish Quarter—and those synagogues, among other sights (all described in more detail later, under "Sights in Toledo")—continue steeply downhill on the cobbled street past the Santo Tomé ticket office. Stay on this lane as it curves sharply left, descending below the bottom end of Plaza del Conde.

In a few minutes, the lane takes you past the entrance of the **El Greco Museum** (on your right). While the best paintings by El

Greco are displayed in three sights we've already passed—the Santa Cruz Museum, the cathedral, and Santo Tomé—this museum offers a more in-depth look at the painter's life and times.

Across the street from the El Greco Museum is a big park (with a giant memorial to the painter). Turn right here, and in 100 yards you'll run right into the entrance to the **Tránsito Synagogue** building, which offers a very rare-in-Spain look inside a historic synagogue and houses a fine museum.

Continue past the Tránsito Synagogue on Calle de los Reyes Católicos, which links up several more sights.

A block past the synagogue, a side street on the left leads to the **Victorio Macho Museum,** with works by Spain's most important 20th-century sculptor (watch for signs to *Real Fundación de Toledo*).

Farther along on the right is a little park with a bus stop. Just beyond that is the **Santa María la Blanca Synagogue,** with a more pristine Mudejar-style interior than the Tránsito Synagogue.

Finally, Calle de los Reyes Católicos passes the huge **San Juan de los Reyes monastery** complex, originally designed to be the final resting place for Isabel and Ferdinand (who wound up being buried in Granada instead). At the very end of the street, the castle-like church exterior displays a variety of chains that were supposedly used by the Moors to shackle Christians in Granada before the Reconquista. The interior of the monastery and its chapel are also worth a look.

• *Our walk is finished. Across the street from the Monastery of San Juan de los Reyes is another stop for bus #12, which you can take on a scenic ride outside Toledo's walls and then back up to Plaza de Zocodover. See the end of the "Sights in Toledo" section for details.*

Sights in Toledo

I've organized Toledo's sights geographically: near Plaza de Zocodover, the cathedral and nearby, and in the town's southwest end. You can link the major sights using my self-guided "Toledo Walk," earlier.

NEAR PLAZA DE ZOCODOVER
▲Santa Cruz Museum (Museo de Santa Cruz)
This stately Renaissance building, formerly an orphanage and hospital, was funded by money left by the humanist and diplomat Cardinal Mendoza when he died in 1495. The cardinal,

confirmed as Chancellor of Castile by Queen Isabel, was so influential that he was called "the third royal." The museum has a good permanent collection (with eight El Grecos) about Spain under Charles V and his offspring, a peaceful cloister with a good ceramics collection, and temporary exhibits.

Cost and Hours: Free; Mon-Sat 10:00-18:00, Sun until 15:00; from Plaza de Zocodover, go through arch to Calle Miguel de Cervantes 3; +34 925 221 402, www.patrimoniohistoricoclm.es.

Visiting the Museum: The building's **facade** still wears bullet scars from the Spanish Civil War. The frilly decorations around the main entrance (as well as the cloister arches and stairway leading to the upper cloister) are fine examples of the Plateresque style, an ornate strain of Spanish Renaissance named for the detailed work of silversmiths of the 16th century. Note the Renaissance-era mathematics—ideal proportions, round arches, square squares, and classic columns.

Inside, as you make your way down the long hall toward the El Grecos, browse the **exhibits** that set the stage. A century before El Greco's heyday in Toledo, the "Catholic Monarchs"—Ferdinand and Isabel—were turning Spain into a militantly religious country. They were aided by Cardinal Mendoza (look for his portrait), who drove the Muslims from Granada, founded this Christian charity hospital, and was buried among kings at the high altar of Toledo Cathedral. In Spain's new ultra-religious climate, paintings of saints and altarpieces were artists' main outlet.

The Catholic Monarchs' grandson, Charles V (see his glittering bust in the left "transept"), spread Spanish Catholicism throughout his worldwide empire. His son, Philip II (see exhibits in the apse, near the El Grecos), was especially devout, battling Protestants in the Counter-Reformation as well as Muslim Turks (see the big blue banner from the Battle of Lepanto, 1571). This was the environment the Greek immigrant El Greco found when he arrived in Spain in 1577 and started working for the introverted ascetic Philip II. It's little wonder that El Greco's main art was designed to express the intense spiritual fervor of 16th-century Spain.

The highlight of the museum is the dozen or so **El Greco** paintings (a rotating display of some permanent, some on loan). El Greco's specialty was capturing ascetic Christian saints in voluminous robes experiencing their moment of epiphany. They tilt their faces heavenward or express their deep feelings with a simple hand gesture. The scenes are rendered in bright, almost florescent colors that give these otherwise ordinary humans a heavenly aura.

Most impressive is *Assumption of Mary,* a spiritual poem on canvas (housed in its own little caged room). This altarpiece, finished one year before El Greco's death in 1614, is the culmination of his unique style. (The *Assumption* more likely depicts the Immac-

ulate Conception, which is how it's labeled.) Bound to earth, the city of Toledo sleeps, but a vision is taking place overhead. An angel in a billowing robe, as if doing the breaststroke with his wings, flies up, supporting Mary, the mother of Christ. She floats up through warped space, to be serenaded by angels and wrapped in the radiant light of the Holy Spirit. Mary flickers and ripples, charged from within by her spiritual ecstasy, caught up in a vision that takes her breath away. No painter before or since has captured the supernatural world better than El Greco. (For more on El Greco, see page 585.)

Nearby is El Greco's *Holy Family*. The tender, otherworldly scene of Mary and Anne adoring the Baby Jesus is given a down-to-earth touch with a stormy Toledo sky and a balding Joseph—probably modeled after the work's patron. Notice the little scrap of paper in the lower-right corner, signed with El Greco's full name in Greek.

El Greco's *San Ildefonso* celebrates Toledo's hometown saint and early bishop of the cathedral. He meditates on the Bible while wearing the ornate robe marking him as Spain's "Primate," or head bishop.

Next, find the doorway in the right "transept" that leads into the peaceful Renaissance **cloister.** Turn left to find a collection of ancient artifacts—Arabic funerary columns, a third-century Roman mosaic that depicts the four seasons, and a marble well bearing an Arabic inscription. Note the grooves in the sides of the well made by generations pulling their buckets up by rope. This well was once located in the courtyard of an 11th-century mosque, which stood where the cathedral does today. The cloister is usually ringed with temporary exhibits (look for signs).

Find the frilly (Plateresque) staircase to the upper level of the cloister and enter the beautiful **Carranza Collection** of tiles and ceramics dating from the end of the Reconquista (1492). Stroll through and see how each region (Valencia, Catalunya) had its own style or color scheme, building up to Toledo's distinctive blue pieces in the final room. From the top level of the courtyard, you may be able to go up a short flight of stairs to a temporary exhibit hall with a view down into the atrium that runs through the navel of the museum.

▲Army Museum (Museo del Ejército)

One of Europe's top military museums, the Army Museum is worth ▲▲ and at least three hours for military history buffs. (Those bored

by weapons and war can skip it.) Much of Spain's history is military, and this museum—housed in the mighty Alcázar fortress that caps Toledo—tells that part of Spain's story from 1492 to the 20th century. You'll see Spanish military collections of armor, uniforms, cannons, guns, paintings, and models. The posted English information is excellent, and the audioguide is a worthwhile supplement. The museum has one major flaw: its skimpy coverage of the Spanish Civil War (1936-1939).

The permanent exhibits fill four floors: thematic exhibits on T1 and T2, and a chronological sweep through Spanish military history on H1 and H2. Read my descriptions before your visit and target what interests you—or follow my once-over-lightly tour of the highlights.

Cost and Hours: €5, free on Sun; free to enter temporary exhibits and archeological ruins—ask for pass at ticket office; open Tue-Sun 10:00-17:00, closed Mon; great audioguide-€3, café/restaurant and view terrace, +34 925 238 800, www.museo.ejercito.es.

❍ Self-Guided Tour: The floor plan is sprawling and confusing—be sure to pick up the English map to navigate. We'll breeze quickly through, but even at that, this huge collection will test your endurance. So buck up, soldier.

• *From the ticket booth, head up a series of escalators (over the excavated ruins of earlier fortifications) to the...*

Permanent Collection (Floor T2): At the top of the escalators, cut through the gift shop to reach the thematic exhibits. We'll skip these for now and head for the far-right corner, where you can take the elevator or stairs to floor H1 to find the "Start of the Historical Tour," a chronological sweep through 500 years of Spanish history.

1492-1843 (Floor H1): In the first room (labeled *The Catholic Monarchs*), it's 1492, the Muslims have been driven out (see Boabdil the Moor's captured sword and robe), and a united Spain emerges as a major military power. Conquistadors like Cortés (see his *Historia*) were conquering the New World, and Emperor Charles V (portrait) assumed the role of policeman for all of Europe.

• *From here, begin the clockwise loop around level H1 (following "historical round" arrows), sweeping through Spain's military history.*

Browse through the flags (*banderas*), weapons, and armor of the period. Next, learn about Spain's many wars in the 1500s, including in the New World (with exhibits of Native American weapons). You'll pass through the open-air **Charles V Courtyard**—

The History of the Alcázar

The Alcázar is the huge former imperial residence that dominates Toledo's skyline. It's built on the site of Roman, Visigothic, Moorish, and early Renaissance fortresses, the ruins of which are a reminder of the city's strategic importance through the centuries. Today the building itself is free to enter to view the archaeological ruins (there's an entry fee for the Army Museum that's housed here).

Today's structure (originally built in the 16th century, then destroyed in the civil war and rebuilt) became a kind of right-wing Alamo. During the civil war, Franco's Nationalists (and hundreds of hostages), commanded by Colonel José Moscardó, were besieged here by Republican troops for two months in 1936. The Republicans kidnapped Moscardó's teenaged son, Luís, and called the colonel, threatening to execute Luís if his father didn't surrender in 10 minutes. Moscardó asked for his son to be put on the line and told him that he would have to be a hero and die for Spain. Moscardó then informed the Republican leader that he didn't need 10 minutes: the choice was made—he would never give up the Alcázar. (While the Nationalists believed Luís was shot immediately, he was actually executed with other prisoners weeks later in a reprisal for an air raid.)

Finally, after many fierce but futile Republican attacks that destroyed much of the Alcázar, Franco sent in an army that took Toledo, a major victory for the Nationalists. After the war, the place was rebuilt and glorified under Franco. Only one room has been left in a tattered ruin since the siege: the office of Nationalist Colonel Moscardó, which you can see if you visit the Army Museum.

Italian-inspired Renaissance in style and adorned with a proud statue of Holy Roman Emperor Charles V (a.k.a. King Charles I of Spain), the ultimate military king and Europe's most powerful 16th-century leader. It's hard to believe that this massive fortress was virtually demolished in the 1930s and later elegantly restored.
• *Continue through floor H1.*

A dozen steps in, find a darkened room with a press-the-button exhibit on the **Battle of Almansa** (1707). Fought by many armies, this battle encapsulates the ultra-confusing War of the Spanish Succession, when all of Europe fought over who should rule Spain. (The Bourbons of France won.) In the next series of rooms, you see how Napoleon overthrew the Bourbons and brought still more turmoil.
• *Cross the stairwell and go into a room labeled* **The Napoleonic War 1808-14.**

On "El Dos de Mayo" (May 2), Napoleon's troops attacked

Madrid. You'll see a tattered uniform of a proud Spanish defender; some swords, hats, and portraits of other Spanish patriots; and small works by the artist Goya, who chronicled the events in famous paintings.

A few steps farther (and a century later), you reach the **Moscardó Room.** It's 1936, in the midst of the Spanish Civil War, and Toledo's Alcázar is under siege. This office was the headquarters of Toledo's fascist forces, led by Nationalist Colonel José Moscardó, holding out against the Republicans. (For more on the siege and the colonel, see the sidebar.) The room is preserved as it was by the end, battered and bullet-ridden. Photos show how the Alcázar was blasted to smithereens.

Complete your tour of this floor by viewing swords, uniforms, and portraits of the Spaniards who fought against Simón Bolívar and other emancipators of Spain's colonies in America.

• *Now take the stairs or elevator up (a half-flight) to floor CI to glimpse the* **Imperial Chapel** *of Philip II, featuring the 16th-century "Charles V tent." Continue up another half-flight to...*

1843-20th Century (Floor H2): Pass through a series of rooms on the **"Liberal State,"** when Spain was in decline and her monarchs battled the forces of democracy. Spain also battled the United States (1898) over **Cuba and the Philippines** (see US Army gear, a video on the sinking of the *Maine,* and insignia from Teddy Roosevelt's charge up San Juan Hill).

Continue to "The 20th Century" and the **Spanish Civil War.** Though the war was *the* event of 20th-century Spanish history, the curators chose to dodge the still-controversial issue by going light on it. Displays trace Primo de Rivera's dictatorship of the 1920s and the rise of the fascist General Francisco Franco in the 1930s. Continue past the displays of 1930s-era weapons and the stairwell to "How the War Unfolded." There you'll find some timelines and maps, a script of Franco's victory speech, and objects rescued from the rubble of the Alcázar—a motorcycle, a telephone, and a daily ration of bread.

Next, it's **World War II.** Though officially neutral, Franco supported Hitler, while many Spaniards became "El Maquis"—guerrillas fighting the fascists. The final exhibits cover the **1970s,** when Franco died (1975) and his powerful military state made a peaceful transition to democracy.

• *Whew. You've finished your 500-year march through history. Now descend (by elevator or stairs) to...*

Thematic Exhibits (Floors T2 and T1): Each room is dedicated to a particular collection: uniforms, medieval armor and swords, cannons and early rifles, toy soldiers collection, medals, wartime photography, and non-European weaponry. The "Crypt" (labeled

on your map) has the stark tomb of Colonel José Moscardó—who led the Nationalists during the siege of the Alcázar in 1936—and his wife and kids. Room T9 has artifacts from the entire history of the Alcázar—from Roman pottery to Charles V to the disastrous 1936 siege. If you like these exhibits, a few similar ones are one floor lower (T1). These cover the evolution of Spain's flag and display weapons—from battle axes, swords, and pikes to cannons, muskets, pistols, German lugers, and machine guns.

Mezquita del Cristo de la Luz

Of Muslim Toledo's 20 mosques, this barren little building (dating from about 1000) is the best survivor. Enter through the modern, rust-colored building just below, buy your ticket, and head into the mosque. Looking up, you'll notice the Moorish fascination with geometry—each dome is a unique design. The lovely keyhole arch faces Mecca. In 1185, after the Reconquista, the mosque was changed to a

church and renamed Iglesia de Cristo de la Luz. In 1187 the Christian apse (with its crude Romanesque art) was added and became the city's first example of Mudejar art and the model for all that would come after it. The small garden, with its fountains, is a reminder of the Quranic image of heaven. At the back of the garden, you can enjoy a view of the Mudejar-style Puerta del Sol gateway. And running along the fence in front of the mosque is a Roman road leading to the city wall (discovered when the mosque was undergoing restoration).

Cost and Hours: €3, Mon-Fri 10:00-18:45, until 17:45 on Sat-Sun and in winter, audioguide-€1, west of Plaza de Zocodover at Cuesta de las Carmelitas Descalzas 10, +34 925 254 191.

THE CATHEDRAL AND NEARBY
▲▲▲Toledo Cathedral

Holy Toledo! Spain's leading Catholic city has a magnificent cathedral. For more than 1,500 years, the people of Toledo have worshipped on this spot. The first were Visigoth Christians, in a small church. Around 711, Islamic Moors conquered the city, tore down that church, and built a magnificent mosque. When Toledo was reconquered (in 1085), Christians started using the mosque for their own services. But in 1226, the now-crumbling structure was dismantled, and construction began on the current cathedral. With

TOLEDO

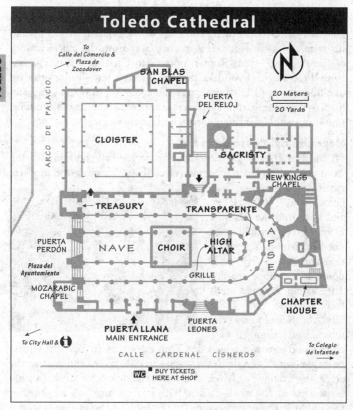

Toledo Cathedral

To Calle del Comercio & Plaza de Zocodover

SAN BLAS CHAPEL

PUERTA DEL RELOJ

20 Meters
20 Yards

ARCO DE PALACIO

CLOISTER

SACRISTY

NEW KINGS CHAPEL

TREASURY

TRANSPARENTE

PUERTA PERDÓN

Plaza del Ayuntamiento

NAVE

CHOIR

HIGH ALTAR

A P S E

GRILLE

MOZARABIC CHAPEL

CHAPTER HOUSE

To City Hall &

PUERTA LLANA
MAIN ENTRANCE

PUERTA LEONES

To Colegio de Infantes

CALLE CARDENAL CISNEROS

WC ■ BUY TICKETS HERE AT SHOP

its long history, Toledo's cathedral is still considered the spiritual heart of Spain.

Over the centuries, the church was decorated with the sights we see today: a five-story Gothic altarpiece, Renaissance-era frescoes, a one-of-a-kind Baroque skylight, a ten-foot-tall golden monstrance, and museum-worthy paintings by El Greco and others. Shoehorned  into the old center, the cathedral's exterior is hard to appreciate. But its rich and lofty interior will have you wandering around like a Pez dispenser stuck open, whispering "Wow."

Cost and Hours: €10 ticket includes multimedia guide and Colegio de Infantes; tickets sold in shop opposite church entrance on Calle Cardenal Cisneros (WC inside shop); open Mon-Sat 10:00-18:30, Sun from 14:00, open earlier for prayer only; +34 925 222 241.

⊃ Self-Guided Tour

• *Begin in the...*

Nave: Wander among the pillars, thick and sturdy as a red-wood forest. Sit under one and imagine a time when the lightbulbs were candles and the tourists were pilgrims—when every window provided both physical and spiritual light.

This cathedral is Spain's purest example of the Gothic style. Enjoy the soaring crisscross ceiling, elaborate wrought-iron work, lavish wood carvings, and windows of 500-year-old stained glass. Though Gothic, the church has some unusual features. It's especially wide (200 feet) relative to the length (400 feet) because it follows the footprint of the earlier mosque. (A few red-tinted columns incorporated into the choir wall may have come from that mosque.) The nave is divided into five aisles (not the usual three), clogged with columns, and filled with the choir—the walled enclosure in the middle. Circling the interior are ornate chapels, purchased by the town's most noble families.

• *Head for the space between the choir and the high altar, with its enormous carved altarpiece.*

High Altar: Climb two steps and grip the iron grille as you marvel at one of the most stunning altarpieces in Spain. Eighty

feet tall and made of real gold on wood, it's one of the country's best pieces of Gothic art. Twenty-seven Flemish, French, and local artists—architects, wood-carvers, painters, and goldsmiths—labored on it for seven years.

Study the wall with the scenes from the **life of Christ,** frame by frame. You can begin in the center with Jesus' birth. On the left side, he's arrested, forced to carry his cross, and crucified. On the right side, he's resurrected and appears to his followers. The images seem to celebrate the colorful Assumption of Mary (upper center), with Mary escorted by six upwardly mobile angels. The crucified Christ on top is nine feet tall—taller than the lower statues—to keep this towering altar approachable.

To the right of the altarpiece is a row of **stone statues** of venerable bishops, saints...and one Muslim. That mellow-looking guy with the cone-shaped hat and beard is the "Wise Moor," who brokered the peaceful handover of the mosque to the Christians in 1085.

To the left of the altarpiece, the two-story **tomb** in the style of a triumphal arch honors the bishop who ushered in the cathedral's golden age in the 1500s. Cardinal Mendoza helped Ferdinand and

Isabel conquer the Moors in Granada, promoted Columbus, and oversaw completion of this Gothic-style church (its construction took 250 years—1226-1493). He then began a new era of building in a new style—Renaissance. Mendoza and his powerful successors left their imprints, adding the grand altarpiece, the choir, and several of the chapels we'll see later. The wide-ranging decor reflects the church's long history: Gothic, Renaissance, Baroque, and Neoclassical.

Take note of the finely worked, gold-plated iron **grille** itself—considered to be the best from 16th-century Spain.

• *About-face to the...*

Choir: This intimate space, lined with 120 carved-wood stalls, is where VIPs and hymn-singing musicians (hence the name "choir") can celebrate Mass near the high altar. Stepping inside, you're greeted by a 700-year-old statue of the **Virgin and Child.** Mary smiles sweetly, her body sways seductively, her deeply creased robe is luxuriant, and Jesus playfully tweaks his mother's chin. This "White Virgin" is thought to be a gift from the French king to Spain.

The choir is ringed by **stone statues**—an alabaster genealogy of Christ—starting with Adam and Eve and working counterclockwise to Joseph and "S. M. Virgo Mater" (St. Mary the Virgin Mother). Compare the stiff, forward-facing statues on the right wall with the more lifelike, twisting, side-posing ones on the left—by Alonso Berruguete, "the Michelangelo of Spain." All this imagery is designed to remind viewers of the legitimacy of the bishop of Toledo's claims to religious power.

The focal point is the archbishop's **throne,** in the center of the far wall. Get close and find the fine alabaster relief just above the throne. It shows the miraculous event that put this cathedral on the map: In the seventh century, Mary came down from heaven to the cathedral to give Toledo's bishop, Saint Ildefonso, a holy robe. This legitimized Toledo as the spiritual capital (and therefore political capital) of the budding nation of Spain. The legend is found in artwork all over the cathedral and the city—including on the music stands nearby and the tympanum outside.

Now turn to the richly carved wooden **stalls,** where worshippers half-sit/half-stand during services. The carvings depict scenes of the Christian Reconquista, specifically the steady one-city-at-a-time finale—the retaking of the towns around Granada. Each castle represents a different town, labeled with its name, besieged

by valiant Christian armies. The assault culminates at the archbishop's throne (the two reliefs to either side), with the final victory at Granada in 1492. The soldiers' clothing, armor, and weaponry are so detailed that historians have studied them to learn the evolution of weaponry.

Also check out the **seat backs,** made of carved walnut and featuring New Testament figures—including Peter (key) and Paul (sword) alongside the archbishop himself. Now turn to the stalls' misericords—the tiny seats that allowed tired worshippers to lean while they "stand." These carvings depict various sins and proverbs. They feature folksy, sexy, secular scenes: animals, mermaids, unicorns, and common laborers. Apparently, since you sat on it, it could never be sacred anyway.

The iron **grille** of the choir is notable for the dedication of Domingo de Céspedes, the Toledo ironworker who built it for 6,000 ducats. The project, which lasted from 1541 until 1548, went way over budget. The medieval Church didn't accept cost overruns, so Domingo sold everything he owned to finish it and went into debt. He died a poor but honorable man.

Before leaving the choir, take a moment to absorb the marvelous complexity, harmony, and cohesiveness of the art around you. Look up. There are two fine **pipe organs:** one (frilly, on the left) is early-18th-century Baroque, and the other (austere and pointy, on the right) is late-18th-century Neoclassical. Music has been a big deal here since medieval times. It's part of the tradition that Toledo's bishops trace back to Saint Ildefonso and the days of the Visigoths.

• *As you leave the choir, face the huge altarpiece and go around it to your right to the door in the back-right corner, where you can enter the...*

Chapter House (Sala Capitular): Under a lavish ceiling, a **fresco** celebrates the humanism of the Italian Renaissance. There's a Deposition (taking crucified Jesus off the cross), a pietà, and a Resurrection on the front wall; they face a fascinating Last Judgment, where the seven sins are spelled out in the gang going to hell: arrogance (the guy striking a pose), avarice (holding his bag of coins), lust (the easy woman with the lovely hair and fiery crotch), anger (shouting at lust), gluttony (the fat guy), envy, and laziness. Think about how instructive this was in 1600.

Below the fresco, a pictorial review of 1,900 years of Toledo archbishops circles the room. The upper row of **portraits** dates from the 16th century. Except for the last two, these were not painted from life (the same face seems to be recycled over and over). The lower portraits were added one at a time from 1515 on and are of more historic than artistic interest. Imagine sitting down to church business surrounded by all this tradition and theology.

The current cardinal—whose portrait will someday grace the

next empty panel—is the top religious official in Spain. When he speaks—especially about controversial topics like divorce, abortion, and contraception—it makes news all over Spain.

As you leave, notice the iron-pumping cupids carved into the pear-tree panels lining the walls.

• *Go behind the high altar to find the...*

Transparente: This towering white, red, and gold altarpiece bursting with statues is a unique feature of the cathedral. But that's just half of this multimedia extravaganza.  Look up. In the 1700s, a hole was cut in the ceiling. The opening faces east, and on the morning of the summer solstice, the sun sends a beam into the church to strike the altarpiece, lighten this space for worship, and remind all that God is light. Natural light pours in and down a radiant tunnel of painted angels, which become 3-D angels molded out of stucco—the whole assembly tumbling toward the altar near ground level. On the altar is a marble statue of Mary holding Baby Jesus, who looks up in wonder. Put these elements together, and the result is a Baroque masterpiece.

Now turn to the **altarpiece** itself. Gape up at this riot of angels doing flip-flops, babies breathing thin air, bottoms of feet, and gilded sunbursts. Carved out of marble from Italy, it's bursting with motion and energy. Appreciate those tough little cherubs who are supporting the whole thing—they've been waiting for help for about 300 years now.

Step back to appreciate the altar's symbolism: The good news of salvation springs from Baby Jesus, up past the archangels (including one in the middle who knows how to hold a big fish correctly) to the Last Supper high above, and beyond into the light-filled dome. Also notice the two red cardinals' hats hanging on chains from the edge of the hole. A perk that only a cardinal enjoys is to choose a burial place in the cathedral and hang his hat over that spot until the hat rots. I guess the cardinals liked the Transparente, too.

• *Continue around the apse. On the right, enter the...*

Chapel of the New Kings (Capilla de Reyes Nuevos): These reclining statues mark the tombs of just some of the monarchs buried in this venerable cathedral. In the 16th century, Emperor Charles V moved these eight tombs of medieval-era kings here. In the short hallway connecting the chapel to the apse, look for a facsimile of an 800-year-old Bible, hand-copied and beautifully illustrated by French monks; it was a gift from St. Louis, the 13th-

century king of France. Imagine looking at these lavish illustrations with medieval eyes. (This is a replica; the fragile lambskin original is preserved out of public view.)

• *Back in the apse, the next door on your right takes you into the...*

Sacristy: The cathedral's sacristy is a mini Prado, with 19 El Grecos and masterpieces by Francisco de Goya, Titian, Diego Velázquez, Caravaggio, and Giovanni Bellini.

First, notice the fine perspective work on the **ceiling,** painted by Neapolitan artist Luca Giordano around 1690. (You can see the artist himself—with his circa-1690 spectacles—in the far-left corner.) It seems all the angels of heaven are hurrying toward the far end of the room, where Mary (in blue) is descending to earth to give the priestly robe to a kneeling Saint Ildefonso.

The most important painting in the collection—framed by marble columns—is **El Greco's** *The Spoliation* (a.k.a. *Christ Being Stripped of His Garments,* 1579). The great Spanish painter was Greek, and this is the first masterpiece he created after arriving in Toledo. It hangs exactly where he intended it to—in the room where priests donned their sacred robes for Mass.

El Greco shows Jesus surrounded by a sinister mob and suffering the humiliation of being stripped in public before his execution. His scarlet robe is about to be yanked off; the women (lower left) avert their eyes, turning to watch a carpenter at work (lower right) boring the holes for nailing Jesus to the cross. While the carpenter bears down, Jesus—the other carpenter—looks up to heaven. The contrast between the motley crowd gambling for his clothes and Jesus' noble face underscores the quiet dignity with which he endures this ignoble treatment. Jesus' delicate white hand stands out from the flaming red tunic with an odd gesture that's common in El Greco's paintings—with his ring finger and middle finger together (the "Reverse Spock"). Some say this was the way Christians of the day swore they were true believers, not merely Christians-in-name-only, such as former Muslims or Jews who converted to survive.

Other El Grecos adorn the room. His various saints show his trademark style: thin, solemn, weathered men on a neutral background, with simple expressive gestures. Close to the entrance is a scene rarely painted: *St. Joseph and the Christ Child.* Joseph is walking with Jesus, just as El Greco enjoyed walking around the Toledo countryside with his sons. Notice Joseph's gentle expression—and the Toledo views in the background.

To the right of *The Spoliation* is a more down-to-earth depiction of Christ's Passion: Francisco de Goya's *Betrayal of Christ.* It shows Judas preparing to kiss Jesus, thus identifying him to the Roman soldiers.

In an adjoining room are more treasures by master artists, in-

cluding Titian's probing portrait of Pope Paul III (a friend of Michelangelo) and Cardinal Mendoza's cross.

• *As you step out of the sacristy, walk through an open-air courtyard and make your way back to the nave. Turn right, and head for the far end. As you go, glance high up to your right at a beautiful* **rose window**—*the oldest stained glass in the church (14th century). Pass a chapel reserved for worship and head toward the far end. You'll pass a freestanding, fenced-in* **chapel**—*supposedly the very spot where the Virgin Mary appeared to Ildefonso.*

Now locate our final stops: The Treasury is in a chapel straight ahead. Through doors near the Treasury, step outside into the...

Cloister: The cloister is worth a visit for its finely carved colonnade. This area was once the open-air courtyard entrance of the mosque that stood here. Take a peaceful detour around the cloister, passing a subtitled film about the construction of the cathedral, then the funerary San Blas Chapel. The ceiling fresco over the alabaster tomb of a bishop is by a student of the 14th-century Italian Renaissance master Giotto.

• *Returning to the cathedral the way you came, turn right to find the...*

Treasury: The star attraction here is a 10-foot-high, 430-pound gold-and-silver **monstrance**—the ceremonial tower designed to hold the Holy Communion wafer (the host) that every year is paraded atop a float through the city during the festival of Corpus Christi ("body of Christ"). Built in 1517 by Enrique de Arfe, it features more than 250 little individual statuettes and details. It's made of 500 pieces held together by 12,500 screws. There are diamonds, emeralds, rubies, and 400 pounds of gold-plated silver. The inner part (which is a century older) is 40 pounds of solid gold. Yeow.

This precious and centuries-old monstrance is still a vital part of civic life, a testament to the Toledo Cathedral's unique position as the religious center of Spain.

• *Your essential cathedral tour is over, but there are several other sights to consider.*

More Cathedral Sights

Mozarabic Chapel (Capilla Mozárabe): Though historic and impressive, this chapel is rarely open to tourists. If you arrive before 10:00 (when the cathedral is open only for prayer; enter from north entrance), you can peek into the otherwise locked chapel. Better yet, attend the 9:00 Mass (daily except Sun) held inside the chapel. This Visigothic Mass (in Spanish) is the oldest surviving Christian ritual in Western Europe. You're welcome to partake in this stirring example of peaceful coexistence of faiths. Toledo's proud Mozarabic community of 1,500 people traces its roots to Visigothic times.

Cathedral View: Exiting the cathedral, turn right and walk a half-block to the Plaza del Ayuntamiento, the square presided over by the City. Here you'll find the best exterior view of the cathedral's prickly tower—a fitting end to your tour.

Colegio de Infantes: This is where the cathedral displays its fine collection of tapestries and vestments (€2 or included in cathedral ticket, daily 10:00-18:00; from the cathedral go down Calle Barco to Plaza Colegio Infantes, +34 925 258 723). Many of the 17th-century tapestries here are still used to decorate the cathedral during the festival of Corpus Christi. You'll also find the lavish-but-faded *Astrolabe Tapestry* (c. 1480, Belgian). It shows a new view of the cosmos at the dawn of the Age of Discovery: God (far left) oversees all, as Atlas (with the help of two women and a crank handle) spins the universe, containing the circular Earth. The wisdom gang (far right) heralds the wonders of the coming era. Rather than a map of Earth, this is a chart showing the cosmic order of things, as the constellations spin around the stationary North Star (center).

▲Visigothic Museum in the Church of San Román (Museo de los Concilios y de la Cultura Visigoda)

Though small, this museum offers a thought-provoking collection of artifacts from Toledo's infancy, displayed in a colorfully deco-

rated church in an untouristed part of Toledo. In the seventh century, Visigoth Christians built a church on this site atop one of Toledo's highest hills. In the 10th century, the church was knocked down and a mosque was built in its place. Three centuries

later, the mosque was replaced by the church you see today.

Cost and Hours: Free, Tue-Sat 10:00-14:00 & 16:00-18:00, Sun 9:00-15:00, closed Mon, no English information, west of the cathedral at Plaza San Román, +34 925 227 872.

Visiting the Museum: Start with the church **interior.** A few Visigoth capitals from the original church were reused and placed atop columns in the nave. The keystone arches, lobed windows, and murals with Christian themes represent the Mudejar mix of Christian and Islamic—each culture both conquering and celebrating their predecessors.

The 13th-century Romanesque **murals** are especially lively. Facing the altar, turn counterclockwise: On the left wall is the ever-popular giant St. Christopher (though this particular fresco is not all that old). In the back corner is an apocalyptic dragon/griffin.

The back wall has rows of saints flanking Islamic-style windows. Next, find naked Eve covering herself by the forbidden tree, while God says, "Put some clothes on." On the long wall is a remarkably literal Resurrection: Angels blow trumpets to wake the dead, who lift their coffin lids to climb out. Finally, find three winged angels (one with a bull's head) representing the Evangelists writing their Gospels. Beneath them is St. Eugene ("EVGENII"), the seventh-century bishop who founded Toledo Cathedral in the days of the Visigoths.

Now turn to the **Visigoth artifacts** from the *"Siglo VII"*—the seventh century. (Some are 1,400-year-old originals; some are replicas.) There are column capitals with Roman-style acanthus leaves and stone slabs with Latin inscriptions. To the Romans, the Visigoths were "barbarians" from Germany who conquered and looted the Empire, but in the long run the Visigoths adopted and preserved Roman culture. As Rome fell (AD 500), the Visigoths settled down in Roman Spain, making Toledo their capital and ruling Spain for two centuries.

The Visigoths adopted Christianity and built churches—as is clear from numerous stone fragments here. A carved relief depicts a row of robed saints and naked Adam and Eve. You'll see early Christian symbols: crosses, doves, and olive branches. The X-shaped symbol flanked by the Greek letters alpha and omega represents how Christ (the X) is the beginning and end of all.

Old coins attest to the Visigoths' thriving Mediterranean trade networks. Manuscripts preserve the Visigoth Law and theological writings that shaped Spanish legal and religious institutions for centuries. (Even Spain's current king traces his lineage—at least, in theory—back to the legendary Visigoth kings.) Pottery, jewelry, and elaborate metal-worked belt buckles give a glimpse into everyday life of these long-ago people.

Most impressive are the **votive crowns** (they look like hanging lanterns). The crowns are made of gold, crusted with gems, dripping with dangling pendants, and filigreed with intricate metalworking. Votive crowns, popular in medieval times, were not designed to be worn. Rather, these ceremonial objects were given to a church or bishop by devoted followers (or nobles needing a favor) to be hung by a chain directly over the altar. Because Toledo was the spiritual center of Spain, the city acquired many. (These crowns are replicas of ones unearthed in a big Visigoth treasure trove 10 miles southwest of Toledo.)

Finally, take in the entire **church**. Imagine it's the year 600, and Toledo is the center of thriving Visigothic Spain. Kings are crowned here in Toledo (including right here in this church). Nobles and bishops from throughout Spain convene here regularly to set policy. They debate whether Jesus was human (as the Arian

Visigoths believed) or part of a three-in-one Trinity (as Roman Catholics believed and the Visigoths eventually converted to). During the Visigoth era, Bishop Ildefonso had his vision of the Virgin Mary.

The Visigoths reigned supreme until the year 711, when the Islamic Moors invaded. Because Toledo was the political, cultural, and spiritual head of Spain, by decapitating Toledo, the Moors quickly took the entire peninsula. They built a mosque on top of a Visigoth church, which was, in turn, knocked down to make room for this medieval Mudejar church. Now artifacts from Visigothic times are on display, bringing the story full circle.

If the church **tower** is open, you can climb the steep stairs for a view of Toledo's rooftops.

SOUTHWEST TOLEDO

These sights cluster at the southwest end of town. For efficient sightseeing, visit them in this order, then return to the center on bus #12 (listed at the end of this section).

▲▲Santo Tomé

A simple chapel on Plaza del Conde holds El Greco's most beloved painting—*The Burial of the Count of Orgaz*—which couples heaven and earth in a way only The Greek could. It feels so right to see a painting in the same church where the artist placed it 400 years ago (though moved slightly to accommodate modern crowds). This 15-foot-tall masterpiece, painted at the height of El Greco's powers, is the culmination of his unique style.

Cost and Hours: €3, daily 10:00-18:45, off-season until 17:45, +34 925 256 098. There's often a line to get in; try going early or late to avoid tour groups.

Visiting Santo Tomé: The year is 1323. Count Don Gonzalo Ruiz of Orgaz, the mayor of Toledo, has died. You're at his burial right here in the chapel that he himself had ordered built. (Count Orgaz's actual granite tombstone is at your feet.) The good count was so holy, even saints Augustine and Stephen have come down from heaven to lower his body into the grave. Meanwhile, above, the saints in heaven wait to receive his blessed soul. (The painting's subtitle is "Such is the reward for those who serve God and his saints.")

More than 250 years later, in 1586, a local priest (depicted on

the far right, reading the Bible) hired El Greco to make a painting of the burial to hang over the count's tomb. The funeral is attended by Toledo's most distinguished citizens. (El Greco used local nobles as models.) The two saints, wearing rich robes, bend over to place Count Orgaz, dressed in his knight's armor, into the tomb. The detail work is El Greco at his best. Each nobleman's face is a distinct portrait, capturing a different aspect of sorrow or contemplation. The saints' robes are intricately brocaded and have portraits of saints on them. Orgaz's body is perfectly foreshortened, sticking out toward us. The officiating priest wears a wispy, transparent white robe. Orgaz's armor is so shiny, you can see St. Stephen's reflection on his chest.

The serene line of noble faces divides the painting into two realms—heaven above and earth below. Above the faces, the count's soul, symbolized by a little baby, rises up through a mystical birth canal to be reborn in heaven, where he's greeted by Jesus, Mary, and all the saints. A spiritual wind blows through as colors change and shapes stretch. This is Counter-Reformation propaganda—notice Jesus pointing to St. Peter, the symbol of the pope in Rome, who controls the keys to the pearly gates. With its surreal colors, wavelike clouds, embryonic cherubs, and elongated forms, heaven is as surreal as the earth is sober. But the two realms are united by the cross at right.

El Greco considered this to be one of his greatest works. It's a virtual catalog of his lifelong techniques: elongated bodies, elegant hand gestures, realistic faces, surreal colors, voluminous robes, and a mix of heaven and earth. The boy in the foreground—pointing to the two saints as if to say, "One's from the first century, the other's from the fourth...it's a miracle!"—is El Greco's own son. On the handkerchief in the boy's pocket is El Greco's signature, written in Greek. The only guy in this whole scene who doesn't seem to be completely engaged in the burial is the seventh figure from the left, looking directly out at the viewer—El Greco himself.

▲El Greco Museum (Museo del Greco)

Housed in a faux 16th-century villa located near the site of El Greco's actual home, this museum offers a look at the genius of his art and Toledo in his day. While you won't find many great works by El Greco here (for those, visit Santo Tomé, the cathedral, and the Santa Cruz Museum), there are a few good ones, along with thoughtful exhibits about his life and work.

Cost and Hours: €3, free Sat afternoon from 14:00 and all day Sun; open Tue-Sat 9:30-19:30 (off-season until 18:00), Sun 10:00-15:00, closed Mon; next to Tránsito Synagogue on Calle Samuel Leví, +34 925 223 665.

Visiting the Museum: From the ticket office, head through

El Greco (1541-1614)

Born on Crete and trained in Venice, Doménikos Theotokópoulos (tongue-tied friends just called him "The Greek") came to Spain to get a job decorating El Escorial. He failed there, but succeeded in Toledo, where he spent the last 37 years of his life. He mixed all three regional influences into his palette. From his Greek homeland, he absorbed the solemn, abstract style of icons. In Italy, he learned the bold use of color, elongated figures, twisting poses, and dramatic style of the later Renaissance. These elements were then fused in the fires of fanatic Spanish-Catholic devotion.

Not bound by the realism so important to his fellow artists, El Greco painted dramatic visions of striking colors and figures—bodies unnatural and lengthened as though stretched between heaven and earth. He painted souls, not faces. His work is on display at nearly every sight in Toledo. Thoroughly modern in his disregard for realism, he didn't impress the austere Philip II. But his art still seems as fresh as contemporary art does today. El Greco was essentially forgotten through the 18th and most of the 19th centuries. Then, with the Romantic movement (and the discovery of Toledo by Romantic-era travelers, artists, and poets), the paintings of El Greco became the hits they are today.

the garden to the museum building. Inside the courtyard, notice the little kitchen, watch the introductory video, and then climb the stairs to begin the one-way route, which shows the evolution of El Greco's art. **Upstairs,** you'll learn about his upbringing in Crete, his training in Venice and Rome, and his arrival in Toledo—each step spurring his style to evolve. One highlight is the long hall lined with portraits of the 12 Apostles, plus Jesus. Compare El Greco's style with Apostles painted by his contemporaries, displayed directly opposite. At the end of the hall is the remarkable *View and Plan of Toledo*, a panoramic map showing the city in 1614—a 400-year-old version of the tourist maps the TI hands out today. It was commissioned to promote the city (suddenly a *former* capital) after the king moved to Madrid. Study the map and list of sights, executed with stunning detail—El Greco must have scratched the writing onto the canvas with a needle dipped in paint.

Continue **downstairs,** where an altar painting of San Bernardine occupies a chapel of its own, under a fine Mudejar ceiling and set inside a simple golden frame El Greco designed himself. The

ascetic Italian preacher seems lost in his huge Franciscan robe. At his feet are bishops' hats, representing the prestigious offices he turned down to preach peace to the poor. The painting's lines—the slender cane, the dangling tassel in the robe, the edge of his Bible—all point upward, and Bernadine's robe tapers as it rises, depicting an idealistic saint who clearly had his head in the clouds.

The exhibit wraps up with a description of El Greco's workshop, creative process, and some of his talented students, including his son Jorge Manuel—the kid in the *Burial of Count Orgaz.*

Nearby: Across the street is a delightful park, with great views of Toledo's rooftops and river and a giant monument to *Dominico Thetocopvli*—better known as El Greco.

▲Tránsito Synagogue and Sephardic Jewish Museum (Sinagoga del Tránsito y Museo Sefardí)

Built in 1361, this is the best surviving slice of Toledo's Jewish past. The austere interior rewards patient visitors with its fine details. Serving as Spain's national Sephardic Jewish museum, the building also displays a modest selection of Jewish artifacts, including traditional costumes, menorahs, and books. Paltry English sheets in each room explain the museum; for more detail, get the audioguide.

Cost and Hours: €3, free Sat afternoon from 14:00 and all day Sun; open Tue-Sat 9:30-19:30 (off-season until 18:00), Sun 10:00-15:00, closed Mon; near El Greco Museum on Calle de los Reyes Católicos, +34 925 223 665.

Background: This 14th-century synagogue was built at the peak of Toledo's enlightened tolerance—constructed for Jews with Christian approval by Muslim craftsmen. Nowhere else in the city does Toledo's three-culture legacy shine brighter than at this place of worship. But in 1391, just a few decades after the synagogue was built, the Church and the Spanish kings began a violent campaign to unite Spain as a Christian nation, forcing Jews and Muslims to convert or leave. In 1492 Ferdinand and Isabel exiled Spain's remaining Jews, and although a third of them left, others converted to Christianity to remain in the country.

Visiting the Synagogue: Your visit comes with three parts: the main hall of the synagogue, a ground floor exhibition space with a history of Spain's Jews, and the women's gallery upstairs, which shows lifestyles and holy rituals among Sephardic Jews.

Pass your bag through an x-ray machine, buy your ticket, and step into the **great hall.** Built as a place for Jews to worship, it still has a few features found in many synagogues today. Men worshipped here on ground level, women in the upper balcony. They all faced the hall's east end (symbolically facing Jerusalem), where a three-arched niche in the wall held the Torah.

But what makes this synagogue unique is that its interior decor looks more Muslim than Jewish. After Christians reconquered the city in 1085, many Moorish workmen stayed on, beautifying the city with the style called Mudejar. The synagogue's intricate, geometrical carving in stucco—nearly all original, from 1360—features leaves, vines, and flowers; there are no human shapes, which are forbidden by the Torah—like the Quran—as being potential objects of idolatry. In the frieze (running along the upper wall, just below the ceiling), the Arabic-looking script is actually Hebrew, quoting psalms (respected by all "people of the book"—Muslims, Jews, and Christians alike).

Move up to the front. Stand close to the holy wall and study the exquisite workmanship (with reminders of all three religions: the coat of arms of the Christian king, Hebrew script, and Muslim decor). Look down. The small rectangular patch of the original floor survived only because the Christian altar table sat there.

The rest of the museum is skippable for most. But if you're interested, head into the **side hall,** with displays about the history of Toledo's Jews and the development of the Jewish Quarter. The Memorial Garden displays Jewish tomb markers from around Spain.

If possible, head upstairs—through a sunny patio—to reach the **women's gallery,** which hosts a small exhibit about Jewish traditions (area may be closed for renovation). You'll see candelabras from Hanukah, fancy Torah scrolls, bar mitzvah clothes, wedding regalia, and a circumcision knife, as well as a model of the synagogue itself. There's a display on the Sephardi—Jews who settled in Spain, dispersed across the globe after 1492, but still retain unique customs, language, and heritage. Together, the exhibits help paint a picture of Jewish life in medieval Toledo and today.

▲Victorio Macho Museum (Museo Victorio Macho)

Overlooking the gorge and Tajo River, this small and attractive museum—once the home and workshop of the early-20th-century sculptor Victorio Macho—offers a delightful collection of his bold Art Deco-inspired work. The museum's theater hosts a gimmicky multimedia show called the Toledo Time Capsule, which isn't worth the extra fee.

Cost and Hours: €3, Sun-Wed 10:00-14:00, Thu-Sat 11:00-18:00, between the two synagogues at Plaza de Victorio Macho 2, ring doorbell to enter, +34 925 284 225.

Background: Victorio Macho (1887-1966) was Spain's first great modern sculptor. When his left-wing Republican (say that three times) politics made it dangerous for him to stay in Franco's Spain, he fled to the USSR, then to Mexico and Peru, where he met his wife, Zoila. They later returned to Toledo, where they lived

and worked until he died in 1966. Zoila eventually gave the house and Macho's art to the city.

Visiting the Museum: The house and its garden are a cool oasis of calm in the city. Entering the complex, belly up to the terrace for a peaceful and expansive **view** (look for *mirador/balcony* signs for the best viewpoint). From here it's clear how the Tajo River served as a formidable moat protecting the city. Imagine trying to attack. The 14th-century bridge (on the right) connected the town with the region's *cigarrales*—mansions of wealthy families, whose orchards of figs and apricots dot the hillside even today. To the left (in the river), look for the stubs of 15th-century watermills; directly below is a riverside trail that's delightful for a stroll or jog.

The door marked *Crypta* leads to *My Brother Marcelo*—the touching tomb Macho made for his brother. Eventually he featured his entire family in his art.

A dozen steps above the terrace, you'll find a single room, marked *Museo*, filled with Macho's art. A pietà is carved expressively in granite. Next to the pietà, several self-portrait sketches show the artist's genius. The bronze head (from 1904) is a self-portrait at age 17. In the next section, exquisite pencil-on-paper studies illustrate how a sculptor must understand the body (in this case, Zoila's body). The sketch of Zoila from behind is entitled *The Guitar* (Spanish artists traditionally think of a woman's body as a guitar). Other statues show the strength of the people's spirit as leftist Republicans stood up to Franco's fascist forces, and Spain endured its 20th-century bloodbath. The highlight is *La Madre* (from 1935), Macho's life-size sculpture of his mother sitting in a chair. It illustrates the sadness and simple wisdom of Spanish mothers who witnessed so much suffering. Upon a granite backdrop, her white marble hands and face speak volumes.

Santa María la Blanca Synagogue (Sinagoga de Santa María la Blanca)

This synagogue-turned-church has Moorish horseshoe arches and wall carvings. It's a vivid reminder of the religious cultures that shared (and then didn't share) this city. While it looks like a mosque, it never was one. Built as a Jewish synagogue by Muslim workers around 1200, it became a church in 1391 when Toledo's Jews were first expelled from the city by Christians—hence the mix-and-match name. After being used as horse stables by Napoleonic troops, it was further ruined in the 19th century. Today, fully renovated and sparkling white, it's beautiful in its

simplicity. In many ways it's a more evocative and architecturally pleasing sight than the Tránsito Synagogue up the street.

Cost and Hours: €3, daily 10:00-18:45, until 17:45 in winter, Calle de los Reyes Católicos 4, +34 925 227 257.

▲Monastery of San Juan de los Reyes (Monasterio de San Juan de los Reyes)

"St. John of the Monarchs" is a grand Franciscan monastery, impressive church, and delightful "Isabeline" cloistered courtyard. The style is late Gothic, contemporaneous with Portugal's Manueline (c. 1500) and Flamboyant Gothic elsewhere in Europe. It was the intended burial site of the Catholic Monarchs, Isabel and Ferdinand. But after the Moors were expelled in 1492 from Granada, their royal bodies were planted there to show Spain's commitment to maintaining a Moor-free peninsula.

Cost and Hours: €3, daily 10:00-18:45, off-season until 17:45, San Juan de los Reyes 2, +34 925 223 802.

Visiting the Monastery: Before entering and getting your ticket, circle around to take in the **facade** (at the downhill end). It is famously festooned with 500-year-old chains. Moors used these to shackle Christians in Granada until 1492. It's said that the freed Christians brought these chains to the church, making them a symbol of their Catholic faith and a sign of victory.

Go to the side door to enter the monastery, head down the stairs, and buy your ticket. Then look up. A skinny monk welcomes you (and reminds us of our mortality).

Head into the cloister, then turn right into the glorious **chapel**—made of creamy stone, with clean lines and intricate trim. It's topped with an octagonal dome with interlacing vaults. Even without the royal tombs that would have dominated the space, the chapel gives you a sense of Spain when it was Europe's superpower. The monastery was built to celebrate the 1476 Battle of Toro, which made Isabel the queen of Castile. Since her husband, Ferdinand, was king of Aragon, this effectively created the Spain we know today. (You could say 1476 is to Spain what 1776 is to the US.) Once united, Spain was able to quickly finish the Reconquista, ridding Iberia of its Moors within the next decade and a half.

Sitting in the chapel, you're surrounded by propaganda proclaiming the Catholic Monarchs' greatness. Their coat of arms—complex because of Iberia's many kingdoms (e.g., a lion for León and a castle for Castile)—is repeated obsessively. Above each

one, the eagle with the halo disk represents St. John, protector of the royal family. The yoke and arrows that flank the coat of arms are the symbols of Ferdinand and Isabel. The letters "F" and "Y" intertwined in the designs are for Ferdinand and Ysabel, and the lions underneath remind people of the power of the kingdoms joined together under Ferdinand and Isabel.

As you leave, look up over the door to see the Franciscan coat of arms, with the five wounds of the Crucifixion (the stigmata—which St. Francis earned through his great faith) flanked by angels with dramatic wings.

Enjoy a walk around the **cloister.** Notice details of the fine carvings. At eye level, you'll find (lurking amid the foliage) vari-

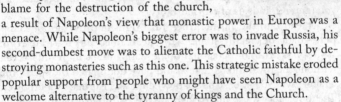

ous animals and fantastic beasts: dragons, lions, eagles, cupids, and naked people. Everything had meaning in the 15th century. In the far corner (kitty-corner across from the entry), just above eye level, find a small monkey—an insulting symbol of Franciscans—on a toilet reading the Bible upside-down. Perhaps a stone carver snuck in a not-too-subtle comment on Franciscan pseudo-intellectualism, with their big libraries and small brains.

Napoleon's troops are mostly to blame for the destruction of the church, a result of Napoleon's view that monastic power in Europe was a menace. While Napoleon's biggest error was to invade Russia, his second-dumbest move was to alienate the Catholic faithful by destroying monasteries such as this one. This strategic mistake eroded popular support from people who might have seen Napoleon as a welcome alternative to the tyranny of kings and the Church.

The skippable **upper cloister** offers a simple walk around the top level of the courtyard under a finely renovated Moorish-style ceiling.

▲Bus #12 Self-Guided Tour (A Sweat-Free Return Trip from Santo Tomé to Plaza de Zocodover)

When you're finished with the sights at the Santo Tomé end of town, you can hike all the way back to Plaza de Zocodover (not fun), or simply catch bus #12 (fun!). The ride offers tired sightseers an interesting 15-minute look at the town walls. You can catch the bus from Plaza del Conde in front of Santo Tomé. This is the end of the line, so buses wait to depart from here twice hourly (at :25 and :55, until 21:25, pay driver €1.40). You can catch the same bus a few stops downhill, at the very bottom of Toledo's sightseeing spine, across the street from the San Juan de los Reyes ticket entrance (a

few minutes after it leaves Plaza del Conde). You can do this tour in reverse by riding bus #12 from Plaza de Zocodover to Plaza del Conde (departing at :25 and :55, same price and hours).

If you start at Santo Tomé, here's what you'll see along your way:

Leaving Plaza del Conde, you'll first ride through Toledo's Jewish Quarter. On the right, you'll pass the El Greco Museum, Tránsito Synagogue, and Santa María la Blanca Synagogue, followed by—on your left—the ornate Flamboyant Gothic facade of the Monastery of San Juan de los Reyes. After squeezing through the 16th-century city gate, the bus follows along the outside of the mighty 10th-century wall. (Toledo was never conquered by force... only by siege.)

Just past the big escalator (which brings people up from parking lots into the city) and the Hotel del Cardenal, the wall gets fancier, as demonstrated by the little old Bisagra Gate. Soon after, you see the big new Bisagra Gate, the main entry into the old town. While the city walls date from the 10th century, this gate was built as an arch of triumph in the 16th century. The massive coat of arms of Emperor Charles V, with the double-headed eagle, reminded people that he ruled a unified Habsburg empire (successor of ancient Rome), and they were entering the capital of an empire that, in the 1500s, included most of Western Europe and much of America. (We'll enter the town next to this gate in a couple of minutes.) Just outside the big gate is a well-maintained and shaded park—a picnic-perfect spot and one of Toledo's few green areas.

After a detour to the bus station basement to pick up people arriving from Madrid, you swing back around Bisagra Gate. As recently as 1960, all traffic into the city at this spot passed through this gate's tiny original entrance.

As you climb back into the old town, you'll pass the fine 14th-century Moorish Puerta del Sol (Gate of the Sun) on your right. Then, on your left is the modern Palacio de Congresos Miradero convention center, which is artfully incorporated into the more historic cityscape. Within moments you pull into Plaza de Zocodover.

Shopping in Toledo

Toledo probably sells more souvenirs than any city in Spain. This is *the* place to buy medieval-looking swords, armor, maces, three-legged stools, lethal-looking letter-openers, and other nouveau antiques. It's also Spain's damascene center, where, for centuries, craftspeople have inlaid black steel with gold, silver, and copper wire. Spain's top bullfighters wouldn't have their swords made anywhere else.

Damascene: You can find artisans all over town pounding gold and silver threads into a steel base to create shiny inlaid plates, decorative wares, and jewelry. The damascene is a real tourist racket, but it's fun to pop into a shop and see the intricate handiwork in action.

El Martes: Toledo's colorful outdoor market is a lively scene on Tuesdays at Paseo de Merchan, better known to locals as "La Vega" (9:00-14:00, outside Bisagra Gate near TI).

Sleeping in Toledo

Day-trippers darken the sunlit cobbles, but few stay to see Toledo's medieval moonrise. Spend the night. Toledo's hotels are modest—it's hard to really splurge here (except for the parador). Most hotels have a two-tiered price system, with prices at least 20 percent higher on Friday and Saturday (I've based my price rankings on weekday rates). Spring and fall are high season; rooms are scarce and prices go up during the Corpus Christi festival as well (usually late May or early June). Most places have an arrangement with parking lots in town that can save you a few euros; ask when you reserve.

DEEP IN TOLEDO, NEAR THE CATHEDRAL

These places hide out on characteristic lanes near the cathedral; because they're not close to bus stops, it's best to take a taxi on arrival.

$ Hotel Santa Isabel, in a 15th-century building two blocks from the cathedral, has 41 clean, modern, and comfortable rooms and squeaky tile hallways (some view rooms, elevator, scenic roof terrace, pay parking—call same day to reserve, drivers enter from Calle Pozo Amargo, Calle Santa Isabel 24, +34 925 253 120, www.hotelsantaisabeltoledo.es, info@hotelsantaisabeltoledo.es).

$ La Posada de Manolo rents 14 tight, rustic, cozy rooms across from the downhill corner of the cathedral. Manolo Junior (and wife Almudena) opened this *hostal* with each of its three

floors themed differently—Moorish, Jewish, and Christian. The place has its quirks, and noise carries through its tiled halls, but it has personality and is popular with European tourists (RS%, view terraces, Calle Sixto Ramón Parro 8, +34 925 282 250, www. laposadademanolo.com, toledo@laposadademanolo.com).

$ Hotel Eurico cleverly fits 23 dated, simple, but well-priced and well-located rooms into a medieval building buried deep in the old town (air-con, Calle Santa Isabel 3, +34 925 284 178, www. hoteleurico.com, reservas@hoteleurico.com).

NEAR PLAZA DE ZOCODOVER

$ Antídoto Rooms, although part of a hotel chain, is an antidote to the epidemic of same-old, same-old hotels in Toledo. Its 10 modern rooms are crafted with concrete floors and pops of color, and each has a tiny balcony. It's ideally located on a back street just a short stroll from Plaza de Zocodover (air-con, elevator, Calle Recoletos 2, +34 925 285 191, www.antidotorooms.com, reservas@ hotelpintorelgreco.com).

$ Hotel Toledo Imperial, sitting efficiently above Plaza de Zocodover, rents 29 nondescript rooms (air-con, elevator, Calle Horno de los Bizcochos 5, +34 925 280 034, www.hoteltoledoim- perial.com, reservas@hoteltoledoimperial.com).

$ Hotel La Conquista de Toledo, with 35 dated but well- priced rooms, gleams with marble—it almost feels more like a hospital than a hotel (family rooms, air-con, elevator, Juan Lab- rador 8, +34 925 210 760, www.hotelconquistadetoledo.com, conquistadetoledo@yithoteles.com).

IN THE JEWISH QUARTER

Most of the hotels I list in Toledo are older and rough around the edges. But the two listed here are slick, more expensive business- class options. They sit lower in the old town—near the Jewish Quarter sights and El Greco Museum—in an area that's less con- venient to the central sights or the train and bus stations, but more historic and appealing than the area near Bisagra Gate.

$$ Hotel Pintor El Greco is a chain hotel with 54 modern, colorful rooms across the street from the El Greco Museum (air- con, elevator, pay parking, Calle Alamillos del Tránsito 13, +34 925 285 191, www.hotelpintorelgreco.com, info@hotelpintorel- greco.com)

$$ Hotel San Juan de los Reyes fills a historic 19th-century brick factory building with 35 cookie-cutter, characterless, but predictably comfortable rooms, on the road between its name- sake monastery and the Tránsito Synagogue (air-con, elevator, pay parking, Calle Reyes Católicos 5, +34 925 283 535, www. hotelsanjuandelosreyes.com, info@hotelsanjuandelosreyes.com).

TOLEDO

Toledo Hotels & Restaurants

Accommodations

1. Hotel Santa Isabel
2. La Posada de Manolo
3. Hotel Eurico
4. Antídoto Rooms
5. Hotel Toledo Imperial
6. Hotel La Conquista de Toledo
7. Hotel Pintor El Greco
8. Hotel San Juan de los Reyes
9. Hacienda del Cardenal
10. Hotel Abad
11. El Hostal Puerta Bisagra
12. To Albergue Juvenil San Servando (Hostel)
13. Oh Oasis Hostel
14. To Parador de Toledo

Eateries & Other

15. Los Cuatro Tiempos Restaurante
16. El Botero Taberna
17. El Trébol
18. Restaurante Ludeña
19. El Nuevo Almacén
20. Madre Tierra Restaurante Vegetariano
21. Restaurante Placido & El Café de las Monjas
22. Mercado Municipal
23. Supermarket
24. Santo Tomé Mazapán Shop (2)

Parque de la Vega

ALFONSO

To CM-40 Ring Road & Parador

PASEO DE RECAREDO

CALLE REAL

CALLE MERCED

Plaza Santo Domingo

S. ILDEFONSO

PUERTO DEL CAMBRÓN

CUESTA SANTA LEOCADIA

Plaza de Padilla

TENDILLAS

SAN MARTÍN

C. PINTOR M. MORENO

COL. DONCELLAS

MARIA PACHECO

Plaza San Román

Plaza San Juan de los Reyes

FACADE

C. DE BULAS

SAN CLEMENTE

VISIGOTHIC MUSEUM

S. ROMÁN

EL

MONASTERY OF SAN JUAN DE LOS REYES

CALLE DEL ÁNGEL

C. GORDO FOLA

C. DE ALFONSO XII

CALLE

CALLE REYES

SANTA MARÍA LA BLANCA SYNAGOGUE

SANTO TOMÉ

CAFÉ

Plaza Barrio Nuevo

JUDERÍA

MAZAPÁN

SANTO TOMÉ

EL SALVADOR

VICTORIO MACHO MUSEUM

SAN JUAN DE DIOS

Plaza del Conde

C. DE SANTA URSULA

EL GRECO MUSEUM

PASEO TRÁNSITO

TALLER MORO

TRÁNSITO SYNAGOGUE

PASEO TRÁNSITO

CALLE DESCALZOS

PASEO SAN CRISTÓBAL

Tajo River

Park

Cliffs

SAN TORCUATO

SAN BART

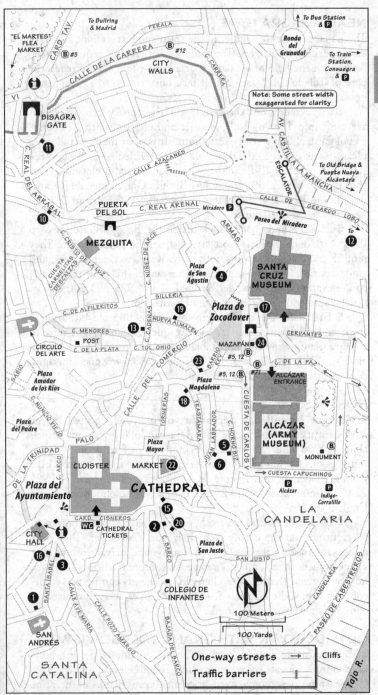

NEAR BISAGRA GATE

These places are a bit handier to the train and bus stations and have easier parking for drivers. The trade-off is that they require a steep hike (with the help of escalators) or a bus or taxi ride to reach the core of Toledo's sightseeing. All face busy roads, so expect street noise.

$$ Hacienda del Cardenal, a 17th-century cardinal's palace built into Toledo's wall, is quiet and elegant, with 27 rooms, a cool garden, and a stuffy restaurant. This poor man's parador—a pleasant oasis next to the dusty old gate of Toledo—is close to the station, but below all the old-town action (air-con, elevator, enter through town wall 100 yards below Bisagra Gate, Paseo de Recaredo 24, +34 925 224 900, www.haciendadelcardenal.com, hotel@haciendadelcardenal.com).

$ Hotel Abad, just a block inside the Bisagra Gate (next to the Puerta del Sol), feels more stylish than the Toledo norm. They rent 28 trendy-rustic rooms with stone walls, wooden rafters, and contemporary furnishings at the higher end of this price range (air-con, elevator, Calle Real del Arrabal 1, +34 925 283 500, www.hotelabadtoledo.com, reservas@hotelabad.com).

$ El Hostal Puerta Bisagra, in a sprawling old building, is fresh and modern inside. It's picturesquely located right next to Bisagra Gate, with 38 comfortable rooms at a good value (air-con, elevator, Calle del Potro 5, +34 925 285 277, www.puertabisagra.com, puertabisagra@yithoteles.com).

HOSTELS

¢ Albergue Juvenil San Servando youth hostel, located in the 10th-century Moorish castle of San Servando, is lavish but affordable, with 96 beds and small rooms for two or four people (swimming pool, 10-minute walk from train station, 15-minute hike from town center, over Puente de Alcántara outside town, +34 925 224 554, reservations +34 925 221 676, alberguesclm@jccm.es, no English spoken).

¢ Oh Oasis Hostel is a fresh, professionally run 21-room hostel right around the corner from Plaza de Zocodover. They have a pleasant rooftop terrace, shared dorms, and private rooms that are even nicer than some more expensive, more traditional *hostales;* however, given the younger clientele, weekends can be noisy (air-con, elevator, Calle Cadenas 5, +34 925 227 650, www.hostelsoasis.com, toledo@hostelsoasis.com).

OUTSIDE TOWN WITH GRAND TOLEDO VIEW

$$$ Parador de Toledo, with 79 rooms, is one of Spain's best-known inns. Guests enjoy a sprawling Toledo view across the Tajo Gorge (some view rooms, fixed-price meals sans drinks in their fine

restaurant overlooking Toledo, 2 windy miles from town at Cerro del Emperador—it may come up as Carretera de Cobisa on mapping apps, +34 925 221 850, www.parador.es, toledo@parador.es).

Eating in Toledo

A day full of El Greco and the romance of Toledo after dark puts me in the mood for game (hunted in the hills to the south, along

the border with La Mancha) and other traditional cuisine. Typical Toledo dishes include partridge *(perdiz)*, venison *(venado)*, wild boar *(jabalí)*, roast suckling pig *(cochinillo asado)*, or baby lamb *(cordero*—similarly roasted after a few weeks of mother's milk). Also popular is the flavorful pork stew called *carcamusas*—everyone seems to have their own recipe. After dinner, find a *mazapán* place for dessert.

Compared to many Spanish cities, Toledo doesn't have a thriving, concentrated tapas scene (its tapas bars are scattered around town). This makes Toledo a good place for a sit-down meal.

MEMORABLE DINING

$$$ Los Cuatro Tiempos Restaurante ("The Four Seasons") specializes in local game and roasts, proficiently served in a tasteful and elegant setting—a mix of traditional and modern. They offer spacious dining with an extensive and inviting Spanish wine list. It's a good choice for a quiet, romantic dinner or a tasty and filling fixed-price lunch (Mon-Sat 13:00-16:00 & 20:30-23:00, Sun 13:00-16:00 only, at downhill corner of cathedral, Calle Sixto Ramón Parro 5, +34 925 223 782).

$$$ El Botero Taberna is a delightful little hideaway. The barman downstairs serves mojitos, fine wine, and exquisite tapas that are well priced and described. Upstairs is an intimate, seven-table restaurant with romantic, white-tablecloth ambience and modern Mediterranean dishes (Wed-Sun 13:30-16:00 & 21:00-23:30, Mon 13:30-16:00 only, closed Tue, a block from cathedral at Calle de la Ciudad 5, +34 925 229 088).

SIMPLE RESTAURANTS

Plaza de Zocodover is busy with eateries serving basic food at affordable prices, and its people-watching scene is great. But my recommended eateries are on side streets a bit off the main drag.

These places are listed roughly in geographical order from Plaza de Zocodover to Santo Tomé. It's worth a few extra minutes—and the navigating challenge—to find places where you'll be eating with locals as well as with tourists. Toledo also has a lively midday tapas scene, and almost every bar you pop into for a stand-up drink will come with a small plate of something to nibble.

$$ El Trébol, tucked peacefully away just a few steps off Plaza de Zocodover, is the place to dine with younger Spaniards. Locals enjoy their *pulgas* (sandwiches), and their mixed grill can feed two. The seating inside is basic, but the outdoor tables are nice (daily 9:00-24:00, Calle de Santa Fe 1, +34 925 281 297).

$$ Restaurante Ludeña is a classic eatery with a dive bar up front, a well-worn dining room in back, and a handful of tables on a sunny courtyard. It's very central. Arrive early, as lots of locals duck in here to pretend there's no tourism in Toledo. They serve up big, stick-to-your-ribs portions of traditional comfort food, including a rich, bright-red *carcamusas* pork stew; their filling fixed-price meals are a good value (Mon-Wed 10:30-16:30, Thu-Sun 10:30-16:30 & 20:00-23:00, Plaza de la Magdalena 10, +34 925 223 384).

$$ El Nuevo Almacén cooks up classic Spanish ingredients in its tapas, pizzas, sandwiches, and hamburgers. They also serve coffee and Spanish-style breakfasts. It's conveniently located just off Plaza de Zocodover (daily 9:00-24:00, Calle Nueva 7, +34 925 283 937).

$$ Madre Tierra Restaurante Vegetariano is Toledo's answer to a vegetarian's prayer. While service is typically slow, the place is bright, spacious, classy, and air-conditioned. Its appetizing vegetarian dishes are based on both international and traditional Spanish cuisine (good tea selection, Wed-Sun 13:00-16:00 & 20:30-23:00, Mon 13:00-16:00 only, closed Tue, 20 yards below La Posada de Manolo just before reaching Plaza de San Justo, Bajada de Tripería 2, +34 925 223 571).

$$ Restaurante Placido, run by high-energy Anna and *abuela* (grandma) Sagrario, serves traditional family-style cuisine on a shady terrace or in a wonderful Franciscan monastery courtyard (open daily for lunch and dinner in summer, lunch only in winter, about a block uphill from Santo Tomé at Calle Santo Tomé 2, +34 925 222 603).

Picnics: Find picnic provisions at the humble city market, **Mercado Municipal,** on Plaza Mayor (on the Alcázar side of cathedral, with a supermarket inside open Mon-Sat 9:00-14:30 & 17:00-20:00 and stalls open mostly in the mornings until 14:00, closed Sun). **Supermarket Unide,** on Plaza de la Magdalena, has groceries and lots of other stuff at good prices (daily 9:30-22:00, just below Plaza de Zocodover). For a picnic with people-watching

on an atmospheric square, consider Plaza de Zocodover or Plaza del Ayuntamiento.

AND FOR DESSERT: *MAZAPÁN*

Toledo's famous almond-fruity-sweet *mazapán* is sold all over town. The nuns living in Toledo's convents were once the main providers of this delight—each piece lovingly shaped by hand—but the number of nuns is dwindling. If you can't track down a convent still selling sweets in the labyrinth of Holy Toledo, visit **El Café de las Monjas,** a pastry and coffee shop around the corner from the Santo Tomé church that brings in *mazapán* from local convents (daily 9:00-21:00, Calle Santo Tomé 2).

The big *mazapán* producer is **Santo Tomé** (several outlets, including near Plaza de Zocodover and at Calle Santo Tomé 3, daily 9:00-21:00). Browse their tempting window displays. They sell *mazapán* goodies individually (*sin relleno*—without filling—is for purists, *de piñon* has pine nuts, *imperiales* is with almonds, others have fruit fillings). Boxes are good for gifts, but if you want an assortment, tell them what you want à la carte. Their *Toledana* is a bigger, nutty, crumbly, not-too-sweet cookie with a subtle thread of squash filling.

For a sweet and romantic evening dessert, pick up a few pastries and head down to the cathedral. Sit on the Plaza del Ayuntamiento's benches (or stretch out on the stone wall to the right of the TI). A fountain is on your right, Spain's best-looking City Hall is behind you, and there before you is her top cathedral—built back when Toledo was Spain's capital—shining brightly against the black night sky.

Toledo Connections

FROM TOLEDO TO MADRID

Madrid and Toledo are very easily connected. The train makes the trip in 30 minutes to Madrid's fairly central Atocha station; buses depart twice as frequently but take nearly twice as long to reach the more distant Plaza Elíptica. Three or four people traveling together can share a taxi economically. To get elsewhere in Spain from Toledo, assume you'll have to transfer in Madrid; see "Madrid Connections" at the end of that chapter.

By Train: Nearly hourly, 30 minutes by AVE or Avant to Madrid's Atocha station (www.renfe.com); early and late trains can sell out—reserve ahead.

By Bus: 2/hour, 1-1.5 hours, bus drops you at Madrid's Plaza Elíptica Metro stop, 1/day direct morning bus to Madrid's Barajas Airport Terminal 4, 1.5 hours, Alsa (www.alsa.es); you can almost always just drop in and buy a ticket minutes before departure.

By Taxi: While it may seem extravagant, if you have limited time, lots of luggage, and a small group, simply taking a taxi from your Toledo hotel to your Madrid hotel is breathtakingly efficient (€90, one hour door-to-door, +34 925 255 050 or +34 925 227 070). You can ask several cabbies for their best "off the meter" rate. A taxi to the Madrid airport costs €110 (find one who will go "off the meter") and takes an hour.

ROUTE TIPS FOR DRIVERS

Toledo to Madrid (45 miles, 1 hour): It's a speedy *autovía* north, past one of La Mancha's classic bull billboards, to Madrid (on A-42). The highways converge into M-30, which encircles Madrid. Follow it to the left (*Nor* or *Oeste*) and take the Plaza de España exit to get to the city center. If you're airport-bound, keep heading into Madrid until you see the airplane symbol (N-II).

To drive to Atocha station in Madrid, take the exit off M-30 for Plaza de Legazpi, then take Delicias (second on your right off the square). Parking for rental-car return is on the north side of the train station. The less-convenient toll road AP-42 will also take you from Toledo to Madrid.

Toledo to Granada (230 miles; 3.5 hours): Driving between Toledo and Granada, you'll pass through **La Mancha,** which shows a side of Spain that you'll see nowhere else—vast and flat. You feel lost in rough seas of olive-green polka dots. Random buildings look like houses and hotels hurled off some heavenly Monopoly board.

This is the setting of Miguel de Cervantes' *Don Quixote*, published in the early 17th century after England sank the Armada and the Spanish Empire began its decline. Cervantes' star character fights doggedly for good, for justice, and against the fall of Spain and its traditional old-regime ideals. Ignoring reality, Don Quixote is a hero fighting a hopeless battle. Stark La Mancha is the perfect stage.

Above Almonacid (8 miles from Toledo), follow the ruined lane past the ruined church up to the ruined castle. The jovial locals hike up with kids and kites.

But the epitome of *Don Quixote* country is the town of **Consuegra** (one hour south of Toledo, www.aytoconsuegra.es). It must be the La Mancha that Cervantes had in mind. Drive up to the ruined 12th-century castle and joust with a windmill. It's hot and buggy here, but the powerful view overlooking the vil-

TOLEDO

lage—with its sun-bleached light-red roofs, modern concrete reality, and harsh, windy silence—makes for a profound picnic. The castle belonged to the Knights of St. John (12th and 13th centuries) and is associated with their trip to Jerusalem during the Crusades. Origi-  nally built from the ruins of a nearby Roman circus, it has been recently restored. Sorry, the windmills are post-Cervantes, only about 250 years old—but you can go inside the Molino de Bolero to see how it works.

GRANADA

For a time, as a thriving Islamic city-state, Granada was the grandest city in Spain. But after the tumult that came with the change from Moorish to Christian rule, it lost its power and settled into a long slumber. Today, Granada seems to specialize in evocative history and good living. Settle down in the old center and explore monuments of the Moorish civilization and its conquest. Taste the treats of a North African-flavored culture that survives here today.

Compared to other Spanish cities its size, Granada is delightfully cosmopolitan—it's worked hard to accept a range of cultures, and you'll see far more ethnic restaurants here than elsewhere in Andalucía. Its large student population (including many students from abroad) also lends it a youthful zest. The Grenadine people are serious about hospitality and have earned a reputation among travelers for being particularly friendly and eager to help you enjoy their historic city.

Granada's magnificent Alhambra palace/fortress was the last stronghold of the Moorish kingdom in Spain. The city's exotically tangled Moorish quarter, the Albayzín, invites exploration. From its viewpoints, romantics can enjoy the sunset and evening views of the grand, floodlit Alhambra.

After visiting the Alhambra and then seeing a blind beggar, a Spanish poet wrote, "Give him a coin, for there is nothing worse in this life than to be blind in Granada." This city has much to see, yet it reveals itself in unpredictable ways; it takes a poet to sort through and assemble the jumbled shards of Granada. Peer through the intricate lattice of a Moorish window. Hear water burbling unseen among the labyrinthine hedges of the Generalife's gardens. Listen

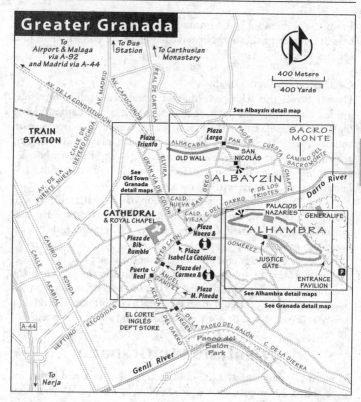

to a flute trilling deep in the swirl of alleys around the cathedral. Don't be blind in Granada—open all your senses.

PLANNING YOUR TIME

You could conceivably hit Granada's highlights in one very busy day, sandwiched between two overnights. With a more relaxed itinerary, Granada is worth two days and two nights. You can easily connect to Granada by direct flight from Barcelona, then continue to other destinations by train or bus.

Note that it's critical to reserve a ticket for the Alhambra well in advance (see "Alhambra Tour," later). In the summer, do what you can to avoid the brutal heat of the early afternoon. Start early, take a break somewhere cool, and stay out late.

Granada in One Day

With just one full day here, fit in the top sights by following this intense plan: In the morning, take my self-guided walk of the old town (visiting the cathedral and Royal Chapel). After a quick lunch, spend the afternoon at the Alhambra (reservation essential).

From the Alhambra, take minibus #C32 (or a taxi) into the Albayzín quarter to the San Nicolás viewpoint for sunset, then find the right place for a suitably late dinner.

Granada in Two Days

Day 1: Stroll the Alcaicería market streets and follow my self-guided tour of the old town, including a visit to the cathedral and its Royal Chapel. Enjoy the vibe at Plaza Nueva, the town's main square. Wander up into the Albayzín Moorish quarter, stopping by a funky teahouse along the way. End your day at the San Nicolás viewpoint—the golden hour before sunset is best, when the Alhambra seems to glow with its own light.

Day 2: Follow my self-guided tour of the Alhambra; you'll see the elaborate and many-roomed Palacios Nazaríes, the Renaissance Palace of Charles V, the refreshing Generalife and its gardens, and more.

On any **evening,** tapa-hop for dinner (consider Gayle's Granada Tapas Tours) or splurge on fine dining at a *carmen*. When the evening cools down, join the paseo. Take in a *zambra* dance in the Sacromonte district. Relax in an Arab bath (Hammam al Andalus) or a *tetería* (tea shop), or both. Slow down and smell the incense.

Orientation to Granada

Modern Granada sprawls (235,000 people), but its main sights are all within a 20-minute walk of Plaza Nueva, where dogs wag their tails to the rhythm of modern hippies and street musicians. Most of my recommended hotels are within a few blocks of Plaza Nueva. Make this the hub of your Granada visit.

Plaza Nueva sits between two hills: On one side is the great Moorish palace, the Alhambra, and on the other is the best-preserved Moorish quarter in Spain, the Albayzín. To the southwest are the cathedral, Royal Chapel, and Alcaicería (Moorish market), where the city's two main drags—Gran Vía de Colón (often just called "Gran Vía") and Calle Reyes Católicos—lead away into the modern city.

TOURIST INFORMATION

The Granada TI is inside City Hall on Plaza del Carmen, a short walk from the cathedral (Mon-Sat 10:00-18:00, Sun until 14:00, longer hours in summer, +34 958 248 280, http://en.granadatur.

com). Another TI, tucked away just above Plaza Nueva near the Santa Ana Church, covers Granada and all of Andalucía. This TI also posts all of Granada's bus departures (Mon-Fri 9:00-20:00, Sat 10:00-19:00, Sun 10:00-15:00, +34 958 575 202).

Sightseeing Pass: The €40 **Granada Card** may get you an Alhambra reservation when the main Alhambra website is sold out. It includes admission to the Alhambra ("Alhambra General" ticket; see "Alhambra Tour," later), entry to the main sights in town (the cathedral, Royal Chapel, Carthusian Monastery), plus nine bus rides and a few other admissions and discounts—and it's good for two days. It can be purchased online three months in advance (http://en.granadatur.com/granada-card).

ARRIVAL IN GRANADA

By Train: Granada's small but modern train station is connected to the center by a €6 taxi ride, frequent buses, or a 30-minute walk down Avenida de la Constitución and Gran Vía. The train station does not have luggage storage.

Taxis wait out front. It's a two-minute walk to reach the bus stop: Exiting the train station, walk straight up tree-lined Avenida de Andaluces (following the Metro tracks). At the first major intersection, find a covered bus stop to the right on Avenida de la Constitución. Buy a ticket from a machine at the stop or purchase a Credibús pass (see "Getting Around Granada," later). Buses #4 and #11 head down Avenida de la Constitución to Gran Vía and stop at the cathedral (Catedral)—three blocks from Plaza Nueva and most of my recommended hotels (stops are shown on monitors).

By Bus: Located on the city outskirts, Granada's bus station *(estación de autobuses)* has a good and cheap cafeteria, ATMs, luggage lockers, and a privately run tourist agency masquerading as an official TI. These services are all downstairs, where you exit the buses.

Upstairs is the main arrivals hall with ticket windows, ticket machines, and a helpful information counter in the main hall that hands out printed schedules. All buses are operated by Alsa (www.alsa.es). To get from the bus station to the city center, it's either a 10-minute taxi ride (€8) or a 25-minute ride on bus #33 (€1.40, pay driver). For Plaza Nueva, get off on Gran Vía at the Catedral stop (check monitors).

By Car: Driving in Granada's historic center is restricted to buses, taxis, and tourists with hotel reservations. (Call ahead and make sure your hotelier registers you with the local traffic police—it's routine, but if they don't do it within 48 hours, you'll be stuck with a steep ticket.) If you have a reservation, simply drive past the sign. Hotels provide parking or have a deal with a central-zone

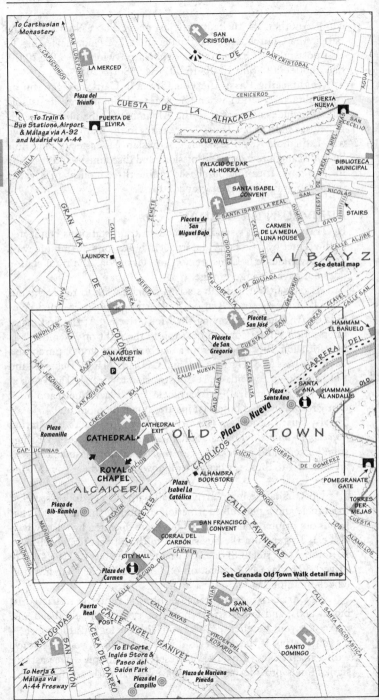

GRANADA

To Carthusian Monastery

C. CAPUCHINOS

SAN ILDEFONSO

SAN CRISTÓBAL

C. DE

C. DE L. SAN CRISTÓBAL

LA MERCED

CENICEROS

Plaza del Triunfo

CUESTA DE LA ALHACABA

PUERTA NUEVA

SAN CECELIO

To Train & Bus Stations, Airport & Málaga via A-92 and Madrid via A-44

PUERTA DE ELVIRA

OLD WALL

TINAJILLA

ZENETE

PALACIO DE DAR AL-HORRA

SANTA ISABEL CONVENT

C. SANTA ISABEL LA REAL

CUESTA DE MARÍA LA MIEL MIRA

SAN

BIBLIOTECA MUNICIPAL

CUESTA DE SAN NICOLÁS

STAIRS

GRAN VÍA

SANTA

CALLE DE ELVIRA

BETETA

Placeta de San Miguel Bajo

C. OIDORES

CALLE TINA

CARMEN DE LA MEDIA LUNA HOUSE

GUMIEL

GATO

CALLE ALJIBE

A L B A Y Z

LAUNDRY

C. SAN JOSÉ ALTA

C. DE QUIJADA

GREGORIO

See detail map

CALLE SAN

TENDILLAS

PAULA

COLON

Placeta San José

Placeta de San Gregorio

CUESTA DE SAN

PORRAS

CLAVEL

HAMMAM EL BAÑUELO

SAN JERÓNIMO

C. SAN AGUSTÍN

BAZAN

SAN AGUSTÍN MARKET

P

GALD. NUEVA

GALD. VIEJA

CARCEL ALTA

CARRERA DEL

OLD

Plaza Romanilla

C. SAN AGUSTÍN

CARCEL BAJA

CATHEDRAL

CATHEDRAL EXIT

SANTA ANA

Plaza Santa Ana

HAMMAM AL ANDALUS

CAP- UCHINAS

O L D

Plaza Nueva

T O W N

ROYAL CHAPEL

OFICIOS

CATÓLICOS

CUCH.

CUESTA DE GÓMEREZ

ALCAICERÍA

ALHAMBRA BOOKSTORE

POMEGRANATE GATE

Plaza de Bib-Rambla

ZACATÍN

C. REYES

Plaza Isabel La Católica

CALLE PAVANERAS

RODRIGO

LOS ALAMILLOS

TORRES BER- MEJAS

CUESTA

ALHÓNDIGA

MESONES

SAN FRANCISCO CONVENT

CORRAL DEL CARBÓN

CITY HALL

CARMEN

Plaza del Carmen

See Granada Old Town Walk detail map

Puerta Real

CALLE ÁNGEL GANIVET

CALLE NAVAS

SAN MATÍAS

SAN MATÍAS

CALLE SANTA ESCOLÁSTICA

POST

RECOGIDAS

SAN ANTON

ACERA DEL DARRO

To El Corte Inglés Store & Paseo del Salón Park

VIRGEN DEL ROSARIO

SANTO DOMINGO

To Nerja & Málaga via A-44 Freeway

Plaza del Campillo

Plaza de Mariana Pineda

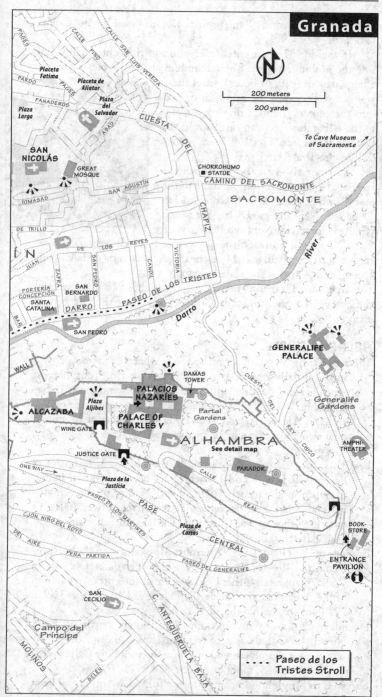

Granada

GRANADA

To Cave Museum
of Sacramonte

Placeta
Fatima

Placeta de
Aliatar

Plaza
del Salvador

Plaza
Larga

CALLE PINO

CALLE SAN LUIS VEREDA

PAGES

PAGES

PARDO

PANADEROS

ABAD

CUESTA

DEL

CHORROHUMO
■ STATUE

SAN
NICOLÁS

GREAT
MOSQUE

SAN AGUSTÍN

CAMINO DEL SACROMONTE

SACROMONTE

TOMASAS

CHAPIZ

DE TRILLO

DE LOS REYES

VICTORIA

CANDIL

River

ÍN

JUAN

ZAFRA

SAN PEDRO

PASEO DE LOS TRISTES

PORTERÍA
CONCEPCIÓN

SAN
BERNARDO

Darro

SANTA
CATALINA

DARRO

SAN PEDRO

GENERALIFE
PALACE

WALL

DAMAS
TOWER

CUESTA

DEL

REY

CHICO

Generalife
Gardens

Plaza
Aljibes

PALACIOS
NAZARÍES

Partal
Gardens

ALCAZABA

WINE GATE

PALACE OF
CHARLES V

ALHAMBRA
See detail map

AMPHI-
THEATER

JUSTICE GATE

Plaza de la
Justicia

ONE WAY

PASE

CALLE

PARADOR

PASEO DE LOS MARTIRES

REAL

CJON. NIÑO DEL ROYO

BOOK-
STORE

DEL AIRE

PEÑA PARTIDA

Plaza de
Carros

CENTRAL

ENTRANCE
PAVILION
&

SAN
CECILIO

PASEO DEL GENERALIFE

Campo del
Príncipe

C. ANTEQUERUELA BAJA

MOLINOS

BELEN

200 meters

200 yards

.... Paseo de los
Tristes Stroll

garage (such as Parking San Agustín, just off Gran Vía del Colón, €26/day).

If you don't have a hotel reservation in the center, park outside the prohibited zone. The Alhambra, above the old town, has a huge pay lot (€19/24 hours); from there you can walk, catch the minibus, or taxi into the center. If you're driving directly to the Alhambra, you can easily avoid the historic center (see "Getting There" under "Alhambra Tour," later).

There are also garages just outside the restricted zone: the Triunfo garage to the east (€20/day, Avenida de la Constitución 5) or the Neptune garage to the south (Centro Comercial Neptuno, €17/day, on Calle Neptuno). To reach the city center from either parking garage, catch the articulated #4 bus nearby (on Avenida de la Constitución) and get off at the Catedral stop.

By Plane: Granada's relaxed airport is about 10 miles west of the city center. See "Granada Connections" near the end of this chapter.

HELPFUL HINTS

Theft Alert: Be on guard for pickpockets wherever there's a crowd and especially late at night in the Albayzín. Your biggest threat is being conned while enjoying drinks and music in Sacromonte. Pushy women, usually hanging out near the cathedral and Alcaicería, may accost you with sprigs of rosemary, then demand payment for fortune-telling services—just say, *"No, gracias."*

Festivals: From late June to early July, the popular **International Festival of Music and Dance** offers classical music, ballet, flamenco, and zarzuela (light opera) nightly in the Alhambra and other historic venues at reasonable prices (visit TI or ticket office in the Corral del Carbón for schedule, www.granadafestival.org).

Bookstore: You'll find the **Alhambra Bookstore** at Calle Reyes Católicos 40—for location, see the "Granada Old Town Walk" map, later. Other branches are at the entrance pavilion of the Alhambra and inside the Palace of Charles V (+34 958 227 846, www.alhambratienda.es).

Laundry: Closest to my recommended hotels north of Plaza Nueva, **La Colada** is a convenient choice (daily 9:00-22:00, self-service, from west end of Plaza Nueva follow Calle de Elvira north to #85, mobile +34 637 834 997).

Farewell to Singlehood: Famed for its fun tapas and cheap beer,

Granada is inundated on weekend evenings with hen and stag parties (called "goodbye to singlehood" parties here). The city can seem busier at midnight than at noon as crazily dressed brides and grooms prowl the streets with gangs of friends looking for fun.

GETTING AROUND GRANADA

With cheap taxis, frisky minibuses, good city buses, and nearly all points of interest an easy walk from Plaza Nueva, you'll get around Granada easily.

Tickets for minibuses and city buses cost €1.40 per ride (buy from curbside machines or driver; must use machine for bus #4 tickets). For schedules and routes, see TransportesRober.com.

Credibús cards save you money if you'll be riding often—or, since they're shareable, if you're part of a group (can be loaded with €5, €10, or €20). To get a €5 card—likely all you'll need—ask for *"un bono de cinco."* These are valid on all buses and include transfers if made within 45 minutes.

By Minibus: Handy little made-for-tourists red minibuses cover the city center; they depart every few minutes from Plaza Nueva, Plaza Isabel La Católica, and Gran Vía (Catedral stop) from 6:00-23:00. For locations of bus stops in the city center, see the "Granada Old Town Walk" map, later.

Bus #C30 is the best for a trip up to the Alhambra, departing 30 yards uphill from Plaza Isabel La Católica, with stops at the Alhambra entrance pavilion and the Justice Gate (Puerta de la Justicia), among others (every 5-7 minutes).

Bus #C31 departs from Plaza Nueva and circles counterclockwise around the Albayzín quarter, navigating the narrow one-way lanes (every 8-10 minutes).

Bus #C32 connects the Alhambra to the Albayzín quarter and goes through the city center. For the Alhambra, catch it from the same spot as #C30 listed above (every 20-30 minutes).

Bus #C34 runs from Plaza Nueva to Sacromonte (every 20 minutes).

Tours in Granada

Hop-On, Hop-Off Tourist Train

For a relaxing and scenic loop through the old town, the touristy hop-on, hop-off train can be time and money well spent (€8/24 hours, daily 9:30-23:00, Nov-March until 19:30, leaves every 25 minutes, includes Alhambra and Albayzín quarter, recorded English narration—use your own earbuds or buy onboard, www. granada.city-tour.com).

Walking Tours

Cicerone offers informative and spirited two-hour city tours describing the fitful and fascinating changes the city underwent over 500 years ago as it morphed from a Moorish capital to a Christian one. The tour includes entry to lesser-known museums and monuments, as well as drinks and tapas, and weaves together bits of the Moorish heritage that survive around the cathedral and in the Albayzín. Tours are offered twice daily in both English and Spanish; reservations are encouraged but not required (€29, RS%—use code "RICKSTEVES10"; basic Granada tours leave from Calle San Jerónimo 10, +34 958 561 810, mobile +34 607 691 676, www.ciceronegranada.com). They also offer small group tours of the Alhambra that include an entry time to Palacios Nazaríes (price based on size of group, ideally reserve at least 1-2 months ahead).

"Free" (Tip-Based) Walking Tours

Students who've memorized a script lead entertaining walks through the historic town center. While you won't get the quality of a licensed guide, the price is right: Just show up, have fun, and tip what you like. With competing advertising umbrellas and enthusiastic welcomes, groups offering these tours daily in English gather at Plaza Nueva and at Plaza Isabel La Católica. Some popular tours are **Feel the City** (www.feelthecitytours.com), **Follow Me Granada** (www.followmegranada.com), **Free Tour Granada** (www.freetour.com/granada), and **Walk in Granada** (www.walkingranada.com).

Local Guides

Margarita Ortiz de Landazuri (mobile +34 687 361 988, www.alhambratours.com) and **Miguel Ángel** (mobile +34 617 565 711, miguelangelalhambratours@gmail.com) are good English-speaking, licensed private guides with lots of experience and a passion for teaching. In addition to the Alhambra, they give tours of Sacromonte, the Albayzín, and other parts of Granada. Guide rates are standard (€130/3 hours, €260/day).

Tapas Tours

Having lived in Granada since 1996, Scottish-born **Gayle Mackie** knows where to find the best food. She and her team at Gayle's Granada Tapas Tours take small groups off the beaten path to characteristic tapas bars, providing cuisine tips and insights into Granada. The various routes offer a moveable feast—amounting to a filling meal—with good wine and craft beer on offer as well as sherry, vermouth, and soft drinks (2.5-3 hours, €50-65/person, tours for 2-8 people, private tours available, daily at 13:00 & 20:00, mobile +34 619 444 984, www.granadatapastours.com). Gayle also offers a food shopping and three-course cooking experience at her

Granada at a Glance

▲▲▲**Alhambra** The last and finest Moorish palace in Iberia, highlighting the splendor of that civilization in the 13th and 14th centuries. **Hours:** Daily 8:30-20:00 (mid-Oct-March until 18:00); also Tue-Sat for nighttime visits (Fri-Sat only in off-season). See page 619.

▲▲**Royal Chapel** Lavish 16th-century chapel with the tombs of Queen Isabel and King Ferdinand. **Hours:** Mon-Sat 10:00-18:30, Sun from 11:00. See page 636.

▲▲**San Nicolás Viewpoint** Breathtaking vista over the Alhambra and the Albayzín—best at sunset. See page 643.

▲**Granada Cathedral** The second-largest cathedral in Spain, with a fine Renaissance interior. **Hours:** Mon-Sat 10:00-18:15, Sun from 15:00. See page 640.

▲**Exploring the Albayzín Walk** Spain's best old Moorish quarter. See page 646.

▲**Great Mosque of Granada** Islamic house of worship featuring a minaret with a live call to prayer and a courtyard with commanding views. **Hours:** Daily 11:00-21:00, shorter hours in winter. See page 646.

home for groups with dishes reflecting the seasons. Wine can be bought en route if desired (3 hours, €55/person, groups of 2-6 people, available for lunch or early dinner).

Granada Old Town Walk

This short self-guided walk covers all the essential old town sights. Along the way, we'll see vivid evidence of the dramatic Moorish-to-Christian transition brought about by the Reconquista—the long and ultimately successful battle to retake Spain from the Muslim Moors and reestablish Christian rule.

• *Start at Corral del Carbón, near Plaza del Carmen.*

❶ Corral del Carbón

A caravanserai (of Silk Road fame) was a protected place for merchants to rest their animals, spend the night, get a bite to eat, and spin yarns. This Moorish structure, the only surviving caravanserai of Granada's original 14, is just a block from the Alcaicería silk market (the next stop on this walk). Stepping through the grand horseshoe-arch entry, you'll find a courtyard with 14th-century

Granada Old Town Walk

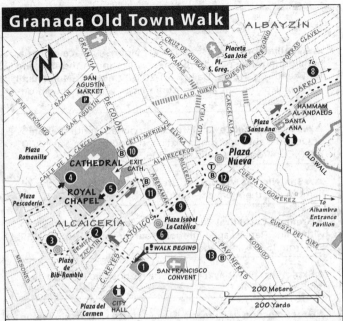

ALBAYZÍN

C. CRUZ DE QUIROS
Placeta
San José
Pl.
S. Greg.
CUESTA S. GREGORIO
PORRAS CLAVEL
GRAN VÍA
C. MARANAS
CALD. NUEVA
CUESTA S. GREGORIO
To **8**
DARRO
C. SAN JERÓNIMO
C. BAZAL
SAN AGUSTÍN MARKET
DE COLÓN
CALLE VIEJA
CARCEL ALTA
HAMMAM AL-ANDALUS
C. SAN AGUSTÍN
C. DE LA CARCEL BAJA
C. DE ELVIRA
Plaza Santa Ana
SANTA ANA
Plaza Romanilla
CATHEDRAL
B **10** EXIT CATH.
CETTI-MERIEM
ALMIRECEROS
BILLERIA
7 **i**
Plaza Nueva
OLD WALL
4
ROYAL CHAPEL
5
ABENAMAR
11
T **B** **12**
CUCH.
CUESTA DE GOMÉREZ
Plaza Pescadería
9
CUESTA DEL AIRE
To Alhambra Entrance Pavilion
ALCAICERÍA
ERMITA
ZACATÍN
3
2
Plaza Isabel La Católica
6
RODRIGO
C. REYES CATÓLICOS
MESONES
Plaza de Bib-Rambla
WALK BEGINS
1
SAN FRANCISCO CONVENT
13
C. PAVANERAS
CITY HALL
Plaza del Carmen
i
200 Meters
200 Yards

Walk
1. Corral del Carbón
2. Alcaicería
3. Plaza de Bib-Rambla
4. Granada Cathedral
5. Royal Chapel Square
6. Plaza Isabel La Católica
7. Plaza Nueva
8. To Paseo de los Tristes & Hammam El Bañuelo

Other
9. Alhambra Bookstore
10. Gran Vía Cathedral Bus Stop (from Train & Bus Stations)
11. Gran Vía del Colón Bus Stop (to Train & Bus Stations)
12. Plaza Nueva Bus Stop (to Albayzín & Sacromonte)
13. Plaza Isabel La Católica Bus Stop (to Alhambra)

Moorish brickwork surrounding a fountain. This plain yet elegant structure evokes the times when traders gathered here with exotic goods and swapped tales from across the Muslim world.

It's a common mistake to think of the Muslim Moors as somehow not Spanish. They lived here for seven centuries and were just as "indigenous" as the Romans, Goths, and Celts. While the Moors were Muslim, they were no more connected to Arabia than they were to France.

After the Reconquista, this space was used as a storehouse for

coal (hence "del Carbón"). These days it houses offices where you can buy tickets for musical events, a handy public WC (to the right as you enter), and sometimes an Alhambra tourist info office.

• *From the caravanserai, exit straight ahead down Puente del Carbón to the big street named Calle Reyes Católicos. The street covers the Darro River, which once ran openly here, spanned by a series of bridges. Today, the modern commercial center is to your left.*

Cross here and continue one block farther to the horseshoe-shaped gate marked Alcaicería. Notice the pedestrian street, Zacatín, just before you reach the gate. It paralleled the Darro River in the 19th century; today it's a favorite paseo destination, busy each evening with strollers. Pass through the Alcaicería gate and walk 20 yards into the old market to the first intersection at Calle Ermita.

❷ Alcaicería

Originally an Arab souk (bazaar) and silk market, this warren of narrow streets is known as the Alcaicería (al-kai-thay-REE-ah).

Offering precious silver, spices, and silk, the market had 10 armed gates and its own guards. Silk was huge in Moorish times, and silkworm-friendly mulberry trees flourished in the countryside. It was such an important product that the sultans controlled and guarded it by constructing this fine, fortified market. After the Reconquista, the Christians realized this market was good for business and didn't mess with it. Later, the more zealous Philip II had it shut down. A terrible fire in 1850 destroyed what was left. Today's Alcaicería is an "authentic fake"—rebuilt in the late 1800s as a tourist attraction to complement the romantic image of Granada popularized by the writings of Washington Irving.

Explore the mesh of tiny shopping lanes: overpriced trinkets, popcorn machines, balloon vendors, leather goods spread out on streets, kids playing soccer, barking dogs, dogged shoe-shine boys, and the whirring grind of bicycle-powered knife sharpeners. You'll invariably meet obnoxious and persistent women pushing their green rosemary sprigs on innocents in order to extort money. Be strong.

• *Turn left down Calle Ermita. After 50 yards, you'll leave the market via another fortified gate and enter a big square crowded with outdoor restaurants. Skirt around the tables to the Neptune fountain, which marks the center of the...*

❸ Plaza de Bib-Rambla

This exuberant square, just two blocks behind the cathedral (from the fountain you can see its blocky bell tower peeking above the big orange building) was once the center of Moorish Granada. Although Moorish rule of Spain lasted 700 years, it declined in its final centuries under weak leadership—even while Christian forces grew more determined. As Muslims fled south from reconquered lands, they flooded into Granada, then held by the last remnants of the Moorish kingdom. By 1400, Granada had an estimated 100,000 people—huge for medieval Europe. This was the main square, the focal point for markets and festivals, but it was much smaller then, hemmed in by the jam-packed city.

Under Christian rule, the Moors who remained were initially tolerated (as they were considered good for business), and this area became their ghetto. Then, with the Inquisition (which peaked under Philip II, c. 1550), ideology trumped pragmatism, and Muslims and Jews were evicted or forced to convert—and some were executed. The elegant square you see today was built, and built big. In-your-face Catholic processions started here. To assert Christian rule, all the trappings of Christian power were layered upon what had been the trappings of Moorish power. Between here and the cathedral were the Christian University (the big orange building) and the adjacent archbishop's palace.

Today Plaza de Bib-Rambla is good for coffee or a meal amid the color and fragrance of flower stalls and the burbling of its Neptune-topped fountain. It remains a multigenerational hangout, where it seems everyone is enjoying a peaceful retirement.

With Neptune facing you, leave the plaza by the left corner (along Calle Pescadería) to reach a smaller, similarly lively square—little Plaza Pescadería, where families spill out to enjoy its many restaurants. For a quick snack, drop into tiny **Cunini Pescadería**—just beyond its namesake restaurant—for a takeaway bite of *pescaito frito*—fried fish.

• *Backtrack from Cunini Pescadería and leave the plaza to the left, on Calle Marqués de Gerona; straight ahead you'll see a small square fronting a very big church.*

❹ Granada Cathedral (Catedral de Granada)

Wow, the cathedral facade just screams triumph. That's partly because its design is based on a triumphal arch, built over a destroyed mosque. Five hundred yards away, there was once open space out-

side the city wall with good soil for
a foundation. But the Christian
conquerors said, "No way." Instead,
they destroyed the mosque and built
their cathedral right here on difficult, sandy soil. This was the place
where the people of Granada had
traditionally worshipped—and now
they would worship as Christians.

Building of the church started
in the early 1500s and didn't finish
until the early 1700s. It began with
a Gothic foundation but over two
centuries the design evolved: The
interior layout is mostly Renaissance, its last altars are Neoclassical,
and its facade, finished by hometown artist Alonso Cano (1601-
1667), is Baroque. Accentuating the power of the Roman Catholic Church, the emphasis here is on Mary rather than Christ. The
facade declares *Ave Maria*. (This was Counter-Reformation time,
and the Church was threatened by Protestant Christians. Mary
was also more palatable to Muslim converts, as she is revered in
the Quran.)

• *To tour the cathedral now, you can enter here (the interior is described
in more detail on page 640). You'll exit on the far side, near the big street
called Gran Vía de Colón.*

*If you're skipping the cathedral interior for now, circle around the
building to the right, keeping the church on your left, until you reach the
small square facing the Royal Chapel.*

❺ Royal Chapel Square

This square was once ringed by important Moorish buildings: a
hammam (public bath), a caravanserai (Days Inn), the silk market,
the leading mosque, and a madrassa (school).

With Christian rule, the **Palacio de la Madraza** (its facade
painted in 3-D Baroque style with faux gray stonework) became
Granada's first City Hall. Five hundred years ago, this was a
Quranic school. If you pay to enter (€2, daily 10:30-20:00) you'll
get a ground-floor peek at an ornate-as-the-Alhambra mini prayer
room and mihrab; upstairs, a modern university lecture room boasts
a circa 1500 Mudejar interlocking wood ceiling, finely painted and
circled by a script celebrating the Christian conquest.

Also on this square is the entrance to the Royal Chapel, where
the coffins of Ferdinand and Isabel were moved in 1521 from the
Alhambra (for details on visiting the chapel, see page 636).

• *Continue up the cobbled, stepped lane to Gran Vía. Turn right, take the
large crosswalk plus two more to stand in the big square just ahead (near*

where minibuses to the Alhambra stop), across the busy Calles Reyes Católicos.

GRANADA

❻ Plaza Isabel La Católica

Granada's two grand boulevards, Gran Vía and Calle Reyes Católicos, meet here at Plaza Isabel La Católica. Above the fountain,

a beautiful statue shows Columbus unfurling a long contract with Isabel. It lists the terms of the explorer's MCCCCLXXXXII voyage: "For as much as you, Columbus, are going by our command to discover and subdue some Islands and Continents in the ocean...." Two reliefs below the figures show the big events in Granada of 1492: Isabel and Ferdinand accepting Columbus' proposal, and a stirring battle scene (which never happened) at the Alhambra walls.

Isabel may have been driven by her desire to spread Catholicism, but Spain's interest was in finding a maritime trade route to the Far East and its spices (Ottoman Turks had cut off the traditional overland route). Columbus himself was driven by his desire for money. As a reward for adding territory to Spain's Catholic empire, Isabel promised Columbus the ranks of Admiral of the Oceans and Governor of the New World. To sweeten the pot, she tossed in one-eighth of all the riches he brought home. Isabel died thinking that Columbus had found India or China. Columbus died poor and disillusioned.

Look back at the fine buildings flanking the start of Gran Vía. With the arrival of cars and the modern age, the people of Granada wanted a Parisian-style boulevard. In the early 20th century, they mercilessly cut through the old town and created Gran Vía and its French-style buildings—in the process destroying everything in its path, including many historic convents. Elegant facades—like the two circa-1910 Paris-inspired buildings facing the square—once ornamented the entire Gran Vía. Now, turn 180 degrees to see the 1970s aesthetic: modern then but perhaps dated (dare I say, ugly) now.

Calle Reyes Católicos, named for the "Catholic Monarchs" Ferdinand and Isabel, leads from this square downhill to the busy intersection called Puerta Real. From there, Acera del Darro takes you through modern Granada to the river, passing the huge El Corte Inglés department store and lots of modern commerce. This area erupts with locals out strolling each night. For one of the best Granada paseos, wander the streets here around 19:00.

• *Follow Calle Reyes Católicos uphill for a couple of blocks until you reach...*

❼ Plaza Nueva

Plaza Nueva is dominated at the far end by the regional Palace of Justice (grand Baroque facade with green & white Andalusian flag). The fountain is capped by a stylized pomegranate—the symbol of the city, always open and fertile. The main action here is the comings and goings of the busy little shuttle buses serving the Albayzín. The local hippie community, nicknamed the *pies negros* (black feet) for obvious reasons, hangs out here and on Calle de Elvira. They squat—with their dogs and guitars—in abandoned caves above those the Roma (Gypsies) occupy in Sacromonte. Many are the children of rich Spanish families from the north, hell-bent on disappointing their high-achieving parents.

• *You could end your walk here—or carry on with a stroll up Carrera del Darro. To continue, leave Plaza Nueva opposite from where you entered, on the little lane that runs alongside the Darro River. This area is particularly enjoyable in the cool of the evening. To trace this stroll, see the map on page 606.*

❽ Paseo de los Tristes Stroll

Carrera del Darro is also called **Paseo de los Tristes**—"Walk of the Sad Ones." It was once the route of funeral processions to the cemetery at the edge of town.

As you leave Plaza Nueva, notice the small Church of Santa Ana on your right. This was originally a mosque—the church tower replaced a minaret. Notice the ceramic brickwork. This is Mudejar art by Moorish craftsmen, whose techniques were later employed by Christians.

Follow Carrera del Darro along the Darro River, which flows around the base of the Alhambra. Six miles upstream, part of the Darro is diverted to provide water for the Alhambra's many fountains—a remarkable feat of Moorish engineering in 1238.

After passing two small, picturesque bridges, the road widens slightly for a bus stop. Here you'll see the broken nub of a once-grand 11th-century **bridge** that led to the Alhambra. Notice two slits in the column: One held an iron portcullis to keep bad guys from entering the town via the river. The second held a solid door that was lowered to dam up water, then released to flush out the riverbed and keep it clean.

Across from the remains of the bridge is the brick facade of the stark but evocative ruins of the **Hammam El Bañuelo** (Arab Baths). This place gives you the chance to explore one of the best-preserved examples of an 11th-century Arab public bath in Spain (€5 to enter, covered by Dobla de Oro card; daily 9:00-14:30 & 17:00-20:30, mid-Sept-April 10:00-17:00; Carrera del Darro 31, www.alhambra-patronato.es). In Moorish times, hammams were a big part of the community (working-class homes didn't have bathrooms). Baths were strictly segregated and were more than places to wash: These were social meeting points where business was done. In Christian times it was assumed that conspiracies brewed in these baths—therefore, only a few of them survive.

Upon entering, you pass through the foyer and into the cold room, the warm room (where services like massage were offered), and finally the hot, or steam, room. Beyond that, you can see the oven that generated the heat, which flowed under the hypocaust-style floor tiles (the ones closest to the oven were the hottest). The romantic little holes in the ceiling once had stained-glass louvers that attendants opened and closed with sticks to regulate the heat and steaminess. Whereas Romans soaked in their pools, Muslims just doused. Rather than being totally immersed, people scooped and splashed water over themselves. Imagine attendants stoking the fires under the metal boiler...while people in towels and wooden slippers (to protect their feet from the heated floors) enjoyed all the spa services you can imagine as beams of light slashed through the mist.

This was a great social mixer. As all were naked, class distinctions disappeared—elites learned the latest from commoners. Mothers found matches for their kids. A popular Muslim phrase sums up the attraction of the baths: "This is where anyone would spend their last coin."

Just across from the baths is a stop for minibus #C31 and #C32—the easy way to head up to the **Albayzín.** Otherwise, continue straight ahead. On your left is **Santa Catalina de Zafra,** a convent of cloistered nuns (they worship behind a screen that divides the church's rich interior in half).

Just past this, on your right is the **Church of San Pedro,** the parish church of Sacromonte's Roma community (across from the Mudejar Art Museum). Within its rich interior is an ornate oxcart used to carry the host on the annual pilgrimage to Rocío, a town near the Portuguese border. A few steps farther along, the **Convento de San Bernardo** sells cookies and monastic wine: Look for the *Venta de Dulces* sign on the corner; goods are sold from behind a lazy Susan.

Our stroll ends at a promenade with bar and restaurant tables

spilling out under the floodlit Alhambra. From here, the road arcs up to the Albayzín and into Sacromonte.

Alhambra Tour

The last and greatest Moorish palace, the Alhambra, is one of Europe's top sights and worth ▲▲▲. Attracting 8,000 visitors a day,

it's the reason most tourists come to Granada. Nowhere else does the splendor of Moorish civilization shine so beautifully.

The last Moorish stronghold in Europe is really a symbol of retreat. As the Christian Reconquista gradually moved south, taking Córdoba (1237) and Sevilla (1248), displaced Muslims relocated to Granada, home of the Nasrids—the last Islamic kingdom in Spain. The Nasrids themselves would fall in 1492, but until that time Granada flourished as an intellectual and artistic center.

As you tour their grand palace, remember that while much of Europe slumbered through the Dark Ages, here Moorish magnificence blossomed—ornate stucco, plaster "stalactites," colors galore, scalloped windows framing Granada views, exuberant gardens, and water, water everywhere. Water—so rare and precious in most of the Islamic world—was the purest symbol of life to the Moors. The Alhambra is decorated with water: standing still, cascading, masking secret conversations, and drip-dropping playfully.

The Alhambra consists of four sights clustered together atop a hill, all covered by the following self-guided tour:

Palacios Nazaríes: Exquisite Moorish palace, the Alhambra's must-see sight (ticket required).

Palace of Charles V: Christian Renaissance palace plopped on top of the Alhambra after the Reconquista, with the fine Alhambra Museum inside (free to enter).

Generalife Palace and Gardens: Small summer palace with fragrant, lovely manicured gardens (ticket required).

Alcazaba Fort: Empty but evocative old fort with tower and views (ticket required).

ALHAMBRA TICKETS IN A NUTSHELL

To ensure you'll see the Palacios Nazaríes, the highlight of the Alhambra, book an "Alhambra General" ticket in advance (includes the Palacios Nazaríes, Alcazaba, and Generalife Palace and its gar-

dens). Demand far exceeds the supply of about 8,000 tickets per day, so buy as far in advance as possible (tickets available one year ahead—but keep in mind that they're nonrefundable and cannot be changed). Tickets covering just the Generalife and Alcazaba are more readily available—but you don't want to miss the Palacios Nazaríes.

When booking tickets online, be prepared to enter the passport number of each visitor in your group; each person will be required to show their passport when entering the sight.

Ticketing options for the Alhambra change frequently. Don't be scammed by unofficial websites selling overpriced tickets. Confirm details only at Alhambra-Patronato.es.

GETTING THERE

There are two entrances to the sprawling Alhambra: the Justice Gate, near the Palacios Nazaríes, and the entrance pavilion, 400 yards farther along at the top of the complex. If you've booked ahead and have tickets in hand, you can go directly to the Justice Gate.

On Foot: From Plaza Nueva, it's a 20-minute hike. Leave the plaza going up Cuesta de Gomérez. Keep going straight—you'll see the Alhambra high on your left. You'll soon reach the Justice Gate, which leads to the Palacios Nazaríes.

By Bus: Just uphill from Plaza Isabel La Católica, catch the #C30 or #C32 minibus, marked *Alhambra*. Stops include *Generalife* (entrance pavilion/ticket office and gardens), *Charles V*, and *Justice Gate*. See "The Alhambra" map on page 623 for stop locations. The ride can take as long as the hike depending on traffic; plan accordingly.

By Taxi: It's a €6 ride from Plaza Nueva.

By Car: If you have a car in town, do not use it to go to the Alhambra. But if you're coming from outside the city, you can drive here without passing through Granada's historic center. From the freeway, take the exit marked *Alhambra*. Signs lead you to a public parking lot, located near the entrance pavilion (€2.80/hour). Overnight and multiday parking is available (€19/24 hours, guarded at night). Leave the same way you came in.

PLANNING YOUR TIME

Alhambra General tickets come with a 30-minute time slot for admission to the Palacios Nazaríes (first entry to palaces at 8:30, last entry one hour before closing). You must enter the Palacios Nazaríes within the 30-minute window, but once inside, you can linger as long as you like. You can see the other Alhambra sights any time during that single day.

Don't miss your appointed time. Ticket checkers at the Pala-

cios Nazaríes are strict. If you're seeing the Generalife Palace and its gardens first, allow at least 15 minutes to walk to the Palacios Nazaríes.

Although you can see the sights in any order, to minimize walking, a good plan is to see the three sights at the lower end first: Start with the Palace of Charles V and the Alcazaba fort, then visit Palacios Nazaríes. When you finish touring the palace, leave through the Partal Gardens, then take a pleasant 15-minute gradual uphill stroll to the Generalife and its gardens.

If you have a long wait for your Palacios Nazaríes appointment, you could do the gardens first, then head down to the other three. Or you can kill time luxuriously on the breezy view terrace of the parador bar within the Alhambra wall.

ORIENTATION TO THE ALHAMBRA

Cost: There are many ticket options for the Alhambra: Be sure to purchase a ticket that includes the Palacios Nazaríes. Expect a surcharge for online purchases.

- **Alhambra General:** €14, covers the Palacios Nazaríes, Alcazaba fort, and Generalife Palace and its gardens.
- **Gardens, Generalife, and Alcazaba:** €7, covers daytime admission to almost everything—but not Palacios Nazaríes.
- **Night Visit to Palacios Nazaríes:** €8, nighttime-only visit to the Palacios Nazaríes.
- **Night Visit to Gardens and Generalife:** €5, nighttime-only visit to the Generalife Palace and its gardens.
- **Alhambra Experiences:** €14, nighttime visit to Palacios Nazaríes, then next-morning entry to the Alcazaba, Generalife, and its gardens.
- **Dobla de Oro General:** €20, valid 3 days, includes Alhambra General ticket (with a timed-entry to Palacios Nazaríes) and several smaller Nasrid sights.
- **Dobla de Oro at Night:** €15, valid 3 days, includes a nighttime-only visit to Palacios Nazaríes and Nasrid sights.
- **Children's and Discounted Tickets:** Children under 12 are free, but still need a reservation booked online in their name.

Hours: The entire Alhambra complex is open daily 8:30-20:00 (mid-Oct-March until 18:00). Last entry is one hour before closing.

Evening Hours: The Palacios Nazaríes and the Generalife are open and nicely lit some evenings (Tue-Sat 22:00-23:30; mid-Oct-March Fri-Sat 20:00-21:30). Note that night tickets include the palace or the Generalife, but not both (as you have only 1.5 hours inside). These tickets are not timed-entry, and it's extremely crowded when the doors open; you must enter no later than one hour before closing.

GRANADA

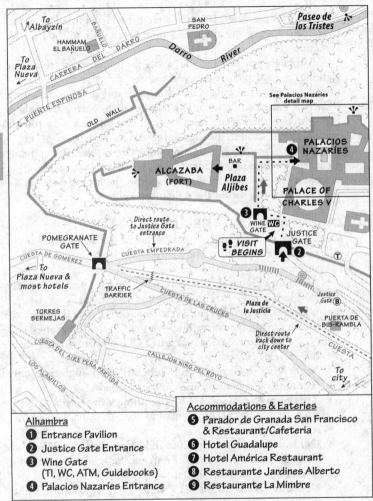

Alhambra
1. Entrance Pavilion
2. Justice Gate Entrance
3. Wine Gate
   (TI, WC, ATM, Guidebooks)
4. Palacios Nazaríes Entrance

Accommodations & Eateries
5. Parador de Granada San Francisco & Restaurant/Cafeteria
6. Hotel Guadalupe
7. Hotel América Restaurant
8. Restaurante Jardines Alberto
9. Restaurante La Mimbre

Information: Visitor info +34 958 027 971, ticket help line +34 858 889 002, https://tickets.alhambra-patronato.es/.

Reservations: Buy tickets online at the official website. Select a ticket, choose a date, then select an entry time for Palacios Nazaríes. When asked for a "document number," use your passport number. Print the ticket or store it on your phone. Tickets are released in intervals throughout the year (at 12 months out, 3 months out, and 1 month out). If tickets appear sold out for a particular date three months in advance, for example, check again one month ahead.

Without Reservations: If you are unable to get a reservation for the Palacios Nazaríes, buy a **Granada Card** sightseeing pass—

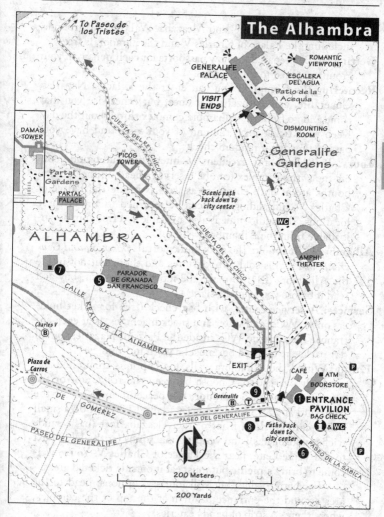

The Alhambra

it may score you a reservation even when the main Alhambra website is sold out; see "Tourist Information" at the beginning of this chapter.

For **in-person ticketing advice**, there are helpful info desks next to the Wine Gate and at the main Alhambra entrance pavilion, close to the bookstore (daily, 8:00-20:00). The TI in town and most hotels are adept at Alhambra issues. An info desk sometimes operates inside the Corral del Carbón in the town center.

If you can't secure a Palacios Nazaríes reservation, you can **enjoy the rest of the Alhambra** with a ticket covering just

the gardens, Generalife, and Alcazaba. Walking the grounds, including the Palace of Charles V and the parador, is free.

Getting In: Be prepared to show passports for each person in your group, matched to their tickets.

Reentering the Complex: You can enter the Palacios Nazaríes, Generalife, and Alcazaba just once, but otherwise you may come and go from the Alhambra complex throughout the day. Keep your ticket until the end of your visit, and have your passport ready for random checks.

Tours: The Alhambra's excellent €6 interactive audioguide covers the entire complex (can be reserved ahead online). Rental booths are at both entrances as well as inside the Palace of Charles V, and audioguides can be returned to any of these locations. The audioguide is also available as a free app, downloadable from the Alhambra website.

Alhambra Guidebook: The slick and colorful *Alhambra and Generalife in Focus* is sold at bookstores and shops but not inside the Alhambra (€11; to make the most of your visit, buy and read it before you tour the sight).

Services: A service center, with bag check (free for ticket holders only), WCs, and water and snack machines, is at each entrance. There are no WCs inside the Palacios Nazaríes. Small day packs are allowed but must be worn in front.

Eating: Within the Alhambra walls, food options are limited and generally overpriced. Choose between the restaurant or the cafeteria at the **$$$ parador;** the peaceful ambience of the courtyard at **$$$ Hotel América** (daily 12:30-17:00); a small **$ bar-café kiosk** in front of the Alcazaba fort (basic sandwiches and snacks); and **vending machines** (at the WC) next to the Wine Gate, near the Palace of Charles V. You're welcome to bring a **picnic** but must eat it outside ticketed areas.

For better-value (but still touristy) options, head to the area around the entrance pavilion at the top of the complex, where there's a strip of handy eateries.

$$$ Restaurante Jardines Alberto, across from the entrance pavilion, has a nice courtyard and offers a charming setting (daily 12:00-23:30, off-season until 18:00; Paseo de la Sabica 1, +34 958 221 661, climb the stairs from the street). The breezy **$$$ Restaurante La Mimbre** offers shade and a break from the crowds. They also serve breakfast (daily 9:30-17:00 & 20:00-23:00, Paseo del Generalife 18, +34 958 222 276).

City Tour from the Alhambra: The hop-on, hop-off tourist train leaves from the top of the Alhambra, offering a convenient hour-long sightseeing tour on the way back to town instead of walking (see "Tours in Granada," earlier.)

GRANADA

◆ SELF-GUIDED TOUR

This tour assumes that you'll visit the Alhambra sights from the bottom of the complex to the top. The first three sights cluster at the bottom end, while the Generalife and its gardens are about a 15-minute walk away, at the top.

▲▲Palace of Charles V

While it's only natural for a conquering king to build his own palace over that of his foe, Holy Roman Emperor Charles V (who

ruled as Charles I over Spain) respected the splendid Moorish palace. And so, to make his mark, he built a modern Renaissance palace for official functions and used the existing Palacios Nazaríes as a royal residence. With a unique circle-within-a-square design by Pedro Machuca, a pupil of Michelangelo, this is Spain's most

impressive Renaissance building. Stand in the circular courtyard surrounded by mottled marble columns, then climb the stairs. Perhaps Charles' palace was designed to have a dome, but it was never finished—his son, Philip II, abandoned it to build El Escorial, his own, much more massive palace outside Madrid (the final and most austere example of Spanish Renaissance architecture). Even without a dome, acoustics are perfect in the center—stand in the middle and sing your best aria. The palace doubles as a venue for the popular International Festival of Music and Dance.

▲Alhambra Museum

On the ground floor of the Palace of Charles V, this museum (Museo de la Alhambra) shows off some of the Alhambra's best surviving Moorish art. Its well-described artifacts—including tiles, characteristic green, blue, and black pottery, lion fountains, and a beautiful carved-wood door—are beautifully displayed (free, Wed-Sat 8:30-20:00, Sun and Tue until 14:30, shorter hours off-season, closed Mon year-round). The **Fine Arts Museum** (Museo de Bellas Artes, upstairs, free) has Christian-era paintings and statues and is of little interest to most.

• *From the front of the Palace of Charles V, the Alcazaba is the towering brick structure across a moat, straight ahead.*

Alcazaba

This fort—the original "red castle" ("Alhambra")—is the oldest and most ruined part of the complex, offering exercise and fine city

views. What you see is from the mid-13th century, but there was probably a fort here in Roman times. Once upon a time, this tower defended a medina (town) of 2,000 Muslims living within the Alhambra walls. It's a huge, sprawling complex—wind your way through passages and courtyards, over uneven terrain, to reach the biggest tower at the tip of the complex. Then climb stairs steeply up to the very top. From there (looking north), find Plaza Nueva and the San Nicolás viewpoint in the Albayzín. To the south are the Sierra Nevada Mountains. Notice the tower's four flags: the blue of the European Union, the green and white of Andalucía, the red and yellow of Spain, and the red and green of Granada.

Speaking of flags, imagine that day in 1492 when the Christian cross and the flags of Aragon and Castile were raised on this tower, and (according to a probably fanciful legend) the fleeing Moorish king Boabdil (Abu Abdullah, in Arabic) looked back and wept. His mom chewed him out, saying, "You weep like a woman for what you couldn't defend like a man." With this defeat, more than seven centuries of Muslim rule in Spain came to an end. Much later, Napoleon stationed his troops at the Alhambra, contributing substantially to its ruin.

• If you're going from the Alcazaba to Palacios Nazaríes, backtrack toward the Palace of Charles V and join the line (to the left, behind the palace) during the 30-minute entry time on your ticket.

▲▲▲Palacios Nazaríes

Crowds crush into the jewel of the Alhambra at the start of each 30-minute entry interval. If your entry time is particularly crowd-

ed, consider lingering at the start to let things quiet down. Once inside, relax. You're no longer under any time constraints. You'll walk through three basic sections: royal offices, ceremonial rooms, and private quarters. Built mostly in the 14th century, this palace offers your best possible look at the refined, elegant Moorish civilization of al-Andalus (the Arabic word for the Moorish-controlled Iberian Peninsula).

You'll visit rooms decorated from top to bottom with carved

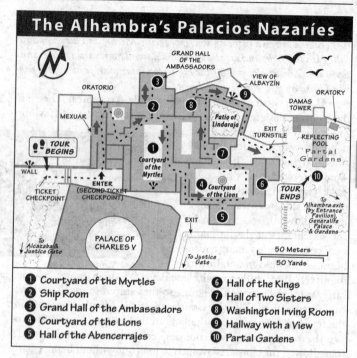

The Alhambra's Palacios Nazaríes

GRAND HALL OF THE AMBASSADORS

ORATORIO

MEXUAR

VIEW OF ALBAYZÍN

DAMAS TOWER

ORATORY

TOUR BEGINS

WALL

Patio of Lindaraja

EXIT TURNSTILE

REFLECTING POOL

Partal Gardens

GRANADA

ENTER (SECOND TICKET CHECKPOINT)

TICKET CHECKPOINT

Courtyard of the Myrtles

Courtyard of the Lions

TOUR ENDS

To Alhambra exit (by Entrance Pavilion), Generalife Palace & Gardens

EXIT

To Alcazaba & Justice Gate

PALACE OF CHARLES V

To Justice Gate

50 Meters
50 Yards

❶ Courtyard of the Myrtles
❷ Ship Room
❸ Grand Hall of the Ambassadors
❹ Courtyard of the Lions
❺ Hall of the Abencerrajes
❻ Hall of the Kings
❼ Hall of Two Sisters
❽ Washington Irving Room
❾ Hallway with a View
❿ Partal Gardens

wood ceilings, stucco stalactites, ceramic tiles, molded-plaster walls, and filigree windows. Open-air courtyards feature fountains with bubbling water, which give the palace a desert-oasis feel. A garden enlivened by lush vegetation and peaceful pools is the Quran's symbol of heaven. The palace is well-preserved and well restored, but the trick to fully appreciating it is to imagine it furnished and filled with Moorish life: Sultans with hookah pipes lounging on pillows upon Persian carpets, heavy curtains on the windows, and ivory-studded wooden furniture. The whole place was painted with bright colors, many suggested by the Quran—blue (heaven), green (oasis), red (blood), and gold (wealth). Throughout the palace, walls, ceilings, vases, carpets, and tiles were covered with decorative patterns and calligraphy, mostly poems and verses of praise from the Quran and from local poets.

As you wander, keep the palace themes in mind: water, a near absence of figural images (they're frowned upon in the Quran), "stalactite" ceilings—and few signs telling you where you are. As tempting as it might be to touch the stucco, don't—it is very susceptible to damage from the oils from your hand. Use this book's map to locate the essential stops listed below.

• Begin by walking through a few administrative rooms (the mexuar, the council of the wise men, where scribes were busy doing the office work

of the state bureaucracy) with a stunning Mecca-oriented prayer room (the oratorio, with a niche on the right facing Mecca, and lacy windows filling it with light and great views) and a small courtyard with a round fountain. Eventually you hit the big rectangular courtyard with a fish-pond lined by two myrtle-bush hedges.

❶ **Courtyard of the Myrtles** (Patio de Arrayanes): The standard palace design included a central courtyard like this. Moors loved their patios—with a garden and water, under the sky. The apartments of the sultan's women looked over this courtyard: two apartments for wives on either side (four was the maximum allowed), and a dorm for the concubines at the far end (a man could have "as many concubines as he could maintain with

dignity"). In accordance with medieval Moorish mores, women rarely ventured outside the home, so they stayed in touch with nature in courtyards like the Courtyard of the Myrtles—named for the fragrant myrtle hedges that add to the courtyard's charm. Notice the wooden screens ("jalousies" erected by jealous husbands) that allowed the cloistered women to look out without being clearly seen. The upstairs was likely for winter use, and the cooler ground level was probably used in summer.

• *Head left from the entry through gigantic wooden doors into the long narrow antechamber called the...*

❷ **Ship Room** (Sala de la Barca): It's understandable that many think the Ship Room is named for the upside-down-hull shape of its fine cedar ceiling. But the name is actually derived from the Arab word *baraka*, meaning "divine blessing and luck." (President Obama's first name came from the same Arabic root word.) As you passed through this room, blessings and luck are exactly what you'd need—because in the next room, you'd be face-to-face with the sultan.

• *Oh, it's your turn. Enter the ornate throne room.*

❸ **Grand Hall of the Ambassadors** (Gran Salón de los Embajadores): The palace's largest room, also known as the Salón de Comares, functioned as the throne room. It was here that the sultan, seated on a throne opposite the entrance, received foreign emissaries. Ogle the room—a perfect cube—from top to bottom. Made from 8,017 pieces inlaid like a giant jigsaw puzzle, the star-studded, domed wooden ceiling suggests the complexity of Allah's infinite universe. Wooden stalactites form the cornice, running around the entire base of the ceiling. The stucco walls, even without their original paint and gilding, are still glorious. The filigree

windows once held stained glass and had heavy drapes to block out the heat. Some precious 16th-century tiles survive in the center of the floor.

A visitor here would have stepped from the glaring Courtyard of the Myrtles into this dim, cool, incense-filled world to meet the silhouetted sultan. Imagine the alcoves functioning busily as workstations, and the light at sunrise or sunset, rich and warm, filling the room.

Let your eyes trace the finely carved Arabic script. Muslims avoided making images of living creatures—that was God's work. But they could carve decorative religious messages. One phrase—"only Allah is victorious"—is repeated 9,000 times throughout the palace. Find the character for "Allah": It looks like a cursive W with a nose on its left side, with a vertical line to the right. The swoopy toboggan blades underneath are a kind of artistic punctuation used to set off one phrase.

In 1492, two historic events likely took place in this room. Culminating a 700-year-long struggle, the Reconquista was completed here as the last Moorish king, Boabdil, signed the terms of his surrender before eventually going into exile in Morocco.

And it was here that Columbus made one of his final pitches to Isabel and Ferdinand to finance a sea voyage to the Far East. Imagine the scene: The king, the queen, and the greatest minds from the University of Salamanca gathered here while Columbus produced maps and pie charts to make his case that he could sail west to reach the east. Ferdinand and the professors laughed and called Columbus mad—not because they thought the world was flat (most educated people knew otherwise), but because they thought Columbus had underestimated the size of the globe, and thus the length and cost of the journey.

But Isabel said, *"Sí, señor."* Columbus fell to his knees (promising to pack light, wear a money belt, and use a good guidebook).

Opposite the Ship Room entrance, photographers pause for a picture-perfect view of the tower reflected in the Courtyard of the Myrtles pool. This was the original palace entrance (before the Palace of Charles V was built).

• *Continue deeper into the palace, to a courtyard where, 600 years ago, only the royal family and their servants could enter. It's the much-photographed...*

❹ **Courtyard of the Lions** (Patio de los Leones): This delightful courtyard is named for the famous fountain at its center with its ring of 12 marble lions—originals from the 14th century.

GRANADA

Conquering Christians disassembled the fountain to see how it worked, rendering it nonfunctional; it finally flowed again in 2012. From the center of the courtyard, four channels carry water outward—figuratively to the corners of the earth and literally to various more private apartments of the royal family. The arched gallery that surrounds the courtyard is supported by 124 perfectly balanced columns. The craftsmanship is first class. For example, the lead fittings between the precut sections of the columns allow things to flex during earthquakes, preventing destruction.

Six hundred years ago, the Muslim Moors could read the Quranic poetry that ornaments this court, and they could understand the symbolism of this lush, enclosed garden, considered the embodiment of paradise or truth. ("How beautiful is this garden / where the flowers of Earth rival the stars of Heaven. / What can compare with this alabaster fountain, gushing crystal-clear water? / Nothing except the fullest moon, pouring light from an unclouded sky.") They appreciated this part of the palace even more than we do today.

• On the right, off the courtyard, the only original door still in the palace leads into a square room called the...

❺ Hall of the Abencerrajes (Sala de los Abencerrajes): This was the sultan's living room, with an exquisite ceiling based on the eight-sided Muslim star.

The name of the room comes from a bloody event that's said to have occurred here in the 16th century. According to legend, the father of Boabdil invited members of the North African Abencerraje family to a banquet—and then promptly massacred them to thwart a threat to his dynasty. He is said to have stacked 36 Abencerraje heads in the pool, under the sumptuous honeycombed stucco ceiling in this hall.

• At the end of the court opposite where you entered is the...

❻ Hall of the Kings (Sala de los Reyes): This hall is famous for its paintings on the goat-leather ceiling depicting scenes of the sultan and his family. The center room's group portrait shows the first 10 of the Alhambra's 22 sultans. The scene is a fantasy, since these people lived over a span of many generations. The two end rooms display scenes of princely pastimes, such

Islamic Art

Rather than making paintings and statues, Islamic artists expressed themselves with beautiful but functional objects. Ce-

ramics (most of them blue and white, or green and white), carpets, glazed tile panels, stucco-work ceilings, and glass tableware are covered with complex patterns. The intricate interweaving, repetition, and unending lines suggest the complex, infinite nature of God, known to Muslims as Allah.

You'll see few pictures of humans, since Islamic doctrine holds that the creation of living beings is God's work alone. However, secular art by Muslims for their homes and palaces was not bound by this restriction; you'll get an occasional glimpse of realistic art featuring men and women enjoying a garden paradise, a symbol of the Muslim heaven.

Look for floral patterns (twining vines, flowers, and arabesques) and geometric designs (stars and diamonds). The decorative motifs (Arabic script, patterns, flowers, shells, and so on) that repeat countless times throughout the palace were made by pressing wet plaster into molds. The most common pattern is calligraphy—elaborate lettering of an inscription in Arabic, the language of the Quran. A quote from the Quran on a vase or lamp combines the power of the message with the beauty of the calligraphy.

as hunting and shooting skeet. In a palace otherwise devoid of figures, these depictions offer a rare look at royal life in the palace.

• *Continue around the lion fountain. Before entering the next room, you'll pass doors leading right and left to a 14th-century WC plumbed by running water and stairs up to the harem. Next is the...*

❼ **Hall of Two Sisters** (Sala de Dos Hermanas): The Sala de Dos Hermanas—nicknamed for the giant twin slabs of white marble on the floor flanking the fountain—has another oh-wow stucco ceiling lit by clerestory windows. This is another royal reception hall, with alcoves for private use and a fountain. Running water helped cool and humidify the room but also added elegance and extravagance, as running water was a luxury most could only dream of.

The room features geometric patterns and stylized Arabic script quoting verses from the Quran. If the inlaid color tiles look "Escher-esque," you've got it backward: Escher is Alhambra-esque. M. C. Escher was inspired by these very patterns on his visit.

Study the geometry of the patterns—they remind us of the Moorish expertise in math. The sitting room (farthest from the entry) has low windows because Moorish people sat on the floor. Some rare stained glass survives in the ceiling. From here the sultana enjoyed a grand view of the medieval city (before a 16th-century wing blocked the view).

• *That's about it for the palace. From here, we enter the later, 16th-century section, and wander past the domed roofs of the old baths down a hallway to a pair of rooms decorated with mahogany ceilings. Marked with a large plaque is the...*

❽ Washington Irving Room: While living in Spain in 1829, Washington Irving stayed in the Alhambra, and he wrote *Tales of the Alhambra* in this room. It was a romantic time, when the palace was home to Roma and donkeys. His "tales" rekindled interest in the Alhambra, causing it to be recognized as a national treasure. A plaque on the wall thanks Irving, who later served as the US ambassador to Spain (1842-1846). Here's a quote from Irving's *The Alhambra by Moonlight:* "On such heavenly nights I would sit for hours at my window inhaling the sweetness of the garden, and musing on the checkered fortunes of those whose history was dimly shadowed out in the elegant memorials around."

• *As you leave, stop at the open-air...*

❾ Hallway with a View: Here you'll enjoy the best-in-the-palace view of the labyrinthine Albayzín—the old Moorish town on the opposite hillside. Find the famous San Nicolás viewpoint (below where the white San Nicolás church tower breaks the horizon—see the crowds of tourists taking pictures of you). Green patches are the gardens of *carmenes* (old noble farms, many that are now romantic restaurants). Below is the river and the Paseo de los Tristes (with its square filled with inviting restaurants). Creeping into the mountains on the right are the Roma neighborhoods of Sacromonte. Still circling old Granada is the Moorish wall (built in the 1400s to protect the city's population, swollen by Muslim refugees driven south by the Reconquista).

The Patio de Lindaraja (with its garden of maze-like hedges) marks the end of the palace visit. Before exiting, you can detour right into the "Secrets Room"—a domed brick room of the former baths with fun acoustics. Whisper into a corner, and your friend—with an ear to the wall—can hear you in the opposite corner. Try talking in the exact center.

• *Step outside into...*

⓾ **The Partal Gardens** (El Partal): The Partal Gardens are built upon the ruins of the Partal Palace. Imagine a palace like the one you just toured, built around this reflecting pond. A fragment of it still stands—once the living quarters—on the cooler north side. Its Mecca-facing oratory (the small building a few steps above the pool) survives. The Alhambra was the site of seven different palaces in 150 years. You have toured parts of just two or three.

• *Leaving the palace, climb a few stairs, continue through the gardens, and follow signs directing you left to the Generalife (or right to the Alcazaba and the rest of the Alhambra grounds, if you haven't already visited them).*

The path to the Generalife and its gardens is a delightful 15-minute stroll through lesser (but still pleasant) gardens, along a row of fortified towers—just follow signs for Generalife. Just before reaching the Generalife, you'll cross over a bridge and look down on the dusty lane called Cuesta del Rey Chico (a handy shortcut for returning to town later).

▲▲Generalife Palace and Gardens

The sultan's vegetable and fruit orchards and the summer palace retreat called the Generalife (heh-neh-rah-LEE-fay) were outside the protection of the Alhambra wall; today, they're a short hike uphill past the entrance pavilion. The thousand-or-so residents of the Alhambra enjoyed the fresh fruit and veggies grown here. But most important, this little palace provided the sultan with a cool and quiet summer escape.

Follow the simple one-way path through the sprawling gardens. You'll catch glimpses of a sleek, modern outdoor theater, built in the 1950s. It continues to be an important concert venue for Granada. From the head of the theater, signs will lead you through manicured hedges, along delightful ponds, and past flowing fountains to the sultan's small summer palace.

Before arriving at the bright white palace, pass through the dismounting room (imagine dismounting onto the helpful stone ledge, and letting your horse drink from the trough here). Enter the most accurately re-created Arabian garden in Andalucía, the **Patio de la Acequia.**

Here in the retreat of the Moorish kings, this garden is the closest thing on Earth to the Quran's description of heaven. It was planted more than 600 years ago—that's remarkable longevity for a European garden. While there were originally only eight

The Alhambra Grounds

As you wander the grounds, remember that the Alhambra was once a city of a thousand people fortified by a 1.5-mile rampart and 30 towers. The zone within the walls was a **medina,** an urban town. The path from the entrance pavilion along the garden-like Calle Real de la Alhambra to the palace passes through the ruins of the medina (destroyed by the French in 1812). This path traces the south wall, with its towers. In the distance are the snow-capped Sierra Nevada peaks—the highest mountains in Iberia. While you need a ticket to visit the highlights of the Alhambra, the medina—with the Palace of Charles V, a church, a line of shops showing off traditional woodworking techniques, and the fancy Alhambra parador—is wide open and free to everyone.

It's especially fun to snoop around the historic **Parador de Granada San Francisco,** which—as a national monument—is open to the public. Once a Moorish palace within the Alhambra, it was later converted into a Franciscan monastery, with a historic claim to fame: Its church is where the Catholic Monarchs (Ferdinand and Isabel) chose to be buried. For a peek, step in through the front door leading to a small garden area and reception. Continue

water jets, most of the details in today's garden closely match those lovingly described in old poems. The flowers, herbs, aromas, and water are exquisite...even for a sultan. Up the Darro River, the royal aqueduct diverted a life-giving stream of water into the Alhambra. It was channeled through this extra-long decorative fountain to irrigate the bigger garden outside, then along an aqueduct into the Alhambra for its thirsty residents. And though the splashing fountains are a delight, they are a 19th-century addition. The Moors liked a peaceful pond instead.

At the end of the pond, you enter the sultan's tiny three-room summer retreat. From the last room, climb 10 steps into the upper Renaissance gardens (c. 1600). The ancient tree rising over the pond inspired Washington Irving, who wrote that this must be the "only surviving witness to the wonders of that age of al-Andalus."

Climbing up and going through the turnstile, you enter the Romantic 19th-century garden. Your visit to the Alhambra is complete, and you've earned your reward. "Surely Allah will make those who believe and do good deeds enter gardens beneath which

straight to see the burial place, located in the open-air ruins of the church (passing the reception-desk area and a delightful former cloister; the history is described in English). The slab on the ground near the altar—a surviving bit from the mosque that was here before the church—marks the place where the king and queen rested until 1521 (when they were moved to the Royal Chapel downtown). Now a hotel, the parador has a restaurant and terrace café—with lush views of the Generalife—open to all.

The medina's main road dead-ended at the **Wine Gate** (Puerta del Vino), which protected the fortress. When you pass through the Wine Gate, you enter a courtyard that was originally a moat, then a reservoir (in Christian times). The well—now encased in a bar-kiosk—is still a place for cold drinks.

You can exit down to the city from the Wine Gate via the Justice Gate, immediately below. From there you'll walk past a Renaissance fountain and pass through the **Pomegranate Gate** (Puerta de las Granadas) into the modern city, close to Plaza Nueva.

rivers flow; they shall be adorned therein with bracelets of gold and pearls, and their garments therein shall be of silk" (Quran 22.23).

• *From here you have can extend your visit to see the highest point of the Generalife from atop a 14th-century staircase, or exit the Alhambra.*

Escalera del Agua and Return to Town

For a little more exercise (and views), turn left at the sign for *continuación de la visita*, and take the half-mile loop up and around to see the staircase called **Escalera del Agua,** whose banisters double as little water canals. From the top, you'll have a chance to enter the "Romantic Viewpoint"—climb up the stairs for a top-floor view over the gardens (pleasant enough, but less impressive than other views at the Alhambra). Then hike back down through the garden and follow *salida* signs, through the long oleander trellis tunnel, to the exit and the minibuses.

But if you're exhausted, skip this detour. Instead, just head to the right and follow *salida* signs toward the gardens' exit (next to

the Alhambra's entrance pavilion). The #C30 and #C32 **minibuses** return from here to Plaza Isabel La Católica.

If you want to **return to town on foot,** there are two direct and scenic routes. One is the easily overlooked **Cuesta del Rey Chico** pathway. It starts under the two stone arches not far from the entrance pavilion, by Restaurante La Mimbre and the minibus stop—a sign just past the restaurant entrance will confirm you're on the right path. You'll walk downhill on a peaceful, cobbled lane scented with lavender and rock rose, beneath the Alhambra ramparts and past the sultan's horse lane leading up to the Generalife. In 15 minutes you're back in town at Paseo de los Tristes, where you can stroll along a level road to Plaza Nueva or continue walking into the Albayzín district (walking downhill on this trail from the Alhambra, you can't get lost).

The other route is the shortest and most common: a straight walk along the **main road** and the base of the fortress wall until you reach a fountain on the left. Follow the shady canopy of trees down, down, down until reaching Cuesta de Gomérez and Plaza Nueva.

More Sights in Granada

IN THE OLD TOWN
▲▲Royal Chapel (Capilla Real)
Without a doubt Granada's top Christian sight, this lavish chapel in the old town holds the dreams—and bodies—of Queen Isabel and King Ferdinand. The Catholic Monarchs were all about the Reconquista. Their marriage united the Aragon and Castile kingdoms, allowing an acceleration of the Christian and Spanish push south. In its last 10 years, the Reconquista snowballed. Symbolic of Ferdinand and Isabel's eventual victory, Granada—the last Moorish capital—was their chosen burial place. This chapel, while smaller and less architecturally striking than Granada's cathedral, is far more historically significant.

Cost and Hours: €5, includes audioguide, Mon-Sat 10:00-18:30, Sun from 11:00; entrance on Calle Oficios, just off Gran Vía del Colón—go through iron gate; +34 958 227 848, www.capillarealgranada.com.

Visiting the Chapel: In the lobby, before you enter the chapel, notice the **painting of Boabdil** (on the black horse) giving the key of Granada to the conquering King Ferdinand. Boabdil wanted to fall to his knees, but the Spanish king, who had great respect for his Moorish foe, embraced him instead. They fought a long and noble war (for instance, respectfully returning the bodies of dead soldiers). Ferdinand is in red, and Isabel is behind him wearing a crown. The painting is flanked by **glass-enclosed exhibits** comparing wood sculptures of the four royal family members buried here

with their marble tomb sculptures (their faces are too high up to see clearly inside the chapel).

Isabel decided to make Granada the capital of Spain (and burial place for Spanish royalty) for three reasons: 1) With the conquest of this city, Christianity had finally overcome Islam in Europe; 2) her marriage with Ferdinand, followed by the conquest of Granada, had marked the beginning of a united Spain; and 3) in Granada, she agreed to sponsor Columbus.

Step into the **chapel.** The light and lacy silver-filigree style is Plateresque Gothic, named for and inspired by the fine silver-work of the Moors. The chapel's interior was originally austere, with fancy touches added later by Ferdinand and Isabel's grand-son, Holy Roman Emperor Charles V. Five hundred years ago, this must have been the most splendid space imaginable. Because of its speedy completion (1506-1521), the Gothic architecture is unusually harmonious.

In front of the main altar, the **four royal tombs** are Renaissance-style. Carved in Italy in 1521 from Carrara marble, they

were sent by ship to Spain. The faces—based on death masks—are considered accurate. **Ferdinand** and **Isabel** are the lower, and humbler, of the two couples. (Isabel fans attribute the bigger dent she puts in the pillow to the weight of her larger brain.) Isabel's contemporaries described the queen as being of medium height, with auburn hair and blue eyes, and possessing a serious, modest, and gentle personality. (Compare Ferdinand and Isabel's tomb statues with the painted and gilded wood statues of them kneeling in prayer, flanking the altarpiece.)

Philip the Fair and **Juana the Mad** (who succeeded Ferdinand and Isabel) lie on the left. Philip was so "Fair" that it drove the insanely jealous Juana "Mad." Philip died young, and Juana, crazy like a fox, used her "grief" over his death to forestall a second marriage, thereby ensuring that their son Charles would inherit the throne. Charles was a key figure in European history, as his coronation merged the Holy Roman Empire (Philip the Fair's Habsburg domain) with Juana's Spanish empire. Charles V ruled a vast empire stretching from Holland to Sicily, and from Bohemia to Bolivia (1519-1556; you can see his palace within the Alhambra complex). Today's Spaniards reflect that while the momentous marriage created their country, it also sucked them into centuries of European squabbling, eventually leaving Spain impoverished.

Granada lost power and importance when Philip II, the son of Charles V, built his El Escorial palace outside Madrid, establishing that city as the single capital of a single Spain. This coincided with the beginning of Spain's decline, as the country squandered its vast wealth trying to maintain an impossibly huge empire. Spain's rulers were defending the romantic, quixotic dream of a Catholic empire—ruled by one divinely ordained Catholic monarch—against an irrepressible tide of nationalism and Protestantism that was sweeping across the vast Habsburg holdings in Central and Eastern Europe. Spain's relatively poor modern history can be blamed, in part, on its people's stubborn unwillingness to accept the end of this old-regime notion. Even Franco borrowed symbols from the Catholic Monarchs to legitimize his dictatorship and keep the 500-year-old legacy alive.

Look at the intricate **carving** on the Renaissance tombs. Dating from around 1520, it's a humanistic statement, with these healthy, organic, realistic figures rising out of the Gothic age. Charles V thought the existing chapel wasn't dazzling enough to honor his grandparents' importance, so he funded decorative touches like the iron screen and the fine 16th-century copy of the Rogier van der Weyden painting *The Deposition* (to the left after passing through the screen). Immediately to the right of the painting, with the hardest-working altar boys in Christendom holding up gilded Corinthian columns, is a chapel with a locked-away relic (an arm) of John the Baptist.

From the feet of the marble tombs, step downstairs to see the actual **coffins.** They are plain. Ferdinand and Isabel were originally buried in the Franciscan monastery up at the Alhambra (in what is today the parador). You're standing in front of the two people who created Spain. The fifth coffin (on right, marked *Príncipe Miguel*) belongs to a young Prince Michael, who would have been king of a united Spain and Portugal. (A sad—but too-long—story...)

The **high altar** is one of the finest Renaissance works in Spain. It's dedicated to two Johns: the Baptist and the Evangelist. In the center you can see the Baptist and the Evangelist chatting as if over tapas—an appropriately humanistic scene. Scenes from the Baptist's life are on the left: John beheaded after Salomé's fine dancing, and (below) John baptizing Jesus. Scenes from the Evangelist's life are on the right: John's martyrdom (a failed attempt to boil him alive in oil), and, below, John on Patmos (where he may have written the last book of the Bible, Revelation). John is talking to the eagle that, according to tradition, flew him to heaven. Flanking both Johns, statues of Ferdinand and Isabel kneel in prayer. A colorful series of reliefs at the bottom level recalls the Christian conquest of the Moors (left to right): a robed processional figure, Boabdil with army and key to Alhambra, Moors expelled from Al-

hambra, conversion of Muslims by tonsured monks (two panels, right of altar table), and another robed figure.

A finely carved Plateresque arch, with the gilded royal initials *F* and *Y*, leads from the chapel into the sacristy/treasury/museum, where you'll see a small glass pyramid. This holds Queen Isabel's silver crown ringed with pomegranates (symbolizing Granada), her scepter, and King Ferdinand's sword. Do a counterclockwise spin around the room to see it all, starting to the right of the entry arch. There you'll see the devout Isabel's prayer book, in which she followed the Mass. The book and its sturdy box date from 1496. According to legend, the fancy box on the other side of the door is supposedly the one that Isabel filled with jewels and gave to bankers as collateral for the cash to pay Columbus. In the corner (also behind glass) is the ornate silver-and-gold cross that Cardinal Mendoza, staunch supporter of Queen Isabel, carried into the Alhambra on that historic day in 1492—and used as the centerpiece for the first Christian Mass in the conquered fortress. Below the cross is Isabel's simple rosary, belt, and other personal items. She embraced Franciscan teaching, gave most of her jewels to the Church and, for a queen, lived quite austerely.

Next, the big silver-and-gold silk tapestry is the altar banner for the mobile campaign chapel of Ferdinand and Isabel, who always traveled with their army. In the case to its left, you'll see the original Christian army flags raised over the Alhambra in 1492.

The next zone of this grand hall holds the first great **art collection** established by a woman. Queen Isabel amassed more than 200 important paintings. After Napoleon occupied Granada (from 1808 until 1812), only 31 remained. Even so, this is an exquisite collection, all on wood, featuring works by Sandro Botticelli, Pietro Perugino, the Flemish master Hans Memling, and some less-famous Spanish masters. (Find the paintings by Perugino and Botticelli ahead on the left.)

Finally, at the end of the room are two **carved sculptures** of Ferdinand and Isabel, the originals from the high altar. Charles V considered these primitive (I disagree) and replaced them with the ones you saw earlier.

To reach the cathedral (described next), exit the treasury behind Isabel, and walk around the block to the right.

▲Granada Cathedral (Catedral de Granada)

Granada's cathedral is the second-largest church in the country (after Sevilla's) and one of the few to exhibit Renaissance features. Its 200-year-long construction saw it begin as a Gothic church, then laid out using Renaissance elements, before being decorated in Baroque style.

Cost and Hours: €5, includes audioguide, Mon-Sat 10:00-18:15, Sun from 15:00, +34 958 222 959, www.catedraldegranada. com.

Visiting the Cathedral: Enter the church from Plaza de las Pasiegas. Before exploring the interior, step into the cathedral's little **museum** (tucked into the corner behind the ticket counter; no photos here). Filling the ground floor of the big bell tower, it's worth seeking out for two pieces of art: a Gothic, hexagonal-shaped monstrance with a Renaissance-era base given to the cathedral by Isabel, and a beautiful bust of San Pablo (Paul, with a flowing beard, carved in wood and painted)—a self-portrait by hometown great Alonso Cano.

Leave the museum and stand in the back of the **nave** for an overview. Survey the church. It's huge. It was designed to be the national church when Granada was the capital of a newly reconquered-from-the-Muslims Spain. High above the main altar are square niches originally intended for the burial of Charles V and his family. But King Philip II changed focus and abandoned Granada for El Escorial, so the niches are now plugged with saintly paintings. High above under the stained glass are seven scenes from the life of Mary (by Alonso Cano).

The cathedral's cool, spacious **interior** is mostly Renaissance—a refreshing break from the closed-in, dark Gothic of so many Spanish churches. In a move that was modern back in the 18th century, the wooden walls of the choir (which dominates the center of most Spanish churches) were taken out so that common people could see as well as hear Mass. At about the same time, a bishop ordered the interior painted with lime (for hygienic reasons, during a time of disease). The people liked it, and it stayed white.

Notice the two rear chapels (sand-colored, on right and left); they're Neoclassical in style and a far cry from the Gothic beginnings of the church. As you explore, remember that the abundance of Marys is all part of the Counter-Reformation. Most of the side chapels are decorated in Baroque style.

As you walk to the front for a closer look at the **altar,** take a small detour to the scale model of the entire complex (left of pews). Examine the cathedral's immensity. The Royal Chapel (right side) is shaped like a small church would be, complete with mini transepts and fitting perfectly into the corner of the cathedral. Resume your walk to the altar, passing two fine Baroque organs with horizontal trumpet pipes, unique to Spain.

Standing before the altar, notice the abundance of gold leaf. It's from Spain's Darro River, which originally attracted Romans here for its gold. As this is a seat of the local bishop, there's a fine wooden bishop's throne on the right.

Between the pairs of Corinthian columns on both sides of the altar are **sculptures** with a strong parenting theme: Inside the thick, round frames at the top are busts of Adam and Eve, from whom came mankind. Around them are the four gold-covered evangelists, who—with the New Testament—brought the Good News of salvation to believers. Completing the big parenting picture (under Adam and Eve) are Ferdinand and Isabel, kneeling in prayer, who brought Catholicism to the land. Their complex coat of arms (beneath each respective statue) celebrates how their marriage united two influential kingdoms to create imperial Spain.

To your right is the ornate carved-stone Gothic door to the **Royal Chapel** (described earlier), with 15th-century decorations that predate the cathedral. The chapel holds the most important historic relics in town—the tombs of the Catholic Monarchs. And, because the chapel and cathedral are run by two different religious orders, this door is always closed and there are separate admission fees for each.

Now examine the chapels on each side of the closed Royal Chapel door. To the left is a politically incorrect version of St. James the Moor-Slayer, with his sword raised high and an armored Moor trampled under his horse's hooves. The chapel to the right features a painting by Cano—but the frame itself is a masterpiece. Cano carved the wooden frame, gilded it, painted over the gold leaf, and scratched through where he wanted the gold to show.

Strolling behind the altar, look for the **giant music sheets:** They're mostly 16th-century Gregorian chants. Notice the sliding C clef. Rather than a fixed G or F clef, the monks knew that this clef—which could be located wherever it worked best on the staff—marked middle C, and they chanted to notes relative to that. Go ahead—try singing a few verses of the Latin.

Step to the center to view the high altar from the rear. The giant four-sided swiveling music rack held these huge sheets, allowing monks to sign in unison in the days before printed hymnals. Look up at the paintings in the dome: Church fathers plugging the

planned royal tombs and, above those, the Cano scenes of Mary's life.

The **sacristy** (between the exit and the St. James altarpiece, in the right corner)—filled with closets and drawers for the robes and garments necessary for the high Church pageantry—is worth a look. It's lush and wide open; its gilded ceilings, mirrors, and wooden cabinets give it a light, airy feel. Two grandfather clocks made in London (one with Asian motifs) ensured that everyone got dressed on time. The highlight of this room is another work by Cano—a small, delicate painted wood statue of the *Immaculate Conception,* under the Crucifixion.

Exit the cathedral through its little **shop** (with a nicely curated selection of religious and secular souvenirs). If you walk straight out, you'll come directly to Gran Vía and the stop for minibus #C32 for the Albayzín (to walk to the Albayzín, head left up Gran Vía for two blocks, then turn right on Calle Cárcel Baja). But first, for a fun detour, make a quick left into the little lane immediately upon exiting the cathedral—you'll be just steps from Medievo, a fine purveyor of bulk spices and teas.

Hammam al Ándalus (Arab Baths)
For an intimate and subdued experience, consider some serious relaxation at these Arab baths where you can enjoy three different-temperature pools and a steam room.

Cost and Hours: €42 for 1.5-hour soak in the baths (more if you add a massage), open daily 10:00-24:00, appointments scheduled every even-numbered hour, coed with mandatory swimsuits, quiet atmosphere encouraged, free lockers and towels available, no loaner swimsuits but you can buy one, just off Plaza Nueva—follow signs a few doors down from the TI to Santa Ana 16, paid reservation required—ask about cancellation policy, +34 958 229 978, https://granada.hammamalandalus.com/en.

▲▲Paseo Without the Tourists
While Granada's old town is great for strolling, it's also fun to just be in workaday Granada with everyday locals. A five-minute walk from Plaza Nueva gets you into a delightful urban slice of Andalucía. To enjoy an evening paseo without tourists, start with a tapas crawl along any of the streets beyond Plaza del Carmen (see "Beyond Plaza del Carmen" under "Eating in Granada," later), then stroll down Carrera de la Virgen, off Plaza del Campillo, where there's always something cultural going on. Carrera de la Virgen leads gracefully down to the Paseo del Salón riverbank park, passing the El Corte Inglés department store.

THE ALBAYZÍN

Spain's best old Moorish quarter, with countless colorful corners, flowery patios, and shady lanes, is worth ▲. While the city center of Granada feels more or less like many other pleasant Spanish cities, the Albayzín is unique. You can't say you've really seen Granada until you've at least strolled a few of its twisty lanes. Climb high to the San Nicolás church for the best view of the Alhambra (see "To San Nicolás on Foot," below). Then, to really get to know this neighborhood, wander through its evocative back streets (following my "Exploring the Albayzín Walk," later).

▲▲San Nicolás Viewpoint (Mirador de San Nicolás)

This popular spot, looking across to the Alhambra from the edge of the Albayzín, is one of Europe's most romantic viewpoints. To

best enjoy it, be here at sunset, when the Alhambra glows red and Albayzín seniors share the benches with lovers, hippies, and tourists. For an overpriced drink with the same million-euro view, step into the bar at the recommended El Huerto de Juan Ranas (restaurant just below the viewpoint and to the left, at Calle de Atarazana 8). Order a drink, tip the Roma musicians who perform here, settle in, and consider it a concert. For more advice on drinking and dining with a view, see "Eating in Granada," later.

Getting There: Ride the bus, hike up, or take a taxi (about €5—ride up and explore downhill). The handy Albayzín **minibuses #C31** and **#C32** make a loop through the quarter, getting you scenically and sweatlessly to the San Nicolás viewpoint. Buses depart about every 10 minutes from the Cathedral/Gran Vía or Plaza Nueva.

To San Nicolás on Foot: It's a steep but fascinating 30-minute walk up (see route on the "Albayzín Neighborhood" map). Start from the west end of Plaza Nueva on Calle de Elvira. When you see a pair of signal lights, turn uphill (90 degrees, right) on Calle Calderería Nueva. Follow this stepped street—a virtual tunnel of vendors of imported North African goods, leading to a

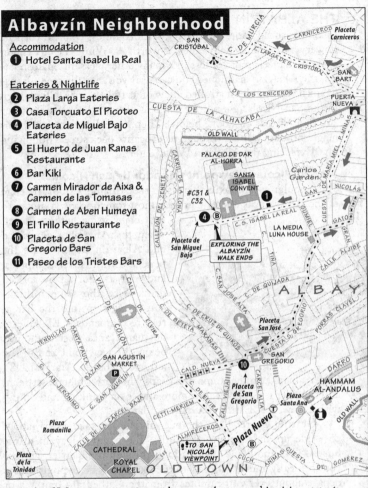

Albayzín Neighborhood

Accommodation

❶ Hotel Santa Isabel la Real

Eateries & Nightlife

❷ Plaza Larga Eateries

❸ Casa Torcuato El Picoteo

❹ Placeta de Miguel Bajo Eateries

❺ El Huerto de Juan Ranas Restaurante

❻ Bar Kiki

❼ Carmen Mirador de Aixa & Carmen de las Tomasas

❽ Carmen de Aben Humeya

❾ El Trillo Restaurante

❿ Placeta de San Gregorio Bars

⓫ Paseo de los Tristes Bars

GRANADA

stretch of Moroccan eateries and pastry shops, and inviting *teterías* (Moorish tearooms). Ahead is the tiny square and Church of San Gregorio.

Placeta de San Gregorio, the tiny junction at the top of Calle Calderería Nueva, has a special hang-loose character. If you're not in a hurry, grab a rickety seat here at Bar las Cuevas, under the classic church facade with potted plants and a commotion of tiled roofs. Enjoy the steady stream of people flowing by. Another fine perch a few steps higher up is Taverna El 22, great for a Reserva 1925 (Granada's best craft beer), *vermut de la casa*, or a sweet sherry (*jerez*).

The **Church of San Gregorio** is the domain of a small group of Franciscan sisters. Step inside for a moment of tranquility and

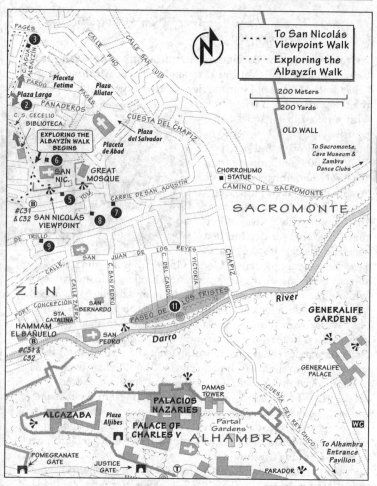

holiness in the midst of this lively town. One of the sisters, dressed in glorious white, kneels at the altar in prayer all day, every day.

Continue your climb up Cuesta de San Gregorio. When you reach the big brick tower of a Moorish-style house, **La Media Luna** (with tall palm trees and a keyhole-style doorway), stop for a photo and a breather, then follow the wall, continuing uphill. At the T-intersection (with the painted black cats on the wall), turn right on Aljibe del Gato. A bit farther on, take the first left onto the stepped Cuesta de María de la Miel. Keep going up, up, up. Take the first right, on Camino Nuevo de San Nicolás, then walk to the street that curves up left. Continue up the curve, and soon you'll see feet hanging from the plaza wall. More steps lead up to the viewpoint. Whew! You made it!

• *Just next to the San Nicolás viewpoint (to your left as you face the Alhambra) is the striking and inviting...*

▲Great Mosque of Granada (Mezquita Mayor de Granada)

Granada has a vital Muslim community. Local Muslims write, "The Great Mosque of Granada signals, after a hiatus of 500 years,

the restoration of a missing link with a rich and fecund Islamic contribution to all spheres of human enterprise and activity." Built in 2003 (with money from the local community and Islamic Arab nations), it has a peaceful view courtyard and a minaret that comes with a live call to prayer five times a day (printed schedule inside). It's stirring to hear the muezzin proclaim "God is Great" from the minaret. Visitors are welcome in the courtyard, which offers Alhambra views without the hedonistic ambience of the more famous San Nicolás viewpoint. Take a look at the video showing the mosque in action.

While many tourists come to Granada to learn about its complex cultural history, not all are aware of the ongoing relevance of its Islamic past. Today, five centuries after the Reconquista, there are almost 2 million Muslims in Spain. Those living in Granada and Andalucía are as Iberian as any modern Spaniard, as were their forebears. When you look out at the Alhambra from the mosque's garden, you are witnessing something built not by outsiders but by the people of Granada, who in that era were Muslim and spoke Arabic. This mosque is an acknowledgment of Islam's great importance to Granada's cultural fabric.

Cost and Hours: Free, daily 11:00-21:00, shorter hours in winter, closes for prayer, +34 958 202 526, www.mezquitadegranada.com.

• *From the San Nicolás viewpoint and the Great Mosque, you're poised to begin my...*

▲Exploring the Albayzín Walk

This little stroll connects two Albayzín viewpoints, the well-known San Nicolás *mirador* and the less-visited San Cristóbal. In the 20 or 30 minutes it takes to complete the walk, you'll see why this hilltop neighborhood is recognized even by the people of Granada as a world apart. To trace the route, see the "Albayzín Neighborhood" map.

Each of the 20 churches in this district sits on a spot once occupied by a mosque. When the Reconquista first arrived in Granada, Christians and Muslims attempted to coexist. But within a short

time, the Christian Spaniards forced Muslims to convert and then expelled them altogether. By 1570 all but a remnant of Granada's Muslim community had been eliminated. What remained, though, was this neighborhood, the oldest part of Granada, with its narrow, cobbled streets and Moorish-style homes called *carmenes*. These large, walled houses with private gardens survive today in the form of the characteristic *carmen* restaurants so popular with visitors.

● **Self-Guided Walk:** From the San Nicolás viewpoint, turn your back to the Alhambra and walk north (passing the Church of San Nicolás on your right and, farther on, the Biblioteca Municipal on your left). The small lane Callejón San Cecilio leads past a white brick arch (on your right)—now a chapel built into the old Moorish wall. You're walking by the scant remains of the pre-Alhambra fortress of Granada.

At the end of the lane, step down to the right through the 11th-century "New Gate" (Puerta Nueva—older than the Alhambra) and into **Plaza Larga.** You're now in the heart of the Albayzín. In medieval times, this tiny square (called "long," because back then it was) served as the local marketplace. It still is a busy market each morning. Casa Pasteles, at the near end of the square, serves good coffee and cakes.

From Plaza Larga, walk up **Calle Agua de Albayzín** (as you face Casa Pasteles, it's to your right). The street, named for the public baths that used to line it, shows evidence of the Moorish plumbing system: gutters. Back when many of Europe's streets were filled with muck, Granada had gutters with drains leading to clay and lead pipes.

At the top of the street, take a left and then another left onto Calle Principal de San Bartolomé, leading you to the **San Bartolomé Church.** This Mudejar church, built on top of a mosque, has a well next to the entrance. Unfortunately, it was one of the many churches set on fire during the Spanish Civil War, and the inside is completely empty.

Now cross the small plaza and continue straight ahead. Take a right onto Calle Larga de San Cristóbal; where the lane ends, look left to see the **San Cristóbal viewpoint.** Lesser known than the San Nicolás viewpoint, this *mirador* presents a great historical view of the Albayzín.

Gazing outward, notice the impressive **old wall** in the middle distance, first built by the Iberians in the 6th century BC and later modified and strengthened by the Romans, Visigoths, and Moors. Behind the wall (and a white fence) is where the initial Roman citadel lay. In the 1200s, as the Nasrid dynasty was under heavy pressure from the Christian kingdoms, it was decided to build a better fortified palace on the hill behind the citadel: the Alhambra. Now notice the white palace farther to the right, behind the old

GRANADA

Safety in the Albayzín

While this charming Moorish district is certainly safe by day, it can be edgy after dark. Most of the area is fine to wander, though many streets are poorly lit, and the maze of lanes can make it easy to get lost and wind up somewhere you don't want to be. Some nervous travelers choose to avoid the neighborhood entirely after dark, but I recommend venturing into the Albayzín to enjoy its restaurants, ideal sunset views, and charming ambience. Just exercise normal precautions: Leave your valuables at your hotel, stick to better-lit streets, and take a minibus or taxi home if you're unsure of your route. Violent crime is rare, but pickpocketing is common.

wall. This is the 15th-century **Palacio de Dar al-Horra,** named after its owner, Aixa la-Horra, who was the mother of Boabdil, the last emir of Granada. (We'll go by this palace later in our walk.) The highest mountain in the Iberian Peninsula is named for Aixa's husband, Sultan Muley Hacén (Abu al-Hasan Ali); legend says he is buried there. You can see the peak, Mulhacén (11,413 feet), from where you stand; it's a pyramid-shaped mountain and usually covered in snow.

From the viewpoint, backtrack to Calle Larga de San Cristóbal and follow it straight ahead to Plaza Larga. From here, walk back through the **Puerta Nueva** gate and down Placeta de las Minas (which becomes Cuesta de María de la Miel) to Camino Nuevo de San Nicolás. Turn right, and you'll soon come to the **Santa Isabel Convent,** where you can buy sweets from the nuns (daily 9:00-18:30). If you need more sustenance, **Placeta de San Miguel Bajo,** just beyond the convent, has options for a meal or a refreshing snack (see "Eating in Granada," later). If you have energy left, a visit to the nearby Palacio de Dar al-Horra (€5, covered by Alhambra Dobla de Oro ticket) is worthwhile for those interested in Spanish-Islamic architecture.

When you are ready to return to the town center, catch minibus #C31 or #C32 from Placeta de San Miguel Bajo, or walk downhill for 10 minutes to Plaza Nueva.

SACROMONTE

The Sacromonte district is home to Granada's thriving Roma community. Marking the entrance to Sacromonte is a statue of Chor-

rohumo (literally, "exudes smoke," and a play on the slang word for "thief": *chorro*). He was a Roma from Granada, popular in the 1950s for guiding people around the city.

While the neighboring Albayzín is a sprawling zone blanketing a hilltop, Sacromonte is much smaller—very compact and very steep. Most houses are burrowed into the cliff wall. Sacromonte has one main street: Camino del Sacromonte, which is lined with caves primed for tourists and restaurants ready to fight over the bill. (Don't come here expecting to get a deal on anything.) Intriguing lanes run above and below this main drag—a steep hike above Camino del Sacromonte is the cliff-hanging, parallel secondary street, Vereda de Enmedio, which is less touristy, with an authentically residential vibe.

Cave Museum of Sacromonte
(Museo Cuevas del Sacromonte)

This hilltop complex, also known as the Center for the Interpretation of Sacromonte (Centro de Interpretación del Sacromonte), is a kind of open-air folk museum about Granada's unique Roma cave-dwelling tradition (though it doesn't have much on the people themselves). Getting there is a bit of a slog for what you'll see—but if you can combine your visit with one of their summertime flamenco and/or classical guitar concerts, it may be worth your while (see museum website for offerings).

The exhibits (with adequate, if not insightful, English descriptions) are spread through a series of whitewashed caves along a ridge, with spectacular views to the Alhambra. As you stroll from cave to cave, you'll see displays on the native habitat (rocks, flora, and fauna); crafts (basket-weaving, pottery making, metalworking, and weaving); and lifestyles (including a look into a typical home and kitchen). There's also an exhibit about other cave-dwelling cultures from around the "troglodyte world," and one about Sacromonte's vital role in the development of Granada's brand of flamenco. As you wander, imagine this in the 1950s, when it was still a bustling community of Roma cave-dwellers.

Cost and Hours: €5, daily 10:00-20:00, off-season until 18:00, Barranco de los Negros, +34 958 215 120, www.sacromontegranada.com.

Getting There: You can ride minibus #C34 from Plaza Nueva (ask driver, *"¿Museo cuevas?"*; departs every 20 minutes) or take a

Granada's Roma (Gypsies)

Both the English word "Gypsy" and its Spanish counterpart, *gitano,* come from the word "Egypt"—from where Europeans once believed these nomadic people originated. Today the preferred term is "Roma," since "Gypsy" has acquired negative connotations (though for clarity's sake, I've used both terms throughout this book).

After migrating from India in the 14th century, the Roma people settled mostly in the Muslim-occupied lands in southern Europe (such as the Balkan Peninsula, then controlled by the Ottoman Turks). Under medieval Muslims, the Roma enjoyed relative tolerance. They were traditionally good with crafts, animals, and blacksmithing.

The first Roma arrived in Granada in the 15th century—and they've remained tight-knit ever since. Today 50,000 Roma call Granada home, many of them in the district called Sacromonte. In most of Spain, Roma are more assimilated into the general population, but Sacromonte has a large, distinct Roma community.

Spaniards, who generally consider themselves to be tolerant, claim that in maintaining such a tight community, the Roma segregate themselves. The Roma call Spaniards *payos* ("whites"). Recent mixing of Roma and *payos* has given birth to the term *gallipavo* (rooster-duck), although who's who depends upon whom you ask.

The Roma challenge is nothing new. Five hundred years ago Queen Isabel issued a proclamation urging the "Gypsies" of her realm to pick and follow a religion, abandon their nomadic ways and settle down, get an honest job, and cease fortune-telling.

The stereotype holds that all Roma are thieves. And sure, some of them are. But others are honest citizens, trying to make their way in the world just like anyone else. Because of the high incidence of petty theft in Granada, it's wise to be cautious when dealing with a Roma person—but it's also important to keep an open mind.

taxi; the bus gives you elevated views. Get off next to the big Venta El Gallo restaurant, along the main road (several *zambra* performance caves line up along here, too—see next). From here, it's a steep 10-minute hike past cave dwellings up to the top of the hill—follow the signs.

Zambra Dance

A long flamenco tradition exists in Granada, and the Roma of Sacromonte are credited with developing this city's unique flavor of the Andalusian art form. Sacromonte is a good place to see *zambra,* a flamenco variation in which the singer also dances. A half-dozen

cave-bars offering *zambra* in the evenings line Sacromonte's main drag. Hotels are happy to book you a seat and arrange the included transfer. Experiencing flamenco in a Roma cave is like seeing art in situ.

Two well-established venues are **Zambra Cueva de la Rocio** (€25, on the hour 20:00-23:00, 1 hour, Camino del Sacromonte 70, +34 958 227 129, www.cuevalarocio.es) and **María la Canastera,** an intimate venue where the Duke of Windsor and actor Yul Brynner came to watch *zambra* (€29 includes drink and bus from hotel, €24 without transport, daily show at 22:00, 1 hour, Camino del Sacromonte 89, +34 958 121 183, www.marialacanastera.com). The biggest operation here is the restaurant **Venta El Gallo,** which has performances of more straightforward flamenco (not specifically *zambra,* €20 includes one drink, daily shows at 21:00 and 22:30, dinner possible beforehand on outdoor terrace, Barranco de los Negros 5, mobile +34 640 147 985, https://cuevaventaelgallo.es). Or consider the summer performances at the Cave Museum (explained earlier).

If you don't want to venture to Sacromonte, try **Casa del Arte Flamenco,** which performs one-hour shows just off Plaza Nueva (€20, at 19:00 and 20:30; Cuesta de Gomérez 11, +34 958 565 767, www.casadelarteflamenco.com).

OUTSIDE THE CITY CENTER
Carthusian Monastery (Monasterio de la Cartuja)

A mile north of town on the way to Madrid, this monastery was built by Carthusian monks between the 16th and 18th centuries. Its unassuming sandstone exterior hides an extraordinarily colorful interior. La Cartuja is sometimes called the "Christian Alhambra" for its elaborate decor.

La Cartuja is a quintessential example of late Spanish Baroque (c. 1650-1750, also known as Churrigueresque). Spanish Baroque took the already-ornate Baroque/Rococo style to even greater heights. With curved lines and odd shapes, it wows the viewer with a multimedia combo of architecture, sculpture, and painting. La Cartuja's unique contribution is to achieve much of that effect with nothing but basic white stucco (plaster) that looks like it was squirted from a can of whipped cream.

Cost and Hours: €5, Daily 10:00-18:00 except closed Sat 12:45- 15:00, +34 958 161 932, www.cartujadegranada.com.

Getting There: It may be easiest to just hop a taxi (about €10). Bus #8 will get you there via its Paseo Cartuja–Monasterio stop. Bus #C34 also gets you very close—couple of long blocks away from the Cristo de la Yedra 33 stop. If the weather is pleasant, the monastery is an easy 25-minute stroll from the city center.

Visiting La Cartuja: In the rooms around the **cloister,** consider monastic life while enjoying paintings of St. Bruno and his Carthusian martyrs placidly meeting their grisly fates. Highlights include Sánchez Cotán's *Last Supper* (in the refectory) and saints Peter and Paul with a trompe l'oeil frame (in the Profundis room).

The highlight is the **church,** which gets increasingly ornate with each step. The **nave** near the entrance (the area for commoners) is impressive enough, covered in white stucco shaped into niches, statues, arches, and garlands. A few steps farther, the **choir** (for the monks) is even more intricately stuccoed with a tangle of vines. The golden choir screen adds a splash of color with paintings by Sánchez Cotán, a Cartuja monk whose work appears throughout. The **altar** (for the priests) is more colorful still. A prickly gold canopy frames a statue of Mary being assumed into heaven. The statue looking on (from the upper right) is St. Bruno, the founder of the contemplative order of Carthusians shown contemplating a cross and a book.

The **sancta sanctorum** (the room behind the altar, seen through the paned-glass window) is the most elaborate of all. With black corkscrew columns supporting a red canopy over a temple for the communion host, the room is an explosion of brilliant art. There's barely a straight line in sight. In the painted dome overhead, the heavens open to reveal the dove of the Holy Spirit surrounded by saints, including St. Bruno hefting the world on his holy shoulders.

The **sacristy** (to the left of the altar) is a white-walled palate cleanser. The stuccoed columns shatter into Baroque fractals of spirals, scallops, waves, and stalactites that recall Moorish decor. At the ripple-ice-cream marble altar, Bruno holds a skull and contemplates it all.

Sleeping in Granada

In July and August, when Granada's streets are littered with sunstroke victims, rooms are plentiful and prices soft. In the crowded months of April, May, September, and October, prices can spike up. Most places offer breakfast for an additional charge.

If you're traveling by car, see "Arrival in Granada" at the beginning of this chapter for driving and parking information.

ON OR NEAR PLAZA NUEVA

Each of these (except the hostel) is professional, plenty comfortable, and perfectly located within a 5- to 10-minute walk of Plaza Nueva.

$$$ **Hotel Casa 1800 Granada** sets the bar for affordable class. Its 25 rooms face the beautiful, airy courtyard of a 17th-century mansion in the lower part of the Albayzín (just steps above Plaza Nueva). Tidy, friendly, and well-run, it has a free, 24-hour refreshments bar and complimentary tea each afternoon (pricier rooms not much different except for the Alhambra views and patios, air-con, elevator, Benalúa 11, +34 958 210 700, www. hotelcasa1800granada.com, info.granada@hotelcasa1800).

$$ **Casa del Capitel Nazarí,** just off the church end of Plaza Nueva, is a restored 16th-century Renaissance manor with 23 tastefully down-to-earth rooms that are intimate, bright, and spacious, most facing a courtyard that hosts art exhibits (RS%, some view rooms, air-con, elevator, afternoon tea/coffee, loaner laptop, pay parking, Cuesta Aceituneros 6, +34 958 215 260, www. hotelcasacapitel.com, info@hotelcasacapitel.com). Their connected annex, $$$ **Mariana Pineda,** has five exquisitely decorated rooms in a former palace.

$$ **Hotel Monjas del Carmen** is a modern hotel with a friendly staff and bright clean rooms. It's nicely located just a few steps off Plaza Nueva (Plaza de los Cuchilleros 13, elevator, pay parking, +34 958 101 619, www.hotelmonjasdelcarmen.com, hotelmonjasdelcarmen@amchoteles.com).

$$ **Hotel Anacapri** is a bright, cool marble oasis with 50 spiffy, clean rooms, a comfortable lounge, and updated bathrooms (family rooms, air-con, elevator, pay parking, 2 blocks toward Gran Vía from Plaza Nueva at Calle Joaquín Costa 7, just a block from cathedral bus stop, +34 958 227 477, www.hotelanacapri.com, reservas@hotelanacapri.com).

$ **Hotel Inglaterra** has with 36 modern, business-style rooms wrapped around a grand central patio in an ideal location. Exterior rooms come with some noise from the popular bars below (air-con, elevator to third floor only, pay parking, Cetti Merien 6, +34 958 221 559, www.hotelinglaterragranada.com, info@hotel-inglaterra. es).

¢ **Oasis Hostel Granada** offers a communal terrace, the scent of fried food, and lots of backpacker bonding, including daily tours and activities on request. It's just a block above the lively Moorish-flavored tourist drag (includes welcome drink with direct booking, pay parking, at the top end of Placeta Correo Viejo at #3, +34 958 215 848, www.oasisgranada.com, granada@hostelsoasis.com).

Granada's Hotels & Restaurants

Accommodations

1. Hotel Casa 1800 Granada
2. Casa del Capitel Nazarí
3. Hotel Monjas del Carmen
4. Hotel Anacapri
5. Hotel Inglaterra
6. Oasis Hostel Granada
7. Hotel Puerta de las Granadas
8. Pensión Landazuri & Cafetería
9. Pensión AlFin
10. Pensión Navarro Ramos
11. OYO Hostal Austria
12. La Bella Granada
13. To Hotel Reina Cristina, Hostals Casa de Reyes & Rodri; Pensión Zurita

Eateries & Tapas Bars

14. Bodegas Castañeda
15. La Auténtica Carmela
16. La Cueva de 1900
17. Arrayanes
18. Los Diamantes
19. B1930
20. Papas Elvira
21. Los Italianos Ice Cream
22. Supermarket (2)
23. Mercado San Agustín
24. La Botillería
25. Taberna La Tana & Bar Los Diamantes II
26. Café Fútbol & La Esquinita de Javi
27. Restaurante Chikito
28. Calle Calderería Nueva Eateries
29. Placeta de San Gregoria Eateries

CHEAP SLEEPS ON CUESTA DE GOMÉREZ

These lodgings, all inexpensive and some ramshackle, are on this street leading from Plaza Nueva up to the Alhambra. Sprinkled among the knickknack stores are the storefront workshops of several guitar makers who are renowned for their handcrafted instruments.

$$ Hotel Puerta de las Granadas rents 36 crisp, clean rooms with a modern vibe. It has a courtyard, a terrace with an Alhambra view, and a handy location (air-con, family rooms, elevator, pay parking, Cuesta de Gomérez 14, +34 958 216 230, www.hotelpuertadelasgranadas.com, reservas@hotelpuertadelasgranadas.com).

$ Pensión Landazuri is run by friendly English-speaking Matilde Landazuri, her son Manolo, and daughters Margarita and Elisa. Their characteristic old house has 15 rooms—ask for a recently renovated one. It boasts hardworking, helpful management and a great roof garden with a splendid Alhambra view (family rooms, no elevator or air-con, pay parking, Cuesta de Gomérez 24, +34 958 221 406, www.pensionlandazuri.com, info@pensionlandazuri.com). The Landazuris also run a good, cheap café open for breakfast and lunch, next door.

$ Pensión AlFin is located just up the street from Pensión Landazuri and run by the same family. Its five high-ceilinged rooms with antique wooden beams and marble columns are colorful and stylish, with Cuban flair. A glass floor in the lobby lets you peer into a well from an ancient house (some rooms with balconies, pay parking, reception at Pensión Landazuri, Cuesta de Gomérez 31, +34 958 228 172, www.pensionalfin.com, info@pensionalfin.com).

¢ Pensión Navarro Ramos is a small cheapie, renting seven quiet, bare bones but clean rooms (5 with private baths) facing away from the street (no elevator, Cuesta de Gomérez 21, +34 958 250 555, www.pensionnavarroramos.com, info@pensionnavarroramos.com, Carmen).

¢ OYO Hostal Austria rents 15 basic, tiny but clean rooms (family rooms, air-con, Cuesta de Gomérez 4, +34 958 227 075, www.oyorooms.com, hola@oyorooms.com).

NEAR THE CATHEDRAL

$ La Bella Granada offers 30 comfortable, business-like rooms (some with balconies) on the charming traffic-free Plaza de Bib-Rambla. The fourth-floor terrace has views of the cathedral and the Alhambra (family rooms, air-con, pay parking, Plaza de Bib-Rambla 4, +34 958 266 712, https://labellasensehoteles.com).

On or near Plaza de la Trinidad

The charming, parklike square called Plaza de la Trinidad, just a short walk west of the cathedral area (Pescadería and Bib-Rambla squares), is home to several good accommodations.

$$ Hotel Reina Cristina has 55 quiet, homey rooms a few steps off Plaza de la Trinidad. Check out the great Mudejar ceiling at the top of the stairwell. The famous Spanish poet Federico García Lorca hid out in this house before being captured and executed by the Guardia Civil during the Spanish Civil War (includes breakfast, cheaper rate without breakfast, air-con, elevator, pay parking, near Plaza de la Trinidad at Tablas 4, +34 958 253 211, www.hotelreinacristina.com, clientes@hotelreinacristina.com).

$$ Hostal Casa de Reyes has 18 well-appointed rooms in two buildings a block off the square. The public areas and rooms are flamboyantly decorated with medieval flair—colorful tiles, wood-carved life-sized figures, and swords (home-cooked dinner available—book in advance, air-con, elevator in one building only, pay parking, Laurel de las Tablas 17, +34 958 295 029, www. hostalcasadereyes.com, info@hostalcasadereyes.com, run with class by Manolo and Carmen).

$ Hostal Rodri has 10 similarly good rooms a few doors down that feel new and classy for their price range. Take in the sun on an "L"-shaped terrace (air-con, elevator, pay parking, Laurel de las Tablas 9, +34 958 288 043, www.hostalrodri.com, info@ hostalrodri.com, run by Manolo's brother José).

$ Pensión Zurita, well-run by personable Francisco and Loli, faces Plaza de la Trinidad. Twelve of the 14 rooms have modern, in-room baths and small exterior balconies. Even with double-pane windows, some rooms may come with night noise from cafés below (air-con, kitchen nook available for guest use, pay parking, Plaza de la Trinidad 7, +34 958 275-020, mobile +34 685 843 745, www. pensionzurita.es, pensionzurita@gmail.com).

IN THE ALBAYZÍN

For the location of this hotel in Granada's most intriguing quarter, see the "Albayzín Neighborhood" map on page 644.

$$$ Hotel Santa Isabel la Real, a handsome 16th-century edifice, has 11 rooms ringing a charming courtyard. Each room is a bit different; basic rooms look to the patio, while pricier rooms have better exterior views. The owners' antiques accentuate the Moorish ambience (breakfast included, air-con, elevator, pay parking, midway between San Nicolás viewpoint and Placeta de San Miguel Bajo on Calle Santa Isabel la Real, minibuses #C31 and #C32 stop nearby, +34 958 294 658, www.hotelsantaisabellareal.com, info@ hotelsantaisabellareal.com).

IN AND NEAR THE ALHAMBRA

To stay on the Alhambra grounds, choose between a famous, overpriced parador and a practical and economical hotel above the parking lot. Both are a half-mile up the hill from Plaza Nueva (see "The Alhambra" map on page 623 for locations).

$$$$ Parador de Granada San Francisco offers 40 designer rooms in a former Moorish palace that was later transformed into a 15th-century Franciscan monastery. It's considered Spain's premier parador—and that's saying something (air-con, free parking, Calle Real de la Alhambra, +34 958 221 440, www.parador.es, granada@parador.es). You must book months ahead to spend the night in this lavishly located, stodgy, and historic palace. Any peasant, however, can drop in for a coffee, drink, snack, or meal. For more about the building's history, see "The Alhambra Grounds" sidebar earlier in this chapter.

$ Hotel Guadalupe, big and modern with 42 sleek rooms, is quietly and conveniently located overlooking the Alhambra parking lot. While it's a 30-minute hike above the town, many—especially drivers—find this to be a practical option (air-con, elevator, special parking rate in Alhambra lot, Paseo de la Sabica 30, +34 958 225 730, www.hotelguadalupegranada.com, reservas@hotelguadalupegranada.com).

Eating in Granada

Restaurants generally serve lunch from 13:00 to 16:00 and dinner from 20:00 until very late (remember, Spaniards don't start din-

ner until about 21:00). Reservations are often required; stop by in advance or call ahead if you're eager to eat somewhere.

Granada's bars pride themselves on serving a small tapas plate free with any beverage—a tradition that's dying out in most of Spain. Save on your food expenses by doing a tapas crawl, and claim your "right" to a free tapa with every drink. Order your drink and wait for the free tapa before ordering food (if you order food too soon, you likely won't get the freebie). Avoid the touristy Calle Navas, right off Plaza del Carmen.

For more budget-eating thrills, buy picnic supplies near Plaza Nueva, and schlep them up into the Albayzín. This makes for a great cheap date at the San Nicolás viewpoint or on one of the scattered squares and lookout points.

In search of an edible memory? A local specialty, *tortilla de Sacromonte*, is a spicy omelet with lamb's brain and other organs. *Berenjenas fritas* (fried eggplant) and *habas con jamón* (small green fava beans cooked with cured ham) are worth seeking out. *Tinto de verano*—a red-wine spritzer with lemon and ice—is refreshing on a hot evening. For tips on eating near the Alhambra, see "Orientation to the Alhambra," earlier.

IN THE ALBAYZÍN

The food scene in the Albayzín can be a mixed bag. Part of the charm of the quarter is the lazy ambience on its squares. My two favorites are Plaza Larga and Placeta de Miguel Bajo. To find a particular square, ask any local, and see the "Albayzín Neighborhood" map on page 644. If dining late, take a taxi back to your hotel; Albayzín back streets can be poorly lit and confusing to follow.

Plaza Larga is extremely characteristic, with tapas bar tables spilling out onto the square, a morning market, and a much-loved pastry shop. Just off Plaza Larga, **$$ Casa Torcuato El Picoteo** is a hardworking eatery serving creative food in a streetside setting. They serve good plates of fresh fish and prizewinning *salmorejo*-style gazpacho (Wed-Sat 12:00-16:00 & 20:00-23:30, Sun 12:00-16:00, closed Mon-Tue, Agua del Albayzín 20, +34 958 292 380). Minibus #C34 stops a block away from the restaurant (or take a €5 taxi from Plaza Nueva).

Placeta de Miguel Bajo, the farthest hike into the Albayzín, boasts a spirited local scene—kids kicking soccer balls, old-timers warming benches, and women gossiping under the facade of a humble church. It's circled by a half-dozen inviting little bars and restaurants—each very competitive with cheap lunch deals. In the evening, the most serious restaurant is **$ Bar Lara** with nice traditional plates, salads, paellas, and fish (closed Wed, Placeta de Miguel Bajo 4, +34 958 209 466). This square is a nice spot to end your Albayzín visit, as there's a viewpoint overlooking the modern city a block beyond the square. Minibus #C31 or #C32 rumbles by every few minutes, ready to zip you back to Plaza Nueva. Or just walk 10 minutes downhill.

Near the San Nicolás Viewpoint

This area is thoroughly touristy—don't expect any local hangouts.

$$$ El Huerto de Juan Ranas Restaurante is a stuffy restaurant below a popular rooftop bar. Packed with a commotion of people taking selfies, sipping cocktails, and paying too much for tapas, it's immediately below the San Nicolás viewpoint and has amazing Alhambra views (daily 11:30-24:00, Calle de Atarazana 8, +34 958 286 925).

$$ Bar Kiki, a laid-back and popular bar-restaurant, is on an unpretentious square with no view but plenty of people-watching. They serve simple dishes outside on rickety tables and plastic chairs. Try their tasty fried eggplant (Thu-Mon 12:00-17:00, closed Tue-Wed, just behind viewpoint at Plaza de San Nicolás 9, +34 958 276 715).

Romantic *Carmenes*

For dinner in a dressy setting and a dreamy Alhambra view, consider dining in a *carmen*, a typical Albayzín house with a garden (buzz to get in). Long ago, wealthy families built these walled mansions with terraced gardens on the hillside. Today, the gardens of many of these *carmenes* host dining tables and romantic restaurants.

$$$ Carmen Mirador de Aixa is small and elegant. You'll pay a little more, but the food is exquisitely presented and the view is worth the price. Try the codfish or ox (Tue-Sat 20:00-23:00, also open for lunch Wed-Sun 13:30-15:30, closed Mon; call to reserve, next to Carmen de las Tomasas at Carril de San Agustín 2, +34 958 223 616).

$$$ Carmen de las Tomasas serves thoughtfully presented gourmet Andalusian cuisine with killer views on three terraces. The service is friendly if slightly formal (Tue-Sat 20:30-24:00, closed Sun-Mon; off-season also open for lunch, closed Mon; reservations required, Carril de San Agustín 4, +34 958 224 108, www.lastomasas.com, Joaquín).

$$ Carmen de Aben Humeya, with outdoor-only seating, is another smart option (daily 12:00-16:00 & 19:00-23:00, reservations required, Cuesta de las Tomasas 12, +34 958 228 345, www.abenhumeya.com).

$$ El Trillo Restaurante is homey, without pretense or big groups. Most tables are in a tranquil garden (with trees but no view); several choice tables upstairs have good Alhambra views. When it's cold, meals are served in their vintage dining room. The menu of modern Mediterranean and Spanish dishes is fun and creative, often with a surprising twist (Wed-Mon generally 20:00-23:00, closed Tue, when reserving ask for garden or terrace; tricky to find—three levels below San Nicolás viewpoint, Calle Aljibe de Trillo 3, +34 958 225 182, www.restaurante-eltrillo.com).

Nightlife

For evening views, try the outdoor bars on **Paseo de los Tristes,** on a terrace over the river gorge: it's like a stage set, with the floodlit Alhambra high above and a happy crowd of locals. While there's no serious restaurant here, the scene is a winner. It's a simple, level, five-minute walk from Plaza Nueva.

NEAR PLAZA NUEVA

For people-watching, consider the many restaurants on Plaza Nueva or Plaza de Bib-Rambla. For locations, see the "Granada's Hotels & Restaurants" map earlier in this section.

$$ Bodegas Castañeda, just a block off Plaza Nueva, has the right mix of lively, central, and cheap. When it's crowded, you need to power your way to the bar to order. When it's quiet, you can order at the bar and grab a little table (same prices). Consider their *tablas combinadas*—variety plates of cheese, meat, and *ahumados* (smoked fish)—and tasty *croquetas de jamón* (breaded and fried béchamel sauce with cured ham). Order a glass of gazpacho. The big kegs tempt you with local vermouths, and wine comes with a free tapa (daily 11:30-16:30 & 19:00-24:00, Calle Almireceros 1, +34 958 215 464). They've expanded with extra tables across the alley (where you can enjoy service and a bit of sanity as you dine), but don't be confused by the neighboring, similar "Antigua Bodega Castañeda" restaurant (run by a relative and not as good).

$$ La Auténtica Carmela, with a casual ambience, is respected for its creative tapas, best enjoyed family-style. You can eat on the outside terrace or take a table in the modern interior (daily 8:00-24:00, just up from Plaza Isabel La Católica at Calle Colcha 13, +34 958 225 794).

$$ La Cueva de 1900, a family-friendly chain on the main drag (with other locations nearby), is appreciated for its simple dishes and quality ingredients. Though it lacks character, it's reliable and low stress. They're proud of their homemade hams, sausages, and cheeses—sold in 100-gram lots and served on grease-proof paper as your free tapa (daily 8:00-23:00, Calle Reyes Católicos 42, +34 958 229 327).

$ Cafetería Landazuri, connected to the recommended Pensión Landazuri, is a smart option for travelers walking down from the Alhambra and anyone who wants quality food at a bargain basement price. Manolo cooks to order; his individual-sized *tortilla española* and salads are good and filling (daily 7:00-16:00, Cuesta de Gomérez 24, +34 958 221 406).

$$ Arrayanes is a good Moroccan restaurant a world apart from my other listings. Brothers Mostafa and Ibrahím treat guests like old friends and will help you choose among the many salads, the *briwat* (chicken-and-cinnamon pastry appetizer), the *pastela* (first-course version of *briwat*), the couscous, or *tajin* dishes. The homemade lemonade with mint pairs well with everything (Wed-Sun 13:30-16:30 & 19:30-23:30, closed Mon-Tue, just off Calle Calderería Nueva—from Church of San Gregorio, walk one block and take first right, uphill to Cuesta Marañas 4 and 7, +34 958 228 401).

$$ Los Diamantes is a modern, packed, high-energy local

favorite for fresh seafood (free tapa with drink, only *raciones* and half-*raciones* on the menu, same price for table seating or bar, daily 12:00-24:00, facing Plaza Nueva at #13, +34 958 075 313).

$ B1930 is a hardworking, bright and basic café serving locals since 1930. It feels like a deli/bakery (but with plenty of alcohol) and serves hearty salads and sandwiches; tapas are served only at the bar. Indoor dining prices are lower than on the terrace. It's great for breakfast (Mon-Fri 7:30-24:00, Sat-Sun from 8:30, air-con, Almireceros 4—just behind Gran Vía but 30 yards off the big street opposite cathedral; +34 958 050 908).

Nightlife: For a happening scene, check out the bars on and around **Calle de Elvira.**

Cheap To-Go Options

A strip of dirt-cheap eateries (including pizza and kebab shops) lines the bottom end of Plaza Nueva. Some have stools, or get your food to go and enjoy it on a sunny plaza bench on the square.

$ Papas Elvira is a popular hole-in-the-wall with fast, cheap food from Morocco and Spain (daily until 24:00, Calle de Elvira 9).

Ice Cream: Italian-run and teeming with locals, popular **Los Italianos** serves ice cream, *horchata* (*chufa*-nut drink), and shakes. For something special, try their *cassata,* a slice (not scoop) of Neapolitan with frozen fruit in a cone. Their photo menu is helpful (daily 9:00-24:00, shorter hours and sometimes closed off-season, across the street from cathedral and Royal Chapel at Gran Vía 4, +34 958 224 034).

Supermarket: Find two handy **Carrefour Express** branches near the cathedral (daily 9:00-22:00, Gran Vía de Colón 11 and Calle Ángel Ganivet 5).

Markets: Though heavy on fresh fish and meat, **Mercado San Agustín** also sells fruits and veggies. If nothing else, it's as refreshingly cool as a meat locker (Mon-Sat 9:00-15:00, closed Sun, very quiet on Mon, a block north of cathedral and a half-block off Gran Vía on Calle Cristo San Agustín). Tucked away in the back of the market is a very cheap and colorful little eatery: **Cafetería San Agustín.** They make their own *churros* and give a small tapa free with each drink (menu on wall). If you are waiting for the cathedral or Royal Chapel to open, kill time in the market.

BEYOND PLAZA DEL CARMEN
Tapas Bars

Granada is a wonderland of happening little tapas bars. As the scene changes from night to night, it's best to simply wander and see what appeals. You'll be amazed at how the vibe changes when you venture just five minutes from the historic and touristic cen-

ter. From Plaza del Carmen, walk through the gauntlet of touristy places along Calle Navas. Calle Navas eventually becomes Calle Virgen del Rosario, with a cluster of fun tapas spots. Consider these places (all within a block of each other):

$$ La Botillería is more relaxed than the standard tapas bar. It has a dressy zone (with nicer tables but the same menu) along with a fun bar scene and tables on a quiet little square. They serve good salads, tasty pork cheeks, and wine by the glass (daily 12:30-24:00, Calle Varela 10, +34 958 224 928).

$$ Taberna La Tana is a tight, intensely Andalusian place with tiny tables and people hanging out in the street. It's well known for its fine tapas, wine, and classic *raciones* (daily 13:00-16:30 & 20:30-24:00, Placeta del Agua 3, +34 958 225 248).

$$ Bar Los Diamantes II is famous for its seafood and happy energy. The menu is easy, prices are great, and locals appreciate fish fried in fresh olive oil. Portions can be huge; prices are the same at the bar, tables, and terrace. The seating in back feels like a fish-and-chips joint. I'd go for the *surtido de pescado* with five kinds of fish (daily 13:00-16:00 & 20:00-23:00, Calle Rosario 12, mobile +34 619 787 828).

$$ Café Fútbol is an old-school classic with an Art Deco vibe, serving basic Spanish dishes. It's the best place in town to finish your pub crawl (or start your day) with a dessert of chocolate and *churros;* a *media-ración* is plenty for two (daily 8:00-24:00 except Sun until 22:30, Plaza de Mariana Pineda 6, +34 958 226 662). It's just two blocks away (to the southwest) from a great local paseo street, Carrera de la Virgen, leading to the river (see "Paseo Without the Tourists," on page 642).

Restaurants for Full Meals

$$ Restaurante Chikito, a venerable classic on a leafy square at the top of a strolling boulevard, serves big plates *(para compartir)* designed to split. Its conservative local clientele appreciates the traditional Spanish cuisine and good prices; Sinatra would enjoy its tapas bar. Originally owned by an Argentine soccer star (see celebrity photos on the walls), it's enthusiastic about its meat. You can dine in the dressy, white-tablecloth interior or on the square (Thu-Tue 12:30-16:30 & 20:00-23:30, closed Wed, Plaza del Campillo 9, +34 958 223 364).

$$ La Esquinita de Javi has a "crank-out-the-fresh-seafood" formula and is run by the same family as Diamantes (listed earlier), but it's more like a normal sit-down restaurant. It has a family-friendly conviviality and an easy menu served in a well-lit, spacious interior and at pleasant tables on the square—where you'll pay more (Tue-Sat 13:00-16:00 & 20:30-23:00, Sun 13:00-16:00,

closed Mon, two locations on Plaza Mariana Pineda, the better one is adjacent to Café Fútbol on downhill side, +34 958 049 142).

Granada Connections

BY PLANE

Granada's airport—Federico García Lorca Granada-Jaén Airport—provides fast connections to Spain's big cities. Iberia and low-cost carrier Vueling offer several direct flights daily to Madrid and Barcelona (code: GRX, +34 913 211 000, www.aena.es, select "F.G.L. Granada-Jaén"). Especially for Barcelona, flying is smart (1.5-hour trip versus 6-14 hours by train or bus).

To get between the airport and downtown, you can take a taxi (€35) or the much cheaper airport bus, timed to leave from directly outside the terminal when flights arrive and depart (€3, 16/day, 45 minutes to/from the Cathedral bus stop at the end of Gran Vía).

BY TRAIN OR BUS

From Granada by Train to: Madrid (5/day, 3.5 hours), **Toledo** (5/day, 4.5 hours, transfer in Madrid), **Málaga** (4/day via AVE, 1 hour; 4/day via cheaper Avant train, 1.5-2 hours, 1 transfer), **Ronda** (1/day, 3 hours), **Barcelona** (4/day, 1 direct, 2 with change in Madrid, 6-8 hours—consider flying instead), **Córdoba** (8/day, 1.5 hours), **Sevilla** (9/day, 2.5 hours). Train info: +34 912 320 320, www.renfe.com.

From Granada by Bus: Almost all buses from Granada are operated by Alsa (www.alsa.es), except the bus to Algeciras, which is run by Avanza (www.avanzabus.com). **Nerja** (6/day, 2-3 hours), **Sevilla** (7/day to Plaza de Armas station, 3 hours), **Córdoba** (6/day, 2.5 hours), **Madrid** (11/day, 5-6 hours; 1 direct to T4 Barajas Airport), **Málaga** (hourly, 1.5-2 hours, several direct to Málaga airport, change  here to continue to La Línea de la Concepción/Gibraltar), **Algeciras** (5/day, 3.5-5.5 hours, Avanza), **Barcelona** (3/day, 14 hours). To reach **Ronda,** change in Antequera; to reach **Tarifa,** change in Algeciras or Málaga.

If there's a long line at the ticket windows, you can use the many ticket machines (press the flag for English).

SEVILLA

Flamboyant Sevilla (seh-VEE-yah) thrums with flamenco music, sizzles in the summer heat, and pulses with passion. It's a place where bullfighting is still politically correct and little girls still dream of being flamenco dancers. While Granada has the great Alhambra and Córdoba has the remarkable Mezquita, Sevilla has soul. As the capital of Andalucía, Sevilla offers a sampler of every Spanish icon, from sherry to matadors to Moorish heritage to flower-draped whitewashed lanes. It's a wonderful-to-be-alive-in kind of place.

As the gateway to the New World in the 1500s, Sevilla boomed when Spain did. The explorers Amerigo Vespucci and Ferdinand Magellan sailed from its great river harbor, discovering new trade routes and abundant sources of gold, silver, cocoa, and tobacco. For more than a century, it all flowed in through the port of Sevilla, bringing the city into a golden age. By the 1600s, Sevilla had become Spain's largest and wealthiest city, home to artists like Diego Velázquez and Bartolomé Murillo, who made it a cultural center. But by the 1700s, Sevilla's golden age was ending, as trade routes shifted, the harbor silted up, and the Spanish empire crumbled.

Nevertheless, Sevilla remained a major stop on the Grand Tour of Europe. European nobles flocked here in the 19th century, wanting to see for themselves the legendary city from story and song: the daring of *Don Giovanni* (Don Juan), the romance of *Carmen*, the spine-tingling cruelty of the Spanish Inquisition, and the comic gaiety of *The Barber of Seville*. To build on this early tourism, Sevilla planned a grand world's fair in 1929. Bad year. But despite the worldwide depression brought on by the US stock market crash, two million visitors flocked to see Sevilla's new parks and new

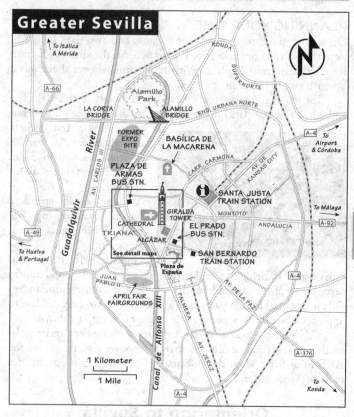

Greater Sevilla

To Itálica & Mérida

RONDA

SUPERNORTE

A-66

Alamillo Park

LA CORTA BRIDGE

ALAMILLO BRIDGE

RND. URBANA NORTE

FORMER EXPO SITE

BASÍLICA DE LA MACARENA

AV. CARLOS III

River

Guadalquivir

PLAZA DE ARMAS BUS STN.

CARR. CARMONA

AV. DE KANSAS CITY

To Airport & Córdoba

A-4

SANTA JUSTA TRAIN STATION

MONTOTO

To Málaga

GIRALDA TOWER

CATHEDRAL

ANDALUCIA

A-92

TRIANA

EL PRADO BUS STN.

A-49

To Huelva & Portugal

ALCÁZAR

See detail maps

SAN BERNARDO TRAIN STATION

Plaza de España

A-4

JUAN PABLO II

AV. DE LA PAZ

APRIL FAIR FAIRGROUNDS

PALMERA

de Alfonso XIII

Canal

1 Kilometer

1 Mile

AV. JEREZ

A-376

A-4

To Ronda

SEVILLA

neighborhoods, which are still beautiful parts of the city. In 1992, Sevilla got a second chance, and this world's fair was an even bigger success, leaving the city with impressive infrastructure: a new airport, six sleek bridges, a modern train station, and the super AVE bullet train (making Sevilla a 2.5-hour side trip from Madrid). In 2007, the main boulevards—once thundering with noisy traffic and mercilessly cutting the city in two—were pedestrianized, enhancing Sevilla's already substantial charm.

Today, Spain's fourth-largest city (pop. 700,000) is Andalucía's leading destination, buzzing with festivals, color, guitars, castanets, and street life, and enveloped in the fragrances of orange trees and jasmine. Sevilla also has its share of impressive sights. It's home to the world's largest Gothic cathedral. The Alcázar is a fantastic royal palace and garden ornamented with Islamic flair. But the real magic is the city itself, with its tangled former Jewish Quarter, riveting flamenco shows, thriving bars, and teeming evening paseo. As James Michener wrote, "Sevilla doesn't *have* ambience, it *is* ambience."

PLANNING YOUR TIME

On a three-week trip, spend three nights and two days here. On even the shortest Spanish trip, I'd zip here on the slick AVE train for a day trip from Madrid. With more time, if ever there was a Spanish city to linger in, it's Sevilla.

The major sights are few and simple for a city of this size. The cathedral and the Alcázar can be seen in about three hours—but

only if you buy tickets in advance. A wander through the Barrio Santa Cruz district takes about an hour.

You could spend a second day touring Sevilla's other sights. Stroll along the bank of the Guadalquivir River and cross Isabel II Bridge to explore the Triana neighborhood and to savor views of the cathedral and Torre del Oro. An evening in Sevilla is essential for the paseo and a flamenco show. Stay out late to appreciate Sevilla on a warm night—one of its major charms.

Córdoba (see next chapter) is the most convenient and worthwhile side trip from Sevilla, or a handy stopover if you're taking the AVE to or from Madrid or Granada. Other side trip possibilities include Arcos or Jerez.

Orientation to Sevilla

For the tourist, this big city is small. The bull's-eye on your map should be the cathedral and its Giralda bell tower, which can be seen from all over town. Nearby are

Sevilla's other major sights, the Alcázar (palace and gardens) and the lively Barrio Santa Cruz district. The central north-south pedestrian boulevard, Avenida de la Constitución, stretches north a few blocks to Plaza Nueva, gateway to the shopping district. A few blocks west of the cathedral are the bullring and the Guadalquivir River, while Plaza de España is a few blocks south. The colorful Triana neighborhood, on the west bank of the Guadalquivir River, has a thriving market and plenty of tapas bars, but no major tourist sights. While most sights are within walking distance, don't hesitate to hop in a taxi to avoid a long, hot walk (they are plentiful and cheap).

TOURIST INFORMATION

Sevilla has provincial tourist offices at the **airport** (Mon-Fri 9:00-19:30, Sat-Sun 9:30-15:00, +34 954 449 128), at **Santa Justa train station** (same hours as airport TI, +34 954 782 002), and near the Alcázar on **Plaza del Triunfo** (Mon-Fri 9:00-19:30, Sat-Sun from 9:30, +34 954 210 005).

At any TI, ask for the English-language magazine *The Tourist* (also available at www.thetouristsevilla.com) and a current listing of sights with opening times. The free monthly events guide—*El Giraldillo*, written in Spanish basic enough to be understood by travelers—covers cultural events throughout Andalucía, with a focus on Sevilla. Helpful websites are www.turismosevilla.org and www.andalucia.org.

Steer clear of orange-and-white "visitor centers" on Avenida de la Constitución (near the Archivo General de Indias) and at Santa Justa train station (overlooking tracks 6-7), which are private enterprises.

ARRIVAL IN SEVILLA

By Train: All long-distance trains arrive at modern **Santa Justa** station, with banks, ATMs, and a TI. Baggage storage is above track 1 (follow signs to *consigna,* security checkpoint open 6:00-24:00). The easy-to-miss TI sits by sliding doors just before the left-hand exit as you leave the station. The plush little AVE Sala Club, designed for business travelers, welcomes those with a first-class AVE ticket and reservation (across the main hall from track 1). The town center is marked by the ornate Giralda bell tower, peeking above the apartment flats (visible from the front of the station—with your back to the tracks, it's at 1 o'clock). To get into the center, it's a flat and boring 25-minute walk or about an €8 taxi ride. By city bus, it's a short ride on #C1 or #21 to the El Prado de San Sebastián bus station (find bus stop 100 yards in front of the train station, €1.40, pay driver), then a 10-minute walk or short tram ride (see next section).

Regional trains use **San Bernardo** station, linked to the center by a tram (see "Getting Around Sevilla," later).

By Bus: Sevilla's two major bus stations—El Prado de San Sebastián and Plaza de Armas—both have information offices, basic eateries, and baggage storage.

The **El Prado de San Sebastián bus station,** or simply "El Prado," covers most of Andalucía (information desk, daily 8:00-20:00, +34 955 479 290, generally no English spoken; baggage lockers/*consigna* at the far end of station, same hours). From the bus station to downtown (and Barrio Santa Cruz hotels), it's about a 15-minute walk: Exit the station straight ahead. When you reach the busy avenue (Menéndez Pelayo) turn right to find a crosswalk

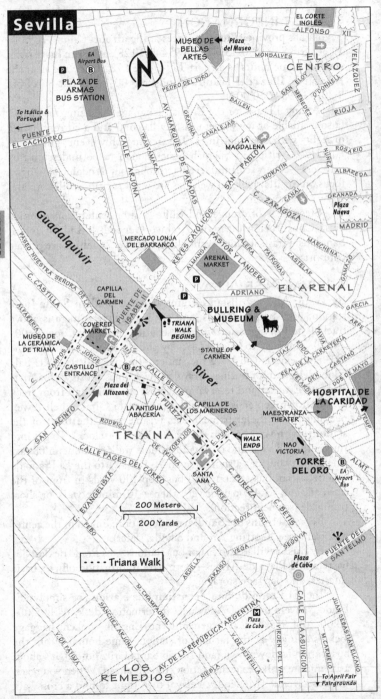

Sevilla

EL CORTE INGLES
C. ALFONSO XII

MUSEO DE BELLAS ARTES
Plaza del Museo

MONSALVES
EL CENTRO
VELAZQUEZ

EA Airport Bus

PLAZA DE ARMAS BUS STATION

PEDRO DEL TORO

SAN ELOY
O'DONNELL

AV. MARQUES DE PARADAS
GRAVINA
CALLE ARJONA
TRASTAMARA
DE MENDEZ
RIOJA

To Itálica & Portugal

PUENTE EL CACHORRO

BAILEN
CANALEJAS
LA MAGDALENA
SAN PABLO
NUÑEZ
ROSARIO
ALBAREDA

Guadalquivir

MOKATIN
CANAL
GRANADA
Plaza Nueva

C. ZARAGOZA
MADRID

PASEO NUESTRA SEÑORA DE LA O

MERCADO LONJA DEL BARRANCO

REYES CATÓLICOS
ALMANSA
PASTOR Y LANDERO
GALERA
PATRONAS

MARCHENA
CASTELAR
GAMAZO

C. CASTILLA
ALFARERIA

ARENAL MARKET

EL ARENAL

CAPILLA DEL CARMEN

ADRIANO
GARCIA
ARFE

MUSEO DE LA CERÁMICA DE TRIANA

COVERED MARKET

PUENTE DE ISABEL II

TRIANA WALK BEGINS

BULLRING & MUSEUM

PAVIA
RODO
CASTAÑO
DOS DE MAYO

CASTILLO ENTRANCE

S. JORGE
CAMPO

B #C3

CALLE BETIS

STATUE OF CARMEN

A. DIAZ
REAL DE LA CARRETERIA
REAL VELARDE

River

HOSPITAL DE LA CARIDAD

Plaza del Altozano

C. PUREZA
LA ANTIGUA ABACERÍA

CAPILLA DE LOS MARINEROS

MAESTRANZA THEATER

C. SAN JACINTO
RODRIGO

TRIANA
DE TRIANA
C. TORRIJOS

E. DUARTE

WALK ENDS

NAO VICTORIA

CALLE PAGES DEL CORRO

SANTA ANA

C. PUREZA
CORREA
C. BETIS

TORRE DEL ORO
B EA Airport Bus
ALMI.

J. EVANGELISTA
J. FEBO

TROYA
FORT
SEGOVIA

200 Meters
200 Yards

VEGA

PUENTE DEL SAN TELMO

- - - - Triana Walk

ARDILLA
PARAISO

Plaza de Cuba

M. CHAMPAGNAT

AV. DE LA REPÚBLICA ARGENTINA

M Plaza de Cuba

CALLE D. LA ASUNCIÓN

SANCHEZ ARJONA
Y. DE FATIMA

NIEBLA
Y. DE SETEFILLA

VIRGEN DEL VALLE

JUAN SEBASTIAN ELCANO
M. CARMELO
VIRGEN DEL VALLE

LOS REMEDIOS

To April Fair Fairgrounds

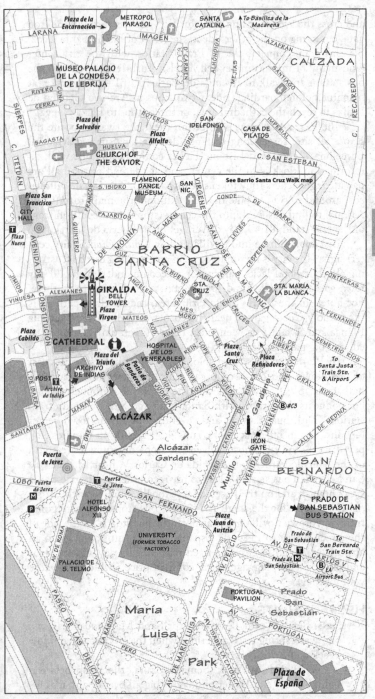

and cross the avenue. Enter the Murillo Gardens through the iron gate, emerging on the other side in the heart of Barrio Santa Cruz. Sevilla's tram connects the El Prado station with the city center (and many of my recommended hotels): Turn left as you exit the bus station and walk to Avenida de Carlos V (€1.40, buy ticket at machine before boarding; ride it two stops to Archivo General de Indias to reach the cathedral area, or three stops to Plaza Nueva).

The **Plaza de Armas bus station** (near the river, opposite the Expo '92 site) serves long-distance destinations such as Madrid, Barcelona, Lagos, and Lisbon. Ticket counters line one wall, an information kiosk is in the center, and at the end of the hall are pay luggage lockers (buy tokens at info kiosk). Taxis to downtown cost around €7. Or, to take the bus, exit onto the main road (Calle Arjona) to find bus #C4 into the center (stop is to the left, in front of the taxi stand; €1.40, pay driver, get off at Puerta de Jerez).

By Car: To drive into Sevilla, follow *Centro Ciudad* (city center) signs. The city is no fun to drive in and parking can be frustrating. If your hotel lacks parking or a recommended plan, I'd pay for a garage (€24/day) and grab a taxi to your hotel from there. For hotels in the Barrio Santa Cruz area, the handiest parking is the Cano y Cueto garage near the corner of Calle Santa María la Blanca and Avenida de Menéndez Pelayo (open daily 24 hours, at edge of big park, underground).

By Plane: Sevilla's San Pablo Airport sits about six miles east of downtown and has several car rental agencies in the arrivals hall (code: SVQ, www.aena.es). The Especial Aeropuerto (EA) bus connects the airport with Santa Justa and San Bernardo train stations, both bus stations, and several stops in the town center (4/hour, less in off-peak hours, runs 4:30-24:00, 40 minutes, €4, pay driver). The two most convenient stops downtown are south of the Murillo gardens on Avenida de Carlos V, near El Prado de San Sebastián bus station (close to my recommended Barrio Santa Cruz hotels); and on the Paseo de Cristóbal Colón, near the Torre del Oro. Look for the small *EA* sign at bus stops. If you're going from downtown Sevilla *to* the airport, the bus stop is on the side of the street closest to Plaza de España. To taxi into town, go to an airport taxi stand to ensure a fixed rate (€25 by day, €27 at night and on weekends, luggage extra, confirm price with driver before your journey).

HELPFUL HINTS

Festivals: Sevilla's peak season is April and May, and it has two one-week spring festival periods when the city is packed: Holy Week and April Fair.

While **Holy Week** (Semana Santa, the week between Palm Sunday and Easter Sunday) is big all over Spain, it's big-

gest in Sevilla. Locals prepare for the event starting up to a year in advance. What would normally be a five-minute walk can take an hour if a religious procession crosses your path, and many restaurants stop serving meat during this time. But any hassles become totally worthwhile as you listen to the *saetas* (devotional songs) and give in to the spirit of the festival.

Then, after taking two weeks off to catch its communal breath, Sevilla holds its **April Fair** (April 23-29 in 2023). This is a celebration of all things Andalusian, with plenty of eating, drinking, singing, and merrymaking (though most of the revelry takes place in private parties at a large fairground).

Book rooms well in advance for these festival times. Prices can be sky-high and many hotels have four-night minimums.

Rosemary Scam: In the city center, and especially near the cathedral, you may encounter women thrusting sprigs of rosemary into the hands of passersby, grunting, *"Toma! Es un regalo!"* ("Take it! It's a gift!"). The twig is free...but then they grab your hand and read your fortune for a tip. Coins are "bad luck," so the minimum payment they'll accept is €5. They can be very aggressive, but you don't need to take their demands seriously—don't make eye contact, don't accept a sprig, and say firmly but politely, *"No, gracias."*

Laundry: Lavandería Tintorería Roma offers quick and economical drop-off service (Mon-Fri 10:00-13:30 & 17:30-20:00, Sat 10:00-13:30, closed Sun, a few blocks west of the cathedral at Calle Arfe 22, +34 954 210 535). Near the recommended Barrio Santa Cruz hotels, **La Segunda Vera Tintorería** has two self-service machines (Mon-Thu 10:00-13:30 & 17:30-20:00, Fri 10:00-13:30, closed Sat-Sun, about a block from the eastern edge of Barrio Santa Cruz at Avenida de Menéndez Pelayo 11, +34 954 536 376). For locations, see the "Sevilla Hotels" map, later.

Bike Rental: This biker-friendly city has designated bike lanes and a public bike-sharing program (€14 one-week subscription, first 30 minutes of each ride free, €2 for each subsequent hour, www.sevici.es). Ask the TI about this and other bicycle-rental options.

Architecture Guidebook: For a more in-depth exploration into Sevilla's trademark brickwork, ceramic, and wrought-iron architecture, consider downloading *Regionalismo,* written by Robert Wright, who leads some of my Spain tours. This guidebook (available as a PDF) features seven 30-minute walks (approximately 15 buildings each) through the city center and to neighborhoods outside the typical tourist circuit (€5.50, www. endlessmile.com).

Sevilla at a Glance

▲▲▲**Flamenco** Flamboyant, riveting music-and-dance performances, offered at clubs throughout town. See page 733.

▲▲**Sevilla Cathedral** The world's largest Gothic church, with Columbus' tomb and climbable bell tower. **Hours:** Mon-Sat 11:00-17:00 (July-Aug until 18:00), Sun 14:30-19:00 (July-Aug from 14:00). See page 686.

▲▲**Royal Alcázar** Palace built by the Moors in the 10th century, revamped in the 14th century, and still serving as royal digs. **Hours:** Daily 9:30-19:00, Oct-March until 17:00. See page 697.

▲▲**Hospital de la Caridad** Former charity hospital (funded by likely inspiration for Don Juan) with gorgeously decorated chapel. **Hours:** Mon-Fri 10:30-19:30, Sat-Sun 14:00-19:00. See page 708.

▲▲**Church of the Savior** Sevilla's second-biggest church and home to some of its most beloved statues used for religious festivals. **Hours:** Mon-Sat 11:00-18:00 (July-Aug from 10:00), Sun 15:00-19:30. See page 713.

▲▲**Basílica de la Macarena** Church and museum with much-venerated Weeping Virgin statue and Holy Week floats. **Hours:** Daily 9:00-14:00 & 18:00-21:30, mid-Sept-May daily 9:00-14:00 & 17:00-21:00 except Sun from 9:30. See page 719.

▲▲**Triana** Energetic, colorful neighborhood on the west bank of the river. See page 722.

▲▲**Bullfight Museum** Guided tour of the bullring and its museum. **Hours:** Daily 9:30-21:00, Nov-March until 19:30, until 15:00 on fight days. See page 726.

▲▲**Evening Paseo** Locals strolling around the city. **Hours:** Best paseo scene 19:00-21:00, until very late in summer. See page 735.

▲**Museo Palacio de la Condesa de Lebrija** 18th-century aristocratic mansion. **Hours:** Daily 10:00-14:15 & 15:15-18:00. See page 715.

▲**Flamenco Dance Museum** High-tech museum on the history and art of flamenco. **Hours:** Daily 10:00-19:00. See page 716.

▲**Museo de Bellas Artes** Andalucía's top paintings, including works by Murillo and Zurbarán. **Hours:** Tue-Sat 9:00-21:00, until 15:00 on Sun and in summer, closed Mon year-round. See page 716.

GETTING AROUND SEVILLA

Most visitors have a full and fun experience in Sevilla without ever riding public transportation. The city center is compact, and most of the major sights are within easy walking distance.

By Taxi: Sevilla is a great taxi town; they're plentiful and cheap. Two or more people should go by taxi rather than public transit. You can hail one showing a green light anywhere, or find a cluster of them parked by major intersections and sights (€1.35 drop rate, €1/kilometer, €3.50 minimum; about 20 percent more evenings and weekends; calling for a cab adds about €3). A quick daytime ride in town will generally fall within the €3.60 minimum. Although I'm quick to take advantage of taxis, note that because of one-way streets and traffic congestion it's often just as fast to hoof it between central points.

By Bus, Tram, and Metro: A single trip on any form of city transit costs €1.40. Skip the various transit cards—they are a hassle to get and not a good value for most tourists. Various #C **buses**, which are handiest for tourists, make circular routes through town (note that all of them except the #C6A eventually wind up at Basílica de la Macarena). For all buses, buy your ticket from the driver. The #C3 stops at Murillo Gardens, Triana, then La Macarena. The #C4 goes the opposite direction, but without entering Triana.

A **tram** *(tranvía)* makes just a few stops in the heart of the city but can save you a bit of walking. Buy your ticket at the machine on the platform before you board (runs about every 7 minutes Sun-Thu until 23:00, Fri-Sat until 1:45 in the morning). It makes five city-center stops (from south to north): San Bernardo (at the San Bernardo train station), Prado San Sebastián (next to El Prado de San Sebastián bus station), Puerta Jerez (south end of Avenida de la Constitución), Archivo General de Indias (next to the cathedral), and Plaza Nueva (beginning of shopping streets).

Sevilla also has a one-line underground **Metro,** but it's of little use to travelers since its primary purpose is to connect the suburbs with the center. Its downtown stops are at the San Bernardo train station, El Prado de San Sebastián bus station, and Puerta Jerez.

Tours in Sevilla

🎧 To sightsee on your own, download my free Sevilla City Walk audio tour.

ON FOOT
Sevilla Walking Tours

A joy to listen to, **Concepción Delgado** is an enthusiastic teacher who takes small groups on English-only walks. Although you can just show up, it's smart to confirm departure times and reserve a spot (4-person minimum, none on Sun and certain holidays, mobile +34 616 501 100, www.sevillawalkingtours. com, info@sevillawalkingtours. com). Because she's a busy mom, Concepción sometimes sends her equally excellent colleagues to lead these tours.

City Walk: This fine two-hour introduction to Concepción's hometown is a fascinating cultural show-and-tell in which she skips the famous monuments and shares intimate insights the average visitor misses. Other than seeing the cathedral and Alcázar, this to me is the most interesting two hours you could spend in Sevilla (€18/person, Mon-Sat at 10:30, check website for Dec-Feb and Aug schedule, meet at statue in Plaza Nueva).

Cathedral and Alcázar Tours: For those wanting to really understand the city's two most important sights, Concepción offers 75-minute visits to the **cathedral** (€12 plus admission) and the **Alcázar** (€28 including admission, must book in advance). These tours are scheduled to fit efficiently after Concepción's city walk (€2 discount if combined). Meet at 13:30 at the statue in Plaza del Triunfo (cathedral tours—Mon, Wed, and Fri; Alcázar tours—Tue, Thu, and Sat).

Other Tours: Concepción offers a Tasty Culture tour covering social life and popular traditions (€26, includes a drink and tapa), and a *Game of Thrones* add-on to the Alcázar tour.

All Sevilla Guided Tours

Licensed guides Susana and Elena offer quality private tours (€170/2.5 hours). They also run a Monuments Tour covering the Sevilla basics: cathedral, Alcázar, and Barrio Santa Cruz (€25/person plus admissions, Mon-Sat at 14:00, 2.5 hours, leaves from Plaza del Triunfo, mobile +34 606 217 194, www.allsevillaguides. com).

Sevilla a la Carta

Julia Rozet adopted Sevilla as her home in 2008 and specializes in themed tours that explore different, lesser-known facets of the city like the old port and connections to the slave trade. If you visit during one of Sevilla's many festivals, Julia can explain the traditions behind all the commotion (€20, families with children welcome, mobile +34 633 083 961, www.sevillalacarta.com).

"Free" Walks

Free tour companies dominate the walking tour scene in Sevilla. They are not "free," as you're aggressively hit up for a tip at the end, and you'll spend a good part of the tour hearing a sales pitch for the companies' paid offerings. The walk spiel is entertaining but with little respect for history or culture, and your "guide" is often a student who has memorized a script. Still—it's "free" and you get what you pay for. You'll see these guides with color-coded umbrellas at various starting points around the city.

Food Tours

For information on tapas tours and cooking lessons, see the sidebar on page 745.

BY BUS AND BUGGY

Hop-On, Hop-Off Bus Tours

Two competing city bus tours leave from the curb near the riverside Torre del Oro. You'll see parked buses and salespeople handing out fliers. Each tour does about an hour-long swing through the city with recorded narration. The tours, which allow you to hop on and off at 14 stops, are heavy on Expo '29 and Expo '92 neighborhoods—of limited interest nowadays. While the narration does its best, Sevilla is most interesting in places buses can't go (daily 10:00-22:00, off-season until 18:00, €22 for red bus: www.city-sightseeing.com; €18 online in advance for green bus: http://sevilla.busturistico.com).

Horse-and-Buggy Tours

A carriage ride is a classic, popular way to survey the city and to enjoy María Luisa Park (€45 for a 45-minute clip-clop, much more during Holy Week and the April Fair, find a likable English-speaking driver for better narration). There are several departure points around town: Look for rigs at Plaza de América, Plaza del Triunfo, the Archivo General de Indias, the Alfonso XIII Hotel, and Plaza de España.

Holy Week (Semana Santa)

Holy Week—the week between Palm Sunday and Easter—is a major holiday throughout the Christian world, but nowhere is it celebrated with as much fervor as in Andalucía, especially Sevilla. Holy Week is all about the events of the Passion of Jesus Christ: his entry into Jerusalem, his betrayal by Judas and arrest, his crucifixion, and his resurrection. In Sevilla, on each day throughout the week, 60 neighborhood groups (brotherhoods, called *hermandades* or *cofradías*) parade from their neighborhood churches to the cathedral with floats depicting some aspect of the Passion story. (With the help of my Sevilla guides and friends, this amazing event was featured in my *Rick Steves' European Easter* public television special, viewable at RickSteves.com/watch-read-listen.)

As the week approaches, anticipation grows: Visitors pour into town, grandstands are erected along parade routes, and TV stations anxiously monitor the weather report. (The floats are so delicate that rain can force the processions to be called off—a crushing disappointment.)

By midafternoon of any day during Holy Week, thousands line the streets. The parade begins. First comes a line of "penitents" carrying a big cross, candles, and incense. The *penitentes* perform their penance publicly but anonymously, their identities obscured by pointy, hooded robes. (The penitents' traditional hooded garb has been worn for centuries—long before such hoods became associated with racism in the American South.) Some processions are silent, but others are accompanied by beating drums, brass bands, or wailing singers.

A hush falls over the crowd as the floats (*los pasos*) approach.

Barrio Santa Cruz Walk

The soul of Sevilla is best found in the narrow lanes of its oldest quarter—the Barrio Santa Cruz. Of Sevilla's once-thriving Jewish neighborhood, only the tangled street plan and a wistful Old World ambience survive. This classy maze of lanes (too tight for most cars), small plazas, tile-covered patios, and whitewashed houses with wrought-iron latticework draped in flowers is a great refuge from the summer heat and bustle of Sevilla. The streets are narrow—some with buildings so close they're called "kissing lanes." A happy result of the narrowness is shade: Locals claim the Barrio Santa Cruz is three degrees cooler than the rest of the city.

First comes a Passion float, showing Christ in some stage of the drama—being whipped, appearing before Pilate, or carrying the cross to his execution. More penitents follow—with hundreds or even thousands of participants, a procession can stretch out over a half-mile. All this sets the stage for the finale—typically a float of the Virgin Mary, who represents the hope of resurrection.

The elaborate floats feature carved wooden religious sculptures, most embellished with gold leaf and silverwork. They can be adorned with fresh flowers, rows of candles, and even jewelry on loan from the congregation. Each float is carried by 30 to 50 men *(los costaleros)*, who labor unseen—although you might catch a glimpse of their shuffling feet. The bearers wear turban-like headbands to protect their heads and necks from the crushing weight (the floats can weigh as much as three tons). Two "shifts" of float carriers rotate every 20 minutes. As a sign of their faith, some men carry the float until they collapse.

As the procession nears the cathedral, many pass through the square called La Campana, south along Calle Sierpes, and through Plaza de San Francisco. (Some parades follow a parallel route a block or two east.) Grandstands and folding chairs are filled by VIPs and Sevilla's prominent families. Thousands of candles drip wax along the well-trod parade routes, forming a waxy buildup that causes shoes and car tires to squeal for days to come.

Being in Sevilla for Holy Week is both a blessing and a curse. It's a remarkable spectacle, but it's extremely crowded. Parade routes can block your sightseeing for hours. Check printed schedules if you want to avoid them. But, if a procession blocks your way, look for a crossing point marked by a red-painted fence, or ask a guard. Even if all you care about on Easter is a chocolate bunny, the intense devotion of the Andalusian people during their Holy Week traditions is an inspiration to behold.

SEVILLA

The *barrio* is made for wandering. Getting lost is easy, and I recommend doing just that. But to get started, here's a self-guided  plaza-to-plaza walk that loops you through the *corazón* (heart) of the neighborhood and back out again. Along the way, we'll get an introduction to some of the things that give Sevilla its unique charm.

🎧 Download my free Sevilla City Walk audio tour, which

Barrio Santa Cruz Walk

1. Plaza de la Virgen de los Reyes
2. Nun Goodies
3. Plaza del Triunfo
4. Patio de Banderas
5. Calle Agua
6. Plaza de Santa Cruz
7. Casa de Murillo & Monasterio de San José del Carmen
8. Calle Reinoso
9. Plaza de los Venerables
10. Plaza de Doña Elvira

complements this walk (following stops at the Sevilla Cathedral and Royal Alcazar).

When to Go: Tour groups often trample the *barrio*'s charm in the morning. I find that early evening—around 19:00—is the ideal time to explore the quarter.

• Start in the square in front of the cathedral, at the lantern-decked fountain in the middle that dates from Expo '29.

1 Plaza de la Virgen de los Reyes

Do a 360-degree spin and take in some of Sevilla's signature sights. There's the gangly cathedral with its soaring Giralda bell tower—

ground zero of the city. To the right is the ornate red Archbishop's Palace, a center of power since Christians first conquered the city from the Moors in 1248. Continuing your spin, the next building is almost a cliché of early 20th-century (and now government-protected) Sevillian architecture—with gold-enrod trim and ironwork balconies. The street stretching away from the cathedral is lined with another Sevillian trademark—tapas bars, housed in more typical Andalusian  buildings with their ironwork. Continuing your spin, there's a row of Sevilla's signature orange trees. Hiding in the orange trees is a statue of Pope John Paul II, who performed Mass here before a half-million faithful Sevillians during a 1982 visit. Finally, you return to the Giralda bell tower.

The Giralda encapsulates Sevilla's 2,000-year history. The large blocks that form the very bottom of the tower date from when Sevilla was a Roman city. (Up close, you can actually read some Latin inscriptions.) The tower's main trunk, with its Islamic patterns and keyhole arches, was built by the Moors (with bricks made of mud from the river) as a call-to-prayer tower for a mosque. The top (16th-century Renaissance), with its bells and weathervane figure representing Faith, was added after Christians reconquered Sevilla, tore down the mosque, built the sprawling cathedral—and kept the minaret as their bell tower.

This square is dedicated to that Christian reconquest, and to the Virgin Mary. Turn 90 degrees to the left as you face the cathedral and find (hiding behind the orange trees) the Virgin of the Kings (see her blue-and-gold tiled plaque on the white wall). This is one of the many different versions of Mary you'll see around town—some smiling, some weeping, some triumphant—each appealing to a different type of worshipper.

Notice the columns and chains that ring the cathedral, as if put there to establish a border between the secular and Catholic worlds. Indeed, that's exactly the purpose they served for centuries, when Sevillians running from the law merely had to cross these chains to find sanctuary—like crossing the county line. Many of these columns are far older than the cathedral, having originally been made for Roman and Visigothic buildings and later recycled by medieval Catholics.

• *Facing the cathedral, turn left and walk toward the next square to find some...*

❷ Nun Goodies

The white building on your left was an Augustinian convent. Step inside the door at #3 to meet (but not see) a cloistered nun behind a fancy *torno* (a lazy Susan the nuns spin to sell their goods while staying hidden). The sisters raise money by selling rosaries, incense, prayer books, and communion wafers (*tabletas*—bland, but like sin-free cookies). Consider buying something here just as a donation. The sisters, who speak only Spanish, have a sense of humor—have fun practicing your Spanish with them (Mon-Sat 9:00-13:00 & 16:45-18:15, Sun 10:00-13:00).

• *Step into the square marked with a statue of the Virgin atop a pillar. This is...*

❸ Plaza del Triunfo

Bordered by three of Sevilla's most important buildings—the cathedral, the walled Alcázar, and the Archivo General de Indias (filled with historic papers)—this place was the center of the action during the golden age of the 16th and 17th centuries. Businessmen from all over Europe gathered here to trade in the exotic goods pouring in from the New World. That wealth produced a flowering of culture, including Sevilla's most beloved painter, Bartolomé Murillo, who is honored at the base of the pillar (the sculptor used a famous painting by Murillo for his model of the Immaculate Conception on top).

The "Plaza of Triumph" is named for yet another Virgin statue atop a smaller pillar at the far end of the square. This Virgin helped the city miraculously "triumph" over the 1755 earthquake that destroyed Lisbon but only rattled Sevilla.

• *Before leaving the square, consider stopping at the TI. Then pass through the arched opening in the Alcázar's spiky, crenellated wall. You'll emerge into a white-and-goldenrod courtyard called the...*

❹ Patio de Banderas

The Banderas Courtyard (as in "flags," not Antonio) was part of the Alcázar, the Spanish king's residence when he was in town. This square was a military parade ground, and the barracks surrounding it housed the king's bodyguards.

Before the Alcázar was the palace of the Christian king, it was the palace of the Muslim Moors who ruled Sevilla. Archaeologists found remains of this palace (as well as 2,000-year-old Roman ruins) beneath the courtyard. They excavated it, then covered the site to protect it.

Orange trees abound. Because they never lose their leaves, they provide constant shade. But forget about eating the oranges. They're bitter and used only to make vitamins, perfume, cat food, and that marmalade you can't avoid in British B&Bs. But when they blossom (for three weeks in spring, usually in April), the aroma is heavenly. (You can identify a bitter orange tree by its leaves—they have a tiny extra leaf between the main leaf and the stem.)

The far-right corner of this square usually has a queue of people waiting to buy Alcázar tickets (which you'll avoid by buying yours online in advance). Head for the arch at the far-left corner, do a 180, and enjoy the view of the Giralda bell tower.

• *Exit the courtyard through the Judería arch. Go down the long, narrow passage still paved with its original herringbone brickwork. Emerging into the light, you'll be walking alongside the red Alcázar wall. Take the first left at the corner lamppost and you'll pass another gate. A gate here was locked each evening—at first to protect the Jewish community (when they were the privileged elite—bankers, merchants, tax collectors) and later during times of persecution to isolate them (until they were finally expelled in 1492). Passing the gate, go right, through a small square, and follow the long narrow alleyway called...*

❺ Calle Agua

This narrow lane is typical of the *barrio*'s tight quarters, born when the entire Jewish community was forced into a small segregated ghetto. As you walk, on your right is one of the older walls of Sevilla, dating back to Moorish times. Glancing to the left, peek through iron gates for occasional glimpses of the flower-smothered patios of restaurants and exclusive private residences (sometimes open for viewing). The patio at #2 is a delight—ringed with columns, filled with flowers, and colored with glazed tiles. The tiles are not merely decorative—they keep buildings cooler in the summer heat. If the gate is closed, try the next door down, or just look up for a hint of the garden's flowery bounty. Admire the expensive ornamental mahogany eaves.

The plaque above and to the left of #2 remembers Washington Irving. He and Romantic novelists, poets, and painters of his era

Sevilla's Jews

In the summer of 1391, smoldering anti-Jewish sentiment flared up in Sevilla. On June 6, Christian mobs ransacked the city's Jewish Quarter (Judería). Approximately 4,000 Jews were killed, and 5,000 Jewish families were driven from their homes. Synagogues were stripped and transformed into churches. The former Judería eventually became the neighborhood of the Holy Cross—Barrio Santa Cruz. Sevilla's uprising spread through Spain (and Europe), the first of many nasty pogroms during the next century.

Before the pogrom, Jews had lived in Sevilla for centuries as the city's respected merchants, doctors, and bankers. They flourished under the Muslim Moors. After Sevilla was "liberated" by King Ferdinand III (1248), Jews were given protection by Castile's kings and allowed a measure of self-government, though they were confined to the Jewish neighborhood. But by the 14th century, Jews were increasingly accused of everything from poisoning wells to ritually sacrificing Christian babies. Mobs killed suspected Jews, and some of Sevilla's most respected Jewish citizens had their fortunes confiscated.

After 1391, Jews were forced to make a choice: Be persecuted (even killed), relocate, or convert to Christianity. The newly Christianized—called conversos (converted) or marranos (swine)—were constantly under suspicion of practicing their old faith in private, and thereby undermining true Christianity. Fanning the mistrust were the perceptions of longtime Christians, who felt threatened by this new social class of converted Jews, who now had equal status.

To root out the perceived problem of underground Judaism, the "Catholic Monarchs," Ferdinand and Isabel, established the Inquisition in Spain (1478). Under the direction of Grand Inquisitor Tomás de Torquemada, these religious courts arrested and interrogated conversos suspected of practicing Judaism. Using long solitary confinement and torture, they extracted confessions.

On February 6, 1481, Sevilla hosted Spain's first auto-da-fé ("act of faith"), a public confession and punishment for heresy. Six accused conversos were paraded barefoot into the cathedral, forced to publicly confess their sins, then burned at the stake. Over the next three decades, thousands of conversos were tried and killed in Spain.

In 1492, the same year the last Moors were driven from Spain, Ferdinand and Isabel decreed that all remaining Jews convert or be expelled. In what became known as the Sephardic Diaspora, Spain's Jews left mostly for Portugal and North Africa (many ultimately ended up in Holland). Spain emerged as a nation unified under the banner of Christianity.

inspired early travelers and popularized the Grand Tour. Aristocrats back in the 19th century had their favorite stops as they gallivanted around Europe, and Sevilla—with its operas (like *Carmen*), bullfighting, and flamenco—was hard to resist.

Emerging at the end of the street, turn around and look back at the openings of two old pipes built into the wall. These 12th-century Moorish pipes once carried fresh spring water to the Alcázar (and today give the street its name—Agua). They were part of a 10-mile-long aqueduct system that was originally built by the ancient Romans and expanded by the Moors, serving some parts of Sevilla until the 1600s. You're standing at an entrance into the pleasant Murillo Gardens (through the iron gate), formerly the fruit and vegetable gardens for the Alcázar.

• *Don't enter the gardens now, but instead cross the square diagonally, and continue 20 yards down a lane to the...*

❻ Plaza de Santa Cruz

Arguably the heart of today's *barrio*, this pleasant square is graced with orange trees and draping vines, with a hedged garden in the center.

This square encapsulates the history of the neighborhood. In early medieval times, it was the *Judería*, with a synagogue standing where the garden is today. When the Jews were rousted in the 1391 pogrom, the synagogue was demolished, and a Christian church was built on the spot (the Church of Santa Cruz). It was the neighborhood church of the Sevillian painter Bartolomé Murillo (and later his burial site). But when the French (under Napoleon) invaded, the church was demolished. A fine 17th-century iron cross in the center of the square now marks the former site of the church. This "holy cross" *(santa cruz),* from a renowned Sevillian forge, has inspired similar-looking crosses still carried in Holy Week processions, and gave this former Jewish Quarter its Christian name.

At #9, you can peek into a lovely courtyard that's proudly been left open so visitors can enjoy it. It's a reminder of the traditional Andalusian home, built around an open-air courtyard. The square is also home to the recommended Los Gallos flamenco bar, which puts on nightly performances (see "Nightlife in Sevilla," later).

• *Exit the square right of Los Gallos, going uphill (north) on Calle Santa Teresa. Notice millstones in the walls. Tour guides like to say this was a way for a wealthy miller to show off (like someone today parking a fancy car in their driveway). Notice also the well-worn ancient column functioning as a cornerstone. With the ruins of Roman Itálica nearby, Sevilla had a ready quarry for such ornamental corner pieces.*

After the kink in the road, find #8 (on the left).

❼ Casa de Murillo and Monasterio de San José del Carmen

Sevilla's famous painter, Bartolomé Esteban Murillo, lived here in the 17th century. Born and raised in Sevilla, Murillo spent his final years here in this plush two-story mansion with a central patio. He soaked in the ambience of street life in this characteristic *barrio* and reproduced it in his paintings of cute beggar children. He also painted iconic versions of local saints and took Sevilla's devotion to the Virgin to another level with his larger-than-life Immaculate Conceptions. Wedding extreme religiosity with down-to-earth street life, he captured the Sevillian spirit.

Directly across from Casa de Murillo is the enormous wooden doorway of the Monasterio de San José del Carmen. This convent was founded by the renowned mystic, St. Teresa of Ávila. When she arrived in Sevilla in 1575, it was Spain's greatest city, and she stayed here for 10 years. Today, the Baroque convent keeps some of Teresa's artifacts and spiritual manuscripts, but it's closed to the public except for early morning Mass (Mon-Fri at 8:45 and Sun at 9:00).

• *Continue north on Calle Santa Teresa, then take the first left on Calle Lope de Rueda (just before the popular Las Teresas café). Here you enter a series of very narrow lanes. Take a left again, then right on...*

❽ Calle Reinoso

This street—so narrow that the buildings almost touch—is one of the *barrio*'s "kissing lanes." A popular explanation suggests the buildings were so close together to provide maximum shade. But the history is more complex than that: This labyrinthine street plan goes back to Moorish times when this area was a tangled market. Later, this was the densely populated Jewish ghetto.

• *Leaving the "kissing zone," just to the left, the street spills onto...*

❾ Plaza de los Venerables

This tiny square is another candidate for "heart of the *barrio*," as it captures the romantic ambience that inspired so many operas in Sevilla (from *Don Giovanni* and *Carmen* to *The Barber of Seville* and *The Marriage of Figaro*). The square also serves as the lively hub for several narrow streets that branch off it, oozing local color. With its vibrant buildings and visitor-oriented businesses, it typifies the *barrio* today: traditional and touristy at the same time.

The harmonious red-and-white Sevillian-Baroque Hospital

de los Venerables (1675) was once a retirement home for old priests (the "venerable" ones). It's now a cultural foundation worth visiting for its ornate church and small but fine collection of Sevillian paintings (see listing later, under "Sights in Sevilla"). The ceramic shop at the far end of the square welcomes tourists to use its bus-tour-friendly WCs.

• *Pass through the square. On Calle de Gloria is an interesting tile map of the Jewish Quarter. (Find yourself in the lower left, second row up, third tile from the left.) Now continue west on Calle de Gloria, where you'll soon emerge into...*

⑩ Plaza de Doña Elvira

This square—with orange trees, tile benches, and a stone fountain—sums up our *barrio* walk. Shops sell work by local artisans, such as ceramics, embroidery, and fans. The plaza has a long history. In the 19th century, aristocrats flocked here to see the supposed home of the legendary lady love of the legendary Don Juan. At night, with candlelight and Spanish guitars playing, this is indeed a romantic place to dine.

But the plaza we see today reflects the fate of much of the *barrio*. After the neighborhood's Jews were expelled in 1492, the area went into slow decline. Napoleon's invasion furthered the destruction. By the early 1900s it was deserted and run down. Sevilla began an extensive urban renewal project, which culminated in the 1929 world's fair. They turned much of the *barrio*, including this plaza, into a showcase of Andalusian style. Architects renovated with traditional-style railings, tile work, orange trees, and other too-cute, Epcot-like adornments. The Barrio Santa Cruz may not be quite as old as it appears, but the new and improved version respects tradition while carrying the neighborhood's 800-year legacy into the future.

• *Our walk is over. To return to the area near the start of this walk, cross the plaza and head north along Calle Rodrigo Caro; keep going until you enter the large Plaza de la Alianza. From here, a narrow lane (Calle Joaquín Romero Murube) leads left back to the Alcázar.*

Sights in Sevilla

▲▲SEVILLA CATHEDRAL

Sevilla's cathedral (Catedral de Sevilla) is the third-largest church in Europe (after St. Peter's at the Vatican in Rome and St. Paul's in London) and the largest Gothic church anywhere. When they ripped down a mosque of brick on this site in 1401, the Reconquista Christians vowed they'd build a cathedral so huge that "anyone who sees it will take us for madmen." When it was finished in 1528, it was indeed the

world's biggest, and remained so for a century until St. Peter's came along. Even today, the descendants of those madmen proudly point to a *Guinness Book of Records* letter certifying, "Santa María de la Sede in Sevilla is the cathedral with the largest area."

On this self-guided tour, we'll marvel at the vast interior, over-the-top altars, world-class art, a wooden crocodile, and the final resting place of Christopher Columbus.

Cost and Hours: €11 combo-ticket also includes Giralda bell tower and entry to the Church of the Savior—buy online in advance for €1 extra; Mon-Sat 11:00-17:00 (July-Aug until 18:00), Sun 14:30-19:00 (July-Aug from 14:00); www.catedraldesevilla.es.

Advance Tickets Recommended: It's smart to buy your ticket online to avoid the long, time-consuming line (dates are available starting seven weeks in advance). If arriving without a ticket, you can still try to buy one online for that day, or consider buying your combo-ticket at the Church of the Savior first (though lines there can also be long).

Tours: The €5 **audioguide** is excellent. The cathedral offers a **guided tour** that provides only a little extra information and is overpriced at €20; consider joining Concepción Delgado's guided tour instead (see "Tours in Sevilla," earlier).

The cathedral offers a 90-minute **guided rooftop visit** (€20, includes cathedral entrance, book online, English tours Tue and Thu at 10:00, Sat at 9:30, meet at west facade 15 minutes before tour). If you booked a rooftop tour, you can enter the cathedral anytime before your scheduled tour. Otherwise, after your tour, the guide can add your name to a list for approved entry the following day. If you do this tour, skip the Giralda tower climb.

∩ My free Sevilla City Walk **audio tour** includes background detail and descriptions of the cathedral exterior, but doesn't cover the interior.

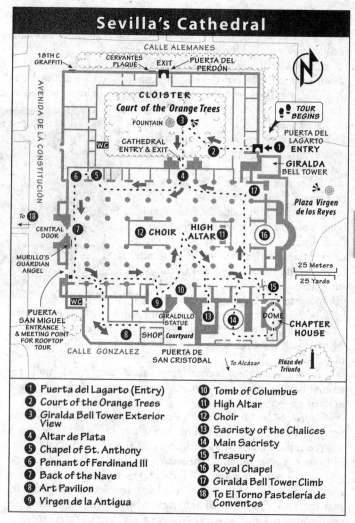

Sevilla's Cathedral

CALLE ALEMANES

18TH C GRAFFITI

CERVANTES PLAQUE · EXIT · PUERTA DEL PERDÓN

AVENIDA DE LA CONSTITUCIÓN

CLOISTER *Court of the Orange Trees*

FOUNTAIN ③

CATHEDRAL ENTRY & EXIT

② WC

TOUR BEGINS

PUERTA DEL LAGARTO ENTRY ①

GIRALDA BELL TOWER

Plaza Virgen de los Reyes

④

⑥ ⑤

⑰

To ⑱

CENTRAL DOOR

⑦

⑫ CHOIR

HIGH ALTAR

⑪

⑯

25 Meters
25 Yards

MURILLO'S GUARDIAN ANGEL

WC

⑨

⑩

⑮

DOME

PUERTA SAN MIGUEL ENTRANCE & MEETING POINT FOR ROOFTOP TOUR

⑧

GIRALDILLO STATUE

⑬

⑭

CHAPTER HOUSE

SHOP Courtyard

CALLE GONZALEZ

PUERTA DE SAN CRISTOBAL

To Alcázar

Plaza del Triunfo

SEVILLA

① Puerta del Lagarto (Entry)
② Court of the Orange Trees
③ Giralda Bell Tower Exterior View
④ Altar de Plata
⑤ Chapel of St. Anthony
⑥ Pennant of Ferdinand III
⑦ Back of the Nave
⑧ Art Pavilion
⑨ Virgen de la Antigua
⑩ Tomb of Columbus
⑪ High Altar
⑫ Choir
⑬ Sacristy of the Chalices
⑭ Main Sacristy
⑮ Treasury
⑯ Royal Chapel
⑰ Giralda Bell Tower Climb
⑱ To El Torno Pastelería de Conventos

Visitor Services: A WC and drinking fountain are by the art pavilion (southwest corner) and also in the courtyard near the exit.

❍ Self-Guided Tour

• *If you arrive early for your timed-entry slot, take time to circle the exterior and study the facades (you can also do this at the end of the tour).*

Exterior

Sevilla's cathedral has an odd exterior that is hard to fully appreciate. As the mosque was square and the cathedral was designed to entirely fill its footprint, the transepts don't show from the outside. And with no great square leading to the church, you hardly know

where the front door is (it's on the west side). The church is circled by pillars and chains, which provided sanctuary to those escaping secular law (but not Christian law) 500 years ago.

East Side: This side is dominated by the Giralda Tower, which stands next to the Puerta del Lagarto gate. If you have a timed-entry ticket, you'll enter at this door. From here, circle the cathedral clockwise.

South Side: The south facade is 19th-century Neo-Gothic and unfinished—notice the empty niches that never got their statues. In the courtyard stands a full-size replica of the Giraldillo statue that caps the bell tower.

West Side: This side faces the trams, horses, and commotion of Avenida de la Constitución. Though this is the main entry to the cathedral, it seems totally ignored. The central door shows the Assumption of Mary, with the beloved Virgin rocketing up to heaven to be crowned by God with his triangular halo (reminding all of the Trinity). While this part wasn't finished until the 19th century, the side doors—with their red terra-cotta saints—date from the 15th century.

At the northwest corner (across from Starbucks) you'll see animal-blood graffiti from 18th-century students celebrating their graduation—revealed in a recent cleaning project.

North Side: On the north side is the Puerta del Perdón, the entry to the mosque's courtyard (and where you'll exit after touring the cathedral). But, as with much of the Moorish-looking art in town, it's now actually Christian—the two coats of arms are a giveaway. The relief above the door shows the Bible story of Jesus ridding the temple of the merchants...a reminder to contemporaries that there will be no retail activity in the church. (German merchants gathered on this street—notice the name: Calle Alemanes.) The plaque on the right honors Miguel de Cervantes, the great 16th-century writer; this is one of many plaques scattered throughout town showing places mentioned in his books. (In this case, the topic was pickpockets.)

• *Circle back to the east side. With your timed-entry ticket, enter at* ❶ **Puerta del Lagarto.** *Why is a crocodile hanging at this gate? It's a reminder of the live crocodile (lagarto) given by the Islamic sultan of Egypt in 1260 to the Christian king Alfonso the Wise as a show of goodwill. Alfonso proudly showed off his croc, and when it died he had the body stuffed for display. When that rotted, it was replaced with this wooden replica. You're now in an open-air courtyard (with WCs at the*

far end). If you get routed through a different entry (as entry procedures are variable), just make your way to the courtyard to join our tour.

❷ Court of the Orange Trees

This courtyard—one of the few things remaining from the original mosque—was the place for ritual ablutions. Muslims would enter through the keyhole-shaped archway, stop at the fountain to wash their hands, face, and feet, then proceed inside to pray. Another remnant is the Puerta del Perdón ("Door of Forgiveness"), the keyhole-arch entrance, with its original green doors of finely wrought bronze-covered wood. The lanes between the courtyard bricks were once irrigation streams—a reminder that the Moors introduced irrigation to Iberia. Otherwise, the Christians completely leveled the site and turned a mosque of brick into a cathedral of stone.

• The biggest remnant of the original mosque ended up becoming the symbol of Sevilla itself—the Giralda bell tower. Find a spot in the courtyard where you can take in the tower.

❸ Giralda Bell Tower Exterior View

This was the mosque's minaret from which Muslims were called to prayer. After the Reconquista, it still called the faithful to prayer...

but as a Christian bell tower. The tower offers a brief recap of the city's history: a strong foundation of precut blocks from ancient Rome; a middle section of brick made by the Moors; and the rebuilt tower from the Christian era (the original fell in 1356 and was rebuilt even higher in the 1550s).

Capping the tower is a 4,000-pound bronze female angel symbolizing the Triumph of Faith—specifically, the Christian faith over the Muslim one. The statue serves as a weather vane. (In Spanish, *girar* means "to rotate"; *la giralda* refers to this figure that turns with the wind.) A ribbon of letters (you can make out *Nomen Die* from this vantage point) proclaims, "The strongest tower is the name of God."

• Now enter the cathedral, where you'll encounter the...

❹ Altar de Plata

This gleaming silver altarpiece is meant to resemble a monstrance—that's the ceremonial vessel that displays a communion wafer in the center. This one is gargantuan, big enough for a card table-sized wafer (and made from more than 5,000 pounds of silver looted from Mexico by Spanish conquistadores in the 16th century). Amid the gleaming silver is a colorful statue of the Virgin. In 2014, Sevilla's celebration of La Macarena's 50th anniversary "jubilee" culminated here, remembering when this beloved icon was granted a canonical coronation by the pope.

• *From here, we'll tour some sights going counterclockwise around the church. Head left from the Altar de Plata, pass a few chapels where people come to pray to their chosen saint, and keep going to the last chapel on the right (with the big, marble baptismal font).*

❺ Chapel of St. Anthony

This chapel (Capilla de San Antonio) holds a special place in the hearts of Sevillians. Many were baptized in the big Renaissance-era font with the delightful carved angels dancing along its base. The chapel is also special for Murillo's tender painting of the *Vision of St. Anthony* (1656). The saint kneels in wonder as Baby Jesus comes down surrounded by a choir of angels. Anthony, one of Iberia's most popular saints, is the patron saint of lost things—so people come here to pray for his help in find-  ing jobs, car keys, and life partners. (In 1874, the cathedral had to find Anthony himself, when thieves stole this painting; it turned up in New York.) Above the *Vision* is *The Baptism of Christ,* also by Murillo. As for the stained glass, you don't need to be an art historian to know that it dates from 1685. The women are Santa Justa and Santa Rufina, the third-century Roman sisters eaten by lions at Itálica because of their faith and now two of Sevilla's four patron saints. Potters by trade, they're easy to identify by their palm branches (symbolic of martyrdom), their pots (at their feet or in their hands), and the Giralda bell tower symbolizing the town they protect. As you tour, keep a lookout for this dynamic hometown duo.

• *Exiting the rear of the chapel, look for the enormous glass display case with the...*

❻ Pennant of Ferdinand III

This 800-year-old battle flag shows the castle of Castile and the lion of León—the two kingdoms Ferdinand inherited, forming the

nucleus of a unified, Christian Spain two centuries later. This pennant was raised here over the minaret of the mosque on November 23, 1248, as Christian forces finally expelled the Moors from Sevilla. For centuries afterward, it was paraded through the city on special days.

• *Continuing on, stand at the...*

❼ Back of the Nave

Face the choir and appreciate the ornate immensity of the church. Can you see the angels trumpeting on their Cuban mahogany? Any birds? On the floor before you (breaking the smooth surface) is the gravestone of Ferdinand Columbus (Hernando Colón), Christopher's second son. Having given the cathedral his collection of 6,000 precious books, he was rewarded with this prime burial spot. Behind you (behind an iron grille, left of the curtain-covered, large door) is Murillo's *Guardian Angel* pointing to the light and showing an astonished child the way.

The church is 137 yards long and 90 yards wide. That's more than two acres, the size of an entire city block in downtown Manhattan. Measured by area, this is still the world's largest church. (The church's footprint needed to be big enough to stamp out every trace of the mosque it replaced.) While most Gothic churches are long and tall, this nave is square and compressed. The pillars are massive. Like other Spanish churches, this nave is clogged in the middle by the huge rectangular enclosure called the choir.

• *Still moving counterclockwise, find a small door that leads to the...*

❽ Art Pavilion

This room features paintings that once hung in the church. You'll see a few by Sevilla's 17th-century master, Bartolomé Murillo, including paintings of beloved local characters who'll crop up again on our tour. King (and saint) Ferdinand III—usually shown with sword, crown, globe, and ermine robe—is the man who took Sevilla from the Moors and made this church possible. Remember you've seen Santa Justa and Santa Rufina before, holding up the Giralda bell tower (in the Chapel of St. Anthony).

• *Return to the church and continue counterclockwise to find a massive wooden candlestick from 1560. That's old, but there's even older stuff here. Find a chapel (opposite the towering organ) with a big wall of statues whose centerpiece is a golden fresco of Mary and Baby Jesus.*

❾ Virgen de la Antigua

In this gilded fresco, the Virgin delicately holds a rose while the Christ Child holds a bird. It's some of the oldest art here (from the 1300s), even older than the cathedral itself. This chapel was once the site of the mosque's mihrab—the horseshoe-shaped prayer niche that points toward Mecca. When Christians moved

SEVILLA

Immaculate Conception

Throughout Sevilla—and all of Spain—you'll see paintings titled *The Immaculate Conception,* all looking quite similar (see the example in the Bartolomé Murillo sidebar, later. Young, lovely, and beaming radiantly, these virgins look pure and untainted... you might even say "immaculate." According to Catholic doctrine, Mary, the future mother of Jesus, entered the world free from the original sin that other mortals share. When she died, her purity allowed her to be taken up directly to heaven (in the Assumption).

The doctrine of Immaculate Conception can be confusing, even to Catholics. It does not mean that the Virgin Mary herself was born of a virgin. Rather, Mary's mother and father conceived her in the natural way. But at the moment Mary's soul animated her flesh, God granted her a special exemption from original sin. The doctrine of Immaculate Conception had been popular since medieval times, though it was not codified until 1854. It was Murillo who painted the model of this goddess-like Mary, copied by so many lesser artists. In Counter-Reformation times (when Murillo lived), paintings of a fresh-faced, ecstatic Mary made abstract doctrines like the Immaculate Conception and the Assumption tangible and accessible to Catholics across Europe.

Most images of the Immaculate Conception show Mary wearing a radiant crown and with a crescent moon at her feet; she often steps on the heads of cherubs. Paintings by Murillo frequently portray Mary in a blue robe with long, wavy hair—young and innocent.

in (1248), they initially used the mosque for their church services, covering the mihrab with this Virgin. The mosque served as a church for about 120 years—until it was completely torn down and replaced by today's cathedral. But the Virgin stayed, thanks to her beauty and her role as protector of sailors—crucial in this port city. Gaze up (above the metal gate) to find flags of all the New World countries where the Virgen de la Antigua is revered.

• *Just past the Virgen de la Antigua chapel is the...*

⑩ Tomb of Columbus

Four royal pallbearers carry the coffin of Christopher Columbus. It's appropriate that Columbus is buried here. His 1492 voyage departed just 50 miles away, and the port of Sevilla became the exclusive entry point for all the New World plunder

that made Spain rich. Columbus' pallbearers represent the traditional kingdoms that formed the core of Spain: Castile, Aragon, León, and Navarre (identify them by their team shirts). The last kingdom, Granada, is also represented: Notice how Señor León's pike is stabbing a pomegranate, the symbol of Granada—the last Moorish-ruled city to succumb to the Reconquista in that momentous year of 1492.

Columbus didn't just travel a lot while alive—he even kept it up posthumously. He died in 1506 in northwestern Spain (in Valladolid) and was buried there. His remains were then moved to a monastery here in Sevilla, then to what's now the Dominican Republic (as he'd requested), then to Cuba. Finally—when Cuba gained independence from Spain in 1902—his remains sailed home again to Sevilla. After all that, are these really his remains? In 2006, a DNA test matched the bones of his son (buried just a few steps from here), giving Sevillians some evidence to substantiate their proud claim.

Columbus' tomb stands, appropriately, at the church entrance reserved for pilgrims, near a 1584 mural of St. Christopher, patron saint of travelers. The clock above has been ticking since 1788.

• *Walk to the center of the church, where you can enjoy a view of the main altar. Look through the wrought-iron Renaissance grille at the...*

⑪ High Altar

This dazzling 80-foot wall of gold covered with statues is considered the largest altarpiece *(retablo mayor)* ever made. Carved from walnut and chestnut, and blanketed by a staggering amount of gold leaf, it took three generations to complete (1481-1564). Its 44 scenes tell the story of Jesus and Mary—left to right, bottom to top. Focus on the main spine of scenes running up the cen-

ter. At the bottom sits a 750-year-old silver statue of Baby Jesus and Mary—the cathedral's patroness since Christians first worshipped here in the old converted mosque. Above Mary, find the scene of Baby Jesus (with cow and donkey) being born in a manger. Above that, Mary (flanked by winged angels) is assumed into heaven. Above that, a shirtless, flag-waving Jesus stands atop his coffin, having been resurrected. And above that, he ascends past his disciples into heaven. Bible scholars can trace the entire story through the miracles, the Passion, and the Pentecost. Look way up to the tippy-top, where a Crucifixion adorns the dizzying summit: That teeny figure is six feet tall.

Bartolomé Murillo (1617-1682)

The son of a barber of Seville, Bartolomé Murillo (mur-EE-yoh) got his start selling paintings meant for export to the frontier churches of the Americas. In his 20s, he be-came famous after he painted a series of saints for Sevilla's Franciscan monastery. By about 1650, Murillo's sugary, simple, and ac-cessible religious style was spreading through Spain and beyond.

Murillo painted street kids with cute smiles and grimy faces, and radiant young Marías with Ivory-soap complexions and rapturous poses (Immaculate Conceptions). His paintings view the world through a soft-focus lens, wrapping everything in warm colors and soft light, with a touch (too much, for some) of sentimentality.

Murillo became a rich, popular family man, and the toast of Sevilla's high society. In 1664, his wife died, leaving him heartbro-ken, but his last 20 years were his most prolific. At age 65, Murillo died after falling off a scaffold while painting. His tomb is lost somewhere under the bricks of Plaza de Santa Cruz.

Now crane your neck skyward to admire the elaborate **ceiling** with its intricate interlacing arches. Though done in the 16th-century Spanish Renaissance style, this stonework is only about 100 years old. You're standing under the cathedral's central dome, which has collapsed three times in the past 500 years.

• *Don't even think about that. Turn around and check out the...*

⑫ Choir

A choir area like this one—enclosed within the cathedral for more intimate services—is where church VIPs can gather close to the high altar. Choirs are common in Spain and England, but rare in churches elsewhere. They're called choirs because singers were also allowed here to accompany services. This one features an organ of more than 7,000 pipes (played Mon-Fri at the 10:00 Mass, Sun at the 10:00 and 13:00 Mass, not in July-Aug, free entry for worship-pers). The big, spinnable book holder in the middle of the room held giant hymnals—large enough for all to chant from in an age when there weren't enough books to go around.

• *Return to Columbus' tomb and find the next chapel.*

⑬ Sacristy of the Chalices

This space is where the priests get ready each morning before Mass. The painting above the altar is remarkable for several reasons: It's

by the well-known artist Goya, it was specifically painted for this room, and it features our old friends Justa and Rufina with their trademark bell tower, pots, and palm leaves. Here they're bathed in a heavenly light, triumphing over a broken pagan statue, while the lion who was supposed to attack meekly licks their toes. Goya daringly portrayed the two third-century Romans dressed like fashionable women of his time.

• *Two chapels farther along is the entrance to the...*

⓮ Main Sacristy

Marvel at the ornate, 16th-century dome of the main room, a grand souvenir from Sevilla's golden age. The intricate masonry,

called Plateresque, resembles lacy silverwork (*plata* means "silver"). God is way up in the cupola. The three layers of figures below him show the heavenly host; relatives in purgatory—hands folded in prayer—looking to heaven in hope of help; and the wretched in hell, including naked sinners engulfed in flames and teased cruelly by pitchfork-wielding monsters.

Dominating the room is a nearly 1,000-pound, silver-plated monstrance (vessel for displaying the communion wafer). This is the monstrance used to parade the holy host through town during Corpus Christi festivities.

• *The next door down leads you through a few rooms, including one with a unique oval dome.*

This is the 16th-century **chapter house** *(sala capitular),* where monthly meetings take place with the bishop (he gets the throne, while the others share the bench). The paintings here are by Murillo: *The Immaculate Conception* (1668, high above the bishop's throne) is one of his finest (and largest) depictions of Mary (in blue and white, standing amid a cloud of cherubs). To the right of her is Ferdinand (with sword and globe), along with more of Sevilla's favorite saints.

• *Now enter the...*

⓯ Treasury

This wood-paneled Room of Ornaments shows off gold and silver reliquaries, which hold hundreds of holy body parts and splinters of the true cross. The star of the collection is Spain's most valuable crown—the Corona de la Virgen de los Reyes. Made in 1904, it sparkles with nearly 12,000 precious stones, including the world's largest pearl—used as the

torso of an angel. This amazing treasure was completely paid for by devoted locals. Not fit for a human head, once a year the crown is taken out and placed on the head of a statue of the Virgin who represents Mary as patron of this cathedral.

• *Leave the treasury and continue around, passing (directly behind the high altar) the closed-to-tourists* ⑯ *Royal Chapel. Though it's only open for worship (access from outside), it's the holy-of-holies of Sevillian history, with the tombs of Sevilla's founder Ferdinand III, his enlightened successor Alfonso the Wise, and Pedro I, who built the Alcázar.*

In the far corner is the entry to the Giralda bell tower. It's time for some exercise (unless you're touring the rooftop later—then you can skip it).

⑰ Giralda Bell Tower Climb

Your church admission includes entry to the bell tower, a former minaret. Notice the beautiful Moorish simplicity as you climb to its top, 330 feet up (35 ramps plus 17 steps), for a grand city view. The graded ramp was designed to accommodate a donkey-riding muezzin, who clip-clopped up five times a day to give the Muslim call to prayer back when a mosque stood here. It's less steep the farther up you go, but if you get tired along the way, stop at balconies for expansive views over the entire city.

Back on the ground, return to the giant silver altar and head outside through the Court of the Orange Trees. Before leaving, take in the whole scene—Giralda tower, courtyard, and the church with its flying buttresses and magnificent Gothic doorways. Enjoy the impressive remnants of the former mosque and the additions of today's church. And appreciate the significance of this site that was sacred to two great world religions.

• *Your cathedral tour is finished. Exit the courtyard through the Puerta del Perdón onto Calle Alemanes. If you haven't already done so, loop around the exterior of the cathedral (described at the start of the tour).*

Or for a truly religious experience, consider one more stop. After exiting the cathedral, make a U-turn left onto Avenida de la Constitución. At #24 (directly across from the church door), enter the passageway marked Plaza del Cabildo, *which leads into a quiet courtyard with a humble little hole-in-the-wall shop.*

⑱ El Torno Pastelería de Conventos

Here, nuns sell handicrafts (such as baptismal dresses for babies) and baked goods (Mon-Fri 10:00-13:30 & 17:00-19:30, Sat-Sun 10:30-14:00, closed Aug). You won't actually see the cloistered sisters, since this shop is staffed by laypeople, but the pastries they make are heavenly—Sevilla's best cookies, bar nun.

▲▲ROYAL ALCÁZAR

This palace has been a lavish residence for Spain's rulers for a thousand years. Originally a 10th-century palace built for the governors

of the local Moorish state, it still functions as one of the royal family's homes—the oldest in Europe that's still in use. The core of the palace features an extensive 14th-century rebuild, done by Muslim workmen for the Christian king, Pedro I (1334-1369). Pedro was nicknamed either "the Cruel" or "the Just," depending on which end of his sword you were on. Pedro's palace embraces both cultural traditions.

Today, visitors can enjoy several sections of the Royal Alcázar. Spectacularly decorated halls and courtyards have distinctive Islamic-style flourishes. Exhibits call up the era of Columbus and Spain's New World dominance. The lush, sprawling gardens invite exploration.

Cost and Hours: €13.50, €1 extra to buy advance tickets online; daily 9:30-19:00, Oct-March until 17:00; +34 912 302 200, www.alcazarsevilla.org. Your ticket gets you free admission to four other museums in Sevilla, including the Antiquarium (in the basement of the *Metropol Parasol*—see page 715) and the Museo de la Cerámica de Triana (see page 723).

Advance Tickets Recommended: You could line up for hours to buy a ticket, but why? The smart move is to buy a timed-entry ticket in advance. Book online as soon as you can, then wait at the entrance along with savvy travelers who did just that (show your printed or digital ticket). Note that groups tend to book the 11:00 entrance time (a good time to avoid).

Tours: The fast-moving **audioguide** gives you an hour of information as you wander (free with ticket purchase; scan QR code for mobile download at ticket office). Or consider Concepción Delgado's **guided tour** (see "Tours in Sevilla," earlier).

🎧 My free Sevilla City Walk **audio tour** includes background information and descriptions of the Royal Alcázar exterior, but not the interior.

Upper Royal Apartments Option (Cuarto Real Alto): With a little planning, you could fit in a visit to the 15 lavish, chandeliered, Versailles-like rooms used by today's monarchs, including the official dining room, living rooms, and stunning Mudejar-style Audience Room. Your group (15 people max) will be escorted on a 30-minute tour while using the included audioguide. It's a delightful and less-crowded part of the palace, but you'll need to book well in advance (€20 combo-ticket with Alcázar, must check bags

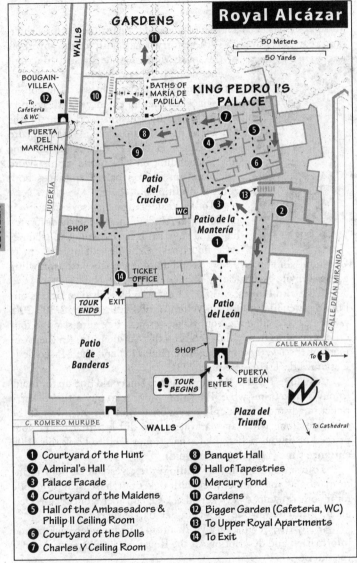

Royal Alcázar

GARDENS

WALLS

50 Meters
50 Yards

BOUGAIN-
VILLEA

BATHS OF
MARÍA DE
PADILLA

KING PEDRO I'S
PALACE

To
Cafeteria
& WC

PUERTA
DEL
MARCHENA

Patio
del
Cruciero

WC

JUDERIA

SHOP

Patio de la
Montería

CALLE DEAN MIRANDA

TICKET
OFFICE

TOUR
ENDS

EXIT

Patio
del León

Patio
de
Banderas

SHOP

CALLE MAÑARA

To

TOUR
BEGINS

ENTER

PUERTA
DE LEÓN

C. ROMERO MURUBE

WALLS

Plaza del
Triunfo

To Cathedral

1 Courtyard of the Hunt
2 Admiral's Hall
3 Palace Facade
4 Courtyard of the Maidens
5 Hall of the Ambassadors &
   Philip II Ceiling Room
6 Courtyard of the Dolls
7 Charles V Ceiling Room

8 Banquet Hall
9 Hall of Tapestries
10 Mercury Pond
11 Gardens
12 Bigger Garden (Cafeteria, WC)
13 To Upper Royal Apartments
14 To Exit

in lockers, check in 15 minutes early, last tour departs at 13:30).
With this ticket, you become an Alcázar VIP and can enter the
complex anytime you like that day (go to the front of the line and
present ticket).

◑ Self-Guided Tour

This royal palace is decorated with a mix of Islamic and Christian
elements—a style called Mudejar. It offers a thought-provoking

glimpse of a graceful al-Andalus world that might have survived its Castilian conquerors...but didn't. The floor plan is intentionally confusing, to make experiencing the place more exciting and surprising. While Granada's Alhambra was built by Moors for Moorish rulers, what you see here is essentially a Christian ruler's palace, built

in the Moorish style by Moorish artisans (after the Reconquista).

• *Just past the entrance, you'll go through the garden-like Lion Patio (Patio del León), with the rough original structure of the older Moorish fortress on your left (c. 913), and through the 12th-century arch into a courtyard called the...*

SEVILLA

❶ Courtyard of the Hunt (Patio de la Montería)

For centuries, this has been the main gathering place in the Alcázar (and it's now where tourists converge). Get oriented. The palace's main entrance is directly ahead, through the elaborately decorated facade.

History is all around you. The Alcázar was built over many centuries, with rooms and decorations from the various rulers who've lived here. Behind you, the courtyard you passed through has remnants of the original 10th-century Moorish palace. The towering entrance facade before you dates from after Sevilla was Christianized, when King Pedro I built the most famous part of the complex. To the right are rooms dedicated to Spain's golden age, when the Alcázar was home to Ferdinand and Isabel and, later, their grandson Charles V (the most powerful man in Europe...the Holy Roman Emperor). Each successive monarch left their mark, adding still more luxury. And today's king and queen still use the palace's upper floor as one of their royal residences.

• *Before entering the heart of the palace, let's get a sense of its history. Start in the wing to the right of the courtyard.*

❷ Admiral's Hall (Salón del Almirante)

In the first room, filled with big canvases, find the **biggest painting** (and most melodramatic). This shows the crucial turning point

in the Alcázar's history: The king who defeated the Moors in 1248, and turned the palace from Moorish to Christian, is kneeling humbly before the bishop, symbolically giving his life to God. Other paintings depict later royalty who made their mark on the Alcázar's history. (This particular room is still used today for fancy government receptions.)

Queen Isabel put her stamp on the Alcázar by building this series of rooms (1503). Having debriefed Columbus after his New World discoveries, she realized the potential business opportunity. She created this wing to administer Spain's New World ventures. In these halls, Columbus recounted his travels, Ferdinand Magellan planned his around-the-world cruise, and Amerigo Vespucci tried to come up with a catchy moniker for that newly discovered continent.

Continue into the pink-and-red Audience Chamber, once the Admiralty's chapel. The **altarpiece painting** is *St. Mary of the Navigators* (*Santa María de los Naveg-*

antes, Alejo Fernández, 1530s). The Virgin—the patron saint of sailors and a favorite of Columbus—keeps watch over the puny ships beneath her. Her cape seems to protect everyone under it—even the Native Americans in the dark background (the first time "Indians" were painted in Europe). Kneeling beside the Virgin (on the right, dressed in gold, almost joining his hands together in prayer) is none other than Christopher Columbus. He's on a cloud and this is heaven (this was painted a few decades after his death). Notice that Columbus is blond. Columbus' son said of his dad: "In his youth his hair was blond, but when he reached 30, it all turned white." Many historians believe this to be the earliest known portrait of Columbus. If so, it's also likely to be the most accurate. The man kneeling on the left side of the painting, with the big gold cape, is King Ferdinand, the husband of Isabel.

Left of the painting is a **model** of Columbus' *Santa María*,

his flagship and the only of his three ships not to survive the 1492 voyage. Columbus complained that the *Santa María*—a big cargo ship, different from the sleek *Niña* and *Pinta* caravels—was too slow. On Christmas Day it ran aground off present-day

Haiti and tore a hole in its hull. The ship was dismantled to build the first permanent structure in America, a fort for 39 colonists. (After Columbus left, the natives burned the fort and killed the colonists.) Opposite the altarpiece (in the center of the back wall) is the family **coat of arms** of Columbus' descendants, who now live in Spain and Puerto Rico. Using Columbus' Spanish name, it reads: "To Castile and to León, a new world was given by Colón."

As you return to the courtyard, don't miss the room (beyond the grand piano) with display cases of ornate **fans** (mostly foreign and well described in English). A long painting (designed to be gradually rolled across a screen and viewed like a primitive movie) shows 17th-century Sevilla during Holy Week. Follow the procession, which is much like today's, with traditional floats carried by teams of men along with a retinue of penitents.

• *Back in the Courtyard of the Hunt, face the impressive entrance to the...*

❸ Palace Facade

This is the entrance to **King Pedro I's Palace** (Palacio del Rey Pedro I), the Alcázar's 14th-century nucleus. Though it looks Islamic—with lobed arches, slender columns, and intricate stucco work— it's a classic example of the palace's Mudejar style. Looking closer you'll see Christian motifs mixed in—coats of arms of Spain's kings and heraldic animals. About two-thirds of the way up, find the inscription dedicated to the man who built the gate (center of the top row)—"Conquerador Don Pedro." The facade's elaborate blend of Islamic tracery and Gothic Christian elements introduces us to the unique style seen throughout Pedro's part of the palace.

• *Enter the palace (wear backpacks in front so as not to damage the walls). Go left through the vestibule (impressive, yes, but we'll see better), and emerge into the big courtyard with a long pool in the center. This is the...*

❹ Courtyard of the Maidens (Patio de las Doncellas)

You've reached the center of King Pedro's palace. It's an open-air courtyard, surrounded by rooms. In the middle is a long, rectangular reflecting pool. Like the Moors who preceded him, Pedro built his palace around water.

King Pedro cruelly abandoned his wife and moved into the Alcázar with his mistress, then hired Muslim workers from Granada to re-create the romance of that city's Alhambra in Sevilla's stark Alcázar. The designers created a microclimate engineered

for coolness: water, sunken gardens, pottery, thick walls, and darkness. This palace is considered Spain's best example of the Mudejar style. Stucco panels with elaborate designs, coffered wooden ceilings, and intricate lobed arches atop slender columns create a refined, pleasing environment. Ceramic tiles on the walls add color. The elegant proportions and symmetry of this courtyard are a photographer's delight.

Pedro's original courtyard was a single story; the upper floors were added by Isabel's grandson, Charles V, in the 16th century. Today, those upper-story rooms are part of the Spanish monarchs' living quarters. See the different styles: Mudejar below (lobed arches and elaborate tracery) and Renaissance above (round arches and less decoration).

• *Let's explore some rooms surrounding the courtyard. Start with the room at the far end of the long reflecting pool—beneath the big octagonal tower. This is the palace's most important room.*

❺ Hall of the Ambassadors (Salón de Embajadores)

Here, in his throne room, Pedro received guests and caroused in luxury. The room is a cube topped with a half-dome, like many important Islamic buildings. In Islam, the cube represents the earth, and the dome is the starry heavens. In Pedro's world, the symbolism proclaimed that he controlled heaven and earth. Islamic horseshoe arches stand atop recycled columns with leafy golden capitals. As you marvel, remember that this is original, from the 1300s.

The stucco on the walls is molded with interlacing plants, geometrical shapes, and Arabic writing. Despite this being a Christian palace, the walls are inscribed with unapologetically Muslim sayings: "None but Allah conquers" and "Happiness and prosperity are benefits of Allah, who nourishes all creatures." The artisans added propaganda phrases, such as "Dedicated to the magnificent Sultan Pedro—thanks to God!" (Perhaps the Allah quotes survived because Muslims and Christians praise the same God, and in Arabic—Muhammad's native language—God is called Allah.)

The Mudejar style also includes Christian motifs. Find the row of kings, high up at the base of the dome, chronicling all of

Castile's rulers from the 600s to the 1600s (portrayed as if on playing cards). Within the intricate patterns inside the dome, you can see a few coats of arms—including the castle of Castile and the lion of León. These symbols (along with another royal symbol with twin columns) are seen throughout the palace. The Mudejar style also incorporates birds, seashells, and other natural objects you wouldn't normally find in Islamic decor, as it traditionally avoids realistic images of nature.

Notice how it gets cooler as you go deeper into the palace. Straight ahead from the Hall of the Ambassadors, in the **Philip II Ceiling Room** (Salón del Techo de Felipe II), look above the arches to find peacocks, falcons, and other birds amid interlacing vines. Imagine day-to-day life in the palace—with VIP guests tripping on the tiny steps.

• *Make your way to the second courtyard (with your back to the Hall of the Ambassadors, circle right). This smaller courtyard (with the skylight) is the...*

❻ Courtyard of the Dolls (Patio de las Muñecas)

This delicate courtyard was reserved for the king's private family life. Originally, the center of the courtyard had a pool, cooling the residents and reflecting decorative patterns that were once brightly painted on the walls. The columns—recycled from ancient Roman and Visigothic buildings— are of alternating white, black, and pink marble. The courtyard's name comes from the tiny doll faces found at the base of one of the arches. Circle the room and try to find them. (Hint: While just a couple of inches tall, they're eight feet up—kitty-corner from where you entered.)

• *Wander around before returning to the big Courtyard of the Maidens. In the middle of the right side an arch leads to the...*

❼ Charles V Ceiling Room (Salón del Techo del Carlos V)

Emperor Charles V ruled Spain at its peak and, flush with New World wealth, expanded the palace. His marriage to his beloved cousin Isabella—which took place in this room—joined vast realms of Spain and Portugal. Devoutly Christian, Charles celebrated his wedding night with a midnight Mass, and later ordered the Mudejar ceiling in this room to be replaced with the less Islamic (but no less impressive) Renaissance one you see today. At the base of the ceiling, find Charles' coat of arms—the black double eagle.

• *When you're ready to move on, return to the Courtyard of the Maidens, then turn right. In the corner, find the small staircase. Go up to rooms decorated with bright ceramic tiles and Gothic vaulting. Pass directly through the chapel (with its majestic mahogany altar on your right) and into a big, long room.*

❽ Banquet Hall (Salón Gótico)

This airy banquet hall is where Charles and Isabella held their wedding reception. Note the huge coats of arms: Charles' double eagle on one end and Isabella's shield of Portugal on the other. Both are painted cloth from the 1500s. Tiles of yellow, blue, green, and orange (from the 16th century) line the room, some decorated with whimsical human figures with vase-like bodies. Imagine a formal occasion here, as elegant guests took in the views of the gardens. To this day, city officials and VIPs still host receptions here.

• *Midhall, on the left, enter the...*

❾ Hall of Tapestries (Salón Tapices)

Next door, the walls are hung with 18th-century Spanish copies of 16th-century Belgian tapestries showing the power, conquests, and industriousness of Charles'

prosperous reign. This series of scenes depicts the pivotal Conquest of Tunisia (1535), which stopped the Muslim Ottomans in North Africa at a time when they were threatening Europe on different fronts. (The highlights are described in Spanish along the top, and in Latin along the bottom.) The map tapestry of the Mediterranean world has south pointing up. Find Genova, Italy, on the bottom; Africa on top; Lisbon (Lisboa) on the far right; the large city of Barcelona in between; and Tunisia (Tunis). The ships of the Holy Roman Empire gather in anticipation of a major battle. The artist included himself (far right) holding the legend—with a scale in both leagues and miles.

At the far end of the room is a big, dramatic portrayal of the Spanish Navy. With cannon-laden warships and a merchant fleet to haul goods and people, Spain ruled the waves—and thereby an empire upon which the sun never set. Its reign lasted from 1492 until the defeat of the Spanish Armada in 1588; after that, Britannia's navy took the helm, and it was her crown that controlled the next global empire.

• *Return to the Banquet Hall, then head outside at the far end to the extensive landscaped gardens. First up is the...*

⑩ Mercury Pond

The Mercury Pond is marked by a tiny bronze statue of the messenger of the gods, with his cute little winged feet. This was a reservoir fed by a 16th-century aqueduct that irrigated the palace's entire garden. As only elites had running water, the fountain was an extravagant show of power. The long stucco-studded wall along one side of the garden was part of the original Moorish

castle wall. In the early 1600s, when fortifications were no longer needed here, that end was redesigned to be a grotto-style gallery.

*• From the Mercury Pond, steps lead into the formal gardens. Just past the bottom of the steps, a tunnel on the right leads under the palace to the coolest spot in the city—the **Baths of María de Padilla**. This long underground pool was a rainwater cistern, named for Pedro of Castile's mistress who frequented the place. Its mysterious medieval atmosphere is like something out of* Game of Thrones—*which actually did use this and other Alcázar settings in several episodes of the television series. Finally, explore the rest of the...*

⑪ Gardens

The intimate geometric zone nearest the palace is the Moorish garden. The far-flung garden beyond that was the backyard of the Christian ruler.

Here in the gardens, as in the rest of the palace, Christian and Islamic traditions merge and mingle. Both cultures used water and nature as essential parts of their architecture. The gardens' pavilions and fountains only enhance this. Wander among palm trees, myrtle hedges, and fragrant roses. While tourists pay to be here, these are actually public gardens, free to locals. They've been that way since 1931, when the king was exiled and Spanish citizens took ownership of royal holdings. In 1975, the Spanish people allowed the king back on the throne—but on their terms...which included keeping these gardens.

From the Moors to Pedro I to Ferdinand and Isabel, and from Charles V to King Felipe VI, we've seen the home of a millennium of Spanish kings and queens. Feel free to explore the exotic landscape they created and create your own *Arabian Nights* fantasies.

• Your Alcázar tour is over. When you're ready to leave these gardens, return to the Mercury Pond and step back into the palace into a small courtyard with palm trees. From here, consider your options:

Just a few steps away, on the other side of the stucco wall, is a mas-

Christopher Columbus (1451-1506)

This Italian wool weaver ran off to sea, was shipwrecked in Portugal, married a captain's daughter, learned Portuguese and Spanish, and persuaded Spain's monarchs to finance his bold scheme to trade with the East by sailing west. On August 3, 1492, Columbus set sail from Palos (near Huelva, 60 miles west of Sevilla) with three ships and 90 men, hoping to land in Asia, which Columbus estimated was 3,000 miles away. Ten weeks—and yes, 3,000 miles—later, with a superstitious crew ready to mutiny after they'd seen evil omens (including a falling meteor and a jittery compass), Columbus landed on an island in the Bahamas, convinced he'd reached Asia. He and his crew traded with the "Indians" and returned home to Palos harbor, where they were received as heroes.

Columbus made three more voyages to the New World and became rich with gold. But he gained a bad reputation among the colonists for ruling with an iron fist. Further tarnishing his legacy was Columbus' mistreatment, forced labor, and enslavement of the indigenous people he encountered—establishing a cruel precedent that would linger for centuries. Eventually, Columbus was arrested and brought back to Spain in chains. Though pardoned, Columbus fell out of favor with the court. On May 20, 1506, he died in Valladolid. His son said he was felled by "gout and by grief at seeing himself fallen from his high estate," but historians speculate that diabetes or syphilis may have contributed. Columbus died thinking he'd visited Asia, unaware he'd opened up Europe to a New World.

sive bougainvillea and a ⑫ **bigger garden with cafeteria and WCs.** Once a farm that provided for the royal community, the garden is now home to a cool and convenient cafeteria with a delightful terrace.

If you've booked a spot to visit the ⑬ **Upper Royal Apartments,** return to the Courtyard of the Hunt, and head upstairs.

Otherwise, follow ⑭ **exit** signs and head out through the **Patio de Banderas,** once the entrance for guests arriving by horse carriage. Enjoy a classic Giralda bell tower view as you leave.

BETWEEN THE CATHEDRAL AND THE RIVER
▲Archivo General de Indias
(General Archives of the Indies)

To the right of the Alcázar's main entrance, the Archivo General de Indias houses historic papers related to Spain's overseas territories. Its four miles of shelving contain 80 million pages documenting a once-mighty empire. While little of interest is actually on show, a visit is free, easy, and gives you a look at the Lonja Palace, one of the finest Renaissance edifices in Spain. Designed by royal architect Juan de Herrera, the principal designer of El Escorial, the

building evokes the greatness of the Spanish empire at its peak (c. 1600).

🎧 Download my free Sevilla City Walk audio tour for background on the Archivo General de Indias.

Cost and Hours: Free, Mon-Sat 9:30-17:00, Sun 10:00-14:00, Avenida de la Constitución 3, +34 954 500 528.

Background: In the early 1500s, as exotic goods began pouring into Sevilla from newly discovered lands, this spot between the cathedral and the Alcázar was an open-air market, where businessmen met to trade. Sevilla was the only port licensed to trade with the New World, and merchants came here from across Europe, establishing the city as a commercial powerhouse. The area evolved as a hub of Spanish power, where the royal palace, business community, and cathedral all came together.

In 1583, this grand building was built as a place for those merchants, moneychangers, and accountants to do their business—an early stock market, or *lonja*. (On the cathedral-facing side of the building stands a stone cross where businessmen would "swear to God" to be honest in their trade.) Mapmakers, sea captains, and navigators also gathered here, as well as lawyers, accountants, and politicians who could administer Spain's far-flung colonies. Herrera designed a no-nonsense Renaissance building of symmetrical doors and windows, balustrades, and distinctive rooftop pinnacles.

By 1785, with Sevilla in decline (a victim of plagues, a silted-up harbor, and the rise of Cádiz as Spain's main port), the building was put to new use as an archive: the storehouse for documents the country was quickly amassing from its discovery, conquest, and administration of the New World.

Visiting the Archives: The **ground floor** houses a small rotating exhibit that tells the story of the building. You may see copies of famous documents here, like the Treaty of Tordesillas (1494, when Spain and Portugal divvied up the New World) or the Capitulations of Santa Fe (the contract Columbus signed with Ferdinand and Isabel for his 1492 voyage). There's often a cannon discovered by American treasure hunter Mel Fisher. He used information in the archives to find a Spanish galleon that sank off the Florida coast in 1616—with a huge treasure onboard. Fisher returned the cannon as a gesture of goodwill.

Upstairs (up an extravagant marble staircase) there are several exhibits clustered near the landing: Don't miss the huge 16th-century security chest—meant to store gold and important documents. Its elaborate locking mechanism (it fills the inner lid) could be opened only by following a set series of pushes, pulls, and twists—an effective way to keep prying eyes and greedy fingers from its valuable contents. Portraits depict some of the explorers whose discoveries made this building possible (Columbus, Cortés,

et al.), scholars who archived the documents, and the powdered-wig administrators *(teniente general)* of the colonial empire. Nearby, find a curtained room with an interesting 15-minute video on Sevilla's New World connections and the archive's work. Then browse the wooden racks with (copies of) documents from the collection. The collection covers both "Indies"—East and West—so you'll see maps of Guatemala and the Philippines, maps by Amerigo Vespucci (who sailed from Sevilla in the 1490s and was one of the first to realize America wasn't India), manuscripts about Magellan's around-the-world voyage and Pizarro's conquest of Peru, and old sketches of indigenous people the explorers encountered.

Finally, make a big circle around the rest of the (mostly empty) upstairs to check out the rows and rows of cedar and mahogany bookshelves, beautifully decorated domes, and whatever rotating exhibit may be on display.

Avenida de la Constitución

Old Sevilla is bisected by this grand boulevard. Its name celebrates the country's 1978 adoption of a democratic constitution, as the Spanish people moved quickly to reestablish their free government after the 1975 death of longtime dictator Francisco Franco (an understandable change, since it was previously named for the founder of Spain's Fascist Party, José Antonio Primo de Rivera).

The busy avenue was converted into a pedestrian boulevard in 2007. Overnight, the city's paseo route took on a new dimension. Suddenly cafés and shops here had fresh appeal. The tram line (infamously short, only about a mile long) was at first controversial, as it violated what could have been a more purely pedestrian zone.

▲▲Hospital de la Caridad

This charity hospital, which functioned as a place of final refuge for Sevilla's poor and homeless, was founded in the 17th century by the nobleman Don Miguel Mañara. Your visit includes an evocative courtyard, a church filled with powerful art, and a good audioguide that explains it all. This is still a working charity, so when you pay your entrance fee, you're advancing the work Mañara started back in the 17th century.

Cost and Hours: €8, includes audioguide, Mon-Fri 10:30-19:30, Sat-Sun 14:00-19:00, Calle Temprado 3, +34 954 223 232, www.santa-caridad.es.

Background: Hospital founder Don Miguel Mañara (1626-1679) was the happy-go-lucky mayor of Sevilla at its peak of prosperity and sophistication. A big-time playboy and enthusiastic sinner, he had a massive change of heart late in life and dedicated his last years to strict worship and taking care of the poor. In 1674, Mañara acquired some empty warehouses in Sevilla's old shipyard and built this 150-ward "place of heroic virtues."

Mañara could well have been the inspiration for Don Juan, the quasi-legendary character from a play set in 17th-century Sevilla, popularized later by Lord Byron's poetry and Mozart's opera *Don Giovanni*. While no one knows for sure, it adds some fun to the visit. Regardless, the hospital's iconography is all built around a Don Juan theme: the sudden realization that, in the face of death, all of life's pleasures are fleeting, and only by doing acts of charity can we gain eternal life.

Visiting the Hospital: Entering the **courtyard** you're greeted by a statue of a woman and two ecstatic cherubs, filled with the love of mankind. It's Charity, the mission of this hospital. The statues come from Genoa, Italy, as Mañara's family were rich Genovese merchants who moved to Sevilla to get in on the wealth from New World discoveries. The Dutch tiles (from Delft), depicting scenes from the Old and New Testament, are a reminder that the Netherlands was under Spanish rule in centuries past. This charming red-and-white courtyard, surrounded by offices, was the administrative hub of the hospital's charitable work and its ongoing assistance to the poor. You're likely to see seniors shuffling in and out, as this is still a home for the poor—Mañara's legacy in action.

The **Sala de Cabildos,** a small room at the end of the courtyard, is Mañara's former office. It has rotating exhibits from Mañara's art collection.

Stepping out of the Sala de Cabildos, the chapel is on your right. But first, head left into a small, evocative courtyard. These arches are part of the 13th-century **shipyards.** Wander around and imagine the huge halls where the ships were produced that enabled Columbus, Vasco da Gama, and Magellan to broaden Europe's horizons and make Portugal a world power.

Next, cross the inner courtyard and head up a few steps into the highlight—the **chapel.** It's an over-the-top masterpiece of Sevillian Baroque—a fusion of architecture, painting, and sculpture. Don Miguel hired Sevilla's three greatest artists (who were also his friends): the painters Bartolomé Murillo and Juan de Valdés Leal and the sculptor Pedro Roldán. Mañara himself worked with them to design the church and its themes.

Start with the painting at the back of the **nave,** on the left wall. Worshippers would be greeted by Leal's *In the Blink of an Eye (In Ictu Oculi).* In it, the Grim Reaper extinguishes the candle of life. Filling the canvas are the ruins of worldly goods, knowledge, power, and position. It's all gone in the blink of an eye—true in the 1670s...and true today. Don Miguel experienced that personally when his wife suddenly died—along with half of Sevilla—in a devastating plague.

Directly opposite is Leal's *The End of the Glories of the World.* The painting shows Mañara and a bishop decaying together in a

crypt, with worms and assorted bugs munching away. Above, the hand of Christ—pierced by the nail—holds the scales of justice: sins ("Nimas," on the left) and good deeds ("Nimanos," on the right). The placement of both paintings gave worshippers plenty to think about during and after their visit.

Strolling up the nave, you'll see paintings and statues that show various good deeds and acts of self-sacrifice and charity performed by Jesus and the saints—the kinds of things that we should emulate to save us from eternal death. Most of the paintings leading up to the altar are replicas of Murillo's pieces, lost during Napoleonic times. On the left wall, Moses strikes a rock to bring water to the needy Israelites. A trademark Murillo beggar-boy atop a horse points at Moses as if saying, "Do what he did." On the right wall, Jesus gives loaves and fishes to thousands of hungry people. Murillo, a devoted member of this charity, was hammering home one of the institution's functions—give food and drink to the poor.

The giant **altar** is carved wood with gold leaf, with a dozen hardworking cupids providing support. Christ's lifeless body has been taken from the cross and some workers are bringing in the dark-gray tombstone. This illustrated the mission of the monks here—to provide a proper Christian burial to society's outcasts, like executed criminals. The carved-and-painted statues by Roldán are realistic and emotional, in the style of his famed *La Macarena* statue. Atop the altar are three female figures representing faith (left), hope (right), and—the star of this place—charity. Notice how the altar's painting blends seamlessly with the statues of his burial below. The rocks and shrubs of the painting morph into sculpted 3-D rocks and shrubs, as the events of the Crucifixion become the more tangible reality of Jesus' very dead body.

As you leave the church, do Don Miguel Mañara a favor. Step on his **tombstone.** It's located in the back, tucked within the big wooden entranceway. Set in the pavement, this tombstone has served as a humble doormat since 1679. He requested to be buried here so everyone would step on him as they entered. The tombstone reads, "Beneath this stone lies the worst man in the world." By focusing on the vanity of his own life and dedicating himself to charity, Don Miguel hoped to be saved from his sins.

Outside, more big shots—many of Sevilla's top families to this day—are featured on tombstones paving the exit.

Across the street from the entry is a park. Pop in and see Don Miguel—wracked with guilt—carrying a poor, sick person into his hospital. One thing's for certain: Don Miguel is on the road to sainthood. But since you need to perform miracles to become a saint, his supporters request that you report any miraculous answers to prayers to the Vatican.

Torre del Oro (Gold Tower) and Naval Museum

Sevilla's historic riverside Gold Tower was the starting and ending point for all shipping to the New World. It's named for the golden reflection of the sun off the Guadalquivir River—not for all the New World booty that landed here. Ever since the Moors built it in the 13th century, it's been part of the city's fortifications, and long anchored a heavy chain that draped from here across the river to protect the harbor. In 1248, King Ferdinand III's ships rammed the chain and broke through, taking the city from the Moors. Today, it houses a skippable, dreary naval museum with a mediocre river view.

Nao Victoria

Magellan may not have returned from his round-the-world expedition, but the *Nao Victoria* did, and this is a full-scale replica of that ship. A small museum and on-deck visit show how Basque navigator Juan Sebastián Elcano took charge of the last of five ships and brought 17 men safely back to Sevilla.

Cost and Hours: €3, Wed-Sun 10:00-18:00 except Fri-Sat until 19:00, closed Mon-Tue, +34 954 470 891, www.espacioprimeravueltaalmundo.org.

BARRIO SANTA CRUZ

For a self-guided walk through this neighborhood, see my "Barrio Santa Cruz Walk," earlier, or 🎧 download my free Sevilla City Walk audio tour.

Hospital de los Venerables

This former charity-run old-folks home and hospital comes with a Baroque church and an exquisite painting gallery that includes the Centro Velázquez, which displays works by one of Spain's premier artists. It merges local history, art, and architecture in one building. Everything is well explained by the audioguide.

Cost and Hours: €10, includes audioguide, Tue-Sat 10:00-18:00, Sun until 15:00, closed Mon, Plaza de los Venerables 8, +34 697 898 659, www.hospitalvenerables.es.

Visiting the Hospital: In the courtyard, you get a sense of how retired priests and Sevilla's needy mingled around its sunken fountain.

The church, which takes you back to the year 1700, is bursting with Baroque decor, one of Spain's best pipe organs, and frescoes

by Juan de Valdés Leal. Of note is the *trompe l'oeil* he painted on the sacristy ceiling, turning a small room into a piece of heaven. The decor exalts the priesthood and Spain's role as standard-bearer of the pope.

The top-notch **painting gallery** is dedicated to one of the world's greatest painters, Diego Velázquez (1599-1660), who was born in Sevilla and worked here as a young man. Velázquez's *Vista de Sevilla* helps you imagine the excitement of this thriving city in 1649 when, with 120,000 people, it was the fourth largest in Europe. You'll recognize landmarks like the Giralda bell tower, the cathedral, and the Torre del Oro. The pontoon bridge leads to Triana—where citizens of all ranks strolled the promenade together, as they still do today.

The Sevilla that shaped Velázquez was the gateway to the New World. There was plenty of stimulation: adventurers, fortune hunters, and artists passed through here, and many stayed for years. Of the few Velázquez paintings remaining in his hometown, three are in this gallery. Upstairs has little of interest, but the staircase dome is worth a look, as is the private box view into the church.

NORTH OF THE CATHEDRAL
Plaza Nueva
The pleasant "New Square" is a five-minute walk north of the cathedral and the end of the line for Sevilla's short tram system (which zips down Avenida de la Constitución to the San Bernardo train station).

At the center of the square is a **statue of King Ferdinand III,** who liberated Sevilla from the Moors in the 13th century and was later sainted. This is another example of Sevilla's devotion to the Virgin. If you look closely at the statue, you can see the horn of the king's saddle is actually his treasured Virgin of the Battles statuette. Made of hollowed ivory, it was carved to fit over the saddle horn, and he rode with it into battle many times. When his 13th-century tomb was opened in the 17th century, they found the same ivory Mary with his incorrupt body. (And that very statue is now in the cathedral's big sacristy).

For centuries after the Christian reconquest, a huge Franciscan **monastery** stood on this site; it was a spiritual home to many of the missionaries who colonized the California coast. But in the 1800s, when the Jesuits threatened the secular government and stood in the way of modern, post-revolutionary thinking, the power of the monasteries was overturned and grand monasteries like this were destroyed.

Running along the square is the relatively modern **City Hall.** Couples use the grand salon upstairs for weekend weddings, then join their photographers on the front steps. For a more interesting

look at this building, circle around to the other end (to the smaller square, called Plaza de San Francisco). This square—the site of the Spanish Inquisition's infamous *auto-da-fé*—has been used for executions, bullfights, and (today) big city events.

▲▲Church of the Savior (Iglesia del Salvador)

Sevilla's second-biggest church, built on the site of a ninth-century mosque, gleams with freshly scrubbed Baroque pride. While the larger cathedral is a jumble of styles, this church is uniformly Andalusian Baroque—the architecture, decor, and statues are all from the same period. The church is home to some of Sevilla's most beloved statues that are paraded through town during religious festivals.

Cost and Hours: €6, includes audioguide, covered by cathedral combo-ticket, best to buy ticket in advance online; Mon-Sat 11:00-18:00 (July-Aug from 10:00), Sun 15:00-19:30; Plaza del Salvador, +34 954 211 679, www.catedraldesevilla.es.

Advance Tickets Recommended: While lines are generally shorter here than at the cathedral, they can still be long and slow. It's smart to purchase your combo-ticket online in advance. Ticket in hand, head straight to the exit, where a guard will let you in.

Visiting the Church and Semana Santa Statues: The spacious **nave** covers the same footprint as the ancient mosque it replaced from the year 830, and because of that it's oddly shaped (square, like the cathedral). This Baroque structure dates from around 1700, built to replace an earlier (run-down) church. The enormous **high altar** features a golden Jesus (being Transfigured) atop an eruption of black clouds. But the artistic stars here are the whirling pair of angels holding lamps with red ropes. Look high above to see frescoes that, once long forgotten, were revealed by a recent cleaning. (It's easy to forget how sooty Europe's art treasures were until the last generation or so.)

The church's many richly decorated **chapels** are the highlight. Each has a distinct statue, generally made of wood, painted, and expressive in the Sevillian style. The realistic statues depict events from the Passion (the week leading up to Easter), showing Jesus being tortured and crucified, and Mary mourning her son. Many are set atop floats during Holy Week—and many are on pedestals, making them portable. The rest of the year, they reside here and are cared for by brotherhoods dedicated to charitable works. (If you visit here just before Holy Week, you might see floats being assembled and bedecked in flowers in the nave.) Some of the better-known statues headquartered here include:

The **Little Donkey,** or *Borriquita* (right of altar), carries a statue of Jesus into Jerusalem to kick off Holy Week on Palm Sunday. All six statues in this corner of the church parade together during

Holy Week. The grippingly beautiful **Christ of Love** (adjacent chapel, left of the donkey), showing the Crucifixion, dates from about 1600 and is one of the oldest in the parade.

Our Lady of the Waters (large chapel, right of the Little Donkey) is a maternal pyramid filling an extravagantly Baroque chapel with a white marble baptismal font in front. She predates this church by about 400 years. Though permanently parked now, for centuries she was paraded through Sevilla in times of drought.

Christ Suffering for the Afflicted (left of the altar) shows Christ laboring under his tortoiseshell and silver cross for souls stranded in purgatory—see groups in flames at the bottom.

Christ of the Passion (left of the altar, in the left transept) shows Jesus carrying the cross to his death. Made in 1619 by Juan Martínez Montañés, this is one of the city's most beloved statues. It's so revered by pilgrims and worshippers that the chapel has a separate entrance (though it's sometimes visible through the bars, if the curtain is open).

To reach the Christ of the Passion **chapel,** exit the church and go right, then right again. Under the stubby tower, go through a small door into a courtyard and then through a small pilgrims' shop (free, daily 10:00-14:00 & 17:00-21:00). For centuries, the faithful have come here to pray, marvel at the sadness that fills the chapel, then kiss Jesus' heel. (To join them, head up the stairs behind the altar.) Jesus is flanked by John the Evangelist and a grieving, red-eyed María Dolorosa, with convincing tears and a jeweled dagger in her heart. Also next to Jesus are two Jesuit missionaries who were martyred in Japan. Their skulls are under their feet. In the adjacent shop (above the cashier), a wall tile shows the Christ of the Passion statue in a circa-1620 procession.

Back outside, in the **courtyard,** you can feel the presence of the mosque that once stood on this spot. Its minaret is now the Christian bell tower and the mosque's arches are now halfway underground.

Nearby: Finish your visit by enjoying **Plaza del Salvador,** a favorite local meeting point. Strolling this square, you become part of the theater of life in Sevilla.

Casa de Pilatos

This 16th-century palace offers a scaled-down version of the Royal Alcázar (with a similar mix of Gothic, Moorish, and Renaissance styles) and a delightful garden. The nobleman who built it was inspired by a visit to the Holy Land, where he saw the supposed mansion of Pontius Pilate. If you've seen the Alcázar, this probably isn't worth the time or money. Your visit comes in two parts: the stark ground floor and garden (a tile lover's fantasy, with good audio-

guide); and a plodding, 25-minute guided English/Spanish tour of the lived-in noble residence upstairs.

Cost and Hours: €12, includes entire house and guided tour; €10 covers just the ground floor and garden; audioguide included in both tickets; daily 9:00-19:00, off-season until 18:00, tours run 2/hour (check schedule at entry); Plaza de Pilatos 1, http://en.fundacionmedinaceli.org.

▲Museo Palacio de la Condesa de Lebrija

This aristocratic mansion takes you back to the 18th century like no other place in town. The Countess of Lebrija was a passionate collector of antiquities. Her home's ground floor is paved with Roman mosaics (that you can actually walk on) from nearby Itálica and lined with musty old cases of Phoenician, Greek, Roman, and Moorish artifacts—mostly pottery. The grand staircase and dining-room tiles came from a former Augustinian convent, and several rooms were even modified to fit the collectibles the countess bought (a good example is the octagonal room built to house an eight-sided Roman floor mosaic). To see a plush world from a time when the nobility had a private priest and their own chapel, take a quickie tour of the upstairs, which shows the palace as the countess left it when she died in 1938.

Cost and Hours: €12, includes English/Spanish tour of "lived-in" upstairs—offered every 45 minutes; open daily 10:00-14:15 & 15:15-18:00, free and obligatory bag check, Calle Cuna 8, +34 954 227 802, www.palaciodelebrija.com.

Plaza de la Encarnación

Several years ago, in an attempt to revitalize this formerly nondescript square, the city unveiled what locals call "the mushrooms": a gigantic, undulating canopy of five waffle-patterned, toadstool-esque, hundred-foot-tall wooden structures. Together, this structure (officially named *Metropol Parasol*) provides shade, a gazebo for performances, and a traditional market hall. While the  market is busy each morning, locals don't know what to make of the avant-garde structure. A ramp under the canopy leads down to ancient-Roman-era street level, where a museum (the Antiquarium) displays Roman ruins found during the building process. From the museum level, a pay elevator takes you up top, where you can do a loop walk along the terrace to enjoy its commanding city views—but I found it not worth the time or trouble. Other views in

town are free and just as good (such as from the rooftop bar of the EME Catedral Hotel, across the street from the cathedral).

Cost and Hours: Plaza level always open and free; viewpoint elevator ride—€5 during the day, €10 at night, runs daily 10:00-23:30, shorter hours off-season; Antiquarium visit free with Alcázar ticket; www.setasdesevilla.com.

▲Flamenco Dance Museum (Museo del Baile Flamenco)

Though small and pricey, this museum is worthwhile for anyone looking to understand more about the dance that embodies the spirit of southern Spain. The main exhibit, on floor 1, takes about 45 minutes to see. It features well-produced videos, flamenco costumes, and other artifacts collected by the grande dame of flamenco, Cristina Hoyos. The top floor and basement house temporary exhibits, mostly of photography and other artwork. On the ground floor and in the basement, you can watch flamenco lessons in progress—or even take one yourself (one hour, first person-€60, €20/person after that, shoes not provided but yours are OK).

Cost and Hours: €10, €26 combo-ticket includes evening flamenco performance (see "Nightlife in Sevilla," later), daily 10:00-19:00, pick up English info sheet at front desk; about 3 blocks east of Plaza Nueva at Calle Manuel Rojas Marcos 3—follow signs for *Museo del Baile Flamenco*; +34 954 340 311, www.museoflamenco.com.

▲Museo de Bellas Artes

Sevilla's passion for religious art is preserved and displayed in its Museum of Fine Arts. While most Americans go for El Greco, Goya, and Velázquez (not a forte of this collection), this museum opens horizons and gives a fine look at other, less well-known Spanish masters: Zurbarán and Murillo. Rather than exhausting, the museum is pleasantly enjoyable.

Cost and Hours: €1.50; Tue-Sat 9:00-21:00, until 15:00 on Sun and in summer, closed Mon year-round; mandatory bag check (€1 deposit), +34 954 786 498, www.museosdeandalucia.es.

Getting There: The museum is at Plaza Museo 9, a 15-minute walk or cheap taxi ride from the cathedral.

Background: As Spain's economic golden age (the 1500s) blossomed into its arts and literature golden age (the 1600s), wealthy Sevilla reigned as the sophisticated capital of culture while Madrid was still a newly built center of government. Several of

Spain's top painters—Zurbarán, Murillo, and Velázquez—lived in Sevilla in the 1600s. They labored to make the spiritual world tangible, and forged the gritty realism that marks Spanish painting. You'll see balding saints and monks with wrinkled faces and sun-burned hands, radiating an inner spirituality. This highly accessible style inspired the Catholic faithful in an age when Protestants were demanding a closer personal relationship with God.

Appropriately, this collection of (mostly) religious art is now displayed in the halls of what once was a convent for friars of the Order of Mercy. The building itself is an attraction: It was a particularly wealthy convent boasting some of the finest courtyards and decorative tiles in the city. In the early 1800s, Spain's ultra-secular government began disbanding convents and monasteries, and secular fanatics had a heyday looting churches. Fortunately, much of Andalucía's religious art was rescued and hung safely here.

○ **Self-Guided Tour:** The permanent collection features 20 rooms in neat chronological order. It's easy to breeze through once with my tour, then backtrack to what appeals to you. Pick up the English-language floor plan, which explains the theme of each room.

• *Enter and follow signs to the permanent collection, which begins in Sala I (Room 1).*

Rooms 1-4: Medieval altarpieces of gold-backed saints, Virgin-and-babes, and Crucifixion scenes attest to the religiosity that nurtured Spain's early art. Spain's penchant for unflinching realism culminates in Room 2 with Michelangelo friend/rival Pietro Torrigiano's 1525 statue of an emaciated San Jerónimo, whose gaze never falters from the cross, and in Room 3 with the painted clay head of St. John the Baptist—complete with severed neck muscles, throat, and windpipe. This warts-and-all naturalism would influence the well-known Sevillian art teacher Francisco Pacheco (also Room 3) as well as his student and son-in-law, Velázquez (Room 4). Velázquez's *Head of an Apostle*—a sober portrait of a bearded, balding, wrinkled man—exemplifies how Sevillian painters could make once-inaccessible saints seem flesh and blood like you and me.

• *Continue through the pleasant outdoor courtyard (the convent's former cloister) to the grand, former church that is now Room 5.*

Room 5: Large-scale religious art now hangs in what was once a church nave. On the left wall is the *Apotheosis of St. Thomas Aquinas (Apoteosis de Santo Tomás de Aquino,* 1631) by **Francisco de Zurbarán** (thoor-ba-RAHN, 1598-1664). This is the artist's most important work, done at the height of his career. Zurbarán presents the pivotal moment when the great saint-theologian experiences his spiritual awakening. He's surrounded by ultra-realistic portraits of other saints, whose stately poses and simple gestures speak vol-

umes. What's unique about Zurbarán is the setting. He strips away any semblance of 3-D background to portray how these real people are having a surreal experience. Thomas has suddenly found himself in a heavenly cloud surrounded by long-dead saints, while his contemporaries below gaze upward, sharing the vision. We'll see more of Zurbarán later in our tour.

As you approach the former church's main altar, you find works of another hometown boy, **Bartolomé Murillo,** including

several paintings of the Virgin Mary, his signature subject (for more on Murillo, see the sidebar on page 694). He portrayed the Immaculate Conception of Mary, the doctrine that she was born without the taint of original sin. Typically, he depicted Mary as young, dressed in white and blue, gazing rapturously.
She stands atop the moon (crescent or full), surrounded by tumbling winged babies. Murillo's tiny *Madonna and Child* (*Virgen de la Servilleta,* 1665), at the end of the room in the center, shows the warmth and appeal of his work.

Murillo's sweet naturalism is quite different from the harsh realism of his fellow artists, so his work was understandably popular. For many Spaniards, Mary is their main connection to heaven. They pray directly to her, asking her to intercede on their behalf with God. Murillo's Marys are always receptive and ready to help.

Besides his *Inmaculadas,* Murillo painted popular saints. They often carry sprigs of plants, and cock their heads upward, caught up in a heavenly vision of sweet Baby Jesus. Murillo is also known for his "genre" paintings—scenes of common folk and rascally street urchins—but the museum has few of these.

• *Now head back outside to enjoy the coolness of the cloister and the beauty of its tiles, then go up the Imperial Staircase to the first floor.*

Rooms 6-9: In Rooms 6 and 7, you'll see more Murillos and Murillo imitators. Room 8 is dedicated to yet another native Sevillian (and friend of Murillo), Juan de Valdés Leal (1622-1690), whose work is also featured in the Hospital de la Caridad (see listing earlier). He adds Baroque motion and drama to religious subjects. His surreal colors and feverish, unfinished style create a mood of urgency. In Room 9, art students will recognize the work of José de Ribera—a Spaniard living in Italy—who merged Spanish realism with Caravaggio's strong dark-light contrast.

Room 10: Here you'll find more Zurbarán saints and monks, and the miraculous things they experienced, with an unblinking, crystal-clear, brightly lit, highly detailed realism. Browse the paint-

ings, enjoying the weathered faces, voluminous robes, and precisely etched details. These photorealistic people are shown against a neutral background, as though existing in the landscape of an otherworldly vision. Monks and nuns could meditate upon Zurbarán's meticulous paintings for hours, finding God in the details.

In Zurbarán's *St. Hugo Visiting the Refectory (San Hugo en el Refectorio)*, white-robed Carthusian monks gather for their simple meal in a communal dining hall. Above them hangs a painting of Mary, Baby Jesus, and John the Baptist. Zurbarán created paintings like this for monks' dining halls. His audience: celibate men and women who lived in isolation, as in this former convent, devoting their time to quiet meditation, prayer, and Bible study. Zurbarán shines a harsh spotlight on many of his subjects, creating strong shadows. Zurbarán's people often stand starkly isolated against a single-color background—a dark room or the gray-white of a cloudy sky. He was the ideal painter for the austere religion of 17th-century Spain as it led the Counter-Reformation, standing strong against the rising tide of Protestantism in Europe.

Adjacent to *St. Hugo*, find *The Virgin of the Caves (La Virgen de las Cuevas)* and study the piety and faith in the monks' weathered faces. Zurbarán's Mary is protective, with her hands placed on the heads of two monks. Note the loving detail on the cape embroidery, the brooch, and the flowers at her feet.

Rest of the Museum: Spain's subsequent art, from the 18th century on, generally followed the trends of the rest of Europe. Room 11 is a hallway with a dozen joyous scenes from the 1700s of carriages and parade floats filing by Sevillian landmarks. Room 12 has creamy Romanticism and hazy Impressionism. You'll see typical Sevillian motifs such as matadors, cigar-factory girls, and river landscapes. Of particular interest is the large *Death of the Master* by José Villegas Cordero, in which bullfighters touchingly express their grief after their teacher, gored in the ring, dies in bed. Enjoy these painted slices of Sevilla, then exit to experience similar scenes today.

FAR NORTH OF THE CATHEDRAL
▲▲Basílica de la Macarena

Sevilla's Holy Week celebrations are Spain's grandest. During the week leading up to Easter, the city is packed with pilgrims wit-

nessing 60 processions carrying about 100 religious floats. If you miss the actual event, you can get a sense of it by visiting the Basílica de la Macarena and its accompanying museum to see the two most impressive floats and the darling of Semana Santa, the statue of the Virgen de la Macarena. Although far from the city center, it's located on Sevilla's ring road and easy to reach. (While La Macarena is the big kahuna, for a more central look at beloved procession statues, consider stopping by the Church of the Savior or Triana's Church of Santa Ana, both described in this chapter.)

Cost and Hours: Church-free, treasury museum-€5; daily 9:00-14:00 & 18:00-21:30, mid-Sept-May daily 9:00-14:00 & 17:00-21:00 except Sun from 9:30, closed a few weeks before Holy Week for float preparation; audioguide-€1, +34 954 901 800, www.hermandaddelamacarena.es.

Getting There: A taxi is about €6 from the city center. The quickest bus routes are #C3 and #C4 from Puerta de Jerez (near the Torre del Oro) or Avenida de Menéndez Pelayo (the ring road east of the cathedral). Buses #C1 and #C2 also go there but take much longer.

Visiting the Church: Despite the long history of the Macarena statue, the Neo-Baroque church was only built in 1949 to give the oft-moved sculpture a permanent home. Grab a pew and study the statue.

Weeping Virgin: La Macarena is known as the "Weeping Virgin" for the five crystal teardrops trickling down her cheeks. She's like a Baroque doll with human hair and articulated arms, and even has underclothes. Sculpted in the late 17th century (probably by Pedro Roldán), she's become Sevilla's most popular image of Mary.

Her beautiful expression—halfway between smiling and crying—is ambiguous, letting worshippers project their own emotions onto her. Her weeping can be contagious—look around you. She's also known as La Esperanza, the Virgin of Hope, and she promises better times after the sorrow.

Installed in the left side chapel is the **Christ of the Judgment** (from 1654), showing Jesus on the day he was condemned. This statue and La Macarena stand atop the two

most important floats of the Holy Week parades. The side chapel on the right has an equally remarkable image of the **Virgen del Rosario,** which is paraded around the city on the last Sunday of October.

Tesoro (Treasury Museum): To see the floats and learn more, head to the museum (to reach the entrance—on the church's left side—either exit the church or go through a connecting door at the rear). This small, three-floor museum tells the history of the Virgin statue and the Holy Week parades. Though rooted in medieval times, the current traditions developed around 1600, with the formation of various fraternities (hermandades). During Holy Week, they demonstrate their dedication to God by parading themed floats throughout Sevilla to retell the story of the Crucifixion and Resurrection of Christ (for more, see the sidebar on page 676). The museum displays ceremonial banners, scepters, and costumed mannequins; videos show the parades in action (some displays in English).

The three-ton **float** that carries the Christ of the Judgment is slathered in gold leaf and shows a commotion of figures acting out the sentencing of Jesus. (The statue of Christ—the one you saw in the church—is placed before this crowd for the Holy Week procession.) Pontius Pilate is about to wash his hands. Pilate's wife cries as a man reads the death sentence. During the Holy Week procession, pious Sevillian women wail in the streets while relays of 48 men carry this float on the backs of their necks—only their feet showing under the drapes—as they shuffle through the streets from midnight until 14:00 in the afternoon every Good Friday. The men rehearse for months to get their choreographed footwork in sync.

La Macarena follows the Christ of the Judgment in the procession. Mary's smaller 1.5-ton float seems all silver and candles—"strong enough to support the roof, but tender enough to quiver in the soft night breeze." Mary has a wardrobe of three huge mantles, worn in successive years; these are about 100 years old, as is her six-pound gold crown/halo. This float has a mesmerizing effect on the crowds. They line up for hours, then clap, weep, and throw roses as it slowly sways along the streets, working its way through town. A Sevillian friend once explained, "She knows all the problems of Sevilla and its people; we've been confiding in her for centuries. To us, she is hope."

The museum collection also contains some **matador paraphernalia.** La Macarena is the patron saint of bullfighters, and they give thanks for her protection. Copies of her image are popular in bullring chapels. In 1912, bullfighter José Ortega, hoping for protection, gave La Macarena the five emerald brooches she wears. It worked for eight years...until he was gored to death in the ring.

For a month, La Macarena was dressed in widow's black—the only time that has happened.

Macarena Neighborhood: Outside the church, notice the best surviving bit of Sevilla's old walls. Originally Roman, what remains today was built by the Moors in the 12th century to (unsuccessfully) keep the Christians out. And yes, it's from this city that a local dance band (Los del Río) changed the world by giving us the popular 1990s song, "The Macarena." He-e-y-y, Macarena!

SOUTH OF THE CATHEDRAL
University

Today's university was yesterday's *fábrica de tabacos* (tobacco factory), which employed 10,000 young female *cigarreras*—including the saucy femme fatale of Bizet's opera *Carmen*. In the 18th century, it was the second-largest building in Spain, after El Escorial. Today it boasts a gallery of reproduced sculpture, a beautiful chapel, and a studious library. It's free to visit outside of school hours (Fri 9:30-12:30 & 16:00-18:00, Sat 9:30-14:00, closed to public Sun-Thu and Aug).

Plaza de España

This square, the surrounding buildings, and the adjacent María Luisa Park are the remains of the 1929 world's fair, where for a year the Spanish-speaking countries of the world enjoyed a mutual-admiration fiesta. With the restoration work here finished, this delightful area—the epitome of world's fair-style architecture—is once again great for people-watching (especially during the 19:00-20:00 peak paseo hour). The park's highlight is this for-  mer Spanish Pavilion. Its tiles—a trademark of Sevilla—show historic scenes and maps from every province of Spain (arranged in alphabetical order, from Álava to Zaragoza). Climb to one of the balconies for a classic postcard view of Sevilla. Wandering around this zone, you may feel like you've been here before: Lots of filming has been done here, including bits of *Star Wars: Episode II* and *Lawrence of Arabia*.

▲▲TRIANA WALK

In Sevilla—as is true in so many other European cities that grew up in the age of river traffic—what was long considered the "wrong side of the river" is now the most colorful part of town. Sevilla's Triana, west of the river, is a proud neighborhood that identifies

with its working-class origins and is famed for its flamenco soul (characterized by the statue that greets arrivals from across the river). Known for their independent spirit, locals describe crossing the bridge toward the city center as "going to Sevilla." To trace the route described next, see the "Sevilla" map on page 668.

• *To reach Triana from downtown Sevilla, head to the river and cross over...*

Puente de Isabel II: Note the bridge's distinctive design as you approach. It was inspired by an 1834 crossing over the Seine River in Paris—look for the circles under each span that lead the way into Triana.

While crossing the Guadalquivir River, to the right you can see Sevilla's single skyscraper—designed by Argentine architect César Pelli of Malaysia's Twin Towers fame. Locals lament the Torre Sevilla because according to city law, no structure should be taller than the Giralda bell tower. But since this building doesn't sit within the city center, developers found a way to avoid that regulation. Today it houses a bank, offices, a swanky shopping center, and a fancy five-star hotel. Surrounding the skyscraper are leftover buildings from the 1992 Expo.

The **Capilla del Carmen** sits at the end of the bridge. Designed by 1929 world's fair architect Aníbal González, the bell tower and chapel add glamour to the entrance to Triana.

• *At the end of the bridge, walk down the staircase on the right.*

Triana's Castle and Market: The **Castillo de San Jorge** is a 12th-century castle that in the 15th century was the headquarters for Sevilla's Inquisition (free small museum and TI kiosk; Mon-Fri 11:00-18:30, Sat-Sun 10:00-15:00). Explore the castle briefly, then retrace your steps to visit the neighborhood's covered market. Built in 2005 in the Moorish Revival style, it sits within the ruins of the castle (you can see its remains as you exit at the other side). The market bustles in the mornings and afternoons with traditional fruit and vegetable stalls as well as colorful tapas bars and cafés. This is a great spot to stop for coffee, watch produce being sold, and see locals catching up on the latest gossip.

• *Exit the market downstairs, out the back door, and turn left.*

Ceramic Museum and Shops: Here you can discover the district's ceramic history, starting with the **Museo de la Cerámica de Triana,** which focuses on tile and pottery production. Located in the remains of a former riverside factory, the museum explains the entire process—from selecting the right type of earth to kiln firing—with a small collection of ceramics and well-produced videos of interviews with former workers (good English translations). Another short video highlights Triana's neighborhood pride (€2, free with Alcázar ticket, Tue-Sat 11:00-18:00, Sun 10:00-15:00, closed Mon, Calle Antillano Campos 14, +34 954 342 737).

After your museum visit, ponder what you can carry home from nearby shops. Walk along Calle Antillano Campos, then turn left on Calle Alfarería. This area is lined with the old facades of ceramic workshops that once populated this quarter. Most have closed up or moved to the outskirts of town, where rent is cheaper. But a few stalwarts remain, including the lavishly decorated Santa Ana and the large showroom Santa Isabel (at Calle Alfarería 12). Several recommended bars are in this area (see "Eating in Sevilla," later).

• Continue down Calle Alfarería to...

Calle San Jacinto: This is the main (pedestrian-only) street of the quarter. It's the hip center of the people scene—a festival of life each evening. Venturing down side lanes, you find classic 19th-century facades with fine ironwork and colorful tiles.

• Walk down Calle San Jacinto in the direction of the bridge. The final cross-street (to the right) is...

Calle Pureza: This street cuts through the historic center of Triana. As you wander, pop into bars and notice how the decor mixes bullfighting lore with Virgin worship. It's easy enough to follow your nose into Dulcería Manu Jara, at Calle Pureza 5, where tempting artisan pastries are made on the spot.

At #12 is La Antigua Abacería. An *abacería* is a traditional neighborhood grocer that also functions as a neighborhood bar. Step inside and feel the presence of the Virgin Mary, flamenco culture, wine, and ham hocks...beautiful ham hocks.

At #28, sculptor José Gómez is busy with his restoration work and sculpting. If it's early in the year, he's likely particularly busy, preparing for Holy Week.

Take a moment to gaze down the street—looking above the shops—and appreciate the real community feel of this colorful line of homes.

Chapel of the Mariners: Across from #54 is the Capilla de los Marineros, home of the beloved Virgin statue called *Nuestra Señora de la Esperanza de Triana* (Our Lady of Hope of Triana). She's a big deal here. In Sevilla, upon meeting someone, it's customary to ask not only which football team they support, but which Virgin Mary they favor. The top two in town are the Virgen de la Macarena and La Esperanza de Triana. On the Thursday of Holy Week, it's a battle royale of the Madonnas, as Sevilla's two favorite Virgins are both in processions on the streets at the same time. Step inside to see her presiding like a queen from the high altar. The adoration is palpable. In the pilgrims' shop adjacent, see the photo of this Mary in the streets being mobbed by what seems like the entire population of Triana. Jesus with his cross is almost second fiddle. The brotherhood of this Virgin runs a delightful (if you're into Mary)

museum where you can see her actual float, lots of regalia, and video clips (€4 entry).

• *Continue down Calle Pureza to explore the...*

Rest of Triana: The next church is the **Church of Santa Ana,** nicknamed the "Cathedral of Triana." The recommended **Bar Santa Ana** (on the corner before the church) is a classic Virgin Mary bar (with a little bullfighting tossed in). Step inside. A sign behind the bar is counting down the days to the next Holy Week.

Walking around the little church, on the far side is a delightful square with two recommended eateries, **Bar Bistec** and **Taberna La Plazuela.** Circling farther around, return to Calle Pureza and the tiny Calle Duarte, which leads to the river. Gazing across the water, imagine the ships that sailed from here to kick off the Age of Discovery. The replica of Magellan's *Nao Victoria* (described on page 711) is anchored on the other shore.

Don't cross the river hungry. Consider making the neighborhood you just explored your destination for a tapas crawl.

NEAR SEVILLA
Itálica

One of Spain's most impressive Roman ruins is found outside the sleepy town of Santiponce, about six miles northwest of Sevilla. Founded in 206 BC for wounded soldiers recuperating from the Second Punic War, Itálica became a thriving town of great agricultural and military importance. It was the birthplace of the famous Roman emperors Trajan and Hadrian. Today its best-preserved ruin is its amphitheater—one of the largest in the Roman Empire—with a capacity for 25,000 spectators (and used as a backdrop for dragons in *Game of Thrones*). Other highlights include beautiful floor mosaics, such as the one in Casa de los Pájaros (House of the Birds), with representations of more than 30 species of birds. In summer, plan your visit to avoid the midday heat—arrive either early or late in the day, and definitely bring water. After being picked clean as a quarry for centuries by Sevillian builders, there's not much left here.

Cost and Hours: €1.50; Tue-Sun 9:00-15:00 (Tue-Sat until 21:00 in April-mid-June), shorter hours off-season, closed Mon; mobile +34 600 141 767, www.museosdeandalucia.es.

Getting There: You can get to Itálica on bus #M-172A or #M-172B from Sevilla's Plaza de Armas station (30-minute trip, 2/hour Mon-Sat, hourly on Sun). If you're driving, head west out of Sevilla in the direction of Huelva; after you cross the second branch of the river, turn north on SE-30, exit on to N-630, and after a few miles, get off at Santiponce. Drive past pottery warehouses and through the town to the ruins at the far (west) end.

Experiences in Sevilla

▲Bullfights

Some of Spain's most intense bullfighting happens in Sevilla's 14,000-seat bullring, Plaza de Toros. The arena hosts about 45 fights each year, which are held (generally at 18:30) on most Sundays in May and June; on Easter and Corpus Christi; daily during the April Fair; and for two weeks in late September (during the Feria de San Miguel). These serious fights, with adult matadors, are called *corrida de toros* and often sell out in advance. On many Thursday

evenings in July, the *novillada* fights take place, with teenage novices doing the killing and smaller bulls doing the dying. *Corrida de toros* seats range from €60 for high seats looking into the sun to €225 for the first three rows in the shade under the royal box; *novillada* seats are half that—and easy to buy at the arena a few minutes before showtime (ignore scalpers outside; get information at a TI, your hotel, by phone, or online; +34 655 430 455, www.taquillaoficial.com).

▲▲Bullring (Plaza de Toros) and Bullfight Museum (Museo Taurino)

This 50-minute tour (escorted with audioguide) takes you through the bullring's strangely quiet and empty arena, its museum, and the chapel where the matador prays before the fight. (Thanks to readily available blood transfusions, there have been no deaths here in three decades.) The two most revered figures of Sevilla, the Virgen de la Macarena and the Jesús del Gran Poder (Christ of All Power), are represented in the chapel. In the museum, you'll see great classic scenes and the heads of a few bulls—awarded the bovine equivalent of an Oscar for a particularly good fight. The city was so appalled when the famous matador Manolete was killed in 1947 that even the mother of the bull that gored him was destroyed. Matadors—dressed to kill—are heartthrobs in their "suits of light." Many girls have their bedrooms wallpapered with posters of cute bullfighters. See page 951 for more on the "art" of bullfighting.

Cost and Hours: €10, includes audioguide, entrance with escorted tour only—no free time inside; 3/hour, daily 9:30-21:00—last tour at 20:30, Nov-March until 19:30; until 15:00 on fight days, when chapel and horse room are closed. While they take groups of up to 50, it's still wise to reserve a spot in the busy season (+34 954 210 315, www.realmaestranza.com).

April Fair

Two weeks after Easter, much of Sevilla packs into its vast fairgrounds for a grand party (April 23-29 in 2023). The fair, seeming to bring all that's Andalusian together, feels friendly, spontaneous, and very real. The passion for horses, flamenco, and sherry is clear—riders are ramrod straight, colorfully clad girls ride sidesaddle, and everyone's drinking sherry spritzers. Women sport outlandish dresses that would look clownish elsewhere but are somehow

brilliant here en masse. Every day for one crazy week, horses clog the streets in an endless parade until about 20:00, when they clear out and the lanes fill with exuberant locals. The party goes on literally 24 hours a day.

Countless private party tents, called *casetas,* line the lanes. Each tent is the private party zone of a family, club, or association. You need to know someone in the group—or make friends quickly—to get in. Because of the exclusivity, it has a real family-affair feeling. In each *caseta,* everyone knows everyone. It seems like a thousand wedding parties being celebrated at the same time.

Any tourist can have a fun and memorable evening by simply crashing the party. The city's entire fleet of taxis (who can legally charge double) and buses seems dedicated to shuttling people from downtown to the fairgrounds. Given the traffic jams and inflated prices, you may be better off hiking: From the Torre del Oro, cross the San Telmo Bridge to Plaza de Cuba and hike down Calle Asunción. You'll see the towering gate to the fairgrounds in the distance. Just follow the crowds (there's no admission charge). Arrive before 20:00 to see the horses, but stay later, as the ambience improves after the *caballos* giddy-up on out. Some of the larger tents are sponsored by the city and open to the public, but the best action is in the streets, where party-goers from the livelier *casetas* spill out. Although private tents have bouncers, everyone is so happy that it's not tough to strike up an impromptu friendship, become a "special guest," and be invited in. The drink flows freely, and the food is fun, bountiful, and cheap.

Flamenco Classes

Energetic performances often leave people wanting more, so Eva Izquierdo shares her passion for flamenco culture with an inspiring **master class** at a studio in the city center. Eva introduces you to the essentials of flamenco: its origins, rhythms, and different styles

(palos). Learn to clap properly—technique is everything—in order to accompany flamenco music and song. Once you've got the beat down, you'll get more out of any show. If flamenco captivates you with its passion and tension, learn some of the basic movements to express those feelings. After basic foot and leg work, Eva will guide you through a unique routine—*olé!* Reservations are required (€25, 1 hour, 1-4 classes daily—contact her for details, Calle Gravina 50, mobile +34 626 007 868, www.ishowusevilla.com).

Shopping in Sevilla

For the best local shopping experience in Sevilla, visit the popular pedestrian streets Sierpes, Tetuán, Velázquez, and Cuna near Plaza Nueva. They, and the surrounding lanes, are packed with people and shops. For details, see my "Shopping Paseo," later in this section.

Clothing and shoe stores stay open all day. Other shops generally take a siesta, closing between 13:30 and 16:00 or 17:00 on weekdays, as well as on Saturday afternoons and all day Sunday. Big department stores such as **El Corte Inglés** stay open (and air-conditioned) right through the siesta. El Corte Inglés on Plaza del Duque also has a supermarket downstairs, a pricey cafeteria, and the Gourmet Experience food court on the fifth floor, with several international options and a view terrace (Mon-Sat 10:00-22:00, closed Sun).

Souvenir Markets

Popular Sevillian souvenir items include ladies' fans, shawls, *mantillas* (ornate head scarves), other items related to flamenco (castanets, guitars, costumes), ceramics, and bullfighting posters. The following markets are worth a browse.

Collectors' markets hop on Sunday. You'll see stamps and coins, and kids trading soccer cards like American kids trade baseball cards, at Plaza del Cabildo (near the cathedral). You can browse art on Plaza del Museo (by the Museo de Bellas Artes).

The arts-and-crafts **Mercado El Postigo,** in an architecturally interesting old market building behind the Hospital de la Caridad, features artisan wares of all types (Mon-Fri 10:00-19:00, Sat-Sun until 20:00, at the corner of Calles de Arfe and Dos de Mayo, +34 954 560 013).

Mercado del Arenal, the covered fish-and-produce market, is perfect for hungry photographers (see "Eating in Sevilla," later).

▲▲Shopping Paseo

Although many tourists never get beyond the cathedral and Barrio Santa Cruz, the lively pedestrianized shopping area north of the cathedral is well worth a wander. The best shopping streets—Calle Sierpes and Calle Cuna—also happen to be part of the oldest section of Sevilla. A walk here is a chance to join one of Spain's liveliest paseos—that bustling celebration of life that takes place before dinner each evening, when everyone is out strolling, showing off their fancy shoes and checking out everyone else's. This walk, if done between 18:00 and 20:00, gives you a chance to experience the paseo scene while getting a look at the town's most popular shops. First, to get warmed up, we'll walk from Plaza Nueva down Calle Tetuán (a pedestrian mall with more trendy fashion). Then we'll double back on the much more interesting (and traditional) Calle Sierpes.

Start on the pedestrianized **Plaza Nueva**—the 19th-century square facing the ornate City Hall. From here wander the length of **Calle Tetuán,** where old-time standbys bump up against fashion-right boutiques. First you'll find the flagship store of **Camper** (#24), the proudly Spanish shoe brand that's become a worldwide favorite. The rest of the street showcases mainly modern Spanish brands, such as Massimo Dutti, Zara, and Mango. Next to the Chico jewelry store (#9) you'll see a large tile panel serving as permanent advertising for a US import that was significant in Sevilla in the 1920s: the **Studebaker**. During the remainder of this walk, make sure to look up occasionally, because the shopping streets are dotted with other surviving ads in tile work.

Calle Tetuán (which changes names to Calle Velázquez) ends five blocks later at La Campana, a big intersection and popular meeting point. The super department store El Corte Inglés is just beyond, on Plaza del Duque de la Victoria.

Turn right at the end of the street. At the corner of Calle Sierpes awaits a venerable pastry shop, **Confitería La Campana,** with a fine 1885 interior...and Sevilla's most tempting sweets (take a break at the outdoor tables, or head to the back of the shop, where you can grab a coffee and pastry at the stand-up bar).

The green newsstand in front of the pastry shop is **Prensa Sierpes.** This traditional newsstand has been in Miguel's family for 100 years, and while times are tough as newspaper sales decrease, he still has his loyal customers.

You may see someone nearby selling lottery tickets to benefit a charity named ONCE (the national organization for the blind of Spain). They not only raise money for the charity this way, but they also provide job opportunities for those in need.

A few steps down Calle Sierpes at #5 is **Papelería Ferrer,** where the Ferrer family has been selling traditional stationery and

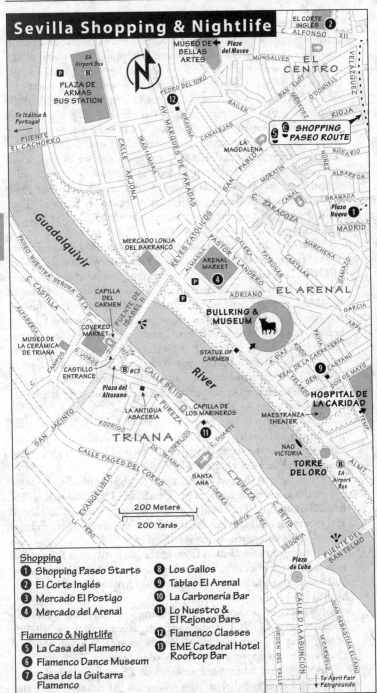

Sevilla Shopping & Nightlife

Shopping
1. Shopping Paseo Starts
2. El Corte Inglés
3. Mercado El Postigo
4. Mercado del Arenal

Flamenco & Nightlife
5. La Casa del Flamenco
6. Flamenco Dance Museum
7. Casa de la Guitarra Flamenco
8. Los Gallos
9. Tablao El Arenal
10. La Carbonería Bar
11. Lo Nuestro & El Rejoneo Bars
12. Flamenco Classes
13. EME Catedral Hotel Rooftop Bar

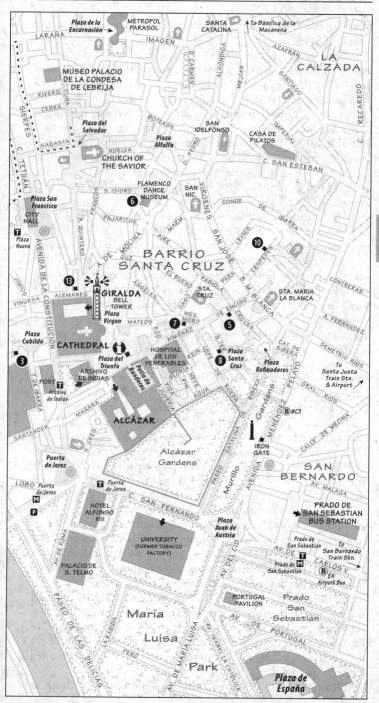

SEVILLA

pens since 1856. Such elegance survives and is appreciated by the people of Sevilla.

Next, at #19, is the clock-covered, wood-paneled **El Cronómetro** shop, where master watchmakers have been doing business since 1901. If you've got a problem with your Rolex, drop in—they're an official retailer of all the luxury brands.

At #33 is a **Juan Foronda** shop, since 1926 carrying traditional ladies' accessories for Sevilla's many festivals. For a fancy festival hat, stop at #40. **Sombrerería Maquedano** is a styling place—especially for men. They claim to be the oldest hat seller in Sevilla. Check out the great selection of wide-brimmed horse-rider hats, perfect for the April Fair. The inventory is huge but hiding—hats are stacked Pringles-style within boxes throughout the store.

If it's teatime, #45 is a handy next stop. Since 1910 **Ochoa** *confitería* and *salón de té* has been tempting locals with a long display case of sweets. In back is a buffet line for tapas and a light lunch.

At the corner of Sierpes and Jovellanos/Sagasta, you'll find several fine shops featuring more Andalusian accessories. **Abanicos Díaz** (#69) has a dazzling selection. Drop in to see how serious locals are about their fans, shawls, *mantillas,* and *peinetas* (combs designed to secure and prop up the *mantilla*). The most valuable *mantillas* are silk, and the top-quality combs are made of tortoiseshell (though people generally opt for much more affordable polyester and plastic). Andalusian women accessorize with fans, matching them to different dresses. The *mantilla* comes in black (worn only on Holy Thursday and by the mother of the groom at weddings) and white (worn at bullfights during the April Fair).

From here turn left down **Calle Sagasta.** Notice that the street has two names—the modern version and a medieval one: Antigua Calle de Gallegos ("Former Street of the Galicians"). With the Christian victory in 1248, the Muslims were given one month to evacuate. To consolidate Christian control during that time, settlers from Galicia, the northwest corner of Iberia, were planted here; this street was the center of their neighborhood.

The first shop on the right is **Lotería Sagasta,** the government-run national lottery. It's well known that the government makes a 30 percent margin on bettors; it's essentially a tax on those who aren't so bright. At Christmas time, a line of those hoping to strike it rich stretches down the street. Wish someone *"buena suerte."*

If you did win, you'd want to dress up. At #5, **Galán Camisería** is a traditional men's store that sells the "uniform" for the older gentlemen of Andalucía. While young men dress casually in T-shirts and jeans, older men still dress up to go out (especially for the Sunday paseo). Do a quick visual survey and see how the old formality persists.

Now jump into **Plaza del Salvador**—it's teeming with life at

the foot of the Church of the Savior (well worth a visit; described earlier, under "Sights in Sevilla").

Finish your shopping stroll by heading left up **Calle Cuna.** At #50 peek into the windows at **Barcarola.** This *boutique infantil* displays pricey but exquisitely made baby clothes—knit, embroidered, starched, and beribboned—along with baptismal gowns with bonnets, tiny crocheted booties, and more. This street is actually more famous for its exuberant flamenco dresses and classic wedding dresses. Local women save up to have flamenco dresses custom-made for the April Fair: They're considered an important status symbol. At #46 a shop displays this year's dress fashions (or last year's at clearance prices). And at #42, **Galerias Madrid** has all the fabric that more talented shoppers need to save money, sew their own dress, and get it just right.

Nightlife in Sevilla

▲▲▲FLAMENCO

This music-and-dance art form has its roots in the Roma (Gypsy) and Moorish cultures. Even at a packaged "flamenco evening," sparks fly. The men do most of the flamboyant machine-gun footwork. The women often concentrate on the graceful turns and smooth, shuffling step of the *soleá* version of the dance. Watch the musicians. Flamenco guitarists, with their lightning-fast finger-roll strums, are among the best in the world. The intricate rhythms are set by castanets or the hand-clapping (called *palmas*) of those who aren't dancing at the moment. In the raspy-voiced wails of the singers, you'll hear echoes of the Muslim call to prayer.

Like jazz, flamenco thrives on improvisation. Also like jazz, good flamenco is more than just technical proficiency. A singer or dancer with "soul" is said to have *duende*. Flamenco is a happening, with bystanders clapping along and egging on the dancers with whoops and shouts. Get into it.

Hotels push tourist-oriented, nightclub-style flamenco shows, but they charge a commission. Fortunately, it's easy to book a place on your own.

Sevilla's flamenco offerings tend to fall into three categories: serious concerts (about €20 and about an hour long), where the singing and dancing take center stage; touristy dinner-and-drinks shows with table service (generally around €40—not including

food—and 90 minutes long); and—the least touristy option—
casual bars with late-night performances, where for the cost of a
drink you can catch impromptu (or semi-impromptu) musicians at
play. Here's the rundown for each type of performance. For venue
locations, see the "Sevilla Shopping & Nightlife" map, earlier.

Serious Flamenco Concerts

While it's hard to choose among these three nightly, one-hour flamenco concerts, I'd say enjoying one is a must during your Sevilla
visit. To the novice viewer, each company offers equal quality. They
cost about the same, and each venue is small, intimate (congested
seating in not-very-comfy chairs), and air-conditioned. For many,
the concerts are preferable to the shows (listed next) because they're
half the cost, length, and size (smaller audience), and generally
start earlier in the evening. Also, shows are not appropriate for kids
under six (or perhaps vice versa).

My recommended concerts are careful to give you a good overview of the art form, covering all the flamenco bases. At each venue
you can reserve by phone and pay upon arrival, or drop by early to
pick up a ticket. While La Casa del Flamenco is the nicest and
most central venue, Flamenco Dance Museum has an exhibit that
can add to the experience.

La Casa del Flamenco is in a delightful arcaded courtyard
right in the Barrio Santa Cruz (€20, RS%—€2 discount with this
book if you book directly and pay cash; shows nightly at 19:00 and
20:30, earlier or later performances added with demand—confirm
on their website or stop by the venue; no drinks, 75 spacious seats,
next to recommended Hotel Alcántara, Calle Ximénez de Enciso
28, +34 955 029 999, www.lacasadelflamencosevilla.com).

Flamenco Dance Museum, while the most congested venue
(with 150 tightly packed seats), has a bar and allows drinks inside, and puts on a bigger production (six performers). It has festival seating—the doors open early so, for earlier performances, you
can grab the seat of your choice, then tour the museum before the
show (€25, nightly at 19:00 and 20:45, earlier or later performances
added with demand; €29 combo-ticket includes the museum—described earlier under "Sights in Sevilla"; reservations smart, +34
954 340 311, www.museoflamenco.com).

Casa de la Guitarra Flamenco is another venue in the tourist zone with cramped seating (75 seats) and a strong performance
(€18, daily at 19:30 and 21:00, no drinks, next to recommended
Restaurante San Marco, Calle Mesón del Moro 12, +34 954 224
093, www.flamencoensevilla.com).

Razzle-Dazzle Flamenco Shows

These packaged shows can be a bit sterile—and an audience
of mostly tourists doesn't help—but I find both Los Gallos and

Tablao El Arenal entertaining and riveting. While El Arenal may have a slight edge on talent, and certainly feels slicker, Los Gallos has a cozier setting, with cushy rather than hard chairs, and is cheaper and less pretentious.

Los Gallos presents nightly 75-minute shows at 19:00 and 20:45 (€35 ticket includes drink, arrive 30 minutes early for best seats, bar, no food served, Plaza de Santa Cruz 11, +34 954 216 981, www.tablaolosgallos.com, owners José and Blanca promise goose bumps). Their box office is open at 11:00 (you'll pass it on my Barrio Santa Cruz Walk).

Tablao El Arenal is more of an old-fashioned dinner show with arguably more professional performers and a classier setting. Dinner customers get preferred seating and servers work throughout the performance (€40 ticket includes drink, €62 includes tapas, €75 includes dinner, 75-minute shows at 19:00 and 21:30, likely later in summer, near bullring at Calle Rodo 7, +34 954 216 492, www.tablaoelarenal.com).

Impromptu Flamenco in Bars

Spirited flamenco singing still erupts spontaneously in bars throughout the old town after midnight—but you need to know where to look. Ask a local for the latest.

La Carbonería Bar, the sangria equivalent of a beer garden, is a few blocks north of the Barrio Santa Cruz. It's a big, open-tented area filled with young locals, casual guitar strummers, and nearly nightly flamenco music from about 22:30 to 24:00. Located just a few blocks from most of my recommended hotels, this is worth finding if you're not quite ready to end the day (no cover, daily 20:00-very late; near Plaza Santa María—find Hotel Fernando III, along the side alley Céspedes at #21; +34 954 214 460).

While the days of Roma performers and flamenco throbbing throughout Triana are mostly long gone, a few bars still host live dancing; **Lo Nuestro** and **El Rejoneo** are favorites (at Calle Betis 31A and 31B).

OTHER NIGHTLIFE
▲▲Evening Paseo

Sevilla is meant for strolling. The paseo thrives every evening (except in winter) in these areas: along either side of the river between the San Telmo and Isabel II bridges (Paseo de Cristóbal Colón and Triana district; see "Eating in Sevilla," later), up Avenida de la Constitución, around Plaza Nueva, at Plaza de España, and throughout the Barrio Santa Cruz. The best paseo scene is about 19:00 to 21:00, but on hot summer nights, even families with toddlers are out and about past midnight. Spend some time rafting through this river of humanity.

Nighttime Views

Savor the view of floodlit Sevilla by night from the Triana side of the river—perhaps over dinner. For the best late-night drink with a cathedral view, visit the trendy top floor of **EME Catedral Hotel** (at Calle Alemanes 27). Ride the elevator to the top, climb the staircases to the cocktail bar, and sit down at a tiny table with a big view (daily 12:00-24:00).

Sleeping in Sevilla

All of my listings are centrally located, mostly within a five-minute walk of the cathedral. The first are near the charming but touristy Barrio Santa Cruz. The last group is just as central but closer to the river, across the boulevard in a less touristy zone.

Room rates as much as double during the two Sevilla fiestas (Holy Week and the April Fair). In general, the busiest and most expensive months are April, May, September, and October. Hotels put rooms on the discounted push list in July and August—when people with good sense avoid this furnace—and from November through February.

If you do visit in July or August, you'll find the best deals in central, business-class places. They offer summer discounts and provide a (necessary) cool, air-conditioned refuge. But be warned that Spain's air-conditioning often isn't the icebox you're used to, especially in Sevilla.

BARRIO SANTA CRUZ

These places are off Calle Santa María la Blanca and Plaza Santa María. The most convenient parking lot is the underground Cano y Cueto garage (see page 670). A self-service launderette is a couple of blocks away up Avenida de Menéndez Pelayo (see "Helpful Hints" on page 671).

$$$$ Casa del Poeta offers peace, quiet, and a timeless elegance that seem contrary to its location in the heart of Santa Cruz. At the end of a side street, Trinidad and Ángelo have lovingly converted an old family mansion with 17 spacious rooms surrounding a large central patio into a home away from home. Evening guitar concerts plus a fantastic view terrace make it a worthwhile splurge (free breakfast if you reserve on their website, family room, air-con, elevator, Calle Don Carlos Alonso Chaparro 3, +34 954 213 868, www.casadelpoeta.es, info@casadelpoeta.es).

$$$$ Hotel Las Casas de la Judería has 178 quiet, classy rooms and junior suites, most of them tastefully decorated with hardwood floors and a Spanish Old World ambience. The service can be too formal, but the rooms, which spread out through three connected buildings surrounding a series of peaceful courtyards, are

a romantic splurge (air-con, elevator, pool in summer, valet parking, Plaza Santa María 5, +34 954 415 150, www.casasypalacios. com, juderia@casasypalacios.com).

$$$$ Hotel Casa 1800, well priced for its elegance, is worth the extra euros. Located dead-center in the Barrio Santa Cruz (facing a boisterous tapas bar that quiets down after midnight), its 33 rooms are accessed via a lovely chandeliered patio lounge, where guests enjoy a daily free afternoon tea. With a rooftop terrace and swimming pool offering an impressive cathedral view, and tastefully appointed rooms with high, beamed ceilings, it's a winner (family rooms, air-con, elevator, Calle Rodrigo Caro 6, +34 954 561 800, www.hotelcasa1800.com, info@hotelcasa1800.com).

$$$ Hotel Amadeus is a classy and comfortable gem, with welcoming public spaces lovingly decorated with musical motifs, and a very charming staff. The 42 recently renovated rooms are situated around small courtyard spaces among four interconnected buildings. Elevators take you to a multitiered roof terrace that covers the entire property and boasts an under-the-stars hot tub and a small pool. Breakfast is plentiful—enjoy it in your room, in the lounge, or on a terrace (air-con, elevator, laundry service, pay parking nearby, Calle Farnesio 6, +34 954 501 443, www. hotelamadeussevilla.com, reservas@hotelamadeussevilla.com, wonderfully run by María Luisa and her daughters Zaida and Cristina).

$$$ Hotel Palacio Alcázar is the former home and studio of John Fulton, an American who moved here to become a bullfighter and painter. This charming boutique hotel has 12 crisp, modern rooms, and each soundproofed door is painted with a different dreamy scene of Sevilla. Triple-paned windows keep out the noise from the plaza (air-con, elevator, rooftop terrace with bar and cathedral views, Plaza de la Alianza 11, +34 954 502 190, www. hotelpalacioalcazar.com, hotel@palacioalcazar.com).

$$$ Hotel Murillo enjoys one of the most appealing locations in Santa Cruz, along one of the very narrow "kissing lanes." Above its elegant, antiques-filled lobby are 64 nondescript, salmon-colored rooms with marble bathrooms (air-con, elevator, Calle Lope de Rueda 7, +34 954 216 095, www.hotelmurillo.com, reservas@ hotelmurillo.com). They also rent apartments with kitchens (see website for details).

$$ El Rey Moro encircles its spacious, colorful patio with 18 rooms. Colorful, dripping with quirky Andalusian character, and thoughtful about including extras (such as free loaner bikes, a welcome drink, afternoon snacks, and private rooftop whirlpool-bath time), it's a class act (air-con, elevator, Reinoso 8, +34 954 563 468, www.elreymoro.com, hotel@elreymoro.com).

$$ Hotel Alcántara offers clean and casual comfort in the

SEVILLA

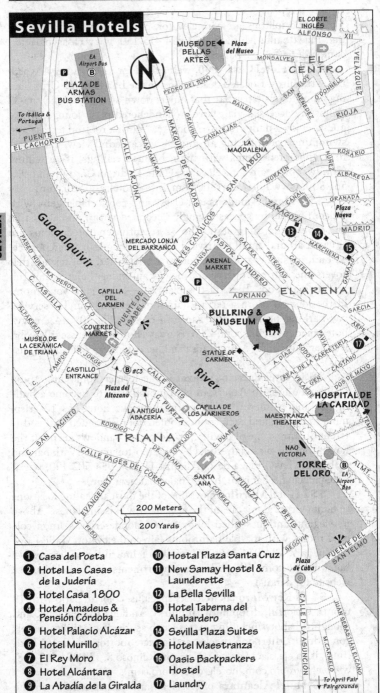

Sevilla Hotels

EL CORTE INGLÉS
C. ALFONSO XII

MUSEO DE BELLAS ARTES
Plaza del Museo

MONSALVES

EL CENTRO

EA Airport Bus

P B

PLAZA DE ARMAS BUS STATION

SAN ELOY
O'DONNELL

PEDRO DEL TORO

VELÁZQUEZ

To Itálica & Portugal

AV. MARQUES DE PARADAS

GRAVINA

CANALEJAS

BAILEN

LA MAGDALENA

SAN PABLO

MORATIN

RIOJA

ROSARIO

ALBAREDA

NÚÑEZ

PUENTE EL CACHORRO

CALLE ARJONA

TRASTAMARA

REYES CATÓLICOS

C. ZARAGOZA

CANAL

GRANADA

Plaza Nueva

MADRID

Guadalquivir

PASEO NUESTRA SEÑORA DE LA O

MERCADO LONJA DEL BARRANCO

PASTOR Y LANDERO

ALMANSA

GALEA

PATRONAS

13

14

15

MARCHENA

C. CASTILLA

ALFARERÍA

CAPILLA DEL CARMEN

PUENTE DE ISABEL II

ARENAL MARKET

P

CASTELAR

EL ARENAL

GARCIA

MUSEO DE LA CERÁMICA DE TRIANA

COVERED MARKET

S. JORGE

CAMPO

CASTILLO ENTRANCE

ADRIANO

P

BULLRING & MUSEUM

GAMAZO

ARFE

17

PAVÍA

RODDO

REAL DE LA CARRETERÍA

A. DIAZ

GEN. CASTAÑO

VELARDE

DOS DE MAYO

B #C3

CALLE BETIS

River

STATUE OF CARMEN

Plaza del Altozano

C. PUREZA

LA ANTIGUA ABACERÍA

CAPILLA DE LOS MARINEROS

HOSPITAL DE LA CARIDAD

MAESTRANZA THEATER

C. SAN JACINTO

RODRIGO DE TRIANA

TRIANA

CALLE PAGES DEL CORRO

E. DUARTE

NAO VICTORIA

TEMP.

TORRE DEL ORO

B

EA Airport Bus

ALMT.

C. EVANGELISTA

C. PELÁO

SANTA ANA

C. PUREZA

CORREA

TROYA

FORT

C. BETIS

200 Meters

200 Yards

SEGOVIA

PUENTE DEL SAN TELMO

Plaza de Cuba

CALLE D. LA ASUNCIÓN

JUAN SEBASTIAN ELCANO

M. CARMELO

To April Fair Fairgrounds

N

1 Casa del Poeta
2 Hotel Las Casas de la Judería
3 Hotel Casa 1800
4 Hotel Amadeus & Pensión Córdoba
5 Hotel Palacio Alcázar
6 Hotel Murillo
7 El Rey Moro
8 Hotel Alcántara
9 La Abadía de la Giralda

10 Hostal Plaza Santa Cruz
11 New Samay Hostel & Launderette
12 La Bella Sevilla
13 Hotel Taberna del Alabardero
14 Sevilla Plaza Suites
15 Hotel Maestranza
16 Oasis Backpackers Hostel
17 Laundry

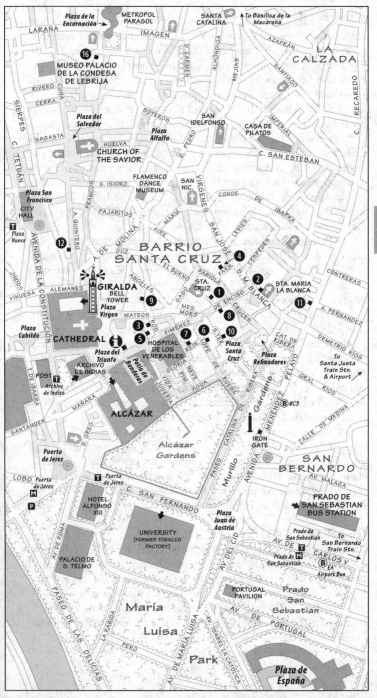

heart of Santa Cruz. Well situated, it rents 23 slick rooms—most with patio views—at a good price (nice buffet breakfast available, air-con, elevator, outdoor patio, Calle Ximénez de Enciso 28, +34 954 500 595, www.hotelalcantara.es, info@hotelalcantara.net). The hotel also functions as the box office for the nightly La Casa del Flamenco show, next door (see "Nightlife in Sevilla," earlier).

$$ La Abadía de la Giralda, once an 18th-century abbots' house, is now a homey 14-room hotel tucked away on a little street right off Calle Mateos Gago, just a couple of blocks from the cathedral. The exterior rooms have windows onto a pedestrian street, and a few of the interior rooms have small windows that look into the inner courtyard; all rooms are basic but neatly appointed (air-con, Calle Abades 30, +34 954 228 324, http://abadiagiralda.alojamientosconencantosevilla.com, giralda@alojamientosconencantosevilla.com).

$ Pensión Córdoba, a homier and cheaper option, has 11 tidy, quiet rooms with cool-tone decor, and a showpiece tiled courtyard (air-con, on a tiny lane off Calle Santa María la Blanca at Calle Farnesio 12, +34 954 227 498, www.pensioncordoba.com, reservas@pensioncordoba.com, twins Ana and María).

$ Hostal Plaza Santa Cruz is a charming little place, with thoughtful touches that you wouldn't expect in this price range. The 17 clean, basic rooms surround a bright little courtyard that's buried deep in the Barrio Santa Cruz, just off Plaza Santa Cruz. They also have nine even-nicer rooms with a common terrace in a renovated residential palace on Calle Ximénez de Enciso (air-con, Calle Santa Teresa 15, +34 954 228 808, http://santacruz.alojamientosconencantosevilla.com, plaza@alojamientosconencantosevilla.com).

¢ New Samay Hostel, on a busy avenue a block from the edge of the Barrio Santa Cruz, is a youthful, well-run slumbermill with 77 beds in 17 rooms (some rooms with private bath available, shared kitchen, air-con, elevator, 24-hour reception, rooftop terrace, Avenida de Menéndez Pelayo 13, +34 955 100 160, www.newsamayhostel.com, info@hostelsamay.com).

NEAR THE CATHEDRAL

$$$ La Bella Sevilla, tidy and sophisticated, rents 11 fresh, slick, updated rooms. Double-pane windows keep it quiet at night, and two rooms have private terraces (air-con, elevator, loaner laptop, just 100 yards from the cathedral at Calle Álvarez Quintero 52, +34 954 293 913, www.labellasensehoteles.com, reservas@labellasensehoteles.com, run by well-dressed, never-stressed Francisco).

WEST OF AVENIDA DE LA CONSTITUCIÓN

$$$$ Hotel Taberna del Alabardero has a special charm with seven spacious rooms occupying the top floor of a poet's mansion (above the classy recommended restaurant, Taberna del Alabardero). It's nicely located, a great value, and the ambience is perfectly circa-1900—notice the original Triana-made tiles in the lobby (air-con, elevator, pay parking, may close in Aug, Zaragoza 20, +34 954 502 721, www.tabernadelalabardero.es, info@tabernadelalabardero.es).

$$$ Sevilla Plaza Suites rents 10 self-catering apartments with wood floors and kitchenettes. It's squeaky clean, family friendly, and well located—and comes with an Astroturf sun terrace with a cathedral view. While service is scaled down, reception is open long hours (9:00-21:00) and rooms are cleaned daily (air-con, inside rooms are quieter, a block off Plaza Nueva at Calle Zaragoza 52, +34 955 038 533, www.suitessevillaplaza.com, info@suitessevillaplaza.com, Javier).

$ Hotel Maestranza, sparkling with loving care and understated charm, has 17 simple, bright, clean rooms well located on a street just off Plaza Nueva. It feels elegant for its price. Double-pane windows help to cut down on noise from the tapas bars below (family rooms available, 5 percent discount if you pay cash, air-con, elevator, Gamazo 12, +34 954 561 070, www.hotelmaestranza.es, sevilla@hotelmaestranza.es, Antonio).

NEAR PLAZA DE LA ENCARNACIÓN

¢ Oasis Backpackers Hostel is a good place for cheap beds, and perhaps Sevilla's best place to connect with young backpackers. Each of the eight rooms, with up to eight double bunks, comes with a modern bathroom and individual lockers. The rooftop terrace—with lounge chairs, a small pool, and adjacent kitchen—is well used (includes breakfast, just off Plaza de la Encarnación on the tiny and quiet lane behind the church at Compañía 1, reception hours vary—confirm check-in time when you book, +34 955 228 287, www.oasissevilla.com, sevilla@hostelsoasis.com).

Eating in Sevilla

Eating in Sevilla is fun and affordable (visitors from more-expensive Madrid and Barcelona find it a wonderful value). Make a point to get out and eat well when you're here.

A dining trend in Sevilla is the rise of gourmet tapas bars, with spiffed-up decor and creative menus, at the expense of traditional restaurants. Old-school places survive, but they often lack energy, and their clientele is aging with them. My quandary: I like the classic *típico* places. But the lively atmosphere and the best food

SEVILLA

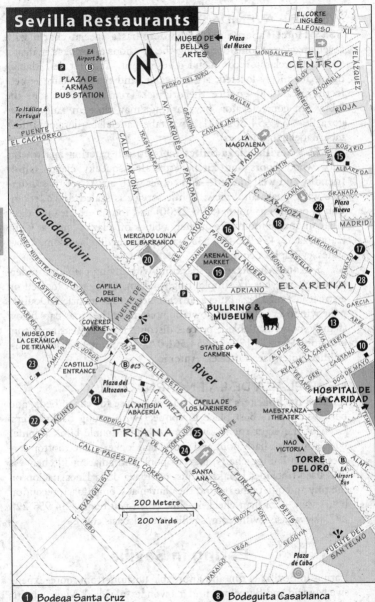

Sevilla Restaurants

EL CORTE INGLÉS
C. ALFONSO XII

MUSEO DE BELLAS ARTES
Plaza del Museo

MONSALVES

EL CENTRO

PLAZA DE ARMAS BUS STATION
EA Airport Bus

PEDRO DEL TORO

SAN ELOY
MENÉNDEZ
O'DONNELL
VELÁZQUEZ

To Itálica & Portugal

PUENTE EL CACHORRO

BAILEN

CANALEJAS

GRAVINA

AV. MARQUÉS DE PARADAS

CALLE ARJONA

TRASTAMARA

LA MAGDALENA

SAN PABLO

MORATIN

RIOJA

ROSARIO

NÚÑEZ

ALBAREDA

GRANADA

Plaza Nueva

MADRID

MARCHENA

CASTELAR

GAMAZO

Guadalquivir

PASEO NUESTRA SEÑORA DE LA O

C. CASTILLA

ALFARERÍA

MUSEO DE LA CERÁMICA DE TRIANA

S. JORGE
CAMPOS

CAPILLA DEL CARMEN

COVERED MARKET

CASTILLO ENTRANCE

MERCADO LONJA DEL BARRANCO

REYES CATÓLICOS

PASTOR Y LANDERO

ALMANSA

ARENAL MARKET

GALERA
PATERNAS

C. ZARAGOZA
CANAL

ADRIANO

EL ARENAL

GARCÍA

ARFE

A. DÍAZ
RODO
REAL DE LA CARRETERÍA
GEN.
CASTAÑO
DOS DE MAYO

BULLRING & MUSEUM

PUENTE DE ISABEL II

Plaza del Altozano

#C5
CALLE BETIS

STATUE OF CARMEN

River

LA ANTIGUA ABACERÍA

C. PUREZA

CAPILLA DE LOS MARINEROS

HOSPITAL DE LA CARIDAD

MAESTRANZA THEATER

TRIANA

C. SAN JACINTO

RODRIGO
DE TRIANA

C. DUARTE

SANTA ANA

NAO VICTORIA

TORRE DEL ORO

EA Airport Bus

CALLE PAGÉS DEL CORRO

C. PUREZA

CORREA

C. EVANGELISTA

C. FEBO

200 Meters

200 Yards

TROYA
FORT.
C. BETIS

VEGA

SEGOVIA

PARAÍSO

PUENTE DEL SAN TELMO

Plaza de Cuba

---

1 Bodega Santa Cruz

2 Donaire Azabache

3 Restaurante San Marco

4 Freiduría Puerta de la Carne

5 Bar Restaurante El 3 de Oro

6 El Monasterio Ice Cream

7 La Canasta

8 Bodeguita Casablanca

9 La Casa del Tesorero

10 El Postiguillo

11 La Isla

12 Bodega Morales

13 Bar Arenal

14 Cervecería Salmedina

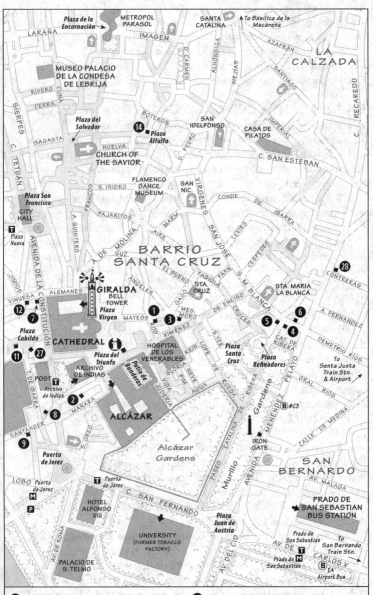

SEVILLA

⑮ Zelai Bar Restaurant
⑯ La Brunilda Tapas
⑰ Abacería Casa Moreno
⑱ Taberna del Alabardero
⑲ Restaurante El Pesquero
⑳ Mercado Lonja del Barranco
㉑ Taberna Miami

㉒ Blanca Paloma Bar
㉓ Las Golondrinas Bar
㉔ Bar Bistec & Taberna La Plazuela
㉕ Bar Santa Ana
㉖ Fish Joints
㉗ El Torno Pastelería de Conventos
㉘ Grocery (3)

are in the new places. One thing's for certain: If you want a good "restaurant" experience, your best value is a trendy tapas bar that offers good table seating—sit and enjoy some *raciones*.

Before heading out, review my "Tapas Menu Decoder" and the drinks vocabulary in the Practicalities chapter.

BARRIO SANTA CRUZ AND CATHEDRAL AREA

For tapas, the Barrio Santa Cruz is *romántico* and *turístico*. Plenty of atmospheric joints fill the neighborhood near the cathedral. Walk up Calle Mateos Gago, where classic old bars—with the day's tapas scrawled on chalkboards—keep the tourists (and a few locals) well fed and watered.

$ Bodega Santa Cruz (a.k.a. **Las Columnas**) is a popular local standby with few tourists, affordable tapas, and an unforgettable scene. You can keep an eye on the busy kitchen from the bar or hang out like a cowboy at the tiny stand-up tables out front. To order, you'll need to muscle your way to the bar—a fun experience in itself (no table service). Separate chalkboards list tapas and *montaditos* (daily 11:30-24:00, Calle de Rodrigo Caro 1A, +34 954 218 618).

$$ Donaire Azabache offers tasty standards from Spain's south like *croquetas* and *salmorejo*, but they shine by inventing new dishes like *canelón ibérico* (cannelloni stuffed with grilled pork, covered with melted cheese) or serving a fancier version of *ensaladilla* with octopus *(pulpo)*. Bar service is quick and attentive, and a few tables are in back for casual dining. Outdoor tables are self-service—order and pick up at the bar window (Mon-Sat 8:00-16:30 & 19:00-24:00, Sun 12:00-17:00, Calle Santo Tomás 11, +34 954 224 702).

$$ Restaurante San Marco serves basic Italian dishes under the arches of what was a Moorish bath (1,000 years ago) and then a disco (in the 1990s). The air-conditioned atmosphere feels upscale, but it's easygoing and family-friendly, with live Spanish guitar nightly after 20:30 (daily 13:00-16:15 & 19:30-24:00, Calle Mesón del Moro 6, +34 954 214 390).

$ Freiduría Puerta de la Carne is a fried-fish-to-go place, with great outdoor seating. Step into the fry shop and order a cheap cone of tasty fried fish, jumbo shrimp, or delicious chicken wings. Study the photos of your options; *un quarto* (250 grams, for €5-7) serves one person. Then head out front and grab a table. If you need a drink or even a small salad, flag down a server—technically from the El 3 de Oro restaurant across the lane, which shares the same owner (Wed-Mon 13:00-17:00 & 20:00-24:30, closed Tue, usually no lunch service in summer; Calle Santa María la Blanca 34, +34 954 426 820).

$$ Bar Restaurante El 3 de Oro is a venerable place with old-

Food Tours and Classes

Sevilla is one of Spain's great eating towns. The city's tourist information website is a great resource for local specialties and where to find them (www.visitasevilla.es). Below are some ways to immerse yourself deeper into the scene.

Tapas Tours: If ever a town was right for a tapas tour, it's Sevilla. Several hardworking little companies offer memorable experiences. For €80-90 you'll typically get four stops in three hours. At each stop your guide corrals a drink and a selection of local specialties, and adds cultural insights. Some tours go through the old center and others around Triana. I find them fun and educational...and time and money well spent. Companies come and go but **Azahar Sevilla Tapas**, run by Canadian Shawn Hennessey, has been into the tapas scene for 30 years offering unique food-and-wine experiences in her adopted city. Tours are kept private to experience a typical *tapeo* the way locals would (€100/person, minimum 2 people, discount for 4 or more). Shawn also provides regional wine and sherry tastings (€50/person, minimum 4 people, mobile +34 608 636 290, www.azahar-sevilla.com).

Cooking Lessons: Taller Andaluz de Cocina offers a fun hands-on shopping/cooking/eating experience each morning in the colorful Triana neighborhood. You'll start your 3.5-hour tour at 10:30 getting supplies in the market, then head to their shiny kitchen (fit for an episode of *Top Chef*), where you'll munch on olives, sip sangria, and whip up a traditional meal (typically a couple of starters, paella, and dessert). You then get to eat what you created (€60/person, Mon-Sat, none on Sun, reserve online, meets on the river side of the market, Mercado de Triana stalls 75-77, mobile +34 672 162 621, www. tallerandaluzdecocina.com). They also offer an evening version without the shopping (€55, starts at 18:00).

school waiters and a fun energy. The menu offers the full range of Andalusian classics (long hours Wed-Mon, closed Tue, Calle Santa María la Blanca 34, +34 954 422 759).

Ice Cream: The neighborhood favorite is **El Monasterio,** where *maestro heladero* Antonino has been making ice cream in Sevilla for the past 40 years, with a focus on fresh, natural, and inventive products. They are generous with samples and creative with their offerings, so try a few wild flavors before choosing. His wife, Cecilia, speaks English and doles out samples (Wed-Sun 14:00-23:30, closed Mon-Tue, Calle Puerta de la Carne 3).

Groceries: Más is close to many of my recommended hotels (Mon-Sat 9:00-21:30, closed Sun, Avenida Menéndez Pelayo 50).

BETWEEN THE CATHEDRAL AND THE RIVER

The area between the cathedral and the river, just across Avenida de la Constitución, is a wonderland of tapas, cheap eats, and fine dining. Calle García de Vinuesa leads past several colorful and cheap tapas places to a busy corner surrounded by an impressive selection of happy eateries (where Calle Adriano meets Calle Antonia Díaz).

$$ La Canasta ("The Basket") is a modern diner facing the cathedral. While not particularly characteristic, it's bright, efficient, and air-conditioned, and the fun and accessible menu offers a nice break from tapas fare. It's also popular for breakfast, a bakery nibble, simple lunches, and smoothies (daily 7:30-23:00, Avenida de la Constitución 16, +34 955 671 654).

$$$ Bodeguita Casablanca is famously the choice of bullfighters—and even the king. Just steps from the touristy cathedral area, this feels like a neighborhood spot, with stylish locals and a great menu. I'm partial to the *solomillo* (tenderloin) and the artichokes. Tapas are available outside Monday through Thursday and inside anytime, while *raciones* are available inside or out. This is a good place to be bold and experiment with your order (Mon-Fri 12:30-17:00 & 20:15-24:00, Sat 12:30-17:30, closed Sun and Aug, reservations smart, across the way from Archivo General de Indias at Calle Adolfo Rodríguez Jurado 12, +34 954 224 114, www.bodeguitacasablanca.com).

$$$ La Casa del Tesorero is a good, dressy alternative to the tapas commotion, with mellow lighting and music (and with a full range of Italian options: salads, pastas, and pizzas). It creates its own world, with a calm, spacious, elegant interior built upon 12th-century Moorish ruins (look through the glass floor) and under historic arches of what used to be the city's treasury (daily 12:30-16:00 & 19:30-23:30, Calle Santander 1, +34 954 503 921).

$$ El Postiguillo has a fun ambience—sort of bullfighting-meets-*Bonanza*—where stuffed heads decorate the walls of a fanciful wooden stable. Locals come for the top-quality, traditional dishes, while tourists like the easy menu and snappy service. Try the *carrillada* (stewed pork cheeks), *rabo de toro* (bulltail stew), or chilled *salmorejo* (a thicker, Córdoba-style gazpacho). Tapas are an option anywhere you sit (daily 12:00-24:00, Calle Dos de Mayo 2, +34 954 565 162).

$$$ La Isla, tucked away in a narrow alley behind the Postigo craft market, is dressy, expensive, and sought out for its food—locals say it serves some of the best seafood and paella in town. A nautical theme reminds diners of seafood specialties—the *albóndigas de pescado* (fish meatballs) are delectable. Classy service is the norm whether dining outside, at the bar, or in the restaurant (Tue-Sun 13:00-16:30 & 20:00-24:00, closed Mon, Calle Arfe 25, +34 954 215 376).

$ Bodega Morales oozes old-Sevilla atmosphere. The front area is more of a drinking bar; for food, go to the back section (use the separate entrance around the corner). Here, sitting among huge adobe jugs, you can munch on affordable tiny sandwiches *(montaditos)* and tapas; both are just €2. Try the *salchicha al vino blanco*—tasty sausage braised in white wine—or the spinach with chickpeas (order at the bar, good wine selection, Mon-Sat 13:00-16:00 & 20:00-24:00, Sun 12:00-17:00, Calle García de Vinuesa 11, +34 954 221 242).

$ Bar Arenal is a classic bull bar with tables spilling out onto a great street-corner setting. It's good for just a drink and to hang out with a crusty crowd. They sell cheap, old-school tapas (Tue-Sun 14:00-24:00, closed Mon, Calle Arfe 2, +34 954 223 686).

Near Plaza Nueva

$$$ Cervecería Salmedina opened during the pandemic with a bang, giving a bright makeover to a closed, traditional space. Tucked into a small corner with nice terrace tables, this place serves the freshest possible seafood from their own providers in Chipiona on the Cádiz coast. Not to be missed: grilled *chipirón* (cuttlefish) served on a bed of sweet onion reduction, the airy cod brandade, and a sweet-and-savory cheesecake (Tue-Sat 12:30-16:30 & 20:30-24:00, Sun 13:30-16:30, closed Mon, reservations smart, near Plaza de la Alfalfa at Calle Guardamino 1, +34 954 213 172).

$$$ Zelai Bar Restaurant is utterly contemporary, without a hint of a historic-Sevilla feel or touristy vibe. Their pricey gourmet tapas and *raciones* are a hit with a smart local crowd, who enjoy the fusion of Basque, Andalusian, and international dishes. Study the English menu, which works in both the bar area and the dressy little restaurant out back, where reservations are generally required (daily 13:00-16:30 & 21:00-23:30, off Plaza Nueva at Calle Albareda 22, +34 954 229 992, www.restaurantezelai.com).

$$ La Brunilda Tapas offers stylish, modern Spanish dishes along with bites from around the world in a comfortable, clean atmosphere. There's something for everyone—their duck confit and desserts get rave reviews (daily 13:30-16:30 & 20:30-23:30, reservations smart, Calle Galera 5, +34 954 220 481, www. labrunildatapas.com).

$$ Abacería Casa Moreno is a classic *abacería*, a neighborhood grocery store that doubles as a standing-room-only tapas bar. Squeeze into the back room and you're slipping back in time—and behind a tall language barrier. They're proud of their top-quality *jamón serrano, queso manchego,* and super-tender *mojama* (cured, dried tuna). Rubbing elbows here with local eaters, under a bull's head, surrounded by jars of peaches and cans of sardines, you feel like you're in on a secret (Mon-Fri 9:00-15:30 & 20:00-22:30, Sat

12:00-15:30, closed Sun, 3 blocks off Plaza Nueva at Calle Gamazo 7, +34 954 228 315).

$$$ **Taberna del Alabardero,** one of Sevilla's top restaurants, serves refined Spanish cuisine in chandeliered elegance. If you order à la carte, it adds up to about €50 a meal. For €33 you can have an elaborate, five-course fixed-price meal with lots of little surprises from the chef, and for €55 (two-person minimum) you can have 10 courses (daily 13:00-17:00 & 20:00-23:30, air-con, reservations smart, Calle Zaragoza 20, +34 954 502 721, www.alabarderosevilla.es).

Groceries: Two handy markets are near Plaza Nueva, but remember that in Spain alcoholic beverages are not sold after 22:00. **Spar Express** has all the basics, plus a takeaway counter for sandwiches, salads, and smoothies (daily until 23:00, Calle Zaragoza 31). **Carrefour Express** is stocked with prepared foods and picnic supplies (daily 9:00-22:30, Calle Harinas 7).

At or near the Arenal Market Hall

Mercado del Arenal, Sevilla's covered fish-and-produce market, is ideal for snapping photos and grabbing a cheap lunch. As with most markets, you'll find characteristic little diners with prices designed to lure in savvy shoppers, not to mention a crispy fresh world of picnic goodies—and a riverside promenade with benches just a block away (Mon-Sat 9:00-14:30, closed Sun, sleepy on Mon, on Calle Pastor y Landero at Calle Arenal, just beyond bullring).

$$$ **Restaurante El Pesquero** is a popular fish restaurant that thrives in the middle of the Arenal Market and stays open after the market closes. In the afternoon and evening, you're surrounded by the empty Industrial Age market, with workers dragging their crates to and fro. It's a great family-friendly, finger-licking-good scene that's much appreciated by its enthusiastic local following. Fish is priced by weight, so be careful when ordering, and double-check the bill (Tue-Sat 13:30-17:00, also open Thu-Sat nights 20:30-24:00, closed Mon, reservations smart for dinner, enter on Calle Pastor y Landero 9, +34 954 220 881).

$$ **Mercado Lonja del Barranco,** an old fish market, is now a food hall with a wide variety of trendy, chain-like eateries filling a 19th-century building designed by Gustave Eiffel (of Parisian tower fame). Every city in Spain seems to have one of these now, but they can be fun. It's just opposite Triana, at the foot of the Isabel II Bridge (daily 12:00-24:00).

TRIANA

Colorful Triana, across the river from the city center, offers a nice range of eating options, especially around trendy Calle San Jacinto

and the neighborhood scene behind the Church of Santa Ana (see my recommendations below).

Other than my listings, consider eating at Triana's covered market, home to a world of tempting lunchtime eateries. Take a stroll, take in the scene, and take your pick (busiest Tue-Sat morning through afternoon). Or consider the riverside fish joints at the Isabel II Bridge—El Mero and María Trifulca. These change names and quality like hats and charge a little extra for their scenic setting, but they're worth considering if you want to eat on the river.

On or near Calle San Jacinto

The area's pedestrianized main drag is lined with the tables of several easy-to-enjoy restaurants.

$$ Taberna Miami is a reliable bet for seafood. Grab a table with a good paseo-watching perch right on the street (daily 12:00-24:00, Calle San Jacinto 21, +34 954 340 843).

$$ Blanca Paloma Bar is a classic wine bar offering a delightful bar (for tapas), plenty of small tables for a sit-down meal (no tapas), and a fine selection of good Spanish wines by the glass (listed on the blackboard). They serve tasty tapa standards such as *pisto con huevo frito* (ratatouille with fried egg) that look and taste homemade (Tue-Sat 12:30-16:30 & 20:00-24:00, lunch only on Mon, closed Sun, at the corner of Calle Pagés del Corro, +34 954 333 640).

$$ Las Golondrinas Bar ("The Swallows") is famed in Triana for its wonderful list of tasty tapas (from a fun and accessible menu). The dining area is limited to big and pricier *raciones* (ideal for groups). For one or two people, the tapas scene in the bar is best. Favorites here are the pork *punta de solomillo* (tenderloin) and *champiñones* (mushrooms). Complement your meat with a veggie plate from the *aliños* section of the menu. Cling to a corner of the bar and watch the amazingly productive little kitchen jam; be aggressive to get your order in. The clatter in the kitchen is the steady pounding of pork being tenderized (daily 13:00-17:00 & 20:00-24:00, Calle Antillano Campos 26, +34 954 338 235).

Behind the Church of Santa Ana

This is a more rustic and casual neighborhood scene, offering a charming setting where you can sit down under a big tree in the shade of the old church and dine with locals.

$$ Bar Bistec, with half of the square's tables, is enthusiastic about their cod fritters, fried zucchini *(calabacín)*, and calamari, and brags about their quail and snails in sauce. Before taking a seat out on the square, consider the indoor seating and the fun action at

the bar (tapas only, Mon-Sat 12:00-24:00, Sun until 16:30, Plazu-ela de Santa Ana, +34 954 274 759).

$ **Taberna La Plazuela,** which shares the same square as Bar Bistec, is simpler, doing fried fish, grilled sardines, and *caracoles* (snails) in spring. They serve from the tapas menu in the bar and at tables on the square (Wed-Mon 8:00-24:00, closed Tue, Plazuela de Santa Ana 1, mobile +34 686 976 293).

$ **Bar Santa Ana,** just a block away alongside the church, is a rustic neighborhood bar—run by the same family for a century—with great seating on the street and a classic neighborhood-bar ambience inside. Peruse the interior, draped in Weeping Virgin and bullfighting memorabilia. It's always busy with the neighborhood gang, who enjoy fun tapas like *delicia de solomillo* (pork tenderloin) and appreciate the bar's willingness to serve even cheap tapas at the outdoor tables. I like to be engulfed in the scene—sitting at the bar, where they keep track of your bill by chalking it directly on the counter (daily 10:00-24:00, facing the side of the church at Calle Pureza 82, +34 954 272 102).

Sevilla Connections

Note that many destinations are well served by both trains and buses.

BY TRAIN

All trains arriving and departing Sevilla, including high-speed AVE trains, leave from the larger, more distant **Santa Justa** station. But many *cercanías* and regional trains heading south to Granada, Jerez, Cádiz, and Málaga also stop at the smaller **San Bernardo** station a few minutes from Santa Justa, which is connected to downtown by tram. Hourly *cercanías* trains connect both stations (about a 4-minute trip). For tips on arrival at Santa Justa, see "Arrival in Sevilla," earlier.

Train Tickets: For schedules and tickets, consult the Renfe website or visit the Renfe Travel Center, at the train station (daily 8:00-22:00, take a number and wait). Train info: +34 912 320 320, www.renfe.com.

From Sevilla by AVE Train to Madrid: The AVE express train is expensive but fast (2.5 hours to Madrid; hourly departures 7:00-21:00). Departures between 16:00 and 19:00 can book up far in advance, and surprise holidays and long weekends can totally jam up trains—reserve as far ahead as possible.

From Sevilla by Train to Córdoba: There are three options for this journey: slow and cheap regional, *media distancia* trains (7/day, 1.5 hours); fast and cheap regional high-speed **Avant** (or Alvia) trains (hourly, 45 minutes, requires reservation); and fast

and expensive **AVE** trains (almost hourly, 45 minutes, requires reservation). Unless you must be on a particular departure, there's no reason to pay more for AVE; Avant trains are just as quick and half the price. However, promotional fares for the AVE can be as cheap as regional trains when booked in advance. (If you have a rail pass, you still must buy a reservation; Avant reservations are about half the cost of AVE.)

Other Trains from Sevilla to: Málaga (5/day, 2 hours on Avant; 4/day, 3 hours on slower regional trains), **Ronda** (1/day, 3 hours, transfer in Antequera), **Granada** (8/day, 2.5 hours), **Jerez** (nearly hourly, 1.25 hours), **Toledo** (hourly, 4 hours, transfer in Madrid), **Barcelona** (3/day direct, more with transfer in Madrid, 5.5 hours). There are no direct trains to **Lisbon,** Portugal; buses or a direct flight to Lisbon are far better (see later).

BY BUS

Sevilla has two bus stations: The El Prado de San Sebastián station, near Plaza de España, primarily serves regional destinations; and the Plaza de Armas station, farther north (past the bullring), handles most long-distance buses. Go to the TI for the latest schedules.

From El Prado de San Sebastián station to Andalucía and the South Coast: Regional buses are operated by Comes (www.tgcomes.es), Damas (https://damas-sa.es), and Autocares Valenzuela (www.grupovalenzuela.com). Connections to **Jerez** are frequent, as many southbound buses head there first (7/day, 1.5 hours, run by all three companies; note that train is also possible—see earlier). Damas runs buses to some of Andalucía's hill towns, including **Ronda** (4/day, 2.5 hours, fewer on weekends) and **Arcos** (2/day, 2 hours; more departures possible with transfer in Jerez). For Spain's South Coast, a Comes bus departs Sevilla three times a day and heads for **Tarifa** (3 hours, but not timed well for taking a ferry to Tangier that same day—best to overnight in Tarifa), then **Algeciras** (3.5 hours), and ends at **La Línea/Gibraltar** (4 hours). However, if **Algeciras** is your goal, Autocares Valenzuela has a much faster direct connection (7/day, fewer on weekends, 2.5 hours). There is one bus a day from this station to **Granada** (3 hours); the rest depart from the Plaza de Armas station with Alsa or Socibus.

From Plaza de Armas station to: Madrid (4/day, 6.5 hours, https://socibusventas.es), **Córdoba** (5/day, 2 hours), **Granada** (7/day, 3 hours), **Málaga** (6/day direct, 3 hours), **Nerja** (1/day direct, more with transfer in Málaga, 5 hours), **Barcelona** (3/day, 16.5 hours, transfer in Granada or Albacete, #1 to El Prat airport).

By Bus to Portugal: The cheapest way to get to **Lisbon** is by bus (12/day, 7 hours, leaves from both Plaza de Armas bus station and Santa Justa train station, arrives at either Lisbon Oriente sta-

tion or Sete Rios bus station, #1 goes directly to airport, all transfer in either Albufeira or Caia, check details on www.alsa.es or https://rede-expressos.pt, two companies share service). The midnight departure continues past Lisbon to **Coimbra** and **Porto** (including the airport). Sevilla also has direct bus service to **Lagos,** on the Algarve (5/day, 5 hours, buy ticket a day or two in advance May-Oct, www.alsa.es). The bus departs from Sevilla's Plaza de Armas bus station and arrives at the Lagos bus station. If you'd like to visit Tavira on the way to Lagos, purchase a bus ticket to Tavira (3-hour trip), have lunch there, then take the train to Lagos.

ROUTE TIPS FOR DRIVERS

Sevilla to Arcos (55 miles/88 km): The remote hill towns of Andalucía are a joy to tour by car with Michelin map 578 or any other good map. Drivers can follow signs to *Cádiz* on the fast toll expressway (blue signs, E-5, AP-4); the toll-free N-IV is curvy and dangerous. About halfway to Jerez, at Las Cabezas de San Juan, take A-371 to Villamartín. From there, circle scenically (and clockwise) through the thick of the Pueblos Blancos—Zahara and Grazalema—to Arcos.

It's about two hours from Sevilla to Zahara. You'll find decent but winding roads and sparse traffic. It gets worse (but very scenic) if you take the tortuous series of switchbacks over the 4,500-foot summit of Puerto de Las Palomas (Pigeons Pass, climb to the viewpoint) on the direct but difficult road (CA-9104) from Zahara to Grazalema (you'll see several hiking trailheads into Sierra de Grazalema Natural Park).

Another scenic option through the park from Grazalema to Arcos is the road (A-372) that goes up over Puerto del Boyar (Boyar Pass), past the pretty little valley town of Benamahoma, and down to El Bosque.

To skirt the super-twisty roads within the park while passing through a few more hill towns, try the road from Ronda to El Gastor, Setenil (cave houses and great olive oil), and Olvera—another picturesque alternative.

CÓRDOBA

Straddling a sharp bend of the Guadalquivir River, Córdoba has a glorious Roman and Moorish past, once serving as a regional capital for both empires. It's home to Europe's best Islamic sight after Granada's Alhambra: the Mezquita, a splendid and remarkably well-preserved mosque that dates from AD 784. When you step inside the mosque, which is magical in its grandeur, you can imagine Córdoba as the center of a thriving and sophisticated culture. During the Dark Ages, when much of Europe was barbaric and illiterate, Córdoba was a haven of enlightened thought—famous for religious tolerance, artistic expression, and dedication to philosophy and the sciences. To this day, you'll still see and feel the Muslim influence in Córdoba.

Beyond the magnificent Mezquita, the city of Córdoba has two sides: the touristy maze of old town streets immediately surrounding the giant main attraction (lined with trinket shops, hotels, and restaurants); and the workaday but interesting modern city (centered on Plaza de las Tendillas). In between are the side lanes of the Jewish Quarter, humming with history. Just a quick walk takes you from a commercialized vibe into real-life Córdoba.

PLANNING YOUR TIME

Ideally, Córdoba is worth two nights and a day. Don't rush the magnificent Mezquita, but consider sticking around to experience the city's other pleasures: wander the evocative Jewish Quarter, enjoy the tapas scene, and explore the modern part of town.

However, if you're tight on time, it's possible to do Córdoba more quickly—especially since it's conveniently located on the AVE bullet-train line (and because, frankly, Córdoba has fewer

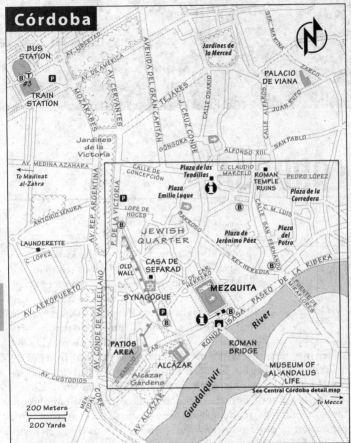

Córdoba

BUS STATION

TRAIN STATION

PALACIO DE VIANA

Jardines de la Merced

AV. LIBERTAD

AV. DE AMÉRICA

AV. CERVANTES

MOZÁRABES

AVENIDA DEL GRAN CAPITÁN

TEJARES

J. CRUZ CONDE

CALLE OSARIO

GÓNGORA CONDE

ZARCO

JUAN RUFO

CALLE ALFAROS

SAN PABLO

STA. MARINA

ALFONSO XIII

Jardines de la Victoria

AV. MEDINA AZAHARA

To Madinat al-Zahra

ANTONIO MAURA

AV. REP. ARGENTINA

LAUNDERETTE

C. LÓPEZ

AV. AEROPUERTO

AV. CONDE DE VALLELLANO

CALLE DE CONCEPCIÓN

Plaza Emilio Luque

LOPE DE HOCES

P. DE LA VICTORIA

SACROBO

JEWISH QUARTER

OLD WALL

CASA DE SEFARAD

SYNAGOGUE

C. DE CAR. HERRERO

Plaza de las Tendillas

C. CLAUDIO MARCELO

ROMAN TEMPLE RUINS

PEDRO LÓPEZ

Plaza de la Corredera

CALLE SAN FERNANDO

Plaza de Jerónimo Páez

C. M. LUIS

Plaza del Potro

REY-HEREDIA

MEZQUITA

ISASA

PASEO DE LA RIBERA

PUENTE DE MIRAFLORES

River

PATIOS AREA

S. BASILIO

CAB.

RONDA

ALCÁZAR

Alcázar Gardens

AV. CUSTODIOS

MENPIDAL

COM...

AV. ALCÁZAR

ROMAN BRIDGE

Guadalquivir

MUSEUM OF AL-ANDALUS LIFE

See Central Córdoba detail map

To Mecca

200 Meters
200 Yards

CÓRDOBA

major sights than the other two big Andalusian cities, Sevilla and Granada). To see Córdoba as an efficient stopover between Madrid and Sevilla (or as a side trip from Sevilla—frequent trains, 45-minute trip), focus on the Mezquita: taxi from the station, spend one hour there, explore the old town for an hour or two, sample the famous local cuisine...and then get on your way.

Orientation to Córdoba

Córdoba's big draw is the mosque-turned-cathedral called the Mezquita (meth-KEE-tah). Most of the town's major sights are nearby, including the Alcázar, a former royal castle. And though the town seems to ignore its marshy Guadalquivir River (a prime bird-watching area), the riverbank sports a Renaissance triumphal arch next to a stout "Roman Bridge." The bridge leads to the town's

old fortified gate (which houses a museum on Moorish culture, the Museum of al-Andalus Life). The Mezquita is buried in the characteristic medieval town. Around that stretches the Jewish Quarter, then the modern city—with some striking Art Deco buildings at Plaza de las Tendillas and more modern architecture lining Avenida del Gran Capitán.

TOURIST INFORMATION

Córdoba has a helpful TI at Plaza de las Tendillas (daily 9:00-14:30, +34 957 471 577, https://turismodecordoba.org). Another option is the Visitor Center near the Mezquita, covering both Córdoba and the Andalucía region (Mon-Sat 9:00-19:00, Sun 9:30-14:30, free WCs in basement along with a few ruins and a reproduction of how the Moorish city of "Qurtuba" looked 1,000 years ago, Plaza del Triunfo, +34 957 355 179, same website as the TI).

ARRIVAL IN CÓRDOBA

By Train or Bus: Córdoba's train station is located on Avenida de América. The modern glass-and-steel station has ATMs, restaurants, shops, an information counter, and a small lounge for first-class passengers of the high-speed AVE train line. Taxis and local buses are just outside, to the left as you come up the escalators from the platforms.

The bus station is across the street from the train station (on the north side of Avenida Vía Augusta). There's no luggage storage at the train station, but the bus station has lockers (next to ticket booth #11, look for *Consigna/Locker* sign and buy token at machine, lockers are around the corner). Car rental agencies are located here.

To get to the old town, hop a **taxi** (€8 to the Mezquita) or catch **bus** #3 (stop is between the train and bus stations, parallel to the taxi line, buy €1.30 ticket on board). The route includes convenient stops for recommended hotels near Plaza de las Tendillas; Calle San Fernando, a short walk to the Mezquita; Puerta del Puente, ideal for the riverfront; and the patio-filled neighborhood of San Basilio.

It's about a 25-minute **walk** from either station to the old town. To walk from the train station to the Mezquita, turn left onto Avenida de América, then right through the pleasantly manicured Jardines de la Victoria park. Near the end of the park, on the left, you'll see a section of the old city walls. The Puerta de Almodóvar gate and a statue of Seneca mark the start of Calle de Cairuán (sometimes signposted as Kairuán). Follow this street downhill, with the wall still on your left, until you reach Plaza Campo de los Santos Mártires. Then head left, past the Alcázar, down Calle Amador de los Rios, which leads directly to the Mezquita and the river.

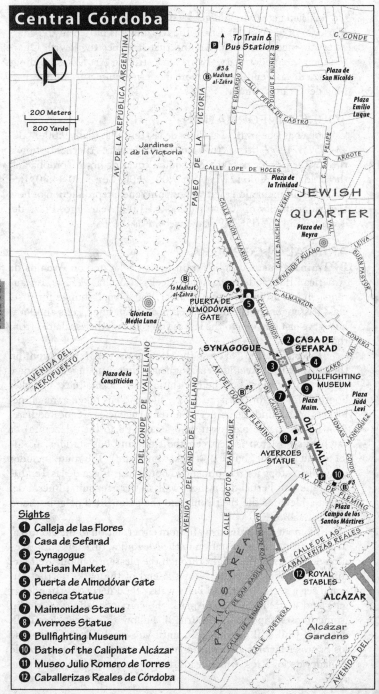

Central Córdoba

To Train & Bus Stations

#3 & Madinat al-Zahra

C. CONDE

Plaza de San Nicolás

Plaza Emilio Luque

200 Meters
200 Yards

AV DE LA REPÚBLICA ARGENTINA

PASEO DE LA VICTORIA

C. DE EDUARDO DATO

CALLE PÉREZ DE CASTRO

CALLE DUQUE F. NÚÑEZ

Jardines de la Victoria

CALLE LOPE DE HOCES

Plaza de la Trinidad

JEWISH QUARTER

C. SAN FELIPE

ARGOTE

CALLE SÁNCHEZ DE FERIA

CALLE TEJÓN Y MARÍN

Plaza del Neyra

TIVOLI

LEIVA

BUEN PASTOR

To Madinat al-Zahra

Glorieta Media Luna

FERNÁNDEZ RUANO

PUERTA DE ALMODÓVAR GATE

C. ALMANZOR

ROMERO

AVENIDA DEL AEROPUERTO

Plaza de la Constitución

AV. DEL CONDE DE VALLELLANO

CALLE JUDÍOS

SYNAGOGUE

CASA DE SEFARAD

CAÑO

CAÑO SAL

Artisan Market

BULLFIGHTING MUSEUM

AV. DEL DOCTOR FLEMING

#3

CALLE DE CAIRUÁN

Plaza Maim.

Plaza Judá Leví

C. TOMÁS MÁRQUEZ

CONDE

AVENIDA DEL CONDE DE VALLELLANO

CALLE DOCTOR BARRAGUER

AVERROES STATUE

OLD WALL

AV. DE DR FLEMING

#3

Plaza Campo de los Santos Mártires

CALLE MARTÍN DE ROA

PATIOS AREA

CALLE DE SAN BASILIO

CALLE DE ENMEDIO

CALLE POSTRERA

ROYAL STABLES

CALLE DE LAS CABALLERIZAS REALES

ALCÁZAR

Alcázar Gardens

AVENIDA DEL

Sights

1 Calleja de las Flores
2 Casa de Sefarad
3 Synagogue
4 Artisan Market
5 Puerta de Almodóvar Gate
6 Seneca Statue
7 Maimonides Statue
8 Averroes Statue
9 Bullfighting Museum
10 Baths of the Caliphate Alcázar
11 Museo Julio Romero de Torres
12 Caballerizas Reales de Córdoba

CÓRDOBA

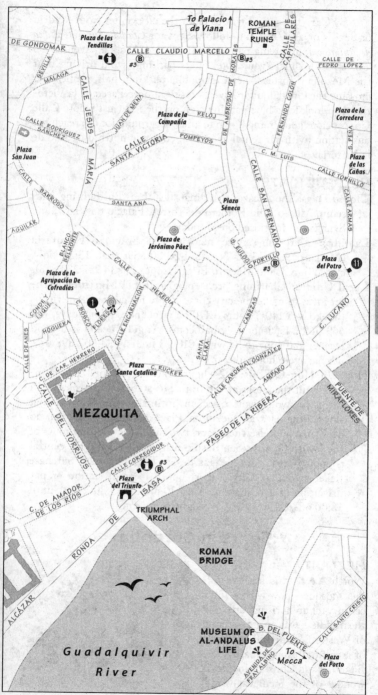

DE GONDOMAR

Plaza de las Tendillas

CALLE CLAUDIO MARCELO

To Palacio de Viana

ROMAN TEMPLE RUINS

CALLE DE CAPITULARES

CALLE DE PEDRO LÓPEZ

SEVILLA

MÁLAGA

CALLE JESÚS Y MARÍA

JUAN DE MENA

Plaza de la Compañía

RELOJ

C. DE AMBROSIO DE MORALES

FERNANDO COLÓN

Plaza de la Corredera

CALLE RODRÍGUEZ SÁNCHEZ

CALLE SANTA VICTORIA

POMPEYOS

C. M. LUIS

S. PEÑA

Plaza San Juan

Plaza de las Cañas

CALLE TORNILLO

CALLE BARROSO

SANTA ANA

Plaza Séneca

CALLE SAN FERNANDO

CALLE ARMAS

AGUILAR

Plaza de Jerónimo Páez

BLANCO BELMONTE

CALLE REY HEREDIA

Plaza de la Agrupación De Cofradías

CONDE LUQUE

C. BOSCO

FLORES

CALLE ENCARNACIÓN

S. EULOGIO

PORTILLO

Plaza del Potro

HOGUERA

C. CABEZAS

CALLE DEANES

C. DE CAR. HERRERO

Plaza Santa Catalina

C. RUCKER

SANTA CLARA

CALLE CARDENAL GONZÁLEZ

AMPARO

C. LUCANO

CALLE DEL TORRIJOS

MEZQUITA

PASEO DE LA RIBERA

PUENTE DE MIRAFLORES

CALLE CORREGIDOR

Plaza del Triunfo

ISASA

C. DE AMADOR DE LOS RÍOS

TRIUMPHAL ARCH

RONDA DE

ROMAN BRIDGE

ALCÁZAR

MUSEUM OF AL-ANDALUS LIFE

B. DEL PUENTE

CALLE SANTO CRISTO

To Mecca

Plaza del Porto

AVENIDA DE FRAY ALBINO

Guadalquivir River

CÓRDOBA

By Car: The easiest way to enter the city center from Madrid or Sevilla on A-4/E-5 is to follow signs for *Córdoba sur* and *Plaza de Andalucía,* following palm-tree-lined A-431 (a.k.a. Avenida del Corregidor). Unless your hotel offers parking, avoid driving near the Mezquita. Instead, head for public parking: half a mile after crossing the Guadalquivir River, veer right onto Paseo de la Victoria, then look for a blue parking sign on the left (just before Calle Concepción) and a ramp down to an underground lot. To reach the bus station (with car rental agencies), continue north on Paseo de la Victoria.

HELPFUL HINTS

Closed Days: The Alcázar, Madinat al-Zahra, Bullfighting Museum, Museo Julio Romero de Torres, Palacio de Viana, and Synagogue are closed on Monday.

Laundry: Find self-service machines at **Solymar Tintoreria** (Mon-Fri 9:30-13:30 & 17:30-20:00, Sat 9:30-13:30 only, closed Sun, Calle Maestro Priego López 2, +34 957 233 818).

Local Guides: Charming archaeologist **Isabel Martínez Richter** loves to make the city come to life for curious Americans (weekdays €140/3 hours, €170 on weekends and holidays, +34 669 369 645, isabmr@gmail.com). **Ángel Lucena** is a good teacher and a joy to be with (€100/3 hours, +34 607 898 079, lucenaangel@hotmail.com).

Hop-On, Hop-Off Bus: A 24-hour ticket is good for a "panoramic" circuit that stops at the train/bus station and generally in places you won't want to see; an "intimate" *microbús* route that stops at the Alcázar, Mezquita, Plaza de las Tendillas, Palacio de Viana, and elsewhere; and two one-hour walking tours of the Jewish Quarter/San Basilio neighborhood and the central shopping area around Plaza de las Tendillas (€20, purchase ticket at orange City Expert booth in train station or pay driver; buses depart about every 30 minutes 9:30-21:00, until 18:00 off-season; www.city-sightseeing.com).

Sights in Córdoba

MEZQUITA

Worth ▲▲▲, this massive former mosque—now with a 16th-century church rising up from the middle—was once the center of Western Islam and the heart of a cultural capital that rivaled Baghdad and Constantinople. A wonder of the medieval world,

it's remarkably well-preserved, giving today's visitors a chance to soak up the ambience of Islamic Córdoba in its 10th-century prime.

Cost: €11, machines attended by helpful staff inside the Patio de los Naranjos, free to enter Mon-Sat 8:30-9:30 (because they don't want to charge a fee to attend the 9:30 Mass; no access to altar, choir, or treasury during free entry period).

Hours: Mon-Sat 8:30-14:00 & 16:00-19:00, Sun 8:30-11:30 & 15:00-19:00; Nov-Feb closes daily at 18:00; Christian altar accessible only after 10:00 unless you attend Mass; usually less crowded after 15:00. During religious holidays, particularly Holy Week, the Mezquita may close to sightseers at certain times of day—check the online events calendar before you go. You can also enjoy the Mezquita on a sound-and-light tour on most summer evenings (described under "Entertainment in Córdoba," later).

Information: +34 957 470 512, www.mezquita-catedraldecordoba.es.

Tours: Detailed but dry audioguide-€4; download the app version for visuals.

Bell Tower Climb: €2, limited to 20 people every half-hour, daily 9:30-18:30, until 17:30 in winter. Reserve a time for your climb when you buy your ticket. Inside you'll see a few remnants of the original minaret that became the base structure for the bell tower, and as you climb, you'll have progressively better views of the mosque-cathedral and the city itself.

Planning Your Visit: Usually one hour is enough to visit the interior of the Mezquita. If you plan to climb the bell tower, save it for last.

◯ Self-Guided Tour

Before entering the patio, take in the exterior of the Mezquita. The mosque's massive footprint is clear when you survey its sprawling walls from outside. At 600 feet by 400 feet, it dominates the higgledy-piggledy medieval town that surrounds it.

❶ Patio de los Naranjos

The Mezquita's big, welcoming courtyard is free to enter. When this was a mosque, the Muslim faithful would gather in this courtyard to perform ablution—ritual washing before prayer, as directed by Muslim law. The courtyard walls display many of the former mosque's carved and painted ceiling panels and beams, which date from the 10th century. The rows of orange trees were added as a continuation of the columns in the prayer hall.

❷ Bell Tower/Minaret

Gaze up through the trees for views of the bell tower (c. 1600), built over the remains of the original Muslim minaret. For four centuries, five times a day, a singing cleric (the muezzin) would ride

Mezquita

N

50 Meters
50 Yards

CALLE HERRERO

PUERTA DEL PERDÓN

2

TICKETS FOR BELL TOWER

TICKET VENDING MACHINES

TICKET COUNTER

AUDIOGUIDES

BELL TOWER

FOUNTAIN

1

Patio de los Naranjos

CALLE DE TORRIJOS

CÓRDOBA

PUERTA DE LAS PALMAS

3 ENTER

EXIT

CALLE GONZÁLEZ FRANCÉS

4

CATHEDRAL

CHOIR

13

12

14

7

8

11

MIHRAB

5

WC

6

9

10

CALLE CORR. LUIS DE LA CERDA

Plaza Triomfo

To River

GRAY SHADING INDICATES APPROX. FOOTPRINT OF 16TH CENTURY CATHEDRAL BUILT WITHIN THE MOSQUE

1 Patio de los Naranjos
2 Bell Tower/Minaret
3 Entrance
4 Visigothic Mosaic
5 Visigothic Ruins
6 Mihrab
7 Villaviciosa Chapel
8 Royal Chapel
9 Treasury
10 Stonemason Marks
11 Chapel of the Conversion of St. Paul
12 Altar
13 Choir
14 Gothic Vaulting

a donkey up the ramp of the minaret, then call to all Muslims in earshot that it was time to face Mecca and pray.

• *Buy your ticket (and, if you wish, rent an audioguide at a separate kiosk to the right). During regular hours, enter the building by passing through the keyhole gate at the far-right corner (pick up an English map-brochure as you enter). During the free entry period, enter through the Puerta de las Palmas.*

❸ Entrance

Walking into the former mosque from the patio, you pass from an orchard of orange trees into a forest of delicate columns (erected here in the eighth century). The more than 800 red-and-blue columns are topped with double arches—a round Romanesque arch

above a Visigothic horseshoe arch—made from alternating red brick and white stone. The columns and capitals (built of marble, granite, and alabaster) were recycled from ancient Roman ruins and conquered Visigothic churches. (Golden Age Arabs excelled at absorbing both the technology and the building materials of the peoples they conquered—no surprise, considering the culture's nomadic roots.) The columns seem to recede to infinity, as if reflecting the immensity and complexity of Allah's creation.

Although it's a vast room, the low ceilings and dense columns create an intimate and reverent atmosphere. The original mosque was brighter, before Christians renovated the place for their use and closed in the arched entrances from the patio and street. The giant cathedral sits in the center of the mosque. We'll visit it after exploring the mosque.

• *From either entrance, count five columns into the building and look for two small walls. Between them, find a glass floor covering a section of mosaic floor below. Look in.*

❹ Visigothic Mosaic

The mosque stands on the site of the early-Christian Church of San Vicente, built during the Visigothic period (sixth century). Peering down, you can see a mosaic that remains from that original church. This is important to Catholic locals, as it proves there was a church

here before the mosque—thereby giving credence to those who see the modern-day church on this spot as a return to the site's original purpose, rather than a violation of the mosque.

• *Continue ahead to the wall opposite the entrance, where you'll find more...*

❺ Visigothic Ruins

On display in the corner are rare bits of carved stone from that same sixth-century church. (Most other stonework here had been scrubbed of its Christian symbolism by Muslims seeking to reuse them for the mosque.) Prince Abd al-Rahman bought the church from his Christian subjects before leveling it to build his mosque. From here, pan to the right to take in the sheer vastness of the mosque. (A hidden WC and drinking fountain are in the corner.)

• *Walk to your left until you come to the mosque's focal point, the...*

❻ Mihrab

The equivalent of a church's high altar, this was the focus of the mosque and remains a highlight of the Mezquita today. Picture the original mosque at prayer time, with a dirt floor covered by a patchwork of big carpets. More than 20,000 people could pray at once here. Imagine the multitude kneeling in prayer, facing the mihrab, rocking forward to touch their heads to the ground, and saying, *"Allahu Akbar, la ilaha illa Allah, Muhammad rasul Allah"*—"Allah is great, there is no God but Allah, and Muhammad is his prophet."

The mihrab, a feature in all mosques, is a decorated niche—in this case, more like a small room with a golden-arch entrance. Dur-ing a service, the imam (prayer leader) would stand here to read scripture and give sermons. He spoke loudly into the niche, his back to the assembled crowd, and the architecture worked to amplify his voice so all could hear. Built in the mid-10th century by al-Hakam II, the exquisite room reflects the wealth of Córdoba in its prime. Three thousand pounds of shimmering multicolored glass-and-enamel cubes panel the walls and domes in mosaics designed by Byzantine craftsmen, depicting flowers and quotes from the Quran. Gape up. Overhead rises a colorful, starry dome with skylights and interlocking lobe-shaped arches.

• *Now turn around so that you're facing away from the mihrab. Ahead of you, and a bit to the left, is a roped-off open area. Gaze into the first chapel built within the mosque after the Christian Reconquista.*

❼ Villaviciosa Chapel

In 1236, Saint-King Ferdinand III conquered the city and turned the mosque into a church. The higher ceiling allowed for clerestory windows and more light, making it feel more church-like. Still, the locals continued to call it "la Mezquita," and left the structure virtually unchanged (70 percent of the original mosque structure survives to this day). Sixteen columns were removed and replaced by Gothic arches to make this first chapel. It feels as if the church architects appreciated the opportunity to incorporate the sublime architecture of the preexisting mosque into their church. Notice how the floor was  once almost entirely covered with the tombs of nobles and big shots eager to make this their final resting place.

• *Immediately to your right (as you face the main entrance of the Mezquita), you'll see the walled-off...*

❽ Royal Chapel

The chapel—designed for the tombs of two Christian kings of Castile, Fernando IV and Alfonso XI—is completely closed off. Peek through the windows here or wander to the right side for the best views. While it was never open to the public, the tall, well-preserved Mudejar walls and dome are easily visible. Notice the elaborate stucco and tile work. The lavish Arabic-style decor dates from the 1370s, done by Muslim artisans after the Reconquista of the city. The floor inside has been raised to accommodate tombs buried beneath it. The fact that a Christian king chose to be buried in a tomb so clearly Moorish in design indicates the mutual respect between the cultures (before the Inquisition changed all that). The remains of both Castilian kings were moved to another Córdoba church in the 1700s, so it remains a mystery why this chapel is still closed to visitors.

• *Return to the mihrab, then go through the big, pink marble door to your immediate left, which leads into the Baroque...*

❾ Treasury (Tesoro)

The treasury is filled with display cases of religious artifacts and the enormous monstrance that is paraded through the streets of Córdoba each Corpus Christi, 60 days after Easter (notice the handles).

The monstrance was an attempt by 16th-century Christians to create something exquisite enough to merit being the holder of the Holy Communion wafer. As they believed the wafer actually

Islamic Córdoba (756-1236): Medieval Europe's Cultural Capital

After political rivals slaughtered his family in 750, the 20-year-old Umayyad prince Abd al-Rahman fled the royal palace at Damascus, headed west across North Africa, and went undercover among the Berber tribesmen of Morocco. For six years he avoided assassination while building a power base among his fellow Arab expatriates and the local Muslim Berbers. As an heir to the title of "caliph" (a civil and religious leader), he sailed north and claimed Moorish Spain as his own, exerting his power by decapitating his enemies and sending their salted heads to the rival caliph in Baghdad. This split in Islam was somewhat like the papal schism that stirred up medieval Christian Europe, when the Church split into factions over who was the rightful pope.

Thus began an Islamic flowering in southern Spain under the Umayyads. They dominated Sevilla and Granada, ruling the independent state of "al-Andalus," with their capital at Córdoba.

By the year 950—when the rest of Europe was mired in poverty, ignorance, and superstition—Córdoba was Europe's greatest city, rivaling Constantinople and Baghdad. It had well over 100,000 people (Paris had a third that many), with hundreds of mosques, palaces, and public baths. The streets were paved and lit at night with oil lamps, and running water was piped in from the outskirts of the city. Medieval visitors marveled at the size and luxury of its mosque (the Mezquita), a symbol that the Umayyads of Spain were the equals of the caliphs of Baghdad.

This golden age was marked by a remarkable spirit of tolerance and cooperation in this region among the three great monotheistic religions: Islam, Judaism, and Christianity. As a proudly Andalusian guide once explained to me, "Umayyad al-Andalus was not one country with three cultures. It was one culture with

was the body of Christ, this trumped any relics. The monstrance is designed to direct your gaze to heaven. While the bottom is silver-plated 18th-century Baroque, the top is late Gothic—solid silver with gold plating courtesy of 16th-century conquistadors. Gaze up at an equally spectacular ceiling.

The big canvas nearest the entrance shows Saint-King Ferdinand III, who conquered Córdoba in 1236, accepting the keys to the city's fortified gate from the vanquished Muslims. The victory ended a six-month siege and resulted in a negotiated settlement: The losers' lives were spared, providing they evacuated. Most went to Granada, which remained Muslim for another 250 years. The same day, the Spaniards celebrated Mass in a makeshift chapel right here in the great mosque.

The black-and-white marble tomb at the entrance opposite Ferdinand III belongs to Fray Pedro de Salazar y Toledo. After

three religions...its people shared the same food, dress, art, music, and language. Different religious rituals within the community were practiced in private. But clearly, Muslims ruled. No church spire could be taller than a minaret, and while the call to prayer rang out five times daily, there was no ringing of church bells."

The university rang with voices in Arabic, Hebrew, and Latin, sharing their knowledge of medicine, law, literature, and *al-jibra*. The city fell under the enlightened spell of the ancient Greeks, and Córdoba's 70 libraries bulged with translated manuscripts of Plato and Aristotle, works that would later inspire medieval Christians.

Ruling over the golden age were two energetic leaders—Abd al-Rahman III (912-961) and al-Hakam II (961-976)—who conquered territory, expanded the Mezquita, and boldly proclaimed themselves caliphs.

Córdoba's Y1K crisis brought civil wars that toppled the caliph (1031), splintering al-Andalus into several kingdoms. Córdoba came under the control of the Almoravids (Berbers from North Africa), who were less sophisticated than the Arab-based Umayyads. Then a wave of even stricter Islam swept through Spain, bringing the Almohads to power (1147) and driving Córdoba's best and brightest into exile. The city's glory days were over, and Sevilla and Granada replaced Córdoba as the center of Iberian Islam. On June 29, 1236, Christians conquered the city. That morning Muslims said their last prayers in the great mosque. That afternoon, the Christians set up their portable road altar and celebrated the church's first Mass. Córdoba's days as a political and cultural superpower were over.

CÓRDOBA

studies in Salamanca, Salazar had the honor of being the main preacher to two Spanish kings, Philip IV and Charles II. In 1686, he was named cardinal by Pope Innocent XI, but his local claim to fame is as founder of one of the first public hospitals in Córdoba, in use today as the School of Philosophy for the local university.

Among the other Catholic treasures, don't miss the ivory crucifix (next room, body carved from one tusk, arms carefully fitted on) from 1665. Get close to study Jesus' mouth—it's incredibly realistic. The artist? No one knows.

• *Just outside the treasury exit, a glass case holds casts that show many...*

⑩ Stonemason Marks

These casts bear the marks and signatures left by those who cut them to build the original Visigothic church and later, the mosque. Try to locate the actual ones on nearby columns. (I went five for

six.) This part of the mosque has the best light for photography, thanks to skylights put in by 18th-century Christians.

The mosque grew over several centuries under a series of rulers. Remarkably, each ruler kept to the original vision—rows and rows of multicolored columns topped by double arches. Then came the Christians.

⓫ Chapel of the Conversion of St. Paul

Sharing a back wall with the Royal Chapel, the church ceded this space for the burial of Pedro Muñiz de Godoy—Grand Master of the Order of Santiago who fought several battles for Castile against the Portuguese in the 1300s. Godoy's descendants recently spent a fortune to painstakingly clean and restore the chapel, which drips with gold and 17th-century sculpture. The chapel is likely by the same architect as the choir you are about to see.

• *Find the towering church in the center of the mosque and step in.*

⓬ Altar

Rising up in the middle of the forest of columns is the bright, restored cathedral, oriented with its altar at the east end, per Christian tradition. Gazing up at the rich, golden  decoration, it's easy to forget that you were in a former mosque just seconds ago. While the mosque is about 30 feet high, the cathedral's space soars 130 feet up. Look at the glorious ceiling.

In 1523 Córdoba's bishop proposed building this grand church in the Mezquita's center. The town council opposed it, but Charles V (called Charles I in Spain) ordered it done. If that seems like a travesty to you, consider what some locals will point out: Though it would have been quicker and less expensive for the Christian builders to destroy the mosque entirely, they respected its beauty and built their church into it instead.

As you take in the styles of these two great places of worship, ponder how they reflect the differences between Catholic and Islamic aesthetics and psychology: horizontal versus vertical, intimate versus powerful, fear-inspiring versus loving, dark versus bright, simple versus elaborate, feeling close to God versus feeling small before God.

The basic structure is late Gothic, with fancy Isabelline-style columns. The nave's towering Renaissance arches and dome emphasize the triumph of Christianity over Islam in Córdoba. The twin pulpits feature a marble bull, eagle, angel, and lion—symbols

of the four evangelists. The modern *cátedra* (the seat of the bishop) is made of Carrara marble.

While churches and mosques normally both face east (to Jerusalem or Mecca), this space holds worship areas aimed 90 degrees from each other, since the mihrab faces south. Perhaps it's because from here you have to travel south (via Gibraltar) to get to Mecca. Or maybe it's because this mosque was designed by the Umayyad branch of Islam, whose ancestral home was Damascus—from where Mecca lies to the south.

• *Facing the high altar is a big, finely decorated wooden enclosure.*

⓭ Choir

The Baroque-era choir stalls were added much later—made in 1750 of New World mahogany. While cluttering up a previously open Gothic space, the choir is considered one of the masterpieces of 18th-century Andalusian Baroque. Each of the 109 stalls (108 plus the throne of the bishop) features a scene from the Bible: Mary's life on one side facing Jesus' life on the other. The lower chairs feature carved reliefs of the 49 martyrs of Córdoba (from Roman, Visigothic, and Moorish times), each with a palm frond symbolizing martyrdom and the scene of their death in the background.

The medieval church strayed from the inclusiveness taught by Jesus: choirs (which were standard throughout Spain) were for clerics (canons, priests, and the bishop). The pews in the nave were for nobles. And the peasants listened in from outside. (Lay people didn't understand what they were hearing anyway, as Mass was held in Latin until the 1960s.) Those days are long over. Today, a public Mass is said—in Spanish—right here most mornings (Mon-Sat at 9:30, Sun at 12:00 and 13:30).

• *Before leaving, walk to the back of the altar to admire the* ⓮ *Gothic vaulting mingled with Moorish arches—a combination found nowhere else in the world.*

NEAR THE MEZQUITA

These sights are all within a few minutes' walk of the Mezquita.

On and near the River

Just downhill from the Mezquita is the Guadalquivir River, which flows on to Sevilla and eventually out to the Atlantic. While silted up today, it was once navigable from here. The town now seems to turn its back

on the Guadalquivir, but the arch next to the Roman Bridge (with its ancient foundation surviving) and the fortified gate on the far bank (now housing a museum, described later) evoke a day when the river was key to the city's existence.

Triumphal Arch and Plague Monument

The unfinished Renaissance arch was designed to give King Philip II a royal welcome, but he arrived before its completion—so the job was canceled. ("Very Andalusian," according to a local friend.) The adjacent monument with the single column is an 18th-century plague monument dedicated to St. Raphael (who was in charge of protecting the region's population from its main scourges: plague, hunger, and floods).

Roman Bridge

The ancient bridge sits on its first-century-AD foundations and retains its 16th-century arches. It was the first bridge built over this river and established Córdoba as a strategic place. As European bridges go, it's a poor stepchild (its pedestrian walkway was unimaginatively redone in 2009), but Cordovans still stroll here nightly. Walk across the bridge for a fine view of the city—especially the huge mosque with its cathedral busting through the center. You'll be steps away from the museum described next.

▲Museum of al-Andalus Life and Calahorra Tower (Museo Vivo de al-Andalus)

This museum fills the fortified gate (built in the 14th century to protect the Christian city) at the far side of the Roman Bridge. Its worthy mission—to explain the thriving Muslim Moorish culture of 9th- to 12th-century Córdoba and al-Andalus—is undermined by its obligatory but clumsy audioguide system. You'll don a headset and wander through simple displays as the gauzy commentary lets you sit at the feet of the great poets and poke into Moorish living rooms. The scale models of the Alhambra and the Mezquita are fun, as are the dollhouse tableaus showing life in the market, mosque, university, and baths. It's worth the climb up to the rooftop terrace for the best panoramic view of Córdoba.

Cost and Hours: €4.50, includes one-hour audio tour; daily 10:00-19:00; Torre de la Calahorra, +34 957 293 929, www.torrecalahorra.es.

Jewish Córdoba

Córdoba's Jewish Quarter dates from the late Middle Ages, after Muslim rule and during the Christian era. These days, little evidence of that time remains. For a sense of the neighborhood in its thriving heyday, first visit the Casa de Sefarad, then the synagogue located a few steps away. For a pretty picture, find **Calleja de**

Córdoba's Jewish Quarter: A 10-Point Scavenger Hunt

Whereas most of the area around the Mezquita is commercial and touristy, some streets of the Jewish Quarter seem somehow almost untouched by tourism and the modern world (as you leave the Mezquita, exit the orange-grove patio to the left, then wander into the narrow back lanes around the synagogue). Explore this district to catch a whiff of Córdoba as it was before the onslaught of tourism and the affluence of the 21st century. Just meander and observe. Here are a few characteristics to look for:

1. **Narrow streets.** Skinny streets make sense in hot climates, as they provide much-appreciated shade. The ones in this area are remnants from the old Moorish bazaar, crammed to fit within the protective city walls.

2. **Thick, whitewashed walls.** Both features serve as a kind of natural air-conditioning—and the chalk ingredient in the whitewash "bugs" bugs.

3. **Colorful doors and windows.** In this famously white city, what little color there is—mostly added in modern times—helps counter the boring whitewash.

4. **Iron grilles.** Historically, these were more artistic, but modern ones are more practical. Their continued presence is a reminder of the persistent gap through the ages between rich and poor. The wooden latticework covering many windows is a holdover from days when women, held to extreme standards of modesty, wanted to be able to see out while still keeping their privacy.

5. **Stone bumpers on corners.** These protected buildings against reckless drivers. Scavenged secondhand ancient Roman pillars worked well.

6. **Scuff guards.** Made of harder materials, these guards sit at the base of the whitewashed walls—and, from the looks of it, are serving their purpose.

7. **Riverstone cobbles.** These stones were cheap and local, and provided drains down the middle of a lane. They were flanked by smooth stones that stayed dry for walking (and now aid the rolling suitcases of modern-day tourists).

8. **Pretty patios.** Cordovans are proud of their patios. Walk up to the inner iron gates of the wide-open front doors and peek in (see "Patios" sidebar, later).

9. **Remnants of old towers from minarets.** Córdoba's Muslim population peaked in the 10th century, which meant lots of neighborhood mosques.

10. **A real neighborhood.** People really live here. There are no tacky shops, and just about the only tourist is...you.

las Flores (a.k.a. "Blossom Lane"). This narrow flower-bedecked street frames the cathedral's bell tower as it hovers in the distance (the view is a favorite for local guidebook covers).

Casa de Sefarad

Set inside a restored 14th-century home directly across from the synagogue, this museum brings to life Córdoba's rich Jewish past. Exhibits in the rooms around a central patio recount Spanish Jewish history, focusing on themes such as domestic life, Jewish celebrations and holidays, and Sephardic musical traditions. Upstairs is an interpretive exhibit about the synagogue, along with rooms dedicated to the philosopher Maimonides and the Inquisition. Along with running this small museum, the Casa de Sefarad is a cultural center for Sephardic Jewish heritage (Sephardic Jews are those from Spain or Portugal). They teach courses, offer a library, and promote an appreciation of Córdoba's Jewish past.

Cost and Hours: €4, Fri-Sat 11:00-18:00, Sun until 14:00, 30-minute guided tours in English by request if guide is available, across from synagogue at corner of Calle de los Judíos and Calle Averroes, +34 957 421 404.

Concerts: The Casa de Sefarad hosts occasional concerts—acoustic, Sephardic, Andalusian, and flamenco—on its patio (€15, usually at 19:00, confirm schedule).

Synagogue (Sinagoga)

This small yet beautifully preserved synagogue was built between 1314 and 1315 and was in use right up until the final expulsion of the Jews from Spain in 1492.

Cost and Hours: Free, Tue-Sat 9:00-21:00, Sun and summer until 15:00, closed Mon year-round; Calle de los Judíos 20, +34 957 202 928, www.turismodecordoba.org/synagogue.

Visiting the Synagogue: The synagogue was built by Mudejar craftsmen during a period of religious tolerance after the Christian Reconquista of Córdoba (1236). During Muslim times, Córdoba's sizable Jewish community was welcomed in the city, though its members paid substantial taxes—money that enlarged the Mezquita and generated goodwill. That goodwill came in handy when Córdoba's era of prosperity and mutual respect ended with the arrival of the intolerant Almohad Berbers. Christians and Jews were repressed, and brilliant minds—such as the philosopher Maimonides, whose statue sits nearby—fled for their own safety.

Its relatively small dimensions lead historians to believe this

was a private or family synagogue. It's one of only three medieval synagogues that still stand in Spain (and the only one in Andalucía). That it survived at all is due to its having been successively converted into a church (look for the cross painted into a niche), a hospital, and a shoemakers' guild. The building's original purpose was only rediscovered in the late 19th century.

Rich Mudejar decorations of intertwined flowers and arabesques plaster the walls. The inscriptions in the main room are nearly all from the Bible's Book of Psalms (in Hebrew, with translations posted on each wall). On the east wall (the symbolic direction of Jerusalem), find the niche for the Ark, which held the scrolls of the Torah (the Jewish scriptures). The upstairs gallery was reserved for women.

Artisan Market (Zoco Municipal)

This charming series of courtyards off Calle de los Judíos was the first craft market in Spain. More than a dozen studios cluster around the pretty patios, where artists work in leather, glass, textiles, mosaics, and pottery. Their products—tiles, notecards, jewelry, leather bracelets, and bags—are sold in the associated retail shop.

Cost and Hours: Free to enter, daily 10:00-20:00, Calle de los Judíos s/n, +34 957 204 033, www.artesaniadecordoba.com.

City Walls

Built upon the foundation of Córdoba's Roman walls, these fortifications date mostly from the 12th century. While the city stretched beyond the walls in Moorish times, these fortifications protected its political, religious, and commercial center. Of the seven original gates, the Puerta de Almodóvar (near the synagogue) is best-preserved today. Along this wall, you'll find statues honoring Córdoba's great thinkers.

Statues of Seneca, Maimonides, and Averroes

Among Córdoba's deepest-thinking residents were a Roman philosopher forced to commit suicide, and a Jew and a Muslim who were both driven out during the wave of intolerance after the fall of the Umayyad caliphate. (Seneca is right outside the Puerta de Almodóvar; Maimonides is 30 yards downhill from the synagogue; Averroes is outside the old wall, where Cairuán and Doctor Fleming streets meet.)

Lucius Annaeus Seneca the Younger (c. 3 BC-AD 65) was born into a wealthy Cordovan family, but was drawn to Rome early in life. He received schooling in Stoicism and made a name for himself in oration, writing, law, and politics. Exiled to Corsica by Emperor Claudius, a remarkable reversal brought him into the role of trusted adviser to Emperor Nero, but eventually Nero accused

Seneca of plotting against him and demanded Seneca kill himself. In true Stoic fashion, Seneca complied with this request in AD 65, leaving behind a written legacy that includes nine plays, hundreds of essays, and numerous philosophical works that influenced the likes of Calvin, Montaigne, and Rousseau.

Moses Maimonides (1135-1204), "the Jewish Aquinas," was born in Córdoba and raised on both Jewish scripture and the philosophy of Aristotle. Like many tolerant Cordovans, he saw no conflict between the two. An influential Talmudic scholar, astronomer, and medical doctor, Maimonides left his biggest mark as the author of *The Guide for the Perplexed*, in which he asserted that secular knowledge and religious faith could go hand-in-hand (thereby inspiring the philosophy of St. Thomas Aquinas). In 1148, Córdoba was transformed when the fundamentalist Almohads assumed power, and young Maimonides and his family were driven out. Today tourists, Jewish scholars, and fans of Aquinas rub the statue's foot in the hope that some of Maimonides' genius and wisdom will rub off on them.

The story of **Averroes** (1126-1198) is a near match of Maimonides', except that Averroes was a Muslim lawyer, not a Jewish physician. He became the medieval world's number-one authority on Aristotle, also influencing Aquinas. Averroes' biting tract *The Incoherence of the Incoherence* attacked narrow-mindedness, asserting that secular philosophy (for the elite) and religious faith (for the masses) both led to truth. The Almohads banished him from the city and burned his books, ending four centuries of Cordovan enlightenment.

Bullfighting Museum (Museo Taurino Córdoba)

This museum, in a beautiful old palatial home of brick arcades and patios, examines Córdoba's bullfighting tradition. The introductory video provides a romanticized rundown of the sport (ask for the English version). Displays explore the landscape where bulls are bred and raised, and pay tribute to great bullfighters of the past (and their remarkably tiny waistlines) and to the tempo and aesthetics of the bullfight. It's high-tech, spacious, and merits a visit if you're interested in learning about an important local tradition. But if you've already seen the bullfight museums in Ronda or Sevilla, give this one a pass.

Cost and Hours: €5; open same hours as Alcázar (see next listing), closed Mon year-round; Plaza de Maimonides s/n, +34 957 201 056, www.museotaurinodecordoba.es.

Alcázar (Alcázar de los Reyes Cristianos)

Tourists line up to visit Córdoba's overrated fortress, the "Castle of the Christian Monarchs," which sits strategically next to the Guadalquivir River. (I think they confuse it with the much more worthy Alcázar in Sevilla.) Upon entering, look to the right to see a big, beautiful garden rich with flowers and fountains. To the left is a modern-feeling, unimpressive fort. While it was built along the Roman walls in Visigothic times, constant reuse and recycling has left it sparse and barren (with the exception of a few interesting Roman mosaics on the walls). Crowds squeeze up and down the congested spiral staircases of "Las Torres" for meager views. Ferdinand and Isabel donated the castle to the Inquisition in 1482, and it became central to the church's effort to discover "false converts to Christianity"—mostly Jews who had decided not to flee Spain in 1492.

Cost and Hours: €5; Tue-Fri 8:15-19:30, Sat 9:30-17:30, Sun until 14:15, shorter hours in summer, closed Mon year-round; +34 957 420 151. On Fridays and Saturdays, you're likely to see people celebrating civil weddings here.

Baths of the Caliphate Alcázar (Baños del Alcázar Califal)

The scant but evocative remains of these 10th-century royal baths are all that's left from the caliph's palace complex. They date from a time when the city had hundreds of baths to serve a population of several hundred thousand. The exhibit teaches about Arabic baths in general and the caliph's in particular. A 10-minute video (normally in Spanish; English on request) tells the story well.

Cost and Hours: €3, open same hours as Alcázar, on Plaza Campo de los Santos Mártires, just outside the wall—near the Alcázar, +34 608 158 893.

AWAY FROM THE MEZQUITA
Plaza de las Tendillas

While most tourists leave Córdoba having seen only the Mezquita and the cute medieval quarter that surrounds it, the modern city offers a good peek at urban Andalucía. For the best glimpse of this area, browse Plaza de las Tendillas and the surrounding streets. The square, with an Art Deco charm, mixes slice-of-life scenes and touristic eateries. On the hour, a clock here chimes the chords of flamenco guitarist Juan Serrano—a Cordovan classic since 1961.

Characteristic cafés and shops abound. For example, **$ Café La Gloria** provides an earthy Art Nouveau experience. Located just down the street from Plaza de las Tendillas, it has an unassuming entrance but a sumptuous interior. Carved floral designs wind around the bar, mixing with *feria* posters and bullfighting memories. Pop in for a beer or coffee with the locals (daily 8:00-24:00,

quiet after lunch crowd clears out, Calle Claudio Marcelo 15—for location see "Hotels & Restaurants in Central Córdoba" map, later, +34 957 477 780).

Roman Temple (Templo Romano)

The remains of this first-century Roman temple, a few minutes' walk from Plaza de las Tendillas, were discovered in the 1950s during a remodeling of City Hall. Today, you can stroll by the site for a free view of the towering columns and base of what was a massive temple in its day. It's particularly striking at night when illuminated (Calle Capitulares).

▲Museo Julio Romero de Torres

A city rich in mystical monuments and colorful patios, Córdoba has produced several fine artists during its long history. Well-to-do Julio Romero de Torres began painting at the age of 10 in 1884, under the tutelage of his father who was also a painter and director of the city's fine-arts museum. Early works resembled those of fellow Impressionists like Joaquín Sorolla, but in the 1920s, inspired by his passion for (or obsession with) flamenco, Julio developed a distinct style. He crafted soulful portraits of the dreamy-eyed, melancholic gaze of the women he loved to paint. After he died in 1930, his family donated many works to the city government and this museum opened one year later. Stroll through six small rooms and discover the sumptuous spirit of Córdoba through this captivating artist's eyes.

Cost and Hours: €4; Tue-Fri 8:15-19:30, Sat 9:30-17:30, Sun 8:15-14:15, shorter hours in summer, closed Mon year-round; Plaza del Potro 1, +34 957 491 909, https://museojulioromero.cordoba.es.

Palacio de Viana

Decidedly off the beaten path, this former palatial estate is a 25-minute walk northeast from the cluster of sights near the

Mezquita. The complex's many renovations over its 500-year history are a case study in changing tastes. A guided tour whisks you through each room of an exuberant 16th-century estate, while an English handout trudges through the dates and origin of each important piece. But the house is best enjoyed by ignoring the guide and gasping at the massive collection of—for lack of a better word—stuff. Decorative-art fans will have a field day. If your interests run more to flowers, skip the house and buy a "patio" ticket: 12 connecting garden patios, each with a differ-

Patios

In Córdoba, patios are taken seriously—even to the point of

competition. In the first half of every May, the city hosts a fiercely fought contest, the Concurso Popular de Patios Cordobeses, to pick the city's most picturesque.

Patios, a common feature of houses throughout Andalucía, have a long history here. The Romans used them to cool off, and the Moors added lush, decorative touches. The patio functioned as a quiet outdoor living room, an oasis from the heat. Inside elaborate ironwork gates, roses, geraniums, and jasmine spill down whitewashed walls, while fountains play and caged birds sing. Some patios are owned by individuals, some are communal courtyards for several homes, and some grace public buildings like museums or convents.

Today homeowners take pride in these mini paradises and have no problem sharing them with tourists. Keep an eye out for square metal signs that indicate historic homes. As you wander Córdoba's back streets, pop your head into any wooden door that's open. The proud owners (who keep inner gates locked) enjoy showing off their picture-perfect patios.

A concentration of patio-contest award-winners runs along Calle de San Basilio and Calle Martín Roa, just across from the Alcázar gardens. Seven of these winners have banded together to open their patios to the public for a single entry fee (€10 tickets available online; +34 654 530 377, www.patiosdesanbasilio.com). A competing neighborhood organization, dePatios, has a ticket office at Calle de San Basilio 14 and offers a look into five patios for €6 (+34 957 941 881, www.depatios.com). Both groups share the same hours (Mon and Wed-Sat 10:00-14:00 & 17:00-20:00, Sun 10:00-14:00 only, shorter hours in summer, patios closed Tue year-round).

ent theme, sprawl around and throughout the residence. It's no Alhambra, but if you won't see the gardens in Granada, these are a wee taste of the Andalusian style.

Cost and Hours: House—€10, patios only—€6; Tue–Sat 10:00-19:00, Sun until 15:00, shorter hours in summer, closed Mon year-round, last entry one hour before closing; Plaza de Don Gome 2—for location see "Córdoba" map on page 754, +34 957 496 741, www.palaciodeviana.com.

NEAR CÓRDOBA

Madinat al-Zahra (Medina Azahara)

Five miles northwest of Córdoba, this once-fabulous palace of the caliph was completely forgotten until excavations of its ruins began

in the early 20th century. Extensively planned, with an orderly design, Madinat al-Zahra was meant to symbolize and project a new discipline on an increasingly unstable Moorish empire in Spain. It failed. Only 75 years later, the city was looted and destroyed. Today, the site is mostly underwhelming—a jigsaw puzzle waiting to be reassembled by patient archaeologists. Check at the TI before committing to a trip, as the most interesting sections of the site may be closed for restoration.

Cost and Hours: €1.50; April-mid-June Tue-Sat 9:00-19:00, Sun until 15:00; mid-June-mid-Sept Tue-Sun 9:00-15:00; off-season until 18:00; the site stays open late some evenings (museum closed) but these hours only work with a car; closed Mon year-round; +34 957 104 933, www.museosdeandalucia.es.

Getting There: Madinat al-Zahra is located on a back road five miles from Córdoba. By **car,** head to Avenida de Medina Azahara (one block south of the train station), following signs for *A-431;* the site is well-signed from the highway. The TI runs a 20-minute **shuttle bus** that leaves twice daily and returns 3 hours later (€9, buy ticket at any TI; year-round Tue-Sat at 10:15 and 11:00; also at 13:45 mid-Sept-Oct; confirm current bus schedule at TI, informative English booklet). Your shuttle bus ticket (show driver) includes a €2.50 minibus that connects the museum with the site (round-trip, departures every 15 minutes, last minibus 1 hour before closing). Catch the shuttle on Paseo de la Victoria at either of two stops shared with the Bus Turístico route (see the "Central Córdoba" map, earlier). You can also take a **taxi**—your driver will wait for three hours as you explore the site, then drive you back into town. Have your hotel call to reserve (Radio Taxi Córdoba, €30 for up to 4 people, +34 957 764 444).

Visiting Madinat al-Zahra: Built in AD 929 as a power center to replace Córdoba, Madinat al-Zahra was both a palace and an entirely new capital city—the "City of the Flower"—covering nearly half a square mile (only about 10 percent has been uncovered).

Excavations of the upper terrace have revealed stables and servants' quarters. Farther downhill, the house of a high-ranking

official has been partially reconstructed. At the lowest level, you'll come to the remains of the mosque—placed at a diagonal, facing true east. The highlight of the visit is an elaborate reconstruction of the caliph's throne room, capturing a moody world of horseshoe arches and

delicate stucco. Legendary accounts say the palace featured waterfall walls, lions in cages, and—in the center of the throne room—a basin filled with mercury, reflecting the colorful walls. The effect likely humbled anyone fortunate enough to see the caliph.

Entertainment in Córdoba

Caballerizas Reales de Córdoba

This equestrian show at the royal stables (just beyond the Alcázar) combines an artful demonstration of different riding styles with flamenco dance. If you're not going to Jerez to see the show at the Royal Andalusian School of Equestrian Art, this is a fun and convenient alternative (€16.50; one-hour shows Wed-Sat at 21:00 or 21:30; mid-Sept-mid-April at 19:30, no shows Sun-Tue; outside in summer, inside in winter, +34 957 497 843, www.cordobaecuestre. com). During the day, you can tour the stables and vintage carriages (Wed-Sat 10:00-13:30 & 16:00-20:30, Sun until 13:00, longer hours in summer, Caballerizas Reales 1).

Flamenco

While flamenco is better in nearby Sevilla, you can see it in Córdoba, too. **Tablao Flamenco Cardenal** is the city's most popular and awarded show, with 120 seats in a beautifully decorated private patio. They also offer a preshow dinner with typical dishes from Córdoba (€23, includes one drink, 1.5-hour shows Mon-Thu at 20:30, Fri-Sat at 21:00, no shows Sun, confirm schedule online, Buen Pastor 2—for location, see the "Hotels & Restaurants in Central Córdoba" map, later; +34 691 217 922, www.tablaocardenal.es).

El Alma de Córdoba

To experience "the soul of Córdoba"—or at least the Mezquita by night—you can take this pricey one-hour audio tour, joining about 80 people to be shepherded around the complex listening via headset to an obviously Christian-produced sound-and-light show (€18, March-Oct Mon-Sat, off-season Fri-Sat only, 1-2 shows a night,

CÓRDOBA

hours vary according to sunset; book at Mezquita or online; http://www.mezquita-catedraldecordoba.es).

Sleeping in Córdoba

NEAR THE MEZQUITA

These are all within a five-minute stroll of the Mezquita.

$$$$ Balcón de Córdoba is an elegant little boutique hotel buried in the old town, just steps away from the Mezquita. With a compassionate staff, 10 stylish rooms, charming public spaces, plenty of attention to detail, and a magnificent rooftop terrace, it's a lot of luxury for the price. It feels both new and steeped in tradition. Look for the original architectural features of the 14th-century convent that once occupied this space. The restaurant serves wonderful cuisine, enhanced by evening views of the Mezquita from the terrace (includes breakfast, air-con, pay parking, restaurant open daily 12:30-16:00 & 19:30-23:00, Calle Encarnación 8, +34 957 498 478, www.balcondecordoba.com, reservas@balcondecordoba.com).

$$$$ Hotel Madinat's 11 rooms have old-world charm with modern comforts. Guests can take advantage of the hotel's Hammam-style spa and the cozy bar (some rooms with Mezquita views, rooftop terrace, air-con, Calle Cabezas 17, +34 975 395 000, www.hotelmadinat.com, info@hotelmadinat.com).

$$ La Llave de la Judería is a nine-room jewel box of an inn, featuring plush furniture, elegant and traditional decor, and attentive service. Quiet and romantic, it's tucked in the old quarter just far enough away from the tourist storm, yet still handy for sightseeing (terrace with Mezquita view, air-con, midway between Puerta de Almodóvar and the Mezquita at Calle Romero 38, +34 957 294 808, www.lallavedelajuderia.es, info@lallavedelajuderia.es). Charming Ana Luna and staff make you feel right at home.

$$ La Casa de la Costurera offers a uniquely Cordovan experience: sleeping in one of the city's prize-winning patios. Araceli and her sister rent four homey and colorful apartments, each with a kitchenette. While some noise might come from patio visitors during the day, the neighborhood is quiet at night and close to several recommended restaurants (air-con, Calle de San Basilio 40, +34 654 530 377, www.lacasadelacosturera.com, info@elpatiodelacosturera.com).

$$ Hotel Mezquita, just across from the Mezquita, rents 32 modern and comfortable rooms (10 with Mezquita views). The grand entrance lobby elegantly recycles an upper-class mansion (air-con, elevator, Plaza Santa Catalina 1, +34 957 475 585, www.hotelmezquita.com, reservas@hotelmezquita.com).

$ Hotel González, with many of its 30 basic rooms facing a

cool and peaceful patio, is humble but very sleepable. It's clean and well run, with a good location and price. Streetside rooms come with a bit of noise at night (air-con, elevator, Calle de los Manríquez 3, +34 957 479 819, www.hotelgonzalez.com, reservas@ hotelgonzalez.com).

¢ **Al-Katre Hostel** is a fun 40-bed hostel run in a casual, homey way by two women. Its rooms (each with shared bathrooms) gather around a cool courtyard, and its terrace feels a world away (Calle Martínez Rucker 14, +34 626 389 706, www.alkatre.com, alkatre@alkatre.com).

IN THE MODERN CITY

While still within easy walking distance of the Mezquita, these places are outside of the main tourist zone—not buried in all that tangled medieval cuteness.

$$ **Hotel Córdoba Centro** sits at a good crossroads between the historic center around the Mezquita and the modern part of the city. Most of its 25 simple but comfortable rooms are interior, assuring a solid night's sleep, while nine rooms face the pedestrian street and coffee shop below (air-con, elevator, Jesús y María 8, +34 957 497 850, www.hotel-cordobacentro.es, reservas@hotel-cordobacentro.es).

$ **Hotel Califa,** a modern 65-room business-class hotel belonging to the NH chain, sits on a quiet street a block off busy Paseo Victoria, on the edge of the jumbled old quarter. Still close enough to the sights, it has a beautiful patio courtyard, and its slick, minimalist rooms can be a great value if you get a deal (air-con, elevator, pay parking, Lope de Hoces 14, +34 957 299 400, www.nh-hotels.com, nhcalifa@nh-hotels.com).

¢ **Arc House Ribera** rents 40 hostel beds in a great neighborhood (private rooms available, air-con, terrace, kitchen, laundry facility, right by Plaza del Potro bus stop—take #3 from station—at Calle Lucano 12, +34 954 913 002, www.archouse.es/córdoba, cordoba@archouse.es).

Eating in Córdoba

Córdoba has a reputation among Spaniards as a great dining town, with options ranging from obvious touristy bars in the old center to enticing, locals-only hangouts a few blocks away. Specialties include *salmorejo*, Córdoba's version of gazpacho. It's creamier, with more bread and olive oil and generally served with pieces of ham and hard-boiled egg on top. Look for winners of the city's yearly oxtail stew *(rabo de toro)* contest and find your favorite. Most places serve white wines from the nearby Montilla-Moriles region; these *finos* are slightly less dry but more aromatic than the sherry pro-

CÓRDOBA

Hotels & Restaurants in Central Córdoba

Accommodations

1. Balcón de Córdoba
2. La Llave de la Judería
3. La Casa de la Costurera
4. Hotel Mezquita
5. Hotel Madinat
6. Hotel González
7. Al-Katre Hostel
8. Hotel Córdoba Centro
9. Hotel Califa
10. Arc House Ribera

Eateries & Other

11. Bodegas Mezquita
12. Bar Santos
13. La Posada del Caballo Andaluz
14. Mesón San Basilio
15. Bodega San Basilio
16. Taberna Restaurante Casa Rubio
17. Casa Pepe Salinas
18. Restaurante Asador El Choto
19. El Churrasco Restaurante
20. Casa Mazal
21. Bodega Guzmán
22. To Bodegas Campos
23. Macsura Gastrotaberna
24. Taberna Salinas
25. To Taberna San Miguel (Casa el Pisto)
26. Taberna La Cazuela de la Espartería
27. Tablao Flamenco Cardenal
28. Café La Gloria
29. Grocery (4)

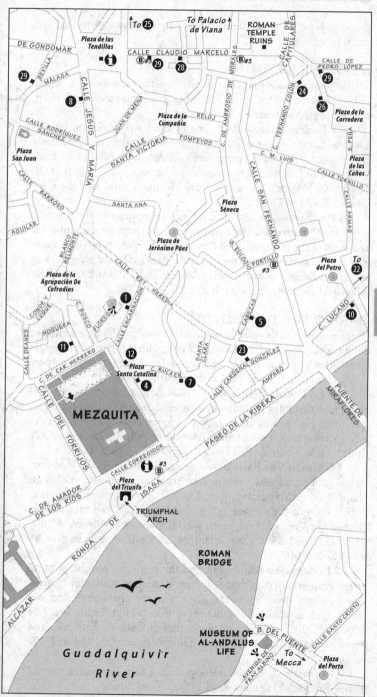

CÓRDOBA

duced in Jerez de la Frontera. Ask for a *fino fresquito* (chilled) and you'll fit right in.

NEAR THE MEZQUITA

Touristy options abound near the Mezquita. By walking a couple of blocks north or east of the Mezquita, you'll find plenty of cheap, accessible places offering a better value.

$$ Bodegas Mezquita is one of the touristy places, but it's easy and handy—a good bet for a bright, air-conditioned place near the mosque. They have a good *menú del día*, or you can order from their menu of tapas, half-*raciones*, and *raciones* (daily 13:00-16:30 & 20:00-23:30, one block above the Mezquita patio at Calle Céspedes 12, +34 957 490 004).

$ Bar Santos, facing the Mezquita, supplies the giant *tortilla de patatas* (potato omelette) that you see locals happily munching on the steps of the mosque. Their "fast" food is served to-go in disposable containers. A hearty tortilla and a beer make for a very cheap meal; add a *salmorejo* and it feels complete (daily 10:00-24:00, Calle Magistral González Francés 3, +34 957 893 220).

BARRIO SAN BASILIO

This delightful little quarter outside the town wall, just a couple of minutes' walk west of the Mezquita and behind the royal stables, is famous for its patios. It's traffic-free, quaint as can be, and feels perfectly Cordovan without the crush of tourists around the Mezquita.

$$ La Posada del Caballo Andaluz is a fresh, modern restaurant with tables delightfully scattered around a courtyard (no bar area). Enjoy tasty traditional Cordovan cuisine at great prices while sitting amid flowers and under the stars (daily 12:30-16:30 & 20:00-23:30, Calle de San Basilio 16, +34 957 290 374).

$$ Mesón San Basilio, just across the street, is the longtime neighborhood favorite, with no tourists and no pretense. Although there's no outside seating, it still offers a certain patio ambience, with a view of the kitchen action and lots of fish and meat dishes (classic fixed-priced meal, lunch special weekdays, Mon-Sat 13:00-16:00 & 20:00-24:00, Sun 20:00-24:00, Calle de San Basilio 19, +34 957 297 007).

$ Bodega San Basilio, around the corner, is rougher around the edges, serving rustic tapas and good meals to workaday crowds. The bullfight decor gives the place a crusty character—and you won't find a word of English here (Wed-Mon 13:00-16:30 & 20:00-23:30, closed Tue, on the corner of Calle de Enmedio and small street leading to Calle de San Basilio at #29, +34 957 297 832).

Groceries: A **Super Alcoop** is at Calle Dr. Barraquer 12 (Mon-Fri 9:00-21:00, Sat until 14:00, closed Sun).

BETWEEN PUERTA DE ALMODÓVAR AND THE JEWISH QUARTER

The evocative Puerta de Almodóvar gate connects a parklike scene outside the wall with the delightfully jumbled Jewish Quarter just inside it, where cafés and restaurants take advantage of the neighborhood's pools, shady trees, and dramatic face of the wall. The first two recommendations are immediately inside the gate; the others are on or near Calle de los Judíos, which runs south from there.

$$ Taberna Restaurante Casa Rubio serves reliably good traditional dishes with smart, prompt service and several zones to choose from: a few sidewalk tables, with classic people-watching; inside, with a timeless interior and lively banter; or on the rooftop, with dressy white tablecloths and a view of the old wall (daily 13:00-16:00 & 19:30-23:00, Puerta de Almodóvar 5, +34 957 420 853).

$$ Casa Pepe Salinas, from the same people who run the highly recommended Taberna Salinas in the modern city, is a more basic place with a fine reputation for quality food at a good price (Thu-Tue 12:30-17:00 & Fri-Sat 19:30-23:30, closed all day Wed; near gate at Puerta de Almodóvar 2, +34 957 941 907).

$$$ Restaurante Asador El Choto is a bright, formal, and dressy steak house buried deep in the Jewish Quarter. With a small leafy patio, it's touristy yet intimate, serving well-presented international dishes with an emphasis on grilled meat. The favorite is kid goat with garlic—*choto al ajillo* (Mon-Sat 13:00-23:30, Sun until 16:30, closed Mon in summer, reservations smart, Calle Almanzor 10, +34 957 760 115, www.restauranteelchotocordoba. es).

$$$ El Churrasco Restaurante is a charmingly old-fashioned place where longtime patrons are greeted by name. The specialty is grilled meat and seafood, cooked simply and deliciously over oak-charcoal braziers in the open kitchen. It's a fun place for tapas in the bar or a meal under the glass roof of the dining room (daily 13:00-16:00 & 20:30-23:30, Calle Romero 16, +34 957 290 819).

$$ Casa Mazal, run by the nearby Casa de Sefarad Jewish cultural center, serves contemporary Jewish cuisine. Small dining rooms sprawl around the charming medieval courtyard of a former house. With a seasonal menu that includes several vegetarian options, it offers a welcome dose of variety from the typical Spanish standards (daily 12:30-16:00 & 19:30-23:00, Calle Tomás Conde 3, +34 957 246 304).

$ Bodega Guzmán could hardly care less about attracting tourists. This bristly, dark holdover from a long-gone age proudly displays the heads of brave-but-unlucky bulls, while serving cold, very basic tapas to locals who burst into song when they feel the

CÓRDOBA

flamenco groove. Notice how everyone seems to be on a first-name basis with the waiters. It may feel like a drinks-only place, but they do serve rustic tapas and *raciones* (ask for the list in English). Choose a table or belly up to the bar and try a glass of local white wine, either dry *(blanco seco)* or sweet *(blanco dulce)*. If it's grape juice you want, ask for *mosto* (daily 12:00-16:00 & 20:00-22:45, Calle Judíos 7, +34 957 290 960).

JUST EAST OF THE MEZQUITA ZONE

$$$ **Bodegas Campos,** my favorite place in town, is a historic and venerable eatery, attracting so many locals it comes with its own garage. It's worth the 10-minute walk from the tourist zone. They have a stuffy and expensive formal restaurant upstairs, but I'd eat in the more relaxed and affordable tavern on the ground floor. The service is great, portions are large, and the menu is inviting. Experiment—you can't go wrong. House specialties are bull-tail stew *(rabo de toro*—rich, tasty, and a good splurge) and anything with *pisto,* the local ratatouille-like vegetable stew. Don't leave without exploring the sprawling complex, which fills 14 old houses that have been connected to create a network of dining rooms and patios, small and large. The place is a virtual town history museum: Look for the wine barrels signed by celebrities and VIPs, the old refectory from a convent, and a huge collection of classic, original *feria* posters and great photos (daily 13:00-16:00 & 20:30-23:00; reservations smart, Calle de Lineros 32, +34 957 497 500, www.bodegascampos.com).

$$ **Macsura Gastrotaberna** serves beautifully presented international dishes for anyone who might need a break from *jamón*—think Asian-Spanish fusion. Choose between bright and white inside seating or watch the locals go by on a triangular patio outside (daily 11:30-23:30, Calle Cardenal González, +34 957 486 004).

IN THE MODERN CITY

These places are a 10- to 15-minute walk and a world apart from the main tourist zone. Combine a meal here with a paseo through the Plaza de las Tendillas area to get a good look at modern Córdoba. If Taberna Salinas is full, as is likely, there are plenty of characteristic bars nearby in the lanes around Plaza de la Corredera.

$$ **Taberna Salinas** seems like a movie set designed to give you the classic Córdoba scene. Though all the seating is indoors, it's still pleasantly patio-esque and popular with locals for its traditional cuisine and exuberant bustle. The seating fills a big courtyard and sprawls through several smaller, semiprivate rooms. The fun menu features a slew of enticing *raciones* (spinach

with chickpeas is a house specialty). Study what locals are eating before ordering. There's no drink menu—just beer, *fino*, or inexpensive wine. If there's a line (as there often is later in the evening), leave your name and throw yourself into the adjacent tapas-bar mosh pit for a drink (Mon-Sat 12:30-16:00 & 20:00-23:30, closed Sun and Aug; from Plaza de las Tendillas walk 3 blocks to the Roman Temple, then go 1 more block and turn right to Tundidores 3; +34 957 482 950).

$$ Taberna San Miguel is nicknamed "Casa el Pisto" for its famous vegetable stew *(pisto)*. Well-respected, it's packed with locals who appreciate regional cuisine, a good value, and a place with a long Cordovan history. There's great seating in its charming interior or on the lively square (tapas at bar only, daily 12:00-16:00 & 20:00-24:00, closed Aug, 2 blocks north of Plaza de las Tendillas at Plaza San Miguel 1, +34 957 470 166).

$$ Taberna La Cazuela de la Espartería offers traditional Andalusian and Cordovan recipes, featuring dishes baked in *cazuelas* (ceramic dishes), such as *berenjenas de barro* (a kind of eggplant lasagna). The specialties pair nicely with the restaurant's numerous Spanish wines. Eat in the rustic dining room or enjoy their tapas and *raciones* at barrel tables in the bar or outdoors. Be sure to check out the "Las Tavernas" room upstairs, with striking bullfighter photos (Mon-Sat 12:30-16:15 & 20:00-24:00, Sun 13:00-16:30, Calle Rodríguez Marin 16, +34 957 488 952).

Groceries: Look for a large branch of **Día** near Plaza de las Tendillas (Mon-Sat 9:00-21:30, closed Sun, Sevilla 4). **Aldi** is also near Plaza de las Tendillas (Mon-Sat 9:00-21:30, closed Sun, Claudio Marcelo 19). **Carrefour Express** is between Plaza de la Corredera and the Roman Temple ruins (daily 9:00-22:00, Calle Rodríguez Marín 13).

Córdoba Connections

From Córdoba by Train: Córdoba is on the slick **AVE** train line (reservations required), making it an easy stopover between **Madrid** (almost hourly, 2 hours) and **Sevilla** (45 minutes). The **Avant** train connects Córdoba to Sevilla just as fast for a lower price (hourly, 45 minutes). The slow *larga distancia* train to Sevilla takes about twice as long, but doesn't require a reservation and is even cheaper (4/day, 4 hours).

Other trains go to **Barcelona** (4/day direct, 5 hours, many more with transfer in Madrid), **Granada** (8/day, 1.5 hours), **Ronda** (1/day direct on Intercity, 2 hours), **Jerez** (6/day direct on *media distancia*, 2.5 hours, transfer in Sevilla), **Málaga** (fast and cheap Avant train, 5/day, 1 hour; more expensive but no faster on

AVE), and **Algeciras** (1/day direct, 4 hours). Train info: +34 912 320 320, www.renfe.com.

By Bus to: Granada (6/day, 2.5 hours, Alsa), **Sevilla** (7/day, 2 hours, Alsa), **Madrid** (4/day, 5 hours, Socibus), **Nerja** (3/day, 4.5 hours, Alsa), **Málaga** (5-6/day, 2-3.5 hours, Alsa). You can check all schedules at www.estacionautobusescordoba.es. Bus info: Alsa, www.alsa.es; Socibus, www.socibusventas.es.

CÓRDOBA

ANDALUCÍA'S WHITE HILL TOWNS

Arcos de la Frontera • Ronda • Zahara & Grazalema • Jerez de la Frontera

Just as the American image of Germany is Bavaria, the Yankee dream of Spain is Andalucía. This is the home of bullfights, flamenco, gazpacho, pristine whitewashed hill towns, and glamorous Mediterranean resorts. The big cities of Andalucía (Granada, Sevilla, and Córdoba) and the south coast (Costa del Sol) are covered in separate chapters. This chapter explores Andalucía's hill-town highlights.

The Route of the White Hill Towns (Ruta de los Pueblos Blancos), Andalucía's charm bracelet of cute villages perched in the sierras, gives you wonderfully untouched Spanish culture. The most substantial and entertaining home base is Ronda, which stuns visitors with its breathtaking setting—straddling a gorge that thrusts deep into the Andalusian bedrock. Ronda's venerable old bullring, smattering of enjoyable sights, and thriving tapas scene round out its appeal. Or, for something quieter and more exotic, spend a night in the romantic queen of the white towns, Arcos de la Frontera. (Towns with "de la Frontera" in their names were established on the front line of the centuries-long fight to recapture Spain from the Muslims, who were slowly pushed back into Africa.) Smaller hill towns, such as Zahara and Grazalema, offer plenty of beauty. As a whole, the hill towns—no longer strategic, no longer on any frontier—are now just passing time peacefully. Except for the cruise groups that wash in from Costa del Sol resorts like the tide, these towns feel a bit bypassed and mysterious.

West of the hill towns, the city of Jerez de la Frontera—teeming with traffic and lacking in charm—is worth a peek for its famous dancing horses and a glass of sherry on a bodega tour.

ANDALUCÍA

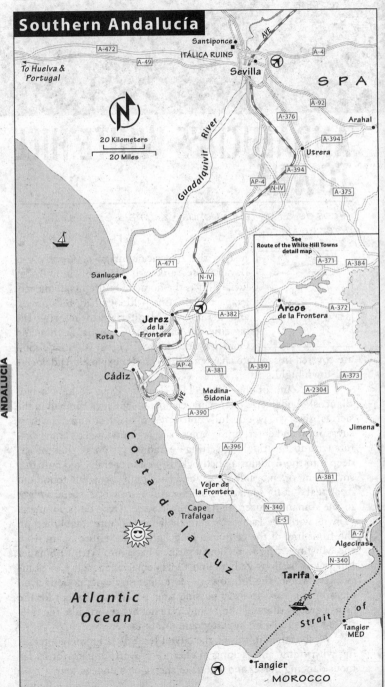

Southern Andalucía

To Huelva & Portugal

A-472

A-49

Santiponce

ITÁLICA RUINS

Sevilla

AVE

A-4

S P A

A-376

A-92

Arahal

A-394

Utrera

A-394

Guadalquivir River

N

20 Kilometers

20 Miles

AP-4

N-IV

A-375

A-471

N-IV

See
Route of the White Hill Towns
detail map

A-371

A-384

Sanlucar

A-382

Arcos
de la Frontera

A-372

Jerez
de la
Frontera

Rota

AP-4

A-381

A-389

A-373

A-2304

Cádiz

AVE

Medina-
Sidonia

Jimena

A-390

A-396

A-381

Vejer de
la Frontera

A-7

Cape
Trafalgar

N-340

E-5

Algeciras

Costa de la Luz

N-340

Tarifa

Atlantic
Ocean

Strait of

Tangier
MED

Tangier

MOROCCO

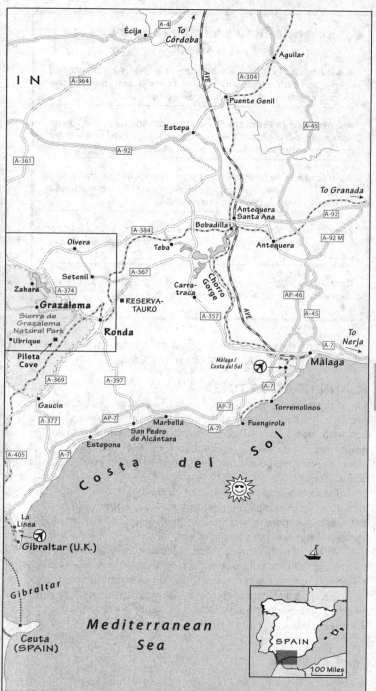

ANDALUCÍA

Andalucía's White Hill Towns at a Glance

▲▲▲**Ronda** Midsize town dramatically overhanging a deep gorge, and home to Spain's oldest bullring, with nearby prehistoric paintings at Pileta Cave. See page 802.

▲▲**Arcos de la Frontera** Queen of the Andalusian hill towns, with a cliff-perched old town that meanders down to a vibrant modern center; well suited as a home base. See page 791.

▲**Jerez de la Frontera** Proud equestrian mecca and birthplace of sherry, with plenty of opportunities to enjoy both in a relatively urban setting. See page 828.

Zahara de la Sierra Tiny whitewashed village scenically set between a rocky Moorish castle and a turquoise reservoir. See page 823.

Grazalema Bright-white town nestled in the green hills of the Sierra de Grazalema Natural Park. See page 826.

To study ahead, visit Andalucia.com for information on festivals, museums, nightlife, and sports in the region.

PLANNING YOUR TIME

On a three-week vacation in Spain, Andalucía's hill towns are worth at least two nights and one day—or more. Ronda (bigger and with more going on) or Arcos (smaller and sleepier) make the best home bases. Ronda is closer to the Costa del Sol. Arcos is closer to Jerez, and conveniently situated halfway between Sevilla and Tarifa.

Ronda can keep you busy for an entire day. Arcos can be experienced in an evening. You could spend a day hopping from town to town in the more remote interior (including Grazalema and Zahara). See Jerez on your way in or out.

Unlike most hill towns, Arcos, Jerez, and Ronda are conveniently reached by public transportation: They have bus connections with surrounding towns, and Ronda is on a train line.

Spring and fall are high season throughout this area. In summer you'll encounter intense heat, but empty hotels, lower prices, and no crowds.

ANDALUCÍA

Arcos de la Frontera

Arcos smothers its long, narrow hilltop and tumbles down the back of the ridge like the train of a wedding dress. It's larger than most other Andalusian hill towns, but equally atmospheric. The old center is a labyrinthine wonderland, a photographer's feast. Viewpoint-hop through town. Feel the wind funnel through the narrow streets as cars inch around tight corners. Join the kids' soccer game on the churchyard patio. Enjoy the moonlit view from the main square.

Though it tries, Arcos is low energy. It doesn't have much to offer other than its basic whitewashed self. The locally produced English guidebook on Arcos waxes poetic and at length about very little. You can arrive late and leave early and still see it all.

Orientation to Arcos

Arcos consists of two parts: the fairy-tale old town on top of the hill and the more commercial lower, or new, town. The **main TI** is on the skinny one-way road leading up into the old town (Sun-Tue 10:00-14:00, Wed-Sat 9:30-14:00 & 15:00-19:30, Cuesta de Belén 5, +34 956 702 264, www.turismoarcos.com). A model there shows Arcos (in Latin, *Arx Arcis*—"high fortress") as it was in 1264 when the Christian Reconquista forces retook it from the Moors. On the floors above the TI is a skippable local history museum (sparse exhibits described only in Spanish).

ARRIVAL IN ARCOS

By Bus: The bus station is on Calle Corregidores, at the foot of the hill. To get up to the old town, catch the **shuttle bus** marked *Centro* from the bus stalls behind the station. Tell the driver the name of your hotel and he'll bring you to the closest stop (€1, pay driver, generally departs at :15 and :45 past the hour, runs roughly Mon-Fri 7:45-21:15, Sat until 14:15, none on Sun). Alternately, hop a taxi (about €6; if none are waiting, call +34 956 704 640), or hike 15 uphill minutes.

By Car: The old town is a tight squeeze with a one-way traffic flow from west to east (coming from the east, circle south of town). The TI and my recommended hotels are in the west. If you miss your target, you must drive out the other end, double back, and try again. Driving in Arcos is like threading needles (many drivers pull in their side-view mirrors to buy a few extra precious inches). Turns are tight, parking is frustrating, and congestion can lead to long jams.

It's less stressful to park in the modern Paseo de Andalucía underground pay lot (€10/day with a hotel-stamped parking ticket)

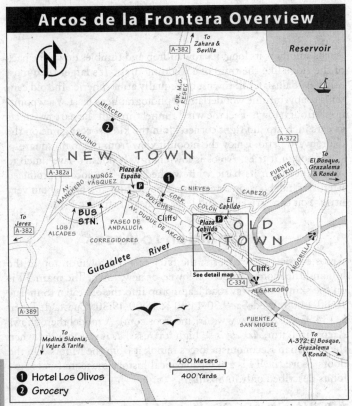

Arcos de la Frontera Overview

To Zahara & Sevilla
A-382

Reservoir

C. DR. M.G. PESCI

MERCED

A-372

MOLINO

NEW TOWN

To El Bosque, Grazalema & Ronda

A-382a

Plaza de España

FUENTE DEL RÍO

MUÑÓZ VÁSQUEZ

AV. MANCHERO

C. NIEVES

CABEZO

BOLICHES

CORR.

COLÓN

El Cabildo

BUS STN.

AV. DUQUE DE ARCOS

Cliffs

Plaza Cabildo

OLD TOWN

To Jerez
A-382

LOS ALCADES

PASEO DE ANDALUCÍA

CORREGIDORES

ANGORILLA

Guadalete River

See detail map

Cliffs

C-334

ALGARROBO

A-389

To Medina Sidonia, Vejer & Tarifa

FUENTE SAN MIGUEL

To A-372: El Bosque, Grazalema & Ronda

400 Meters

400 Yards

❶ Hotel Los Olivos
❷ Grocery

at Plaza de España in the new town and hike 15 uphill minutes to the old town. Or catch a taxi or the *Centro* shuttle bus—see "By Bus" earlier (as you're looking uphill, the bus stop is to the right of the traffic circle). Many hotels offer discounts at this lot; inquire when booking your room.

Small cars capable of threading the narrow streets of the old town can park in the main square at the top of the hill (Plaza del Cabildo) for free. However, there are only 50 spots and the plaza is often full.

HELPFUL HINTS

Money: There are no ATMs in the old town. You'll find several ATMs in the new town along Calle Corredera and near the Paseo de Andalucía underground parking lot.

Groceries: You'll find smaller stores with a basic selection of groceries in the old town or close to the TI. For a bigger grocery store head to the **Mercadona** in the new town (Mon-Sat 9:00-21:30, closed Sun, Avenida San Juan Bautista de la Salle).

Shuttle Bus Joyride: The old town is easily walkable, but it's fun to take a circular ramble on the shuttle bus. The little minibus constantly circles through the town's one-way system and around the valley (see "Arrival in Arcos," earlier, for details). For a 30-minute tour, just hop on. In the old town, you can catch it just below the main church near the mystical stone circle (generally departs at :20 and :50 past the hour). Sit in the front seat for the best view of the tight squeezes and the school kids hanging out in the plazas. After passing under a Moorish gate, you enter a modern residential neighborhood, circle under

the eroding cliff, and return to the old town by way of the bus station and Plaza de España.

Views: For drivers, the best town overlook is from a tiny park just beyond the new bridge on the El Bosque road. In town, there are some fine viewpoints (for instance, from the main square), but the church towers are no longer open to the public.

Arcos Old Town Walk

This self-guided walk will introduce you to virtually everything worth seeing in Arcos. (Avoid this walk during the hot midday siesta.)

• *Start at the top of the hill, in the main square dominated by the church.*

Plaza del Cabildo

Stand at the viewpoint opposite the church on the town's main square. Survey the square, which in the old days doubled as a bullring. On your right is the parador, a former palace of the governor. It flies three flags: green for Andalucía, red and yellow for Spain, and blue and yellow for the European Union. On your left is City Hall, below the 11th-century Moorish castle where Ferdinand and Isabel held Reconquista strategy meetings (castle privately owned and closed to the public).

Now belly up to the railing and look down at the dramatic view. The people of Arcos boast that only they see the backs of

Arcos de la Frontera

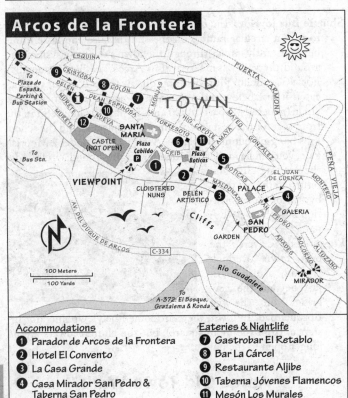

Accommodations
1. Parador de Arcos de la Frontera
2. Hotel El Convento
3. La Casa Grande
4. Casa Mirador San Pedro & Taberna San Pedro
5. Rincón de las Nieves
6. Pension & Bar San Marcos

Eateries & Nightlife
7. Gastrobar El Retablo
8. Bar La Cárcel
9. Restaurante Aljibe
10. Taberna Jóvenes Flamencos
11. Mesón Los Murales
12. Alcaraván
13. Tabanco Lalola

the birds as they fly. Ponder the parador's erosion concerns (it lost part of its lounge in the 1990s when it dropped right off), the orderly orange groves, and the fine views toward the southernmost part of Spain. The city council considered building an underground parking lot to clear up the square, but nixed it because of the land's fragility. You're 300 feet above the Guadalete River.

• *Looming over the square is the...*

Church of Santa María

After Arcos was retaken from the Moors in the 13th century, this church was built atop a mosque. Notice the church's fine but chopped-off bell tower. The old one fell in the earthquake of 1755 (famous for destroying Lisbon). The replacement was intended to be the tallest in Andalucía after Sevilla's, but money ran out. It looks like someone lives on an upper floor. Someone does—the church guardian resides there.

Cost and Hours: €2, €3 combo-ticket includes Church of San Pedro, Mon-Fri 10:30-13:30 & 16:30-18:30, Sat 11:00-17:00, Sun until 18:00, shorter hours in winter.

Visiting the Church: Buy a ticket and step inside, where you can see they've packed a lot of decoration into a small space. Work

your way between the pews to examine the beautifully carved choir. Its organ was built in 1789 with that many pipes. At the very front of the church, the nice Renaissance high altar, carved in wood, covers up a Muslim prayer niche that survived from the older mosque. The altar shows God with a globe in his hand (on top), and scenes from the life of Jesus (on the right) and Mary (left). On the left wall past the altar is a fine surviving 14th-century Andalusian Gothic fresco.

Continue circling the church and notice the elaborate chapels. Although most of the architecture is Gothic, the chapels are decorated in the Baroque and Rococo styles that were popular when the post-earthquake remodel began. The ornate statues are used in Holy Week processions. Sniff out the "incorruptible body" (miraculously never rotting) of St. Felix—a third-century martyr (directly across from the entry). Felix may be nicknamed "the incorruptible," but take a close look at his knee. He's no longer skin and bones...just bones and the fine silver mesh that once covered his skin. Rome sent his body here in 1764, after recognizing this church as the most important in Arcos. In the back of the church, near a huge fresco of St. Christopher (carrying his staff and Baby Jesus), is a gnarly Easter candle from 1767.

• *Back outside, circle clockwise around the church and examine the church exterior.*

Down four steps, find the third-century Roman votive altar with a carving of the palm tree of life directly in front of you. Though the Romans didn't build this high in the mountains, they did have a town and temple at the foot of Arcos. This carved stone was discovered in the foundation of the original Moorish mosque, which stood here before the first church was built. This has long been considered a fertility stone (women would come here to help with pregnancy).

Head down a few more steps and come to the main entrance (west portal) of the church (always closed). This is a good example of Plateresque Gothic—Spain's last and most ornate kind of Gothic.

In the pavement, notice the 15th-century magic circle with

12 red and 12 white stones—the white ones have various "constellations" marked (though they don't resemble any of today's star charts). When a child would come to the church to be baptized, the parents stopped here first for a good Christian exorcism. The exorcist would stand inside the protective circle and cleanse the baby of any evil spirits. While locals no longer do this (and a modern rain drain now marks the center), many Sufi Muslims still come here in a kind of pilgrimage every November. (Down a few more steps, you can catch the public minibus for a circular joyride through Arcos; see "Helpful Hints," earlier.)

Go down the next few stairs to the street and circle right. Peer down the next narrow path to the left called Cuesta de las Monjas. The security grille (over the window above) protected cloistered nuns when this building was a convent. Look at the arches that prop up the houses downhill; all over town, arches support earthquake-damaged structures.

Continue straight under the **flying buttresses.** Notice the scratches of innumerable car mirrors on each wall (and be glad you're walking). The buttresses were built to shore up the church when it was damaged by an earthquake in 1699. (Thanks to these supports, most of the church survived the bigger earthquake of 1755.)

• *Now make your way...*

From Santa María to the Church of San Pedro

Completing your circle around the Church of Santa María (huffing back uphill), turn left under more arches built to repair earthquake damage and walk east down the bright, white Calle Escribanos ("Street of the Scribes"). Although it changes names, you'll basically follow this lane until you come to the town's second big church (San Pedro).

After a block, you hit Plaza Boticas. On your right is the last remaining **convent** in Arcos. Notice the no-nunsense, spiky window grilles high above, with tiny peepholes in the latticework for the cloistered nuns to see through. If you're hungry, check out the list and photos of the treats the nuns provide. Then step into the lobby under the fine portico to find their one-way mirror and a spinning cupboard that hides the nuns from view. Push the buzzer, and one of the eight sisters (several are from Kenya and speak English well) will spin out some boxes of excellent, freshly baked cookies—made from pine nuts, peanuts, almonds, and other nuts—for you to consider (€7-8, open daily but not reliably 8:30-14:30 & 17:00-19:00; be careful—if you stand big and tall to block out the

light, you might see the sister through the glass). If you ask for *magdalenas*, bags of cupcakes will swing around (€3.50). These are traditional goodies made from natural ingredients. Buy some treats to support their church work and give them to kids as you complete your walk.

• *As you exit the convent, turn right and go right again down Calle Boticas.*

Be on the lookout for ancient columns tucked into building corners. All over town, these columns—many actually Roman, appropriated from their original ancient settlement at the foot of the hill—were put up to protect buildings from reckless donkey carts (and tourists in rental cars).

As you continue straight, notice that the walls are scooped out on either side of the windows. These are a reminder of the days when women stayed inside but wanted the best possible view of any action in the streets. In that more restrictive age, these "window ears" also enabled suitors to lean inconspicuously against the wall to chat up eligible young ladies.

Across from the old chapel facade ahead, find the **Palacio del Mayorazgo,** which houses the Association of San Miguel. Duck right, past a bar, into one of the oldest courtyards in town—you can still see the graceful Neo-Gothic lines of this noble home from 1850. Enjoy any art exhibits and the garden. The bar is a club for retired men—always busy when a bullfight's on TV or during card games. The guys are friendly, and drinks are cheap. You're welcome to flip on the light and explore the old-town photos in the back room.

• *Just beyond, facing the elegant front door of that noble house, is Arcos' second church...*

Church of San Pedro

Enter through the small door to the left of the main entrance (€2, €3 combo-ticket includes Church of Santa María, same hours as Church of Santa María).

You know it's the Church of San Pedro because San Pedro, mother of God, is the centerpiece of the facade. Let me explain. This really is the town's second church, having had an extended battle with Santa María for papal recognition as the leading church in Arcos. When the pope finally favored Santa María (he declared it a minor basilica in 1993), San Pedro's parishioners changed their

prayers. Rather than honoring "María," they wouldn't even say her name. They prayed "San Pedro, mother of God." Like Santa María, it's a Gothic structure, filled with Baroque decor (including a stunning organ covered with cherubs), many Holy Week procession statues, and humble English descriptions. Santa María may have won papal recognition, but this church has more relic skeletons in glass caskets (flanking both sides of the main altar are St. Fructuoso and St. Víctor, martyrs from the third century AD). The music stand in the choir illustrates how the entire chorus can sing from just four hymnals.

• Back outside, explore...

Back Lanes, Artisan Workshops, and Courtyards

In the cool of the evening, the tiny square in front of the church—about the only flat piece of pavement around—serves as the old-town soccer field for neighborhood kids. This church once had a resident bellman—notice the cozy balcony halfway up. He was a basket-maker and a colorful character, famous for bringing a donkey into his quarters that grew too big to get back out. Finally, he had no choice but to kill and eat the donkey.

Twenty yards beyond the church, step into the humble **Galería de Arte San Pedro,** featuring artisans in action and their reasonably priced paintings, engravings, and pottery (Mon-Fri 10:00-21:00, Sat-Sun until 19:00, shorter hours in winter).

Crossing behind the church to the next lane, signs direct you to a **mirador**—a tiny square 100 yards downhill that affords a commanding view of Arcos. The reservoir you see to the northeast of town is used for water sports in the summertime. Looking south, among the rolling fields you'll see a power plant that local residents protested—to no avail—based on environmental concerns. Wind-driven generators blink along the horizon at night. Relax on a bench and take in this spectacular view.

• Return to the Church of San Pedro, then circle down and right along Calle Maldonado as we head back toward the main square.

Just below San Pedro's is a delightful little **Andalusian garden** (formal Arabic style, with aromatic plants such as jasmine, rose, and lavender, and water in the center). About 100 yards farther along on Maldonado (on the right after the dip), peek into the **Belén Artístico,** a little cave-like museum, which highlights a popular Spanish tradition of setting up a Nativity scene during Christmas using miniature figures (free but donations accepted, daily 10:30-13:30).

• This street eventually leads you back to Plaza Boticas (and those cloistered nuns selling cookies).

The lanes that run steeply down behind Plaza Boticas and the Church of Santa María offer both exercise and a chance to see into

Arcos' lovely courtyards. The lane called Higinio Capote is particularly picturesque with its many geraniums. Peek discreetly into the private patios. These wonderful, cool-tiled courtyards filled with plants, pools, furniture, and happy family activities are typical of Arcos. Except in the mansions, these patios are generally shared by several families. Originally, each courtyard served as a catchment system, funneling rainwater to a drain in the middle, which filled the well. You can still see tiny wells in wall niches with now-decorative pulleys for the bucket.

Nightlife in Arcos

Arcos is a quiet town. When I ask locals about nightlife, they say, "We sleep." But you'll find a tiny pulse of nocturnal energy here and there. The newer part of Arcos has a modern charm. In the cool of the evening, all generations enjoy life out around Plaza de España (15-minute walk from the old town).

The old town is pretty quiet after hours. But the fun little bar, **Taberna San Pedro** (next to the Church of San Pedro), seems to be spoiling for a party. It's a tiny, cozy joint with typical tapas, a proud selection of wines from Cádiz, and a mishmash of paintings, matador photos, and *fútbol* banners (closed Tue). And **Tabanco Lalola** (down the hill, past the TI at Corredera 11) is great for drinks, tapas, and "Flamenquito" Fridays with a guitarist and *cajón* player.

Sleeping in Arcos

Hotels in Arcos consider April, May, August, September, and October to be high season. Note that some hotels double their rates during the motorbike races in nearby Jerez de la Frontera (usually April or May) and during Holy Week before Easter.

IN THE OLD TOWN

Drivers should obtain a parking pass from their hotel to park overnight on the main square. (The pass does not exempt you from daytime rates.) Otherwise, park in the Paseo de Andalucía lot at Plaza de España in the new town and walk or catch a taxi or the shuttle bus up to the old town (see "Arrival in Arcos," earlier).

$$$ Parador de Arcos de la Frontera is royally located, with 23 elegant and reasonably priced rooms (eight have balconies). The terraces offer splendid views of the town and the valley

below (air-con, elevator, Plaza del Cabildo, +34 956 700 500, www.
parador.es, arcos@parador.es).

$$ Hotel El Convento, deep in the old town just beyond the
parador, is the best value in town. Run by a hardworking family
and their wonderful staff, this cozy hotel offers 13 delicately ro-
mantic rooms—all with great views, most with balconies. In 1998
I enjoyed a big party here with most of Arcos' big shots as they
dedicated a fine room with a grand view balcony to "Rick Steves,
Periodista Turístico." Guess where I sleep when in Arcos... (RS%,
communal terrace, usually closed Nov-Feb, Maldonado 2, +34 956
702 333, www.hotelelconvento.es, reservas@hotelelconvento.es).

$$ La Casa Grande is a lovingly appointed *Better Homes and
Moroccan Tiles* kind of place that rents eight rooms with big-view
windows. As in a lavish yet authentic old-style inn, you're free to
enjoy its fine view terrace and homey library or have a traditional
breakfast (extra) on the atrium-like patio. They also offer massage services (family rooms, air-con, Wi-Fi in public areas only,
Maldonado 10, +34 956 703 930, www.lacasagrande.net, info@
lacasagrande.net, Elena).

$$ Casa Mirador San Pedro, in the shadow of the Church of
San Pedro, has seven rustically cozy rooms and a whimsical rooftop
terrace with great Arcos views. The windows are single pane, but
the street noise quiets down in the evening (apartment available,
air-con, El Juan de Cuenca 2—around the corner from Taberna
San Pedro, +34 635 189 005, miradorjuandecuenca@hotmail.com).

$ Rincón de las Nieves, with simple Andalusian charm, has a
cool inner courtyard filled with plants and ceramics surrounded by
three rooms. Two rooms have their own outdoor terraces with ob-
structed views, and all have high ceilings and access to the rooftop
terrace (the highest in town) with nearly 360-degree views (air-con,
Boticas 10, also rents an apartment, +34 956 701 528, +34 656 886
256, www.rincondelasnieves.com, rincondelasnieves@gmail.com,
Paqui).

¢ Pensión San Marcos, above a neat little bar in the heart
of the old town, offers five air-conditioned rooms and a great sun
terrace with views of the reservoir (air-con, Marqués de Torresoto
6, +34 956 105 429, +34 675 459 106, www.pensionsanmarcosdear-
cos.es, sanmarcosdearcos@hotmail.com, José Luis speaks some
English).

IN THE NEW TOWN

See the "Arcos de la Frontera Overview" map, earlier, for this new
town accommodation.

$$ Hotel Los Olivos is a bright, cool, and airy place with
19 rooms, an impressive courtyard, roof garden, generous public
spaces, bar, view, friendly folks, and easy pay parking. The four

view rooms can be a bit noisy in the afternoon, but—with double-pane windows—are usually fine at night (RS%, includes breakfast, Paseo de Boliches 30, +34 956 700 811, www.hotel-losolivos.es, reservas@hotel-losolivos.es, Raquel, Marta, and Miguel Ángel).

Eating in Arcos

VIEW DINING

$$$ The **Parador** (described earlier, under "Sleeping in Arcos") has a formal restaurant and a cafeteria with a cliff-edge setting. Its tapas and *raciones* are reasonably priced, and even just a drink and a snack on the million-dollar-view terrace at sunset is a nice experience (daily 13:00-16:00 & 20:00-23:00, shorter hours off-season, on main square, +34 956 700 500).

CHEAPER EATING IN THE OLD TOWN

Several decent bar-restaurants are in the old town, within a block or two of the main square and church. Most serve tapas and *raciones* both at the bar and at their tables.

$$ **Gastrobar El Retablo** has gained a reputation for great dining since opening in 2018. Chef Antonio José Armario trained in coastal restaurants, which explains his excellent prep of tuna, either *crudo* or grilled. Creamy cod dishes are also a hit whether enjoyed inside or on street-side tables (Wed-Mon 12:00-17:30 & 19:30-24:00, closed Tue, Calle Dean Espinosa 6, +34 856 041 614).

$$ **Bar La Cárcel** ("The Prison"), down the street, celebrates seafood and local meats with friendly, attentive staff. Their small bar draws a local crowd catching up on all the gossip (Tue-Sun 12:00-24:00, closed Mon, Calle Dean Espinosa 18, +34 956 700 410).

$$ **Restaurante Aljibe** takes diners farther south with Andalusían dishes and decor inspired by both Spain and Morocco (Thu-Sun 12:30-16:00 & 19:00-24:00, closed Mon-Wed, Carretera de Belén 10, +34 622 836 527).

$$ **Taberna Jóvenes Flamencos** offers a fun and accessible menu and is high energy for Arcos. Try their specialties—*abajao*, an egg-and-asparagus dish, and *perolitos*, an egg scramble in a minipan (Thu-Tue 12:00-24:00, closed Wed, Calle Dean Espinosa 11, +34 657 133 552).

$$ **Mesón Los Murales** serves tasty, affordable tapas, *raciones*, and fixed-price meals in their simple bar or at tables in the square outside. Don't confuse it with the competition next door (Fri-Wed 10:00-24:00, closed Thu, Plaza Boticas 1, +34 678 064 163).

$$ **Alcaraván,** run by the same owners as La Cárcel, does double duty as a café with scrumptious sweets during the day and as a cocktail bar by night. A fun ambience fills its medieval vault

in the castle's former dungeon (Fri-Sun 16:00-24:00, closed Mon-Thu, Calle Nueva 1, +34 956 700 410).

$$ Bar San Marcos is a tiny, homey bar with five tables and an easy-to-understand menu offering hearty, simple home cooking (Sun-Mon 9:00-16:30, Tue-Sat 8:00-24:00, Marqués de Torresoto 6, +34 956 700 721).

Arcos Connections

BY BUS

If you're traveling by bus, plan ahead for leaving Arcos: Some trips leave late, schedule information boards can be inaccurate, and the ticket window usually isn't open (luckily, you can buy tickets onboard and often online). Buses run less frequently on weekends. The closest train station to Arcos is Jerez.

Two bus companies—Damas and Comes—share the Arcos bus station. If your Spanish is good, you can call the Jerez offices for departure times—otherwise ask your hotelier or the TI for help. To find out about the Arcos-Jerez schedule, make it clear you're coming from Arcos (Damas, www.damas-sa.es; Comes, www.tgcomes.es). Also try Movelia.es for bus schedules and routes.

From Arcos by Bus to: Jerez (hourly, 40 minutes, Damas), **Ronda** (2/day, 2 hours, Comes), **Sevilla** (1-2/day, 2 hours, more departures with transfer in Jerez, Damas).

ROUTE TIPS FOR DRIVERS

Arcos to Sevilla (55 miles/90 km): The trip to **Sevilla** takes about 1.5 hours if you pay €7 for the toll road that starts near Jerez. To continue to **southern Portugal,** follow the freeway to Sevilla, and skirt the city by turning west on the SE-30 ring road in the direction of Huelva. It's a straight shot from there on A-49/E-1.

Arcos to Tarifa (80 miles/130 km): If you're going to Tarifa, take the tiny A-389 road at the Jerez edge of Arcos toward Paterna and Medina Sidonia, where you'll pick up A-381 to Algeciras, then on to Tarifa. Another option is to continue through Medina Sidonia to Vejer on A-396, from where you can cut south to Tarifa.

Ronda

With more than 34,000 people, Ronda is one of the largest white hill towns. It's also one of the most spectacular, thanks to its gorge-straddling setting.

Approaching the town from the train or bus station, it seems flat...until you reach the New Bridge and realize that it's clinging to

ANDALUCÍA

the walls of a canyon. During Moorish times, this was a tight fortified town of 9,000—a bastion second only to Granada during the last years of Moorish rule in southern Spain. (It fell to Christian forces only in 1485—seven years before Granada.) The cliffside setting is now more inspirational than practical, and the old town remains home to 1,000 lucky people.

Ronda's main attractions are its gorge-spanning bridges, the oldest bullring in Spain, and an intriguing old town. Spaniards know Ronda as the cradle of modern bullfighting and the romantic home of 19th-century *bandoleros* (bandits). But the real joy of Ronda these days lies in exploring its back streets and taking in its beautiful balconies, exuberant flowerpots, wispy gardens, and panoramic views. Walking the streets, you feel a strong local pride and a community where everyone seems to know everyone.

While day-trippers from cruise ships and the touristy Costa del Sol clog Ronda's streets during the day, locals retake the town in the early evening, making nights peaceful. Since it's served by train and bus, Ronda makes a relaxing break for nondrivers traveling between Granada, Sevilla, and Córdoba. Drivers can use Ronda as a convenient base from which to explore many of the other *pueblos blancos*.

Orientation to Ronda

Ronda's breathtaking ravine divides the town's labyrinthine Moorish quarter and its new, noisier, and more sprawling Mercadillo quarter. A massive-yet-graceful 18th-century bridge connects these two neighborhoods. Most things of touristic importance (TI, hotels, bullring) are clustered within a few blocks of the bridge. The *paseo* (early evening stroll) happens in the new town, on Ronda's major pedestrian and shopping street, Carrera Espinel.

TOURIST INFORMATION

Ronda's hardworking **TI**, across the square from the bullring, covers not only the town but all of Andalucía. It gives out good, free maps of the town, the region's roads, Granada, Sevilla, and the Route of the White Towns. The TI also organizes a creative array of activities such as tours, concerts, and walks, all described in helpful lists (Mon-Fri 9:30-19:00, Sat-Sun until 18:00, shorter

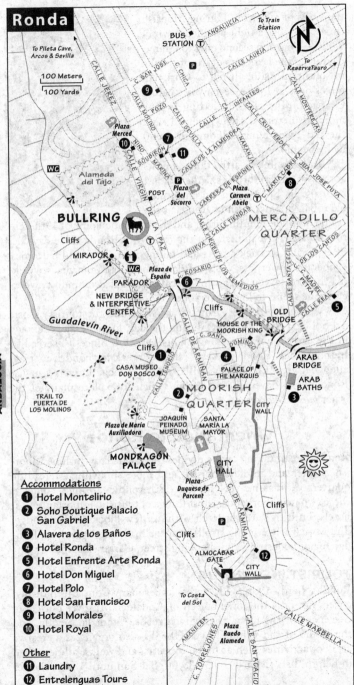

Ronda

To Pileta Cave,
Arcos & Sevilla

CALLE JEREZ

ANDALUCÍA

To Train
Station

BUS
STATION Ⓣ

ANDALUCÍA

To
ReservaTauro

N

100 Meters
100 Yards

C. SAN JOSÉ

C. CHICA

CALLE LAURIA

Ⓟ

CALLE MOLINO

CALLE SEVILLA

CALLE
INFANTES

CALLE NARANJA

CALLE CRUZ VERDE

CALLE MONTEREJAS

❾

CALLE DE LA ALMENDRA

Plaza
Merced

❿

POZO

❼

❶❶

CALLE MARINA

CALLE MARÍA CABRERA

JUAN JOSÉ PUYA

WC

Alameda
del Tajo

SOUDIRÓN

POST

Ⓟ

Plaza
del
Socorro

CARRERA DE ESPINEL

Plaza
Carmen
Abela

Ⓣ

❽

CALLE VIRGEN DE LA PAZ

NUEVA

CALLE TIENDAS

CALLE VIRGEN DE LOS REMEDIOS

CALLE SANTA CECILIA

CALLE DE LOS CANTOS

MERCADILLO
QUARTER

BULLRING

Cliffs

MIRADOR
ℹ
WC

Plaza de
España

ROSARIO

❻

C. MADRE
PEDRA

CALLE REAL

PARADOR

NEW BRIDGE
& INTERPRETIVE
CENTER

Guadalevín River

Cliffs

HOUSE OF THE
MOORISH KING

OLD
BRIDGE

❺

Cliffs

❶

CALLE DE ARMIÑAN

C. SANTO
DOMINGO

ARAB
BRIDGE

CASA MUSEO
DON BOSCO

CALLE TENORIO

❹

PALACE OF
THE MARQUIS

ARAB
BATHS

❸

TRAIL TO
PUERTA DE
LOS MOLINOS

❷

MOORISH
QUARTER

CITY
WALL

Plaza de María
Auxiliadora

JOAQUÍN
PEINADO
MUSEUM

SANTA
MARÍA LA
MAYOR

MONDRAGÓN
PALACE

CITY HALL

☀

Plaza
Duquesa de
Parcent

Cliffs

CALLE DE ARMIÑAN

Ⓟ

Cliffs

ALMOCÁBAR
GATE

❶❷

CITY WALL

To Costa
del Sol

C. AMANECER

C. TORREJONES

Plaza
Ruedo
Alameda

CALLE SAN ACACIO

CALLE MARBELLA

Accommodations

❶ Hotel Montelirio
❷ Soho Boutique Palacio
   San Gabriel
❸ Alavera de los Baños
❹ Hotel Ronda
❺ Hotel Enfrente Arte Ronda
❻ Hotel Don Miguel
❼ Hotel Polo
❽ Hotel San Francisco
❾ Hotel Morales
❿ Hotel Royal

Other

❶❶ Laundry
❶❷ Entrelenguas Tours

hours Oct-late March, Paseo Blas Infante, +34 952 187 119, www.turismoderonda.es).

Sightseeing Pass: The **Bono Turístico** city pass comes in three price tiers (€12, €20, and €24) and gets you into many sights including the Arab Baths, Joaquín Peinado Museum, Mondragón Palace, and the New Bridge Interpretive Center. It's generally only worth purchasing if you want to see absolutely everything in Ronda.

ARRIVAL IN RONDA

By Train: The small station has ticket windows, a train information desk, and a café, but no lockers (though you will find them at the nearby bus station; see "Helpful Hints," below).

From the station, it's a 15-minute **walk** to the center: Exit the station, turn right onto Avenida de Andalucía, and walk to the large roundabout (you'll see the bus station on your right). Continue straight down the street (now called San José) until you reach Calle Jerez. Turn left and walk downhill past a church and the Alameda del Tajo park. Keep going, passing the bullring, to reach the TI and the famous bridge.

By Bus: To get to the center from the bus station, leave the station walking to the right of the roundabout, then follow the directions for train travelers described above. Baggage storage is available (see "Helpful Hints" below).

By Car: Street parking away from the center is often free. The handiest place for paid parking is the underground lot at Plaza del Socorro (one block from the bullring). Narrow lanes and tight turns can be challenging for even medium-size vehicles, and some access is restricted for nonresidents. Be sure to get driving and parking instructions from your hotel.

HELPFUL HINTS

Baggage Storage: A few coin-fed lockers are available in the bus station, across from the WC.

Laundry: There's one self-service machine at **HigienSec,** which also offers full-service options including delivery to your hotel (same-day service if you drop off early enough; Mon-Fri 10:00-14:00 & 17:00-20:30, Sat 10:00-14:00, closed Sun, two blocks north of the bullring at Calle Molino 6, +34 952 875 249).

Souvenirs: Worth a browse is **Taller de Grabados Somera,** a printmaking studio near the New Bridge. Their inexpensive, charming prints of Ronda's iconic scenery and famous bulls are hand-pulled right in their shop (Tue-Sat 10:30-14:30, closed Sun-Mon, Calle Rosario 4, just across from the parador).

Tours in Ronda

Walking Tours

Many local guides work in conjunction with the **TI** to offer two-hour city walks (€10, Mon-Thu at 12:00, also at 17:30 in summer). Reserve and pay at the TI.

Entrelenguas is a cultural center in Ronda that offers much more than Spanish language lessons. Alex and Mar guide visitors around Ronda, focusing on monuments (€55) or cultural immersion and local businesses (€75). They can do wine tastings (€35), vineyard tours (€60), or even put together a cooking class for groups of up to six people (Calle Espíritu Santo 9, +34 951 083 862, www.slowronda.com).

Local Guide

Energetic and knowledgeable **Antonio Jesús Naranjo** will take you on a two-hour walking tour of the city's sights (€130, reserve early, +34 639 073 763, http://guiajesus.wixsite.com/local-tours-of-ronda).

Sights and Experiences in Ronda

IN THE NEW TOWN
Alameda del Tajo Park

One block away from the bullring, the town's main park is a great breezy place for a picnic lunch, people-watching, a snooze in the shade, or practicing your Spanish with seniors from the nearby old-folks' home. Don't miss letting loose a few butterflies in your stomach at its tiny view terrace. It overlooks the scenic Serranía de Ronda mountains—and a drop of about 650 feet...straight down.

▲▲Bullring (Real Maestranza de Caballería de Ronda)

Ronda is the birthplace of modern bullfighting, and this was the first great Spanish bullring. Philip II initiated bullfighting as war training for knights in the 16th century. Back then, there were two kinds of bullfighting: the type with noble knights on horseback, and the coarser, man-versus-beast entertainment for the commoners (with no rules...much like when WWE wrestlers bring out the folding chairs). Ronda practically wor-

ships Francisco Romero, who melded the noble and chaotic kinds of bullfighting with rules to establish modern bullfighting right here in the early 1700s. He introduced the scarlet cape, held un-

furled with a stick. His son Juan further developed the ritual (local aficionados would never call it a "sport"—you'll read newspaper coverage of fights not on the sports pages but in the culture section), and his grandson Pedro was one of the first great matadors (killing nearly 6,000 bulls in his career).

To tour the ring, stables, chapel, and museum, buy a ticket at the back of the bullring.

Cost and Hours: €8; Mon 10:00-15:00 year-round; Tue-Sun 10:00-20:00, March and Oct until 19:00, Nov-Feb until 18:00, +34 952 874 132, www.rmcr.org.

Tours: The excellent €1.50 audioguide describes everything and is essential to fully enjoy your visit (drop it at the gift shop as you leave).

Bullfights: Bullfights are scheduled only for the first weekend of September during the *feria* (fair). Whereas every other *feria* in Andalucía celebrates a patron saint, the Ronda fair glorifies legendary bullfighter Pedro Romero. As these fights are so limited and sell out immediately, Sevilla and Madrid are more practical places for a tourist to see a bullfight.

❷ Self-Guided Tour: Ronda's bullring and museum rivals Sevilla's as Spain's most interesting.

• *Walk through the stables and the bulls' entry into the **bullpen**.*

There are six bulls per fight (plus two backups) and three matadors. Before the fight, the bulls are penned up in this bovine death row, and ropes and pulleys safely open the right door at the right time. Climb the skinny staircase and find the indoor arena *(picadero)*. If you're here on a weekday, you may see thoroughbred Spanish **horses** training (they're from the Equestrian School of the Real Maestranza).

• *Exit down the stairs and head left.*

Here's your chance to play *toro*, surrounded by 5,000 empty seats. The two-tiered **arena** was built in 1785— on the 300th anniversary of the defeat of the Moors in Ronda. As you leave the museum and walk out on the sand, look ahead to see the ornamental columns and painted doorway marking the royal box

where the king and dignitaries sit (over the gate where the bull enters). Opposite the VIP box is the place for the band (marked *música*), which, in the case of a small town like Ronda, is most likely a high school band. Notice the 136 classy columns, creating a kind of 18th-century theater. Lovers of the "art" of bullfighting

will explain that the event is much more than the actual killing of the bull. It celebrates noble heritage and Andalusian horse culture.
• *Return to where you entered the bullring, follow the inner wall, and head right to...*

The **horse gear exhibit** makes the connection with bullfighting and the equestrian upper class. As throughout Europe, "chivalry" began as a code among the sophisticated, horse-riding gentry. (In Spanish, the word for "gentleman" is the same as the word for "horseman"—*caballero*.)

Cross the hallway to enter the **history exhibit.** It's a shrine to bullfighting and the famous Romero family. First it traces the long history of bullfighting, going all the way back to the ancient Minoans on Crete. Historically, there were only two arenas built solely for bullfighting: in Ronda and Sevilla. Elsewhere, bullfights were held in town squares—you'll see a painting of Madrid's Plaza Mayor filled with spectators for a bullfight.

(For this reason, to this day, even a purpose-built bullring is generally called *plaza de toros*—"square of bulls.") You'll also see stuffed bull heads, photos, "suits of light" worn by bullfighters, and capes (bulls are colorblind, but the traditional red cape was designed to disguise all the blood). One section explains some of the big "dynasties" of fighters. At the end of the hall are historical posters from Ronda's bullfights (all originals except the Picasso). Running along the left wall are various examples of artwork glorifying bullfighting, including original Goya engravings.
• *Head up the stairs for a grand overview of the bullring. Explore the spectators' seating before exiting through the gift shop. From here, you can stroll to the **Mirador de Ronda** viewpoint and then walk along the cliffside (behind the Parador) to the New Bridge.*

▲▲▲The Gorge and New Bridge (Puente Nuevo)

The ravine called El Tajo—over 300 feet deep and just about 200 feet wide—divides Ronda into the whitewashed old city (Moorish Quarter) and the new town (El Mercadillo) that was built after the Christian reconquest in 1485. The New Bridge mightily spans the gorge. A different bridge was built here in 1735, but it fell after six years. This one was built from 1751 to 1793. Look down from the bridge viewpoint. Spit.

You can see the foundations of the original bridge and a super view of the New Bridge from the walkway between the gorge and the parador—the town's former Town Hall-turned-hotel—which

overlooks the gorge and bridge from the new-town side.

From the new-town side of the bridge (just outside the parador), you'll see the entrance to the **New Bridge Interpretive Center,** where you can pay to climb down and enter the structure of the bridge itself (€2.50; Mon-Sat 10:00-14:00 & 15:00-18:00, Sun until 15:00, closes earlier off-season). The empty-feeling hall has modest audiovisual displays about the bridge's construction and famous visitors to Ronda.

The views of the bridge and gorge from the outside are far more thrilling than anything you'll find inside.

IN THE OLD TOWN
▲Church of Santa María la Mayor (Iglesia de Santa María)
This church (built from the 15th to the 17th century) has a fine Mudejar bell tower and shares a parklike square with orange trees and City Hall. It was built on and around the remains of Moorish Ronda's main mosque (which was itself built on the site of an ancient Roman temple to Julius Caesar). With a pleasantly eclectic interior that features some art with unusually modern flair, and a good audioguide to explain it all, it's worth a visit.

Cost and Hours: €4.50, daily April-Sept 10:00-20:00, closed Sun 13:00-14:00 for Mass, closes earlier off-season, includes audioguide, Plaza Duquesa de Parcent in the old town.

Visiting the Church: In the room where you purchase your ticket, look for the rare surviving door to the Moorish mosque (that's a mirror; look back at the actual door). The mihrab faced not Mecca, but Gibraltar—where you'd travel to get to Mecca. Partially destroyed by an earthquake, the church was reconstructed with the fusion (or confusion) of Moorish, Gothic, Renaissance, and Baroque styles you see today.

Inside the church, look left and marvel at the magnificent Baroque **Altar del Sagrario** with a statue of the Immaculate Conception in the center. The smaller altar (adjacent on the right) is a good example of Churrigueresque architecture, a kind of Spanish Rococo in which the decoration consumes the architecture—notice that you can hardly make out the souped-up columns. Its fancy decor provides a frame for the artistic highlight of the town, the Dolorosa ("Virgin of the Ultimate Sorrow"). The big fresco of St. Christopher with Baby Jesus on his shoulders (left, above the door

ANDALUCÍA

where you entered) shows the patron saint both of Ronda and of travelers.

In the center of the church is an elaborately carved **choir** with a series of modern reliefs depicting scenes from the life of the Virgin

Mary. Similar to the Via Crucis (Way of the Cross), this is the Via Lucis (Way of the Light), with 14 stations focusing on the Resurrection and its aftermath (such as #13—the Immaculate Conception, and #14—Mary's assumption into heaven) that serve as a worship aid to devout Catholics. The centerpiece is an ethereal Mary as the light of the world (with the moon, stars, and sun around her).

Head to the left around the choir, noticing the bright **paintings** along the wall by French artist Raymonde Pagegie. He gave sacred scenes a fresh twist—like the Last Supper attended by female servants, or the scene of Judgment Day, when the four horsemen of the apocalypse pause to adore the Lamb of God.

The **treasury** (at the far-right corner, with your back to the choir) displays vestments that look curiously like matadors' brocaded outfits—appropriate for this bullfight-crazy town. Before exiting the treasury, find a spiral staircase. Climb the 73 steps to a U-shaped **terrace** around the church's rooftop. Survey the entire deck (ducking under the buttresses) for great views. The highlight is actually inside: Find a tiny door that leads to a breathtaking perch high above the elaborate main altar. (Imagine walking around this ledge before there was a railing.)

Mondragón Palace City Museum (Palacio de Mondragón)

This beautiful, originally Moorish building was erected in the 14th century and is the legendary (but not actual) residence of Moorish kings. The building was first restored in the 16th century (notice the Mudejar tiled courtyard), and its facade dates only from the 18th century. Upstairs is Ronda's Municipal Museum, focusing on prehistory and geology. Wander through its many kid-friendly rooms. Peruse the exhibits on Neolithic toolmaking and early metallurgy (like a seventh-century BC mold for making a sword from molten metal), and brief descriptions of local Roman history. If you plan to visit the Pileta Cave (see "Sights near Ronda," later), find the panels that describe the cave's formation and shape. Linger in the two small gardens with wonderful panoramic views.

Cost and Hours: €4; Mon-Fri 10:00-19:00, Sat-Sun until

15:00, closes earlier and midday off-season; on Plaza Mondragón, +34 952 870 818.

Nearby: Leaving the palace, wander left a few short blocks to the nearby Plaza de María Auxiliadora for more views and a look at the two rare *pinsapos* (resembling extra-large Christmas trees) in the middle of the park; this part of Andalucía is the only region in Europe where these ancient trees still grow.

Plaza de María Auxiliadora leads to **the best Ronda view at sunset** from a viewpoint where windmills once stood. Photographers go crazy reproducing the most famous postcard view of Ronda—the entirety of the New Bridge. Look for the tiled *Puerta de los Molinos* sign and head down, down, down. This pathway is not for the faint of heart, and a bad idea in the heat of the afternoon sun. Wait until just before sunset for the best light and cooler temperatures.

▲Joaquín Peinado Museum (Museo Joaquín Peinado)

Housed in an old palace, this fresh museum features an overview of the life's work of Joaquín Peinado (1898-1975), a Ronda native and pal of Picasso. Because Franco killed creativity in Spain for much of the last century, nearly all of Peinado's creative work was done in Paris. His style evolved through the big "isms" of the 20th century, ranging from Expressionism to Cubism, and even to eroticism. Peinado's works follow the major trends of his time—understandable, as he was friends with one of the art world's biggest talents. The short movie that kicks off  the display is only in Spanish, though there are good English explanations throughout the museum. Find a famous Cubist version of Don Quixote upstairs and a few Picasso pieces downstairs. It's an interesting modern art experience with no crowds, and fun to be exposed to a lesser-known but very talented artist in his hometown.

Cost and Hours: €4, Mon-Fri 10:00-17:00, Sat until 15:00, closed Sun, Plaza del Gigante, +34 952 871 585, www.museojoaquinpeinado.com.

▲Walk Through Old Town to Bottom of Gorge

From the New Bridge you can descend down Cuesta de Santo Domingo into a world of whitewashed houses, tiny grilled balconies, and winding lanes—the old town. To get started, cross the bridge from the new town into the old and take the first left just beyond the former Dominican convent, once the headquarters of the In-

quisition in Ronda. Be ready for lots of ups and downs—this is not a flat walk.

A couple of blocks steeply downhill (on the left), you'll see the **House of the Moorish King** (Casa del Rey Moro). It was never home to a king; it was given its fictitious name by the grandson of President McKinley, who once lived here. Although the house is closed and its once-fine belle époque garden is overgrown, it does offer visitors entry to the **"Mine,"** an exhausting series of 280 slick, dark, and narrow stairs (like climbing down and then up a 20-story building) leading to the floor of the gorge. The Moors cut this zig-zag staircase into the wall of the gorge in the 14th century to access water when under siege, then used Spanish slaves to haul water up to the thirsty town (€8, daily 10:00-20:00).

Fifty yards downhill from the garden is the **Palace of the Marquis of Salvatierra** (Palacio del Marqués de Salvatierra, closed to public). As part of the "distribution" of spoils following the Reconquista here in 1485, the Spanish king gave the land for this grand house to the Salvatierra family (who live here to this day). The facade is rich in colonial symbolism from Spanish America—note the pre-Columbian-looking characters (four Peruvian Indians) flanking the balcony above the door and below the family coat of arms.

Just below the palace, stop to enjoy the view terrace. Look below. There are two old bridges, with the Arab Baths just to the right.

Twenty steps farther down, you'll pass through the Philip V gate, for centuries the main gate to the fortified city of Ronda.

Continuing downhill, you come to the **Old Bridge** (Puente Viejo), rebuilt in 1616 upon the ruins of an Arabic bridge. Enjoy the views from the bridge (but don't cross it yet—we'll do that after visiting the baths below). Then continue down the old stairs past a small, Moorish-inspired electric substation. Swing  around the little chapel at the bottom of the staircase to look back up to the highly fortified Moorish city walls. A few steps ahead is the oldest bridge in Ronda, the Arab Bridge (a.k.a. the San Miguel Bridge). For centuries, this was the main gate to the fortified city. In Moorish times, you'd purify both your body and your soul here before entering the city, so just outside the gate was a little mosque (now the chapel) and the Arab Baths.

The **Arab Baths** (Baños Árabes), worth ▲, are evocative ruins that warrant a quick look. They were located half underground

to maintain the temperature and served by a donkey-powered water tower. You can still see the top of the shaft (30 yards beyond the bath rooftops, near a cypress tree, connected to the baths by an aqueduct). Water was hoisted from the river below to the aqueduct by ceramic containers that were attached to a belt powered by a donkey walking in circles. Inside the baths, two of the original eight columns scavenged from the Roman ruins still support brick vaulting (€4.50, credit

card only; generally open Mon-Fri 10:00-19:00, Sat-Sun until 15:00, shorter hours off-season). A delightful 10-minute video brings the entire complex to life—Spanish and English versions run alternately. Ask about the next English showing as you go in.

From here, hike back to the new town along the other side of the gorge: Climb back up to the Old Bridge, cross it, and take the brick stairs immediately on the left, which lead scenically along the gorge through the wonderful **Jardines de Cuenca** hillside park. Exit the park going left and then uphill on Calle Virgen de los Remedios to the recommended Bar El Lechuguita. Stop here for a much-deserved break, then continue on Calle Rosario to return to the New Bridge.

▲▲ Ronda Guitar Concert

Local Spanish guitar artist Paco Seco performs a 45-minute solo concert in the historic Casa Museo Don Bosco each evening Monday through Saturday at 19:00. It's an intimate affair with Paco describing his three guitars (historic, classical, and flamenco) and the pieces he performs by celebrated composers as well as his own compositions. Travelers who show this guidebook get a free glass of Ronda wine to enjoy during the show. Seating is first-come, first-seated, and the venue opens at 18:00 so ticket holders can explore the cliffside house and enjoy the fine mountain views. Buy tickets in person at Casa Museo Don Bosco, by phone, or online (€15, Calle Tenorio 20, closed in Jul-Aug & Dec-Feb, +34 660 280 720, www.rondaguitarmusic.com).

Sights near Ronda

▲Pileta Cave (Cueva de la Pileta)

The Pileta Cave, set in a dramatic, rocky limestone ridge at the eastern edge of Sierra de Grazalema Natural Park, offers Spain's most intimate look at Neolithic and Paleolithic paintings that are

ANDALUCÍA

more than 30,000 years old. Farmer José Bullón and his family live down the hill from the cave—which was discovered by Bullón's grandfather in 1905. The caves are open only to escorted groups, as guides (speaking English and Spanish) take up to 25 visitors at a time deep into the mountain. Because the number of cave visitors is strictly limited, Pileta's rare paintings are among the best-preserved in the world.

Cost and Hours: €10; tours run daily in summer Mon-Fri at 10:30, 11:30, 13:00, 16:30 and 18:00; Sat-Sun on the hour from 11:00-13:00 & 16:00-18:00; fewer departures late Oct-April; €3 interpretive map, €10 guidebook; +34 677 610 500 (phone answered 10:00-13:00), www.cuevadelapileta.es.

Reservations and Getting In: Call at least a day ahead, then arrive at least 15 minutes before your reserved time. Budget in a 10-minute steep hike to the ticket booth from the parking lot.

Getting There: Pileta Cave is 14 miles from Ronda, past the town of Benaoján, at the end of an access road easily reached between Ronda and Grazalema.

From Ronda, you can get to the cave by taxi—it's about a half-hour drive on twisty roads—and have the driver wait (€70 round-trip). If you're driving, it's easy: Leave Ronda through the new part of town and take A-374 towards Sevilla. After a few miles, exit left toward Benaoján on MA-7401. Go through Benaoján (MA-7401 changes names to MA-8400), then take a sharp left onto MA-8401 and follow signs (reading *Cueva de la Pileta*) to the cave. Leave nothing of value visible in your car.

Visiting the Cave: Arrive early and be flexible. Bring a sweater and sturdy shoes. You need a good sense of balance to take the tour. The 10-minute hike from the parking lot up a stone-stepped trail to the cave entrance is moderately steep. Inside the cave, it can be difficult to keep your footing on the slippery, uneven floor while being led single file, with only a lantern light illuminating the way.

As you walk the cool half-mile, your guide explains the black, ochre, and red drawings, which are more than 30,000 years old—that's five times as old as the Egyptian pyramids. Among other animals, you'll see horses, goats, cattle, and a rare giant fish, made from a mixture of clay and fat by finger-painting prehistoric people. Surprisingly, the plain-looking stick drawings in black are more recent than the discernible animal shapes. The 200-foot main hall is cavernous and feels almost sacred. Throughout the site, mineral monoliths look adorned in lace and drapery. Stalagmites and stalactites reach toward one another as they have for a million years or so in these caves, and some formations lend themselves to appropriate names like "The Organ" and "The Castle."

Eating near the Cave: Nearby, the lovely village of Mon-

ANDALUCÍA

tejaque (much nicer than Benaoján) has several good restaurants clustered around the central square.

▲ReservaTauro

As the birthplace of modern bullfighting, Ronda attracts plenty of *aficionados* and even bullfighters themselves. Rafael Tejada worked as an engineer for many years but eventually switched gears to train as a bullfighter. In 2011, he bought land in the nearby *serranía* to raise horses, cows, and stud bulls, and now welcomes visitors to experience his working farm. A visit here allows you to get up close and personal with bulls and horses, as well as try out some matador skills in a practice ring (no bulls, no worries...just the capes). The two-hour option also lets you help the herdsman in one of his daily tasks, such as feeding the free-range bulls, and concludes with a surprise snack.

Cost and Hours: €28/person for 70 minutes, €40/person for 2 hours, €90/person for 2-3 hour private tour; visits offered daily at 12:00 & 16:30, winter afternoon visit at 16:00; reservations required, +34 951 166 008, www.reservatauro.com.

Getting There: Drivers should leave Ronda through the new part of town and take A-367 (Carretera Ronda-Campillos) toward Campillos. After about 5.5 miles, turn right into a stone gate marked by a small black-and-white, arrow-shaped sign labeled *RESERVATAURO*. If you're visiting without a car, request a special taxi (€25) for round-trip transportation when you book your tour by phone or email.

Sleeping in and near Ronda

Ronda has plenty of reasonably priced, decent-value accommodations. It's crowded only during Holy Week (the week leading up to Easter) and the first week of September (for bullfighting season). Most of my recommendations are in the new town, a short stroll from the New Bridge and about a 10-minute walk from the train station. In cheaper places, ask for a room with a *ventana* (window) to avoid the few interior rooms. Breakfast is usually not included. If arriving by car, email your hotel for driving and parking instructions. For locations, see the "Ronda" map on page 804.

IN THE OLD TOWN

Clearly the best options in town, these hotels are worth reserving early. Soho Boutique Palacio San Gabriel is right in the heart of the old town, while Alavera de los Baños is a steep 15- to 20-minute hike below, but still easily walkable to all the sights (if you're in good shape) and in a bucolic setting.

$$$ Hotel Montelirio perches on the cliffs of the western

side of the Moorish quarter with dramatic views of the valley and the new town. The former palace of a 17th-century count, it feels both traditional and plush with its 15 classically tasteful rooms (the view rooms are worth the splurge) and its elegant common areas (air-con, elevator, pool, sun deck, terrace dining with views even for nonguests, Tenorio 8, +34 952 873 855, www.hotelmontelirio. com, recepcion@hotelmontelirio.com).

$$ Soho Boutique Palacio San Gabriel has 22 pleasant rooms, a kind staff, public rooms filled with art and books, a cozy wine cellar, and a fine garden terrace. It's a large 1736 labyrinth of a townhouse that's been converted into a characteristic hotel, marinated in history. If you're a cinephile, kick back in the charming TV room—with seats from Ronda's old theater and a collection of DVD classics—then head to the breakfast room to check out photos of big movie stars (and, ahem, a certain travel writer) who have stayed here (air-con, incognito elevator, Calle Marqués de Moctezuma 19 at Plaza del Gigante, +34 952 190 392, www.sohohoteles. com, palaciosangabriel@sohohoteles.com).

$$ Alavera de los Baños, a delightful oasis located next to ancient Moorish baths at the bottom of the hill, has nine comfortable rooms, two spacious suites, and big inviting public places. This hotel offers a swimming pool, a peaceful Arabic garden, and an eclectic aura of Mediterranean, Moorish, and modern decor. Enjoy the pastoral views of the vast countryside and the horses just beyond the garden (includes breakfast, some rooms have balconies, free parking, closed mid-Dec-Jan, steeply below the heart of town at Calle Molino de Alarcón, +34 952 879 143, www. alaveradelosbanos.com, hotel@alaveradelosbanos.com, well run by personable Christian and Inma).

$ Hotel Ronda provides an interesting mix of minimalist and traditional Spanish decor in a refurbished mansion that is both quiet and homey. Although its five rooms are without views, the small, lovely rooftop deck overlooks the town (air-con, Ruedo Doña Elvira 12, +34 952 872 232, www.hotelronda.net, reservas@hotelronda. net, some English spoken by kind and gentle Sra. Nieves).

IN THE NEW TOWN

More convenient than charming (except the Hotel Enfrente Arte Ronda—in a class all its own), these hotels put you in the thriving new town.

$$ Hotel Enfrente Arte Ronda, on the edge of things a steep 10- to 15-minute walk below the heart of the new town, is relaxed and funky. The 12 rooms are spacious and exotically decorated, but dimly lit. The hotel features a sprawling maze of public spaces with offbeat and repurposed decor, a peaceful bamboo garden, a game and reading room, small swimming pool, sauna, and terraces

with sweeping countryside views. Guests can help themselves to free drinks from the self-service bar. This one-of-a-kind place is in all the guidebooks, so reserve early (includes buffet breakfast, air-con, elevator, Calle Real 40, +34 952 879 088, enfrentearte@gmail.com).

$$ Hotel Don Miguel, facing the gorge next to the bridge, can seem like staying in a cave, but it couldn't be more central. Of its 30 sparse but comfortable rooms, 20 have gorgeous views. Street rooms come with a little noise (air-con, elevator, pay parking a block away, Plaza de España 4, +34 952 877 722, www.hoteldonmiguelronda.com, reservas@dmiguel.com).

$ Hotel Polo is a boutique gem run by the Puya family in the heart of the new town. Each of its 36 bright and spacious rooms features a watercolor painted by Miguel Puya. Inviting common spaces like the social "Food Corner" and the vast rooftop terrace provide a tranquil respite and cool views (family rooms, air-con, elevator, honesty bar, pay parking, Padre Mariano Souvirón 8, +34 952 872 447, www.hotelpolo.net, reservas@hotelpolo.net).

$ Hotel San Francisco offers 27 small, nicely decorated rooms and rooftop terrace a block off the main pedestrian street in the town center. Their public cafeteria doubles as the breakfast room (family rooms available, air-con, elevator, pay parking, María Cabrera 18, +34 648 943 695, www.hotelsanfrancisco-ronda.com, recepcion@hotelsanfrancisco-ronda.com).

$ Hotel Morales has 18 simple but prim-and-proper rooms, and friendly Lola helps you feel right at home. Interior rooms can be a bit dark, so request to be streetside. There's little traffic at night (air-con, elevator, pay parking nearby, Sevilla 51, +34 952 871 538, www.hotelmorales.es, reservas@hotelmorales.es).

¢ Hotel Royal has a dark reception hall but friendly staff and 29 clean, spacious, simple rooms—many on the main street that runs between the bullring and bridge. Thick glass keeps out most of the noise, while the tree-lined Alameda del Tajo park is just across the way (air-con, pay parking, Calle Virgen de la Paz 42, +34 952 871 141, www.hotelroyalronda.com, hroyal@ronda.net).

IN THE COUNTRYSIDE NEAR PILETA CAVE

A good base for visiting Ronda and the Pileta Cave (as well as Grazalema) is **$$ Cortijo las Piletas.** Nestled at the edge of Sierra de Grazalema Natural Park (just a 15-minute drive from Ronda, with easy access from the main highway), this spacious family-run country estate has eight rooms and plenty of opportunities for exploring the surrounding area (includes breakfast, dinner offered some days—book in advance, +34 605 080 295, www.cortijolaspiletas.com, info@cortijolaspiletas.com, Pablo and Elisenda). Another countryside option is **$La Guzmana de Ronda**

Guest House. Six brightly appointed rooms surround an open patio at this renovated estate house (includes breakfast, +34 600 006 305, www.laguzmana.com, info@laguzmana.com). Both hotels offer bird-watching, swimming, and hiking.

Eating in Ronda

Plaza del Socorro, a block in front of the bullring, is an energetic scene, bustling with tourists and local families enjoying the square and its restaurants. The pedestrian-only **Calle Nueva** is lined with hardworking eateries. To enjoy a drink or a light meal with the best view in town, consider the terraces of Hotel Don Miguel just under the bridge.

Sweets: For coffee and pastries, locals like the elegant little $ **Confitería Daver,** where they say "once you step inside...it's too late" (Tue-Sun 9:00-21:00, closed Mon, Calle Virgen de los Remedios 6).

Groceries: The **Día** supermarket is conveniently in the new town (Mon-Sat 9:00-21:30, closed Sun, Calle Cruz Verde 18). **Maskom** is two blocks from Alameda del Tajo park (Mon-Sat 9:00-21:00, Sun 9:30-14:30, Calle Molino 36).

TAPAS IN THE CITY CENTER

Ronda has a fine tapas scene. You won't get a free tapa with your drink as in some other Spanish towns, but these bars have accessible tapas lists, and they serve bigger plates. Each of the following places could make a fine solo destination for a meal, but they're close enough that you can easily try more than one.

$$ **Taberna El Almacén** offers a modern take on traditional tapas from many Spanish regions in an industrial chic setting. Friendly, approachable staff can explain the day's specials that are *fuera de carta* (not listed on the menu). Even veggie haters rave over their *pisto*—a type of ratatouille where all ingredients are first cooked separately, then mixed together and served with a fried egg on the side. This is a good spot to try local wines as well (Tue-Sat 13:00-16:00 & 20:30-23:00, Sun 13:00-16:00, closed Mon, Calle Virgen de los Remedios 7, +34 951 489 818).

$$ **Tragatá** serves creative and tasty tapas in a stainless-steel minimalist bar. There's just a handful of tall tiny tables and some bar space inside, with patio seating on the pedestrian street (same menu), and an enticing blackboard of the day's specials. You'll pay more, but if you want to sample Andalusian gourmet (such as asparagus on a stick sprinkled with grated manchego cheese), this is the place to do (Wed-Sun 13:00-16:00 & 20:00-23:00, closed Mon-Tue, Calle Nueva 4, +34 952 877 209).

$ **Bar El Lechuguita,** a traditional hit with locals, serves

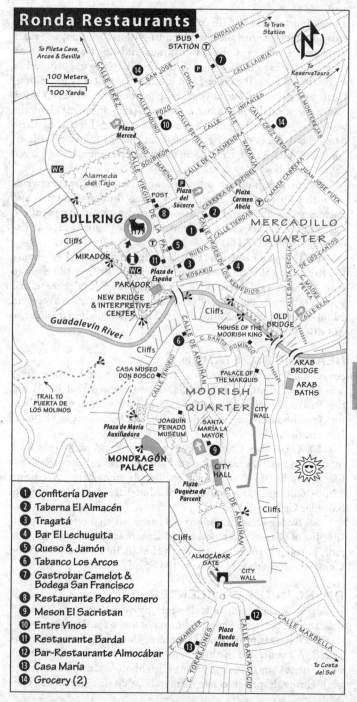

Ronda Restaurants

To Pileta Cave, Arcos & Sevilla

100 Meters
100 Yards

To Train Station

ANDALUCIA

To ReservaTauró

BUS STATION

CALLE JEREZ

C. SAN JOSE

C. CHICA

CALLE LAURIA

CALLE MONTEREJAS

Plaza Merced

CALLE MOLINO

POZO

CALLE SEVILLA

CALLE INFANTES

CALLE CRUZ VERDE

CALLE DE LA ALMENDRA

NARANJA

NIÑO SOLIBIEON

CALLE VIRGEN DE LA PAZ

CALLE MARINA

CARRERA DE ESPINEL

Plaza Carmen Abela

CALLE MARIA CABRERA

JUAN JOSE PUYA

WC

Alameda del Tajo

POST

Plaza del Socorro

Plaza de España

CALLE TIENDAS

NUEVA

MERCADILLO QUARTER

CALLE SANTA CECILIA

C. DE LOS SANTOS

C. MADRE PETRA

BULLRING

Cliffs

MIRADOR

WC

PARADOR

NEW BRIDGE & INTERPRETIVE CENTER

CALLE VIRGEN DE LOS REMEDIOS

C. ROSARIO

CALLE REAL

Cliffs

OLD BRIDGE

Guadalevín River

Cliffs

CALLE DE ARMIÑAN

CALLE SANTO DOMINGO

HOUSE OF THE MOORISH KING

ARAB BRIDGE

ARAB BATHS

CASA MUSEO DON BOSCO

CALLE TENORIO

PALACE OF THE MARQUIS

TRAIL TO PUERTA DE LOS MOLINOS

Plaza de María Auxiliadora

JOAQUÍN PEINADO MUSEUM

SANTA MARÍA LA MAYOR

MOORISH QUARTER

CITY WALL

MONDRAGÓN PALACE

Plaza Duquesa de Parcent

CITY HALL

C. DE ARMIÑAN

Cliffs

Cliffs

ALMOCÁBAR GATE

CITY WALL

C. AMANECER

C. TORREJONES

Plaza Ruedo Alameda

CALLE SAN ACACIO

CALLE MARBELLA

To Costa del Sol

1 Confitería Daver
2 Taberna El Almacén
3 Tragatá
4 Bar El Lechuguita
5 Queso & Jamón
6 Tabanco Los Arcos
7 Gastrobar Camelot & Bodega San Francisco
8 Restaurante Pedro Romero
9 Meson El Sacristan
10 Entre Vinos
11 Restaurante Bardal
12 Bar-Restaurante Almocábar
13 Casa María
14 Grocery (2)

a long and tasty list of €1 tapas. Rip off a tapas inventory sheet, cross-reference it with the laminated English translation, and mark which ones you want. Be adventurous and don't miss the bar's namesake, *lechuguita* (a wedge of lettuce with vinegar, garlic, and a secret ingredient). The order-form routine makes it easy to communicate and get exactly what you like, plus you know the exact price. This place is small—just a bar and some stand-up ledges along the wall, plus some rustic tables with stools outside. Ideally, be there when the doors open and grab a spot at the bar (Mon-Sat 12:30-16:00 & 20:00-23:00, closed Sun and Wed evenings, Calle Virgen de los Remedios 35).

$ Queso & Jamón is my pick for quality *bocadillos* (sandwiches) with your choice of cheeses and hams. Brothers Antonio and Paco can also advise you on different cured meats, dairy products, oils, and marmalades for a customized foodie picnic (Plaza de España 1, +34 952 877 114).

$$ Tabanco Los Arcos bustles underneath the arches—hence the name—on the old town side of the New Bridge. Go early to snag a "gorge-ous" view table while sampling local cheese and wine. Staff bustle between tables and are eager to serve (Wed-Sun 13:00-16:00 & 20:30-24:00, closed Mon-Tue, Calle Armiñán 6, +34 610 705 897).

NEAR THE BUS STATION

Away from the tourist crowds, there's a strip of bustling tapas bars along Calle Comandante Salvador Carrasco that locals call the *Pasillo Marítimo* (Maritime Corridor). Pop into any of them for typical Spanish and Andalusian shareable bar snacks and local conversation.

$$ Gastrobar Camelot goes a step beyond with their sleek interior and tasty, great-value seafood and meat dishes. *Ronderos* like to say it's "food from here for people from here" (Wed-Sun 12:00-16:00 & 20:00-24:00, closed Mon-Tue, Calle Comandante Salvador Carrasco 2).

$$ Bodega San Francisco is a rustic bar that offers an accessible list of *raciones* and tapas, as well as serious plates and big split-table portions if you're waiting on the bus (daily 11:00-24:00, Calle Comandante Salvador Carrasco, +34 952 878 162).

DINING IN THE CITY CENTER

Ronda is littered with upscale-seeming restaurants that toe the delicate line between a good dinner spot and a tourist trap.

$$$ Restaurante Pedro Romero, though touristy and overpriced, is a venerable institution in Ronda. It's named for Ronda's most famous son, the first great bullfighter. Assuming a shrine to bullfighting draped in *el toro* memorabilia doesn't ruin your appe-

tite, rub elbows with the local bullfighters or dine with the likes (well, photographic likenesses) of Orson Welles, Ernest Hemingway, and Francisco Franco (daily 12:00-15:30 & 19:00-22:30, aircon, across from bullring at Calle Virgen de la Paz 18, +34 952 871 110).

$$$ Meson El Sacristan is a well-respected restaurant serving classical and innovative dishes with a focus on meat (many prepared in the wood-fired oven). Their 12-hour *rabo de toro* oxtail stew is a favorite. It's a good place to slow down—enjoy the helpful waiters and the rustic setting, either inside or on the quiet square. Their tasting menus are enticing, and the savory homemade *croquetas* are exceptional (Thu-Mon 12:00-23:00, closed Tue-Wed, reservations smart, Plaza Duquesa de Parcent 14, +34 952 875 684, www.mesonelsacristan.com).

$$ Entre Vinos only seats a few people but offers good quality tapas and highlights Ronda's wines at a reasonable price. Friendly staff can help you choose among many options by the glass (additional tables streetside, Tue-Sat 12:30-16:30 & 20:00-24:00, closed Sun-Mon, Calle Pozo 2, +34 672 284 146).

$$$$ Restaurante Bardal has the only Michelin two-star rating in town. Local-wonder chef Benito Gómez serves two tasting menus (16 tiny courses-€85, 20 courses-€100, wine extra). While almost comically fancy, this is a delicious experience featuring morsels based on local ingredients. Benito serves about 20 people each lunch and dinner, and all are treated like VIPs (Wed 20:00-24:00, Thu-Sat 13:15-18:00 & 20:00-24:00, Sun 12:00-16:30, closed Mon-Tue, reserve ahead, Calle José Aparicio 1, +34 951 489 828, www.restaurantebardal.com).

OUTSIDE THE ALMOCÁBAR GATE

To entirely leave the quaint old town and bustling city center with its tourists and grand gorge views, hike 10 minutes out to the far end of the old town, past City Hall, to a big workaday square that goes about life as if the world didn't exist outside Andalucía.

$$ Bar-Restaurante Almocábar is a favorite eatery for many Ronda locals. Its restaurant—a cozy eight-table room with Moorish tiles and a window to the kitchen—serves up tasty, creative, well-presented meals from a menu that's well described in English (plus a handwritten list of the day's specials). Many opt for the good salads—rare in Spain. At the bar up front, choose from gourmet tapas like the *serranito* (a pork, roast pepper, and tomato mini sandwich) or you can order from the dining-room menu (Wed-Mon 13:00-16:00 & 19:30-23:00, closed Tue, reservations smart, Calle Ruedo Alameda 5, +34 952 875 977).

$$$ Casa María is a delightful, family-run place managed by Elias and Isabel, daughter Maria, and Lucero the dog. There's no

menu—only the promise of a wonderful meal. Just sit down, and for a set price around €30 you'll be treated to a full home-cooked feast: salad, vegetables, fish, meat, and dessert. It's worth making a reservation for this adventure. In summer, their tables spill out onto the plaza (daily 13:00-15:30 & 20:00-23:00, facing Plaza Ruedo Alameda at #27, +34 951 083 663).

Ronda Connections

Some destinations are linked with Ronda by both bus and train. Direct bus service to other hill towns can be sparse (as few as one per day), and train service usually involves a transfer in Antequera. It's worth spending a few minutes comparing schedules online to plan your departure. Your options improve from major transportation hubs such as Málaga.

From Ronda by Bus to: Algeciras (1/day, 3 hours, Comes), **La Línea/Gibraltar** (no direct bus, transfer in Algeciras; Algeciras to La Línea/Gibraltar—2/hour, 45 minutes, buy ticket on bus, Comes), **Arcos** (1/day, 2 hours, Comes), **Zahara** (2/day, Mon-Fri only, 75 minutes, Comes), **Sevilla** (4/day, 2.5 hours, fewer on weekends, Damas; also see trains), **Málaga** (6/day Mon-Fri, 7/day Sat-Sun, 2 hours, Damas; access other Costa del Sol points from Málaga), **Marbella** (3/day, 1.5 hours, Avanza), **Nerja** (4 hours, transfer in Málaga; can take train or bus from Ronda to Málaga, bus is better). If traveling to **Córdoba,** it's easiest to take the train since there are no direct buses. Bus info: Damas (www.damas-sa.es), Avanza (www.avanzabus.com), and Comes (www.tgcomes.es).

By Train to: Algeciras (3/day, 1.5 hours), **Málaga** (2/day, 2.5 hours, transfer in Antequera), **Sevilla** (2/day, 3 hours, transfer in Antequera), **Granada** (2/day, 2.5 hours, transfer in Antequera), **Córdoba** (1/day direct, 2 hours; 2 more with transfer in Antequera, 2 hours), **Madrid** (1/day direct, 4 hours; 1 more with transfer in Antequera). Any transfer is a snap and time-coordinated; with four trains arriving and departing simultaneously, double-check that you're jumping on the right one. Train info: +34 912 320 320, www.renfe.com.

ROUTE TIPS FOR DRIVERS

Ronda to the South Coast: Drivers who want to dip down to the coast from Ronda can catch A-397 and head over the mountains and down to San Pedro de Alcántara (about 30 miles/50 km). Many trucks use this route as well, so the going may be slow if following a convoy. The longer, winding A-369/A-377 route (about 50 miles/80 km) offers a scenic alternative to reach the coastal town of Estepona. You'll go through gorgeous countryside and a series of whitewashed villages, but note that the A-377 stretch of this road

(from Gaucín to the coast), while perfectly drivable, is in rough shape—expect to go slowly.

Zahara and Grazalema

There are plenty of interesting hill towns to explore. Public transportation is frustrating, so I'd do these towns only by car. Useful information on the area is rare. Fortunately, a good map, the regional tourist brochure (pick it up in Sevilla or Ronda), and a spirit of adventure work fine.

Along with Arcos, Zahara de la Sierra and Grazalema are my favorite white villages. While Grazalema is a better overnight stop, Zahara is a delight for those who want to hear only the sounds of the wind, birds, and elderly footsteps on ancient cobbles.

ZAHARA DE LA SIERRA

This tiny town in a tingly setting under a Moorish castle (worth ▲) has a spectacular view over a turquoise reservoir. While the big church facing the town square is considered one of the richest in the area, the smaller church has the most-loved statue: The Virgin of Dolores is Zahara's answer to Sevilla's Virgin of Macarena (and is similarly paraded through town during Holy Week).

The **TI** is located in the main plaza (Tue-Sun 10:00-14:00, closed Mon, gift shop, Plaza del Rey 3, +34 956 123 114, www.zaharadelasierra. es). Upstairs from the TI are Spanish-only displays about the flora and fauna of nearby Sierra de Grazalema Natural Park. A map posted nearby shows the tour and trail system.

Drivers can park for free in the main plaza, or continue up the hill to the parking lot at the base of the castle, just past the recommended Hotel Arco de la Villa. It's one way up and one way down, so follow *salida* signs to depart. The street that connects both churches, Calle de San Juan, is lined with tapas bars and cafés.

Sights in Zahara: During Moorish times, Zahara lay within the fortified castle walls above today's town. It was considered the gateway to Granada and a strategic stronghold for the Moors by the Christian forces of the Reconquista. Locals tell of the Spanish conquest of the Moors' castle (in 1482) as if it happened yesterday: After the Spanish failed several times to seize the castle, a clever

Route of the White Hill Towns

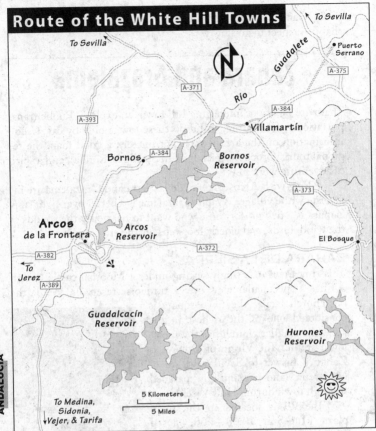

To Sevilla

To Sevilla

Guadalete

Puerto Serrano

A-375

A-371

Río

A-384

Villamartín

A-393

Bornos

A-384

Bornos Reservoir

A-373

Arcos de la Frontera

Arcos Reservoir

A-372

El Bosque

A-382

To Jerez

A-389

Guadalcacín Reservoir

Hurones Reservoir

5 Kilometers

5 Miles

To Medina, Sidonia, & Vejer, & Tarifa

Spanish soldier noticed that the Moorish sentinel would check if any attackers were hiding behind a particular section of the wall by tossing a rock and setting the pigeons in flight. If they flew, the sentinel figured there was no danger. One night a Spaniard hid there with a bag of pigeons and let them fly when the sentinel tossed his rock. Upon seeing the birds, the guard assumed he was clear to enjoy a snooze. The clever Spaniard then scaled the

wall and opened the door to let in his troops, who conquered the castle. Ten years later Granada fell, the Moors retreated to North Africa, and the Reconquista was complete.

Skip the church, but it's a fun climb up to the remains of the

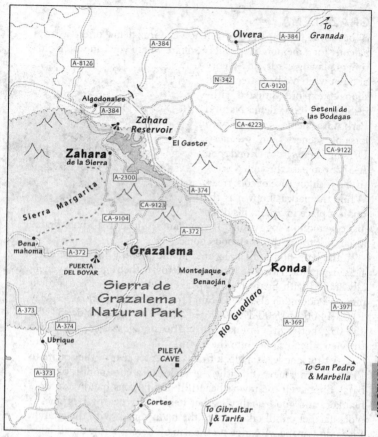

castle (free, tower always open). Start at the paved path across from the town's upper parking lot. It's a moderately steep 15-minute hike past some Roman ruins and along a cactus-rimmed ridge to the top, where you can enter the tower. Use your phone's flashlight or feel along the stairway to reach the roof, and enjoy spectacular views from this almost impossibly high perch far above the town. As you pretend you're defending the tower, realize that what you see is quite different from what the Moors saw: the huge lake dominating the valley is a reservoir—before 1991, the valley had only a tiny stream.

Sleeping and Eating in Zahara: The town's only real hotel is **$ Hotel Arco de la Villa** (16 small modern rooms, Wi-Fi in common areas only, +34 956 123 230, in the hotel menu at www.tugasa. com, arco-de-la villa@tugasa.com). The hotel's very good **$ restaurant** offers a reasonably priced *menú del día*, along with reservoir and mountain views.

GRAZALEMA

A beautiful postcard-pretty hill town, Grazalema offers a royal balcony for a memorable picnic, a square where you can watch old-timers playing cards, and plenty of quiet whitewashed streets and shops to explore. Situated within Sierra de Grazalema Natural Park, Grazalema is graced with lots of scenery and greenery. Driving here from Ronda on A-372, you pass through a beautiful parklike grove of cork trees. While the park is known as the rainiest place in Spain, it's often just covered in a foggy mist. If you want to sleep in a small Andalusian hill town, this is a good choice.

The bare-bones **TI** is located at the parking lot at the cliffside viewpoint, Plaza de los Asomaderos. When open, it's generally staffed with Spanish-only speakers who can give you a town map and not much else (Wed-Sun June-Sept 9:00-15:00, Oct-May 10:00-14:00 & 15:00-17:30, closed Mon-Tue year-round, +34 956 132 052, better info online at http://turismo.grazalema.es). Enjoy the view, then wander into the town.

A tiny lane leads a block from the center rear of the square to Plaza de Andalucía (filled by the tables of a commotion of tapas bars). Shops sell the town's beautiful and famous handmade wool blankets and good-quality leather items from nearby Ubrique. A block farther uphill takes you to the main square with the church, Plaza de España. A coffee on the square here is a joy. Small lanes stretch from here into the rest of the town.

For outdoor gear and adventures, including hiking, caving, and canoeing, contact **Horizon** (summer Mon-Sat 9:00-14:00 & 17:00-20:00, closed Sun, shorter hours off-season, off Plaza de España at Calle las Piedras 1, +34 956 132 363, +34 655 934 565, www.horizonaventura.com).

Sleeping in Grazalema: Your best bet is **$ La Mejorana Guesthouse**—if you can manage to get one of its nine rooms. This beautifully perched garden villa, with royal public rooms, overlooks the valley from the top of town (includes breakfast, pool, on tiny lane below Guardia Civil headquarters at Santa Clara 6, +34 956 132 527, +34 649 613 272, www.lamejorana.net, info@lamejorana. net, Ana and Andrés can help with local hikes).

¢ Casa de Las Piedras, just a block from the main square, has 16 comfortable en suite double rooms with air-con. The beds feature the town's locally made wool blankets (RS% with 2-night minimum, Calle de las Piedras 32, +34 956 132 014, www.

Grazalema

To Zahara
(via CA-531)
& Ronda

A-372

Accommodations
1 To La Mejorana Guesthouse
2 Casa de Las Piedras

Eateries & Other
3 Plaza de Andalucía Eateries
4 El Torreón
5 Mesón El Simancón
6 To Gastrobar La Maroma
7 Supermarket
8 Horizon Adventure Tours

C. DE LOS ANGELES
C. ARRIBA
PUERTA DE LA VILLA
C. DE LA EMPEDRADA
C. DEL DOCTOR MATEOS GAGO
C. JIMENEZ
AV. POMAR
PUERTA DE LA VILLA
Plaza de los Asomaderos
CALLE DEL AGUA
CALLE DE LAS PIEDRAS
Plaza de España
CHURCH
CALLE DE LAGUNETA
CALLE DE CORRALES SEGUNDOS
CALLE JUAN DE LA ROSA
C. CORRALES TERCEROS
CALLE DE LAS PARRAS
A-372

100 Meters
100 Yards

casadelaspiedras.es, reservas@casadelaspiedras.net, Caty and Rafi). They also rent nearby apartments that sleep 2-8 people.

Eating in Grazalema: Tiny Plaza de Andalucía has several good bars for tapas with umbrella-flecked tables spilling across the square, including **$$ Zulema** (big salads), **$ La Posadilla,** and **$ Travesía.** To pick up picnic supplies, head to the **Eroski** supermarket (Mon-Sat 9:00-14:00 & 17:00-21:00, closed Sun, Calle las Piedras 12).

$$ El Torreón specializes in local cuisine such as lamb and game dishes, plus many vegetarian options. Diners are warmed by the woodstove while deer heads keep watch (Thu-Tue 12:00-16:00 & 19:00-23:00, closed Wed, Calle Agua 44, +34 956 132 313).

$$ Mesón El Simancón serves well-presented cuisine typical of the region in a romantic setting. While a bit more expensive, it's considered the best restaurant in town (Wed-Mon 12:00-16:00 & 19:30-23:00, closed Tue, Plaza de los Asomaderos 54, +34 956 132 421).

$ Gastrobar La Maroma serves home-cooked regional specialties at affordable prices (Fri-Sun 13:00-16:00 & 20:00-22:30,

closed Mon-Thu, Calle Santa Clara, near La Mejorana Guest-house, +34 956 132 279).

Grazalema Connections: By Bus to Ronda (2/day, 45 min-utes), **El Bosque** (1/day, 45 minutes). Bus service is provided by Damas (www.damas-sa.es).

Jerez de la Frontera

With more than 200,000 people, Jerez de la Frontera is your typi-cal big-city mix of industry and dusty concrete suburbs, but it has a lively old center and two claims to touristic fame: horses and sherry. Jerez is ideal for a noontime visit on a weekday. See the famous horses, sip some sherry, wander through the old quarter, and swag-ger out. For the most efficient visit if arriving by bus or train, taxi from the train station right to the Royal Andalusian School for the equestrian performance, then walk around the corner to the San-deman bodega for the next English tour.

Orientation to Jerez

Thanks to its complicated medieval street plan, there is no easy way to feel oriented in Jerez—so ask for directions liberally.

The helpful **TI** is on Plaza del Arenal (Mon-Fri 9:00-15:00 & 16:30-18:30, Sat-Sun 9:30-14:30, +34 956 149 863, www. turismojerez.com).

ARRIVAL IN JEREZ

By Bus or Train: The bus and train stations are located side by side, near the Plaza del Minotauro (with an enormous headless statue). Unfortunately, you can't store luggage at either one. You can stow bags for free in the Royal Andalusian School's *guardaropa* (coat room) if you attend their equestrian performance, but only for the duration of the show.

Cheap and easy **taxis** wait in front of the train station (€5 to TI; about €9 to the horses). Otherwise, it's a 20-minute **walk** from the stations to the center of town and the TI: Angle across the brick plaza (in front of the stations, with two black smokestacks) to find Calle Diego Fernández de Herrera. Follow this street for sev-eral blocks until you reach a little square (Plaza de las Angustias). Leave the square at the far left side down Calle Corredera. In a few minutes you'll arrive at Plaza del Arenal (ringed with palm trees, with a large fountain in the center); the TI is in the arcaded build-ing across the plaza.

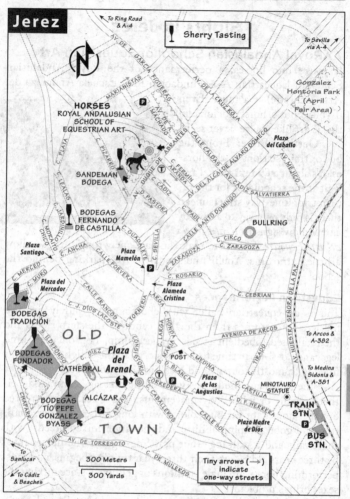

By Car from Arcos: Driving in Jerez can be frustrating. The outskirts are filled with an almost endless series of roundabouts. Continuing straight through each one (you'll see a rail bridge) and follow traffic and signs to *Centro Ciudad*. The circuitous route will ultimately take you into Plaza Alameda Cristina; park in one of the many underground garages (at Plaza Alameda Cristina or Plaza Arenal, €2/hour) and catch a cab or walk. For street parking, blue-line zones require prepaid parking (€0.80/hour, 2-hour maximum, put ticket on dashboard; Mon-Fri 9:00-13:30 & 17:00-20:00, Sat 9:00-14:00; free to park outside these hours, Sun mornings, and mornings in July-Aug).

Sights in Jerez

▲▲Royal Andalusian School of Equestrian Art

If you're into horses, a performance of the Royal Andalusian School of Equestrian Art (Fundación Real Escuela Andaluza del Arte Ecuestre) is a must. Even if you're not a horse aficionado, this is art like you've never seen.

Getting There: From the bus or train stations to the horses, it's about a €9 **taxi** ride. Taxis wait at the school exit for the return trip. One-way streets mean there is only one way to arrive by **car:** Follow signs to *Real Escuela de Arte Ecuestre*. Expect to make at least one wrong turn, so allow a little extra time. You'll find plenty of free parking behind the school.

Equestrian Performances

This is an equestrian ballet with choreography, purely Spanish music, and costumes from the 19th century. The stern riders and their talented, obedient steeds prance, jump, hop on their hind legs, and do-si-do in time to the music, all to the delight of an arena filled with mostly tourists and local horse aficionados.

The riders cue the horses with subtle dressage commands, either verbally or with body movements. You'll see both purebred Spanish horses (of various colors, with long tails, calm personalities, and good jumping ability) and the larger mixed breeds (with short tails and a walking—not prancing—gait). The horses must be three years old before their three-year training begins, and most performing horses are male (stallions or geldings), since mixing the sexes brings problems.

The equestrian school is a university, open to all students in the EU, and with all coursework in Spanish. Tightly fitted mushroom hats are decorated with different stripes to show each rider's level. Professors often team with students and evaluate their performance during the show.

Cost and Hours: €23 general seating, €30 "preference" seating; 1.5-hour shows run at 12:00 Tue and Thu (March-July and Oct-Dec), Tue and Thu-Fri (Aug-Sept), and Thu (Jan-Feb); additional shows one Sat a month (twice in June-July); +34 956 922 580, best to buy tickets in advance online at www.realescuela.org. General seating is fine; some "preference" seats are too close for good overall views. The show explanations are in Spanish.

Training Sessions

The public can get a sneak preview at training sessions on nonperformance days. Sessions can be exciting or dull, depending on what the trainers are working on. Afterward, you can take a 1.5-hour guided tour of the stables, horses, multimedia and carriage museums, tack room, gardens, and horse health center. Sip sherry in the arena's bar to complete this Jerez experience.

Cost and Hours: €12, Mon 10:00-14:00, last entry at 12:00, tours depart when a large enough group forms. A shorter €7 tour covers only the museums and saddlery.

▲▲Sherry Bodega Tours

Spain produces more than 10 million gallons per year of the fortified wine known as sherry. The name comes from English attempts to pronounce Jerez. Although sherry was traditionally the drink of England's aristocracy, today's producers have left the drawing-room vibe behind. Your tourist map of Jerez is speckled with *venencia* symbols, each representing a sherry bodega that offers tours and tasting. (*Venencias* are specially designed ladles for dipping inside the sherry barrel, breaking through the yeast layer, and getting to the good stuff.) For all the bodegas, it's smart to confirm tour times before you go, as schedules can be changeable.

Bodegas Tradición

Although founded in 1998, this winery continues family winemaking traditions that date back to 1650. Their guided tours do a remarkable job of explaining the sometimes difficult-to-understand method of producing sherry. Aficionados claim that their award-winning sherries are not to be missed. Art lovers will get an extra treat: a museum-worthy private collection of works by Murillo, Velázquez, El Greco, Zurburán, Goya, and many others.

Cost and Hours: €40 for 1.5-hour tour, includes 5 sherries, always available in English for up to 12 people; Mon-Fri 10:00 & 16:00; reservations required, private tours available, Calle Cordobeses 3, +34 956 168 618, www.bodegastradicion.com.

Bodegas Rey Fernando de Castilla

Founded in the 1960s by a family with 200 years of winemaking experience, this *bodega* has become a powerhouse, focusing on producing amazing sherry, brandies, and vinegars. Of note are their Palo Cortado and Pedro Ximénez varieties.

ANDALUCÍA

Sherry

Spanish sherry is not just the sweet dessert wine sold in the States as sherry. In Spain, sherry is (most commonly) a chilled and very dry fortified white wine, often served with appetizers such as tapas, seafood, and cured meats.

British traders invented the sherry-making process as a way of transporting wines so they wouldn't go bad on a long sea voyage. Some of the most popular brands (such as Sandeman and Osbourne) were begun by Brits, and for years it was a foreigners' drink. But today, sherry is typically Spanish.

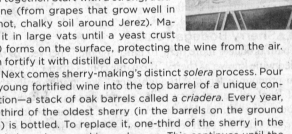

Sherry is made by blending wines from different grapes and vintages, all aged together. Start with a strong, acidic wine (from grapes that grow well in the hot, chalky soil around Jerez). Mature it in large vats until a yeast crust *(flor)* forms on the surface, protecting the wine from the air. Then fortify it with distilled alcohol.

Next comes sherry-making's distinct *solera* process. Pour the young fortified wine into the top barrel of a unique contraption—a stack of oak barrels called a *criadera*. Every year, one-third of the oldest sherry (in the barrels on the ground level) is bottled. To replace it, one-third of the sherry in the barrel above is poured in, and so on. This continues until the top barrel is one-third empty, waiting to be filled with the new year's vintage.

Fino is the most popular type of sherry (and the most different from Americans' expectations)—white, dry, and chilled. The best-selling commercial brand of *fino* is Tío Pepe; *manzanilla* is a regional variation of *fino*, as is *montilla* from Córdoba. Darker-colored and more complex varieties of sherry include *amontillado* and *oloroso*. And yes, Spain also produces the thick, sweet cream sherries served as dessert wines. A good raisin-y, syrupy-sweet variety is Pedro Ximénez (often marked just "PX"), made from sun-dried grapes of the same name.

Cost and Hours: €15 for tour and tasting; English tours available Mon-Fri 10:00-14:00—reservations required; Jardinillo 7, +34 956 182 454, www.fernandodecastilla.com, bodegas@fernandodecastilla.com.

Sandeman

Just around the corner from the equestrian school is the venerable Sandeman winery, founded in 1790 and the longtime drink of English royalty. This tour is the aficionado's choice for its knowledgeable guides and their quality explanations of the process. Each

stage is explained in detail, with visual examples of *flor* (the yeast crust)
in backlit barrels, graphs of how different blends are made, and a quick
walk-through of the bottling plant.
The finale is a chance to taste three
varieties.

Cost and Hours: €12 regular
sherries, €18 rare sherries, tour/tast-
ing lasts 1-1.5 hours; English tours
run Mon-Fri 3/day, fewer in winter, Sat by appointment only, closed
Sun and all of Jan—check schedules
online; reservations not required,
Calle Pizarro 10, +34 675 647 177, www.sandeman.com.

Tío Pepe González Byass

The makers of the famous Tío Pepe offer a tourist-friendly tour,
with more pretense and less actual sherry-making on display (that's
done in a new, enormous plant outside town). But the grand circle
of sherry casks signed by a *Who's Who* of sherry drinkers is worthwhile. Taste two sherries at the end of the 2-hour tour.

Cost and Hours: €19.50 for tour/tasting, €23.50 for light tapas
lunch with tour; tours run daily at 12:30; additional times may be
available—confirm online; Manuel María González 12, +34 956
357 016, www.tiopepe.com. Drivers can park in the underground
Alameda Vieja lot at the skippable Alcázar (€2/hour).

Other Sherry Bodegas

You'll come across many other sherry bodegas in town, including
Fundador, located near the cathedral. This bodega, founded by
Pedro Domecq, is the oldest in Jerez and the birthplace of the city's
brandy. Tastings here are generous (€15 for 3 sherries plus 1 brandy,
€25 with light tapas; Tue-Sat 12:00, reservations required; Calle
San Ildefonso 3, +34 956 151 552, http://bodegasfundador.site).

Jerez Connections

Jerez's bus station is shared by multiple bus companies, each with
its own schedule. The big ones serving most southern Spain destinations are Damas (www.damas-sa.es), Comes (www.tgcomes.es),
and Socibus (https://socibusventas.es). Shop around for the best
departure time and most direct route. While here, clarify routes for
any further bus travel you may be doing in Andalucía—especially
if you're going through Arcos de la Frontera, where the ticket office
is often closed. Also try Movelia.es for bus schedules and routes.

From Jerez by Bus to: Tarifa (1/day on Algeciras route, 2.5

ANDALUCÍA

hours, more frequent with transfer in Cádiz, Socibus), **Algeciras** (1/day, 2.5 hours, Socibus) **Arcos** (hourly, 40 minutes, Damas), **Ronda** (2/day, 2.5-3 hours), **La Línea/Gibraltar** (1/day, 2.5 hours), **Sevilla** (4/day, 1-1.5 hours), **Granada** (1/day, 4.5 hours).

By **Train to: Sevilla** (hourly, 1 hour), **Madrid** (3/day direct, 4 hours; nearly hourly with change in Sevilla, 4 hours), **Barcelona** (nearly hourly, 7-8 hours, all with change in Sevilla and/or Madrid). Train info: tel.+34 912 320 320, www.renfe.com.

Near the Hill Towns

If you're driving between Arcos and Tarifa, here are several sights to explore.

YEGUADA DE LA CARTUJA

This breeding farm, which raises Hispanic Arab horses according to traditions dating back to the 15th century, offers a 2-hour guided visit and show on Saturday at 11:00 (€23 for best seats in *tribuna* section, €17 for seats in the stands, Finca Fuente del Suero, Carretera Medina-El Portal, +34 956 162 809, www.yeguadacartuja. com). From Jerez, take the road to Medina Sidonia, then turn right in the direction of El Portal—you'll see a cement factory on your right. Drive for five minutes until you see the farm.

MEDINA SIDONIA

This town is as whitewashed as can be, surrounding its church and hill, which is topped with castle ruins. I never drive through here without a coffee break and a quick stroll. Signs to *centro urbano* route you through the middle to Plaza de España (lazy cafés, bakery, plenty of free parking just beyond the square out the gate). If it's lunchtime, consider buying a picnic, as all the necessary shops are nearby and the plaza benches afford a solid workaday view of a perfectly untouristy Andalusian town. According to its own TI, the town is "much appreciated for its vast gastronomy." Small lanes lead from the main square up to Plaza Iglesia Mayor, where you'll find the church and TI (+34 956 412 404, www.medinasidonia. com). At the church, an attendant will show you around for a tip. Even without giving a tip, you can climb yet another belfry for yet another vast Andalusian view. The castle ruins just aren't worth the trouble.

VEJER DE LA FRONTERA

Vejer, south of Jerez and just 30 miles north of Tarifa, will lure all but the very jaded off the highway. Vejer's strong Moorish roots

give it a distinct Moroccan (or Greek Island) flavor—you know, black-clad women whitewashing their homes, and lanes that can't decide if they're roads or stairways. The town has no real sights—other than its remarkable views—and very little tourism, making it a pleasant stop. The TI is at Calle de los Remedios 2 (+34 956 451 736, www.turismovejer.es).

The coast near Vejer has a lonely feel, but its pretty, windswept beaches are popular with windsurfers and sand flies. The Battle of Trafalgar was fought just off Cabo de Trafalgar (only a nondescript lighthouse today). I drove the circle so you don't have to.

Sleeping in Vejer: A newcomer on Andalucía's tourist map, the old town of Vejer has just a few hotels. **$$ Hotel La Botica de Vejer** provides 13 comfortable rooms in what was once a local apothecary. Homey decor and view patios add to the charm (Calle Canalejas 13, near Plaza de España, +34 956 450 225, www.laboticadevejer.com). **$$ Hotel Convento San Francisco** is a poorman's parador with spacious rooms in a refurbished convent (Calle Plazuela, +34 956 451 001, www.tugasa.com).

ANDALUCÍA

SPAIN'S SOUTH COAST

Nerja • Gibraltar • Tarifa

Much of Spain's south coast is so bad, it's interesting. To northern Europeans, the sun is a drug, and this is their needle. Anything resembling a quaint fishing village has been bikini-strangled and Nivea-creamed. Oblivious to the concrete, pollution, ridiculous prices, and traffic jams, tourists lie on the beach like the local sardine skewers—cooking, rolling, and sweating under the sun. It's a fascinating study in human nature.

The most famous stretch of coast is the Costa del Sol, where human lemmings make the scene and coastal waters are so polluted that hotels are required to provide swimming pools. And where Europe's most popular beach isn't crowded by high-rise hotels, most of it's in a freeway chokehold.

But the south coast holds a few gems. If you want a place to stay and play in the sun, unroll your beach towel at Nerja, the most appealing resort town on the coast.

And remember that you're surprisingly close to jolly olde England: The land of tea and scones, fish-and-chips, pubs, and bobbies awaits you—in Gibraltar. Though a British territory, Gibraltar has a unique cultural mix that makes it far more interesting than the anonymous resorts lining the coast.

Beyond "The Rock," the whitewashed port of Tarifa—the least-developed piece of Spain's generally overdeveloped southern coast—is a workaday town with a historic center, broad beaches, and good hotels and restaurants. Most important, Tarifa is the perfect springboard for a quick trip to Tangier, Morocco (see next chapter).

These three places alone—Nerja, Gibraltar, and Tarifa—make Spain's south coast worth a trip.

Spain's South Coast

To Córdoba

To Sevilla

SPAIN

Granada

AVE

Jerez • Arcos ☺☺

Lanjarón

Cádiz ☺

PUEBLOS

Ronda ☺☺

☺☺ Frigiliana • CAVES

Motril

BLANCOS

AVE

Costa del Sol

Nerja ■ Almuñécar

Salobreña

Vejer ☺☺

Costa

Málaga ☺☺

S. Pedro ☺

Marbella ☺

Torremolinos ☺☺

30 Kilometers

de

Estepona ☺☺

Fuengirola ☺☺

30 Miles

la

La

Cape
Trafalgar

Luz

Algeciras ☺

Línea ☺☺

Gibraltar
(U.K.) ☺☺

Mediterranean
Sea

☺☺ Tarifa

Tangier ☺☺

Tangier
Med

Ceuta ☺☺
(SPAIN)

☺☺ DELIGHTFUL

☺☺ TOLERABLE

☺☺ AWFUL

MOROCCO

PLANNING YOUR TIME

My negative opinions on the "Costa del Turismo" are valid for peak
season (mid-July to mid-Sept). If you're there during a quieter time
and you like the ambience of a beach resort, it can be a pleasant
stop. Off-season it can be neutron-bomb quiet, with many hotels
and restaurants closed until their clients return for the sun.

The whole 150 miles of coastline takes six hours by bus or
three hours to drive with no traffic jams. You can resort-hop by bus
across the entire Costa del Sol and reach Nerja for dinner. If you
want to party on the beach, it can take as much time as it would to
get to Mazatlán.

To day-trip to Tangier, Morocco, head for Tarifa.

Nerja

Despite cashing in on the fun-in-the-sun culture, Nerja (NE-

HR-hah) has kept much of its
Old World charm. It has good
beaches, a fun evening paseo
(strolling scene) that culminates
at the Balcony of Europe viewpoint, enough pastry shops and
nightlife to keep you fed and
entertained, and locals who get
more excited about their many
festivals than the tourists do.

Although Nerja's popula-

tion swells from about 22,000 in winter to about 90,000 in the summer, it's more of a year-round destination and a real town than many other resorts. Spaniards have a long tradition of vacationing here, and pensioners from northern Spain move here—enjoying long life spans, thanks in part to the low blood pressure that comes from a diet of fish and wine. While they could afford to travel elsewhere in summer, to escape the brutal heat of inland Spain many Spanish parents take turns with their kids in family condos on the south coast. Whoever stays home to work gets to "be Rodriguez" *(estar de Rodríguez),* an idiom whose closest English equivalent is "when the cat's away, the mice will play."

For the average traveler coming from Madrid or Barcelona, walking Nerja's streets, where everyone seems to have all the time in the world, is a psychological adjustment—but that's why you're here.

Orientation to Nerja

The tourist center of Nerja is right along the water and crowds close to its famous bluff, the Balcony of Europe (Balcón de Europa). Fine strings of beaches flank the bluff, stretching in either direction. The old town is just inland from the Balcony, while the more modern section slopes up and away from the water.

Tourist Information: The helpful English-speaking TI has bus schedules, tips on beaches and side trips, and brochures for nearby destinations, such as the Caves of Nerja, Frigiliana, Málaga, and Ronda (generally Mon-Fri 10:00-14:00 & 16:30-20:00, Sat-Sun 10:00-13:45; morning only off-season; 100 yards from the Balcony of Europe and a half-block inland from the big church, +34 952 521 531, http://turismo.nerja.es). They also stock the local newspaper *SUR in English,* and their free *Route on Walks* booklet describes good local walks.

ARRIVAL IN NERJA

By Bus: The Nerja station is just a bus stop with an info kiosk on Avenida de Pescia (Mon-Tue 6:00-20:15, Wed-Sun 7:00-12:15 & 14:45-19:00, schedules posted, Alsa, www.alsa.es). To travel from Nerja, buy tickets at the kiosk; if the kiosk is closed, buy them on the bus. If uncertain, ask which side of the street your bus departs from. Because many buses leave at the same times, arrive at least 15 minutes before departure to avoid having to elbow other tourists.

By Car: To find the old-town center and the most central parking, follow *Balcón de Europa, Centro Urbano,* or *Centro Ciudad* signs, and then pull into the big underground municipal lot beneath the Plaza de España (which deposits you 200 yards from the Balcony of Europe; €2/hour, €22/24 hours). The enormous

Costa del Sol History

Many Costa del Sol towns come in pairs: the famous beach town with little history, and its smaller yet much more historic partner established a few miles inland—safely out of reach of the Barbary pirate raids that plagued this coastline for centuries. Nerja is a good example of this pattern. Whereas it has almost no history and was just an insignificant fishing village until tourism hit, its more historic sister, Frigiliana, hides out in the nearby hills. The Barbary pirate raids were a constant threat. In fact, the Spanish slang for "the coast is clear" is *"no hay moros en la costa"* (there are no Moors on the coast).

Decadence and lots of skin on the beach are rather new here. During the time of the dictator Franco, the Catholic Church and the Spanish government made society very conservative. Beaches were generally gender segregated. When Raquel Welch starred in *Fathom,* a spy comedy filmed here in 1966, a babe in a bikini was pretty shocking.

Tourism is also a relatively new thing in Nerja. Its first hotels (Balcón de Europa and Portofino) date from after World War II, but tourism didn't start picking up until the 1980s, when the phenomenal Spanish TV show *Verano Azul (Blue Summer)* was set here. This post-Franco program featured the until-then off-limits topics of sexual intimacy, marital problems, adolescence, and so on in a beach-town scene (imagine combining *All in the Family, Baywatch,* and *The Hills*). To this day, when Spaniards hear the word "Nerja," they think of this TV hit.

Despite the fame, development didn't really take off until about 2000, when the expressway finally and conveniently connected Nerja with the rest of Spain. (Granada is now just an easy hour away.) Thankfully, a building code prohibits any new buildings higher than three stories in the old town.

aboveground Parking Carabeo, just east of the Balcony, is slightly cheaper but exposed to brutal sun (€1.80/hour, €18/24 hours). The handiest free parking is about a 10-minute walk farther out, next to the bridge over the dry riverbed (near the town bus stop, just off N-340). Street parking in Nerja can be very tight. Blue lines mean it's metered (pay and display); white lines indicate it's generally free. If you do find a space, read signs carefully—on certain days of the month you're required to move your car. It's best to ask your hotelier if your street spot is OK.

HELPFUL HINTS

Laundry: Full-service launderette **Bubbles Burbujas** is run by friendly Jo from England (same-day service if you drop off in the morning, no self-service; Mon-Fri 10:00-14:00, Sat until

Nerja

N

100 Meters
100 Yards

To Nerja Caves, Aqueduct,
Cantarriján Beach
& Granada

N-340

C. JOAQUÍN HERRERA

AV. PESCIA

CALLE DE

CALLE DE

BUS
INFO

WC

B

B

T

Plaza
Cantarero

CALLE A. BUENO

PAS. S. JUAN

AVENIDA DE PESCIA

N-340

To
Málaga

P
Free

M. NÚÑEZ

CALLE DE LA PINTADA

9

28

CALLE COLÓN

CALLE ALFONSO XII

CALLE DE ALMIRANTE FERNÁNDEZ

30

C. SAN MIGUEL

C. INGENIO

Plaza
Ermita

T

CALLE DE ANGUSTIAS

8

11

C. NUEVA

17

19

BRONCE

C. DE LA CRUZ

31

26

27

14

18

Río Chillar

Parque
Verano
Azul

P

CALLE ANTONIO FERRANDIS CHANQUETE

CALLE DE CHAPARIL

12

CALLE DE CASTILLA
PÉREZ

ANIMAS

To
P

NERJA
MUSEUM

Plaza
de
España

GLORIA

CALLE DE LA PINTADA

15

7

13

16

POST

CALLE

24

MANUEL MARÍN

CALLE DE GRANADA

32

4

i

10

Cliffs

30

C. DIPUTACIÓN PROVINCIAL

2

Plaza de
Cavana

29

"TUTTI
FRUTTI"
AREA

32

5

CALLE EL BARRIO

C. CARMEN

6

CALLE ANT. MILLÓN

EL
SALVADOR

23

1

C. MÁLAGA

CALLE DE CHAPARIL

DOCTOR FERRÁN

To
El Playazo
Beach

La Torrecilla
Beach

Del Salón
Beach

BALCONY OF
EUROPE

Plaza Balcón
de Europa

Cliffs

Mediterranean   Sea

SOUTH COAST

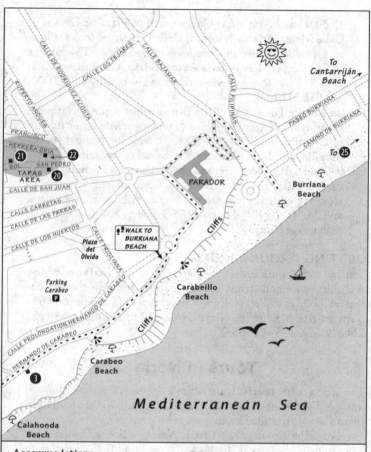

Accommodations

1. Hotel Balcón de Europa
2. Hotel Plaza Cavana
3. Hotel Carabeo
4. Hotel Mena Plaza
5. Hostal Don Peque
6. Hostal & Cafetería Marissal
7. Pensión Sevillano
8. Hostal Dianes
9. Hostal Lorca

Eateries & Other

10. Anahí Café
11. Café Las 4 Esquinas
12. Good Stuff Café
13. Oliva
14. Rincón del Sevillano & Bar Redondo #2
15. Bar Redondo #1
16. El Pulguilla Fish Bar & Restaurant
17. Los Barriles
18. Haveli
19. Coach & Horses Pub
20. El Chispa (Bar Dolores)
21. La Puntilla Bar Restaurante
22. La Taberna de Pepe
23. Cochran's Terrace Bar Restaurant
24. La Marina
25. To Ayo & Educare Aventura
26. Bar El Molino
27. El Burro Blanco
28. Bodega Los Bilbainos
29. Heladería Valenciano
30. Grocery (2)
31. Foodstore Andaluz
32. Launderette (2)

13:00, closed Sun; a few blocks north of Plaza de Cavana at Calle Manuel Marín 1, just off Calle Granada—look for Pasaje Granada pedestrian passage on left, +34 665 539 256). For self-service, try **Lavandería Autoservicio Axarquia** on Calle Castilla Pérez (coins only—no change given, daily 8:00-21:00, +34 952 522 104).

British Media: For a taste of the British expat scene, pick up the monthly magazine *Street Wise* (www.streetwise.es) or tune in to Coastline Radio at 97.6 FM. To imagine being a retired Scandinavian here, have a look at *Soltalk* (www.soltalk.com).

Local Guide: Excellent licensed guide **Carmen Fernández** has vast regional knowledge extending from tailored cityscapes to stunning natural areas around Nerja, Frigiliana, Antequera, and Málaga (€90/3 hours, €125/5 hours, +34 610 038 437, mfeyus@gmail.com).

GETTING AROUND NERJA

You can easily **walk** anywhere you need to go. **Taxis** are widely available; you'll find stands at Plaza Ermita and near the bus station on Avenida de Pescia. Expect to pay €5-15 (for example, €6 to Burriana Beach, €9 to the Nerja Caves, €12 to Frigiliana, +34 952 524 519 or +34 952 520 537).

Tours in Nerja

The little generic **tourist train** offers a 25-minute ramble through town, but there's not a lot to say or see (€4, daily 10:00-18:00 from Plaza Cavana, recorded multilanguage narrations).

For offbeat tours, try **6 Thrills Nerja,** which offers 1.5-hour town tours on Segway (€50), bike (€9), and foot (€25). Drop in to see what's on (small groups, generally English only, erratic departures, just off Plaza Cavana at Calle Iglesia 2, +34 663 811 514, www.sixthrills.com).

Educare Aventura offers kayak and paddleboard rental at Burriana Beach, either on your own (€15/2 hours) or with a guide (€24/2.5 hours). They also have 4x4 tours and hiking trips into the nearby Sierra de Tejeda and Sierra Nevada mountains (office located just behind the recommended Ayo restaurant at Camino de Burriano 28, +34 952 039 026, www.educare-aventura.com).

Sights in Nerja

▲▲Balcony of Europe (Balcón de Europa)

The bluff, jutting happily into the sea, is completely pedestrianized. It's the center of Nerja's paseo and a magnet for street performers. The mimes, music, and puppets can draw bigger crowds than the

Balcony itself, which overlooks the Mediterranean,
miles of coastline, and
little coves below.

But this happy bluff
was the site of a castle for
a thousand years (from the
ninth century until a big
earthquake in 1884). The
Nerja castle was part of
a 16th-century lookout system. After the Christian Reconquista
drove Muslim Moors into exile in 1492, pirate action from Muslim countries in North Africa picked up. Lookout towers were stationed within sight of one another all along the coast. Warnings
were sent whenever pirates threatened (smoke by day, flames by
night). To the east (left), if you look closely, you can see two towers
breaking the horizon on the distant bluffs.

Later, a Spanish fort built here in the 16th century was destroyed by the English in the early 1800s to keep it from being
captured by Napoleon. Its cannons tumbled into the sea, where
they sat rusting for about a century. Two were salvaged, cleaned
up, and placed here, pointing east and west. Study the beautifully
aged metalwork.

Joining the promenade crowds is a cute statue of King Alfonso
XII, reminding locals of this popular sovereign—the great-great-

grandfather of today's King Felipe VI—who came here after the
devastating earthquake of 1884
(a huge number of locals died).
He mobilized the local rich to
dig out the community and put
things back together. Standing
on this promontory amid the
ruins of the earthquake-devas-
tated castle, he marveled at the
view and coined its now-famous name, Balcón de Europa.

Walk beneath the Balcony for views of the scant remains
(bricks and stones) of the ninth-century Moorish castle. Locals
claim an underground passage connected the Moorish fortress
with the mosque that existed where the Church of El Salvador
stands today.

Church of El Salvador (Iglesia de El Salvador)

Just a block inland from the Balcony, this church was likely built on
the ruins of a mosque (in around 1600). You can visit it briefly before the daily 19:00 Mass starts or possibly find it open during the

afternoon (no set hours). Its wooden ceiling is Mudejar—made by Moorish artisans working in Christian times, with a woodworking technique similar to that featured in the Alhambra in Granada. Inlaid tiles depicting the stations of the cross ring the walls, and a modern mural of the Annunciation (by local artist Paco Hernandez) decorates the rear of the nave. In front, on the right, is a niche featuring Jesus with a young St. Isidoro, the patron saint of Madrid, Nerja, and farmers (sugarcane farming was the leading industry here before tourism hit). The towering tree in front of the church was brought here from Chile in 1885 and is a symbol of the city. From the porch of the church, look inland (left) to see City Hall, marked by four flags (Andalucía's is green for olive trees and white for the color of the houses in this part of Spain).

Nerja Museum (Museo de Nerja)

This museum, with modern exhibits well described in English, is a good option on a rainy day or if you've had too much sun. It's run in association with the Nerja Caves (described under "Sights near Nerja"). Exhibits focus on the history of Nerja and the surrounding region, from prehistoric times through its sugar cane heritage. A highlight is the exhibit on the nearby Nerja Caves, including prehistoric tools, weapons, and a skeleton found there. Don't miss the 10-minute video (on repeat in the theater) that shows a Franco-era newsreel about the discovery of the caves in 1959 by farm boys looking for bats.

Cost and Hours: €3, €12 combo-ticket with Nerja Caves; open Tue-Sun 10:00-16:30, July-Aug until 19:00, closed Mon year-round; Plaza de España 4, +34 952 527 224, www.cuevadenerja.es.

Town Strolls

Nerja was essentially destroyed after the 1884 earthquake—and at the time there was little here beyond the castle anyway. So there's not much to see in the town itself. However, a few of its main streets are worth a ramble. From the Balcony of Europe head inland. Consider first grabbing some ice cream at **Heladería Valenciano,** a local favorite. You could try the refreshing *chufa*-nut specialty drink called *horchata*.

A block farther beyond the *heladería,* the old town's three main streets come together. The oldest and most picturesque street, Calle Hernando de Carabeo, heads off to your right (notice how buildings around here are wired on the outside). On the left, Calle Pintada heads inland. Its name means "the painted street," as it was spiffed up in 1885 for the king's visit. Today it's the town's best shopping street, especially the stretch below Calle de la Gloria. And between Calles Carabeo and Pintada runs Calle Almirante Ferrándiz, Nerja's restaurant row, which is particularly lively in the evenings.

BEACHES

The single best thing to do on a sunny day in Nerja is to hit the beach: swim, sunbathe, sip a drink, go for a hike along the rocky coves...or all of the above.

Many of Nerja's beaches are well equipped with bars and restaurants, free showers, and rentable lounge chairs and umbrellas

(€4-5/person for chair and umbrella, same cost for 10 minutes or all day). Nearby restaurants rent beach furniture, and you're welcome to take drinks and snacks out to your spot. Spanish law requires all beaches to be open to the public. While there are some nude beaches (such as Cantarriján, described later), keep in mind that in Europe, any beach can be topless. Watch out for red flags on the beach, which indicate when the seas are too rough for safe swimming (blue=safe, orange=caution, red=swimming prohibited). Keep a careful eye on your valuables—or better yet, leave them in the hotel.

During the summer, Spanish sun worshippers pack the beach from about 11:00 until around 13:30, when they move into the beach restaurants for relief from the brutal rays. The most typical Spanish beach cafés are called *chiringuitos*—shacks selling drinks and simple, cheap-but-good eats. Considering practically every beach has one, *chiringuitos* are a way of life along the coast. When Spaniards play on the *playa* they simply say "see you at the *chiringuito*" to meet friends for a beer and *espetos*—fish, usually sardines, skewered whole, stacked tepee style, and cooked over coal in large barbeque pits.

Beaches lie west and east of the Balcony of Europe. For each area, I've listed beaches from nearest to farthest. Even if you're not swimming or sunbathing, walking along these beaches (and the trails that connect them, if open) is a delightful pastime.

West of the Balcony of Europe

A pleasant series of beaches begin just beneath the Balcony of Europe and stretch on toward sunset. The first is a singular cove, while the next are accessed from the end of Calle Málaga, a five-minute walk through town, and are connected by a promenade and trails.

Del Salón Beach (Playa del Salón)

The sandiest (and most crowded) beach in Nerja is down the walkway to the right of Cafetería Marissal, just west of the Balcony of

SOUTH COAST

Europe (to the right as you look out to sea). For great drinks with a view, stop by the recommended Cochran's Terrace on the way down.

Playa la Torrecilla and Playa el Chucho

Farther west is another sandy beach, **Playa la Torrecilla,** crowded with sunbathers, shops, and restaurants. From here, a waterfront promenade brings you to the beach **Playa el Chucho,** popular with families for its shallow water.

El Playazo ("Big Beach")

A short hike west of Playa el Chucho, this beach is preferred by locals, as it's less developed than the more central ones (no showers, bring your own everything). It offers a couple of miles of wide-open spaces that allow for fine walks and a chance to "breathe in the beach."

East of the Balcony of Europe

An appealing walkway called the Paseo de los Carabineros once connected the enticing beaches east of the Balcony, but it's been closed for several years due to erosion and a lack of funds to restore it. For that reason, you'll walk through the modern town above the coast to reach the beaches east of the Balcony of Europe.

Calahonda Beach (Playa Calahonda)

Directly beneath the Balcony of Europe (to the left as you face the sea) is one of Nerja's most characteristic little patches of sun. This pebbly beach is full of fun pathways, crags, and crannies. To get to the beach from the Balcony, simply head down through the arch across from the Heladería Valenciano ice cream stand...you'll be on the beach in seconds. Outside of July and August, this beach is relaxed and inviting.

Carabeo and Carabeillo Beaches (Playa Carabeo/Playa Carabeillo)

Tiny and barely developed, these two beaches are wedged into wee coves between the bustling Calahonda and Burriana beaches. For many, their lack of big restaurants and services is a deal-breaker. For others, it's a plus. To reach them, walk along Calle Hernando de Carabeo. The stairs down to Carabeo Beach are at a little view-point on the right (with a big wall map of the area). A bit farther along, a larger view plaza has stairs down to Carabeillo.

Burriana Beach (Playa de Burriana)

Nerja's leading beach is a 20-minute walk east from the Balcony of Europe. Big, bustling, crowded, and fun, it's understandably a top attraction. Burriana is ideal for families, with a grand promenade, paddleboats, kayaks, playgrounds, volleyball courts, and other en-

tertainment options. The beach is also lined with a wide range of inviting cafés and restaurants serving fresh seafood and *espetos*. The recommended Ayo *chiringuito* is a destination for its legendary lunchtime paella feast.

Getting There: It's an easy walk or a €6 taxi ride. To walk, follow Calle Hernando de Carabeo to the viewpoint plaza above Carabeillo Beach. At the roundabout, go up the first street to the right (you'll see a no-entry sign for cars), jog left (up Calle Cómpeta) alongside Nerja's boxy parador, then walk around the parador, following the signs for *Playa Burriana*. The path will curl right, then twist down a switchbacked path to the beach.

Cantarriján Beach (Playa del Cantarriján)

The only beach listed here not within easy walking distance of Nerja, this is the place if you're craving a more desolate beach (and have a car). Drive about four miles (15 minutes) east (toward Herradura) to the Cerro Gordo exit, and follow *Playa Cantarriján* signs (paved road, just before the tunnel). Park at the viewpoint and hike 30 minutes down to the beach (or, in summer, ride the shuttle bus). Down below, rocks and two restaurants separate two pristine beaches—one for people with bathing suits (or not); the other, more secluded, more strictly for nudists. As this beach is in a natural park and requires a long hike, it provides a fine—and rare—chance to experience the Costa del Sol in some isolation.

SIGHTS NEAR NERJA

The area around Nerja has its own charms, with caves, hiking, and the appealing whitewashed village of Frigiliana.

▲Nerja Caves (Cueva de Nerja)

These caves (2.5 miles east of Nerja), with an impressive array of stalactites and stalagmites, are a classic roadside attraction. The huge caverns, filled with backlit formations, are a big hit with cruise-ship groups and Spanish families—so it's best to go in the morning, when crowds are usually lighter. The visit involves a 45-minute audioguide tour, during which you'll climb deep into the mountain, up and down 400 dark stairs. At the end you reach the Hall of the Cataclysm, where you'll circle the world's largest stalactite column (certified by the *Guinness Book of World Records*). Someone figured out that it took one trillion drops to make the column. The caves, discovered in 1959, have hosted human beings for at least 30,000 years; prehistoric paintings here go back nearly

that far (to preserve the paintings, the cave art is not viewable by the public). If you're fascinated by what you see here, the museum in town has a good exhibit on the caves.

Cost and Hours: €11, €12 combo-ticket with Nerja Museum; daily 9:30-16:30, July-Aug until 19:00, timed entry on the hour and half-hour—book ahead online, last entry one hour before closing; guided tours and science-oriented or nighttime tours also available; easy pay parking, +34 952 529 520, www.cuevadenerja.es.

Getting There: A taxi costs around €9 one-way. To go by public transit, catch a bus across the street from Nerja's main bus stop (Alsa bus, €1.20, roughly hourly, 10-minute ride—get schedule from TI or the Nerja Museum, or check www.alsa.es). Drivers will find the caves well signed (exit 295 on A-7)—just follow the *Cueva de Nerja* signs right to the parking lot. As a little bonus, a footbridge behind the ticket window crosses over a free botanical garden before descending into the pleasant sea village of Maro.

Hiking Around Nerja

Europeans visiting the region for a longer stay generally use Nerja as a base from which to hike. The TI can describe a variety of hikes (ask for the free trails booklet). One of the most popular hikes, Rio Chillar, is a refreshing walk up a river (at first through a dry riverbed, and later up to your shins in water; 7 miles one-way, 2-3 hours total, access the riverbed from Calle de Joaquín Herrera, behind the bus station). Another, more demanding hike takes you to the 5,000-foot summit of El Cielo for the most memorable king-of-the-mountain feeling this region offers.

An easy, somewhat dull two-mile walk ends with a surprisingly impressive sight with an interesting history—the Eagle Aqueduct (Acueducto del Águila). Heading east from town, follow the green-and-white stone sidewalk all the way along Avenida de Pescia. Thirty minutes outside Nerja, you'll pass Capistrano Playa (above Burriana Beach), where you can enjoy views of the coastline, Nerja, and El Cielo in the distance. Half a mile later you'll see the ruins of a 19th-century sugar mill (on the left).

Shortly after the ruins, look for the *Cala Barranco del Maro* sign pointing to the right. Follow the path downhill past the Old Maro Bridge to the base of the aqueduct. Thirty-six arches support four levels; it was built in the 1870s to supply water to the ruined sugar mill you passed on the way here. Look for the double-headed eagle weathervane that gives the aqueduct its name. Bombed during Spain's civil war, the structure was restored in 2011. From here you can cross the Old Maro Bridge and continue on to Maro, a whitewashed, seaside, cliff-top village sitting just below the Nerja Caves (connected over N-340 by a pedestrian footbridge) and above

two popular beaches. Alternately, backtrack to Nerja the way you came.

Nightlife in Nerja

Bar El Molino offers live Spanish folk singing nightly in a rustic cavern that's actually an old mill—the musicians perform where the mules once trod. It's touristy but fun (starts at 19:00 but pretty dead before 23:00, fewer shows off-season, no cover—just buy a drink, Calle San José 4). The local sweet white wine, *vino del terreno*—made up the hill in Frigiliana—is popular here (€3/glass).

El Burro Blanco is a touristy flamenco bar that's enjoyable and intimate, with shows nightly in the summer from 21:30 (off-season shows run Tue, Thu, and Sat-Sun at 20:00). Keeping expectations low, they advertise "The Best Flamenco Show in Nerja" (€15 admission includes a drink, four dancers; recorded music Sun-Thu, live music Fri-Sat; 00; on corner of Calle Pintada and Calle de la Gloria, www.flamencoennerja.com, +34 615 153 961).

Bodega Los Bilbainos is a classic, dreary old dive—a favorite with local men and communists (tapas and drinks, Calle Alejandro Bueno 8).

For more nightlife, check out the pub bars and dance clubs on Antonio Millón and Plaza Tutti Frutti.

Sleeping in Nerja

The entire Costa del Sol is crowded during August and Easter Week, when prices are at their highest. Reserve in advance for peak season—basically mid-July through mid-September—which is prime time for Spanish families to hit the beaches. Any other time of year, Nerja has plenty of available comfy, easygoing low-rise resort-type hotels and rooms.

Compared to the pricier hotels, the better *hostales* are an excellent value. Hostal Don Peque and Pensión Miguel are within a few blocks of the Balcony of Europe.

CLOSE TO THE BALCONY OF EUROPE

$$$$ Hotel Balcón de Europa is the most central place in town, right on the water and the square, with the prestigious address Balcón de Europa 1. It has 108 rooms with modern style, plus all the comforts—including a pool and an elevator down to the beach. It's popular with groups. All the suites have seaview balconies, and most regular rooms also come with views (air-con, elevator, gym, sauna, pay parking, +34 952 520 800, www.hotelbalconeuropa. com, reservas@hotelbalconeuropa.com).

$$$ Hotel Plaza Cavana, with 40 rooms, overlooks a plaza

lily-padded with cafés. It feels a bit institutional, but if you'd like a central location, marble floors, modern furnishings, an elevator, and a small unheated rooftop swimming pool, dive in (RS%, breakfast included for Rick Steves readers, some view rooms, family rooms, air-con, mini fridge, elevator, pay parking, 2 blocks from Balcony of Europe at Plaza de Cavana 10, +34 952 524 000, www. hotelplazacavana.com, info@hotelplazacavana.com).

$$ Hotel Carabeo is a boutique hotel with seven classy rooms on the cliff east of downtown—less than a 10-minute walk away, but removed from the bustle of the Balcony of Europe (closed mid-Nov-March, five view rooms, includes continental breakfast, air-con, Calle Hernando de Carabeo 34, +34 952 525 444, www. hotelcarabeo.com, info@hotelcarabeo.com).

$$ Hotel Mena Plaza is clean, bright, and friendly, offering 34 rooms on the lethargic Plaza de España right by the Nerja Museum. Some rooms have views and wide balconies (family room, air-con, elevator, pay parking, pool, rooftop terrace, +34 952 520 965, www.hotelmenaplaza.es, info@hotelmenaplaza.es).

$ Hostal Don Peque, an easy couple of blocks' walk from the Balcony of Europe, has 14 bright, colorful, and cheery rooms (eight with balconies—a few with sea views). Owners Roberto and Clara moved here from France and have infused the place with their personalities. They lend beach equipment, and their bar-terrace with a hot tub and views over rooftops and the sea is enticing (family room, breakfast April-Oct only, air-con, Calle Diputación 13, +34 952 521 318, +34 640 778 988, www.hostaldonpeque.com, info@ hostaldonpeque.com).

$ Hostal Marissal has an unbeatable location next door to the fancy Hotel Balcón de Europa, and 23 modern, spacious rooms with old-fashioned furniture and balconies (some overlooking the Balcony of Europe action). Their cafeteria and bar, run by helpful staff, make the Marissal even more welcoming (family room, some view rooms, apartment, double-paned windows, air-con, elevator, Balcón de Europa 3, reception at Cafetería Marissal—staffed mornings only in off-season but they'll send you a code to access your room, +34 952 520 199, www.hostalmarissal.com, reservas@ hostalmarissal.com).

$ Pensión Sevillano offers nine sunny and airy rooms in the heart of "Restaurant Row" (some street noise in front rooms). Breakfast is served on the pretty green terrace with mountain views (family suite, no air-con but fans and fridges, laundry service, beach equipment, Calle Almirante Ferrándiz 31, +34 952 524 138, +34 679 046 122, www.pensionsevillano.com, info@pensionsevillano. com).

$ Hostal Dianes is a simple place—there's no elevator, no breakfast, no balconies, or views—with 10 airy, old-fashioned

rooms and a pleasant rooftop terrace. Its location, straddling the residential and nightlife districts, is close enough to the action but far enough away to provide a friendly welcome, good value, and a peaceful night's slumber (large family room, air-con, Calle Pintada 67, +34 952 528 116, www.hostaldianes.com, info@hostaldianes.com).

IN A RESIDENTIAL NEIGHBORHOOD

$ Hostal Lorca is in a quiet residential area a five-minute walk from the center, three blocks from the bus stop, and close to a small, handy grocery store. Run by a friendly, energetic Dutch couple, Femma and Rick, this *hostal* has nine modern, comfortable rooms and an inviting backyard with a terrace and a small pool. You can use the microwave and take drinks (on the honor system) from the well-stocked fridge. This quiet, homey place is a winner (family room, no air-con but fans, look for a house with flags at Calle Méndez Núñez 20, +34 952 523 426, www.hostallorca.com, hostallorcanerja@gmail.com).

Eating in Nerja

There are three Nerjas: the private domain of the giant beachside hotels; the central zone, packed with fun-loving (and often tipsy) expats and tourists eating and drinking from trilingual menus; and the back streets, where local life goes on as if there were no tourists. The whole old town (around the Balcony of Europe) is busy with lively restaurants. And you're just a 10-minute taxi ride from the whitewashed hill town of Frigiliana, with several lovely restaurants tucked away in its back lanes and perched on its viewpoints.

To pick up picnic supplies, head to the **Mercadona** supermarket (Mon-Sat 9:00-21:30, closed Sun, inland from Plaza Ermita on Calle San Miguel). There's also a handy **Carrefour Express** closer to town at the corner of Castilla Pérez and Manuel Marín (daily). For an interesting selection of imported foods, check out Frank and Marianne's **Foodstore Andaluz,** a Dutch-run grocery that stocks especially good chocolates and sweets (Mon-Sat 10:00-20:00, closed Sun, Calle Pintada 46, +34 681 327 841).

Breakfast: Many hotels here overcharge for breakfast. Don't hesitate to go elsewhere, as lots of places serve breakfast for more reasonable prices. For breakfast with a front-row view of the promenade action on the Balcony of Europe, head to one of the first two listed here.

$$ Cafetería Marissal (in the recommended *hostal* of the same name) features wicker seats under the palm trees (options include English breakfasts and a buffet, daily from 8:30).

$ Anahí Café serves tempting pastries and cheap breakfasts

to early risers on a tiny balcony overlooking Calahonda Beach—they also sell picnic-perfect loaves of bread to go (daily 8:00-21:00, Calle Puerta del Mar 6, +34 952 521 457).

$ Café Las 4 Esquinas is where the chef fries up hot *churros* to dip into a hot pudding-like chocolate drink (daily 7:00-23:00, *churros* 7:00-12:30 & 17:00-20:00, Calle Pintada 57, on the corner of Calle Angustias, +34 626 126 564).

If you're up for a short hike before breakfast, a great target is the recommended **$ Ayo** on Burriana Beach (see "Paella Feast on Burriana Beach," later).

At the **$ Good Stuff Café,** Adam makes savory quiches and pies, and Irene makes scones, brownies, carrot cake, banana bread, and Victoria sponge cake (Mon-Sat 9:00-15:00, closed Sun and August; Calle Castilla Perez 4, +34 606 512 586).

ALONG RESTAURANT ROW

Strolling up Calle Almirante Ferrándiz (which some locals call "Cristo" at its far end), you'll find a good variety of eateries, albeit filled with tourists. The presence of expats means you'll find places serving food earlier in the evening than the Spanish norm.

$$$ Oliva feels like a premium restaurant on a cruise ship—white-tablecloth ambience and a gourmet twist on international fusion cuisine made from local products. It's tucked away through a courtyard off the Calle Pintada and has seating both inside and on a quiet back square (daily 13:00-16:00 & 19:00-23:00, Calle Pintada 7, +34 952 522 988).

$$ Rincón del Sevillano, an elegant fixture in a sea of high-energy tapas bars, serves the hungry on both sides of Calle de la Gloria. While they have a standard bar offering free tapas with each drink, for formal dining try the ground-floor dining room or the second-floor rooftop section on the uphill side (daily, Calle de la Gloria 15 and 17, +34 951 325 119).

$$ Bar Redondo, a sloppy place popular with locals and visitors alike, is a colorfully tiled *taparía* and watering hole. Bartenders work from within the completely round, marble-topped bar; if you can't find room there, grab a spot at a wine-barrel table on the street. Buy any drink and choose a free tapa from their enticing list of 25 options. Their bigger dishes, like the *ensalada redondo,* are worth considering. Their second venture, directly across the sidewalk, serves seafood and keeps the same format: round bar and free tapas with your drink (daily 12:30-24:00, Calle de la Gloria 10, +34 952 523 344).

$$ El Pulguilla Fish Bar and Restaurant is a great scene for Spanish cuisine, fish, and tapas. Its two distinct zones (tapas bar up front and more formal restaurant out back) are jammed with enthusiastic locals and tourists. The lively no-nonsense stainless-steel

tapas bar doubles as a local pickup joint later in the evening. Drinks come with a free small plate of clams, mussels, shrimp, chorizo sausage, or seafood salad. For a sit-down meal (same menu and cost), head all the way back to one of two gigantic terraces (one under a canopy and the other under the stars). Enjoy an exhibit of old black-and-white town photos as you pass through the middle room. Half-portions *(media-raciones)* are available for many items, allowing you to easily sample different dishes (Tue-Sun 12:30-15:45 & 19:00-23:45, closed Mon—"to give our clients a day off," Calle Almirante Ferrándiz 26, +34 952 521 384).

$$ Los Barriles is a family-run bar where Rafa, Carmen, and their son serve up drinks and a short, simple menu of *raciones,* including a fiery chorizo sausage. Your best bet is to order a drink and wait for the tapa that comes with it. Locals flock here and tourists are treated like locals (Mon-Sat 19:30-24:00, closed Sun, Calle San José 2).

$$ Haveli, run by Amit and his Swedish wife, Eva, serves good Indian cuisine in a dressy first-floor dining room and on a sunny rooftop terrace. For more than three decades, it's been a hit with Brits, who know their Indian food (Thu-Mon 18:30-22:30, closed Tue-Wed, Calle Almirante Ferrándiz 44, +34 952 524 297).

$$ Coach & Horses Pub is a little bit of old England run by no-nonsense British expat Catherine—this is where to find bangers and mash. Although she serves the only real Irish steaks in town, she also caters to vegetarians, with daily specials that go beyond the usual omelet. In fine weather, enjoy the terrace seating (Tue-Sun 14:00-22:00, closed Mon, Calle Almirante Ferrándiz 70, +34 952 520 071).

TAPAS BARS ON OR NEAR CALLE HERRERA ORIA

A 10-minute gentle uphill hike from the water takes you into the residential thick of things, where the sea views come thumbtacked to the walls, prices are lower, and locals fill the tables. These three tapas bars are within a block of one another. Each is a colorful local hangout with different energy levels on different nights. Survey all three before choosing one or have a drink and tapa at each. These places offer table-service meals during normal dining hours, but the action is at the bar, which is generally open all day for tapas and drinks.

Remember that in Nerja, tapas are snack-size portions, generally not for sale but free with each drink. To turn them into more of a meal, ask for the menu and order a full-size *ración* or half-size *media-ración.* The half-portions are generally much bigger than you'd expect.

$ El Chispa (a.k.a. Bar Dolores) is big on seafood, which lo-

Britain's Home Away from Home

Particularly in the resorts around Málaga, many of the foreigners who settle in for long holidays are British—you'll find beans on your breakfast plate and Adele for Muzak. Spanish visitors complain that some restaurants have only English menus, and indeed, the typical expats here actually try *not* to integrate. I've heard locals say of the British, "If they could, they'd take the sun back home with them—but they can't, so they stay here." The Brits enjoy their English TV and radio stations, and many barely learn a word of Spanish. (Special school buses take their children to private English-language schools that connect with Britain's higher-education system.) For an insight into this British community, read the free local expat magazines.

cals enjoy on an informal terrace adjacent to the bar (enter directly from the street). Their *tomate ajo* (garlic tomato) is tasty, and their piping-hot *berenjena* (fried and salted eggplant) is worth considering—try it topped with *miel de caña*, molasses-like sugarcane syrup. They serve huge portions—*media-raciones* are enough for two (daily, Calle San Pedro 12, +34 952 523 697).

$ **La Puntilla Bar Restaurante** fills the corner with a boisterous, tiled bar and a more formal restaurant with outdoor tables spilling onto the cobbles (show this book and get a free *digestivo*, daily 12:00-24:00, a block in front of Los Cuñaos at Calle Bolivia 1, +34 952 528 951).

$ **La Taberna de Pepe** is a family-run, sit-down restaurant (with a few outdoor tables), though it does have a small bar with tapas. The tight, cozy (almost cluttered) interior is decorated with old farm tools and crammed with happy eaters choosing from a short menu of well-executed seafood. It feels a cut above its neighbors (Fri-Wed 12:00-16:00 & 19:00-24:00, closed Thu, Calle Herrera Oria 30, +34 952 522 195).

NEAR THE BALCONY OF EUROPE

$$ **Cochran's Terrace Bar Restaurant,** just behind Hostal Marissal, serves mediocre meals in a wonderful seaview setting, overlooking Del Salón Beach (daily 11:00-19:00). They also offer breakfast from 8:30 to 10:30 and drinks all day.

$$ **La Marina,** away from the tourist zone, is a neighborhood seafood joint bustling with locals and worth the walk. Their *gambas* plate spills onto nearly every butcher-paper tablecloth in the restaurant (Thu-Tue 12:00-16:30 & 19:30-24:00, closed Wed, Calle Castilla Pérez 20, +34 952 521 299).

SOUTH COAST

PAELLA FEAST ON BURRIANA BEACH

$ Ayo is famous for its character of an owner and its beachside paella feast at lunchtime. For 30 years, Tito (a.k.a. Ayo, a Spanish term of endearment similar to "grandfather") has been feeding locals. A lovable ponytailed bohemian who promises to be here until he dies, Ayo is a very big personality. He's one of the five kids who discovered the Nerja Caves, formerly a well-known athlete, and now someone who makes it a point to hire hard-to-employ people as a community service. The paella fires get stoked up at about noon and continue through mid-to-late afternoon. Grab one of a hundred tables under the canopy next to the rustic open-fire cooking zone and enjoy the beach setting in the shade with a jug of sangria. It's a 20-minute walk from the Balcony of Europe, at the east end of Burriana Beach—look for Ayo's rooftop pyramid (open daily "sun to sun" with a full menu, paella served only in the afternoon, cash only, Playa de Burriana, +34 952 522 289).

Breakfast at Ayo's: Consider arriving at Ayo's at 9:00. Locals order the *tostada con aceite de oliva* (toast with olive oil and salt). Ayo also serves toasted ham-and-cheese sandwiches and good coffee.

Nerja Connections

While there are some handy direct bus connections from Nerja to major destinations, many others require a transfer in the town of **Málaga**. The closest train station is in Málaga. Fortunately, connections between Nerja and Málaga are easy, and the train and bus stations in Málaga are right next to each other (for more about Málaga, see "Coastal Towns," later).

Almost all buses from Nerja are operated by Alsa (www.alsa.es), except the local bus to Frigiliana, which is run by Grupo Fajardo (ask for schedule at TI).

From Nerja by Bus to: Málaga (1-2/hour, 1.5 hours), **Nerja Caves** (1/hour, 10 minutes), **Frigiliana** (about hourly, 15 minutes), **Granada** (6/day, 2 hours), **Sevilla** (1/day direct, more with transfer in Málaga, 5 hours). To reach **Ronda, Gibraltar,** or **Tarifa,** you'll transfer in Málaga.

To Málaga Airport (about 40 miles west): Take a direct Alsa bus (2/day, 1.5 hours). Otherwise, catch a bus to the Málaga bus station, then take the local Line A express airport bus (also called L-75, 2/hour, 15 minutes, €3, buy ticket on board) or commuter train C1 (2-3/hour, 10 minutes, €1.80; Málaga's train station is a five-minute walk across the street from the bus station). A taxi from Nerja costs about €65 or ask your Nerja hotelier about airport shuttle transfers.

ROUTE TIPS FOR DRIVERS

Nerja to Granada (60 miles, 95 km, 100 views): Drive east along the coast toward Motril or take the faster A-7, then head north to Granada on the slower N-323 or the quicker A-44. While scenic side trips may beckon, don't arrive late in Granada without a confirmed hotel reservation. See the Granada chapter ("Arrival in Granada/By Car") for tips on how to avoid getting a traffic ticket when driving into the city center.

Frigiliana

The picturesque whitewashed village of Frigiliana (free-hee-lee-AH-nah), only four miles inland from Nerja, makes for a wonderful side trip. A thousand feet above sea level, full of history, and feeling like it dropped in from the mountains of Morocco, it's a striking contrast to its beach resort sister.

Getting There: It's easy: Catch the hourly bus from the stop on Avenida de Pescia in Nerja (€1.20, 15 minutes, https://grupofajardo.es; or hop in a taxi (around €12 one-way).

Getting Oriented: Your landing pad is **Plaza del Ingenio,** a utilitarian hub dividing the old and the new towns. At this little square you'll find the bus stop, taxi stand, tourist train departure point, free WC, and start of my self-guided old town walk. The TI is a 100-yard walk uphill, in the new town (daily 10:00-14:00, sometimes later; +34 952 534 261, www.turismofrigiliana.es). Pick up a map and the translations of the tiles you'll see displayed around town. The TI shares a building with the free **archaeological museum,** with artifacts and tools unearthed near Frigiliana (including the fifth-century BC skull of a 10-year-old child). Above the TI, situated on a bluff, is an old tower with a grand view.

Frigiliana has many characteristic and romantic little **restaurants,** some with commanding views. As the town is most charming in the evening, consider coming up for an early evening walk and dinner (ride the bus up and catch a cab home). Local specialties to try are *berenjenas con miel de caña* (fried eggplant with local cane syrup) and *tortillas de bacalao con miel de caña* (cod cakes with cane syrup).

FRIGILIANA OLD TOWN WALK

This 30-minute stroll—rated ▲▲—comes with lots of ups and downs, commanding views, and delightful back lanes. (It's easier to follow with the fine little town map from the TI.) If you're planning to catch a bus back to Nerja, note departure times before you start.

Begin by climbing from Plaza del Ingenio up to the terrace in front of the **factory** *(ingenio)*—the blocky, un-whitewashed, dou-

ble-smokestack building that dominates the town. Dating from the 16th century, this still produces molasses-like sugarcane syrup, *miel de caña* (factory closed to public).

From the left end of the factory terrace, hike up the steep street (Calle Real) past **shops** tempting you with local wine, cork products, and *miel de caña*. At the fork, stay right on the stepped lane (Calle Hernando el Darra) with its black-and-white pavement. At #10 (on the right), notice the **tile** in the wall—the first in a series of a dozen around town that describe, in poetic Spanish, the story of the 1568 Battle of Peñón.

A few steps before the top of the lane (at #26), turn right into a covered passageway. Climb 100 yards to a **viewpoint** on the right (above the romantic Garden Restaurant). The valley was once filled with sugarcane; it's been replaced in recent decades by avocado and mango trees.

Circle uphill and to the left. The street plan dates to medieval times, when the Moors tucked their village here, high in the hills away from coastal raiders. The **white-wash** dates to the 18th century, when a plague killed 40 percent of the population. To sterilize the town, everything was burned or slathered in lime to kill the germs. It turned out that the white-wash reflected the sun, keeping things cool. People liked it, and it remains to this day. While houses must be white, the trim is your choice. Enjoy the traffic-free tranquility, small restaurants, big views, and flowers.

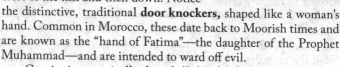

Follow the lane straight over the crest of the hill and then down. Notice the distinctive, traditional **door knockers,** shaped like a woman's hand. Common in Morocco, these date back to Moorish times and are known as the "hand of Fatima"—the daughter of the Prophet Muhammad—and are intended to ward off evil.

Continuing scenically downhill, head left down the stepped and steep **El Zacatin** lane. This means "little souk," and you can imagine it in Moorish times bustling with shops.

El Zacatin ends at Calle Real. At the T-intersection, go a few steps to the right to the inviting café-lined plaza in front of **Church of San Antonio of Padua.** The church was built in 1679 and whitewashed in the 1700s to defend against the plague. Step inside. At the top of two arches, the church retains some of its original painted decor from 1679. Skulls (with bishop's miter and royal crown) are a reminder that death is the great equalizer. The second arch is colorfully dedicated to Virgin Mary with her "Ave

SOUTH COAST

Maria" logo under the crown. The wooden ceiling is Mudejar style (done by Moorish craftsmen after the Christian reconquest). Many of the altarpieces are floats that hit the streets for a procession each Semana Santa (Holy Week, leading up to Easter). In the left front chapel, notice the dozen masks—one for each of the apostles—worn during Semana Santa.

Leaving the church, turn left and follow **Calle Real** (the only lane in the old town wide enough to fit a car) back to where you started.

Coastal Towns

Buses take five hours to make the Nerja-Gibraltar trip, including a transfer in Málaga, where you may have to change bus companies. Along the way, buses stop at each of the following towns (see map on page 837).

MÁLAGA

Málaga's busy airport is the gateway to the Costa del Sol, and taking a long layover in this seaside city may be worth your while. It has spruced itself up in recent years and deserves at the very least a lengthy stroll and visits to the two impressive museums.

Tourist Information: The TI has a branch at the center of the train station (in front of tracks 1-8; Mon-Sat 10:00-14:00 & 16:00-20:00, Sun 10:00-13:00, shorter hours off-season) and a larger office at the marina (daily 9:00-20:00, Plaza de la Marina 11, +34 951 926 020, www.malagaturismo.com).

Arrival in Málaga: One of Spain's busiest airports, Málaga-Costa del Sol Airport (code: AGP, www.aena.es) is five miles southwest of Málaga. The easiest and fastest way to get from the airport to the city center is by train (€1.80, 12 minutes, get off at Málaga Centro Alameda). You can also take a taxi (about €15, 15 minutes) to the *casco viejo* (old town). The Line A express bus (also called L-75, €3, pay cash on bus, 15-20 minutes) takes you blocks from the cathedral—get off at Paseo del Parque–Plaza de la Marina, a long tree-lined plaza with florist stalls. From there you can easily wander into the old town's pedestrianized zone, which is easy to navigate thanks to signposts on almost every corner indicating tourist sights.

The bus and train stations—a block apart at the western edge of the town center—both have pickpockets and lockers. You'll want to store your bags in the more modern lockers at the train station. For more details, see "Málaga Connections," later.

Sights in Málaga: The **Museo Picasso Málaga** holds over 200 paintings, sculptures, and ceramics spanning the artist's life and artistic styles. Pablo Picasso was born in Málaga and first dis-

cussed establishing a museum here in 1953. It finally opened 50 years later, thanks to a donation by the artist's daughter-in-law and grandson (€9, includes audioguide; daily July-Aug 10:00-20:00, March-June & Sept-Oct until 19:00, Nov-Feb until 18:00; Calle San Agustín 8, a block away from the cathedral; +34 952 127 600, www.museopicassomalaga.org).

For a look at Spanish art just prior to Picasso, visit the **Museo Carmen Thyssen Málaga,** which features 19th-century paintings with mostly Andalusian themes from the collection of Carmen Cervera. (A former Miss Spain, she's the widow of industrial tycoon Hans Heinrich von Thyssen-Bornemisza, whose famous art collection is housed in Madrid.) There are more than 250 works by Sorolla, Fortuny, Zuloaga, Zurbarán, and other Spanish artists exhibited in the restored 16th-century Palace of Villalón (€10, includes audioguide; Tue-Sun 10:00-20:00, closed Mon; Plaza Carmen Thyssen/Calle Compañía 10; +34 902 303 131, www.carmenthyssenmalaga.org).

Málaga Connections: The slick, modern **train station** is a five-minute walk away: Exit at the far corner of the bus station, cross the street, and enter the big shopping mall (with a food court upstairs) labeled *Estación María Zambrano*—walk a few minutes through the mall to the train station. Modern lockers are by the entrance to tracks 10-11 (security checkpoint), and car-rental offices are by the entrance to tracks 1-8. A TI kiosk is in the main hall, just before the shopping mall. To go from the train station to the bus station, enter the mall by the TI kiosk and follow signs to *estación de autobuses.*

Málaga's big, airy, U-shaped **bus station,** on Paseo de los Tilos, has long rows of counters for the various bus companies. In the center of the building is a helpful info desk that can print out schedules for any destination and point you to the right ticket window (daily 7:00-22:00, tel.+34 952 350 061, estabus.malaga.eu). Flanking the information desk on either side are old-fashioned pay lockers (buy a token—*una ficha*—from the automat, no access overnight). The station also has several basic eateries, newsstands, and WCs.

From Málaga by Train to: Ronda (1/day, 2 hours, 1 more with transfer in Antequera), **Algeciras** (1/day, 4 hours, transfer in Algeciras—same as Ronda train, above), **Madrid** (hourly, 3 hours on AVE), **Córdoba** (5/day, 1 hour; more expensive but no faster on AVE), **Granada** (4/day, 1.5-3.5 hours, 1 transfer—bus is better), **Sevilla** (5/day, 2 hours on Avant; 4/day, 3 hours on slower regional trains), **Jerez** (4/day, 4 hours, transfer in Córdoba or Sevilla), **Barcelona** (6/day on AVE, 6 hours; 1 direct). Train info: +34 912 320 320, www.renfe.com.

From Málaga by Bus to: Nerja (1-2/hour, 1.5 hours, Alsa),

Ronda (15/day Mon-Fri, 8-10/day Sat-Sun, 2 hours, Damas and S. Nieves), **Algeciras** (hourly, 2-3 hours, Avanza), **La Línea de Concepción/Gibraltar** (5/day, 3 hours, Avanza), **Tarifa** (2/day, 2.5-4 hours, Avanza), **Sevilla** (6/day direct plus 2/day from Málaga's airport, 3 hours, Alsa), **Granada** (hourly, 1.5-2 hours, Alsa), **Córdoba** (4/day, 2-3.5 hours, Alsa), **Madrid** (6/day, 6 hours, Interbus/Daibus), **Marbella** (hourly, 1 hour, Avanza). Bus info: Alsa (www.alsa. es), Damas (www.damas-sa.es), Interbus/Daibus (www.interbus. es), Avanza (www.avanzabus.com).

FUENGIROLA AND TORREMOLINOS

The most built-up part of the region, where those most determined to be envied settle down, is a bizarre world of Scandinavian package tours, flashing lights, pink flamingos, multilingual menus, and all-night happiness. Fuengirola is like a Spanish Mazatlán with a few older, less-pretentious budget hotels between the main drag and the beach. The water here is clean and the nightlife fun and easy. The once-idyllic Torremolinos has been strip-malled and parking-metered.

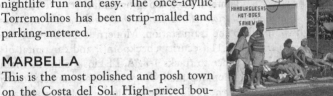

MARBELLA

This is the most polished and posh town on the Costa del Sol. High-priced boutiques, immaculate streets set with intricate pebble designs, and beautifully landscaped squares testify to Marbella's position on the world-class-resort scene. Have a *café con leche* on the beautiful Plaza de Naranjos in the old city's pedestrian section. Wander down to modern Marbella and the high-rise beachfront apartment buildings to walk along the wide promenade lined with restaurants. Check out the beach. Marbella is an easy stop on the Algeciras-Málaga bus route (as you exit the bus station, take a left to reach the center of town). You can also catch a handy direct bus here from the Málaga airport (€9.50, roughly every 1-2 hours, fewer off-season, 45 minutes, www.avanzabus.com).

SAN PEDRO DE ALCÁNTARA

This town's relatively undeveloped sandy beach is popular with young travelers. San Pedro's neighbor, Puerto Banús, is "where the world casts anchor." This luxurious, Monaco-esque jet-set port, complete with casino, is a strange mix of Rolls-Royces, yuppies, boutiques, rich Arabs, and budget browsers.

Gibraltar

One of the last bits of the empire on which the sun never set, Gibraltar is an unusual mix of Anglican propriety, "God Save the Queen" tattoos, English bookstores, military memories, and tourist shops. It's understandably famous for its dramatic Rock of Gibraltar, which rockets improbably into the air from an otherwise flat terrain, dwarfing everything around it. If the Rock didn't exist, some clever military tactician would have tried to build it to keep an eye on the Strait of Gibraltar.

Britain has controlled this highly strategic spit of land since taking it by force in 1704, in the War of Spanish Succession. In 1779, while Britain was preoccupied with its troublesome overseas colonies, Spain (later allied with France) declared war and tried to retake Gibraltar; a series of 14 sieges became a way of life, and the already-imposing natural features of the Rock were used for defensive purposes. During World War II, the Rock was further fortified and dug through with more and more strategic tunnels. In the mid- to late-20th century, during the Franco period, tensions ran high—and Britain's grasp on the Rock was tenuous.

Strolling Gibraltar, you can see that it was designed as a modern military town (which means it's not particularly charming). But in recent decades the economy has gone from one dominated by the military to one based on tourism (as, it seems, happens to many empires). On summer days and weekends, the tiny colony is inundated by holiday-goers, primarily the Spanish (who come here for tax-free cigarettes and booze) and British (who want a change in weather but not in culture). Glitzy high-rise resorts have sprouted up between the stout fortresses and ramparts, as if trying to create a mini-Monaco.

Though it may be hard to imagine a community of about 30,000 that feels like its own nation, real Gibraltarians, as you'll learn when you visit, are a proud bunch. They were evacuated during World War II, and it's said that after their return, a national spirit was forged. If you doubt that, be here on Gibraltar's main holiday—September 10—when everyone's decked out in red and white, the territory's colors.

Gibraltarians have a mixed and interesting heritage. Spaniards call them Llanitos (yah-NEE-tohs), meaning "flat" in Spanish, though the residents live on a rock. The locals—a fun-loving

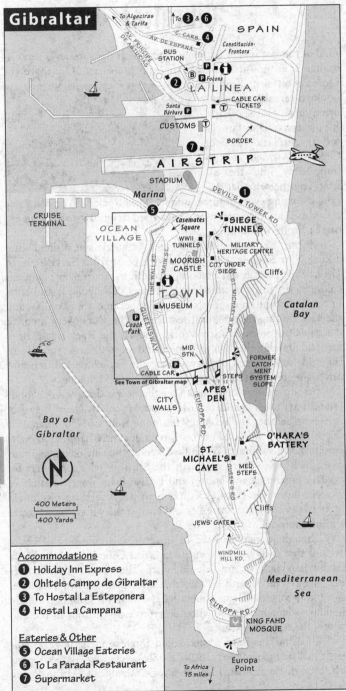

Gibraltar

To Algeciras & Tarifa

SPAIN

To ❸ & ❻

C. CARB.

AV. DE ESPAÑA

AV. PRINCIPE DE ASTURIAS

❹

Constitución-Frontera

BUS STATION

P

P ❷ B

Focona

Santa Bárbara

P

LA LINEA

CABLE CAR TICKETS

CUSTOMS T

BORDER

❼

AIRSTRIP

STADIUM

Marina

DEVIL'S TOWER RD.

❶

CRUISE TERMINAL

❺

OCEAN VILLAGE

Casemates Square

WWII TUNNELS

SIEGE TUNNELS

MILITARY HERITAGE CENTRE

CITY UNDER SIEGE

Cliffs

MOORISH CASTLE

LINE WALL RD.

MAIN ST.

TOWN

MUSEUM

QUEENSWAY

Coach Park

MID. STN.

CABLE CAR

P

ST. MICHAEL'S RD.

Catalan Bay

FORMER CATCH-MENT SYSTEM SLOPE

STEPS

APES' DEN

CITY WALLS

EUROPA RD.

See Town of Gibraltar map

Bay of Gibraltar

O'HARA'S BATTERY

ST. MICHAEL'S CAVE

QUEEN'S RD.

MED. STEPS

400 Meters

400 Yards

Cliffs

JEWS' GATE

WINDMILL HILL RD.

Mediterranean Sea

EUROPA RD.

KING FAHD MOSQUE

To Africa 15 miles

Europa Point

Accommodations
❶ Holiday Inn Express
❷ Oh!tels Campo de Gibraltar
❸ To Hostal La Esteponera
❹ Hostal La Campana

Eateries & Other
❺ Ocean Village Eateries
❻ To La Parada Restaurant
❼ Supermarket

SOUTH COAST

and tolerant mix of British, Spanish, and Moroccan, virtually all of whom speak the Queen's English—call their place "Gib."

From a traveler's perspective, Gibraltar—with its quirky combination of Brits, monkeys, and that breathtaking Rock—is an offbeat detour that adds some variety to a Spanish itinerary. If you're heading to Gibraltar from Spain (as you almost certainly are), be aware most Spaniards still aren't thrilled with this enclave of the Commonwealth on their sunny shores. They basically ignore the place—so, for example, if you're inquiring about bus schedules, don't ask how to get to Gibraltar, but rather to La Línea de la Concepción, the neighboring Spanish town. A passport is required to cross the border.

PLANNING YOUR TIME

Make Gibraltar a day trip (or just one overnight); rooms are expensive compared to Spain. Avoid visiting on a Sunday, when just about everything except the cable car is closed.

Before you walk across the border, decide whether you want to take the cable car to the top of the Rock or visit it via a private taxi tour, which you can book online or hire on the spot at a taxi stand just inside the border (see "By Taxi Tour" under "Sights in Gibraltar," later). Skip the heavily advertised big-bus tour.

If you decide on the cable car, stop at the Gibraltarinfo window on the left before passport control, next to the La Línea taxi stand. If the cable car is running, buy tickets here and take the free shuttle directly to the cable-car station, where you can join the Fast Track line and avoid some of the wait. Ride to the peak for Gibraltar's ultimate top-of-the-rock view.

Then, either walk down—taking in the Apes' Den, siege tunnels, and other sights—or ride the cable car back into town. From the lower cable-car station, follow my self-guided town walk all the way back to Casemates Square. Spend your remaining free time in town before returning to Spain. Note that all the old walls and fortresses make Gibraltar tricky to navigate. Ask for directions: Locals speak English.

Tourists who stay overnight find Gibraltar a peaceful place in the evening, when the town can just be itself. No one's in a hurry. Families stroll, kids play, seniors window shop, and everyone chats...but the food is still not that great.

There's no reason to take a ferry from Gibraltar to visit Morocco—for many reasons, it's a better side trip from Tarifa (specifics covered on page 901).

SOUTH COAST

Orientation to Gibraltar

Gibraltar is a narrow peninsula (three miles by one mile) jutting into the Mediterranean. Virtually the entire peninsula is dominated by the steep-faced Rock itself. The locals live down below in the long, skinny town at the western base of the mountain (much of it on reclaimed land).

For tips on little differences between Gibraltar and Spain—from area codes to electricity—see "Helpful Hints," later.

Tourist Information: Gibraltar's main TI is at John Mack-intosh Square, a 10-minute walk south of Casemates Square, near City Hall. Pick up a free map and—if it's windy—confirm that the cable car is running (Mon-Fri 9:00-16:30, Sat 9:30-15:30, closed Sun, +350 200 45000, www.visitgibraltar.gi). At the border, there's a TI window in the customs building (Mon-Fri 9:00-16:30, closed Sat-Sun, +350 200 50762).

ARRIVAL IN GIBRALTAR

No matter how you arrive, you'll need your passport to cross the border. These directions will get you as far as the border; from there, see "Getting from the Border into Town."

By Bus: Spain's La Línea de la Concepción bus station is a five-minute walk from the Gibraltar border. To reach the border, exit the station and bear left toward the Rock (you can't miss it). If you need to store your bags, you can do so at the Gibraltar Airport (see "Helpful Hints," later).

By Car: You don't need a car in Gibraltar. It's simpler to park in La Línea and just walk across the border.

Freeway signs in Spain say *Algeciras* and *La Línea*, often pre-tending that Gibraltar doesn't exist until you're very close. After taking the La Línea-Gibraltar exit off the main Costa del Sol road, your best bet is to follow signs for *Aduana de Gibraltar* (Gibraltar customs).

The Santa Bárbara parking lot is closest to the border, with room for 650 cars. Ignore anyone who claims to be a cashier and only pay as you leave, at machines or the official booth (€2.20/hour, €10/day). If Santa Bárbara is full, try a bit farther away at ei-ther Parking Constitución-Frontera or Parking Focona. La Línea's main square—Plaza de la Constitución—covers a huge under-ground parking garage; just look for the blue "P" signs (€18.20/day). The Focona underground lot is also handy (€2.40/hour, €16.50/day, on Avenida 20 de Abril, near the bus station). You'll also find blue-

Spain vs. Gibraltar

Spain has been annoyed about Gibraltar ever since Great Britain nabbed this prime 2.5-square-mile territory in 1704 (during  the War of Spanish Succession) and was granted it through the Treaty of Utrecht in 1713. Although Spain long ago abandoned efforts to reassert its sovereignty by force, it still tries to make Gibraltarians see the error of their British ways. Over the years Spain has limited Gibraltar's air and sea connections, choked traffic at the three-quarter-mile border, and even messed with the local phone system in efforts to convince Britain to give back the Rock. Still, given the choice—which they got in referenda in 1967 and 2002—Gibraltar's residents steadfastly remain Queen Elizabeth's loyal subjects, voting overwhelmingly (99 percent in the last election) to continue as a self-governing British dependency. Brexit has raised new questions about the relationship, since 96 percent of the territory unsuccessfully voted to remain in the EU. Gibraltar continues to negotiate with Spain to prevent a hard border and stay within the Schengen Area.

lined pay parking spots in this area (signs give time limits). From the square, it's a five-minute stroll to the border, where you can catch a bus or taxi into town (see "Getting from the Border into Town," below).

If you do drive into Gibraltar, customs checks at the border create a bottleneck. There's often a 30-minute wait during the morning rush hour into Gibraltar and during the evening rush hour back out. Once in Gibraltar, drive along the harbor side of the ramparts (on Queensway—but you'll see no street name). There are big parking lots here and at the cable-car terminal. Parking is generally free—if you can find a spot (it's tight during weekday working hours). By the way, while you'll still find English-style roundabouts, cars here stopped driving on the British side of the road in the 1920s.

Getting from the Border into Town

The "frontier" (as the border is called) is a chaotic hubbub of travel agencies, confused tourists, crafty pickpockets, and duty-free shops (you may see people standing in long lines, waiting to buy cheap cigarettes). The guards barely even look up as you flash your pass-

port. Note that as soon as you cross the border, the currency changes from euros to pounds (see "Helpful Hints," next).

To reach downtown, you can walk (20 minutes), catch a bus, or take a taxi. To get into town by **foot,** walk straight across the runway (look left, right, and up), then head down Winston Churchill Avenue. Angle right at the second roundabout, then walk along the fortified Line Wall Road to Casemates Square.

From the border, you can ride **bus #5** (regular or London-style double-decker, runs every 15 minutes, €2.10/£1.40 one-way) three stops to Market Square (just outside Casemates Square) or stay on to Cathedral Square, at the center of town. From Market Square, Gibraltar **city buses** head to various points on the peninsula—a useful route for most tourists is bus #2 (€2/£1.80 one-way, €9/£6 all-day ticket) which goes to the cable-car station and Europa Point, Gibraltar's southernmost point. Border buses and city buses have different, nontransferable tickets (drivers accept either currency and give change).

A **taxi** from the border is pricey (€9/£6 to the cable-car station). If you plan to join a taxi tour up to the Rock (see "Sights in Gibraltar," later), note that you can book one right at the border.

HELPFUL HINTS

Gibraltar Isn't Spain: Gibraltar, a British colony, uses different coins, currency (see below), and stamps than those used in Spain. Note that British holidays such as the Queen's (official) birthday (on a Saturday in June) and Bank Holidays are observed, along with local holidays such as Gibraltar's National Day (Sept 10).

Use Pounds, not Euros: Gibraltar uses the British pound sterling (£1 = about $1.30). Like other parts of the United Kingdom, Gibraltar mints its own Gibraltar-specific banknotes and coins featuring local landmarks, people, and historical events—offering a colorful history lesson. Gibraltar's pounds are not generally accepted in the UK, so try to use up your Gibraltar bills before you leave.

Merchants in Gibraltar also accept euros...but at an unfavorable exchange rate. You'll save money by hitting up an ATM and taking out what you'll need (look along Main Street). Before you leave, stop at an exchange desk and change back what you don't spend (at about a 5 percent loss), since Gibraltar currency is hard to change in Spain.

On a quick trip, don't bother drawing out cash; you can buy things with your credit card or use euros (though you may get pounds back in change).

Phones: To dial a Gibraltar phone number, use the local calling code 350 (not rather than 34 (Spain).

Hours: Even though it's part of the UK, Gibraltar follows a siesta schedule, with some businesses closing from 13:00 to 15:00 on weekdays and shutting down at 14:00 on Saturdays until Monday morning.

Electricity: Gibraltar uses the British three-pronged plugs (not the European two-pronged ones). Your hotel may be able to loan you an adapter.

Baggage Storage: There's no luggage storage at the bus station, but there is a bag check at the Gibraltar Airport, which is right across the border (£3-6/item; go to airport info desk in departures hall).

John Mackintosh Hall: This is your classic British effort to provide a cozy community center. Without a hint of tourism, the upstairs library welcomes drop-ins to enjoy local newspapers and free Wi-Fi (Mon-Fri 9:30-19:30, closed Sat-Sun, 308 Main Street, +350 200 78000).

Activities: The **King's Bastion Leisure Centre** fills an old fortification (the namesake bastion) with a modern entertainment complex just outside Cathedral Square. On the ground floor is a huge bowling alley; upstairs are an ice-skating rink and a three-screen cinema (www.leisurecinemas.com). Rounding out the complex are bars, restaurants, discos, and lounges (daily 9:00-24:00, +350 200 44777, www.kingsbastion.gov.gi).

Monkey Alert: The monkeys, which congregate at the Apes' Den on the Rock, have been spoiled by being fed by tourists, and can be aggressive. Keep your distance and don't feed them; it's best to have no food with you when you visit the Rock.

Gibraltar Walk

Gibraltar town is long and skinny, with one main street (called Main Street). Stroll the length of it from the cable-car station to Casemates Square, following this little self-guided walk. A good British pub and a room-temperature pint of beer await you at the end.

From the cable-car terminal, turn right (as you face the harbor) and head into town. Soon you'll come to the **Trafalgar Cemetery,** a reminder of the colony's English military heritage; two of the seamen who died of wounds after the 1805 Battle of Trafalgar are buried here, and those who perished during the battle were consigned to the sea. (Of course, Lord Nelson was

Town of Gibraltar

Accommodations
1. The Eliott Hotel
2. To Hoilday Inn Express
3. Bristol Hotel

Eateries
4. The Clipper Pub
5. The Star Bar
6. The Living Room
7. Gauchos Steakhouse
8. All's Well Pub
9. Market Place & Produce Market
10. Supermarket
11. Marks & Spencer; Bon Bon Cash & Carry
12. The Waterfront & other eateries

Other
13. John Mackintosh Hall
14. Governor's Residence
15. Convent Guard Room
16. John & Yoko's Wedding Site
17. King's Bastion Leisure Centre

SOUTH COAST

To Ocean Village
To Airstrip & Border
WATERPORT
GLACIS RD.
CORRAL RD.
SMITH DORRIEN AVE.
FISHMARKET LN.
Casemates Square
To Siege Tunnels
MOORISH CASTLE
COOP
QUEENSWAY
RECLAMATION RD.
LINE WALL ROAD
PARLIAMENT LN.
IRISH TOWN
TUCKEY'S
MAIN ST.
ENGINEER LN.
TARIK PASSAGE
CASTLE RD.
WILLIS'S RD.
MARKET
BELL LN.
CORNWALL'S
John Mackintosh Square
COLLEGE LN.
KING ST.
ST. MARY
GOVERNOR'S ST.
P. EDWARD'S RD.
SYNAGOGUE
GIBRALTAR MUSEUM
Common-wealth Park
LIBRARY
LIBRARY RAMP
GEORGE'S
Cathedral Square
GOV. LN.
MAIN ST.
QUEENSWAY
Queensway Quay & Marina
TOWN RANGE
PRINCE EDWARD'S RD.
FLAT BASTION RD.
CHARLES V WALL
Trafalgar Cemetery
SOUTHPORT GATES
ROSIA RD.
BOYD RD.
EUROPA RD.
To Top of the Rock
CABLE CAR STATION
Botanical Gardens
To St. Michael's Cave

100 Meters
100 Yards

taken to London and buried in St. Paul's Cathedral.) Nearby is the **Charles V wall**—a reminder of Gibraltar's Spanish military heritage—built in 1540 by the Spanish to defend against marauding pirates. Gibraltar was controlled by Moors (711-1462), Spain (1462-1704), and then the British (since 1704). Passing through the Southport Gates, you'll see one of the many blue-and-white history plaques posted about town.

Heading into town, you pass the tax office, then **John Mackintosh Hall,** which has free Wi-Fi and a copy of today's *Gibraltar Chronicle* upstairs in its library. The *Chronicle* comes out Monday through Friday and has covered the news since 1801. For a low-key weekday lunch with the locals, the recommended **Living Room** café is just down the street in the Methodist church.

The pedestrian portion of Main Street begins near the **governor's residence.** The British governor of Gibraltar took over a Franciscan convent, hence the name of the local White House: The Convent. The formally classic Convent Guard Room, facing the governor's residence, is good for photos.

Gibraltar's courthouse stands behind a **small tropical garden,** where John and Yoko got married back in 1969 (as the ballad goes, they "got married in Gibraltar near Spain"). Sean Connery did, too. Actually, many Brits like to get married here because weddings are cheap, fast (only 48 hours' notice required), and legally recognized as British.

Main Street now becomes a **shopping drag.** You'll notice lots of colorful price tags advertising tax-free booze, cigarettes, and sugar (highly taxed in Spain). Lladró porcelain, while made in Valencia, is popular here (because it's sold without the hefty Spanish VAT—Value-Added Tax). The Catholic cathedral retains a whiff of Arabia (as it was built on the remains of a mosque), while the big **Marks & Spencer department store** helps vacationing Brits feel at home.

Continue several more blocks through the bustling heart of Gibraltar. If you enjoy British products, this is your chance to stock up on Cadbury chocolates, digestive biscuits, wine gums, and Weetabix—but you'll pay a premium, since it's all "imported" from the UK.

The town (and this walk) ends at **Casemates Square.** While a lowbrow food circus today, it originated as a barracks and place for ammunition storage. When Franco closed the border with Spain in 1969, Gibraltar suffered a labor shortage, as Spanish guest workers could no longer commute into Gibraltar. The colony countered by inviting Moroccan workers to take their place—ending a nearly 500-year Moroccan absence, which began when the Moors fled in 1462. As a result, today's Moroccan community dates only from the 1970s. Whereas the previous Spanish labor force simply com-

muted in to work, the Moroccans needed apartments, so Gibraltar converted the Casemates barracks for that purpose. Cheap Spanish labor has crept back in, causing many locals to resent store clerks who can't speak proper English.

If you go through the triple arches at the end of the square, you'll reach the covered **produce market** and food stalls. Across the busy road a few minutes' walk farther is the well-marked entrance to the **Ocean Village** boardwalk and entertainment complex (described later, under "Eating in and near Gibraltar").

Sights in Gibraltar

IN TOWN

▲Gibraltar Museum

Built atop a Moorish bath, this museum tells the story of a chunk of land that has been fought over for centuries. Start with the cheerleading 15-minute video overview of the story of the Rock—a worthwhile prep for the artifacts (such as ancient Roman anchors made of lead) you'll see in the museum. Then wander through the remains of the 14th-century Moorish baths. Upstairs you'll see military memorabilia, a 15-foot-long model of the Rock (compare it with your map to see all the changes), wonderful century-old photos of old Gibraltar, paintings by local artists, and, in a cave-like room off the art gallery, a collection of prehistoric remains and artifacts. The famous skull of a Neanderthal woman found in Gibraltar is a copy (the original is in the British Museum in London). Unearthed in Forbes' Quarry (at the north end of the Rock) in 1848, this was the first Neanderthal skull ever discovered. No one realized its significance until a similar skull found years later in Germany's Neanderthal Valley was correctly identified—stealing the name, claim, and fame from Gibraltar.

Cost and Hours: £5, Mon-Fri 10:00-18:00, Sat until 14:00, closed Sun, on Bomb House Lane near the cathedral, www.gibmuseum.gi.

ON THE ROCK OF GIBRALTAR

The actual Rock of Gibraltar—specifically, the Upper Rock Nature Reserve—is the colony's best sight. Its main draws are the stupendous view from the very top and the temperamental resident monkeys you'll encounter on the way down. Other attractions include a hokey cave (St. Michael's), a glass "skywalk" and a suspension bridge, and the impressive Great Siege Tunnels drilled into the rock.

Visiting the Rock: You have two options for touring the Rock—take a taxi tour or ride the cable car.

The **taxi tour** includes entry to St. Michael's Cave and the

Great Siege Tunnels, a couple of extra stops, and running commentary from your licensed cabbie/guide. Because the cable car doesn't get you very close to the cave and tunnels (and doesn't cover cave and tunnel admission), take the taxi tour if you'll be visiting these sights and don't want to walk.

The **cable car** takes you to the very top of the Rock (which the taxi tours don't). You can then take a long, steep, scenic walk down, connecting the various sights by foot as you stroll along paved lanes (it's a pleasant walk down).

There's no reason to take a big-bus tour (advertised and sold all over town) considering how fun and easy the taxi tours are. Private cars are not allowed high on the Rock.

Taxi Tour of the Rock

Minivans driven by cabbies trained and licensed to lead these 1.5-hour trips stand by at the border and at various points in town (including Cathedral Square, John Mackintosh Square, Casemates Square, Trafalgar Cemetery, and near the cable-car station). They charge £31/person (likely 4-person minimum, includes nature reserve and sights ticket, +350 200 70027, www.

gibraltartaxiassociation.com). Taxi tours and big buses do the same 1.5-hour loop tour with four stops: a Mediterranean viewpoint (called the Pillar of Hercules), St. Michael's Cave (15-minute visit), a viewpoint near the top of the Rock where you can get up close to the monkeys, and the Great Siege Tunnels (20-minute visit). Buddy up with other travelers and share the cost.

Cable Car to the Summit

Buy your tickets for the six-minute cable-car ride at the GibraltarInfo kiosk just before the border, at the cable-car station, or online at GibraltarInfo.gi/Cable-Car. Tickets bought at the Gibraltarinfo kiosk or online include Fast Track entry as well as shuttle service to and from the border. The cable car won't run if it's windy or rainy; if the weather is questionable, ask at the Gibraltarinfo kiosk or the TI before heading to the station.

To take in all the sights, I recommend **hiking down** instead of taking the cable car back. Simply hiking down without visiting the sights is enjoyable, too. Approximate hiking times: from the top of the cable car to St. Michael's Cave—25 minutes; from the cave to the Apes' Den—20 minutes; from the Apes' Den to the Great

...nels—30 minutes; from the tunnels back into town, pass-...e Moorish Castle—20 minutes. Total walking time, from top ...bottom: about 1.5 hours (on paved roads with almost no traffic), not including sightseeing. For hikers, I've connected the dots with directions later.

In winter (Nov-March), the cable car stops halfway down for those who want to get out, gawk at the monkeys, and take a later car down—but you'll probably see monkeys at the top anyway.

Cost: A round-trip ticket is £18, but you won't be able to leave the upper cable-car area. If you plan to ride up and walk down, you'll need to buy a £32 one-way cable car plus Nature Reserve ticket (includes entry to all sights).

Hours: The cable car runs every 10 minutes, or continuously in busy times (daily from 9:30; April-Oct last ascent at 19:15, last descent at 19:45; Nov-March last ascent at 17:15, last descent at 17:45). Lines can be long if a cruise ship is in town.

Information: http://gibraltarinfo.gi/cable-car.

Multimedia Guide/App: The included multimedia guide explains what you're seeing from the spectacular viewpoints up top (pick it up at the well-marked booth at the summit—must leave ID and return before leaving the summit—or download the guide using free Wi-Fi).

Sights on the Rock

The various sights on the Rock keep the same hours: Daily 9:30-19:15, until 18:15 late Oct-late March.

▲▲▲The Summit

The cable car takes you to the real highlight of Gibraltar: the summit of the spectacular Rock itself. The limestone massif is nearly

a mile long, rising 1,400 feet with very sheer faces. According to legend, this was one of the Pillars of Hercules (paired with Djebel Musa, another mountain across the strait in Morocco), marking the edge of the known world in ancient times. Local guides say that these pillars are the only places on the planet where you can see two seas and two continents at the same time.

In AD 711, the Muslim chieftain Tarik ibn Ziyad crossed over from Africa and landed on the Rock, beginning the Moorish conquest of Spain and naming the Rock after himself—Djebel-Tarik ("Rock of Tarik"), which became "Gibraltar."

At the cable-car terminal at the top of the Rock you'll find view terrace and a café. From here you can explore old ramparts and drool at the 360-degree view of Morocco (including the Rif Mountains and Djebel Musa), the Strait of Gibraltar, the bay stretching west toward Algeciras, and the twinkling Costa del Sol arcing eastward. The views are especially crisp on brisk off-season days. Below you (to the east) stretches a vast, vegetation-covered slope—part of a giant catchment system built by the British in the early 20th century to collect rainwater for use by the military garrison and residents. Broad sheets once covered this slope, catching the rain and sending it through channels to reservoirs carved inside the rock. (Gibraltar's water is now provided through a desalination system.)

• *Up at the summit, you'll likely see some of the famed...*

▲▲Apes of Gibraltar

The Rock is home to about 200 "apes" (actually, tailless Barbary macaques—a type of monkey). Taxi tours stop at the Apes' Den, but if you're on your own, you'll probably see them at the top and at various points on the walk back down (basically, the monkeys cluster anywhere that tourists do—hoping to get food). The males are bigger, females have beards, and newborns are black. They live about 15 to 20 years. Legend has it that

as long as the monkeys remain here, so will the Brits. (According to a plausible local legend, when word came a few decades back that the ape population was waning, Winston Churchill made a point to import reinforcements.) Keep your distance from the monkeys. Guides say that for safety reasons, "they can touch you, but you can't touch them." And while guides may feed them, you shouldn't—it disrupts their diet and encourages aggressive behavior, not to mention it's illegal and there's a £500 fine. Beware of the monkeys' kleptomaniac tendencies; they'll ignore the peanut in your hand and claw after the full bag in your pocket. Because the monkeys associate plastic bags with food, keep your bag close to your body: Tourists who wander by absentmindedly, loosely clutching a bag, are apt to have it stolen by a purse-snatching simian.

• *If you're hiking down, you'll find that your options are clearly marked at most forks. I'll narrate the longest route down, which passes all the sights en route.*

From the top cable-car station, exit and head downhill on the well-

(toward Africa). You'll go by the viewpoint for taxi tours
monkeys hanging around, waiting for tour groups to come feed
em), pass under a ruined observation tower, and eventually reach a
wide part of the road. Most visitors will want to continue to St. Michael's Cave (skip down to that section), but you also have an opportunity to hike (or ride a shuttle bus) steeply up to...

O'Hara's Battery

At 1,400 feet, this is the actual highest point on the Rock. A massive 9.2-inch gun sits on the summit, where a Moorish lookout post
once stood. The battery was built after World War I, and the last
test shot was fired in 1974. Locals are glad it's been mothballed—
during test firings, they had to open their windows, which might
otherwise have shattered from the pressurized air blasted from this
gun. You can go inside to see not only the gun but the powerful
engines underneath that were used to move and aim it. The iron
rings you see every 30 yards or so along the military lanes around
the Rock once anchored pulleys used to haul up guns like the huge
one at O'Hara's Battery.

• From the crossroads below O'Hara's Battery, the right (downhill) fork
leads down to a restaurant and shop, then the entrance to...

▲St. Michael's Cave

Studded with stalagmites and stalactites, eerily lit, and echoing
with classical music, this cave is dramatic, corny, and slippery when
wet. Considered a one-star sight since Neolithic times, the cave
was alluded to in ancient Greek legends—when it was believed to
be the Gates of Hades (or the entrance of a tunnel to Africa). All
taxi tours stop here (entry included in cost of taxi tour). This sight
requires a long walk for cable-car riders. Walking through takes
about 15 minutes; you'll pop out at the gift shop.

• From here, most will head down to the Apes' Den (see next paragraph),
but serious hikers can curl around to **Jews' Gate** at the tip of the Rock,
then circle around the back of the Rock on the strenuous **Mediterranean
Steps** (leading back up to O'Hara's Battery). To do this, turn sharply
left after St. Michael's Cave and head for Jews' Gate, the closest thing in
Gibraltar to "wilderness." If this challenging 1.5-to-2-hour hike sounds
enjoyable, get details at the TI before setting out.

The more standard route is to continue downhill. At the three-way
fork, you can take either the middle fork (more level) or the left fork (hill-
ier, but you'll see monkeys at the Apes' Den) to the Great Siege Tunnels.
The **Apes' Den**, at the middle station for the cable car, is a scenic terrace
where monkeys tend to gather, and where taxi tours stop for photo ops.

Continue on either fork (they converge), following signs for Great
Siege Tunnels, for about 30 more minutes. Eventually you'll reach a
terrace with flags of the United Kingdom and Gibraltar (until Brexit,
the EU flag flew as well) and a fantastic view of Gibraltar's airport,

the "frontier" with Spain, and the Spanish city of La Línea de la Concepción. From here, the Military Heritage Centre is beneath your feet (described later), and it's a short but steep hike up to the...

▲Great Siege Tunnels

Also called the Upper Galleries, these chilly tunnels were blasted out of the rock by the Brits during the Great Siege by Spanish and French forces (1779-1783).

The clever British, safe inside the Rock, wanted to chip and dig to a highly strategic outcrop called "The Notch," ideal for mounting a big gun. After blasting out some ventilation holes for the miners, they had an even better idea: Use gunpowder to carve out a whole network of tunnels with shafts that would be ideal for aiming artillery. Eventually they excavated St. George's Hall, a huge cavern that housed seven guns. These were the first tunnels inside the Rock; more than a century and a half later, during World War II, 30 more miles of tunnels were blasted out. Hokey but fun dioramas help recapture a time when Brits were known more for conquests than for crumpets.

• *Hiding out in the bunker below the flags (go down the stairs and open the heavy metal door—it's unlocked) is the...*

Military Heritage Centre

This small, one-room collection features old military photographs from Gibraltar. The second room features a poignant memorial to the people who "have made the supreme sacrifice in defense of Gibraltar."

• *From here, the road switchbacks down into town. At each bend in the road you'll find one of the next three sights.*

City Under Siege

This hokey exhibit is worth a quick walk-through if you've been fascinated by all this Gibraltar military history. Displayed in some of the first British structures built on Gibraltar soil, it re-creates the days of the Great Siege, which lasted more than three and a half years (1779-1783)—one of 14 sieges that attempted but failed to drive the Brits off the Rock. With evocative descriptions, some original "graffiti" scratched into the wall by besieged Gibraltarians, and some dioramas, the exhibit explains what it was like to live on the Rock, cut off from the outside world, during those challenging times.

War II Tunnels

...ovember 1942, American Army General Dwight D. Eisen-...wer took charge of Operation Torch, the Allies' plan to occupy French North Africa. From a network of passageways deep within the Rock of Gibraltar, Eisenhower and British admiral Andrew Browne Cunningham conducted the first major collaboration between British and American forces in World War II.

During the war, Britain added 30 miles of tunnels beneath this strategic rock. It was enough space to accommodate an entire city—including a water distillation plant, barracks, generators, repair shops, hospitals, and a telephone exchange—for soldiers and civilians engaged in wartime operations against the Nazis.

Tours of the tunnels leave approximately hourly and are accompanied by an audioguide (included in the nature reserve ticket). You can simply show up and join the next available tour, or check at the TI or Gibraltar info kiosk about reserving a time.

Moorish Castle

Actually more a tower than a castle, this recently restored building is basically an empty shell. (The tourist board recently tried to change the name to the more diplomatic "Medieval Castle"...but it *is* Moorish, so the name didn't stick.) It was constructed on top of the original castle built in AD 711 by the Moor Tarik ibn Ziyad, who gave his name to Gibraltar.

• *The tower marks the end of the Upper Rock Nature Reserve. Heading downhill, you begin to enter the upper part of modern Gibraltar. While you could keep on twisting down the road, keep an eye out for staircase shortcuts into town (most direct are the well-marked Castle Steps).*

Nightlife in Gibraltar

Compared to the late-night bustle of Spain, where you'll see young parents out strolling with their toddlers at midnight, Gibraltar is extremely quiet after-hours. Main Street is completely dead (except for a few lively pubs, mostly a block or two off the main drag). Head instead to the **Ocean Village** complex, a five-minute walk from Casemates Square, where the boardwalk is lined with bars, restaurants, and a casino. Another waterfront locale—a bit more sedate—is the **Queensway Quay Marina.** (Both areas are described later, under "Eating in and near Gibraltar.") Kids love the **King's Bastion Leisure Centre** (see "Helpful Hints," earlier).

Some pubs, lounges, and discos—especially on Casemates Square—offer live music (look around for signs, or ask at the TI). The **Eliott Hotel** hosts free live jazz on Thursday and Saturday evenings.

SOUTH COAST

Sleeping in and near Gibraltar

Gibraltar is not a good value for accommodations. There are only a handful of hotels and (disappointingly) no British-style B&Bs. As a general rule, rooms are either bad or overpriced. The places I list here range from about £95 to more than £200 a night.

As an alternative, consider staying at one of my recommended accommodations in La Línea de la Concepción, across the border from Gibraltar in Spain, where hotels can be are a better value.

IN GIBRALTAR TOWN

$$$$ The Eliott Hotel, with four stars, boasts a rooftop pool with a view, a fine restaurant, bar, terrace, inviting sit-a-bit public spaces, and 123 modern, stylish business-class rooms—all with balconies (air-con, elevator, pay parking, centrally located at 2 Governor's Parade, up Library Street from main drag, +350 200 70500, www.eliotthotel.com, eliott@ocallaghancollection.com).

$$$ The **Holiday Inn Express**, near the north end of the Rock, has 120 reliably comfortable rooms (air-con, elevator, limited free parking, 21 Devil's Tower Road, +350 200 67890, www.ihg.com, reservations@hiexgibraltar.com).

$$ Bristol Hotel offers 60 basic, slightly worn English rooms in the heart of Gibraltar—noise can be a problem (air-con, elevator, swimming pool; limited free parking; 10 Cathedral Square, +350 200 76800, www.bristolhotel.gi, reservations@bristolhotel.gi).

ACROSS THE BORDER, IN LA LÍNEA

Staying in Spain—in the border town of La Línea de la Concepción—offers an affordable, albeit less glamorous, alternative to sleeping in Gibraltar. The streets north of the bus station are lined with inexpensive *hostales* and restaurants. These options are just a few blocks from the La Línea bus station and an easy 15-minute walk to the border—get directions when you book. All but Oh!tels Campo are basic, family-run *hostales,* offering simple, no-frills rooms at a good price for a mix of tourists and refinery and port laborers.

$$$ Oh!tels Campo de Gibraltar is a huge blocky building, with 227 cookie-cutter rooms spread over seven floors. It's a big, friendly business-class hotel that is just blocks from the border, around the corner from the bus station. It's also easy to access by car as it's on the main road coming into town. Stay here if you rented a car to avoid lining up to cross the border. Ask for a room on the top floors with expansive views of the Rock (air-con, elevator, pool, large patio, underground pay parking, at the intersection of Avenida Príncipe de Asturias and Avenida del Ejército, +34 956 178 213,

www.ohtelscampodegibraltar.es,   recepcion.campodegibraltar@
ohtels.es).

$ Hostal La Campana has 17 rooms at budget prices. Run by
Ivan and his dad Andreas, this place is simple, clean, and friendly
but lacks indoor public areas except for its breakfast room (air-
con, elevator, limited free street parking, pay parking in nearby
underground garage, just off Plaza de la Constitución at Calle
Carboneros 3, +34 956 173 059, www.hostalcampana.es, info@
hostalcampana.es).

$ Hostal La Esteponera is a budget option in the center of
La Línea. The rooms are very basic, but the communal lounge has
a microwave and fridge available for guests to use (ceiling fans, pay
air-con, cheaper rooms with shared bath, Calle Carteya 10, +34
956 176 668, book on Booking.com).

Eating in and near Gibraltar

IN GIBRALTAR TOWN

Take a break from *jamón* and sample some English pub grub: fish-
and-chips, meat pies, jacket potatoes (baked potatoes with fillings),
or a good old greasy English breakfast. Eng-
lish-style beers include chilled lagers and
room-temperature ales, bitters, and stouts.
In general, the farther you venture away
from Main Street, the cheaper and more
local the places become; I've listed a few of
my favorites. Or explore one of Gibraltar's
more upscale developments at either end of
the old town: Ocean Village or Queensway
Quay.

Downtown, near Main Street

$ The Clipper pub offers filling meals—in-
cluding some salads and all-day breakfast—
and Murphy's stout on tap (Mon-Sat 9:00-22:00, Sun from 10:00,
on Irish Town Lane, +350 200 79791).

$$ The Star Bar, which claims to be Gibraltar's oldest bar, is
on a quiet side street with an unpubby, modern interior (Mon-Sat
8:00-23:00, Sun 9:00-16:00, 12 Parliament Lane, off Main Street
and across from Corner House Restaurant, +350 200 75924).

$ The Living Room is a fast, cheap-and-cheery café run by
the Methodist church with a missionary's smile. It's upstairs in the
Methodist church on Main Street (Mon-Fri 10:00-16:00, closed
Sat-Sun and Aug, volunteer-run, no alcohol, 100 yards past the
governor's residence at 297 Main Street, +350 200 77491).

$$$ Gauchos is a classy, atmospheric steakhouse just outside

Casemates Square (Mon-Sat 18:30-23:00, Sun 12:00-16:00, 1 Fish Market Lane, +350 200 59700).

Casemates Square Food Circus: The big square at the entrance of Gibraltar contains a variety of restaurants, ranging from fast food (fish-and-chips joint, Burger King, and Pizza Hut) to inviting pubs spilling out onto the square. The **$$ All's Well** pub serves everything from a full English breakfast to salads or fish-and-chips, and offers pleasant tables with umbrellas under leafy trees (food served daily 10:00-19:00, open later for drinks, +350 200 72987). Fruit stands and cheap takeout food stalls bustle just outside the entry to the square at the **Market Place** (Mon-Sat 9:00-14:00, closed Sun).

Groceries: The Spanish supermarket chain **Eroski** has two locations in Gibraltar: between the border and the airstrip at 12 Winston Churchill Avenue; and in the ICC building, just outside Casemates Square on Line Wall Road (daily 8:00-21:00, ICC location closed Sat). The **Bon Bon Cash & Carry** minimarket is on the main drag, off Cathedral Square (daily 9:30-19:00, Main Street 239). Nearby, **Marks & Spencer** has a small food market on the ground floor, with fresh-baked pastries and lots of UK snacks (Mon-Fri 9:00-19:00, Sat 9:30-17:00, closed Sun).

Ocean Village

This development is the best place to get a look at the bold new face of Gibraltar. Formerly a dumpy port, it's been turned into a swanky marina fronted by glassy high-rise condo buildings. The boardwalk arcing around the marina is packed with shops, restaurants, and bars—Indian, Mexican, sports bar, pizza parlor, Irish pub, fast food, wine bar, and more. Anchoring everything is

Gibraltar's casino. While the whole thing can feel a bit corporate, it offers an enjoyable 21st-century contrast to the "English village" vibe of Main Street (which can be extremely sleepy after-hours).

Queensway Quay Marina

To dine in yacht-club ambience, stroll the marina and choose from a string of restaurants serving the boat-owning crowd. When the sun sets, the quay-side tables at each of these places are prime dining real estate. **$$$ The Waterfront Restaurant** serves upscale bistro fare in its lounge-lizard interior and at great marina-side

tables outside (daily 10:00-22:00, +350 200 45666). Other options include Indian, Italian, trendy lounges, and (oh, yeah) Spanish.

IN LA LÍNEA

The pedestrian street Calle Real, several blocks north of the La Línea bus station, is lined with inexpensive cafeterias, restaurants, and tapas bars. La Línea doesn't offer anything out of the ordinary, but you could try the local indoor/outdoor ambience of **La Parada** for *pescadito frito*—typical Andalusian batter-fried fish (Calle Duque de Tetuán 2, Plaza de la Iglesia, +34 856 121 669).

Gibraltar Connections

BY BUS

The nearest bus station to Gibraltar is in La Línea de la Concepción in Spain, five minutes from the border—ask at the Gibraltar TI for schedules. The nearest train station is at Algeciras, which is the region's main transportation hub (for Algeciras connections, see the end of this chapter).

From La Línea de la Concepción by Bus to: Algeciras (2/hour, fewer on weekends, 45 minutes), **Tarifa** (6/day, 1 hour), **Málaga** (5/day, 3 hours), **Ronda** (no direct bus, transfer in Algeciras; Algeciras to Ronda: 1/day, 3 hours), **Granada** (3/day, 6-7 hours, change in Malaga), **Sevilla** (5/day, 4.5 hours), **Córdoba** (1/day, 5 hours), **Madrid** (1-2/day, 8 hours).

BY PLANE

From Gibraltar, you can fly to various points in Britain and Morocco: British Airways flies to London Heathrow (www.britishairways.com) and EasyJet connects to several UK airports (www.easyjet.com). The airport is easy to reach; you can't enter town without crossing its runway (code: GIB, www.gibraltarairport.gi).

ROUTE TIPS FOR DRIVERS

Gibraltar to Nerja (125 miles/200 km): Barring traffic problems, the trip along the Costa del Sol is smooth and easy by car—much of it on a new toll highway. Just follow the coastal highway east. After Málaga, follow signs to *Almería* and *Motril*.

Tarifa

Mainland Europe's southernmost town is whitewashed and Arab-feeling, with a lovely beach, an old castle, restaurants swimming in fresh seafood, inexpensive places to sleep, enough windsurfers to sink a ship, and best of all, hassle-free boats to Morocco. Though Tarifa is pleasant, the main reason to come here is to use it as a springboard to Tangier, Morocco—a remarkable city worth ▲▲.

As I stood on Tarifa's town promenade under the castle, looking across the Strait of Gibraltar at the almost-touchable Morocco, my only regret was that I didn't have this book to steer me clear of gritty Algeciras on earlier trips. Tarifa, with 35-minute boat transfers to Tangier departing about every hour, is the best jumping-off point for a Moroccan side trip, as its ferry route goes directly to Tangier Ville Port in the city center. (For details on taking the ferry to Tangier from Tarifa—or joining an easy belly-dancing-and-shopping excursion-type tour—see the Morocco & Tangier chapter.)

In Tarifa, don't expect blockbuster sights or a Riviera-style beach resort. Tarifa is a seaside town where you just feel good to be on vacation. Its atmospheric old town and long, broad stretch of wild Atlantic beachfront more than compensate for the more functional parts of this port city. The town is a hip and breezy mecca among windsurfers, drawn here by the strong winds created by the bottleneck at the Strait of Gibraltar.

Tarifa is mobbed with young adventure seekers in July and August (but can be quiet off-season). This crowd from all over Europe (and beyond) makes Tarifa one of Spain's trendiest-feeling towns. It has far more artsy, modern hotels than most Spanish towns its size, a smattering of fine boutique shopping, and restaurant offerings that are atypically eclectic for normally same-Jane Spain—you'll see vegetarian and organic, Italian and Indian, gourmet burgers and teahouses, and on each corner, it seems, there's a stylish bar-lounge with techno music, mood lighting, and youthful Europeans just hanging out.

SOUTH COAST

Orientation to Tarifa

The old town, surrounded by a wall, slopes gently up from the water's edge (and the port to Tangier). The modern section stretches farther inland from Tarifa's fortified gate.

Tourist Information: The TI faces the port at the top of Paseo de la Alameda (Mon-Fri 10:00-13:30 & 16:00-18:00, Sat-Sun 10:00-13:30; hours may be longer in summer and shorter on slow or bad-weather days, +34 956 680 993, www.turismodetarifa.com).

Experiencia Tarifa: This organization, run by can-do Quino of the recommended Hostal Alborada, produces a good free magazine with a town map featuring hotels, restaurants, a wide array of activities, and bus schedules.

ARRIVAL IN TARIFA

By Bus: The bus station is on Calle Batalla del Salado, about a five-minute walk from the old town. (The TI also has bus schedules.) Buy tickets directly from the driver if the station is closed (Mon-Thu 7:30-12:30 & 14:15-18:00, Fri 8:30-12:30 & 14:15-16:45, Sun 14:00-20:00, closed Sat, bus station +34 956 684 038, Comes bus company +34 902 199 208, www.tgcomes.es). To reach the old town, walk away from the wind turbines perched on the mountain ridge.

By Car: If you're staying in the center of town, follow signs for *Alameda* or *Puerto,* and continue along Avenida de Andalucía to Tarifa's one traffic light. Take the next left after the light, down Avenida de la Constitución, to find the TI, ferry ticket offices, and the port. Look for free street parking throughout the town, including just beyond the port customs building (on the harbor, at the base of the castle). During the busiest summer months (July-Aug), these street spaces fill up, in which case you'll need to use a pay lot or park farther out, in the new town (for more on parking, see "Helpful Hints," next).

HELPFUL HINTS

Laundry: Find a clean self-service machine at the welcoming **Eco Lavandería Bio Market** just behind the bus station in the new town (daily 7:00-22:00, staff available Mon-Sat 9:30-14:00, Calle Mar del Norte 2, +34 603 755 618).

Tickets and Tours to Morocco: Two ferry companies—FRS and InterShipping—make the crossing between Tarifa and Tangier. You can buy tickets for either boat at the port. FRS also has a couple of offices in town (see page 901 for information on buying ferry tickets). If taking a tour to Tangier, you can book through a ferry company, your hotel, or one of several travel agencies in Tarifa (for details, see page 882).

Long-Term Parking: Tangier day-trippers looking to leave their cars for the day or overnight can try one of these four long-term lots: on Calle San Sebastián, just off Avenida de Andalucía (€15/24 hours, long-stay discounts, secured garage); east of the old-town wall (guarded lot just behind the church, €12.45/24 hours); between the bullring and Avenida de Andalucía on Calle Numancia (€15/24 hours, guarded lot); or the port facility (€18/24 hours—show your ferry ticket for a €4 discount).

You can also park for free. Many drivers leave their cars for a few days on the street, especially in free spaces lining the road alongside the port customs building (under the castle). For any street parking, observe the curb color: yellow lines are no-parking areas for visitors. If it's white or unmarked, it's free.

Excursions: Check with **Girasol Adventure** for mountain-bike rentals (€25/day with helmet), guided bike tours, national park hikes, rock-climbing classes, tennis lessons, and, when you're all done...a massage (€30-60). They also offer tours of Tarifa and Bolonia. Activities generally last a half-day and cost around €25-50. Ask Sabine or Chris for details (Mon-Fri 10:00-14:00 & 18:30-20:30, Sat-Sun 11:00-14:00, Calle Colón 12, +34 956 627 037, www.girasol-adventure.com).

Sights in Tarifa

Church of St. Matthew (Iglesia de San Mateo)

Tarifa's most important church, facing its main drag, is richly decorated for being in such a small town. Most nights, it seems life squirts from the church out the front door and into the fun-loving Calle Sancho IV el Bravo.

Cost and Hours: Free, Mon-Sat 8:30-13:00 & 18:00-21:00, Sun 10:00-13:00 & 19:00-21:00; English-language leaflets may be inside on the right.

Visiting the Church: Find the fragment of an **ancient tombstone**—a tiny square (eye-level, about the size of this book) in the wall on the right—next to a chapel with a small iron gate (the third one off the right nave). Probably the most important historical item in town, this stone fragment proves there was a functioning church here during Visigothic times, before the Moorish conquest. The tombstone reads, in a kind of Latin Spanish (try reading it), "Flaviano lived as a Christian for 50 years, a little more or less. In death he received forgiveness as a servant of God on March 30, 674. May he rest in peace." If that gets you in the mood to light a candle, switch on an electric "candle" by dropping in a coin. (It works.)

Head back out into the main nave and face the high altar. A

SOUTH COAST

Accommodations

1 Hotel La Mirada
2 Hostal Alborada
3 La Sacristía
4 Hotel Misiana
5 Dar Cilla Guesthouse & Apartments
6 Casa Blanco
7 Hostal La Calzada
8 Hostal Alameda
9 Hostal Africa
10 Hospedaje Villanueva Tarifa

Eateries & Nightlife

11 El Puerto & El Ancla
12 Rist. La Trattoria
13 Restaurante Morilla
14 Almedina Bar (Flamenco)
15 Mandrágora
16 To Rest. Souk & Surla
17 Bar El Francés
18 Café Bar Los Melli & Bar El Pasillo
19 El Otro Melli
20 Café Central & FIRMM
21 Casino Tarifeño
22 Mesón El Picoteo
23 Confitería La Tarifeña
24 Café Azul
25 Churrería La Palmera
26 Chilimosa

Other

27 Supermarket (2)
28 Mercado (Farmers Market)
29 Girasol Adventure
30 Turmares Tarifa
31 FRS Ferry Office (2)

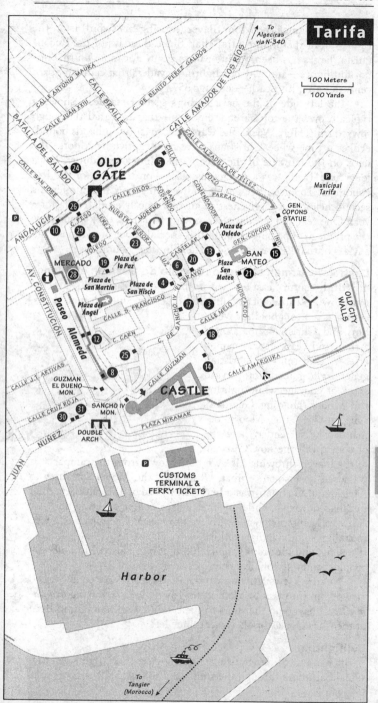

Tarifa

100 Meters
100 Yards

To Algeciras via N-340

OLD GATE

OLD CITY

SAN MATEO

Plaza de Oviedo

Plaza San Mateo

GEN. COPONS STATUE

Municipal Tarifa

OLD CITY WALLS

MERCADO

Plaza de la Paz

Plaza de San Martín

Plaza de San Hiscio

Plaza del Ángel

GUZMAN EL BUENO MON.

SANCHO IV MON.

DOUBLE ARCH

CASTLE

PLAZA MIRAMAR

CUSTOMS TERMINAL & FERRY TICKETS

Harbor

To Tangier (Morocco)

SOUTH COAST

relief of **St. James the Moor Slayer** (missing his sword) is on the right wall of the main central altar. Since the days of the Reconquista, James has been Spain's patron saint. For more on this important figure—and why he's fighting invaders that came to Spain centuries after his death—see page 357.

The left side of the nave harbors several **statues**—showing typically over-the-top Baroque emotion—that are paraded through town during Holy Week. The **Captive Christ** (with hands bound) evokes a time when Christians were held captive by Moors. The door on the left side of the nave is the **"door of pardons."** For a long time Tarifa was a dangerous place—on the edge of the Reconquista. To encourage people to live here, the Church offered a second helping of forgiveness to anyone who lived in Tarifa for a year. One year and one day after moving to Tarifa, they would have the privilege of passing through this special "door of pardons" and a Mass of thanksgiving would be held in their honor.

Castle of Guzmán el Bueno (Castillo de Guzmán el Bueno)

This 10th-century castle is set on the edge of Europe's southernmost town—a strategically important location since Roman times,

acting as a stronghold for Muslims and Christians for almost a thousand years. It was named after a 13th-century Christian general who gained fame in a sad show of courage while fighting the Moors. Holding Guzmán's son hostage, the Moors demanded he surrender the castle or they'd kill the boy. Guzmán refused, even throwing his own knife down from the ramparts. It was used on his son's throat. Ultimately, the Moors withdrew to Africa, and Guzmán was a hero. *Bien.* Today, the ramparts offer fine harbor views while an interpretive center explains how the castle was constructed and displays a modest collection of artifacts, including some original clothing.

Cost and Hours: €4; daily 10:00-16:00, closed Mon off-season; last entry 45 minutes before closing.

Nearby Views: If you skip the castle, you'll get equally good views from the plaza just left of the Town Hall. Following *ayuntamiento* signs, go up the stairs to the ceramic frog fountain in front of the Casa Consistorial, and continue left.

Bullfighting

Tarifa has a third-rate bullring where novices botch fights on occasional Saturdays through the summer. Professional bullfights take

place during special events in August and September. The ring is a short walk from town. You'll see posters everywhere.

▲Whale Watching

Several companies in Tarifa offer daily whale- and dolphin-watching excursions. Over the past four decades, people in this area went from eating whales to protecting them and sharing them with 20,000 visitors a year. The Spanish side of the Strait of Gibraltar is protected as part of El Estrecho Natural Park.

For any of the tours, it's wise (but not always necessary) to reserve one to three days in advance. You'll get a multilingual tour and a two-hour boat trip. Sightings occur on nearly every trip: Dolphins and pilot whales frolic here any time of year (they like the food), sperm whales visit from March through July, and orcas pass through in July and August. In bad weather, trips may be cancelled, or boats may leave instead from Algeciras (in which case, drivers follow in a convoy, people without cars usually get rides from staff, and you'll stand a lesser chance of seeing whales).

The best company is the Swiss nonprofit **FIRMM** (Foundation for Information and Research on Marine Mammals), which gives a 30-minute educational talk before departure. To reserve, call ahead or stop by one of their two offices (€45-65/person, 1-5 trips/day April-Oct, sometimes also Nov, one office around the corner from Café Central at Pedro Cortés 4, second office inside the ferry port, offices open 9:00-21:00, +34 956 627 008, +34 678 418 350, www.firmm.org). If you don't see any whales or dolphins on your tour, you can join another trip for free.

Turmares Tarifa offers a two-hour whale-watching trip March through October (€30) and a three-hour orca trip in July and August (€45; Calle del Alcalde Juan Núñez 3, +34 956 680 741, www.turmares.com).

Isla de las Palomas

Extending out between Tarifa's port and beaches, this island connected by a spit is the actual "southernmost point in mainland Europe." Walk along the causeway, with Atlantic Ocean beaches stretching to your right and a bustling Mediterranean port to your left. Head to the tip, which was fortified in the 19th century to balance the military might of Britain's nearby Rock of Gibraltar. The actual tip, still owned by the Ministry of Defense, is closed to the public, but a sign at the gate still gives you that giddy "edge of the world" feeling.

▲▲Beach Scene

Tarifa's vast, sandy, and untamed beach stretches west from Isla de las Palomas for about five miles. You can walk much of its length on the Paseo Marítimo, a wide, paved walkway that fronts the sand

and surf. Beach cafés and benches along the way make good resting or picnicking stops. Pick up the paseo where the causeway leads out to Isla de las Palomas, near Playa Chica. You'll join dog walkers, runners, and neighbors comparing notes about last night's rainstorm (they get some doozies here). Keep in mind that this is the Atlantic—the waves can be wild and the wind strong (if you're looking for calm, secluded coves, spend your beach time in Nerja instead). On windy summer

days, the sea is littered with sprinting windsurfers, while kitesurfers' kites flutter in the sky. Paddleboarding is also popular.

Those with a car can explore farther (following the N-340 road toward Cádiz). It's a fascinating scene: A long string of funky beach resorts is packed with vans and fun-mobiles from northern Europe under mountain ridges lined with modern energy-generating windmills. The various resorts each have a sandy access road, parking, a cabana-type hamlet with rental gear, beachwear shops, a bar, and a hip, healthy restaurant. I like Valdevaqueros beach (five miles from Tarifa), with a wonderful thatched restaurant serving hearty salads, paella, and burgers. Torre de la Peña also has some fun beach eateries.

In July and August, inexpensive buses do a circuit of nearby campgrounds, all on the waterfront (€2, departures about every 1-2 hours, confirm times with TI). Trying to get a parking spot in August can take the joy out of this experience.

Nightlife in Tarifa

You'll find plenty of enjoyable nightspots—the entire town seems designed to cater to a young, international crowd of windsurfers and other adventure travelers. Just stroll the streets of the old town and dip into whichever trendy lounge catches your eye. For something more sedate, the evening paseo fills the parklike boulevard called Paseo de la Alameda (just outside the old-town wall); the Almedina bar hosts flamenco shows every Thursday at 22:30 (at the south end of town, just below Plaza de Santa María, +34 956 680 474); and the theater next to the TI sometimes has musical performances (ask at the TI or look for posters).

SOUTH COAST

Sleeping in Tarifa

Room rates vary with the season: lowest in winter and highest during Easter and from mid-June through September. Many hotels are closed in winter months and reopen the first week of March.

OUTSIDE THE CITY WALL

These hotels are about five blocks from the old town, close to the main drag, Batalla del Salado, in the plain, modern part of town. While in a drab area, they are well-run oases that are close to the beach and the bus station, with free and easy street parking.

$$ Hotel La Mirada, which feels sleek and stark, has 25 mod and renovated rooms—most with sea views at no extra cost. While the place lacks personality, it's well priced and comfortable, with a large roof terrace with views and inviting lounge chairs (elevator, Calle San Sebastián 41, +34 956 680 626, www.hotel-lamirada. com, reservas@hotel-lamirada.com).

$$ Hostal Alborada is a squeaky-clean, family-run 37-room place with two attractive courtyards and modern conveniences. Father Rafael—along with sons Quino (who speaks English and is generous with travel tips), Fali, and Carlos—are happy to help make your Morocco tour or ferry reservation, or arrange any other activities you're interested in. If they're not too busy, they'll even give you a free lift to the port (RS%, air-con, pay laundry, Calle San José 40, +34 956 681 140, www.hotelalborada.com, info@ hotelalborada.com).

INSIDE OR NEXT TO THE CITY WALL

The first three listings are funky, stylish boutique hotels in the heart of town—*muy* trendy and a bit full of themselves.

$$$ La Sacristía, formerly a Moorish stable, now houses travelers who want stylish surroundings. It offers 10 fine and uniquely decorated rooms, mingling eclectic elements of chic Spanish and Asian style. They offer spa treatments, custom tours of the area, and occasional special events—join the party since you won't sleep (sometimes includes breakfast, air-con, massage room, sauna, small roof terrace, very central at San Donato 8, +34 956 681 759, www. lasacristia.net, tarifa@lasacristia.net).

$$$ Hotel Misiana has 15 comfortable, recently remodeled, spacious rooms above a bar-lounge. Their designer gave the place a mod pastel boutique-ish ambience. To avoid noise from the lounge below, which is open until 3:00 in the morning, request a room on a higher floor (minimum stays of 2-4 nights in high season, double-paned windows, elevator, 100 yards directly in front of the church at Calle Sancho IV el Bravo 16, +34 956 627 083, www. misianahotel.com, info@misianahotel.com).

SOUTH COAST

$$$ Dar Cilla Guesthouse & Apartments is a Moroccan-influenced *riad* (or guesthouse), built into the town wall and remodeled into eight chic apartments surrounding a communal courtyard. Each apartment has a kitchen and is decorated in modern Moroccan style, with earth-tone walls, terracotta-tiled floors, and Moroccan rugs (family rooms; 2-, 4-, and 7-night minimums; air-con, large roof terrace with remarkable bird's-eye view over the old town to the sea and Moroccan coastline, just east of the old-town gate at Calle Cilla 7, +34 653 467 025, www.darcilla.com, info@darcilla.com).

$$ Casa Blanco, where minimalist meets Moroccan, is a newer, reasonably priced designer hotel. Each of its seven rooms (all with double beds) is decorated (and priced) differently. The place is decked out with practical amenities (minifridges in premium rooms) as well as romantic touches—loft beds, walk-in showers, and subtle lighting (small roof terrace, reception open 9:00-14:00 only, off main square at Calle Nuestra Señora de la Luz 2, +34 956 681 515, +34 622 330 349, www.hotelcasablanco.es, info@hotelcasablanco.es).

$$ Hostal La Calzada has eight airy, well-appointed rooms right in the lively old-town thick of things, though the management is rarely around (closed Dec-March, air-con, 20 yards from church at Calle Justino Pertinez 7, +34 956 681 492, www.hostallacalzada.com, reservashostallacalzada@gmail.com).

$$ Hostal Alameda, overlooking a square where the local children play, glistens with pristine marble floors and dark red decor. The main building has 11 bright rooms and the annex has 16 more modern rooms; both face the same delightful square (air-con, Paseo de la Alameda 4, +34 956 681 181, www.hostalalameda.com, info@hostalalameda.com, Antonio).

$ Hostal Africa, with 13 bright rooms and an inviting roof terrace, is buried on a very quiet street in the center of town. Its dreamy blue-and-white color scheme and stripped-down feel give it a Moorish ambience (RS%, laundry service, storage for boards and bikes, Calle María Antonia Toledo 12, +34 956 680 220, +34 606 914 294, www.hostalafrica.com, info@hostalafrica.com, charming Eva and Miguel keep the reception desk open 9:00-24:00).

¢ Hospedaje Villanueva Tarifa offers 17 remodeled rooms at budget prices. It's simple, clean, and friendly. It lacks indoor public areas but has an inviting terrace overlooking the old town on a busy street. Reconfirm your reservation by phone the day before you arrive (just west of the old-town gate at Avenida de Andalucía 11, access from outside the wall, +34 956 684 149, www.hospedajevillanuevatarifa.com, hostalvillanueva@hotmail.com).

SOUTH COAST

Eating in Tarifa

I've grouped my recommendations below into two categories: Sit down to a real restaurant meal or enjoy a couple of the many characteristic tapas bars in the old town.

RESTAURANTS
Near the Port

$$$ El Puerto, in an untouristy area near the causeway out to Isla de las Palomas, has a great reputation for its pricey but very fresh seafood. Locals swear that it's a notch or two above the seafood places in town (daily 12:00-16:00 & 20:00-23:30, Avenida Fuerzas Armadas 13, +34 956 681 914).

$$$ Next door, El Ancla offers a more casual seafood alternative and is especially known for the local specialty *croquetas de choco*—delectable hot-and-fluffy croquettes made with squid ink (Tue-Sat 13:00-16:30 & 21:00-23:30, Sun lunch only, closed Mon; Avenida Fuerzas Armadas 15, +34 956 680 913).

$$$ Ristorante La Trattoria is a good option on the Alameda, with cloth-napkin class, friendly staff, and ingredients from Italy. Sit inside, near the wood-fired oven, or out along the main strolling street (June-Sept daily 13:00-16:00 & 19:30-23:00; off-season Thu-Tue dinner only, closed Wed; Paseo de la Alameda, +34 956 682 225).

Near the Church

$$ Restaurante Morilla, facing the church, is on the town's prime piece of people-watching real estate. This is a real restaurant (tapas sold only at the stand-up bar and sometimes at a few tables), with good indoor and outdoor seating. It serves tasty local-style fish, grilled or baked—your server will tell you about today's fish; it's sold by weight, so confirm the price carefully (daily 8:30-24:00, Calle Sancho IV el Bravo 2, +34 956 681 757).

$$$ Mandrágora serves a stylish fusion of Moroccan, Mediterranean, and Asian flavors: lamb shanks with plums and almonds, classic tagines and couscous, generous salads, and the best-anywhere *berenjenas* (eggplant drizzled with honey). It's a sophisticated white-tablecloth place, but casual attire is fine (dinner from 18:30 Mon-Sat, closed Sun, tucked just behind the church at Calle Independencia 3, +34 956 681 291).

In the New Town

These two restaurants are in a residential area just above the beach, about a 15-minute walk along the Paseo Marítimo (or an easy car or taxi ride) from the old town. They're worth a detour for their great food and the chance to see another part of Tarifa. As you

walk the promenade, keep going until you pass the park and public swimming pool, then turn right into the passageway after the
parking lot. You'll find Surla just ahead on the left (in a corner of
the large beige building). Souk is straight ahead, across the street
and up two flights of stairs. To drive there, head up Calle San Sebastián, which turns into Calle Pintor Pérez Villalta. You'll see the
Surla building on the left.

$$ Restaurante Souk serves a tasty mix of Moroccan, Indian,
and Thai cuisine in a dark, exotic, romantic, purely Moroccan am-
bience. The ground floor (where you enter) is a bar and atmospheric
teahouse, while the dining room is downstairs (daily 20:00-24:00,
closed Tue off-season; good wine list, Mar Tirreno 46, +34 956 627
065, friendly Claudia).

$$ Surla, a hipster surfer bar, serves up breakfast, lunch, and
dinner, including wonderfully executed, shareable sushi platters,
along with good coffee. Situated just a few steps above the beachfront walkway, it's at the center of a sprawling zone of après-surf
hangouts. They also offer delivery (daily 9:00-18:00, Sat-Sun until
20:00, dinner served Thu-Mon, Calle Pintor Pérez Villalta 64—
look for the surfboard nailed to the building, +34 956 685 175).

TAPAS

$$ Bar El Francés is a thriving place where "Frenchies" (as the
bar's name implies) Marcial and Alexandra serve tasty little plates
of tapas. This spot is popular for its fine *raciones*—especially octo-
pus *(pulpo a la brasa),* fish in brandy sauce *(pescado en salsa al cognac),*
and garlic-grilled tuna *(atún a la plancha)*—and cheap tapas. It's
standing-and-stools only inside, but the umbrella-shaded terrace
outside has plenty of tables and is an understandably popular spot
to enjoy a casual meal (no tapas on terrace; order off regular menu).
Show this book and Marcial will be happy to bring you a free glass
of sherry (open Fri-Tue long hours June-Aug; closed Thu and Dec-
Feb; Calle Sancho IV el Bravo 21A—from Café Central, follow
cars 100 yards to first corner on left; +34 685 857 005).

$$ Café Bar Los Melli is a local favorite for feasts on barrel tables set outside. This family-friendly place, run by Ramón
and Juani, is a hit with locals and offers a good chorizo sandwich
and *patatas bravas*—potatoes with a hot tomato sauce served on a
wooden board (Thu-Tue 12:00-16:00 & 20:00-23:00, closed Wed;
across from Bar El Francés—duck down the little lane next to the
Radio Alvarez sign and it will be on your left at Calle Guzmán el
Bueno 16, +34 605 866 444). **$$ Bar El Pasillo,** next to Los Melli,
also serves tapas (closed midday and Mon). **$$ El Otro Melli,** run
by Ramón's brother José, is a few blocks away on Plaza de San Mar-
tín.

$$ Café Central is *the* perch for all the cool tourists. With a decidedly international vibe, it's less authentically Spanish than the others I've listed. The bustling ambience and appealing setting in front of the church are better than the food, but they do have breakfast with eggs, good salads, and impressive healthy fruit drinks when fruit is in season (daily 9:00-14:00, off Plaza San Mateo, near the church at Calle Sancho IV el Bravo 9, +34 956 682 877).

$$ Casino Tarifeño is just to the sea side of the church. It's an old-boys' social club "for members only" but offers a musty Andalusian welcome to visiting tourists, including women. Wander through. It has a low-key bar with tapas, a TV room, a card room, and a lounge. There's no menu, but prices are standard. Just point and say the size you want: tapa, *media-ración,* or *ración.* A far cry from some of the trendy options around town, this is a local institution (daily 10:00-22:00).

$$ Mesón El Picoteo is a small, characteristic bar popular with locals and tourists alike for its good tapas and *montaditos.* Eat in the casual, woody interior or at one of the barrel tables out front (Wed-Sun 12:00-16:30 & 20:00-24:00, Mon lunch only, closed Tue; a few blocks west of the old town on Calle Mariano Vinuesa, +34 956 681 128).

OTHER EATING OPTIONS

Breakfast or Dessert: Sweet-tooth destination **$ Confitería La Tarifeña** serves super pastries and flan-like *tocino de cielo* (daily 9:00-21:00, at the top of Calle Nuestra Señora de la Luz, near the main old-town gate).

$ Breezy Café Azul is blissful place to get energized for the day with their generously portioned fruit bowls, Spanish toasts, and fresh juice (daily 9:00-15:00, Calle Batalla del Salado 8).

$ Churrería La Palmera serves breakfast before most hotels and cafés have even turned on the lights—early enough for you to get your coffee fix and/or bulk up on *churros* and chocolate before hopping the first ferry to Tangier (daily 7:00-13:00, Calle Sanchez IV el Bravo 34).

Vegetarian: Literally a small hole in the old town wall, **$ Chilimosa** serves fresh and healthy vegetarian options, homemade desserts, and a variety of teas. It's a rare find in meat-loving Spain. Eat at one of the few indoor tables, or get it to go and find a bench on the nearby Paseo de la Alameda (daily 13:00-16:00 & 19:30-23:00, closed Feb; just west of the old-town gate on Calle del Peso 6, +34 956 685 092).

Windsurfer Bars: If you have a car, head to the string of beaches west of town. Many have bars and fun-loving thatched

restaurants that keep the wet-suit gang fed and watered (see "Beach Scene," earlier).

Picnics: Stop by the *mercado municipal* (farmers market, Mon-Sat 8:00-14:00, closed Sun, in old town, inside gate nearest TI). Other options include the **Supeco** supermarket near my recommended hotels in the new town (Mon-Sat 9:00-22:00, closed Sun, at Callao and San José) or the **Día** supermarket (daily, Calle San Sebastián 30).

Tarifa Connections

TARIFA

From Tarifa by Bus to: La Línea/Gibraltar (6/day, 1 hour), **Algeciras** (hourly, fewer on weekends, 45 minutes, Comes), **Jerez** (1/ day, 2.5 hours, more frequent with transfer in Cádiz, Comes), **Sevilla** (4/day, 2.5-3 hours), and **Málaga** (2/day, 2.5-4 hours, Avanza). Bus info: Comes (www.tgcomes.es), Avanza (www.avanzabus. com).

Ferries from Tarifa to Tangier, Morocco: Two boat companies make the 35-minute journey to Tangier Ville Port about every hour (see the Morocco & Tangier chapter for details).

ALGECIRAS

Algeciras (ahl-*h*eh-THEE-rahs) is only worth leaving. It's useful to the traveler mainly as a transportation hub, with trains and buses to destinations in southern and central Spain (it also has a ferry to Tangier, but it takes you to the Tangier MED port about 25 miles from Tangier city—going from Tarifa is much better). If you're headed for Gibraltar or Tarifa by public transport, you'll almost certainly change in Algeciras at some point.

Everything of interest is on Juan de la Cierva, which heads inland from the port. The **TI** is about a block in (+34 670 948 731), followed by the side-by-side **train station** (opposite Hotel Octavio) and **bus station** three blocks later.

Trains: If arriving at the train station, head out the front door: The bus station is ahead and on the right; the TI is another three blocks (becomes Juan de la Cierva when the road jogs), also on the right; and the port is just beyond.

From Algeciras by Train to: Madrid (2/day, 1 direct, 5.5-6 hours, arrives at Atocha), **Ronda** (3/day, 1.5-2 hours), **Granada** (2/ day, 4-5 hours), **Sevilla** (2/day, 5-6 hours, transfer at Antequera, bus is better), **Córdoba** (1/day direct on Intercity, 3 hours; more with transfer in Antequera, 4 hours), **Málaga** (2/day, 4 hours, transfer in Antequera; bus is faster). With the exception of the route to Madrid, these are particularly scenic trips; the best (though slow) is the mountainous journey to Málaga via Antequera.

SOUTH COAST

Buses: Algeciras is served by five bus companies, all located in the same terminal (called San Bernardo Estación de Autobuses) next to Hotel Octavio and directly across from the train station. The companies generally serve different destinations, but there is some overlap. Lockers are near the platforms—purchase a token at the machines.

From Algeciras by Bus: Comes (www.tgcomes.es) runs buses to **La Línea/Gibraltar** (2/hour, fewer on weekends, 45 minutes), **Tarifa** (hourly, fewer on weekends, 45 minutes), **Sevilla** (4/day, 3-4 hours), **Jerez** (2/day 2.5 hours). Interbus (www.interbus.es) travels to **Madrid** (1/day, overnight, 9 hours).

Avanza (www.avanzabus.com) offers buses to **Málaga** (hourly, 2-3 hours), **Málaga Airport** (6/day, 2 hours), and **Granada** (5/day, 3.5-5.5 hours).

Autocares Valenzuela (www.grupovalenzuela.com) runs the most frequent direct buses to **Sevilla** (7/day, fewer on weekends, 2.5-3 hours) and **Jerez** (6/day, fewer on weekends, 1.5 hours).

Ferries from Algeciras to Tangier, Morocco: Although it's possible to sail from Algeciras to Tangier, the ferry takes you to the Tangier MED Port, which is 25 miles east of Tangier city and a hassle. You're better off taking a ferry from Tarifa, which sails directly to the port in Tangier. If you must sail from Algeciras, buy your ticket at the port; companies sailing this route include FRS (www.frs.es) and Balearia (www.balearia.com). Official offices of the boat companies are inside the main port building, directly behind the helpful little English-speaking info kiosk (8-22 ferries/day, port open daily 6:45-21:45).

ROUTE TIPS FOR DRIVERS

Tarifa to Gibraltar (28 miles/45 km): This short drive takes you past a silvery-white forest of windmills, from peaceful Tarifa past Algeciras to La Línea (the Spanish town bordering Gibraltar). Passing Algeciras, continue in the direction of Estepona. At San Roque, take the La Línea-Gibraltar exit.

MOROCCO

Morocco Practicalities

Money: The local currency is the Moroccan dirham (10 dh or MAD = about $1), but euros work here, as do dollars and pounds. For a day trip, bring lots of €1 and €0.50 coins for tips, small purchases, and camel rides. If you plan to do anything independently, change some money into Moroccan dirhams or find an ATM upon arrival.

Language: The native language is Arabic (for useful phrases, see the "Moroccan Mix" sidebar, later), but French is also spoken.

Emergencies and Travel Advisories: Dial 190 for police, medical, or other emergencies. For US State Department travel advisories, see www.travel.state.gov.

Time Zone: Morocco is on Greenwich Mean Time (like Great Britain), so it is an hour behind Spain. It observes Daylight Saving Time with Europe, except during the month of Ramadan, when it is two hours behind Spain (meaning that daylight fasting hours end earlier).

Closed Days and Ramadan: Friday is the Muslim day of rest, when most of the country—except Tangier—closes down. On the final day of the holy month of Ramadan, Muslims celebrate Eid (an all-day feast and gift-giving holiday), and travelers may find some less touristy stores and restaurants closed.

Marijuana Alert: In Morocco, marijuana (*kif*) is as illegal as it is popular. As a general rule, just walk right by those hand-carved pipes in the marketplace. Some dealers sell marijuana cheap—and make their profit after you get arrested. Cars and buses are stopped and checked by police routinely throughout Morocco, especially in the north and in the Chefchaouen region, which is Morocco's *kif* capital.

Health: Take commonsense precautions: Eat in clean—not cheap—places. Peel fruit, eat only cooked vegetables, and drink reliably bottled water (Sidi Ali and Sidi Harazem are two good brands). Carry hand sanitizer. When you do get diarrhea—and you should plan on it—adjust your diet (small and bland meals) or fast for a day, and make sure you replenish lost fluids.

Embassies: In Rabat—US embassy +212 537 637 200 (Km 5.7, Avenue Mohamed VI, https://ma.usembassy.gov); Canadian embassy +212 537 544 949 (66 Mehdi Ben Barka Avenue, www.morocco.gc.ca).

Phoning: I've listed phone numbers as you would dial them from a US mobile phone. Morocco's country code is 212. To dial from a Moroccan landline, drop 212 and add a zero before the number. To call from a Spanish landline, dial 00 (Europe international access code), 212 (Morocco country code), and then the number.

Tipping: Most Moroccan waiters expect about a 10 percent tip. For a taxi driver, round up the fare a bit.

Tourist Information: www.visitmorocco.com.

MOROCCO & TANGIER

al-Maghreb • Tanja

Go to Africa. A young country with an old history, Morocco is a photographer's delight and a budget traveler's dream. It's exotic, and easier and more appealing than ever. Along with a rich culture, Morocco offers plenty of contrast—from beach resorts to bustling desert markets, from jagged mountains to sleepy, mud-brick oasis towns. And a visit to Morocco—so close to Europe, yet embracing the Arabic language and Muslim faith—lets a Westerner marinated in anti-Muslim propaganda see what Islam aspires to be...and can be.

From the town of Tarifa in southern Spain, it's just 35 minutes by boat to the Moroccan port city of Tangier, the focus of this chapter. Tangier defies expectations. Ruled by Spain in the 19th century and France in the 20th, it's a rare place where signs are in three languages and English doesn't make the cut. In this Muslim city, you'll find in close proximity a synagogue, Catholic and Anglican churches, and the town's largest mosque. Wind your way from the port to the Grand Socco, pause in the medina's colorful market, and peek through keyhole gates as you follow twisty lanes up to the Kasbah. In Tangier, the roosters, even more than the minarets' call to prayer, make sure the city wakes up early.

For me, this is the most exciting day trip in Europe: You'll get a legitimate taste of North Africa and an authentic slice of an Islamic culture. As you step off the boat, you realize that, culturally, the crossing has taken you farther than your trip from the US to Spain. Morocco needs no museums; its sights are living in the streets.

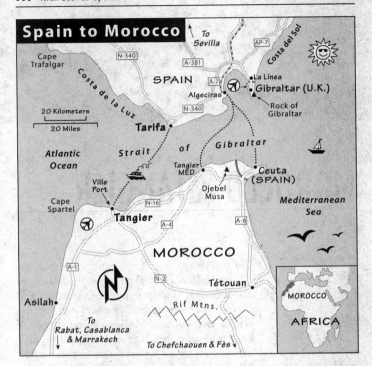

Spain to Morocco

To Sevilla

Cape Trafalgar

N-340

A-381

SPAIN

A-7

Algeciras

La Línea

Gibraltar (U.K.)

Rock of Gibraltar

Costa de la Luz

N-340

20 Kilometers

20 Miles

Tarifa

Atlantic Ocean

Strait of Gibraltar

Tangier MED.

Ceuta (SPAIN)

Ville Port

Djebel Musa

Mediterranean Sea

Cape Spartel

N-16

Tangier

A-4

A-6

MOROCCO

A-1

N-2

Tétouan

Asilah

Rif Mtns.

To Rabat, Casablanca & Marrakech

To Chefchaouen & Fès

MOROCCO

AFRICA

Morocco in a Day?

Though Morocco ("Marruecos" in Spanish; "al-Maghreb" in Arabic) certainly deserves more than a day, many visitors touring Spain see it in a side trip. Guided excursions to Tangier from Tarifa make day-tripping foolproof, if clichéd. But it's just as easy to take a boat on your own and meet a local guide at the port. And, though such a short sprint through Tangier is only a tease, a day or overnight in Tangier gives you a good introduction to the country and its people. All you need is a passport (no visa or shots required) and about €80 for either a tour package or the round-trip ferry crossing.

WITH A TOUR OR ON YOUR OWN?

Your big decisions are whether to visit Tangier solo or with a guided tour, and how long to stay (day trip or overnight). Ask yourself: Do you want the safety and comfort of having Morocco handed to you on a user-friendly platter? Or do you want the independence to see what you want, with fewer cultural clichés and less forced shopping?

Taking a **package tour** is easier but less rewarding. On a package tour, visitors are met at the ferry dock by a guide, toured around town by bus and on foot, shepherded through lunch and a shopping

excursion, then hustled back down to the boat where—five hours after they landed—they return to the First World thankful they don't have diarrhea.

The alternative is to see Tangier **on your own.** Independent adventurers get to see all the sights and avoid all the kitsch. You can catch a morning boat and return to Spain that evening; extend with an overnight in Tangier; or even head deeper into Morocco (see the end of this chapter for ideas).

My preferred approach is a **hybrid:** Get to Tangier "on your own," but arrange in advance to meet a local guide to ease your culture shock and accompany you to your choice of sights (I list a few reliable guides under "Tours in Tangier," later in this chapter). While you'll pay a bit more than joining a package tour, ultimately the cost difference (roughly €20-40 more per person) is pretty negligible, considering the dramatically increased cultural intimacy.

ON YOUR OWN FROM TARIFA

While the trip to Tangier can be made from various Spanish ports, only the Tarifa ferry takes you to the Tangier Ville Port, in the city center (what Spaniards call *Puerto Viejo,* "Old Port"). Note that ferries also travel to Morocco from Algeciras and Gibraltar, but they arrive at the Tangier MED Port, 25 miles from downtown (connected to the Tangier Ville Port by a cheap one-hour shuttle bus). But the most logical route for the typical traveler is the one I'll describe here—sailing from Tarifa to Tangier Ville Port.

Ferry Schedule and Tickets: Two companies make the 35-minute crossing from Tarifa to Tangier; confirm schedules

online for the latest. **FRS** ferries leave Tarifa on odd hours (9:00, 11:00, and so on, except none at 15:00; +34 956 681 830, www.frs.es). **InterShipping** ferries depart Tarifa on even hours (8:00, 12:00, 16:00, and 20:00; +34 956 684 729, www.intershipping.es). Return boats from Tangier to Tarifa typically run from about 8:00 to 22:00. A few crossings a year are canceled due to storms or wind, mostly in winter. Tarifa's modern little terminal has a cafeteria and WCs. **Prices** are roughly €40 each way.

Tickets are easy to get: Buy them online, at the Tarifa ferry terminal (both companies have offices there), through your hotel in Tarifa, or from a Tarifa travel agency. FRS also has offices in Tarifa itself: One is just outside the old-town wall, at the corner of Avenida de Andalucía and Avenida de la Constitución (closed Sun, +34 956 681 830); another is near the port on Calle Alcalde Juan

Time Change

Morocco is one hour behind Spain, except during the month of Ramadan, when it's two hours behind. In general, ferry and other schedules correspond to the local time in each port (if your boat leaves Tangier "at 17:00," that means 5:00 p.m. Moroccan time—not Spanish time). Be sure to change your watch when you get off the boat in Tangier.

Núñez 2 (open daily; see the "Tarifa" map on page 885 of the South Coast chapter for both locations).

Reservations and Check-In: You may need to reserve tickets in advance, especially in July and August and during the month of Ramadan. The popular 8:00 and 9:00 departures can also fill up. You may also need to check in an hour or more before departure—check ferry websites for the latest guidance. Check-in is available online and via the FRS Travel app for FRS ferries.

Ferry Crossing to Tangier: The ferry from Tarifa is a fast Nordic hydrofoil that theoretically takes 35 minutes to cross. In practice, it often leaves late, and the ferries advise passengers to arrive well in advance (up to 1.5 hours) to clear customs. You'll go through Spanish customs at the port and Moroccan customs on the ferry. Whether taking a tour or traveling on your own, you *must* get a stamp in your passport (only available on board): After you leave Tarifa, find the Moroccan immigration officer on the boat (usually in a corner booth that's been turned into an impromptu office) and get a stamp in your passport and an entry paper (which they keep). The ferry is equipped with WCs, a shop, and a snack bar.

Hiring a Guide: To book a local guide to show you around Tangier, see my recommendations under "Tours in Tangier," later.

Returning to Tarifa: Arrive well before your ferry departs (check ferry website for specifics). For the return trip, you must complete a passport-control form and get an exit stamp at the Tangier terminal before you board. Back in Tarifa, you'll show your passport once more to reenter Spain and the European Union.

WITH A PACKAGE TOUR FROM TARIFA

A typical day-trip tour includes a round-trip crossing and a guide who meets your big group at a prearranged point at the Tangier

port, then hustles you through the hustlers and onto your tour bus. All tours offer essentially the same five-hour Tangier experience: a city bus tour, a drive through the ritzy palace neighborhood, a walk through the medina (old town), and an overly thorough look at a sales-starved carpet shop (where prices include a commission for your guide and tour company; some carpet shops are actually owned by the ferry company). Longer tours may include a trip to the desolate Atlantic Coast for some rugged African scenery

and a short camel ride. Any tour wraps up with lunch in a palatial Moroccan setting with live music and belly dancing, topped off by a final walk back to your boat through a gauntlet of desperate merchants.

Sound cheesy? It is. But no amount of packaging can gloss over the depth and richness of this culture.

Tour Prices: Tour tickets are priced roughly the same no matter where you buy them: about €70-95 (sometimes less than the cost of a round-trip ferry ticket—the tours make their margin in shopping kickbacks). Don't worry about which company you select. (They're all equally bad.)

Tour Schedules: Tours leave Tarifa on a variable schedule throughout the day: For example, one tour may depart at 9:00 and return at 15:00, the next could run 11:00-19:00, and the next 13:00-19:00. If you're an independent type on a one-day tour, you could stay with your group until you return to the ferry dock, and then just slip back into town, thinking, "Freedom!"

Overnight Options: If you want a longer visit, you can book a package through the ferry company that includes a one-night stay in a Tangier hotel. There are also two-day options with frills (all meals and excursions outside the city) or no-frills (no guiding or meals—€85 for a basic overnight, €10-17 extra in peak season; two-day options-€95-115).

Booking a Tour: You rarely need to book a package tour more than a day in advance, even during peak season. Book directly with the **ferry company** (see contact information earlier, under "Plan Your Trip"/"Explore Morocco," or visit their offices at the port in Tarifa) or through your **hotel.** There's not much reason to book with a **travel agency,** but offices all over southern Spain and in Tarifa sell ferry tickets and seats on tours.

MOROCCO & TANGIER

Moroccan Mix

While Morocco is clearly a place apart from Mediterranean Europe, it doesn't really seem like Africa either. It's a mix, reflecting its strategic position between the two continents. Situated on the Strait of Gibraltar, Morocco has been flooded by waves of invasions over the centuries: The Berbers, the native population, have had to contend with the Phoenicians, Carthaginians, Romans, Vandals, and more.

The Arabs brought Islam to Morocco in the seventh century AD and stuck around, battling the Berbers in various civil wars. A series of Berber and Arab dynasties rose and fell; the Berbers won out and still run the country today. From the 15th century on, European countries carved up much of Africa. By the early 20th century, most of Morocco was under French control, and strategic Tangier was jointly ruled by multiple European powers as a freewheeling international zone. The country finally gained independence in 1956.

As throughout the Arab world, Morocco has had its share of political unrest in recent years. Widespread but mostly peaceful protests in 2011, influenced by the Arab Spring, called for greater democracy and economic reforms. A new constitution, adopted later that year, gave more power to the legislative branch and the prime minister (although some say King Mohammed VI retained the actual authority). Since that time, crackdowns on protesters (demanding vital services for all) and news-media critics (calling for respect for constitutional rights) have occasionally threatened the country's stability.

Morocco is also struggling to reconcile tensions between Islamist and secular factions within its government and in the region. Bombings attributed to Islamic fundamentalists in 2003 and in 2011 prompted an array of initiatives to counter extremism.

Americans pondering a visit may wonder how they'll be received in this Muslim nation. Al Jazeera blares from televisions in all the bars, but I've sensed no animosity toward American individuals (even on a visit literally days after US forces killed Osama bin Laden). It's culturally enriching for Westerners to experience Morocco—a Muslim monarchy succeeding on its own terms without embracing modern Western "norms."

A feast for the senses, Morocco provides a good dose of culture shock—both good and bad. It's cheap, relatively safe, and private guides are affordable. You'll also encounter sometimes

oppressive friendliness, pushy hustlers and aggressive beggars, brutal heat, and the unfamiliarity of the Arabic language. Annoyingly persistent but generally harmless men make a sport of harassing female travelers. Many visitors develop some intestinal problems by the end of their visit. And in terms of efficiency, Morocco makes Spain look like Sweden. When you cruise south across the Strait of Gibraltar, leave your busy itineraries and split-second timing behind. Morocco must be taken on its own terms. Here things go smoothly only *"Inshallah"*—if God so wills.

A Few Words of Arabic

With its unique history of having been controlled by many different foreign and domestic rulers, Tangier is a babel of languages. Most locals speak Arabic first and French second (all Moroccans learn it in school); sensing that you're a foreigner, they'll most likely address you in French. Spanish ranks third, and English a distant fourth. Communication can be tricky for English-speaking travelers. A little French goes a long way, but learn a few words in Arabic. Have your first local friend help you with the pronunciation:

English	Arabic
Hello ("Peace be with you")	*Salaam alaikum* (sah-LAHM ah-LAY-koom)
Hello (response: "Peace also be with you")	*Wa alaikum salaam* (wah ah-LAY-koom sah-LAHM)
Please	*Min fadlik* (meen FAHD-leek)
Thank you	*Shokran* (SHOH-kron)
Excuse me	*Ismahli* (ees-SMAH-lee)
Yes/No	*Yeh* (EE-yeh)/*Lah* (lah)
Give me five (kids enjoy this)	*Ham sah* (hahm sah)
OK	*Wah hah* (wah hah)
Very good	*Miz yen biz ef* (meez EE-yehn beez ehf)
Goodbye	*Maa salama* (mah sah-LEM-ah)

Moroccans have a touchy-feely culture. Expect lots of hugs if you make an effort to communicate. When greeting someone, a handshake is customary, followed by placing your right hand over your heart. It helps to know that *souk* means a particular market (such as for leather, yarn, or metalwork), while a *kasbah* is loosely defined as a fortress (or a town within old fortress walls). In markets, I sing, "la la la la" to my opponents (*lah shokran* means "No, thank you").

Tangier

Artists, writers, and musicians have always loved Tangier. Delacroix and Matisse were drawn by its evocative light. The Beat generation, led by William S. Burroughs and Jack Kerouac, sought the city's multicultural, otherworldly feel. Paul Bowles found his sheltering sky here. From the 1920s through the 1950s, Tangier was an "international city," too strategic to give to any one nation, and jointly governed by as many as nine different powers, including France, Spain, Britain, Italy, Belgium, the Netherlands...and Morocco. The city was a tax-free zone (since there was no single authority to collect taxes), which created a booming free-for-all atmosphere, attracting playboy millionaires, bon vivants, globetrotting scoundrels, con artists, and expat romantics. Tangier enjoyed a cosmopolitan golden age that, in many ways, shaped the city visitors see today.

Because so many different colonial powers have had a finger in this city, it goes by many names: In English, it's Tangier; in French, Tanger (tahn-zhay); in Arabic, it's Tanja (TAHN-zhah); in Spanish, Tánger (TAHN-hair). Unless you speak Arabic, French is the handiest second language, followed by Spanish and (finally) English.

Because of its international-zone status, Morocco's previous king effectively disowned the city, denying it national funds for improvements. Over time, neglected Tangier became the armpit of Morocco, and the once-grand coastal city earned a reputation as the "Tijuana of Africa." But that has changed. When King Mohammed VI was crowned in 1999, the first city he visited was Tangier. He's enthusiastic about the city and continues to implement his vision to restore Tangier to its former glory.

While the city (with a population of more than one million and growing quickly) still has a ways to go, restorations are taking place on a grand scale: the beach has been painstakingly cleaned, the Kasbah is getting spruced up, pedestrian promenades are popping up, gardens bloom with lush new greenery, and a futuristic soccer stadium hosts professional matches. The city-center port (Tangier Ville) is in the midst of a years-long renovation project that will transform it into a huge, slick marina complex capable of handling mega cruise ships, yachts, and ferries from Tarifa, while more directly connecting the port and old town.

I'm uplifted by the new Tangier—it's affluent and modern

without having abandoned its roots. Many visitors are impressed by the warmth of the Moroccan people. Notice how they touch their right hand to their heart after shaking hands or saying thank you—a kind gesture meant to emphasize sincerity.

PLANNING YOUR TIME

If you're not on a package tour, arrange for a guide to meet you at the ferry dock, hire a guide upon arrival, or head on your own to the big square called the Grand Socco to get oriented (you could walk, but it's easier to catch a taxi from the port; see "Arrival in Tangier," later). Get your bearings with my Grand Socco spin tour, then delve into the old town (the lower medina, with the Petit Socco, market, and American Legation Museum; and the upper medina's Kasbah, with its museum and residential lanes). With more time, take a taxi to sightsee along the beach and through the urban new town on Avenue Mohammed VI before heading back to the port. You'll rarely see other tourists outside the regular tour-group circuit.

Orientation to Tangier

Like almost every city in Morocco, Tangier is split in two: old and new. From the ferry dock you'll see the old town (medina)—encircled by its medieval wall. The old town has the markets, the Kasbah (with its palace and the mosque of the Kasbah—marked by the higher of the two minarets you see), cheap hotels, characteristic guesthouses, homes both decrepit and recently

renovated, and 2,000 wannabe guides. The twisty, hilly streets of the old town are caged within a wall accessible by keyhole gates. The larger minaret (on the left) belongs to the modern Mohammed V mosque—the biggest in town.

The new town, with the TI and modern international-style hotels, sprawls past the port zone to your left. The big square, Grand Socco, is the hinge between the old and new parts of town.

Note that while tourists (and this guidebook) refer to the twisty old town as "the medina," locals consider both the old and new parts of the city center to be medinas.

The city could use more street signs, but it's laid out simply, and maps are posted at the major gates. In the mazelike medina, you'll sometimes find street names on ceramic plaques on the cor-

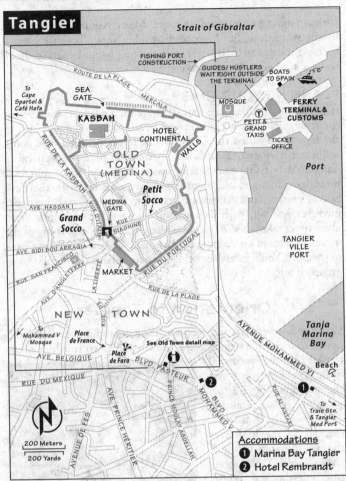

Tangier

Strait of Gibraltar

FISHING PORT
CONSTRUCTION

GUIDES/ HUSTLERS
WAIT RIGHT OUTSIDE
THE TERMINAL

BOATS
TO SPAIN

ROUTE DE LA PLAGE — MERCALA

MOSQUE

FERRY
TERMINAL &
CUSTOMS

To
Cape
Spartel &
Café Hafa

SEA
GATE

KASBAH

PETIT &
GRAND
TAXIS

HOTEL
CONTINENTAL

TICKET
OFFICE

RUE DE LA KASBAH

WALLS

OLD
TOWN
(MEDINA)

Port

AVE. HASSAN I

MEDINA
GATE

Petit
Socco

Grand
Socco

RUE D'ITALIE

RUE
SIAGHINE

AVE. SIDI BOU ARRAQIA

RUE DU PORTUGAL

TANGIER
VILLE
PORT

RUE SAN FRANCISCO

MARKET

RUE DE LA PLAGE

AVE. D'ANGLETERRE

RUE DE LA LIBERTE

RUE FES

To
Mohammed V
Mosque

NEW TOWN

Place
de France

See Old Town detail map

AVENUE MOHAMMED VI

Tanja
Marina
Bay

AVE. BELGIQUE

Place
de Faro

BLVD. PASTEUR

Beach

PRINCE MOULAY ABDELLAH

BLVD. MOHAMMED V

RUE AL ANTAKI

RUE DU MEXIQUE

2

1

To
Train Stn.
& Tangier
Med Port

AVENUE DE FES

AVENUE PRINCE HÉRITIER

N

200 Meters
200 Yards

Accommodations
1 Marina Bay Tangier
2 Hotel Rembrandt

ners of buildings, as well as signs directing you to sights in the Kasbah. You're bound to get turned around, but take heart: Nothing listed under "Sights in Tangier" is more than a 20-minute walk from the port, which is always downhill. Petit Taxis (see under "Getting Around Tangier") are a remarkably cheap godsend for the hot and tired tourist. Use them liberally.

TOURIST INFORMATION

The TI, about a 15-minute gradual uphill walk from the Grand Socco, is not particularly helpful (English is in short supply, but a little French goes a long way). But at least you can pick up the free *Tanger Pocket* guide—in French only—with a town map (Mon-Fri

9:00-16:30, closed Sat-Sun, in new town at Boulevard Pasteur 29, +212 539 948 050).

Travel information, English or otherwise, is rare here, but a good English guidebook available locally is *Tangier and Its Surroundings* by Juan Ramón Roca.

ARRIVAL IN TANGIER
By Ferry

If you're taking a tour, just follow the leader. If you're on your own, head for the Grand Socco to get oriented. Note that ongoing construction at the port may cause some changes from the way things are described here.

Given the hilly nature of the city, a small, cheap, blue **Petit Taxi** is the best way to get into town (described later, under "Getting Around Tangier"). Confirm what you'll pay before you hop in. An honest cabbie will charge you 20-30 dh (about $3) for a ride from the ferry into town; less scrupulous drivers will try to charge closer to 100 dh.

If you're determined to **walk,** it's about 10 gently uphill but potentially confusing minutes through the colorful lanes of the medina. Head out through the port entrance gate (by the mosque), cross the busy street, and head left toward the open lot. Then turn *left* to follow the old city walls, keeping the landmark Hotel Continental on your right. After passing the Hotel Continental, look for a street ramp at the end of the lot. Go up this ramp onto Rue de Portugal, and follow it as it curves around the old city wall. At the corner of the wall, take the first right onto Rue de la Plage. This will lead you past the market and into the Grand Socco.

Another option is the **staircase** on the northern edge of the city wall, which leads steeply but directly up from just across the port to the top of the Kasbah (handy for travelers sleeping in one of my recommended guesthouses). Exit the port as described earlier, then—from the open lot—turn *right* to follow the city walls and find the never-ending stone staircase on your left, just beyond the row of cannons. At the top, head through a gate in the old town walls and emerge in the Place de la Kasbah.

By Plane

The Tangier Ibn Battuta Airport (code: TNG) is small but well organized, with ATMs and cafés. Air Arabia, Iberia, Royal Air

MOROCCO & TANGIER

Maroc, Ryanair, and others fly from here to destinations in Spain and throughout Europe.

Taxis between the airport and downtown Tangier run about 150 dh and take 30 minutes. If spending the night, ask your hotel to book a taxi and confirm the fare in advance (generally the same price as hiring a taxi yourself).

GETTING AROUND TANGIER

Avoid the big, beige Mercedes "Grand Taxis," which don't use their meters (they're meant for longer trips outside the city center and are OK for the airport, but have been known to take tourists for a ride in town...in more ways than one). Look instead for the cheap **Petit Taxis**—blue with a yellow stripe (they fit 2-3 people). These generally use their meters in town, but from the port, they charge whatever they can get, so it's essential to agree on a price up front.

Be aware that Tangier taxis sometimes "double up"—if you're headed somewhere, the driver may pick up someone else who's going in the same direction. However, you don't get to split the fare: Each of you pays full price (even if the other passenger's route takes you a bit out of your way).

When you get in a taxi, be prepared for a white-knuckle experience. Drivers, who treat lanes only as suggestions, prefer to straddle the white lines rather than stay inside them. Pedestrians add to the mayhem by fearlessly darting out every which way along the street. It's best to just close your eyes.

HELPFUL HINTS

Hustler Alert: Unfortunately, most of the English-speaking Moroccans the typical tourist meets are vendors, hustling to make a buck. Haggle when appropriate; prices skyrocket for tourists (see the "Bargaining Basics" sidebar later in this chapter). You'll attract hustlers like flies at every famous tourist site or whenever you pull out a guidebook or map. In the worst-case scenario, they'll lie to you, get you lost, blackmail you, and pester the heck out of you. Wear your money belt, and

assume that con artists are cleverer than you. Never leave your baggage where you can't get back to it without someone else's "help." Consider hiring a guide, since it's helpful to have a translator, and once you're "taken," the rest seem to leave you alone (be aware that anything you buy in a guide's company gets him a hefty commission).

Money: If you're on a tour or only day-tripping, you can stick with euros—most businesses happily take euros or even dollars. But if you're on your own, it's fun to get a pocketful of dirhams. You'll find ATMs in the parking lot of the port (along with exchange services), around the Grand Socco (look just to the left of the archway entrance into the medina), and near the TI along Boulevard Pasteur. ATMs work as you expect them to and are often less hassle than exchanging money. Banks and ATMs have uniform rates.

If you can't find an ATM, exchange desks are quick, easy, and fair. Just understand the buy-and-sell rates—they should be within 10 percent of each other with no other fee. (If you change €50 into dirhams and immediately change the dirhams back, you should have about €45.) Look for the official *Bureaux de Change* offices, where you'll get better rates than at the banks. There are some on Boulevard Pasteur and a handful between the Grand and Petit Soccos. The official change offices all offer the same rates, so there's no need to shop around.

Convert your dirhams back to euros before catching the ferry—it's cheap and easy to do here but very difficult once you're back in Spain.

Keeping Your Bearings: Tangier's maps and street signs are frustrating. I ask in French for the landmark: *"Où est...?"* (Where is...?), pronounced "oo ay," as in *"oo ay medina?"* or *"oo ay Kasbah?"* It can be fun to meet people this way. However, most people who offer to help you (especially those who approach you) are angling for a tip—young and old, locals see dollar signs when a traveler approaches. To avoid getting unwanted company, ask for directions only from people who can't leave what they're doing (such as the only clerk in a shop) or from women who aren't near men. Be aware that most locals tend to navigate by landmarks and don't know the names of the smaller streets (which don't usually have signs). Ask three times and go with the consensus. If there's no consensus, it's time to hop into a Petit Taxi.

Eating with Your Hands: In Islam, the right hand is seen as pure and the left hand as impure. Moroccans who eat with their hands—as many civilized people do in this part of the world—always eat with their right hand; the left hand is for washing.

Mosques: Tangier's mosques (and virtually all of Morocco's) are closed to non-Muslim visitors.

Antiques and Souvenirs: Near the Place de France, **Bazar Tindouf** is a fun place to browse and practice your bargaining skills, with three labyrinthine levels of wall-to-wall, floor-to-ceiling antiques, carpets, pottery, tiles, old photographs, and Moroccan bric-a-brac. Even if you aren't into shopping, it's in-

teresting to browse everyday articles long abandoned by their original owners (daily 10:30-20:30, 64 Rue de la Liberté, +212 539 931 525).

Tours in Tangier

PACKAGE TOURS

For information on guided day-trip tours including the ferry to Tangier from Tarifa in Spain, see "With a Package Tour from Tarifa," earlier.

LOCAL GUIDES

If you're on your own in Tangier, you'll be to street guides what a horse's tail is to flies...all day long. Seriously—it can be exhausting to constantly deflect come-ons from anyone who sees you open a guidebook. If only to have your own translator and a shield from less scrupulous touts who hit up tourists constantly throughout the old town, I recommend hiring a guide.

Getting the Tour You Want: When hiring a guide, be very clear about your interests. Guides, hoping to get a huge commis-

sion from your purchases, can cleverly turn your Tangier day into the Moroccan equivalent of the Shopping Channel. Truth be told, some of these guides would work for free, considering all the money they make on commissions when you buy stuff. State outright that you want to experience the place, its people, and the culture—not its shopping. Request an outline of what your tour will include, and confirm whether the principal guide will be working with you or if you'll be passed off to another team member. Once your tour is under way, if your guide deviates from your expectations, speak up.

What to Expect: While each local guide has specific itineraries, the two basic options are more or less the same: a half-day walking tour around the medina and Kasbah (generally 3-5 hours); or a full-day grand tour that includes the walk around town as well as a minibus ride to outlying viewpoints such as the Caves of Hercules and Cape Spartel (7-8 hours, lunch is generally at your expense in a restaurant the guide suggests). Prices are fairly standard from guide to guide.

If you want, your guide can reserve ferry tickets for you for the same cost as booking directly: He'll give you a reference number

and you'll pick up your tickets at the ferry office in Tarifa (you'll reimburse him when you meet in Tangier).

Recommended Guides: The guides that I've worked with and recommend here speak great English, are easy to get along with, will meet you at the ferry dock in Tangier, and charge fixed rates. Any of them will make your Tangier experience more enjoyable for a negligible cost. If you're very pleased with your guide, he'll appreciate a tip. If you're displeased with your guide, please let me know at RickSteves.com.

Aziz ("Africa") Benami is energetic and fun to spend the day with. He or a reliable member of his guiding team will happily tailor a tour to your interests (half-day walking tour from €15/person, full-day minibus and walking tour from €35/person, traditional Moroccan lunch-€15/person, market visit and cooking class-€65/person or €55 if added to walking tour, RS%—10 percent discount with this book, free cancellation up to one day before travel for Tangier tours, also offers day and multiday trips with flexible itineraries to destinations across Morocco, can arrange ferry tickets from Tarifa with RS%, +212 661 263 335, from the US or Canada dial toll-free +1 888 745 7305, www.abtravels.com, info@abtravels.com).

Aziz Begdouri is an old friend who runs private tours of Tangier and the area, and seems to be on a first-name basis with everyone in town. He also manages the recommended hotel La Maison Blanche. Contact him in advance to decide how he can create a tour for you (€45/person, +212 661 639 332, aziztour@hotmail.com).

Ahmed Taoumi, who has been guiding for more than 35 years, has a friendly and professorial style (half-day walking tour including short panoramic car ride up into town-€18/person, full-day grand tour with minibus-€35/person, also offers minibus side trips to nearby destinations and discounted ferry tickets, +212 661 665 429, taoumitour@hotmail.com).

Abdellatif ("Latif") Chebaa is personable and is dedicated to making visitors comfortable. In addition to Tangier tours, his offerings include cooking classes, a visit to a traditional Berber house, and a trip to a Berber food market outside Tangier (half-day walking tour-€15/person, grand tour-€35/person, other experiences-€25-55/person, +212 661 072 014, visittangier@gmail.com).

Other Options: I've had good luck with the **private guides who meet the boat.** If you're a decent judge of character, try interviewing guides when you get off the ferry to find one you click with, then check for an official license and negotiate a good price. These hardworking, English-speaking guides offer their services for the day for €15.

Tangier's Old Town (Medina)

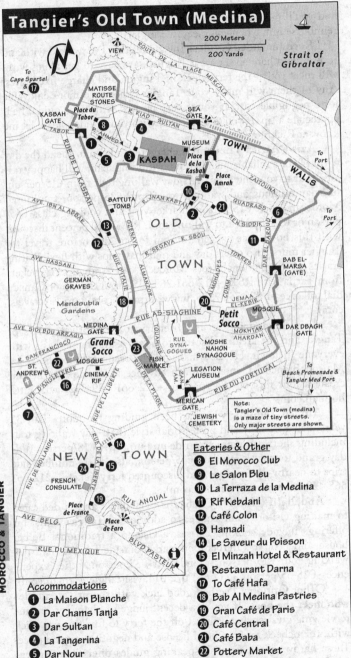

200 Meters
200 Yards

Strait of Gibraltar

ROUTE DE LA PLAGE MERCALA

VIEW

To Cape Spartel & **17**

MATISSE ROUTE STONES

KASBAH GATE

Place du Tabor

R. TABOR

8

1

R. AHMED

5

3

R. RIAD

SULTAN

4

SEA GATE

MUSEUM

Place de la Kasbah

KASBAH

Place Amrah

9

10

TOWN

WALLS

ZAITOUNA

To Port

RUE DE LA KASBAH

AVE. IBN AL ABBAR

BATTUTA TOMB

R. JNAN KABTAN

2

21

QUADRASS

BEN SIDDIK

6

DAR EL BAROUD

13

12

GZENAYA

R. SEGAYA   R. SBOU

OLD

TOWN

TORRES

11

To Port

BAB EL-MARSA (GATE)

AVE. HASSAN I

GERMAN GRAVES

Mendoubia Gardens

AVE. SIDI BOU ARRAQIA

R. SAN FRANCISCO

ST. ANDREW'S

7

22

AVE. D'ANGLETERRE

MEDINA GATE

Grand Socco

MOSQUE

16

CINEMA RIF

RUE D'ITALIE

18

ALMANZOR

RUE AS-SIAGHINE

TOUAHINE

RUE DE LA PLAGE

FISH MARKET

23

RUE SYNA- GOGUES

MOSHE NAHON SYNAGOGUE

ALMOHADES

COMM.

JEMAA EL-KEBIR

20

Petit Socco

MOKHTAR AHARDAN

MOSQUE

DAR DBAGH GATE

LEGATION MUSEUM

RUE DU PORTUGAL

To Beach Promenade & Tangier Med Port

AV. JNAN

MERICAN GATE

JEWISH CEMETERY

Note:
Tangier's Old Town (medina) is a maze of tiny streets. Only major streets are shown.

RUE DE ROLLANDE

14

NEW

TOWN

RUE DE LA LIBERTE

15

24

FRENCH CONSULATE

19

Place de France

AVE. BELG.

Place de Faro

RUE ANOUAL

BLVD PASTEUR

RUE DU MEXIQUE

i

MOROCCO & TANGIER

Accommodations

- **1** La Maison Blanche
- **2** Dar Chams Tanja
- **3** Dar Sultan
- **4** La Tangerina
- **5** Dar Nour
- **6** Hotel Continental
- **7** Grand Hotel Villa de France

Eateries & Other

- **8** El Morocco Club
- **9** Le Salon Bleu
- **10** La Terraza de la Medina
- **11** Rif Kebdani
- **12** Café Colon
- **13** Hamadi
- **14** Le Saveur du Poisson
- **15** El Minzah Hotel & Restaurant
- **16** Restaurant Darna
- **17** To Café Hafa
- **18** Bab Al Medina Pastries
- **19** Gran Café de Paris
- **20** Café Central
- **21** Café Baba
- **22** Pottery Market
- **23** Produce Market
- **24** Bazar Tindouf (Antiques)

Sights in Tangier

GRAND SOCCO AND NEARBY
▲▲Grand Socco

This big, bustling square is a transportation hub, market, popular meeting point, and the fulcrum between the new town and the old town (medina). A few years ago, it was a pedestrian nightmare and a perpetual traffic jam. But now, like much of Tangier, it's on the rise. Many of the sights mentioned in this spin tour are described in more detail later in this chapter.

◐ **Self-Guided Spin Tour:** The Grand Socco is a good place to get oriented to the heart of Tangier. Stand on the square between the fountain and the mosque (the long building with arches and the tall tower). We'll do a slow clockwise spin.

Start by facing the **mosque,** with its long arcade of keyhole arches and colorfully tiled minaret. Morocco is a decidedly Mus-

lim nation, though its take on Islam is moderate, likely owing to the country's crossroads history. Five times a day, you'll hear the call to prayer echo across the rooftops of Tangier, from minarets like this one. Unlike many Muslim countries, Morocco doesn't allow non-Muslims to enter its mosques (with the exception of its biggest and most famous one, in Casablanca). This custom may have originated decades ago, when occupying French foreign legion troops spent the night in a mosque, entertaining themselves with wine and women. Following this embarrassing desecration, it was the French government—not the Moroccans—who instituted the ban that persists today.

Locals say that in this very cosmopolitan city, anytime you see a mosque, you'll find a church nearby. Sure enough, peeking up behind the mosque, you can barely make out the white, crenellated top of the **Anglican church tower** (or at least the English flag above it—a red cross on a white field). A fascinating hybrid of Muslim and Christian architecture, this house of worship is worth a visit (see listing following this section).

Also behind the mosque, you can see parts of a sprawling

Women in Morocco

Some visitors to Tangier expect to see women completely covered head-to-toe by their kaftans. In fact, not all Moroccan women adhere strictly to this religious dress code, especially in cities. Some cover only their hair (allowing their face to be seen), while others eliminate the head scarf altogether. Some women wear only Western-style clothing. This change in dress visibly reflects slowly changing Moroccan attitudes about women's rights.

Morocco is one of the more progressive Muslim countries. As in any border country, contact with other cultures fosters the growth of new ideas. Bombarded with Spanish television and visitors like you, change is inevitable. Another proponent of change is King Mohammed VI, who was only 35 years old when he rose to the throne in 1999. For the first time in the country's history, the king personally selected a female adviser to demonstrate his commitment to change. However, sexual mores are still traditional: Sex outside of marriage is illegal in Morocco, as is homosexual behavior.

But recent times have brought some transformations for women in Morocco. Schools are now coed, although many more boys than girls are enrolled, especially in rural areas. The legal age for women to marry is now 18 instead of 15 (although arranged marriages are still commonplace). Other changes make it more difficult for men to have a second wife. Verbal divorce and abandonment are no longer legal—disgruntled husbands, including the king (who married a commoner for...get this...*love*), must now take their complaints to court. And for the first time, women can divorce their husbands. If children are involved, whoever takes care of the kids gets the house.

Morocco took another step forward with its 2011 constitutional reforms, which guarantee women "civic and social" equality. But it will take time for any progressive changes in the law to be thoroughly translated into practice.

market (featuring pottery and other everyday goods; the far more colorful produce, meat, and fish market is across the square from where you're standing). Traditionally the Grand Socco was Tangier's hub for visiting merchants. The town gates were locked each evening, and vendors who arrived too late spent the night in this area. (Nearby were many caravanserai—old-fashioned inns.) But King Mohammed VI dramatically renovated this square and gave

it a new name: "April 9th 1947 Square," commemorating the date when an earlier king appealed to his French overlords to grant his country its independence. (France eventually complied, peacefully, in 1956.) Mohammed VI tamed the traffic, added the fountain you're standing next to, and turned this into a delightfully people-friendly space.

Spin a few more degrees to the right, where you'll see the crenellated gateway marked *Tribunal de Commerce*—the entrance to the **Mendoubia Gardens,** a pleasant park with a gigantic tree and a quirky history that reflects the epic story of Tangier (see listing following this section). At the top of the garden gateway, notice the Moroccan flag: a green five-pointed star on a red field. The five points of the star represent the five pillars of Islam, green is the color of peace, and red represents the struggles of hard-fought Moroccan history.

Spinning farther right, you'll see the **keyhole arch** marking the entrance to the medina. (If you need cash, an ATM and exchange booths are just to the left of this gateway.) To reach the heart of the medina—the Petit Socco (the café-lined little brother of the square you're on now)—you'd go through this arch and take the first right.

In front of the arch, you'll likely see **day laborers** looking for work. Each one rests next to a symbol of the kind of work he specializes in: a bucket of paintbrushes for a painter, a coil of wiring for an electrician, and a loop of hose for a plumber.

Speaking of people looking for work, how many locals have offered to show you around? ("Hey! What you looking for? I help you!") Get used to it. While irritating, it's understandable. To these very poor people, you're impossibly rich—your pocket change is at least a good day's wage. If someone pesters you, you can simply ignore them, or say *"Lah shokran"* (No, thank you). But be warned: The moment you engage with anyone, you've just prolonged the sales pitch.

Back to our spin tour: To the right of the main arch, and just before the row of green rooftops, is the low-profile archway entrance to another **market** *(souk)*. A barrage on all the senses, this is a fascinating place to explore. The row of green rooftops to the right of the market entrance leads toward Rue de la Plage, with even more market action.

Continue spinning another quarter-turn to the tall, white

building at the top of the square labeled **Cinema Rif.** This historic movie house still plays films (in Arabic, French, and occasionally English). The street to the left of the cinema takes you to Rue de la Liberté, which eventually leads through the modern town to the TI (about a 15-minute walk). Just to the right of the cinema, notice the yellow terrace, which offers the best view over the Grand Socco (just go up the staircase). It's also part of a café, where you can order a Moroccan tea (green tea, fresh mint, and lots of sugar), enjoy the view over the square, and plot your next move.

▲St. Andrew's Church

St. Andrew's Anglican Church, tucked behind a showpiece mosque, embodies Tangier's mingling of Muslim and Christian tradition.

The land on which the church sits was a gift from the sultan to the British community in 1881, during Queen Victoria's era. Shortly thereafter, this church was built. Although fully Christian, the church is designed in the style of a Muslim mosque. The Lord's Prayer rings the arch in Arabic, as verses of the Quran would in a mosque. Knock on the door—Ali or his son Yassin will greet you and give you a "thank you very much" tour. The garden surrounding the church is a tranquil, parklike cemetery. On Sundays and Thursdays, an impromptu Berber farmers market occupies the sidewalk out front (about 9:00-13:00).

Cost and Hours: 20 dh tip appreciated; open daily 9:30-12:30 & 14:30-sunset, closed during Sun services.

Mendoubia Gardens

This pleasant park, accessed through the castle-like archway off the Grand Socco, is a favorite place for locals to hang out. Walk through the gateway to see the trunk of a gigantic banyan tree, which, according to local legend, dates from the 12th century. Notice how the extra supportive roots have grown from the branches down to the ground.

The large building to the left—today the business courthouse *(Tribunal de Commerce)*—was built in the early 20th century to house the representative of the Moroccan king. In those days, back when Tangier was officially an international zone administered by various European

powers, Morocco needed an ambassador of sorts to keep an eye out for the country's interests.

The smaller house on the right (behind the giant tree) is currently a courthouse used exclusively for marriages and divorces, but it was once the headquarters of the German delegation in Tangier. When France established Morocco's protectorate status in 1912, Germany was kept out of the arrangement in exchange for territory along the Congo River. But in 1941, when Germany was on the rise in Europe and allied with Spain's Franco, it joined the mix of ruling powers in Tangier. Although Germans were only here for a short time (until mid-1942), they have a small cemetery in what's now the big park in front of you. Go up the stairs and around the blocky Arabic monument. At the bases of the trees beyond it, you'll find headstones of German graves...an odd footnote in the very complex history of this intriguing city.

Boulevard Pasteur

In the oldest part of the new town, this street is the axis of cosmopolitan Tangier. The street is lined with legendary cafés, the most storied of which is the **Gran Café de Paris,** which has been doing business here since 1920 (daily early until late, at Place de France, just across from the French consulate). Moroccans call this the "tennis" street because while sitting at an al fresco café, your head will be constantly swiveling back and forth to watch the passing parade.

A block farther along is the beautiful Place de Faro terrace, with its cannons and views back to Spain. It's nicknamed "Terrace of the Lazy Ones": instead of making the trek down to the harbor, family members came here in the old days to see if they could spot ships returning with loved ones who'd been to Mecca.

MEDINA (OLD TOWN)

Tangier's medina is its convoluted old town—a twisty mess of narrow stepped lanes, dead-end alleys, and lots of local life spilling out into the streets. It's divided roughly into two parts: the lower medina, with the Petit Socco, synagogue, market, American Legation Museum, and bustling street life; and, at the top, the more tranquil Kasbah.

Lower Medina

A maze of winding lanes and tiny alleys weave through the old-town market area. In an effort to help

orient hopelessly turned-around tourists, Tangier has installed map signboards with suggested walking tours at the major medina gates. Write down the name of the gate you came in, so you can enjoy being lost—temporarily.

Petit Socco

This little square, also called Souk Dahel ("Inner Market"), is the center of the lower medina. Lined with tea shops and cafés, it has a romantic quality that has long made it a people magnet. In the 1920s, it was the meeting point for Tangier's wealthy and influential elite; by the 1950s and '60s, it drew Jack Kerouac and his counterculture buddies. Nursing a coffee or a mint tea here, it's easy to pretend you're a Beat Generation rebel, dropping out from Western society and delving deeply into an exotic, faraway culture.

The Petit Socco is ideal for some casual people-watching over a drink. You can go to one of the more traditional cafés, but **Café Central**—with the large awnings and look of a European café—is accessible, and therefore the most commercialized and touristy (coffees, fruit drinks, and meals; long hours daily).

Moshe Nahon Synagogue

Steps away from the Petit Socco, down a narrow, dead-end alley, is the Moshe Nahon Synagogue (closed Sat, Rue Synagogues 3). When Sephardic Jews were expelled from Spain in 1492, many fled to Morocco. This area was the Jewish quarter in Tangier, and this is one of the oldest synagogues in the city (it's open to the public—ring the bell outside). Built in the late 19th century by a Jewish scholar, the ornately decorated synagogue draws inspiration from Spanish, Islamic, and Jewish design, reminding visitors how the three cultures are historically connected. Plaques on the wooden benches bear the names of members who paid an annual fee for seats—a mark of wealth and privilege. The wooden panel behind the lectern opens to reveal the Torah, written on leather over 600 years old and protected by a traditional cloth covering. To the left is the circumcision altar, and upstairs is the women's gallery (accessed by a staircase in the courtyard), lined with Hebrew scripture proclaiming, "God for everyone" and decorated with marriage embroideries from the early 1900s.

▲▲Market (Souk)

The medina's market, just off the Grand Socco, is a highlight. Wander past piles of fruit, veggies, and olives, countless varieties of bread, and fresh goat cheese wrapped in palm leaves. Phew! You'll find everything but pork.

Entering the market through the door from the Grand Socco, turn right to find butchers, a cornucopia of produce (almost all of it from Morocco), more butchers, piles of olives slathered with an

aromatic and lustrous topcoat of oil, and yet more butchers. The chickens are plucked and hung to show they have been killed according to Islamic guidelines (halal): Animals are slaughtered with a sharp knife in the name of Allah, head toward Mecca, and drained of their blood. The far aisle (parallel and to the left of where you're walking) has more innards and is a little harder to stomach.

Scattered around the market are Berber tribeswomen, often wearing straw hats decorated with ribbons or colorful striped skirts; they ride donkeys to the city from the nearby Rif Mountains, mostly on Tuesdays and Thursdays. (Before taking photos of these women, or any people you see here, it's polite to ask permission.)

Eventually you'll emerge into the large, white fish market;

with the day's catch from both the Mediterranean and the Atlantic, this place is a textbook of marine life.

The door at the far end of the fish market pops you out on the Rue de la Plage; a right turn takes you back to the Grand Socco, but a left turn leads across the street to the (figurative and literal) low end of the market—a world of very rustic market stalls under a corrugated plastic roof. While just a block from the main market, this is a world apart, and not to everyone's taste. Here you'll find cheap produce, junk shops, ragtag electronics, old ladies sorting bundles of herbs from crinkled plastic bags, and far less sanitary-looking butchers than the ones inside the main market hall (if that's possible). Peer down the alley filled with a twitching poultry market, which encourages vegetarianism.

The upper part of the market (toward the medina and Petit Socco) has a handful of food stands but more nonperishable items, such as clothing, cleaning supplies, toiletries, and prepared foods. Scattered around this part of the market are spice-and-herb stalls (usually marked *hérboriste*), offering a fragrant antidote to the meat stalls. In addition to cooking spices, these sell homegrown Berber cures for ailments. Pots hold a dark-green gelatinous goo—a kind of natural soap.

If you're looking for souvenirs, you won't have to find them... they'll find you, in the form of aggressive salesmen who approach you on the street and push their conga drums, T-shirts, and other trinkets in your face. Most of the market itself is more focused on locals, but the medina streets just above the market are loaded with souvenir shops. Aside from the predictable trinkets, the big-ticket items here are tilework (such as vases) and carpets. You'll notice

Bargaining Basics

No matter what kind of merchandise you buy in Tangier, the shopping style is pure Moroccan. Bargain hard! The first price you're offered is simply a starting point, and it's expected that you'll try to talk the price way down. Bargaining can become an enjoyable game if you follow a few basic rules:

Determine what the item is worth to you. Before you even ask a price, decide what the item's value is to you. Consider the hassles involved in packing it or shipping it home.

Determine the merchant's lowest price. Many merchants will settle for a nickel profit rather than lose the sale entirely. Work the cost down to rock bottom, and when it seems to have fallen to a record low, walk away. That last price the seller hollers out as you turn the corner is often the best price you'll get.

Look indifferent. As soon as the merchant perceives the "I gotta have that!" in you, you'll never get the best price.

Employ a third person. Use your friend who is worried about the ever-dwindling budget or who is bored and wants to return to the hotel. This can help to bring the price down faster.

Show the merchant your money. Physically hold out your money and offer him "all you have" to pay for whatever you are bickering over. He'll be tempted to just grab your money and say, "Oh, OK."

If the price is too much, leave. Never worry about having taken too much of the merchant's time. They are experts at making the tourist feel guilty for not buying. It's all part of the game.

many shops have tiles and other, smaller souvenirs on the ground floor, and carpet salesrooms upstairs.

▲▲▲Exploring the Medina

Appealing as the market is, one of the most magical Tangier experiences is to simply lose yourself in the lanes of the medina. A first-time visitor cannot stay oriented—so don't even try. I just wander, knowing that going uphill will eventually get me to the Kasbah and going downhill will lead me to the port. Expect to get a little lost...going around in circles is part of the fun. Pop in to see artisans working in their shops: mosaic tilemakers, thread spinners, tailors. Shops are on the ground level, and the family usually lives upstairs. Doors indicate how many families live in the homes be-

hind them: one row of decoration for one, another parallel row for two.

Many people can't afford private ovens, phones, or running water, so there are economical communal options: phone desks (called *teleboutiques*), baths, and bakeries. If you smell the aroma of baking bread, look for a hole-in-the-wall bakery, where locals drop off their ready-to-cook dough (as well as meat, fish, or nuts to roast). You'll also stumble upon communal taps, with water provided by the government, where people come to wash. Cubbyhole rooms are filled with kids playing video games on old TVs—they can't afford their own at home, so they come here instead.

Go on a photo safari for ornate "keyhole" doors, many of which lead to neighborhood mosques (see photo). Green doors are the color of Islam and symbolize peace. The ring-shaped door knockers double as a place to hitch a donkey.

As you explore, notice that some parts of the medina seem starkly different, with fancy wrought-iron balconies. Approximately 20 percent of the town was built and controlled by Spaniards and Portuguese living here (with the rest being Arabic and Berber). The two populations were separated by a wall, the remains of which you can still trace running through the medina. It may seem at first glance that these European zones are fancier and "nicer" compared to the poorer-seeming Arabic/Berber zones. But the Arabs and Berbers take more care with the insides of their homes—if you went behind these humble walls, you'd be surprised how pleasant the interiors are. While European cultures externalize resources, Arab and Berber cultures internalize them.

The medina is filled with surprises for which serendipity is your best or only guide. As you wander, keep an eye out for the legendary **Café Baba** (up a few stairs on Rue Doukkala—not far from Place Amrah, daily 10:30-23:30). Old, grimy, and smoky, it's been around since the late 1940s and was a hippie hangout in the 1960s and '70s—the Rolling Stones smoked hash here (on the wall there's still a battered picture of Keith Richards holding a pipe). Enjoy a mint tea here and take in the great view over the old

quarter, including a lush mansion just across the way formerly owned by American heiress Barbara Hutton.

One of the few sights revered by Moroccans that can be entered by non-Muslim visitors is the **tomb of Ibn Battuta.** Hiding at the top of a narrow residential lane (Rue Ibn Battuta—look for tile signs pointing the way), this simple mausoleum venerates the man considered the Moroccan Marco Polo. What started as a six-month pilgrimage to Mecca in 1325 stretched out to some 30 years for Ibn Battuta, as he explored throughout the Islamic world and into India and China. (If you visit the tomb, remove your shoes before entering, and leave a small tip for the attendant.) No one really knows if it's actually Ibn Battuta interred here, but that doesn't deter locals from paying homage to him.

▲Tangier American Legation Museum

Located at the bottom end of the medina (just above the port), this unexpected museum is worth a visit. Morocco was one of the first

countries to recognize the newly formed United States as an independent country (in 1777). The original building, given to the United States by the sultan of Morocco, became the fledgling government's first foreign acquisition. It was declared a US National Historic Landmark in 1983.

Cost and Hours: 20 dh, Mon-Fri 10:00-17:00, Sat until 15:00; during Ramadan daily 10:00-15:00, otherwise closed Sun year-round; Rue d'Amérique 8, +212 539 935 317, www.legation.org.

Visiting the Museum: This 19th-century mansion was the US embassy (or consulate) in Morocco from 1821 to 1961, and it's still American property—our only National Historic Landmark overseas. Today this nonprofit museum and research center is a strangely peaceful oasis within Tangier's intense old town. It offers a warm welcome and lots of interesting artifacts—all well described in English. The ground floor is filled with an art gallery. In the stairwell, you'll see photos of kings with presidents, and a letter with the news of Lincoln's assassination. Upstairs are more paintings, as well as model soldiers playing out two battle scenes from Moroccan history. These belonged to American industrialist Malcolm Forbes, who had a home in Tangier (his son donated these dioramas to the museum). Rounding out the upper floor are wonderful old maps of Tangier and Morocco. A visit here is a fun reminder of how long the US and Morocco have had good relations.

• *When you've soaked in enough old-town atmosphere, make your way*

Islam 101

Islam has more than a billion adherents worldwide, and traveling in an Islamic country is an opportunity to better understand the religion. This admittedly basic and simplistic outline (written by a non-Muslim) is meant to help travelers from the Christian West understand a very rich but often misunderstood culture. Just as it helps to know about spires, feudalism, and the saints to comprehend European sightseeing, a few basics on Islam help make your sightseeing in Morocco more meaningful.

Muslims, like Christians and Jews, are monotheistic. They call God "Allah." The most important person in the Islamic faith is the prophet Muhammad, who lived in the sixth and seventh centuries. The holy book of Islam is the Quran, believed by Muslims to be the word of Allah as revealed to Muhammad. The "five pillars" of Islam are the core obligations of the faith that followers must satisfy:

1. Say and believe this basic statement of faith: "There is no god but God, and Muhammad is his prophet."
2. Pray five times a day.
3. Give to the poor (annually, about 2.5 percent of one's income).
4. Fast during daylight hours through the month of Ramadan. Fasting develops self-control and awareness, and is a step toward achieving selflessness.
5. Make a pilgrimage (hajj) to Mecca. Muslims who can afford it and are physically able are required to travel to Mecca at least once in their lifetimes.

to the Kasbah (see map on page 914). Within the medina, head uphill, or exit the Medina Gate and go right on Rue de la Kasbah, which follows the old wall uphill to Bab Kasbah (a.k.a. Porte de la Kasbah or Kasbah Gate), a gateway into the Kasbah.

Kasbah

Loosely translated as "fortress," a *kasbah* is an enclosed, protected residential area near a castle that you'll find in hundreds of Moroccan towns. Originally this was a place where a king or other leader could protect his tribe. Tangier's Kasbah, comprising the upper quarter of the old town, has twisty lanes and some nice guesthouses.

It is a bit more sedate and less claustrophobic than parts of the medina near the market below.

Way finding here has always been a challenge for visitors. Look for tile signs with street names and arrows pointing to main sights posted on many corners, and spray-painted blue numbers marking each intersection. Eventually, these numbers will be painted over... once, and if, a permanent system is decided on.

▲Kasbah Museum of Mediterranean Cultures

On Place de la Kasbah, you'll find a former sultan's palace, Dar el-Makhzen, that's now a history museum with a few historical artifacts. While there's not a word of English, some of the exhibits are still easy to appreciate, and the building itself is beautiful.

Cost and Hours: 20 dh, Wed-Mon 10:00-18:00, closed for prayer Fri 12:00-13:30 and all day Tue, ask for English brochure, +212 539 932 097.

Visiting the Museum: Enter straight past the ticket booth. Most of the exhibits surround the central, open-air courtyard; rooms proceed roughly chronologically as you move counterclockwise, from early hunters and farmers to prehistoric civilizations, Roman times, the region's conversion to Islam, and the influence of European powers. Duck through the far-right corner of the courtyard to find a two-story space with a second-century mosaic floor depicting the journey of Venus. A 12th-century wall-size map shows the Moorish view of the world: with Africa on top (Spain is at the far right). Mirrors help visitors see the intricate details on the ceiling. Nearby is an explanation of terra-cotta production (a local industry), and upstairs is an exhibit on funerary rituals. Near the entrance to the courtyard, look for signs to *jardin* and climb the stairs to reach a chirpy (if slightly overgrown) garden courtyard. Striking tilework is featured throughout the 17th-century building.

PLACE DE LA KASBAH

The square in front of the Kasbah Museum attracts more than its share of tourists, and that means it's a vivid gauntlet of amusements: snake charmers, squawky dance troupes, and flamboyant water vendors. These

colorful Instagram-worthy hustlers make their living off the many tour groups passing by daily. (As you're cajoled, remember that the daily minimum wage here for men as skilled as these beggars is $10. That's what the gardeners you'll pass in your walk earn each day. In other words, a €1 tip is an hour's wage for these people.) If you draft behind a tour group, you won't be the focus of the hustlers. But if you take a photo, you must pay.

Before descending from the Kasbah, don't miss the ocean viewpoint—as you stand in the square and face the palace, look to the right to find the rebuilt city wall and Bab Bahr, the "Sea Gate." This leads out to a large natural terrace with fine views over the port, the Mediterranean, and Spain. From here, you can descend a lengthy staircase all the way back to the port.

The lower gate of the Kasbah (as you stand in Place de la Kasbah facing the palace, it's on your left) leads to a charming little alcove between the gates, where you can see a particularly fine tile fountain: The top part is carved cedarwood, below that is carved plaster, and the bottom half is hand-laid tiles.

Matisse Route

The artist Henri Matisse traveled to Tangier in 1912-13. The culture, patterns, and colors that he encountered here had a lifelong effect on the themes in his subsequent art. The diamond-shaped stone patterns embedded in the narrow lane leading up along the left side of the palace mark a route that the famous artist regularly walked through the Kasbah, from the lower gate to the upper; those who know his works will spot several familiar scenes along this stretch. Just off the Grand Socco, on Rue de la Liberté, is the instantly recognizable Grand Hotel Villa de France, where Matisse lived and painted while in Tangier (for more on this hotel, see the listing under "Sleeping in Tangier," later).

TANGIER BEACH AND MARINA

Tanja Marina Bay, inaugurated in 2018 as part of the port's rejuvenation project, offers cafés, shops, over 1,400 berths, modern underground parking, and a home for the Royal Yacht Club of Tangier. Stretching gracefully eastward from the marina, the chic La Corniche promenade rests above a stretch of fishy eateries and entertaining nightclubs as it follows the curve of the wide, white-sand crescent beach (Plage de Corniche). The locals call it by the Span-

ish word *playa*. It's packed with
locals doing what people around
the world do at the beach—with
a few variations. Traditionally
clad moms let their kids run
wild. You'll see people—young
and old—covered in hot sand to
combat rheumatism. Early, late,
and off-season, the beach becomes a popular venue for soccer

teams. But while Tangier is making great efforts to upgrade the
entire area, and the beach is cleaner than it once was, if you have a
beach break in mind, do it on Spain's Costa del Sol.

Nightlife in Tangier

Nighttime is great in Tangier. If you're staying overnight, don't
relax in a fancy hotel restaurant. Get out and about in the old town
after dark. In the cool of the evening, the atmospheric squares and
lanes become even more alluring. It's an entirely different experience and a highlight of any visit. The Malataba area in the new
town (along Avenue Mohammed VI) is an easy cab ride away and
filled with modern nightclubs. (But remember, this isn't night-owl
Spain—things die down by around 22:00.)

El Minzah Hotel hosts traditional music most nights for
those having dinner there. The **El Morocco Club** has a sophisticated piano bar. For details on both, see "Eating in Tangier," later.

Cinema Rif, the landmark theater at the top of the Grand
Socco, shows movies in French—which the younger generation is
required to learn—Arabic, and occasionally English. The cinema is
worth popping into, if only to see the Art Deco interior. As movies
cost only 25 dh, consider dropping by to see a bit of whatever's on
(closed Mon, +212 539 934 683).

Sleeping in Tangier

I've recommended two vastly different types of accommodations
in Tangier: cozy Moroccan-style (but mostly French-run) guesthouses in the maze of lanes of the Kasbah neighborhood, and
modern international-style hotels, most in the urban new town, a
10- to 20-minute walk from the central sights. June through mid-
September is high season, when rooms may be a bit more expensive
and reservations are wise.

Although the local currency is the dirham, nearly every hotel
gives prices in euros, too. I've ranked the hotels below as **$** Budget:

500-900 dh; **$$** Moderate: 900-1300 dh; **$$$** Pricier: 1300-1700 dh; and **$$$$** Splurge: Over 1700 dh. All include breakfast.

GUESTHOUSES AND A HOTEL IN THE KASBAH

In Arabic, *riad* means "guesthouse." You'll find these in the atmospheric old town (medina). While the lower part of the medina is dominated by market stalls and tourist traps—and can feel a bit seedy after dark—the upper Kasbah area is more tranquil and residential. My recommendations are buried in a labyrinth of lanes that can be difficult to navigate; the map of "Tangier's Old Town (Medina)," earlier, gives you a vague sense of where to go, but it's essential to ask for very clear directions when you reserve. If you're hiring a guide in Tangier, ask him to help you find your *riad*. (If you're on your own, you can try asking directions when you arrive—but be forewarned that locals may see that as an invitation to tag along and hound you for tips.) The communal nature of *riad*s means that occasional noise from other guests can be an issue; bring your earplugs.

When you arrive at your *riad*, don't look for a doorbell—the tradition is to use a door knocker. The guesthouses listed here are in traditional old houses, with rooms surrounding a courtyard atrium, and all have rooftop terraces where you can relax and enjoy sweeping views over Tangier. Besides breakfast, many also serve good Moroccan dinners, which cost extra and should be arranged beforehand, typically that morning. Some also offer hammams (Turkish-style baths) with massages and spa treatments. Some lack stand-alone showers; instead, in Moroccan style, you'll find a handheld shower in a corner of the bathroom.

$$$ La Maison Blanche ("The White House"), run by Aziz Begdouri, one of my recommended guides, has nine rooms in a restored traditional Moroccan house. Modern and attractively decorated, each room is dedicated to a personality who's spent time in Tangier—including a travel writer I know well. With its friendly vibe, great view terrace, and lavish setting, this is a worthwhile splurge (all with bathtubs, air-con, just inside the upper Kasbah gate at Rue Ahmed Ben Ajiba 2, +212 539 375 188, +212 661 639 332, www.lamaisonblanchetanger.com, info@lamaisonblanchetanger.com).

$$$ Dar Chams Tanja, just below the lower Kasbah gate, has seven elegant, new-feeling rooms (named after women from Morocco) that surround an inner courtyard with lots of keyhole windows. It's impeccably decorated, has a proper French-expat ambience, and boasts incredible views from its rooftop terrace (air-con, hammam, massage service, Rue Jnan Kabtan 2, +212 539 332 323 or +212 654 935 175, www.darchamstanja.com, darchamstanja@gmail.com).

$$$ **Dar Sultan** rents seven romantically decorated rooms on a pleasant street in the heart of the Kasbah with a small rooftop terrace (some rooms with balconies, Rue Touila 49, +212 539 336 061, +212 671 181 580, www.darsultan.com, dar-sultan@menara.ma).

$$ **La Tangerina,** run by Jürgen (who's German) and his Moroccan wife, Farida, has 10 comfortable rooms that look down into a shared atrium. At the top is a gorgeous rooftop sea-view balcony (cash only, wood-fired hammam, turn left as you enter the upper Kasbah gate and hug the town wall around to Riad Sultan 19, +212 539 947 731, www.latangerina.com, info@latangerina.com).

$$ **Dar Nour,** run with funky French style by Philippe, Jean-Olivier, and Catherine, has an "Escher-esque" floor plan that sprawls through five interconnected houses (it's "labyrinthine like the medina," says Philippe). The 10 homey rooms feel very traditional, with lots of books and lounging areas spread throughout, and a fantastic view terrace and cocktail bar on the roof (Wi-Fi in lobby only, Rue Gourna 20, +212 662 112 724, www.darnour.com, contactdarnour@yahoo.fr).

$$ **Hotel Continental**—sprawling at the bottom of the old town, facing the port—is the grand Humphrey Bogart option. It has lavish, atmospheric, and recently renovated public spaces, a chandeliered breakfast room, and 53 spacious bedrooms with rough hardwood floors and new bathrooms. Jimmy, who's always around and runs the shop adjacent to the lobby, says he offers everything but Viagra. When I said, "I'm from Seattle," he said, "206." Test him—he knows your area code (family rooms, Dar Baroud 36; follow my directions for walking into town from the port, but take a right through the yellow gateway—Bab Dar Dbagh—marked *1339,* then turn right again and follow the signs, +212 539 931 024, hcontinental@menara.ma). This hotel's terrace aches with nostalgia. Back during the city's glory days, a ferry connected Tangier and New York. American novelists would sit out on the terrace of Hotel Continental, never quite sure when their friends' boat would arrive from across the sea.

MODERN HOTELS IN THE MODERN CITY

These hotels are centrally located, near the TI, and within walking distance of the Grand Socco, medina, and market.

$$$$ **Grand Hotel Villa de France,** perched high above the Grand Socco, has been around since the 19th century, when Eugène Delacroix stayed here and started a craze for Orientalism in European art. Henri Matisse was a guest in 1912-13, painting what he saw through his window. After sitting empty for years, the hotel was restored and reopened. Lavish public spaces, including a restaurant and view terrace, have more charm than most of the 58 modern, updated rooms, but a Matisse-inspired leaf design echoes

throughout and adds a bit of character to an otherwise businesslike hotel. Suites have a more Moroccan vibe but are not quite worth the splurge (intersection of Rue Angleterre and Rue Hollande, +212 539 333 111, www.leroyal.com, reservation@ghvdf.com).

$$$ Marina Bay Tangier, restored to its 1970s glamour, is a worthy splurge. Offering 127 plush, modern rooms, sprawling public spaces, a garden, pool, and grand views, it feels like an oversized boutique hotel. Overlooking the harbor, the great lounge—named for Winston Churchill—compels you to relax (some view rooms, air-con, elevator, 3 restaurants, spa and sauna, Avenue Mohammed VI 152—see the "Tangier" map near the beginning of this chapter, +212 539 349 300, www.hotelsatlas.com, htoula@hotelsatlas.com).

$ Hotel Rembrandt feels just like the 1950s, with a restaurant, a bar, and a swimming pool surrounded by a great grassy garden. Its 70 rooms are outdated and simple but clean and comfortable, and some come with views (air-con, elevator, a 5-minute walk above the beach in a busy urban zone at Boulevard Mohammed V 1—see the "Tangier" map near the beginning of this chapter, +212 539 333 314, www.rembrandthoteltanger.com, reservation@hotelrembrandt.ma).

Eating in Tangier

Moroccan food is a joy to sample. First priority is a glass of refreshing "Moroccan tea"—green tea that's boiled and steeped once, then combined with fresh mint leaves to boil and steep some more, before being loaded up with sugar. Tourist-oriented restaurants have a predictable menu. For starters, you'll find a Moroccan tomato-based vegetable soup *(harira)* or Moroccan salad (a combination of fresh and stewed vegetables). Main dishes include couscous (usually with chicken, potatoes, carrots, and other vegetables and spices); *tagine* (stewed meat served in a fancy dish with a cone-shaped top); and *briouates* (small savory pies). Everything comes with Morocco's distinctive round, flat bread. For dessert, it's pastries—typically, almond cookies.

I've mostly listed places in or near the medina. If you'd prefer the local equivalent of a yacht-club restaurant, survey the places along the beach.

IN THE MEDINA
$$$ El Morocco Club has three distinct zones. Outside, it's an inexpensive **terrace** café, serving a light menu of sandwiches, quiches, and salads in the shade of a rubber tree. At night a bouncer lets you into the pricier **fine restaurant** with a Med-Moroccan menu of grilled fish, roasted lamb, and creamy risottos. Guests at the restaurant have entrée to the wonderfully grown-up **piano bar:** a

sophisticated lounge with vintage Tangier photos and zebra-print couches (café Tue-Fri and Sun 9:00-18:00, Sat 13:00-16:00; restaurant and piano bar Tue-Sun 19:30-late; all closed Mon; Place du Tabor, just inside the upper Kasbah gate, +212 539 948 139).

$$ Le Salon Bleu has decent Moroccan food and some of the most spectacular seating in town: perched on a whitewashed terrace overlooking the square in front of the Kasbah Museum, with 360-degree views over the rooftops. Hike up the very tight spiral staircase to the top level, with the best views and lounge-a-while sofa seating. Run by the French owners of the recommended Dar Nour guesthouse, it offers a simple menu of Moroccan fare—the appetizer plate is a good sampler for lunch or to share for an afternoon snack. While there is some indoor seating, I'd skip this place if the weather's not ideal for lingering on the terrace (daily 9:00-19:00, Place de la Kasbah, +212 662 112 724). You'll see it from the square in front of the Kasbah; to reach it, go through the gate to the left (as you face it), then look right for the stairs up.

$$ La Terraza de la Medina has two floors of spacious dining areas and an outdoor terrace with views. If you're looking for a low-stress restaurant in the heart of the Kasbah, you'll find it here, just behind the recommended hotel Dar Chams Tanja. They serve traditional Moroccan fare such as *pastella*—a savory-sweet chicken pastry, *harira*, couscous, and *tagines* (Tue-Thu 11:30-23:00, Fri-Sun from 9:00, closed Mon, Rue Dakakine 6, +212 539 332 386).

$$ Rif Kebdani is a cozy, not-too-touristy place with colorful Moroccan tiles and Berber decor that's matched by a simple yet appetizing menu. With solid *tagine* options plus a variety of seafood dishes at reasonable prices, it's an especially good choice for lunch (daily 12:00-17:00 & 19:00-23:00, Rue Dar Baroud, +212 539 371 760).

$ Café Colon is a window into the real, present-day Tangier, where locals come to play cards and pass the day drinking coffee and tea. There's no food, almost no tourists, and drinks come with a customary glass of water (astute waiters bring bottled mineral water for travelers). Stopping here fills your cultural sustenance tank. As you idly watch passersby from a sidewalk table, you'll feel a part of keeping traditions—and Tangier—alive (long hours daily, Rue d'Italie 54).

Touristy Places in the Medina: Tangier seems to specialize in touristy restaurants designed to feed and entertain dozens or even hundreds of tour-group members with overpriced Moroccan classics and belly dancing. The only locals you'll see are the waiters. But for day-trippers who just want a safe, comfortable break in the heart of town, these restaurants' predictability and Moroccan clichés are just perfect. **$$ Hamadi,** as luxurious a restaurant as a tourist can find in Morocco, has good food at reasonable prices

(long hours daily, check bill carefully, Rue de la Kasbah 2, +212 539 934 514).

IN THE NEW TOWN

These places, while technically in the new town, are clustered just beyond the Grand Socco.

$$$ Le Saveur du Poisson is an excellent bet for the more adventurous, featuring one room cluttered with paintings adjoining a busy kitchen. There are no choices here. Just sit down and let owner Hassan take care of the rest. You get a rough hand-carved spoon and fork. Surrounded by lots of locals and unforgettable food, you'll be treated to a multicourse menu. Savor the delicious fish dishes—Tangier is one of the few spots in Morocco where seafood is a major part of the diet. The fruit punch—a mix of seasonal fruits brewed overnight in a vat—simmers in the back room. Ask for an explanation, or even a look. The desserts are full of nuts and honey. The big sink is for locals who prefer to eat with their fingers (Sat-Thu 13:00-17:00 & 19:00-22:30, closed Fri and during Ramadan; from El Minzah Hotel (described next), walk down Rue de la Liberté roughly a block toward the Grand Socco, look for the stairs leading down to the market stalls, and go down until you see fish on the grill, Escalier Waller 2, +212 539 336 326).

$$$ El Minzah Hotel offers a fancy yet still authentic experience. Classy but low stress, it's where unadventurous tourists and local elites dine. Dress up and choose between two dining zones: The white-tablecloth continental (French) dining area, called El Erz, is stuffy; while in the Moroccan lounge, El Korsan, you'll be serenaded by live traditional music (music nightly 20:00-23:00, belly-dance show at 20:30 and 21:30, no cover). There's also a cozy wine bar here—a rarity in a Muslim country—decorated with photos of visiting celebrities. At lunch, light meals and salads are served poolside (all dining areas open daily 13:00-16:00 & 20:00-22:30, Rue de la Liberté 85, +212 539 333 444).

$ Restaurant Darna, operated by the Maison Communautaire des Femmes, a community center for women, is open to everyone and offers a tasty, hearty, 60-dh two-course lunch. Profits support the work of the center (Mon-Sat 12:00-16:00, closed Sun, last order at 15:30, also open 9:00-11:00 & 15:30-17:00 for cakes and tea, cash only, pleasant terrace out back, near slipper market just outside Grand Socco, Place du 9 Avril, +212 539 947 065).

MOROCCO & TANGIER

ON THE WATER WEST OF THE MEDINA

$ Café Hafa, a basic outdoor café cascading down a series of cliff-hugging terraces, is a longtime Tangier landmark. Find your way here with a taxi or your guide, but don't rush—you'll want to settle in to sip your tea and enjoy the fantastic sea views. Tangier's most famous expat, the writer Paul Bowles, used to hang out here (simple pizzas and brochettes, daily 9:00 until late, in the Marshan neighborhood west of the medina on Avenue Hadi Mohammed Tazi).

PASTRIES

Moroccan pastries and cookies are often offered with mint tea in cafés or hotels and are served for dessert after meals. But those with a serious sweet tooth should step into a *pâtisserie* to choose from the variety of local sweets made with almonds, pistachios, cashews, pine nuts, peanuts, dates, honey, and sugar. Ask for *"une boîte petite"* (a little box), and point to what you want to fill it—you'll pay by weight. One easy and delicious spot is **$ Bab Al Medina,** just off the Grand Socco (daily 6:00-22:00, Rue d'Italie 28, +212 667 151 779). It has two sections: a café with pizzas and shawarma, and a bakery that offers Moroccan and French pastries, bread, and Moroccan *crêpes* (called *baghrir,* these have nooks and crannies similar to a crumpet). Eat at the café's tables or on your hotel terrace for a sweet sunset.

Morocco Beyond Tangier

Morocco gets much better as you go deeper into the interior. The country is incredibly rich in cultural thrills, though you'll pay a price in hassles and headaches—it's a package deal. But if adventure is your business, Morocco is a great option. Moroccan trains are quite good—and a high-speed line connects Tangier with Casablanca. Second class is cheap and comfortable. Buses connect all smaller towns very well. By car, Morocco is easy.

To plan a trip that extends beyond Tangier, you'll need a supplemental guidebook. Lonely Planet, Moon, and Rough Guide all publish good ones, available at home and in Spain. To get you started in your planning, I've listed a few of my favorite Moroccan destinations here.

MOROCCAN TOWNS

Chefchaouen

Just two hours by bus or car from Tétouan, this is the first pleasant town beyond the north coast. Monday and Thursday are colorful market days. Wander deep into the atmospheric old town from the main square and admire the colorful buildings that inspired the nickname "blue pearl of Morocco."

Rabat

Morocco's capital and most European city, Rabat is the most comfortable and least stressful place to start your North African trip. You'll find a colorful market (in the old neighboring town of Salé), bits of Islamic architecture (Mausoleum of Mohammed V), the king's palace, mellow hustlers, and fine hotels.

Fès

More than just a funny hat that tipsy Shriners wear, Fès is Morocco's religious and artistic center, bustling with craftspeople, pilgrims, shoppers, and shops. Like most large Moroccan cities, it has a distinct new town from the French colonial period, as well as an exotic (and stressful) old walled Arabic town (the medina), where you'll find the market.

For 12 centuries, traders have gathered in Fès, founded on a river at the crossroads of two trade routes. Soon there was an irrigation system; a university; resident craftsmen from Spain; and a diverse population of Muslims, Christians, and Jews. When France claimed Morocco in 1912, they made their capital in Rabat, and Fès fizzled. But the Fès marketplace is still Morocco's best.

Marrakech

Morocco's gateway to the south, Marrakech is where the desert, mountain, and coastal regions merge. This market city is a constant folk festival, bustling with Berber tribespeople and a colorful center. The new city has the train station, and the main boulevard (Mohammed V) is lined with banks, airline offices, a post office, a tourist office, and comfortable hotels. The old city features the mazelike market and the huge Djemaa el-Fna, a square seething with people—a 43-ring Moroccan circus.

Over the Atlas Mountains

Extend your Moroccan trip several days by heading south over the Atlas Mountains. Take a bus from Marrakech to Ouarzazate (short stop), and then to Tinerhir (great oasis town, comfy hotel, overnight stop). The next day, go to Er Rachidia and take the overnight bus to Fès.

By car, drive from Fès south, staying in the small mountain town of Ifrane, and then continue deep into the desert country past Er Rachidia, and on to Rissani (market days: Sun, Tue, and Thu). Explore nearby mud-brick towns still living in the Middle Ages. Hire a guide to drive you past where the road stops, and head cross-country to an oasis village (Merzouga), where you can climb a sand dune and watch the sun rise over the vastness of Africa. Only a sea of sand separates you from Timbuktu.

SPAIN: PAST & PRESENT

The distinctive Spanish culture has been shaped by the country's parade of rulers. Roman emperors, Muslim sultans, hard-core Christians, conquistadors, French dandies, and Fascist dictators have all left their mark on Spain's art, architecture, and customs. Start by understanding the country's long history of invasions and religious wars, and you'll better appreciate the churches, museums, and monuments you'll visit today.

History

The sunny weather, fertile soil, and ports of the Iberian Peninsula made it a popular place to call home. A mix from various migrations and invasions, the original "Iberians" crossed the Pyrenees around 800 BC. The Phoenicians established the city of Cádiz around 1100 BC, and Carthaginians settled there around 250 BC.

ROMANS (200 BC-AD 400)

The future Roman Emperor Augustus finally quelled the last Iberian resistance in 19 BC, making the province of "Hispania" an agricultural breadbasket (olives, wheat) to feed the vast Roman Empire. Romans brought the Latin language, a connection to the wider world, and (in the fourth century) Christianity. When the empire began crumbling around AD 400, Spain made a peaceful transition, ruled by Christian Visigoths from Germany who had strong Roman ties. Roman influence remained for centuries after, in the Latin-based Spanish language, irrigation methods, and building materials and techniques. The Romans' large farming estates would change hands over the years, passing from Roman senators to Visigoth kings to Islamic caliphs to Christian nobles. And, of course, the Romans left wine.

Six Dates that Changed Spain

711: Arab Muslims ("Moors") from North Africa invade and occupy Iberia.

1492: Under the Catholic Monarchs Isabel and Ferdinand, Columbus sails Spain into a century of wealth and power. This same year, Spain conquers the last Moorish stronghold in Granada, expels its Jews, and ramps up the Inquisition to root out "heretics."

1588: Spain's Armada is routed by the English, and the country's slow decline begins.

1898: Thrashed by the US in the Spanish-American War, Spain reaches a low ebb.

1936: The Spanish Civil War begins, hundreds of thousands are killed during its three-year span, and more than three decades of Franco's fascist rule follow.

1975: Juan Carlos I becomes king; he later leads the nation to democracy and the European Union.

MOORS (711-1492)

In AD 711, 12,000 zealous members of the world's newest religion—Islam—landed on the Rock of Gibraltar and, in three short years, conquered the Iberian Peninsula. These North African Muslims—generically called "Moors"—dominated Spain for the next 700 years. Though powerful, they were surprisingly tolerant of the people they ruled, allowing native Jews and Christians to practice their faiths, so long as the infidels paid extra taxes.

The Moors themselves were an ethnically diverse culture, including both simple Berber tribesmen from Morocco and sophisticated rulers from old Arab families. From their capital in Córdoba, various rulers of the united Islamic state of "al-Andalus" formed their own caliphate, separate from those in Syria, Baghdad, or Morocco.

With cultural ties that stretched from Spain to Africa to Arabia to Persia and beyond, the Moorish culture in Spain (especially around AD 800-1000) was perhaps Europe's most advanced—a beacon of learning in Europe's so-called Dark Ages. Mathematics, astronomy, literature, and architecture flourished. Even winemaking was encouraged, though for religious reasons the Muslims didn't drink alcohol. The Moorish legacy lives on today in architecture (horseshoe arches, ceramic tiles, fountains, and gardens), language (the Spanish *el* comes from Arabic *al*)...and wine.

Spain Almanac

Official Name: Reino de España (Kingdom of Spain)

Locals Call It: España

Size: 195,000 square miles, including the Canary and Balearic islands, and small enclaves in Morocco. Population 47 million.

Geography: The interior of Spain is a high, flat plateau (the Meseta Central), with hot, dry summers and harsh winters. Surrounding the plateau are mountains (including the Pyrenees in the north) and 2,000 miles of coastline. The 600-mile Tajo River runs westward from Toledo through Portugal to the Atlantic. The Guadalquivir irrigates Andalucía and made Sevilla an oceangoing port city...until the dockyards silted up.

Latitude and Longitude: 40°N and 4°W (similar latitude to New York).

Regions: Spain is divided into 17 autonomous regions (e.g., Andalucía, Catalunya, Castile-La Mancha, Madrid), which in time will have full responsibility for health care, social programs, and education.

Major Cities: Madrid (the capital, 3 million), Barcelona (1.6 million), Valencia (810,000), and Sevilla (700,000).

Economy: The Gross Domestic Product is $1.8 trillion; the GDP per capita is about $38,400. Major moneymakers include tourism, textiles, shoes, fishing, olives, wine, oranges, cars, and ships.

Government: Spain is a parliamentary monarchy, guided symbolically by King Felipe VI. The prime minister is elected but appointed by the king. Some of the 600-plus legislators (in two houses) are elected directly, some by regional parliaments.

Flag: Three horizontal bands of red, yellow, and red, with the coat of arms.

Soccer: The two perennial powerhouses in La Liga (The League) are Real Madrid and FC Barcelona. The country has five daily newspapers dedicated to the sport.

RECONQUISTA (711-1492)

For more than 700 years, the Moors were a minority ruling a largely Christian populace. Pockets of independent Christians remained, particularly in the peninsula's mountainous north. Local Christian kings fought against the Moors whenever they could, whittling away at the Muslim empire, "reconquering" more and more land in what's known as the Reconquista. The last Moorish stronghold, Granada, fell to the Christians in 1492.

The slow, piecemeal process of the Reconquista split the peninsula into many independent kingdoms and dukedoms, some Christian, some Moorish. The Reconquista picked up steam after AD

Historical Spaniards

Hadrian (AD 76-138): Roman emperor, one of three born in Latin-speaking Hispania (along with Trajan, reigned 98-117, and Theodosius I, reigned 379-395).

El Cid (1040?-1099): A real soldier-for-hire who inspired fictional stories and Spain's oldest poem, *El Cid* (The Lord). He fought for both Christians and Muslims during the wars of the Reconquista, and is best known for liberating Valencia from the Moors.

St. Teresa of Ávila (1515-1582): Mystic nun whose holiness and writings led to convent reform and to her sainthood. Religiously intense Spain produced other saints, too, including Dominic (1170-1221), who founded an order of wandering monks, and Ignatius of Loyola.

Ferdinand (1452-1516) and **Isabel** (1451-1504): Their marriage united much of Spain, ushering in its golden age. The Catholic Monarchs drove out Moors and Jews, and financed Columbus' lucrative voyages to the New World.

Francisco Pizarro (1476-1541): Conquistador who vanquished the Incan Empire in the 1530s and then founded Peru's current capital, Lima.

Juan Ponce de León (1460-1521): Although he sailed on Columbus' second voyage to the New World, Ponce de León is primarily known for being the first European to explore Florida. His quest for the Fountain of Youth is a myth popularized by American author Washington Irving three centuries later.

1000, when al-Andalus splintered into smaller regional states—Granada, Sevilla, Valencia—each governed by a local ruler. Toledo fell to the Christians in 1085. By 1249 the neighboring Christian state of Portugal had the borders it does today, making it the oldest unchanged state in Europe. The rest of the peninsula was a battleground. Heavy stone castles dotted the interior region of Castile, as lords and barons duked it out. Along the Mediterranean coast (from the Pyrenees to Barcelona to Valencia), three Christian states united into a sea-trading power, the kingdom of Aragon.

In 1469, Isabel of Castile married Ferdinand II of Aragon. These so-called Catholic Monarchs (Reyes Católicos) united the peninsula's two largest kingdoms, instantly making Spain a European power. In 1492, the Catholic Monarchs drove the Moors out of Granada and expelled the country's Jews, creating a unified, Christian, militaristic

Hernán Cortés (1485-1547): A minor Spanish nobleman seeking his fortune, Cortés conquered Mexico in 1521. Along with fellow conquistadors Francisco Pizarro and Vasco Núñez de Balboa (who discovered the Pacific), Cortés and other Spaniards explored the New World and exploited its indigenous peoples.

Ignatius of Loyola (1491-1556): After being wounded on a battle-field, this devout Basque founded the Society of Jesus—a.k.a. the Jesuits, a Catholic order of "intellectual warriors" and a leading force in the Counter-Reformation.

Miguel de Cervantes (1547-1616): Author of the classic satirical romance *Don Quixote,* Cervantes was also a poet and a playwright whose works shaped Spanish literature and the language itself.

Charles I/V (1500-1558): The Flanders-born grandson of Ferdinand and Isabel assumed the Spanish throne in 1516 (as King Charles I) and led the Holy Roman Empire from 1519 (as Emperor Charles V), ruling over much of Western Europe, the Far East, and the Americas. He abdicated in 1556, retiring to a monastery.

Francisco Franco (1892-1975): As the general who led the military uprising against the elected Republic, Franco helped spark Spain's Civil War (1936-1939). After victory, he ruled Spain for more than three decades as an absolute dictator, maintaining its Catholic, aristocratic heritage while slowly modernizing the country (see "The 20th Century," on page 944).

nation-state, fueled by the religious zeal of the Reconquista. Soon after, Columbus explored the seas under Ferdinand and Isabel's flag.

THE GOLDEN AGE (1500-1600)

Spain's bold sea explorers changed the economics of Europe, opening up a New World of riches and colonies. The Spanish flag soon flew over most of South and Central America. Gold, silver, and agricultural products (grown on large estates with cheap labor) poured into Spain. In return, the stoked Spaniards exported Christianity, converting the American natives with persistent Jesuit priests and cruel conquistadors.

Ferdinand and Isabel's daughter (Juana the Mad) wed a Ger-

man prince (Philip the Fair), and their son Charles (1500-1558) inherited not only their crowns but that of his grandfather, the Holy Roman Emperor Maximilian I. Known as King Charles I of Spain, and as Emperor Charles V, he was the most powerful man in the world, ruling an empire that stretched from Holland to Sicily, and from Bohemia to Bolivia. The aristocracy and the clergy were swimming in money. Art and courtly life flourished during this golden age, with Spain hosting the painter El Greco and the writer Miguel de Cervantes.

But Charles V's Holy Roman Empire was torn by different languages and ethnic groups, and by protesting Protestants. He spent much of the empire's energies at war with Protestants, encroaching Muslim Turks, and Europe's rising powers. When an exhausted Charles announced his abdication (1556) and retired to a monastery, his sprawling empire was divvied up among family members, with Spain and its possessions going to his son, Philip II (1527-1598).

Philip II inherited Portugal in 1581 due to a succession crisis, moved Spain's capital to Madrid, built El Escorial, and continued fighting losing battles across Europe (the Netherlands, France) that drained the treasury of its New World gold. In the summer of 1588, Spain's seemingly unbeatable royal fleet of 125 ships—the Invincible Armada—sailed off to conquer England, only to be unexpectedly routed in battle by bad weather and Sir Francis Drake's cunning. Just like that, Britannia ruled the waves, and Spain spiraled downward, becoming a debt-ridden, overextended, flabby nation.

SLOW DECLINE (1600-1900)

Easy money from the colonies kept Spain from seeing the dangers at home. The country stopped growing its own wheat and neglected its fields. Great Britain and the Netherlands were the rising sea-trading powers in the new global economy. During the centuries when science and technology developed as never before in other European countries, Spain was preoccupied by its failed colonial politics. (Still, 1600s Spain produced the remarkable painter Diego Velázquez.)

By 1700, once-mighty Spain lay helpless while rising powers France, England, and Austria fought over the right to pick Spain's next king in the War of the Spanish Succession (1701-1714). Spanish king Charles II didn't have an heir, so he willed his kingdom to Louis XIV's grandson, Philip of Anjou, who was set to inherit

The *Other* Spanish Languages

What we call "Spanish" *(español)*, many Spaniards call "Castilian" *(castellano)*—the language of the people of Castile. That's because Spanish isn't the only language spoken in Spain.

Catalunya, in the northeast corner of the country (around Barcelona), speaks **Catalan,** which sounds like a mix of Spanish and French. For example, "Please" is *Si us plau* (see oos plow), and "Thank you" is *Gracies* (grah-see-es). Since Catalan doesn't use the *ñ* letter, they spell the name of their region "Catalunya" rather than "Cataluña" (as Spanish speakers do).

Galego (*gallego* in Spanish), which sounds like a blend of Spanish and Portuguese, is spoken in the northwest province of Galicia. The biggest change is that *el* and *la* become *o* and *a* (for example, the city of La Coruña is called "A Coruña" locally). The Spanish greeting *"Buenos días"* becomes *"Bos días"* in Galego, and *"plaza"* (town square) becomes *praza*. If you want to impress a local, say *graciñas* (grah-theen-yahs)—a super-polite thank-you.

The Basque region (a chunk of north-central Spain and southwest France) speaks **Euskara,** the Basque language. While Galego and Catalan are closely related to Spanish, Basque is a complete oddball that's distinct from every other European language. With its seemingly impossible-to-pronounce words filled with k's, tx's, and z's (restrooms are *komunak: gizonak* for men and *emakumeak* for women), Euskara makes speaking Spanish seem easy.

If this sounds intimidating, never fear. In each of these regions, everyone also speaks Spanish, generally as a first language. But if you hear unfamiliar conversations in certain corners of Spain, tune in for an earful of Spain's other languages.

both France and Spain. But the rest of Europe didn't want powerful France to become even stronger. The war ended in compromise: Philip became king of Spain (Spain lost several possessions), but he had to renounce claims to any other thrones. The French-born, French-speaking Bourbon King Philip V (1683-1746) ruled Spain for 40 years. He and his heirs made themselves at home, building the Versailles-like Royal Palace in Madrid and La Granja near Segovia.

The French invaded Spain under Napoleon, who installed his brother as king in 1808. The Spaniards rose up (chronicled by Goya's paintings of the second and third of May 1808), sparking the Peninsular War—called the War of Independence by Spaniards—that decisively won Spain's independence from French rule.

Nineteenth-century Spain was a backward nation, with internal wars over which noble family should rule (the Carlist Wars), liberal revolutions put down brutally, and political assassinations.

Spain gradually lost its global possessions to other European powers and to South American revolutionaries. Spain hit rock bottom in 1898, when the upstart United States picked a fight and thrashed them in the Spanish-American War, taking away Spain's last major possessions: Cuba, Puerto Rico, and the Philippines.

THE 20TH CENTURY

A drained and disillusioned Spain was ill-prepared for modern technology and democratic government.

The old ruling class (the monarchy, Church, and landowners) fought new economic powers (cities, businessmen, labor unions) in a series of coups, strikes, and sham elections. In the 1920s, a military dictatorship under Miguel Primo de Rivera kept the old guard in power. In 1930, he was ousted, and an open election brought a modern democratic Republic to power. But the right wing regrouped under the Falange (fascist) party, fomenting unrest and sparking a military coup against the Republic in 1936, supported by General Francisco Franco (1892-1975).

For three years (1936-1939), Spain fought a bloody civil war between Franco's Nationalists (also called Falangists) and the Republic (also called Loyalists). Some 500,000 Spaniards died (due to all causes), and Franco won. (For more on the Spanish Civil War, see page 526.) For nearly the next four decades, Spain was ruled by Franco, an authoritarian, church-blessed dictator who tried to modernize the backward country while shielding it from corrupting modern influences. Spain was officially neutral in World War II, and the country spent much of the postwar era as a world apart. (On my first visit to Spain, in 1973, I came face-to-face with fellow teenagers—me in backpack and shorts, the Spaniards in military uniforms, brandishing automatic weapons.)

Before Franco died, he handpicked his protégé, King Juan Carlos I, to succeed him. But to everyone's surprise, the young, conservative, mild-mannered king stepped aside, settled for a figurehead title, and guided the country quickly and peacefully toward democratic elections (1977).

Spain had a lot of catching up to do. Culturally, the once-conservative nation exploded and embraced new ideas, even plunging to wild extremes. In the 1980s Spain flowered under left-leaning prime minister Felipe González. Spain showed the world its new modern face in 1992, hosting both a World Exhibition at Sevilla and the Summer Olympics at Barcelona.

SPAIN TODAY

From 1996 to 2004, Spain was led by Prime Minister José María Aznar. He adopted conservative policies to minimize the stress on the country's young democracy, fighting problems such as unem-

ployment and foreign debt with reasonable success. However, his support of the United States' war in Iraq was extremely unpopular. In spring of 2004, the retiring Aznar supported a similarly centrist successor, Mariano Rajoy, who seemed poised to win the election. On the eve of the election, on March 11, three Madrid train stations were bombed at the height of rush hour, killing 191 people. The terrorist group claiming responsibility denounced Spain's Iraq policy, and three days later, Aznar's party lost the election.

The next prime minister, left-of-center José Luis Rodríguez Zapatero, quickly began pulling Spain's troops out of Iraq, as well as enacting sweeping social changes. But Zapatero and his party were shown the door in 2011, a casualty of the economic crisis. The more-conservative Popular Party regained the majority, and Mariano Rajoy finally got his turn to be prime minister. Elections in 2015 created the most fragmented Spanish parliament ever, transforming the country's politics from a two-party system to a multi-party one. Months of disagreement among the four dominant parties regarding how to form a coalition government ended in a stalemate and calls for new elections.

In June 2016, Spaniards handed the People's Party the most seats in parliament—though not a majority—followed by the Spanish Socialist Workers' Party and Unidos Podemos, a party born from the 2011 protests. Mariano Rajoy took power, but less than two years later, his People's Party became mired in a corruption scandal. He was ousted from office in a no-confidence vote, replaced by Socialist Pedro Sánchez.

Spain enjoyed a strong economy through the late 1990s and early 2000s, thanks in part to a thriving tourism industry and a boom in housing construction. But the country was hit hard by the 2009 global economic downturn, and its economy entered a recession that lasted until 2014. Spain's banks stopped lending, those who couldn't meet their mortgage payments lost their homes, and by 2013 unemployment had soared to 25 percent.

Under pressure from the EU to cut its national debt, Spain's government limited payouts to new parents, scaled back government pensions and salaries, and made cuts in education and health care. These "austerity measures," which have eased since Rajoy was ousted in 2018, drew criticism from unions and the public, and Spain's mainstream politicians have become deeply unpopular. The effects of the austerity measures were felt strongly when the Covid-19 pandemic hit, exposing Spain's weakened health care system, leading to one of Europe's worst outbreaks.

Surprisingly, the once-admired King Juan Carlos lost popular support with some ill-timed, expensive hijinks even while Spain's economic woes mounted. After almost 40 years on the throne, he

PAST & PRESENT

1000 Years	Each dashed line = 500 years	Each dashed line =100 years	Each dashed

1000 0 500 1000 1100 1200 1300 1400 1500 1600

ROYAL LINEAGE ➤

FERDINAND & ISABEL

CHARLES I (V)

PHIL. III

PHILIP II

JUANA THE MAD & PHILIP THE FAIR

HABSBURG

CÁDIZ FOUNDED

PHOENICIAN

CARTH.

Trajan
Hadrian

ROMAN

VISIGOTH

SEVILLA RETAKEN

RECONQUISTA

TOLEDO RETAKEN

CÓRDOBA RETAKEN

GRANADA RETAKEN 1492

ARMADA

PUNIC WARS

Hannibal

MOORS ARRIVE 711

PEAK

MOORISH EMPIRE

CATHOLIC MONARCHS

MADRID BECOMES CAPITAL

GOLDEN AGE

MOHAMMED

KINGDOM OF ARAGON FOUNDED

MARRIAGE OF FERDINAND & ISABEL

INQUISITION BEGINS

St. Ignatius

St. Teresa of Avila

St. James

El Cid

UNIV. OF SALAMANCA FOUNDED

LUTHER'S 95 THESES

Jesus

PEAK OF TOLEDO'S CULTURAL DIVERSITY

REFORMATION & RELIGIOUS WARS

Cortés
Pizarro

PERU (INCAS) CONQ.

COLUMBUS REACHES AMERICA

AGE OF EXPLORATION

GREECE

TREATY OF TORDESILLAS

FLORIDA

MEXICO (AZTECS) CONQUERED

BATTLE OF BATALHA

MAGELLAN'S VOYAGE

PORTUGAL

← To Pileta & Altamira Cave Painting

MOORS DEFEATED

HENRY THE NAVIGATOR

MANUELINE PERIOD

UNDER SPANISH CONTROL

Segovia Aqueduct

ROMAN

Italica

VISIGOTHIC

Mezquita Córdoba

Alhambra

Alcázar Sevilla Rebuilt

Don Quixote

MOORISH

El Greco

Churches in Segovia & along the Camino

Sevilla Cath.

Burial of Count of Orgaz

ROMANESQUE

GOTHIC

El Escorial

Toledo Cath.

Barcelona Cathedral

RENAISSANCE

Salamanca Univ. Entrance

Charles V Palace

Lonja Sevilla

S. MARIA LA BLANCA SYNAGOGUE

PLATERESQUE

MUDEJAR

MOZARABIC

TRANSITO SYNAGOGUE

Juan de Herrera

1000 0 500 1000 1100 1200 1300 1400 1500 1600

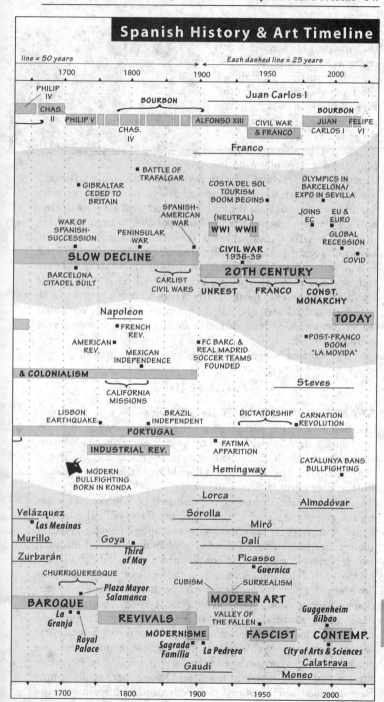

Spanish History & Art Timeline

line = 50 years — Each dashed line = 25 years

| 1700 | 1800 | 1900 | 1950 | 2000 |

PHILIP IV
CHAS. II
PHILIP V
CHAS. IV
BOURBON
ALFONSO XIII
CIVIL WAR & FRANCO
Juan Carlos I
BOURBON
JUAN CARLOS I
FELIPE VI
Franco

- BATTLE OF TRAFALGAR
- GIBRALTAR CEDED TO BRITAIN
- COSTA DEL SOL TOURISM BOOM BEGINS
- OLYMPICS IN BARCELONA/ EXPO IN SEVILLA
- SPANISH-AMERICAN WAR
- (NEUTRAL) WWI WWII
- JOINS EC
- EU & EURO
- WAR OF SPANISH-SUCCESSION
- PENINSULAR WAR
- CIVIL WAR 1936-39
- GLOBAL RECESSION
- COVID

SLOW DECLINE

- BARCELONA CITADEL BUILT
- CARLIST CIVIL WARS

20TH CENTURY

UNREST   FRANCO   CONST. MONARCHY

Napoleón
- FRENCH REV.
AMERICAN REV.
MEXICAN INDEPENDENCE
- FC BARC. & REAL MADRID SOCCER TEAMS FOUNDED

TODAY

- POST-FRANCO BOOM "LA MOVIDA"

& COLONIALISM

CALIFORNIA MISSIONS

Steves

LISBON EARTHQUAKE
BRAZIL INDEPENDENT
DICTATORSHIP
CARNATION REVOLUTION

PORTUGAL

INDUSTRIAL REV.
- FATIMA APPARITION

MODERN BULLFIGHTING BORN IN RONDA

Hemingway

CATALUNYA BANS BULLFIGHTING

Lorca
Sorolla
Almodóvar

Velázquez
- Las Meninas
Miró

Murillo
Goya
Dalí

Zurbarán
- Third of May
Picasso
- Guernica

CHURRIGUERESQUE
CUBISM   SURREALISM

- Plaza Mayor Salamanca

BAROQUE   **MODERN ART**

La Granja   **REVIVALS**   VALLEY OF THE FALLEN

Guggenheim Bilbao

Royal Palace   **MODERNISME**   **FASCIST**   **CONTEMP.**

Sagrada Família   La Pedrera   City of Arts & Sciences
Calatrava
Gaudí   Moneo

| 1700 | 1800 | 1900 | 1950 | 2000 |

PAST & PRESENT

abdicated in 2014, turning over the crown to his son, who now reigns as King Felipe VI.

Meanwhile, Catalunya, the Basque Country, and other regions of Spain have called for more autonomy or outright independence. In October 2017, the regional parliament of Catalunya held a referendum on independence (despite the Spanish government declaring it illegal). Though independence won overwhelmingly, most of those who would have voted against it simply boycotted what they considered an illegal vote—making the results impossible to interpret. Madrid sent in police, protests broke out (with occasional flashes of violence), several politicians were arrested (and sentenced to long prison terms), the Catalan president fled the country to evade arrest, and Spain wrestled with a constitutional crisis. Some years later, in a bid to ease tensions, the Spanish government in 2021 pardoned and released the jailed separatists. However, separatist leaders who avoided prosecution by fleeing the country were still considered fugitives.

It's clear that in Spain, history is unfolding in front of us.

Architecture

SPANISH HISTORY SET IN STONE

The two most fertile periods of architectural innovation in Spain were during the Moorish era and the golden age. Otherwise, Spanish architects marched obediently behind the rest of Europe. But in the modern era, Spain's architects have brought the country back to the forefront of construction and design.

Spain's Christian history is dominated by 700 years of a territorial give-and-take with Muslim Moors (711-1492). Throughout Spain, it seems every old church was built upon a mosque (Sevilla's immense cathedral, for one, and Córdoba's remarkable Mezquita, which preserved the mosque but plopped a cathedral right in the middle of it). Granada's Alhambra is the best example of the secular Moorish style. It's an *Arabian Nights* fairy tale: finely etched domes, lacy arcades, stalactite-studded ceilings, keyhole arches, and lush gardens. At its heart lies an elegantly proportioned courtyard, where the designers created an ingenious microclimate: water, plants, pottery, thick walls, and darkness...all to be cool. The stuccoed walls are ornamented with a stylized Arabic script, creating a visual chant of verses from the Quran. Meanwhile, simple Romanesque churches dotted the northern part of Spain not con-

Spain's Artists

El Greco (1541-1614) exemplifies the spiritual fervor of much Spanish art. Known for his ethereal paintings of "flickering" saints, the drama, surreal colors, and intentionally unnatural distortion of his compositions have the intensity of a religious vision. (For more on El Greco, see page 585.)

Diego Velázquez (1599-1660) went to the opposite extreme. His masterful royal court portraits are studies in camera-eye realism and cool detachment from his subjects. Velázquez was unmatched in using a few strokes of paint to suggest details.

Francisco de Goya (1746-1828) lacked Velázquez's detachment. He let his liberal tendencies shine through in unflattering portraits of royalty and in emotional scenes of abuse of power. He unleashed his inner passions in the eerie, nightmarish canvases of his last, "dark" stage. (For more on Goya, see page 460.)

Bartolomé Murillo (1617-1682) painted a dreamy world of religious visions. His pastel, soft-focus works of cute Baby Jesuses and radiant Virgin Marys helped keep Catholic doctrine palatable to the common folk while illustrating core doctrines of the Counter-Reformation. (For more on Murillo, see page 694.)

Pablo Picasso, Joan Miró, and Surrealist **Salvador Dalí** made their marks in the 20th century. Great museums featuring all three are in or near Barcelona. Although Picasso (1881-1973) lived most of his adult life in France, the 20th century's greatest artist explored Spanish themes, particularly in his inspirational antiwar *Guernica* mural (described on page 469). A flamboyant, waxed-mustachioed Surrealist painter, Salvador Dalí (1904-1989) and a fellow Spaniard, filmmaker Luis Buñuel, made the landmark art film *Un Chien Andalou* (see page 169).

trolled by the Moors (such as along the Camino de Santiago and in the folds of the Picos de Europa).

As the Christians slowly reconquered Iberian turf, they turned their fervor into stone, building churches in the lighter, heaven-reaching stained-glass Gothic style (as in León, Toledo, and Sevilla). Gothic was a French import, trickling into conservative Spain long after it had swept through Europe.

As Christians moved in, many Muslim artists and architects stayed, giving the new society the Mudejar style—Moorish in appearance, but commissioned by Catholics. (Mudejar means "those who stayed.") In Sevilla's Alcázar, the Arabic script on the walls refers not to the Quran, but to New Testament verses and Christian propaganda, such as "Dedicated to the magnificent Sultan, King Pedro—thanks to God!"

The money reaped and raped from Spain's colonies in the

Typical Church Architecture

History comes to life when you visit a centuries-old church. Even if you wouldn't know your apse from a hole in the ground, learning a few simple terms will enrich your experience. Note that not every church has every feature, and a "cathedral" isn't a type of church architecture, but rather a designation for a church that's a governing center for a local bishop.

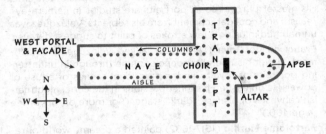

Aisles: Long, generally low-ceilinged arcades that flank the nave

Altar: Raised area with a ceremonial table (often adorned with candles or a crucifix), where the priest prepares and serves the bread and wine for Communion

Apse: Space behind the altar, sometimes bordered with small chapels

Barrel Vault: Continuous round-arched ceiling that resembles an extended upside-down U

Choir: Intimate space reserved for clergy and choir, located within the nave near the high altar and often screened off

Cloister: Covered hallways bordering a square or rectangular open-air courtyard, traditionally where monks and nuns got fresh air

Facade: Exterior of the church's main (west) entrance, usually highly decorated

Groin Vault: Arched ceiling formed where two equal barrel vaults meet at right angles

Narthex: Area (portico or foyer) between the main entry and the nave

Nave: Long central section of the church (running west to east, from the entrance to the altar) where the congregation sits or stands during the service

Transept: One of the two parts forming the "arms" of the cross in a traditional cross-shaped floor plan; runs north-south, perpendicularly crossing the east-west nave

West Portal: Main entry to the church (on the west end, opposite the main altar)

golden age (1500-1600) spurred new construction. Churches and palaces borrowed from the Italian Renaissance and the more elaborate Baroque. Ornamentation reached unprecedented heights in Spain, culminating in the Plateresque style of stonework, so called because it resembles intricate silver *(plata)* filigree work (see, for example, the facade of the University of Salamanca).

The 1500s were also the era of religious wars. The monastery/palace of El Escorial, built in sober geometric style, symbolizes the austerity of a newly reformed Catholic Church ready to strike back. King Philip II ruled his empire and directed the Inquisition from here, surrounded by plain white walls, well-scrubbed floors, and simple furnishings. El Escorial was built at a time when Catholic Spain felt threatened by Protestant heretics, and its construction dominated the Spanish economy for a generation (1563-1584). Because of this bully in the national budget, Spain has almost nothing else to show from this most powerful period of her history.

Over the next two centuries (1600-1800), Spain followed the rest of Europe in an explosion of extravagant Baroque designs, especially in Sevilla and Madrid in the 1700s. The 1800s were not much for innovation, but as Europe leapt from the 19th into the 20th century, it celebrated a rising standard of living and nearly a hundred years without a major war. Art Nouveau architects forced hard steel and concrete into softer organic shapes. Barcelona's answer to Art Nouveau was Modernisme, and its genius was Antoni Gaudí, with his asymmetrical "cake-in-the-rain" Barcelona buildings such as La Pedrera (a.k.a. Casa Milà) and Sagrada Família.

Much of Spain's 20th-century architecture—the minimal fascist style of the Valley of the Fallen and ugly concrete apartments—follows patterns seen elsewhere in Europe. But Spain today produces some of Europe's most interesting structures. Santiago Calatrava (from Valencia, born 1951) uses soaring arches and glass to create bridges (such as the iconic one in Sevilla, and similar copies around the world), airports, and performance halls (including Valencia's Opera House). One of the world's most striking and well-known buildings in recent years—Frank Gehry's Guggenheim Museum—is in Bilbao, and similarly innovative structures are popping up everywhere.

Bullfighting

AUTHENTIC RITUAL OR CRUEL SPECTACLE?

The Spanish bullfight is as much a ritual as it is a sport. Not to acknowledge the importance of the bullfight is to censor a venerable part of Spanish culture. But it also makes a spectacle out of the cruel killing of an animal. Should tourists boycott bullfights? I don't know.

When the day comes that bullfighting is kept alive by tourist dollars rather than by the local culture, then I'll agree with those who say it's immoral and that tourists shouldn't encourage it by buying tickets. Consider the morality of supporting this gruesome aspect of Spanish culture before buying a ticket. If you do decide to attend a bullfight, here's what you'll see:

While no two bullfights are the same, they unfold along a strict pattern. The ceremony begins punctually with a parade of participants across the ring. Then the trumpet sounds, the "Gate of Fear" opens, and the leading player—*el toro bravo*—thunders in. A ton of angry animal is an awesome sight, even from the cheap seats (with the sun in your eyes).

The fight is divided into three acts. Act I is designed to size up the bull and wear him down. With help from his assistants, the matador (literally, "killer") attracts the bull with a shake of the cape, then directs the animal past his body, as close as his bravery allows. The bull sees only things in motion and (some think) in red. After a few passes, the picadores enter, mounted on horseback, to spear the swollen lump of muscle at the back of the bull's neck. This tests the bull, causing him to lower his head and weakening the thrust of his horns.

In Act II, the matador's assistants (banderilleros) continue to enrage and weaken the bull. They charge the charging bull and—leaping acrobatically across its path—plunge brightly-colored barbed sticks into the bull's vital neck muscle.

After a short intermission, during which the matador may, according to tradition, ask permission to kill the bull and dedicate the kill to someone in the crowd, the final, lethal Act III begins.

The matador tries to dominate and tire the bull with hypnotic cape work. A good pass is when the matador stands completely still while the bull charges past. Then the matador thrusts a sword between the animal's shoulder blades for the kill. A quick kill is not always easy, and the matador may have to make several bloody thrusts before the sword stays in and the bull finally dies. (One of the matador's assistants may go in at the end to finish the job

with a dagger between the eyes.) Mules drag the dead bull out, and his meat is in the market *mañana* (barring "mad cow" concerns—and if ever there was a mad cow...). *Rabo del toro* (bull-tail stew) is a delicacy.

Throughout the fight, the crowd shows its approval or impatience. Shouts of *"¡Olé!"* or *"¡Torero!"* mean they like what they

Man vs. Bull Through History

The exact origins of bullfighting are impossible to trace, but men have battled bulls since antiquity. In ancient Crete, Minoan athletes sprang somersaults over bulls' horns (c. 1500 BC). In Asia and Italy, worshippers of Mithras and Artemis slaughtered bulls in ritual sacrifice (c. 500 BC-AD 500). And in ancient Rome, animal fights were popular warm-up acts for the gladiator games, performed in large arenas while thousands cheered. (In an interesting counterpoint, in many cultures—including, some would argue, Spain—bulls are respected or even revered, from those who would worship a golden calf in Moses' time, to the people of contemporary India.)

The Romans likely introduced bullfights to Spain. In the Middle Ages (historians speculate), bullfighting became a sport for knights, both Christian and Moorish, who held tournaments on feast days. They fought on horseback with lances, assisted by squires.

It was in the town of Ronda, around 1726, that the charismatic Francisco Romero transformed bullfighting from a sport of nobles on horseback to one of commoners on foot, armed only with a sword and cape. The mounted picador became the support player, and the matador became the star. Successive matadors thrilled crowds by allowing the bull to come ever closer.

From Spain, bullfighting spread to southern France and Latin America (where it continues today). In the 20th century, the dictator Franco made bullfighting the national pastime. Since Franco's death, it's become increasingly unpopular. Today, only a third of Spaniards follow it at all. Calling bullfights unsuitable for children, the government has banned live broadcasts on state-run TV, though private channels continue to cover the events.

Today's matadors remain the brave-but-pretty cover boys gracing the tabloids. But the sport's brutality was underscored in 2016 when a matador died after being gored by a bull—the first bullfighter to die in the ring in more than 30 years. The debate continues to divide the country: In 2010, bullfighting was banned in Catalunya, but in 2016 the national government overturned that ruling, saying it violated Spain's cultural heritage (though bullfights haven't resumed in Catalunya since).

see. Whistling or rhythmic hand-clapping greets cowardice and incompetence.

You're not likely to see much human blood spilled. For example, in 200 years of bullfighting in Sevilla, only 30 fighters have died (and only three were actually matadors). If a bull does kill a fighter, the next matador comes in to kill him. Historically, even the bull's mother is killed, since the evil qualities are assumed to have come from her.

After an exceptional fight, the crowd may wave white handkerchiefs to ask that the matador be awarded the bull's ear or tail. A brave bull, though dead, gets a victory lap from the mule team on his way to the slaughterhouse. Then the trumpet sounds, and a new bull charges in to face a fresh matador.

Fights are held on most Sundays from Easter through September (at 18:30 or 19:30). Serious fights with adult matadors are called *corridas de toros*. These are often sold out in advance. Summer fights are often *novillada*, with teenage novices doing the killing. *Corrida de toros* seats range from €20 for nosebleed seats in the sun to €140 for front-row seats in the shade. *Novillada* seats are half that, and generally easy to get at the arena a few minutes before showtime. A few Spanish women consider bullfighting sexy. They swoon at the dashing matadors who are sure to wear tight pants (with their *partes nobles*— noble parts—in view, generally organized to one side, farthest from the bull).

A typical bullfight lasts about two hours and consists of six separate fights—three matadors (each with his own team of picadores and banderilleros) fighting two bulls each. If you're curious to see a bullfight without making an expensive and time-consuming trip to the ring, keep an eye out for televised bullfights in bars. For a closer look at bullfighting by an American aficionado, read Ernest Hemingway's classic *Death in the Afternoon*.

well before you depart, and again a few days before your trip. See the websites listed above for current requirements.

ETIAS Registration: The European Union may soon require US and Canadian citizens to register online with the European Travel Information and Authorization System (ETIAS) before entering Spain and other Schengen Zone countries (quick and easy process). For the latest, check www.etiasvisa.com.

Tourist Information: Spain's national tourist office **in the US** will fill brochure requests and answer your general travel questions by email (newyork.information@tourspain.es). Scan their website (www.spain.info) for practical information and sightseeing ideas; you can download many brochures free of charge. If you're going to Barcelona, also see www.barcelonaturisme.cat.

In Spain, a good first stop in any town is generally the *Oficina de Turismo*, the tourist information office (abbreviated **TI** in this book). TIs are in business to help you spend money in their town—which can color their advice—but I still swing by to pick up a city map and get info on public transit, walking tours, special events, and nightlife. Some TIs have information on the entire country—or at least the region, so you can pick up maps and other info for destinations you'll be visiting later in your trip.

Emergency and Medical Help: For any emergency service—ambulance, police, or fire—call **112** from a mobile phone or landline (operators typically speak English). If you get sick, do as the locals do and go to a pharmacist for advice. Or ask at your hotel for help—they'll know the nearest medical and emergency services.

Theft or Loss: To replace a passport, you'll need to go in person to an embassy or consulate (see next). If your credit and debit cards disappear, cancel and replace them (see "Damage Control for Lost Cards" on page 961). File a police report, either on the spot or within a day or two; you'll need it to submit an insurance claim for lost or stolen items, and it can help with replacing your passport or credit and debit cards. For more information, see RickSteves.com/help.

US Embassy: Madrid—passport and nonemergency services by appointment only, Mon-Fri 08:00-13:00, +34 915 872 200 (Calle de Serrano 75, https://es.usembassy.gov).

US Consulates: Barcelona—nonemergency services by appointment only, Mon-Fri 9:00-13:00, +34 932 802 227, after-hours emergency +34 915 872 200 (Passeig de la Reina Elisenda de Montcada 23, https://es.usembassy.gov); Sevilla—no emergency passport services, +34 954 218 751 (Plaza Nueva 8B, https://es.usembassy.gov).

Canadian Embassy: Madrid—passport services by appointment only, Mon-Thu 8:30-17:30, Fri and Aug weekdays 8:30-

PRACTICALITIES

This chapter covers the practical skills of European travel: how to get tourist information, pay for things, sightsee efficiently, find good-value accommodations, eat affordably but well, use technology wisely, and get between destinations smoothly. For more information on these topics, see RickSteves.com/travel-tips.

Travel Tips

Travel Advisories: Before traveling, check updated health and safety conditions, including restrictions for your destination, on the travel pages of the US State Department (www.travel.state.gov) and Centers for Disease Control and Prevention (www.cdc.gov/travel). The Spanish government has an English-language website with all the updated requirements for travel to Spain (https://www.spth.gob.es). The US embassy website for Spain is another good source of information (see below).

    Covid Vaccine/Test Requirements: It's possible you'll need to present proof of vaccination against the coronavirus and/or a negative Covid-19 test result to board a plane to Europe or back to the US. Carefully check requirements for each country you'll visit

14:30, +34 913 828 400 (in Torre Espacio skyscraper at Paseo de la Castellana 259D, www.espana.gc.ca).

Canadian Consulate: Barcelona—passport services by appointment only, Mon-Fri 9:00-12:30, +34 932 703 614, after-hours emergency in Ottawa—call collect +1 613 996 8885 (Plaça de Catalunya 9, www.spain.gc.ca, click "Contact Us," then "Consulate of Canada in Barcelona").

Time Zones: Spain, like most of continental Europe, is generally six/nine hours ahead of the East/West coasts of the US. The exceptions are the beginning and end of Daylight Saving Time: Europe "springs forward" the last Sunday in March (two weeks after most of North America), and "falls back" the last Sunday in October (one week before North America). For a handy time converter, use the world clock app on your phone or download one (see www.timeanddate.com).

Business Hours: For visitors, Spain is a land of strange and frustrating schedules. Many businesses respect the afternoon siesta. When it's 100 degrees in the shade, you'll understand why. The biggest museums stay open all day. Smaller ones often close for a siesta. Shops are generally open from about 9:30 to 14:00 and from 17:00 to 21:00, longer for big chain shops or touristy places. Small shops are often open on Saturday only in the morning, and closed all day Sunday.

Watt's Up? Europe's electrical system is 220 volts, instead of North America's 110 volts. Most electronics (laptops, phones, cameras) and appliances (newer hair dryers, CPAP machines) convert automatically, so you won't need a converter, but you will need an adapter plug with two round prongs, sold inexpensively at travel stores in the US.

Rip up this book! Turn chapters into mini guidebooks: Break the book's spine and use a utility knife to slice apart chapters, keeping gummy edges intact. Reinforce the chapter spines with clear wide tape; use a heavy-duty stapler; or make or buy a cheap cover (see the Travel Store at RickSteves.com), swapping out chapters as you travel.

Discounts: Discounts for sights are generally not listed in this book. However, seniors (age 65 and over), youths under 18, and students and teachers with proper identification cards (obtain from www.isic.org) can get discounts at many sights—always ask. Some discounts are available only to European citizens.

Online Translation Tips: Google's Chrome browser instantly translates websites; Translate.google.com and DeepL.com are also handy. The Google Translate app converts spoken or typed English into most European languages (and vice versa) and can also translate text it "reads" with your phone's camera.

Going Green: There's plenty you can do to reduce your envi-

PRACTICALITIES

ronmental footprint when traveling. When practical, take a train instead of a flight within Europe, and use public transportation within cities. In hotels, use the "Do Not Disturb" sign to avoid daily linen and towel changes (or hang up your towels to signal you'll reuse them). Bring a reusable shopping tote and refillable water bottle (Europe's tap water is safe to drink). Skip printed brochures, maps, or other materials that you don't plan to keep—get your info online instead. To find out how Rick Steves' Europe is offsetting carbon emissions with a self-imposed carbon tax, see RickSteves.com/about-us/climate-smart.

Money

Here's my basic strategy for using money wisely in Europe. I pack the following and keep it all safe in my money belt.

Credit Card: You'll use your credit card for purchases both big (hotels, advance tickets) and small (little shops, food stands). Many European businesses have gone cashless, making a card your only payment option. A "tap-to-pay" or "contactless" card is widely accepted and simplest to use.

Debit Card: Use this at ATMs to withdraw a small amount of local cash. Wait until you arrive to get euros (European airports have plenty of ATMs); if you buy euros before your trip, you'll pay bad stateside exchange rates. While most transactions are by card these days, cash can help you out of a jam if your card randomly doesn't work, and can be useful to pay for things like tips and local guides. But don't take out too much, or you may find you can't use it all.

Backup Card: Some travelers carry a third card (debit or credit; ideally from a different bank) in case one gets lost or simply doesn't work.

Stash of Cash: I carry $100-200 in US dollars as a cash backup, which comes in handy in an emergency (for example, if your debit card gets eaten by the machine).

BEFORE YOU GO

Know your cards. For credit cards, Visa and MasterCard are universal while American Express and Discover are less common. US debit cards with a Visa or MasterCard logo will work in any European ATM.

Go "contactless." Get comfortable using contactless pay options. Check to see if you already have—or can get—a tap-to-pay version of your credit card (look on the card for the tap-to-pay symbol—four curvy lines), and consider setting up your smartphone for contactless payment (see next section for details). Both options are widely used in Europe and are more secure than a physical credit

Exchange Rate

1 euro (€) = about $1.10

To convert prices in euros to dollars, add about 20 percent: €20 = about $22, €50 = about $55. Like the dollar, one euro is broken into 100 cents. Coins range from €0.01 to €2, and bills from €5 to €200 (bills over €50 are rarely used).

Check www.oanda.com for the latest exchange rates.

card: Instead of recording your credit card number, a one-time encrypted "token" enables the purchase and expires shortly afterward.

Know your PIN. Make sure you know the numeric, four-digit PIN for each of your cards, both debit and credit. Request it if you don't have one, as it may be required for some purchases. Allow time to receive the information by mail—it's not always possible to obtain your PIN online.

Report your travel dates. Let your bank know that you'll be using your debit and credit cards in Europe, and when and where you're headed.

Adjust your ATM withdrawal limit. Find out how much you can withdraw daily and ask for a higher daily limit if you want to get more cash at once. Note that European ATMs will withdraw funds only from checking accounts, not savings accounts.

Find out about fees. For any purchase or withdrawal made with a card, you may be charged a currency conversion fee (1-3 percent) and/or a Visa or MasterCard international transaction fee (less than 1 percent). If you're getting a bad deal, consider getting a new card. Reputable no-fee cards include those from Capital One, as well as Charles Schwab debit cards. Most credit unions and some airline loyalty cards have low or no international transaction fees.

IN EUROPE
Using Credit Cards and Payment Apps

Tap-to-Pay or **Contactless Cards:** These cards have the usual chip and/or magnetic stripe, but with the addition of a contactless symbol. Simply tap your card against a contactless reader to complete a transaction—no PIN or signature is required. This is by far the easiest way to pay and has become the standard in much of Europe. Some small businesses (such as market stalls or food stands) accept *only* tap cards, and sometimes don't accept cash.

Payment Apps: Just like at home, you can pay with your smartphone or smartwatch by linking a credit card to an app such as Apple Pay or Google Pay. To pay, hold your phone near a con-

PRACTICALITIES

tactless reader; you may need to verify the transaction with a face scan, fingerprint scan, or passcode. If you've arrived in Europe without a tap-to-pay card, you can easily set up your phone to work in this way.

Other Card Types: Chip-and-PIN cards have a visible chip embedded in them; rather than swiping, you insert the card into the payment machine, then enter your PIN on a keypad. In Europe, these cards have largely been supplanted by tap-to-pay cards, but you may be asked to use chip-and-PIN for certain purchases. **Swipe-and-sign** credit cards—with a swipeable magnetic stripe, and a receipt you have to sign—are increasingly rare.

Will My US Card Work? Usually, yes. On rare occasions, at self-service payment machines (such as transit-ticket kiosks, toll-booths, or fuel pumps), some US cards may not work. Usually a tap-to-pay card does the trick in these situations. Just in case, carry cash as a backup and look for a cashier who can process your payment if your card is rejected. Drivers should be prepared to move on to the next gas station if necessary. (In some countries, gas stations sell prepaid gas cards, which you can purchase with any US card). When approaching a toll plaza or ferry ticket line, use the "cash" lane.

Using Cash

Cash Machines: European cash machines work just like they do at home—except they spit out local currency instead of dollars, calculated at the day's standard bank-to-bank rate. In most places, ATMs are easy to locate—in Spain ask for a *cajero automático*. When possible, withdraw cash from a bank-run ATM located just outside that bank.

If your debit card doesn't work, try a lower amount—your request may have exceeded your withdrawal limit or the ATM's limit. If you still have a problem, try a different ATM or come back later.

Avoid "independent" ATMs, such as Travelex, Euronet, Moneybox, Your Cash, Cardpoint, and Cashzone. These have high fees, can be less secure, and may try to trick users with "dynamic currency conversion" (see next).

Dynamic Currency Conversion: When withdrawing cash at an ATM or paying with a credit card, you'll often be asked whether you want the transaction processed in dollars or in the local currency. Always refuse the conversion and *choose the local currency*. While DCC offers the illusion of convenience, it comes with a poor exchange rate, and you'll wind up losing money.

Exchanging Cash: Minimize exchanging money in Europe; it's expensive (you'll generally lose 5 to 10 percent). In a pinch you can find exchange desks at major train stations or airports. Banks generally do not exchange money unless you have an account with them.

Security Tips

Pickpockets target tourists. Keep your cash, credit cards, and passport secure in your money belt, and carry only a day's spending money in your front pocket or wallet.

Before inserting your card into an ATM, inspect the front. If anything looks crooked, loose, or damaged, it could be a sign of a card-skimming device. When entering your PIN, carefully block other people's view of the keypad.

Avoid using a debit card for purchases. Because a debit card pulls funds directly from your bank account, potential charges incurred by a thief will stay on your account while your bank investigates.

To access your accounts online while traveling, be sure to use a secure connection (see the "Tips on Internet Security" sidebar, later).

Damage Control for Lost Cards

If you lose your credit or debit card, report the loss immediately to the respective global customer-assistance centers. With a mobile phone, call these 24-hour US numbers: Visa (+1 303 967 1096), MasterCard (+1 636 722 7111), and American Express (+1 336 393 1111). From a landline, you can call these US numbers collect by going through a local operator.

You'll need to provide the primary cardholder's identification-verification details (such as birth date, mother's maiden name, or Social Security number). You can generally receive a temporary card within two or three business days in Europe (see RickSteves. com/help for more).

If you report your loss within two days, you typically won't be responsible for unauthorized transactions on your account, although many banks charge a liability fee.

TIPPING

Tipping in Spain isn't as automatic and generous as in the US. For special service, tips are appreciated, but not expected. As in the US, the proper amount depends on your resources, tipping philosophy, and the circumstances, but some general guidelines apply.

Restaurants: If eating at the counter of a tapas bar, there's no need to tip, though it's respectable to round up the bill. At restaurants with table service, if a service charge is included in the bill,

add about 5 percent; if it's not, leave 10-15 percent. If paying with a credit card, be prepared to tip separately with cash or coins; credit card receipts don't often have a tip line. For more details on tipping in restaurants and tapas bars, see pages 979 and 981.

Taxis: For a typical ride, just round up your fare a bit (for instance, if the fare is €4.85, pay €5). If the cabbie hauls your bags and zips you to the airport to help you catch your flight, you might want to toss in a little more.

Services: In general, if someone in the tourism or service industry does a super job for you, a small tip of a euro or two is appropriate...but not required. If you're not sure whether (or how much) to tip, ask a local for advice.

GETTING A VAT REFUND

Wrapped into the purchase price of your Spanish souvenirs is a Value-Added Tax (VAT) of 21 percent (in Spain, it's called IVA—*Impuesto sobre el Valor Añadido*). You're entitled to get most of that tax back if you purchase more than €90 worth of goods at a store that participates in the VAT-refund scheme. Typically, you must ring up the minimum at a single retailer—you can't add up your purchases from various shops to reach the required amount. (If the store ships the goods to your US home, VAT is not assessed on your purchase.)

Getting your refund is straightforward...and worthwhile if you spend a significant amount.

At the Merchant: Have the merchant completely fill out the refund document (they'll ask for your passport; a photo of your passport usually works). Keep track of the paperwork and your original sales receipt. Note that you're not supposed to use your purchased goods before you leave Europe.

At the Border or Airport: Process your VAT document at your last stop in the European Union (such as at the airport) with the customs agent who deals with VAT refunds (allow plenty of extra time to deal with this process). At some airports, you'll have to go to a customs office to get your documents stamped and then to a separate VAT refund service (such as Global Blue or Planet) to process the refund. At other airports, a single VAT desk handles the whole thing. (Note that refund services typically extract a 4 percent fee, but you're paying for the convenience of receiving your money in cash immediately or as a credit to your card). Otherwise, you'll need to mail the stamped refund documents to the address given by the merchant.

CUSTOMS FOR AMERICAN SHOPPERS

You can take home $800 worth of items per person duty-free, once every 31 days. Many processed and packaged foods are allowed, in-

cluding cheeses, dried herbs, jams, baked goods, candy, chocolate, oil, vinegar, condiments, and honey. Fresh fruits and vegetables and most meats are not allowed, with exceptions for some canned items. As for alcohol, you can bring in one liter duty-free (it can be packed securely in your checked luggage, along with any other liquid-containing items).

To bring alcohol (or liquid-packed foods) in your carry-on bag on your flight home, buy it at a duty-free shop at the airport. You'll increase your odds of getting it onto a connecting flight if it's packaged in a "STEB"—a secure, tamper-evident bag. But stay away from liquids in opaque, ceramic, or metallic containers, which usually cannot be successfully screened (STEB or no STEB).

For details on allowable goods, customs rules, and duty rates, visit http://help.cbp.gov.

Sightseeing

Sightseeing can be hard work. Use these tips to make your visits to Spain's finest sights meaningful, fun, efficient, and painless.

In the wake of the pandemic, be prepared for changes to hours or entry procedures; call ahead to confirm details if it seems like a museum's website hasn't been updated recently.

MAPS AND NAVIGATION TOOLS

A good map is essential for efficient navigation while sightseeing. The maps in this book are concise and simple, designed to help you locate recommended destinations, sights, hotels, and restaurants. In Europe, simple maps are generally free at TIs and hotels.

You can also use a mapping app on your mobile device, which provides turn-by-turn directions for walking, driving, and taking public transit. Google Maps, Apple Maps, and CityMaps2Go allow you to download maps for offline use; ideally, download the areas you'll need before your trip. For certain features, you'll need to be online—either using Wi-Fi or an international data plan.

PLAN AHEAD

Set up an itinerary that allows you to fit in all your must-see sights. For a one-stop look at opening hours, see this book's "At a Glance" sidebars for major destinations (Barcelona, Madrid, Toledo, Granada, Sevilla, Camino de Santiago, and Basque Country). Most sights keep stable hours, but you can easily confirm the latest by checking at the TI or on museum websites.

Don't put off visiting a must-see sight—you never know when a place will close unexpectedly for a holiday, strike, or restoration. Many museums are closed or have reduced hours at least a few ' a year, especially on holidays such as Christmas, New Year's,

Covid Changes: What to Expect Post-Pandemic

The Covid-19 pandemic caused many disruptions and changes to the way museums and other sights operate—some of which were temporary, others of which may turn out to be permanent. Depending on what's happening during your visit, hours may be modified; reservations may be required (or strongly recommended) to control crowd flow; and paper maps and audioguides may have been replaced by apps.

For any must-see sight on your list, check in advance on its official website (listed throughout this book) to fully understand the current situation. You may learn that it's required to prebook, for example, or you may be able to download an app so you'll have an up-to-date museum map and audioguide on your phone when you arrive.

Labor Day (May 1). A list of holidays is in the appendix; check for possible closures during your trip. In summer, some sights may stay open late. Off-season hours may be shorter.

Going at the right time helps avoid crowds. This book offers tips on the best times to see specific sights. Try visiting popular sights very early or very late. Evening visits (when possible) are usually more peaceful, with fewer crowds. Late morning is usually the worst time to visit a popular sight.

If you plan to hire a local guide, reserve ahead by email. Popular guides can get booked up.

Study up. To get the most out of the sight descriptions in this book, read them before you visit.

RESERVATIONS, ADVANCE TICKETS, AND PASSES

Many popular sights in Europe come with long lines—not to get in, but to buy a ticket. Visitors who buy tickets online in advance (or who have a museum pass covering these key sights) can skip the line and waltz right in. Advance tickets are generally timed-entry, meaning you're guaranteed admission on a certain date and time.

For some sights, buying ahead is required (tickets aren't sold at the sight and it's the only way to get in). At other sights, buying ahead is recommended to skip the line and save time. And for many sights, advance tickets are available but unnecessary: At these uncrowded sights you can simply arrive, buy a ticket, and go in.

Don't confuse the reservation options: available, recommended, and required. Use my advice in this book as a guide. Note any must-see sights that sell out long in advance and be prepared to

buy tickets early. If you do your research, you'll know the smart strategy.

Given how precious your vacation time is, I'd book in advance where it's required (as soon as your dates are firm) and where it will save time in a long line (in some cases, this can be done even on the day you plan to visit). For Spain-specific recommendations, see page 25.

Several cities offer sightseeing passes that are worthwhile values for serious sightseers; do the math to see if they'll save you money.

AT SIGHTS

Here's what you can typically expect:

Entering: You may not be allowed to enter if you arrive too close to closing time. And guards start ushering people out well before the actual closing time, so don't save the best for last.

Many sights have a security check. Allow extra time for these lines. Some sights require you to check day packs and coats. (If you'd rather not check your day pack, try carrying it tucked under your arm like a purse as you enter.)

At churches—which often offer interesting art (usually free) and a cool, welcome seat—a modest dress code (no bare shoulders or shorts) is encouraged though rarely enforced.

Photography: If the museum's photo policy isn't clearly posted, ask a guard. Generally, taking photos without a flash or tripod is allowed. Some sights ban selfie sticks; others ban photos altogether.

Audioguides and Apps: I've produced free, downloadable audio tours for neighborhood walks in Barcelona, Madrid, and Sevilla; look for the 🎧 in this book. For more on my audio tours, see page 26.

Some sights offer audioguides with dry-but-useful recorded descriptions in English. In some cases, you'll rent a device to carry around (if you bring your own plug-in earbuds, you'll enjoy better sound). Increasingly, museums and sights instead offer an app you can download with their audioguide (often free; check websites from home and consider downloading in advance as not all sights offer free Wi-Fi).

Temporary Exhibits: Museums may show special exhibits in addition to their permanent collection. Some exhibits are included in the entry price, while others come at an extra cost (which you may have to pay even if you don't want to see the exhibit).

Expect Changes: Artwork can be on tour, on loan, out sick, or shifted at the whim of the curator. Pick up a floor plan as you enter and ask the museum staff if you can't find a particular item. Say the title or artist's name, or point to the photograph in this

book, and ask, "*¿Dónde está?*" (DOHN-day eh-STAH; meaning, "Where is?").

Services: Important sights usually have a reasonably priced on-site café or cafeteria (handy and air-conditioned places to rejuvenate during a long visit). The WCs at sights are free and generally clean.

Before Leaving: At the gift shop, scan the postcard rack or thumb through a guidebook to be sure you haven't overlooked something that you'd like to see. Every sight or museum offers more than what is covered in this book. Use the information I provide as an introduction—not the final word.

Sleeping

Extensive and opinionated listings of good-value rooms are a major feature of this book's Sleeping sections. Rather than list accommodations scattered throughout a town, I choose hotels in my favorite neighborhoods that are convenient to your sightseeing.

My recommendations run the gamut, from dorm beds to luxurious rooms with all the comforts. I like places that are clean, central, relatively quiet at night, reasonably priced, friendly, small enough to have a hands-on owner or manager, and run with a respect for Spanish traditions. I'm more impressed by a handy location and fun-loving philosophy than oversized TVs and a fancy gym. Most of my recommendations fall short of perfection. But if I can find a place with most of these features, it's a keeper.

In Spain, high season *(temporada alta)* is from July to September—except for a dip in August in hot inland cities like Madrid and Salamanca. Low season *(temporada baja)* runs from November through March. Barcelona can be busy any time of year with festivals and trade fairs. Book your accommodations as soon as your itinerary is set, especially if you want to stay at one of my top listings or if you'll be traveling during busy times (such as Semana Santa—Holy Week—particularly in the south). See the appendix for a list of major holidays and festivals.

Some people make reservations a few days ahead as they travel. This approach fosters spontaneity, and booking sites make it easy to find available rooms, but—especially during busy times—you run the risk of settling for lesser-value accommodations.

RATES AND DEALS

I've categorized my recommended accommodations based on price, indicated with a dollar-sign rating (see sidebar). Room prices can fluctuate significantly with demand and amenities (size, views, room class, and so on), but relative price categories remain con-

Sleep Code

Hotels in this book are categorized according to the average price of a standard double room without breakfast in high season.

$$$$	**Splurge:**	Most rooms over €170
$$$	**Pricier:**	€130-170
$$	**Moderate:**	€90-130
$	**Budget:**	€50-90
¢	**Backpacker:**	Under €50
RS%	**Rick Steves discount**	

Unless otherwise noted, credit cards are accepted, hotel staff speak basic English, and free Wi-Fi is available. Comparison-shop by checking prices at several hotels (on each hotel's own website, on a booking site, or by email). For the best deal, *book directly with the hotel.* Ask for a discount if paying in cash; if the listing includes **RS%,** request a Rick Steves discount.

stant. Hoteliers are encouraged to quote prices with the IVA tax included—but it's smart to ask when you book your room.

Booking Direct: Once your dates are set, compare prices at several hotels. You can do this by checking hotel websites and booking sites such as Hotels.com or Booking.com. After you've zeroed in on your choice, book directly with the hotel itself. This increases the chances that the hotelier will be able to accommodate special needs or requests (such as shifting your reservation). And when you book on the hotel's website, by email, or by phone, the owner avoids the commission paid to booking sites, giving them wiggle room to offer you a discount, a nicer room, or a free breakfast (if it's not already included).

Getting a Discount: Some hotels extend a discount to those who pay cash or stay longer than three nights. And some accommodations offer a special discount for Rick Steves readers, indicated in this guidebook by the abbreviation **"RS%."** Discounts vary: Ask for details when you reserve. Generally, to qualify for this discount, you must book direct (not through a booking site), mention this book when you reserve, show this book upon arrival, and sometimes pay cash or stay a certain number of nights. In some cases, you may need to enter a discount code (which I've provided in the listing) in the booking form on the hotel's website. Rick Steves discounts apply to readers with either print or digital books. Understandably, discounts do not apply to promotional rates.

TYPES OF ACCOMMODATIONS
Hotels

In this book, the price for a double room ranges from about $60

Using Online Services to Your Advantage

From booking services to user reviews, online businesses are playing a greater role in travelers' planning than ever before. Take advantage of their pluses—and be wise to their downsides.

Booking Sites

Booking websites such as Booking.com and Hotels.com offer one-stop shopping for hotels. While convenient for travelers, they're both a blessing and a curse for small, independent, family-run hotels. Without a presence on these sites, small hotels become almost invisible. But to be listed, a hotel must pay a sizable commission...and promise that its own website won't undercut the price on the booking-service site.

Here's the work-around: Use the big sites to research what's out there, then book directly with the hotel by email or phone, in which case hotel owners are free to give you whatever price they like. Ask for a room without the commission markup (or ask for a free breakfast if not included, or a free upgrade). If you do book online, be sure to use the hotel's own website. The price will likely be the same as via a booking site, but your money goes to the hotel, not agency commissions.

As a savvy consumer, remember: When you book with an online service, you're adding a middleman who takes a cut. To support small, family-run hotels whose world is more difficult than ever, book direct.

Short-Term Rental Sites

Rental juggernaut Airbnb (along with other short-term rental sites) allows travelers to rent rooms and apartments, often providing more value, space, and amenities than a cookie-cutter hotel. Airbnb fans appreciate feeling part of a real neighborhood and getting into a daily routine as "temporary Europeans." Some places are run by thoughtful hosts, allowing you to get to know a local and keep your money in the community; but beware: Others are impersonally managed by large, absentee agencies.

(very simple, toilet and shower down the hall) to $400 (maximum plumbing and more), with most clustering at about $150.

Some hotels can add an extra bed (for a small charge) to turn a double into a triple; some offer larger rooms for four or more people (I call these "family rooms" in the listings). If there's space for an extra cot, they'll cram it in for you. In general, a triple room is cheaper than the cost of a double and a single. Three or four people can economize by requesting one big room.

Spain has stringent restrictions on smoking in public places. Smoking is not permitted in common areas, but hotels can designate 10 percent of their rooms for smokers.

Arrival and Check-In: Hotels and B&Bs are sometimes lo-

Critics of Airbnb see it as a threat to "traditional Europe." Landlords can make more money renting to short-stay travelers, driving rents up—and local residents out. Traditional businesses are replaced by ones that cater to tourists. And the character and charm that made those neighborhoods desirable to the tourists in the first place goes too. Some cities have cracked down, requiring owners to obtain a license and to occupy rental properties part of the year (and staging disruptive "inspections" that inconvenience guests).

As a lover of Europe, I share the worry of those who see residents nudged aside by tourists. But as an advocate for travelers, I appreciate the value Airbnb can provide in offering the chance to stay in a local building or neighborhood with potentially fewer tourists.

User Reviews

User-generated review sites and apps such as Yelp and TripAdvisor can give you a consensus of opinions about everything from hotels and restaurants to sights and nightlife. If you scan reviews of a restaurant or hotel and see several complaints about noise or a rotten location, you've gained insight that can help in your decision-making.

As a guidebook writer, my sense is that there is a big difference between the uncurated information on a review site and the vetted listings in a guidebook. A user review is based on the limited experience of one person, who stayed at just one hotel in a given city and ate at a few restaurants there. A guidebook is the work of a trained researcher who forms a well-developed basis for comparison by visiting many restaurants and hotels year after year.

Both types of information have their place, and in many ways, they're complementary. If something is well reviewed in a guidebook and it also gets good online reviews, it's likely a winner.

cated on the higher floors of a multipurpose building with a secured door. In that case, look for your hotel's name on the buttons by the main entrance. When you ring the bell, you'll be buzzed in.

Hotel elevators are common, though small, and some older buildings still lack them. You may have to climb a flight of stairs to reach the elevator (if so, you can ask the front desk for help carrying your bags up).

The EU requires hotels to collect your name, nationality, and ID number. At check-in, the receptionist will normally ask for your passport and may keep it for several hours. If you're not comfortable leaving your passport at the desk, bring a copy to give them instead.

If you're arriving in the morning, your room probably won't

Hotels in Spain: Know the Code

No national regulation exists to classify hotels, but regional governments divide accommodations into several broad categories. Look for a blue-and-white plaque by the hotel door indicating the category:

Hotel (H): The most comfortable and expensive accommodation option (rated with stars).

Parador: A government-run inn, often in a refurbished castle or palace. They can be expensive unless you qualify for a discounted rate.

Hostal (Hs): Less expensive than a hotel, but still rated by stars. Don't confuse *hostales* with youth hostels.

Pensión (P), Casa de Huéspedes (CH), and **Fonda (F):** Cheaper, usually family-run places.

Albergue: Basic hostel.

Casa Particular: Private home renting budget rooms.

Casa Rural: Country house renting rooms, ranging from basic to fancy.

be ready. Check your bag safely at the hotel and dive right into sightseeing.

In Your Room: Most hotel rooms have a TV and free Wi-Fi, which can vary in strength and quality. Simpler places rarely have a room phone.

Some hotels don't use central heat before November 1 and after April 1 (unless it's unusually cold); prepare for cool evenings if you travel in spring and fall. Summer can be extremely hot. Consider air-conditioning, fans, and noise (since you'll want your window open). Many rooms come with mini refrigerators. Conveniently, expensive business-class hotels in big, nonresort cities often drop their prices in July and August, just when the air-conditioned comfort they offer is most important.

Checking Out: While it's customary to pay for your room upon departure, it can be a good idea to settle your bill the day before, when you're not in a hurry and while the manager's in.

Hotelier Help: Hoteliers can be a good source of advice. Most know their city well and can assist you with everything from public transit and airport connections to finding a good restaurant, the nearest launderette, or a late-night pharmacy.

Hotel Hassles: Even at the best places, mechanical breakdowns occur: sinks leak, hot water turns cold, toilets may gurgle or smell, the Wi-Fi goes out, or the air-conditioning dies when you need it most. Report your concerns clearly and calmly at the front desk.

Light sleepers struggle more in Spain than just about anywhere in Europe. Street noise is loud (Spaniards are notorious night owls, and traffic can rumble and screech until very late), and walls and doors tend to be very thin. Earplugs are a necessity. Always ask to see your room first. If you suspect night noise will be a problem, request a quiet *(tranquilo)* room in the back, on the courtyard, and/ or on an upper floor *(planta alta)*. In most cases, view rooms *(con vista)* come with street noise. You'll often sleep better and for less money in a room without a view.

To guard against theft in your room, keep valuables out of sight. Some rooms come with a safe, and other hotels have safes at the front desk. I've never bothered using one and in a lifetime of travel, I've never had anything stolen from my room.

For more complicated problems, don't expect instant results. Any legitimate place in Spain is legally required to have a complaint book *(libro de reclamaciones)*. A request for this book will generally prompt the hotelier to solve your problem to keep you from writing a complaint. Above all, keep a positive attitude. If your hotel is a disappointment, spend more time out enjoying the place you came to see.

Hostales and Pensiones

Budget hotels—called *hostales* and *pensiones*—are easy to find, inexpensive, and, when chosen properly, a fun part of the Spanish cultural experience. These places are often family-owned, and may or may not have amenities such as private bathrooms and air-conditioning. Don't confuse a *hostal* with a hostel—a Spanish *hostal* is an inexpensive hotel, not a hostel with bunks in dorms.

Paradores

Spain has a system of luxurious, government-sponsored, historic inns called *paradores*. These are often renovated castles, palaces, or monasteries, many with great views and stately atmospheres. While full of Old World character, they are usually run in a sterile, bureaucratic way. They are generally pricier than hotels but do offer discounts for travelers 30 and younger, and 55 and older ($100-300 doubles; for details, bonus packages, and family deals, see www. parador.es). If you're not eligible for any deals, you'll get a better value by sleeping in what I call "poor-man's *paradores*"—elegant hotels that offer double the warmth and Old World intimacy for half the price of these palaces.

Casas Rurales

Located mainly in rural areas throughout Spain, *casas rurales* can be furnished rooms, whole farmhouses, villas, or sprawling ranches. Some are simple, but others are luxurious, and they are mostly used

Making Hotel Reservations

Reserve your rooms as soon as you've pinned down your travel dates. For busy national holidays (and, in Barcelona, trade fairs), it's wise to reserve far in advance (see the appendix).

Requesting a Reservation: For family-run hotels, it's generally best to book your room directly via email or phone. For business-class and chain hotels, or if you'd rather book online, reserve directly through the hotel's official website (not a booking website). Almost all of my recommended hotels take reservations in English.

Here's what the hotelier wants to know:

- Type(s) of room(s) you want and number of guests
- Number of nights you'll stay
- Arrival and departure dates, written European-style as day/month/year (18/06/24 or 18 June 2024)
- Special requests (en suite bathroom, cheapest room, twin beds vs. double bed, quiet room)
- Applicable discounts (such as a Rick Steves discount, cash discount, or promotional rate)

Confirming a Reservation: Most places will request a credit-card number to hold your room. If the hotel's website doesn't have a secure form where you can enter the number directly, share this info via a phone call.

Canceling a Reservation: If you must cancel, it's courteous—and smart—to do so with as much notice as possible, especially for

by Spaniards, so you'll really be going local. Many are in the countryside, so you will need a car. For more information and reservations, try www.ecoturismorural.com or www.micasarural.com.

Short-Term Rentals

A short-term rental—whether an apartment, a house, or a room in a private residence—is a popular alternative, especially if you plan to settle in one location for several nights. For stays longer than a few days, you can usually find a rental that's comparable to—and cheaper than—a hotel room with similar amenities. Plus, you'll get a behind-the-scenes peek into how locals live.

Many places require a minimum stay and have strict cancellation policies. And you're generally on your own: There's no reception desk, breakfast, or daily cleaning service.

Finding Accommodations: Websites such as Airbnb, FlipKey, Booking.com, and VRBO let you browse a wide range of properties. In Barcelona, you can check to see if your choice is licensed by visiting the www.fairtourism.barcelona website. Alternatively, rental agencies such as InterhomeUSA.com and RentaVilla.

From: rick@ricksteves.com
Sent: Today
To: info@hotelcentral.com
Subject: Reservation request for 19-22 July

Dear Hotel Central,

I would like to stay at your hotel. Please let me know if you have a room available and the price for:
• 2 people
• Double bed and en suite bathroom in a quiet room
• Arriving 19 July, departing 22 July (3 nights)

Thank you!
Rick Steves

smaller family-run places. Cancellation policies can be strict; read the fine print before you book. Many discount deals require pre-payment and can be expensive to change or cancel.

Reconfirming a Reservation: Always call or email to reconfirm your room reservation a few days in advance. For B&Bs or very small hotels, I call again on my arrival day to tell my host what time to expect me (especially important if arriving late—after 17:00).

Phoning: For tips on how to call hotels overseas, see page 988.

com can provide a more personalized service (their curated listings are also more expensive).

Before you commit, be clear on the location. I like to virtually "explore" the neighborhood using Google Street View. Also consider the proximity to public transportation and how well connected the property is with the rest of the city. Ask about amenities (elevator, air-conditioning, laundry, Wi-Fi, parking, etc.). Reviews from previous guests can help identify trouble spots.

Think about the kind of experience you want: Just a key and an affordable bed...or a chance to get to know a local? Some hosts offer self check-in and minimal contact; others enjoy interacting with you. Read the description and reviews to help shape your decision.

Confirming and Paying: Many places require payment in full before your trip, usually through the listing site. Be wary of owners who want to take your transaction offline; this gives you no recourse if things go awry. Never agree to wire money (a key indicator of a fraudulent transaction).

Apartments or Houses: If you're staying in one place several nights, it's worth considering an apartment or rental house (shorter

Keep Cool

If you're visiting Spain in the summer, you'll want an air-conditioned room. Most hotel air-conditioners come with a remote control that generally has similar symbols and features: fan icon (click to toggle through wind power, from light to gale); temperature (20 degrees Celsius is comfortable); louver icon (choose steady airflow or waves); snowflake and sunshine icons (cold air or heat, depending on season); and clock ("O" setting: run X hours before turning off; "I" setting: wait X hours to start). When you leave your room for the day, do as the environmentally conscious Europeans do, and turn off the air-conditioning.

stays aren't worth the hassle of arranging key pickup, buying groceries, etc.). Apartment and house rentals can be especially cost-effective for groups and families. European apartments, like hotel rooms, tend to be small by US standards. But they often come with laundry facilities and small, equipped kitchens, making it easier and cheaper to dine in.

Rooms in Private Homes: Renting a room in someone's home is a good option for those traveling alone, as you're more likely to find true single rooms—with just one single bed, and a price to match. These can range from air-mattress-in-living-room basic to plush-B&B-suite posh. While you can't expect your host to also be your tour guide—or even to provide you with much info—some are interested in getting to know the travelers who pass through their home.

Other Options: Swapping homes with a local works for people with an appealing place to offer (don't assume where you live is not interesting to Europeans). Good places to start are HomeExchange.com and LoveHomeSwap.com. To sleep for free, Couchsurfing.com is a vagabond's alternative to Airbnb. It lists millions of outgoing members, who host fellow "surfers" in their homes.

Hostels

A hostel *(albergue juvenil)* provides cheap beds in dorms where you sleep alongside strangers for about €20-30 per night. Travelers of any age are welcome if they don't mind dorm-style accommodations and meeting other travelers. Most hostels offer kitchen facilities, guest computers, Wi-Fi, and a self-service laundry. Hostels almost always provide bedding, but the towel's up to you (though you can usually rent one). Family and private rooms are often available.

Independent hostels tend to be easygoing, colorful, and informal (no membership required; www.hostelworld.com). You may

pay slightly less by booking directly with the hostel. **Official hostels** are part of Hostelling International (HI) and share an online booking site (www.hihostels.com). HI hostels typically require that you be a member or else pay a bit more per night.

Eating

Spanish cuisine is hearty, and meals are served in big, inexpensive portions. You can eat well in restaurants for about €15-20—or even more cheaply and more varied if you graze on appetizer-sized tapas in bars.

For listings in this guidebook, I look for restaurants that are convenient to your hotel and sightseeing. When restaurant-hunting, choose a spot filled with locals, not the place with the big neon signs boasting, "We Speak English and Accept Credit Cards." And avoid any restaurant that posts big photographs of its food. Venturing even a block or two off the main drag leads to higher-quality food for a better price.

The Spanish eating schedule—lunch from 13:00 to 16:00, dinner after 21:00—frustrates many visitors. Most Spaniards eat one major meal of the day—lunch *(comida)*—
around 14:00, when stores close, schools let out, and people gather with their friends and family for the siesta. Because most Spaniards work until 19:30, supper *(cena)* is usually served at about 21:00 or 22:00. And, since few people want a heavy meal that late, many Spaniards eat a light tapas dinner.

Generally, no self-respecting *casa de comidas* ("house of eating"—when you see this label, you can bet it's a good, traditional eatery) serves meals at American hours. If you're looking for a "nontouristy restaurant," remember that a spot filled with tourists at 20:00 will be an entirely different—and more authentic—scene at 22:00, when the locals take over.

Survival Tips for Spanish Eating Schedules: To bridge the gap between their coffee-and-roll breakfast and late lunch, many Spaniards eat a light meal at about 11:00 *(merienda)*. This can be a light lunch at a bar or a *bocadillo* (baguette sandwich)—hence the popularity of fast-food *bocadillo* chains such as Pans & Company. Besides *bocadillos*, bars often have slices of *tortilla española* (potato omelet) and fresh-squeezed orange juice. For your main meal of the day, you can either eat a late lunch at a restaurant at around 15:00, then have a light tapas snack for dinner; or reverse it, having a tapas

Restaurant Code

Eateries in this book are categorized according to the average cost of a typical main course. Drinks, desserts, and splurge items can raise the price considerably.

    $$$$ **Splurge:** Most main courses over €25
    $$$ **Pricier:** €18-25
    $$ **Moderate:** €12-18
    $ **Budget:** Under €12

In Spain, takeout food is **$**; a basic tapas bar or no-frills sit-down eatery is **$$**; a casual but more upscale tapas bar or restaurant is **$$$**; and a swanky splurge is **$$$$**.

meal in the afternoon, followed by a late restaurant dinner. Either way, tapas bars are the key to eating well at any hour.

RESTAURANT PRICING

I've categorized my recommended eateries based on the average price of a typical main course, indicated with a dollar-sign rating (see sidebar). Obviously, expensive specialties, fine wine, appetizers, and dessert can significantly increase your final bill.

The categories also indicate the personality of a place: **Budget** eateries include street food, takeaway, order-at-the-counter shops, basic cafeterias, and bakeries selling sandwiches. **Moderate** eateries are nice (but not fancy) sit-down restaurants, ideal for a pleasant meal with good-quality food. Most of my listings fall in this category—great for a taste of local cuisine at a reasonable price.

Pricier eateries are a notch up, with more attention paid to the setting, presentation, and (often inventive) cuisine. **Splurge** eateries are dress-up-for-a-special-occasion swanky—typically with an elegant setting, polished service, and pricey and refined cuisine.

BREAKFAST

Hotel breakfasts are generally handy, optional, and pricey. Start your day instead at a corner bar or at a colorful café near a market hall. Ask for the *desayunos* (breakfast special, usually only available until noon), which can include coffee, a roll (or sandwich), and juice—much cheaper than ordering them separately. Sandwiches can either be on white bread (called "sandwich") or on a baguette (*bocadillo*).

A basic and standard savory breakfast item is *tostada con aceite*, toasted bread with olive oil (and often with a tomato/garlic spread called *pan con tomate*). For something more substantial, look for a slice of *tortilla española* (potato omelet). In Andalucía, get your

morning protein with the *mollete con jamón y aceite,* a soft bread roll with Spanish ham and olive oil (and sometimes cheese).

Those with a sweet tooth will find various sweet rolls (*bollos* or *bollería*). If you like a doughnut and coffee in American greasy-spoon joints, try the Spanish equivalent: *churros* (or the thicker *porras*) that you dip in thick hot chocolate or your *café con leche.*

Here are some other key breakfast words (some with their Catalan variant):

Bikini: Grilled ham-and-cheese sandwich (popular in Catalunya)

Bocadillo (bocata) con jamón/queso/mixto: Baguette sandwich with ham/cheese/both

Bocadillo (bocata) mixto con huevo: Baguette sandwich with ham and cheese and an over-easy egg on top

Caracola: "Snail"-shaped pastry, similar to a cinnamon roll

Croissant a la plancha: Croissant grilled and slathered with butter

Palmera: Palm-shaped pastry, like a French *palmier* or "elephant ear"

Pan (pa) de molde/de barra: Bread (sandwich bread/baguette)

Rosquilla: Hard doughnut

Sandwich, tostado: White bread sandwich, toasted

Tortilla española (truita de patates): Potato omelet

SPANISH RESTAURANTS

While Spain's tapas bars offer small plates throughout the afternoon and evening, formal restaurants have a standard à la carte menu (no tapas) and start their service much later than the American norm. But many eateries blur the distinction between a bar and a restaurant, boasting both a bar in front and some sit-down tables in the back or outside on the *terraza.*

Don't expect "My name is Carlos and I'll be your waiter tonight" cheery service. Service is often *serio*—it's not friendly or unfriendly...just white-shirt-and-bow-tie proficient.

At both restaurants and bars, smoking is banned in enclosed public spaces.

Ordering: While menus at formal restaurants are generally broken down by courses or categories, more casual eateries (and tapas bars) may feature dishes served in portions called *raciones* (*racions* in Catalan), or the smaller half-servings, *media-raciones* (*mitja racions* in Catalan). Smaller tapas plates are more commonly served at bars than at sit-down restaurants.

Typically, couples or small

Sampling *Jamón*

The staple of Spanish cuisine, *jamón* (hah-MOHN) is prosciut-to-like ham that's dry-cured and aged. It's generally sliced thin (right off the hock) and served at room temperature. *Jamón* can be eaten straight, served in a *bocadillo* sand-wich, or mixed into a wide variety of dishes. Bars proudly hang ham hocks from the rafters as part of the decor. *Jamón* is more than a food—it's a way of life. Spaniards treasure memories of Grandpa at Christmas, thinly carving a *jamón* supported in a special ham-hock holder, just as Americans savor the turkey carving at Thanksgiving.

Like connoisseurs of fine wine, Spaniards debate the merits of different breeds of pigs, the pig's diet, and the quality of the curing. The two major types of ham are *jamón serrano,* from white pigs whose meat is cured in the mountains of Spain, and the higher-quality *jamón ibérico,* made with the back legs of black-hooved pigs. These Iberian *pata negra* ("black foot") pigs are said to be fatter and happier (slaughtered much later than other pigs), thereby pro-ducing particularly fine ham. Another indication of quality is *de bellota,* which means the pig was raised on acorns. *Jamón ibérico de bellota* is, to Spanish eaters, as good as it gets: free-range, black-footed pigs who ate only acorns. (Ham labeled *Jamón ibérico de recebeo* or *de cebo* is still good, but comes from pigs that are grain-fed.)

To sample this delicacy without the high price tag you'll find in bars and restaurants, go to the local market. Ask for 100 grams of top-quality ham (*cien gramos de jamón ibérico;* about €80/kilo, so your *ración* will run about €8), and enjoy it as a picnic with red wine and a baguette. To round out the pic-nic, also pick up 100 grams each of *salchichón* (salami), *cho-rizo* (spicy sausage), and *manchego* or *cabrales* cheese, along with some olives and pickles.

groups can share a few *raciones,* making this an economical way to eat and a great way to explore the regional cuisine. Ordering *media-raciones* may cost a bit more per ounce, but you'll broaden your tast-ing experience. Two people can fill up on four *media-raciones.*

For a budget meal in a restaurant, try a *plato combinado* (com-bination plate), which usually includes portions of one or two main dishes, a vegetable, and bread for a reasonable price; or the *menú del día* (menu of the day), a substantial three- to four-course meal that comes with a drink.

Spanish cuisine has many regional specialties (see "Spanish

Regional Specialties" sidebar), but the most famous Spanish dish is probably paella. Featuring saffron-flavored rice as a background for seafood, chicken, peppers, or whatever the chef wants to mix in, an authentic paella takes time to prepare—expect a wait. In a tapas bar, jump (like everyone else) at the opportunity to snare a small plate of paella when it appears hot out of the kitchen. Avoid the paella shown in pretty pictures on a separate menu—it's from the microwave.

Spanish cuisine can be a bit meat-centered for Americans more accustomed to salads, fruits, and grains. Main meat and fish courses are usually served with only a garnish, not a side of vegetables. Good vegetarian and lighter options exist, but you'll have to seek them out. The secret is to choose the creamed vegetable soup, *parrillada de verduras* (sautéed vegetables), *ensalada mixta,* or other green option available as a first course. (Spaniards rarely eat salads as a main course, so they tend to be small and simple—just lettuce, tomatoes, and maybe olives and tuna.) Fruit is often considered a dessert and a healthy choice at the end of a meal.

Tipping: At restaurants with table service, a service charge is sometimes included in the bill (*servicio incluido; servei inclós* in Catalan). Spaniards traditionally tipped nothing or next to nothing beyond that, but times are changing. There's a growing tendency to tip for good service, especially in cities like Barcelona. Leaving 10-15 percent for excellent service is appreciated. Tip in cash—there's generally no option for adding a tip to your bill when paying with a credit card. At most places, you can leave the tip on the table. At an outdoor café, hand the tip to your server to avoid having it swiped by a passerby.

TAPAS BARS

I can't resist stopping in local tapas bars to munch on tasty small portions of seafood, meat-filled pastries, deep-fried morsels, and other delicious bites (typically costing around €4). Best of all, I can eat well any time of day in a tapas bar.

Chasing down a particular bar for tapas nearly defeats the purpose and spirit of such places— they are impromptu. Just drop in at any lively bar. Some are sit-down, while others are more stand-up. I look for the noisy spots with lots of customers, the TV blaring soccer games or Spanish soaps, and piles of napkins and food debris on the floor (it's considered unsanitary

to put trash back on the bar; go local and toss your napkins on the floor, too).

There is nothing wrong with ordering a tapa or two to start before deciding whether to stay at the same bar or move on. In fact, Spaniards rarely settle into just one place. Part of the joy of eating at a tapas bar is turning it into a mobile feast, visiting two or three bars during a single meal.

The authentic tapas experience is not for shrinking violets. You'll elbow up to a bar crowded with pushy locals, squint at a hand-scrawled chalkboard menu, and try to order from a typi-cally brusque bartender. In some locales, a small, free tapa may be included with your drink. (Notice what locals are being served.) Order your drink first with the expectation of the freebie; then order additional food as you like.

Basque-style bars have an array of tapas (called *pintxos* or *pin-chos*) already laid out and can be less intimidating, as you simply point to or grab what you want. To find this type of bar, look for a place with *vasca* or *euskal* (both mean "Basque") in the name.

When to Go: Bars can be extremely crowded with locals, and visitors can find it hard to get in an order—or even find a place to sit. You'll have more room, and get better service, by showing up before the local crowd. Try to be there by 13:30 for lunch, and 20:00-20:30 for dinner. For less competition at the bar, go on a Monday or Tuesday.

Where to Sit: Eating and drinking at a bar is usually cheapest if you sit or stand at the counter *(barra)*. You may pay a little more to sit at a table *(mesa* or *salón)* and still more for an outdoor table *(terraza)*. Traditionally, tapas are served at the bar, and *raciones* (and *media-raciones*) are served at tables, where food can be shared fam-ily style. If you're eating a free tapa with your drink, you can't oc-cupy a table.

It's bad form to order food at the bar, then take it to a table. If you're standing and a table opens up, it's OK to move as long as you signal to the waiter; anything else you order will be charged at the higher *mesa/salón* price. In the right place, a quiet snack and drink on a terrace is well worth the extra charge. But the cheapest seats sometimes get the best show. Sit at the bar and study your bartender—he's an artist.

Ordering: To figure out what you want, read the posted or printed menu. Use the "Tapas Menu Decoder," later, to sort through your options. You can also just point to items in the display case or at your neighbor's plate to get what you

want. Handwritten signs that start out *"Hay"* mean "Today we have," as in *"Hay caracoles"* ("Today we have snails").

Hang back and observe before ordering. When you're ready, be assertive or you'll never be served. Your bartender isn't a "waiter"—he wants to take your order, period. To grab his attention, say *"por favor"* (please; *"si us plau"* in Catalan); you can also say *"perdona"* (excuse me; *"perdó"* in Catalan).

Some bars push *raciones* (dinner plate-sized) portions rather than smaller tapas (saucer-sized). Ask for the smaller tapas portions or a *media-ración* (listed as ½ *ración* on a menu)—that way you can try more things.

If you don't know what to order, try an inexpensive sampler plate. Ask for *una tabla de canapés variados* to get a plate of various little open-faced sandwiches. Or ask for a *surtido de* (an assortment of) *charcutería* (a mixed plate of meat) or *queso* (cheese). *Un surtido de jamón y queso* means a plate of different hams and cheeses. Order bread and two glasses of red wine on the right square, and you've got a romantic (and inexpensive) dinner for two.

Paying and Tipping: Don't worry about paying until you're ready to leave; the bartender is keeping track of your tab. To get the bill, ask for *"¿La cuenta?"* (*"El compte?"* in Catalan). If you're sampling tapas at a counter, there's no need to tip (though you can round up the bill).

DESSERTS AND PASTRIES

In Spain, desserts are often an afterthought; here are a few items you may see on menus or in a bakery window:

Arroz con leche: Rice pudding

Bamba de nata: Cream puff

Brazo de gitano: Sponge cake filled with butter cream; literally "Gypsy's arm"

Crema catalana: Catalan take on crème brûlée (Barcelona)

Flan de huevo: Flan (crème caramel)

Fruta de la estación/fruta de temporada: Fruit in season

Helados, variados: Ice cream, various flavors

Mel i mató: Light Catalan cheese with honey (Barcelona)

Músic de fruits secs: Selection of nuts and dried fruits (Barcelona)

Napolitana: Rolled pastry, filled with chocolate (similar to French *pain au chocolat*) or *crema* (cream)

Queso: Cheese

Torrijas: Sweet fritters, like French toast, available during Lent and Easter

SPANISH DRINKS
Wine and Spirits

Spain is one of the world's leading producers of grapes, and that

Tapas Menu Decoder

You can often just point to what you want on the menu or in the display case, say *por favor* (Spanish) or *si us plau* (Catalan), and get your food, but these words will help. I've given both Spanish and Catalan (in parentheses), when applicable.

a la parrilla (a la graella)	barbecued
a la plancha (a la planxa)	grilled (on a flat-top griddle)
aceitunas (olives)	Olives
al ajillo	with garlic
albóndigas (mandonguilles)	spiced meatballs with sauce
almejas (cloïsses), a la marinera	clams, in paprika sauce
almendras (ametlles)	almonds (usually fried)
anchoas (anxoves)	cured anchovies (salted or in oil)
atún (tonyina)	Tuna
bacalao (bacallà)	Cod
banderilla	mini skewer (often olives, fish, and pickled veggies)
bocadillo (entrepà/bocata)	basic baguette sandwich
bombas (bombes)	fried meat-and-potato ball
boquerones (seitons), en vinagre	fresh anchovies, marinated in olive oil, vinegar, and garlic
brocheta (broqueta)	shish kebab (on a stick)
cabrillas	big snails, served in a tomato sauce
calamares fritos (calamars fregits)	fried squid rings
callos	tripe stew
canapé	tiny open-faced sandwich
caracoles (cargols)	small tree snails (May-Sept)
cazón en adobo	salty marinated dogfish
champiñones (xampinyons)	mushrooms
charcutería (xarcuteria)	cured meats
chorizo (xoriço)	spicy sausage
croquetas (croquetes)	croquettes—breaded, fried béchamel with fillings like ham
empanadillas (crestes)	meat or seafood hand pies
ensaladilla rusa (ensalada russa)	potato salad with lots of mayo, peas, and carrots
espinacas, con garbanzos (espinacs, amb cigrons)	spinach, with garbanzo beans
flauta	sandwich on flute-thin baguette
frito (fregit)	Fried
fuet	Catalan salami-like sausage
gambas, con cáscara (gambes, amb closca)	shrimp, with shell
gazpacho	cold tomato soup
guiso (estofat)	Stew
jamón (pernil)	cured ham (like prosciutto)

judías verdes (mongetes tendres)	green beans
lomo (llom)	pork tenderloin
mejillones (musclos)	mussels
merluza (lluç)	hake (whitefish)
montadito	tapa on bread, mini sandwich in Sevilla
morcilla (botifarró)	blood sausage
morro	pig snout
paella	saffron rice dish with seafood and meat
pan (pa)	Bread
patatas bravas (patates braves)	fried potatoes with spicy tomato sauce
pescaditos fritos (peixet fregit)	assortment of fried little fish
picos	little breadsticks
pimiento, relleno (pebrot, farcit)	pepper, stuffed
pimientos de Padrón (pebrots de Padró)	fried small green peppers, a few of which are jalapeño-hot
pinchos morunos (pintxos morunos)	skewer of spicy lamb or pork
pisto (samfaina)	mixed sautéed vegetables
pollo, alioli (pollastre, all i oli)	chicken, with garlic olive-oil sauce
pulga, pulguita, or pepito (entrepà petit)	a small baguette sandwich
pulpo (pop)	octopus
queso (formatge)	cheese
queso manchego (formatge manxec)	classic Spanish sheep-milk cheese
rabas (rabes)	squid rings
rabo de toro (cua de bou)	bull's-tail stew (fatty and tender)
revuelto, de setas (remenat, de bolets)	scrambled eggs, with wild mushrooms
salchichón (llonganissa)	salami-like sausage
sandwich (sandvitx)	American-style sandwich on soft bread
sardinas (sardines)	sardines
sesos	lamb brains
surtido de (assortit)	assortment of
tabla serrana (assortit d'embotits i formatges)	hearty plate of meat and cheese
tortilla española (truita de patata)	potato omelet
tortilla de jamón/queso (truita de pernil/formatge)	potato omelet with ham/cheese
tortillitas de camarones	shrimp fritters (Andalucía)
variado de fritos (peixet fregits)	mix of various fried fish

means lots of excellent wine, both red *(tinto)* and white *(blanco)*. Major wine regions include Valdepeñas (both red and white wines made in Don Quixote country south of Toledo); Penedès (cabernet-style wines from near Barcelona); Rioja (spicy, lighter reds from the tempranillo grape, from the high plains of northern Spain); and Ribera del Duero (reds from northwest of Madrid).

For a basic glass of red wine, you can order *un tinto*. But for quality wine, ask for *un crianza* (old), *un reserva* (older), or *un gran reserva* (oldest). For good, economical wine, I always ask for **un crianza**—for little or no extra money than a basic *tinto*, you'll get a quality, aged wine.

Cava is Spain's answer to champagne. For variety, consider ordering a **tinto de verano** (red wine with lemon soda—similar to sangria) or try a local **vermut** (vermouth, generally sweet). For nondrinkers, **mosto** is excellent Spanish grape juice that hasn't been fermented (available in both red and white).

Sherry, a fortified wine from the Jerez region, is a shock to the taste buds if you're expecting a sweet dessert drink. Named for its city of origin, *jerez* ranges from dry *(fino)* to sweet *(dulce)*—Spaniards drink the *fino* and export the *dulce* (mostly to the UK and the Netherlands in the form of cream sherry). You'll also see *amontillado* and *manzanilla* sherries; both are variants of *fino*. *¡Salud!* Cheers!

Beer

Spaniards rarely ask for a "cerveza." Instead, they usually specify a size or type when ordering, such as a *caña* (small draft beer).

Most places just have the standard local beer—a light lager—on tap. Cruzcampo—which is very light so that hot, thirsty drinkers can consume more—is big in the south, whereas San Miguel is big in the north, and Madrid's Mahou is the choice in central Spain. In Barcelona, local options include Estrella Damm, the trendier Moritz, and various craft beers. One of the most-appreciated Spanish lagers is Estrella Galicia, from the Galicia region.

Caña (canya): Small glass of draft beer (7-8 ounces)
Cerveza (cervesa): Beer
Cerveza sin (Cervesa sense): Nonalcoholic beer
Clara con limón/casera: Small beer with lemonade/soda (shandy)
Doble: Typically double the size of a *caña*
Mediana: Bottle of beer (*quinto* is a small bottle)
Sidra: Dry, alcoholic cider
Tubo: Tall, thin glass of beer (about 10 ounces)

Spanish Regional Specialties

Asturias: Squeezed between the Picos de Europa mountains and the North Atlantic, Asturias combines seafood with sturdy mountain foods—including *fabas* (giant, white, fava-like beans); the powerful, white, Roquefort-like *Cabrales* cheese; and *sidra* (hard cider), used both for drinking and for cooking.

Galicia: The green, rainy northwest of Spain is known for its octopus (*pulpo,* specifically *pulpo a la gallega,* served in pieces and sprinkled with paprika) and its many pork dishes (such as *orejas,* fried pig's ears). Other specialties include *pimientos de Padrón* (deep-fried, small green peppers) and Ribeiro white wine, traditionally served in little ceramic bowls.

Andalucía: Gazpacho and *salmorejo,* Andalusian specialties, are chilled tomato-based soups, served with chunks of bread or *jamón* and chopped egg. (Gazpacho sometimes adds other ingredients, such as peppers or cucumbers.) Both are refreshing on a hot day and are commonly available as soon as the weather heats up. Many dishes in this region rely on *sofrito*—a base of onion, tomatoes, and peppers.

Castilla y León: This high, central plateau of Spain was the home of vast flocks of sheep in the Middle Ages. This influence—in the form of lamb and the famous *manchego* (from La Mancha) sheep's cheese—persists today. Other popular Castilian and Leonese meats are sausages, *cochinillo asado* (roast suckling pig), and *cecina* (beef that's cured like *jamón serrano*).

Catalunya: Like its culture and language, Catalan food is a fusion of Spanish and French. Every meal starts with *pan con tomate* (or *pa amb tomaquet* in Catalan): a baguette rubbed with crushed tomatoes, garlic, and olive oil. Favorite dishes include *fideuà,* a thin, flavor-infused noodle served with seafood, and *arròs negre,* rice cooked in black squid ink.

Basque Country: Most consider this region to be the culinary capital of Spain, with *pintxos* (tapas) bars that display a mouth-watering array of choices (just grab what you like from the platters at the bar, and pay on the honor system). Look for *txangurro* (spider crab), *antxoas* (tasty anchovies), *marmitako* (tuna stew), *ttoro* (seafood stew), and *txakolí* (fresh white wine, poured from high up). *Cazuelas* are stews meant for sharing.

Water, Coffee, and Other Nonalcoholic Drinks

If ordering mineral water in a restaurant, request a *botella de agua grande* (big bottle). For a glass of tap water, specify *un vaso de agua del grifo*. If you insist on *del grifo*, not *embotellada* (bottled), you'll usually get it. Note that tap water in Barcelona does not taste particularly good, and some places would rather not serve it to their customers (though it is safe to drink).

Hurdling the Language Barrier

Imported from the Old World throughout the New, Spanish is the most widely spoken Romance language in the world. With its straightforward pronunciation, Spanish is also one of the simplest languages to learn. Many Spanish people—especially those in the tourist trade and in big cities—speak English. Still, many people don't. Learn the key phrases (see "Spanish Survival Phrases" in the appendix). Travel with a phrase book, particularly if you want to interact with the Spanish people. You'll find that doors open more quickly and with more smiles when you can speak a few words of the language.

For more tips on hurdling the language barrier, consider the *Rick Steves Spanish Phrase Book & Dictionary* (available at RickSteves.com).

Spain's bars often serve fresh-squeezed orange juice. For something completely different, try the sweet and milky *horchata*, traditionally made from chufa (a.k.a. tigernuts or earth almonds).

Here are some common additional beverage phrases (with Catalan variants where applicable):

Agua con/sin gas (aigua amb/sin gas): Water with/without bubbles

Café con leche (café amb llet): Espresso with hot milk

Café solo: Shot of espresso, sometimes with hot water added

Cortado (tallat): Espresso with a little milk

Jarra de agua: Pitcher of tap water

Leche: Milk

Refresco (Refresc): Soft drink (common brands are Coca-Cola, Fanta—*limón* or *naranja,* and Schweppes—*limón* or *tónica*)

Té/infusion: Tea

Zumo: Juice

Zumo de naranja, natural: Orange juice, freshly squeezed

Staying Connected

One of the most common questions I hear from travelers is, "How can I stay connected in Europe?" The short answer is? More easily and affordably than you might think.

The simplest solution is to bring your own device—phone, tablet, or laptop—and use it much as you would at home, following the money-saving tips below, such as getting an international plan or connecting to free Wi-Fi whenever possible. Another option is to buy a European SIM card for your mobile phone. Or you can use European landlines and computers to connect. More details are at RickSteves.com/phoning.

Tips on Internet Security

Make sure that your device is running the latest versions of its operating system, security software, and apps. Next, ensure that your device and key programs (like email) are password-protected. On the road, use only secure, password-protected Wi-Fi. Ask the hotel or café staff for the specific name of their network, and make sure you log on to that exact one.

If you must access your financial info online, use a bank-ing app rather than accessing your account via a browser, and use a cellular connection, not Wi-Fi. Never log on to personal finance sites on a public computer. If you're very concerned, consider subscribing to a VPN (virtual private network).

USING YOUR PHONE IN EUROPE

Here are some budget tips and options.

Sign up for an international plan. To stay connected at a lower cost, sign up for an international service plan through your carrier. Most providers offer a simple bundle that includes calling, messaging, and data. Your normal plan may already include inter-national coverage (for example, T-Mobile's covers data and text, but not voice calls).

Before your trip, research your provider's international rates. Activate the plan a day or two before you leave, then remember to cancel it when your trip's over.

Use free Wi-Fi whenever possible. Unless you have an un-limited-data plan, save most of your online tasks for Wi-Fi (pro-nounced *wee-fee* in Spanish). Most accommodations in Europe offer free Wi-Fi. Many cafés (including Starbucks and McDon-ald's) offer hotspots for customers; ask for the password when you buy something. You may also find Wi-Fi at TIs, city squares, major museums, public-transit hubs, airports, and aboard trains and buses.

Minimize the use of your cellular network. The best way to make sure you're not accidentally burning through data is to put your device in "airplane" mode (which also disables phone calls and texts) and connect to Wi-Fi as needed. When you need to get on-line but can't find Wi-Fi, simply turn on your cellular network (or turn off airplane mode) just long enough for the task at hand.

Even with an international data plan, wait until you're on Wi-Fi to Skype or FaceTime, download apps, stream videos, or do other megabyte-greedy tasks. Using a navigation app such as Google Maps over a cellular network can require lots of data, so download maps when you're on Wi-Fi, then use the app offline.

Limit automatic updates. By default, your device constantly checks for a data connection and updates app content. Check your

How to Dial

Here's how to dial from anywhere in the US or Europe, using the phone number of one of my recommended Madrid hotels as an example (915 212 900). If a number starts with 0, drop it when dialing internationally (except when calling Italy).

From a US Mobile Phone

Phone numbers in this book are presented exactly as you would dial them from a US mobile phone. For international access, press and hold the 0 (zero) to get a + sign, then dial the country code (34 for Spain) and phone number.

▶ To call the Madrid hotel from any location, dial +34 915 212 900.

From a US Landline

Replace + with 011 (US/Canada access code), then dial the country code (34 for Spain) and phone number.

▶ To call the Madrid hotel from your home landline, dial 011 34 915 212 900.

From a European Landline

Replace + with 00 (Europe access code), then dial the country code (34 for Spain, 1 for the US) and phone number.

▶ To call the Madrid hotel from a German landline, dial 00 34 915 212 900.

▶ To call my US office from a Spanish landline, dial 00 1 425 771 8303.

From One Spanish Phone to Another

To place a domestic call (from a Spanish landline or mobile), drop +34 and dial the phone number.

▶ To call the Madrid hotel from Barcelona, dial 915 212 900.

More Dialing Tips

Local Numbers: European phone numbers and area codes can vary in length and spacing, even within the same country. Mobile phones use separate prefixes (for instance, in Spain, landlines begin with 8 or 9, and mobile numbers begin with 6 or 7).

Toll and Toll-Free Calls: It's generally not possible to dial European toll or toll-free numbers from a US mobile or landline (although you can sometimes get through using Skype). Look for a direct-dial number instead.

Calling the US from a US Mobile Phone, While Abroad: Dial +1, area code, and number.

More Phoning Help: See HowToCallAbroad.com.

device's settings menu for ways to turn this off, and change your email settings from "auto-retrieve" to "manual" (or from "push" to "fetch").

Use Wi-Fi calling and messaging apps. Skype, WhatsApp, FaceTime, and Google Meet are great for making free or low-cost calls or sending texts over Wi-Fi worldwide. Just log on to a Wi-Fi network then connect with friends, family members, or local contacts who use the same service.

Buy a European SIM card. If you anticipate making a lot of

local calls, need a local phone number, or your provider's international data rates are expensive, consider buying a SIM card in Europe to replace the one in your (unlocked) US phone or tablet. SIM cards are sold at department-store electronics counters and some newsstands (you may need to show your passport), and vending machines. If you need help setting it up, buy one at a mobile-phone shop. There are generally no roaming charges when using a European SIM card in other EU countries, but confirm when you buy.

WITHOUT A MOBILE PHONE

It's less convenient but possible to travel in Europe without a mobile device. You can make calls from your hotel, and check email or get online using public computers.

Most **hotels** charge a fee for placing calls. You can use a prepaid international phone card (*tarjeta telefónica con código*, usually available at newsstands, tobacco shops, and train stations) to call out from your hotel.

Some hotels have **public computers** in their lobbies for guests to use; otherwise you can find them at public libraries (ask your hotelier or the TI for the nearest location). On a European keyboard, use the "Alt Gr" key to the right of the space bar to insert the extra symbol that appears on some keys. If you can't locate a special character (such as @), simply copy and paste it from a web page.

MAIL

You can mail one package per day to yourself worth up to $200 duty-free from Europe to the US (mark it "personal purchases"). If you're sending a gift to someone, mark it "unsolicited gift." For details, visit www.cbp.gov, select "Travel," and search for "Know Before You Go." The Spanish postal service works fine, but for quick transatlantic delivery (in either direction), consider services such as DHL (DHL.com).

Transportation

Figuring out how to get around in Europe is one of your biggest trip decisions. **Cars** work well for two or more traveling together (especially families with small kids), those packing heavy, and those delving into the countryside. **Trains** and **buses** are best for solo travelers, blitz tourists, city-to-city travelers and those who want to leave the driving to others. Short-hop **flights** within Europe can creatively connect the dots. Be aware of the potential downside of each option: A car is an expensive headache in any major city; with trains and buses you're at the mercy of a timetable; flying entails a trek to and from a usually distant airport and leaves a larger carbon footprint.

If your itinerary mixes cities and countryside, my advice is to connect cities by train (or bus) and to explore rural areas by rental car. Arrange to pick up your car in the last big city you'll visit, then use it to lace together small towns and explore the countryside. For more detailed information on transportation throughout Europe, see RickSteves.com/transportation.

TRAINS

Renfe is the Spanish national train system. For information and reservations, visit Renfe.com or dial Renfe's number (+34 912 320 320) from anywhere in Spain. You'll find tips on buying tickets later in this section.

Types of Trains

Trains generally get more expensive as they pick up speed, but all are cheaper per mile than their northern European counterparts. Spain loves to name trains, so you may encounter types of trains not listed here.

The high-speed train called the **AVE** (AH-vay, stands for *Alta Velocidad Española*) whisks travelers between Madrid and Toledo in 30 minutes, and between Madrid and Sevilla, Barcelona, Granada, Málaga, or Santiago de Compostela in 3-4 hours. AVE trains are priced according to their time of departure. Peak hours *(punta)* are most expensive, followed by *llano* and *valle* (quietest and cheapest times). Tickets for these trains typically go on sale two months in advance. AVE trains are almost entirely covered by the Eurail Pass (book ahead, seat reservation fee from Madrid to Sevilla costs Eurailers about $12). It's smart to bring your passport (ticket checkers may ask for identification, especially if you have a rail pass).

A related high-speed train, the **Alvia,** runs on AVE lines but can switch to Iberian tracks without stopping. On the Madrid-San Sebastián route, for example, it reaches the Basque Country in five hours.

Avlo is a low-cost version of AVE, running a few times per day between Madrid, Zaragoza, and Barcelona, with all second-class seating and fewer services. Non-refundable tickets are sold online only (and rail passes are not accepted). Avlo has competition on these routes from a similar, no-frills version of France's TGV called **OUIGO Spain** (www.ouigo.com/es/en/destinations). However, these cheap trains don't yet cross the French border.

Avant trains are also high-speed—typically about as fast as

AVE—but designed for shorter distances. They also tend to be cheaper than AVE, even on the same route. If you're on a tight budget, compare your options before buying.

Intercity and **Media Distancia** trains fall just behind Avant in speed, comfort, and expense. **Cercanías** and **Rodalies** are commuter trains for big-city workers and small-town tourists.

Your ticket for an AVE or Larga Distancia train also allows you to connect by Cercanías, Rodalies, and the Alicante TRAM network within four hours of your ticketed departure and arrival times. Collect a *Combinado Cercanías* ticket at self-service machines and station ticket offices by scanning the barcode or entering the code on your train ticket. (In Madrid, you can scan your ticket directly at the Cercanías turnstile.)

Overnight Trains: Overnight trains are not expected to resume operation in Spain. Their removal leaves no convenient train to/from Portugal (aside from twice daily service between Vigo and Porto).

Rail Passes

The single-country Eurail Spain Pass can be a reasonable value if you'll be taking three or more long train rides in Spain. But otherwise, it's unlikely to save you money. A rail pass doesn't provide much hop-on convenience in Spain, since most trains require paid seat reservations. Buying individual train tickets in advance or as you go in Spain can be less expensive and gives you better access to seat reservations (which are limited for rail-pass holders). For most trains, point-to-point ticket prices already include seat reservations when required (for instance, for fast trains and longer distances).

Renfe also offers its own "Renfe Spain Pass," which works entirely differently. It counts trips instead of calendar days, requires reservations to be made in chronological order, and is sold only on their website.

If your trip extends beyond Spain, consider the Eurail Global Pass, covering most of Europe (trains crossing the Spanish border only accept passes that cover your entire trip). If you buy separate passes for neighboring countries, note that you'll use a travel day on each when crossing the border. Even if you have a rail pass, use buses when they're more convenient and direct than the trains.

Rail-pass holders can book seat reservations directly at Spanish stations up to departure, if still available, or in Eurail's Rail Planner app. Making those reservations before you leave home is advisable for any train you cannot afford to miss, for routes with limited schedules (such as one or two direct trains per day) and for busy times (for example, Friday and Sunday afternoons, Saturday mornings, weekday rush hours, and holiday weekends—see "Holidays and Festivals" in the appendix).

Iberia's Public Transportation

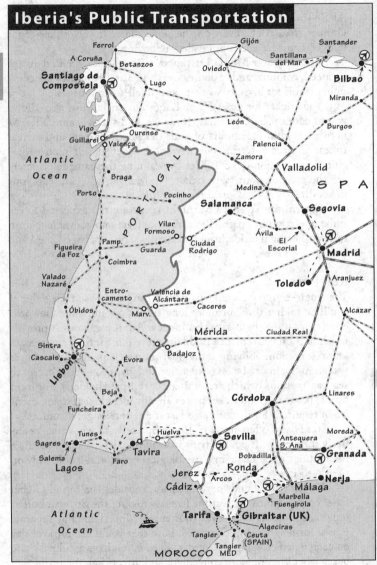

For more detailed advice on figuring out the smartest rail-pass options for your train trip, visit RickSteves.com/rail.

Buying Train Tickets

Trains can sell out, and high-speed AVE ticket prices increase as your departure date draws closer, so it's smart to buy tickets at least a day in advance—even for short rides. You have several options for buying train tickets: at the station or a Renfe office, at a travel

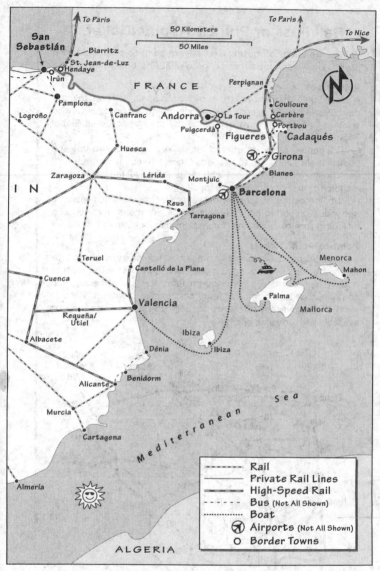

Rail
Private Rail Lines
High-Speed Rail
Bus (Not All Shown)
Boat
Airports (Not All Shown)
Border Towns

agency, online, or by phone. Since station ticket offices can get very crowded, some travelers will find it easiest to go to a travel agency, most of which charge a nominal service fee.

At the Station: You will likely have to wait in a line to buy your ticket (and pay a five percent service fee). First find the correct line—at bigger stations, there might be separate windows for short-distance, long-distance, advance, and "today" *(para hoy)* tickets. You might have to take a number—watch others and follow

PRACTICALITIES

Rail Pass or Point-to-Point Tickets?

Will you be better off buying a rail pass or point-to-point tickets? It pays to know your options and choose what's best for your itinerary.

Rail Passes

A Eurail Spain Pass lets you travel by train in Spain for three to eight days (consecutively or not) within a one-month period. Spain is also covered (along with most of Europe) by the classic Eurail Global Pass.

Discounted rates are offered for seniors (age 60 and up) and youths (ages 12-27). Up to two kids (ages 4-11) can travel free with each adult-rate pass (but not with senior rates). All rail passes offer a choice of first or second class for all ages.

While most rail passes are delivered electronically, it's smart to get your pass sorted before leaving home. For more on rail passes, including current prices and purchasing, visit RickSteves.com/rail.

Point-to-Point Tickets

If you're taking just a couple of train rides, buying individual point-to-point tickets may save you money over a pass. Use this map to add up approximate pay-as-you-go fares for your itinerary, and compare that to the price of a rail pass plus reservations. Keep in mind that significant discounts on point-to-point tickets may be available with advance purchase.

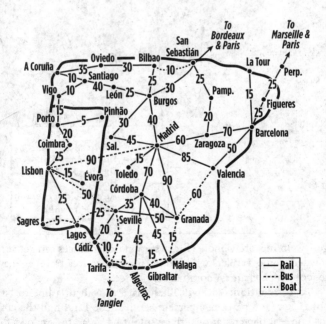

Map shows approximate costs, in US dollars, for one-way, second-class tickets on faster trains.

their lead. Renfe ticket machines usually take US credit cards but in some cases you may have to enter your PIN.

You can also buy tickets or reservations at the Renfe offices located in more than 100 city centers. These are more central and multilingual—also less crowded and confusing—than most train stations.

Travel Agency: The easiest choice for most travelers is to buy tickets at an English-speaking travel agency (look for a train sticker in agency windows). El Corte Inglés department stores (with locations in most Spanish cities) often have handy travel agencies inside.

Online: Although the Renfe website is useful for confirming schedules and prices, you may have trouble buying tickets online unless you use PayPal. (The website sometimes rejects attempts to use a US card.) But with patience and enough Spanish language skill, you may nab an online discount of up to 60 percent (limited seats at these prices, available two weeks to two months ahead of travel). Online vendors based in the US include RickSteves.com/rail and Petrabax.com (expect a small fee from either) or use the European vendor Trainline.eu.

By Phone: You can purchase your ticket by phone (+34 912 240 202), then pick it up at the station by punching your confirmation code *(localizador)* into one of the machines. Discounts up to 40 percent off are offered a week or more ahead by phone (and at stations).

You can also reserve tickets by phone, then buy them at the station, which you must do a few days before departure (at a ticket window, usually signed *"venta anticipada"*). You can't pay for reserved tickets at the station on your day of travel.

BUSES

Bus travel in Spain gives you a glimpse at *España profunda* ("deep Spain"), where everyone seems to know each other and no one's in a hurry. The system can be confusing to the uninitiated, as a number of different companies operate throughout the country, sometimes running buses to the same destinations and using the same transfer points. The aggregator website Movelia.es is a good place to begin researching schedules and companies; local TIs also have bus information for their region.

Among the major companies are Alsa (www.alsa.es), Avanza (www.avanzabus.com), Comes (www.tgcomes.es), and Damas (www.damas-sa.es), but you will see many other regional carriers. Ticket desks are usually clustered within one bus station, and larger stations have a consolidated information desk with all schedules. In smaller stations, check the destinations and schedules posted on each office window.

Remember to double-check the codes on bus schedules to confirm service on the day you want to travel: for example, "12:00S" means 12:00 daily except Saturday. Bus service on holidays, Saturdays, and especially Sundays can be less frequent. Departures are listed under *salidas*, and arrivals are *llegadas*. Whenever possible, choose a faster *directo* route over a slower *ruta* option (with more stops along the way).

Some routes can require a transfer; typically (but not always) your onward connection will be run by the originating company. Spend some time at the station upon arrival to check your departure options and buy a ticket in advance if necessary (and possible). If you're downtown, need a ticket, and the bus station isn't central, save time by asking at the TI about travel agencies that sell bus tickets.

On the Bus: You can (and most likely will be required to) stow your luggage under the bus. Your ticket comes with an assigned seat; if the bus is full, you should take that seat, but if it's uncrowded, most people just sit where they like. Buses are nonsmoking.

Drivers and station personnel may not speak English. Buses generally lack WCs, but they stop every two hours or so for a short break. Drivers announce how long the stop will be, but if in doubt, ask, "How many minutes here?" *("¿Cuántos minutos aquí?")*. Listen for the bus horn as a final call before departure.

TAXIS AND RIDE-BOOKING SERVICES

Most European taxis are reliable and cheap. In many cities, two people can travel short distances by cab for little more than the cost of bus or subway tickets. If you like ride-booking services such as Uber, their apps usually work in Europe just like they do in the US: Request a car on your mobile phone (connected to Wi-Fi or data), and the fare is automatically charged to your credit card. However, as of this writing, Uber is available only in

Madrid. For more about tipping your cabbie, see page 961.

RENTING A CAR

It's cheaper to arrange most car rentals from the US, so research and compare rates before you go. Most of the major US rental agencies (including Avis, Budget, Enterprise, Hertz, and Thrifty) have offices throughout Europe. Also consider the two major Europe-based agencies, Europcar and Sixt. Consolidators such as Auto Eu-

rope (AutoEurope.com—or the sometimes cheaper AutoEurope. eu) compare rates at several companies to get you the best deal.

Wherever you book, always read the fine print. Check for add-on charges—such as one-way drop-off fees, airport surcharges, or mandatory insurance policies—that aren't included in the "total price."

Rental Costs and Considerations

Figure on paying roughly $275 for a one-week rental for a basic compact car. Allow extra for supplemental insurance, fuel, tolls, and parking. To save money on fuel, request a diesel car. Be warned that international trips—say, picking up in Madrid and dropping off in Lisbon—can be expensive if the rental company assesses a drop-off fee for crossing a border.

Manual vs. Automatic: Almost all rental cars in Europe are manual by default—and cars with stick shift are generally cheaper. If you need an automatic, reserve one specifically. When selecting a car, don't be tempted by a larger model, as it won't be as maneuverable on narrow, winding roads (such as in Andalucía's hill towns) or when squeezing into tight parking lots.

Age Restrictions: Some rental companies impose minimum and maximum age limits. Young drivers (25 and under) and seniors (69 and up) should check the rental policies and rules section of car rental websites.

Choosing Pick-up/Drop-off Locations: Always check the hours of the location you choose: Many rental offices close from midday Saturday until Monday morning and, in smaller towns, at lunchtime.

When selecting an office, confirm the location on a map. A downtown site might seem more convenient than the airport but could actually be in the suburbs or buried deep in big-city streets. Pedestrianized and one-way streets can make navigation tricky when returning a car at a big-city office or urban train station. Wherever you select, get precise details on the location and allow ample time to find it.

Have the Right License: If you're renting a car in Spain, bring your driver's license. You're also technically required to have an International Driving Permit—an official translation of your license (sold at AAA offices for about $20 plus the cost of two passport-type photos; see AAA.com). How this is enforced varies: I've never needed one.

Picking Up Your Car: Before driving off in your rental car, check it thoroughly and make sure any damage is noted on your rental agreement. Rental agencies in Europe tend to charge for even minor damage, so be sure to mark everything. Find out how your car's gearshift, lights, turn signals, wipers, radio, and fuel cap

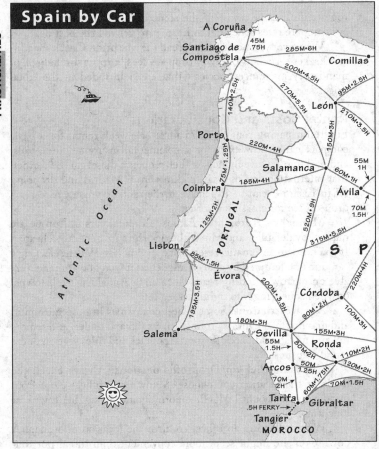

Spain by Car

function, and know what kind of fuel the car takes (diesel is common in Europe). When you return the car, make sure the agent verifies its condition with you.

Car Insurance Options

When you rent a car in Europe, the price typically includes liability insurance, which covers harm to other cars or motorists—but not the rental car itself. To limit your financial risk in case of damage to the rental, choose one of these options: Buy a Collision Damage Waiver (CDW; also called "loss damage waiver" or LDW by some firms) with a low or zero deductible from the car-rental company (roughly 30-40 percent extra), get coverage through your credit card (free, but more complicated), or get collision insurance as part of a larger travel-insurance policy.

Basic **CDW** costs $15–30 a day and typically comes with a $1,000-2,000 deductible, reducing but not eliminating your finan-

cial responsibility. When you reserve or pick up the car, you'll be offered the chance to "buy down" the deductible to zero (for an additional $10–30/day; this is sometimes called "super CDW" or "zero-deductible coverage").

If you opt for **credit-card coverage,** you must decline all coverage offered by the car-rental company—which means they can place a hold on your card to cover the deductible. In case of damage, it can be time-consuming to resolve the charges. Before relying on this option, quiz your card company about how it works.

If you're already purchasing a **travel-insurance policy** for your trip, adding collision coverage can be an economical option. For example, Travel Guard (TravelGuard.com) sells affordable renter's collision insurance as an add-on to its other policies; it's valid everywhere in Europe except the Republic of Ireland, and some Italian car-rental companies refuse to honor it, as it doesn't cover you in case of theft.

For more on car-rental insurance, see RickSteves.com/cdw.

Navigation Options

If you'll be navigating using your phone or a GPS unit from home, remember to bring a car charger and device mount.

Your Mobile Phone: The mapping app on your phone works fine for navigating Europe's roads. To save on data, most apps allow you to download maps for offline use (do this before you need them, when you have a strong Wi-Fi signal). Some apps—including Google Maps—also have offline route directions, but you'll need mobile data access for current traffic. For more on using a mapping app without burning through data, see "Using Your Phone in Europe," earlier.

GPS Devices: If you want a dedicated GPS unit, consider renting one with your car (about $20/day, or sometimes included—ask). These units offer real-time turn-by-turn directions and traffic without the data requirements of an app. The unit may come loaded only with maps for its home country; if you need additional maps, ask. Make sure you know how to use the device—and that the language is set to English—before you drive off.

Paper Maps and Atlases: Even when navigating primarily with a mobile app or GPS, I always have a paper map, ideally a big, detailed regional road map. It's invaluable for getting the big picture, understanding alternate routes, and filling in if my phone runs out of juice. The free maps you get from your car-rental company usually don't have enough detail. It's smart to buy a better map before you go, or pick one up at local gas stations, bookshops, newsstands, and tourist shops.

Driving

Driving in rural Spain is great—traffic is sparse and roads are generally good. But a car is a pain in big cities. Drive defensively. If you're involved in an accident, you will be in for a monumental headache. Spaniards love to tailgate. Don't take it personally; let impatient drivers pass you and enjoy the drive. In smaller towns, following signs to *Centro Ciudad* will get you to the heart of things.

Freeways and Tolls: Spain's freeways come with tolls, but save huge amounts of time. Each toll road *(autopista de peaje)* has its own pricing structure, so tolls vary. Near some major cities, you must prepay for each stretch of road you drive; on other routes, you take a ticket where you enter the

freeway, and pay when you exit. Payment can be made in cash or by credit or debit card (credit-card-only lanes are labeled *"vias automáticas"*; cash lanes are *"vias manuales"*).

Because road numbers can be puzzling and inconsistent, be ready to navigate by city and town names. Memorize some key road words: *salida* (exit), *de sentido único* (one way), *despacio* (slow), and *adelantamiento prohibido* (no passing). Mileage signs are in kilometers.

Road Rules: Seatbelts are required by law. Children under 12 must ride in the back seat and use a child's car seat (type varies with age/weight; check with your rental company for details). It's recommended that children over 12 ride in the back when possible.

You must put on a reflective safety vest any time you get out of your car on the side of a highway or unlit road (most rental-car companies provide one—check when you pick up the car). Those who use eyeglasses are required by law to have a spare pair in the car.

Be aware of typical European road rules; for example, many countries require headlights to be turned on at all times, and nearly all forbid handheld mobile-phone use. In Europe, you're not allowed to turn right on a red light unless a sign or signal specifically authorizes it, and on expressways it's illegal to pass drivers on the right. You should also stay in the right lane unless you are passing.

Ask your car-rental company about these rules, or check the "International Travel" section of the US State Department website (www.travel.state.gov, search for your country in the "Learn About Your Destination" box, then click "Travel and Transportation").

Traffic Cops: Watch for traffic radars and expect to be stopped for a routine check by the police. Small towns come with speed traps and corruption. Tickets, especially for foreigners, are issued and paid for on the spot. Insist on a receipt *(recibo)*, so the money is less likely to end up in the cop's pocket.

Fuel: Gas and diesel prices are controlled and the same everywhere—about $5 a gallon for gas and $4 a gallon for diesel. Unleaded gas *(gasolina sin plomo)* is either *normal* or *super*. Note that diesel is called *diesel* or *gasóleo*—pay attention when filling your tank. Some pumps are color-coded: Unleaded pumps are green and labeled "E," while diesel pumps (often yellow or black) are labeled "B."

Theft: Thieves easily recognize rental cars and assume they are filled with a tourist's gear. Be sure all your valuables are out of sight and locked in the trunk, or even better, with you or in your room. Parking attendants all over Spain holler, *"Nada en el coche"* ("Nothing in the car"). And they mean it. In cities you can park safely but expensively in guarded lots or garages.

FLIGHTS

To compare flights, begin with an online travel search engine: Kayak is the top site for flights to and within Europe, easy-to-use Google Flights has price alerts, and Skyscanner includes many inexpensive flights within Europe. To avoid unpleasant surprises, before you book be sure to read the small print about refunds, changes, and the costs for "extras" such as reserving a seat, checking a bag, or printing a boarding pass.

Flights to Europe: Start looking for international flights about four to six months before your trip, especially for peak-season travel. Depending on your itinerary, it can be efficient and no more expensive to fly into one city and out of another. If your flight requires a connection in Europe, see our hints on navigating Europe's top hub airports at RickSteves.com/hub-airports.

Flights Within Europe: Flying between European cities is surprisingly affordable. Before buying a long-distance train or bus ticket, check the cost of a flight on one of Europe's airlines, whether a major carrier or a no-frills outfit like EasyJet or Ryanair. Be aware that flying with a discount airline can have drawbacks, such as minimal customer service, time-consuming treks to secondary airports, and a larger carbon footprint than a train or bus.

Flying to the US and Canada: Because security is extra tight for flights to the US, be sure to give yourself plenty of time at the airport (see www.tsa.gov for the latest rules).

Resources from Rick Steves

Begin Your Trip at RickSteves.com

My mobile-friendly **website** is *the* place to explore Europe in preparation for your trip. You'll find thousands of fun articles, videos, and radio interviews; a wealth of money-saving tips for planning your dream trip; travel news dispatches; a video library of travel

talks; my travel blog; our latest guidebook updates (RickSteves. com/update); and the free Rick Steves Audio Europe app. You can also follow me on Facebook, Instagram, and Twitter.

Our **Travel Forum** is a well-groomed collection of message boards where our travel-savvy community answers questions and shares their personal travel experiences—and our well-traveled staff chimes in when they can be helpful (RickSteves.com/forums).

Our **online Travel Store** offers bags and accessories that I've designed to help you travel smarter and lighter. These include my popular carry-on bags (which I live out of four months a year), money belts, totes, toiletries kits, adapters, guidebooks, and planning maps (RickSteves.com/shop).

Our website can also help you find the perfect **rail pass** for your itinerary and your budget, with easy, one-stop shopping for rail passes, seat reservations, and point-to-point tickets (RickSteves. com/rail).

Rick Steves' Tours, Guidebooks, TV Shows, and More

Small Group Tours: Want to travel with greater efficiency and less stress? We offer more than 40 itineraries reaching the best destinations in this book...and beyond. Each year about 30,000 travelers join us on about 1,000 Rick Steves bus tours. You'll enjoy great guides and a fun bunch of travel partners (with small groups of 24 to 28 travelers). You'll find European adventures to fit every vacation length. For all the details, and to get our tour catalog, visit RickSteves.com/tours or call us at +1 425 608 4217.

Books: This book is just one of many books in my series on European travel, which includes country and city guidebooks, Snapshots (excerpted chapters from bigger guides), Pocket Guides (full-color little books on big cities), "Best Of" guidebooks (condensed, full-color country guides), and my budget-travel skills handbook, *Rick Steves Europe Through the Back Door.* A complete list of my titles—including phrase books, cruising guides, and travelogues on European art, history, and culture—appears near the end of this book.

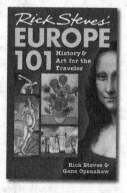

TV Shows and Travel Talks: My public television series, *Rick Steves' Europe,* covers Europe from top to bottom with over 100 half-hour episodes—and we're working on new shows every year (watch full episodes at my website for free). My free online video library, Rick Steves Classroom Europe, offers a searchable data-

PRACTICALITIES

base of short video clips on European history, culture, and geography (Classroom.RickSteves.com). And to raise your travel I.Q., check out the video versions of our popular classes (covering most European countries as well as travel skills, packing smart, cruising, tech for travelers, European art, and travel as a political act—RickSteves.com/travel-talks).

Audio Tours on My Free App: I've produced dozens of free, self-guided audio tours of the top sights in Europe. For those tours and other audio content, get my free **Rick Steves Audio Europe app,** an extensive online library organized by destination. For more on my app, see page 26.

Radio: My weekly public radio show, *Travel with Rick Steves,* features interviews with travel experts from around the world. It airs on 400 public radio stations across the US. An archive of programs is available at RickSteves.com/radio.

Podcasts: You can enjoy my travel content via several free podcasts. The podcast version of my radio show brings you a weekly, hour-long travel conversation. My other podcasts include a weekly selection of video clips from my public television show, my audio tours of Europe's top sights, and live recordings of my travel classes (RickSteves.com/watch-read-listen/audio/podcasts).

APPENDIX

Holidays and Festivals

This list includes selected festivals in major cities, plus national holidays observed throughout Spain. Many sights and banks close

on national holidays—keep this in mind when planning your itinerary. Before planning a trip around a festival, verify the dates with the festival website, the national tourist office (www.spain. info), or my "Upcoming Holidays and Festivals in Spain" web page at RickSteves.com/europe/spain/festivals.

Be prepared for big crowds during these holiday periods: Holy Week (Semana Santa) and Easter weekend, especially in Sevilla; April Fair in Sevilla; the San Isidro festival in Madrid; Labor Day (May 1); Dos de Mayo, Madrid; Ascension Day; Pentecost weekend; Assumption weekend; Spanish National Day; Constitution Day, followed closely by the Feast of the Immaculate Conception—both the previous and following weekends may be busy; and

Christmas and New Year's. Look out for any local holiday that falls on a Tuesday or Thursday—the Spanish will often take Monday or Friday off as well to have a four-day weekend.

Jan 1	New Year's Day
Jan 6	Epiphany
Early Feb	La Candelaria, Madrid (religious festival)
Feb 28	Andalucía Day (some closures, Andalucía only)
March/ April	Holy Week (Semana Santa): April 2-9, 2023; March 24-31, 2024
March/ April	Easter Sunday and Monday (Sunday-only in Andalucía): April 9-10, 2023; March 31-April 1, 2024
Two weeks after Holy Week	April Fair (Feria de Abril), Sevilla
April 23	St. George's Day, Barcelona (flowers and books)
May 1	Labor Day (closures)
May 2	Dos de Mayo, Madrid
May 3	Fiesta de las Cruces, Granada and Córdoba (religious festival)
Mid-May	Feria del Caballo, Jerez (horse pageantry)
May 15	San Isidro, Madrid and Nerja (religious festival)
Late May	La Patum, Berga (near Barcelona; religious festival)
May	Ascension Day: May 18, 2023; May 9, 2024
May/June	Pentecost and Whit Monday: May 28-29, 2023; May 19-20, 2024
May/June	Corpus Christi: June 8, 2023; May 30, 2024
June 24	Festival of St. John the Baptist (bonfires and fireworks)
June-July	International Festival of Music and Dance, Granada
July 6-14	Running of the Bulls (Fiesta de San Fermín), Pamplona
July 25	Feast Day of St. James, Santiago de Compostela
Aug	Gràcia Festival, Barcelona
Aug 15	Assumption of Mary (religious festival); Verbena de la Paloma, Madrid (folk festival)
Sept	Autumn Festival, Jerez (flamenco, bullfights)
Late Sept	La Mercé, Barcelona (week-long festival of parades and live music); Feria de San Miguel, Sevilla (bullfights); Little San Fermín, Pamplona (concerts, parades)

Oct 12	Spanish National Day
Nov 1	All Saints' Day
Nov 9	Feast of the Almudena, Madrid (religious festival)
Dec 6	Constitution Day
Dec 8	Feast of the Immaculate Conception
Dec 25	Christmas
Dec 31	New Year's Eve

Books and Films

To learn more about Spain's past and present, check out a few of these books or films.

Nonfiction

Barcelona (Robert Hughes, 1992). This is an opinionated journey through the city's tumultuous history, with a focus on art and architecture.

Barcelona: The Great Enchantress (2004) is a condensed version of Hughes' love song to his favorite city.

Barcelona: A Thousand Years of the City's Past (Felipe Fernandez-Armesto, 1992). A historical and artistic perspective on Barcelona, this book also details the tensions between the city and the rest of Spain.

The Basque History of the World (Mark Kurlansky, 2001). This is an essential history for understanding the Basque region and its people.

The Battle for Spain (Antony Beevor, 2006). A prize-winning account of the disintegration of Spain in the 1930s, Beevor's work is the best overall history of the bloody civil war.

Discovering Spain: An Uncommon Guide (Penelope Casas, 1992). Casas, a well-known Spanish cookbook author, insightfully blends history, culture, and food in this personal guide.

Driving Over Lemons (Chris Stewart, 2001). In this real-life account, the one-time drummer of Genesis and his family relocate to Spain and adjust to new cultures and traditions.

Following the Milky Way (Elyn Aviva, 1989). In 1982, Aviva explored the nature of pilgrimage along the famous Camino de Santiago trail in northern Spain—before its newfound popularity.

Ghosts of Spain: Travels Through Spain and Its Silent Past (Giles Tremlett, 2007). Spain comes to grips with its past under Franco in this evocative account—part social history and part travelogue.

Hell and Good Company: The Spanish Civil War and The World It

Made (Richard Rhodes, 2015). Reporters, writers, artists, and doctors who witnessed the Spanish Civil War tell their extraordinary stories.

Homage to Barcelona (Colm Toibin, 1990). This rich history of Barcelona includes anecdotes from the author's time in the city.

Homage to Catalonia (George Orwell, 1938). Orwell writes a gripping account of his experiences in the Spanish Civil War fighting Franco's fascists.

Hotel Florida: Truth, Love, and Death in the Spanish Civil War (Amanda Vaill, 2014). In this popular history, Vaill reconstructs events of the Spanish Civil War through the letters, diaries, and photographs of the war correspondents who covered it.

Into the Arena: The World of the Spanish Bullfight (Alexander Fiske-Harrison, 2011). The author examines the controversial sport from the perspective of the bullfighter, trainer, and fan—and even gets in the ring himself.

The New Spaniards (John Hooper, 2006). Hooper surveys all aspects of modern Spain, including its transition from dictatorship to democracy, its cultural traditions, and its changing society.

The Ornament of the World (María Rosa Menocal, 2002). Menocal gives a vivid depiction of how Muslims, Jews, and Christians created a culture of tolerance in medieval Spain.

Sister Queens: The Noble, Tragic Lives of Katherine of Aragon and Juana, Queen of Castile (Julia Fox, 2011). This dual biography of the daughters of Ferdinand and Isabel tells how they each lost positions of power—one to madness and the other to England's Henry VIII.

South from Granada (Gerald Brenan, 1957). The eccentricities of village life in the mountains of Andalucía are lovingly detailed in this British expat's tribute.

Spain in Our Hearts: Americans in the Spanish Civil War, 1936-1939 (Adam Hochschild, 2016). This moving narrative follows the idealistic Americans who fought in and wrote about the Spanish Civil War.

Travelers' Tales: Spain (Lucy McCauley, 1995). Taken together, this collection of essays from numerous authors builds an appealing overview of Spain and its people.

Fiction

The Blind Man of Seville (Robert Wilson, 2003). Wilson's popular police thrillers, including this one, are set in Spain and Portugal.

The Carpenter's Pencil (Manuel Rivas, 2001). The psychological cost of Spain's Civil War is at the heart of this unsentimental tale of a revolutionary haunted by his past.

Don Quixote (Miguel de Cervantes, 1605). This classic tale of a deluded nobleman trying to revive chivalry in early-16th-century Spain is one of the world's greatest novels.

For Whom the Bell Tolls (Ernest Hemingway, 1940). After reporting on the Spanish Civil War from Madrid, Hemingway wrote his iconic novel about an American volunteer fighting Franco's fascist forces.

The Heretic (Lewis Weinstein, 2000). Sevilla is the backdrop for this tale exploring the brutality and intolerance of the Spanish Inquisition.

The Last Jew (Noah Gordon, 2000). This sweeping saga recounts one man's survival in Inquisition-era Spain.

The Queen's Vow (C. W. Gortner, 2012). The life and times of Queen Isabel are vividly re-created in this historical novel.

The Shadow of the Wind (Carlos Ruiz Zafón, 2005). This best-selling thriller is set in 1950s Barcelona; sequels include *The Angel's Game* and *The Prisoner of Heaven*.

Stories from Spain (Genevieve Barlow and William Stivers, 1999). Readers follow nearly 1,000 years of Spanish history in brief short stories printed in Spanish and English.

The Sun Also Rises (Ernest Hemingway, 1926). A bullfight enthusiast, Hemingway chronicles the running of the bulls in Pamplona in this novel about the "Lost Generation." He also wrote about the spectacle in *Death in the Afternoon* (1932) and *The Dangerous Summer* (1960).

Tales of the Alhambra (Washington Irving, 1832). In this timeless classic, Irving weaves fact and mythical tales into his descriptions of the Alhambra.

Three Tragedies (Federico García Lorca, 1933-36). Written in the last years of the poet's life, these plays about repression, ritual, desire, and tradition are a fine introduction to Lorca's genius.

Films

L'Auberge Espagnole (2002). This comedy-drama chronicles the loves and lives of European students sharing an apartment in Barcelona.

Barcelona (1994). Two Americans try to navigate the Spanish singles scene and the ensuing culture clash.

Blancanieves (2012). An homage to silent films, this melodramatic black-and-white film recasts Snow White as a female bullfighter trying to overcome her evil stepmother in the 1920s.

Carlos Saura's Flamenco Trilogy. The first film, *Blood Wedding* (1981), adapts Federico García Lorca's play about a wedding imposed on a bride in love with another man. *Carmen* (1983) follows a Spanish cast rehearsing the well-known French opera. *El Amor Brujo* (1986) is a ghostly love story.

Carol's Journey (2002). A Spanish-American girl travels to Spain for the first time in the turbulent spring of 1938.

Un Chien Andalou (*The Andalusian Dog*, 1928). Dalí collaborated with Luis Buñuel on this classic Surrealist short film.

El Cid (1961). Sophia Loren and Charlton Heston star in this epic about an 11th-century hero's effort to unite Spain.

Goya's Ghosts (2006). Focusing on the last phases of the Spanish Inquisition, this film by Milos Forman is part satire and part soap opera.

Juana la Loca (*Mad Love*, 2001). This historical drama set in the early 16th century combines sex and politics in the time of Queen Juana the Mad.

Man of La Mancha (1972). Peter O'Toole and Sophia Loren star in this musical version of *Don Quixote*.

Manuale d'Amore (2005). The four episodes of this film follow the love stories of four couples, with Barcelona and Rome as backdrops.

The Mystery of Picasso (1956). Picasso is filmed painting from behind a transparent canvas, allowing a unique look at his creative process.

Ocho Apellidos Vascos (*Spanish Affair*, 2014). Two of Spain's most different cultures collide as a dumped bride-to-be from the Basque Country goes ahead with her bachelorette party...in Sevilla. Eventually the south vs. north conflict is amorously resolved.

Open Your Eyes (1997). Set in Madrid, Alejandro Amenábar's film was the inspiration for the Tom Cruise thriller *Vanilla Sky*, in which a car accident sets off an intricate series of events.

Pan's Labyrinth (2006). Exploring the dark times of fascist Spain in World War II, this film is a rich excursion in magic realism.

Vicky Cristina Barcelona (2008). In this Woody Allen film, a macho Spanish artist (Javier Bardem) tries to seduce two American women when his stormy ex-wife (Penélope Cruz) suddenly re-enters his life.

Women on the Verge of a Nervous Breakdown (1988). This film, about a woman's downward spiral after a breakup, is one of several piquant Pedro Almodóvar movies about relationships in the post-Franco era. Others include *All About My Mother* (1999), *Talk to Her* (2002), *Volver* (2006), and *Broken Embraces* (2009).

Books for Kids

Building with Nature: The Life of Antoni Gaudí (Rachel Rodriguez and Julie Paschkis, 2009). Beautiful, folksy illustrations enliven the biography of Barcelona's most famous architect.

Carmelita de Andalucía (Charlotte Brokaw Powers, 2001). In this charming story, a young girl wants her very own red flamenco shoes.

Diego Velazquez (Mike Venezia, 2004). Full-color images of Velazquez's art combine with humorous cartoons to engage young readers.

Katie and the Spanish Princess (James Mayhew, 2006). Katie goes to an art museum to find inspiration for her perfect princess dress.

Kids' Travel Guide—Spain (Flying Kids, 2019). In this activity travel guide, kids explore Spain with a mix of interactive quizzes, tips, and coloring pages alongside their personal tour guide, Leonardo.

Lola's Fandango (Anna Witte and Micha Archer, 2011). A girl discovers her talent when her father gives her secret lessons in this traditional Spanish dance.

Medio Pollito: A Spanish Tale (Eric A. Kimmel and Valeria Docampo, 2010). This traditional Spanish folktale relates the adventures of a unique chicken who ventures to the big city.

Molly and the Magic Suitcase: Molly Goes to Barcelona (Chris Oler and Amy Houston Oler, 2013). With the help of a magic suitcase, Molly and her brother trek to Barcelona in search of adventure.

Picasso and Minou (P.I. Maltbie and Pau Estrada, 2005). This beautifully illustrated book shares the story of Picasso and his work through the eyes of his cat, Minou.

The Prince of Mist (Carlos Ruiz Zafón, 1993). For more mature young readers, this mystery tells of a family's move to a haunted house in coastal Spain.

Princess Prissypants Goes to Spain (Ashley Putnam Evans and Martha-Elizabeth Furguson, 2009). A princess learns to appreciate foreign customs and language.

Shadow of a Bull (Maia Wojciechowska, 1965). A Spanish boy longs to become a doctor—despite family expectations that he be a bullfighter like his father.

Soccer World Spain: Explore the World Through Soccer (Ethan Zohn and David Rosenberg, 2011). A look at Spain through its most famous sport.

The Story of Ferdinand (Munro Leaf and Robert Lawson, 1936). Ferdinand the bull would rather sit and smell the flowers than fight like the other bulls.

Conversions and Climate

Numbers and Stumblers

- Europeans write a few of their numbers differently than we do. 1=1, 4 =4, 7 =7.
- In Europe, dates appear as day/month/year, so Christmas 2024 is 25/12/24.
- Commas are decimal points and decimals are commas. A dollar and a half is $1,50, one thousand is 1.000, and there are 5.280 feet in a mile.
- When counting with fingers, start with your thumb. If you hold up your first finger to request one item, you'll probably get two.
- What Americans call the second floor of a building is the first floor in Europe.
- On escalators and moving sidewalks, Europeans keep the left "lane" open for passing. Keep to the right.

Metric Conversions

A **kilogram** equals 1,000 grams (about 2.2 pounds). One hundred **grams** (a common unit at markets) is about a quarter-pound. One **liter** is about a quart, or almost four to a gallon.

A **kilometer** is six-tenths of a mile. To convert kilometers to miles, cut the kilometers in half and add back 10 percent of the original (120 km: 60 + 12 = 72 miles). One **meter** is 39 inches—just over a yard.

1 foot = 0.3 meter	1 square yard = 0.8 square meter
1 yard = 0.9 meter	1 square mile = 2.6 square kilometers
1 mile = 1.6 kilometers	1 ounce = 28 grams
1 centimeter = 0.4 inch	1 quart = 0.95 liter
1 meter = 39.4 inches	1 kilogram = 2.2 pounds
1 kilometer = 0.62 mile	32°F = 0°C

Clothing Sizes

When shopping for clothing, use these US-to-European comparisons as general guidelines (but note that no conversion is perfect).

Women: For pants and dresses, add 32 in Spain (US 10 = Spanish 42). For blouses and sweaters, add 8 for most of Europe (US 32 = European 40). For shoes, add 30-31 (US 7 = European 37/38).

Men: For shirts, multiply by 2 and add about 8 (US 15 = European 38). For jackets and suits, add 10. For shoes, add 32-34.

Children: Clothing is sized by height—in centimeters (2.5

cm = 1 inch), so a US size 8 roughly equates to 132-140. For shoes up to size 13, add 16-18, and for sizes 1 and up, add 30-32.

Spain's Climate

First line, average daily high; second line, average daily low; third line, average days without rain. For more detailed weather statistics for destinations in this book (as well as the rest of the world), check Wunderground.com.

	J	F	M	A	M	J	J	A	S	O	N	D
SPAIN												
Madrid												
	47°	52°	59°	65°	70°	80°	87°	85°	77°	65°	55°	48°
	35°	36°	41°	45°	50°	58°	63°	63°	57°	49°	42°	36°
	23	21	21	21	21	25	29	28	24	23	21	21
Barcelona												
	55°	57°	60°	65°	71°	78°	82°	82°	77°	69°	62°	56°
	43°	45°	48°	52°	57°	65°	69°	69°	66°	58°	51°	46°
	26	23	23	21	23	24	27	25	23	22	24	25
Sevilla												
	61°	64°	69°	72°	79°	88°	96°	96°	91°	79°	68°	62°
	43°	45°	48°	51°	55°	62°	66°	66°	64°	57°	50°	46°
	25	23	26	25	28	29	31	31	28	26	25	25
MOROCCO												
Tangier												
	61°	63°	64°	66°	72°	77°	82°	84°	81°	75°	68°	63°
	48°	48°	50°	52°	55°	61°	66°	66°	64°	61°	54°	50°
	12	19	21	21	24	27	30	29	27	22	20	19

Fahrenheit and Celsius Conversion

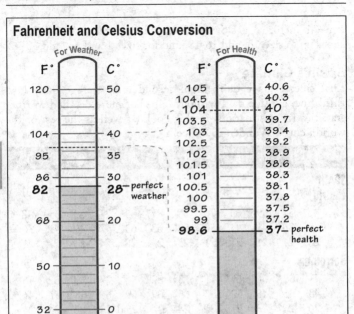

Europe takes its temperature using the Celsius scale, while we opt for Fahrenheit. For a rough conversion from Celsius to Fahrenheit, double the number and add 30. For weather, remember that 28°C is 82°F—perfect. For health, 37°C is just right. At a launderette, 30°C is cold, 40°C is warm (usually the default setting), 60°C is hot, and 95°C is boiling. Your air-conditioner should be set at about 20°C.

APPENDIX

Packing Checklist

Whether you're traveling for five days or five weeks, you won't need more than this. Pack light to enjoy the sweet freedom of true mobility.

Clothing

- ❑ 5 shirts: long- & short-sleeve
- ❑ 2 pairs pants (or skirts/capris)
- ❑ 1 pair shorts
- ❑ 5 pairs underwear & socks
- ❑ 1 pair walking shoes
- ❑ Sweater or warm layer
- ❑ Rainproof jacket with hood
- ❑ Tie, scarf, belt, and/or hat
- ❑ Swimsuit
- ❑ Sleepwear/loungewear

Money

- ❑ Debit card(s)
- ❑ Credit card(s)
- ❑ Hard cash (US $100-200)
- ❑ Money belt

Documents

- ❑ Passport
- ❑ Other required ID: Vaccine card/Covid test, entry visa, etc.
- ❑ Driver's license, student ID, hostel card, etc.
- ❑ Tickets & confirmations: flights, hotels, trains, rail pass, car rental, sight entries
- ❑ Photocopies of important documents
- ❑ Insurance details
- ❑ Guidebooks & maps

Electronics

- ❑ Mobile phone
- ❑ Camera & related gear
- ❑ Tablet/ebook reader/laptop
- ❑ Headphones/earbuds
- ❑ Chargers & batteries
- ❑ Phone car charger & mount (or GPS device)
- ❑ Plug adapters

Toiletries

- ❑ Basics: soap, shampoo, toothbrush, toothpaste, floss, deodorant, sunscreen, brush/comb, etc.
- ❑ Medicines & vitamins
- ❑ First-aid kit
- ❑ Glasses/contacts/sunglasses
- ❑ Face masks & hand sanitizer
- ❑ Sewing kit
- ❑ Packet of tissues (for WC)
- ❑ Earplugs

Miscellaneous

- ❑ Daypack
- ❑ Sealable plastic baggies
- ❑ Laundry supplies: soap, laundry bag, clothesline, spot remover
- ❑ Small umbrella
- ❑ Travel alarm/watch
- ❑ Notepad & pen
- ❑ Journal

Optional Extras

- ❑ Second pair of shoes (flip-flops, sandals, tennis shoes, boots)
- ❑ Travel hairdryer
- ❑ Picnic supplies
- ❑ Disinfecting wipes
- ❑ Water bottle
- ❑ Fold-up tote bag
- ❑ Small flashlight
- ❑ Mini binoculars
- ❑ Small towel or washcloth
- ❑ Inflatable pillow/neck rest
- ❑ Tiny lock
- ❑ Address list (to mail postcards)
- ❑ Extra passport photos

APPENDIX

Pronunciation Guide for Place Names

Spanish	Pronunciation
Algeciras	ahl-*heh*-**thee**-rahs
Andalucía	ahn-dah-loo-**thee**-ah
Arcos de la Frontera	**ar**-kohs day lah frohn-**teh**-rah
Atapuerca	ah-tah-**pwehr**-kah
Ávila	**ah**-vee-lah
Barcelona	bar-theh-**loh**-nah
Bayonne	bai-**ohn**
Bilbao	bil-**bow**
Burgos	**boor**-gohs
Cadaqués	kah-dah-**kehs**
Cantabria	kahn-**tah**-bree-ah
Catalunya	kah-tah-**loon**-yah
Ciudad Rodrigo	thee-oo-**dahd** roh-**dree**-goh
Comillas	koh-**mee**-yahs
Córdoba	**kor**-doh-bah
El Escorial	ehl ehs-kor-ee-**ahl**
Figueres	fee-**gehr**-ehs
Frigiliana	free-*hee*-lee-**ah**-nah
Fuenterrabía	fwehn-teh-rah-**bee**-ah
Galicia	gah-**lee**-thee-ah
Gibraltar	*hee*-brahl-tar
Granada	grah-**nah**-dah
Grazalema	grah-zah-**lay**-mah
Guernica	**gehr**-nee-kah
Hendaye	**hehn**-day
Hondarribia	hohn-dah-**ree**-bee-ah
Jerez de la Frontera	*heh*-**reth** day lah frohn-**teh**-rah
La Mancha	lah **mahn**-chah
León	lay-**ohn**
Lequeitio	leh-**kay**-tee-oh
Madrid	mah-**dreed**
Marbella	mar-**bay**-yah
Montserrat	mohnt-seh-**raht**
Nerja	**nehr**-*hah*
O Cebreiro	oh theh-**bray**-roh
Orreaga	oh-ray-**ah**-gah
Pamplona	pahm-**ploh**-nah
Picos de Europa	**pee**-kohs day eh-ew-**roh**-pah
Potes	**poh**-tehs
Rioja	ree-**oh**-*hah*
Roncesvalles	rohn-thes-**va**-yes
Ronda	**rohn**-dah
Salamanca	sah-lah-**mahn**-kah
San Sebastián	sahn seh-bah-stee-**ahn**
Santiago de Compostela	sahn-tee-**ah**-goh day kohm-poh-**steh**-lah
Santillana del Mar	sahn-tee-**yah**-nah del mar
Segovia	seh-**goh**-vee-ah
Sevilla	seh-**vee**-yah
Sitges	**seet**-jehz
Tarifa	tah-**ree**-fah
Toledo	toh-**lay**-doh
Zahara	tha-**ah**-rah

Spanish Survival Phrases

Good morning.	Buenos días.	**bweh**-nohs **dee**-ahs
Good afternoon.	Buenas tardes.	**bweh**-nahs **tar**-dehs
Do you speak English?	¿Habla usted inglés?	**ah**-blah oo-**stehd** een-**glays**
Yes. / No.	Sí. / No.	see / noh
I (don't) understand.	(No) comprendo.	(noh) kohm-**prehn**-doh
Please. / Thank you.	Por favor. / Gracias.	por fah-**bor** / **grah**-thee-ahs
I'm sorry.	Lo siento.	loh see-**ehn**-toh
Excuse me.	Perdone.	pehr-**doh**-nay
No problem.	No hay problema.	noh i proh-**bleh**-mah
Good. / OK.	Bueno. / Vale.	**bweh**-noh / **bah**-lay
Goodbye.	Adiós.	ah-dee-**ohs**
one / two / three	uno / dos / tres	**oo**-noh / dohs / trehs
four / five / six	cuatro / cinco / seis	**kwah**-troh / **theen**-koh / says
seven / eight	siete / ocho	see-**eh**-tay / **oh**-choh
nine / ten	nueve / diez	**nweh**-bay / dee-**ehth**
How much is it?	¿Cuánto cuesta?	**kwahn**-toh **kweh**-stah
Write it?	¿Me lo escribe?	may loh eh-**skree**-bay
Is it free?	¿Es gratis?	ehs **grah**-tees
Is it included?	¿Está incluido?	eh-**stah** een-kloo-**ee**-doh
Where can I buy / find...?	¿Dónde puedo comprar / encontrar...?	**dohn**-day **pweh**-doh kohm-**prar** / ehn-kohn-**trar**
I'd like / We'd like...	Me gustaría / Nos gustaría...	may goo-stah-**ree**-ah / nohs goo-stah-**ree**-ah
...a room.	...una habitación.	**oo**-nah ah-bee-tah-thee-**ohn**
...a ticket to ___.	...un billete para ___.	oon bee-**yeh**-tay **pah**-rah ___
Is it possible?	¿Es posible?	ehs poh-**see**-blay
Where is...?	¿Dónde está...?	**dohn**-day eh-**stah**
...the train station	...la estación de trenes	lah eh-stah-thee-**ohn** day **treh**-nehs
...the bus station	...la estación de autobuses	lah eh-stah-thee-**ohn** day ow-toh-**boo**-sehs
...the tourist information office	...la oficina de turismo	lah oh-fee-**thee**-nah day too-**rees**-moh
Where are the toilets?	¿Dónde están los servicios?	**dohn**-day eh-**stahn** lohs sehr-**bee**-thee-ohs
men	hombres, caballeros	**ohm**-brehs, kah-bah-**yeh**-rohs
women	mujeres, damas	moo-**heh**-rehs, **dah**-mahs
left / right	izquierda / derecha	eeth-kee-**ehr**-dah / deh-**reh**-chah
straight	derecho	deh-**reh**-choh
When do you open / close?	¿A qué hora abren / cierran?	ah kay **oh**-rah **ah**-brehn / thee-**ehr**-ahn
At what time?	¿A qué hora?	ah kay **oh**-rah
Just a moment.	Un momento.	oon moh-**mehn**-toh
now / soon / later	ahora / pronto / más tarde	ah-**oh**-rah / **prohn**-toh / mahs **tar**-day
today / tomorrow	hoy / mañana	oy / mahn-**yah**-nah

In a Spanish Restaurant

I'd like / We'd like...	Me gustaría / Nos gustaría... may goo-stah-**ree**-ah / nohs goo-stah-**ree**-ah
...to reserve...	...reservar... reh-sehr-**bar**
...a table for one / two.	...una mesa para uno / dos. **oo**-nah **meh**-sah **pah**-rah **oo**-noh / dohs
Non-smoking.	No fumador. noh foo-mah-**dor**
Is this table free?	¿Está esta mesa libre? eh-**stah** eh-stah **meh**-sah **lee**-bray
The menu (in English), please.	La carta (en inglés), por favor. lah **kar**-tah (ehn een-**glays**) por fah-**bor**
service (not) included	servicio (no) incluido sehr-**bee**-thee-oh (noh) een-kloo-**ee**-doh
cover charge	precio de entrada **preh**-thee-oh day ehn-**trah**-dah
to go	para llevar **pah**-rah yeh-**bar**
with / without	con / sin kohn / seen
and / or	y / o ee / oh
breakfast / lunch / dinner	desayuno / almuerzo / cena deh-sah-**yoo**-noh / ahl-**mwehr**-zoh / **seh**-nah
menu (of the day)	menú (del día) meh-**noo** (dehl **dee**-ah)
specialty of the house	especialidad de la casa eh-speh-thee-ah-lee-**dahd** day lah **kah**-sah
tourist menu	menú turístico meh-**noo** too-**ree**-stee-koh
combination plate	plato combinado **plah**-toh kohm-bee-**nah**-doh
appetizers	tapas **tah**-pahs
bread	pan pahn
cheese	queso **keh**-soh
sandwich / soup	bocadillo / sopa boh-kah-**dee**-yoh / **soh**-pah
salad	ensalada ehn-sah-**lah**-dah
meat / poultry	carne / aves **kar**-nay / **ah**-behs
fish / seafood	pescado / marisco peh-**skah**-doh / mah-**ree**-skoh
fruit / vegetables	fruta / verduras **froo**-tah / behr-**doo**-rahs
dessert	postre **poh**-stray
tap water	agua del grifo **ah**-gwah dehl **gree**-foh
mineral water	agua mineral **ah**-gwah mee-neh-**rahl**
(orange) juice	zumo (de naranja) **thoo**-moh (day nah-**rahn**-hah)
coffee / tea / milk	café / té / leche kah-**fay** / tay / **leh**-chay
wine / beer	vino / cerveza **bee**-noh / thehr-**beh**-thah
red / white	tinto / blanco **teen**-toh / **blahn**-koh
glass / bottle	vaso / botella **bah**-soh / boh-**teh**-yah
Cheers!	¡Salud! sah-**lood**
More. / Another.	Más. / Otro. mahs / **oh**-troh
The same.	El mismo. ehl **mees**-moh
The bill, please.	La cuenta, por favor. lah **kwehn**-tah por fah-**bor**
tip	propina proh-**pee**-nah
Delicious!	¡Delicioso! deh-lee-thee-**oh**-soh

For hundreds more pages of survival phrases for your trip to Spain, check out *Rick Steves Spanish Phrase Book*.

INDEX

INDEX

INDEX

MAP INDEX

MAP INDEX

Our website enhances this book and turns

Explore Europe

At ricksteves.com you can browse through thousands of articles, videos, photos and radio interviews, plus find a wealth of money-saving travel tips for planning your dream trip. And with our mobile-friendly website, you can easily access all this great travel information anywhere you go.

TV Shows

Preview the places you'll visit by watching entire half-hour episodes of *Rick Steves' Europe* (choose from all 100 shows) on-demand, for free.

your travel dreams into affordable reality

Radio Interviews

Enjoy ready access to Rick's vast library of radio interviews covering travel tips and cultural insights that relate specifically to your Europe travel plans.

Travel Forums

Learn, ask, share! Our online community of savvy travelers is a great resource for first-time travelers to Europe, as well as seasoned pros.

Travel News

Subscribe to our free Travel News e-newsletter, and get monthly updates from Rick on what's happening in Europe.

Classroom Europe®

Check out our free resource for educators with 500 short video clips from the *Rick Steves' Europe* TV show.

Save time and energy

This guidebook is your independent-travel toolkit. But for all it delivers, it's still up to you to devote the time and energy it takes to manage the preparation and logistics that are essential for a happy trip. If that's a hassle, there's a solution.

Rick Steves Tours

A Rick Steves tour takes you to Europe's most interesting places with great

great tours, too!

with minimum stress

guides and small groups. We follow Rick's favorite itineraries, ride in comfy buses, stay in family-run hotels, and bring you intimately close to the Europe you've traveled so far to see. Most importantly, we take away the logistical headaches so you can focus on the fun.

Join the fun

This year we'll take thousands of free-spirited travelers—nearly half of them repeat customers—along with us on 50 different itineraries, from Athens to Istanbul. Is a Rick Steves tour the right fit for your travel dreams?

Find out at ricksteves.com, where you can also check seat availability and sign up. Europe is best experienced with happy travel partners. We hope you can join us.

See our itineraries at ricksteves.com

BEST OF GUIDES

Full-color guides in an easy-to-scan format. Focused on top sights and experiences in the most popular European destinations

Best of England
Best of Europe
Best of France
Best of Germany
Best of Ireland
Best of Italy
Best of Scotland
Best of Spain

COMPREHENSIVE GUIDES

City, country, and regional guides printed on Bible-thin paper. Packed with detailed coverage for a multi-week trip exploring iconic sights and venturing off the beaten path

Amsterdam & the Netherlands
Barcelona
Belgium: Bruges, Brussels,
  Antwerp & Ghent
Berlin
Budapest
Croatia & Slovenia
Eastern Europe
England
Florence & Tuscany
France
Germany
Great Britain
Greece: Athens & the Peloponnese
Iceland
Ireland
Istanbul
Italy
London
Paris
Portugal
Prague & the Czech Republic
Provence & the French Riviera
Rome
Scandinavia
Scotland
Sicily
Spain
Switzerland
Venice
Vienna, Salzburg & Tirol

THE BEST OF ROME

me, Italy's capital, is studded with
an remnants and floodlit-fountain
res. From the Vatican to the Colos-
, with crazy traffic in between, Rome
nderful, huge, and exhausting. The
ts, the heat, and the weighty history

of the Eternal City where Caesars walked
can make tourists wilt. Recharge by taking siestas, gelato breaks, and after-dark
walks, strolling from one atmospheric
square to another in the refreshing evening air.

d *Pantheon*—which
st dome until the
ry 2,000 years old
y over 1,500).

of Athens in the Vat-
dies the humanistic
ce.

ladiators fought
nother, entertaining

POCKET GUIDES
Compact color guides for shorter trips

Amsterdam
Athens
Barcelona
Florence
Italy's Cinque Terre
London
Munich & Salzburg
Paris
Prague
Rome
Venice
Vienna

SNAPSHOT GUIDES
Focused single-destination coverage

Basque Country: Spain & France
Copenhagen & the Best of Denmark
Dublin
Dubrovnik
Edinburgh
Hill Towns of Central Italy
Krakow, Warsaw & Gdansk
Lisbon
Loire Valley
Madrid & Toledo
Milan & the Italian Lakes District
Naples & the Amalfi Coast
Nice & the French Riviera
Normandy
Northern Ireland
Norway
Reykjavík
Rothenburg & the Rhine
Sevilla, Granada & Southern Spain
St. Petersburg, Helsinki & Tallinn
Stockholm

CRUISE PORTS GUIDES
Reference for cruise ports of call

Mediterranean Cruise Ports
Scandinavian & Northern European
  Cruise Ports

Complete your library with...

TRAVEL SKILLS & CULTURE
*Study up on travel skills and gain
insight on history and culture*

Europe 101
Europe Through the Back Door
Europe's Top 100 Masterpieces
European Christmas
European Easter
European Festivals
For the Love of Europe
Italy for Food Lovers
Travel as a Political Act

PHRASE BOOKS & DICTIONARIES
French
French, Italian & German
German
Italian
Portuguese
Spanish

PLANNING MAPS
Britain, Ireland & London
Europe
France & Paris
Germany, Austria & Switzerland
Iceland
Ireland
Italy
Scotland
Spain & Portugal

Credits

RESEARCHERS

For help with this edition, Rick relied on...

Amanda Buttinger

Amanda came to Madrid 20 years ago for what was to be a short adventure. But she's still there today, living with her husband and two energetic boys (the handsomest *chulapos* in Madrid). She maintains her American roots while enjoying *madrileño* and Spanish traditions, and leading Rick Steves tours through Spain and the Basque Country.

Pål Bjarne Johansen

A tour guide and guidebook researcher for Rick Steves' Europe (covering Scandinavia and Spain), Pål grew up in the Norwegian countryside near Oslo. He discovered his passion for travel and adventure at a young age and has backpacked much of the world. He first visited Spain with his family when he was four and has been back numerous times since, to this land that he considers his second home. When he's not working for Rick Steves, you'll find Pål skiing the Norwegian woods in winter and sailing the seven seas in summer.

Robert Wright

Raised in Memphis, Robert funded his first dream trip to Europe in 1998 by selling his entire *Star Wars* collection—proof that where there's a will, there's a way. He fell in love with Spain and Portugal and constantly returned, all while living for 14 years in Argentina. In the end, Robert married a *sevillano* and moved to Spain. He enjoys exploring small-town Iberia and uncovering long-lost connections between Spain and Portugal's intertwined history.

CONTRIBUTOR
Gene Openshaw

Gene has co-authored more than a dozen books with Rick, specializing in Europe's art, history, and culture. In particular, their *Europe 101: History and Art for the Traveler* and *Europe's Top 100 Masterpieces* have helped bring European art to life. Gene also writes for Rick's television shows, produces the audio tours, and is a regular guest on Rick's radio show. For public TV, Gene has co-authored *Rick Steves Fascism in Europe* and the ambitious six-hour series *Rick Steves Art of Europe*. Outside of the travel world, Gene has composed an opera called *Matter*, a violin sonata, and dozens of songs. His latest book is *Michelangelo at Midlife*. Gene lives near Seattle, where he roots for the Mariners in good times and bad.

ACKNOWLEDGMENTS

Thanks to Cameron Hewitt for writing this book's original chapters on the Camino de Santiago, Santiago de Compostela, and Cantabria. Thanks to guidebook researcher Robert Wright for writing this book's original chapter on Córdoba. And thank you to Risa Laib for her 25-plus years of dedication to the Rick Steves guidebook series.

Photo Credits

Front Cover: La Mezquita in Cordoba © Matteo Colombo / Getty Images
Back Cover (left to right): Ronda © Sean Pavone | Dreamstime.com; Spanish paella © Glesik | Dreamstime.com; Park Güell, Barcelona © Pitatatu | Dreamstime.com

Title Page: Waiter at Plaza Mayor, Madrid © Dominic Arizona Bonuccelli

Alamy: 87, 88 Album/Art Resource, NY; 90 Keystone Pictures USA

Dreamstime: 651 © Leochen66; 959 © Areg43

Public Domain via Wikimedia Commons: 442, 454 (left), 454 (right), 455 (left), 455 (right), 457, 459 (top and bottom), 460 (bottom), 461 (top), 462, 463, 542, 583, 694

Additional Credits: 7 (bottom) © Shutterstock/Studioimagen73

Additional Photography: Dominic Arizona Bonuccelli, Rich Earl, Cameron Hewitt, Dave Hoerlein, Suzanne Kotz, Pat O'Connor, Gene Openshaw, Jessica Shaw, Robyn Stencil, Rick Steves, Robert Wright. Photos are used by permission and are the property of the original copyright owners.

Avalon Travel
Hachette Book Group
1700 Fourth Street
Berkeley, CA 94710

Printed in Canada by Friesens
18th Edition. First printing September 2022

ISBN 978-1-64171-465-5

For the latest on Rick's talks, guidebooks, tours, public television series, and public radio show, contact Rick Steves' Europe, 130 Fourth Avenue North, Edmonds, WA 98020, +1 425 771 8303, RickSteves.com, rick@ricksteves.com.

Rick Steves' Europe
Managing Editor: Jennifer Madison Davis
Assistant Managing Editor: Cathy Lu
Editors: Glenn Eriksen, Julie Fanselow, Suzanne Kotz, Rosie Leutzinger, Teresa Nemeth, Jessica Shaw, Carrie Shepherd
Editorial & Production Assistant: Megan Simms
Researchers: Amanda Buttinger, Pål Bjarne Johansen, Robert Wright
Contributor: Gene Openshaw
Graphic Content Director: Sandra Hundacker
Maps & Graphics: Orin Dubrow, David C. Hoerlein, Lauren Mills, Mary Rostad

Avalon Travel
Senior Editor and Series Manager: Madhu Prasher
Associate Managing Editor: Jamie Andrade
Editor: Rachael Sablik
Proofreader: Kelly Lydick
Indexer: Stephen Callahan
Production & Typesetting: Lisi Baldwin, Jane Musser
Cover Design: Kimberly Glyder Design
Maps & Graphics: Kat Bennett

COLOR MAPS

Spain • Barcelona • Madrid • Granada • Sevilla

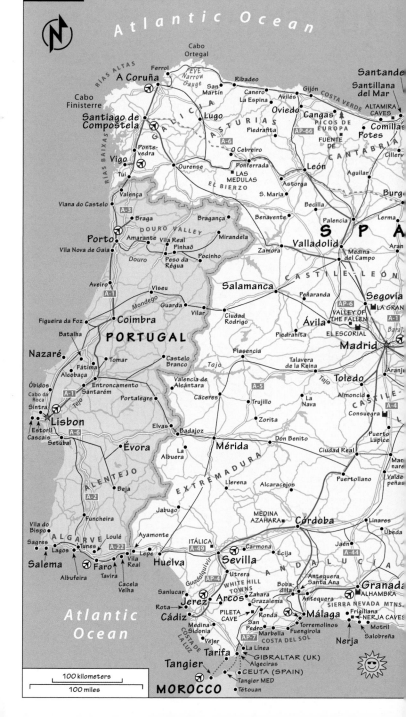

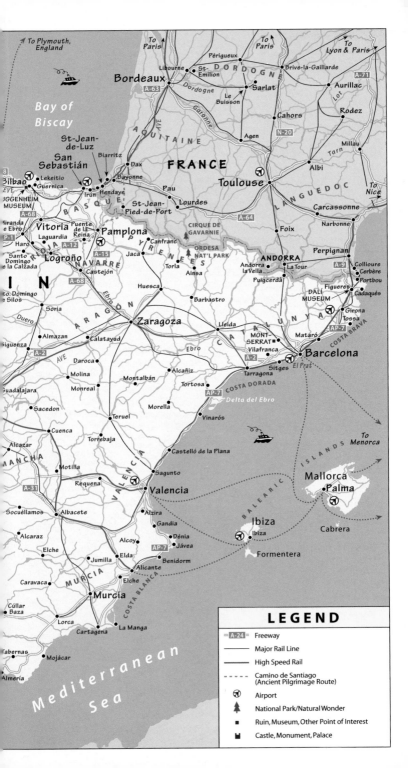

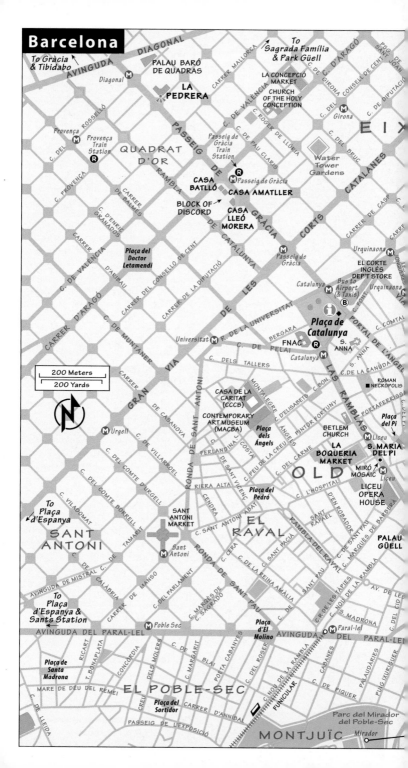

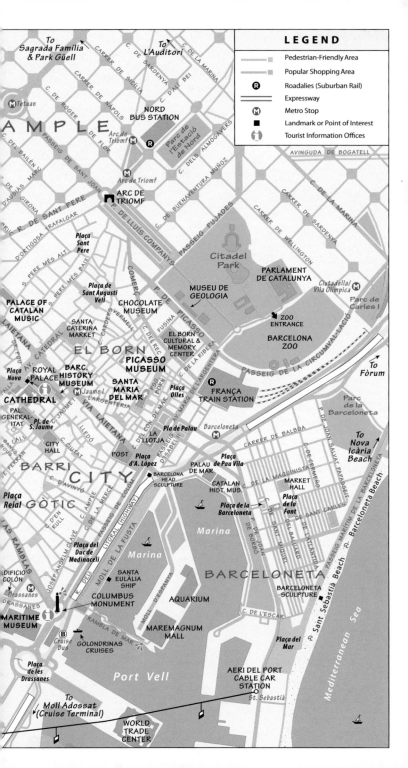

LEGEND

▬ ▬	Pedestrian-Friendly Area
▬ ▬	Popular Shopping Area
ℝ	Roadalies (Suburban Rail)
═══	Expressway
Ⓜ	Metro Stop
■	Landmark or Point of Interest
🛈	Tourist Information Offices

To Sagrada Família & Park Güell

To L'Auditori

Ⓜ Tetuan

AMPLE

NORD BUS STATION

Arc de Triomf Ⓜ ℝ

Parc de l'Estació de Nord

AVINGUDA DE BOGATELL

Arc de Triomf Ⓜ

■ ARC DE TRIOMF

Plaça Sant Pere

Plaça de Sant Augustí Vell

Citadel Park

PARLAMENT DE CATALUNYA

Ciutadella/ Vila Olímpica Ⓜ

Parc de Carles I

PALACE OF CATALAN MUSIC

SANTA CATERINA MARKET

CHOCOLATE MUSEUM

EL BORN

MUSEU DE GEOLOGIA

ZOO ENTRANCE

BARCELONA ZOO

To Fòrum

Plaça Nova

ROYAL PALACE

BARC. HISTORY MUSEUM

PICASSO MUSEUM

EL BORN CULTURAL & MEMORY CENTER

CATHEDRAL

Ⓜ Jaume I

SANTA MARIA DEL MAR

Plaça Olles

ℝ FRANÇA TRAIN STATION

Parc de la Barceloneta

PAL. GENERAL-ITAT

Pl. de S. Jaume

CITY HALL

LLEDÓ

POST

Plaça d'A. López

Pla de Palau

Barceloneta

To Nova Icària Beach

BARRI CITY

GÒTIC

BARCELONA HEAD SCULPTURE

PALAU DE MAR

CATALAN HIST. MUS.

Plaça de Pau Vila

MARKET HALL

Plaça de la Font

Plaça Reial

LA LLOTJA

Plaça de la Barceloneta

Barceloneta Beach

Plaça del Duc de Medinaceli

Marina

SANTA EULÀLIA SHIP

Marina

BARCELONETA

Sant Sebastià Beach

DIFICIO COLÓN Ⓜ Drassanes

COLUMBUS MONUMENT

AQUARIUM

BARCELONETA SCULPTURE

MARITIME MUSEUM

Ⓑ Cruise Bus

GOLONDRINAS CRUISES

MAREMAGNUM MALL

Plaça del Mar

Mediterranean Sea

Plaça de les Drassanes

Port Vell

AERI DEL PORT CABLE CAR STATION

St. Sebastià

To Moll d'Adossat (Cruise Terminal)

WORLD TRADE CENTER

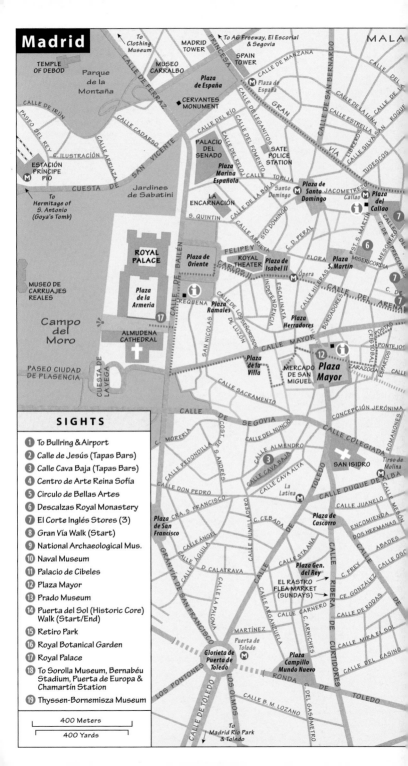

Madrid

TEMPLE OF DEBOD

Parque de la Montaña

To Clothing Museum

MADRID TOWER

SPAIN TOWER

To A6 Freeway, El Escorial & Segovia

MALA

CALLE DE MANZANA

MUSEO CARRALBO

Plaza de España

CERVANTES MONUMENT

CALLE DE SAN BERNARDO

CALLE DE LA

CALLE DE TERRAZ

CALLE DE IRÚN

PASEO DEL REY

C. ILUSTRACIÓN

CALLE CADARSO

CALLE DEL RÍO

Plaza de España

GRAN VÍA

CALLE DE LA LUNA

CALLE ESTRELLA SAN ROQUE

CALLE DE LEGANITOS

CALLE DEL FOMENTO

CALLE SILVA

LIBREROS

TUDESCOS

CALLE DE SAN VICENTE

CALLE ARRIAZA

PALACIO DEL SENADO

CALLE DEL RELOJ

SATE POLICE STATION

VÍA

ESTACIÓN PRINCIPE PÍO

CUESTA DE SAN VICENTE

Jardines de Sabatini

Plaza Marina Española

CALLE

TORIJA

Santo Domingo

Plaza de Santo Domingo

JACOMETREZO

Callao

Plaza del Callao

To Hermitage of S. Antonio (Goya's Tomb)

LA ENCARNACIÓN

CALLE DE LA BOLA

STO. DOMINGO

S. QUINTIN

C.D. PERAL

CALLE S. MARTIN

STS. S. MARTIN

MESONERO

CALLE DE PRECIADOS

ROYAL PALACE

FELIPE V

CALLE ARRIETA

FLORA

Plaza S. Martin

MISERICORDIA

Plaza de Oriente

ROYAL THEATER

CARLOS II

Plaza de Isabel II

CALLE HILERAS

C. DE

MUSEO DE CARRUAJES REALES

Plaza de la Armería

CALLE DE BAILÉN

REQUENA

Plaza Ramales

Ópera

CALLE DEL ARENAL

C. DE

Plaza Herradores

CALLE DE LOS-BORDADORES

BORDADORES

INDEPENDENCIA

ESCALINATA

Campo del Moro

ALMUDENA CATHEDRAL

SAN NICOLAS

CALLE DE LUZÓN

CALLE MAYOR

COSTA

CRISTOBAL

PONTEJOS

PASEO CIUDAD DE PLASENCIA

CUESTA DE LA VEGA

Plaza de la Villa

Plaza de Cibeles

MERCADO DE SAN MIGUEL

Plaza Mayor

ZARAZOGA

CALLE

CALLE SACRAMENTO

CALLE DE SEGOVIA

CONCEPCIÓN JERÓNIMA

ESPARTEROS

SIGHTS

1 To Bullring & Airport

2 Calle de Jesús (Tapas Bars)

3 Calle Cava Baja (Tapas Bars)

4 Centro de Arte Reina Sofía

5 Círculo de Bellas Artes

6 Descalzas Royal Monastery

7 El Corte Inglés Stores (3)

8 Gran Vía Walk (Start)

9 National Archaeological Mus.

10 Naval Museum

11 Palacio de Cibeles

12 Plaza Mayor

13 Prado Museum

14 Puerta del Sol (Historic Core) Walk (Start/End)

15 Retiro Park

16 Royal Botanical Garden

17 Royal Palace

18 To Sorolla Museum, Bernabéu Stadium, Puerta de Europa & Chamartín Station

19 Thyssen-Bornemisza Museum

C. MORERIA

CALLE DEL NUNCIO

CALLE ALMENDRO

ROMANONES

CALLE COLEGIADA

Tirso de Molina

C. REDONDILLA

C. COSTU DE S ANDRES

Plaza CAVA BAJA

SAN ISIDRO

CALLE REDONDILLA

CALLE CAVA ALTA

CALLE DON PEDRO

La Latina

TOLEDO

CALLE DUQUE DE ALBA

CALLE JUANELO

Plaza de San Francisco

CRA. S. FRANCISCO

CALLE ANGEL

CALLE AGUILA

D. CALATRAVA

GRANVÍA DE SAN FRANCISCO

Plaza de Cascorro

CALLE STA ANA

Plaza Gen. del Rey

CALLE

CALLE MESÓN DE

ENCOMIENDA

DOS HERMANAS

ABADES

C. FREY

CALLE OSC

CALLE LA PALOMA

CALLE HUMILLDERO

CALLE CEBADA DE

EL RASTRO FLEA MARKET (SUNDAYS)

CE. GONZALEZ

CALLE CARNERO

CALLE DE RODAS

MARTÍNEZ

Puerta de Toledo

Glorieta de Puerta de Toledo

RONDA

LOS PONTONES

LOS OLMOS

CALLE DE TOLEDO

CALLE B. M. LOZANO

To Madrid Río Park & Toledo

CALLE AGANZUELA

C. ARNICHES

CALLE MIRA EL SOL

CALLE DEL CASINO

Plaza Campillo Mundo Nuevo

RIBERA DE CURTIDORES

DE

TOLEDO

C. DEL GASÓMETRO

400 Meters

400 Yards

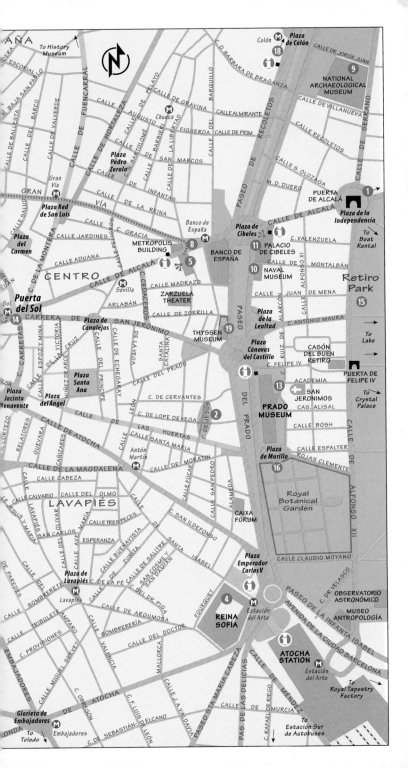

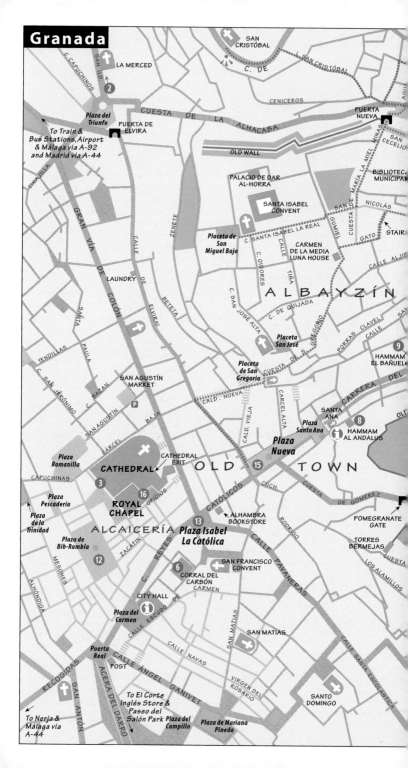

Granada

SAN CRISTÓBAL

C. DE

C. SAN CRISTÓBAL

LA MERCED

C. Capuchinos

SAN ILD

2

Plaza del Triunfo

PUERTA DE ELVIRA

CUESTA DE LA ALHACABA

PUERTA NUEVA

To Train & Bus Stations, Airport & Málaga via A-92 and Madrid via A-44

OLD WALL

SAN CECILIO

PALACIO DE DAR AL-HORRA

SANTA ISABEL CONVENT

BIBLIOTECA MUNICIPAL

ZENETE

GRAN VÍA DE COLÓN

CALLE DE ELVIRA

NICOLÁS

STAIR

Placeta de San Miguel Bajo

C. SANTA ISABEL LA REAL

CALLE TIÑA

CARMEN DE LA MEDIA LUNA HOUSE

CALLE ALJIBE

FINAJILA

C. OIDORES

LAUNDRY

SANTA PAULA

C. BAZAN

C. SAN JERÓNIMO

TENDILLAS

BETETA

C. SAN JOSÉ ALTA

C. DE QUIJADA

A L B A Y Z Í N

Placeta San José

PORRAS

CLAVEL

CALLE

HAMMAM EL BAÑUELO

9

Placeta de San Gregorio

CUESTA DE S.

SAN AGUSTÍN MARKET

CALD. NUEVA

CALD. VIEJA

CARCEL ALTA

SANTA ANA

HAMMAM AL ANDALUS

8

SAN AGUSTÍN

BAJA

Plaza Santa Ana

Plaza Nueva

CARRERA DEL

OLD

Plaza Romanilla

CARCEL

CATHEDRAL EXIT

3

CATHEDRAL

16

O L D

15

T O W N

CUESTA

DE GOMÉREZ

CAPUCHINAS

CUCH

Plaza Pescadería

ROYAL CHAPEL

OFICIOS

CATÓLICOS

RODRIGO

POMEGRANATE GATE

Plaza de la Trinidad

ALCAICERÍA

ALHAMBRA BOOKSTORE

TORRES BERMEJAS

Plaza de Bib-Rambla

Plaza Isabel La Católica

13

CALLE PAVANERAS

LOS ALAMILLOS

CUESTA

12

ZACATÍN

C. REYES

6

CORRAL DEL CARBÓN

SAN FRANCISCO CONVENT

MESONES

CARMEN

CITY HALL

CALLE ESCUDO DE

ALHÓNDIGA

Plaza del Carmen

SAN MATIAS

SAN MATIAS

CALLE SANTA ESCOLÁSTICA

Puerta Real

POST

CALLE ÁNGEL GANIVET

CALLE NAVAS

RECOGIDAS

SAN ANTÓN

ACERA DEL DARRO

VIRGEN DEL ROSARIO

SANTO DOMINGO

To Nerja & Málaga via A-44

To El Corte Inglés Store & Paseo del Salón Park

Plaza del Campillo

Plaza de Mariana Pineda

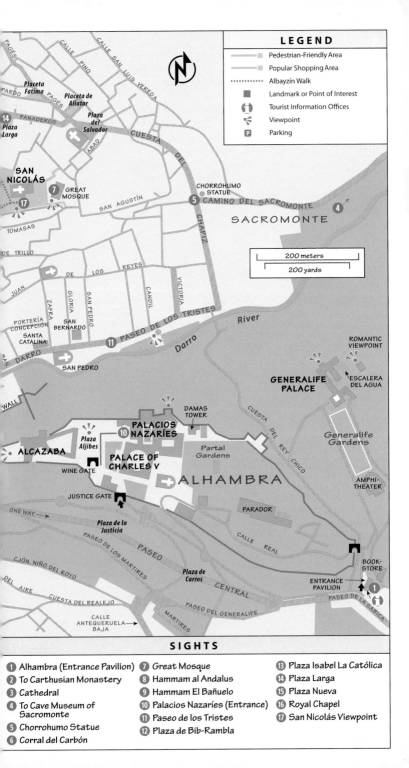

LEGEND

- ▦ Pedestrian-Friendly Area
- ▦ Popular Shopping Area
- ▪▪▪▪ Albayzín Walk
- ■ Landmark or Point of Interest
- ⚧ Tourist Information Offices
- ⋌ Viewpoint
- Ⓟ Parking

200 meters
200 yards

SIGHTS

- ① Alhambra (Entrance Pavilion)
- ② To Carthusian Monastery
- ③ Cathedral
- ④ To Cave Museum of Sacromonte
- ⑤ Chorrohumo Statue
- ⑥ Corral del Carbón
- ⑦ Great Mosque
- ⑧ Hammam al Andalus
- ⑨ Hammam El Bañuelo
- ⑩ Palacios Nazaríes (Entrance)
- ⑪ Paseo de los Tristes
- ⑫ Plaza de Bib-Rambla
- ⑬ Plaza Isabel La Católica
- ⑭ Plaza Larga
- ⑮ Plaza Nueva
- ⑯ Royal Chapel
- ⑰ San Nicolás Viewpoint

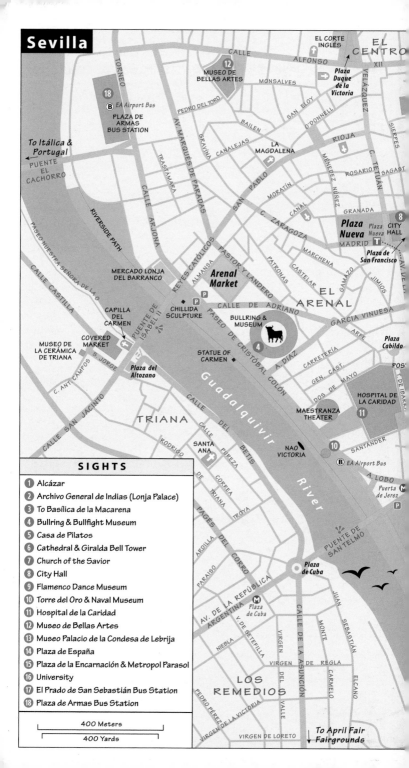

Sevilla

EL CORTE INGLÉS
EL CENTRO
CALLE ALFONSO XII
Plaza Duque de la Victoria
MONSALVES
SAN ELOY
BAILEN
O'DONNELL
LA MAGDALENA
RIOJA
MENÉNDEZ NÚÑEZ
ROSARIO
GRANADA
C. TETUÁN
SAGASTA
SIERPES
VELÁZQUEZ

CALLE
TORNEO
MUSEO DE BELLAS ARTES
PEDRO DEL TORO
GRAVINA
CANALEJAS
AV. MARQUÉS DE PARADAS
TRASTÁMARA
CALLE ARJONA
SAN PABLO
MORATÍN
C. ZARAGOZA
CANAL
Plaza Nueva
Plaza Nueva
CITY HALL
MADRID
MARCHENA
CASTELAR
PÁTRONAS
Plaza de San Francisco
AV. DE LA
JIMIOS
GAMAZO

PLAZA DE ARMAS BUS STATION
EA Airport Bus

To Itálica & Portugal
PUENTE EL CACHORRO
PASEO NUESTRA SEÑORA DE LA O
RIVERSIDE PATH
CALLE CASTILLA
MERCADO LONJA DEL BARRANCO
REYES CATÓLICOS
ALMANSA
PASTOR Y LANDERO
Arenal Market
CALLE DE ADRIANO
EL ARENAL
GARCÍA VINUESA
ARFE
Plaza Cabildo

CAPILLA DEL CARMEN
CHILLIDA SCULPTURE
PUENTE DE ISABEL II
PASEO DE CRISTÓBAL COLÓN
BULLRING & MUSEUM
CARRETERÍA
GEN. CAST.
DOS DE MAYO
POS

MUSEO DE LA CERÁMICA DE TRIANA
COVERED MARKET
C. ANT CAMPOS
S. JORGE
Plaza del Altozano
STATUE OF CARMEN
A. DÍAZ
HOSPITAL DE LA CARIDAD
DE IBARRA

CALLE SAN JACINTO
TRIANA
CALLE DEL BETIS
RODRIGO
SANTA ANA
CALLE PUREZA
Guadalquivir
MAESTRANZA THEATER
NAO VICTORIA
SANTANDER
EA Airport Bus
A. LOBO
Puerta de Jerez

DE TRIANA
CORREA
TROYA
PAGÉS DEL CORRO
ARDILLA
River
PUENTE DE SAN TELMO

SIGHTS

1. Alcázar
2. Archivo General de Indias (Lonja Palace)
3. To Basílica de la Macarena
4. Bullring & Bullfight Museum
5. Casa de Pilatos
6. Cathedral & Giralda Bell Tower
7. Church of the Savior
8. City Hall
9. Flamenco Dance Museum
10. Torre del Oro & Naval Museum
11. Hospital de la Caridad
12. Museo de Bellas Artes
13. Museo Palacio de la Condesa de Lebrija
14. Plaza de España
15. Plaza de la Encarnación & Metropol Parasol
16. University
17. El Prado de San Sebastián Bus Station
18. Plaza de Armas Bus Station

PARAÍSO
AV. DE LA REPÚBLICA ARGENTINA
Plaza de Cuba
Plaza de Cuba
V. DE SETEFILLA
NIEBLA
VIRGEN DEL VALLE
VIRGEN DE LA VICTORIA
LOS REMEDIOS
PEDRO PÉREZ
VIRGEN DE REGLA
VIRGEN DE LA ASUNCIÓN
CARMELO
MONTE
CALLE DE LA ASUNCIÓN
JUAN SEBASTIÁN
ELCANO

400 Meters
400 Yards

To April Fair Fairgrounds
VIRGEN DE LORETO

More for your trip!
Maximize the experience with Rick Steves as your guide

Guidebooks
Make side-trips smooth and affordable with Rick's Barcelona and Portugal guides

Phrase Books
Rely on Rick's Spanish Phrase Book & Dictionary

Rick's TV Shows
Preview your destinations with a wide variety of shows covering Spain

Rick's Audio Europe™ App
Get free self-guided audio tours for Barcelona, Madrid, and Sevilla

Small Group Tours
Take a lively, low-stress Rick Steves tour through Spain

For all the details, visit ricksteves.com

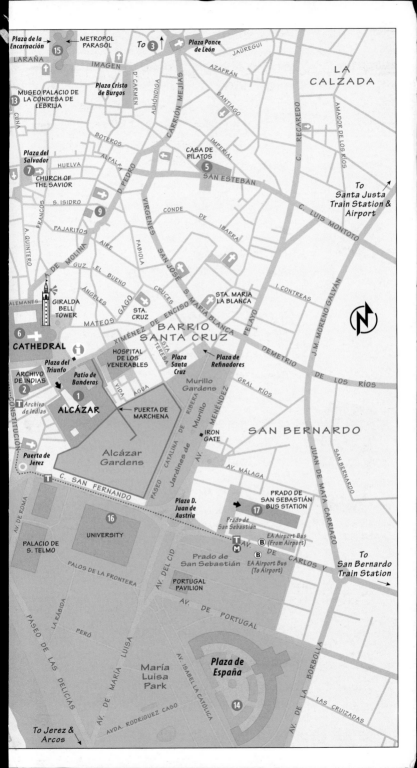

Rick Steves®

SPAIN